# The Popular Encyclopedia of Christian Counseling

General Editors

DR. TIM CLINTON
& DR. RON HAWKINS

Managing Editors

George Ohlschlager and Pat Springle

Contributing Editors

Ryan Carboneau
Joshua Straub
Laura Faidley
Hitomi Makino

HARVEST HOUSE PUBLISHERS
EUGENE, OREGON

*Cover by Koechel Peterson & Associates, Inc., Minneapolis, Minnesota*

*Cover photo © Thomas Northcut / Digital Vision / Thinkstock*

**THE POPULAR ENCYCLOPEDIA OF CHRISTIAN COUNSELING**

Published by Harvest House Publishers
Eugene, Oregon 97402
www.harvesthousepublishers.com

Library of Congress Cataloging-in-Publication Data
The popular encyclopedia of Christian counseling / Tim Clinton and Ron Hawkins, general editors.
p. cm.
Includes bibliographical references.
ISBN 978-0-7369-4356-7 (hardcover)
1. Counseling—Religious aspects—Christianity—Handbooks, manuals, etc. I. Clinton, Timothy E., 1960-
II. Hawkins, Ronald E.
BR115.C69P67 2011
253.5—dc22

2011013247



**Printed in the United States of America**

15 16 17 18 19 / LB-SK / 10 9 8 7 6 5 4 3

# CONTENTS

## PART 3: VARIOUS KINDS OF DISORDERS



## PART 4: MODES AND APPLICATIONS OF CHRISTIAN COUNSELING

## PART 5: COUNSELOR SKILLS, THEORIES, AND THERAPIES

## PART 6: SYSTEMIC AND ETHICAL ISSUES, EDUCATION, AND RESEARCH

# PREFACE

WE ARE PLEASED TO share the new *Popular Encyclopedia of Christian Counseling* with our members in the American Association of Christian Counselors (AACC), our students at Liberty University and Light University, and Christian counselors worldwide. This is the first such encyclopedic work that focuses on Christian counseling in the history of the AACC—and just in time to celebrate the silver anniversary of the AACC.

The encyclopedia includes more than 300 items arranged in 26 topical groupings that largely follow the outline of our field. We were determined to create a clear and comprehensive layout of Christian counseling in a logical progression that enhances counselors' knowledge, skill, and ethical dedication in the delivery of faith-enriched help to others. Time and resource limits shaped a *popular* encyclopedia—an exhaustive corpus of everything in our dynamic field was never our goal.

We were determined to make this book as useful as possible for practicing counselors and pastors. Students and new counselors will be especially blessed by this revealing project, but experienced therapists and academicians will also find much to learn and ponder in its pages. Moreover, in addition to the contents, which are arranged according to practice topics and issues, we have also attached an alphabetical index at the end of the book so you can reference articles in both ways—by topical relationship and by alphabetical guide.

More than one hundred contributors, representing some of the best clinical practitioners, teachers, researchers, pastors, pastoral counselors, ministry leaders, and even some graduate students, contributed to the content of this new encyclopedia. Seasoned professionals as well as many new writers have contributed to this project. We are encouraged—excited, in fact—to witness a whole new vanguard of young and accomplished Christian counselors who are being raised up by God to contribute to the advancement of our field.

Christian counseling will come of age—it will fully mature—as an influential ministry-profession, likely in the first half of this $21^{st}$ century. As it does, millions of lives will be touched by the transforming power of God in Christ, working by the Holy Spirit. We believe that Christian counseling will be a healing force in countless lives that are broken by the ways of this world and that it will facilitate the maturity of a multitude of Christian believers, making disciples and advancing the Great Commission in dozens of countries where freedom allows this kind of ministry.

Our prayer is that you will embrace Christian counseling if this is what God is calling you to do. Study and soak it in with all your powers of learning. Deliver it with grace and truth that comes from God and from his work in and through you on behalf of those who come for help. Practice it with all dedication and ethical excellence. Research and contribute to its application to a $21^{st}$-century world.

Praise God and thank him for raising up a ministry-profession that is given to the world for such a time as this. And celebrate it with your friends and colleagues every time you have the opportunity to get together with other Christian counselors.

*Part 1*

# Christian Counseling Definitions and Foundations

# 1

# CHRISTIAN COUNSELING DESCRIBED AND DEFINED

## CHRISTIAN COUNSELING

Christian counseling is a worldwide enterprise—a ministry-profession that is maturing in complexity and in membership. It consists of professional clinicians, pastoral counselors, and many others who deliver counseling and care-giving services to a wide range of clients from a distinctively Christian worldview. It is a triadic form of counseling that implicitly or explicitly honors Jesus Christ and believes the Holy Spirit is always present in the counseling relationship with the counselor and the client. Christian counseling has many goals, including helping people deal with severe losses, conflicts, and disorders, but it has one ultimate concern: helping clients become more like Christ and grow into a deeper intimacy with God and with one another.

**Definitions and Purposes.** Christian counseling has grown into a "big tent" that encompasses a wide range of definitions and practices. A pioneer Christian counselor, Gary Collins (1993), found that...

> attempts to define or describe Christian counseling tend to emphasize the *person* who does the helping, the *techniques* or skills that are used, and the *goals* that counseling seeks to reach. From that perspective the Christian counselor is:
>
> - a deeply committed, spirit-guided (and Spirit-filled) servant of Jesus Christ
> - who applies his or her God-given abilities, skills, training, knowledge, and insights
> - to the task of helping others move to personal wholeness, interpersonal competence, mental stability, and spiritual maturity (Collins, 1993, p. 21).

Another pioneer, Larry Crabb (1977), argued that the goal of Christian counseling should not be to make clients happy, but to promote Christian maturity (both spiritual and psychological) and to "free people to better worship and serve God by helping them become more like the Lord" (p. 20). He suggested that effective counseling needs both "a caring relationship and an understanding of human functioning" (p. 14) and that counseling insights and skills should be filled with Christ's love.

Everett Worthington (1999) offered this careful, cryptic, and comprehensive definition:

> Christian counseling is an explicit or implicit agreement for the provision of help for a client, in which the counselor has at heart the client's psychological welfare, but also the client's Christian spiritual welfare and tries to promote those goals through counseling methods, and the client can trust the counselor not to harm and to try to help the client psychologically and spiritually (Worthington, 1999, p. 189).

In *Competant Christian Counseling* (Clinton & Ohlschlager, 2002), we wrote that:

we propose...a Paracentric focus that... melds two crucial aspects of Christian counseling.... Our yieldedness to the Paraklete of God—the Holy Spirit—who is the invisible God present in counseling...[and our commitment] to Paraklesis...to "come alongside someone to help." These terms describe Spirit-directed and Christ-centered people committed to assisting others across a wide range of needs, from consolation to encouragement to confrontation.... A Paracentric focus represents a centered convergence in Christ as our exalted model, and on the client as the clinical and ethical object of our ministry. This focus...conveys the full arc of the helping process...

- The competent Christian counselor, yielded to an active, holy, and merciful God (1 Corinthians 1:18), meets the client at his or her point of need (diverging and becoming all things to all people [1 Corinthians 9:19, 2]), and connects with the client to create a working alliance.
- This activity includes comforting the brokenhearted, supporting the weak, encouraging the discouraged, exhorting those who are motivated, entreating and guiding the misdirected, and warning the rebel and sinner (the full scope of Spirit-led counselor behavior is described in 1 Thessalonians 5:14 and 2 Corinthians 1:3-7).
- The counselor serves to refocus, facilitate, instruct, and reinforce client action toward growing up into maturity (Ephesians 4:12-16) and living in more intimate relationship (John 17:9-13) with the divine object of our faith, Jesus Christ. This involves de-centering ourselves (Lamentations 3:20-24) and converging or centering on the Author and Finisher of our faith (Hebrews 12:2).

Christian counseling must be a biblical-clinical process that facilitates case-wise client sanctification. It is built on the sure foundation of Scripture, dependent on the inspired leading of the Holy Spirit, and selectively using the best of helping ministry resources and the bio-psycho-social sciences (Clinton & Ohlschlager, 2002, pp. 50-51).

The revised edition of *Psychology and Christianity* (Johnson, 2010) has five core paradigms through which to view the content and process of Christian counseling, up from the four views of the original edition.

- *The biblical counseling model* holds that the Bible alone is the source of all wisdom and revelation in counseling, and any reliance on psychology or extra-biblical resources has a high likelihood of tainting the counseling endeavor.
- *The levels-of-explanation model* holds that Christian religion and psychology are two different fields that are best left and approached as they are, without any mixing.
- *The integration model* attempts to synthesize psychology and theology with the Bible as the controlling source. Any psychology in contravention of the Bible is rejected as unacceptable for integration.
- *The Christian psychology model* asserts that psychology from every era and history is worthy of study, especially that done by church leaders and saints from throughout history.
- The newest model, *the transformative worldview,* conceives of doing psychology and theology in an embodied redemption, in the power of the Holy Spirit. Sanctified scientists make a huge difference in the doing of psychology.

Possibly the best one-sentence description of Christian counseling was given recently by Siang-Yang Tan (2011, p. 363), emphasizing the role and work of the Holy Spirit: "Christian counseling or psychotherapy can be simply described as counseling conducted by a Christian who is Christ-centered, biblically based, and Spirit filled" (p. 363).

**Theory-Building and Research.** Everett Worthington (1993) has analyzed Christian counseling theory building from three distinct conceptualizations.

*Academic and research-based theories.* Beutler and Bergan (1991) have shown not only the value-laden nature of psychotherapy but also how values similarity influences client identification with a counselor, and how values differences (faith-based vs. secular approaches) impact counseling outcomes. Worthington (1988) suggested three dimensions of values (i.e., the role of authority of human leaders, Scripture or doctrine, and religious group norms) essential in working with religiously committed clients. Allen Bergin (1980) identified and contrasted theistic values with nonreligious clinical and humanistic values.

*Religious versions of secular theories.* The many adaptations of secular models revealed the strong reliance of cognitive therapies transformed into sources of "renewing the mind." These included counseling models by Larry Crabb (1977), Robert McGee (1990), Norm Wright (1981), Everett Worthington (1989), and Bill Backus (1985). Also noted were eclectic attempts at integration, such as models by Smith (1990) and the leaders of the Minirth-Meier Clinic in their heyday (Minirth, Meier, & Wichern, 1982). Jones and Buttman's (1991) analysis of secular theories from a Christian worldview is also an important contribution.

*Specifically religious theories.* Some theories have been developed superficially as Christian approaches. These theories are represented by Paul Tournier's (1965) *The Healing of Persons*, Charles Solomon's (1977) spirituotherapy, Jay Adam's (1973) nouthetic counseling, and Gary Collins' *Helping People Grow* (1980) and *Case Studies in Christian Counseling* (1991). After evaluating the various theories and their construction, Worthington notes, "the challenge before our profession [is] to fashion a truly integrated set of Christian counseling theories, supported by Scripture, experience, and research" (1993, p. 33). Recent developments, such as Mark McMinn and Clark Campbell's (2007) social cognitive theory and Siang-Yang Tan's (2011) Christian counseling development reflect Worthington's concern and integrate Scripture, theory, experiences, and science.

**Current Status.** Currently, many levels of care can be given to clients based on the professional proficiency of the helper.

- *Professional counselors and clinicians* are licensed professionals across the disciplines of psychology, social work, mental-health counseling, marriage and family therapy, and the two medical disciplines, psychiatry and nursing.
- *Pastoral and biblical counselors* work largely in the church.
- *Recovery counselors* work largely in the addictions field.
- *Lay and peer counselors* also work mostly in the church.

In *Caring for People God's Way* (Clinton, Hart, & Ohlschlager, 2005), we outlined seven synthesizing traits that we believe anchor most of what is done in Christian counseling today.

1. *Scripturally anchored.* True Christian counseling is as dependent on Scripture as people are on food and water to live. The Scriptures are, in fact, the food and water of spiritual life.
2. *Spiritual forming.* Christian counselors are called to help form the Spirit

of God into the lives of those who come to us for help.

3. *Short-term (initially).* Nearly all clients terminate counseling in six to ten sessions. Brief therapy is mandatory for all clients, but long-term therapy is discretionary, chosen by those who want it and can afford it.

4. *Solution-focused.* Solution-focused therapy arose as did brief therapy, with counselor and clients looking for solutions that have worked before and work partially on the client's behalf.

5. *Strength-based.* Intimate sibling to solution-focused and brief forms of therapy, strength-based assessment involves searching for and magnifying client strengths, which, as they grow stronger, crowd out any room for problems to fester and grow.

6. *Storied narratives.* Human beings live by stories, tell about their lives in stories, and relate to God and others primarily in storied forms. God reveals himself to us primarily in the way of a grand story of creation-Fall-redemption that cycles over and over throughout history. Therapy at its best is a lived narrative.

7. *Scientific.* In a scientific world, all truth claims are submitted to the rigors of the empirical way. Christian counseling must do the same and has nothing to fear by doing so.

We then noted the seven stages through which the Christian counseling process passes from beginning to end.

- *Intake.* The therapeutic alliance begins with the first handshake, so it is important to instill hope and inspire confidence in the client, who usually has voices inside telling him or her to turn and run.
- *Assessment.* Assessment also begins from the first meeting, a flexible process of detailing both problems and strengths to define where the client is now and where she or he wants to go when counseling is done.
- *Gaining insight.* Clients must be able to make connections that have not yet been made that increase their understanding of why they are where they are and what must be done to get where they want to go.
- *Yielding to God's healing touch.* As with salvation and every step of growth and sanctification, all healing is the gracious work of God in Christ through the power of the Holy Spirit. All that is required of us is that we yield in faith, believing that God will do a good and godly work within.
- *Active change (brief therapy for all).* Interventions that facilitate active changes in thinking and behavior—in pursuit of at least one agreed goal—are the objectives of brief therapy for everyone. A strength-based approach involves strengthening what the client is already doing partially or has done before.
- *Transformative change (long-term therapy for some).* Some clients will pursue longer-term goals of deep spiritual and character change, either by continuing in long-term therapy or by engaging a coach or mentor.
- *Counseling as discipleship.* We recognize Christian counseling as an intensive form of case-based discipleship. The pursuit of spiritual maturity in Christ shows that the goals of discipleship and Christian counseling are synonymous.

TIM CLINTON
RON HAWKINS
GEORGE OHLSCHLAGER

## REFERENCES


Adams, J. E. (1970). *Competent to Counsel: Introduction to Nouthetic Counseling.* Grand Rapids, MI: Zondervan.

Adams, J. E. (1973). *The Christian Counselor's Manual.* Nutley, NJ: Presbyterian and Reformed.

American Association of Christian Counselors. (2004). *AACC Christian Counseling Code of Ethics.* Forest, VA: Author.

Backus, W. (1985). *Telling Truth to the Troubled People.* Minneapolis, MN: Bethany House.

Bergin, A. E. (1980). Psychotherapy and religious values. *Journal of Consulting and Clinical Psychology, 48,* 95-105.

Beutler, L., & Bergan, J. (1991). Value change in counseling and psychotherapy: A search for scientific credibility. *Journal of Counseling Psychology, 38,* 16-24.

Clinton, T., Hart, A., & Ohlschlager, G. (2005). *Caring for People God's Way: Personal and Emotional Issues, Addictions, Grief, and Trauma.* Nashville, TN: Thomas Nelson.

Clinton, T., & Ohlschlager, G. (1997). *Law, Ethics, and Values in Christian Counseling: Practice and Advocacy in a Brave New World.* Presentation at the 1997 World Conference on Christian Counseling, Dallas, TX.

Clinton, T., & Ohlschlager, G. (2002). *Competent Christian Counseling: Foundations and Practice of Compassionate Soul Care.* Colorado Springs, CO: WaterBrook Press.

Collins, G. R. (1980). *Practical Approaches to Christian Counseling.* Santa Ana, CA: Vision House.

Collins, G. R. (1991). *Case Studies in Christian Counseling.* Dallas, TX: Word.

Collins, G. R. (1993). *The Biblical Basis of Christian Counseling for People Helpers.* Colorado Springs, CO: NavPress.

Crabb, L. (1977). *Effective Biblical Counseling.* Grand Rapids, MI: Zondervan.

Croucher, R. (1991). Spritual formation. *Grid (A Publication of World Vision Australia), 1*(2).

Hawkins, R., & Clinton, T. (2011). *The New Christian Counselor: A Fresh Biblical and Transformational Approach.* Eugene, OR: Harvest House Publishers.

Johnson, E. L. (2010). *Psychology and Christianity: Five Views.* Downers Grove, IL: InterVarsity Press.

Jones, S. L., & Butman, R. E. (2001). *Modern Psychotherapies: A Comprehensive Christian Appraisal.* Downers Grove, IL: InterVarsity Press.

Koenig, H. G. (2004). Religion, spirituality, and medicine: Research findings and implications for clinical practice. *Southern Medical Journal, 97,* 1194-1200.

McGee, R. S. (1990). *The Search for Significance* (2nd ed.). Houston, TX: Rapha.

McMinn, M. R., & Campbell, C. D. (2007). *Integrative Psycotherapy: Toward a Comprehensive Christian Approach.* Downers Grove, IL: InterVarsity Press.

Minirth, F., Meier, P., & Wichern, F. (1982). *Introduction to Psychology and Counseling: Christian Perspectives and Applications.* Grand Rapids, MI: Baker.

Ohlschlager, G., & Mosgofian, P. (1992). *Law for the Christian Counselor. A Guidebook for Clinicians and Pastors.* Dallas, TX: Word Books.

Pargament, K. I. (2007). *Spiritually Integrated Psychotherapy: Understanding and Addressing the Sacred.* New York, NY: Guilford Press.

Powlison, D. (1997). Critical issues in biblical counseling. In D. Powlison (Ed.), *Counseling the Word: A Selection of Readings from the Journal of Biblical Counseling.* Glenside, PA: Christian Counseling and Education Foundation.

Richards, P. S., & Bergin, A. E. (2005). *A Spiritual Strategy for Counseling and Psychotherapy.* Washington, DC: American Psychological Association.

Smith, D. (1990). *Integrative Therapy: A Comprehensive Approach to the Methods and Principles of Counseling and Psychotherapy.* Grand Rapids, MI: Baker.

Solomon, C. (1977). *Counseling with the Mind of Christ.* Old Tappan, NJ: Revell.

Sweet, L. (1999). *Soul Tsunami: Sink or Swim in the New Millennium Culture.* Grand Rapids, MI: Zondervan.

Tan, S.-Y. (2011). *Counseling and Psychotherapy: A Christian Perspective.* Grand Rapids, MI: Baker Books.

Tournier, P. (1965). *The Healing of Persons.* New York, NY: Harper & Row.

Worthington, E. L., Jr. (1988). Understanding the values of religious clients: A model and its application to counseling. *Journal of Counseling Psychology, 35,* 166-174.

Worthington, E. L., Jr. (1989). *Marriage Counseling: A Christian Approach for Counseling Couples.* Downers Grove, IL: InterVarsity.

Worthington, E. (Ed.). (1993). *Psychotherapy and Religious Values.* Grand Rapids, MI: Baker Books.

Worthington, E. L., Jr. (1999). Christian counseling and psychotherapy. In D. Benner & P. Hill (Eds.), *Baker Encyclopedia of Psychology and Counseling* (2nd ed.). Grand Rapids, MI: Baker Books.

Wright, H. N. (1981). *Marital Counseling: A Biblical, Behavioral, Cognitive Approach.* San Francisco, CA: Harper and Row.


## SOUL CARE

**Definition.** The definition of soul care is vast and varied. The word *soul* is translated from the Greek word *psuche,* meaning "the breath, breath of life" (Vine, Unger, & White, 1996, p. 588). The Latin words for the care of souls are *cura animarum. Cura* means the "care of" or "cure for," and *animarum* means "breath, breeze, air, wind." Soul care, according to the strictest sense of the words, involves literally caring for and curing the very breath that gives us life. It is tending to the deepest needs of the soul.

**History.** The Bible is filled with examples of soul-care ministry (Ex. 3:16; 1 Sam. 3:9; 2 Sam. 12:7; Mt. 14:13; Mk. 1:35; Gal. 6:2; Jas. 5:16). Soul care is originally a monastic concept in which men would teach others the deep mysteries of God as well as draw away from their communities and seclude themselves in solitude. Merton (1960) also connected soul care to spiritual direction (Demarest, 2003; Imbach, 2007; Johnson, 2007; Nouwen, 2006).

According to Merton (1960), the purpose of spiritual direction is to dig beneath the surface underneath the typical Christian facade and bring people to their inmost truth, the center of their soul, which strives for the likeness of Christ. Benner (2002) described spiritual direction as a process whereby "a person seeking help in cultivating a deeper personal relationship with God meets with another for prayer and conversation that is focused on increasing awareness of God in the midst of life experiences and facilitating surrender to God's will" (p. 188). The goal of spiritual direction (soul care) is spiritual formation. Rowland Croucher speaks of spiritual formation as "the dynamic process whereby the Word of God is applied by the Spirit of God to the heart and mind of the child of God so that he or she becomes more like the Son of God" (1991). Nouwen (2006) defined it as the capacity to live a spiritually disciplined life from our hearts and souls. Foster (2002) says that the spiritual disciplines of the faith are "instruments of human transformation."

Soul care, however, is not at the top of many Christians' lists of things to work toward. Research by the Barna Group (2001) found that four out of ten "born again" Christians do not attend church or read the Bible in a typical week, three out of ten say they are not "absolutely committed to the Christian faith," and seven out of ten are not involved in small groups that meet for spiritual purposes.

**Counseling and Spiritual Direction.** Being both counselor and spiritual director is an attainable goal. "The boundaries between spiritual counseling and mental-health counseling cannot be drawn easily or clearly" (Buford, 1997, p. 112). Often, counselors work to help mature people so that they are free to grow in Christ, and spiritual directors then are given the challenge of helping persons take on the character and the imitation of Christ. Both the counseling and spiritual direction worlds move along the same path of spiritual transformation when they fully expect the Holy Spirit to intervene and cause supernatural change in the life of the client (Clinton & Ohlschlager, 2002; Moon & Benner, 2004). This process could be understood as the "transformation of the spirit" (Willard, 2002), the divine process of becoming an apprentice of Jesus (Moon, 2009).

According to Clebsch & Jaekle (1964), soul care involves four primary elements: healing, sustaining, reconciling, and guiding. Many researchers believe the church is to be a spiritual hospital, caring for those hurting and debilitated by mental and spiritual disorders (Clinton & Ohlschlager, 2005; Crabb, 1999). The church is absolutely critical to the care and solace of those suffering with problems in this world (Crabb, 2009).

In soul care the triune God and the Christian helper work together to bring the sojourner to a deeper level of union and communion with God (Johnson, 2007). Crabb (1999) states that "life is a journey toward a land we have not yet seen along a path we sometimes cannot find. It is a journey of the soul toward its destiny and its home" (p. 182).

**Application.** The apostle Paul's words in 2 Corinthians 1:3-4 are instructive here: "Praise be to the God and Father of our Lord

Jesus Christ...who comforts us in all our troubles, so that we can comfort those in any trouble with the comfort we ourselves receive from God." Soul care helps conform lives to the life of Jesus Christ so they reflect the image of God (Demarest, 2003; Johnson, 2007). All believers are hastened toward soul care with the command, "Above all else guard your heart, for everything you do flows from it" (Proverbs 4:23). Ultimately, the spiritual journey is navigated with the purpose of accomplishing what is at the heart of Paul's words in 2 Corinthians—to reach out and comfort others with the comfort that we ourselves receive from God.

TIM CLINTON
RON HAWKINS
RYAN CARBONEAU

## REFERENCES


Barna Group. (2001). *Annual Study Reveals America Is Spiritually Stagnant.* Retrieved from www.barna.org

Benner, D. G. (2002). *Sacred Companions: The Gift of Spiritual Friendship and Direction.* Downers Grove, IL: InterVarsity Press.

Buford, R. K. (1997). Consecrated counseling: Reflections on the distinctives of Christian counseling. *Journal of Psychology and Theology, 25*(1), 111-122.

Clebsch, W. A., & Jaekle, C. R. (1964). *Pastoral Care in Historical Perspective.* New York, NY: Seabury.

Clinton, T. E. (2005). Introduction to Christian counseling: The 21st century state of the art. In T. Clinton, A. Hart, & G. Ohlschlager (Eds.), *Caring for People God's Way: Personal and Emotional Issues, Addictions, Grief, and Traumas* (pp. 3-25). Nashville, TN: Nelson.

Clinton, T. E., & Ohlschlager, G. (2002). *Competent Christian Counseling: Foundations and Practice of Compassionate Soul Care* (Vol. 1). New York, NY: WaterBrook.

Crabb, L. J. (1999). *Becoming a True Spiritual Community: A Profound Vision of What the Church Can Be.* Nashville, TN: Thomas Nelson.

Crabb, L. J. (2009). *Real Church: Does It Exist? Can I Find It?* Nashville, TN: Nelson.

Croucher, R. (1991). Spiritual formation. *Grid (a publication of World Vision Australia),* 1-2.

Demarest, B. (2003). *Soul Guide: Following Jesus as Spiritual Director.* Colorado Springs, CO: NavPress.

Foster, R. J. (2002). *Celebration of Discipline: The Path to Spiritual Growth.* New York, NY: HarperCollins.

Imbach, J. D. (2007). *The River Within: Loving God, Living Passionately.* Abbotsford, BC, Canada: Fresh Wind Press.

Johnson, E. L. (2007). *Foundations for Soul Care: A Christian Psychology Proposal.* Downers Grove, IL: InterVarsity Press.

Merton, T. (1960). *Spiritual Direction and Meditation.* Collegeville, MN: The Order of St. Benedict.

Moon, G. W. (2009). *Apprenticeship with Jesus: Learning to Live Like the Master.* Grand Rapids, MI: Baker Books.

Moon, G. W., & Benner, D. G. (2004). Spiritual direction and Christian soul care. In G. W. Moon & D. G. Benner (Eds.), *Spiritual Direction and the Care of Souls* (pp. 11-28). Downers Grove, IL: InterVarsity Press.

Nouwen, H. J. M. (2006). *Spiritual Direction: Wisdom for the Long Walks of Faith.* New York, NY: Harper Collins.

Vine, W. E., Unger, M. F., & White, W. (1996). *Vine's Complete Expository Dictionary of Old and New Testament Words.* Nashville, TN: Nelson.

Willard, D. (2002). *Renovation of the Heart: Putting On the Character of Christ.* Colorado Springs, CO: NavPress.


## PSYCHOTHERAPY AND VALUES

**UNDERSTANDING VALUES.** Counseling is a discipline that cannot be separated from its moral and philosophical roots (Christopher, 1996). One of the most important aspects of becoming a counselor is awareness of one's own values and their influence in the counseling process. Counselors' recognition of their beliefs and values, where they came from, and why they hold them is crucial to understanding how those values may or may not be exposed or even imposed on their clients (Corey, 2008). Whether we realize it or not, our values impact nearly every facet of the therapeutic process, including intake and assessment, goal setting, problem solving, therapeutic technique, outcomes, and evaluation (Corey; Ellis, 1973). In fact, research has shown that clients can and do often assume the values of the counselor (Richards, Rector, & Tjeltveit, 1999). Many authoritative figures in the field of counseling have attested that there is no such thing as values-neutral psychotherapy (Corey; Falender & Shafranske, 2004; Jones, 1994; Tan, 2011). To assume that we can enter into the therapeutic relationship without our values influencing the client is presumptuous. Corey (2008) suggests that counselors avoid two extremes regarding values in the counseling setting: (a) holding to an absolute position on a particular value whereby they impose that value onto the client in a forceful or proselytizing manner (for example, if a client has decided to get an abortion and the therapist gets into an ethical debate with the client about this position and threatens to end the treatment relationship if the client does not agree to refrain from obtaining the abortion); and (b) holding to a position of values-free counseling, whereby their fear is having too much influence on clients, thereby rendering themselves ineffective (e.g. in the above situation the counselor refuses to discuss values with the client and therefore does not address some of the possible negative consequences of abortion).

**Religious Values.** Research suggests that both clients and therapists have religious values and preferences. For instance, Fouque and Glachan (2000) found that 42% of people seek help from clergy first for their emotional problems, showing the desire for their faith to be addressed when in need. Furthermore, according to Hage (2006), two thirds of Americans reported that they prefer to be treated by therapists who have spiritual beliefs. A majority of therapists also acknowledge their religious beliefs and values; for example, 80% of professional therapists (psychologists and psychiatrists excluded) claim a religious preference, and 77% "try to live according to their religious beliefs" (Bergin & Jensen, 1990). While the numbers for psychiatrists and psychologists are lower, these statistics on therapists is encouraging, for it seems to meet many clients' desire for faith-based or spiritual psychotherapies.

**The Significance of Congruence.** Even when the client identifies himself or herself as having the same religious background or denomination as the therapist, the therapist should not assume that their beliefs are exactly the same (Bergin & Jensen, 1990). However, when these values and beliefs are explored, respected, and agreed upon, such value congruence between therapist and client leads to richer therapeutic outcomes. For example, several studies showed that the use of Christian cognitive-behavioral therapy (with explicit use of Christian beliefs, prayer, and Scripture) was not only as effective as traditional cognitive-behavioral therapy but also more effective in enhancing clients' spiritual health, which includes a sense of well-being as it relates to God, life satisfaction, and life purpose (Tan & Johnson, 2005).

**Exposing Versus Imposing Personal Values.** The psychotherapeutic climate and setting should be characterized by a sense of safety, including unconditional positive regard and respect for clients' value systems. Within a safe environment, clients can freely express their thoughts, beliefs, feelings, and behaviors without feeling judged or ridiculed. Effective therapy allows for the processing of these behaviors to be evaluated on the basis of clients' quality of life.

As a professional counselor, the goal of therapy should not be to impose your values on clients in an attempt to get them to believe what you think is right, but to help them determine whether they are living up to their own values and whether those beliefs are leading to behaviors that negatively affect their lives and relationships with others. Helping clients discern these behaviors based on their own value systems may require them to reevaluate their core beliefs. Clients can define and refine their value systems, choose their own actions, and then evaluate those actions based on their therapeutic goals. Psychotherapists will inevitably expose their values based on their own theoretical approaches, goals for therapy, and evaluation of the client's progress, but they must remain aware of their value system so as not to impose their values on the client (Corey, 2008; Tan, 2011).

**Client Right to Self-Determination.** As mentioned, it is unrealistic to think that a counselor-client relationship can be values-neutral. Richards and Bergin's (1997) suggestion regarding the ethical principles of values in counseling is applicable. For instance, the counselor should respect the client's right to self-determination in the counseling process when it comes to spirituality and religious values, even if the client and counselor hold to different faith backgrounds. If a client's choices and behaviors are valuably different, it is an ethical violation to condemn, judge, or punish the client for those choices. Those choices can be discussed as they relate to the client's presenting problems and impact on therapeutic goals, but if they ever cross a point whereby the therapeutic relationship is negatively affected as a result, the counselor and client must begin discussing the possibility of referral to another counselor. Only when the client is interested in pursuing spiritual, religious, or related interventions and informed consent is provided should a counselor utilize these interventions in professional psychotherapy.

**Value Conflicts: Protocol and Procedure.** Counselors and clients need to understand and respect clients' rights. For instance, if you are a professional Christian counselor and a Muslim client comes in to seek help for an issue related primarily to his Islamic faith, it would behoove you to refer that client to a Muslim therapist who can address his faith issues more effectively than you can.

There has been considerable debate on this issue, especially as it pertains to seeing clients who value living a homosexual lifestyle. Counselors with faith backgrounds who feel conflicted about counseling people living a gay lifestyle are ethically responsible to refer to professional counselors who can best help those clients obtain their goals in therapy. Conversely, if a Christian client is conflicted over same-sex behavior and wants to lead a celibate heterosexual lifestyle that conflicts with the beliefs and practices of a gay-affirming therapist, the preferred ethic is to refer the client to a competent professional counselor who will affirm the desires and religious beliefs of the client.

A great deal of controversy related to these issues has been raised recently with the expulsion of two graduate counseling students who had a conflict of values with the practice of same-sex behavior. (For more information on these cases, refer to links in reference section.) Leading experts (Corey, 2008; Richards & Bergin, 1997; Tan, 2011) believe that when values conflicts are clearly found in therapeutic relationships, competent referrals should be made to mental-health professionals who can better help the clients reach their goals. This same standard is upheld by the American Counseling Association code of ethics in Section A.11.b., Inability to Assist Clients:

> If counselors determine an inability to be of professional assistance to clients, they avoid entering or continuing counseling relationships. Counselors are knowledgeable about culturally and clinically appropriate referral resources and suggest these alternatives. If clients decline the suggested referrals, counselors should discontinue the relationship.

This ethical standard is consistent with the American Association of Christian Counselors code of ethics found in section I-222 Referral Practice:

> Referral shall be made in situations where client need is beyond the counselor's ability or scope of practice or when consultation is inappropriate, unavailable, or unsuccessful. Referrals should be done only after the client is provided with informed choices among referral sources. As much as possible, counselors referred to shall honor prior commitments between client and referring counselor or church.

Such professional behavior demonstrates

a clear respect of client self-determination and honors our freedom to worship God and embrace our faith of choice within the mental-health profession.

Tim Clinton
Joshua Straub
Gary Sibcy

## REFERENCES


American Association of Christian Counselors. (2004). *AACC Christian Counseling Code of Ethics.* Retrieved from http://www.aacc.net/about-us/code-of-ethics/

American Counseling Association (2005). *ACA Code of Ethics.* Retrieved from http://www.counseling.org/Resources/CodeOfEthics/TP/Home/CT2.aspx

Bergin, A. E., & Jensen, J. P. (1990). Religiosity of psychotherapists: A national survey. *Psychotherapy, 27*(1), pp. 3-7.

Christopher, J. C. (1996). Counseling's inescapable moral visions. *Journal of Counseling & Development, 75*(1), 17-25.

Corey, G. (2008). *Theory and Practice of Counseling and Psychotherapy.* Belmont, CA: Thomson Brooks/Cole.

Ellis, A. (1973). *Humanistic Psychotherapy.* New York, NY: McGraw-Hill.

Falender, C. A., & Shafranske, E. P. (2004). *Clinical Supervision: A Competency-Based Approach.* Washington, DC: American Psychological Association.

Fouque, P., & Glachan, M. (2000). The impact of Christian counseling on survivors of sexual abuse. *Counseling Psychology Quarterly, 13,* 201-220.

Hage, S. (2006). A closer look at spirituality in psychology training programs. *Professional Psychology: Research and Practice, 37*(3), 303-310. doi:10.1037/0735-7028.37.3.303.

Jones, S. L. (1994). A constructive relationship for religion with the science and profession of psychology: Perhaps the boldest model yet. *American Psychologist, 49*(3), 184-199.

Richards, P. S., & Bergin, A. E. (1997). *A Spiritual Strategy for Counseling and Psychotherapy.* Washington, DC: American Psychological Association.

Richards, P. S., Rector, J. M., & Tjeltveit, A. C. (1999). Values, spirituality, and psychotherapy. In W. R. Miller (Ed.), *Integrating Spirituality in Treatment: Resources for Practitioners* (pp.133-160). Washington, DC: American Psychological Association.

Tan, S.-Y. (2011). *Counseling and Psychotherapy: A Christian Perspective.* Grand Rapids, MI: Baker Books.

Tan, S.-Y., & Johnson, W. B. (2005). Spiritually oriented cognitive-behavioral therapy. In S. Len. & E. P. Shafranske (Eds.), *Spiritually Oriented Psychotherapy* (pp. 77-103). Washington, DC: American Psychological Association. doi:10.1037/10886-004


## REFERENCES REGARDING THE DISMISSAL OF COUNSELING STUDENTS


Schmidt, P. (2010, July 27). Federal judge upholds dismissal of counseling student who balked at treating gay clients. *The Chronicle of Higher Education.* Retrieved from http://chronicle.com/article/Judge-Upholds-Dismissal-of/123704/

Schmidt, P. (2010, July 22). Augusta State U. is accused of requiring a counseling student to accept homosexuality. *The Chronicle of Higher Education.* Retrieved from http://chronicle.com/article/Augusta-State-U-Is-Accused-of/123650/


## PSYCHOLOGY OF RELIGION

**Description.** The psychology of religion is the study of religious traditions and practices and people's beliefs through the lenses of psychological approaches and interpretation. The psychological study of religion concerns itself with three primary tasks:

- defining the terms, observances, rituals, and individual experiences related to religion, beginning with the very word *religion* itself
- explaining from a psychological perspective why religion and its related observances and experiences came to prominence in society
- describing the positive and negative outcomes of religious practices on individuals and the community and culture at large (Wulff, 2010).

**Confusion of Terms.** A primary concern in the psychology of religion is the difficulty defining the term *religion* and differentiating it from the term *spirituality* (Schlehofer, Omoto, & Adelman, 2008). Part of the problem includes the way the term *religion* has changed in its definition and practice over the course of centuries (Smith, 1963). In recent years, the term *spirituality* has risen to prominence to describe people's experience in light of a postmodern culture. Therefore, the need to develop and use objective measures to determine empirical validation of these religious phenomena cannot be underestimated (Hill, 2005).

**Early Proponents.** William James, known as the father of psychology, is one of many writers in the field to describe the extent to which religion can help people function more effectively throughout life because of the security and confidence it provides. Sigmund Freud (1927/1961) also saw religion as a place of security and comfort for believers. Freud's value-laden theoretical approach, however, used terminology such as *regression* and *dependence* to negatively characterize a believer's relationship with God.

Carl Jung had more appreciation of religion than did Freud. He put more weight on the individual experience of religious symbols and believed a psychologist could not resolve the issue of God (Jung, 1969). Alfred Adler theorized that people primarily seek to overcome a sense of inferiority. He saw religion as a way of people overcoming their inferiority by desiring to become unified with a more superior, perfect God. In *The Individual and His Religion* (1950), Gordon Allport described how people use their religion in both mature and immature ways. Erich Fromm, in his work *Psychoanalysis and Religion* (1950), wrote a response to Freud's theories in an attempt to explain that religious devotion had less to do with a sexual motivation than with a motivation to remain close to a stable and protective parental figure.

**Contemporary Proponents.** Researchers such as Allen Bergin, Robert Emmons, and James Hillman are key contemporary contributors to the psychology of religion. Kenneth Pargament (1997) has also been a key researcher in the past few years on developing measures to study religious coping strategies. In conjunction with Pargament, attachment theorists have recently taken John Bowlby's approach to describe God as an attachment figure. Lee Kirkpatrick (1992, 1999) first conceptualized religion as an attachment process; later studies by Kirkpatrick and another researcher named Pehr Granqvist (2005) have supported the idea of God as an attachment figure. Since these findings, Richard Beck and Angie McDonald (2004) developed the Attachment to God Inventory to empirically document the way one relates to God.

The major studies presently taking place in the psychology of religion primarily involve religious coping strategies (Pargament, 1997) and God attachment (Kirkpatrick, 1992; Granqvist, 2005). In recent studies in the psychology of religion, researchers have found that in times of distress, people of faith seek proximity to God in ways similar to those in which an infant seeks closeness to the caregiver (Kirkpatrick, 1999). Kirkpatrick argues that even the imagery and language used in the Judeo-Christian faith is representative of attachment relationships. Coping with distress in life is much easier when Christians speak of Jesus being by our side, holding our hand, or holding us in his arms (Kirkpatrick & Shaver, 1990, p. 319).

Prayer is a second way people turn to God (Spilka, Hood, Hunsberger, & Gorsuch, 2003). Research supports the claim that people seek God as a safe haven during times of stress (Granqvist, 2005). Other studies have shown that higher religious commitment and intrinsic religious orientation are positively correlated with more active problem-solving skills (Pargament, Steele, & Tyler, 1979), a sense of internal locus of control (Kahoe, 1974; Strickland & Shaffer, 1971), a sense of personal competence (Ventis, 1995), and a more optimistic and hopeful outlook on the future (Myers, 1992). As a whole, attachment to God seems to increase a person's ability to handle both present and future challenges (Sim & Loh, 2003).

Joshua Straub

## REFERENCES

Allport, G. (1950). *The Individual and His Religion.* New York, NY: MacMillan.

Beck, R., & McDonald, A. (2004). Attachment to God: The attachment to God inventory, tests of working model correspondence, and an exploration of faith group differences. *Journal of Psychology and Theology, 32,* 92-103.

Emmons, Robert A. (1999). *The Psychology of Ultimate Concerns: Motivation and Spirituality in Personality.* New York, NY: Guilford.

Freud, S. (1927/1961). *The Future of an Illusion* (J. Strachey, Trans.). New York, NY: Norton.

Fromm, E. (1950). *Psychoanalysis and Religion.* New Haven, CT: Yale University Press.

Granqvist, P. (2005). Building a bridge between attachment and religious coping: Tests of moderators and mediators. *Mental Health, Religion & Culture, 8*(1), 35-47.

Hill, P. C. (2005). Measurement in the psychology of religion and spirituality: Current status and evaluation. In R. F. Paloutzian & C. L. Park (Eds.), *Handbook of the Psychology of Religion and Spirituality.* New York, NY: Guilford Press.

Jung, C. G. (1969). *On the Nature of the Psyche.* Princeton, NJ: Princeton University Press.

Jung, C. G., Hull, R. F., & Adler, G. (1969). *On the Nature of the Psyche* (C.W.8, Aphorisms 362, 420). Princeton, NJ: Princeton University Press.

Kahoe, R. D. (1974). Personality and achievement correlates of intrinsic and extrinsic religious orientations. *Journal of Personality and Social Psychology, 29,* 812-818.

Kirkpatrick, L. A. (1992). An attachment-theoretical approach to the psychology of religion. *International Journal for the Psychology of Religion, 2*(1), 3-28.

Kirkpatrick, L. A. (1999). Toward an evolutionary psychology of religion and personality. *Journal of Personality, 67,* 921-952.

Kirkpatrick, L. A., & Shaver, P. R. (1990). Attachment theory and religion: Childhood attachments, religious beliefs, and conversion. *Journal for the Scientific Study of Religion, 29,* 315-334.

Myers, D. G. (1992). *The Pursuit of Happiness.* New York, NY: Morrow.

Pargament, K. I. (1997). *The Psychology of Religion and Coping: Theory, Research, Practice.* New York, NY: Guilford Press.

Pargament, K. I., Steele, R. E., & Tyler, F. B. (1979). Religious participation, religious motivation, and individual psychosocial competence. *Journal for Scientific Study of Religion, 18,* 412-419.

Schlehofer, M. M., Omoto, A. M., & Adelman, J. R. (2008). How do "religion" and "spirituality" differ? Lay definitions among older adults. *Journal for the Scientific Study of Religion, 47,* 411-425.

Sim, T. N., & Loh, B. S. M. (2003). Attachment to God: Measurement and dynamics. *Journal of Social and Personal Relationships, 20,* 373-389.

Smith, W. C. (1963). *The Meaning and End of Religion: A New Approach to the Religious Traditions of Mankind.* New York, NY: Macmillan.

Spilka, B., Hood, R. W., Jr., Hunsberger, B., & Gorsuch, R. (2003). *The Psychology of Religion: An Empirical Approach* (3rd ed.). New York, NY: Guilford Press.

Strickland, B. R, & Shaffer, S. (1971). I-E, I-E, and F. *Journal for the Scientific Study of Religion, 10,* 366-369.

Ventis, W. L. (1995). The relationships between religion and mental health. *Journal of Social Issues, 51,* (2), 33-48.

Wulff, D. M. (2010). Psychology of religion. In D. A. Leeming, K. Madden, & S. Marian (Eds.), *Encyclopedia of Psychology and Religion* (pp. 732-735). New York, NY: Springer.

## SPIRITUALITY IN COUNSELING

Currently, *spirituality* is vying for recognition as the "fifth force" in counseling. Until recently, however, spirituality was neglected as a legitimate domain of client inquiry in professional counseling. This rapid transition from outcast to important treatment consideration has caught some clinicians unaware. We need a clear definition of Christian spirituality, information to contrast the religiosity of the public and of mental-health professionals, and an understanding of the ethical and empirical support for the inclusion of spirituality in counseling.

**Spirituality Defined.** The counseling literature continues to debate the specific definition of spirituality, often separating spirituality and religion as constructs (Aten & Leach, 2009). For Christians, however, these concepts are intertwined. Christian spirituality focuses on cultivating an intimate relationship with Jesus Christ that progressively transforms one's values, sense of purpose, beliefs, and lifestyle in the context of a faith community.

**Contrasts in Faith Characteristics.** Gallup polls consistently find more than 90% of U.S. citizens believe there is a God, more than 80% try to live according to their faith, and about 85% self-identify as Christians. These percentages suggest that the majority of clients coming to therapy will have a spiritual perspective.

The statistics for mental-health professionals differ substantially. For example, Delaney, Miller, and Bosonó (2007) found that only 46% of clinical psychologists identified themselves as Christian, 38% endorsed other religions, and 16% stated they were agnostic, atheists, or had no religious faith. Such contrasting views highlight the complexity of ethically incorporating spirituality in therapy.

**Ethical Support for Spirituality in Counseling.** These statistical differences and the historical tendencies to pathologize religion in early psychology led theorists (e.g., Freud, Skinner, etc.) to a "don't ask, don't tell" policy in previous decades regarding a client's faith. Increasingly, however, religion and spirituality have become recognized as important aspects of a client's culture. Accordingly, the ethics codes of all professional mental-health organizations now include religion and spirituality as important components of culturally sensitive treatment.

**Empirical Support for Spirituality in Counseling.** Numerous studies indicate spirituality can positively impact a person's physical and mental health (Koenig, 2004). For example, church involvement can provide critical social support that decreases loneliness. Devotional meditation has been helpful in treating hypertension, cardiac conditions, and anxiety.

Research has also suggested that at times spirituality can lead to harmful effects on a client's health. For instance, people who use spirituality more extrinsically (for self-focused reasons, such as inclusion in the right social circles, etc.) appear more vulnerable to a variety of mental-health problems.

Finally, clients who are deeply committed to their faith appear to prefer clinicians who can incorporate prayer, Scripture, and other faith resources in therapy (Wade, Worthington, & Vogel, 2007). They also expect the therapist to bring up the subject of prayer in therapy rather than having to bring it up themselves (Weld & Eriksen, 2007).

**Spiritual Assessment and Interventions in Counseling.** The cited empirical evidence supports including faith in treatment; however, therapists who misjudge a client's spirituality or impose their values on clients jeopardize the therapeutic relationship. Consequently, careful assessment and informed consent are needed before incorporating spirituality in therapy. Such assessment can begin with two simple questions: "Are spiritual resources important in your coping?" If the answer is yes, the second question is appropriate. "Would you like to discuss them in treatment when relevant?" (Richards & Bergin, 2005). Further assessment might involve exploring childhood experiences of religion, conversion, the role of prayer and Scripture in the client's life, positive and negative experiences of church, spiritual struggles, and disengagement from faith-related activities (Pargament, 2007).

A wide variety of spiritual interventions exist for appropriately religious clients. These include prayer, discussions of Scripture themes, Scripture study, devotional meditation, forgiveness, therapist spiritual self-disclosure, confrontation of sin, values exploration, church involvement, encouragement of confession, spiritual books and websites, spiritual direction, and pastoral consultation and referral (Richards & Bergin, 2005). As with other interventions, counselors should evaluate their competency and seek additional training and consultation when necessary.

**Training.** Many clinicians graduated from programs that did not include spirituality as a key instructional component; therefore, they need additional training. A wide variety of Christian spiritual formation, spiritual direction, and Christian counseling organizations exist to provide such training. For example, the American Association of Christian Counselors offers conferences, webinars, and has certificate training programs in biblical counseling, addiction and recovery, stress and trauma, etc.

**Conclusion.** The characteristics of the U.S. population, the ethical mandate for culturally sensitive treatment, and empirical findings on the role of faith in mental health justify the inclusion of spirituality in counseling. If careful assessment and informed consent procedures are followed, therapists have a wide variety of spiritual interventions to consider. Proper training should be sought for using these strategies. Truly, spirituality should be considered the fifth force in counseling and psychotherapy.

**Fernando Garzon**

### REFERENCES

Aten, J. D., & Leach, M. M. (Eds.). (2009). *Spirituality and the Therapeutic Process: A Comprehensive Resource from Intake to Termination.* Washington, DC: American Psychological Association.

Delaney, H. D., Miller, W. R., & Bisonó, A. M. (2007). Religiosity and spirituality among psychologists: A survey of clinician members of the American psychological Association. *Professional Psychology: Research & Practice, 38*(5), 538-546.

Koenig, H. G. (2004). Religion, spirituality, and medicine: Research findings and implications for clinical practice. *Southern Medical Journal, 97,* 1194-1200.

Pargament, K. I. (2007). *Spiritually Integrated Psychotherapy: Understanding and Addressing the Sacred.* New York: Guilford Press.

Richards, P. S., & Bergin, A. E. (2005). *A Spiritual Strategy for Counseling and Psychotherapy.* Washington, DC: American Psychological Association.

Wade, N., Worthington, E. L., Jr., & Vogel, D. (2007). Effectiveness of religiously tailored interventions in Christian therapy. *Pychotherapy Research, 17,* 91-105.

Weld, C. & Eriksen, K. (2007). Christian clients' preferences regarding prayer as a counseling intervention. *Journal of Psychology and Theology, 35*(4) 328-341.

## CHRISTIAN PSYCHOLOGY

All sciences are conducted within and guided by a worldview, a set of foundational assumptions regarding reality (Naugle, 2002). Psychology is the science of the immaterial aspect of individual human beings. Among its activities are research, theory building, education and publication (the dissemination of its findings and conclusions), and counseling and psychotherapy.

Currently, the dominant model of psychology in the West is called *modern* psychology, and it arose in the late 1800s. This version was patterned on the natural sciences (physics and chemistry) and based on the worldview of *naturalism,* so it restricts itself to publicly verifiable empirical descriptions and theoretical statements about human beings that are supposedly devoid of beliefs regarding the nature of human beings, including what humans should be. As a result, it does not permit any reference to supernatural beings (such as God) or ethical values (such as righteousness or sin). Over the past 140 years, modern psychology has developed an extremely rich and varied literature describing human beings. However, in keeping with its underlying naturalistic worldview, it is thoroughly secular.

By contrast, *Christian* psychology is based on and shaped by a Christian worldview. Like modern psychology, it is interested in empirical descriptions and theoretical statements, but in keeping with a Christian worldview, it also utilizes biblical and theological teaching and Christian philosophical reflection on human beings. As a result, a Christian psychology includes statements about human beings that refer to God, sin, and salvation (see Charry, 2010; Evans, 1990; Johnson, 2007; Roberts & Talbot, 1997).

Given Christianity's broader sources of psychological knowledge, some of the distinctives of Christian psychology include the concept of the image of God and the belief that it is humanity's most important psychological characteristic, the ultimate loves (and objects of worship) of humans, uniquely Christian motivation, the profound alienation of humans from their Creator and each other due to sin, the nature and effects of original sin, the development of sins and vices, the nature of salvation (and its soul-healing benefits), stages of Christian spiritual development, the indwelling of the Holy Spirit in the Christian, the causal role of God in human good and especially in the Christian life, Christian self-representations (including the old self and new self), the nature of human personhood and Christian maturity, uniquely Christian virtues (including faith, hope, humility, and agape love) and uniquely Christian understandings of human strengths (a Christian positive psychology), the relation between the body/brain and the soul, ethical and spiritual psychopathology, distinctive means of counseling and psychotherapy that make use of salvation in Christ (including healing prayer and utilization of the cross of Christ), and unique perspectives on social dynamics and relationships (such as the nature of love and spiritual communion). There is a tremendous need to do psychological research and build theories in such areas (Roberts and Watson, 2010).

At the same time, Christians do not need to redo work that non-Christians have already done well (Kuyper, 1898, p. 159). Also, in many areas of psychology, one's worldview makes little difference on one's observations and theoretical formulations (for example, in neuropsychology, sensation and perception, animal learning, and cognition). In such areas, Christians will be able to incorporate the findings of non-Christians and contribute to mainstream psychology without much difficulty. Christian psychology is more likely to differ from psychologies based on other worldviews in areas that have greater human significance and existential import, such as personality theory, distinctly human motivation, psychopathology, counseling and psychotherapy, and social psychology. Nonetheless, even in these areas, Christians will usually benefit greatly from reading well-done non-Christian psychology, confident that God enables all humans to understand his creation scientifically through what is called *common grace* or *creation grace*. However, because modern psychology is formulated according to secular standards of knowledge, such interpretive work may be more difficult than the term *integration* implies. From a Christian standpoint, modern psychology is less distorted by what it asserts than by what it leaves out, and the distortions that result from leaving God and Christian teachings out of psychological theory are difficult to assess without a deep and detailed familiarity with the relevant teachings of the Christian faith. To cite one such hole in modern social psychology, attribution theory studies humans' beliefs about what causes human behavior (like success on a test). Modern psychology has focused exclusively on natural causes, such as personal ability and effort, other people, or unique circumstances, but it does not consider the possibility of God's involvement.

As a result, careful Christian reading of non-Christian psychology texts in more worldview-dependent areas might be more like translation than integration (Johnson, 2007; MacIntyre, 1988). Good Christian translation is a complex interpretive task, involving a faithful rendering of the truths of a non-Christian text into Christian discourse, and this requires an expert knowledge of both language systems and a personal commitment to the Christian way of life (Coe and Hall, 2010).

Some might worry that Christian psychology will result in a Christian intellectual ghetto that would marginalize Christians in the field. However, Christian psychologists are committed to collaboration with other psychologists on research, theory building, and practice in areas where worldview differences are not very influential. Moreover, as modern psychologists become more aware of modern psychology's antitheistic bias (Slife and Reber, 2009), it will become increasingly possible for Christians to make a distinctive impact on contemporary psychology *as Christians*—for example, by getting articles published in mainstream journals on Christian theories of the self, motivation, and counseling techniques. Nonetheless, the development of distinctively Christian psychological theory, research, and practice for the Christian community will be of primary importance. The Society for Christian Psychology, a division of the AACC, was established in 2003 to advance just such an agenda (visit www.Christianpsych.org).

**Eric L. Johnson**

## REFERENCES


Calvin, J. (1960). *Institutes of the Christian Religion*. (F. L. Battles, Trans.). Philadelphia, PA: Westminster.

Charry, E. (2010). *God and the Art of Happiness*. Grand Rapids, MI: Eerdmans.

Coe, J. H., & Hall, T. W. (2010). *Psychology in the Spirit: Contours of a Transformational Psychology*. Downers Grove, IL: InterVarsity.

Evans, C. S. (1990). *Søren Kierkegaard's Christian Psychology*. Grand Rapids, MI: Baker.

Johnson, E. L. (2007). *Foundations for Soul Care: A Christian Psychology Proposal*. Downers Grove, IL: InterVarsity.

Kuyper, A. (1898). *Encyclopedia of Sacred Theology: Its Principles*. New York, NY: Scribner.

MacIntyre, A. (1988). *Whose Justice? Which Rationality?* South Bend, IN: University of Notre Dame Press.

Naugle, D. K. (2002). *Worldview: The History of a Concept*. Grand Rapids, MI: Eerdmans.

Roberts, R. C., & Talbot, M. R. (1997). *Limning the Psyche: Explorations in a Christian Psychology*. Grand Rapids, MI: Eerdmans.

Roberts, R. C., & Watson, P. J. (2010). A Christian psychology view. In E. L. Johnson (Ed.). *Psychology and Christianity: Five Views*. Downers Grove, IL: InterVarsity Press.

Slife, B. D., & Reber, J. S. (2009). Is there a pervasive bias against theism in psychology? *Journal of Theoretical and Philosophical Psychology, 29*(2), 1-15.


## CHRISTIAN COUNSELING EFFICACY

**Description.** Religious people often prefer approaches to their psychological healing that are explicitly tailored to their beliefs and values (Aten, McMinn, and Worthington, 2011; Worthington, Kurusu, McCullough, & Sandage, 1996). The Christian Scriptures do not explicitly discuss psychotherapy. Likewise, psychological science is limited in the extent to which it can address theological or moral issues. In recent years, there have been numerous attempts to develop counseling treatments that fit within a Christian worldview. A few recent studies evaluate the efficacy of Christian counseling.

**History.** Concern over treatment effectiveness intensified when managed mental-health care took hold in the late 1980s. Mental-health costs had gotten out of hand. For example, the hourly rate for psychotherapy was more than $100. (Adjusted for inflation, this would correspond to approximately $200 today.) Research also showed that most improvement occurred within the first seven sessions, and additional sessions of psychotherapy suffered diminishing, marginal returns (Howard, Kopta, Krause, and Orlinsky, 1986). Consequently, managed care companies often decided to pay for brief treatments with demonstrated effectiveness. Christian counselors still operate under this pressure to show that their treatments are effective.

**Assessment.** Treatment effectiveness is usually assessed by a clinical trial. Most common is the randomized clinical trial (RCT), in which participants are randomly assigned to a specific treatment, control, or alternative condition. Although the RCT is the gold standard, this type of research design has limitations. For example, clinical trials sometimes recruit participants who differ from real clients who seek treatment. For example, individuals paid to participate in a study may differ from individuals who would pay to attend counseling at a private practice. Also, research-based treatments sometimes diverge from psychotherapy that occurs naturally in real-life settings. For example, RCTs often rely on treatment manuals that guide what the therapist does, which may stifle some of the spontaneity that occurs in other settings.

Even the ideal RCT (such as one that uses real clients and counselors) cannot provide utterly trustworthy results. Every study, no matter how rigorous, has many biases and limitations. Qualitative literature reviews investigate patterns found within outcome research. For example, Hook et al. (2010) detailed which Christian-accommodated treatments were effective in two or more independent labs and were therefore empirically supported treatments (ESTs). Even better, meta-analytic reviews quantitatively summarize studies by converting results from each study to a common metric (an *effect size*) and aggregating across studies.

A meta-analysis was recently conducted on religiously accommodated treatments (Worthington, Hook, Davis, & McDaniel, 2011). Generally, the results showed that when theoreticians or counselors have adapted religious treatments, clients have reduced psychological symptoms, and the effects are at least as strong as with secular treatments. Religiously accommodated treatments have produced more positive spiritual changes. The most consistently effective psychotherapies or couple treatments have been Christian-oriented cognitive and cognitive-behavioral therapies (which are ESTs) and forgiveness therapies based on Worthington's REACH forgiveness model (an EST). Christian PREP and the hope-focused approach to enrichment have been found to be efficacious, and both have been designated ESTs.

**Biblical and Spiritual Issues.** A word of caution is warranted. Counseling is a modern invention. It is not something that Scripture even mentions. In fact, there was no parallel to professional counseling—and perhaps not even pastoral counseling—in the history of the church prior to 1900. Thus, sincere and thoughtful Christians disagree about its scriptural support. Some Christians denigrate the value of psychological science to inform counseling theories, methods, or approaches. Others are extremely cautious to say that anything can be learned from the Bible to apply to modern counseling. We think humility is warranted (see Worthington, 2010). Theology is a human enterprise, susceptible to all the distortion of sin and human nature. Likewise, psychological science cannot address issues of right and wrong. That said, as Christian counselors, we can evaluate the fruits of our work with psychological science.

Everett L. Worthington Jr.
Don E. Davis
Joshua N. Hook

## REFERENCES


Aten, J., McMinn, M. R., & Worthington, E. L., Jr. (Eds.). (2011). *Spiritually Oriented Interventions for Counseling and Psychotherapy*. Washington, DC: American Psychological Association.

Hook, J. N., Worthington, E. L., Jr., Davis, D. E., Gartner, A. L., Jennings, J., & Hook, J. P. (2010). Empirically supported religious and spiritual therapies. *Journal of Clinical Psychology, 1*, 46-72.

Howard, K. I., Kopta, S. M., Krause, M. S., & Orlinsky, D. E. (1986). The dose-effect relationship in psychotherapy. *American Psychologist, 41*, 159-164.

Worthington, E. L., Jr. (2010). *Coming to Peace with Psychology: What Christians Can Learn from Psychological Science*. Downers Grove, IL: InterVarsity Press.

Worthington, E. L., Jr., Hook, J. N., Davis, D. E., & McDaniel, M. (2011). Religion and spirituality. *Journal of Clinical Psychology: In Session, 67*(4), 204-214.

Worthington, E. L., Jr., Kurusu, T. A., McCullough, M. E., & Sandage, S. J. (1996). Empirical research on religion and psychotherapeutic processes and outcomes: A 10-year review and research prospectus. *Psychological Bulletin, 199*, 448-487.

# THEOLOGICAL FOUNDATIONS

## DOCTRINE OF GOD

**Description.** The knowledge of God is drawn from a variety of sources, including the created order, which bears witness to the Creator's glory and handiwork. We reflect on this in its macroscopic display of God's immensity and microscopically in relation to the intricate order, design, and balance that point to a wise and purposeful Creator. This knowledge in turn assures us that the universe and all that is in it is rational, orderly, and predictable. That is to say, we can do science. The Christian doctrine of God draws on this knowledge and its epistemic implications, but it also moves beyond it to include God's self-revelation in the Bible.

God is the supreme subject of the Bible as well as its supreme object, before whom all creation bows. Scripture begins with the words "In the beginning God." Here there is no prolegomenon, no apologetic. It is simply affirmed. The apostle John captures the import of this at the beginning of his Gospel, where, contrary to many translations, the definite article is not used. The apostle writes, "In [any] beginning [one may contemplate] was the Word, and the Word was with God, and the Word was God."

Concerning this God, Scripture has much to say. God can be known. "We know also that the Son of God has come and has given us understanding, so that we may know him who is true. And we are in him who is true by being in his Son Jesus Christ. He is the true God and eternal life" (1 Jn. 5:20). Jesus spoke about the nature of God: "God is spirit, and his worshipers must worship in the Spirit and in truth" (Jn. 4:24). Paul adds to our understanding of God, "who alone is immortal and who lives in unapproachable light, whom no one has seen or can see" (1 Tim. 6:16).

Yet this transcendent God is also personal. "Do we not all have one Father? Did not one God create us?" (Mal. 2:10). Jesus answered the doubts of one of his disciples by asking, "Don't you not know me, Philip, even after I have been among you such a long time? Anyone who has seen me has seen the Father. How can you say, 'Show us the Father'?" (Jn. 14:9).

God is infinite and unchanging. "Great is our Lord and mighty in power; his understanding has no limit" (Ps. 147:5). In Exodus, we read these piercing questions: "Who among the gods is like you, Lord? Who is like you—majestic in holiness, awesome in glory, working wonders?" (Ex. 15:11). Through Malachi, God explained, "I the Lord do not change. So you, the descendants of Jacob, are not destroyed" (Mal. 3:6).

The God of the Bible is also a Trinity. "Therefore go and make disciples of all nations, baptizing them in the name of the Father and of the Son and of the Holy Spirit" (Mt. 28:19). "May the grace of the Lord Jesus Christ, and the love of God, and the fellowship of the Holy Spirit be with you all" (2 Cor. 13:14). The exact nature of the Trinity remains a mystery, but recent scholarship has given special attention to the Trinity as it bears on the relationality of God.

**Application.**

> Belief in God...comes not merely from a perceived need to explain the existence of the cosmos, nor merely from a need to have a grounding of morality in an ultimate arbiter of what is right. It stems as well from a desire to understand who we are and why we are here. It arises from a need for a friend in times of trouble, a friend who not only sympathizes with our plight but is able to do something to change it. It arises from a need for someone with knowledge and wisdom beyond even the collective wisdom of all humanity to guide us as we face the changing circumstances of life. But most of all, belief in God issues from the fact that there is a God and he has revealed himself to mankind (Feinberg, 2001, p. 37).

Scripture reveals the triune God as the answer to humanity's deepest needs. Those who will experience the greatest fulfillment in this life will be those who embrace with the command, "Love the Lord your God with all your heart and with all your soul and all your strength" (Dt. 6:5), and who, with God's grace, emulate his character as his image-bearers. Among the so-called "communicable attributes" of God, Scripture shows that God is all-knowing (Heb. 4:13), wise (Ps. 104:24; Dan. 2:20-21), good (Ps. 86:5; 118:29), loving (Jn. 3:16; 1 Jn. 4:8), gracious (Neh. 9:17; Rom. 3:24), merciful (Rom. 9:18; Eph. 2:4-5), longsuffering (Num. 14:18; Rom. 2:4), holy, righteous, and true (Ex. 15:11; Num. 23:19; Ps. 89:14; 2 Tim. 2:13).

Living in rebellion against God, or worse, acting as if God did not exist, distorts and perverts people's perception of existence. In our secular milieu, the idea that life has meaning, purpose, and significance has been lost, and in their place are the poor counterfeits of ambition, success, and material accumulation. But these pursuits distort meaning and destroy relationships. When we choose to reject God's plan for our lives, we abandon our destiny as well. All hope is lost. The Christian God is both the source and the end of our existence.

Shults (2005, p. 91) styles this "the promising presence of God." He suggests three themes from the Hebrew Bible that are especially relevant. "First, the name of God revealed to Moses (Exod. 3:14) evokes a leaning into the future of this one who calls Israel to freedom.... Second, the idea of the 'kingdom of God' runs throughout Israel's religious experience, and is taken up in the message of Jesus and the apostles" (Shults, p. 92). Even as we were taught to pray, "Thy kingdom come," his kingdom in contrast to earthly kingdoms breaks into our present from the future, enabling us to share now in his kingdom yet to be realized. Third, the experience of the "face of God also bears on the idea of the divine presence. The longing for the divine countenance which brings grace and peace (Num. 6:24-26)" (Shults; see also Shults and Sandage, 2003). It is in this "promising presence" that real healing comes—and with it, freedom and hope.

**Daniel R. Mitchell**

## REFERENCES


Charry, E. T. (2001). Theology after psychology. In M. R. McMinn & T. R. Phillips (Eds.), *Care for the Soul.* Downers Grove, IL: InterVarsity Press.

Collins, G. (1993). *The Biblical Basis of Christian Counseling for People Helpers.* Colorado Springs, CO: Navpress.

Feinberg, J. S. (2001). *No One Like Him.* Wheaton, IL: Crossway Books.

Lewis, G. R., & Demarest, B. A. (1987). *Integrative Theology.* Grand Rapids, MI: Zondervan.

Shults, F. L. (2005). *Reforming the Doctrine of God.* Grand Rapids, MI: Eerdmans.

Shults, F. L., & Sandage, S. J. (2003). *The Faces of Forgiveness.* Grand Rapids, MI: Baker.


## DOCTRINE OF CHRIST

**Description.** No one ever provoked more questions about himself than Jesus Christ. His own disciples struggled to understand him, yet they knew he was no ordinary man. They saw and heard too much to believe any less. During his three-year public ministry, he was the topic of conversation everywhere in Israel. Who is he? Where did he come from? How does he do those miracles?

> When Jesus came to the region of Caesarea Philippi, he asked his disciples, "Who do people say the Son of Man is?"
>
> They replied, "Some say John the Baptist, others say Elijah, and still others, Jeremiah or one of the prophets."
>
> "But what about you?" he asked. "Who do you say I am?"
>
> Simon Peter answered, "You are the Messiah, the Son of the living God."
>
> Jesus replied, "Blessed are you, Simon son of Jonah, for this was not revealed to you by flesh and blood, but my Father in heaven" (Mt. 16:13-17).

Jesus had asked the most important question in life, and Peter's confession secured for him and all who join with him a relationship with Christ that lasts for time and eternity. J. I. Packer comments on the significance of our relationship with Christ when he says, "The essence of Christianity is neither beliefs nor behavior patterns. It is the reality of communion here and now with Christianity's living founder, the mediator, Jesus Christ" (Packer, 1995, p. 60). The theology of Christ—known as *Christology*—considers his miraculous birth, his person, his words and works, his death and the atonement, his resurrection, his ascension, his high priestly ministry of intercession, and his second coming to destroy Satan and his evil minions (Collins, 1993; Johnson, 2007; Stott, 1986).

**The Incarnation.** There is only one God (Dt. 6:4; Mk. 12:29), but he exists in three persons—the Father, Son, and Holy Spirit. Jesus Christ is the Son of God, the exact representation of the Father (Heb. 1:3), eternally existing with God (Jn. 8:58), and he asserted that whoever had seen him had seen the Father (Jn. 14:9). In his Incarnation (literally, his *in-flesh-ment*) he took on human flesh and was born as a man, but he did not give up his divine nature to do so. He was born miraculously of the virgin Mary, who was impregnated by the Holy Spirit. From his conception and birth to his death and resurrection, Jesus was both true God and true man.

The humanity of Jesus meant that he experienced life on this earth as we do. He had a human body that knew hunger and thirst (Jn. 19:28), fatigue and exhaustion (Jn. 4:6), loneliness and pain, anger and the full range of human feelings (Mk. 3:5; Jn. 12:27), suffering, and a horrible death (Jn. 19:30; Heb. 2:9). He cared for his mother and family (Jn. 19:27), paid taxes (Mt. 17:24-25), and faced victoriously the temptations that we all struggle with (Heb. 4:15). The only difference is this: Jesus experienced it all without sin (2 Cor. 5:21; 1 John 3:5).

**The Work of Redeeming Humanity.** John 3:16, possibly the most familiar verse in all of the Scriptures, sums up the nature and work of Christ: "God so loved the world that he gave his one and only Son, that whoever believes in him shall not perish but have eternal life." This work of substitutionary atonement (or payment, redemption, or sacrifice) for the sins of mankind was finished by Christ himself in his death and resurrection. Two realities made this atonement necessary. First, mankind was so lost in sin and depravity that we could do nothing to save ourselves (that is still the case). Second, God's perfect holiness demanded a judicial remedy for sin—someone has to pay, and it is either the sinner who pays, or Christ, who took our place and paid the deadly penalty. British theologian John Stott (1986, p. 159) may have said it best: "In order to save us in such a way as to satisfy himself, God through Christ substituted himself for us. Divine love triumphed over divine wrath by divine self-sacrifice."

It is the most amazing story of all history—God himself coming in the flesh to willingly take on the penalty for the sins of all mankind for all time because he loves us beyond measure. Beginning with the prophetic foretelling of his life and purpose in the Old Testament, continuing through his birth and three years of ministry, and culminating in his death, resurrection, and ascension, there is no story on this planet that compares to the story of Jesus. Christian counselors are empowered in their interaction with wounded and broken people with a story of redemption and restoration that is designed to bring hope where there is despair and life where once only death and darkness existed.

The sinner who believes on the Lord Jesus Christ is born anew from above through the work of the Holy Spirit. That believing sinner is then empowered by that same Spirit, who works through the Scriptures and a community of believers to engage in a process of transformation that results in Christ being made visible through the life and witness of the redeemed sinner.

On the journey toward Christlikeness, disciples are encouraged by two powerful truths found in the Scriptures. First, Jesus Christ, who has ascended to the right hand of the Father, makes intercession for us from his position of honor. Better than that, he has established a throne of grace and bids us come boldly to him and present our every need in order that we might have his help in our times of need (Heb. 4:14-16). What an encouragement to the anxious and depressed who come to us for help. Second, Jesus Christ is coming again. He is coming in power to establish his kingdom on a restored earth and to put down evil in all of its forms. Our destiny includes no tears or crying (Rev. 19–22). What a powerful message of hope he has given to all of us living in this profoundly fallen place.

**Application.** The parable of the prodigal son best captures the heart of God the Father and the Lord Jesus Christ. In this parable we witness the grand cycle of humanity's fall, redemption, and restoration, which is central to the task of Christian counseling. The self-absorbed younger brother had no appreciation of his life and the love of his wealthy father. He demanded and received, with his father's sadness, his inheritance, which he proceeded to squander on riotous living. Coming to his senses in the pigsty, he reasoned that even the lowest employee of his father received three square meals a day, so he began his journey home. Seeing him from far away, the father was elated by his son's return and threw a huge party to celebrate. As an example of our heavenly Father, the father in the story graciously and extravagantly welcomed his wayward son home and reinstated him as his beloved son.

**Imitating Christ.** The highest goal in life, to imitate Christ, requires us to walk, think, pray, entreat, speak, love, believe...to act in every way as Jesus did. This is the legitimate metagoal of Christian counseling. This cannot be achieved without spiritual maturity, and spiritual maturity in turn cannot be achieved without a deep understanding and persistent application of the truths and virtues of the Bible (Clinton, Hindson, & Ohlschlager, 2001).

All we know, all we understand, all we believe, and all we do about the truths of the Bible must come together into patterns of living that become habitual. These new habits must break into and replace the pattern of old, dead habits that reflect the carnal or unredeemed state of our being. Then we must follow through in word and deed. Of course, we have not been left alone in this objective of reaching maturity and achieving a life of virtuous thinking and acting. God has given us himself—the virtuous life of our master, Jesus Christ, whose Spirit enables us to accomplish this high call. He has also provided an extensive support system to aid us in our task in all facets of the church.

**Conclusion.** The doctrine of Christ makes possible the Christian counselor's ability to engage in the ministry of extending reconciliation (2 Cor. 5:18-19), which the Father so deeply desires for everyone on the planet. God's incomparable grace works internally to forgive our sins and heal our wounds, and it enables us to make peace with God and with others. As we experience his love and grace, we are set free from our own greed and self-centeredness, and we are enabled by God's Spirit to love and care for others in the same way God cares for us.

**Ron Hawkins**
**George Ohlschlager**
**Ed Hindson**

## REFERENCES

Clinton, T., Hindson, E., & Ohlschlager, G. (2001). *The Soul Care Bible*. Nashville, TN: Thomas Nelson.

Collins, G. R. (1993). *The Biblical Basis of Christian Counseling for People Helpers*. Colorado Springs, CO: NavPress.

Johnson, E. L. (2007). *Foundations for Soul Care*. Downers Grove, IL: InterVarsity Press.

Packer, J. I. (1995). *Knowing Christianity*. Wheaton, IL: Shaw.

Stott, J. R. W. (1986). *The Cross of Christ*. Downers Grove, IL: InterVarsity Press.

## DOCTRINE OF THE HOLY SPIRIT

The doctrine of the Holy Spirit, or *pneumatology*, is a vast and fascinating subject. The Holy Spirit is the third person of the triune God (Father, Son, and Holy Spirit) and has a crucial and central role in Christian counseling (see Tan, 1999; Tan, 2011, pp. 363-67). Scripture describes the Holy Spirit as the Counselor, Helper, Comforter, or Advocate (Jn. 14:16-17). Adams (1973) has pointed out that at least three persons are involved in every counseling situation: the counselor, the client, and the Holy Spirit, who is the Counselor par excellence. Christian counselors need to depend on the Spirit's presence and healing power and have a basic understanding of the ministry of the Holy Spirit.

**The Ministry of the Holy Spirit.** Scripture describes the Holy Spirit's work or ministry in three major ways: the Spirit's power and gifts, the Spirit's truth, and the Spirit's fruit (see Tan, 1999, p. 568).

*The Spirit's power and gifts.* The power of the Holy Spirit is essential in Christian life and ministry, especially in evangelism and witnessing (Acts 1:8). We are commanded to be continually filled with the Holy Spirit (Eph. 5:18) and to yield to the Spirit's control so that we are empowered by him to become more like Jesus in character and ministry, including counseling.

The Holy Spirit also sovereignly gives us spiritual gifts, or droplets of grace, to empower us to have effective ministries (see Rom. 12, 1 Cor. 12, Eph. 4, and 1 Pet. 4). Spiritual gifts that are relevant for an effective counseling ministry include exhortation or encouragement, healing, wisdom, knowledge, discerning of spirits, and mercy (see Tan, 1999, p. 568). Wagner (1994) has provided helpful definitions of 27 spiritual gifts and a questionnaire that Christians can use to discover their spiritual gifts in order to minister to others and glorify God.

*The Spirit's truth.* The Holy Spirit, as the Spirit of truth, will teach and guide us into all truth (Jn. 14:26; 16:13). Scripture, as God's Word, is inspired by the Spirit. The Spirit will therefore not contradict the truth of Scripture, properly interpreted, in counseling or any other context. The Spirit will always uphold the moral and ethical dimensions of biblical truth in the process of Christian counseling.

*The Spirit's fruit.* The fruit of the Spirit, produced by the Holy Spirit working in the heart and life of a Christian, is essentially *agape* or Christlike love and is characteristic of mature Christlikeness (Rom. 8:29). This fruit can be further described as love, joy, peace, patience, kindness, goodness, faithfulness, gentleness, and self-control (Gal. 5:22-23). Agape love is powerfully therapeutic and healing in the context of counseling ministries.

These three major aspects of the Spirit's ministry in biblical balance are central and essential in Christian life as well as in Christian counseling. Power without truth can lead to heresy. Power without love can lead to abuse. Power, used with love and biblical truth, can bring deep and lasting healing and wholeness to broken lives.

**The Work of the Holy Spirit in Counseling.** The Holy Spirit can work in a variety of ways during a counseling session, whether quietly and implicitly, overtly and explicitly, or in a combination of these (see Tan, 2011).

Explicit integration in Christian counseling deals directly and openly with religious and spiritual issues and uses spiritual and religious interventions such as prayer and Scripture with clients who give their informed consent. In this environment, the Holy Spirit can work in at least five ways (Tan, 1999).

First, the Spirit can directly help the Christian counselor discern the root issues and problems of the client by giving the counselor specific words of knowledge and wisdom. Swindoll (1994) has described such experiences as "inner promptings" or nudges of the Spirit within the pastor or Christian counselor who prayerfully depends on the guidance of the Spirit in a counseling context.

Second, the Spirit can provide spiritual direction and guidance to clients and counselors during a counseling session as they explicitly engage in prayer, discussion of Scripture, and open exploration of spiritual issues. The Spirit can also do this more quietly and implicitly.

Third, the Spirit can directly minister to a client in the counseling session with his healing grace and power. This can happen spontaneously in the Spirit's own sovereign way and time. However, the explicit use of prayer and inner-healing prayer for the healing of memories can be particularly helpful in opening up to the direct healing touch of the Spirit (see Tan, 2003).

Fourth, the Spirit can help the Christian counselor discern the presence of demonization or demonic oppression, giving the counselor the spiritual gift of discerning of spirits or distinguishing between what is human, divine, or demonic (1 Cor. 12:10). This can be especially helpful in the distinguishing between demonization and mental illness, or discerning that both may be present in the client. The Spirit can also enable the Christian counselor to pray powerful and effective prayers for deliverance and protection from the demonic (if this is appropriate and if the client has given informed consent). A referral to prayer ministry teams in a local church context may, however, be more appropriate in certain counseling situations.

Fifth, the Spirit can deepen spiritual formation into greater Christlikeness in both the client and the Christian counselor through the practice of the spiritual disciplines (including prayer, Bible study, fellowship, solitude, surrender, and service) in the power of the Holy Spirit (Tan and Gregg, 1997). Some of these disciplines can be practiced in the counseling session (especially prayer and the use of Scripture), and others can be assigned for the client to practice as homework between sessions (such as solitude, silence, and fasting). As the client and counselor practice the spiritual disciplines as means of grace and not legalistically, the Spirit can bring about transformation and spiritual growth.

**Conclusion.** The role of the Holy Spirit in Christian counseling is of paramount importance. Christian counselors require training and competence in counseling skills, but they will first and foremost prayerfully depend on the Holy Spirit in his work as the Counselor, Advocate, and Helper.

SIANG-YANG TAN

## REFERENCES


Adams, J. E. (1973). *The Christian Counselor's Manual.* Grand Rapids, MI: Baker.

Swindoll, C. R. (1994). Helping and the Holy Spirit. *Christian Counseling Today, 2*(1), 16-19.

Tan, S.-Y. (1999). Holy Spirit: Role in counseling. In D. G. Benner & P. C. Hill (Eds.), *Baker Encyclopedia of Psychology and Counseling* (2nd ed.). Grand Rapids, MI: Baker Academic.

Tan, S.-Y. (2003). Inner Healing Prayer. *Christian Counseling Today, 11*(4), 20-22.

Tan, S.-Y. (2011). *Counseling and Psychotherapy: A Christian Perspective.* Grand Rapids, MI: Baker Academic.

Tan, S.-Y., & Gregg, D. H. (1997). *Disciplines of the Holy Spirit.* Grand Rapids, MI: Zondervan.

Wagner, C. P. (1994). *Your Spiritual Gifts Can Help Your Church Grow* (Rev. ed.). Ventura, CA: Regal.


## DOCTRINE OF MAN

The doctrine of man, or anthropology, is an area of critical importance in Christian counseling. Effective Christian counseling requires an adequate understanding of anthropology generally and especially biblically.

**DEFINITION.** Anthropology is the study of human beings and their origins, bio-psycho-social characteristics, religions, and cultures. Within a biblically informed Christian worldview, anthropology focuses on humanity's origin, nature, and relationships with God, self, and others. A biblically derived model presents man as a fallen being created in the divine image and likeness of God (Collins, 1989).

**KEY ISSUES.** In this discipline, several important factors must be considered, especially for Christian counselors.

*Types of anthropology.* A distinction can be made between scientific and theological anthropology while respecting the value of both endeavors for Christian counseling. McClintock and Strong (1981) identify anthropology as a part of "scientific theology" and distinguish scientific or physiological anthropology from theological anthropology. There are legitimate differences in their purposes, emphases, and spheres of consideration. Scientific anthropology is primarily concerned with the physical dimension of humanity in the context of nature. Theological anthropology is principally concerned with the religious and psychological nature of humanity and its relation to God. Bromiley (2006) identifies various objects of biblical anthropology, including man in relation to the rest of creation, man in relation to man, and man in relation to God.

Biblical anthropology must also take into account the nature of man and his relationships prior to sin, during this age when sin is still present, and once sin and its effects are finally eradicated. Erikson makes the following observation concerning humanity: "If we investigate the Bible's depiction of humanity, we find that people today are actually in an abnormal condition. The real human is not what we now find in human society. The real human is the being that came from the hand of God, unspoiled by sin and the fall. In a very real sense, the only true human beings were Adam and Eve before the fall, and Jesus" (Erikson, 2001, p. 171).

*Man's creation and dignity.* The God of Scripture created all that exists in our world as evidence of his power and for his glory. Everything that he created, including Scripture and all creation, was good. It exists for his glory and is a revelation of his person and power. This principle is well established throughout the Bible, especially in Romans 1:20: "For since the creation of the world God's invisible qualities—his eternal power and divine nature—have been clearly seen, being understood from what has been made, so that people are without excuse."

Nowhere in all of creation is God's glory more fully revealed than in the creation of man as male and female. In a unique way, humanity as male and female is invested with majesty and dominion and is a revelation of the nature and character of God. Erikson states, "A key expression used in describing the original form of humanity is that God made humankind in his own image and likeness. This distinguished human beings from all the other creatures, for only of humans is this expression used. There has been a great amount of discussion on the subject; in fact, some would say it has been discussed too much. Actually, however, the concept is critical because the image of God is what makes us human" (Erikson, 2001, p. 171). "The precise characteristics—the human capabilities—bound up with our possession of the image of God include above all our rationality and moral nature, to which some proponents add our capacity for holiness" (Grenz, 1994, p. 169).

*Constitution of man.* The constituent parts of God's image bearers has been described, discussed, and debated for centuries. Dichotomists stress that persons are immaterial (soul and spirit) and material (body). Trichotomists hold that man is body, soul, and spirit. Interestingly, on two occasions recorded in the Gospels, Jesus used a total of four different terms when referring to individuals serving God with the entirety of their beings. Matthew 22:37 uses *heart, soul,* and *mind,* and Mark 12:30 adds the term *strength.* In 1 Thessalonians 5:23, Paul refers to spirit, soul, and body after expressing his hope that the God of peace would sanctify his readers entirely.

**The Dilemma of Man.** The dignity and value of every human is clearly evidenced by the biblical witness that we bear the image of our divine Creator. However, the dilemma of humanity is also clearly alluded to in passages like Romans 3:23 and 6:23. As humans, we still bear the image of God, but "we simply cannot come to a biblical understanding of man...if we do not come to grips with the awfulness of man in rebellion, separation and death, we are profoundly fallen" (Allen, 1984, p. 102). "The Christian counselor must be able to diagnose correctly the theological malady that is at the core of humanity's dilemma. Created upright and empowered with the imagination resident in the divine image at the core of human personality, male and female are free to dwell on what-ifs (Genesis 3:1-6; Ecclesiastes 6:9). In the service of autonomy, desire is free to wander, and because of our sinful bent, the tragic result is idolatry, rebellion, and disobedience to divine commandment. Unless we repent and turn, we will become destructive, abandon our postings, and vandalize the very *shalom* of God (Ecclesiastes 10:4)" (Hawkins, Hindson, and Clinton, 2002, p. 108).

**The Destiny of Man.** All men are now in the process of dying as a consequence of Adam's sin and our inheritance of the consequences of that rebellion. However, those who have experienced redemption through Christ are destined for heaven. Heaven is the place God has prepared for those who by faith have received his forgiveness and imputed righteousness through Jesus Christ. Jesus reminded his disciples that he was going to prepare a place for them and that where he was, they would one day be (Jn. 14:1-6). Paul reminded the Thessalonians that although Christians sorrow at the death of loved ones, we do not sorrow as those do who are outside of Christ because we have the hope of the resurrection and eternity in the presence of God (1 Thess. 4:13-18).

**Implications for Christian Counseling.** Anthropology anchored in Scripture emphasizes that all people have dignity and are to be highly valued, honored, and respected because they bear the image of their divine Creator (Ps. 8:4-6).

Biblical anthropology, while taking into account the dignity of all human beings, also recognizes the depths of human depravity as a result of sin. Thus, dealing with the effects of personal sin, sin of others, and sin in the world must be an integral part of Christian counseling. Only by way of the cross of Christ can sin's influence and effects be decisively overcome in the lives of counselors and clients alike. Because of this, the hope of redemption and the power of the Holy Spirit to transform persons must also be paramount in the counseling process. The Father takes great joy when we are transformed by the Holy Spirit's power into greater conformity to the likeness of Jesus Christ in our primary relationships.

Ron Hawkins
David E. Jenkins

## REFERENCES

Allen, R. B. (1984). *The Majesty of Man: The Dignity of Being Human.* Portland, OR: Multnomah.

Bromiley, G. W. (2006). Anthropology. In G. W. Bromiley (Ed.), *International Standard Bible Encyclopedia* (Revised ed.). Grand Rapids, MI: Eerdmans.

Clinton, T. C., & Oschlager, G. O. *Competent Christian Counseling.* Colorado Springs, CO: WaterBrook Press.

Collins, G. R. (1989). *The Rebuilding of Psychology: An Integration of Psychology and Christianity.* Wheaton, IL: Tyndale House.

Erikson, M. J. C (2001). *Introducing Christian Doctrine.* Grand Rapids, MI: Baker Academic.

Grenz, S. J. (2000). *Theology for the Community of God.* Nashville, TN: Broadman and Holman.

Hawkins, R. E., Hindson, E., & Clinton, T.C. (2002). Theological roots. In T. Clinton & G. Ohschlager (Eds.), *Competent Christian Counseling.* Colorado Springs, CO: WaterBrook Press.

McClintock, J., & Strong, J. (1981). Anthropology. In *McClintock and Strong's Cyclopedia of Biblical, Theological, and Ecclesiastical Literature.* Grand Rapids, MI: Baker Book House.

## DOCTRINE OF SALVATION

Salvation is the grand theme of the Bible. It encompasses the salvation of the human soul, deliverance from divine wrath, and the redemption of society itself. In Christian theology, the doctrine of salvation, or *soteriology*, is the full expression of God's glory, grace, and mercy to provide forgiveness, redemption, justification, and transformation to all who will accept God's gift of saving grace.

In the Old Testament, the Hebrew word *Yasa'* expresses the concept of salvation from danger, with an overtone of undeserved grace and mercy. In the New Testament, the Greek term *soteria* not only indicates deliverance and preservation from danger but also implies "wholeness" or "soundness." Thus, the biblical doctrine of salvation includes God's total provision for the deepest needs of the human condition.

**Parallel Doctrines.** The biblical doctrine of salvation is closely related to the doctrine of sin (*hamartiology*). It presumes that all human beings are sinners who have fallen short of the glory of God (Rom. 3:23). We are incapable of saving ourselves and are therefore in need of divine intervention to save us from the natural consequences of our fallen sinful nature.

The doctrine of Christ (*Christology*) is also closely related to the doctrine of salvation. Jesus Christ is presented in the Bible as the Savior, whose atoning death on the cross provides salvation to all who put their faith in the sufficiency of his sinless sacrifice on our behalf (2 Cor. 5:17-21). The cross of Christ was the climax of history. Then and there God settled the issue of our salvation. At the Place of the Skull (*Golgotha*), the sin debt was paid once for all. When Jesus died on the cross, he took the punishment we deserved. He received the full fury of God's wrath in our place.

John Stott (1986, p.167) expressed it like this: "Moved by the perfection of his holy love, God in Christ substituted himself for us sinners." A new day dawned—the day of salvation. A new hope was born—eternal life. This is the good news of the gospel: the death, burial, and resurrection of Christ. He completed all he set out to accomplish. He took our place, paid for our sins, settled the matter of our eternal destiny, and secured for us a home in heaven.

All other biblical doctrines revolve around the control theme of salvation. His triumph is our triumph. His victory is our victory. The apostle Paul said it this way: "In all these things we are more than conquerors through him who loved us" (Rom. 8:37).

**Personal Responses.** The doctrine of salvation includes the personal responses of repentance and faith, which result in our conversion and regeneration. Erickson (1985, p. 929) calls them the "subjective aspects" of the Christian experience. They result in a change in our spiritual condition and a transformation of our inward nature. Conversion views that change from the human perspective, whereas regeneration views it from God's perspective. Both include the transformative experience of the new birth (Jn. 3:3-7).

Unbelievers are called to repent and believe God's offer of personal salvation (Rom. 10:13). Biblical repentance is described in terms of "turning" (Hebrew, *shub*) and "changing one's mind" (Greek, *metanoeō*). In one of the earliest Christian sermons, the apostle Peter urges, "Repent and turn to God so that your sins may be wiped out" (Acts 3:19).

In a similar appeal, the apostle Paul urges, "Believe in the Lord Jesus and you will be saved" (Acts 16:31). *Faith* is the noun form of the verb *believe* (Greek, *pisteauō*). J. I. Packer explains that biblical faith is more than acknowledging Jesus as teacher or miracle worker, "but as God incarnate whose atoning death is the sole means of salvation" (cited in Elwell, 1984, p. 401). Saving faith rests in the work of Christ as the object of our faith. Thus, *what* we believe and in *whom* we believe determines our attitudes and behavior (Ferguson & Wright, 1988, p. 246).

**Practical Application.** The doctrine of salvation is central to the concept of Christian counseling. Calvin Linton observed, "When God's love is permitted through faith, to permeate existence, life manifests the qualities inherent in divine creation: harmony, beauty, holiness and joy" (cited in Henry, 1962, p. 200). Apart from God, humans wander in moral darkness and spiritual death. Therefore the Christian counselor accepts the limitations of human self-improvement on the part of unbelievers. We may certainly bring the light of biblical truth to the client, but we cannot bring about permanent transformation apart from the work of God in the human heart.

At the same time, Christian counselors recognize the life-changing power of the living Christ. Salvation not only changes one's eternal destiny but also his or her personal experience. Those who genuinely repent of their sins honestly face their failures and by faith in Christ find real hope for life's journey. Believers may not be perfect, but they realize they have been *forgiven*, and that sets them free to live as God intends for them to live. We have been saved by grace through faith (past) to do good works (present); thus we are at peace with God (forever).

The task of the Christian counselor includes the challenge of presenting the beauty of the gospel of salvation and its transformative power to those who need to know God personally and intimately by faith in Jesus Christ. Charles Spurgeon concluded, "We may safely lay our trouble where God has laid his help" (Cited in Lee & Hindson, 1998, p. 294). Jesus came to rescue us, save us, and transform us. In the meantime, we walk by faith and grow in grace as we continue to experience so great salvation.

**Edward E. Hindson**

## REFERENCES

Elwell, W. A. (1984). *Evangelical Dictionary of Theology.* Grand Rapids, MI: Baker.

Erickson, M. J. (1985). *Christian Theology*. Grand Rapids, MI: Baker.

Ferguson, S. & Wright, D. (1988). *New Dictionary of Theology*. Downers Grove, IL: InterVarsity Press.

Henry, C. F. H. (1962). *Basic Christian Doctrines*. New York, NY: Holt, Rinehart & Winston.

Lee, R., & Hindson, E. (1998). *No Greater Savior*. Eugene, OR: Harvest House.

Stott, J. (1986). *The Cross of Christ*. Downers Grove, IL: InterVarsity Press.

## DOCTRINE OF THE BIBLE

**Description.** Christian counselors share a great affection for the Bible and view it as the primary source for truth regarding God and all things human. Without the Scriptures, we would be left to draw information regarding God and humanity from our observation of the world, history, and human reason. The Bible provides a rich body of truth that equips the Christian counselor to engage the myriad of problems people face in our profoundly fallen world (Collins, 2007).

**God's Nature.** In the Bible we meet a God who is both sovereign Creator and grace-oriented communicator. Additionally, as we read the pages of Scripture, we are compelled to confess that the God revealed in its pages has a passion for communication. In fact, it's his nature; Jesus is the Word who became flesh. Though the God of the Bible is one, he exists in a community of the Trinity (Father, Son, and Holy Spirit), where we witness the high value placed on relational holiness. In Genesis we see this heart for connection in and with the triune Godhead in the words "Let us make man in our image." We witness the passion of Jesus the God-man for in-depth communion with the Father when he prays for all who would believe in him, "that they may be one as we are one—I in them and you in me" (Jn. 17:22-23). God's communication with humans is laced with grace, as witnessed in his quest for and question to fallen Adam when he asks, "Where are you?"

The giving of the Scriptures represents an action by God that was predictable and congruent with his nature. In addition, because the Bible is second only to the Incarnation in God's attempts to communicate truth to humans, we would be right to expect that this communication would be both inerrant and authoritative. To assure the absolute trustworthiness of the Bible, God utilized a process called *inspiration*. Paul describes the process when he writes to Timothy, "All Scripture is God-breathed" (2 Tim. 3:16). By the *inspiration* of Scripture, we mean the supernatural influence of the Holy Spirit upon the writers, who rendered in their writings an accurate record of the revelation, with the result that what they wrote was the Word of God (Erikson, 2001, p. 6).

**Application.** Professor and author J. I. Packer summarizes the responsibility of clients and counselors to the Scriptures:

> What is called for now...is the humility which bows before the Scriptures and accepts them as instruction from God. They are God preaching, God telling, God talking, God instructing, God setting before us the right way to think and speak about Him. The Scriptures are God showing us Himself: God communicating to us who He is and what He has done so that in the response of faith we may truly know Him and live our lives in fellowship with Him (Packer, 1995, p. 16).

Counselors must know the Bible. In knowing Scripture well, we are equipped to impart to others the resources they need to be set free from the idolatries and bondage that contribute to the brokenness in the human community.

Christian counselors who know the Bible well are equipped with special wisdom. Paul speaks of that wisdom when he reminds Timothy, "From infancy you have known the Holy Scriptures, which are able to make you wise for salvation through faith in Jesus Christ" (2 Tim. 3:15). Paul reminds us that wisdom given by God as a gift through Scripture and supernatural endowment has the special benefit of providing direction in the midst of difficult challenges (2 Tim. 3:16). This wisdom gives counselors insight to discern the proper time, the proper procedure, and the proper message to share with clients. Christian counselors pray for the direction that is the fruit of God-given wisdom. Wisdom provides guidance for counselors as they seek to develop an intervention that is appropriate for specific clients. As counselors use Scripture in a variety of ways, they do well to follow Paul's directions to provide warnings, encouragement, support, and patience (1 Th. 5:14).

Paul goes further in his instruction to Timothy, citing four specific uses of Scripture that Christian counselors will find useful (2 Tim. 3:16-17). First, Christian counselors experiencing the direction of divine wisdom will know when it is time for the use of doctrine to teach truth about the nature of God, people, and situations. There are times in counseling when truth must be spoken into the lives of clients for the purpose of instruction designed to produce growth or to confront sin and error. Scripture thoroughly resources the Christian counselor for such a task. "The one who trusts the Bible knows what God did, does, and will do, what God commands, and what God promises. This confidence produces liberated living—living, that is, which is free from uncertainty, doubt and despair" (Packer, 1995, p. 41).

Second, Christian counselors utilizing doctrine in their interaction with clients will discover errors in thought and habituated, sinful patterns of behavior that need to be reproved. To reprove is to point out to clients that they are thinking or behaving in ways that do not meet the requirements of godliness and truth in Scripture. Reproof is loving confrontation laced with encouragement to embrace a better way that leads to obedience and advancement in Christlikeness. The objective is repentance from disobedience to faithful obedience and a renewed commitment to reshaping thoughts and behaviors into conformity with the truth discovered in Scripture.

Third, Christian counsel never ends with reproof. It proceeds to correction. Setting the stumbling or fallen on their feet so they may walk uprightly with purpose and peace is always uppermost in the Christian counselor's mind. Reproof is always followed with the message of God's redemptive and sanctifying grace, making clear the way to move forward in fulfillment of scriptural truth. Instruction on right thinking and acting is always coupled with the encouragement that we are in this together and change is possible.

Fourth, the end in view in Christian counseling is the use of the Bible for the cultivation of a relational environment in which counselees embrace ongoing instruction that thoroughly equips them to reach maturity in Christ and perform with joy the good works that God has ordained for them.

**Ron Hawkins**

## REFERENCES

Collins, G. R. (2007). *Christian Counseling: A Comprehensive Guide* (3rd ed.). Wheaton, IL: Tyndale House.

Erikson, M. J. (2001). *Introducing Christian Doctrine* (2nd ed.). Grand Rapids, MI: Baker Academic.

Packer, J. I. (1995). *Knowing Christianity.* Wheaton, IL: Shaw.

## DOCTRINE OF SIN

**Description.** *Sin* is exclusively a theological term. "It is basically an offense against God" (Sabourin, 1993, p. 696). More formally, sin is any lack of conformity to the law of God in act, disposition, or state. Sin is not merely a bad choice or a descriptor for certain evil acts. Rather, *sin* in its biblical and theological setting describes behaviors, motives, and a state of alienation from God. This condition is universal. Paul wrote, "All have sinned and fall short of the glory of God" (Rom. 3:23). As unbelief, sin is the distrust of God's Word. As transgression, sin is willfully breaking God's command. As godlessness, sin acts without fear of the Almighty. As a state or condition, sin corrupts our entire nature and every faculty of our being.

In modern thought, however, the concept of sin has suffered much the same fate as the concept of soul. It has become secularized. As soul has become the *self*, sin has become a phenomenon. It goes without saying that a secular culture has little place for a concept that requires explicit reference to God for its meaning. Nevertheless, as both O. Hobart Mowrer and Karl Menninger realized several decades ago, when we ignore the reality of sin in the psychotherapeutic arena, we do so to our own peril (Mowrer, 1960; Menninger, 1973).

**History and Assessment.** Since the debates between Augustine and Pelagius, Christians have disputed the cause, nature, and consequences of sin. Specifically at issue was the extended impact of the original sin of Adam both *internally* (with respect to the subsequent condition of each individual before a holy God), and *externally* (with respect to the residual moral capacity of fallen humanity). These disputes spilled over into other theological concerns regarding the nature and extent of atonement for sin, reconciliation with God, and restoration of the sinner's capacity for holiness and righteousness. These issues inevitably bring us to Jesus Christ and to his living and dying to resolve the catastrophic effects of sin.

Since the so-called Copernican Revolution, Western thought has been "under the spell of the new world consciousness associated with the Enlightenment and romanticism" (Bloesch, 1984, p. 1014). For theological reflection, this means that one begins "from below" (with the human condition) rather than "from above" (with God, as in classical thought). As the French mathematician Laplace famously said to Napoleon in regard to the absence of any mention of God in his five-volume *Mécanique Céleste* (1799–1825), "*Je n'avais pas besoin de cette hypothèse-là*" ("I have no need of that hypothesis"). In the 19th century, theologians Schleiermacher and Ritschl led the way in seeking more natural explanations for what came to be considered the phenomenon of sin.

In the 20th century, Emil Brunner and Karl Barth reengaged the Calvinist-Arminian debate regarding the capacity for sinful humans to apprehend and respond to God's gracious offer extended in the gospel. Others, such as Reinhold Niebuhr and Paul Tillich, interpreted sin in the language of sociology and psychology more than biblical terms or motifs. More recently, various "designer theologies" have reworked their theological systems around demographic underclasses, such as oppressed ethnic groups, the poor, and women. In these systems, sin is perpetrated by the powerful on hapless victims. The victims, in turn, are given a pass to nurture sinful attitudes and sinful behavior in retaliation.

Theological reflection in the early 21st century is largely influenced by the postmodern turn with new (some might say renewed) interest in relationality over against substance metaphysics. This has opened up conceptual space to consider sin in relation to the broader systems in which human life is experienced.

**Assessment.** Whether one defines sin in ontological terms (as in classic theology) or in phenomenological terms (as in modern and postmodern systems), it is evident that the reality and consequences of sin remain potent forces. Regardless of whether one denies the God who gives sin its fierce meaning, there is no denying what Ted Peters styles "radical evil in soul and society" (Peters, 1998). In the biblical account, God warned the first family that when they disobeyed, they would die. They would experience alienation from their Creator God that very day. But there is more. They would go on to experience alienation from one another, as is evident in their blame game when confronted with their sin. They were banished from the garden, and life thereafter would be harsh and foreboding. The Bible declares that God would curse the ground for their sake (Gen. 3:17). Even nature itself "has been groaning as in the pains of childbirth right up to the present time" (Rom. 8:22). Paul contemplates the alienation of sinful humanity with effects in nature itself.

**Application.** It is important to observe the correlation between the way sin is understood and the way one responds to it. If sin is understood *vertically* as an offense against a holy God, then only a holy God can resolve it. If it is understood *horizontally* as a problem between individuals or communities in society, then social therapeutic strategies are needed. If it is an *internal* problem such as alienation, depression, guilt, and the like, then perhaps behavioral or cognitive therapy might be in order. A more comprehensive appraisal will have to acknowledge that all three of these perspectives are in play when dealing with sin.

Collins rightly observes, "Few topics could be more relevant than the issue of sin. The problems that characterize all of our lives, counselors included, have come because of the pervading and penetrating influence of sin in nature and the environment, in the societies and communities where we live, and in the inner core of every human being.... How we view the issue of sin will have a significant influence on how we counsel and on the effectiveness of our counseling" (Collins, 1993, p. 110). It is a mistake to focus on just one of these factors to the exclusion of the others. Invariably, sinful behavior is symptomatic of the condition of sin into which every human being is born. And when sin happens there are consequences, often including innocent victims.

**Biblical and Spiritual Factors.** The Christian counselor recognizes the existential and phenomenological dimensions to sin, which require a critical and informed response. But we dare not neglect the spiritual dimension. The writer James challenged his persecuted readers, who were tempted to respond to their victimization by victimizing others. He wrote, "Submit yourselves, then, to God. Resist the devil, and he will flee from you. Come near to God and he will come near to you. Wash your hands, you sinners, and purify your hearts, you double-minded. Grieve, mourn and wail. Change your laughter to mourning and your joy to gloom. Humble yourselves before the Lord, and he will lift you up" (Jas. 4:7-10). The Christian counselor recognizes that ultimate cleansing and deliverance from sin come from the One who has the greatest investment in our restoration, reconciliation, and healing—the ultimate victim of sin—God himself.

**Daniel R. Mitchell**

## REFERENCES

Bloesch, D. G. (1984). Sin. In W. Elwell (Ed.), *The Evangelical Dictionary of Theology.* Grand Rapids, MI: Baker.

Collins, Gary R. (1993). *The Biblical Basis of Christian Counseling for People Helpers.* Colorado Springs, CO: NavPress.

Menninger, Karl. (1973). *Whatever Became of Sin?* New York, NY: Hawthorne Books.

Mowrer, O. H. (1960). Sin, the lesser of two evils. *American Psychologist, 15,* 303.

Mowrer, O. H. (1972). Integrity groups: Basic principles and objectives. *The Counseling Psychologist, 3,* 7-32.

Peters, Ted. (1998). *Radical Evil in Soul and Society.* Grand Rapids, MI: Eerdmans.

Sabourin, L. (1993). Sin. In B. M. Metzger, & M. D. Coogan (Eds.), *The Oxford Companion to the Bible.* New York, NY: Oxford University Press.

## THEOLOGY OF SUFFERING

**Description.** What is suffering? Before we

define the term, consider some of its synonyms: pain, affliction, agony, torment, distress, and trauma. These descriptors alone reveal why the word *suffering* often generates feelings of fear, dread, discomfort, and uneasiness. As Thomas and Habermas (2008) observe, "There is nothing more central to the human experience than our capacity to feel, and no aspect of this is as deep as our capacity to suffer" (p. 8). These strong, adverse feelings or reactions to suffering are especially common in people from Western cultures, where "creature comforts" are adored and suffering is avoided at any cost.

Suffering is characterized by something unpleasant, such as loss, injury, distress, or pain. Suffering can be experienced physically or emotionally, yet regardless of how it is experienced, it hurts. No wonder the apostle Paul referred to his suffering as a *thorn* (2 Cor. 12:7), a word that means "a sharply pointed stake" (Swindoll, 2002, p. 99) and that drips with pain. Put another way, suffering "offers a *general* message of warning to all humanity that something is wrong with this planet and that we need radical outside intervention" (Yancey, 1997, pp. 83-84).

**Prevalence and Causes.** In addition to being inherently painful and something many try desperately to avoid, our experience of suffering is not new or unique, regardless of how we may feel. Rather, suffering began with Adam and Eve in the Garden of Eden as a direct result of their sin (Gen. 3) and has been a constant thread in the fabric of human history ever since (see Job 5:7). Suffering is a universal experience; no one is exempt from it, including (or perhaps particularly) Christians. This fact is often missed by some who mistakenly believe that because they are children of God, they are immune from suffering. Such thinking runs contrary to scriptural teaching. In fact, according to the apostle Peter, Christians should assume suffering will happen to them, and when it does, they can rejoice that they are able to participate with Christ in his sufferings (1 Pet. 4:12-13).

All of this begs the question, what are the causes of and reasons for suffering? Clinton and Hawkins (2007) offer several explanations: (a) personal sin and failure, (b) the sin and failure of someone else, (c) forces outside an individual's control, and (d) antagonistic responses to a person's faith (persecution) (p. 244). Scripture is replete with illustrations of those who experienced suffering for such reasons.

- As a direct result of his own moral failure and sin—including adultery, deception, and murder—King David suffered the death of his infant son, a broken relationship with God, and a tainted reputation with the people of his kingdom (Ps. 51).
- Joseph was sold into slavery, wrongfully accused of a heinous crime, and unjustly imprisoned. His suffering originated with his brothers' sins of hated, envy, anger, resentment, and bitterness (Gen. 37–50).
- In Jesus' day, a tower in Siloam collapsed for some reason beyond anyone's control, killing 18 people and leaving an untold number of family members and friends suffering grief and loss (Lk. 13:4).
- The apostle Paul was regularly persecuted for his faith. He was beaten, flogged, pelted with stones, imprisoned, and eventually martyred (2 Cor. 11:22-29).

**Biblical and Spiritual Issues.** Ministering to the suffering is a privilege and an obligation all members of the body of Christ share equally (1 Cor. 12). As Paul clearly states, every believer in Christ is to "rejoice with those who rejoice, and weep with those who weep" (Rom. 12:15 NASB). To that end, Clinton and Hawkins (2007) challenge those who minister to the suffering to cultivate a theology of suffering (p. 245). A theology of suffering is a practical and biblically consistent approach to looking at and responding to pain in oneself and in others. More specifically, this approach views suffering as...

- an opportunity for God to be glorified (Jn. 9:1-3)
- a chance for sufferers to grow personally and spiritually (2 Cor. 12:9-10)
- a channel for developing perseverance and endurance (Jas. 1:3)
- an occasion to trust God more deeply (1 Pet. 4:19)
- a means by which sufferers learn to effectively minister to others who encounter similar pain (2 Cor. 1:3-5)

**Conclusion.** How then can someone effectively minister to the suffering? The book of Job offers three simple yet powerful strategies for helping the hurting.

1. *Be present.* One of the best things anyone can do for those who are suffering is simply be present. More often than not, in times of pain, nothing is better or more comforting than friends who are willing to just "be there" (Job 2:11).
2. *Be silent.* Amazingly, in Job's time of need, his three friends not only came to be with him, they sat with him for seven days and seven nights and never said a word (Job 2:13)! Sometimes, the best thing to say to someone who's suffering is nothing at all (Jas. 1:19).
3. *Be encouraging.* Those who effectively minister to the suffering seek concrete ways to encourage them. They realize that the primary goal in helping the hurting is not to provide answers, explanations, personal opinions, or advice, but rather to mourn with them and offer comfort and encouragement to them (Job 2:11).

Fred Milacci

### REFERENCES

Clinton, T., & Hawkins, R. (2007). *Biblical Counseling: A Quick Reference Guide.* Nashville, TN: Thomas Nelson.

Swindoll, C. (2002). *Paul: A Man of Grit and Grace.* Nashville, TN: W Publishing Group.

Thomas, J., & Habermas, G. (2008). *What's So Good About Feeling Bad? Finding Purpose and a Path Through Your Pain.* Carol Stream, IL: Tyndale House.

Yancey, P. (1997). *Where Is God When It Hurts?* Grand Rapids, MI: Zondervan.

## SANCTIFICATION AND SPIRITUAL GROWTH

**Description and Prevalence.** The term *sanctification* comes from the same root as the words *saint* and *holy,* meaning "separate" or "set apart," usually for sacred or religious purposes. In Scripture, *sanctification* often denotes an act of God setting apart a person, place, or thing for his use. In the book of Genesis, for example, God set apart the seventh day as his holy Sabbath day of rest (2:3). Similarly, the Lord used his glory as the means of sanctifying the tabernacle as the place of worship for the nation of Israel (Ex. 29:43). And according to the author of Hebrews (10:10), believers in Jesus are divinely set apart at the moment of salvation by Christ's sacrifice on the cross (Ryrie, 1995).

The act by which God sets apart a person at salvation is referred to as *positional* sanctification because it highlights the Christian's "position or standing before God. [In] positional sanctification, the believer is accounted holy before God [and] declared a saint" (Enns, 1997, p. 329). It should be noted, however, that for the Christian, sanctification does not end with salvation; rather, positional sanctification is just the first step in what should be a lifelong process of being transformed. This process is called *progressive* or *experiential* sanctification (Ryrie, 1995) and emphasizes that Christians are set apart to live lives that are characterized by holiness (1 Pet. 1:16) and conformed to the image of Jesus Christ (Rom. 8:29).

It is important that Christians recognize the significance of both aspects of sanctification (positional and progressive/experiential). Specifically, they must understand that whereas the *position* of being set apart is solely God's work, the *process* of becoming more like Jesus includes believers' own responsibility and the Spirit's work in them (Phil. 2:12-13). They therefore must take ownership for their role in their own sanctification.

Of course, becoming more like Jesus is no easy task because, unlike the places and things sanctified by God in the Bible, people—even and especially sanctified Christians—have the capacity to sin (Gal. 5:17). This, however, is where Christian counseling can provide some help by instilling in counselees hope that transformation is possible as they begin "to put God first in their lives" (Hawkins, 2010, p. 104). In this way, counseling can be a tool God uses to assist the sanctification process, enabling people to be more Christlike and supporting them in their spiritual growth.

**Biblical and Spiritual Issues.** Though it represents a vital theological concept, the word *sanctification* is largely absent from most people's daily vocabulary. A more familiar term, however, is *spiritual growth*. Though the two terms are not synonymous, there is a strong link between them, especially with regard to spiritual growth and the progressive/experiential side of sanctification. Simply stated, the pursuit of sanctification manifests itself in positive spiritual growth for the Christian.

Though much could be written on the subject of spiritual growth, only a few more salient features are needed here. As is true in any type of growth or development process, spiritual growth happens gradually, almost imperceptibly. Though one may desire to grow quickly, spiritual growth, like sanctification, is a lifelong process with highs and lows, successes and failures. In the end, what matters most is that over the long haul, spiritual growth does in fact happen.

In order to experience this process, one must be familiar with the core elements of spiritual growth. Most notable among these elements are the Word of God, prayer, and worship.

- The Bible is a primary means of relating, interacting, and communicating with God, and is therefore essential to spiritual growth (1 Pet. 2:2). As the apostle Paul teaches, true spiritual growth is contingent upon time spent in thoughtful study of and meditation on Scripture (2 Tim. 3:16-17).
- Prayer is also vital to experiencing spiritual growth. Believers pray for themselves (Ps. 119:17-24) and for others (Eph. 3:14-19). More specifically, prayer brings a person closer to God, provides comfort in hardship, and gives strength to overcome sin—all essential to spiritual growth.
- Worship aids spiritual growth by drawing attention away from oneself and focusing it on God (Is. 6). Corporate worship also places the person in fellowship with other believers who are in the growth process, and together, they mutually edify each other, facilitating more growth and transformation.

Another indispensable yet often missing component in spiritual growth is the Holy Spirit. As Ortberg (2010) notes, "A frequent problem in the way we talk about spiritual growth is that there is not much spirit in it—God's Holy Spirit, that is" (p. 55). Since only God makes things grow (Ortberg), any attempt at spiritual growth outside of the Spirit will certainly lead to failure.

Finally, it is important to understand that ultimately, there is no one-size-fits-all approach to spiritual growth. Rather, every person is uniquely created by God in his image, so God's plan for the spiritual growth of one person "will not look the same as his plan to grow someone else.... The key is... finding the unique conditions that help each creature grow" (Ortberg, 2010, p. 51). The growth that these unique conditions produce in the individual Christian *is* the daily process of sanctification.

**Ron Hawkins**
**Fred Milacci**

## REFERENCES

Enns, P. (1997). *The Moody Handbook of Theology.* Chicago, IL: Moody Press.

Hawkins, S. (2010). Counseling. In K. Spann & D. Wheeler (Eds.), *Nelson's Church Leader's Manual for Congregational Care.* Nashville, TN: Thomas Nelson.

Ortberg, J. (2010). *The Me I Want to Be: Becoming God's Best Version of You.* Grand Rapids, MI: Zondervan.

Ryrie, C. (1995). *A Survey of Bible Doctrine.* Chicago, IL: Moody Press.

# PSYCHOSOCIAL DEVELOPMENT AND NEUROBIOLOGY

## DEVELOPMENTAL PSYCHOLOGY

**Description.** Developmental psychology is the study of how people change psychologically throughout the life span. Typically, it incorporates a foundational understanding of child development (further subdivided into conception, prenatal, infancy, toddler, preschool, and school-age development). Developmental psychology has specialized subfields also in early, middle, and late adolescence. Emerging or early adulthood usually examines developmental tasks of college-age and post college-age people. Middle adulthood includes career development, mating, family development, and leisure. Later adulthood can involve the elderly (early sixties up to the time of limited self-care) and the old-old (those whose self-care is limited).

Theories of developmental psychology include steady-state development, stage theories, and transition theories.

*Steady-state theories.* These treat learning, growing, and developing as continuously building knowledge, skills, and physical, mental, and emotional attributes. Continuous theories include learning theories—Pavolvian classical conditioning, Skinnerian operant conditioning, and social learning theories.

*Stage theories.* These are characterized by rapid change between periods of life when capabilities are vastly different. For example, early adolescence is marked by dramatic hormonal changes as well as significant changes in people's social environment and relationships with parents and peers. The stage of early adolescence is starkly different from the preceding stage of school-aged childhood. There are several well-known stage theorists. Freud proposed psychosocial and psychodynamic stages of oral, anal, phallic, latency, and mature genital stages. Piaget suggested stages of mental development (sensori-motor, preoperational, concrete operational, and formal operational). Erik Erikson proposed eight stages of psychosocial development throughout the lifespan (trust versus mistrust, identity versus role confusion, or generativity versus stagnation). Some theorists, such as Evelyn Duvall, have described stages of family development.

*Transitional theories.* These theories acknowledge that stages happen and continuous learning and development occur during the stages, but they focus on times when people move from stage to stage. Dramatic changes and healing can occur during these transitions. For example, Daniel Levinson proposed a theory of transition characterizing adults. Most people are familiar with his idea of the midlife crisis. Of course, research shows that midlife crises, much like adolescent storm-and-stress, actually happen only about ten percent of the time.

**History.** Developmental psychology was originally thought of as synonymous with child development. Under Freud's influence, childhood events were considered the formative events of life, and adulthood was seen as an almost inevitable unfolding of those events.

Throughout the history of developmental

psychology, as the field has relied less on armchair theorizing and more on actual empirical findings, the tide has steadily shifted. Now each life stage and life transition is thought of as having its unique character. Yes, the past undoubtedly affects people, but developmental psychology has shown that other things do as well, including genetics and genetic expression, life situations (family, school, career, and non-normative events like crises or wars or economic booms or busts), and physical, mental, and social stresses and coping mechanisms.

None of these, however, is definitive. For example, one can have the genetics of Arnold Schwarzenegger for bodybuilding, but if one does not lift weights, is born during a famine, or suffers a spinal injury limiting mobility, then the person will not build bodybuilder muscles. Genetics is one among other significant factors.

**Assessment.** Developmental psychology studies differences, similarities, and developments that occur across the life span, that differ at different stages, or that emerge or deteriorate during transitions between stages. As a psychological discipline, developmental psychology has unique methods (Myers, 2010). Cross-sectional studies take cross-sections of different ages of participants. However, although they tell a lot about how people at different ages are different, this research model has problems. For example, people who were 10 in 2001 are 20 in 2011 (when we are writing this). They have lived their entire reasoning and meaning-making life under Homeland Security's Code Orange, the Afghanistan and Iraqi conflicts, and Facebook interconnections. Their experience of adolescence is certainly different from that of people who grew through adolescence in the *Leave It to Beaver* era (the 1950s) with telephones and televisions at the forefront of technology in the home. Furthermore, consider the changes in the definition of marriage and the family over time. Cross-sectional assessment methods cannot account for effects of history and culture.

For this reason, developmental psychologists prefer longitudinal studies, which sample people and follow them for many years, watching as they move through different stages of life and trying to separate development from culture. Ultimately, that is impossible. Lewis Terman (1915) studied gifted children in the early 1900s. Those "Termites" were followed for about 90 years. But surely someone who was a child at the beginning of World War I (about 1914–1917) is different from the child of 2011. Still, longitudinal studies are much more helpful than cross-sectional studies.

The two methods are combined in the cross-lagged sequential design. It samples a cross-section of different cohorts and follows them over time, adding additional cohorts as they come of age.

**Treatment.** When treating clients, counselors do well to carefully consider a few things. First, we must be careful not to assume that children are like little adults or that children of different ages have similar capabilities. Second, we must be aware that developmental psychology is often consumed with capabilities, yet people do not always behave according to their capabilities. We are all capable of logical thought, but we know we most often think emotionally instead of logically. The younger the adolescent, the less often he or she thinks logically. Third, developmental psychology describes what most children or adults do, but every client who sits in front of a counselor is a unique person and might not do what most people do at that age. It is important to understand developmental differences but to use them only as a beginning point for assessing and treating clients.

**Biblical and Spiritual Issues.** In the application of developmental psychology, numerous biblical issues arise. Some of these produce fierce debate. When does life begin? Is stem-cell research with newly spontaneously aborted embryos ethical and consistent with the Bible? Should spanking be used to discipline children? Should people divorce? Should they remarry? Does God call people to specific jobs—ministry or otherwise? When an adult loses cognitive functioning due to severe dementia (such as Alzheimer's), is he or she still a person? The difficult issues across the life span are the stuff of modern life, and they fuel the culture wars of today. Furthermore, in all of these questions, we find sincere Christian believers arguing on the basis of Scripture on each side of each issue. We may easily think that we have a hammerlock on the truth, believe that our theology is the only logical one, and be convinced that if a person argues on the other side of an issue from us, the person must be deceived by Satan. We believe that there is biblical truth, but theology can distort our understanding of it, regardless of how well intentioned and studious we are. In dealing with developmental issues, we plead for humility and discernment and the leading of the Holy Spirit.

Everett L. Worthington Jr.
R. Kirby Worthington

## REFERENCES

Myers, D. G. (2010). *Psychology* (9th ed.). New York, NY: Worth Publishers.

Terman, L. M. (1915). The mental hygiene of exceptional children. *Pedagogical Seminary, 22*, 529-537.

## SOCIAL INFLUENCE THEORY

**Description.** Most humanities and social sciences have studied the fact that people influence each other. Notably, both social psychology and communication studies have studied social influence. From a social-psychological perspective, *social influence* is a label for what happens when one's behavior is changed by other people and groups, including changes in behavior due to conformity (receiving new information or simply fitting in), social comparison (evaluating ourselves in light of others), norms (expectations of groups), compliance (acquiescing to the requests of others), and obedience (following orders of legitimate authority figures).

Communication studies inform theology by viewing the Scriptures as a message communicated to a needy audience by a loving and sovereign God. This communication is overseen by the Holy Spirit, who exerts influence by persuading and convicting humans of God's love. Examples of human social influence also include witnessing (testifying to God's influence in one's life) and apologetics (making persuasive arguments connecting Scripture and reasoning).

**History.** Personality psychologists tend to emphasize the internal causes for behavior, and social psychologists tend to emphasize the external causes. In classic experiments, social psychologists like Solomon Asch (1951) and Stanley Milgram (1974) showed the power of external, situational cues. Counseling psychologist Stanley R. Strong (1968) suggested that counseling could be thought of as social influence, opening the door for using basic social psychology to inform therapists how to counsel their clients. Strong identified three counselor conditions that affected outcome, and within 20 years of the paper, more than 200 studies had investigated counselor expertness, attractiveness, and trustworthiness as important attributes of good counseling (for a review of the first ten years, see Corrigan, Dell, Lewis, & Schmidt, 1980). Strong's work spawned the social psychology–clinical psychology interface, which is best exemplified by the *Journal of Social and Clinical Psychology.*

**Assessment.** Today, social influence research from both basic psychology and applied psychology bears on counseling.

For instance, in recent years, Beach, Fincham, Hurt, McNair, and Stanley (2008) have studied the use of prayer in counseling couples. Worthington and Wade (1999) reviewed research on forgiving and its applicability to counseling. Hall and Fincham (2005) proposed a theory of self-forgiveness. Social-clinical interface researchers also have studied such topics as shame, guilt, regret, and low self-control as being due to ego depletion, meaning in life, and existential anxiety, which affect the behavior of clients. They have studied such social psychological methods as priming, which suggest ways that counselors' sometimes seemingly insignificant comments can influence clients.

**Application.** Social influence is not actually a theory or an approach to counseling. It is a recognition that God's world can be discovered (Worthington, 2010). When one looks at a picture by Picasso, one can know some things about Picasso. Similarly, seeing God's social creation can reveal something about God and about the people God created. People can be persuaded rationally at times—if a counselor's approach allows for client self-discovery and does not seem coercive. But humans also are influenced for good or ill in ways of which they are not aware. Some of those counseling influences are due to the ways counselors act, even if they are not doing so intentionally. For instance, counselors can help clients seek to discern God's will or drive them away through clumsy counseling behavior.

**Biblical and Spiritual Issues.** Social influence is as old as Eve influencing Adam to take a bite of forbidden fruit. Discernment is needed to know when social influence is for godly good or satanic perversion. In addition we must stay in dialogue with those in science, social sciences, and the humanities, and we must seek the guidance of the Holy Spirit. Biblical social influence is a product of how we live our lives and how we seek and find the triune God.

**Additional Issues.** Social influence goes to the heart of the ethics of counseling. People are often influenced by factors outside of their awareness, and counselors can influence people negatively if they blithely assume that one size fits all, even if the one size can be justified by a particular theology or religious tradition.

Everett L. Worthington Jr.
Daryl R. Van Tongeren

## REFERENCES

Asch, S. E. (1951). Effects of group pressure upon the modification and distortion of judgment. In H. Guetzkow (Ed.), *Groups, Leadership and Men.* Pittsburgh, PA: Carnegie Press.

Beach, S. R. H., Fincham, F. D., Hurt, T. R., McNair, L. M., and Stanley, S. (2008). Prayer and marital intervention: A conceptual framework. *Journal of Social and Clinical Psychology, 27,* 641-69.

Corrigan, J. D., Dell, D. M., Lewis, K. N., and Schmidt, L. D. (1980). Counseling as a social influence process: A review. *Journal of Counseling Psychology, 27*(4), 395-441.

Hall, J. H., and Fincham, F. D. (2005). Self-forgiveness: The stepchild of forgiveness research. *Journal of Social and Clinical Psychology, 24*(5), 621-37.

Milgram, S. (1974). *Obedience to Authority.* New York, NY: Harper & Row.

Strong, S. R. (1968). Christian counseling. *Counseling and Values, 20,* 151-60.

Worthington, E. L., Jr. (2010). *Coming to Peace with Psychology: What Christians Can Learn from Psychological Science.* Downers Grove, IL: InterVarsity Press.

Worthington, E. L., Jr., & Wade, N. G. (1999). The social psychology of unforgiveness and forgiveness and implications for clinical practice. *Journal of Social and Clinical Psychology, 18,* 385-418.

## ATTACHMENT THEORY

**Description.** Attachment theory has increasingly become a dominant theory in various lines of developmental research and in the broad literature on counseling and psychotherapy. In Christian counseling and Christian psychology, attachment theory has become popular because it provides a powerful, integrative framework for how social-emotional development, neurobiology, and spirituality interact (Clinton & Sibcy, 2002).

The core tenets of attachment theory address the way early relationship experiences powerfully influence social-emotional development, neurobiology, and the way core beliefs about God are formed and maintained (Clinton & Straub, 2010).

**The Secure-Base System.** How do early relationships shape the brain and form core beliefs about self, world, and others? The secure-base system is a powerful way to conceptualize and understand the various components of attachment relationships (Bowlby, 1977, 1988). In this system, children form emotionally charged beliefs (also referred to as *schemas* or *internal working models*) about themselves and others in the context of intimacy and caregiving. In addition, core assumptions about emotions and emotional/relational needs (referred to as *meta-emotions*) are shaped in the crucible of the secure-base system. These assumptions powerfully influence the way we interpret and respond to our own feelings and those of others.

The secure-base system has four core components that unfold in a feedback loop. To visualize this process, imagine a mother and her toddler in a strange room filled with toys and other interesting objects. The mother sits in a chair, and the child initially sits in her lap as she looks around the room (Ainsworth, Blehar, Waters, & Wall, 1978). The first component in the secure-base system is the *secure-base experience.* This refers to the child's felt sense of security and is tied directly to her felt sense that the parent or caregiver is available and accessible. Also, the secure-base experience refers to the child's felt sense of emotional and physical regulation.

Once a secure-base is established, the child's *exploration system* is activated. The child crawls off her mother's lap and curiously explores her surroundings, frequently referring back to her mother as a way of sharing the experience and checking to make sure her mother is available. Exploration is the developmental precursor to a future sense of self-confidence. It is an internal sense of "I can do..." accompanied by a sense of curiosity and a striving for autonomy. Note that in this model, self-confidence and autonomy seeking are inherently relational and begin with confidence in the attachment figure.

Should something threaten the child's felt sense of security, such as a stranger entering the room or the parent leaving the room, the exploration system immediately turns off, and the *attachment behavior system* is activated. Attachment behavior is propelled by intense emotion, usually some mixture of anxiety and anger. There are at least two kinds of attachment behavior: *proximity seeking* and *signaling.* Proximity seeking is any behavior that helps the child obtain physical closeness to the caregiver. It can take many forms, including crying, whining, crawling, running, or even screaming. Signaling is the way the child communicates with or alerts the parent that there is a problem.

Finally, the caregiver and child work together in a *goal-corrected partnership* to achieve a sense of safety and calmness, which is referred to as the *safe-haven experience.* This experience then resets the stage for the child's exploration system to restart, completing what is called the *circle of security* (Cooper, Hoffman, Powell, & Marvin, 2005).

Throughout childhood, many thousands of secure-base scenarios unfold. The basic theme of these experiences has an enormous influence on the developing child in two important ways: (a) how the child's brain develops and how well she learns certain core neuro-cognitive skills, such as emotion regulation, social skills, cognitive flexibility, empathy and compassion, and social problem-solving skills; and (b) the development of core beliefs (the schemas or internal working models) about the self ("Am I lovable?" "Am I capable?"), about others ("Are you reliable?" "Are you accessible and trustworthy?"), about the world ("Is the world a safe place, or do I need to be on a constant lookout for danger?"), and about emotions ("Are my emotions tolerable, and can they help me relate to the world and others more deeply, or are they toxic and always destructive?") (Clinton & Straub, 2010). These working models are stored in the limbic system (also known as the emotional brain) as implicit memories. These memories are emotionally charged, preverbal structures that strongly influence a child's behavior long before he or she develops explicit, verbal, autobiographical memories of the experiences that shaped them.

**Secure Models of Attachment.** Secure models of attachment are formed when parents help their children achieve a secure base from which the children can explore the world (Weinberg, Sroufe, Egeland, & Carlson, 1999). These parents are comfortable with their children's exploration and autonomy. Also, when the child becomes distressed and the attachment system is activated (the child is upset, seeking proximity and signaling that there is a problem), the parent accurately reads the distress and sensitively and effectively responds in a way that helps the child achieve a state of safe haven. These repeated experiences become encoded as secure working models of attachment, with a positive view of self ("I am worthy of love and care; my needs are legitimate, and I am capable of getting these needs met") and a positive view of others ("Others are reliable and dependable; they take my needs seriously and will work with me to help me in times of need"). The secure working model also contains beliefs and rules about emotion ("My emotions, such as curiosity, autonomy, anger, anxiety, and sadness, are valuable, and they tell me something about what I need and what others need. It is okay for me to express my emotions, and my caregivers will help me calm them down"). Secure models extend into a person's internal image of God as a reliable, accessible, responsive being who provides both a secure base from which to explore the world and a safe haven during times of trouble.

**Attachment Gone Bad.** *Avoidant* or *dismissing* working models develop when caregivers tend to overemphasize the exploration and autonomy system and minimize, punish, or reject attachment behavior (Sroufe, 2005). The caregivers tend to misinterpret children's signaling and proximity-seeking behavior (such as crying, anger, or anxiety) as forms of weakness or manipulation. As a result, those with avoidant or dismissing models of attachment develop self-beliefs that overemphasize autonomy and independence ("I just need to rely on myself to deal with problems. My self-worth is tied to what I do and what I have") and an overly negative view of others' ability to help them in times of distress ("I can't rely on others to be there for me. I can take care of others and their needs, but I can't trust them to help me"). Avoidant/dismissing individuals also develop negative views of attachment needs and unpleasant emotions ("Emotions are signs of weakness and vulnerability"), and therefore, avoidant individuals are cut off from their own needs. Because of their compulsive self-reliance and discomfort with their own attachment needs, avoidant/dismissing individuals tend to jettison their need for relational intimacy and closeness and replace them with a spectrum of addictive behaviors related to video games, food, gambling, sexual addiction, drugs, alcohol, and the like. In a more subtle way, avoidant/dismissing individuals can also become compulsive caregivers (some may become social workers, counselors, medical professionals, and clergy), taking care of others' needs while ignoring or rejecting their own. In terms of religious beliefs, such individuals are prone to wander away from God as a secure base, lose interest in their faith, and be drawn to hedonistic practices (Clinton & Straub, 2010).

In contrast, *ambivalent* or *preoccupied* models of attachment unfold in the context of caregivers who are emotionally immature and unstable. The caregivers often engage in subtle forms of role reversal, making themselves the objects of their children's attention and expecting their children to meet their psychological and emotional needs (Sroufe & Fleeson, 1988). In such contexts, a child's exploration system is minimized as the parent discourages exploration by communicating to the child that the world is dangerous, and the attachment system is hyperactivated so that the child is preoccupied with the parent's whereabouts for fear of being abandoned or left behind. In contrast to the avoidant/dismissing working models, ambivalent/preoccupied models develop powerful, negative beliefs about the self ("I am unworthy; I am basically flawed and inept; I cannot do things on my own") and a somewhat mixed and unstable set of beliefs about the other ("I must have your constant support and availability to survive; I must be vigilant of your whereabouts or you will leave me; I must take care of you so you won't abandon me or be angry with me"). Spiritually, these individuals are prone to develop various types of religious doubt; they frequently question their faith and worry about losing their salvation.

Finally, *fearful/disorganized* working models often develop in the context of abusive, chaotic, and neglectful home environments. In these homes, children are faced with a relational paradox. The attachment figures, who are the children's solution to stress and anxiety, become the very source of the children's fear. Thus the caregivers are both the source and the solution to the children's extreme distress. As a result, the children's brains are faced with irresolvable conflict, which causes circuits to disintegrate as high levels of cortisole and adrenaline are released throughout the body. Psychologically, the child disconnects from experience and becomes frozen, which becomes the precursor to dissociation, as both the exploration system and the attachment system come to a screeching halt and the child is transfixed in a state of fear. Dissociation occurs when the conscious self disconnects from its overwhelming experiences as a way of coping with unbearable emotion. Research is discovering more about how these types of experiences cause disintegration between the circuits in the brain responsible for thinking, feelings, and sensations, and those circuits involved in self-awareness, narrative memory, and rational problem solving (Schore, 2001).

Those with fearful/disorganized models of attachment have negative views about the self, others, and the world. They are also more prone to have severe problems with mood regulation, behavior control, and coping with relationships. Spiritually, they are prone to doubt God's goodness, and while they want to be close to God, they find themselves flooded with fear of punishment and alienation.

**Gary Sibcy**

## REFERENCES

Ainsworth, M. D. S., Blehar, M. C., Waters, E., & Wall, S. (1978). *Patterns of Attachment: A Psychological Study of the Strange Situation.* Hillsdale, NJ: Lawrence Erlbaum Associates.

Bowlby, J. (1977). The making and breaking of affectional bonds: I. Aetiology and psychopathology in the light of attachment theory. *British Journal of Psychiatry, 130,* 201-210.

Bowlby, J. (1988). *A Secure Base: Clinical Applications of Attachment Theory.* London, England: Routledge.

Clinton, T., & Sibcy, G. (2002). *Attachments: Why You Love, Feel, and Act the Way You Do.* Brentwood, TN: Integrity Press.

Clinton, T., & Straub, J. (2010). *God Attachment: Why You Believe, Act and Feel the Way You Do About God.* New York, NY: Howard Books.

Cooper, G., Hoffman, K., Powell, B., & Marvin, R. (2005). The circle of security intervention: Differential diagnosis and differential treatment. In L. J. Berlin, Y. Ziv, L. M. Amaya-Jackson, & M. T. Greenberg (Eds.), *Enhancing Early Attachments: Theory, Research, Intervention, and Policy* (pp. 127-151). New York, NY: Guilford Press.

Schore, A. N. (2001). The effects of early relational trauma on right brain development, affect regulation, and infant mental health. *Infant Mental Health Journal, 22*(1-2), 201-269.

Sroufe, L. A. (2005). Attachment and development: A prospective, longitudinal study from birth to adulthood. *Attachment and Human Development, 7*, 349-367.

Sroufe, L. A., & Fleeson, J. (1988). The coherence of family relationships. In R. A. Hinde & J. Stevenson (Eds.), *Relationships Within Families: Mutual Influences* (pp. 27-47). Oxford, UK: Oxford University Press.

Weinberg, N. S., Sroufe, L. A., Egeland, B., & Carlson, E. A. (1999). The nature of individual differences in infant-caregiver attachment. In J. Cassidy & P. R. Shaver (Eds.), *Handbook of Attachment: Theory, Research, and Clinical Applications* (pp. 68-88). New York, NY: Guilford Press.

## INTERPERSONAL NEUROBIOLOGY

**Description.** Interpersonal neurobiology is a rapidly expanding field that draws from a dozen different areas of science to help paint a more complete picture of human growth and development. It may eventually be the fulcrum for integrating Christian counseling and psychology, along with contemporary neuroscience and theology. Siegel's (2010a) Triangle of Well-Being helps clarify the relationship between the mind, the brain, and relationships. To apply the principles of interpersonal neurobiology, we will identify five core findings from neuroscience and interpersonal neurobiology and discuss some ways they provide powerful insights into counseling and psychotherapy from a biblical perspective.

**Seigel's Triangle.** Seigel's Triangle of Well-Being integrates three important spheres of human functioning: the mind, the brain, and relationships. He defines the *mind* as an embodied process that regulates the flow of both energy and information. The *brain*, on the other hand, is the neurocircuitry through which both energy and information flow. Although most of these neurons are contained in the skull, they extend throughout the entire body, including the gut. The gut is a very important part of this neurocircuitry and is sometimes referred to as "the second brain" because it contains many of the same neurotransmitters as does the brain. These neurocircuits are responsible for "heartfelt reactions" and gut-level intuition. *Relationships* are how energy and information are shared and regulated between persons through the processes of connection and communication. Relationships play a very powerful role in the regulation of energy and information, not only between two people but also within each person (Siegel, 2010a).

*Neuroplasticity.* This refers to the brain's ability to be modified, not only through pure biological processes, such as medication, diet, and exercise, but also through relationships and by the mind. More specifically, relational experiences, such as empathy and forgiveness, as well as mind-related experiences, including cognitive restructuring and the use of certain kinds of meditation and prayer, can cause the brain to develop new neural pathways. Counselors and therapists can help clients create conditions that challenge the brain to enhance, expand, and strengthen neurocircuits. Siegel (2010a) refers to this process as SNAGing (stimulating neuronal activation and growth) the brain.

*Mindsight.* This refers to a capacity of the mind to intentionally focus attention; to monitor thoughts, feelings, and physical sensations; and to ultimately direct the flow of energy and information within the triangle of well-being (Siegel, 2010a). It can be an internal process of intentional attention to one's own thoughts and feelings, or it can unfold in the context of close interpersonal relationships in which the mind of one person can help shape the flow of energy and information in the mind of another. Attachment relationships are examples of this interpersonal shaping, especially parent-child and counselor-client relationships. The concept fits well within the Christian worldview, especially in terms of the way God and the Holy Spirit can influence the way we think, feel, and respond. Becoming a believer begins a process of reshaping of the flow of energy and information throughout the Triangle of Well-Being.

*Mirror neurons.* These brain cells mirror or map what is happening in the brain of another person. For example, if person *A* eats a plum, the specific neurons in his motor cortex needed to execute that behavior will light up. This is not a big surprise. However, if person *A* simply watches person *B* eat a plum, the same motor neurons in person *A*'s brain will light up just as if he were actually eating the plum himself. This becomes a powerful concept for explaining how we can map the minds of others (see below). Some researchers believe it's the key to understanding how empathy develops (Allen, Fonagy, & Bateman, 2008; Wallin, 2007).

*Differentiation and integration.* The brain develops from the bottom to the top and from the right hemisphere to the left hemisphere. Bottom-to-top development begins with the brain stem, which is responsible for the regulation of somatic states. The limbic system is responsible for the generation and regulation of affect, motivation, drives, attachment, and the rapid appraisal of incoming stimuli (Cozolino, 2010). The prefrontal cortex rests above the limbic system just behind the eyes and is responsible for a number of important functions, including attuned communication, emotional regulation, empathy, insight, intuition, and even morality (Cozolino, 2006, 2010).

At birth, the brain has billions of neurons that are relatively undifferentiated. Based on the types of experiences with the environment, the neurons begin to differentiate into specialized circuits for accomplishing specific functions. The goal of development is for each of these specialized regions to become linked together and interconnected. This is referred to as "an integrated system." A highly integrated brain is one in which the neurocircuits designed for thinking, feeling, communicating, relating, and problem solving all work together in a goal-directed, collaborative fashion. In *vertical integration*, the higher brain circuits (e.g., the frontal and prefrontal cortex neurocircuits) are interlinked with the low neurocircuits of the limbic system and the brain stem. *Horizontal integration* refers to the integration of the nonverbal/emotional right hemisphere with the verbal/logical left hemisphere (Siegel, 2010b). The process of integrating these specialized neurocircuits entails creating conditions (or SNAGing the brain) whereby the brain is challenged to direct the flow of energy and information through mindsight (Siegel, 2010a).

*Memory and the brain.* A memory is any past experience that influences the way we think, feel, behave, and relate (Siegel, 2008). Notice that this definition does not necessarily require that the experience be consciously "remembered." Understanding the different structures of memory may help clarify this point. There are two broad divisions in our memory system. The first is *implicit memory*, which begins forming at birth. These memories are encoded into the brain based on repeated sequences of experiences that can include packages of behaviors, feelings, sensations, and perceptions. It's important to note that many implicit memories, especially those about relationships, are stored in the limbic system. They do not require the activation of the hippocampus, which does not come online until later in development. Implicit memories can be encoded into the brain even when we are not directly focusing our attention on the event being encoded (Siegel, 2010b). Also, based on these stored sequences of experiences, more general rules or *mental models* are formed about how to do things (e.g., procedural memories about how to put on clothing or how to ride a bicycle). Implicit memories also store patterns of relationship experiences (Siegel, 2010a, 2010b). For example, a child may associate crying with being comforted, or she may associate crying with anger and rejection. Based on these patterns or themes, more general rules about the self, others, intimacy, and emotions are formed. For example, "I can express my emotions effectively, and my caregivers will respond in a way that helps me feel better." Interestingly, the caregiver's response to the child is likely to be encoded into mirror neurons such that the child will automatically and without awareness respond to her own emotions and behaviors in a way that reflects the way the caregiver has responded to her. A very important feature about implicit memory is that when it is recalled, it is not accompanied by an internal sensation of being "remembered." Therefore, past experiences can very powerfully influence the way we think, feel, behave, relate, and perceive events without an awareness of how the past is influencing the present.

In contrast, *explicit memory* is what typically comes to mind when people talk about memory. There are many different types of explicit memory, including both factual and autobiographical. Factual memory concerns consciously recalled pieces of information (like what is a bicycle or a flower). Autobiographical or narrative memory has to do with memories of ourselves in time. The capacity to form autobiographical memories does not come on line until about age two. Both forms of explicit memory are stored and recalled as verbal information, and they both require conscious attention for the encoding process (Siegel, 2008, 2010a, 2010b). In many ways, all our experiences can be encoded as implicit memories. A special part of the brain, the hippocampus, assembles implicit memories like a jigsaw puzzle and transforms them into explicit, verbal memories that can either become factual (you recall what a bicycle is) and/or autobiographical (you remember your dad teaching you how to ride a bicycle).

Autobiographical memory is sometimes called *narrative memory*. This is a very important part of our lives and represents some of the most complex functions in the brain, as the prefrontal cortex integrates our implicit, emotionally charged memories with our explicit autobiographical memory and forms stories about our lives and relationships. The very essence of secure adult attachment is the ability to understand our lives. It's a coherent story that includes the good, the bad, and the ugly events and integrates them into an understanding of why we are the way we are.

**Biblical and Spiritual Issues.** In an important way, Scripture tells the story of God's dealings with humankind, and each of our testimonies is our way of understanding how God has worked in our lives and continues to do so even today. Counseling and psychotherapy may be seen as our effort to help people develop more coherent narratives as they come to an understanding of their lives.

**Gary Sibcy**

## REFERENCES

Allen, J. G., Fonagy, P., Bateman, A. W. (2008). *Mentalizing in Clinical Practice*. Arlington, VA: American Psychiatric Publishing.

Cozolino, L. (2006). *The Neuroscience of Human Relationships: Attachment and the Developing Social Brain*. New York, NY: Norton.

Cozolino, L. (2010). *The Neuroscience of Psychotherapy: Healing the Social Brain* (2nd ed.). New York, NY: Norton.

Siegel, D. (2007). *The Mindful Brain: Reflection and Attunement in the Cultivation of Well-Being*. New York, NY: Norton.

Siegel, D. (2008). *The Neurobiology of We* [Audio book]. Louisville, CO: Sounds True Inc.

Siegel, D. (2010a). *Mindsight: The New Science of Personal Transformation*. New York, NY: Bantam Books.

Siegel, D. (2010b). *The Mindful Therapist: A Clinician's Guide to Mindsight and Neural Integration.* New York, NY: Bantam Books.

Wallin, D. J. (2007). *Attachment in Psychotherapy.* New York, NY: Guilford Press.

## BRAIN IMAGING

Brain imaging is of two types, anatomical and functional. The former is like a photograph and provides information about shape and structure. The latter gives information about activity in different parts of the brain. Multimodal imaging is best because function can be accurately located on the anatomy of the same patients' brains.

**Anatomical.** *Computed tomography* (CT), invented in 1971, uses two-dimensional X-rays to create a three-dimensional picture. It is 100 times more accurate than X-rays in detecting abnormalities in soft tissue such as the brain. Unlike *magnetic resonance imaging* (MRI), CT cannot accurately detect lesions smaller than 1.5 centimeters. However, CT is quicker, quieter, less expensive, less claustrophobic, and safer for patients with metal in their bodies. A CT scanner costs between $650,000 and $1.6 million, and a scan costs about $1,000.

*Magnetic resonance imaging*, invented in 1977, does not involve any adverse effects of radiation. Hydrogen atoms, which had been randomly spinning, are lined up by the MRI magnetic field. Specific radio waves are sent into the patient's head, causing many hydrogen protons to spin at a particular frequency and in a particular direction. When the waves are turned off, the hydrogen atoms return to their previous alignment, releasing energy that is picked up by the MRI and turned into a picture. MRI machines cost between $1 and $3 million, and a brain scan costs between $1,500 and $3,500, depending on the requirements.

*Diffusion tensor imaging* (DTI), invented in 1991 and derived from MRI using cellular water diffusion, provides information about white matter connectivity of the brain. DTI software costs about $50,000, increasing the cost of a scan slightly compared with standard MRI.

**Functional.** *Electroencephalography* (EEG), invented in 1924, is the recording of the brain's electrical activity and is somewhat similar to an electrocardiogram of the heart. The electricity, measured in millionths of a volt, has to penetrate brain coverings, fluid, skull bone, and scalp, causing smearing and poor spatial resolution. However, temporal resolution is excellent, timing individual brain activities in thousandths of a second. Standard EEGs, read visually by a physician, are mainly used for the diagnosis of seizure disorders. An EEG machine costs about $20,000, and an EEG test is about $500.

*Quantified EEG* (QEEG) is an extension of standard EEG. Tracings are digital and can be analyzed by computer. Colored statistical maps determine localized abnormalities, which would not be apparent to the human eye. *Source localization,* using multichannel EEG recordings, can more accurately determine the locus of a seizure. *Evoked responses* to sensory input are derived by averaging portions of the EEG, timed from the moment of sensory input. Random waves cancel out, leaving only the waveform caused by the event. This method provides many probes of mental function. Early waves relate to the arrival of the input, and later waves relate to how the brain deals with it. For examples, the P50 (positive wave at 50 milliseconds) measures sensory gating, the P300 (positive wave at 300 milliseconds) measures attention, and the N400 (negative wave at 400 milliseconds) measures incongruity.

*Magnetoencephalography* (MEG), invented in 1969, is very similar to EEG. Magnetic fields are not distorted by tissue and bone, resulting in much better spatial resolution and a clearer brain map. Since the magnetic field is at right angles to the electric field, it provides complementary information about cortical surfaces not contributing to the EEG. The disadvantage is the expense; an MEG machine costs about $2.5 million, and a single scan costs about $2,500.

*Functional MRI* (fMRI), invented in 1991, is based on blood-oxygen-level dependence (BOLD). Brain activity results in increased blood flow to deliver oxygen. Paradoxically, deoxyhemoglobin (hemoglobin without oxygen) is reduced because oxygen extraction does not match increased blood flow. Deoxyhemoglobin is paramagnetic and is the source of the signal for cortical functions. The cost of software to upgrade an MRI is about $50,000.

*Single photon emission computed tomography* (SPECT), invented in 1976, requires an injection of a radioactive tracer, which binds to specific tissues and emits gamma rays, which are detected by the SPECT camera. Most SPECT scans are functional, but some are anatomical. A SPECT machine costs between $200,000 and $800,000, and a scan costs between $1,500 and $3,000.

*Positron emission tomography* (PET), invented in 1970, also detects gamma rays after an injection of a radioactive tracer. However, unlike SPECT, PET detects two gamma photons that originate simultaneously at 180 degrees opposite from one another. This results in a much clearer and more accurate image. PET machines cost between $600,000 and $1.6 million, and a scan costs about $2,000. Combined PET/CT units, invented in 1996, allow simultaneous acquisition and coregistration of anatomical (CT) and functional (PET) data. They cost about $1.6 million.

*Near-infrared spectroscopy* (NIRS), invented about 1987, shines the near-infrared range of light through the skull, and the degree of attenuation of the remerging light is measured. This attenuation determines the amount of hemoglobin in the blood, and thus oxygen and brain activity in different brain areas. NIRS is non-invasive, safe, relatively inexpensive, and portable. The machine costs between $250,000 and $370,000. As it is still a research tool, the cost of a clinical scan is not known.

Norman C. Moore

## PSYCHOPHARMACOLOGY

**Description.** Drugs are substances that alter the normal bodily functions of living organisms. Pharmacology is the study of the interaction of drugs within the body to affect biological functions. Psychopharmacology is the study of psychotropic or psychoactive substances that can cross the blood-brain barrier and affect brain function. They impact alertness, perception, consciousness, cognition, mood, and behavior.

**History.** The roots of pharmacology and psychopharmacology predate recorded history. Over the millennia, cultures have developed various substances for medicinal, recreational, and spiritual purposes. Natural substances, primarily plant extracts, became useful for treating illnesses. Some cultures used natural substances (such as mushrooms and cacti) for purposeful altering of consciousness individually or in rituals. Byproducts of farming included opium, cannabis, and alcohol derived from the fermentation of cereals and fruits. An *entheogen* ("God inside us") is a psychoactive substance used in a religious or spiritual context. The use of psychoactive substances pervades our cultures today.

Hippocrates of Cos (ca. 460–370 BC), a Greek physician, is known as the father of medicine. He acknowledged the brain-body connection and suggested that body physiology may contribute to mental illness. Hippocratic medicine focused on the healing power of nature. Treatment was gentle and kind to the patient, and drugs were used sparingly. Pedanius Dioscorides (ca. 40–90 AD) was a Greek physician, pharmacologist, and botanist. He wrote a five-volume pharmacopeia of herbal and related medicinal substances that remained in use until around 1600. William Withering and others sparked a resurgence of pharmacology in the nineteenth century.

In the 1950s, three areas of endeavor led to modern psychopharmacology: the development of Thorazine and other early psychotropic drugs, the discovery of the synapse and neurochemical transmission, and genetic studies. The result has been the development of numerous psychotropic medications, algorithms for diagnosis and medication management, and specific neurophysiologic targets for intervention in psychiatric illness. Research seeks to identify the specific neuroscience (such as neurotransmitter production, function, and destruction) leading to psychiatric symptoms and conditions and develop psychotropic agents to target them.

**Classification.** There are six major classes of psychopharmacological agents (*psychotropics*, previously known as *phrenotropics*):

1. Antipsychotic agents (also known as *neuroleptics*, *ataractics*, or major tranquilizers) treat psychosis, schizophrenia, mania, and aggression. The conventional antipsychotics include Thorazine and Haldol and have significant side effects including extrapyramidal (Parkinson-like) effects and tardive dyskinesia. The atypical antipsychotics include aripiprazole (Abilify), asenapine (Saphris), clozapine (Clozaril), iloperidone (Fanapt), lurasidone (Latuda), olanzapine (Zyprexa), paliperidone (Invega), quetiapine (Seroquel), risperidone (Risperdal), and ziprasidone (Geodon). These atypicals produce fewer muscle movement disorders than conventionals, but they may produce weight gain and metabolic issues.

2. Antidepressants (also known as psychic energizers or *thymoleptics*) improve depression and anxiety, and many may impact pain. Tricyclic antidepressants (TCAs) and monoamine oxidase inhibitors (MAOIs) are older and less utilized. TCAs include amitriptyline (Elavil, Endep), clomipramine (Anafranil), doxepin (Adapin, Sinequan), imipramine (Tofranil), trimipramine (Surmontil), desipramine (Norpramin), nortriptyline (Pamelor, Aventyl), and protriptyline (Vivactil). MAOIs include isocarboxazid (Marplan), moclobemide (Aurorix, Manerix), phenelzine (Nardil), selegiline (Eldepryl, Emsam), and tranylcypromine (Parnate). Inhibitors of selective or multiple neurochemicals including serotonin, norepinephrine, and dopamine are commonly used. Selective serotonin reuptake inhibitors (SSRIs) include Prozac, Zoloft, Paxil, Celexa, Luvox, and Lexapro. Serotonin-norepinephrine reuptake inhibitors (SNRIs) include desvenlafaxine (Pristiq), duloxetine (Cymbalta), milnacipran (Ixel), and venlafaxine (Effexor). Norepinephrine-dopamine reuptake inhibitors (NDRIs) include bupropion (Wellbutrin, Zyban).

3. Mood stabilizers treat bipolar disorder, schizoaffective disorder, and aggression. Lithium and many antiepileptic medications (Depakote, carbamazepine, and Lamictal) are useful as mood stabilizers.

4. *Anxiolytics* (also known as minor tranquilizers or *psycholeptics*) treat anxiety disorders, compulsions, tension, and agitation. Many have potential for dependency. Benzodiazepines, SSRIs, BuSpar (buspirone), hydroxyzine, pregabalin (Lyrica), and other agents are useful in the treatment of anxiety disorders.

5. Psychostimulants (amphetamines and methylphenidate) treat disorders such as attention-deficit disorder and narcolepsy and are used to suppress the appetite. They improve alertness and motivation, and they impact executive function in the prefrontal cortex.

6. Depressants are used as hypnotics, sedatives, and anesthetics.

**Assessment and Treatment.** Prior to psychopharmacotherapy, a comprehensive evaluation is essential. This includes patient and collateral input regarding psychiatric, physical, medical, social, psychological, spiritual, and educational/occupational function and impairment. The evaluation identifies *differential diagnoses* (conditions that may appear like each other) and *comorbid conditions* (conditions co-occurring at the same time in an individual). A physical examination and baseline laboratory review determine medical conditions that may impact the current clinical picture and subsequent treatment.

Following evaluation, a treatment plan determines the indicated nonpharmacologic interventions for the diagnoses. The clinician must determine the risks and benefits of medication for specific medication targets for each diagnosis or symptom compared to nonmedication approaches, or in combination with them. Patient (and family) education is important to produce understanding, medication compliance, and enhanced response. The clinician must review the risks, benefits, adverse effects, and precautions of medications with the patient (and family) and obtain informed consent.

Medication trials require monitoring for beneficial effects and adverse side effects. It is often necessary to switch medications that are ineffective or inadequate or that produce intolerable adverse effects. Although it is best to avoid polypharmacy (more than one medication at a time), combinations of medications may be necessary to attain optimization of response or remission of illness. Many conditions are comorbid or co-occurring with other conditions, with each condition requiring specific medication treatment. Once response is achieved, continuation or maintenance of medication is often necessary for six months to many years, depending on the individual circumstances of the patient. Withdrawal of medication often requires close monitoring for withdrawal effects and relapse of symptoms.

Many mild conditions respond to nonmedication approaches. For moderate to severe impairment, medication is often necessary. Studies indicate that medication alone may be sufficient for a few individuals. More commonly, an integrative approach is necessary to achieve optimum results. This includes (a) psychotherapy (individual, group, family, substance abuse, and so on) specific to the circumstances of the patient, (b) lifestyle changes (nutrition, exercise, sleep, social network) to improve overall health and well-being, (c) spiritual counseling, practice, and support, (d) occupational or educational accommodations or remediation, and (e) coordination of care with the primary care physician and various care givers and support persons.

E. John Kuhnley

## ANTIANXIETY DRUGS

**Description.** Anxiety is normal. It is the apprehensive anticipation of present or future danger or misfortune. Worry implies persistent doubt or fear—to torment oneself with or suffer from disturbing thoughts. An anxiety disorder occurs when anxiety and worry are excessive, recurrent, and long-lasting, and they cause distress, dysfunction, and inflexibility. Common diagnoses include generalized anxiety disorder (GAD), social anxiety disorder, separation anxiety disorder, obsessive compulsive disorder, posttraumatic stress disorder, and panic disorder (DuPont, Spencer, & Dupont, 2003).

**Assessment and Treatment.** Anxiety management strategies, lifestyle changes, spiritual counseling, and cognitive-behavioral therapy are effective methods for treating mild to moderate anxiety disorders (DuPont, Spencer, & Dupont, 2003; Hart, 1999; Sperry, 1995). When these measures are insufficient to relieve the anxiety, medication may be helpful. The more severe the anxiety disorder, the more likely medication will be necessary to relieve it. However, nonmedication treatments are necessary to produce lasting changes and relief. Consequently, multimodal or combination therapy is most effective (Sperry, 1995).

Medication management requires a comprehensive evaluation, including patient and collateral input regarding psychiatric, physical, medical, social, psychological, spiritual, and educational/occupational function and impairment (Sperry, 1995; Cohen, 2003). A physical examination and baseline laboratory review determine medical conditions that may impact the current clinical picture and subsequent treatment. The clinician must determine the risks and benefits of medication and educate the patient (and the family) to produce understanding and compliance with the medication prescribed for optimum results. The clinician must review the risks, benefits, adverse effects, and precautions of medications with the patient (and family) and obtain informed consent. Medication trials require monitoring for beneficial effects and adverse side effects. It is often necessary to switch medications that are ineffective or inadequate or that produce intolerable adverse effects. Although it is best to avoid polypharmacy (more than one medication at a time), combinations of medications may be necessary to attain optimization of response or remission of illness. Withdrawal of medication often requires close monitoring for withdrawal effects and relapse of symptoms (Cohen, 2003).

**Types of Medications.** Antianxiety medications (also known as *anxiolytics*, minor tranquilizers, or *psycholeptics*) treat anxiety disorders, compulsions, tension, and agitation. Some have potential for dependency. Benzodiazepines, antidepressants (especially selective serotonin reuptake inhibitors [SSRIs]), buspirone, hydroxyzine, pregabalin, and other agents are useful in the treatment of anxiety disorders (Hollander & Simeon, 2008).

Benzodiazepines produce a calming effect on neurons by enhancing the effect of the neurotransmitter gamma-aminobutyric acid (GABA). They have sedative, hypnotic, anxiolytic, muscle relaxant, and anticonvulsant effects (Hollander & Simeon, 2008). Common side effects include drowsiness, dizziness, diminished concentration and coordination, decreased libido, impaired memory, confusion, and depression. Risks include development of dependence, tolerance, and withdrawal effects (Hollander & Simeon, 2008, 2011). Generally, they are prescribed for short-term management of anxiety. They act within an hour and are useful for overwhelming anxiety and panic attacks. Since other medications may take weeks to reach therapeutic effect, clinicians may start the other agent and a benzodiazepine together for a few weeks until achieving response and then gradually withdraw the benzodiazepine. Common benzodiazepines include Xanax (alprazolam), Klonopin (clonazepam), Valium (diazepam), Ativan (lorazepam), and Librium (chlordiazepoxide) (Chew, Hales, & Yudofsky, 2009).

Pregabalin (Lyrica) is a structural analogue of GABA. It is effective and quick-acting for GAD. Somnolence and dizziness are the most frequent side effects. There is no withdrawal syndrome. Gabapentin (Neurontin, Gabarone) is an anticonvulsant (*antiepileptic*) for epilepsy, neuropathic pain, and anxiety disorders. It is structurally related to GABA. Side effects include sleepiness, dizziness, nausea, and fatigue (Sadock & Sadock, 2007).

Buspirone (BuSpar) is a mild, slow-acting tranquilizer. It increases serotonin and decreases dopamine. Common side effects include nausea, headaches, dizziness, drowsiness, and upset stomach (Sadock & Sadock, 2007).

Hydroxyzine (Atarax, Vistaril) is an antihistamine that can reduce anxiety and tension short-term (less than four months). Common side effects include headaches, dizziness, drowsiness, upset stomach, and disturbed coordination (Sadock & Sadock, 2007).

Antidepressants are the mainstay for

the treatment of anxiety disorders. These include SSRIs, tricyclic antidepressants (TCAs), monoamine oxidase inhibitors (MAOIs), and the newer atypical antidepressants (that is, they do not fit into other classes) (Hollander & Simeon, 2008).

The antidepressants most widely prescribed for anxiety are the SSRIs, which include Paxil (paroxetine), Prozac (fluoxetine), Zoloft (sertraline), Luvox (fluvoxamine), Celexa (citalopram), and Lexapro (escitalopram). They work by regulating serotonin levels in the brain to elevate mood and have been used to treat panic disorder, OCD, and GAD. Common side effects include nausea, nervousness, headaches, sleepiness, sexual dysfunction, dizziness, stomach upset, and weight gain (Sadock & Sadock, 2007; Diamond, 2009).

Serotonin-norepinephrine reuptake inhibitors (SNRIs) include desvenlafaxine (Pristiq), duloxetine (Cymbalta), milnacipran (Ixel), and venlafaxine (Effexor). Norepinephrine-dopamine reuptake inhibitors (NDRIs) include bupropion (Wellbutrin, Zyban) (Sadock & Sadock, 2007; Diamond, 2009).

Monoamine oxidase inhibitors (MAOIs) include Marplan (isocarboxazid), Nardil (phenelzine), Emsam (selegiline), and Parnate (tranylcypromine). They increase availability of monoamine neurotransmitters by inhibiting the monoamine oxidase enzyme from breaking them down. Consumption of foods containing tyramine can lead to hypertensive crises for persons taking MAOIs (Sadock & Sadock, 2007; Diamond, 2009).

**Conclusion.** For optimal response, medication prescription and monitoring must be part of a comprehensive and integrated treatment approach. Effective communication among providers and with the patient (and collateral individuals) is essential for the best results.

E. John Kuhnley

## REFERENCES


Chew, R. H., Hales, R. E., & Yudofsky, S. C. (2009). *What Your Patients Need to Know About Psychiatric Medications.* Arlington, VA: American Psychiatric Publishing.

Cohen, B. J. (2003). *Theory and Practice of Psychiatry.* New York, NY: Oxford University Press.

Diamond, R. J. (2009). *Instant Psychopharmacology* (2nd ed.). New York, NY: Norton.

Dupont, R. L., DuPont, E., & DuPont, C. M. (2003). *The Anxiety Cure: An Eight-Step Program for Getting Well* (2nd ed.). Hoboken, NJ: Wiley & Sons.

DuPont, R. L., Spencer, E. D., & Dupont, C. M. (2003). *The Anxiety Cure: An Eight-Step Program for Getting Well.* Hoboken, NJ: Wiley & Sons.

Hart, A. D. (1999). *The Anxiety Cure: You Can Find Emotional Tranquility and Wholeness.* Nashville, TN: Nelson.

Hollander, E., & Simeon, D. (2008). Anxiety disorder. In R. E. Hales, S. C. Yudofsky, & G. O. Gabbard (Eds.), *The American Psychiatric Publishing Textbook of Psychiatry* (pp. 505- 608). Arlington, VA: American Psychiatric Publishing.

Hollander, E., & Simeon, D. (2011) Anxiety disorder. In R. E. Hales, S. C. Yudofsky, & G. O. Gabbard. (Eds.), *The Essentials of Psychiatry* (pp. 255-270). Arlington, VA: American Psychiatric Publishing.

Sadock, B. J., & Sadock, V. A. (2007). *Kaplan and Sadock's Synopsis of Psychiatry: Behavioral Sciences/Clinical Psychiatry* (10th ed.). Philadelphia, PA: Lippincott Williams & Wilkins.

Sperry, L. (1995). *Psychopharmacology and Psychotherapy Strategies for Maximizing Treatment Outcomes.* New York, NY: Brunner/Mazel.


## ANTIDEPRESSANT DRUGS

**History.** The pharmacological treatment of depression dates back to the 1950s, when it was observed that two antituberculosis drugs also had the effect of stimulating the mood of depressed patients as a side effect. Imipramine was developed in the late 1950s as a targeted treatment for depression and opened the door to two decades of intense research into medications for depression. By 2005, antidepressants had become the most widely prescribed medications in the United States. Despite this, it is still estimated that only 25% of depressed patients are appropriately treated.

**Appropriate Uses.** Antidepressants are FDA approved to treat mood disorders (such as major depression and dysthymia), anxiety disorders (obsessive-compulsive disorder, panic disorder, generalized anxiety disorder), premenstrual dysphoric disorder, fibromyalgia, diabetic peripheral neuropathy pain, low back pain, and musculoskeletal pain from osteoarthritis. They are used "off-label" (not FDA approved) for headaches, irritable bowel syndrome, insomnia, ADHD, perimenopausal syndrome, bulimia, and adjunctively with mood stabilizers for bipolar depression, smoking cessation, trichotillomania, weight loss in obese patients, phobias, and to decrease relapse in substance-abuse patients with a history of depression.

**Mechanism of Action.** It is not fully known how these medications work. It has been speculated that they work by raising the amounts of neurotransmitters (serotonin, norepinephrine, and dopamine) that are available to neurons in the brain. However, this effect can be measured after hours or days on these medications with therapeutic benefit taking weeks to months. Current thinking is that depression is caused by a constellation of factors, including genetic modulation and expression, inflammatory damage by cytokines, stress induction of cortisol systems, inhibition of brain "fertilizers" (brain derived neurotrophic factor), atrophy of key brain areas (hippocampus), nutritional issues (such as a deficiency of vitamin D and folate), and other neurochemical effects, such as glutamate, GABA, endogenous opiates, and substance P. Researchers believe antidepressants start a cascade of effects that may involve multiple aspects of these mechanisms of action.

**Types.** Antidepressants are grouped by known mechanisms of action on neurotransmitter systems in the brain. Selective serotonin reuptake inhibitors (SSRIs) enhance serotonin transmission and include Prozac, Paxil, Zoloft, Celexa, Lexapro, and Luvox. Serotonin norepinephrine reuptake inhibitors (SNRIs) are represented by Pristiq, Cymbalta, and Effexor. Tricyclic antidepressants enhance serotonin and norepinephrine along with other systems that predict more side effects (histamine and acetylcholine). They include Elavil, Pamelor, Sinequan, Surmontil, Norpramine, and Anafranil. Wellbutrin enhances dopamine and norepinephrine. Remeron, Serzone, and Desyrel interact with receptor systems that result in enhancement in multiple neurotransmitter systems. MAO inhibitors target enzymes (monoamine oxidase) that metabolize serotonin, norepinephrine, and dopamine, with resultant widespread and potent effects. However, they also affect the same enzymes in the gastrointestinal tract that keep dietary toxins out of the system. Therefore, patients on Parnate, Nardil, Marplan, or higher dosage Emsam patches would have to adhere to a diet that is absent of the tyramine, which can dramatically increase blood pressure. These different classes of antidepressants are combined to complement different mechanisms of action. Other types of medications are added to antidepressants to enhance their productivity. These "augmenters" include Zyprexa, Abilify, Seroquel, Buspar, Lithium, thyroid, Deplin, Provigil, and psychostimulants. There are potential side effects to all of these options that must become a part of the risk benefit decision-making calculation.

**Controversies.** Some concerns revolve around the use of antidepressants. These are some common complaints and responses:

- They are addictive. Response: None of the FDA approved antidepressants cause craving or true withdrawal; however, most of these drugs, like most pharmaceuticals, should be tapered, not stopped abruptly.
- They do not work. Response: When compared to placebo, the benefits of

antidepressants are not impressive in mild cases of depression. The more severe the depression, the greater the chances of efficacy.

- You cannot get off of them. Response: Most patients take antidepressants for less than a year. Only about 20% of patients take these medications long term.
- They cause long-term damage. Response: Long-term exposure is associated with a risk for weight gain, sexual dysfunction, and emotional blunting. However, the failure to treat depression is associated with long-term risks of heart disease, diabetes, disability, divorce, and more.
- Taking them will take the place of spiritual and psychological growth. Response: These medications can relieve dysfunctional symptoms, such as depression and anxiety, but they do not promote love, joy, peace, patience, and hope. To expect otherwise is to invite disappointment.

**Michael R. Lyles**

## REFERENCES

Banov, M. (2010). *Taking Antidepressants: Your Comprehensive Guide to Starting, Staying On, and Safely Quitting.* North Branch, MN: Sunrise River Press.

Preston, J. & Johnson, J. (2009). *Clinical Psychopharmacology Made Ridiculously Simple.* Miami, FL: MedMaster.

Stahl, S. (2009). *The Prescriber's Guide (Essential Psychopharmacology Series).* New York, NY: Cambridge University Press.

## ANTIPSYCHOTIC DRUGS

**Description.** Antipsychotic drugs are medications designed to treat psychoses, including hallucinations, delusions (fixed false beliefs), and disorganized and disordered thoughts (Craighead & Nemeroff, 2001).

**History.** For thousands of years, the herb *Rauwolfia serpentina* was used to treat psychosis (Craighead & Nemeroff, 2001). In 1952, reserpine, a pharmaceutical used to treat high blood pressure, was isolated from *Rauwolfia* and discovered to cause high rates of depression. The same year, French anesthesiologists observed that patients given a pre-anesthesia drug, chlorpromazine, were calmer after surgery and had a certain indifference to life. This led to a "chemical" hypothesis of mental illness and to the use of chlorpromazine as a tranquilizer, with subsequent discovery that it effectively treated psychosis. In 1954, chlorpromazine was the first drug to receive FDA approval as an antipsychotic.

Shortly thereafter, other first-generation or *typical* antipsychotics were developed and approved for use in the United States, including fluphenazine and thioridazine in 1959 and haloperidol in 1967. Beginning in the 1990s and continuing today, second-generation or *atypical* antipsychotics have been developed and approved for use in the United States. Second-generation antipsychotics include, in order of their approval for use in the United States, clozapine, risperidone, olanzapine, quetiapine, ziprasidone, aripiprazole, paliperidone, asenapine, iloperidone, and lurasidone (Shorter, 2005).

**Awareness.** In order to understand the functional difference between the first- and second-generation antipsychotics, we first need to understand basic brain circuits. The brain has many neurotransmitters—chemical messengers that communicate between neurons. One of these transmitters is a chemical called dopamine. In the brain there are four primary dopamine circuits, or pathways (groups of neurons that operate by using dopamine as their primary messenger):

1. *Mesolimbic.* This is found deep beneath the temporal portion of the brain (Deligiannidis & Rothschild,

2010). Too much dopamine here is thought to cause the psychotic symptoms of hallucination, delusions, violent aggression, and rapid, racing, and disorganized thoughts. Blocking dopamine in this pathway is what treats psychosis.

2. *Mesocortical.* This is the dopamine pathway terminating in the brain region right behind the forehead. Blocking dopamine in this pathway contributes to side effects such as slowed thinking, depression, loss of creativity, and zombielike states (Howland & Thase, 1999; Diamond, 2009).

3. *Nigrostriatal.* This pathway is deep inside the brain and is responsible for smooth muscle movement. Loss of neurons in this pathway causes Parkinson's disease. Therefore, blocking dopamine in this pathway would cause Parkinson-like symptoms of muscle stiffness, tremor, and rigidness (Muller, 2007). Chronic blockage here can lead to permanent involuntary movement problems (tardive dyskinesia). Such things as lip smacking and constant tongue movement are most common (Stahl, 2008).

4. *Tuberoinfundibular.* This dopamine pathway into the pituitary gland controls prolactin release. Prolactin is a hormone that causes the breast to produce milk. Dopamine prevents prolactin release and thus milk production (Stahl, 2008). Therefore, blocking dopamine in this pathway can cause the side effect of milk production.

The factor that determines whether a medication is considered a first-generation (typical) or second-generation (atypical) antipsychotic is the way the drug interacts with neuronal receptors. All currently known antipsychotics block the dopamine receptors wherever those receptors are found. By blocking dopamine receptors in all the pathways, these medications not only treat psychosis but also cause various side effects (Mizenberg, Yoon, & Carter, 2011).

The second-generation antipsychotics, in addition to blocking dopamine receptors, also block receptors found on the dopamine-producing neurons that are sensitive to serotonin (Mizenberg et al., 2011). Why is this important? Serotonin modulates the activity of the dopamine neurons. When serotonin stimulates the receptors on the dopamine neurons, a braking signal is sent, telling the dopamine neuron to stop releasing dopamine (Diamond, 2009). The newer agents block these specific serotonin receptors on the dopamine neurons, which results in continued dopamine release. Fortunately, all the dopamine pathways *except* the mesolimbic pathway have these serotonin receptors (Cohen, 2003). Because of the serotonin blockade on all the other pathways, the atypical drugs reduce psychosis and have fewer of the traditional side effects than do the typical antipsychotics.

**Treatment Application.** Antipsychotic medications are used to treat all psychotic disorders, such as schizophrenia, and are also used to treat bipolar disorder and, as augmenting agents in treatment-resistant depression, to control agitation in dementia patients, calm individuals in delirium and drug-induced agitated states, and treat obsessive-compulsive disorder (Cohen, 2003; Diamond, 2009; Stahl, 2008). These are the most common side effects:

*Typical drugs.* Sedation, Parkinson-like movement problems, dry mouth, constipation, sluggishness, prolactin elevations with milk production, tardive dyskensia, and sexual dysfunction (Stahl, 2008).

*Atypical drugs.* Sedation, increased appetite, weight gain, elevated cholesterol, increased risk diabetes mellitus, dry mouth, sexual dysfunction, and to a much lesser degree, movement problems (Mizenberg et al., 2011).

**Biblical Issues.** More than 6,000 years from Eden, God's creation is marred with many biological defects, including defects of brain structure and function. Sometimes these defects result in alterations in our ability to reason, think clearly, and accurately perceive reality. In such a state, it is more difficult to discern truth and come to the knowledge of God. To the degree we can intervene with medication and restore the ability to reason clearly and perceive reality accurately, we increase the ability to know God and work with the Holy Spirit to restore the image of God in man. Antipsychotic medications are tools we can utilize to help those suffering with physical brain illness to think and function more clearly.

**Timothy R. Jennings**

### REFERENCE


Cohen, B. J. (2003). *Theory and Practice of Psychiatry.* New York, NY: Oxford University Press.

Craighead, W. E., & Nemeroff, C. B. (Eds.). (2001). *The Corsini Encyclopedia of Psychology and Behavioral Science.* New York, NY: Wiley & Sons.

Deligiannidis, K. M., & Rothschild, A. J. (2010). Mood and anxiety disorders. In A. J. Rothschild (Ed.), *Evidence-Based Guide to Psychotic Medications* (pp. 45-92). Washington, DC: American Psychiatric Publishing.

Diamond, R. J. (2009). *Instant Psychopharmacology* (2nd ed.). New York, NY: Norton.

Howland, R. H., & Thase, M. E. (1999). Affective disorders: Biological aspects. In M. Theodore, P. H. Blaney, & R. D. Davis (Eds.), *Oxford Textbook of Psychopathology* (pp.166-202). New York, NY: Oxford University Press.

Mizenberg, M. J., Yoon, J. H., & Carter, C. S. (2011). Schizophrenia. In R. E. Hales, S. C. Yudofsky, & G. O. Gabbard (Eds.), *Essentials of Psychiatry* (pp. 111-150). Washington, DC: American Psychiatric Publishing.

Muller, T. (2007). Drug treatment of motor symptoms in Parkinson's disease. In A. Lajtha, M. Youdin, P. Riederer, S. A. Mandel., & L. Battistin (Eds.), *Handbook of Neurochemistry and Molecular Neurobiology: Degenerative Disease of the Nervous System* (3rd ed, pp. 103-122). Orangeburg, NY: Springer.

Shorter, E. (2005). *A Historical Dictionary of Psychiatry.* New York, NY: Oxford University Press.

Stahl, S. M (2008). *Antipsychotics and Mood Stabilizers: Stahl's Essential Psychopharmacology* (3rd ed.). New York, NY: Cambridge University Press.

Stein, D. J., Kupfer, D. J., & Schatzberg, A. F. (Eds.). (2005). *The American Psychiatric Publishing Textbook of Mood Disorders* (pp. 292-304). Washington, DC. American Psychiatric Publishing.


## PSYCHOACTIVE DRUGS

**Description.** A psychoactive drug is any substance that alters brain functioning, and subsequently, a person's behavior. Ashley and O'Rourke (2002) describe how these drugs "alter emotions, perceptions, and imagination so that the patient is able to pursue a more normal pattern of behavior" (p. 162).

According to the Substance Abuse and Mental Health Services Administration, alcohol, caffeine, and nicotine are the three most commonly used legal psychoactive drugs (U.S. Department of Health and Human Services, 2006). Illegal drug use is also prevalent and destructive; statistics estimate that 45% of Americans have used a psychoactive substance illegally at some point (U.S. Department of Health and Human Services). In the mental-health field, psychoactive drugs have been used to effectively treat a variety of disorders. They have been called various names—psychiatric drugs, psychotherapeutic drugs, and treatments in psychopharmacology. These drugs are comprised of many drug types—psycho-stimulants, antidepressants, antianxiety drugs, antipain drugs, antipsychotic drugs, mood stabilizers, muscle relaxants, and sleep-inducing medications, just to name a few.

**History.** Psychiatric medications have been used since ancient times to produce feelings of relaxation or to provide energy (Kahn & Fawcett, 2008). Opioids are identified in literature as early as 300 BC. Scientific advancements in recent years have led to the development of many new drugs for the treatment of specific disorders (Ashley & O'Rourke, 2002), including chloral hydrate (1860), meprobamate (1935), amphetamine (1936), lithium carbonate (1948), Thorazine (1954), Tofranil (1958), Librium

(1960), Tegretol (1974), Prozac (1987), Risperdal (1994), and Latuda (2011).

**Biblical and Spiritual Issues.** Some Christians are skeptical of the use of any medications; however, Scripture does makes clear reference to medications and the care of physicians (Mt. 9:12; Lk. 4:23; Col. 4:14). Beginning with God's provision of "every seed-bearing plant" to eat (Gen. 1:29) and clear diet regulations in Old Testament law, Scripture presents a holistic view of care. It is interesting to see how many recent medical findings line up with biblical guidelines for health. For example, the book of Genesis refers to fish as an important dietary element. Today, the omega-3 fatty acids present in fish oil have been found beneficial to the heart and brain (Siddiqui et al., 2004). In other words, an ordinary substance like fish oil could be considered a psychiatric drug.

The apostle Paul notes the importance of helping the whole person, referencing the spirit (the theological), soul (the psychological), and body (the physiological) (1 Th. 5:23). One may argue that the spiritual is most important, which is an accurate assessment. Nothing is as important as where one spends eternity; the temporal pales in comparison to the spiritual. One may also argue that the psychological is more important than the physiological, and this might also be accurate. A sound mind, stable emotions, and a strong will for Christ can decrease physiological problems.

**Benefits.** For years, physicians and counselors minimized the role of psychiatric medications. Although still controversial, the importance of psychoactive drugs today cannot be denied. Research suggests that mental-health professionals are becoming more accepting of new psychoactive drugs, as newer drugs are more refined and produce fewer side effects (Coppock & Hopton, 2000). The use of psychoactive drugs is becoming widely accepted, with obvious benefits to thousands, especially in the past 60 years.

Psychoactive drugs are often used when stress plays a role in shifting the stability of the central nervous system. Stress also plays a strong role in the induction of medical disorders in other organs (cardiovascular disease is the number one killer, and immune system disease is number two). Psychoactive drugs have been used to successfully treat patients with schizophrenia, depression, anxieties, and phobias, to name a few (Kahn & Fawcett, 2008). With antipsychotics, people have left mental hospitals by the thousands; with antidepressants, suicides have been abated; with psychostimulants, many have been able to pay attention for the first time in their lives; with mood stabilizers, convulsions have been quelled and moods are less extreme. In addition, patients have benefited from the introduction of imaging devices, such as the positron emission tomography (PET) scans in 1975 and the completion of indelible genome studies starting in 1980 and continuing into the 21st century.

However, "psychoactive drugs can never be the total answer to mental health because there are so many social factors involved in psychological development" (Ashley & O'Rourke, 2002, p. 162). Psychoactive drugs are powerful substances and can be addictive. Therefore, it is essential that mental-health professionals stay up-to-date with the latest research on the effectiveness and suitability of medications (Ghodse, 2010). Additionally, it is important that such drugs not be viewed as substitutes for deeper issues for healing that may need to be addressed.

Ultimately, the issue is not so much whether clients are taking psychoactive drugs, but rather, whether they are maintaining a functional lifestyle and are being effective for Christ. Sometimes, psychoactive drugs can be instrumental in providing stability so people can think clearly and follow Christ wholeheartedly.

**Frank Minirth**

## REFERENCES

Ashley, B., & O'Rourke, K. (2002). *Ethics of Health Care.* Washington, DC: Georgetown University Press.

Coppock, V., & Hopton, J. (2000). *Critical Perspectives on Mental Health.* New York, NY: Routledge.

Ghodse, H. (2010). *Godhse's Drugs and Addictive Behavior: A Guide to Treatment.* New York, NY: Cambridge University Press.

Kahn, A. P., & Fawcett, J. (2008). *The Encyclopedia of Mental Health* (3rd ed.). New York, NY: Infobase.

Siddiqui, R., Shaikh, S., Sech, L., Yount, H., Stillwell, W., & Zaloga, G. (2004). Omega 3-fatty acids: Health benefits and cellular mechanisms of action. *Mini Review in Medicinal Chemistry, 4*(8), 859-87.

U.S. Department of Health and Human Services, Substance Abuse and Mental Health Services Administration. (2006). *National Survey on Drug Use and Health.* Retrived from http://oas.samhsa.gov/NSDUH/2k9NSDUH/2k9ResultsP.pdf

# 4

# CHRISTIAN COUNSELING AS MINISTRY AND PROFESSION

## LAY COUNSELING

**Description.** Lay helpers are caring individuals without professional credentials who seek to aid spiritually and emotionally distressed people in church or ministry environments. Although they typically have limited training in mental health or pastoral care, most have received instruction in a specific model of how to care for hurting people. They may minister in a clear organizational structure, such as a lay help center in a church, or in more informal venues, such as a person's house, a park, a coffee shop, and the like. This article addresses the utility of lay helpers, guidelines for lay helper ministry, the variety of lay help approaches, and how experiences with lay helpers may shape the people's expectations for professional treatment.

**Why Have Lay Helpers?** Lay helpers provide an important complementary ministry to traditional mental-health services. Many people do not have insurance to cover professional counseling services, managed care often limits access to care, and state mental-health systems are overburdened. Some pastors have limited training or feel too busy to minister effectively to hurting people. In these situations, lay helpers can fill an important need as long as proper guidelines are implemented. Preliminary research supports the efficacy of lay help approaches, but true experimental studies are needed to confirm these initial results (Garzon & Tilley, 2009).

**Lay-Helper Guidelines.** Lay helpers should work within the limits of their competency, and ideally, they should be supervised by a licensed mental-health professional (Tan, 1991). High-risk situations that include the possibility of suicide or homicide, psychotic thinking, personality disorders, and complex trauma (such as dissociative identity disorder) should be referred to licensed therapists. In these situations, lay helpers can complement mental-health services by being supportive friends of hurting people rather than seeking to resolve the distress.

**Lay-Helper Approaches.** Numerous lay-helper models exist. Garzon, Worthington, Tan, and Worthington (2009) offer four categories:

- Stephen Ministry (www.stephenministries.org) provides an example of an *active listening* lay helper approach. Such models combine Rogerian principles, such as unconditional positive regard, empathy, and basic listening skills, with prayer and Scripture.
- *Cognitive and solution-focused* lay approaches stress the role of automatic thoughts, problem-solving skills, and client strengths in working with people. Backus (1985) and Holland (2007) provide examples of these models.
- *Inner healing* approaches consist of "a range of 'journey back' methodologies that seek, under the Holy Spirit's leading, to uncover personal, familial, and

ancestral experiences that are thought to contribute to the troubled present" (Hurding, 1995, p. 297). These have similarities to psychodynamic and experiential therapies, but they emphasize prayer-focused encounters with Christ as the mechanisms of change. The Sandfords' model (www.elijahhouse.org) is one type of this strategy.

- Light University from the American Association of Christian Counselors (www.aacc.net/courses/biblical-counseling) exemplifies a *mixed approach,* including a broad range of psychological and spiritual formation perspectives. Light University utilizes a variety of highly qualified Christian mental-health professionals in the development of its training resources. Online training with this approach is also available.

**Lay Helper Impact on Clinical Therapy.** People who have experienced lay help may come to professional therapy with specific expectations. For example, they sometimes believe the clinician should be an expert in prayer or Scripture who uses similar but more advanced strategies. Given this possibility, clinicians should assess for previous lay help experiences as part of the intake process and clarify how they actually do therapy as part of informed consent (Garzon et al., 2009).

Therapists also may have training in lay help models and incorporate these into their practice. Competency issues and expanded informed-consent procedures should be considered in such cases. These include noting the empirical status of the approach, describing any potential for increased emotional distress, and indicating alternative treatment options (Hunter & Yarhouse, 2009).

**Conclusion.** Lay helpers provide an important resource for the Christian community that complements traditional mental-health services. Appropriate guidelines for lay help ministry have been developed, and a wide variety of lay help models are present. Lay help experiences can impact client expectations for what occurs in therapy, so assessment of this area should be included in treatment.

**Fernando Garzon**

## REFERENCES


Backus, W. (1985). *Telling the Truth to Troubled People.* Minneapolis, MN: Bethany House.

Garzon, F., & Tilley, K. (2009). Do lay Christian counseling approaches work? What we currently know. *Journal of Psychology and Christianity, 28,* 130-140.

Garzon, F., Worthington, E., Tan, S.-Y., & Worthington, R. (2009). Lay Christian counseling and client expectations for integration in therapy. *Journal of Psychology and Christianity, 28,* 113-120.

Holland, J. (2007). Solution-focused lay pastoral care. *Journal of Family and Community Ministries, 22*(2), 22-30.

Hunter, L., & Yarhouse, M. A. (2009). Considerations and recommendations for use of religiously based interventions in a licensed setting. *Journal of Psychology and Christianity, 28,* 159-166.

Hurding, R. F. (1995). Pathways to wholeness: Christian journeying in a postmodern age. *Journal of Psychology and Christianity, 14,* 293-305.

Tan, S.-Y. (1991). *Lay Counseling: Equipping Christians for a Helping Ministry.* Grand Rapids, MI: Zondervan.


# SPIRITUAL DISCIPLINES

**Description.** Spiritual disciplines can include any activity for the purpose of gaining a closer relationship with God. Through the ages, various Christian traditions have adopted an array of acts of commission and omission in an attempt to encourage these efforts. Various approaches have emerged that range from simple categories of behavior to expansive lists. The common thread among them is the process by which one decreases his "worldly" mindedness and becomes more like Christ. These approaches are integral to one's perception of spiritual formation as a whole and deserve some attention in the counseling room. Although generally seen as healthy, adaptable ways for Christians to relate to God and experience transformation, these acts can also be telltale signs of pathological thinking or maladaptive coping.

**Spiritual Formation.** As in the psychodynamic process, in which healthy emotional experiences and maladaptive schemas create psychodynamic conflict within the mind (see McCullough et al., 2003), the Christian is in a constant state of spiritual conflict, contending with natural "fleshly" desires and a regenerated mind and heart indwelt by the Holy Spirit. This is the battle the spiritually disciplined seek to win.

The goal, therefore, behind spiritual disciplines is the very formation of the Christ-centered life. It is no wonder that men and women through the ages have fought so hard to articulate effective strategies and call others to arms. The use of spiritual disciplines varies in organization, vantage point, and approach, but the majority of approaches are similar in content. Nearly all approaches, such as the contemplative, spiritual formation, and emerging approaches, all include attention to prayer, the reading of Scripture, repentance, fellowship, and forgiveness, to name only a few (see Ortberg, 1997; Dennis, 2005; Foster, 1998; Barton, 2006; and Calhoun, 2005). Regardless of the approach, all these authors address the importance of the heart's motivation in performing such activities. The perceived outcome and the expectations involved in being disciplined are keys to their success.

**Spiritual Considerations.** John Ortberg (1997) brings a particularly important point to light when he notes the distinction between training and trying. Ortberg suggests that a key to accomplishing the goal of spiritual formation through disciplines is to view the process as a long-term event, much like training for a marathon. He notes that running a marathon, particularly for competition, is not something one can try successfully. Most runners require years of training to accomplish such a feat. Spiritual formation and the use of disciplines should be viewed in a similar way. The regular exercise, even in the smallest ways, produces a long-term effect so that disciples accomplish great change over their lifetimes and are able to see themselves as works in progress.

**Considerations in Counseling.** At first glance, all acts of spiritual discipline may seem to come from a healthy heart and mind, but the counselor should not make this assumption. Disciplines of relating to God for forgiveness, fellowship, and praise can be vital and adaptive ways to connect with God and other people, and they can be signs of a healthy individual. However, even the most basic of religious activities can emerge as a compulsion resulting from feelings of intense anxiety (see Pargament, 1997). For this reason, the practice of disciplines as a process of coping can become either adaptive or maladaptive.

In the counseling room, spiritual disciplines can be useful treatment tools as well as telltale signs of psychodynamic conflict. The difference, as with many behaviors, may be identified by exploring the personal gains involved, the intensity and repetition by which the behavior is carried out, and the various perceptions surrounding intent and expected outcomes. For example, does a woman pray multiple times a day for a friend because she cares for her, or is she incapable of disentangling her fearful thoughts from her daily routine? Is it openhearted love with no strings attached, or is it a compulsive behavior?

In counseling, spiritual disciplines can be powerful, practical ways of treatment for the Christian, or they can be hurdles for both client and clinician. Counselors should be aware of their own perceptions of spiritual formation in order to avoid imposing personal or denominational influences into the counseling relationship. Relating to God is a very personal and unique experience that can be influenced by heritage, culture, tradition, and even personality (see Thomas, 1996).

The goal for implementing spiritual disciplines into one's life is to grow in faith, encourage Christlikeness, and through repentance overcome perceived weaknesses. The process by which a client forms these personal goals and carries them out in daily life can be a powerful area of exploration for the counselor and grounds for gaining personal insight for the counselee. As with every counseling opportunity, respect for personal preference and culture should always be considered.

**Mark Myers**

## REFERENCES


Barton, R. H. (2006). *Sacred Rhythms: Arranging Our Lives for Spiritual Transformation.* Madison, WI: InterVarsity Press.

Calhoun, A. A. (2005). *Spiritual Disciplines Handbook: Practices That Transform Us.* Downers Grove, IL: InterVarsity Press.

Dennis, J. (2005). *The Jesus Habits: Exercising the Spiritual Disciplines of Jesus.* Nashville, TN: Broadman & Holman.

Foster, R. J. (1998). *Celebration of Discipline.* New York, NY: HarperCollins.

McCullough, L., Kuhn, N., Andrews, S., Kaplan, A., Wolf, J., & Hurley, C. (2003). *Treating Affect Phobia: A Manual for Short-Term Dynamic Psychotherapy.* New York, NY: Guilford Press.

Ortberg, J. (1997). *The Life You've Always Wanted.* Grand Rapids, MI: Zondervan.

Pargament, K. I. (1997). *The Psychology of Religion and Coping.* New York, NY: Guilford Press.

Thomas, G. (1996). *Sacred Pathways.* Nashville, TN: Thomas Nelson.


## SPIRITUAL SUPPORT SYSTEMS

**Description.** Spiritual support systems are means of sustaining, undergirding, healing, and empowering people through divine intervention. Unlike natural support systems, which provide assistance from human sources, such as individual, family, and social relationships and organizations, spiritual support systems in Christian counseling originate in the divine purposes, prerogatives, provisions, and interventions of God. Christian counselors recognize that God is ultimately responsible for all of life and that we are to seek him in all our endeavors. He provides counseling resources that minister biologically, socially, psychologically, and spiritually to the whole person and that build up his church.

Diverse examples of church support ministries and organizations exist, including preaching and pastoral care, music and worship, administration, training and discipleship, counseling, social services, health care, and age- and gender-related church groups. These entities may become conduits of spiritual support but only as they engage the source of spiritual truth and power.

**History.** In Scripture, the word *spiritual* (Greek *pneumatikos*) is found primarily in Paul's letters, where it indicates evidence of the working of the Holy Spirit. It is used to describe a gift from God (1 Cor. 12); to indicate a person—a *pneumatikos* (1 Cor. 2:13,15), or one whose thoughts, words, and discerning judgment manifest the Holy Spirit; and to refer to objects, such as spiritual things or spiritual blessings (1 Cor. 9:11) (Mounce, 2006). The one time the term is used outside of Paul is in 1 Peter 2:5, where the Christian community is described as "being built into a spiritual house" and "offering spiritual sacrifices acceptable to God through Jesus Christ." So spiritual support systems can incorporate spiritual gifts, the embodiment of the spiritual in individuals, spiritual blessings, and spiritual communities of faith.

**Assessment.** The primary source for empowerment and expression of a Christian spiritual support system is the Holy Spirit. The Bible describes the Holy Spirit as a counselor or helper who teaches and reminds us of the words of Christ (Jn.

14:26). The Spirit fills and empowers Christians (Acts 1:5,8; Eph. 5:18) and is revealed in the spiritual fruit of love, joy, and peace (which strengthen the individual believer); patience, gentleness, and goodness (which nurture relationships with others); and faithfulness, meekness, and self-control (which emulate the conduct of Christ) (Gal. 5:22-23). The Spirit unites believers into one body (1 Cor. 12:13,27), forming the basic spiritual support system.

**Application.** The church—the universal (Eph. 1:22-23) and local (Acts 8:1; 13:1) body of Christ—provides Christians with a fundamental spiritual support system. "Where two or more gather in my name, there am I with them," said the Lord (Mt. 18:20). The Bible uses the image of a shepherd and sheep (Jn. 10:1-18), the vine and branches (Jn. 15:1-17), a building (Eph. 2:19-22), a bride and bridegroom (Rev. 19:7-8), and a body (Col. 1:24) to show the spiritual provision, nurture, protection, unity, and development of the people called and sanctified in Christ (1 Cor. 1:2).

Examples of expressions of spiritual support systems are found in the multiple roles, gifts, and activities identified in Scripture. Within the church, people are called to care for one another through a variety of roles, each of which is considered valuable, making a contribution to the unity and health of the body (1 Cor. 12). Spiritual gifts and ministries particularly related to spiritual support in counseling include prophecy, teaching, exhortation or encouragement, evangelism, serving, giving, healing, miracles, wisdom, knowledge, faith, discernment, helps, pastoring, and hospitality (Rom. 12:4-8; 1 Cor. 12; Eph. 4:1-16; 1 Pet. 4:8-11). Spiritual gifts have less to do with special abilities and more to do with service and ministry in strengthening the body of Christ (Kuen, 1971; Hemphill, 1988; Berding, 2006).

A number of biblical traits and spiritual disciplines or practices are related particularly to counseling and spiritual support systems. These include love, gentleness, self-control (1 Cor. 13; Gal. 5:22-23), walking with the Lord (1 Jn. 1:7), using the armor of God (Eph. 6:10-18), knowledge of God's Word (Josh. 1:8; Ps. 119), working toward biblical goals (Mt. 6:31-34; Lk. 16:17), giving God the glory (Num. 14:11-20; Phil. 1:11), purity in heart (Mt. 5:8), renewing the mind (Rom. 12:2), placing thoughts obedient to Christ (2 Cor. 10:5), wisdom (Eph. 1:17; Col. 3:16), discernment (Phil. 1:9-11), biblical morality (Jas. 1:22-25), acceptance (Rom. 15:16), compassion (Col. 3:12), empathy (Heb. 4:15), forgiveness (Eph. 4:32), peacemaking (Mt. 5:9; Jas. 3:18), prayer (Mt. 6:5-13; 1 Th. 5:17-18), service (Mt. 20:26-28; 1 Pet. 4:10), and ministering to all needs (Mt. 25:31-46) (Jones, 2006). With Paul, we should long to impart a spiritual gift, through spiritual support systems, to Christians in the local church so that they may be strengthened and "mutually encouraged by each other's faith" (Rom. 1:12).

Ian Jones

## REFERENCES


Berding, K. (2006). *What Are Spiritual Gifts?: Rethinking the Conventional View.* Grand Rapids, MI: Kregel.

Hemphill, K. S. (1988). *Spiritual Gifts: Empowering the New Testament Church.* Nashville, TN: Broadman Press.

Jones, I. F. (2006). *The Counsel of Heaven on Earth: Foundations for Biblical Christian Counseling.* Nashville, TN: B&H.

Kuen, A. (1971). *I Will Build My Church* (R. Lindblad, Trans.). Chicago, IL: Moody Press.

Mounce, W. D. (Ed.). (2006). *Mounce's Complete Expository Dictionary of Old and New Testament Words.* Grand Rapids, MI: Zondervan.


## AMERICAN ASSOCIATION OF CHRISTIAN COUNSELORS

The American Association of Christian Counselors (AACC) is the largest Christian mental-health membership organization in the world and is committed to assisting the entire community of care, including licensed clinicians, educators, pastors, and caring church members with little or no formal training. The AACC exists to resource and educate people helpers who practice from a Christian perspective and care about faith issues in the counseling setting.

**Mission Statement.** The intention of the AACC is to equip clinical, pastoral, and lay caregivers with biblical truth and psychosocial insights that minister to hurting persons and help them move to personal wholeness, interpersonal competence, mental stability, and spiritual maturity. The AACC is anchored on five key principles:

> *Our source.* We are committed to honor Jesus Christ and glorify God, remaining flexible and responsive to the Holy Spirit in all that he has called us to be and do.
>
> *Our strength.* We are committed to biblical truths and to clinical excellence and unity in the delivery of all our resources, services, training, and benefits.
>
> *Our service.* We are committed to effectively and competently serve the community of care worldwide—both our membership and the church at large—with excellence and timeliness and by over-delivery on our promises.
>
> *Our staff.* We are committed to value and invest in our people as partners in our mission to help others effectively provide Christ-centered counseling and soul care for hurting people.
>
> *Our stewardship.* We are committed to profitably steward the resources God gives to us in order to continue serving the needs of hurting people.

**History.** The AACC has long promoted the metaphor of Christian counseling as a train running on two tracks—the track of pastoral care and counseling that has its genesis in the early church 2,000 years ago, and the modern iteration of professional Christian counseling as a post-WWII development (Clinton & Ohlschlager, 2002). Below is a timeline of the first 25 years of the AACC.

> 1986. A Mississippi psychologist named Joe Dunn officially begins the AACC.
>
> 1991. Gary Collins and Tim Clinton assume control of the AACC. Membership is 700.
>
> 1992. The AACC reaches its first goal of 3,000 members and launches its flagship magazine, *Christian Counseling Today*, at the second International Congress in Atlanta.
>
> 1993. The AACC obtains continuing-education approval status with APA, NBCC, and various states. The AACC website is launched (www.aacc.net).
>
> 1995. The AACC introduces the provisional draft of the Christian Counseling Code of Ethics (see AACC, 2004); AACC cosponsors with Focus on the Family the International Congress on the Family in Denver.
>
> 1996. Membership reaches 17,000.
>
> 1997. The AACC launches *Marriage and Family: A Christian Journal* and holds its first World Conference in Dallas with 2,200 attendees.
>
> 1998. Tim Clinton assumes presidency and establishes new executive board.
>
> 1999. More than 3,000 attend the first bi-annual World Conference at the Opryland Hotel in Nashville, Tennessee, the largest single gathering of Christian counselors to that date. Membership reaches nearly 30,000. The AACC launches *Caring for People God's Way*, its first course in the biblical counselor training program later coined Light University.
>
> 2001. Membership reaches 40,000, with more than 5,000 attendees at the World Conference. E-women is

launched. More than a thousand pastors and crisis workers are trained for the aftermath of 9/11 in New York City. *The Soul Care Bible* is published.

2002. Tim Clinton and George Ohlschlager publish *Competent Christian Counseling.*

2003. Membership reaches nearly 50,000, with 6,000 attendees at the World Conference. Tim Clinton and Gary Sibcy publish *Attachments: Why You Love, Feel, and Act the Way You Do.*

2005. 7,000 members attend the World Conference in Nashville. *Caring for People God's Way* is published by Tim Clinton, Archibald Hart, and George Ohlschlager.

2006. The east (Myrtle Beach) and west (Denver) National Christian counseling events are sold out.

2007. 7,000 members attend the World Conference.

2008. The east (Orlando) and west (Dallas) National Christian counseling conferences once again sell out.

2009. 7,000 attend the World Conference.

2010. AACC moves from holding two regional conferences to one National Conference in the off year of the World Conference. Nearly 1,700 attend the first National Christian Counseling Conference in Branson, Missouri. Tim Clinton and Joshua Straub publish *God Attachment: Why You Believe, Act, and Feel the Way You Do About God.*

2011. The AACC holds its 25$^{th}$ anniversary World Conference in Nashville.

**AACC Christian Counseling Code of Ethics.** A code of ethics is a systematic statement of ethical standards that represent the moral convictions and guide the practice behavior of a group—in this case, Christian counselors. Every one of the primary counseling disciplines—psychiatry, psychology, social work, marriage and family therapy, and professional counseling—has an ethics code. In 1995, the AACC led the way in developing Christian counseling ethical codes. The preliminary draft of 1995 has been revised and updated. The latest edition of the *AACC Christian Counseling Code of Ethics* is the primary code of ethics in the Christian counseling field (AACC, 2004).

**Membership.** The AACC consists of nearly 50,000 members and includes the following categories of people helpers:

- Clinicians and educators, including psychiatrists, psychologists, social workers, licensed counselors, educators, and others who have advanced training in one of the mental-health professions.
- Religious leaders, including pastors, youth leaders, missionaries, pastoral counselors, Christian educators, and others with theological and/or counseling training.
- Lay counselors, including church members of parachurch organizations, spouses of professionals or religious leaders, and others who are interested in Christian counseling but who have little or no professional training.

**Member Services.** The AACC offers a variety of member benefits to help educate and inform members of various issues in the field of Christian counseling.

1. *Christian Counseling Today* (a quarterly magazine)
2. *Christian Counseling Connection* (a quarterly newsletter)
3. Counsel CDs (a quarterly interview with a Christian counseling leader, hosted by Tim Clinton)
4. professional conferences and trainings

5. *AACC eNews Monthly* (a monthly online publication)
6. *AACC Weekly Biblical Insights* (delivered online weekly)
7. opportunities for continuing education
8. listing in the National Membership Registry
9. online community (www.aacc.net)
10. an established professional code of ethics
11. Christian Care Referral Network

**Light University.** Starting in 1999 with the overwhelming launch of *Caring for People God's Way,* Light University began with a vision to provide academically sound, clinically excellent, and distinctively Christian resources to educate, equip, and serve people helpers in their professional, ministerial, and/or caregiving roles. Light University's joint vision with the AACC is to train one million leaders worldwide in counseling, coaching, and crisis and trauma intervention. More than 160,000 students are enrolled. Light University offers both certificate and diploma programs in the School of Counseling and Psychology, the School of Professional Life Coaching, and the School of Professional Development and Continuing Education. The newly innovated Light University Online offers world-renowned faculty, a robust and interactive online learning experience, proactive student support, and a relevant curriculum to help ensure students' success. Students enjoy interaction with peers around the world, flexibility in time and place of study, achievable five-week terms, and small, tight-knit virtual classes.

Tim Clinton
George Ohlschlager
Joshua Straub
Ryan Carboneau

## REFERENCES

American Association of Christian Counselors. (2004). *AACC Christian Counseling Code of Ethics.* Forest, VA: Author.

Clinton, T., & Ohlschlager, G. (2002). *Competent Christian Counseling: Foundations and Practice of Compassionate Soul Care.* Colorado Springs, CO: WaterBrook Press.

## ADVOCACY

**Description.** *Advocacy* has been defined as "the process or act of arguing or pleading for a cause or proposal" (Lee, 1998, p. 8). Client advocacy involves supporting, recommending, or pursuing a cause on behalf of a client. This effort also can be directed to reform unfair laws or regulations and bureaucratic processes. Counselors, pastors, and lay leaders can be effective in their respective ministries by providing both care and advocacy.

Professional effectiveness is undermined by advocating for one's client but not for the profession (Myers, Sweeney, & White, 2002, p. 400). Effectiveness is enhanced when counselors are respected by the persons and institutions with power to resolve clients' situations.

**History.** As early as the 1700s, health workers recognized the need for mental-health advocacy. (Myers et al., 2002, p. 395). Later, federal law established programs for mental-health advocacy in response to a Congressional investigation. (See the Protection and Advocacy for Mentally Ill Individuals Act, 42 U.S.C. §10801 et seq. [1985].)

Over the years, emerging professional associations have enabled counselors to advocate for laws and regulations protecting the public. In 2003, the American Counseling Association (ACA) endorsed advocacy competencies that stress the role of counselors through student and client empowerment, community collaboration, and sociopolitical intervention (Lewis, Arnold, House, & Toporek, 2002).

**Application.** Many different individuals

and groups can benefit from advocacy, including crime victims, the elderly, people with disabilities, the homeless, prisoners, and students. A counselor's role can range from making a telephone call to assisting legislators with drafting and promoting passage of a statute. If appropriate, counselors should teach their clients how to advocate for themselves so they gain confidence and useful skills.

Counselors can often advocate more effectively than clients can. A substance-abuse counselor watching a trend of addiction to prescription painkillers can help alleviate the underlying problem by working with state legislators to develop guidelines for licensing pain-management clinics. Counselors can also use their professional position to advocate for informed-consent laws and other stricter regulation of abortion clinics, support legislation encouraging premarital and predivorce counseling, or protect children by advocating for adoption laws requiring the prospective parents to be a married man and woman.

Effective working relationships between counselors and other professionals, such as physicians, attorneys, and politicians, can enhance advocacy for shared goals and values. Networking helps counselors transition into the advocacy role when needed.

**Biblical and Spiritual Issues.** An advocate is "one who pleads another's cause, who helps another by defending or comforting him" (Easton, 1897). Advocating and comforting are closely related in Scripture. Christ called the Holy Spirit an Advocate three times (Jn. 14:16; 15:26; 16:7). The Greek word (*parakletos*) is translated "Comforter" in some versions, although in 1 John 2:1, the same Greek word is translated "Advocate" when applied to Christ.

Isaiah challenged Israel, "Seek justice. Defend the oppressed. Take up the cause of the fatherless; plead the case of the widow" (1:17). Counselors find unique opportunities in these areas. They can help clients find deeper meaning in trials and suffering as they overcome evil by advocating for social change (Rom. 12:21).

**Legal and Ethical Concerns.** The American Association of Christian Counselors developed guiding principles for Christian counselors, ministers, and other people helpers in the *AACC Christian Counseling Code of Ethics*. Section 1-820 of the Code states that Christian counselors advocate for clients in relationship to the church, the community, and the government. The Code contains other references to client advocacy, including in the areas of managed care and privacy (see AACC Code 1-113, 1-470). Counselors are also reminded not to "advocate for, or assist the harmful actions of clients" (see AACC Code 1-120).

Counselor advocates and attorneys face similar challenges. As one legal writer observed, "Under the guise of zealous representation of a client's best interests, lawyers too often usurp the individual's power of self-determination, preempt the client's decisions, and destroy the client's dignity and humanity in the process" (Gutierrez, 1996, p. 115). In advocacy, as in other situations, counselors should take care to not inappropriately cross personal boundaries (Gregoire & Jungers, 2007, p. 13).

In client advocacy, as in all forms of service, competent counselors follow the admonition of the apostle Paul: "Do not be overcome by evil, but overcome evil with good."

**Anita L. Staver**

## REFERENCES

American Association of Christian Counselors. (2004). *AACC Christian Counseling Code of Ethics*. Retrieved from http://www.aacc.net/about-us/code-of-ethics/

Easton, M. G. (1987). *Illustrated Bible Dictionary* (3rd ed.). Nashville, TN: Thomas Nelson.

Gregoire, J., & Jungers, C. (2007). *The Counselor's Companion*. London, England: Psychology Press.

Gutierrez, F. J. (1996). Who is watching big brother when big brother is watching mental health advocacy programs? *Law & Psychology Review, 20,* 57.

Lee, C. C. (1998). Counselors as agents of social change. In C. C. Lee & G. W. Walz (Eds.), *Social Action: A Mandate for Counselors.* Alexandria, VA: American Counseling Association.

Lewis, J. H., Arnold, M. S., House, R., & Toporek, R. I. (2002). *ACA Advocacy Competencies.* Retrieved from http://counseling.org/Publications/

Myers, J. E., Sweeney, T. J., & White, V. E. (2002). Advocacy for counseling and counselors: A professional imperative. *Journal of Counseling & Development, 80*(4), 394-443.

## PROFESSIONAL IDENTITY AND DISCLOSURE

**Counselor Professional Identity.** For the professional Christian counselor, professional identity is an important element of a larger identity as a Christian and has profound implications on what it means to be a Christian counselor. Foremost, it means our professional identity must be synergized with our personal identity. We cannot compartmentalize our professional roles from our personal lives. In this sense, our professional identity emerges from who we are in Christ.

As professional Christian counselors, we are bringing our professional identities under the authority of Christ. We do not perform our counseling duties primarily to please our state licensing board, to please the ethics committee of our profession, or even primarily to please our clients. We primarily seek to please Christ, following Paul's admonition, "Do your work heartily, as for the Lord" (Col. 3:23 NASB). In fact, when we perform our profession by pleasing him, the other individuals and institutions will be usually pleased with our work because we do our work as ministry with excellence and integrity.

In the future as our culture changes, there may come a time when the profession demands that we hold certain views or perform our craft in ways that violate our Christian views and values. At this time we will need to take the apostle Peter's approach and "obey God rather than human beings" (Acts 5:29). Although I don't believe we are to that place yet, I do see some troubling conflicts emerging on the horizon.

As professional Christian counselors, our identity isn't only being followers of Christ but also being followers of Christ in a profession. Being professionals means that we have a higher level of expertise and training than do those who are paraprofessional or untrained. Therefore, professionals are protected by most states. If we are to be professionals of excellence and integrity, we need to be fully trained, licensed, and certified to perform our craft. Partially due to the historic perceived conflict between Christianity and psychology, some Christian counselors unfortunately have not done the hard work of being academically trained, licensed by the state, and certified to work with populations they are counseling. Today, with all the options for being academically trained, licensed, and certified in institutions and organizations that counsel from a Christian worldview, offering professional counsel without appropriate credentialing is unacceptable.

Following the ethical code of our profession assists the Christian counselor in gaining clarity about what behavior is acceptable. One critical aspect of the ethical code that directly relates to counselor professional identity is the category of "Competence in Christian Counseling" as found in the American Association of Christian Counselors' *AACC Christian Counseling Code of Ethics* (2004). This section addresses such issues as "Honoring the Call to Competent Christian Counseling," "Duties to Study and Maintain Expertise," "Maintaining Integrity in Work, Reports, and Relationships," and "Protective Action When Personal Problems Interfere."

**Disclosure.** Professional Christian counselors have the same responsibility as any other professional counselor to disclose to the community and the clients they serve information regarding their professional identity as well as client rights. As part of the responsibility to provide informed consent, both the AACC and American Counseling Association (2005) ethically require that professional counselors provide the following information:

- the purposes, goals, techniques, procedures, limitations, potential risks, and benefits of services
- the counselor's qualification, credentials, and relevant experience
- continuation of services upon the incapacitation or death of a counselor
- implications of diagnosis, the intended use of tests and reports, fees, and billing arrangements
- clients' right to confidentiality and to an explanation of its limitations, to obtain clear information about their records, to participate in the ongoing counseling plans, and to refuse any services or modify change and to be advised of the consequences of such refusal

Additionally, the ethics code of the AACC addresses disclosure for "Biblical-Spiritual Practices in Counseling" not directly addressed in ACA guidelines. This code states, "Christian counselors do not presume that all clients want or will be receptive to explicit spiritual interventions in counseling. We obtain consent that honors client choice, receptivity to these practices, and the timing and manner in which these things are introduced: prayer for and with clients, Bible reading and reference, spiritual meditation, the use of biblical and religious imagery, assistance with spiritual formation and discipline, and other common spiritual practices."

The AACC guidelines additionally point out the need for "Special Consent for More Difficult Interventions." In these cases, close or special consent is obtained for more difficult and controversial practices. These include but are not limited to deliverance and spiritual warfare activities; cult deprogramming work; recovering memories and treatment of past abuse or trauma; use of hypnosis and any kind of induction of altered states; authorizing (by MDs) medications, electroconvulsive therapy, or patient restraints; use of aversive, involuntary, or experimental therapies; engaging in reparative therapy with homosexual persons; and counseling around abortion and end-of-life issues. These interventions require more detailed discussions with clients or their representatives to explain the procedures, risks, and treatment alternatives. They also require detailed written agreement for the procedure.

**Gene A. Sale**

## REFERENCES

American Association of Christian Counselors. (2004). *AACC Christian Counseling Code of Ethics*. Retrieved from www.http://www.aacc.net

American Counseling Association. (2005). *ACA Code of Ethics*. Retrieved from www.http://counseling.org

*Part 2*

# Change in and Process of Christian Counseling

5

# CHANGE AND RESISTANCE TO CHANGE

## COUNSELOR-CLIENT RELATIONSHIP

**Description.** The relationship a counselor establishes with a counselee is the cornerstone on which the entire counseling process is built. Although a connection with a client is not an end goal, it is the means by which counseling goals are accomplished. Through the counselor-client relationship, exploration, experimentation, and growth are either facilitated or hindered.

God is a relational God who lives in perfect relationship. The very nature of God is face-to-face community. God put in us, his image-bearers, a craving to relate—first to himself and then to others. In the counseling office, the counselor creates a relationship with the client that provides an incarnational relationship through which counselees are exposed to God's character displayed by the counselor. The relationship is a context in which a counselee receives agape love, a need that is deep within every human heart.

The bond that occurs between the counselor and counselee is known as *rapport*, a term that captures the concepts of goodwill, confidence, trust, and caring. The Trinity could be characterized as the perfect model of rapport. The relationships between the Father, Son, and Holy Spirit are sustaining, trusting, and harmonious. The eternal and immutable rapport allows God to be all of who he is.

Therapeutically, rapport provides a context for clients to learn their true identity—to begin to understand that their worth makes them irreplaceable. It helps clients sense that God made them in his image for a special plan and purpose that only they can accomplish.

Clients often develop close relationships with their counselors through the sharing of their stories. Counselors care deeply for their clients. In fact, the intensity of this interaction gives the counselor the power to significantly impact the client positively or negatively. Though a counseling relationship might have similarities to a friendship, it is actually a one-way street, whereas friendship is mutual. The focus of the counselor-client relationship is on the needs of the client, not the counselor.

**Theories and Efficacy.** Virtually all counseling theories view the counselor-client relationship as integral to outcome, though each theory places a different emphasis on it. For example, in cognitive-behavioral counseling, the relationship is viewed as a collaborative process aimed at helping the client in self-discovery, but the vehicle of change is technique, not the relationship. In contrast, Rogerians hold that the counselor's primary effectiveness is through the relationship.

Theorists emphasize the importance of the counselor-client relationship because research consistently shows that it is one of the most important factors in counseling outcome (Asay & Lambert, 1999; Hubble, Duncan, & Miller, 1999; Kim, Ng, & Ahn, 2005). Moreover, the similarities between counselors' and clients' attitudes, beliefs, and values is considered the strongest predictor of outcome (Beutler, 1991; Beutler, Crago, & Arizmendi, 1986; Reis & Brown, 1999).

Given the salient nature of the counselor-client relationship, counselors must be skilled at establishing a bond with their clients. Thomas and Sosin (2011) recommend three means by which a counselor-client relationship can be established and maintained: (a) Create a safe haven, (b) establish presence with the counselee by actively listening, and (c) communicate empathy. When the counselee experiences the helping relationship as a safe haven, free disclosure is more likely to occur. A secure and stable helping relationship allows counselees the opportunity to struggle, fail, and learn without fear of losing the relationship.

**Characteristics.** The effective counseling relationship is exemplified by several crucial characteristics.

*Unconditional positive regard* includes warmth and agape love. The client needs to know that the counselor cares about him or her as an individual, regardless of personal circumstances or other differences. The counselor is firmly committed to the client; the counselor is for rather than against the client.

A second necessary characteristic is *acceptance*. The client believes the counselor is acting in his or her best interest.

Third, *empathy* demonstrates that the counselor understands the client's difficulties. The counselor must be able to get into his or her client's world, understand it, and communicate that understanding back to the client. In Hebrews 13:3, the writer captures the idea of empathy: "Remember those in prison as if you were together with them in prison, and those who are mistreated as if you yourselves were suffering." The Christian counselor feels with the client to the degree that he or she can fully relate to the experience.

Fourth, through *genuineness* or *authenticity*, the counselor sincerely believes what is said to the client.

Finally, the relationship must be characterized by *trust*. Over time, a developing trust allows the client the ability to share more deeply and authentically as the counselor proves himself or herself to be trustworthy. As Christian counselors, we want to be able to say, "Our conscience testifies that we have conducted ourselves...in our relations with you, with integrity and godly sincerity" (2 Cor. 1:12).

John C. Thomas

## REFERENCES

Asay, T. P., & Lambert, M. J. (1999). The empirical case for the common factors in therapy: Quantitative findings. In M. A. Hubble, B. L. Duncan, & S. D. Miller (Eds.), *The Heart and Soul of Change: What Works in Therapy*. Washington, DC: American Psychological Association.

Beutler, L. E. (1991). Have all won and must all have prizes? Revisiting Luborsky et al.'s verdict. *Journal of Counseling and Clinical Psychology, 59*, 226-232.

Beutler, L. E., Crago, M., & Arizmendi, T. G. (1986). Therapist variables in psychotherapy process and outcome. In S. L. Garfield & A. E. Bergin (Eds.), *Handbook of Psychotherapy and Behavior Change* (3rd ed.). New York, NY: Wiley & Sons.

Hubble, M. A., Duncan, B. L., & Miller, S. D. (Eds.). (1999). *The Heart and Soul of Change: What Works in Therapy* (pp. 23-55). Washington, DC: American Psychological Association.

Kim, B. S. K., Ng, G. F., & Ahn, A. J. (2005). Effects of client expectation for counseling success, client-counselor worldview match, and client adherence to Asian and European American cultural values on counseling process with Asian Americans. *Journal of Counseling Psychology, 52*(1), 67-76.

Reis, B. F., & Brown, L. G. (1999). Reducing psychotherapy dropouts: Maximizing perspective convergence in the psychotherapy dyad. *Psychotherapy, 36*, 123-136.

Thomas, J. C., & Sosin, L. (2011). *Therapeutic Expeditions: Equipping the Christian Counselor for the Journey*. Nashville, TN: B&H.

## CHANGE READINESS

How do people grow and change, especially when struggling with repetitive, negative behavior patterns, such as addictions, marital conflict, overeating, self-harm, and risky sexual behaviors? What does it mean when clients resist efforts to help them change?

**Description.** Effective counselors assess client readiness for change to enable them to provide the right kind of care. James Prochaska, Carlo DiClemente, and James Norcross (1992) attempt to explain the process of behavior change in their development of the transtheoretical model of change

(TTM). At the heart of this model is their conceptualization of identifiable stages individuals proceed through as they modify unwanted, unhelpful, or risky behaviors. These stages are identified as *precontemplation* (not considering change despite external pressures), *contemplation* (considering action but ambivalent about change), *preparation* (planning for change in the future), *action* (making changes), and *maintenance* (maintaining gains and preventing relapses).

**Assessment.** When clients fail to make progress in counseling, or they relapse after making initial changes, it is essential to assess why progress has stalled. Counselors who fail to make this assessment may fall prey to the fundamental attribution error (attributing characterological reasons for the behaviors) and conclude their clients lack the motivation or desire for change (Ross, Lepper, & Hubbard, 1975). Even as clients begin to change, counselors may find it helpful to make ongoing assessment of the commitment to change during treatment because client resolve may fluctuate over time. The consideration of a client's readiness for change has been found to reduce premature terminations (Brogan, Prochaska, & Prochaska, 1999) and may increase successful outcomes by providing stage-appropriate interventions (Levesque, Driskell, Prochaska, & Prochaska, 2008).

**Application.** Effective counseling begins and continues with assessment of client needs, abilities, and levels of change readiness. Clients who have yet to wrestle with the need to change problematic behaviors tend to be passive or defensive clients, rationalize their lack of effort, and be noncompliant with any prescribed homework. Therapists may find that avoiding exhortation and emotional pressure while expressing empathy and exploring barriers to change lead many of these clients to consider the possibility of change. Therapists should avoid giving these clients homework, but rather, ask them to take notice of possible benefits of committing to therapy.

Clients who *contemplate* a commitment to change often struggle with feelings of ambivalence due to the perception of significant risk and cost associated with the process. Their counselors will do well to focus on honest exploration of the risks and rewards of change and to develop additional incentives.

Clients who exhibit a growing commitment to change but have yet to begin are in the *preparation* stage of change. They have begun to see the need and value of change, but their enthusiasm often lacks specific strategies for growth. Counselors who support and validate these desires for change and who devise specific initial strategies tend to be successful in removing potential barriers that might derail the process.

Clients in the *action* stage of change take observable steps toward a goal. During this stage, they may experience a significant decrease in temptations to revert to old behaviors. Counselors of these clients cheerlead change efforts, avoid becoming too directive, and begin to focus on building insight, empathy for others, and self-awareness.

When clients achieve significant behavioral change, they move into a *maintenance* mode. During this time, they may take stock of unexpected costs and consequences of change and experience periods of discouragement and/or episodes of relapse. Counselors help these clients develop new life goals and address guilt or discouragement from relapses in order to recycle quickly to their new behavior pattern.

**Biblical and Spiritual Issues.** Through his letters to the Romans and Ephesians, Paul teaches that all are dead in their sins (Rom. 3:12; Eph. 2:1) and that God alone saves and sanctifies (Rom. 5:6; Eph. 2:5). And yet Paul often exhorts believers to pursue holiness and reject sinful behavior. God already lives in his children by means of the indwelling of the Holy Spirit, but Christians are not yet glorified. We all have a long way to go as we trust God to change us. In Paul's letters and in counseling offices, the human experience of change varies with levels of understanding, desire, and motivation. To remedy this human weakness, God empowers members of the church community to support each other.

Rather than assume that struggles to change are simply the result of lack of desire, counselors need to consider change readiness and encourage clients with interventions designed to activate their innate desire to put off the old self, renew their minds, and put on new, healthy habits of life (Eph. 4:17-24). Following Jesus' example in his relationships with "sinners," counselors often utilize caring questions and acts of mercy, but they rarely rebuke people when trying to increase their motivation.

**Philip G. Monroe**

### REFERENCES

Brogan, M. M., Prochaska, J. O., & Prochaska, J. M. (1999). Predicting termination and continuation status in psychotherapy by using the transtheoretical model. *Psychotherapy, 36,* 105-113.

Levesque, D. A., Driskell, M., Prochaska, J. M., & Prochaska, J. O. (2008). Acceptability of stage-matched expert system intervention for domestic violence offenders. *Violence and Victims, 23,* 432-445.

Prochaska, J. O., DiClemente, C. C., & Norcross, J. C. (1992). In search of how people change: Applications to addictive behaviors. *American Psychologist, 47,* 1102-1114.

Ross, L., Lepper, M., & Hubbard, M. (1975). Perseverance in self-perception and social perception: Biased attributional processes in the debriefing paradigm. *Journal of Personality and Social Psychology, 32,* 880-892.

## DENIAL

**Description.** Denial, one of the best-known defense mechanisms, is the conscious, subconscious, or unconscious refusal to admit to one's self that something negative has occurred in one's life. For some people the pain of loss or the challenge of an alternate belief is so great that they look for ways to deny the truth for a while. Although change is a fundamental building block of human experience, people sometimes perceive negative change as too great, and they resist it intellectually or psychologically.

Denial functions as an ego protector or buffer zone to protect people from things they cannot cope with, such as anxiety or pain. Denial requires significant energy, but it temporarily resolves emotional conflict by disavowing the thoughts, feelings, needs, or wants from people's external reality that are consciously intolerable at the time. Typically, individuals experience denial initially and then begin to realize that the change cannot be ignored.

**History.** Sigmund Freud first postulated denial as a defense mechanism, but Anna Freud was the first to seriously research the psychoanalytic theory of denial. She referred to denial as "a mechanism of the immature mind" because it is incapable of learning from and coping with reality. Denial is one of the easiest defense mechanisms to verify, even for nonspecialists, but it can also be interpreted incorrectly. A thorough assessment must be made before determining that a person is in denial.

**Assessment.** Denial is most often utilized in regard to dying, death, one's health, rape, organizational change, or substance abuse. It is specifically addressed in 12-step programs (in steps 1, 4, 5, 8, and 10) to help accept the reality of an addiction. Victims of sexual abuse often cannot face that trauma and deny the incident through repression or suppression. Reactions to organizational changes are frequently met with resistance and the use of denial as well.

Elisabeth Kübler-Ross (1997) identified denial as the first of five stages in the process of dying. Denial, since then, has been applied in reaction to a person's sickness and impending death, as well as for those who mourn after the person has died. During early grieving, the bereaved may cognitively acknowledge the death but be unable to believe it emotionally.

Seven types of denial have been identified. The most common are denial of fact, responsibility, impact, or accountability.

**Treatment.** Suggested counseling strategies to help counselees overcome the temptation to deny the reality of various losses include talking through the loss by going over the details to make it become "real," doing the hard stuff like viewing the deceased's body or filing a rape charge, talking about forthcoming changes within one's work site or organization, participating in 12-step meetings, and journaling thoughts and feelings regarding the unwanted situation (Stroebe, Hansson, Stroebe, & Schut, 2001).

**Biblical and Spiritual Issues.** The Bible is filled with accounts of people living in denial of God's warnings and instructions on how to live a Spirit-filled life. Adam and Eve denied the seriousness of God's warning about the consequences of eating of the tree of good and evil. The Israelites engaged in a form of denial of fact, responsibility, and impact when they strayed multiple times from God's commands to serve only him. The rich young ruler, in hearing Christ's response to his question about eternal life, denied the serious impact of continuing his own self-absorbed lifestyle. Christians are healthiest when they look at difficulty as a challenge, believing they can get through it as God holds them in the palm of his hand.

Susan J. Zonnebelt-Smeenge
Robert C. DeVries

## REFERENCES

Hooyman, N. R., & Kramer, B. J. (2006). *Living Through Loss: Interventions Across the Life Span.* New York, NY: Columbia University Press.

Kübler-Ross, E. (1997). *On Death and Dying.* New York, NY: Scribner.

Stroebe, M. S., Hansson, R. O., Stroebe, W., & Schut, H. (2001). *Handbook of Bereavement Research: Consequences, Coping, and Care.* Washington, DC: American Psychological Association.

## DEFENSE MECHANISMS

**Description.** Defense mechanisms are the unconscious processes that ward off unacceptable mental content. Defense mechanisms help individuals cope with stress, anxiety, fear, and other negative emotions while creating some level of emotional stability. Many times, defense mechanisms distort reality. Everyone uses defense mechanisms on a daily basis; however, when taken to an extreme, these defenses can hamper people's ability to accurately perceive and respond to reality (Johnson, 2004).

**History.** Sigmund Freud first developed the concept of defense mechanisms to explain the unconscious process whereby individuals avoid unwanted mental content. Defense mechanisms, therefore, are those unconscious abilities utilized to protect self (ego) from content that would be perceived as inducing anxiety or distress (Seaward, 2006). Sigmund Freud identified nine primary defenses, and Anna Freud added a tenth. Today there are many opinions on just how many defenses there are, but all agree on their basic purpose—to protect ego from unwanted mental content (Murdock, 2009).

**Awareness.** Defense mechanisms are classically divided into four categories:

1. *Pathological* defenses are almost always harmful and result in the distortion of reality in ways that allow individuals to avoid dealing with reality. Individuals will appear irrational or insane when they use these defense mechanisms:

- delusional thinking (false beliefs about reality)
- denial (refusal to believe or arguing against reality)

- distortion (twisting reality to fit one's own needs)
- splitting (dividing the world into all good and all bad camps; black and white thinking)

2. *Immature* defenses are a normal part of child and adolescent development, but when they persist into adulthood, they become dysfunctional and interfere with adaptation. Adults are seen as immature, undesirable, and difficult to deal with because of these defenses:

- acting out (direct behavior that acts out of the unconscious impulse)
- passive aggressive (expressing aggression through passive actions, such as doing an assigned job slowly or with poor quality)
- projection (seeing one's own defects in others)
- projective identification (responding to projection in accord with the material projected)
- fantasy (retreat from reality into a fantasy world)
- idealization (unconsciously seeing others with more positive qualities than reality would merit)
- somatization (experiencing mental stress as physical symptoms)

3. *Neurotic* defenses are common in adults and are utilized when stress is high. They can provide short-term ability to cope, but if used long-term, they generally cause impairment in relationships and functioning.

- displacement (This separates emotions from the real object and places them on another. The classic example is of a man who is angry at his boss but comes home and kicks the dog.)
- dissociation (temporary disconnect from events in reality)
- hypochondriasis (excessive preoccupation with having a serious medical problem)
- isolation (separating feelings and facts, such as describing the death of a loved one in great detail but without apparent emotion)
- rationalization (twisting reality to justify one's behavior in one's own mind; frequent convenient excuse making)
- reaction formation (converting unacceptable unconscious desires into their opposite external behavior)
- regression (temporary reversion to an earlier stage of developmental functioning, such as a child wetting the bed)
- repression (the unconscious blockade of undesirable memories or thoughts)
- undoing (undoing undesirable thoughts or feelings by engaging in contrary behavior)

4. *Mature* defenses are found among mentally and emotionally healthy adults and are considered to help adaptation and functioning.

- altruism (helping others)
- anticipation (realistic planning for future problems)
- humor (turning distressing tension into humorous expression)
- identification (modeling oneself after another)
- introjection (internalizing ideas or principles into oneself)
- sublimation (transforming negative desires into acceptable expressions,

such as a child's murderous desire toward a sibling being sublimated as the child eventually becomes a law enforcement officer)
- thought suppression (the conscious choice to avoid thinking of distressing thoughts)

**Treatment Applications.** Awareness of these defense mechanisms can provide insight into the treatment of patients. The therapist, with these insights, may consciously choose to not respond to immature or neurotic defenses as the untrained person would, but instead to look beneath the defense and understand the underlying issues and then calculate responses designed to result in conflict resolution.

**Biblical Issues.** Defense mechanisms originated with sin and stem from our selfish need to protect self. As soon as Adam sinned, he said, "It wasn't me; it was the woman you gave me," (denial, distortion, projection, and externalization) (see Genesis 3:12). McMinn (2008) writes, "Defense mechanisms...make sense from a Christian perspective. Theologians speak of the noetic effects of sin, meaning that our sin binds us in various ways from an honest look at ourselves and our need for God" (p. 51). All defense mechanisms, including the mature defenses, function to protect self.

Freudian theory of defenses is predicated on evolutionary self-survival motivation and undermines Christian understanding of the need to die to self, be renewed in mind and heart, and live for Christ. Defense mechanisms are motivated by survival instincts, which are contrary to Christ's principles of selfless love: "Greater love has no one than this: to lay down one's life for one's friends" (Jn. 15:13). Such self-sacrificing love occurs when we no longer seek to save or defend self but completely surrender self into Christ's hands, experience a regenerate heart and mind, and become motivated by God's Spirit. When Christ returns and we are fully reconciled to him, defense mechanisms will be needless because we will be completely selfless, loving, and transparent in the perfect unity of love.

In the reality of this earthly life, defense mechanisms can serve both a positive and negative function. Some defenses are necessary as healthy boundaries, but many clients' defenses distort their reality. Newman (2008) describes three critical factors to the evaluation of defense mechanisms in the counseling process.

1. The client must have the courage to change.
2. The client must be dedicated to the truth, regardless of how painful it is.
3. The client must accept responsibility for the situation.

**Additional Issues.** Classic psychodynamic psychotherapy requires years of professional training and should not be attempted by counselors early in their careers. Dangers of such therapy include overidentification with the patient, boundary violations, introduction of harmful mental concepts, and undermining defenses before adequate alternative defenses are in place, resulting in decompensation.

**Timothy R. Jennings**

## REFERENCES

Johnson, S. L. (2004). *Therapist's Guide to Clinical Intervention* (2nd ed.). San Diego, CA: Elsevier.

McMinn, M. R. (2008). *Sin and Grace in Christian Counseling: An Integrative Paradigm*. Downers Grove, IL: InterVarsity Press.

Murdock, N. (2009). *Theories of Counseling and Psychotherapy: A Case Approach*. Upper Saddle River, NJ: Prentice Hall.

Newman, W. C. (2008). *Biblical Teaching About Christian Counseling: Theory and Practice*. Tacoma, WA: Newman International.

Seaward, B. L. (2006). *Managing Stress: Principles and Strategies for Health and Wellbeing*. Sudbury, MA: Jones and Bartlett.

## RESISTANCE

**Description and History.** *Resistance* is a term initially used by Sigmund Freud to refer to patients blocking memories from conscious memory. Later, Freud described five different forms of resistance, and they became associated with various analytic structures. Mainly due to Freudian influence, the early theories of resistance assumed that patients repress certain memories (Freud, 1959).

The belief that certain memories are part of the conscious mind and others a part of the unconscious mind is still prevalent today. The therapeutic theory is that if a patient can become aware of what has been unconscious, healing will proceed. However, this theory also teaches that what has been unconscious may be painful, and therefore, the patient automatically (that is, without consciously thinking about it) resists knowing it. Theories of resistance therefore led to theories of "primary and secondary gains" (Leahy, 2001). A *primary gain* occurs when the client avoids painful feelings such as anxiety or anger. A *secondary gain* occurs when the client avoids social, financial, or relational "demands." That is, a client uses his illness to avoid responsibility.

*Resistance* eventually came to mean anything a client did to make therapy or a particular intervention less effective. In this perspective, resistance can be defined as defensiveness in response to the confrontation or suggestion of change (Miller & Rollnick, 2002). This development shifts the definition away from processes of the mind to a description of the patient. Virtually all counselors have complained, "I have a very difficult [resistant] patient." Perhaps we should wonder, along with Jay Haley, if the problem is not resistant patients, but incompetent therapists.

Resistance can take several forms, including these:

- resistance to the recognition of feelings, fantasies, and motivation
- resistance to the authority or personality of the pastor or counselor, a condition which is referred to as *negative transference*
- resistance as a way of demonstrating, "I can do this myself"
- resistance demonstrated as a client's reluctance to change
- resistance to others who are perceived by the client as lacking empathy for the client's pain

**Assessment.** Resistance is not a clinical diagnosis to which a code can be applied. It is an awareness that the counselor is dealing with a "tough case." As such, a counselor is wise to assess personal feelings toward the client, called *countertransference*, such as, "I don't like this person," or "I don't look forward to her coming in," or "I would like to transfer this person to some other counselor." In extreme cases, resistant clients might even trigger dramatic feelings in the counselor to want to do physical harm to the person. Resistant clients can also trigger feelings of shame in the counselor, who may conclude, "I'm a bad therapist."

Common examples of resistance include the client canceling or rescheduling appointments, avoiding consideration of identified themes, and forgetting to complete homework assignments. These attitudes and behaviors make it difficult for the therapist to work with the client, but observing these traits provide him with valuable information about the client.

1. What internal feelings, such as shame, anxiety, or anger might be creating resistance?
2. What responsibilities is the person avoiding by remaining stuck in the presenting problems?
3. Is the client rebelling against the counselor and others, such as a spouse, God, or the church?

**Treatment Issues.** Resistance is a common dynamic in all mental health and spiritual conditions, and it cuts across all cultural and gender differences. It also blocks effective treatment. Therefore, it is often essential to address resistance before further treatment can be accomplished. Confronting resistance requires helping a person to feel safe in the therapeutic process. The personality of the counselor, the counseling office, and office staff must work together to create a positive mood, which is vital to achieving safety. Also, it is often helpful for a person to participate in some form of group therapy or support group so other people can model the sense of safety, the courage to confront pain, and the hope of progress.

**Spiritual and Biblical Issues.** As Christians, we believe that God uses both internal and external conflict to help people grow spiritually and emotionally. Innumerable passages of Scripture speak to this point. Pastor Rick Warren observed, "Character is both developed and revealed by tests, and all of life is a test. You are always being tested. God constantly watches your response to people, problems, success, conflict, illness, disappointment, and even the weather! He even watches the simplest actions, such as when you open a door for others, when you pick up a piece of trash, or when you're polite toward a clerk or waitress" (Warren, 2002).

It is often helpful to begin therapy or treatment with the story of Jesus' healing of the man who is an invalid man at the pool of Bethesda (Jn. 5:1-11). Jesus asks, "Do you want to be made well?" The man had been there for 38 years and may have had primary and secondary gain for being an invalid. Certainly he was accustomed to the role. The Greek words used in this passage for *invalid* or *infirmity* and *well* or *whole* carry the meaning of being weak in body or mind and well in body and mind. There is no healing without the cooperation of the soul and mind of the client. Jesus' profound question penetrates and reveals any resistance, and it can be used to begin every counseling session. Answering Jesus' invitation to wellness is always the beginning of the breakdown of resistance.

**Mark R. Laaser**

## REFERENCES

Freud, S. (1959). *Freud's Psychoanalytic Procedure* (pp. 261-262). London, England: Standard Edition.

Leahy, R. L. (2001). *Overcoming Resistance in Cognitive Therapy*. New York, NY: Guilford Press.

Miller, W. R., & Rollnick, S. (2002). *Motivational Interviewing*. (2nd ed.). London, England: Guilford Press.

Warren, R. (2002). *The Purpose-Driven Life*. Grand Rapids, MI: Zondervan.

## REFRAMING

**Description.** *Reframing* is a technique used in various types of counseling to facilitate change in people who are stuck in a problematic way of viewing a situation. Reframing can be defined in many different ways. One of the more widely cited definitions comes from the work of Watzlawick, Weakland, and Fisch (1974):

> To reframe, then, means to change the conceptual and/or emotional setting or viewpoint in relation to which a situation is experienced and to place it in another frame which fits the "facts" of the same concrete situation equally well or even better, and thereby changes its entire meaning (p. 95).

Many well-known therapists, including Erickson (in Haley, 1993), Satir (1972), Minuchin (1974), Burns (1981), and Haley (1991), use reframing to help individuals, couples, and families make positive changes. Numerous Christian counselors, including Capps (1990), Habermas (1998), and Arterburn (2007) have explored the use of reframing in helping people grow spiritually.

**Biblical Reframing.** Perhaps the most

important version of reframing from a Christian perspective is the challenge in Scripture to "set your minds on things above, not on earthly things" (Col. 3:2). This is what Habermas (1998) calls "top-down thinking" and what Clinton & Ohlschlager (2002) call the "heavenly reframe." Christians often frame their lives from a worldly (secular and temporal) perspective rather than a heavenly (sacred and eternal) one. Framing life from a secular perspective leads to anxiety, depression, and bitterness. Framing life from a sacred perspective allows us to be "content in any and every situation" (Phil. 4:12) and experience "the peace of God, which transcends all understanding" (verse 7).

Suffering is a crucial issue that many people need to reframe from an eternal perspective. If we put an earthly frame around suffering, we see it as universally bad and to be avoided at all costs. If, however, we put a heavenly frame around suffering, "we also glory in our sufferings, because we know that suffering produces perseverance; perseverance, character; and character, hope" (Rom. 5:3-4). Though an event may be very painful or a product of genuine evil, the biblical reframing of suffering allows us to see it as constructive because it can lead to a more Christlike character and a closer relationship with God.

Christ reframed many things in his interactions with people. He reframed the concept of greatness as the humble willingness to serve others (Mt. 20:26). He reframed worries about food and clothing as a lack of faith in the goodness of God (Mt. 6:25-34). The Pharisees taught that God was narrow, harsh, legalistic, and delighted in condemning people, but Jesus reframed God as the loving Father who joyfully runs out to welcome home the son who was once lost but is now found (Lk. 15:11-32). Christ, first and foremost, came to die for people's sins, but he also came to radically reframe *everything* about how people looked at God, themselves, and what the well-lived life really is.

**A Case Study.** Allow me to share what I hope was a Holy Spirit inspired attempt to reframe a situation for a client of mine. Sam (not his real name) came to me struggling with a great deal of anger toward God, whom he believed was all about rules and who delighted in punishing people when they violated the rules. Sam believed that God was cruel to have given us so many rules to live by. He admitted to feeling hatred toward God about it, and he decided years ago that he wanted no part of this kind of God.

I suggested, "Sam, have you ever thought that all the rules God gives us reflect how much he loves us?"

"I'm not sure I'm following you," Sam admitted. "What do you mean?"

"Well, I'm a father of three children, and it is because I love my children that I gave them rules to live by when they were growing up. I knew that if my children chose to live by the rules I gave them, they would be a lot healthier and happier. As a father, I came to see that the most unloving thing I could have done would have been to not have any rules for them."

As long as Sam continued to frame God as being about rules rather than relationship and as being mean rather than loving, he was going to stay bitter and resentful. Reframing God's rules as reflective of just how much God loves us and showing Sam that God "has plans to prosper you, not to harm you" (Jer. 29:11) put things in a whole new light for Sam. As our work together progressed, Sam's hatred and resentment toward God transformed into a thirst to draw closer to God and get to know him better.

**Conclusion.** Reframing involves putting a situation in a whole new light so that a person can get unstuck and make needed changes in his or her life. It is a powerful tool to help people grow into the "fullness of Christ Jesus" (Eph. 4:13). If the truth sets people free, reframing is an important vehicle for seeing the truth more clearly and becoming freer than we have ever been.

**Chris Thurman**

## REFERENCES

Arterburn, S. (2007). *Reframe Your Life: Transforming Your Pain into Purpose.* Nashville, TN: Faith Words.

Burns, D. (1981). *Feeling Good: The New Mood Therapy.* New York, NY: Signet.

Capps, D. (1990). *Reframing: A New Method in Pastoral Care.* Minneapolis: Fortress.

Clinton, T., & Ohlschlager, G. (2002). The empowered helping relationship. In T. Clinton & G. Ohlschlager (Eds.), *Competent Christian Counseling: Foundations and Practice of Compassionate Soul Care.* Colorado Springs, CO: WaterBrook Press.

Habermas, G. (1998). Top-down thinking: Heaven and problems on earth. *Christian Counseling Today, 6*(2), 26-28, 66-67.

Haley, J. (1991). *Problem-Solving Therapy* (2nd ed.). San Francisco, CA: Jossey-Bass.

Haley, J. (1993). *Uncommon Therapy: Psychiatric Techniques of Milton H. Erickson, M.D.* New York, NY: Norton.

Minuchin, S. (1974). *Families and Family Therapy.* Cambridge, MA: Harvard University Press.

Satir, V. (1972). *Peoplemaking.* Palo Alto, CA: Science and Behavior Books.

Watzlawick, P., Weakland, J., & Fisch, R. (1974). *Change: Principles of Problem Formation and Problem Resolution.* New York, NY: Norton.

## GOAL SETTING

**Description.** Goal setting is a key part of the change process and is essential in helping people bring about desired behaviors and extinguish undesired ones (Egan, 2010). Simply put, a goal is a result or achievement toward which effort is directed (Random House, 1995). A goal can be a compass to direct one toward a positive, healthy path. Without goals, people can wander aimlessly through life—and also through the counseling process.

Goal setting is also a major tool for developing treatment plans in counseling. It may seem counterintuitive for people to seek counseling to change bad behaviors and then resist the very change they are seeking, but this phenomenon is very common. One of the best ways to help people overcome their own conscious and unconscious resistance is to have them set effective goals.

There is a saying in behavioral therapy: "If nothing changes, nothing changes" (Stuart, 1980). In other words, goal setting needs to bring about genuine change in behaviors, thoughts, and actions, or it is impotent. Egan (2010) says that goal setting is a "critical part of the self-regulation system" (p. 298). Hughes adds, "We are nothing more than what we do, and can become nothing more than what we see ourselves achieving in terms of goals" (Hughes, 1965).

A more spiritual approach to goal setting focuses not only on what we do but also on what we think and believe (McMinn, 1996). Goal setting is a key to helping these behavioral and spiritual changes occur. However, studies show that people need to avoid rigidity in setting goals. In the counseling process, they may need to actively adapt their goals: to reprioritize them, postpone them, or reduce their effort in order to maintain personal flexibility and emotional health (Egan, 2010; Konig, Wendelien, & Burch, 2010).

**History and Awareness.** The roots of goal setting go back to the beginning of recorded history. Various goal setting methods have been applied to countless areas of life, from increasing sales of products to weight loss. But goal setting became far more popular and lucrative (for some) after the 1960s with the onset of the human potential movement. The more Christian-based experts, such as Zig Ziglar (2000) and Denis Waitley (1993), stressed committing goals to writing and actually visualizing success in meeting them. The seeds of their work continue to bear fruit today.

**Application.** Effective goal setting is designed to help people overcome their resistance to change. In order to help people make substantial progress, counselors must first look at reasons why clients resist change, such as these:

- fear of failure that is rooted in past hurt or soul wounds
- fear of the unknown
- feeling uncomfortable or unworthy of success or happiness, perhaps because of negative messages from childhood (Rodgers & Rodgers, 2006)

Experts agree that effective performance depends on the validity of goals themselves and on the goal-setting process used (Egan 2010, Hughes, 1965). Several guidelines can make goals more achievable.

- Create specific goals, not global ones.
- Write out the goals and examine them regularly.
- Formulate a step-by-step plan of action.
- Anticipate problems and have a plan for overcoming them.
- Develop performance standards and measurement criteria (Hughes, 1965).

**Biblical and Spiritual Issues.** The Bible does not use the term *goal setting*, but many passages indicate that it is an important part of spiritual growth and development. Scripture admonishes us to consider the cost of our choices. Jesus says, "Suppose one of you wants to build a tower. Won't you first sit down and estimate the cost to see if you have enough money to complete it? For if you lay out the foundation and are not able to finish it, everyone who sees it will ridicule you" (Lk. 14:28-29). Christ is pointing out our human tendency to move ahead without proper planning, which includes setting clear, attainable goals.

James underscores this assertion in his letter. "Now listen, you who say, 'Today or tomorrow we will go to this or that city...carry on business and make money.' Why, you do not even know what will happen tomorrow...you ought to say, 'If it is the Lord's will, we will do this or that'" (Jas. 4:13-15). Rather than asking God to rubber stamp our goals, it is far better to ask God for his wisdom and plan accordingly.

Proverbs sums up the issue of change and goal setting: "In their hearts humans plan their course, but the Lord establishes their steps" (Pr. 16:9). Clearly, when it comes to matters of goal setting and change—and even resistance to change—change will be much healthier and much more suited to our best outcomes when we entrust the process to the Lord.

**Conclusion.** Proverbs 3:5-6 summarizes, "Trust in the Lord with all your heart and lean not on your own understanding; in all your ways [including goal setting] submit to him, and he will make your paths straight."

**Bev Rodgers**
**Tom Rodgers**

## REFERENCES


Egan, G. (2010). *The Skilled Helper: A Problem-Management and Opportunity-Development Approach to Helping* (9th ed.). Belmont, CA: Brooks/Cole.

Hughes, C. L. (1965). *Goal Setting: Key to Individual and Organizational Effectiveness.* American Management Association.

Konig, C. J., Wendelien, V. E., & Burch, A. (2010). Predictors and consequences of daily goal adaptation, a diary study. *Journal of Personal Psychology, 9*(1), 50-56.

McMinn, M. (1996). *Psychology, Theology, and Spirituality in Christian Counseling.* Wheaton, IL: Tyndale House.

Random House. (1995). *Webster's College Dictionary.* New York, NY: Author.

Rodgers B., & Rodgers, T. (2006). *Soul Healing Love: Turning Relationships That Hurt into Relationships That Heal.* Bristol, TN: Selah.

Stuart, R. (1980). *Helping Couples Change: A Social Learning Approach to Marital Therapy.* New York, NY: Guilford Press.

Waitley, D. (1993). *Seeds of Greatness.* Grand Rapids, MI: Fleming Revell.

Ziglar, Z. (2000). *See You at the Top.* Gretna, LA: Pelican.

# ASSESSMENT, DIAGNOSIS, AND TREATMENT PLANNING

## CLINICAL ASSESSMENT

**Description.** The Christian counselor must learn to accurately evaluate the visible and invisible elements of people's lives and discern how God evaluates us. Knowing your clients well and having a full and accurate picture of their lives makes your intervention more focused, more helpful, more potent, and especially, more accepted and embraced by the client (Clinton & Ohlschlager, 2003).

**Assessment and Alignment.** Counseling, like medicine, begins with accurate assessment. Assessment that is part of a refined sense of clinical judgment is invaluable because you can't treat what you don't see, and if you can't see it accurately, you can't treat it properly. Furthermore, creating a therapeutic alliance with clients—aligning with clients so they believe that you understand and are for them—is not an end in itself. Like a good doctor-patient relationship in medicine, the purpose of a good counseling relationship is to...

- facilitate an accurate and comprehensive evaluation of the problem(s) and the resources available to "cure" or manage it properly, and
- devise an effective treatment plan that the client can understand, own, and do (Clinton & Ohlschlager, 2003; Gladding, 2009).

**What Is Clinical Assessment?** Clinical assessment accomplishes five objectives in counseling (Aten & Leach, 2009; Clinton & Ohlschlager, 2003; Gladding, 2009):

- identify and understand the client's complaints and problem issues
- gather data on and understand the client's world and way of seeing things
- learn about family history, developmental events, and relationship issues
- identify client strengths and weaknesses across the bio-psycho-social-spiritual spectrum
- begin the process that leads to goal definition and treatment planning

On a broad scale, clinical assessment is divided into objective and subjective forms. Subjective assessment is the process of making evaluative inferences—educated and experienced hunches—based on interview and observational data about someone. Objective assessment is a more formal process—usually involving standardized tests—that controls the variability of subjective evaluation (Clinton & Ohlschlager, 2003). All counselors use subjective methods of assessments, especially direct interviewing procedures, but not all use more objective and standardized tests and measures. Competent clinicians usually have a variety of assessment tools and use selected ones with clients to get a more complete and individually unique portrait of them (Aten & Leach, 2009; Clinton & Ohlschlager, 2003; Cormier, Nurius, & Osborn, 2009).

**Types of Assessment.** There are several types of assessments (Clinton & Ohlschlager, 2003).

*Clinical interview.* This baseline assessment tool is used by nearly all counselors with all clients. Whether conducted in a formal office setting or over a cup of coffee, the interview is guided by a conversation with a goal. Clinical interviewing involves asking a logical train of systematic questions designed to elicit as much information about the client as possible (Cormier et al., 2009).

*Client observation.* This is an ongoing clinical process as the counselor observes and assesses client behavior in context. Most often, this is in the context of the client's own behavior—both verbal and nonverbal cues—but it also includes observing the client interpersonally. Sometimes, what counselors see in context is quite different from what clients describe in sessions about that context (Cormier et al., 2009).

*Secondhand reports.* These are useful corollaries to client observation. They are the reports about the client given by those closest to the client—family, friends, employers, and colleagues. These can be valuable insights about client behavior and confirm or disconfirm client reports, but they can be just as biased and inaccurate as a self-serving client report might be (Cormier et al., 2009).

*Self-assessment.* These are conducted by teaching clients to journal, fill out questionnaires, and write autobiographies, self-coding reports, and narrative reports. The key difference between self-assessed descriptions and client reports gained by interview is that in self-assessment clients are trained to write down events and self-evaluations soon after events take place. Clients are trained to maintain a log of life experience around problem events or people in a way that produces insights and resources for change that aren't often recalled in an interview. Self-monitoring is often the left hand to the right hand of counselor assessment (Cormier, Cormier, & Hackney, 2011; Fitzsimons & Finkel, 2010).

*Acted-out and expressive tools.* These provide opportunities to go beyond talking. Some clients are so angry, withdrawn, regressed and afraid, or young and nonverbal that you will not get good data using verbal, sit-down assessments. The best way to connect with these people is to have them draw pictures, paint with a brush, play in a sand tray, use the house-tree-person tool, play with toys, run through a ropes and obstacle course, or use a variety of other active modes of expression. In fact, these methods are often the preferred course of interaction with many children and adolescents, with highly regressed and fearful trauma victims, and with certain psychotic patients.

*Checklists and questionnaires.* These nonstandardized question-and-answer tools can give quick and often useful information about clients in particular areas.

*Genograms.* These family-systems assessment tools indicate the interactive web of family relations and their strengths and weaknesses (see the article on Genograms) (Marlin, 1989).

*Multimodal inventories.* These global assessment inventories reflect a comprehensive and technical eclecticism. The BECHRISTLIKE multimodal assessment for Christian counselors follows the pattern of the BASICID metamodel that Arnold Lazarus developed (Lazarus, 1981).

*Standardized psychological tests.* These are considered the cream of assessment tools because they have been refined to measure behavior, aptitude, ability, or personality with a high degree of objectivity and consistency (Anastasi & Urbina, 1997). They are used whenever predicting a person's outcome is important.

**Misusing Tests and Assessment.** Any test results must be evaluated, balancing their power to reveal with the knowledge that no test ever equals the dignity or reveals a complete picture of any one person. The *AACC Christian Counseling Code of Ethics* includes this regarding testing:

*1-530 Ethics in Testing, Assessment, and Clinical Evaluation*

Christian counselors do clinical evaluations of clients only in the context of professional relations, in the best interests of clients, and with the proper training and supervision. Christian counselors avoid (1) incompetent and inaccurate evaluations, (2) clinically unnecessary and excessively expensive testing, and (3) unauthorized practice of testing and evaluation that is the province of another clinical or counseling discipline. Referral and consultation are used when evaluation is desired or necessary beyond the competence and/or role of the counselor.

*1-531 Use of Appropriate Assessments*

Christian counselors use tests and assessment techniques that are appropriate to the needs, resources, capabilities, and understanding of the client. We apply tests skillfully and administer tests properly and safely. We substantiate our findings, with knowledge of the reliability, validity, outcome results, and limits of the tests used. We avoid both the misuse of testing procedures and the creation of confusion or misunderstanding by clients about testing purposes, procedures, and findings.

*1-532 Reporting and Interpreting Assessment Results*

Christian counselors report testing results in a fair, understandable, and objective manner. We avoid undue testing bias and honor the limits of test results, ensuring verifiable means to substantiate conclusions and recommendations. We recognize the limits of test interpretation and avoid exaggeration and absolute statements about the certainty of client diagnoses, behavior predictions, clinical judgments, and recommendations. Due regard is given to the unique history, values, family dynamics, sociocultural influences, economic realities, and spiritual maturity of the client. Christian counselors will state any and all reservations about the validity of test results and present reports and recommendations in tentative language and with alternative possibilities.

*Testing abuse.* Maybe you or someone you know has been a victim of testing abuse—discrimination based on an IQ score, the results of a polygraph test, or a personality profile that is less than stellar. As a Christian counselor, be a human rights advocate—never confuse the people in front of you with their test scores. Tests can reveal important clues and dynamics about someone, but they can never fully reveal an accurate composite of the entire person. Watch out for these pitfalls:

- labeling others
- assuming the absolute accuracy of any test
- racial, ethnic, and gender bias
- the "tunneling" effect of testing
- violations of client privacy

**Competent Assessment in Christian Counseling.** It is recommended that counselors use a global, multimodal client assessment that is narrowed to specific issues targeting change. Flowing from this, the client's presenting problem and understanding of problem dynamics (or lack of it) takes on a greater weight in relation with a formal diagnosis. Indeed, counselors must, with a high level of agreement with clients, find common ground in our assessment of clients' problems so the clients will more fully receive and implement our prescription for change (Clinton & Ohlschlager, 2003).

**BECHRISTLIKE Assessment Tool.** We (Clinton & Ohlschlager, 2003) have developed an assessment and treatment system using an acronym—BECHRISTLIKE—to describe the modes of human experience. The apostle Paul often used the phrase "in Christ." To be Christlike reflects a primary goal in Christian counseling.

We have been influenced in this model by Arnold Lazarus (1981) and his multimodal therapy (the BASIC-ID modalities), by social work's development of the global Person-in-Environment (PIE) system of assessment (Corcoran & Walsh, 2010), and by our commitment to prescriptive therapies that tie client assessment to specific treatment planning and practice. This Christ-centered multimodal assessment includes 12 items.

*Behavior.* Focuses on observable behavior and assesses whether helpful or harmful. Defines key behavior patterns around problem issues. Assesses antecedents and consequences of behavior. Notes behavioral strengths and deficits.

*Emotions.* Assesses primary emotional disturbance and the emotional patterns. Describes desired feelings. How do clients value emotions in relation to beliefs, thoughts, and behavior? How do emotional themes reveal relations with God?

*Cognition.* Assesses thought content and process. What are the lies and distortions that animate this client? Reasoning ability? Psychotic or delusional symptoms? Self-talk? Is client imagery helpful or traumatic? What is the content, intensity, and frequency of imagery?

*Health.* What is the client's overall health status? Notes medical problems and physician's care. Notes sensory/somatic complaints and psychosocial interactions, whether for better or for worse. Assesses sleeping, eating, and exercise habits and conditions. Is a physician referral called for?

*Religion.* What is the client's relationship with Christ? Saved or not? Maturing or not? Assesses church life and Christian practices. Conducts a biblical analysis of problem behavior. Assesses receptivity versus resistance to spiritual interventions.

*Idols and false beliefs.* What desires and values compete with God and his priorities? What values line up biblically and need strengthening? How are problems related to value conflicts and discrepancies, biblically understood?

*Substances.* Assesses what drugs client is taking, both prescribed and/or illicit. What are drug interactions? Does the client need a physician referral for psychotropic meds? Does the client need a program for detox and substance-abuse treatment?

*Teachability.* Is the client motivated or resistant, and is the motivation global or specific, dependent on the problem or other variables? Hope versus hopelessness? Does the client trust the counselor? Are there racial, ethnic, or gender differences that need to be bridged?

*Law and ethics.* Assesses whether the client is a danger to self or others. Any current legal trouble? Any other red-flag issues that demand immediate attention? Does the client need to be referred to a lawyer?

*Interpersonal relations.* Describes current issues and history with family and friends—is the web rich or deficient? Who is the best and worst family member? Best and worst friend? What are the best and worst traits in the father and mother? Describe spousal relations, satisfying and dissatisfying. Describe sexual behavior and problems.

*Knowledge.* Does client have sufficient knowledge and skill to change? Assesses skill strengths and deficits. Notes formal education and what, if anything, client does to improve knowledge. Considers resources for further learning, formal and informal.

*Environment.* What are the external obstacles and reaction triggers? What strengths and resources are available to the client? What is the client's locus of control—does he perceive he is controlled by events or free to influence them?

**The Christian Global Assessment System (C-GAS).** Taking the BECHRISTLIKE acronym, we have developed a global assessment matrix that frames the entire clinical process in a single page (Clinton & Ohschlager, 2003). It is a heuristic device that focuses on key issues and actions that lead to constructive change. It is useful for the practicing counselor, for the client's self-knowledge, and for supervisors and colleagues consulting with helpers.

**Christian Global Assessment System**

| | Problem | Goal | Intervention | Evaluation |
|---|---|---|---|---|
| B—Behavior | | | | |
| E—Emotions | | | | |
| C—Cognition | | | | |
| H—Health | | | | |
| R—Religion | | | | |
| I—Idols | | | | |
| S—Substances | | | | |
| T—Teachability | | | | |
| L—Law/ethics | | | | |
| I—Interpersonal | | | | |
| K—Knowledge | | | | |
| E—Environment | | | | |

Tim Clinton
George Ohlschlager

## REFERENCES


American Association of Christian Counselors. (2004). *AACC Christian Counseling Code of Ethics*. Forest, VA: Author.

Anastasi, A., & Urbina, S. (1997). *Psychological Testing* (7th Ed.). Upper Saddle River, NJ: Prentice Hall.

Aten J. D., & Leach, M. M. (Eds.). (2009). *Spirituality and the Therapeutic Process: A Comprehensive Resource from Intake to Termination*. Washington DC: American Psychological Association.

Clinton, T., & Ohlschlager, G. (2003). *Competent Christian Counseling: Foundations and Practice of Compassionate Soul Care*. Colorado Springs, CO: WaterBrook Press.

Corcoran, J., & Walsh, J. (2010). *Clinical Assessment and Diagnosis in Social Work Practice* (2nd ed.). New York, NY: Oxford University Press.

Cormier, S., Nurius, P. S., & Osborn, C. J. (2009). *Interviewing and Change Strategies for Helpers: Fundamental Skills and Cognitive Behavioral Interventions* (6th ed.). Belmont, CA: Brooks/Cole.

Cormier, W. H., Cormier, L. S., & Hackney, H. (2011). *Counseling Strategies and Interventions* (8th ed.). Columbus, OH: Merrill.

Cronbach, L. J. (1990). *Essentials of Psychological Testing* (5th ed.). New York, NY: HarperCollins.

Fitzsimons, G. M., & Finkel, E. J. (2010). Interpersonal influences on self-regulation. *Current Directions in Psychological Science, 19*(2), 101-105.

Gladding, S. T. (2009). *Counseling: A Comprehensive Profession*. (6th ed.). Upper Saddle River, NJ: Prentice Hall.

Lazarus, A. (1981). *The Practice of Multimodal Therapy*. New York, NY: Springer.

Marlin, E. (1989). *Genograms: The New Tool for Exploring the Personality, Career, and Love Patterns You Inherit*. Chicago, IL: Contemporary Books.


## GENOGRAMS

**Definition.** A genogram is a psychological tool diagramming a family structure over three generations or more. It has been developed for the main purpose of understanding relational and behavioral patterns within a family (McGoldrick, Gerson, & Petry, 2008, p. 1). Murray Bowen, founder of Bowen family systems therapy, first conceptualized genograms in the late 1970s to help analyze family structures and generational patterns. The genogram differs from a family tree in that it includes information about occupations, ages, personality types, education, mental illness, causes of death, religious devotion, quality of relationships, and more to assess for patterns that may exist and be passed through the generations. These characteristics are important to both the clinician and the client because they strategically reveal how the client is connected to the family lineage on a variety of levels (Marlin, 1989).

**Why Do a Genogram?** Genograms provide both the counselor and the client with the ability to see the bigger picture of the family lineage, revealing spoken or unspoken rules or standards about belief systems, family expectations, and ways of relating. The biblical concept of the sins of the fathers (Ex. 20:5-6) is shown in a genogram through the dysfunctional patterns that transcend generations (Scazzero, 2003). These "scripts" can be a pleasant activity for clients to learn why they like a certain activity, food, or tradition; why they may be like one family member over another; or how the family developed a knack for success, wealth, courage, or motivation. More significantly, these "scripts" can also be invaluable for assessing and unraveling dysfunctional family patterns that have been the source of pain for generations. As a result, they can help clients learn how to recognize and put an end to unhealthy behaviors in their own family system (Marlin, 1989, p. 5).

**How to Do a Genogram.** A genogram is designed using symbols to denote individuals and relationships. For instance, a circle is used for a female and a square is used for a male. If that particular individual is deceased, an X is placed through the corresponding symbol. Demographic data can include name; age; date and place of birth; if deceased, the cause and date of death; occupation(s); educational levels; religion; dates of marriage, separation, and divorce; and children's names, sex, and birth dates. Data pertaining to family function can also be included and covers issues such as personality types, legal history, medical complications, behavioral problems, mental illness, or emotional issues. In addition, significant family events, including major geographical moves, job changes, promotions, unexpected deaths, and divorce could all be built into the genogram to help assess patterns and changes in family functioning (Marlin, 1989).

**Three Types of Genograms.** There are three types of genograms. *The basics genogram* provides the essential demographic facts similar to a family tree, including gender, age, dates, and names. *The distances genogram* goes beyond the objective facts of particular individuals and maps out the subjective quality of the interpersonal relationships within the family system. This type signifies the depth of emotional connections, including close relationships, conflicted relationships, and individuals who are cut off, estranged, or scapegoated. *The details genogram* uses more specific data to recognize patterns of behavior, addiction, medical or physical complications, traditions, religious beliefs, critical family events, and more. In building a genogram, one important caution—whether for the clinician or the client—is to be careful not to include too many details, which would complicate the exercise and run the risk of getting lost in the data (Marlin, 1989).

**Joshua Straub**
**Laura Faidley**

## REFERENCES

Marlin, E. (1989). *Genograms: The New Tool for Exploring the Personality, Career, and Love Patterns You Inherit.* Chicago, IL: Contemporary Books.

McGoldrick, M., Gerson, R., & Petry, S. (2008).

*Genograms: Assessment and Intervention.* New York, NY: Norton.

Scazzero, P. (2003). *The Emotionally Healthy Church.* Grand Rapids, MI: Zondervan.

## INTERVIEWING

**Description.** Clinical interviewing is a fundamental area of mental-health training. It is one of the most important ports of entry into a client's world, an opportunity for the clinician to make a clinical diagnosis, obtain a relatively accurate assessment of the client's current level of functioning, establish a working therapeutic relationship, engender a sense of hope, and begin the process of treatment planning (Turner, Hersen, & Heiser, 2003).

**Core Components.** Though the clinical interview is complex and multifaceted, six core components are essential.

*The chief complaint.* The interview typically begins with the chief complaint, which reflects the client's perception of the primary purpose for seeking out therapy (Jacobson & Jacobson, 2001). This can usually be written in quotations, such as "I've been feeling depressed." This is a crucial first step because it provides the clinician insight into the type of motivation clients have for seeking therapy (internal vs. external) and the degree of insight they have into their condition. It is important to note how clients present their concerns. For example, some clients may say they are coming to therapy because they've been feeling depressed, but other clients may say that they are coming because of conflict in a relationship or because of problems in performance at work or school.

*The history of present illness.* The history of present illness works from the chief complaint to other areas affected by the client's core concerns. It's important for the clinician to follow the client's lead. If clients begin with symptoms (e.g., depression), clinicians should assess the nature and severity of the symptoms (e.g., sad mood, anhedonia, poor concentration, changes in appetite, changes in sleep patterns, etc.) and then assess the impact of the symptoms on various aspects of the clients' daily functioning (e.g., close relationships, work, recreational activities, health, spiritual well-being). On the other hand, if clients begin with an issue-focused complaint (e.g., difficulties in marriage or problems at school), clinicians would explore the nature of these problems or issues and then assess their impact on the clients' mental health. For example, with a client who has just described a very difficult conflict in a marriage, a clinician might ask, "How does all of this affect the way you've been feeling lately?" This type of transitional question may effectively lead the clinician to explore symptoms of depression and anxiety as well as methods of coping (Carlat, 2005).

In the course of discussing symptoms of one disorder, the therapist can also scan for other types of problems. For example, when interviewing a client for symptoms of depression, those symptoms may become gateways to explore other possible disorders. Questions about appetite may prompt questions about body image and a history of eating disorders. Problems with concentration could lead to a history of attention problems that were present before the depressed mood. Feelings of hopelessness may be linked to suicidality and destructive behaviors (such as cutting) and impulsive behaviors (such as speeding and sexual acting out). During the history of present illness, keep alert for other possible disorders.

*Physical health.* A brief discussion of one's physical health is always important because underlying medical problems can produce an array of psychological disorders (Morrison, 2007). For example, clients with panic disorder symptoms may actually have heart problems. In such cases, it is important to ensure that clients see a physician and sign a release so that you may collaborate with that health-care provider to make sure that any underlying medical diagnoses are appropriately ruled out.

*Social history.* Obtaining a full social history in an initial clinical interview is not usually possible. However, some important markers are needed to get a better assessment of clients' global functioning and a basic history of their emotional health (Jacobson & Jacobson, 2001). For example, did their parents divorce? How did they do in school? Did they graduate? Did they attend college? Did they drop out of school? What's their basic employment status? How long have they been working? Do they have close friendships? Do they feel as if they have enough friends? Do they want more friends? What kind of hobbies do they enjoy? What kind of recreational activity do they have? We sometimes refer to this as the "three Rs" of social functioning: relationships, recreation, and work. Look for imbalances in these three areas because they reflect pathology. For example, some people work too much and cannot find time to relate or recreate, but others are so social and into having fun that they cannot focus on getting necessary work done.

*Loss and trauma.* It is also important to screen for any significant losses or traumas. Therapists should not probe too deeply in the first session. If clients open up and disclose prior traumas, clinicians should pursue them. If they do not, and you suspect trauma is present, make note to return to this issue at another point in the therapy.

*Mental status exam.* Although we mention the mental status exam as a final point, the mental status exam begins the first time you see the client in the waiting room. The social history and the history of present illness give you more of a longitudinal view of the person's functioning, but the mental status exam gives you a cross-sectional view, a snapshot of the client's mental function. This involves gathering information about key mental functions based on the overall interview itself, not necessarily just at the end or beginning of the interview. These are a few of the key mental status functions that are assessed in the clinical interview.

1. *Mood and affect.* While you are investigating each component, you are simultaneously gathering information about mood. Mood is the person's stable emotional state and involves the following feelings: sad, anxious, worried, resentful, angry, and irritable. Conversely, affect has to do with the nonverbal expression of emotion or the range of emotion, such as body movement and the rhythm of voice (Daniel & Crider, 2003). Is the affect consistent with the emotion? This is an important question. If people are feeling sad and depressed but are laughing and giggly, they are exhibiting an incongruent affect (Daniel & Gurcznski, 2010).

2. *Speech. Duration of utterance* is one of the many dimensions of speech. High duration talkers are quite verbal and gregarious, giving much more information than what is asked (sometimes indicative of bipolar disorder or ADHD). Low duration of utterance might be one- or two-word answers and can evidence depression or social anxiety. Another marker is *response time latency*, which is the delay between your question and the person's response. Very low response time is characteristic of a person who answers a question before you finish asking it, which may point to impulsivity, ADHD, or bipolar disorder. A very long response time could suggest depression, or in some cases, it may reflect psychotic state.

3. *Thought content.* This identifies the major themes in their narrative (Carlat, 2005). Do they have paranoid ideas? Are they worried about infidelity? Are they worried about phobias? Do they have obsessions? Do they have suicidal ideation? Are they concerned about somatic complaints?

4. *Thought process.* This has to do with the logic and goal directedness of the client's speech (Carlat, 2005). For example, circumstantial speech occurs when people give excessive detail and they take a long time to get to their point. This is common in anxiety disorders, especially OCD (Daniel & Gurcznski, 2010). People who are tangential get

lost by following rabbit trails and never get to the point.

5. *Judgment.* This describes clients' ability to make decisions that not only are in their best interest but also conform to appropriate social standards of behavior (Jacobson & Jacobson, 2001).

6. *Impulse control.* This assessment identifies clients' ability to filter their thoughts and control behavior in the context of high frustration. Those with low impulse control tend to live as creatures of the moment, acting on whatever they feel at the moment. Judgment can sometimes vary according to negative emotion and impulse control.

**Conclusion.** This is the basis for clinical interviewing. The introduction phase of a clinical interview involves clearly communicating the issue of confidentiality and basic education regarding the therapist's style and orientation. The opening statement will assist in orienting the client, the body of the interview sustains the theoretical orientation and examines the presenting problem, and the closing must manage information and emotions. The clinical interview is a critical component to building a successful client-therapist relationship.

Gary Sibcy

## REFERENCE

Carlat, D. J. (Ed.). (2005). *The Psychiatric Interview* (2nd ed.). Philadelphia, PA: Lippincott Williams & Wilkins.

Daniel, M. D., & Crider, C. J. (2003). The mental status examination. In M. Hersen & S. M. Turner (Eds.), *Diagnostic Interviewing* (3rd ed., pp. 21-46). New York, NY: Kluwer Academic.

Daniel, M., & GurczNski, J. (2010). Mental status examination. In D. L. Segal & M. Hersen (Eds.), *Diagnostic Interviewing* (4th ed., pp. 61-88). New York, NY: Kluwer Academic.

Jacobson, J. L., & Jacobson, A. M. (2001). *Psychiatric Secrets* (2nd ed.). Philadelphia, PA: Hanley & Belfus.

Morrison, J. (2007). *Diagnosis Made Easier: Principles and Techniques for Mental Health Clinicians.* New York, NY: Guilford Press.

Turner, S. M., Hersen, M., & Heiser, N. (2003) The interviewing process. In M. Hersen & S. M. Turner (Eds.), *Diagnostic Interviewing* (3rd ed., pp. 3-20). New York, NY: Kluwer Academic.

## PSYCHOLOGICAL TESTING

**Description.** Psychological testing is an applied activity within the broader field of psychometrics. Samples of expression from behavioral, cognitive, emotional, social, and spiritual domains are used in the measurement of constructs such as intelligence, personality, attitudes, abilities, and aptitudes. Fernández-Ballesteros et al. (2001) define a psychological test as "an evaluative device or procedure in which a sample of the examinee's behavior in a specified domain is obtained and subsequently evaluated and scored using a standardized process" (p. 188). Tests can be evaluated based on considerations of theoretical orientation, practicality, standardization, reliability, and validity (Groth-Marnat, 2009). Psychological testing is most effective and relevant when it occurs as part of the more comprehensive process of psychological assessment, which integrates information from various sources, including interviews, observation, collateral contacts, and previous records as well as results from psychological testing. The testing process can focus on aspects of pathological, normal, or optimal functioning. It is important to note that the primary guiding ethical consideration in the use of psychological testing is the best interest and welfare of the client.

**Types of Psychological Testing.** Psychological testing can measure human functioning and ability across a number of modalities, including cognitive, personality, and neuropsychological domains. Cognitive areas can include intelligence, aptitude, and memory. Measures of personality are generally divided into two primary types. *Objective personality tests* have a structured set and range of possible responses and usually consist of true-false and multiple choice items or ratings on an ordinal scale. An individual's score is compared with the normative sample used to standardize the test. *Projective personality tests* involve the use of ambiguous stimuli that are intended to elicit verbal or graphomotor responses. *Neuropsychological tests* are used to evaluate brain-behavior relationships in such areas as memory, attention, concentration, speech, intelligence, academic achievement, problem solving, perception, and motor abilities.

**Key Issues.** Because the ethical use of psychological tests occurs in the context of a more comprehensive assessment process, it is important to identify key aspects of an assessment interview before describing five of the most commonly used tests. Basic counseling skills, such as empathy, motivation, and client engagement are vital to an effective assessment interview prior to testing. In addition to typical information regarding client demographics, the referral question, presenting issues, and background information and history, the interview will often include the use of behavioral assessment, cognitive-behavioral measures, and client self-report questionnaires. Additionally, a mental status examination is frequently included in order to assess areas of general appearance and behavior, affect and mood, perception, orientation, memory, attention, concentration, insight, judgment, and thought content. Many of these tools are brief but invaluable means of gathering information used to help better understand the client and his or her life context. Psychological testing can then be properly interpreted and utilized. Counselors using psychological tests should be competent to do so, and they should be skillful when working with issues of diversity and cultural sensitivity.

**The Five Most Commonly Used Psychological Tests**

1. *Wechsler Intelligence Scales.* The Wechsler Intelligence Scales use a battery format of 15 subtests and include individually administered versions for adults (WAIS-IV) and children (WISC-IV) (Wechsler, 2008a, 2008b). In addition to the full-scale intelligence quotient (IQ), the Wechsler Intelligence Scales provide four index scores: verbal comprehension, working memory, perceptual reasoning, and processing speed. The newest versions of these scales have resulted in a theory of intelligence that reflects the importance of fluid intelligence and general intellectual ability expressed through functions and processes measured by the four indexes. The Wechsler scales have demonstrated high reliability and validity coefficients, meaning that the scales are stable and accurate measures of intellectual ability. An important development in the WAIS-IV is that it has normed linkages to the Wechsler Memory Scale-IV (WMS-IV), which is the seventh most commonly used psychological test. The WAIS-IV and the WMS-IV have also been conormed with the Wechsler Individual Achievement Test-II (WIAT-II). Thus, intellectual ability, memory function, and achievement can be systematically evaluated as independent yet overlapping constructs (Groth-Marnat, 2009). Additionally, the Wechsler scales are often used as foundational components of neuropsychological testing.

2. *Minnesota Multiphasic Personality Inventory (MMPI-2).* The MMPI-2 is the second most commonly used psychological test and the most widely used and researched objective personality inventory assessing psychopathology. The intent of the original developers of the MMPI was to create one inventory of a wide sampling of behavior based on a large pool of items used to construct various scales that measure facets of personality (Greene, 2000). Their approach was empirical rather than theoretical, thus adding to the objectivity of the test. Criterion groups (individuals with a particular psychiatric diagnosis) and normative groups (individuals without a diagnosis) were compared across the item pool. In this way, items that statistically distinguished

one group from the other were refined and retained until 8 of the 10 clinical scales were constructed. Scales 5 and 0 were constructed in a different manner but still were empirically derived.

The MMPI-2 consists of 567 statements with responses of "true," "false," or "cannot say." The items make up 10 clinical scales and numerous subscales, with four validity scales to help assess how the individual approached taking the test. An individual's scores on each of the scales is plotted on a profile and compared to the standard scale score. Significant elevations on scales and subscales are the primary sources of interpretation, but low scores can also help clarify the clinical picture. The MMPI-2 was restandardized and released in 1989, providing current norms that include appropriate representation of ethnic minorities and updated item content where needed (e.g., eliminating gender bias) (Greene, 2000). The Restructured Clinical Scales and the Personality Pathology Five (PSY-5) Scales are significant refinements that help isolate the core features of the clinical scales and identify relevant, understandable personality constructs (Groth-Marnat, 2009).

The MMPI-2 can be used in softcover, hardcover, and computer-generated forms with both hand scoring and computer-generated scoring and interpretation available. Additionally, the MMPI-A can be used with adolescents.

Other objective personality tests include the Millon Clinical Multiaxial Inventory (MCMI-III) and the California Psychological Inventory (CPI). The MCMI-III is specifically designed to help diagnose Axis II personality disorders and is the ninth most commonly used psychological test. The CPI is an objective measure of normal personality and focuses on practicality, relevance, and accuracy in behavioral predictions. It is the tenth most commonly used psychological test.

3. *Rorschach.* The Rorschach, commonly referred to as the inkblot test, consists of ten bilaterally symmetrical inkblots. Although concerns about the Rorschach's psychometric properties and utility persist, it is still the third most commonly used psychological test. As the classic example of a projective test, Groth-Marnat (2009) states the central thesis of Rorschach interpretation: "The process by which persons organize their responses to the Rorschach is representative of how they confront other ambiguous situations requiring organization and judgment" (p. 385). The area of the inkblot focused on in the response (location), the specific properties of the inkblot used (determinants), and the general class of objects identified (content) are categories used in scoring responses. Contrary to popular opinion, the Rorschach is only partially concerned with the content of responses to the inkblots.

There are several primary scoring and interpretive systems for the Rorschach, but the Exner Comprehensive System is the most psychometrically sound, and it integrates the best of the other scoring systems. Probably its greatest asset is the Rorschach's bypassing of a person's conscious resistance and the test's resistance to faking. Acceptable reliability and validity have generally been achieved, but the Rorschach does have a few limitations, including complexity in scoring and interpretation and significant training demands for those who would use the test in a competent manner (Groth-Marnat, 2009).

4. *Bender Visual Motor Gestalt Test (Bender).* The Bender has been used as a screening for neuropsychological impairment since its inception. The original version consisted of nine designs to be reproduced on a single sheet of blank paper. Principally, it assesses a client's visuomotor constructive abilities, which are then rated according to various scoring systems for accuracy and integration (Groth-Marnat, 2009). Although not fully supported, the Bender has also been used as a projective drawing test in combination with the House-Tree-Person (Ogden, 2001). Its

recent revision (Bender-Gestalt II) includes updated norms, the same scoring system for children and adults, and formal procedures for the recall phase (Groth-Marnat).

5. *Thematic Apperception Test (TAT).* The TAT is a projective personality test in which the client gives verbal responses to a series of pictures. The client's stories are to include the thoughts and feelings of the characters, the events that led up to the situation depicted, and the outcomes. Responses are then evaluated for the following: length, identification of the heroes, environmental forces, outcomes, simple and complex themes, and motives, trends, and feelings of the heroes. Because of variability in administration, sequence and types of cards presented, and scoring, the TAT is often used in conjunction with other personality and psychological tests (Groth-Marnat, 2009). The basic premise is that the TAT stories reveal drives, emotions, complexes, and conflicts that clients might otherwise not be willing or able to admit.

**Conclusion.** Psychological testing has a rich and varied history. Used as part of a comprehensive assessment process, psychological testing can help facilitate case formulation, differential diagnosis, and treatment planning. Recent work within the positive psychology movement has begun to use principles of psychological testing to identify character strengths and virtues. Competent Christian counselors will skillfully use psychological testing when appropriate to help further the growth and healing of those committed to their care.

David E. Jenkins

### REFERENCES

Fernández-Ballesteros, R., DeBruyn, E. E. J., Godoy, A., Hornke, L. F., TerLaak, J., Vizcarro, C.,...Zaccagnini, J. L. (2001). Guidelines for the assessment process (GAP): A proposal for discussion. *European Journal of Psychological Assessment, 17,* 187-200.

Greene, R. L. (2000). *The MMPI-2: An Interpretive Manual* (2nd ed.). Needham Heights, MA: Allyn & Bacon.

Groth-Marnat, G. (2009). *Handbook of Psychological Assessment* (5th ed.). Hoboken, NJ: Wiley & Sons.

Ogden, D. P. (2001). *Psychodiagnostics and Personality Assessment: A Handbook* (3rd ed.). Los Angeles, CA: Western Psychological Services.

Wechsler, D. (2008a). *Wechsler Adult Intelligence Scale* (4th ed.). San Antonio, TX: NCS Prentice Hall.

Wechsler, D. (2008b). *WISC-IV Administration and Scoring Manual.* San Antonio, TX: NCS Prentice Hall.

## PSYCHOPATHOLOGY

**Description.** Psychopathology (including abnormal psychology, mental illness, and psychological disorders) is the study of the various mental disorder designations, their symptoms, and how they manifest in the population (Maxmen & Ward, 1995). They can occur as one predominant problem, such as schizophrenia, or as multiple independent diagnoses across a broad spectrum of areas, a phenomenon known as *comorbidity* (Morrison, 2007). In those instances, a client may be clinically depressed, abusing alcohol, and have a personality disorder while suffering with diabetes and going through a divorce.

Prevalence rates for psychopathology have ranged from around 1% to 51% among children (Roberts, Attkisson, & Rosenblatt, 1998). It is estimated that approximately 39% of older adolescents have some kind of psychopathology (Wittchen, Nelson, & Lachner, 1998). One national sample put the rates above 48% in 15- to 54-year-olds (Kessler et al., 1994). These numbers have remained steady over the past several decades.

**How Psychopathologies Develop.** "Pathological syndromes are dynamic patterns of intercorrelated symptoms and signs that have a characteristic evolution over time" (Jablensky & Kendall, 2002, p. 7). Simply put, mental disorders display certain qualities and characteristics that have a tendency to become more severe without some type of intervention. Kay and Tasman (2006) write that intrapersonal (focusing on themselves) "manifestations of psychiatric illness can be grouped into five broad domains of human functioning: (a) consciousness, orientation, memory, and intellect; (b) speech, thinking, perception, and self-experience; (c) emotions; (d) physical functioning; and (e) behavior and adaptive functioning" (p. 118). When combined with problematic interpersonal functioning (focusing on relationships with others) in the client's workplace, social, and family relationships, psychopathology can cover every facet of a client's life and therefore can be debilitating.

There is no one accepted manner of how mental illness occurs, but it has been linked to developmental factors (De Pauw & Mervielde, 2010), along with dysfunctional emotional and external factors (Leising, Grade, & Faber, 2010). Briggs-Gowan et al. (2010) maintain that traumatic events experienced in childhood may be contributing factors, especially in light of the growing body of evidence that early childhood psychopathology remains highly stable as people progress into adolescence and beyond (Sterba et al., 2010). This suggests a childhood trauma is not outgrown, but is merely "in hiding" until a triggering event revives the early emotional dysregulation so that the client reexperiences the original trauma. For example, an adult female client involved in a relationship may come in for help because she is reexperiencing the feelings of trauma she had when she was sexually abused as a child.

However, adults who had a normal upbringing may experience a painful incident, trauma, or life stressor that sends them into a depressive mood state or ratchets up their feelings of anxiety, requiring them to seek counseling and possible medication intervention. Research has also focused on the role that emotional regulation, cognitive biases, and temperament play in discovering why some individuals seem to be more susceptible to psychological disorders than others (Sontag & Graber, 2010).

**Assessment.** Diagnosing mental illness requires appropriate study and research into the various signs, symptoms, and syndromes and their possible causes, as well as knowledge of appropriate treatment to relieve the worst manifestations of the disorder. The most widely accepted research has been organized into the fourth edition of the *Diagnostic and Statistical Manual of Mental Disorders* (American Psychiatric Association, 2000), which is used to assist in recognition and diagnosis (but not in direct treatment planning), enabling an easier understanding of the complexities surrounding mental illness in people.

**General Treatment Planning Considerations.** Seligman and Reichenberg (2007) maintain that the "fundamental reason for treatment planning is to facilitate effective delivery of mental health services" (p. 2). This requires solid clinical interviewing and assessment for good diagnosis and treatment planning. Consideration should also be made when selecting one's theoretical approach in treatment formulation. There are many choices, but Berman (2010) proposes that treatment effectiveness may be maximized by letting the client's characteristics and presenting concerns guide the theoretical approach choice rather than the counselor's personal preferences (p. 5).

With the exceptions of schizophrenia and the bipolar disorders, Axis I disorders in most instances can be treated in varying degrees so that the client experiences symptom relief and resumption of a normal lifestyle. Depending on the severity and risk to the client, treatment may need to be inpatient (for example, in a psychiatric hospital) or outpatient (for example, in a private practice or community social services). This may involve different types of psychotherapy (cognitive-behavioral, family, solution-focused, and so on) or medication interventions (antidepressants, anxiolytics, etc.) or a combination of the two. Adjuncts to therapy may include wraparound services such as support groups (such as Alcoholics Anonymous), spiritual strengthening through the client's place of worship or pastoral counseling, parenting classes taught by a community agency, or in-home counseling for stabilizing the family.

In the past, Axis II personality disorders have been considered to be permanent and not seen as treatable toward complete dysfunctional symptom relief. However, several promising therapies (except in cases of mental retardation), such as dialectical behavior therapy and pharmacotherapy, may bode well in helping individuals who have prominent personality disorder diagnoses (Crits-Christoph & Barber, 2004). Other issues to consider are "a wide range of factors shared across disorders, including the biological (e.g., disturbed sleep), the psychological (e.g., elevated perfectionism), and social domains (e.g., expressed emotion)," that are referred to as "transdiagnostic" (Mansell, 2011, p. 190). This is a reminder to think holistically during the diagnostic and treatment phases of client care and to consider any other factors that may have an impact on client symptomatology.

CLAY PETERS

## REFERENCES

American Psychiatric Association. (2000). *Diagnostic and Statistical Manual of Mental Disorders* (4th ed., text rev.). Washington, DC: Author.

Berman, P. S. (2010). *Case Conceptualization and Treatment Planning: Integrating Theory with Clinical Practice.* Thousand Oaks, CA: Sage.

Briggs-Gowan, M. J., Carter, A. S., Clark, R., Augustyn, M., McCarthy, K. J., & Ford, J. D. (2010). Exposure to potentially traumatic events in early childhood: Differential links to emergent psychopathology. *Journal of Child Psychology and Psychiatry, 51*(10), 1132-1140.

Crits-Christoph, P., & Barber, J. P. (2004). Empirical research on the treatment of personality disorders. In J. J. Magnavita (Ed.), *Handbook of Personality Disorders: Theory and Practice* (pp. 513-527). Hoboken, NJ: Wiley & Sons.

De Pauw, S. S. W., & Mervielde, I. (2010). Temperament, personality and developmental psychopathology: A review based on the conceptual dimensions underlying childhood traits. *Child Psychiatry and Human Development, 41,* 313-329.

Jablensky, A., & Kendell, R. E. (2002). Criteria for assessing a classification in psychiatry. In M. Maj, W. Gaebel, J. J. Lopez-Ibor, & N. Sartorius (Eds.), *Psychiatric Diagnosis and Classification* (pp. 1-24). Chichester, UK: Wiley & Sons.

Kay, J., & Tasman, A. (2006). *Essentials of Psychiatry.* Chichester, UK: Wiley & Sons.

Kessler, R. C., McGonagle, K. A., Zhao, S., Nelson, C. B., Hughes, M., Eshleman, S., ... & Kendler, K. S. (1994). Lifetime and 12-month prevalence of DSM-III-R psychiatric disorders in the United States: Results from the National Comorbidity Survey. *Archives of General Psychiatry, 51,* 8-19.

Leising, D., Grade, T., & Faber, R. (2010). A longitudinal study of emotional experience, expressivity, and psychopathology in psychotherapy inpatients and psychologically healthy persons. *Journal of Clinical Psychology, 66*(10), 1027-1043.

Mansell, W. (2011). Core processes of psychopathology and recovery: "Does the Dodo bird effect have wings?" *Clinical Psychology Review, 31,* 189-192.

Maxmen, J. S., & Ward, N. G. (1995). *Essential Psychopathology and Its Treatment* (2nd ed.). New York, NY: Norton.

Morrison, J. (2007). *Diagnosis Made Easier: Principles and Techniques for Mental Health Clinicians.* New York, NY: Guilford Press.

Roberts, R. E., Attkisson, C. C., & Rosenblatt, A. (1998). Prevalence of psychopathology among children and adolescents. *The American Journal of Psychiatry, 155,* 715-725.

Seligman, L., & Reichenberg, L. W. (2007). *Selecting Effective Treatments: A Comprehensive, Systematic Guide to Treating Mental Disorders* (3rd ed.). San Francisco, CA: Wiley & Sons.

Sontag, L. M, & Graber, J. A. (2010). Coping with perceived peer stress: Gender-specific and common pathways to symptoms of psychopathology. *Developmental Psychology, 46* (6), 1605-1620.

Sterba, S. T., Copeland, W., Egger, H. L., Costello, E. J., Erkanli, A., & Angold, A. (2010). Longitudinal dimensionality of adolescent psychopathology: Testing the differentiation hypothesis. *Journal of Child Psychology and Psychiatry, 51* (8), 871-884.

Wittchen, H. U., Nelson, C. B., & Lachner, G. (1998). Prevalence of mental disorders and psychosocial impairments in adolescents and young adults. *Psychological Medicine, 28,* 109-126.

## DIAGNOSIS OF MENTAL DISORDERS

**DESCRIPTION.** The fourth edition of the *Diagnostic and Statistical Manual of Mental Disorders* (*DSM*) (American Psychiatric Association [APA], 2000) categorizes and distinguishes one mental illness from another. It allows for the communication of diagnostic impressions using a numeric code and descriptive title in order to enhance client assistance across the spectrum of care, and it helps guide the clinician toward the most effective treatment plan. The *DSM* is "primarily a medical-diagnostic document" (Mayer, 2006, p. 443) and conceptualizes mental disorders as any clinically significant behavior or psychological syndromes or patterns that cause distress, deviance, dysfunction, and/or disability.

**Structure of the DSM.** The *DSM* diagnostic system is divided into five *axes*, or components, that enable the clinician to document psychopathology from several different facets of an individual's life in a succinct, manageable format. The system ranges from the client's presenting problem to personality or developmental concerns to medical conditions to psychosocial stressors to current coping behavior. The *DSM* relies on the categorical approach to divide mental disorders into types based on criterion sets with defining characteristics, which allows for "additional nuance, such as severity ratings [and] codes for the presence/absence of special features" (Langenbucher & Nathan, 2006, p. 3). The clinician evaluates clients to see if they meet a certain number of criteria in a designated period of time. For instance, for clients to be diagnosed with major depression, they would need to meet five or more of the criteria within the past two weeks, and they would need to have either a loss of interest or pleasure and/or depressed mood (APA, 2000). It does this without emphasizing one theoretical perspective over another (such as the psychodynamic, behavioral, or cognitive), seeking instead to be as practical as possible (Segal & Coolidge, 2001).

**Axis I.** This axis covers the traditional diagnoses most seen in psychopathology and is for recording *clinical disorders* and other conditions that may be a focus of clinical attention (APA, 2000). The majority of clients who come for counseling and therapy will be complaining of one or more of these disorders as the presenting problems, which in turn become the focus of treatment and symptom reduction. These psychopathologies are included under Axis I:

- disorders first diagnosed in infancy, childhood, or adolescence
- delirium, dementia, amnestic, and other cognitive disorders
- mental disorders due to a general medical condition
- substance-related disorders
- schizophrenia and other psychotic disorders
- mood disorders
- anxiety disorders
- somatoform disorders
- factitious disorders
- dissociative disorders
- sexual and gender identity disorders
- eating disorders
- sleep disorders
- impulse-control disorders not classified elsewhere
- adjustment disorders
- other conditions that may be a focus of clinical attention

**Axis II.** Here, *personality disorders* and *mental retardation* are recorded, as well as any prominent maladaptive personality features and defense mechanisms. Disorders written here are considered to be lifelong, and while they may be manageable, they are not seen as treatable toward complete dysfunctional symptom relief in the same manner that can be attained on Axis I. These psychopathologies are covered under Axis II:

- mental retardation
- paranoid personality disorder
- schizoid personality disorder
- schizotypal personality disorder

- borderline personality disorder
- histrionic personality disorder
- narcissistic personality disorder
- antisocial personality disorder
- avoidant personality disorder
- dependent personality disorder
- obsessive-compulsive personality disorder
- personality disorder not otherwise specified

**Axis III.** This section denotes a client's "current *general medical condition* that is potentially relevant to the understanding and management of the individual's mental disorder" (APA, 2000, p. 29). Counselors are not trained in the practice of medicine, but this axis is used to list known or reported physical conditions that may be *causative* (kidney failure causing delirium, which is then noted on Axis I as "Mental disorder [delirium] due to general medical condition [kidney failure]"), conditions that are the *result* of a mental disorder (cirrhosis of the liver stemming from long-term alcohol abuse), or conditions that are completely *unrelated* to a mental disorder, such as diabetes, cancer, or arthritis (Kaplan, Sadock, & Sadock, 2007, p. 306).

**Axis IV.** *Environmental* and *psychosocial stressors* that have an impact on the diagnosis, treatment, and prognosis of the disorders listed in Axis I and/or Axis II are detailed here (APA, 2000). These stressors can be negative (death in the family, job loss, divorce, discrimination, etc.) or positive (job promotion, planned pregnancy, marriage, etc.). Noting these stressors and how they are affecting clients and their presenting problems is an important step in treatment planning. These general areas of stress are contained under Axis IV:

- problems with primary support group
- problems related to the social environment
- educational problems
- occupational problems
- housing problems
- economic problems
- problems with access to health care services
- problems related to interaction with the legal system or crime
- other psychosocial and environmental problems

**Axis V.** The final section used in diagnosing mental illness can be one of the more difficult areas, since it relies on the clinician's *reasoned opinion* of a client's overall level of functioning (APA, 2000). This refers to the *Global Assessment of Functioning*, or GAF scale, and is "a composite of three major areas: social functioning, occupational functioning, and psychological functioning" (Kaplan et al., 2007, pp. 306-307). The GAF is divided into ten ranges of functioning, from 1 (persistent danger of severely hurting self or others) up to 100 (superior functioning in a wide range of activities). A 0 means there is not enough information to make an informed rating.

Unfortunately there is not a standard, accepted, objective method for rating an individual's level of functioning. Instead, this rating relies on the clinician's experience and subjective best judgment based on the clinical interview and observation of the client. However, this score can be rendered more accurate by discussing the past and present clinical, familial, educational, developmental, military, and occupational history of the client (Morrison, 2007). Two scores are often posted—one for an approximate guess of functioning during the past year, and another score for the current level of functioning. This allows the clinician to estimate whether the client's functioning is getting better or growing worse.

**Limitations.** The *DSM* is limited in many respects. It concentrates on "individuals rather than addressing family or social systems," and it focuses on "the what, when, and where rather than the why" (Parent & Clinton, 2009, p. 328). Also, categorical systems are a yes-no method to diagnosing, relying on the "presence or absence of a disorder" (Jones, 2011, p. 24). There is also the problem that some clients do not seem to fit perfectly into the *DSM*-identified categories or do not meet the minimum specified criteria but are still manifesting severe symptoms (Jones). In addition, some question its appropriateness due to, among other things, its lack of cultural considerations (Del Barrio, 2004).

**Future Directions.** Changes are coming with the development of the *DSM-V*, but the present categorical system will be retained, and a dimensional system may be added to serve as an adjunct to diagnosis (Jones, 2011). Instead of a "yes they have it, no they don't" approach, the dimensional method may use a system of rating scales, where symptom severity will be measured on a four- or five-point scale (Jones). Having both of these approaches may enhance clinicians' ability to be more precise in their diagnoses and to develop better treatment plans for quality client care.

Clay Peters

## REFERENCES


American Psychiatric Association. (2000). *Diagnostic and Statistical Manual of Mental Disorders* (4th ed., text rev.). Washington, DC: Author.

Del Barrio, V. (2004). Diagnostic and statistical manual of mental disorders. In C. Spielberger (Ed.), *Encyclopedia of Applied Psychology* (Vol. 1, pp. 607-614). Burlington, MA: Academic Press.

Jones, K. D. (2011). Inside the DSM-5: Dimensional assessment. *Counseling Today, 53*(9), 24-25.

Kaplan, H. I., Sadock, B. J., & Sadock, V. A. (2007). *Kaplan and Sadock's Synopsis of Psychiatry: Behavioral Sciences, Clinical Psychiatry* (10th ed.). Philadelphia, PA: Williams & Wilkins.

Langenbucher, J., & Nathan, P. E. (2006). Diagnosis and classification. In M. Hersen & J. C. Thomas (Eds.), *Comprehensive Handbook of Personality and Psychopathology: Adult Psychopathology* (Vol. 2, pp. 3-20). Hoboken, NJ: Wiley & Sons.

Mayer, J. D. (2006). A classification of *DSM-IV-TR* mental disorders according to their relation to the personality system. In M. Hersen & J. C. Thomas (Eds.), *Comprehensive Handbook of Personality and Psychopathology: Personality and Everyday Functioning* (Vol. 1, pp. 443-453). Hoboken, NJ: Wiley & Sons.

Morrison, J. (2007). *Diagnosis Made Easier: Principles and Techniques for Mental Health Clinicians.* New York, NY: Guilford Press.

Parent, M. S., & Clinton, T. (2009). Clinical diagnosis and treatment planning: Uses and limits of the DSM system. In T. Clinton & G. Ohlschlager (Eds.), *Competent Christian Counseling: Foundations of Compassionate Soul Care* (Vol. 1, pp. 324-346). Colorado Springs, CO: WaterBrook Press.

Segal, D. L., & Coolidge, F. L. (2001). Diagnosis and classification. In M. Hersen & V. B. Van Hasselt (Eds.), *Advanced Abnormal Psychology* (2nd ed., pp. 5-22). New York, NY: Kluwer Academic/Plenum.


## SUICIDE ASSESSMENT AND INTERVENTION

Friedrich Nietzsche, the famous 19th-century German philosopher, asserted in *Beyond Good and Evil*, "The thought of suicide is a great consolation; with the help of it one gets successfully through many a bad night." This statement reveals a number of reasons why suicide is such a fierce paradox. Suicidal thinking in times of crisis is fairly common and may even be attractive to the desperate person.

Facing a suicidal client or parishioner is one of the counselor's or pastor's most stressful and fearful experiences. The suicide of a client is surely one of counseling's most difficult occupational hazards. Clients or parishioners who kill themselves not only devastate family and friends but also adversely impact counselors long after the event (Chemtob, Bauer, Hamada, Pelowski, & Muraoka, 1989; Ohlschlager & Mosgofian, 1992; Ohlschlager, Shadoan, & Stewart, 2005).

**Prevalence.** Suicide has become the eighth leading cause of death in the United States. Tragically, it is the third leading cause of death among teenagers. Approximately 750,000 suicide attempts take place in America every year—more than 2,000 people attempt to kill themselves every day (Evans & Norman, 2003). Eighty-five of these succeed—35,000 die every year, or about 4% of those who make attempts (Sadock & Sadock, 2010). Roughly 40% of these deaths are by persons over 65 years of age, most suffering in pain from terminal and debilitating disease. A quarter of all suicides are by young people between the ages of 15 and 24. The rate of suicide within this age group has tripled in the past 25 years.

The dynamics of suicide are highly complex. Simple explanations and easy solutions do not exist. It is not just a matter of acute and severe depression, although the National Institute of Mental Health considers depression the leading cause. It requires more than restraining or avoiding lethal behavior, although individuals must act aggressively to kill themselves. Though options always exist, suicidal people are overcome by constricting choices, sabotaged by a perverse tunnel vision: "It became the only thing left to do."

Finally, it is not just a problem of meaningless and existential despair, although Aaron Beck and his colleagues (Beck, Brown, Berchick, Stewart, & Steer, 1990; Beck, Resnik, & Lettieri, 1974; Weishaar & Beck, 1992) have shown that hopelessness is even more influential than depression in completed suicides.

> Suicide is primarily, although not entirely, a spiritual problem. Persons who are suicidal are asking, either explicitly or implicitly, such critical existential questions as: Does my life have meaning or purpose? Do I have any worth? Is forgiveness possible? Is there any hope for a new life beyond this current mess? (Sullender & Malony, 1990, p. 204).

**Suicide Assessment.** Assessment of suicidal risk involves gathering information from multiple sources across a number of key variables (Posner, Oquendo, Gould, Stanley, & Davies, 2007). Suicide assessment essentially asks two questions: Is this person at risk for committing suicide? And if so, how serious is the risk?

Competent counselors will assess this risk according to history, trait, mood, personality, and situational factors. We incorporate questions about suicide (and homicidal and assaultive behavior) in our clinical intake forms. This gives us direct access to these issues at the start of professional relations and allows us to intervene early when these issues are pressing. Structuring assessments this way and addressing these questions on the initial interview puts clients more at ease as they see it as part of the routine we follow with all new clients. Evaluate suicide risk across these seven key variables:

- past suicide attempts and their seriousness
- communication of intent or denial of intent
- assessing the nonviolent-depressed-hopeless person
- assessing the violent-angry-impulsive person
- other changes in personality and behavior
- environmental stressors
- demographic factors

**Suicide Intervention.**

- Discuss suicide openly and matter-of-factly.
- Expand alternate thinking and options to suicide.
- Respect and use the fears that block suicide.
- Increase clinical or counseling intervention.

- Act assertively to protect in crisis situations.
- Make referrals to people you know and trust.
- Remove access to lethal weapons and means of death.
- Contract for "no suicide" and community care.

Psychiatric research (Kroll, 2000) has called into question the reliability of no-suicide contracts, showing that 41% of psychiatrists who used them had patients kill themselves or make serious attempts. We have found that the most useful contracts are those that incorporate and gain commitment from many people to work in the prevention circle.

A group of caring people who covenant to stay close to, pray for, call on, and visit an at-risk person provide a major aid to prevention. Contracting against suicide in this manner is an effective and flexible procedure that increases protection and aids the clinical process through the crisis period.

**Case Management.**

*Monitor your clients closely.* Staying with clients or congregants is essential through a suicidal crisis. Even if you refer, they will likely return to you, so your legal duty does not end with referral. It is usually necessary to walk a "second mile" with them, sacrificing some time and energy to ensure their safe passage through "the valley of the shadow of death."

*Help hospitalize suicidal people.* Hospitalizing suicidal people may be necessary to save their lives. Seek agreement to admit themselves to a hospital voluntarily and refer them. Take them to the nearest Christian or other inpatient facility. If they will not agree to admit voluntarily, seek involuntary admission for crisis assessment and intervention. If admission criteria is met—serious mental illness and danger to self—most states allow a person to be held for 48 to 72 hours initially.

**Conclusion.** If Nietzsche is right and suicide is "great consolation," it could only be so to the hopeless and desperate few. For most, especially for those who loved the deceased, it is a tragedy that brings lifelong heartache. Even though never fully washed away, the grief of suicide can be redeemed by the crucified and risen Savior, the "man of sorrows" who was and is well acquainted with grief. Counselors who lose a client or congregant to suicide are sometimes devastated but must still go on in the work of ministry. We need God's healing comfort, wisdom, and strength to grieve, overcome the fear that it will happen again, and live without overt anger or repressed hostility toward the deceased.

(Do not rely on this article or any others when facing a suicidal patient or client. Make referral to a psychiatrist or a clinician competent in suicide assessment and intervention.)

George Ohlschlager
Tim Clinton
Scott Hawkins

## REFERENCES


Beck, A., Brown, G., Berchick, R., Stewart, B., & Steer, R. (1990). Relationship between hopelessness and ultimate suicide: A replication with psychiatric outpatients. *American Journal of Psychiatry, 147*(2), 190-195.

Beck, A., Resnik, H., & Lettieri, D. (Eds.). (1974). *The Prediction of Suicide.* Bowie, MD: Charles Press.

Chemtob, C., Bauer, G., Hamada, R., Pelowski, S., & Muraoka, M. (1989). Patient suicide: Occupational hazard for psychologists and psychiatrists. *Professional Psychology: Research and Practice, 20* (5), 294-300.

Evans, G., & Norman, L. F. (Eds.). (2003). *The Encyclopedia of Suicide.* (2nd ed.). New York, NY: Facts on File.

Kroll, J. (2000). Use of no-suicide contracts by psychiatrists in Minnesota. *American Journal of Psychiatry, 157*(10), 1684-1686.

Ohlschlager, G., & Mosgofian, P. (1992). *Law for the Christian Counselor: A Guidebook for Clinicians and Pastors.* Dallas, TX: Word Books.

Ohlschlager, G., Shadoan, M., & Stewart, G. (2005).

Suicide intervention. In T. Clinton, A. Hart, & G. Ohlschlager (Eds.), *Caring for People God's Way: Personal and Emotional Issues, Addictions, Grief, and Traumas.* Nashville, TN: Nelson.

Posner, K., Oquendo, M. A., Gould, M., Stanley, B., & Davies, M. (2007). Columbia classification algorithm of suicide assessment (C-CASA): Classification of suicidal events in the FDA's pediatric suicidal risk analysis of antidepressants. *The American Journal of Psychiatry, 164,* 1035-1043.

Sadock, B. J., Sadock, V. A. (Eds.). (2010). *Kaplan and Sadock's Pocket Handbook of Clinical Psychiatry* (5th ed.). Philadelphia, PA: Lippincott Williams & Wilkins.

Sullender, R. S., & Malony, H. N. (1990). Should clergy counsel suicidal persons? *The Journal of Pastoral Care, 44*(3), 203-211.

Weishaar, M., & Beck, A. (1992). Clinical and cognitive predictors of suicide. In R. Maris, A. Berman, J. Maltsberger, & R. Yufit (Eds.), *Assessment and Prediction of Suicide.* New York, NY: Guilford Press.

## TREATMENT PLANNING

**Description.** Treatment planning in counseling is "the process of plotting out the counseling process so that both counselor and client have a road map that delineates how they will proceed from their point of origin (the client's presenting concerns and underlying difficulties) to their destination, alleviation of troubling and dysfunctional symptoms and patterns, and establishment of improved coping mechanisms and self-esteem" (Seligman, 1996, p. 157). The essence of treatment planning is having a starting point, a destination, and a plan for journeying between the two.

**History and Rationale.** Historically, clinical treatment planning was informal, verbal, therapist initiated, vague, and dynamic, changing week to week in accord with client concerns. Changes in consumer awareness and expectations, the advent of managed care, mandated documentation, bureaucratic oversight, increasing litigation, and professional accreditation have revised the process to reflect mutual involvement by client and counselor, written documentation, competent assessment, ongoing evaluation of progress, and external accountability.

Formal treatment planning is also an ethical responsibility. "Counselors and their clients work jointly in devising integrated counseling plans that offer reasonable promise of success and are consistent with abilities and circumstances of clients. Counselors and clients regularly review counseling plans to assess their continued viability and effectiveness, respecting the freedom of choice of clients" (American Counseling Association [ACA] *Code of Ethics*, 2005, A.1.c.).

**Application.** "From intake to termination, clinicians must gather and analyze case information, formulate hypotheses, and implement treatment decisions. Given the quantity and ambiguity of information presented, this is a daunting task" (Falvey, 2001, p. 293). Treatment planning models vary, but most include the following components in some measure (see Parent, 2002).

**Case Conceptualization: Defining the Problem.** Problem definition begins with comprehensive assessment. Listening carefully to the client describe the presenting concern, assessing secondary issues, attending to the contexts of person and issues, and evaluating the need for formal testing are all elements of the assessment phase.

In today's mental-health climate, a valid, formal diagnosis is a necessary (although not sufficient) condition of accurate mental-health assessment. For licensed professionals, this means using the *Diagnostic and Statistical Manual of Mental Disorders* (*DSM*) as a source of common terminology and criteria. A *DSM* diagnosis may be perceived as insurance driven, but it also brings clarity to the therapeutic process for both client and therapist by providing a basis for the treatment plan.

Assessment must be multidimensional, including physical, psychological, social, and spiritual aspects. In any situation, one of these may take precedence, but a holistic understanding of the individual is essential to accurately evaluate concerns, interventions, and resources. Therapists traditionally receive training in assessing physical and psychological aspects, often ignoring social and spiritual concerns. Cultural shifts have forced greater attention to multicultural competency, helping counselors to become aware of their biases and to facilitate understanding of their clients' cultural and social contexts. Spiritual assessment still remains a relatively unexplored area in treatment planning. It is ethically appropriate and therapeutically sound, but counselors are still reluctant to assess spiritual/religious history despite its importance (Hathway, Scott, & Garver, 2004, cited in Corey, Corey & Callanan, 2011).

The counselor's theoretical approach gives meaning to presenting issues and determines the general framework for interventions. The goals emphasized in counseling, the techniques presented, the division of responsibility, and other issues all reflect the counselor's operating theory. Practitioners may be appropriately eclectic, but they need to be able to articulate a therapeutic rationale for change. Major theoretical schools have different assumptions about how change takes place: through insight, changing behavior, disputing irrational or dysfunctional thoughts, by providing a safe and accepting relationship, or by intervening in a systemic manner. Treatment goals and interventions are based on theoretical assumptions.

**Case Management: Making a Plan.** Goal setting is usually the primary focus in formulating the plan, but it must be preceded by careful consideration of counselor/client variables. Counseling is, at heart, a relational process, and a good match between client and therapist is essential. Both client and counselor resources and responsibilities need to be evaluated. Practical commitments of time, finances, and social and occupational responsibilities need to be factored into the treatment plan. Multiple role benefits, potential value conflicts, and diversity competency need careful attention.

The writing of good treatment goals and objectives has been facilitated in recent years by a variety of forms, books, and computer programs designed to standardize treatment (e.g., Jongsma & Peterson, 1995), provide structured frameworks (e.g., Seligman, 1996), and generally save the clinician time. These are especially helpful in increasing the quality and conformity of documentation but may fail to reflect the uniqueness of the client's situation. Many are good tools, but tools are inevitably subject to the understanding and ability of the user.

Mutually determined goals and objectives facilitate the therapeutic relationship and provide for measurable outcomes. Goals are generally abstract and conceptual, setting the larger agenda. They need to be understandable, realistic, and prioritized (U-R-P) if therapy is to proceed effectively. Objectives are the concrete representations of the goal. They represent the stepwise progressions toward accomplishment. Objectives need to be concrete, measurable, and observable (C-M-O). They are the links to interventions and are reflected in progress notes in light of the current goal.

Interventions and strategies need to be tied to objectives and dictated by issues of competency and informed consent. Good counselors are creative and eclectic in their use of techniques, relating them to the overall approach to change. The rise of empirically supported treatments (ESTs) for many situations has facilitated this aspect of treatment planning. Their use as a singular treatment planning criterion can be problematic, but recent discussion has focused on using ESTs within the context of evidence-based practice (EBP) (American Psychological Association Presidential Task Force on Evidence-Based Practice, 2006).

Appropriate intervention includes more than specific techniques. It includes making decisions regarding modality (e.g., family or group), setting, duration, and frequency. Ongoing treatment planning may necessitate a change in some portion of the plan as clients' situations change. Likewise, counselors need to be aware of the community resources available and be willing to make appropriate referrals.

**Case Evaluation: Evaluating the Process.** Both client and counselor need to know when and if progress is being made. A "progress review is an opportunity for both therapist and client to look at how therapy is going, with an eye toward potentially modifying the treatment plan, moving to a new phase of treatment, or ending therapy" (Wood, Detweiler-Bedell, Teachman, & O'Hearn, 2003). Insurance companies and accreditation standards (such as JCAHO) require outcome measures to be noted and assessed. This type of accountability ultimately facilitates treatment. When treatment planning is done well, knowing when goals are accomplished follows naturally. Good outcome assessment may lead to renegotiating the counseling contract and formulation of other treatment goals.

Providing appropriate termination and follow-up planning brings closure to the therapeutic process. Planning for the end of counseling is an essential part of treatment planning. Follow-up policies are essential to specify the nature of continuing or future contact. All human beings require closure, which should be as individualized as the client. Documentation of this final phase of treatment planning is as essential as the initial case write-up. The final aspect of evaluation involves counselor self-evaluation. This may be as simple as writing a closing summary and addressing the successes and failures of treatment. Difficult clients may require processing with a colleague, supervisor, or consultant.

**Conclusion.** Treatment planning is a creative and dynamic process. It must remain flexible enough to adjust to changing situations and needs, yet structured enough to provide ongoing direction, feedback, and accountability. The need to balance empirically driven models with solid clinical reasoning will continue to be a challenge for competent practitioners.

**Miriam Stark Parent**

## REFERENCES


American Counseling Association. (2005). *Code of Ethics.* Washington, DC: Author.

American Psychiatric Association. (2000). *Diagnostic and Statistical Manual of Mental Disorders* (4th ed., text rev.). Washington, DC: Author.

American Psychological Association Presidential Task Force on Evidence-Based Practice. (2006). Evidence-based practice in psychology. *American Psychologist, 61*(4), 271-285.

Corey, G., Corey, M., & Callanan, M. (2011). *Issues and Ethics in the Helping Professions* (8th ed.). Florence, KY: Brooks/Cole.

Falvey, J. E. (2001). Clinical judgment in case conceptualization and treatment planning across mental health disciplines. *Journal of Counseling & Development, 79*(3), 292-303.

Jongsma, A. E., & Peterson, L. M. (1995). *The Complete Psychotherapy Treatment Planner.* New York, NY: Wiley & Sons.

Parent, M. Stark (2002). Clinical diagnosis and treatment planning. In T. Clinton & G. Ohlschlager (Eds.), *Competent Christian Counseling: Foundations and Practice of Compassionate Soul Care.* Colorado Springs, CO: WaterBrook Press.

Seligman, L. (1996). *Diagnosis and Treatment Planning in Counseling* (2nd ed.). New York, NY: Plenum Press.

Wood, S., Detweiler-Bedell, J., Teachman, B., & O'Hearn, T. (2003). *Treatment Planning in Psychotherapy: Taking the Guesswork out of Clinical Care.* New York, NY: Guilford Press.

# INTERVENTIONS

## BEHAVIORAL INTERVENTIONS

**Description.** Behavioral interventions are counseling techniques designed to modify behavior without necessarily addressing the thoughts, feelings, or motivations associated with that behavior. These types of interventions are often used as a first step toward long-term behavior change and have been effective for treating a range of problems from changing bad habits (Michie, Abraham, Whittington, McAteer, & Gupta, 2009) to improving symptoms of serious mental illness (Bellus, Vergo, Kost, Stewart, & Barkstrom, 1999). Examples of behavioral interventions include systematic desensitization, token economies, and reinforcement paradigms (Coffey & Brumback, 2006).

The underlying process for behavioral interventions involves these steps: Identify the target behavior(s), determine behavior goals, select the intervention approach, and evaluate the result of the intervention. For instance, a counselor might instruct a client with self-injurious behaviors to self-monitor his or her most common self-injurious actions (such as cutting) and report back the number of times he or she participates in that behavior in a given day. A behavioral goal might be to reduce this number by 10% in the following week. The counselor then might plan a behavioral intervention, such as having the client journal when feeling an impulse to cut and verbally praising the client when he or she chooses to journal instead of cut. After some time, the counselor and client evaluate progress to determine if the target behavior has decreased. At this point, the counselor and client decide if this same intervention should be continued, discontinued, or modified.

**History.** The roots of behavioral interventions can be traced to 1913 when John B. Watson coined the term "behaviorism" (Watson, 1913). Behaviorism views psychology as a science of behavior rather than a science of "mind or conscious experience" (Skinner, 1963, p. 951). Behaviorists believe that all behavior can be explained in terms of environmental adjustment. In other words, all behavior is a product of environmental stimuli (Watson, 1917). The concepts of behaviorism were first seen in the counseling field through the development of behavior therapy, which became popular in the 1950s as a response to some clinical practices of that time that were not based on scientific evidence (Hayes, 2004). Behavior therapy provided a way for counselors to operationally define and measure treatment progress by observing clients' behavior before, during, and after interventions. In subsequent years, most of these therapies have been modified to also include cognitive and emotional components.

**Assessment.** Identifying the target behavior(s) and corresponding goals is the first step to create and evaluate a behavioral intervention. Common behavioral assessment methods include behavioral observation, self-monitoring, self-report, and psychophysiological assessment (Haynes & O'Brien, 2000). These strategies are often easy to perform, and many are used in a variety of settings, including a counseling room, waiting room, home, workplace, school, playground, prison, cafeteria, or shopping mall. An optimal behavioral assessment strategy is selected based on the population and behavior, and the results of the assessment are translated into relevant behavioral goals. At times, behavioral assessments are unable to be performed completely or accurately. Knowing one is being observed might alter the very behavior that is being measured, or a client may not be able, willing, or available to participate. If a desired behavioral assessment is not completed, a behavioral intervention must be planned using the information that is given.

**Treatment.** Behavioral interventions are often utilized as part of more comprehensive treatments, such as behavioral therapies and cognitive-behavioral therapies. Activity recording and activity scheduling are common tools used in behavioral activation treatment plans for depression and other mood disorders. In this intervention, the client looks back in time at a list of daily events to process how depression might have influenced his or her choices (activity recording) and plan the following days to break down large tasks into smaller, obtainable goals (activity scheduling) (Barlow, 2008).

In vivo exposure techniques such as systematic desensitization and flooding are useful tools in behavioral therapies for panic disorder and agoraphobia. In these interventions, the client is gradually (systematic desensitization) or suddenly (flooding) exposed to that which triggers his or her panic. For example, if the ultimate behavioral goal for the agoraphobic client is to go shopping in a crowded mall, using systematic desensitization, the client would first get in the car, then drive to the mall, then walk to the door of the mall, and so on over several sessions. When done repeatedly and safely, the conditioned anxiety response to each stage of the process will be extinguished.

Token economies have been found helpful as part of larger school-counseling initiatives in helping children with ADHD and other attentional and behavioral issues (DuPaul & Weyandt, 2006). Students are given tokens throughout the week when engaging in appropriate behavior, and these tokens can later be exchanged for desired rewards. This reinforces students' positive behavior and promotes harmony in the classroom.

**Spiritual Issues.** Christianity focuses on a change of heart that manifests itself in changed behavior. This philosophy is woven throughout the Bible in such concepts as "the fruit of the Spirit" (Galatians 5:22-23) and in the stories of people who experienced radical transformation, such as the apostle Paul. Matthew 12:34 says, "The mouth speaks what the heart is full of," indicating that change occurs from the inside out. However, sanctification is a lifelong and habitually difficult process. Paul explains in Romans 7 that although he loves God with all his heart and wants to do what is right, sin is still at war within him. This is a universal struggle in Christianity and is often a presenting problem in clients. Behavioral interventions are tools that counselors can use to help clients align their external actions with their internal convictions.

**Allison K. Wilkerson**
**Joshua N. Hook**

## REFERENCES


Barlow, D. H. (Ed.). (2008). *Clinical Handbook of Psychological Disorders* (4th ed.). New York, NY: Guilford Press.

Bellus, S. B., Vergo, J. G., Kost, P. P., Stewart, D., & Barkstrom, S. R. (1999). Behavioral rehabilitation and the reduction of aggressive and self-injurious behaviors with cognitively impaired, chronic psychiatric inpatients. *Psychiatric Quarterly, 70*, 27-37.

Coffey, C. E., & Brumback, R. A. (Eds.). (2006). *Pediatric Neuropsychiatry* (1st ed.). Philadelphia: Lippincott Williams & Wilkins.

DuPaul, G. J., & Weyandt, L. L. (2006). School-based intervention for children with attention deficit hyperactivity disorder: Effects on academic, social, and behavioral functioning. *International Journal of Disability, Development and Education, 53,* 161-176.

Hayes, S. C. (2004). Acceptance and commitment therapy, relational frame theory, and the third wave of behavioral and cognitive therapies. *Behavior Therapy, 35,* 639-665.

Haynes, S. N., & O'Brien, W. H. (2000). *Principles and Practice of Behavioral Assessment.* New York, NY: Kluwer Academic.

Michie, S., Abraham, C., Whittington, C., McAteer, J., & Gupta, S. (2009). Effective techniques in healthy eating and physical activity interventions: A Meta-Regression. *Health Psychology, 28,* 690-701.

Skinner, B. F. (1963). Behaviorism at fifty. *Science, 140,* 951-958.

Watson, J. B. (1913). Psychology as the behaviorist views it. *Psychological Review, 20,* 158-177.

Watson, J. B. (1917). An attempted formulation of the scope of behavior psychology. *Psychological Review, 24,* 329-352.

## EXPOSURE THERAPY

**Description.** Exposure therapy (ET) is a clinical intervention involving a group of procedures that are part of a broader cognitive-behavioral approach to counseling. Brady and Raines (2009) defined ET as "deliberately confronting some ordinarily avoided stimulus that provokes an undesired response, in order to reduce the strength of that response" (p. 51). Most commonly used in the treatment of anxiety disorders, ET targets avoidance of feared or avoided stimuli, including objects, images, people, or situations with the goal of modifying maladaptive fear memories and behaviors through habituation to cues that elicit the fear response (Allen, 1996; Baschnagel, Coffey, & Rash, 2006; Brady & Raines, 2009; Henslee & Coffey, 2010). ET can involve exposure that is imaginal or in vivo, as well as repeated or prolonged. There is growing evidence for the efficacy of ET using virtual reality as the exposure component (Myerbröker & Emmelkamp, 2010). When conducted well and according to protocol, ET is probably one of the best-supported therapeutic interventions for a variety of mainly anxiety disorders, including posttraumatic stress disorder (PTSD), panic disorder, obsessive-compulsive disorder, generalized anxiety disorder, and phobias. But ET has also been helpful with depression, chronic pain, and difficult bereavement. Generally, if a clinical condition involves the constellation of fear arousal, phobic avoidance, and distorted cognitions, ET should be considered as a possible treatment component of counseling.

**Awareness.** Allen (1996) identified several domains of new associations that must be established in temporal, cognitive, behavioral, and interpersonal domains. Riggs, Cahill, and Foa (2006) identified two basic propositions of ET: "(1) Anxiety disorders reflect the existence of pathological fear structures in memory, which are activated when information represented in the structures is encountered; and (2) successful treatment modifies the pathological elements of the fear structure, such that information that used to evoke anxiety symptoms no longer does so" (pp. 69-70).

One of the primary therapeutic mechanisms of ET is to gradually habituate the client to heightened arousal in response to the feared or avoided stimulus. A second primary mechanism is using cognitive dissonance to help modify cognitions that have prevented counselees from overcoming their fears. It is important to remember that exposure alone, without modifying arousal and its influence on physiology, thoughts, feelings, and behaviors, may strengthen client avoidance rather than extinguish it. Exposure therapy must include appropriate counselee education about anxiety and avoidance, how exposure can help, relaxation techniques, cognitive dissonance, and practice outside of sessions.

**Application.** In many ways, counselees direct the ET process and how it unfolds. Their involvement is needed to clarify the arousal-avoidance response cycle; to develop the graded hierarchy of arousal and anxiety;

to actively practice relaxation and other adaptive strategies; to direct the type, timing, and amount of exposure; to process in-session thoughts and feelings related to exposure; and to practice ET outside of formal counseling sessions (Riggs et al., 2006; Henslee & Coffey, 2010; Baschnagel et al., 2006; Brady & Raines, 2009). ET is known as one of the most effective treatments for posttraumatic stress disorder and in trauma-focused treatment of substance use disorders.

Over the course of several sessions, counselees should be educated about arousal, avoidance, cognitive distortions and dissonance, classical and operant conditioning, graded and repeated exposure, and in cases where PTSD is involved, the nature and effects of, response to, and recovery from trauma. Throughout the ET process, great care and concern should be given for counselees' welfare and motivation for participation. The counseling alliance can be maintained and strengthened by providing a clear description and rationale of ET, conveying empathy for changing avoidance, communicating caring, acknowledging the challenge of ET, and recognizing counselee courage and resolve (Riggs et al., 2006). Intentionally eliciting and heightening painful arousal without appropriate preparations and safeguards is inconsistent with ethical clinical practice and is not reflective of biblical principles of love and regard for those under our watchful care.

**Biblical and Spiritual Issues.** Genesis 3 records the first responses to the first sin of the first man and woman, which involved fear, shame, denial, concealment, and blame. It is apparent that painful arousal, phobic avoidance, and cognitive distortion were emotional, behavioral, and cognitive effects that resulted. Rather than enjoy intimate fellowship with their Creator, the man and woman hid (avoidance) out of fear (arousal) that was elicited by the sound of God (cognitive distortion).

It is instructive to consider the role of exposure in God's response. What did he do? He prompted his now-fallen image bearers to come out from hiding (exposure) among the trees of the garden. This is not to say God was doing ET. But we do see that, even in the first two human beings, God was aware of the effects fear can have on his children and their relationships with him, themselves, and each other. Perfect love drives out fear, and truth sets us free (see Jn 8:31-36; 1 Jn 4:18). May Christian counselors equip themselves biblically and clinically to help those who are bound by fear and falsehood.

David E. Jenkins

## REFERENCES


Allen, J. G. (1996). Neurobiological basis of posttraumatic stress disorder: Implications for patient education and treatment. *Bulletin of the Menninger Clinic, 60*(3), 377-395.

Baschnagel, J. S., Coffey, S. F., & Rash, C. J. (2006). Treatment of co-occurring PTSD and substance use disorders using trauma-focused exposure therapy. *International Journal of Behavioral and Consultation Therapy, 2*(4), 498-508. Retrieved from http://www.baojournal.com/IJBCT/IJBCT-index.html

Brady, A., & Raines, D. (2009). Dynamic hierarchies: A control paradigm for exposure therapy. *The Cognitive Behaviour Therapist, 2*, 51-62. doi:10.1017/S1754470X0800010X

Henslee, A. M., & Coffey, S. F. (2010). Exposure therapy for posttraumatic stress disorder in a residential substance use treatment facility. *Professional Psychology: Research and Practice, 41*, 34-40. doi:10.1037/a0018235

Myerbröker, K., & Emmelkamp, P. M. G. (2010). Virtual reality exposure therapy in anxiety disorders: A systematic review of process-and-outcome studies. *Depression and Anxiety, 27*, 933-944. doi:10.1002/da.20734

Riggs, D. S., Cahill, S. P., & Foa, E. B. (2006). Prolonged exposure treatment of posttraumatic stress disorder. In V. C. Follette & J. I. Ruzek (Eds.), *Cognitive-Behavioral Therapies for Trauma* (2nd ed., pp. 65-95). New York, NY: Guilford Press.


## OPERANT CONDITIONING

**Description.** Operant conditioning is a learning process involving voluntary behaviors in which the consequences of one's behavior affect how likely one is to behave the same way in the future. Responses from one's environment (including other people)

create consequences that will either increase or decrease the likelihood of that behavior in the future. Reinforcement increases the potential likelihood of that behavior in the future. Positive reinforcement introduces something positive to increase behavior (e.g., using ice cream to reward a child who earns good grades), whereas negative reinforcement removes something negative to increase desired behavior (e.g., a child who finishes her vegetables does not have to make her bed). Positive and negative refer not to morality or social preferences, but rather to the presentation or a removal of a stimulus. Punishment, on the other hand, decreases the potential likelihood of that behavior in the future. Positive punishment decreases behavior by introducing a negative stimulus (e.g., spanking a child who cursed to deter swearing), whereas negative punishment decreases behavior by removing something cherished (e.g., revoking TV privileges for fighting to deter aggression).

**History.** Operant conditioning was part of the behaviorism tradition and was influenced by pioneers such as John Watson (1913), E. L. Thorndike (1911), and B. F. Skinner (1938). Behaviorism focuses on observable behavior and avoids references to inner mental states.

**Awareness.** Operant conditioning is effective for changing the likelihood of performing voluntary behaviors—those behaviors of which an individual is aware. It is less effective for changing involuntary behaviors. For example, operant conditioning would not be effective in changing one's hunger, but it could be effective in changing behavior in response to one's hunger (eating fruit versus eating chocolate). Moreover, individuals have differential preferences for what they consider rewarding; the most effective reinforcers (i.e., primary reinforcers) are those which are related to basic human drives, such as hunger, sex, or belonging. Secondary reinforcers are not biologically rewarding but are things that are still nonetheless desirable, such as encouragement or money.

**Application.** The use of operant conditioning can be effective in counseling individuals (e.g., cessation of problem behaviors or encouraging new behaviors) or couples (e.g., rewarding communicating well and reducing conflict), or in inpatient settings (e.g., token economies). For example, individuals can reward themselves for each day they do not smoke by putting money in a "splurge" jar, or couples can treat themselves to a nice dinner out after a week of effective communication. *Shaping* is a technique in which people are rewarded increasingly as they demonstrate closer approximations to the desired behavior, such as increasing rewards when overcoming social phobia depending on the degree of exploration and involvement in the outside world.

**Spiritual Issues.** Jesus told his followers, "If you love me, keep my commands" (John 14:15). Whether we desire to learn new behaviors or stop certain behaviors to bring our lives in line with his commands, our understanding how to effectively change can bring God glory. By using behavioral change techniques such as operant conditioning, individuals can enhance their relationships with others as well as their relationship with God, which can ultimately improve their own lives and the lives of others. Obedience—which involves aligning one's behavior with God's commandments, learning new behaviors, and changing old ones—is part of that process.

**Additional Issues.** Reinforcement (i.e., increasing positive behaviors) appears to be more effective in learning a desired behavior than punishment (i.e., decreasing negative behaviors). Specifically, reinforcement communicates the exact behavior that is desired, whereas punishment simply conveys that a certain behavior is undesirable (or wrong) without communicating a preferred (or correct) behavior.

Daryl R. Van Tongeren
Joshua N. Hook

## REFERENCES

Skinner, B. F. (1938). *The Behavior of Organisms.* New York, NY: Appleton-Century-Crofts.

Thorndike, E. L. (1911). *Animal Intelligence: Experimental Studies.* Oxford: Macmillan.

Watson, J. B. (1913). Psychology as the behaviorist views it. *Psychological Review, 20,* 158-177.

## STRESS REDUCTION AND RELAXATION

**Description.** The American Psychological Association (APA) annual report from their *Stress in America* survey looks at the way people manage stress and the impact it has on their lives. According to recent results, we are more stressed out than we even realize, and many of us are not coping with this stress effectively. We pay for it in both physical and emotional ill-health. Too much stress can also be destructive to our spiritual lives and marital relationships. These are some of the key findings of the APA stress survey:

- One third of parents reported that their stress level was extremely high.
- 69% of participants in the study said that managing stress was either "very" or "extremely" important.
- Only 32% felt that they were doing an adequate job of controlling stress.
- 86% of children said that their parents' stress affected them also, but most parents didn't realize this at all.

Stress can put people at risk for developing chronic illnesses such as heart disease, diabetes, and depression. Chronic stress contributes significantly to some of the leading causes of death.

What is really troubling is that most people, including Christians, have difficulty implementing the changes they know they need to make to decrease the effects of stress and improve their health. Our healthcare system does not provide the behavioral health treatment strategies necessary to reduce the effects of chronic stress. We also fail to realize that we have to drastically change our lifestyle and set boundaries to our use of computers, the Internet, cell phones, and other digital gadgets that have sped up our lives and intensified our stress levels.

**What Is Stress?** To assess the extent to which stress is disrupting a client's life, counselors must understand what modern stress is all about (see Hart, 1995). Unfortunately, many mistakenly believe that stress is associated only with the bad or troubling things of life, such as losing a job or having difficulties at home or at school. Over-engagement in an interesting project can also cause adrenal hyperarousal. In an ideal world, we could get away from stressful situations or change them. But too often we can't do that, so we must learn to control our responses to those situations.

The two major stress hormones are adrenaline and cortisol. They mobilize our cardiac and other systems, the heart beats faster, blood pressure rises...all to deal with what the brain perceives to be an emergency. Prolonged cortisol arousal can cause depression, panic anxiety, and anhedonia (see Hart, 2007). Modern lifestyle, with its frenetic pace, has pushed this arousal system over the edge. This problem is compounded by the loss of recovery time because computers and cell phones demand our attention throughout the day. In essence, stress is hyperarousal of our adrenal system, and our lifestyle does not provide adequate recovery time. This leads us to the importance of the *relaxation response.*

**Understanding the Relaxation Response.** What can we Christians do to prevent or even cure our stress and anxiety problems? One of the simplest, cheapest, and most effective antidotes is to utilize what God has built into us: relaxation. By mastering several relaxation techniques, we can significantly reduce the effects of stress on our mental, physical, and spiritual health. All counselors need to master several relaxation techniques that can create the relaxation response so they can teach these to their clients.

The scientific evidence supporting the power of relaxation to counter the ravaging effects of stress diseases is overwhelming (Smith, 2007). Relaxation, intentionally and regularly practiced, is a powerful healing agent because it goes right to the root of the problem. It helps our body shut down its stress hormones and provides the right environment for the healing of the damage done by too much stress. A close companion of relaxation is Christian meditation (I am not a fan of other forms, such as Eastern varieties), which is a powerful antidote for stress. When relaxation (which is primarily the lowering of arousal in the body) is combined with meditation (which is primarily a lowering of arousal in the mind), one has a powerful cure for both stress and anxiety. Relaxation techniques can reduce stress symptoms by...

- slowing your heart rate
- lowering your blood pressure
- slowing your breathing rate
- increasing your blood flow to major muscles
- reducing your muscle tension and chronic pain
- improving your concentration
- reducing your anger and frustration
- boosting your confidence to handle problems

(A complete *Relaxation and Christian Meditation* audio CD with an accompanying booklet that can be used by counselors and clients is available through my website, www.hartinstitute.com. On this CD, I provide a series of relaxation and meditation exercises that are thoroughly Christian in content and direction.)

Offering your client a more natural way for treating anxiety and stress problems provides a long-term solution. Relaxation and meditation exercises are good not only for the person's body and mind but also for the spiritual life. In our rapid, always-on culture, we are rapidly losing our capacity for contemplation, but relaxation can help restore our sense of God's presence. We need to follow God's injunction to the psalmist: "Be still, and know that I am God" (Ps. 46:10). For many of us, life is a little too hurried and hassled for our own good.

**Archibald Hart**

## REFERENCES

Hart, A. (1995). *The Hidden Link between Adrenaline and Stress.* Nashville, TN: Thomas Nelson.

Hart, A. (2007). *Thrilled to Death.* Nashville, TN: Thomas Nelson.

Smith, C. (2007). A randomized comparative trial of relaxation to reduce stress and anxiety. *Complementary Therapies in Medicine* 2007, 15-77.

## SCHEMA-BASED INTERVENTIONS

**Description.** The basic assumption behind cognitive therapy is that our emotions are largely determined by our thoughts. That is, we view the world through our own unique system of beliefs, attitudes, interpretations, biases, and expectations. Negative emotions arise from our own automatic negative thoughts (ANTS). Clients are taught to identify the common varieties of ANTS, such as all-or-none thinking, overgeneralization, fortune-telling, mind reading, labeling, and others. Having identified their ANTS, clients are encouraged to develop more helpful ways of thinking.

Cognitive therapy may seem to be too

simplistic and to only scratch the surface of the client's inner experience. This is far from the truth. After working with a client for some time, you will invariably notice that certain themes arise over and over. Usually these themes will reveal a client's *schemas.* A schema is a deeply held core belief or hidden assumption that guides the way one interprets events. We often are not aware of our schemas until someone points them out.

**An Example.** A client with social anxiety describes his thoughts while in an uncomfortable situation: "These people don't like me. I don't fit in here. I look foolish." Thoughts such as these are examples of the ANT of mind reading. That is, the client is focusing on what he imagines the other people are thinking of him. Traditional cognitive restructuring techniques help the client challenge these ANTS. The counselor asks questions that gently challenge the client's thinking and encourage him to think more positively. The client might eventually learn to think, "There really isn't any evidence that the people didn't like me. Some people smiled at me. More people might have greeted me had I spoken to them." As he begins to think differently, he feels more confident that he can navigate social events.

But that is not the end of the story. The next week he comes in and describes a similar situation with identical ANTS. You might think, "Wasn't he paying attention last week?" You might repeat the same cognitive restructuring techniques—or you might decide to look for schemas. A great tool for this is the *vertical-arrow* technique. Rather than trying to dispute the ANTS, you assume, for the moment, that they are true. You then ask the powerful question, "If that were true, what would that mean to you?" Continue asking this question until you bump up against a schema. For our socially anxious client, the conversation might look like this:

> Client: "Those people didn't like me."
>
> Therapist: "If that were true, what would it mean to you?"
>
> Client: "It would mean that I'm not good at making friends."
>
> Therapist: "If that were true, what would it mean to you?"
>
> Client: "It means that I can't please people."
>
> Therapist: "If that were true, what would it mean to you?"
>
> Client: "I'd be worthless."

Now you have touched on a schema. Your job is to gently and humbly check in with your client to see if he agrees. The conversation might continue like this:

> Therapist: "It sounds like you believe that your worth is completely based on pleasing everyone else. Do you think that might be true?"
>
> Client: "I don't like to think that I believe that, but maybe I do."

You now have a lot to talk about. You might want to explore the historical roots of the schema. How did he come to believe this? What life events have led him to think this way? These discussions can help the client develop insight into his problem. However, in cognitive therapy we are not content with just achieving insight. We want to see if the client is willing to change it.

**Cost-Benefit.** A great way to encourage schema change is the *cost-benefit analysis.* The client is asked to consider how this core belief helps and how it hurts. Returning to our socially anxious client, it might look like this:

> Therapist: "What are the benefits of believing your worth is completely based on pleasing other people?"
>
> Client (possible responses): "It makes me try harder to get people to like me,"

or "I won't get conceited or too proud," or "It gives me an excuse to avoid being social."

Therapist: "What are the costs of thinking this way?"

Client: "It makes me feel miserable most of the time," or "It makes me too scared to be around people," or "It isn't consistent with what God thinks about my worth."

If the client sees the costs of the belief outweighing the benefits, ask him if he can think of a less negative core belief. In this case, it might be, "My worth is given to me by God. It isn't based on pleasing others." Of course, that could bring up a new problem:

Client: "I'd like to believe that, but I don't know if I really do."

Therapist: "That's perfectly understandable. What if you just 'tried out' this belief for a week? What if you did your best to act as if it were true?"

Clients are often astounded to discover that they have the power to choose their schemas. However unhealthy or destructive our thinking might have been, we can trust in a God who told us, "You will know the truth, and the truth will set you free" (Jn 8:32).

**Stanley E. Hibbs**

## REFERENCES


Backus, W., & Clark, M. (2000). *Telling Yourself the Truth*, Minneapolis: Bethany House.

Burns, D. (1989). *The Feeling Good Handbook*. New York, NY: Penguin Books.

Clark, D. A., & Beck, A. T. (2010). *Cognitive Therapy of Anxiety Disorders*. New York, NY: Guilford Press.

Hibbs, Stanley E. (2007). *Anxiety Gone: The Three C's of Anxiety Recovery*. Mustang, OK: Dare2Dream Books.


## FAMILY AND SYSTEMS INTERVENTIONS

**Description.** A family and systems perspective focuses on the human condition and family members' relationship to each other and to their physical and contextual world. Therapeutic intervention increases in effectiveness when the effects of systemic influences are not only considered but also utilized to promote change. System perspectives often include a logical integration of numerous theoretical models, values, and beliefs that can include some combination of individual, couple, family, and larger system intervention. A family system approach is not a practice theory or a particular therapy; instead, it is an overarching way of thinking about family problems and their solutions (see DiBlasio, 2000 for more details about system thinking in family therapy).

A systemic perspective usually accounts for the relatedness and interaction of a complex array of variables. Using it as a framework, clinicians attempt to make sense of the human experience and decide how to bring about change in dysfunctional behaviors. It is a view of the world that studies people's interconnection with each other and with the environmental and biological forces that influence the total life process. People are always affecting and being affected by the world around them. The human condition is defined in part by personality and other internal factors, and in part by a complex web of external factors. Family and systems approaches promote thinking in multilinear models about subsystems, boundaries, hierarchy, power, open and closed systems, and so forth.

Each family is a system, and within this system are various subsystems. For example, marital partners and siblings are two typical subsystems found in two-parent families. Even the individual is considered a subsystem. Consequently, work with the individual has ramifications for the larger system. Systemic-oriented therapists have varying views concerning the power of external systemic dynamics versus internal ones. Although common patterns can exist, each system must be understood for its uniqueness.

**Application.** For the most part, the traditional focus of family therapy models has been on intervening in the "here and now" to address symptoms displayed by one or more of its members. A typical family therapy case might address the acting out of a defiant son. The son's negative behavior is put into a system's context and explored to see if the defiant behavior serves a purpose to help keep a homeostatic balance in the family. If the parents join together to share and commiserate with each other over the son's problem, this produces a special type of spousal teaming that offsets some of the stress, especially if the marriage is in crisis. The inverse is also usually true: The parents' conflict with one another implicitly influences the son to act out. In this case, the son would be referred to as the *identified patient.* Although he is the focus of attention, his acting out is seen as being influenced by a number of dysfunctional contributions within the family system.

Sometimes this method of relating is well ingrained and can last for many years. The therapist attempts to untangle the "triangulation" of the son with his parents, to free the son from the need of a symptom, and to give the parents a healthy way to resolve their marital conflict.

**History.** Mary Richmond, a social worker in the late 1880s, was the first known professional to consider families as interconnected systems. She advocated that attempts to improve the mental, emotional, and physical needs of family members must consider the interactive effects that each has on the other (Richmond, 1917). However, Freud (1923) overshadowed this early systems thinking by his emphasis on treating the individual. Psychoanalysis became the primary school of therapeutic thought through the first half of the 1900s. In the 1950s and 1960s, different models that considered individuals in their family context became increasingly popular. Among these were *structural family therapy* (Minuchin & Fishman, 1981), *strategic family therapy* (Haley, 1987; Madanes, 1981), *Bowen's family systems model* (Bowen, 1966), and *experiential family therapy* (also known as the *communications model*) (Satir, 1987). Bowen's and Satir's work made significant contributions to the understanding of system dynamics, but structural family therapy and strategic family therapy have more significantly influenced the techniques of family therapy.

*Structural family therapy.* This approach focused on interrupting the sequences of dysfunctional behavior and replacing them with a functional structure. For example, if parents are in constant arguments with the child, the therapist will interrupt this old pattern and will provide a directive for a new approach. He may ask the parents if they will first do some parent business with each other, discuss the approach they want to take as a team, and then to present it to their son. Instead of the son interrupting them as he was accustomed to do, the therapist engages him in quiet conversation so that he cannot interrupt. The intervention reinforces the hierarchical, superior position of parents as the family executors, and it keeps the son in an appropriate position as their child.

The work of a systems approach is primarily accomplished by using the *enactment* of the patterns and sequences of behavior in therapy. An enactment is a time in the session when the family members begin to manifest the dysfunctional pattern. The therapist will interrupt the dysfunctional pattern and provide a directive for the family to respond to each other in a more functional way. Although attempting to achieve insight and talking about why a dysfunctional pattern is dysfunctional can be appropriate at times, family therapy focuses on the constant correction of the live material that family members enact. Through interrupting the dysfunctional sequences of behavior and altering the structure through constant repetition of healthy behaviors, new functional patterns develop and become habituated.

*Strategic family therapy.* Haley, a family therapy pioneer (who worked with both the well-known Palo Alto, California, group in the 1950s and Minuchin in Pennsylvania in the late 1960s and early 1970s) and his then wife Madanes (a former consulting psychologist with the Minuchin group) moved to the Maryland area in the mid-1970s to develop and train from their own version of system work—strategic family therapy. Their emphasis was that family therapy ought to first and foremost resolve the presenting problem in the quickest way possible. They taught that the "theory of etiology" was less important than the "theory of intervention." If a theory of intervention would lead to strategies that resolved the presenting problem, then the etiological explanation is not as relevant. After a short period of wild and dramatic strategies of the 1970s, they have promoted traditional and safe strategies for the past 30 years. (Unfortunately, some people still associate them with wild and unsafe strategies of the 1970s.) A typical strategic intervention might be to help put parents in charge of children who are acting out and at the same time promote parents to be more nurturing and spend more positive time with their children.

**Biblical and Spiritual Issues.** The Christian counselor who wants to influence Christlike solutions in Christian families should study the two family therapy models emphasized above and filter their methods through prayerful and scriptural understanding. For example, in addition to telling parents and children how to act in love toward one another in counseling, the system-oriented Christian counselor can actually influence structural changes in relationships where Christlike sequences occur on a repetitive basis. Instead of just talking about the changes needed in relationships, the therapy becomes a live laboratory where the dysfunctional behaviors are directly observed and interrupted, new ways are practiced, and problems are solved.

**Frederick A. DiBlasio**

## REFERENCES


Bowen, M. (1966). The use of family theory in clinical practice. *Comprehensive Psychiatry, 7,* 345-374.

DiBlasio, F. A. (2000). Systemic thinking and therapeutic intervention. *Journal of Marriage and the Family: A Christian Journal, 3,* 281-300.

Freud, S. (1923). The ego and the id. In *The Standard Edition of the Complete Psychological Works of Sigmund Freud* (Vol. 19). London, England: Hogarth Press.

Haley, J. (1987). *Problem Solving Therapy* (2nd ed.). San Francisco, CA: Jossey-Bass.

Madanes, C. (1981). *Strategic Family Therapy.* San Francisco, CA: Jossey-Bass.

Minuchin, S., & Fishman, H. (1981). *Family Therapy Techniques.* Cambridge, MA: Harvard University Press.

Richmond, M. (1917). *Social Diagnosis.* New York, NY: Russell Sage Foundation.

Satir, V. (1987). *Conjoint Family Therapy* (3rd ed.). Palo Alto, CA: Science and Behavior Books.


## CHALLENGING UNBIBLICAL THINKING

Many Christian counselors incorporate cognitive techniques in their therapeutic approach. When unbiblical thinking is identified through the counseling process, Christian therapists traditionally challenge clients by pointing out relevant passages of Scripture. However, there are many other creative and interactive ways to help clients understand the truths of Scripture and apply them to current situations (Vernick, 2010). Effective strategies to challenge wrong thinking include a well-timed question, an illustration, and a story.

**Questions.** Jesus masterfully wielded the right questions in order to bring individuals into greater awareness of spiritual truth, to challenge wrong thinking, and to confront sinful attitudes and actions.

*Teaching questions.* Instead of telling someone what to believe, Jesus often used questions to bring about greater awareness of a spiritual truth. To teach the client about the character of God, the counselor may quote this passage: "Which of you, if your son asks for bread, will give him a stone? Or if he asks for a fish, will give him a snake?" (Mt. 7:9).

Jesus used this question to challenge the belief that all problems are the result of personal sin: "Do you think that these Galileans were worse sinners than all the other Galileans because they suffered this way?" (Lk. 13:2).

Or a counselor may read Romans 12:21 and ask these questions: "What do you think it means to not be overcome with evil, but instead to overcome evil with good? What would that look like for you in this situation?"

*Challenging questions.* Jesus asked questions to challenge and cast light on deeply entrenched beliefs to invite people toward greater truth and healing. For instance, he asked a question with an obvious answer: "Do people pick grapes from thornbushes, or figs from thistles?" (Mt. 7:16; see also 12:11,26-29). Similarly, a counselor might ask, "When your thoughts and feelings are contrary to what God says, who wins?"

*Confrontation questions.* Christian counselors are not only truth seekers but also truth tellers. Jesus often used piercing questions to confront particular sins or heart attitudes. In his most famous sermon, he asked, "Why do you look at the speck of sawdust in your brother's eye and pay no attention to the plank in your own eye?" (Mt. 7:3). And in another message, he raised the issue of hypocrisy: "Why do you call me 'Lord, Lord,' and do not do what I say?" (Lk. 6:46).

A counselor may read a passage like Ephesians 5:21-33 and ask questions like these: "Where does it say in this passage on headship and submission or biblical authority that you get to have your way all the time?" "What happens to you when you don't get what you want?"

**Illustrations.** One picture can say (and in counseling, perhaps save) a thousand words (Barker, 1996). Jesus used illustrations common to his culture (including fig trees, soil, birds, and yeast) to challenge people to think truthfully. The Pharisees were irate when they thought Jesus broke the Sabbath, so he used the illustration of a child falling into a well to challenge their legalistic and unloving attitudes (Lk. 14:5).

In my counseling office there is a water bottle with a tiny bit of soil settled on the bottom. When an individual or couple is stuck in the blame game, saying, "I did this because of you" instead of correcting their wrong thinking with words, I usually reach for the bottle of water, holding it from the bottom (hiding the dirt settled there). Next, I vigorously shake it and ask, "Did shaking this bottle make it dirty?" I quietly wait for the truth to register. When comprehension comes, I say, "Of course not. Shaking it just exposed the dirt that was already there. In the same way, Jesus tells us, 'The mouth speaks what the heart is full of' [Lk. 6:45]. People don't make us respond a certain way; they just expose what is already in our hearts." This illustration usually leads to insightful discussion that alleviates blame shifting.

**Stories.** Jesus used many parables and stories to challenge the Pharisees' thinking. The Good Samaritan story challenged the religious leaders' wrong thinking about who was righteous and who was a true neighbor. The story's ending shocked them and turned their thinking upside down. The self-righteous religious leaders were named the sinners, and the supposed sinner (the hated Samaritan) was the righteous one.

In another example, Nathan the prophet confronted King David's sin and self-justifying thoughts about his right to take Bathsheba and murder her husband to cover it up. Nathan told David a story to bypass David's resistance. David was outraged until he realized the story was about him (2 Sam. 11–12).

Stories, illustration, and questions bypass

clients' natural defensiveness (Abbatiello, 2006) and are indirect ways counselors can help clients see and accept corrections to their thinking.

LESLIE VERNICK

## REFERENCES


Abbatiello, G. (2006) Cognitive-Behavioral Therapy and Metaphor. *Perspectives in Psychiatric Care, 42*(3), 208-210.

Barker, P. (1996). *Psychotherapeutic Metaphors: A Guide to Theory and Practice.* New York, NY: Brunner/Mazel.

Vernick, L. (2010). Creativity in Counseling, Parts 1, 2, & 3 [Blog post]. Retrieved from http://christianpsych.org/wp_scp/2010/03/

Vernick, L., & Thurman, C. (2002). Change in process: Working from a biblical model of TRUTH in action. In T. Clinton & G. Ohlschlager (Eds.), *Competent Christian Counseling: Foundations and Practice of Compassionate Soul Care.* Colorado Springs, CO: WaterBrook Press.


## USING THE BIBLE IN COUNSELING

How many times have you met people who were sincere about specific issues but sincerely wrong? Obviously, their personal opinions were not based on purest wisdom. Likewise, all people want to know at least one wise person, one person to go to for wise counsel, one person who will present wise answers. All counselors are expected to be wise, yet some are and some are not.

**BUILDING A CASE FOR THE BIBLE.** In counseling, knowledge is important for imparting information and assessment. However, wisdom means knowing how to apply the knowledge we have. Ultimately, wisdom is being able to see life's problems and solutions from God's point of view. It denotes deep understanding, keen discernment, and sound judgment. If you want to give wise counsel, follow this logic:

- Who is the source of wisdom? God himself.
- If you could think like God thinks, would you be wise? Undoubtedly.
- Where can you find God's thoughts? In the Bible.

Therefore, the more you rely on the Word of God, the more you will apply the wisdom of God. The Bible says, "Get wisdom, get understanding; do not forget my words or turn away from them" (Pr. 4:5). The Bible describes itself as "useful for teaching, rebuking, correcting and training in righteousness" (2 Tim. 3:16). The wise counselor uses the Bible because...

- *The Bible sheds light for living.* This is exactly why we go to the Bible. It is the source of wisdom. The Bible is not just a literary source to be quoted or a spiritual source to be sought. It is *the* source of wisdom for day-to-day living. The book of Psalms says, "Your word is a lamp for my feet, a light on my path" (Ps. 119:105).
- *The Bible has supernatural power.* Many counselors use only their own words when helping others. But consider the added benefit of using pertinent, well-chosen Scriptures: "The word of God is alive and active. Sharper than any double-edged sword, it pierces even to dividing soul and spirit, joints and marrow; it judges the thoughts and attitudes of the heart" (Heb. 4:12).
- *The Bible offers victory over self-defeating sin.* When you encourage those you are helping to personalize certain Scriptures, many of them will experience lasting victory for the first time. The psalmist says, "I have hidden your word in my heart that I might not sin against you" (Ps. 119:11).

**BUILDING THE BIBLE INTO YOUR COUNSELING.** Knowing which of God's 774,746 words to apply to which issue can be daunting because the Bible isn't organized topically. For that reason, mining the Bible for the best verses that relate to real problems is essential. Many counselors are willing to use the Bible but do not know where to begin. Here are some ideas:

- *Survey the pressing problems.* Write them down and ask, *does the Bible say anything about this issue*? If there is nothing specific, then ask, is there a pertinent biblical principle? The Bible gives this priority: "First seek the counsel of the Lord" (1 Ki. 22:5).
- *Select several Scriptures relating to that subject.*
- *Systematize your own mini concordance.* Organizing Scriptures and principles topically is an invaluable aid for counselors (Hunt, 2008a). Many counselors add these lists to the back of their Bibles. (See Pr. 2:1-11.)

**Broadening Your Use of Scripture.** The Bible says we are transformed by the renewing of our minds (Rom. 12:2). Mindless, legalistic repetition is useless, but repeating Scripture with an attitude of taking God at his word can produce life-changing results.

- *Repeat one phrase, emphasizing a different word each time.* For example, if fear is the primary problem, direct the person to say aloud, "The Lord is my Shepherd." Repeat it five times, each time emphasizing a different word. Then repeat the exercise using the phrase "He restores my soul."
- *Read one chapter each day.* If a counselee has an anger problem, give this assignment: "Read one chapter a day in the book of Proverbs, beginning in chapter 10. Write out every verse that shows any misuse of the tongue." At the conclusion of the assignment, have the counselee read aloud every verse. Then ask, "Is this the person you want to be?" (This is a great motivation for change!)
- *Review three verses every day for a month.* Those in counseling need to have hope that change can and will take place in their lives. Usually wrong beliefs need to be exchanged for right beliefs. It often takes just 21 days to form a habit, so repeating these biblical truths for 31 days can help form a new habit. Here are some examples:
  - Adultery: Proverbs 6:27, 32; Hebrews 13:4
  - Anxiety: Matthew 11:29-30; Philippians 4:6-7; 1 Peter 5:7
  - Depression: Psalm 42:5; Ecclesiastes 3:1,4; Isaiah 43:2
  - Domestic violence: Proverbs 19:19; 22:24; 27:12
  - Fear: Deuteronomy 31:8; Psalm 56:3; Isaiah 41:10
  - Forgiveness: Matthew 6:14-15; Romans 12:17-19; Colossians 3:13
  - Grief: Psalm 34:18; 71:20; 118:5
  - Habits: Proverbs 14:12; Matthew 19:26; 2 Peter 2:19
  - Stress: Psalm 46:1; Matthew 11:28; 2 Corinthians 4:8-9
  - Suicide: Ecclesiastes 9:4; Jeremiah 29:11; Hebrews 10:36
  - Temptation: Proverbs 28:13; 1 Corinthians 10:13; Philippians 4:13
  - Victimization: Romans 8:37; Galatians 5:1; 2 Timothy 1:7
  - Worry: Proverbs 3:5-6; Matthew 6:25,33

When the people you are helping personalize each verse—putting themselves into each verse—or thank God for what he has said, these Scriptures become a living hope for them.

**Conclusion.** Jesus, the Wonderful Counselor (Is. 9:6), frequently quoted Old Testament verses. He understood the power of Scripture to bring clarity and comfort to a crushed, captive people. Quoting Isaiah 61, he said about himself, "The Spirit of the Lord is on me, because he has anointed me to proclaim good news to the poor. He has sent me to proclaim freedom for the prisoners and recovery of sight for the blind, to set the oppressed free" (Lk. 4:18-19). Ultimately, the method God used to heal hurting hearts in biblical times is the same method we can use today. Unlike our natural words, his Word offers supernatural healing, for "he sent out his word and healed them" (Ps. 107:20).

June Hunt

## REFERENCES

Hunt, J. (2008a). *Counseling Through Your Bible Handbook.* Eugene, OR: Harvest House.

Hunt, J. (2008b). *How to Handle Your Emotions* (p. 173). Eugene, OR: Harvest House.

## CLIENT HOMEWORK IN COUNSELING

**Description.** There is no specific definition of client homework. It is generally perceived as any specified out-of-session activity upon which the client and counselor agree and that is designed to move the client toward the stated goals of the counseling. Some therapists have found the term *homework* too evaluative or likely to raise thoughts of boring busywork. Terms such as *directives, action homework,* or simply *follow-up activities* are often used instead.

**History and Rationale.** The concept of client homework is most closely identified with cognitive-behavioral therapy (CBT). It emerges out of behavioral, in which activities practiced outside the counseling session are designed to promote generalization of targeted behaviors across environments. In recent years it has become apparent that the practice of assigning homework in psychotherapy is prevalent and is not confined to CBT practice. Client homework has become a common factor in psychotherapy and is now seen as a legitimate practice for psychotherapy independent of theoretical orientation (Kazantzis & Ronan, 2006).

Research has consistently shown that learning that has taken place during the counseling session is easily lost if it is not quickly transferred to daily life (Ivey, Ivey, & Zalaquett, 2010). Homework assignments are especially effective in helping clients sustain and build on work done in the counseling session. Positive treatment outcomes are directly related to the use and completion of homework assignments, and clients who do the most homework improve the most (Scheel, Hanson, & Razzhavaikina, 2004).

**Application.** In cognitive therapy, which is often time-limited, clients are expected to actively work outside the therapy sessions. In the early stages of counseling, assignments focus on recognizing the connections between thoughts, feelings, and actions. Recording automatic thinking in moments of crisis or distress might be suggested. Self-monitoring activities are designed to extend the learning that takes place in the counseling room into the real world of the client. Clients may be asked to keep logs of self-defeating thoughts or to identify activities triggered by such thinking. In later stages of therapy, clients may be asked to confront irrational or dysfunctional beliefs by doing the very thing they fear. Someone who has difficulty setting boundaries, believing that to do so will lead to complete rejection, may be asked to say no to three requests from significant individuals during the time between sessions.

The nature and design of homework assignments is limited only by the counselor's creativity and the client's resources and motivations. Any activity linked to the furtherance of the counseling goals can be useful. Workbooks and CBT treatment plans abound and contain numerous ideas for out-of-session activities related to specific therapeutic goals and objectives (e.g., Jongsma & Peterson, 1995).

Collins (2008) lists seven broad categories of suggested activities: written activities, discussion and study guides, behavior assignments, reading, Internet resources, recordings, and other computer resources. Written and behavioral activities are the most common, but creative use of other venues, especially computer-based ones, is increasing. The ease of video recording allows for role-play practice that can be reviewed and expanded upon outside of session. Bibliotherapy (e.g., Christian literature) can be a useful adjunct, especially when it leads to further insight or client understanding of a particular situation or opens the door for more in-depth discussion in session. Computers and Internet resources (e.g., detailed Bible study) provide a rich environment for creative assignments, although these resources must be handled with care.

Not only the content of the assignment but also the delivery and recommendation process must be carefully considered. Good homework assignments are collaborative, with both client and counselor participating in the creation. Initially in therapy, the counselor may be more directive. However, as counseling progresses, the client should assume more responsibility for identifying problems and solutions and creating appropriate homework assignments. Assignments should be goal-related with the rationale for the assignment clearly stated. Assignments need to be perceived as moving the client forward in counseling.

Assessing the client's resources and motivations is essential to task completion. Matching the client's level of ability to the recommended task capitalizes on the client's strengths. The therapist should be clear and concise with directions. The more specific the task instructions, the more likely it is to be completed. Lastly, the therapist should be sure to follow up by asking about the assignment and incorporating that material into the next session. Forgetting about an assignment is a sure way to give the message that it was not really important.

**Conclusion.** As with any technique, care must be taken to consider a client's values and abilities. Assignments that do not fit within a client's cultural or religious context are not likely to be beneficial. Similarly, creatively incorporating appropriate rituals (e.g., Scripture memory) or cultural activities may significantly enhance both the learning and the probability of assignment completion. Given the preference for CBT strategies by some culturally diverse groups, it is important to factor worldview into the creation of any homework assignment or directive.

**Miriam Stark Parent**

### REFERENCES

Collins, G. (2008). *Christian Counseling: A Comprehensive Guide* (3rd ed.). Nashville, TN: Thomas Nelson.

Ivey, A., Ivey, M., & Zalaquett, C. (2010). *Intentional Interviewing and Counseling: Facilitating Client Development in a Multicultural Society* (7th ed.). Pacific Grove, CA: Brooks/Cole, Cengage Learning.

Jongsma, A., & Peterson, L. M. (1995). *The Complete Psychotherapy Treatment Planner.* New York, NY: Wiley & Sons.

Kazantzis, N., & Ronan, K. (2006). Can between-session (homework) activities be considered a common factor in psychotherapy? *Journal of Psychotherapy Integration, 16*(2), 115-127.

Scheel, M., Hanson, W., & Razzhavaikina, T. (2004). The process of recommending homework in psychotherapy: A review of therapist delivery methods, client acceptability, and factors that affect compliance. *Psychotherapy: Theory, Research, Practice, Training, 41*(1), 38-55.

## CONFESSION AND REPENTANCE

**Description and Prevalence.** Apart from any particular setting, the term *confession* seems ambiguous and is generally defined as any type of admission, concession, acknowledgment, or declaration in a matter that (loosely) pertains to the self. However, when linked with *repentance,* the word takes on a very unambiguous, introspective, and uncomfortable dimension. Now it is clear: A wrong has been done, a sin has been committed, and someone is at fault. In this context, confession needs to be made so that restoration can take place and forgiveness can be received.

Introducing repentance, sin, and transgression, however, seems to present a barrier to practicing confession, especially in today's world. As Plantinga (1995) observes, in the past, "Christians hated sin, feared it, fled from it, grieved over it" (p. ix). But today, things are different: The subject of sin is rarely mentioned, and when it is, it is often trivialized, excused, explained away, or dismissed completely. In addition, most people avoid taking any blame whatsoever for any wrongdoing. In this environment, the practice of true, substantive confession as a spiritual discipline is in danger of extinction in the 21st-century church.

Another hindrance to true confession occurs when someone mistakenly thinks of it as a one-time event or single act (Ortberg, 2002). A more accurate perspective sees confession as a process containing several steps, including recognition and personal admission of guilt to oneself (Ps. 51:3), acknowledgment of guilt to God (Ps. 51:4; 1 Jn. 1:9), and admission of guilt to the one wronged (Lk. 15:21). The good news is that when someone understands confession and goes through this process, two things occur: First, transgressors are freed from guilt, and second, they are now less likely to repeat the same offense in the future because "sin will look and feel less attractive" (Ortberg, p. 130).

This pattern and practice reveal the true value of practicing confession. On the surface, confession may appear to benefit the offended person or God, but the real beneficiary is the offender. As Ortberg (2002) rightly notes, confession is *not* "something God has us do because he needs it, [rather] we need to confess in order to heal and be changed" (p. 129). This notion of change brings the focus of the discussion back to confession's companion: repentance.

**Biblical and Spiritual Issues.** There seems to be some confusion about what repentance is and isn't. In the New Testament, the English word "repent" is a translation of the Greek verb *metanoeo*, which means "to change one's mind" and "pictures someone heading in one direction who, because of a change of mind, starts going in another direction" (Jeffress, 1992, p. 58). Clearly, then, repentance is neither an emotion nor a matter of just feeling sorry for doing wrong. The truth is, feeling sorry alone "is no guarantee of authentic repentance and [in fact] can be highly destructive" (Ortberg, 2002, p. 135). Instead, true repentance is an attitude or mind-set that leads to substantive change in behavior.

Many people feel sorry for their sins but then find themselves repeating the same offense over and over again. In other words, their sorrow did not lead to any real change. Consider the following biblical examples.

- Pharaoh claimed to feel sorry for enslaving and abusing the Israelites, but his sorrow lasted only as long as he was facing a crisis. Once each crisis (plague) was averted, he reverted back to his cruel, stubborn ways (Ex. 9:27-35).

- Achan felt remorse for all the pain and death he had brought onto his countrymen by coveting and stealing several items from the spoils he found in Jericho, but his sorrow came only after he was caught with the goods. By then it was too late (Josh. 7).

- Saul was sorry that he yielded to popular opinion and went against the direct commandment of God. However, his sorrow was triggered by a

> visit from Samuel, who confronted the king with his disobedience and cornered him into making his confession (1 Sam. 15).

The apostle Paul sheds light on this issue by differentiating between two kinds of sorrow. One he calls "worldly sorrow [that] brings death"; this is the kind felt and displayed by Pharaoh, Achan, and Saul. The other Paul identifies as "godly sorrow," which produces change and repentance, ultimately leading to salvation and deliverance from guilt (2 Cor. 7:8-10). This is the heart of biblical repentance.

The stark difference in these two types of sorrow and repentance can be seen in the story of two of Jesus' disciples, Peter and Judas Iscariot. Both men sold Jesus out in his hour of need, and both men felt sorry for their betrayal and confessed their sins. But in the end, only Peter was restored (Mt. 26:75). Judas was overcome by remorse and committed suicide (Mt. 27:4-5). The difference was repentance.

FRED MILACCI

### REFERENCES

Jeffress, R. (1992). *Choose Your Attitudes, Change Your Life.* Wheaton, IL: Victor Books.

Ortberg, J. (2002). *The Life You've Always Wanted.* Grand Rapids, MI: Zondervan.

Plantinga, C. (1995). *Not the Way It's Supposed to Be: A Breviary of Sin.* Grand Rapids, MI: Eerdmans.

## FORGIVENESS

**DESCRIPTION.** Forgiveness involves mental, motivational, and emotional changes in a victim after experiencing a transgression—a violation of physical, emotional, or psychological boundaries. Forgiveness has been defined as being of two types—decisional and emotional forgiveness (Worthington, 2003). *Decisional forgiveness* is making a behavioral intention statement that gives up pursuit of revenge and intends to treat the offender as a valuable person. *Emotional forgiveness* prevents or replaces unforgiveness, which is an emotional complex of resentment, bitterness, hatred, aggression, anger, and fear. Forgiveness is differentiated from reconciliation, which is the reestablishment of a relationship, with or without communicating forgiveness (because one can say one forgives without actually reestablishing the relationship or one can maintain the relationship with the offender without actually forgiving).

**HISTORY.** Forgiveness is a core concept in the Christian faith and has been studied by theologians since the beginning of Christianity, which understands forgiveness differently than Jewish theology does (Dorff, 1998). Jewish theology, which emphasizes the external more than the internal life, locates forgiveness as an embedded process conditioned by an offender's *tseuvah* (i.e., repentance, or return to the path of God). Jesus, and later Paul, conceptualized forgiveness as more internal—as a decision about one's own future behavior and as an emotional coming to peace.

**ASSESSMENT.** Forgiveness is assessed on three levels. The *trait level* measures consistency across time and different relationships, often using the Trait Forgiveness Scale (Berry, Worthington, O'Connor, Parrott, & Wade, 2005) or the Heartland Forgiveness Scale (Thompson et al., 2005). The *relationship level* measures consistency over time and across one relationship, such as marriage (Paleari, Regalia, & Fincham, 2009). The *event level* measures change over time in the level of decisional and emotional forgiveness (Worthington, Hook, Utsey, Williams, & Neil, 2007). McCullough et al. (1998) assessed unforgiving or forgiving motivation, and Enright (1994) assessed affect, behavior, and cognition around forgiveness. Forgiveness might also be assessed as the presence of positive (or the absence of negative) thoughts, motives, or feelings (Rye et al., 2001).

In addition to the forgiveness by the victim, it is important also to consider the offender. Some people are interested in forgiveness of the offender by God (Toussaint, Williams, Musick, & Everson, 2001) or the offender's anger at God (Wood et al., 2010). Others have looked at the offender's sense of guilt, shame, and remorse resulting in self-condemnation or self-forgiveness, which can be assessed at the trait level (Thompson et al., 2005) or the event level (Fisher & Exline, 2006; Wohl, DeShea, & Wahkinney, 2008). Measurement of forgiveness has been done with great psychometric support for most measures.

**Treatment.** The most research-supported model of forgiveness therapy with psychopathology is Enright's process model (Enright & Fitzgibbons, 2000), which conceptualizes forgiveness in 20 steps grouped in four phases of treatment. It has been done with individual clients or in groups and typically produces successful outcomes. Other models used for psychotherapy, but less investigated, are by Luskin, Ginzberg, & Thoresen (2005), Worthington (2006), and for couples counseling, Gordon, Baucom, & Snyder (2004). Other therapies for recovery from affairs are Worthington's model for enrichment, enhancement, and couple therapy, and DiBlasio's model (DiBlasio & Benda, 2008). Only DiBlasio's and Worthington's models have been tested explicitly with Christians. For group psychoeducation, Worthington's REACH model has been shown to be effective in more than five published studies with secular populations and five studies with Christians—it is the only enrichment treatment that has been tested with Christians.

**Biblical and Spiritual Issues.** Forgiveness is one of the two principles that are foundational for Christianity (the other is love). Thus, the verses supporting it are found throughout Scripture, most familiarly in connection with the Lord's prayer (Mt. 6:12-15) and Peter's question about how often Christians must forgive (Mt. 18:21-22).

**Additional Issues.** Some disagreement about forgiveness occurs within the Christian community.

- Should forgiveness be unilateral or conditioned on the offender's repentance? Almost all believe it is unilateral.
- Should forgiveness require willingness or efforts toward the reestablishment of a damaged relationship? Almost all believe that forgiveness is independent of relationship repair, though it often can lead to steps of reconciliation.
- Are any acts unforgivable? Most believe that all offenses are forgivable, though many are extremely difficult to forgive.
- Does complete forgiveness require total and constant emotional peace?

Regarding this last question, most believe that decisional forgiveness is an unwavering decision to treat the other as a valuable person and not to pursue harmful responses, such as revenge. However, most believe that emotional forgiveness is more difficult to experience, is subject to daily and event-related moods, and is not the forgiveness being spoken about in Matthew 6:14-15. There, Jesus requires interpersonal forgiveness (likely decisional forgiveness) as a condition for forgiveness from God. (Note: The forgiveness from God described in this passage is not the forgiveness of justification, which would make justification a matter of our work of forgiving rather than of God's grace. More likely, this passage refers to the fact that harboring resentment effectively blocks our experience of God's love and forgiveness.)

Everett L. Worthington Jr.
Chelsea L. Greer
Yin Lin

## REFERENCES


Berry, J. W., Worthington, E. L., Jr., O'Connor, L., Parrott, L., III, & Wade, N. G. (2005). Forgiveness, vengeful rumination, and affective traits. *Journal of Personality, 73,* 1-43.

DiBlasio, F. A., & Benda B. B. (2008). Forgiveness intervention with married couples: Two empirical analyses. *Journal of Psychology and Christianity, 27,* 150-158.

Dorff, E. N. (1998). The elements of forgiveness: A Jewish approach. In E. L. Worthington (Ed.), *Dimensions of Forgiveness: A Research Approach* (pp. 29-55). West Conshohocken, PA: Templeton Press.

Enright, R. D. (1994). *The Enright Forgiveness Inventory.* Available at www.ForgivenessInstitute.org.

Enright, R. D., & Fitzgibbons, R. P. (2000). *Helping Clients Forgive: An Empirical Guide for Resolving Anger and Restoring Hope.* Washington, DC: American Psychological Association.

Fisher, M. L., & Exline, J. J. (2006). Self-forgiveness versus excusing: The roles of remorse, effort, and acceptance of responsibility. *Self and Identity, 5,* 127-146.

Gordon, K. C., Baucom, D. H., & Snyder, D. K. (2004). An integrative intervention for promoting recovery from extramarital affairs. *Journal of Marital and Family Therapy, 30,* 213-231.

Luskin, F., Ginzberg, K., & Thoresen, C. E. (2005). The efficacy of forgiveness intervention in college age adults: Randomized controlled study. *Humboldt Journal of Social Relations, 29,* 163-184.

McCullough, M. E., Rachal, K. C., Sandage, S. J., Worthington, E. L., Jr., Brown, S. W., & Hight, T. L. (1998). Interpersonal forgiveness in close relationships II: Theoretical elaboration and measurement. *Journal of Personality and Social Psychology, 75,* 1586-1603.

Paleari, F. G., Regalia, C., & Fincham, F. D. (2009). Measuring offence-specific forgiveness in marriage: The marital offence-specific forgiveness scale (MOFS). *Psychological Assessment, 21,* 194-209. doi:10.1037/a0016068

Rye, M. S., Loiacono, D. M., Folck, C. D., Olszewski, B. T., Heim, T. A., & Madia, B. P. (2001). Evaluation of the psychometric properties of two forgiveness scales. *Current Psychology, 20,* 260-277.

Thompson, L. Y., Snyder, C. R., Hoffman, L., Michael, S. T., Rasmussen, H. N., Billings, L. S.,...Roberts, D. E. (2005). Dispositional forgiveness of self, others, and situations. *Journal of Personality, 73,* 319-359.

Toussaint, L. L., Williams, D. R., Musick, M. A., & Everson, S. A. (2001). Forgiveness and health: Age differences in a U.S. probability sample. *Journal of Adult Development, 8,* 249-257.

Wohl, M. J. A., DeShea, L., & Wahkinney, R. L. (2008). Looking within: Measuring state self-forgiveness and its relationship to psychological well-being. *Canadian Journal of Behavioural Science, 40,* 1-10.

Wood, B. T., Worthington, E. L., Jr., Exline, J. J., Yali, A. M., Aten, J. D., & McMinn, M. R. (2010). Development, refinement, and psychometric properties of the Attitudes toward God Scale (ATGS-9). *Psychology of Religion and Spirituality, 2*(3), 148-167.

Worthington, E. L., Jr. (2003). *Forgiving and Reconciling: Bridges to Wholeness and Hope.* Downers Grove, IL: InterVarsity Press.

Worthington, E. L., Jr. (2006). *Forgiveness and Reconciliation: Theory and Application.* New York, NY: Brunner-Routledge.

Worthington, E. L., Jr., Hook, J. N., Utsey, S. O., Williams, J. K., & Neil, R. L. (2007, October). *Decisional and Emotional Forgiveness.* Paper presented at the International Positive Psychology Summit. Washington, DC.


## FORGIVENESS COUNSELING SESSION

Christians often seek out pastors and other mental-health counselors because they are hurting and want solutions to their emotional and interpersonal difficulties. Central to their problems are unresolved issues, especially bitterness and unforgiveness that have infiltrated their relationships with loved ones. Decision-based forgiveness sessions have been effective in helping Christians seek and grant forgiveness. This model has been documented in the practice literature and recently has shown promise in the empirical literature (DiBlasio, 2000, 2010; DiBlasio & Benda, 2008). For people seeking help, counseling intervention that starts with a structured forgiveness session has brought forgiveness and restored intimacy.

The actual forgiveness session is lengthy (usually three to five hours) and includes 13 steps. The steps are organized into three sections: (a) defining and preparing (steps 1–3), which involve a discussion between the counselees and counselor, (b) seeking and granting forgiveness (steps 4–12), and (c) designing the ceremonial act (step 13).

*Step 1: Discuss definitions of forgiveness.* Before taking people through a process of forgiveness, it helps to establish their objective thoughts about forgiveness and what it means to them. The counselor requests permission to take a few moments to discuss the topic of forgiveness and to explore ideas and beliefs. In the process, the counselor presents the definition of decision-based forgiveness (a willful commitment to let go of resentment, bitterness, and need for vengeance) and asks if the counselees agree with the thought that the decision to forgive includes not only the cognitive letting go (Eph. 4:31) but also the self-sacrificing acts of forgiveness and love, just as Christ has forgiven and loved them (Eph. 4:32–5:2). The counselor may also consider these points:

- Forgiveness is an act of the will.
- People can have emotional pain but determine to control revengeful thinking.
- Emotional pain and hurt will be addressed throughout the duration of counseling.
- A forgiveness decision is a beginning to counseling, not an end.
- There are internal and interpersonal benefits of making a forgiveness decision.
- Each person must make his or her own decision about forgiveness issues.

*Step 2: Focus on each person's opportunity to seek forgiveness.* In this step, counselees can choose whether to confess their wrongdoing to each other. One releases control and expectations of the other's hurtful behavior and concentrates instead on his or her own culpability. This is a welcome relief from routine counseling, where loved ones take turns revealing all the problems and sins of their mates, leaving counselors often feeling like referees.

*Step 3: Introduce the forgiveness treatment and let each person decide whether or not to participate.* Because the session has a task orientation, it is best to review the sequential stages so that people can make informed decisions about whether to participate. If counselees desire to participate, then one person completes steps 4 through 12, followed by another person, and so forth.

*Step 4: The offender states the offense.* Here people can be very clear about the hurtful behavior they inflicted on the other. By verbally stating the offense, the person implicitly demonstrates awareness that he or she has done something wrong.

*Step 5: The offender provides an explanation.* The counselor makes clear that most offenses in relationships have explanations but that the explanations are sometimes lost because previous communication between the offender and offended person is defensive and negative. The counselor cautions that the explanation will *not* be considered an excuse, but rather a search for information that will allow a thorough understanding and assessment of the offense.

*Step 6: All parties ask questions and offer answers about the offense.* The hurt associated with the offense usually results in a reduction of both intimacy and communication. When defensiveness and sarcasm are added to the dialogue, family members rarely get enough objective information needed to answer their questions. If the proceeding steps of the forgiveness session have been successful, an atmosphere of objectivity and love has been established. Accurate information is important in bringing clarity and avoiding more negative imagination or assumptions. Giving the answers and facts about the offense also provides the offender with a sense of cleansing.

*Step 7: The offended person gives emotional reactions.* Intimacy includes the sharing of one's heart with another, even if the content shared is hurtful. Humans find connection as they share their hurt, fear, anger, and other deep emotions. Offended people want their offenders to hear and understand their hurt. Considerable care and time is spent focusing on the hurt feelings.

*Step 8: The offender shows empathy and remorse for the hurt he or she caused the other.* Normally in relational conflict, both people are hurting, making empathy for the other a difficult task. However, the conduct of the session puts people in a new position of understanding and love and therefore creates unity. A by-product of unity is empathy, and empathy increases unity. The offender can thoughtfully reflect the hurt, which acknowledges that the other's suffering is understood.

*Step 9: The offender develops a plan to stop or prevent hurtful behavior.* Obviously, seeking true forgiveness means that the offender plans to stop the offensive behavior and prevent it from happening in the future. Forgiveness of the offended person and repentance by the offender is facilitated when a process of corrective action is planned and a system of accountability is established.

*Step 10: The offended person shows empathy for the offender's hurt.* This step promotes empathy that in turn encourages a sense of restored love. The realization and humility that offended persons are human and also have made mistakes contribute to their ability to be empathetic toward offenders (Jn. 8:1-11).

*Step 11: The counselor emphasizes the choice and commitment involved in letting go.* The counselor reminds participants of the discussion in step 1 concerning love and forgiveness and the decision-based approach to forgiveness. If the offended person chooses to forgive, the commitment comes with a decision to purposely let go of the offense and not use it as a weapon in the future. The intent is to "take captive every thought to make it obedient to Christ" (2 Cor. 10:5) and not to bathe in resentment and bitterness over the offense.

*Step 12: The offender formally requests forgiveness.* The biblical pattern for offenses is for the offender or the offended to initiate a face-to-face encounter to resolve the problem (Mt. 5:23-24; 18:15) and to pursue peace (Rom. 14:19; Heb. 12:14; 1 Pet. 3:11). To make the forgiveness clear, the participants put into words the request and the granting of the request. The formal request reinforces that a concrete forgiveness decision was made with the counselor as witness.

*Step 13: Engage a ceremonial act.* Across cultures, ceremonies seal lifelong commitments. In a forgiveness ceremony, an outward act between people reinforces the time of forgiveness they shared and helps to cognitively, emotionally, and spiritually solidify their decisions. The ceremonial act is a symbolic expression that the offense has been formally and permanently forgiven.

**Frederick A. DiBlasio**

### REFERENCES

DiBlasio, F. A. (1999). Scripture and forgiveness: Interventions with families and couples. *Marriage and Family: A Christian Journal, 3,* 257-267.

DiBlasio, F. A. (2000). Decision-based forgiveness treatment in cases of marital infidelity. *Psychotherapy, 37,* 149-158.

DiBlasio, F. A. (2010). Christ-like forgiveness in marital counseling: A clinical follow-up of two empirical studies. *Journal of Psychology and Christianity, 29,* 291-300.

DiBlasio, F. A., & Benda, B. B. (2008). Forgiveness intervention with married couples: Two empirical analyses. *Journal of Psychology and Christianity, 27,* 150-158.

## INNER HEALING

**Description.** Inner healing, also known as inner-healing prayer or healing of memories, is a particular type of prayer "designed to facilitate the client's ability to process affectively painful memories through vividly recalling those memories and asking for the presence of Christ (or God) to minister in the midst of this pain" (Garzon & Burkett, 2002, p. 42). Garzon and Burkett (2002) summarized four major models of inner-healing prayer as developed by Seamands (1985), Tan (1996), Payne (1991), and Smith (2002, 2005) and pointed out their commonalities and differences. The history of the healing of memories actually goes back to the work of Agnes Sanford in the 1950s, followed by others like Ruth Carter Stapleton, Francis MacNutt, and John and Paula Sandford.

Inner-healing prayer is a unique Christian form of prayer that can also be used as a spiritual intervention in Christian therapy. It is explicit in its integration of Christian faith and clinical practice when appropriate.

Inner healing can be of particular help to clients who struggle with painful memories from their past. Such memories may include painful experiences of physical or sexual abuse, abandonment, deprivation or neglect, rejection, criticism or harsh treatment, and even trauma of different kinds. It is not typically used as a spiritual intervention on its own, but it is usually employed as part of the process of ongoing pastoral care and counseling or psychotherapy (Tan, 2003; see also Tan, 2011, pp. 345-351).

Inner-healing prayer requires the informed consent of the client and should be conducted in a clinically sensitive way in prayerful dependence on the Holy Spirit. Garzon and Burkett (2002) emphasize that with clients who suffer from thought disorders, severe depression, substance abuse problems, or burnout, inner-healing prayer should either not be used at all or used only with great caution. Thorough client assessment, careful timing, and comprehensive treatment are crucial in such cases.

**A Seven-Step Model for Inner-Healing Prayer.** One example of inner healing is a seven-step model for inner-healing prayer first described by Tan in 1992 and subsequently developed and elaborated on (see Tan, 2003; Tan, 2011; Tan & Ortberg, 2004, pp. 64-71). This model or approach focuses on prayer and the Holy Spirit's presence and ministry during the process of inner-healing prayer. It emphasizes waiting on the Lord to minister to the client in whatever way the Holy Spirit leads during the prayer session. It therefore does not have a set script for inner-healing prayer for the client and does not instruct the client to imagine specific visualizations of Jesus and what he would do or say (such as hug the client and say, "I love you"), unlike some other forms of healing of memories (see Seamands, 1985).

1. Begin with prayer for protection from evil and ask for the power and healing ministry of the Holy Spirit to take control of the session.
2. Guide the client into a relaxed state, usually by brief relaxation strategies (such as slow, deep breathing, calming self-talk, pleasant imagery, prayer, and Bible imagery).
3. Guide the client to focus attention on a painful past event or traumatic experience and to feel deeply the pain, hurt, anger, and so forth.
4. Prayerfully ask the Lord, by the power of the Holy Spirit, to come to the client and minister his comfort, love, and healing grace (even a gentle rebuke where necessary). This may include imagery of Jesus or other healing imagery, music (song or hymn), Scriptures, a sense of his presence or warmth, or other manifestations of the Spirit's working. No specific guided imagery or visualization is provided or directed at this point.
5. Wait quietly on the Lord to minister to the client with his healing grace and truth. Guide and speak only if necessary and led by the Holy Spirit. In order to follow or track with the client, the counselor will periodically and gently ask, "What's happening? What are you feeling or experiencing now?"
6. Close in prayer.
7. Debrief and discuss the inner-healing prayer experience with the client (Tan, 2003, pp. 20-21).

This seven-step model can be adapted or modified if necessary. Clients can also be asked to use it as a homework assignment in their own times of prayer in between counseling sessions.

Clients who do not experience any significant level of healing after an inner-healing prayer session will need to be reassured that the Lord has promised sufficient grace to meet their need, even if significant healing or relief is not experienced at that time (see 2 Cor. 12:9-10).

**Conclusion.** The crucial role of forgiveness in the process of inner healing also needs to be addressed. Inner-healing prayer is therefore not a panacea or quick solution for all painful memories and complex problems. However, it can be a helpful spiritual intervention in explicit forms of Christian counseling and therapy, including Christian cognitive behavior therapy (Tan, 2007). It can help to deepen emotional processing as well as solidify cognitive restructuring in a more experiential and spiritual context. Controlled outcome research specifically on the effectiveness of inner-healing prayer for past painful memories and related problems is lacking and needed (Garzon & Burkett, 2002).

Siang-Yang Tan

### REFERENCES

Garzon, F., & Burkett, L. (2002). Healing of memories: Models, research, future directions. *Journal of Psychology and Christianity, 21*, 42-49.

Payne, L. (1991). *Restoring the Christian Soul: Overcoming Barriers to Completion in Christ Through Healing Prayer.* Grand Rapids, MI: Baker.

Seamands, D. A. (1985). *Healing of Memories.* Wheaton, Il: Victor Books.

Smith, E. M. (2002, 2005). *Healing Life's Hurts Through Theophostic Prayer.* Campbellsville, KY: New Creation.

Tan, S.-Y. (1996). Religion in clinical practice: Implicit and explicit integration. In E. P. Shafranske (Ed.), *Religion and the Clinical Practice of Psychology* (pp. 365-387). Washington, DC: American Psychological Association.

Tan, S.-Y. (2003). Inner healing prayer. *Christian Counseling Today, 11*(4), 20-22.

Tan, S.-Y. (2007). Use of prayer and Scripture in cognitive-behavioral therapy. *Journal of Psychology and Christianity, 26*, 101-111.

Tan, S.-Y. (2011). *Counseling and Psychotherapy: A Christian Perspective.* Grand Rapids, MI: Baker Academic.

Tan, S.-Y., & Ortberg, J. (2004). *Coping with Depression* (Rev. ed.). Grand Rapids, MI: Baker.

## MINDFULNESS

**Description.** Mindfulness, or mindful awareness, is the ability to focus on a present-moment experience in an open and accepting way. This ability can be cultivated by various formal and informal practices, including meditation and prayer. Although articulated and integrated into Buddhist psychology, various forms of the experience can be seen in writings of ancient philosophies and religions, including Christian practices (see Kabat-Zinn, 1990; Siegel, 2007).

**History.** The importance of mindful awareness is only recently being understood in the scientific world. In the last 20 years, studies have shown positive effects of mindfulness in the treatment of depression, attention, anxiety, personality disorders, obesity, fibromyalgia, dependency, and other problems. Recent brain studies show evidence of decreased activity in areas responsible for emotional response and increases in areas of evaluative functioning, including left prefrontal areas responsible for openness and exploration. Structural changes in the brain have been noted after only eight weeks of participation in a mindfulness-based stress-reduction program (see Seigel, 2007; Holzel et al., 2011; Smalley & Winston, 2010).

**Mindfulness as a Form of Consciousness.** Being aware of present-moment experience, such as breathing or sensations within the body, allows the mind to focus on events that occur moment by moment. As thoughts and feelings enter the scope of awareness, practitioners are told not to resist them or judge them in any way. For example, if the thought of missing an appointment were to come to mind, the person would simply note the thought and any feelings that come along with it and return to focusing on breathing. Many times, the mind preoccupies itself with judgmental thoughts. The goal is to allow thoughts to come and go from the mind like leaves floating down a stream. The moment of mindful awareness occurs when the person becomes aware of a judgmental thought and is able to return to the present experience. The content of the thought is not the focus of mindfulness; instead, the goal is to observe the present-moment experience. This approach does not seek to confront or resist negative thoughts, but to maintain a nonjudgmental, accepting state of mind when they appear.

Mindfulness can be both trait (evident within the personality) and state (evident from moment to moment). Individuals can experience moments that are more mindful than others and yet have a consistent level of trait-like mindful awareness over time. It is unknown if mindfulness is genetic or purely a product of environment. This is currently being researched. However, it is known that mindful awareness can be cultivated through practice. Trait mindfulness can be measured to some degree through self-report measures and is shown to increase over time when participants engage in mindful practice, such as meditation (see Brown & Ryan, 2003; Baer et al., 2006; Lau et al., 2006; Baer, Smith, & Allen 2004; Feldman et al., 2007; Buchheld, Grossman, & Walach, 2001; Cardaciotto, Herbert, Forman, Moitra, & Farrow, 2008; Chawla et al., 2010). Regular practice, such as 45-minute intervals daily, can bring about increases in trait mindfulness after only weeks of participation. Even structural changes in areas of the brain associated with such things as awareness and emotion regulation have been noted after only eight weeks of practice (see Holzel et al., 2011).

**Mindfulness in Therapy.** Therapeutic approaches have been developed around mindfulness practice (see Chiesa & Malinowski, 2011). Mindfulness programs have been used in both inpatient and outpatient settings as well as in individual and group settings. Stand-alone mindfulness programs may be utilized as a part of therapy or for personal growth. These usually include weekly classes, sometimes including daylong or weeklong retreats of silence. Currently, University of Massachusetts, Duke University, University of Virginia, UCLA, Oxford, and other universities have mindfulness centers for research and education.

In therapy, mindful practice can enhance self-awareness, cultivate evaluative thinking, decrease entanglement of emotion, and provide for a more objective exploration of intrusive thought patterns. Since this construct is a core cognitive process, this experience can be adapted to fit within the scope of a wide range of theoretical approaches in counseling.

**Spiritual Concerns.** For many Christians, the idea of meditation or Yoga conjures up fears of Buddhist or New Age influences. This is an important consideration for every Christian client. Although mindfulness can be isolated as a human experience outside the realm of religion or culture and is a strongly empirical phenomenon, perceptions of New Age or Buddhist influence are certainly possible. This is due to the fact that Buddhist teachings and some New Age practices have integrated mindfulness into their routines and popularized the experience. This can be observed by a single search of the word *mindfulness* on the Internet.

For the Christian counselor, this concern should not be taken lightly. A client may be highly offended by what he perceives to be an ungodly approach to therapy. Christian counselors may find that this approach challenges their own perception of integrating science and faith in practice. This is certainly a healthy struggle and an opportunity for therapists to articulate their integrative approach to clients.

Of particular concern when integrating any technique or model into the Christian counseling process is the issue of epistemology. Where is truth coming from? In the case of mindful awareness as researched in clinical settings, the construct of cultivating present-moment awareness is isolated primarily to the client's awareness of his current reality: bodily sensations, emotional states, and thought processes at the time. No outer influence of doctrine or culture is being introduced. The client and therapist are then freely open to explore these thoughts and sensations in the context of the Christian or clinical setting. The Christian therapist may find that careful integration of present-moment awareness into therapy is a very valuable addition to treatment and possibly a very meaningful experience for the Christian client.

Mark Myers

## REFERENCES


Baer, R. A., Smith, G. T., & Allen, K. B. (2004). Assessment of mindfulness by self-report: The Kentucky inventory of mindfulness skills. *Assessment, 11*(3), 191-206.

Baer, R. A., Smith, G. T., Hopkins, J., Krietemeyer, J., & Toney, L. (2006). Using self-report assessment methods to explore facets of mindfulness. *Assessment, 13*(1), 27-45.

Brown, K. W., & Ryan, R. M. (2003). The benefits of being present: Mindfulness and its role in psychological well-being. *Journal of Personality and Social Psychology, 84*(4), 822-848.

Buchheld, N., Grossman, P., & Walach, H. (2001). Measuring mindfulness in insight meditation (vipassana) and meditation-based psychotherapy: The development of the Freiburg mindfulness inventory (FMI). *Journal for Meditation and Meditation Research, 1*(1), 11-34.

Cardaciotto, L., Herbert, J. D., Forman, E. M., Moitra, E., & Farrow, V. (2008). The assessment of present-moment awareness and acceptance: The Philadelphia mindfulness scale. *Assessment, 15*(2), 204.

Chawla, N., Collins, S., Bowen, S., Hsu, S., Grow, J., Douglass, A., & Marlatt, G. A. (2010). The mindfulness-based relapse prevention adherence and competence scale: Development, interrater reliability, and validity. *Psychotherapy Research, 4*, 1-10.

Chiesa, A., & Malinowski, P. (2011). Mindfulness-based approaches: Are they all the same? *Journal of Clinical Psychology, 67*(4), 404-424.

Feldman, G., Hayes, A., Kumar, S., Greeson, J., & Laurenceau, J.-P. (2007). Mindfulness and emotion regulation: The development and initial validation of the cognitive and affective mindfulness scale-revised (CAMS-R). *Journal of Psychopathology and Behavioral Assessment, 29*(3), 177-190.

Holzel, B. K., Carmody, J., Vangel, M., Congleton, C., Yerramsetti, S. M., Gard, T., & Lazar, S. W. (2011). Mindfulness practice leads to increases in regional brain gray matter density. *Psychiatry Research: Neuroimaging, 191*, 36-43.

Kabat-Zinn, J., & University of Massachusetts Medical Center–Worcester. (1990). *Full Catastrophe Living: Using the Wisdom of Your Body and Mind to Face Stress, Pain, and Illness.* New York, N.Y: Delacorte Press.

Lau, M. A., Bishop, S. R., Segal, Z. V., Buis, T., Anderson, N. D., Carlson, L.,...Devins, G. (2006). The Toronto mindfulness scale: Development and validation. *Clinical Psychology, 62*(12), 1445.

Siegel, D. J. (2007). *The Mindful Brain: Reflection and Attunement in the Cultivation of Well-Being.* New York, NY: Norton.

Smalley, S. L., & Winston, D. (2010). *Fully Present: The Science, Art and Practice of Mindfulness.* Cambridge, MA: Da Capo Lifelong.


## PRAYER IN COUNSELING

**Definition.** The effective use of prayer in counseling begins with understanding the nature and function of prayer. *Merriam-Webster's* defines prayer as "an address (or a petition) to God or a god in word or thought" and the act of praying as "to entreat, implore, often used as a function word in introducing a question, request, or plea." However, a Christian understanding of prayer assumes an intimate relationship with God (such as fellowship with God, resting in God, communing with God, etc.) and is usually expressed in a conversation with God (such as worshipping, praising, confessing sins, requests, etc.). Prayer is an expression of worship and dependency on God, and it unleashes the power of the Holy Spirit.

Though much of psychology has often dismissed the role of prayer in counseling, studies conducted on the psychological effects of prayer have identified several themes: Prayer has been found to be associated with a personal feeling of well-being and a greater sense of significance and purpose in life. Prayer has also been shown to help clients in coping with pain and medical problems and even to have an effect on physical health (McCullough & Larson, 1999; McMinn, Ruiz, Marx, Wright, & Gilbert, 2006; McMinn, 1996).

When attempting to help a person through a problem or difficulty, a Christian counselor instinctively asks the question, what is the role of prayer? I suggest a threefold role of prayer in counseling: (a) praying as the counselor for the client, (b) directing the client to pray for himself or herself, and (c) praying for the actual healing process.

**Prayer by the Counselor.** When a counselor invokes God's presence and power to solve a problem, healing takes on a divine dimension. Paul prayed for those he sought to help (see 1 Cor. 1:3; Phil. 1:4; 1 Th. 1:2), and he asked for prayer as he attempted to minister to others (see Rom. 15:30; 1 Th. 5:25; 2 Th. 3:1). A counselor should pray for insight into the person and the difficulty he faces, and then he should pray for clarity of mind to properly diagnose the problem. Next, he should pray for wisdom to determine the solution(s) that would help the client and ask for God to lead him in the counseling process as he uncovers more truth about the issues at hand. The counselor should be yielded to the Holy Spirit so, when changes in the direction of therapy arise from the counseling conversation, prayer will help lead to a successful solution.

Some skeptics feel that the counselor should not ask for God's divine intervention, or miracles, because prayer cannot upset or overrule the natural world. They believe natural laws are the controlling power of life's events, and praying for divine help could not override or abdicate any law of nature without throwing the entire system into chaos. Christians, though, believe that the natural world is created by God for his honor and glory. He has the ability to step into time and space, and indeed, the Scriptures promise that he delights in intervening in the lives of those who trust him. He is a God of miracles.

**Prayer by the Client.** There are many reasons why a client should pray and why a therapist should pray with a client. Prayer is a relationship with God, so clients' prayers connect them with his love, forgiveness, and purposes, and the clients experience hope (Ps. 25:4-5; Pr. 24:13-14), peace (Ps. 34:14; Is. 26:3; John 16:33; Phil. 4:6-7), renewed joy (1 Chron. 16:27; Is. 51:11; Rom. 5:3; Phil. 4:4), and a stronger self-identity and self-determination.

Clients' faith will grow as they talk with God, worship him, and please him. Obviously, there are times of weak faith (Rom. 14:1) and little faith (Mt. 14:31), but prayer will strengthen faith (Rom. 1:17).

**Prayer for Healing.** In praying for people who need healing or help, it is critical to examine whether their sickness or emotional problems are caused by sin in their lives. In these cases, the promise of healing is attached to the condition of confession, forgiveness, and repentance. "The prayer of faith will make the sick person well...and if they have sinned, they will be forgiven. Therefore confess your sins to each other and pray for each other so that you may be healed" (Jas. 5:15-16). Why does the Bible connect sickness to sin? For two reasons: First, certain sins cause physical illness. We know that cigarette smoking leads to cancer, excessive alcohol drinking leads to cirrhosis of the liver, and a sexually immoral lifestyle can lead to STDs. Sin can be the direct cause of a person's illness, or it can be an indirect cause through circumstances that bring about illness—sin destroys a person's self-discipline, and an immoral lifestyle introduces germs and infections into the body. Second, their illness may be a judgment of God.

If the cause of suffering is personal sin, God offers cleansing, assurance of pardon, and healing. Notice again that the passage says, "Confess your sins to each other...that you may be healed." In these situations, sins must be dealt with before God administers healing and wholeness. James introduced the section on praying for sick people by pointing us to the consequences of sin: "Otherwise you will be condemned" (Jas. 5:12).

When praying for healing and wholeness, ask God to give the person spiritual and physical life. "Every good gift and every perfect gift is from above" (Jas. 1:17). God is the one who gives wholeness.

Finally, the key to healing is not merely personal faith or the severity of the person's sickness. Healing power is with God. When you exercise the "prayer of faith," remember that the faith is in the source of healing—God—and not in your prayer or in faith itself. Trust in what God can do. God can do all things, so he can heal anyone.

One of the most common difficulties encountered in prayer is unanswered prayer. Quite often, people are impatient and insistent that God answer in their way and in their timing, but God often uses delays to teach us to seek him more than we seek the answer. As we pray for and with hurting people, we cling to the character of God, seek him more, and humbly ask for wisdom and strength to do his will (Towns, 2009). With Jesus in his hour of need in the garden, we pray, "Not my will, but yours be done" (Lk. 22:42).

**Ethical Issues.** Counselors must be aware of and sensitive to the religious beliefs of their clients. This information can often be gained as part of the intake process (McMinn et al., 2006). It is unethical for counselors to push their values or faith on clients, so verbal prayers in the counseling session should be used only with the consent of the client (Abernethy, Houston, Mimms, & Boyd-Franklin, 2006). Covert prayer is always appropriate (praying for clients outside of the counseling session or silently during the session), but overt prayer (praying aloud with a client in the counseling session) must be handled with care. Abernethy et al. suggest that to be ethically appropriate, verbal prayers in the counseling session should (a) be consistent with the client's faith, (b) use terminology that is understandable and applicable, (c) focus on the positive, and (d) have a real, practical purpose.

**Elmer Towns**

### REFERENCES

Abernethy, A. D., Houston, T. R., Mimms, T., & Boyd-Franklin, N. (2006). Using prayer in psychotherapy: Applying Sue's differential to enhance culturally competent care. *Cultural Diversity and Ethnic Minority Psychology, 12*(1), 101-114.

McCullough, M. E., & Larson, D. B. (1999). Prayer. In W. R. Miller (Ed.), *Integrating Spirituality into Treatment: Resources for Practitioners* (pp. 85-110). Washington, DC: American Psychological Association.

McMinn, M. R. (1996). *Psychology, Theology, and Spirituality in Counseling.* Forest, VA: American Association of Christian Counselors.

McMinn, M. R., Ruiz, J. N., Marx, D., Wright, J. B., & Gilbert, N. B. (2006). Professional psychology and the doctrines of sin and grace: Christian leaders' perspectives. *Professional Psychology: Research and Practice, 37*(3), 295-302.

Towns, E. (2009). *How God Answers Prayer.* Shippensburg, PA: Destiny Image.

## WORSHIP

**Description.** Simply stated, worship is an act of reverence. More specifically, worship is about offering or expressing reverence and honor to a sacred object or person. Moreover, worship reveals the true priorities and secret desires of the heart. People worship what they love. For the Christian, then, the sole object of love, reverence, and worship should be the Lord (see Dt. 6:5).

Whaley (2009) performed an in-depth study on all of the Hebrew and Greek terms associated with worship in Scripture and concluded that *worship* means "to kneel, stoop, prostrate oneself, or throw oneself down, in reverence...to celebrate God foolishly and boast about His attributes...to express deep respect or adoration...to praise God...[and] to revere" (pp. xiv-xv). He summarizes his findings by stating, "It all boils down to love; that is what we were made for—to love God... [and ultimately] to *worship* Him" (p. xv).

**Relevance.** If worship is about loving

and revering God, the obvious question is, what does worship have to do with counseling, and how, if at all, are these concepts related? McMinn (1996) indirectly points to one connection by challenging Christian counselors to understand the spiritual lives of clients. In so doing, they can discern if a client's problem is "simply a behavioral habit to be eliminated [or] a reflection of deep, inner yearnings for intimacy with God and others" (p. 270)—yearnings which are best addressed and met through worship.

A second link between worship and counseling may exist in the therapeutic value of worship. Interestingly, more than 60 years ago, two independent studies explored this topic. Boisen (1948) experimented "with worship services as a therapy in mental hospitals, [arguing that patients] can in group worship have re-orientation, re-affirmation and re-creation of religious faith with therapeutic results." Haas (1950) advocated for corporate worship as a form of group therapy that could potentially "(1) focus attention outside of pre-occupation with self, (2) bring comfort, (3) reduce anxiety, (4) alleviate the sense of guilt, and (5) strengthen inner resources."

Additionally, counseling and worship share a common emphasis on relationships. According to Crabb (1997),"The deepest urge in every human heart is to be in relationship with someone who absolutely delights in us...The longing to connect defines our dignity as human beings" (p. 45). This statement by Crabb on interpersonal relationships in the counseling context parallels that by Whaley (2009) connecting worship to one's relationship with God: "[Worship] is what we were made for. God created man because He wanted relationship. It's what He's about, and...the only way to an intimate relationship with God is through worship" (pp. 333-334).

**Biblical and Spiritual Issues.** True worship causes people to see God in his rightful place: on his throne, above all else. The worshipper then responds by giving God glory for who he is. When worshipping, people are reminded "to stay focused on the God of wonder...[worship] is our expression of love to the Father, Son, and Holy Spirit, lived out in [daily life]" (Whaley, 2009, p. 334). By focusing on God, worshippers are able to see things differently, which in turn can lead to positive, personal change.

This was the experience of the prophet Isaiah, who, during a particularly difficult time in his life, saw the Lord in all of his glory, "high and exalted, seated on a throne" (Is. 6:1). The vision of God in all his majesty invoked Isaiah's worship, and he was forever changed, most notably in his perceptions. Specifically, worship enabled Isaiah to...

- *See his circumstances differently.* Prior to seeing the Lord, Isaiah's world seemed bleak, but now he saw things from heaven's perspective, and that view was glorious.
- *See himself differently.* The sight of a holy God convicted Isaiah of his own wickedness and caused him to cry out in despair (Is. 6:5). No matter how good a person thinks he is, all fall short of the glory of God (Rom. 3:23).
- *See his world differently.* Upon encountering God's glory, the prophet's eyes were opened to the brokenness of the world around him (Is. 6:5) and to the needs of the people in that world (6:8); now he was ready to go and meet those needs.

Positive, personal change: That's what worship and counseling are all about.

**Fred Milacci**

## REFERENCES

Boisen, A. (1948). The service of worship in a mental hospital: Its therapeutic significance. *Journal of Clinical Pastoral Work, 1*, 19-25.

Crabb, L. (1997). *Connecting: Healing for Ourselves and Our Relationships.* Nashville, TN: W Publishing Group.

Haas, A. (1950). The therapeutic value of hymns. *Pastoral Psychology, 1*(9), 39-42. doi:10.1007/BF01785640

McMinn, M. (1996). *Psychology, Theology, and Spirituality in Christian Counseling.* Wheaton, IL: Tyndale House.

Whaley, V. (2009). *Called to Worship: The Biblical Foundation of Our Response to God's Call.* Nashville, TN: Thomas Nelson.

## RELATIONAL SPIRITUALITY AND TRANSFORMATION

In our book *Transforming Spirituality* (Shults & Sandage, 2006), we have described our approach as *relational integration,* in which attending to our own relational dynamics as psychologist and theologian is an integral part of the process. We have assumed that like any good relationship, integration requires a balance between respecting disciplinary boundaries and encouraging mutual influence. In this way we tried to avoid the snares of power and control, in which one discipline is allowed to trump or close off influence from the other. However, this article briefly summarizes some of the contours of our model emphasizing the psychological side of integration.

**Relational Spirituality.** Spirituality has been defined in a myriad of ways. We have defined relational spirituality as "ways of relating to the sacred" (Shults & Sandage, 2006, p. 161). People relate to the sacred in many ways (e.g., trust, avoidance, commitment, disappointment, surrender, and fear). An emphasis on relational categories does not ignore the content of a person's spirituality, but it helps situate spirituality in a relational context and resonates especially well with theistic traditions, such as Christianity.

Contemporary philosophy and theology have also experienced a shift toward emphasizing relational categories. Instead of the modernistic focus on persons (human and divine) as individual rational substances, one finds more robustly Trinitarian views of God and more relational concepts of human being-in-relation in the image of God. In many ways, this represents a return to relationality that shaped earlier resources in the biblical tradition (Shults, 2003).

Social scientists have increasingly construed the self as constituted in and through relationships in contrast to a modernistic focus on the decontextualized individual subject. A large body of empirical research on psychotherapy also supports relational factors (e.g., therapeutic alliance) as effective sources of change (Norcross, 2002). And a relational model is useful for working with couples and families, where spiritual differences within the system can create formidable challenges of triangulation for counselors and therapists.

**Relational Development.** We have found it helpful to consider the developmental nature of relational spirituality. The ways in which a person relates to the sacred often change over the course of life in conjunction with developmental transitions. In the history of Christianity, this is reflected in the writings of many contemplatives, such as St. Theresa of Avila and St. John of the Cross, who recounted the intense challenges of pursuing spiritual intimacy with God. Some of these contemplative writings retain worldview assumptions that are problematic for contemporary readers. But we have sought to recover some of their useful intuitions about spirituality as a developmental process that can potentially move toward the goal of greater intimacy.

In our relational framework, we view development as unfolding through a dialectical process of attachment and differentiation. Humans have a need to connect within the safety of trusted relationships that provide a holding environment for the anxiety of growth (Balswick, King, & Reimer, 2005; Kegan, 1982). And mature human systems (individuals, couples, and groups) are characterized by differentiation, which facilitates the complexity for accepting differences.

Differentiation of self is a good maturity construct because people who are high in this trait tend to (a) accept the anxiety necessary for growth, (b) regain well-being through self-regulation, and (c) cultivate capacities for deeper intimacy with others. But the developmental journey of moving toward greater differentiation of self requires attachment figures who can help contain the transformative process.

**Relational Transformation.** Relationships can shape a crucible for spiritual transformation. A crucible is a container for holding the intense heat and pressure that can transform raw materials and catalytic agents into new forms. Couples therapist David Schnarch defines a crucible as a "resilient vessel in which metamorphic processes occur" (Schnarch, 1991). Numerous clinical theorists, most notably Schnarch, have applied the crucible metaphor to the dynamics of relational transformation in couples and families by highlighting the roles of stress and conflict as opportunities for growth (Allender & Longman, 1995; Holeman, 1999; Napier & Whitaker, 1978).

The resilience and nonreactivity of the container is central to the transformative process. Containers with melting points lower than the chemical reaction inside will crack under pressure and spill out the potential transformative process. Models of therapy and pastoral care that emphasize the differentiation and non-anxious presence of the therapist or minister fit with this insight.

A crucible has also been described as a trial by fire. Transformation requires the intensification of anxiety and arousal as a system heats up. The imagery of heat and fire is a common biblical symbol of spiritual transformation. The transformative process involves a dialectic of arousal and soothing, as fire is balanced by water (Rolheiser, 1999). The Holy Spirit convicts and comforts.

Promoting transformation is a lot like cooking in that it is challenging to get the temperature just right (Maddock & Larson, 1995). Early in my (Steve) therapy career, I leaned on the side of empathically soothing clients. This was helpful for many clients, but I struggled with overly controlled couples who lacked sufficient heat in their relationship to catalyze change. It was helpful to begin to rebalance this by personally tolerating the anxiety of heating up such systems and then offering appropriate levels of soothing as steps of progress were made.

I (LeRon) started with the opposite imbalance early in my teaching career. I tended to heat up my theology classrooms too quickly by introducing an overload of new perspectives and by challenging students' assumptions from the outset. Parallel to Steve's experience, this worked well for students who were eager to be stretched in new ways, but other students felt "overcooked" and raised their defenses. I learned that I needed to first build more trust with such students so they would allow me to help them explore new terrain.

*The crucible of change.* Schnarch's crucible theory of couples therapy fits with our integrative model of transformation. He views intimate relationships as involving a systemic balancing of cycles of growth and stability. Relational systems, such as marriage, maintain states of equilibrium through familiar forms of relating. The relationship might be unsatisfying, but a sense of safety can come from the stability of known patterns. At a certain point of destabilization that Schnarch refers to as "critical mass," one or both partners face a deep integrity dilemma and become willing to tolerate the anxiety that is necessary for a transformative growth cycle (Schnarch, 2009). This typically means going through a "dark night of the soul" as anxiety intensifies and partners are challenged to grow toward greater differentiation.

*Counselors as stewards of transformation.* A similar pattern can be seen in episodes of spiritual transformation. A person experiences an awakening that arouses intense spiritual seeking. This quest often requires a journey beyond the familiar ways of relating to God into the ambiguity of "unknowing" before the presence of God is illuminated again. Biblical narratives depict many of these dark containers of spiritual transformation—dungeons, caves, wells, a cooking pot, a fiery furnace, a belly of a whale, and, of course, a tomb. Death precedes rebirth.

Those of us who are called to be stewards of transformative space—counselors, clinicians, pastors, and lay helpers—have the risky vocation of sitting with people in these dark places. Our own relational integration requires assessing whether we have personal and professional relationships that help us hold the process well. If we do, the work can be integral to our own ongoing transformation.

STEVEN J. SANDAGE
F. LERON SHULTS

## REFERENCES


Allender, D. B., & Longman, T., III. (1995). *Intimate Allies.* Wheaton, IL: Tyndale House.

Balswick, J. O., King, P. E., & Reimer, K. S. (2005). *The Reciprocating Self: Human Development in Theological Perspective.* Downers Grove, IL: InterVarsity Press.

Holeman, V. T. (1999). Mutual forgiveness: A catalyst for relationship transformation in the moral crucible of marriage. *Marriage & Family: A Christian Journal, 2,* 147-158.

Kegan, R. (1982). *The Evolving Self: Problem and Process in Human Development.* Cambridge, MA: Harvard University Press.

Loder, J. E. (1989). *The Transforming Moment.* Colorado Springs, CO: Helmers & Howard.

Maddock, J. W., & Larson, N. L. (1995). *Incestuous Families: An Ecological Approach to Understanding and Treatment.* New York, NY: Norton.

Napier, A. Y., & Whitaker, C. A. (1978). *The Family Crucible.* New York, NY: Harper & Row.

Norcross, J. C. (Ed.). (2002). *Psychotherapy Relationships that Work: Therapist Contributions and Responsiveness to Patients.* New York, NY: Oxford University Press.

Rolheiser, R. (1999). *The Holy Longing: The Search for a Christian Spirituality.* New York, NY: Doubleday.

Schnarch, D. M. (1991). *Constructing the Sexual Crucible: An Integration of Sexual and Marital Therapy* (p. xv). New York, NY: Norton.

Schnarch, D. M. (2009). *Passionate Marriage: Keeping Love and Intimacy Alive in Committed Relationships* (p. 366). New York, NY: Norton.

Shults, F. L. (2003). *Reforming Theological Anthropology: After the Philosophical Turn to Relationality.* Grand Rapids, MI: Eerdmans.

Shults, F. L., & Sandage, S. J. (2006). *Transforming Spirituality: Integrating Theology and Psychology.* Grand Rapids, MI: Baker Academic.

# CORE SKILLS AND CHARACTER TRAITS TO TEACH AND STRENGTHEN IN CLIENTS

## ASSERTIVENESS

**Description.** Assertiveness is a mode of communication characterized by the ability to share one's personal feelings, thoughts, and needs in an honest and safe way. Assertiveness training traditionally suggests that there are three ways, or modes, that people can use to communicate with one another. A person can be aggressive, passive, or assertive. Assertiveness is considered the most psychologically healthy and effective means of communicating with others. Therefore, counselors and other helping professionals try to cultivate assertiveness in their clients. This also helps counselors decrease their clients' aggressive or passive communication.

The skill of assertiveness helps people have healthy boundaries for themselves and to respect healthy boundaries in others. Those with a passive communication style often allow others to abuse or manipulate them and are unable to stand up for themselves. Individuals with an aggressive communication style do not respect the personal boundaries of others. They may use intimidation, fear, or even violence to influence others. Assertiveness is a behavioral middle ground that allows people to express thoughts and feelings effectively and forthrightly without violating the rights or boundaries of others (O'Donohue & Fisher, 2008).

**History.** Assertiveness training was popularized in the field of psychology by psychologist Joseph Wolpe in his 1958 book *Psychotherapy by Reciprocal Inhibition* (Wolpe, 1958). Wolpe explored assertiveness as a way of treating anxiety. He theorized that a person could not be simultaneously assertive and anxious. Therefore, being assertive would inhibit anxiety. Since that time, assertiveness has been a commonly used intervention in behavior therapy. It experienced increased popularity in the 1970s, particularly with women and women's groups as women were entering the workforce and academic programs in greater numbers. It was thought that assertiveness training could teach them skills to stand up for themselves and their rights in these settings. Today, assertiveness is a behavioral and communication skill taught by personal development experts as well as behavior and cognitive-behavioral therapists. It is used in diverse settings from corporate boardrooms and schools to psychiatric and substance-abuse treatment facilities.

**Assessment.** Assessing a client's level of assertiveness is really about determining their ability to communicate their thoughts, feelings, and needs to others in a balanced and healthy way. As mentioned, assertiveness is contrasted with aggressive or passive forms of communicating. Those who are passive may struggle with being manipulated and even abused because of their inability to stand up for themselves. In contrast, those with an aggressive communication style may struggle with anger and inappropriate conduct. Either of these groups would benefit from training in assertiveness.

**Treatment and Resources.** In Christian

counseling, the most foundational work addressing the issue of assertiveness is *Boundaries* by Henry Cloud and John Townsend. The book and accompanying materials are often used in church or ministry settings as a group resource to teach assertiveness and healthy communication techniques. One of the challenges of teaching assertiveness is that these skills, like others, require practice. As people are learning new assertive communication techniques, they commonly overdo the new skills and veer into aggressive communication. It is also important to help clients understand that assertiveness may look different in various settings. Role-playing is an effective tool when teaching assertiveness so that clients have the opportunity to practice and polish their new skills in a safe environment. Groups can be an effective mode for teaching assertiveness.

Assertiveness training also promotes the use of "I" statements in stating one's concerns and needs to others. Rather than saying, "You make me so angry when you..." assertiveness teaches clients to say, "I feel disrespected when you...."

**Spiritual Issues.** Christians may confuse assertiveness with being selfish and misinterpret passivity as being selfless. However, Christians have the perfect example of healthy assertiveness in Jesus Christ. Christ was never passive in his communication style, nor was he aggressive. He stated the truth without violating the rights or boundaries of others.

**Conclusion.** Helping clients develop the skill of assertiveness will likely decrease stress, improve self-esteem, and improve relationships at home, in the church, and in the workplace.

**Jennifer Cisney**

## REFERENCES


Cloud, H., & Townsend, J. (1992). *Boundaries: When to Say Yes, When to Say No to Take Control of Your Life.* Grand Rapids, MI: Zondervan.

O'Donohue, W. T., & Fisher, J. E. (Eds.). (2008). *Cognitive Behavior Therapy* (5th ed.). Belmont, CA: Thomson Wadsworth.

Wolpe, J. (1958). *Psychotherapy by Reciprocal Inhibition.* Palo Alto, CA: Stanford University Press.


## BOUNDARIES

**Description.** Boundaries are necessary parts of a person's healthy functioning and ability to relate at meaningful levels. Simply put, a boundary is a property line. It helps the individual delineate what aspects of life she must own in order to take responsibility for herself as well as protect and develop herself. These include values, thoughts, emotions, behaviors, beliefs and attitudes, talents, desires, choices, time, and energy. The Bible teaches, "Above all else, guard your heart, for everything you do flows from it" (Pr. 4:23). Boundaries assist in that process.

Internal boundaries, which are part of the intrapsychic structure, are the aspects of the self that maintain one's differentiation and preserve autonomy. When an individual experiences herself as distinct from and yet connected to others, she can freely make choices for herself and shows signs of well-constructed internal boundaries. Jesus' instruction to "Let your 'Yes' be 'Yes,' and your 'No,' 'No'" (Mt. 5:37 NASB) is an example of this ability. In short, being connected to someone does not keep the person from feeling free to say or do what she needs to say or do. Boundaries preserve freedom in relationships.

**Development.** Boundaries are developed from early childhood. An infant has very few internal boundaries. He is in a state of symbiosis, or perceived oneness, with his mother and is almost totally unable to experience himself as distinct from his mother, who is protecting and nurturing him in the early weeks and months of life. However, although the mother is always present in some ways, after the first year, the process of separation and individuation increases. During this time, the infant, having been connected and nurtured sufficiently by his mother, and having developed basic trust and ability to connect (Ps. 22:9), is now able to experience himself as more separate from her, with his own feelings and perceptions and power. The word *no* begins to emerge as he hatches from the symbiotic union.

Throughout childhood and all through life, one's boundaries are to develop, clarify, and assist in the abilities to be autonomous, have healthy relationships, make the right choices, and ultimately find the mission and purpose God has designed for him in life.

**Assessment.** When a person has difficulty maintaining his differentiation and sense of self, this is a sign that his boundaries are not working properly. Boundary dysfunctions include the inability to experience one's distinct identity, impulse problems, rescuing and enabling others in codependent relationships, guilt, overcompliance, conflict avoidance, people pleasing, fears of abandonment, fears of autonomy, and in the clinical arena, some types of depressions, anxiety disorders, and addictive problems, to name a few.

**Treatment.** On a treatment level, when the therapist has diagnosed that boundary issues are part of what is driving the client's symptomatology, she can help the internal boundaries to be repaired and strengthened by creating healthy boundaries in the therapeutic frame, allowing the individual to have permission to experience himself in the relationship, to own his own anger, to push against the therapist, and to make his own choices. This is often a very emotional part of therapy because the client can be deeply afraid of being honest about his differentiation, or because he is very angry at those in his life who have been punitive or manipulative with his boundary development.

Another helpful part of therapy is helping the client establish external boundaries, such as saying no; having confrontational conversations, such as "speaking the truth in love" (Eph. 4:15); withdrawing from toxic relationships; and using other people to help him protect himself. These external boundaries become internalized and metabolized in the therapeutic relationship, ultimately becoming part of the intrapsychic structure, thus completing and repairing what went wrong developmentally.

Henry Cloud
John Townsend

## COMMUNICATION TRAINING

The ability to communicate well is the cornerstone of healthy relationships. In the workplace, at home, and in society, the ability to verbalize one's thoughts and feelings in a positive yet assertive manner is key to emotional stability and life satisfaction.

**Description.** It is imperative that counselors have the ability to train their clients to develop effective communication skills (Craighead & Nemeroff, 2001; Guerney, 1974; Long, Angera, Carter, Nakamoto, & Kalso, 1999). Quite often, clients enter the counseling process because they are experiencing conflict in their relationships. At the core of this conflict and subsequent pain is their inability to effectively identify interpersonal feelings and communicate them (Ladd, 2007). Therefore, the need to develop strong skills in communication is essential for successful therapeutic outcomes.

**Key Components and Concepts.** These are five of the key components to healthy communication:

1. The ability to clearly identify interpersonal feelings. Learning to correctly name and identify feelings is a skill that takes consistent practice (Burns, 1999). The therapeutic tool of keeping a feelings journal or feelings log can aid in this process.

2. The ability to actively listen to the other person's point of view (Burns, 1999;

Gottman & DeClaire, 2001). Counselors are trained in the art of active and reflective listening. This skill involves focusing one's attention on what is being said and then repeating accurately what one heard the other person say. Providing this training to clients within the counseling session through role play can help improve clients' ability to hear what is being said and demonstrate respect to others.

3. The use of "I" statements versus "you" statements. Using such phrases as "*I* felt angry and hurt when you said the house is always dirty. *I* don't know if you meant to hurt me or not, but *I* needed to let you know how *I* felt." This method of communicating diffuses the hearers' defense mechanisms (Burns, 1999).

4. Paying attention to body language. It is important not only to pay attention to other people's body language but also to initiate direct eye contact when speaking. Talking too loud or too soft can also help or hinder the flow of communication and desired outcomes.

5. Paying attention to the physical surroundings in which the conversation is taking place. For example, a husband and wife discussing the family's current financial status in the middle of their son's basketball game would be very difficult and probably heighten the conflict. Making sure to discuss issues of importance in quiet, private, and neutral settings ensures the undivided attention of each party involved.

**Treatment.** Cognitive-behavioral therapy has proven to be successful in training clients to evaluate connections between thoughts, feelings, and behavior—key factors in the development of healthy communication (Butler, Chapman, Forman, & Beck, 2006; Chambless & Ollendick, 2001). Negative feelings or incorrect perceptions of the world around us often propel thinking that is incorrect, leading to verbal and physical behavioral reactions that are often unexpected and undesired. Helping clients learn to connect thinking and behavior will strengthen their ability to effectively communicate with the world around them.

**Spiritual Issues.** The apostle Paul is clear about the importance of learning to guard ourselves in the area of communication. He describes the way believers are transformed by the grace of Christ and the power of the Spirit. He instructs his readers to put away some behaviors and put on others: "But now you must put them all away: anger, wrath, malice, slander, and obscene talk from your mouth. Do not lie to one another, seeing that you have put off the old self with its practices and have put on the new self, which is being renewed in knowledge after the image of its creator" (Col. 3:8-10 ESV).

King David was no stranger to conflict. Several times in the book of Psalms, he mentions the importance of guarding the mouth. "Keep your tongue from evil and your lips from speaking deceit" (Ps. 34:13 ESV). "Set a guard, O LORD, over my mouth; keep watch over the door of my lips!" (Ps. 141:3 ESV). David knew his heart. He knew the power of feelings and was aware of his weaknesses. He also knew the power and effectiveness of right communication in dealing with the people in his life.

**Conclusion.** Both counselor and client can benefit from joining with David in his prayer in Psalm 19:14 (ESV): "Let the words of my mouth and the meditation of my heart be acceptable in your sight, O LORD, my rock and my redeemer."

**Amy Feigel**

## REFERENCES

Burns, D. (1999). *The Feeling Good Handbook.* New York, NY: A Plum Book.

Butler, A. C., Chapman, J. E., Forman, E. M., & Beck, A. T. (2006). The empirical status of cognitive-behavioral therapy: A review of meta-analyses. *Clinical Psychology Review, 26*(1), 17-31.

Chambless, D. L., & Ollendick, T. H. (2001). Empirically supported psychological interventions: Controversies and evidence. *Annual Review of Psychology, 52*, 685-716.

Craighead, W. E., & Nemeroff, C. B. (Eds). (2001). *The Corsini Encyclopedia of Psychology and Behavioral Science* (3rd ed., Vol. 1). New York, NY: Wiley & Sons.

Gottman, J. M, & DeClaire, J. (2001). *The Relationship Cure: A Five-Step Guide to Strengthening Your Marriage, Family, and Friendships.* New York, NY: Three Rivers Press.

Guerney, B. G. (1974). *Relationship Enhancement: Skill-Training Programs for Therapy, Problem Prevention, and Enrichment.* San Francisco, CA: Jossey-Bass.

Ladd, P. D. (2007). *Relationships and Patterns of Conflict Resolution: A Reference Book for Couples Counseling.* Lanham, MD: University Press of America.

Long, E. C., Angera, J. J., Carter, S. J., Nakamoto, M., & Kalso, M. (1999). Understanding the one you love: A longitudinal assessment of an empathy training program for couples in romantic relationships. *Family Relationships, 48*, 235-242.

## FAITH

**Description.** Faith is an unshakable confidence placed in the trustworthiness of Christ regardless of current emotions or experiences. There are many views today of faith; some say "It is intellectual assent to propositional statements" (Myers, 2010, p. 36). Christians, however, must see it as much more than this. Calvin (1816) described faith as "a steady and certain knowledge of the Divine benevolence towards us… revealed to our minds, and confirmed to our hearts, by the Holy Spirit" (p. 19).

**Assessment.** Faith is a gift from God. Paul writes, "Think of yourself with sober judgment, in accordance with the faith God has distributed to each of you" (Rom. 12:3). Over time, a Christian's faith should increase in measure, for "faith comes from hearing the message, and the message is heard through the word about Christ" (Rom. 10:17). Finally, every person's faith in Christ will be put to the test because "the testing of your faith produces perseverance" (Jas. 1:3).

**Personal Application.** When I was a teenager and broke my neck in a diving accident, my permanent paralysis nearly crushed my faith in Christ. My faith was already small, and when a severed spinal cord left my body limp and useless, it nearly snuffed it out. Lying in bed paralyzed, I asked God, "If you're so loving, why treat your children so mean?"

That was more than four decades ago. Not once in those years has God been mean. What's more, he has shored up my faith with such a softness and sweetness of fellowship with the Savior that I wouldn't trade the experience for anything—not even walking. The fact that my life as a quadriplegic is nestled safely under God's overarching decrees is, to me, the best of all comforts. God has shown me that when accidents happen, it's okay to call them accidents. Even the Bible does. When babies die, when whole populations starve, and when young girls break their necks, God weeps for his world, "for he does not willingly bring affliction or grief to anyone" (Lam. 3:33). My spinal cord injury was a terrible accident.

But the Bible simultaneously insists on another truth. When suffering and difficulties happen, God has not taken his hands off the wheel for a nanosecond. Psalm 103:19 tells us, "His kingdom rules over all." He considers these awful and often evil things to be tragedies, and he takes no delight in misery. Nevertheless, he is determined to steer suffering for his own ends. And those ends are remarkable. God is heaven-bent on inviting us to share in his joy, peace, and power.

But there's a catch. God shares his joy only on his terms, and those terms call for us, in some measure, to suffer as his beloved Son did while he was on earth. This is where faith is put to the test. Peter reminds us, "To this you were called, because Christ suffered for you, leaving you an example, that you should follow in his steps" (1 Pet. 2:21). Those steps lead us into the fellowship of Christ's sufferings, where we become "like him in his death" (Phil. 3:10); that is, we daily take up our cross and die *to* the sins he died *for* on his cross (Lk. 9:23). When suffering sandblasts us to the core, the true stuff of which we are made is revealed, and then God can use our afflictions to shape our lives and make us holy. We are never more like Christ, never more filled with his joy and peace, than when fear, doubt, and anxieties are replaced with a stronger, more vibrant faith in the Lord.

I don't know why God allowed my accident to happen. That's not the point. The point is that my suffering has taught me to be "done with sin" (1 Pet 4:1), putting behind me the peevishness, small-minded, self-focused Joni to mature into the Joni God has destined me to be, honed and polished by years of quadriplegia.

I'm not saying it's easy. Actually, it's getting harder as time goes by. These thin, tired bones are beginning to bend under the weight of decades of paralysis. But I have to remember that the core of God's plan is to rescue me from sin, even up to my dying breath. God's purpose isn't to make my life happy, healthy, and free of trouble, but to teach me to hate my transgressions and to encourage me to grow in faith as I draw near to Jesus.

"God specifically tells His followers—even followers with great faith—to expect hardship" (Tada, 2009, p. 175). My faith is especially bolstered when I consider Paul's insight: "Our light and momentary troubles are achieving for us an eternal glory that far outweighs them all" (2 Cor. 4:17). My response to my wheelchair has a direct bearing on my capacity for joy, worship, and service in heaven. Of all the things I may waste here on earth, I do not want to waste my quadriplegia. Earth provides my one chance to give Jesus a "sacrifice of praise" (Heb. 13:15), demonstrating that Christ is supremely worthy of my faith.

I've been served best by those counselors who have gently guided me into these rugged, robust truths, reminding me that one day God will close the curtain on all suffering and sorrow. Until then, I can anticipate that God will continue to test, refine, and strengthen my faith in him. God permits what he hates in order to accomplish what he loves. And what he loves is Christ in me, the hope of glory. Having Christ in me is worth anything—even a lifetime of quadriplegia.

**Joni Eareckson Tada**

## REFERENCES

Calvin, J. (1816). *Institutes of the Christian Religion* (Vol. 2). Philadelphia, PA: William Fry.

Myers, R. R. (2010). *Saving Jesus from the Church.* New York, NY: HarperOne.

Tada, J. E. (2009). *A Lifetime of Wisdom; Embracing the Way God Heals You.* Grand Rapids, MI: Zondervan.

## HOPE

**Description.** Hope is "the feeling that what is desired is also possible" (Obayuwana & Carter, 1982). It anchors our souls to the certainty of God's promises, regardless of the circumstances. "Hope is faith waiting for tomorrow. Faith requires belief, and believing is what we do with our minds. Faith requires commitment, and committing is what we do with our wills. But faith must also have hope, and hope is what we do with our hearts" (Ortberg, 2008). Without hope the heart becomes sick (Pr. 13:12). Many people who seek counseling do so because they do not have hope, so helping clients experience hope is an integral part of the counseling process.

**History.** Hope is as old as Scripture itself. Noah had hope that God would send rain, so he built an ark. Moses had hope that the Israelites' enslavement would end. Isaiah had hope that Judah would return to God, and Jeremiah proclaimed that God's people had a future and a hope. The writer of Hebrews gave us a catalog of hope when he listed those who trusted God even in the midst of their darkest moments. In chapter 11, the "hall of faith," he described Abel's more excellent sacrifice, Enoch's translation into heaven, Abraham's obedient sacrifice, and David's courage, all rooted in one thing—hope.

**Application.** Severely wounded clients often have difficulty finding hope. Many have lost hope in life, in relationships, and in God. Their despair may be a result of personal failure, broken relationships, or trauma they experienced as children (Rodgers & Rodgers, 2001). The shame of their childhood abuse can blind them from seeing who God really is—a God of hope (Smedes, 1993).

In recent years, research has demonstrated the value of teaching and imparting resilience, a trait that enables clients to bounce back from adversity and deal with their wounds from the past. In the therapeutic process, clients learn and develop new thoughts, behaviors, and actions. Resilient people feel pain and loss, but they cling to hope in the face of despair (Eberly, 2006). The job of the Christian counselor is to teach resilience and the hope that accompanies it.

The Lord is intimately involved in our character development and wants to teach us this hope. Often he does this through suffering. For this reason we have to teach clients two things: a healthy view of God and a healthy view of suffering.

The religiously minded client cannot separate his or her self-image from the image of God (Hill & Hall, 2002). Counselors must teach clients the loving character of God, that he is a God who offers hope for life's troubles. Counselors can do this by creating an environment of openness, trust, and respect for clients' spiritual expression (Eck, 2002). Just as Christ often modeled in his encounters, counselors can ask probing questions to help people become aware of the hidden places in their hearts that cause them to be hopeless. Through this door of insight, counselors can enable clients to enter into a deeper relationship with God (Coe & Hall, 2010).

We do not mislead clients into thinking that the Christian life will be easy. Romantic idealism has no place in good counseling. Instead, we teach them about God's powerful but often mysterious purpose in their suffering and help them find hope for their future (Whitney, 1991).

**Spiritual and Biblical Issues.** Hopeless clients often have trouble seeing God as good. In their hopelessness they may even feel that God is punishing them. The Bible, however, is full of references about God's heart and how he wants to give hope to his children. Perhaps the key verse is Jeremiah 29:11: "For I know the plans I have for you... plans to prosper you and not to harm you, plans to give you hope and a future." This is God's heart—a heart of hope. Using this and other Scriptures to teach clients about the true character of God can be very effective.

The apostle Paul corrects the faulty perspective that suffering is always a form of punishment. "We also glory in our sufferings, because we know that suffering produces perseverance; perseverance, character; and character, hope" (Rom. 5:3-4). In Paul's letters and throughout the Bible, hope is almost always contrasted with some kind of suffering. Suffering builds character, which in turn produces hope.

**Conclusion.** For Christians, developing hope is becoming most like God. He is the model, goal, and ideal in this developmental process, and ultimately our hope indeed comes from him. "Now may the God of hope fill you with all joy and peace as you trust in him, so that you may overflow with hope by the power of the Holy Spirit" (Rom. 15:13).

**Bev Rodgers**
**Tom Rodgers**

## REFERENCES

Coe, J. H., & Hall, T. W. (2010). *Psychology in the Spirit: Contours of Transformational Psychology.* Downers Grove, IL: IVP Academic.

Eberly, M. (2006). Resiliency bouncing back from adversity. *Christian Counseling Today, 14*(4), 36-39.

Eck, B. E. (2002). An exploration of the therapeutic use of spiritual disciplines and clinical practice. *Journal of Psychology & Christianity, 21*(4), 365-372.

Hill, P. C., & Hall, T. W. (2002). Relational schemas in processing one's image of God and self. *Journal of Psychology & Christianity, 21*(4), 355-371.

Obayuwana, A. & Carter, A. L. (1982). The anatomy of hope. *Journal of the National Medical Association, 74*(3), 229-234.

Ortberg, J. (2008). *Faith and Doubt.* Grand Rapids, MI: Zondervan.

Rodgers, B. & Rodgers, T. (2001). The severely wounded client. *Christian Counseling Today, 9*(1), 32-38.

Smedes, L. (1993). *Shame and Grace: Healing the Shame We Don't Deserve.* San Francisco, CA: HarperCollins.

Whitney, D. S. (1991). *Spiritual Disciplines for the Christian Life.* Colorado Springs, CO: NavPress.

## HUMILITY

**Description.** *Webster's* defines *humility* as "the state or quality of being humble; absence of pride or self-assertion." Typical definitions include other concepts, such as modesty and meekness. However, many definitions tend to define humility by comparing it with what it is not, such as not believing that one is superior to others or lacking pretense. Therefore, it may be helpful to consider antonyms of humility, including arrogance, assumption, conceit, egoism, haughtiness, loftiness, lordliness, pomposity, pompousness, presumptuousness, pretense, pride, pridefulness, superciliousness, and superiority.

Perhaps the best understanding of humility comes from a close observation of the scriptural portrayal of the life of Jesus. We often confuse humility with timidity, but this is not scriptural. Biblical characters who embody humility also stood boldly in the face of danger. They spoke and acted courageously, even at the risk of their lives. Humility may be understood from a biblical perspective in three possible interpretations: pious submission to God, intellectual humility, and modesty as a social skill (Dawes, 1991).

**History.** Over the years, there has been little focus from the psychological community on issues of humility in counseling and psychology. However, from a spiritual perspective, humility has historically been a valued attribute in those deemed to be saints or highly esteemed religious historical figures in the early Christian faith. Many historians and sociologists ascribe the rise of humility as a virtue to the example of Christ and the rise of Christianity. However, some, including S. B. Dawes, challenge this claim, arguing that humility as a social virtue finds its roots in the Hebrew Bible. The apostle Paul, speaking to the congregation in the Roman colony at Philippi, provides a radical perspective in the context of the Greco-Roman ethic. In this honor-shame culture, Paul extorts believers, "In humility value others above yourselves" (Phil. 2:3).

Sadly, sometimes humility appears to be scarce among religious leaders, and the Christian subculture too often has worshipped the cult of personality in its leaders. Pride and self-absorption is woven into the fabric of our culture, with the focus on fulfilling one's needs, personal peace and affluence, being right, achievement, and self-growth rather than an attitude of humility and caring for others.

**Assessment.** Helping clients acquire an accurate awareness of their behaviors and attitudes is foundational to promoting change. However, as with most issues, people are often blind to their shortcomings and frequently fail to realize how others perceive them. Perhaps the best way to help individuals assess humility in their lives is by having them prayerfully review the relevant attributes of humility portrayed in Scripture, and in addition, having those closest to them give their honest perception as well.

**Treatment.** God has designed us as relational beings, and we must be in right relationship with God and other people before we can be healthy and whole. You cannot give a person a humility pill. This virtue must be learned and developed by reflection, honesty, and repentance. It is often only through the medicine of adversity, pain, and loss that we are able to humble ourselves before God and others. Zephaniah 2:3 instructs a prideful nation to obey God and to seek righteousness and humility to avoid destruction. The admonition to submit oneself not only to God but also to one another is common in the Bible. We are to take intentional action to clothe ourselves with humility. In counseling it is critical to address issues of humility when there is relational conflict. More broadly, clients without a proper attitude of humility are unlikely to experience emotional, relational, or spiritual growth.

**Biblical and Spiritual Issues.** The Scriptures provide valuable reminders to guard against pride and our human tendency to be self-seeking. The culmination of these Scriptures is Philippians 2:6-11, which portrays the humility of Christ. As we observe and follow his example, we value others as more important than ourselves and sacrifice for them the way Christ sacrificed for us.

**Biblical Passages on Humility**

| | |
|---|---|
| Dt. 8:2 | Zeph. 2:3 |
| 2 Sam. 22:28 | Zech. 9:9-10 |
| 2 Chron. 6:26 | Mt. 5:23-24 |
| Ps. 25:9 | Phil. 2:1-3 |
| Pr. 11:2; 15:1,31-33; 18:10-12,27; 22:4 | Eph. 4:29-32<br>1 Pet. 5:5 |

**Kevin L. Ellers**

## REFERENCES

Dawes, S. B. (1991). Humility: Whence this strange notion? *The Expository Times, 103*(3), 72.

## SOCIAL JUSTICE

**The Call to Justice.** The biblical call to justice is based foremost in the context of love. The Gospel of Matthew specifically declares that the greatest commandment is to "love the Lord your God with all your heart and with all your soul and with all your mind" (Mt. 22:37). The second commandment is like it: "Love your neighbor as yourself" (Mt. 22: 39). Though these verses may seem familiar to many Christians, true soul care is about understanding the power of love and living it out to help those we counsel. True love that comes from Christ compels us to take action to help those who are hurting: "It is the source of our true self-worth and identity before God" (Cannon, 2009, p. 17). The apostle John explains that our ability to love others comes out of the love that God first gave us (1 Jn. 4:7-12). Knowing and living out this love is based in right action. John also described love in action: "This is how we know what love is: Jesus Christ laid down his life for us. And we ought to lay down our lives for our brothers and sisters. If anyone has material possessions and sees a brother or sister in need but has no pity on them, how can the love of God be in that person?" (1 Jn. 3:16-17). From material possessions to emotional and spiritual care of others, the Bible clearly defines an inherent correlation between beliefs and actions.

**The Responsibility of Justice.** Biblically speaking, we are called to love others (Mt. 22:39) and make disciples (Mt. 28:19-20). We are instructed to do this by feeding the hungry, providing shelter to the homeless, clothing the naked, and freeing and satisfying the needs of the emotionally and physically oppressed (Is. 58:6-10). In fact, James goes as far as to say, "Religion that God our Father accepts as pure and faultless is this: to look after orphans and widows in their distress and to keep oneself from being polluted by the world" (Jas. 1:27).

Justice is about stepping into other people's stories of brokenness. It is experiencing their pain and empathizing with them. As Christian counselors consider their role in carrying out justice in the world, they must recognize their susceptibility to compassion fatigue. Biblical justice avoids compassion fatigue when it flows from the love of God for us, not out of our own false motives to help. The responsibility of justice is truly about God's glory alone and bringing about his redemption in the world (Skillen, 2009).

**Opportunities.** Christians can often become isolated from or blinded to the injustices taking place in their own backyard. Christian counselors must recognize how justice can be carried out in Jerusalem (the community), Judea (locally), Samaria (nationally), and the outermost parts of the earth (globally). These opportunities happen in the counseling office on a daily basis and are increasingly becoming public policy issues as well. The way we balance these issues as counselors or advocates will determine our success in helping the clients we serve (Skillen, 2009). Such issues include drug abuse, sexual addiction, sexual abuse, interpartner violence, poverty, marital issues, incarceration, anxiety, depression, verbal abuse, and more (Ivey & Zalaquett, 2011). On a national level, ministries and counseling centers are reaching out to fight such problems as teen suicide, teenage pregnancy, alcohol and drug abuse, and cutting, and they are proactively promoting justice for healthy families (Ivey & Zalaquett). In recent years, new areas of opportunity are arising for counselors on a global level, including helping trauma victims in third-world countries, fighting the AIDS pandemic, counseling sex-trafficked kids and teens, counseling former child soldiers, counseling victims of natural disasters, and engaging in such cross-cultural issues as racial and tribal reconciliation (Ivey & Zalaquett). Christian counselors, in addition to being advocates for justice within the counseling office, need to also become more aware of the issues of injustice in our society and advocate even within the government and society, putting into action their Christian beliefs toward justice (Ahmed, Wilson, Henrickson, Jr., & WindWalker Jones, 2011). There is a growing movement in the counseling field for all counselors to become more multiculturally competent (Ahmed et al.) and to understand the issues related to neuroscience for victims of injustice (Ivey & Zalaquett). This latter body of research is bringing awareness to the way the stress of poverty and injustice negatively impacts the brain and mental health (Ivey & Zalaquett). Today's counseling leaders are now suggesting that such learning and growing promotes justice and that ignorance of these issues enables injustice (Ahmed et al.).

**Accountability Factor.** The accountability of Christian counselors to carry out justice falls on a balance between social justice and moral righteousness (Keller, 2010). Immediately after James declares that true religion is taking care of orphans and widows in their distress, he clearly directs his readers to avoid being polluted by the world (Jas. 1:27). The entire Bible relates justice to moral righteousness. The two cannot be separated. For Christian counselors, this means abiding by the ethical practices and standards set forth by professional counseling organizations, including the American Association of Christian Counselors and the agencies we work for.

Joshua Straub

## REFERENCES

Ahmed, S., Wilson, K. B., Henrickson, Jr., R. C., & Windwalker Jones, J. (2011, Spring). What does it mean to be a culturally-competent counselor? *Journal for Social Action in Counseling and Psychotherapy, 3*(1), 17-28.

Cannon, M. (2009). *Social Justice Handbook: Small Steps for a Better World.* Downers Grove, IL: InterVarsity Press.

Ivey, A. E., & Zalaquett, C. P. (2011, Spring). Neuroscience and counseling: Central issue for social justice leaders. *Journal for Social Action in Counseling and Psychotherapy, 3*(1), 103-116.

Keller, T. (2010). *Generous Justice: How God's Grace Makes Us Just.* New York, NY: Dutton.

Skillen, J. W. (2009). Genuine public pluralism and the establishment of justice. *Edification Journal, 3*(2), 34-38.

## PROBLEM SOLVING AND DECISION MAKING

Counseling is about change, and at the heart of change are problem-solving strategies wrapped in decision-making capabilities (Egan, 2009). The way we help our clients make decisions affects their ability to make changes in their lives and their psychological and emotional and spiritual well-being.

**Description.** Maintaining a positive perspective in life is not about the absence of problems in our lives, but has to do with the way we handle the difficult situations we face every day. Successful decision making depends on our ability to effectively handle stress and conflict. This is the reason why people seek counseling to begin with—life has become so difficult or problematic that they are unable to make rational decisions. They come to counseling to be relieved of their suffering (Clinton & Ohlschlager, 2002)

**Purpose.** The purpose of this step is to help clients evaluate the best way to solve their problems and make good decisions (Cormier & Cormier, 2008). Most clients know about the problems they face but are simply unable to solve their problems without help. Counselors help their clients determine the best way to go about solving the problems that brought them to counseling in the first place.

**Eight-Step Plan.** It is important to recognize that although there are many plans to help clients make decisions, the will of God for their lives takes precedence above all else. Teaching clients to listen for the voice of God in their lives and to look for his leading will help first and foremost when making important life decisions. Corey, Corey, and Callanan (2007) have also developed an eight-step procedure to help clients in the decision-making process.

1. Identify the problem, including its ambiguity.
2. Outline the various elements and potential issues of the problem.
3. Review the relevant ethical codes that apply in the matter.
4. Know the applicable laws and regulations affecting the issue.
5. Consult with your client and with knowledgeable colleagues.
6. Consider possible and probable courses of action.
7. Define the consequences of various courses of action.
8. Decide on the best course of action for you and your client.

**Core Components.** There are several core components to problem solving and decision making. When training clients how to effectively solve problems, the *GRACE* acronym offers people a proven and successful five-step model.

*Goals.* It is difficult for clients to make decisions if they are unsure of their goals. Helping clients set meaningful, achievable goals will give them the confidence they need to begin making more and better decisions in their lives.

*Resources.* Providing a list of resources to clients such as books, articles, homework, or online assessments will give them the tools they need to effectively solve their problems and achieve their goals.

*Alternatives.* Many clients are cognitively unable to successfully navigate their way through the normal decision-making process. Providing alternatives and other problem-solving options for clients will help them stay grounded and feel empowered to make decisions.

*Commitment to action.* Talking about problems all day does not do anything to help solve them unless there is a plan in place to act. Getting clients to commit to a plan of action will help ensure growth toward their goals.

*Evaluation.* Every plan of action also needs a commitment to evaluate that plan. Taking time to evaluate and sometimes tweak the course of action developed in counseling will help clients stay on track and continue making progress in their ability to solve problems (Stone, 1999).

**Conclusion.** The decision-making and problem-solving processes can be quite difficult, particularly for those struggling with emotional and psychological problems. Professional counselors must step into the pain, suffering, and confusion of their clients' lives and be positive, godly influences to help them make biblically based decisions.

Ryan A. Carboneau
Laura Faidley

### REFERENCES

Clinton, T., & Ohlschlager, G. (2002). *Competent Christian Counseling: Foundations and Practice of Compassionate Soul Care* (Vol. 1). New York, NY: WaterBrook Press.

Corey, G., Corey, M., & Callanan, P. (2007). *Issues and Ethics in the Helping Professions* (7th ed.). Pacific Grove, CA: Brooks/Cole.

Cormier, W. H., & Cormier, L. S. (2008). *Interviewing Strategies for Helpers: Fundamental Skills and Cognitive Behavioral Interventions* (6th ed.). Pacific Grove, CA: Brooks/Cole.

Egan, G. (2009). *The Skilled Helper: A Problem Management Approach to Helping* (9th ed.). Pacific Grove, CA: Brooks/Cole.

Stone, H. (1999). Problem Solving. In D. G. Benner & P. C. Hill (Eds.), *Baker Encyclopedia of Psychology and Counseling* (2nd ed.). Grand Rapids, MI: Baker Books.

## RESPONSIBILITY

**Description.** Responsibility incorporates self-discipline, follow-through, and pursuing excellence in one's activities and obligations. Covey (2004) defines *responsibility* as having the ability to choose one's own responses, owning them rather than blaming people or circumstances for them. Because responsibility is inextricably linked to the privilege of freedom, one must bear the burden of responsibility. Acting responsibly requires behavioral constraint while attending to fairness, expectancies, and social rules (Bierhoff & Auhagen, 2001), whereas avoiding responsibility reduces the burden of self-control and accountability. Regarded as a sign of maturity (Cloud & Townsend, 2001; Greenberger, Josselson, Knerr, & Knerr, 1974) and mental health (Jensen & Bergin, 1988), responsibility has clinical merit (Doherty, 1995; Nicholas, 1994).

*Personal responsibility.* Each person is endowed with personal responsibility as a result of being created in God's image and bestowed the right to steward the earth on God's behalf. Jones and Butman (1991) call this *responsible dominion.* Specifically, personal responsibility can be categorized into three types (Dworkin, 1981): *role responsibility*, or taking ownership and possessing self; *causal responsibility*, in which choices influence or determine the well-being of self or another; and *liability responsibility*, in which one's choices may have undesirable consequences. Jesus also indicated personal responsibility by linking all feelings, thoughts, and actions as the sprout of the heart. A responsible person recognizes that other people and circumstances do not create one's attitude; rather, they reveal it. Even though we have the ability to self-manage, the Fall conceived a penchant for avoiding responsibility (see Gen. 3:9-12), so we justify our actions and make excuses to shield ourselves of culpability. Our fallen nature, in concert with our character, influences whether we are prone to accept responsibility. Research shows that we often accept responsibility only when it is a last alternative (Baumeister, Chesner, Sanders, & Tice, 1988).

*Social responsibility.* Human social responsibility has been examined with prosocial behavior and victim responsibility. Prosocial behavior refers to voluntary actions targeted at benefiting another. Latané and Darley (1970) investigated why people help others and found that participants who believed they were the only ones able to help felt responsible and provided assistance. People are less likely to hold a victim responsible if they relate to the victim (Bell, Kuriloff, & Lottes, 1994) but may respond with disgust if they consider the victim at fault (Weiner, 1980). Sadly, this same pattern is common with highly conservative religious individuals (Jackson & Esses, 1997).

**In Counseling.** Responsibility holds significance among most counseling approaches, though its definition is not always the same. Doherty (1995) argued that counselors value moral responsibility over the current values of unrestricted, autonomous self-expression. Seligman (1994) notes that all effective counseling has two things in common: a forward-looking perspective and requiring that the client assume responsibility.

Because of personal responsibility, we are in a position to constructively change, yielding hope. Therefore, counselors are tasked with helping clients recognize their ability to choose (i.e., free will) where they have control, identifying situations where responsibility is being shunned, examining and removing justifications for actions, and encouraging them to own their internal experiences and behavior. Christian counselors also help clients identify sinful thoughts so the clients may confess and repent in order to bring about change. In fact, the act of confession alone forces one to assume responsibility.

The value of teaching personal and social responsibility has been championed from diverse perspectives. Britzman (2005) advocated for responsibility to be taught in the schools, and it has been included among the six pillars of character in the educational program Character Counts (charactercounts.org). Stelter and Whisner (2007) describe a successful program to build personal and social responsibility for criminal offenders suffering with mental illness.

John C. Thomas

## REFERENCES


Baumeister, R. F., Chesner, S. P., Sanders, P. S., & Tice, D. M. (1988). Who's in charge here? Group leaders do lend help in emergencies. *Personality and Social Psychology Bulletin, 14,* 17-22.

Bell, S. T., Kuriloff, P. J., & Lottes, I. (1994). Understanding attributions of blame in stranger rape and date rape situations: An examination of gender, race, identification, and students' social perceptions of rape victims. *Journal of Applied Social Psychology, 24,* 1719-1734.

Bierhoff, H. W., & Auhagen, A. E. (2001). Responsibility as a fundamental human phenomenon. In A. E. Auhagen & H. W. Bierhoff (Eds.), *Responsibility: The Many Faces of a Social Phenomenon.* New York, NY: Routledge.

Britzman, M. J. (2005). Improving our moral landscape via character education: An opportunity for school counselor leadership. *Professional School Counseling, 8*(3), 293-295.

Cloud, H., & Townsend, J. (2001). *How People Grow: What the Bible Reveals About Personal Growth.* Grand Rapids, MI: Zondervan.

Covey, S. (2004). *The 7 Habits of Highly Effective People.* New York, NY: Free Press.

Doherty, W. J. (1995). *Soul Searching: Why Psychotherapy Must Promote Moral Responsibility.* New York, NY: Basic Books.

Dworkin, G. (1981). Voluntary health risks and public policy. *Hastings Center Report, 11*(5), 26-31.

Giacalone, R. A., & Thompson, K. R. (2006). Business ethics and social responsibility education: Shifting the worldview. *Academy of Management, Learning, & Education, 5,* 266-277.

Greenberger, E., Josselson, R., Knerr, C., & Knerr, B. (1974). The measurement and structure of psychosocial maturity. *Journal of Youth and Adolescence, 4,* 127-143.

Jackson, L. M., & Esses, V. M. (1997). Of scripture and ascription: The relation between religious fundamentalism and intergroup helping. *Personality and Social Psychology Bulletin, 23,* 893-906.

Jensen, J. P., & Bergin, A. E. (1988). Mental health values of professional therapists: A national interdisciplinary survey. *Professional Psychology: Research and Practice, 19,* 290-297.

Jones, S. L., & Butman, R. E. (1991). *Modern Psychotherapies.* Downers Grove, IL: IVP Academic.

Latané, B., & Darley, J. M. (1970). *The Unresponsive Bystander: Why Doesn't He Help?* New York, NY: Appleton-Century-Crofts.

Nicholas, M. W. (1994). *The Mystery of Goodness and the Positive Moral Consequences of Psychotherapy.* New York, NY: Norton.

Seligman, M. (1994). *What You Can Change and What You Can't.* New York, NY: Knopf.

Stelter, L., & Whisner, S. M. (2007). Building responsibility for self through meaningful roles: Occupational adaptation theory applied in forensic psychiatry. *Occupational Therapy in Mental Health, 23*(1), 69-84.

Weiner, B. (1980). *Judgments of Responsibility: A Foundation for a Theory of Social Conduct.* New York, NY: Guilford Press.

## RESTITUTION

**Description.** Restitution, a biblical principle discussed in both the Old and New Testaments, involves a wrongdoer providing compensation for loss or damage to the individual who was wronged. Restitution is also a basic principle of justice in our American legal system. By an offender making amends for wrongs done, restitution can help to promote reconciliation between the parties.

**Biblical Guidance.** The Old Testament law includes very specific guidance on the type of restitution required for various wrongs, including damage to property, fraud, and personal injury. "The one who takes the life of an animal shall make it good, life for life. If a man injures his neighbor, just as he has done, so it shall be done to him: fracture for fracture, eye for eye, tooth for tooth; just has he has injured a man, so it shall be inflicted to him" (Lev. 24:18-20 NASB). "Speak to the sons of Israel, When a man or woman commits any of the sins of mankind, acting unfaithfully against the Lord, and that person is guilty, then he shall confess his sins which he has committed, and he shall make restitution in full for his wrong and add to it one-fifth of it, and give it to him whom he has wronged" (Numbers 5:6-7 NASB).

Jesus acknowledged the principle behind the Old Testament law of restitution. Luke 19:1-10 describes the conversion of Zaccheus, a rich tax collector who had defrauded many. Luke records Zaccheus' determination to be a different man and Jesus' response to his offer of restitution: "Zaccheus stopped and said to the Lord, 'Behold, Lord, half of my possessions I will give to the poor, and if I have defrauded anyone of anything, I will give back four times as much.' And Jesus said to him, 'Today, salvation has come to this house, because he, too, is a son of Abraham'" (NASB). Zaccheus' act of restitution was more than the Old Testament law required. His action evidenced his salvation.

The apostle Paul wrote to Philemon, a wealthy slave owner who had previously found Christ's forgiveness under Paul's ministry. Onesimus, one of Philemon's slaves, had stolen valuables from Philemon and had run away to Rome, where he met Paul and was converted. In this short epistle, Paul urged Philemon to forgive Onesimus, but he also offered to pay any necessary restitution: "But if he has wronged you in any way or owes you anything, charge that to my account" (Phlm. 18 NASB).

**Application.** The counselor should teach the counselee biblical concepts of confession of sin, God's forgiveness of sin, and the importance of biblical restitution. A counselee should be encouraged to consider how restitution may be applicable to compensate or make whole an injured party as a result of the counselee's wrongful behavior.

Restitution can help to relieve a counselee of guilt associated with wrongful behavior, and it offers a path to heal broken relationships. Educate and encourage the counselee about the importance of restitution in interpersonal relationships. Dr. Everett Worthington cites studies showing that a person's emotional forgiveness could be stimulated as a result of a wrongdoer's sincere apology and fair restitution for his or her wrongs (Worthington, 2003, pp. 209-210). According to author Gary Chapman, research findings show restitution as being the "strongest evidence of the sincerity of an apology" (Chapman & Thomas, 2006, p. 56).

Finally, offer hope to the counselee who has wronged someone else. Explain that God can cause all things to work together for good in all situations and in ways we cannot imagine. Even though a wrong has been done, God can use the incident for his glory and to bless others. Remind the counselee of how Joseph consoled his brothers who sold him into slavery: "As for you, you meant evil against me, but God meant it for good in order to bring about this present result, to preserve many people alive" (Gen. 50:20 NASB).

JOHN SANDY

## REFERENCES

Bock, D. L. (1996). *Luke*. In Muck, T., Longman, T., III, Walton, J. H., Hubbard, J., Dearman, A., Peterson, E.,...Snodgrass, K. (Eds.), *The NIV Application Commentary*. Grand Rapids, MI: Zondervan.

Chapman, G., & Thomas, J. (2006). *The Five Languages of Apology*. Chicago, IL: Northfield.

McMinn, M. (1996). *Psychology, Theology and Spirituality in Christian Counseling*. Wheaton, IL: Tyndale.

Sande, K. (2004). *The Peacemaker* (3rd ed.). Grand Rapids, MI: Baker Books.

Worthington, E. L., Jr. (2003). *Forgiving and Reconciling*. Downers Grove, IL: InterVarsity Press.

## SELF-MONITORING

**DEFINITION.** Clients self-monitor when they observe their own behavior and record the emotional and environmental factors surrounding that behavior. Self-monitoring can help clients recognize and overcome triggers and cues related to such issues as weight loss, nutritional programs, addiction, time management, academic behaviors, procrastination, and anxiety. In self-monitoring exercises, clients record the problem behaviors (B), the controlling antecedents (A), and the consequences of the behaviors (C) (Cormier, Nurius, & Osborn, 2009; Cormier, Cormier, & Hackney, 2011).

**WHY IS SELF-MONITORING IMPORTANT?** Self-monitoring not only helps clients recognize the circumstances surrounding their problem behaviors but also helps them substantiate or even change the stories they tell their counselors about the problems and their severity. Any change program requires a full understanding of what is taking place before a therapeutic plan is developed to address the issue. In order for proper assessment to take place, it is always best to maintain the recorded behavior over a period of time. The record functions as a baseline from which to gauge behavior, and it also provides a platform for evaluation. Simply keeping track of one's behaviors has been found to be enough to change it. In fact, researchers have found self-monitoring to be an effective agent of change (Cormier et al., 2009).

**TWO FACTORS OF SELF-MONITORING.**

*Reliability.* The reliability and accuracy of the behavior being recorded can be crucial, especially when using self-monitoring as a way to reach goal behaviors (Cormier et al., 2009).

*Reactivity.* On the other hand, self-monitoring can be used as a treatment option to help clients facilitate change in behavior because of its potential reactivity. When this is the case, the reliability of the data is not as important. *Reactivity* means that the mere act of carefully studying one particular behavior over time is enough to promote change in it. For example, if a client is asked to monitor negative interactions with others, those negative interactions may begin to decline when the recording device (a voice recorder) is turned on. One of the difficulties with using self-monitoring for change is that the behavior typically changes only as long as the self-monitoring continues. Once the self-monitoring stops, so does the change in behavior (Cormier et al., 2009; Cormier et al., 2011).

**VARIABLES TO ENHANCING REACTIVITY.** Nelson (1977) defined eight variables that tend to increase the level and longevity of reactivity in self-monitoring.

1. *Motivation.* Clients willing to change recorded behavior will more likely show reactivity.
2. *Valence of target behaviors.* When the client perceives a behavior as positive, that behavior tends to increase. The inverse is also true; when a client perceives a behavior as negative, it tends to decrease.
3. *Type of target behaviors.* The kind of behavior being monitored can impact reactivity.
4. *Goals, reinforcement, and feedback.* Change is more likely to occur when a client sets a target goal and is reinforced with positive feedback for effective efforts.
5. *Timing of self-monitoring.* The timing of the recording can also play a role in enhanced reactivity. If behaviors are recorded long after they happen, important antecedents could be forgotten or minimized.
6. *Devices used for self-monitoring.* Highly visible devices for recording behavior tend to enhance reactivity more than do less visible ones.
7. *Number of target responses monitored.* The fewer behaviors that are monitored, the higher the reactivity.
8. *Schedule for self-monitoring.* Clients who record behavior more frequently are more likely to experience change than those who are less consistent (Cormier et al., 2009; Cormier et al., 2011).

Social psychologists have historically been concerned about intrapersonal processes that enhance reactivity, but recent research has focused more on the way interpersonal variables also play a key role in self-monitoring (Fitzsimons & Finkel, 2010; Kalavana, Maes, & De Gucht, 2010). Some studies suggest that interpersonal factors can decrease the chances of goal attainment because of social pressures that negatively affect self-control, or they can increase the probability of achieving self-monitoring goals because of the support of friends and loved ones (Fitzsimons & Finkel). In fact, self-regulation cognitions have been found to influence healthy and unhealthy eating habits of teenagers. One particular study has found that interpersonal factors (such as family environment and peer relationships) as well as intrapersonal variables of self-monitoring should be considered for enhancing adolescent eating habits (Kalavana et al.).

**Joshua Straub**

## REFERENCES


Cormier, S., Nurius, P. S., & Osborn, C. J. (2009). *Interviewing and Change Strategies for Helpers: Fundamental Skills and Cognitive Behavioral Interventions* (6th ed.). Belmont, CA: Brooks/Cole.

Cormier, W. H., Cormier, L. S., & Hackney, H. (2011). *Counseling Strategies and Interventions* (8th ed.). Columbus, OH: Merrill.

Fitzsimons, G. M., & Finkel, E. J. (2010). Interpersonal influences on self-regulation. *Current Directions in Psychological Science, 19*(2), 101-105.

Kalavana, T. V., Maes, S., & De Gucht, V. (2010). Interpersonal and self-regulation determinants of healthy and unhealthy eating behavior in adolescents. *Journal of Health Psychology, 15*(1), 44-52.

Nelson, R. O. (1977). Methodological issues in assessment via self-monitoring. In J. D. Cone & R. P. Hawkins (Eds.), *Behavioral Assessment: New Directions in Clinical Psychology.* New York, NY: Brunner/Mazel.


## SELF-EFFICACY AND GENERALIZATION

Generalization is the transferring of information and learning from one situation to another (Cormier, Nurius, & Osborn, 2009; Hill, 2009). Self-efficacy is people's belief in their own ability to control the way they function regardless of the environmental influences in their lives. Counseling creates a microcosm of what is happening in clients' lives and tests new ideas for change. Once clients develop a sense of mastery (self-efficacy), counselors encourage them to test out the new skills and strategies. This process, which brings things learned from the session into real, everyday life, is called *generalization*. Bandura is best known for his work on the social learning theory, an approach to human behavior and personality that attempts to bring together behaviorism and cognitive psychology (Bandura, 1986). Further research by Bandura developed into the idea of modeling and self-efficacy.

**Description.** Although self-efficacy and self-esteem appear to be related, they are conceptually distinct. Self-efficacy is based on the idea that people who perform effectively have high yet realistic expectations for themselves, while self-esteem has to do with individuals failing to recognize their worth (Cormier et al., 2009). For example, professional athletes visualize their success on the playing field, but those with low self-efficacy may only be able to think of what might go wrong. Their fear often debilitates them and causes a propensity to fail and to shy away from new attempts rather than succeeding in life. A person can have high self-efficacy and, at the same time, a low sense of self-esteem (Cormier & Cormier, 2008; Cormier et al., 2009).

**Purpose.** Counselors help clients grasp the idea of generalization and gain self-efficacy in order to give them the skills they need to become more confident about their ability to handle external influences in their lives. Generalization has to do with the way clients' past experiences affect their present behavior in similar circumstances. Counseling helps to generalize learning that takes place in the session and move it to everyday life (Hill, 2009; Young, 2009).

**Core Components.** Bandura (1997) suggested that self-efficacy is developed by four major sources: (a) actual performance accomplishments, (b) mind-body states, such as emotional arousal, (c) environmental experiences, such as vicarious learning, and (d) verbal instillation as a prelude to treatment. Developing self-efficacy from these four areas will produce change in clients' lives and empower them to become effective.

**Conclusion.** Working with clients to help generalize their learning and self-efficacy skills will bring lasting change to their lives. Changing people's self-efficacy changes their beliefs about themselves, and changing people's beliefs about themselves changes their destiny.

**Ryan A. Carboneau**

## REFERENCES


Bandura, A. (1986). *Social Foundations of Thought and Action: A Social Cognitive Theory.* Englewood, CA: Prentice-Hall.

Bandura, A. (1997). *Self-Efficacy: The Exercise of Self-Control.* New York, NY: Freeman.

Cormier, S., Nurius, P. S., & Osborn, C. J. (2009). *Interviewing and Change Strategies for Helpers: Fundamental Skills and Cognitive-Behavioral Interventions* (6th ed.). Belmont, CA: Brooks/Cole.

Cormier, W. H., & Cormier, L. S. (2008). *Interviewing Strategies for Helpers: Fundamental Skills and Cognitive-Behavioral Interventions* (6th ed.). Pacific Grove, CA: Brooks/Cole.

Hill, C. E. (2009). *Helping Skills: Facilitating Exploration, Insight, and Action* (3rd ed.). Washington, DC: American Psychological Association.

Young, M. E. (2009). *Learning the Art of Helping: Building Blocks and Techniques* (4th ed.). Upper Saddle River, NJ: Merrill.


## RESILIENCE

**Description.** Resilience is the process of adapting well in the face of adversity, trauma, tragedy, threats, and significant sources of stress. It is the ability to bounce back from difficult circumstances. Resilience is not a trait that people either have or do not have. Instead, resilience involves behaviors, thoughts, and actions that can be learned and cultivated (Higgins, 1994). Resilience is a skill and strength that is forged through adversity, not despite it. And as believers in Christ, we acknowledge God's intense and intimate participation in this process.

**Background.** Crises and difficult circumstances can potentially elicit the best in people. Higgins' (1994) study of resilient adults revealed hardiness developed because individuals were sorely tested through suffering and emerged stronger than they believed they would have otherwise been. As a result, they valued life greatly. Their behaviors reflected this change: They became more socially active, contributed in meaningful ways to their communities, and helped others facing adversity. Interestingly, half of these resilient people became professional counselors.

Strengths-based therapies are gaining recognition as increasing research in psychology, psychiatry, and sociology combine to show that most people, including young people, can bounce back from stress, risks, crises, and trauma to experience successful lives (Higgins, 1994; Kaufman & Zigler, 1987; Ungar, 2006; Walsh, 2002). Researchers have concluded that many people have a self-righting tendency that operates best when people have experienced resilience-building conditions during their lives.

**Assessment.** Incorporating resilience into counseling means that clients hear less about their susceptibility to harm and more about their ability to rebound effectively from adversity. We mental-health practitioners are tempted to stay focused on people's problems, including pathology and diagnosis. With problem-focused treatment models, we may see clients only as damaged persons in need of repair. They may also see themselves this way. Wolin and Wolin (1993), critical of this approach, called this conceptualization "the damage model." They describe how psychiatric instruction in the 1970s and 1980s taught that the cumulative effect of coping with life's difficulties takes an inevitable toll, resulting in symptoms and behavior problems described in the *Diagnostic and Statistical Manual of Mental Disorders*. In adolescence and adulthood, pathologies are layered upon each other, and eventually people are no better off than their troubled parents were.

Those who critique the damage model believe that "ultimately, the child-as-victim image diverted survivors away from the hard work of changing. The model left many who had traveled a considerable distance from the past, feeling like walking time bombs" (Wolin & Wolin, 1993). The premise that family troubles inevitably repeat themselves from one generation to the next, coupled with the model's omission of resilience, perhaps frightened survivors more than it helped them. There are remnants of this model lurking in the counseling field today. Pathogenic family labels, such as *enmeshed*, *alcoholic*, and *codependent*, may have helped to identify problems within family structures and increased clinical understanding and empathy, but they have done less about offering solutions. We move beyond such stereotypes when we search for individuals' and families' strengths and vulnerabilities, recognizing that healthy family systems are a tapestry of many colors, both dark and light.

In recognizing resilience within individuals or families, we assess for both risk and protective factors. Risk factors, such as low self-esteem, domestic violence, or substance abuse, interfere with one's ability to cope during stress. Research suggests that these factors, as well as certain physiological factors, contribute to poor problem solving, inability to recognize dangerous cues, and difficulty considering alternative options (Anthony, 2008; Fraser, Richman, & Galinsky, 1999; Martinez-Torteya, Bogat, von Eye, & Levendosky, 2009). On the other hand, protective or resiliency factors are strengths that help people cope with stressful life circumstances and increase the likelihood of rebounding from difficult situations. Protective factors include faith, morality, a sense of humor, insight, independence, the ability to connect/attach to others appropriately to form relationships, initiative, and creativity (Ungar & Liebenberg, 2008; Peters, Leadbeater, & McMahon, 2010). These resiliencies form a framework that gives individuals and families an edge in combating adversity.

Kobasa and colleagues (1985) found evidence that persons with hardy personalities possess three general characteristics: (a) the belief that they can control or influence events in their experience, providing a higher level of self-efficacy; (b) an ability to feel deeply involved or committed to the activities in their lives, including faith-based activities; and (c) anticipation of change as an exciting challenge to further development. Counseling techniques used to support the development of these characteristics involve cognitive strengthening skills, such as reframing.

**Treatment.** Walsh (1993, 2006) encourages a life-cycle perspective on individual and family development to fully understand resilience. She also points out that although adaptive functioning in childhood and adolescence is a good predictor of future adult outcomes, the role of early life experience in determining adult capacity to overcome adversity may be less important than previously assumed. These longitudinal studies suggest that adaptations that serve well at one stage of development may not be useful at later stages. New resiliencies are needed and learned along the way. Gender differences also present vulnerabilities at different developmental stages, with the greater risk occurring for boys in childhood and girls in adolescence (Elder, Caspi, & Nguyen, 1985; Werner & Smith, 1982). A pressing question remains: Why do some children leave troubled homes to lead satisfying lives and contribute to society in meaningful ways, and why do some not make this transition?

The difference is found in strengths and traits they discovered within—ones that were encouraged from without by those who role modeled, took an interest in them, and mentored them along the way. Therefore, the relational nature of individual resilience should not be underrated. Children's resilience to hardship is greater when they have access to at least one caring parent or caregiver or another supportive adult in their extended family or social world (Walsh, 1998, 2006; Peters et al., 2010). As Werner (1993) emphasizes, self-esteem and self-efficacy are promoted principally through supportive relationships.

Counselors are not the only people who can point out strengths and resiliencies to those in trouble, but they may be some of the first to do so. Assessment tools are available to help the clients and families identify their individual and corporate strengths (Rawana & Brownlee, 2009). As clients begin to recognize that amid their problems they also have God-given strengths, they are able to harness hope and confidence that healing and restoration can happen for them. The result is a demonstration of competence and an escape from lifelong mental distress.

Oftentimes persons are unaware of their resiliencies and either ignore or downplay them. But as counselors listen to clients' narratives, they can identify resiliencies and, through open-ended questioning, help clients discover the manifestations of these qualities. Helping clients reframe their stories to include application of their faith and belief in their identity in Christ catapults the ability to identify strengths, resiliencies, and responsibilities, and it ultimately leads to improved problem solving and a change in their behavior. Resilience is the picture of one's faith lived out in the midst of difficult circumstances, supported by moral and conscientious decision making.

**Cross-Cultural Issues.** In cross-cultural research, Coles noted the importance of moral and spiritual convictions that provide the courage people need to rise above hardships (Dugan & Coles, 1989; Peters et al., 2010). Similarly, in a landmark resilience study of at-risk Kauai children, Werner and Smith (1982) discovered that by their high school years, despite continual household chaos (including substance abuse, violence, and poverty), youth developed a belief that obstacles could be overcome. The vast majority went on to live productive lives. Werner and Smith discovered that despite the early childhood developmental challenges these children faced, they developed internal and external protective factors yielding long-term resilience.

**Spiritual Issues.** Crises and difficulties have the potential either to transform or to destroy us. God uses the fallout from difficult life circumstances and crises to refine and hone our understanding of his great love for us and his sovereignty in our lives. Although a crisis illumines our existing perspective on God, sometimes people determine what they believe about him based on their immediate crises or on their judgment of God's performance in their crises (Wright, 1997). As a result, a spiritual crisis can produce another opportunity to correct faulty theology or replace a potential abandonment of faith with renewed trust in one's Creator. God created each of us with the capacity to be resilient in the face of adversity. We need not look far in the Scriptures to see this.

Job is often the first example that arises when we think of adversity. Among many resilient responses, Job demonstrated insight in that he understood his friends were not giving him wise counsel. The independence, creativity, and initiative Esther mustered to manage her situation and carry out God's will is evidence of resiliency combined with deep understanding of the love of God for his people. Our theology and our understanding of psychology integrate as we consider these biblical models and so many others, and we recognize how God, in his sovereignty, provides us with the ability to respond in resilience to life's circumstances. The essence of his grace provides us with resiliency, the ability to bounce back and recover from adversity in life.

In light of biblical integration and as believers in Christ, resiliency assumes these truths:

1. God created us in his image (Gen. 1:27; 5:3).
2. We are of great value to God (Ps. 8:4-9; Mt.10:31).
3. God is sovereign and good (Ps. 31:19; 73:1; Eph. 1:23).
4. God seeks the best for us (Ps. 20:4; Jer. 29:11).
5. God in his wisdom allows human suffering (1 Pet. 4:12-13).
6. We have hope (Rom. 12:12, Eph. 1:18; Heb. 6:19; 10:23).
7. In our obedience, we surrender to the lordship of Christ (Pr.16:20; Phil. 3:13-14).

The Christian who incorporates resiliency into counseling seeks to uncover the strengths God has provided—those which people so often lose sight of—and helps others to see those strengths.

Inevitably, as we address life's difficulties, we simultaneously address the issue of suffering. Louis Smedes reminds us that the news is not all bad:

> We need to suffer the cussed wrongness of life in order to find its deep righteousness. We have to feel pain we do not want to feel, carry burdens we do not want to carry, put up with misery we do not want to put up with, cry tears we do not want to shed. If we feel no hurt now, we will, when it is all said and done, be the most miserable of all

people...in the end it will be alright with us only if we have felt some of life's wrongness (Smedes, 1982, p. 88).

These words ring true; in suffering we experience the conflict of knowing God has allowed it and not knowing how we will make it through apart from his mercy and grace. In suffering we have the opportunity to discover the dialectic of suffering hardship as we explore God's personal gifts to us of resilience.

**Marian C. Eberly**

## REFERENCES


Anthony, E. L. (2008). Cluster profiles of youths living in urban poverty: Factors affecting risk and resilience. *Social Work Research, 32*(1), 6-17.

Dugan, T., & Coles, R. (Eds.). (1989). *The Child in Our Times: Studies in the Development of Resiliency*. New York, NY: Brunner/Mazel.

Dunst, C. J., Trivette, C. M., & Deal, A. G. (1988). *Enabling and Empowering Families: Principles and Guidelines for Practice*. Cambridge, MA: Brookline Books.

Elder, G., Caspi, A., & Nguyen, T. V. (1985). Resourceful and vulnerable children: Family influences in hard times. In R. K. Silbereisen & K. Eyferth (Eds.), *Development in Context*. New York, NY: Springer.

Felsman, J. K., & Vaillant, G. (1987). Resilient children as adults: A 40-year study. In E. J. Anthony & B. Cohler (Eds.), *The Invulnerable Child*. New York, NY: Guilford Press.

Fraser, M. W., Richman, J. M., & Galinsky, M. J. (1999). Risk, protection, and resilience: Toward a conceptual framework for social work practice. *Social Work Research, 23*(3), 131-143.

Higgins, G. O. (1994). *Resilient Adults: Overcoming a Cruel Past*. San Francisco, CA: Jossey-Bass.

Kaufman, J., & Zigler, E. (1987). Do abused children become abusive parents? *American Journal of Orthopsychiatry, 57*, 186-192.

Kobasa, S. (1985). Stressful life events, personality, and health: An inquiry into hardiness. In A. Monat & R. Lazarus (Eds.), *Stress and Coping* (2nd ed.). New York, NY: Columbia University Press.

Martinez-Torteya, C., Bogat, G. A., von Eye, A., & Levendosky, A. A. (2009). Resilience among children exposed to domestic violence: The role of risk and protective factors. *Child Development, 80*(2), 562-577.

Peters, R. D., Leadbeater, B., & McMahon, R. J. (2010). *Resilience in Children, Families, and Communities: Linking Context to Practice and Policy*. New York, NY: Plenum.

Prince-Embury, S. (2007). *Resiliency Scales for Adolescents: A Profile of Personal Strengths* (2006). San Antonio, TX: Harcourt Assessment.

Rawana, E., & Brownlee, K. (2009). Making the possible probable: A strength-based assessment and intervention framework for clinical work with parents, children, and adolescents. *Families in Society, 90*(3), 255-260.

Smedes, L. (1982). *How Can It Be All Right When Everything Is All Wrong?* San Francisco, CA: Harper & Row.

Ungar, M. (2006). *Strengths-Based Counseling with At-Risk Youth*. Thousand Oaks, CA: Corwin Press.

Ungar, M., & Liebenberg, L. (2008). *Resilience in Action: Working with Youth Across Cultures and Contexts*. Toronto, Canada: University of Toronto.

Walsh, F. (1993). Conceptualization of normal family processes. In F. Walsh (Ed.), *Normal Family Processes* (2nd ed.). New York, NY: Guilford Press.

Walsh, F. (1998). *Strengthening Family Resilience*. New York, NY: Guilford Press.

Walsh, F. (2002). A family resilience framework: Innovative practice applications. *Family Relations, 51*(2), 130-137.

Walsh, F. (2006). *Strengthening Family Resilience* (2nd ed.). New York, NY: Guilford Press.

Werner, E. E. (1993). Risk, resilience, and recovery: Perspectives from the Kauai longitudinal study. *Development and Psychopathology, 5*, 503-515.

Werner, E. E., & Smith, R. S. (1982). *Vulnerable but Invincible: A Study of Resilient Children*. New York, NY: McGraw-Hill.

Wolin, S. J., & Wolin, S. (1993). *The Resilient Self: How Survivors of Troubled Families Rise Above Adversity*. New York, NY: Villard.

Wright, H. N. (1997). *Resilience: Rebounding When Life's Upsets Knock You Down*. Ann Arbor, MI: Servant/Vine Books.

*Part 3*

# Various Kinds of Disorders

9

# COUNSELING BIBLICAL AND SPIRITUAL ISSUES

## ABORTION

**Normal Processes.** Abortion rates in America have gone down over the past 20 years. According to research by the Guttmacher Institute (2011) 1.21 million abortions were performed in 2008, down from 1.31 million in 2000. The abortion rate of American women was 1.9% in 2005, down from 2.7% in 1990 (Jones, Zolna, Henshaw, & Finer, 2008).

Pregnancy is not a disease or an illness, but a natural event. Women's bodies are designed to nurture and sustain the gift of life. The psychological relationship between the mother and her unborn child is triggered by the woman's internal physical and hormonal changes and also by her external support system and culture.

For most women, the first trimester is a time of either anticipation and excitement about the pregnancy or anger and fear that it has occurred. Ambivalent feelings are common: The mother marvels at the mysterious fact that her body is capable of producing life, yet she may also feel overwhelmed by the responsibilities of caring for another human being. As the pregnancy progresses, the mother may have both positive and negative feelings about the changes in the shape of her body.

The third trimester may include anxiety about the birth, the health of the baby, the family's adjustment, and finances. At the same time, the woman feels excitement and anticipation about the birth of her baby and the beginning of a new phase in her life.

By the moment of birth, when the child is placed in a mother's arms, the mystery, wonder, and excitement all culminate in a powerful bonding process as the mother joyfully welcomes a precious new life into the world. We could say that women require the full nine months of pregnancy to embark on the emotional and psychological process that accompanies motherhood. Together, mother and child experience a dramatic and rapid developmental transformation.

**Culture and Prevalence.** When we look behind the rhetoric of choice, we can more honestly ask, whose choice is it? Research indicates that in 95% of all abortions, the male partner plays a central role in the decision. Other studies reveal that up to 80% of women would give birth if given support. In a hearing, a former clinic security guard testified that women were routinely threatened or abused by the men who brought them to clinics. Too often, abortion is the choice of someone else in a woman's life. In fact, most women say they had no choice but abortion (Political Research Associates [PRA], 2007).

Shockingly, murder is the number one cause of death among pregnant women. Men who have been convicted of the murder of their pregnant partners cite not wanting to pay child support as the primary motive. Such disturbing national statistics clearly indicate a high level of coercion driving women into unwanted abortions. Without the consistent support of the baby's father, the mother's own family, or a counselor or a crisis pregnancy center, many mothers fear they will not have the resources to provide for their children. Given the poverty rates among single parents and the challenges they face, this is a major contributing problem (PRA, 2007).

In far too many cases, behind every woman having an abortion we find a host of people who are very much involved in her "choice" and are often manipulative in their persuasion. For instance, a younger woman's parents may threaten her with a withdrawal of love or even eviction if she does not abort. School, mental health, or clinic workers may use the power of their positions to make abortion seem the only rational and mature decision. This is especially problematic when there is a hint of health problems with the unborn child. In these cases, the pressure is often quite strong to abort. Incredibly, 95% of women who are faced with severe fetal deformities and who are offered perinatal hospice choose this form of support as more humane and emotionally desirable. This avoids the complicated grief brought on by late-term abortions, which is a horrific experience for both mother and baby (Ring-Cassidy & Gentles, 2002).

**The Trauma of Abortion.** When a mother is abruptly and violently disconnected from her child, a natural trauma occurs. She undergoes an unnatural death event. In many cases, she has violated her moral ethics and natural instincts. There has been a crushing blow to her image of a mother who nurtures, protects, and sustains life. Countless women have been shattered by the trauma of abortion, which they experience as a cruel and degrading procedure. They commonly suffer grief, sadness, heartache, guilt, shame, and anger (Burke & Reardon, 2002).

To cope with the pain, they may try to numb themselves with alcohol and drugs, or they may attempt to master their trauma through repetitions of it. Some reenact their abortion pain through promiscuity and repeat abortions, trapped in traumatic cycles of abandonment and rejection. Others stuff their feelings through eating disorders or suffer panic attacks, mental depression, anxiety, and thoughts of suicide. Some have suffered permanent physical and reproductive damage that rendered them unable to have children in the future. The Silent No More Awareness Campaign (www.silentnomoreawareness.org) has compelling personal testimonies of abortion's negative impact.

Abortion is a death experience. It is the demise of human potential, relationship, responsibility, maternal attachment, connectedness, and innocence. Such a loss is rarely experienced without conflict and ambivalence (Ring-Cassidy & Gentles, 2002). It would be foolish to think that getting over it could be free from complication.

**Treatment.** Abortion touches on three central issues of a woman's self-concept: her sexuality, morality, and maternal identity (Burke & Reardon, 2002). It also involves the loss of a child, or at least the loss of an opportunity to have a child. In either case, this loss must be confronted, processed, and grieved.

Because abortion is legal, it is presumed to be safe. Indeed, it is commonly identified as a woman's right. This right, or privilege, is supposed to liberate women from the burden of unwanted pregnancies. Abortion promises to provide them with relief, not grief and depression. However, when women are assaulted by their own natural reactions to their loss, they don't understand what's wrong with them. Many women go into treatment for depression, anxiety, or addictions, but they simply don't understand the roots of their illness. In many cases they are diagnosed and drugged but not led on a path to healing and recovery (Ring-Cassidy & Gentles, 2002).

Unresolved memories and feelings about the abortion may erupt years later in unexpected ways. Suppressed and unresolved emotions will demand one's attention sooner or later, often through the development of subsequent emotional or behavioral disturbances.

Professor David Fergusson, a researcher at Christchurch School of Medicine in New Zealand, wanted to prove that abortion doesn't have any psychological consequences. He was surprised to find that women who have had abortions were 1.5 times more likely to suffer mental illness and 2 to 3 times more likely to abuse alcohol and/or drugs. Fergusson followed 500 women from birth to age 25. He noted, "Those having an abortion had elevated rates of subsequent mental health problems, including depression (46% increase), anxiety, suicidal behaviors and substance use disorders" (Fergusson, 2006, p. 16). This research was published in the *Journal of Child Psychiatry and Psychology*.

An exhaustive review of many other studies and clinical experience indicates that for many women, the souvenir coping styles that followed their traumatic experiences with abortion included sexual dysfunctions, eating disorders, increased smoking, panic and anxiety disorders, and an addiction to abusive relationships (Ring-Cassidy & Gentles, 2002).

**Biblical and Spiritual Issues.** Women and men who have suffered the loss of a child through abortion need to know that hope and healing are available. They need to know they are not alone and that the Lord in his love desires to comfort the brokenhearted and restore peace and joy.

Rachel's Vineyard is the largest postabortion ministry in the world. This healing program offers a unique sensory-based treatment that integrates emotional, psychological, and spiritual dimensions. This distinct program provides an exceptional and effective recovery process for victims of trauma—even those who have spent years in talk therapy but still struggle to move beyond their traumatic experience.

Other ministries offering help to those seeking pro-life options include crisis pregnancy centers, pregnancy support centers, and Christian pro-life organizations. Heartbeat International and Care Net provide the largest network of crisis pregnancy centers in North America with more than 1,100 facilities offering lifesaving services and support to reach the hurting and broken with the hope of Jesus Christ. In addition, the Silent No More Awareness Campaign holds events and offers online resources and support to hurting men and women and raises awareness to the entire Christian community about the effects of abortion.

Ultimately, women who have suffered an abortion do need therapy for the soul. They need to know and live in the reality that "there is now no condemnation for those who are in Christ Jesus" (Rom. 8:1). The process of healing begins with accepting God's forgiveness and learning to forgive themselves. It is critical that postabortive women be accepted into the healing community of the body of Christ. Christian counselors have an unprecedented opportunity to lead the church in responding with Christlike love and acceptance rather than judgment.

**Theresa Burke**

### REFERENCES


Burke, T., & Reardon, D. (2002). *Forbidden Grief: The Unspoken Pain of Abortion.* Warren, MI: Acorn Books.

Fergusson, D. M. (2006). Abortion in young women and subsequent mental health. *Journal of Child Psychology and Psychiatry, 47*(1), 16-24.

Guttmacher Institute. (2011). *State Facts About Abortion: New York.* Retrieved from http://www.guttmacher.org/pubs/sfaa/new_york.html

Jones, R. K., Zolna, M. R. S., Stanley, K., & Finer, L. B. (2008) Abortion in the United States: Incidence and access to services, 2005. *Perspectives on Sexual and Reproductive Health,* 40(1), 6-16.

Political Research Associates. (2007). *Forced Abortion in America.* Retrieved from http://www.stopforcedabortions.org/docs/ForcedAbortions.pdf

Ring-Cassidy, E., & Gentles, I. (2002). *Women's Health After Abortion: The Medical and Psychological Evidence.* Toronto, Canada: The deVeber Institute.


## ABUSE

**Description.** Abuse knows no boundaries—racial, gender, age, or economic. Its damage cuts a broad swath of destruction across every culture. And within each category of abuse—physical, emotional, verbal, sexual, and spiritual—people can be victimized in a myriad of ways. The body, soul, and spirit are all impacted.

Whatever the abuse, one common thread links a victim to all other victims—feeling powerless. For the abused, this thread is often perceived as an unbreakable bond. The victim lives with a sense of powerlessness long after the victimization stops and thus adopts a victim mentality.

Victimized children are truly powerless to prevent abuse, but as adults they needlessly assume the same powerless state. They live as though "once a victim, always a victim." Consequently, victims live with a wounded sense of self-worth, always exaggerating abusers' power and their own helplessness. This understandable but flawed dynamic sets up further incidences of abuse.

Abuse is severe misuse or mistreatment that injures or damages a person. All forms of abuse damage people's sense of dignity and God-given worth. Abuse is intentional, not accidental.

Abuse can be either covert or overt: *Covert* abuse is displayed by uncaring parents who repeatedly ignore their children. *Overt* abuse is demonstrated by cruel parents who belittle or even beat their children. For example, King David's daughter, Tamar, suffered overt abuse when Amnon raped her. She suffered covert abuse when David failed to execute justice and hold Amnon accountable (2 Sam. 13). All forms of abuse wound the spirit of a person. Proverbs, the biblical book of wisdom, poses this rhetorical question: "A crushed spirit who can bear?" (Pr. 18:14).

**Emotional Abuse.** Emotional abuse is the unseen fallout from all other forms of abuse—physical, mental, verbal, sexual, and spiritual. Such abuse strikes at the very core of who we are, whittling away at our sense of worth, suffocating our spirits, and crushing our confidence. The Bible says, "A cheerful heart is good medicine, but a crushed spirit dries up the bones" (Pr. 17:22).

Emotional abuse, or psychological mistreatment, is any ongoing, negative behavior used to control or hurt another person. The damage from emotional abuse can last far longer than damage from any other kind of abuse. A broken arm will soon heal, but a broken heart may last a lifetime. After extended periods of emotional abuse, many victims lose hope, feeling that life is not worth living. The Bible states it this way: "Hope deferred makes the heart sick" (Pr. 13:12).

Emotional abuse can be passive-aggressive—a means of indirect, underhanded control. These abusers express their anger through nonassertive, covert behavior. To gain control in a relationship, they often use manipulation as a means of placing themselves in a position of dependence. Then, with underlying anger, they become faultfinders of the very people on whom they depend (Bustanoby & Bustanoby, 1981, p. 148).

Victims of passive-aggressive abusers feel perplexed and dismayed at being the target of such manipulative, punitive behavior. Friends of passive-aggressive abusers often become enmeshed in trying to comfort or console abusers in response to their claims of unjust treatment and their inability to handle life on their own. Passive-aggressive abusers need to recognize and resolve their very real anger and take to heart God's warning: "Do not be quickly provoked in your spirit, for anger resides in the lap of fools" (Eccle. 7:9).

**Verbal Abuse.** Verbal abuse is a form of overt emotional abuse. A skilled lumberjack carefully wields the ax, repeatedly chopping the same spot until the tall tree falls. Similarly, a skilled verbal abuser uses his tongue like a sharp weapon to hack away at another person, striking blow after blow, wielding derogatory words that cut the heart and sever the soul. Psalm 52:2 paints the picture well: "You who practice deceit, your tongue plots destruction; it is like a sharpened razor."

Verbal abuse is the systematic, ongoing use of harmful words or degrading tones in an attempt to control or dominate another person. The psalmist cries out, "You love every harmful word, you deceitful tongue!" (Ps. 52:4).

Verbal abusers injure the feelings of others with reviling, insulting, or contemptuous words. The Hebrew word for "revile" is *gadaph*, from a root word that means "cut" or "wound." The psalmist said, "I live in disgrace all day long, and my face is covered with shame at the taunts of those who reproach and revile me" (Ps. 44:15-16). These abusers often seek to injure the hearts of others using such tactics as backbiting, barbs, belittling talk, sarcasm, slander, and slurs. The Bible says this about verbal abusers: "You love evil rather than good, falsehood rather than speaking the truth" (Ps. 52:3).

**Spiritual Abuse.** Spiritual abuse is the mistreatment of a person by someone in a position of spiritual authority, diminishing that person's spiritual vitality and growth (Johnson & VanVonderen, 1991, p. 20). At the core of spiritual abuse is excessive control of others, such as religious leaders who use manipulation to compel attendance, use guilt to get people to give more money, take emotional or sexual advantage in the name of comfort or compassion, accuse those who disagree with them of being rebellious against God, or demand absolute, unquestioned obedience regardless of whether it is reasonable or biblical.

Spiritual abuse is the use of religious words or acts to manipulate someone for personal gain or to achieve a personal agenda, thereby harming that person's walk with God.

Spiritual abuse is often broadly defined as any misuse of Scripture where truth is twisted. The victim in this case may not be an individual, but truth itself. For example, when cult leaders use the Scripture "love one another" (Jn. 13:34) to justify having sexual relations with other men's wives, they are guilty of Scripture twisting—they take the Scripture out of context. This is clearly adultery, which is forbidden by God

**Childhood Sexual Abuse.** When a child is a victim of sexual abuse, the damage has long-reaching tentacles that can strangle the life of a child. Nothing wounds the heart of a child more than this type of abuse.

Sexual abuse of a child is any physical, visual, or verbal interaction with a minor by an older child or adult whose purpose is sexual stimulation or sexual satisfaction. This betrayal is almost always committed by someone the child knows or with whom the child has frequent contact (Hancock & Burton Mains, 1997, p. 22). Such close contact sets the stage for a child to be all the more vulnerable to a perpetrator. The Bible is not silent about such a perpetrator: "Like a lion in cover he lies in wait. He lies in wait to catch the helpless; he catches the helpless and drags them off in his net" (Ps. 10:9).

Incest is sexual interaction with a child or an adolescent by a member of the child's family: any blood relative, adoptive relative, or relative by marriage or remarriage (Hancock and Burton Mains, 1997, pp. 16-17). The Bible is not silent about the act of incest: "No one is to approach any close relative to have sexual relations" (Lev. 18:6).

Child victims have no choice about being abused and no ability to stop the abuse unless they are trained to resist. They feel overwhelmed, powerless, and totally alone, and they are defenseless against the resulting emotional pain. The Bible describes God's concern for victims: "You, God, see the trouble of the afflicted; you consider their grief and take it in hand. The victims commit themselves to you;...You, Lord, hear the desire of the afflicted; you encourage them, and you listen to their cry" (Ps. 10:14,17).

**Conclusion.** The challenge of every victim is not just to move from sufferer to survivor (a survivor could be someone half-dead, barely washed up on the beach!), but rather to move from victim to victor. When victims allow Christ to take control of their lives, they can experience his power to become overcomers, for Jesus said, "In this world you will have trouble. But take heart! I have overcome the world" (Jn. 16:33).

Victims relive their past by moving from one abusive relationship to another. They live in denial and refuse to face the dark hidden secret of the past. They don't know how to find help and healing and have little hope of receiving either.

Survivors realize their need to face the past in order to heal from the past. They are not yet healed but are working to resolve false guilt, shame, unforgiveness, and anger. They are seeking to gain mental, emotional, and spiritual healing. Recovery, then, often requires targeted help and support and may occur incrementally for as long as hidden wounds surface.

Victors have conquered the past and are no longer in bondage to the pain. They develop an intimate relationship with Christ, giving him control, and they experience the desire and reality of reaching out and ministering to others. The Bible promises the hope of victory for every victim of abuse: "We are more than conquerors through him who loved us" (Rom. 8:37).

June Hunt

## REFERENCES

Bustanoby, A., & Bustanoby, F. (1981). *Just Talk to Me: The Principles and Practice of Communication in Marriage.* Grand Rapids, MI: Zondervan.

Hancock, M., & Burton Mains, K. (1997). *Child Sexual Abuse: Hope for Healing* (Rev. ed.). Wheaton, IL: Shaw.

Johnson, D., & VanVonderen, J. (1991). *The Subtle Power of Spiritual Abuse: Recognizing and Escaping Spiritual Manipulation and False Spiritual Authority Within the Church.* Minneapolis, MN: Bethany House.

## ANGER

**Description.** Anger is a God-given emotion that can be experienced and expressed in ways that can be healthy or unhealthy. The Bible has a lot to say about the emotion of anger. In fact, next to love, anger is the most frequently mentioned emotion in the Bible (Oliver & Oliver, 2007). It is first mentioned in Genesis 4:5, and the last reference to anger is found in Revelation 19:15. In the Old Testament alone, anger is mentioned 455 times, usually in reference to God's anger.

Anger is the most powerful and the least understood of all the emotions (Carter, 2003). Of all of the God-given emotions, anger is the one most likely to be viewed as negative and dangerous. Virtually all of the headlines involving anger relate to its destructive effects. This leads many to assume that all anger is negative and unhealthy; they don't understand that there can be healthy expressions of anger (Oliver & Oliver, 2007; Lowenstein, 2004).

**Common Disguises.** Of all the emotions, anger is the one most likely to be labeled as something else. What are some of the most common disguises anger can take? When we begrudge, scorn, insult, and disdain others; or when we are annoyed, offended, bitter, fed up, repulsed, irritated, infuriated, incensed, mad, sarcastic, uptight, or cross; or when we experience frustration, indignation, fury, wrath, or rage, we are probably experiencing some form of anger. Anger can also manifest itself in criticism, silence, intimidation, hypochondria, numerous petty complaints, depression, gossip, sarcasm, blame, and passive-aggressive behaviors, such as stubbornness, halfhearted efforts, forgetfulness, and laziness (Oliver & Oliver, 2007).

**Physiological Effects.** Unhealthy anger also has physical effects. A rapidly growing body of research strongly suggests that ignoring anger has detrimental effects on your health. Blood vessels constrict and heart rate and blood pressure increase, eventually leading to the destruction of heart muscle

(Hightower, 2005). A 12-year longitudinal study of 10,000 people revealed that those who suppressed anger were more than twice as likely to die of heart disease as those who expressed anger in healthy ways. A 25-year study showed that people with high hostility scores had higher incidence of heart disease; they were also six times more likely to die by age 50 from all causes of disease than their low-scoring counterparts. Other research over a 20-year period correlated higher hostility scores with increased rates of not only coronary heart disease but also cancer, accidents, and suicide (Wright & Oliver, 2005).

**Anger and Sin.** Of all the emotions, anger is the one most likely to be labeled a sin. However, Paul destroys the myth that all anger is sin when he says, "Be angry, and yet do not sin; do not let the sun go down on your anger, and do not give the devil an opportunity" (Eph. 4:26-27 NASB). Paul makes it clear that it is normal to experience anger and that we can choose to express that anger in ways that are not sinful (Chapman, 2007; Oliver & Oliver, 2007).

**Assessment.** What is anger? Anger is a strong feeling of irritation or displeasure. It is a state of readiness. Anger is energy that can involve emotional, physical, and mental arousal. When we experience the emotion of anger, adrenalin and noradrenalin are pumped into our central and peripheral nervous systems. Our body goes on the alert.

What causes anger? Anger is almost always a secondary emotion that is experienced in response to one or more primary emotions, including hurt (usually from the past), frustration (usually because of something in the present), and/or fear (usually of something in the future). It can often be perceived as a threat to the self, to someone we love, or to something that is important to us. When people experience anger, they tend to react to that secondary emotion rather than identify and respond to the primary emotion that is the source of the anger (Oliver & Oliver, 2007).

The impact of anger on ourselves and those around us depends on the degree to which we allow the anger-energy to control us. A more healthy response is to invest that same energy in identifying and understanding the cause and to choose a healthy solution. Unhealthy anger reacts and is often driven by bitterness, revenge, resentment, and desire for getting even with or punishing others. Allowing the secondary emotion of anger to control our thinking or our behavior is always unhealthy. Anger can be dealt with in passive ways such as stuffing, suppressing, repressing, denying, or ignoring both the anger and the primary emotions that are causing it (Oliver & Oliver, 2007). Active, unhealthy reactions to anger include turning it in on yourself or dumping it on someone else.

**Healthy Expressions.** To deal with anger effectively, start by being aware of it. When are you most likely to experience it, and how are you most likely to express it? Determine at the outset whether you are going to let the anger energy control you and push you to react or you are going to listen to your emotions and find out what the anger might really be about, which will help lead to a healthy response. The next step is to define it—identify the primary emotion and triggers. Then choose your response (Carter, 2003).

Healthy anger responds rather than reacts. It is constructive. It is proactive and not merely reactive. It sheds more light than heat. The energy of anger, when wisely invested, can provide greater focus and intensity and lead to greater productivity. Martin Luther said, "When I am angry I can write, pray, and preach well, for then my whole temperament is quickened, my understanding sharpened, and all mundane vexations and temptations are gone."

Gary J. Oliver

## REFERENCES


Carter, L. (2003). *The Anger Trap: Free Yourself from the Frustrations that Sabotage Your Life.* San Francisco, CA: Jossey-Bass.

Chapman, G. (2007). *Anger: Handling a Powerful Emotion in a Healthy Way.* Chicago, IL: Northfield.

Hightower, N. (2005). *Anger Bursting 101: The New ABCs for Angry Men and the Women Who Love Them.* Houston, TX: Bayou.

Lowenstein, L. F. (2004). Anger—has it a positive as well as negative value?: Recent research into causes, associated features, diagnosis and treatment, 1998–2003. *Journal of Human Behavior in the Social Environment, 93*(3), 21-40.

Oliver, G., & Oliver, C. (2007). *Mad About Us.* Minneapolis, MN: Bethany House.

Wright, H. N., & Oliver, G. J. (2005). *A Woman's Forbidden Emotion.* Ventura, CA: Regal Books.


## BITTERNESS

**Description and Prevalence.** *Bitterness* is a word frequently associated with a person's sense of taste and is often used to describe something that has an acrid, distasteful, or disagreeable flavor. Beyond this understanding, however, the term has also come to refer to a negative emotion people frequently experience when faced with distressing circumstances and/or mistreatment from others. It is an "attitude of *extended and intense anger and hostility*...often accompanied by resentment and a desire to 'get even'" (Clinton & Hawkins, 2007, p. 36).

Key components of bitterness include unresolved anger, the inability to grieve, an inability or unwillingness to face the reality that a certain relationship is never going to fulfill all of one's needs or hopes, and a lack of control (Clinton & Hawkins, 2007). Bitterness can manifest itself in a number of ways, such as obsessive thoughts of revenge, resentment, sarcasm, self-righteousness, unkind or critical comments, conflicts with others, controlling behavior, aggressiveness in relationships, and hostility (Clinton & Hawkins).

How does bitterness develop? Simply stated, bitterness is the direct result of a person's refusal, inability, or unwillingness to forgive another of an offense. This inability to forgive, if left unchecked, allows hurt and anger to grow until pain and resentment cloud the person's view of life (Lutzer, 1988). In reality, others may never do what one desires or expects them to, and they cannot be made to comply. One can only control himself or herself. If people were to accept these truths, much bitterness could be avoided.

Furthermore, bitterness is insidiously destructive on all levels: emotionally, physically, and spiritually (Getz, 1996). Like a cancer, bitterness "grows and grows until it destroys everything around it" (Jeffress, 1992, p. 95). Ironically, bitterness ultimately does less harm to the offender than it does to the person who has been offended, eventually "eating away at [what was a] soft heart and turning it into stone—hard and unyielding (Clinton & Hawkins, 2007, p. 41).

**Biblical and Spiritual Issues.** For a vast majority of people, bitterness appears to be the default reaction to being mistreated—even among Christians. The Bible provides a number of examples of those who succumbed to bitter feelings, including Job (Job 10:1), Esau (Gen. 27:34), Joseph's brothers (Gen. 49:23), Naomi (Ruth 1:20), and Jonah, to name but a few. Scripture further indicates that the bitterness these people experienced was either accompanied by or directly led to a number of other negative effects, such as rage, malice, envy, slander, hatred, and even attempted murder (see Eph. 4:31).

Forgiveness is the antithesis of and antidote for bitterness. As Jeffress (1992) observes, the Greek word often translated *forgiveness* in the Bible means "to release." This, he argues, presents a vivid picture of forgiveness, showing that whereas "bitterness holds on to an offense, forgiveness releases it" (p. 95). Consequently, bitterness can be conquered only through forgiveness.

Outside of Christ himself, the person who best epitomizes forgiveness was the Old Testament character Joseph. Shamefully mistreated by his brothers (who sold him into slavery when he was 17), wrongfully accused of a heinous crime and thrown into prison, abandoned and forgotten, betrayed and disappointed by someone he helped and who promised to help him, Joseph had, humanly speaking, every reason to cultivate a "root of bitterness" in his heart (see Heb. 12:15). And yet years later, when the tables finally turned and he found himself in a position to execute revenge on the very ones who had caused his pain (his brothers), Joseph responded not with bitterness or retaliation, but with kindness, mercy, and grace, which provided undeniable proof that he had completely forgiven them (see Gen. 50:15-20).

Joseph's story provides a case study of what Jeffress (1992) refers to as an attitude that chooses forgiveness over bitterness (p. 106). People with this type of attitude do not ignore the fact that they have been hurt, but endeavor to see that pain from an eternal perspective and understand that a "willingness to forgive others is evidence that God has forgiven [them]" (Jeffress, p. 106).

Finally, the person who chooses forgiveness over bitterness lives each day mindful of this admonition from the apostle Paul: "Let all bitterness, wrath, anger, clamor, and evil speaking be put away from you, with all malice. And be kind to one another, tenderhearted, forgiving one another, even as God in Christ forgave you" (Eph. 4:31-32 NKJV).

Fred Milacci

### REFERENCES


Clinton, T., & Hawkins, R. (2007). *Biblical Counseling: A Quick Reference Guide.* Nashville, TN: Thomas Nelson.

Getz, G. (1996). *Joseph: Overcoming Obstacles Through Faithfulness.* Nashville, TN: Broadman and Holman.

Jeffress, R. (1992). *Choose Your Attitudes, Change Your Life.* Wheaton, IL: Victor Books.

Lutzer, E. (1988). *Managing Your Emotions.* Wheaton, IL: Victor Books.


## DOUBT

**Description.** Few issues more regularly plague believers than religious doubt. Very commonly, this questioning takes on emotional overtones. I will address biblical parameters that closely approximate current psychological and counseling strategies, such as cognitive-behavioral models. I recognize that some cases are so overwhelming or traumatizing that they require medical intervention. (I am not a psychiatrist, psychologist, or professional counselor. My comments here fall into the realm of biblical and pastoral advice.)

**Aspects of Emotional Doubt.** Religious doubt commonly concerns uncertainty regarding God or our relationship to him and is revealed in questions about the truthfulness of religious beliefs, salvation assurance, personal suffering, or God's apparent silence. Though unbelievers may experience many similar quandaries, I am addressing Christian believers.

Three subspecies of religious doubt are factual, emotional, and volitional. *Factual doubt* often concerns evidential issues of a philosophical or historical nature, such as God's existence, the veracity of Scripture, or Jesus' resurrection. Answers to relevant questions provide the greatest relief.

*Emotional doubt* is much more closely related to one's feelings and is often manifested by distraught affective expressions. Questions frequently surface as "what if" queries, concentrating not on actual evidence as much as the mere possibility that believers could somehow be mistaken.

More advanced forms of *volitional doubt* generally do not concentrate so much on theology and may not be expressed emotionally but may have progressed to a lack of motivation to practice one's religious beliefs. Often after a significant experience of hurt, the volitional doubter avoids religious engagement and expression, sometimes due to anger at God.

Factual expressions of doubt are usually uncomplicated in counseling terms, though the subject matter may be more intellectual.

Emotional doubt is the most common form, it is often the most painful, and it frequently tends to invite more intervention. The more advanced volitional doubt can be the most difficult and also the most dangerous variety, viewed in spiritual terms. How do we motivate those who seem not to possess motivation?

Christians frequently harbor many misconceptions about religious doubt, such as concluding that it always opposes faith or always constitutes sin. Further, doubters sometimes wonder if they are the only ones who are plagued or if their uncertainty can ever be a path toward real and vibrant faith. Or they fail to recognize the many biblical examples of saints who doubted.

Due to the large numbers of persons who suffer, sometimes painfully, from emotional doubt, I recommend a biblical strategy for substantial healing.

**Establishing a Biblical Approach.** Among the many psychological models for treating forms of anxiety and depression, Albert Ellis' A-B-C technique is one of the best known. Like certain other cognitive-behavioral strategies, it emphasizes that genetics, life events, calamities, and others' maliciousness do not influence our emotions as much as what we tell ourselves *about* such things. The latter, often termed *misbeliefs*, *lies*, or *cognitive distortions*, are what must be treated so that one may experience greater emotional peace and less dissatisfaction. Through the practice of disputing and replacing these misrepresentations, one may gain substantial relief from unwanted emotional interruptions.

*Replacing misbeliefs with truth*. Paul often wrote about the importance of renewing the mind. Christian counselors understand the importance of this directive—it is the chief model taught in Scripture. However, some might wonder whether this is merely contemporary psychological theory or actually what is taught in God's Word.

In dozens of Scripture passages, believers are told to discontinue their worry and downcast demeanors regarding the unpleasantness of life and to replace these thoughts with God's truth, promises, prayer, worship, or meditation. Many other times, we are commanded to reject reckless words, anxiety, envy, and fixations that lead to heartache. Instead, we are to teach ourselves and each other truthful and uplifting things, bringing healing and peace. Many of these passages describe what we have called religious doubt.

*A heavenly replacement*. Jesus taught that life's anxieties should be purposely exchanged for the pursuit of heavenly treasures with the single-minded purpose of seeking God (Mt. 6:19-34). This eternal message specifically replaces earthly worry (a contrast that accounts for the "therefore" of verse 25).

While cataloging a long list of sins (Rom. 1:21-32), Paul warned that some people had traded God's truth for lies (1:25). In contrast, believers were to act differently, transforming their minds by changing their thinking (Rom. 12:1-2). We are commanded neither to sin nor to lie to each other. We should exhibit renewed minds that meditate on eternity (Col. 3:1-10).

*Paul's four remedies*. In Philippians 4:6-9, the Greek text indicates that Paul's readers were experiencing anxiety (v. 6), so the apostle presents options for breaking these bonds. Though Paul does not specifically address doubt, his suggestions are liberating for the emotional variety of doubts that are the seeds of anxiety and worry. Healing the patterns of worry would be extremely helpful in treating emotional doubt.

Paul's response is fourfold. He commands the Philippians to pray and make their needs known to God. Peter provides similar guidance to anxious believers, instructing them to cast their worries on God (1 Pet. 5:7).

For Paul, these prayers should also include thanksgiving and praise (v. 6,8). This dimension combats emotional distress like few others and can be an exceptionally powerful antidote to worry.

In the most cognitive verse in this passage (v. 8), Paul commands his readers to exchange their current anxiety-driven emotions for God-honoring thoughts. The term *think* indicates a prolonged habit and is perhaps best translated as *meditate* (NKJV). Believers were to think steadily, deeply, and single-mindedly about God's truths, internalizing these concepts instead of the ruminations that led to their anxiety.

Lastly, Paul encourages a behavioral component: habitually practicing these truths (v. 9). It does not follow that these four steps must always be taken and in this exact order. Other passages encourage similar moves, either alone or with other practices.

**Applying Paul's Advice to Emotional Doubt.** How may Paul's cognitive and behavioral proposals be more specifically applied to religious doubt? We have suggested that these patterns can provide a pastoral or personal model for treating worry (even as other biblical texts provide similar advice for sadness and despair) and address the heart of emotional uncertainty.

Some doubters give their worries to God most effectively in prayer, discovering that concentrated times of trusting God with their issues are very useful ways to abandon their concerns. Other cognitive strategies may provide excellent reinforcements.

Thanksgiving and praise are among the most powerful tools for reorienting our thinking to God's eternal perspective and may provide almost immediate relief to doubts. While lecturing, I usually ask listeners what happens when they practice worship during even intense periods of doubt. The immediate response is that in several ways, the doubt lessens. What a powerful tool! Long-term success depends much on practicing this response until it becomes our habit.

The repeated commands of Paul and other biblical writers to replace our anxieties with God's truth and promises point to what is perhaps the strongest weapon of all. Christian counselors report that changing our thinking by arguing against misbeliefs can root out the very causes of religious doubt.

Paul's final point about practice is also crucially important. The best time for us to practice is precisely while we are experiencing raging doubt. The next best time is when we are *not* presently hurting! Preventative therapy continues to keep doubt's weeds out of life's lawn.

In hundreds of discussions with religious doubters, I am told regularly that when these techniques are applied, doubt generally subsides. Conversely, when they fail to act, doubt remains.

Changing hearts is God's business (Phil. 1:6), through his power and spiritual weapons (2 Cor. 10:3-4). God accomplishes the change, even though we are called to act (Gal. 5:19-26; 2 Pet. 1:3-11).

Emotional doubt is widespread and often very painful. Though sometimes difficult to eliminate entirely, its effects often can be severely reduced. The biblical key is the habitual application of spiritual principles to our mistaken thinking and behavior.

Gary R. Habermas

## REFERENCES


Backus, W., & Chapian, M. (2000). *Telling Yourself the Truth.* Minneapolis, MN: Bethany House.

Ellis, A. (1994). *Reason and Emotion in Psychotherapy: A Comprehensive Method of Treating Human Disturbances* (Rev. ed.). New York, NY: Carol.

Habermas, G. R. (1990). *Dealing with Doubt.* Chicago, IL: Moody.

Habermas, G. R. (1998). *The Thomas Factor: Using Your Doubts to Grow Closer to God.* Nashille, TN: Broadman & Holman.

Stoop, D. (1996). *You Are What You Think.* Grand Rapids, MI: Revell.


## SHAME

**Description.** Shame is a strong, unpleasant, and humiliating emotion accompanied by anxious feelings of inadequacy, failure, dishonor, and a degrading view of self. Unhealthy shame is a problem of a distorted, toxic, internal personal identity. Shame is often confused with guilt. Guilt is experienced when people do things they believe they shouldn't do, or when they fail to do something they believe they should do. Shame is an emotional, internal condemning judgment. Guilt acknowledges, "Something I've done is bad." Shame condemns, "I am a bad person."

In contrast to unhealthy shame, the Bible addresses the reality of healthy shame. God has established and clearly communicated a way of living that honors God's glory and man's dignity as a bearer of the image of God. When a Christian lives in violation of God's design, law, and will, an inner sense of godly shame is healthy and can lead to repentance.

**Historical and Biblical Origin of Shame.** The word *shame* comes from a root that means "to cover or hide an exposure" (Benner & Hill, 1999). The Bible paints a vivid picture of shame in action. "Adam and his wife were both naked, and they felt no shame" (Gen. 2:25). But when they willfully disobeyed God, "the eyes of both of them were opened, and they realized they were naked; so they sewed fig leaves together and made coverings for themselves." In this narrative, the first man and woman had enjoyed a season of innocence. Once they acted against what they believed to be true, they suddenly saw their nakedness as a threat. In a desperate attempt to cover their shame, Adam and Eve turned to their own futile resources to attempt to hide their vulnerable, unprotected selves. Externally, nothing about their physical bodies had changed, but internally, their souls were in chaos.

Men and women since then have experienced the fear of being seen for who they truly are. In response, people have found creative, crafty, seemingly positive, addictive, and destructive ways to sew their own fig leaves together in an attempt to cover their perceived inadequacies. In the end, all of their elaborate defenses, disguises, and personality traits are held in bondage to the goal of not being known because to be known is to be caught naked and defenseless (Allender, 1995). Their efforts, however, are ultimately futile because they are attempting to find an external solution to their internal problem.

**Assessment.** Often, addictions are described as "shame based." There is typically a painful core reality that the addict tries to medicate with his addiction. This numbing of shame may be manifested through addictions to alcohol, drugs, sex, food, gambling, financial disorder, workaholism, and in some cases, zealous or legalistic religious commitment and activities. The underlying shame is so strong that the addict becomes willing to obliterate, medicate, or ignore reality (Carnes, 2005).

Childhood sexual abuse traumatizes in ways that introduce shame at a deep level. The lingering impact of the toxic shame of sexual abuse can paralyze people with distorted beliefs that they somehow actually invited the abuse or at least failed to stop it. Again, distorted identity is in play here, and people hear their internal voice saying, "I am a failure; I am dirty; I am damaged goods." External shameful abuse has become internal shameful identity.

Other types of abuse, including abandonment, rejection, and neglect, play a profound and poisonous role in the formation of shame in an individual's life. Verbal, emotional, and physical abuse leave scars on a person's self-image. The shaming voices of abusers, harsh and condemning parents, and toxic authority figures can resonate for decades in a person's mind. He may grow up with an internal shame belief that he is not worthy of anyone's love, time, or attention.

Psychological research finds a relationship between shame and a number of different psychological problems or disorders, including depression, anxiety, eating disorders, subclinical sociopathy, and low self-esteem (VandenBos, 2007).

**Treatment and Application.** Just as God provided a covering for Adam and Eve's shame, God today invites people to stop hiding behind their futile fig leaves of self-effort and self-protection and to be clothed in the righteousness of Christ. Genesis 1:26-27 declares people are created in the image of God. Psalm 8:5 proclaims that men and women are "crowned with glory and honor." Ephesians 4:24 counsels Christians to "put on the new self, created to be like God in true righteousness and holiness." Romans 8:1 pronounces, "Therefore, there is now no condemnation for those who are in Christ Jesus." When the internal voices of unhealthy shame begin to tell Christians who they are, they must practice Paul's admonition in 2 Corinthians 10:5 and replace lies with truth and "take captive every thought to make it obedient to Christ." These are only a few of the many verses in the Bible that describe a Christian's true identity.

The person struggling with shame should be on a healing journey that includes healthy, authentic Christian relationships, regular worship of God, study of the Bible, and memorizing of key Scriptures dealing with one's identity in Christ. Individual Christian counseling, group counseling, and specific books, workshops, and conferences addressing the healing of trauma, abuse, and abandonment are key components to helping a person move from the bondage of shame to the freedom of truth, grace, acceptance, and love.

Jim Cress

### REFERENCES

Allender, D. (1995). *The Wounded Heart.* Colorado Springs, CO: NavPress.

Benner, D., & Hill, P. (Eds.). (1999). *Baker Encyclopedia of Psychology & Counseling* (2nd ed.). Grand Rapids, MI: Baker Books.

Carnes, P. (2005). *Facing the Shadow* (2nd ed.). Carefree, AZ: Gentle Path Press.

Mathes, E. W., & Severa, N. (1981). Jealousy, romantic love, and liking: Theoretical considerations and preliminary scale development. *Psychological Reports, 49*(1), 23-31.

VandenBos, G. R. (Ed.). (2007). *The APA Dictionary of Psychology.* Washington, DC: American Psychological Association.

## JEALOUSY

**Description.** In Pines' 1992 survey of marriage counselors, respondents stated that approximately one third of their clients were plagued with jealousy. Several studies revealed that the discomfiting feeling of jealousy is experienced by men and women alike, both in frequency and intensity (Buss, 2000; Buunk, 1995; Shakelford, LeBlanc, & Drass, 2000). The majority of respondents in another survey (Pines & Aronson, 1983) viewed themselves as jealous and projected their belief that about 75% of everyone is jealous. Jealousy can be viewed as functional because it spurs activities that are "designed to prevent the loss of one's partner to a rival" (Mathes, 1992). It may even be part of human nature, as we serve a jealous God (Ex. 34:14; Josh. 24:19).

Jealousy can also be viewed as dysfunctional because it is often associated with psychopathologies, such as low self-esteem, neuroticism, insecurity, and anxiety. One of these elements may result from comparing oneself to the previous, real, or mistakenly perceived partner. Since the comparison is not likely to be considered favorable, it can lead to attempts to improve one's position by losing weight, cleaning the house, or plying one's partner with gifts.

Jankowiak and Fischer (1992), in an analysis of 166 cultures, found that formal marriage between one man and one woman is predominant worldwide and that people who "value conventional styles of marriage tend to report greater relational satisfaction." Kelly, Mathes, and Kurz (2010) found that partners who reported not only strong faith but also confidence in their spouse's faith were considerably less plagued with romantic jealousy. According to their research, a strong Christian marriage is a noteworthy "antidote to jealousy resulting from the possibility of losing the partner to a rival."

*Normal jealousy.* In his book on jealousy, Mathes (1992) defines *normal romantic jealousy* as "the negative emotion from the actual or threatened loss of a romantic partner to a rival." Such feelings may spur the individual into actions designed to preserve the relationship, paralyzing inactivity, or a combination of the two, depending on the overall mental health of the individual.

*Morbid jealousy.* Morbid jealousy is characterized by excessive, irrational preoccupation with the unfounded or incorrect evidence leading to belief in the partner's infidelity. Such aberrations are often coupled with unacceptable, excessive, or extreme behaviors. The morbidly jealous tend to conclude there is evidence of infidelity from random or irrelevant occurrences and persist in their mistaken beliefs when presented with conflicting information. They also accuse their partners of many instances of infidelity without evidence of such activity.

*Pathological jealousy.* Pathological jealousy, sometimes called delusional jealousy, is often evident in individuals with paranoid personality disorder, preventing them from being in relationships based on trust. The fear that people are trying to trick, deceive, or harm them prompts them to be unforgiving and to hold on to grudges. Accusations of cheating can occur spontaneously or be set off by insignificant events. The fear that whatever they might divulge in the course of therapy could be used against them often prevents them from seeking help.

*Retroactive jealousy.* Retroactive jealousy is the state of upset regarding a mate's previous partners. The former partners may be perceived as more successful, advantaged, or physically or sexually attractive. Intrusive, irrational thoughts based on history versus current information have predictably detrimental effects on present relationships.

**Assessment.** Subjective inventories are useful when determining the extent of jealous feelings. A standard in the field is Mathes and Severa's (1981) Interpersonal Jealousy Scale, a 28-item inventory. Subjects are asked to supply the name of a current, past, or imaginary dating partner and keep that person in mind while completing the survey.

**Treatment.** Treatment options for pathological jealousy are available but have no likelihood of effectiveness unless the subject admits something might be out of kilter. Childhood experiences and genetic factors may be contributing factors, but the cause of pathological jealousy, especially in paranoid personality disorders, is unclear. The main treatment is psychotherapy, with the possible addition of medication. The biggest challenge in treating pathological jealousy is moving past the initial stage of distrust between the subject and the mental-health worker.

The apostle Paul wrote, "You are still worldly. For since there is jealousy and quarreling among you, are you not worldly? Are you not acting like mere humans?" (1 Cor. 3:3). Perhaps like God, all individual image bearers also have similar elements of jealousy woven within them.

Lynn Ellyn Robinson

## REFERENCES


Buss, D. M. (2000). *The Dangerous Passion: Why Jealousy Is as Necessary as Love and Sex.* New York, NY: The Free Press.

Buunk, B. (1995). Sex, self-esteem, dependency and extradyadic sexual experiences as related to jealousy responses. *Journal of Social and Personal Relationships, 12,* 147-153.

Jankowiak, W., & Fischer, E. (1992). A cross-cultural perspective on romantic love. *Ethnology, 31,* 149-155.

Kelly, K., Mathes, E., & Kurz, M. (2010) Christian marriage as an antidote to partner loss jealousy. *Journal of Psychology and Christianity, 29*(3), 218.

Mathes, E. W. (1992). *Jealousy: The Psychological Data.* New York, NY: University Press of America.

Pines, A., & Aronson, E. (1983). Antecedents, correlates, and consequences of sexual jealousy. *Journal of Personality, 51,* 108-136.

Shakelford, T. K., LeBlanc, G. J., & Drass, E. (2000). Emotional reactions to infidelity. *Cognition and Emotion, 14*, 643-659.

## LUST

Definition. The word *lust* has a variety of definitions, uses, and interpretations. "1. Intense or unrestrained sexual craving, 2. a. An overwhelming desire or craving: *a lust for power,* b. Intense eagerness or enthusiasm: *a lust for life*" (Houghton Mifflin, 2009). "1. a strong desire for sexual gratification, or 2. a strong desire or drive" (HarperCollins, 2003).

The Greek word for lust, *epithumeo*, most commonly refers to excessive or extreme desire. It is often referred to as an intense longing. The concept includes lusting after or coveting something that belongs to another, which is consistent with the Hebrew word *chamad*, used in the 10th commandment. However, *chamad* is most often translated as *covet* rather than *lust*. Whether coveting or lusting, the consistent admonition is to not let it lead to evil. The implication is that lust carries with it the intention to act (Bromiley, 1988).

From a Christian perspective, Harris (2005) describes it this way: "To lust is to want what you don't have and weren't meant to have. Lust goes beyond attraction, and appreciation of beauty, or even a healthy desire for sex—it makes these desires more important than God. Lust wants to go outside God's guidelines to find satisfaction" (p. 4).

**Historical and Biblical Context.** In the Old Testament, the primary term describing inordinate desire is *covetousness*. The 10th commandment states, "You shall not covet your neighbor's house. You shall not covet your neighbor's wife, or his male or female servant, his ox or donkey, or anything that belongs to your neighbor" (Ex. 20:17). This passage is referred to again in Deuteronomy 5:21 with the same emphasis on not coveting what belongs to another.

Jesus specifically addressed sexual lust when he said, "You have heard that it was said, 'You shall not commit adultery.' But I say to you that anyone who looks at a woman lustfully has already committed adultery with her in his heart" (Mt. 5:27-28). This passage follows the beatitudes and Jesus' teaching that he came not to destroy the Law, but to fulfill it, and it is followed by Jesus telling the listeners to pluck out an eye or cut off a hand if either should cause them to sin. He makes clear that if we lust, we deserve the same judgment as those who commit adultery. Earlier in the chapter, Jesus similarly compared being angry with murder.

There is no indication that Matthew 5:28 is an indictment against healthy sexual desire or arousal. In fact, it is clear throughout Scripture and from how our bodies are designed that sexual desire and response are innate—we were created that way in the image of God. Thus, it is important that we not equate *chamad* (to covet) or *epithumeo* (to lust) with normal sexual responsiveness. Rather, both seem to refer to conscious, intentional pursuit of something belonging to another that leads to evil and destroys relationships with God and others.

> To "lust after" a person must have something to do with fanning desire into a flame of specific intent. Eros, the longing for personal fulfillment, must not be confused with lust, the untamed desire for another's body. Nor is every feeling of attraction toward an exciting person the spark of lust. It would be odd indeed if the Creator put attractive people in the world and forbade us to notice them (Smedes, 1994, p. 188).

James 1:14-15 reads, "But each one is tempted when they are drawn away by their own evil desire [lust] and enticed. Then, after desire [lust] has conceived, it gives birth to sin; and sin, when it is full-grown, gives birth to death."

What about fantasy? When we fantasize, do we lust? Fantasies are dreams or imaginations. We have been created in the image of God with the capacity to create mental pictures. Thoughts, pictures, and dreams often come into our minds, but we are responsible to nurture the positive images and stop the ones that might lead to lust.

"Sexual drives are strong, but marriage is strong enough to contain them and provide for a balanced and fulfilling sexual life in a world of sexual disorder" (1 Cor. 7:3 MSG). Sexual intimacy and fulfillment were designed for marriage. Therefore, our images and actions are not to distort or distract from the oneness of sex in marriage.

**Assessment and Awareness.** Lust is about gaining sexual pleasure through inappropriate means. The topic of lust is not popular because "most Americans reject the very notion that there are any pleasures that we are not meant to have" (Mohler, 2004). Lust may interfere with people's ability to function intimately in relationships and may lead them to isolate themselves. Obsessive desire for what belongs to another or a focus on images that are not real will leave a person empty and lonely.

Clients may reveal their concerns with lust in their initial assessment, but more likely, these issues will surface as trust is built in the therapy process. Lust may present as...

- a sexual addiction accompanied by an intimacy disorder
- discontentment—longing to have what others have or be what they are
- inhibited personal sexual development and/or sexual freedom in marriage due to a false understanding of lust

**Treatment.** The assessment will inform the treatment plan. Sexual addictions and intimacy disorders require understanding, treatment of the underlying causes, and implementation of a program for control and accountability. The sexual therapy process is most helpful for guiding people toward attachment as the means to finding the true longings of their hearts.

With clients who are dissatisfied with life, counselors must address issues with the families of origin and other contributing factors that keep clients focused on distracting longings.

For those who are sexually underdeveloped, are unable to form relationships with significant others, or are unable to experience sexual fulfillment in marriage due to false beliefs about lust, counselors must incorporate the true messages of Scripture in their therapy process.

Clifford Penner
Joyce Penner

## REFERENCES


Bromiley, G. W. (Ed.). (1988). *The International Standard Bible Encyclopedia.* Grand Rapids, MI: Eerdmans.

HarperCollins. (2003). *Collins English Dictionary.* New York, NY: Author.

Harris, J. (2005). *Sex Is Not the Problem (Lust Is): Sexual Purity in a Lust-Saturated World.* Sisters, OR: Multnomah.

Houghton Mifflin. (2009). *The American Heritage Dictionary of the English Language* (4th ed.). Boston, MA: Author.

Mohler, R. A. (2004, July 15). *Another Look at Lust: A Christian View.* Retrieved from http://www.crosswalk.com/news/al-mohler/another-look-at-lust-a-christian-view-1340429.html?ps=0

Smedes, L. B. (1994). *Sex for Christians.* Grand Rapids, MI: Eerdmans.


## SELF-ESTEEM AND OTHER ESTEEM

**Description.** How am I supposed to feel about myself? Is the concept of so-called self-esteem consistent with Scripture's teaching? As a Christian in the mental-health field, what should I teach others about how they should view themselves? These are important questions because much confusion revolves around the whole idea of self-esteem.

Some critics argue that the notion of

self-esteem violates Scripture's view of how we view and value ourselves. They believe it is a sneaky way of exalting pride over humility. They also suggest that our obsession with feeling good about ourselves has resulted in a culture of narcissism. Our unending preoccupation with self-esteem, they assert, reflects the heart and denial of our sin problem.

On the other hand, some Christians claim that not only is it acceptable to pursue a high sense of regard for oneself but also that sin is actually nothing more than a low sense of self-esteem. The real reason for people's bad behavior, according to this view, is that they have suffered some emotional hurt in the past and feel badly about themselves. Fix people's self-esteem problem, they suggest, and you have fixed their sin problem.

So what should be our understanding here? Our psychology should be rooted in good theology, but even some Christian believers have ignored their theology in this important area.

**History.** Some years ago, *Time* magazine published an edition focusing on the idea of self-esteem. Looking back on its origin, the article featured on the cover stated, "We gave it a name and created a monster!" They were referring to the frantic attempt at that time to solve all our social problems by fixing our young people's low self-esteem.

It is appropriate for Christian counselors to question the validity of our previous understanding of self-esteem and to look more closely at how modern psychology views the concept. This development has opened up a meaningful integration dialogue.

**Application.** After decades of believing that people can become more successful and happy by boosting their sense of self-worth, psychologists are now challenging this myth. In the upheaval of the late 1960s and early 1970s, the popular psychological world blamed all social ills and even mental illness on the problem of low self-esteem. It became the driving force that sent teachers and parents scurrying to find ways to increase children's self-esteem. The states of California and New York rushed to set up task forces on self-esteem. It had become a national preoccupation. However, it ended as a hopeless quest. Research has now conclusively shown that such efforts do little to improve social problems, academic performance, or success in the workplace. They don't even enhance our happiness (Baumeister, Campbell, Krueger, & Vohs, 2005). We now know that a healthy self-esteem is the consequence of accomplishing something significant in life, not the cause of these accomplishments.

A good example of how misleading the quest for self-esteem had become was cited by the renowned psychologist Martin Seligman, a significant leader in the new positive-psychology movement. He denounced several sacred cows of psychotherapy during his presidential address at the August 1994 American Psychological Association annual meeting—one of them being that in order to reduce the incidence of mental illness we should try to increase the self-esteem of our children.

**Solution.** A more acceptable approach to understanding the phenomenon of self-esteem has emerged (Lerner, 1996). In trying to understand the origins of self-esteem, a major paradox has to be explained: Why are so many successful people plagued by so-called feelings of low self-esteem? The answer is that somewhere behind the external achievements is an internal filtering device that denies the successes and hoards the failures.

The article goes on to suggest that the key to building a healthy sense of self-esteem is mainly about creating a healthy and honest internal filtering system. Of course, from a Christian perspective, we also need to factor in salvation and the regenerating work of Christ. A deeper exploration of these critical components is essential to building a healthy self-attitude and can be found in my book *Me, Myself, and I* (Hart, 1992).

Also, we need to pay more attention to the wisdom Paul expresses in his letter to the Romans. It is replete with all we need to know about the self-esteem problem, even though its focus is not so much on low self-esteem, but rather on an inflated and distorted sense of self. He wrote, "By the grace given me I say to every one of you: Do not think of yourself more highly than you ought, but rather think of yourself with sober [honest] judgment, in accordance with the faith God has distributed to each of you" (Rom. 12:3).

**Archibald Hart**

### REFERENCES

Baumeister, R. F., Campbell, J. D., Krueger, J. I., & Vohs, K. D. (2005). Exploding the self-esteem myth. *Scientific American, 292*(1), 84-91.

Hart, A. D. (1992). *Me, Myself, & I: How Far Should We Go in Our Search for Self-Fulfillment?* Ann Arbor, MI: Vine Books.

Lerner, B. (1996). Self-esteem and excellence: The choice and the paradox. *American Educator, 20*(2), 9-13,41-42.

## SIN AND REDEMPTION

**Description.** Some differences between psychology conducted apart from the Christian faith and that done from a Christian perspective are subtle and hard to detect. Both approaches benefit from the same theories and use many of the same methods and strategies. However, other differences between these two approaches stand in stark contrast. Two such constructs that stand out in bold relief as unique to the Christian perspective are the concepts of sin and redemption.

The field of psychology uses terms such as *dysfunctional* and *unhealthy* to describe undesirable thinking or behavior, but Christian psychology adds a moral appraisal by using the term *sin,* or more literally, "missing the mark." Some thoughts and behaviors are not only unwise but also morally wrong. Examining the role of sin in counseling, McMinn (2008) writes, "A comprehensive view of sin emphasizes the human condition of sin, sinful personal choices and the consequences of sin (both the consequences of our personal sin and the consequences of others' sin)" (p. 33). According to Christian doctrine, a holy God reserves the right to determine what is right and what is wrong. Furthermore, because his holiness is the final arbiter, sin is not only wrong, it is also offensive. Because sin is such a serious matter, it behooves Christian counselors to understand what constitutes sin and the remedy for it.

**The Nature of Sin.** According to the Bible, sin has permeated every aspect of human thinking and behavior. As Powlison (2003) puts it, "Sinners sin instinctively" (p. 206). Objectively, Scripture lists many sinful actions, such as murder (Ex. 20:13), stealing (Eph. 4:28), sexual immorality (Col. 3:5), and lying (Rev. 21:8), just to name a few. A Christian counselor should be well versed in what activities the Bible clearly and objectively identifies as sin.

Though these sinful actions are damaging, Jesus warned that the most insidious sin originates in the human heart even before it is expressed in behavior. He even goes so far as to declare the *inside* of a person more corrupt than anything occurring on the outside (Mt. 15:15-20). Thus, the struggle with sin is not just with outward enemies but also with an inward malignancy that is even more resistant to change. Paul describes his battle with sinful thoughts in military terms when he writes, "We demolish arguments and every pretension that sets itself up against the knowledge of God, and we take captive every thought to make it obedient to Christ" (2 Cor. 10:5).

Because sin originates in the human heart, people will have slightly different ways of prosecuting their own private war within. Often, legitimate desires are twisted into idolatry of the heart (Powlison, 2003). This subjective element of sin can be difficult to detect, but the mature Christian counselor receives divine wisdom. Discernment is needed, but confrontation is sometimes necessary in truly biblical counseling, for "both law and grace are necessary components of the gospel of Christ" (McMinn & Phillips, 2001, p. 208).

The author of Hebrews describes mature believers who have exercised their senses to discern good and evil (5:14). Apparently, some Christians have an advanced form of radar that can detect the motivation or direction of a behavior even if that behavior appears benign on the surface. For example, one person may use humor to deflect the direction of a conversation that is leading to conviction. Another person may use tears to evoke an emotional response when instead right thinking and discernment are needed. These judgment calls are hard to make. There is no chapter and verse in the Bible to identify these sins because there is nothing wrong with making a joke or tearing up. The motives behind these actions determine their sinfulness. This is where spiritual discernment is required. If all aspects of good and evil were easy to detect, there would be no need for the maturity called for by the author of Hebrews.

**Redemption.** These facts—that all people are sinners and that sin permeates every aspect of the human heart—can be very discouraging. But the divine narrative does not conclude with sin. The story describes what God did to defeat sin (and its ultimate result—death). Christ's death and resurrection paved the way for fallen human beings to be restored to their Creator. Upon repentance and a belief that what Christ accomplished is indeed enough, any person can be forgiven of sin and can enjoy a renewed relationship with God, both in this life and the next.

Scripture uses many terms to describe God's act of salvation from sin. Some refer to the process of childbirth; those who have accepted Christ are *born again*. Other terms are forensic, such as *justification* and *propitiation,* which emphasize the change in legal standing that results from conversion. *Redemption* is yet another way of describing what happens at salvation. The word is of economic origin. In biblical times, commodities were regularly bought and sold in the marketplace, and sometimes slaves were purchased and sold as property. Those who found themselves hopelessly in debt or in some other unfortunate situation became temporarily owned by others, which included the possibility of being sold again. For those who had no chance of paying off their debt, the situation was permanent, and slavery became their life. The picture of redemption is of God paying the debt a slave could never pay and "buying back" that which was his to begin with. This payment was nothing less than the death of Christ on the cross, a display of love that compels those who are purchased and set free to want to glorify the one who bought them (1 Cor. 6:20).

Being freed from sin, the old owner, the slave is now free to serve God, the new owner (Rom. 6:22). Paradoxically, there is a new and profound freedom in being a servant of God. The slave is no longer under a crushing burden to pay back the heavy debt. Rather, the slave is free to please the new and permanent owner, comforted by the fact that the new owner not only owns him but also loves him. The journey of the Christian life is a process of redemption and sanctification, which requires humble reliance on the Lord. As Sells & Yarhouse (2011) put it, "The faith system of those who follow after Jesus is centered on need and dependence" (p. 60). Rather than living in denial of sin, the believer's continual repentance and awareness of daily need for God's mercy grows a desperate dependence and deeper intimacy with God.

**Applications.** Applications of these concepts to Christian counseling are many because sin and redemption color every relationship and every situation in life. Describing the healing work of God in the counseling process, Langberg (2003) writes, "Therapy...becomes the working out of redemption in a life shattered and scared by evil. As therapists enter into the life experience of their clients, bearing the image of the Lord Jesus Christ in their person, they will see the work of redemption unfold" (p. 58).

Each situation is unique, but the Christian counselor can be assured of two truths: First, sin goes much deeper than mere dysfunctional or unhealthy behavior, and second, redemption so completely pays the purchase price that whatever debts sin has built up, those debts have been completely paid. Nothing else is owed but to freely serve the God who bought us.

**Bryan N. Maier**

## REFERENCES


Langberg, D. M. (2003). *Counseling Survivors of Sexual Abuse.* Longwood, FL: Xulon Press.

McMinn, M. R. (2008). *Sin and Grace in Christian Counseling: An Integrative Paradigm.* Downers Grove, IL: InterVarsity Press.

McMinn, M. R., & Phillips, T. R. (Eds.). (2001). *Caring for the Soul: Exploring the Intersection of Psychology and Theology.* Downers Grove, IL: InterVarsity Press.

Powlison, D. (2003). *Seeing with New Eyes.* Phillipsburg, NJ: P&R.

Sells, J. N., & Yarhouse, M. A. (2011). *Counseling Couples in Conflict: A Relational Restoration Model.* Downers Grove, IL: InterVarsity Press.


## PERFECTIONISM

**Description and History.** Throughout history, philosophers and theologians have espoused many views on the nature of perfection and whether it is achievable in this life. Not until the late 1930s was the word *perfectionist* commonly used to describe a person who has a strong tendency to be satisfied only by the highest standards.

The word *perfect* derives from the Latin word *perficere* (to make thorough or complete). Dictionary definitions include such terms as these: complete in all respects, without defect or omission, in a condition of complete excellence, accurate, precise, and the highest degree of proficiency. Two leading researchers in this field, Gordon Flett and Paul Hewitt, define perfectionism as "the striving for flawlessness" and the strong desire "to be perfect in all aspects of life."

**Assessment.** In business, academia, athletics, and beauty, setting high standards and striving for excellence are the norm as people search for an edge in a very competitive world. But counselors are familiar with the dark side of this striving for perfection.

In academic and popular psychology, some disagreement exists regarding the danger of striving for excellence. Some see all perfectionism as unhealthy and bad, but most see perfectionism on a spectrum where only certain degrees and types of perfectionism are unhealthy or neurotic.

In the spectrum view, normal, healthy perfectionists are enthusiastic, have a positive self-image, and rarely procrastinate when making decisions. They are realistic about their own strengths and weaknesses, enjoy high standards, and pursue excellence. Many great scientific achievements and works of art, music, and literature are the creative products of perfectionists. Such people are driven more by a positive motivation to achieve than by a negative fear of failure.

Neurotic, unhealthy perfectionists set unrealistically high standards. Their sense of self-worth depends entirely on their appearance, performance, or production. They are plagued by continuous self-criticism, feeling their best efforts are not good enough. They often endure shame over mistakes, and self-doubts nag their consciences.

Nonperfectionists are people who have little shame or guilt about failing to reach high standards or to be completely organized. They are relaxed, easygoing, and fun, though perhaps sometimes so laid-back that they may be disorganized, unreliable, and undisciplined.

Many people are perfectionists in only one area of life—usually some aspect of appearance, performance, productivity, or relationships. Some, however, are all-around perfectionists (Elliot and Meltsner, 1991).

Research on perfectionism describes three main types. Self-oriented perfectionists try to live up to their own standards, which are sometimes impossibly high. Socially prescribed perfectionists have "ghosts" of critical parents looking over their shoulders or voices from the outside driving them to meet the expectations of others and telling them that they are not acceptable unless they reach those standards. Other-oriented perfectionists think, "Why can't people live up to my standards and do things the way they *should* be done?"

The negative and unhealthy aspects of perfectionism can be crippling and destructive. Problems arise when we live under the tyranny of believing that perfection is possible and when our self-worth depends on reaching unrealistic standards. Perfectionism often underlies anxiety, phobias, indecision, procrastination, dissatisfaction, envy, broken relationships, obsessive-compulsive tendencies, eating disorders, depression, and suicidal impulses.

**Treatment.** There are many practical strategies to confront unhealthy perfectionism. For those who suffer with it, learning to live with imperfection requires that the pros and cons of perfectionism be rigorously examined. Perfectionists are convinced that their way of thinking protects them from mediocrity, mistakes, and the risk of failure. Healing comes by recognizing all-or-nothing thought patterns ("I must do everything right or not at all"). Counselors may encourage perfectionists to keep a journal to identify both old and new habitual thoughts and feelings. Cognitive therapy in a relationship of acceptance, challenge, and grace is very effective, although helping someone to live in the unfamiliar and frightening world between all and nothing is a gradual process (Anthony & Swinson, 2009). When perfectionism is accompanied by clinical depression or merges into obsessive compulsive disorder, medication may be helpful.

**Biblical and Spiritual Issues.** The deepest and most important part of the cure for perfectionism is found in our beliefs about God. Many religions prescribe rules and rituals that render followers acceptable to a deity. Christianity is profoundly and wonderfully different because the Bible tells us that we are accepted, forgiven, loved, and valued not for what we achieve or how we look, but because of Christ's perfect sacrifice for us. As we embrace the transforming truth of the gospel, we are set free to pursue excellence and high standards without fear of failure or rejection and with gratitude to God. He is more interested in the inner development of character than in appearance or performance. In Jesus' command to be perfect (Mt. 5:48), the word *perfect* means "mature" or "complete." We are called to cooperate with the Spirit of God to produce the qualities of Christ in us (see Col. 3:1-14).

But in the process of spiritual growth, the old habits of perfectionist thinking die hard. Insecurity, feelings of insignificance, the desire to control, fear of rejection and failure...these are based on lies that must be replaced with truth. Our minds are renewed gradually as we allow the powerful blend of God's Spirit, God's truth, and God's people to work his love, forgiveness, and purpose deeply in us (Rom.12:2).

Good and grace-filled friendships and the acceptance of the church family are important sources of healing. In these rich, real relationships, we no longer live behind masks, and we experience grace and truth. We all need a safe place to take risks and to fail without fear of rejection.

As the Holy Spirit works in us to change us little by little, we have the promise that one day in the new heaven and new earth, God will give us the perfection that we long for and that he so desires. Meanwhile we wait eagerly and patiently for that day (Rom. 8:23; 2 Cor. 3:18).

**Richard Winter**

## REFERENCES

Many points in this article are gleaned from Richard Winter, *Perfecting Ourselves to Death: The Pursuit of Excellence and the Perils of Perfectionism* (Downers Grove, IL: InterVarsity Press, 2005). Used with permission of the publisher.

Anthony, M., & Swinson, R. (2009). *When Perfect Isn't Good Enough: Strategies for Coping with Perfectionism.* Oakland, CA: New Harbinger.

Elliot, M., & Meltsner, S. (1991). *The Perfectionist Predicament: How to Stop Driving Yourself and Others Crazy.* New York, NY: William Morrow.

Flett, G. L., & Hewitt, P. L. (2002). Perfectionism and maladjustment: An overview of theoretical, definitional, and treatment issues. In G. Flett & P. Hewitt (Eds.), *Perfectionism: Theory, Research and Treatment.* Washington, DC: American Psychological Association.

## LEGALISM

**Description and Prevalence.** "Christian legalism is seeking to attain, gain, or maintain acceptance with God, or achieve spiritual growth, through keeping a written or unwritten code or standard of performance" (Anderson, Miller, & Travis, 2003, p. 37). The term *legalism* describes the well-intentioned but ill-fated efforts of those who think they can rise to the standard of God's law. Such people characterize their success in the Christian life by their ability to live up to a set of prescribed rules and regulations. Many people work so hard to live up to their (or someone else's) expectations that they suffer from chronic depression, fatigue, and even burnout. The most extreme example is the obsessive-compulsive person, whose life becomes so rigid that he or she no longer even has a choice in the most mundane of daily activities.

Self-righteous legalists will often adopt a strategy of denial. Like the Pharisees of Jesus' day, they concentrate on the exterior to cover up the cesspool of resentment, greed, and lust that lies below the surface. Sometimes the legalist is a church leader who seeks to control others through a grid of do's and don'ts. More often however, legalists are people who are truly sincere and scrupulous in their devotion to God and desire to walk worthy of his name. But, as Paul Travis notes, "God's people by and large have got things wrong, and the spiritual effects are deadly. Like a virus infecting a Bible software program, legalism can corrupt even the noblest of spiritual endeavors. It causes confusion and drivenness, a feeling like being trapped in a maze where every seeming exit ends up a dead end" (Anderson et al., 2003, p. 31).

As a weapon against sin, the use of law is perhaps the most natural default position in families. From their children's infancy, parents "lay down the law" for one type of moral infraction or another. Such laws provide principled virtues and protection for children, and in turn, they form the foundation and guideposts for their lives as adults.

**Biblical Principles.** Laws such as the Ten Commandments function similarly to guide the growth of personal character in the direction of integrity and holiness and to delimit appropriate human action. Such laws also serve God's purpose by establishing limits to sinful behavior and its consequences. The law, then, is not evil. Rather, "the law is holy, and the commandment is holy, righteous and good" (Rom. 7:12). The psalmist understood this when he wrote, "Blessed is the one who does not walk in step with the wicked or stand in the way of sinners or sit in the company of mockers, but whose delight is in the law of the Lord, and who meditates on his law day and night" (Ps. 1:1-2). The greatest principle of law is the law of love. Jesus expressed this when he said we are to love God and our neighbor (Mt. 22:34-40)—which for Jesus included even our enemies (Mt. 5:44). Perhaps it is here that some of the difficulty in complying with God's law becomes evident.

**Assessment.** As wonderful and gracious as the law is, serious problems are encountered when a person attempts to order life strictly on this basis. Law exposes sin more than it enables one to live by its precepts. Paul reflects the frustration generated in the well-intentioned legalist when he says: "For I do not do the good I want to do, but the evil I do not want to do—this I keep on doing" (Rom. 7:19). The legalist fails to comprehend the magnitude of the grace of God. At root, the term *grace* means "beautiful." *Grace* is used in Scripture to signify God's goodness and favor toward humankind—*sinful* humanity at that. The God of grace is the God of love. He loves even sinners. The legalist actually engages in a form of unbelief by refusing to believe that God is trustworthy, gracious, forgiving, and accepting of those who come to him in simple faith. "Sin… involves a cover-up that slanders God's character by reducing him to a God of law, by depicting him as a God of punishment for lawbreakers, by implying that God is ugly" (Peters, 1998, p. 270). Legalists engage in sinful self-deception in attempting to justify themselves before God in order to be accepted, and they fail to appreciate that God is willing to justify by grace, not by works.

**Application.** The antidote to legalism is the recognition of this grace. It is acknowledging that, like it or not, the sinner stands naked before God, with every blemish exposed before him. Sinners come to God, not to give to God or prove themselves worthy, but to receive. Deliverance from sin is not achieved by human effort, but by God's unmerited favor. Jesus was speaking to those who were in bondage to the legalism of the Pharisees when he said, "Come to me, all you who are weary and burdened, and I will give you rest. Take my yoke upon you and learn from me, for I am gentle and humble in heart, and you will find rest for your souls. For my yoke is easy and my burden is light" (Mt. 11:28-30).

Daniel R. Mitchell

### REFERENCES


Allison, C. F. (1966). *The Rise of Moralism: The Proclamation of the Gospel from Hooker to Baxter.* Vancouver, Canada: Regent College.

Anderson, N. T., Miller, R., & Travis, P. (2003). *Breaking the Bondage of Legalism: When Trying Harder Isn't Enough.* Eugene, OR: Harvest House.

Hirsch, F. E., & Fensham, F. C. (1988). Law in the OT and Law in the NT. In G. W. Bromiley (Ed.), *The International Standard Bible Encyclopedia* (pp. 76-91). Grand Rapids: Eerdmans.

Kaye, B. N., & Wenham, G. J. (Eds.). (1978). *Law, Morality and the Bible.* Leicester and Downers Grove, IL: InterVarsity Press.

Kevan, Ernest F. (2003). *The Grace of Law: A Study in Puritan Theology.* London, England: Soli Deo Gloria Ministries.

Peters, Ted. (1998). *Radical Evil in Soul and Society.* Grand Rapids, MI: Eerdmans.


## SPIRITUAL WARFARE AND DELIVERANCE MINISTRY—POSSESSION AND OPPRESSION

**Description.** The concept of spiritual warfare—and the understanding that Satan is a very real spiritual being who hates and wants dominion over all human beings—is normative for every Christian seeking to know and mature in Christ. It is based on the biblical understanding that evil spiritual forces are actively attempting to thwart the purposes and presence of God by bringing about the destruction of all of humankind and all of creation. C. S. Lewis writes, "There are two equal and opposite errors into which our race can fall about devils. One is to disbelieve in their existence. The other is to believe, and to feel an excessive and unhealthy interest in them. They themselves are equally pleased with both errors" (Lewis, 1961, p. 41). This article will review the challenges of spiritual warfare at various levels of demonic attack.

There are few things more controversial at the intersection of faith and mental health than the issue of spiritual warfare and, in particular, deliverance, or the removal of demonic spirits. Few Christians can argue the practice is unbiblical; we have no difficulty in acknowledging, as the apostle Paul did, that the battle experienced by believers is both cosmic and personal. However, we are not always sure what that means or what we should do about it. "Our struggle is not against flesh and blood, but against the rulers, against the authorities, against the powers of this dark world and against the spiritual forces of evil in the heavenly realms" (Eph. 6:12).

**Possession.** To be demonized—or *daimonizomai* in the Greek (Vine, Unger, & White, 1996)—is to be possessed by an evil spirit and to sometimes act under the control of that spirit (Mt. 4:24; 8:16; 12:22; Mk. 5:15-16; Lk. 8:36). Etiologically, demonization is most often seen following long-term drug abuse and addictions of various kinds, after being victimized by severe and repeated trauma, or after dabbling in the occult.

The Scriptures tell us that demonic spirits seek to steal, kill, and destroy the believer (Jn. 10:10). We know that they work to deny the benefits provided the believer by Jesus' death and resurrection. The physical, psychological, and spiritual realms all experience the onslaught. When clients seek a closer relationship with God, they feel separated from him and unworthy of his presence. Love, peace, joy, and self-control elude them, and the torment is unrelenting. Counseling often doesn't work well because it is usually not oriented toward the demonic. However, knowledge of the presence of evil spirits can help us recognize their intentions and schemes (2 Cor. 2:11). We readily acknowledge the fact that Jesus and his disciples cast out demons (Mt. 10:8; Mk. 3:14-15; Lk. 9:1-2), and that, as a result of the indwelling and empowering of the Holy Spirit, it is Christ who does so today.

**The Work of Deliverance.** Deliverance is a spiritual process in which the minister takes on the role of "serving, cooperating with the Holy Spirit, sharing in the ministry of Jesus" (Lozano, 2003, p. 248). Ultimately, the deliverance process invites Jesus the Deliverer to come and set the individual free, just as Jesus said, "Without me you can do nothing" (Jn. 15:5).

When we see something that a demon would do, it is important to consider the possibility that a demon is doing it (Appleby, 2009). When those in our care believe they are being assaulted by demonic spirits, whether it is true or not, it does demand investigation. Therefore, we are looking for behaviors and emotions that...

- bring unrelenting shame and guilt
- are destructive to the person physically, psychologically, and spiritually
- separate the person from God
- constantly torment the person
- do not usually respond well to either medication or counseling (Appleby, 2009, p. 92)

A normal deliverance session will typically include two or three people who meet for one or more hours with the person seeking deliverance. The process consists of the following elements:

- breaking the power of generational curses, ungodly oaths, and ungodly attachments (soul ties)
- addressing the issues of unforgiveness
- determination of the name and purpose of the demon and all associated demonic spirits

- renunciation of the demonic spirits
- prayers asking for forgiveness
- a command by the client that the demonic spirit leave
- casting out the demonic spirit

The deliverance process is repeated until there are no demonic spirits present (Appleby, 2009).

MacNutt (2009) emphasizes the importance of spiritual maturity as a qualification for conducting deliverance ministry. Otherwise, pride and impetuousness may impede the work of the Spirit. A minister of deliverance must be someone who can "combine simple faith with an awareness of difficulties; someone who can join a knowledge of psychology and human frailty with the exercise of the gifts of the Holy Spirit (like discernment)" (p. 149). Thus, deliverance ministry should be approached with prayer, wisdom, and seriousness.

**Oppression and Attack.** A balanced approach to Christian counseling acknowledges the legitimacy of demonic assault and the influence of spiritual warfare but also gives attention to other psychological needs. Peter admonishes all believers to "be self-controlled and alert. Your enemy the devil prowls around like a roaring lion looking for someone to devour. Resist him, standing firm in the faith" (1 Pet. 5:8-9). James 1:12-14 also affirms the power of spiritual resistance when undergoing various trials and temptations. It reveals that evil is quick to attach itself to our sinful habits and unseemly desires, especially when we embrace those desires rather than allow God to purge them from our lives.

Much spiritual attack, therefore, is deterred by resisting the evil one. When Jesus was assaulted by the enemy while in the wilderness, he resisted by directly quoting the Word of God. Resistance will also be empowered by surrounding prayers by committed and praying believers. The dependent believer will always seek God for the power and resources to overcome evil and temptation. And God will always deliver on his promise—and will not allow believers to be tempted beyond their ability to resist (1 Cor. 10:13). Those who feel particularly tormented and oppressed may even find relief by undergoing the deliverance process outlined above. God will provide whatever means are necessary to experience victory in Christ so as to live confidently in the fruit of the Holy Spirit.

**Spiritual Warfare and Mental Health.** Most Christians do not question the legitimacy of these scriptural revelations about Satan and demonic forces, but the presence of demonization in modern times is often looked on skeptically. Within secular psychiatry and psychology, demonization is nearly always denied (but see section on Additional Issues below). Instead, the sufferer is viewed as psychotic, may be unjustly hospitalized, and is heavily medicated. Even many Christians react to the idea of possession because of misrepresentations and misuse of "deliverances" in Western media and movies that focus on bizarre and impossible behavior, personal glory, and the greater relative strength of evil, rather than the leading of the Spirit of God.

Christians working in the mental-health field cannot ignore the influence of the spiritual realm. Misdiagnosis is rampant among unbelieving professionals who deem confrontations with the demonic as being psychotic behavior, and pastors and Christian leaders witnessing psychotic behavior that they deem to be demonic. In cases of DID and other, milder forms of dissociation, alternate personalities are confused with demons, and some demons (who are liars about their identity) are viewed as alter personalities. The Holy Spirit should be invited to assist a consultative process of accurate differential diagnosis when dealing with these cases.

**Strategic Referral.** In spite of the biblical teaching, licensed mental-health professionals run a very real risk of having their licenses removed by state licensing boards and are cautioned against doing any kind of direct deliverance work (Ohlschlager & Mosgofian, 1992). Licensure board research that Ohlschlager reviewed from 1992 to 2000 indicated license revocation in every case in the U.S. involving deliverance by a mental-health professional. This was true even when the client praised the success of the intervention or when the practitioner had dual status as both an ordained minister and a mental-health professional.

Nevertheless, Ohlschlager believes that mental-health professionals must sometimes make competent, risk-managed referrals to pastoral counselors and deliverance specialists who are very good at what they do. He suggests that every licensed counselor have at least one reputable deliverance expert whose faith and track record with deliverance ministry have been thoroughly vetted. Then get out of the way and prayerfully intercede for your client. And since the client will likely return to you, you then have the opportunity to seek and test out the fruit of the deliverance. Aftercare issues will likely be significant—the client may be enabled to grow like never before and will need your support and direction to mature in a healthy way and at a capable pace.

**Additional Issues.** It is interesting to note that the *Diagnostic and Statistical Manual of Mental Disorders* (*DSM-IV-TR*) arguably deals with demonic issues in Appendix B—Criteria Sets and Axes Provided for Further Study, which includes research criteria for what is called Dissociative Trance Disorder. One of the criteria for this diagnosis is a presumed possessing agent that is defined as being spiritual in nature (e.g. spirits of the dead, supernatural entities, gods, demons). Complications associated with this disorder include suicide attempts, self-mutilation, and accidents (American Psychiatric Association, 2000).

In spite of a manifest desire within the mental-health community to be culturally sensitive, treatment (deliverance) that reflects the biblical belief system of the client is considered an aberrant protocol not worthy of professional respect. This puts the Bible-believing therapist in a quandary. If both the therapist's and client's worldviews allow for the reality of demonic influence and affirm that such interventions would be in the best interest of the client, counselors should not be prohibited from serving their clients without fear of losing their means of livelihood. Since the *DSM-IV-TR* recognizes the syndrome, licensed therapists should be allowed to address these issues in an ethical manner that is consistent with the beliefs of the client and the therapist.

Tim Clinton

## REFERENCES


American Psychiatric Association. (2000). *Diagnostic and Statistical Manual of Mental Disorders* (4th ed., text rev.). Washington, DC: Author.

Anderson, N.T. (1995). *Helping Others Find Freedom in Christ.* Ventura, CA: Regal.

Appleby, D. (2009). *It's Only a Demon: A Model of Christian Deliverance.* Winona Lake, IN: BMH Books.

Bufford, R. (1989). *Counseling and the Demonic.* Nashville: W Publishing Group.

Lewis, C. S. (1961). *The Screwtape Letters.* New York, NY: Simon & Schuster.

Lozano, N. (2003). *Unbound: A Practical Guide to Deliverance.* Royal Oak, MI: Chosen Books.

MacNutt, F. (2009). *Deliverance from Evil Spirits.* Grand Rapids, MI: Baker.

Murphy, E. (2003). *The Handbook for Spiritual Warfare.* Nashville, TN: Thomas Nelson.

Ohlschlager, G. & Mosgofian, P. (1992). *Law for the Christian Counselor: A Guidebook for Clinicians and Pastors.* Dallas, TX: Word Books.

Vine, W.E., Unger, M., & White, W., Jr. (1996). *Vine's Complete Expository Dictionary of Old and New Testament Words.* Nashville, TN: Thomas Nelson.

# COUNSELING CLINICAL DISORDERS

## ADJUSTMENT DISORDER

The diagnosis of adjustment disorder (AD) is widely recognized, covering a broad area of depressed mood, anxiety, and behaviors. The importance of properly recognizing and treating adjustment disorder had been acknowledged by its inclusion in all editions of the *Diagnostic and Statistical Manual of Mental Disorders* (Casey, 2009) and its frequent clinical use. The diagnosis is reported in up to 12% of patients attending to psychiatric settings (Balon, 2010; Casey, 2009; American Psychiatric Association [APA], 2000).

**Definition, Description and Prevalence.** The two major diagnostic classification systems, the *Diagnostic and Statistical Manual of Mental Disorders* (*DSM-IV-TR*) (APA, 2000) and the *International Classification of Diseases* (*ICD-10*) (World Health Organization [WHO], 1992), tend to provide broad and somewhat vague definitions for these disorders (Dobricki, Komproe, de Jong, & Maercker, 2010; Casey, 2009). According to the *DSM-IV-TR*, an adjustment disorder is a symptomatic "psychological response to an identifiable stressor or stressors" (APA, 2000). The *ICD-10* definition is no more concise: "States of subjective distress and emotional disturbance" (WHO, 1997). The *DSM-IV-TR* adds the need for symptoms to appear within three months of the onset of precipitating stressors, but usually not lasting more than six months, considered acute in the shorter duration and chronic if it lasts longer (APA, 2000).

**Assessment.** The criteria for diagnosing this disorder emphasize the occurrence of a common life-stressful event—such as unemployment or relocation to another state or country—resulting in the presence of a social or occupational impairment or a more-than-expected distressful response. In addition, the symptoms must not be the result of another Axis I disorder—such as anxiety or mood disorder—or bereavement. However, the *DSM-IV-TR* states that AD may be diagnosed in conjunction with an Axis I or II disorder if this second diagnosis is not the response to the symptoms occurring after the stressor.

The *DSM-IV-TR* identifies several types of possible stressors (APA, 2000). Stressors can include a single event, such as divorce, or multiple events, such as a loved one's terminal illness followed by death. The stressor can be recurrent, such as seasonal business crises, or continuous, such as poverty. Stressors can also affect an individual or an entire community, or they can be attached to a normal developmental stage, such as a transition from preschool to elementary school. The gravity of the stressor is not a good predictor of the intensity of the disorder (Sadock & Sadock, 2007) because other variables may also contribute to the specific response.

Six subtypes reflect the predominant symptoms (APA, 2000):

- with depressed mood, characterized by depressive features, tearfulness, or hopelessness

- with anxiety, typically showing nervousness, worry or fear
- with mixed anxiety and depressed mood, combining symptoms from both depression and anxiety
- with disturbance of conduct, when the behaviors violate the right of others or major societal norms or rules
- with mixed disturbance of emotions and conduct, when there is a combination of both emotional and behavioral symptoms
- unspecified, for maladaptive reactions to stressors that are not classifiable by any other subtype

A few studies report that in the context of primary care, family practitioners tend to diagnose AD in 11% to 18% of cases coming through their clinics with mental-health problems (Casey, 2009). Among those who visited secondary care psychiatric services, AD was diagnosed in 19.2% of women and 14.5% of men (Casey, 2009). In another multicenter study, AD was diagnosed as a sole diagnosis in 7.8% of patients and accounted as a "rule out" diagnosis in 10.6% of other cases (Strain et al., 1998). These reports confirm the relevancy of AD in clinical practice and the importance of a solid and accurate diagnosis procedure.

**Treatment.** An accurate diagnosis is essential for effective treatment for AD. Unfortunately, only a few structured interviews include items to assess for AD (Casey, 2009). Clinicians should rely on their clinical experience and perform a thorough evaluation of the stressors and the respective reactions. Following the symptoms outlined by the *DSM-IV-TR* and the *ICD-10* could provide helpful guidelines in determining the diagnosis and distinguishing from other related psychiatric disorders.

Psychotherapy continues to be the most effective way of treating AD (Sadock & Sadock, 2007). Clients dealing with this disorder benefit from group counseling as well, especially when the other members of the group share similar situations or have dealt with similar stressors. The support of family members in the context of family counseling is also helpful. Other individual modalities that have shown success in treating mood and anxiety disorders can also be beneficial for these clients. There are no reports of the efficacy of psychotropic interventions to treat AD; however, some medications may be very helpful for treating specific symptoms (Sadock & Sadock, 2007).

**Conclusion.** Adjustment disorders develop as a maladaptive response to stressors that, in other conditions, may not produce such unexpected and debilitating reactions. Christian clinicians should encourage and coach clients under stress to develop healthy avenues to prevent or address those challenges and join the psalmist David by enjoying the green pastures and quiet waters of our Great Shepherd.

**J. Javier Sierra**

## REFERENCES

American Psychiatric Association. (2000). *Diagnostic and Statistical Manual of Mental Disorders* (4th ed., text rev.). Washington, DC: Author.

Balon, R. (2010). Proposal to introduce adjustment disorder with distorted sexual functioning into the revised classification of DSM and ICD. *Journal of Sex and Marital Therapy 36*, 1-5.

Casey, P. (2009). Adjustment disorder: Epidemiology, diagnosis and treatment. *CNS Drugs, 23*(11), 927-938.

Dobricki, M., Komproe, I. H., de Jong, J. T. V. M., & Maercker, A. (2010). Adjustment disorders after severe life-events in four post-conflict settings. *Social Psychiatry and Psychiatric Epidemiology, 45*, 39-46.

Sadock, B. J., & Sadock, V. A. (2007). *Kaplan and Sadock's Synopsis of Psychiatry: Behavioral Sciences/Clinical Psychiatry* (10th ed.). Philadelphia, PA: Lippincott Williams & Wilkins.

Strain, J. J., Smith, G. C., Hammer, J. S., McKenzie, D. P., Blumenfield, P. M., Newstadt, G.,...Schleifer, S. S. (1998). Adjustment disorder: A multisite study of its utilization and interventions in the consultation-liaison psychiatry setting. *General Hospital Psychiatry, 20*(3), 139-149.

World Health Organization. (1992). *The ICD-10 Classification of Mental and Behavioural Disorders: Clinical Description and Diagnostic Guidelines.* Geneva, Switzerland: Author.

World Health Organization. (1997). *Composite International Diagnostic Interview.* Geneva, Switzerland: Author.

## ANXIETY DISORDERS

**Description.** Anxiety disorders, not to be confused with the general fear and anxiety experienced by all humans, represent a wide range of disorders characterized by disabling fear, worry, dread, and anxiety. "Anxiety disorders represent a malfunction of the system for activating and terminating a defensive response…symptoms are expressions of the excessive functioning of a person's systems" (Beck, Emery, & Greenberg, 2005, p. 22). Mental symptoms of anxiety include anticipation, apprehension, rumination, intrusive thoughts and images, confusion, disassociation, feeling as if things are not real, or fear of dying or going crazy. Physical symptoms include muscle tension, nausea, diarrhea, dizziness, racing heart, chest pain or pressure, rapid or difficult breathing, tremulousness, numbness, tingling, and hot flashes and sweating.

**Prevalence.** Anxiety disorders are the most common of all mental illnesses. The lifetime prevalence of the United States adult population is 28.8%, and the one-year prevalence is 18.1%. Women are 60% more likely than men to experience anxiety disorders; blacks are 20% less likely and Hispanics 30% less likely than Caucasians to experience anxiety disorders. Only 36.9% of individuals with anxiety disorder receive any treatment, and only 12.7% receive minimally adequate treatment (National Institutes of Mental Health [NIMH], 2005).

**Assessment.** Multiple reliable screening tools are available to assist in identifying individuals likely to be suffering with anxiety disorders, but the diagnosis requires careful clinical interviewing and history taking. The exact specific diagnostic criteria for each disorder can be found in the *Diagnostic and Statistical Manual of Mental Disorders* (*DSM-IV-TR*). Following is an overview of the various anxiety disorders and their general symptoms.

*Generalized anxiety* is a state of excessive worry, anxiety, or apprehension most days for a six-month period. A diagnosis requires that the anxiety interferes with functioning and has at least three of the following symptoms:

- feeling wound-up, tense, or restless
- easily becoming fatigued or worn-out
- concentration problems
- irritability
- significant tension in muscles
- difficulty with sleep

*Panic disorder* is characterized by recurrent panic attacks, worry and fear of the future, and four or more of the following:

- palpitations, pounding heart, or accelerated heart rate
- sweating panic attacks (sudden onset of severe fear) that interfere with functioning
- trembling or shaking
- shortness of breath or sensation of smothering
- feeling of choking
- chest pain or discomfort
- nausea or abdominal distress
- feeling dizzy, unsteady, lightheaded, or faint
- feelings of unreality (derealization) or being detached from oneself (depersonalization)

- fear of losing control or going crazy
- fear of dying
- numbness or tingling sensations (paresthesias)
- chills or hot flushes

*Acute stress disorder* occurs in the aftermath of a traumatic event and causes significant functional impairment. It is associated with reexperiencing the traumatic event, avoidance of stimuli that remind the person of the event, emotional numbing, feeling as if things are not real, and marked anxiety. The condition persists for at least two days but no longer than four weeks and occurs within four weeks of the trauma.

*Posttraumatic stress disorder* is a chronic anxiety disorder that is experienced in the aftermath of trauma in which the trauma is reexperienced through intrusive thoughts, nightmares, and flashbacks, causing disturbance of function. This disorder is associated with impaired relationships, emotional numbing, loss of interest, sense of foreshortened future, increased startle response, sleep disturbance, hypervigilance, impaired concentration, and irritable or angry outbursts.

*Specific phobias* are marked and unreasonable fears that are associated with a specific object or experience and that interfere with functioning.

*Social phobia* is marked and unreasonable fear of social or performance situations. The person recognizes the fear is unreasonable but avoids settings that would induce the fear.

*Obsessive-compulsive disorder* is an anxiety disorder of either obsessions or compulsions that cause marked distress, are time consuming, and interfere with functioning.

- Obsessions are recurrent and persistent impulses or images that are intrusive and inappropriate and that cause marked anxiety or distress. These are irrational and out of proportion to routine life stressors. Persons with this disorder will attempt to resist or neutralize these obsessions with some thought or action and recognize these thoughts and their response as products of their own mind.
- Compulsions are repetitive behaviors (e.g., hand washing, ordering, checking) or mental acts (e.g. praying, counting, repeating words silently) in which the person feels driven to perform in response to an obsession. The person recognizes that the obsessions and compulsions are excessive or unreasonable.

**Treatment.** Anxiety disorders are generally treated in the outpatient setting and usually involve a combination of psychotherapy and medication. Psychotherapies are integral to treating anxiety disorders, with cognitive behavior therapy demonstrating the most robust improvements.

Medications are also beneficial. The medications most commonly used in anxiety disorders are the serotonin reuptake inhibitors (fluoxetine, sertraline, paroxetine, citalopram, escitalopram), the serotonin norepinephrine reuptake inhibitors (venlafexine, desvenlafexine, duloxetine), the benzodiazapines (diazepam, alprazolam, clonazepam, etc.), and in severe cases, the antipsychotic medications. Studies have shown that a combination of psychotherapy and pharmacotherapy achieve better outcomes than either modality by itself.

Other factors that contribute to anxiety include sleep deprivation, caffeine and illegal drugs, family conflict, belief in angry and punishing God concepts, and living a self-centered life. Thus, addressing each of these factors will result in anxiety reduction.

**Biblical and Spiritual Issues.** As soon as Adam and Eve sinned, they ran and hid because they were afraid. Fear and anxiety are part of the infection of sin. Fear is the primary motivator toward selfish behavior and is the engine that drives the "survival of the fittest" instinct. This instinct is known in Scripture as the law of sin and death (Rom. 7:23–8:2) and is overcome in our lives by Christ's work to restore God's law of love into our hearts (Heb. 8:10). As Scripture says, "Perfect love drives out fear" (1 Jn. 4:18).

Research has shown that meditation and prayer can offer effective treatments for anxiety (Lee, Zaharlick, & Akers, 2011). Furthermore, recent advances in neuroscience have confirmed the biblical wisdom that love eradicates fear. The part of the brain in which fear is generated is called the amygdala, whereas the part of the brain in which we experience altruistic love, compassion, empathy, and sympathy is called the anterior cingulate cortex (ACC). Dr. Newberg at the University of Pennsylvania has shown that when individuals aged 60 to 65 meditated 12 minutes a day for 30 days on a God of love, they experience growth in the ACC as measured by MRI brain scans, reductions in heart rate and blood pressure, and improvement in memory testing. Meditating on any other God concept, such as an angry, wrathful, distant, or punitive god did not result in these positive outcomes (Newberg & Waldman, 2009). This means that growth in the ACC from meditating on a God of love calms and reduces the firing of the brain's fear center (the amygdala).

Because of sin, when we encounter a stressful experience, the brain's alarm circuitry (amygdala) will fire, causing the release of adrenalin and stress hormones (glucocorticoids). During an immediate threat, such as a dog attack, this system quickly prepares the body for survival. It will shunt blood out of the digestive organs and into the muscles; cause the heart rate and respirations to increase, increasing oxygen and blood flow to the muscles; dilate the pupils; raise the blood pressure; and alert the brain. We become more aroused and prepared for action. The glucocorticoids cause glucose to be dumped into the bloodstream for energy to either fight or take flight. Additionally, the immune system is primed, or turned on, and inflammatory cytokines are released in order to protect the body against any bacterial or viral invaders if the skin should be pierced.

All of this sounds rather good in the short term, but when one stays stressed, these pathways stay activated and cause significant problems to the body and brain. Anxiety disorders "reflect either the hyperactivity of the behavioral system or else its inhibition," neither of which is healthy long-term (Beck et al., 2005, p. 24). Chronic anxiety results in increased risk of obesity, heart attack, stroke, diabetes mellitus, bone loss, and mental illnesses, such as depression (Gorman, 2004).

TIMOTHY R. JENNINGS

### REFERENCES


American Psychiatric Association. (2000). *Diagnostic and Statistical Manual of Mental Disorders* (4th ed., text rev.). Washington, DC: Author.

Beck, A. T., Emery, G., & Greenberg, R. (2005). *Anxiety Disorders and Phobias: A Cognitive Perspective.* Cambridge, MA: Basic Books.

Gorman, J. L. (Ed.). (2004). *Fear and Anxiety: Benefits of Translational Research.* Washington, DC: American Psychiatric Association.

Lee, M. Y., Zaharlick, A., & Akers, D. (2011). Meditation and treatment of female trauma survivors of interpersonal abuses: Utilizing clients' strength. *Families in Society, 92*(1), 41-49.

National Institutes of Mental Health. (2005). *Statistics: Any Anxiety Disorder Among Adults.* Retrieved from http://www.nimh.nih.gov/statistics/1ANYANX_ADULT.shtml

Newberg, A., & Waldman, M. R. (2009). *How God Changes Your Brain: Breakthrough Findings from a Leading Neuroscientist.* New York, NY: Ballantine Books.


## GENDER IDENTITY DISORDER

**DESCRIPTION AND PREVALENCE.** To meet criteria for a formal diagnosis of gender identity disorder (GID), the *Diagnostic and Statistical Manual of Mental Disorders* (*DSM*)

requires that an individual have a "strong and persistent cross-gender identification" as well as "persistent discomfort with one's assigned sex" (American Psychiatric Association [APA], 2000, p. 576). This often manifests in children when they insist they are the other sex; prefer the roles, clothing, and activities of the opposite gender; display a preference for playmates of the other sex; and express disgust toward their own genitals. Adolescents and adults may attempt to publicly pass as their desired gender, and some people's experience of gender dysphoria is acute enough that they pursue hormonal treatment and sex reassignment surgery.

There are three common subtypes of individuals with GID: (a) female to male, (b) male to female, androphilic type, who develop sexual attraction to males, and (c) male to female, autogynephilic type, who are sexually attracted to females and have an interest in cross-dressing and envisioning themselves as female (Yarhouse, Butman, & McRay, 2005). The best estimates indicate that 1 in 11,000 men and 1 in 30,000 women seek treatment for gender identity disorder (Bakker, van Kesteren, Gooren, & Bezemer, 1993). The higher rate in males may be partly due to the greater stigma that exists for gender atypical behavior in boys as compared to girls.

Currently, the cause of GID is unknown. There exists some evidence that genetic factors, differences in brain structures, and prenatal exposure to certain hormones may contribute. However, these results are far from definitive (Carroll, 2007). Psychoanalytic theorists have hypothesized that problems result from the dynamics of children's relationship with their opposite-gendered parent (see Beitel, 1985; Stoller, 1985), but others hold that opposite-gendered behaviors were likely reinforced and learned during childhood.

**Relevant History.** Although various forms of gender dysphoria appear in early historical accounts of various cultures, professional terminology describing this issue came into existence in the 1950s. Formal diagnoses to capture such experiences were first included in the *DSM-III* in 1980, though the nomenclature has changed as knowledge in this area has advanced. Similarly, standards for assessment and treatment have evolved as a result of increased research and the work of such organizations as the Harry Benjamin International Gender Dysphoria Association, now called the World Professional Association for Transgender Health (WPATH).

**Assessment.** After ruling out possible medical conditions, a thorough psychological assessment of GID should include an extensive gender history and sexual history (Carroll, 2007), as well as an exploration of possible family issues, social issues, and potential psychopathology (WPATH, 2001). Assessment of these areas will aid helpers in fully understanding the nature of the problem, in determining the person's motivations for treatment, and in identifying possible comorbid conditions—such as anxiety or depression—that may obscure clear thinking and exacerbate feelings of dysphoria.

**Treatment.** WPATH (2001) guidelines for care of individuals with GID suggest but do not require that individuals seeking sex reassignment surgery seek therapy. Ultimately, such individuals are required to present letters from clinicians in order to be provided with medical interventions. Ethically, professionals who do not wish to write such letters should inform individuals of this before counseling begins. Therapeutic goals with adolescents and adults could include enhancing self-understanding, connecting individuals with resources for transgender individuals, exploring the various options available for resolving their dysphoria (ranging from accepting one's biological sex, to intermittent cross-dressing, to surgery), helping them to weigh the risks and benefits of these options, and resolving comorbid issues (Carroll, 2007). Goals might also include facilitating reflection on possible conflicts involving religious values and beliefs. For children, treatment might consist of helping parents learn how to implement behavioral techniques to ignore gender atypical behavior and reinforce behaviors aligned with a child's biological sex. In addition, helping children cope with being teased by peers and develop healthy relationships with others their age may be helpful. Professionals providing counsel in this area should familiarize themselves with the WPATH standards.

Emerging trends in treatment revolve around introducing medications at around age 12 that delay puberty. A few years later, at about age 16, the adolescent then makes a decision about whether to begin to take hormones of the preferred sex. This practice is controversial for many reasons but has been practiced for over a decade in the Netherlands and for several years now in the United States.

**Biblical and Spiritual Issues.** Though variations in gender are becoming more acceptable in society, a traditional Christian view would still agree with the current presumption in mental health that such variations are disordered, perhaps reflecting the condition of the Fall of humankind rather than individual sin (Yarhouse et al., 2005). From the creation story, Christians can affirm that God created both male and female and that this difference serves a purpose in men and women living out their relational and communal nature (Yarhouse et al., 2005). Yet Christians also hold the responsibility of supporting fellow believers who may have enduring conditions that they did not choose to experience, including them in a nurturing community, and bearing them up as they strive to live out their faith before God.

Mark A. Yarhouse
Heidi J. Erickson

## REFERENCES

American Psychiatric Association. (2000). *Diagnostic and Statistical Manual of Mental Disorders* (4th ed., text rev.). Washington, DC: Author.

Bakker, A., van Kesteren, P. J., Gooren, L. J. G., & Bezemer, P. D. (1993). The prevalence of transsexualism in the Netherlands. *Atca Psychiatrica Scandinavica, 87*, 237-238.

Beitel, A. (1985). The spectrum of gender identity disturbances: An intrapsychic model. In B. W. Steiner (Ed.), *Gender Dysphoria: Development, Research, Management*. New York, NY: Plenum Press.

Carroll, R. A. (2007). Gender dysphoria and transgender experiences. In S. R. Leiblum (Ed.), *Principles and Practice of Sex Therapy* (4th ed., pp. 477-506). New York, NY: Guilford Press.

Stoller, R. J. (1985). *Presentations of Gender.* New Haven, CT: Yale University Press.

World Professional Association for Transgender Health. (2001). The standards of care for gender identity disorders (6th ed.). *International Journal of Transgenderism, 5*(1). http://www.wpath.org/documents2/socv6.pdf

Yarhouse, M. A., Butman, R. E., & McRay, B. W. (2005). *Modern Psychopathologies: A Comprehensive Christian Appraisal.* Downers Grove, IL: InterVarsity Press.

## MOOD DISORDERS

The diagnostic category of mood disorders (or affective disorders) includes five primary disorders (American Psychiatric Association [APA], 2000) that are commonly referred to as depression and manic-depression. These five disorders are found in two types: unipolar mood disorders (major depressive and dysthymia) and bipolar disorders (bipolar I, bipolar II, and cyclothymic). Some symptoms of mood disorders overlap with other disorders and frequently co-occur with anxiety or substance abuse disorders (National Institute of Mental Health [NIMH], 2011).

**Description and Prevalence.** This set of disorders is primarily concerned with a person's level and type of emotional experience. Mood varies in life depending on personality, life history, physical health, and circumstances. Transient episodes of strong emotions—deep sadness or despair, elation or exuberance—do not constitute a mood disorder, nor does the common description of moodiness. Rather, mood disorders are characterized by extreme, chronic, elevated or depressed moods that indicate pathology.

Symptoms of mood disorders include feelings of discouragement or elation, hopelessness or unrealistic optimism, loss of or abundance of energy, sense of worthlessness or grandiosity, irritability, excessive guilt, and somatic symptoms. *Reactive* or *exogenous* depression is an older designation for depression that occurs in response to stressful life circumstances. *Endogenous* depression refers to depression that has a physiological basis. This distinction is no longer used in the *Diagnostic and Statistical Manual of Mental Disorders* (*DSM-IV-TR*) (APA, 2000) because mood disorders are best understood as a combination of biological and environmental interactions.

Approximately 9.5% of adults in the U.S. have a mood disorder in a given year, and the median age of onset is 30 (NIMH, 2011). Mood disorders cause significant impairment, with major depressive disorder accounting for 75% of hospitalizations for mental disorders. This may be the most lethal mental disorder because of the suicide risk. Mood disorders are among the top ten worldwide causes of disability (Seligman & Reichenberg, 2007).

Social and cultural dimensions of mood disorders impact prevalence and recovery. The prevalence of certain mood disorders tends to vary across cultures, but rates of bipolar disorders tend to be similar, regardless of cultural background. Approximately 70% of those diagnosed with a depressive disorder are women, regardless of culture, but equal numbers of males and females are diagnosed with bipolar disorder across cultures. Adolescents and the elderly may be more susceptible to mood disorders than those in other life stages.

The etiology of mood disorders is typically characterized as biological vulnerability leading to psychological vulnerability. These predispositions make individuals more susceptible to stressful life events, resulting in compromised brain functioning (hormones and neurotransmitters), negative attributions (cognitions and cognitive schemas), interpersonal problems, and lack of social support (Durand & Barlow, 2010). The root of mood disturbances may lie in experiences of bereavement, loss, and trauma. Early life losses and memories of those losses triggered by current stresses in life are considered to be significant factors in adult depression.

**Assessment.** Primary assessment tools are psychological tests and diagnostic or clinical interviews based on *DSM-IV-TR* criteria. Physiological aspects, family and social support, suicidality, life functioning, and spirituality should be examined.

The *DSM-IV-TR* specifiers help to provide a complete clinical picture. Specifiers include acute or chronic; partial or full remission; and presence of psychotic, catatonic, melancholic, atypical, postpartum, seasonal, and rapid cycling features. Hence, there are many different but related clinical presentations of these disorders.

The *DSM-IV-TR* makes a critical distinction between episodes of extreme mood, such as depression or mania, and the actual disorders. Thus major depressive, manic, mixed, and hypomanic episodes each have distinct features, and each disorder is comprised of one or more episodes.

The following graph illustrates the variety of mood disorders and suggests that (a) there is normal variation in mood that does not constitute an episode or disorder, (b) specific disorders consist of one or more episodes of mania and/or depression, and (c) the differential diagnosis of mood disorders is both complex and easily misunderstood.

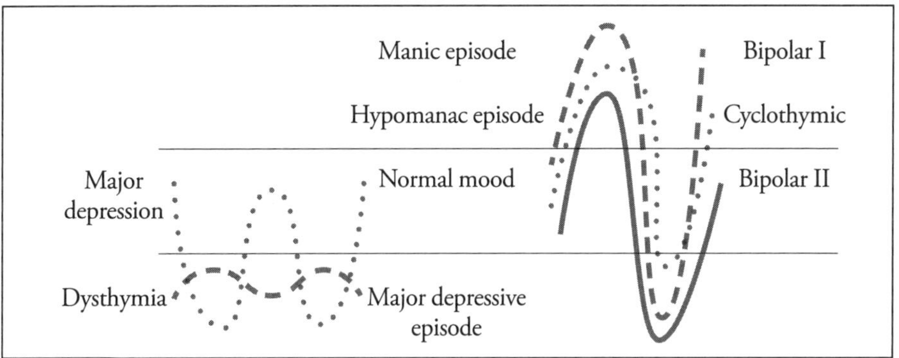


**Treatment.** Possible treatments include medications (antidepressants, mood stabilizers [such as lithium], antipsychotics, and anticonvulsants), electroconvulsive therapy, cognitive-behavioral therapy, dialectical behavior therapy, interpersonal intervention, relapse prevention, and mood maintenance (Ghaemi, 2007; Power, 2006). Accurate diagnosis and the utilization of empirically validated treatments have proven to be helpful in restoring people to normal emotional functioning and greater life satisfaction. Medications are commonly prescribed and are a major focus of research and development for the pharmaceutical industry.

**Spiritual Issues.** The Psalms are perhaps the clearest window to view the full range of human emotions. In these poems, the writers express their highest ecstasy and their deepest heartache. We cannot make a clinical diagnosis based on these writings, but we can certainly appreciate their honesty about the joy of knowing God as well as the disappointments, personal failures, sins, political setbacks, famine, and attacks they endured. In the New Testament, we see that Jesus was, as Isaiah foretold, "a man of sorrows and acquainted with grief." As Paul planted churches around the Roman Empire, he suffered deep discouragement. He wrote the believers in Corinth, "We do not want you to be uninformed, brothers and sisters, about the troubles we experienced in the province of Asia. We were under great pressure, far beyond our ability to endure, so that we despaired of life itself" (2 Cor. 1:8).

The biblical and spiritual writers of previous generations sometimes described depression and mania as closely related to one's relationship with God, sometimes even as a result of God's disfavor. Elijah (1 Ki. 19), David (Ps. 13; 88), Job (Job 3–4), and Jonah (Jon. 4) are commonly cited as biblical characters who struggled with depression.

King Saul is perhaps the clearest example in Scripture of a person with bipolar tendencies. The text describes the symptoms of major depressive and manic episodes, though the source is reported to be an evil spirit. Of course, it is dangerous to diagnose anyone with such limited information, and the causes are often complex.

St. John of the Cross refers to a particular spiritual form of depression, which he called "the dark night of the soul" (May, 2004). It refers to a depth of anguish and despair in which individuals feel, as did the psalmist David and other biblical writers, that at times God has completely abandoned them. This is in dramatic contrast to stories of people who felt that they had received a special touch from God and experienced extreme joy, a sense of well-being, and deep communion with God. Both experiences, anguish and joy, express the range of emotion described in mood disorders, but the question is whether these are mental disorders or beneficial forms of religious experience.

The Bible makes it clear that the goal of the Christian life is to follow in Christ's footsteps in joy and in sorrow, to stay connected to the one who cares and will never leave us, and to continue to examine ourselves, including our mood, to understand how God is working in and through our emotions to bring us closer to him and to others. As David expressed in his psalms, our emotions are under the sovereignty of God and are embraced in his loving and compassionate understanding.

**Conclusion.** Whether the extremes of mood are disorders or spiritual experiences, the challenge is the same: How does one stay in relationship with God, depend on him, embrace one's emotions, and seek God's comfort and healing through the various options he provides? The causes are likely a complex interaction of bio-psycho-social-spiritual factors, and the resolution is probably found through a combination of medical, clinical, and spiritual interventions. The complexity of the variations of disorders under this umbrella requires deeper understanding, differential diagnosis, research on etiology and treatment outcomes, and development of more helpful counseling strategies.

Fred Gingrich
Heather Davediuk Gingrich

## REFERENCES


American Psychiatric Association. (2000). *Diagnostic and Statistical Manual of Mental Disorders* (4th ed., text rev.). Washington, DC: Author.

Durand, M., & Barlow, H. (2010). *Essentials of Abnormal Psychology* (5th ed.). Pacific Grove, CA: Wadsworth-Thomson Learning.

Ghaemi, S. N. (2007). *Mood Disorders: A Practical Guide* (2nd ed.). Philadelphia, PA: Lippincott Williams & Wilkins.

May, G. G. (2004). *The Dark Night of the Soul: A Psychiatrist Explores the Connection Between Darkness and Spiritual Growth.* San Francisco, CA: Harper.

National Institute of Mental Health (2011). *The Numbers Count: Mental Disorders in America.* Retrieved from http://www.nimh.nih.gov/health/publications/the-numbers-count-mental-disorders-in-america/index.shtml

Power, M. (Ed.). (2006). *Mood Disorders: A Handbook of Science and Practice.* New York, NY: Wiley & Sons.

Seligman, L., & Reichenberg, L. W. (2007). *Selecting Effective Treatments: A Comprehensive, Systematic Guide to Treating Mental Disorders* (3rd ed.). San Francisco, CA: Wiley & Sons.


## MAJOR DEPRESSION

**Description.** Major depression, also known as clinical depression, is a complex biomedical, psychosocial, and spiritual disorder (American Psychiatric Association [APA], 2007). Depression may occur by itself or in combination with other physical or mental disorders. Depression co-occurs with anxiety more than 50% of the time and is often misdiagnosed as an anxiety disorder (Sadock & Sadock, 2002). Other common co-occuring disorders include chronic pain, dementia among the elderly, and drug and alcohol abuse.

The term *major depressive disorder* was selected by the APA to represent a mood disorder in the third version of the *Diagnostic and Statistical Manual of Mental Disorders* (APA, 1980). Major depression is a disabling condition that adversely affects a person's family, work or school life, sleeping and eating habits, and general health. In the United States, approximately 3.4% of people with major depression commit suicide, and up to 60% of people who commit suicide have depression or another mood disorder (APA, 2007).

**Assessment.** Major depressive disorder is characterized by a pervasive low mood, accompanied by low self-esteem and loss of interest or pleasure in normally enjoyable activities. It is referred to as "the common cold" of mental health, but this benign description belies the fact that major depression is arguably the most serious—the most adversely life-affecting—mental-health problem people suffer. Major depression can occur not only in adults but also in children and teenagers, who can also receive much benefit from treatment.

Major depression is more severe and debilitating than dysthimia—a milder and more functional kind of depression—and more serious than any prolonged grief or sadness. Major depression is also different from the depressive side of a bipolar disorder, and differential diagnosis here is often missed. The key symptoms of a clinical depression are: (a) anhedonia (the loss of pleasure or satisfaction in life), (b) the rise of numerous bodily and physiological problems, (c) presence of the "cognitive triad of depression" (worthless/helpless/hopeless obsessions), and (d) the debilitating impact of the disorder on one's relationships, work life, and self-care (APA, 2000).

Many researchers believe depression is caused by chemical imbalances in the brain, which may be hereditary but may also interact with stressful and traumatic events in a person's life (which is known as *endogenous* [biologically based] versus *exogenous* [reactive] depression). Depression sometimes runs in families, but it can also occur in people who have no such family history. Stressful life changes or events can trigger depression in some people. Usually, a complex combination of many factors is involved. Major depression is reported about twice as frequently in women as in men, and women attempt suicide more often, although men are at higher risk for completing suicide (see Barlow & Durand, 2005).

**Treatment.** Most depressed patients are treated with a combination of antidepressant medication and psychotherapy or counseling (Hart, 2001; Sadock & Sadock, 2002). Hospitalization may be necessary in cases with associated self-neglect or a significant risk of harm to self or others (suicide is the most common risk requiring hospitalization). A small minority of people who suffer severe depressive symptoms are treated with electroconvulsive therapy (ECT) and other forms of somatic therapy. Increasingly, people use self-help methods, including support groups, exercise, and nutritional supplementation.

Counseling for depression often involves a threefold focus: (a) increasing exercise or physical activity, (b) repairing broken or impaired relationships, and (c) cognitive restructuring—reducing and renouncing worthless/helpless/hopeless thinking, replacing it with worthwhile and helpful self-talk, and renewing hope in Christ. Depression also advances in isolation, so receptivity to and more time spent with others is often essential in breaking the grip of depression.

**Biblical and Spiritual Issues.** Depressed persons often believe they are alienated from God. Significant feelings of distance from God are noted rather than closeness to him (Hart, 2001; McMinn & Campbell, 2007). Depressed persons commonly report their conviction that God is angry with them or has somehow rejected and abandoned them for a myriad of different reasons. The social alienation and withdrawal that is characteristic of the depressed is often reinforced and compounded by this acute sense of divine alienation.

In this alienating equation, depressed people often believe they are being punished by God, that the punishment is usually deserved or just (sometimes there is a powerful obsession with having committed the unpardonable sin), and that there will never be a complete reconciliation—God has abandoned them for all time, and hell is inevitable (see Ohlschlager & Clinton, 2002).

Social histories of depressed persons often reveal a family history that is not grace based, but instead is performance oriented and legalistic. The individual often feels flawed and condemned for failing to live up to projected family or religious standards.

Rather than continuing to seek the impossible (as does the obsessive perfectionist), the depressed person instead retreats into a world of alienating cynicism that seems, at first, to be self-protecting. This spiritual estrangement—believing in a core alienation in every relationship, including with God—fuels the hopelessness that may drive an individual to suicide. For if it were true that God had abandoned someone with no hope of forgiveness or reconciliation, what would be the reason for living? Such existential pain—a pain that is believed to have no real cure—can be understood to motivate the upside-down logic of suicide, in which death is then viewed as the only escape from unending pain.

Existential therapists believe that depressed persons have retreated from or are living in denial of the core challenge of effective living—to properly reconcile the ongoing paradox of being alone in the universe and yet also being connected to others in a sea of relationships. The spiritual-existential challenge of living, it is argued, is to resolve the competing forces of aloneness and relatedness. Although relationships have proven to be very painful, and those who feel alienated engage in a fragile and frustrating ego defense, it is even more painful to withdraw from every relationship in the hope of avoiding further pain. "The charge [of self-induced alienation] is complex because the human self does not exist in isolation. Depressed people often are alienated from others; they are typically nonparticipant spectators to life" (Wetzel, 1984, p. 216).

Often, a newly discovered or rediscovered relationship with God stops the vicious downward cycle of despair and begins to turn a depressed person to an upward healing path. "The reconciliation of aloneness and relationship is the atonement (at-onement) of persons and God" (Wetzel, 1984, p. 217). The gospel tells us that God has supernaturally broken into the realm of alienation and disbelief. When he shows up in a person's present experiences and proves that he is truly present in love and grace, the person experiences a moment of renewal and relief from the legacy of alienating despair. Contrary to the long-held prejudice among many mental-health professionals about the inherent pathology of religious belief, the power of a healthy and intrinsic religious faith has been overwhelmingly supported in the research in the past quarter century (Koenig, 2007; Hook & Worthington, 2007; Richards & Bergin, 2005).

Deeply held religious beliefs—the resilient operation of an active and intimate faith in God—has long been shown to be resistant to depression. Moreover, a wide range of depressive symptoms are less likely to occur and are quicker to remit among those who are intrinsically rather than extrinsically religious—that is, among those who have internalized their beliefs as opposed to living out a rule-regulated religious performance. It is not always clear which factors are causes or which are effects of depression, but depressed persons who are able to make corrections in their thinking patterns often show improved mood and self-esteem (Koenig, 2007, 2001).

Finally, the combination of the proper medicine with good and effectual counseling—which includes renewing and strengthening the client's relationship with God in Christ—can turn the tide on many depressive episodes in two to four months for many sufferers. However, a significant minority of depressive sufferers may experience abated symptoms in six months by doing little to nothing to change.

**George Ohlschlager**

## REFERENCES

American Psychiatric Association. (1980). *Diagnostic and Statistical Manual of Mental Disorders* (3rd ed.). Washington, DC: Author.

American Psychiatric Association. (2000). *Diagnostic and Statistical Manual of Mental Disorders* (4th ed., text rev.). Washington, DC: Author.

American Psychiatric Association. (2007). *Practice Guidelines for the Treatment of Patients with Major Depressive Disorder* (2nd ed.). Washington, DC: Author.

Barlow, D. H., & Durand, V. M. (2005). *Abnormal Psychology: An Integrative Approach* (5th ed.). Belmont, CA: Thomson Wadsworth.

Hart, A. (2001). *Unmasking Male Depression.* Nashville, TN: W Publishing Group.

Hart, A. (2007). *Thrilled to Death: How the Endless Pursuit of Pleasure Is Leaving Us Numb.* Nashville, TN: Thomas Nelson.

Hook, J., & Worthington, E. L., Jr. (2007). The God factor: Evidence from outcome studies of psychological treatments. *Christian Counseling Today, 15*(2), 16-18.

Koenig, H. G. (2001). *The Handbook of Religion and Health.* Oxford: Oxford University Press.

Koenig, H. G. (2007). *Spirituality in Patient Care* (2nd ed.). West Conshohocken, PA: Templeton Press.

McMinn, M., & Campbell, C. (2007). *Integrative Psychotherapy: Toward a Comprehensive Christian Approach.* Downers Grove, IL: IVP Academic.

Ohlschlager, G., & Clinton, T. (2002). Change as Paradox: Overcoming client resistance and fear of change. In T. Clinton & G. Ohlschlager (Eds.), *Competent Christian Counseling: Foundations and Practice of Compassionate Soul Care.* Colorado Springs, CO: WaterBrook Press.

Richards, P. S., & Bergin, A. (2005). *A Spiritual Strategy for Counseling and Psychotherapy* (2nd ed.).Washington, DC: American Psychological Association.

Sadock, B. J., & Sadock, V. A. (2002). *Kaplan and Sadock's Synopsis of Psychiatry: Behavioral Sciences/ Clinical Psychiatry* (9th ed.). Philadelphia, PA: Lippincott Williams & Wilkins.

Wetzel, J. (1984). *Clinical Handbook of Depression.* New York, NY: Gardner Press.

## SLEEP DISORDERS

**Description.** A sleep disorder is essentially a disorder of a person's sleeping pattern. Some sleep disorders are serious enough to interfere with normal physical, mental, and emotional functioning, and most certainly can have a negative impact on a person's spirituality. Sleep disorders can be caused by a variety of issues. People who have difficulty falling or staying asleep suffer from insomnia. Excessive sleep is called hypersomnia. When a sleep disorder is secondary to mental or physical disorders, the treatment is primarily medical and must focus on the underlying disease. However, many sleep disorders are the result of poor sleep habits, excessive stimulation, or a troublesome lifestyle. Such disorders require intensive counseling or psychotherapy to correct the underlying behavioral causes.

**Assessment.** To determine the nature of a sleep disorder, a counselor must discover both the type and cause of the disorder. A *polysomnography* is a test commonly ordered for sleep and is usually performed at a sleep clinic. A counselor can evaluate the sleep disorder, its seriousness, and its cause by having the client keep a detailed sleep chart. (See Hart, 2010—the appendix provides several assessment tools and charts that can be used for this purpose.)

These are the major types of sleep disorders:

- *Bruxism*, or the involuntarily grinding or clenching of the teeth while sleeping.
- *Delayed sleep phase syndrome* (DSPS), or the inability to awaken and fall asleep at socially acceptable times (a common problem in teenagers).
- *Narcolepsy*, or excessive daytime sleepiness, often culminating in falling asleep spontaneously at inappropriate times.
- *Night terrors*, or the abrupt awakening while experiencing a bout of terror.
- *Parasomnias*, or disruptive sleep-related events involving inappropriate actions during sleep, such as sleepwalking and night terrors.
- *Restless legs syndrome* (RLS), or an irresistible urge to move the legs while sleeping or trying to sleep.
- *Circadian rhythm* sleep disorders, such as shift work and jet lag.
- *Obstructive sleep apnea* (OSA), which occurs when the airway is obstructed during sleep, causing a sudden

wakening because of oxygen deprivation.

- *Somnambulism*, or sleepwalking.
- *Nocturia*, or a frequent need to go to the bathroom to urinate at night.

**Health Issues.** Most people do not realize that sleep disturbances can be dangerous. Experts tell us that lack of sleep is taking a heavy toll on American families. Sleep deprivation disorders have shown a dramatic increase since the Internet has become universal, and misleading myths about not needing as much sleep as we are getting are rampant. This is probably the main reason why many people do not seek help for sleep problems. The consequences, however, can be significant: obesity, type 2 diabetes, heart disease, depression, learning difficulties, irritability, lack of joyfulness, increased risk of accidents, a dramatic reduction in productivity, and disordered relationships (even divorce) to name but a few!

**Spiritual Issues.** Sleep disorders also have a negative impact on our spirituality. We are designed to sleep for one-third of our lives, so it would be ridiculous to think that the Christian gospel and God's purpose for us are in no way connected to how we sleep. Sleep is as important to the soul as is our experience of God in our waking moments. There is something incredibly spiritual about sleep, so it is no wonder that Scripture makes many references to it. For instance, fulfilling sleep is the gateway to an exquisite, sublime state of serenity—a wondrous peacefulness that only God can give. Neglecting sleep can rob people of the experience of God's peace.

**Archibald Hart**

### RESOURCES

Hart, A. (2010). *Sleep: It Does a Family Good.* Colorado Springs, CO: Tyndale House.

## SOMATOFORM DISORDERS

**Description.** People with somatoform disorders have primary symptoms of a medical disorder, but no medical cause can be found. Clients with these disorders are not faking their symptoms or using them primarily to gain attention. The symptoms are real, but their source is psychological rather than medical. The symptoms are also not the result of substance abuse or another mental disorder (American Psychiatric Association [APA], 2000).

Somatoform disorders include somatization disorder, undifferentiated somatoform disorder, conversion disorder, somatoform pain disorder, hypochondriasis, and body dysmorphic disorder.

**History.** The disorder was first recognized in 1859 by French doctor Paul Briquet. It was called Briquet's syndrome and was considered a form of hysteria (Lamberty, 2008). Hysteria combined somatoform and dissociative disorders into a single diagnosis until 1980, when separate diagnoses were developed (APA, 1980).

**Assessment and Prevalence.** An important warning: Some somatoform disorders are difficult to diagnose because there may be a hidden physical cause. For example, some symptoms have been misdiagnosed as a somatoform disorder when they were actually signs of multiple sclerosis. It is imperative that a thorough physical examination be made by qualified medical personnel prior to psychological treatment.

According to the *Diagnostic and Statistical Manual of Mental Disorders* (*DSM-IV-TR*) (APA, 2000), somatoform disorders are assessed by the following symptomology:

- *Somatization disorder.* This begins before age 30, extends for a period of years, and is characterized by a combination of pain, gastrointestinal, sexual, and suggested neurological symptoms. It is found in .5% to 1% of the general population.

- *Undifferentiated somatoform disorder.* Unexplained physical complaints last at least six months. It is a less severe but more extensive and common form of somatization disorder.
- *Conversion disorder.* Unexplained symptoms or deficits affect voluntary motor or sensory function associated with psychological factors (e.g. numbness, blindness, inability to walk, etc.).
- *Pain disorder.* Pain is the focus of clinical attention, and psychological factors play an important role in onset, severity, exacerbation, or maintenance.
- *Hypochondriasis.* These are preoccupations with the fear of having (or the idea that one has) a serious disease based on the person's misinterpretation of bodily symptoms or functions.
- *Body dysmorphic* (abnormality) *disorder.* This is a preoccupation with an imagined or exaggerated defect in personal appearance.

**Treatment.** Nathan and Gorman (2007) cite empirical data favoring some form of cognitive behavior therapy as the treatment of choice for most somatoform disorders. Recommended general treatment principles for somatoform disorders include these:

- Help clients determine what the pain they are experiencing means to them (e.g. something is seriously physically wrong, related to stress, etc.).
- Establish with clients that the symptoms are real and not just in their heads.
- Use a symptom-management approach with the realistic goal of reducing discomfort levels. Becoming pain free may be unrealistic.
- Coordinate care between counseling and medical providers.
- Be alert to clients also experiencing depression and anxiety.

Specific treatments for each of the somatoform disorders can be found in Nathan and Gorman (2007). As a counseling provider, encourage clients' continued, regular contact with a physician to avoid unnecessary diagnostic testing and to minimize the use of new medications. Jongsma and Peterson (1999) offer a treatment plan for somatization that includes long-term goals, short-term objectives, and therapeutic interventions for treatment planning.

**Spiritual Issues.** Some have suggested that many somatoform disorders are anxiety based, so strengthening the client's faith in dealing with these fears is helpful. It is beneficial for clients to learn to entrust their well-being to God and his sovereignty, walk by faith daily, and not be preoccupied with doubts and fears about the future.

**Cultural Dimensions.** In many cultures with limited understanding of medical issues, some somatoform disorders, particularly conversion disorders, are perceived as being related to spirits or demons (e.g. voodoo). However, conversion disorder symptoms tend to dissipate after two weeks.

Gene A. Sale

## REFERENCES

American Psychiatric Association. (1980). *Diagnostic and Statistical Manual of Mental Disorders* (3rd ed.). Washington, DC: Author.

American Psychiatric Association. (2000). *Diagnostic and Statistical Manual of Mental Disorders* (4th ed., text rev.). Washington, DC: Author.

Jongsma, A. E., and Peterson, L. M. (1999). *The Complete Adult Psychotherapy Treatment Planner.* New York, NY: Wiley & Sons.

Lamberty, G. J. (2008). *Understanding Somatoform Disorders in the Practice of Clinical Neuropsychology.* New York, NY: Oxford University Press.

Nathan, P. E., & Gorman, J. M. (2007). *A Guide to Treatments that Work* (3rd ed.). New York, NY: Oxford University Press.

Simon, G. E. (2002). Management of somatoform and factitious disorders. In P. W. Nathan & J. M. Gorman, (Eds.), *A Guide to Treatments that Work* (2nd ed., pp. 447-461). New York, NY: Oxford University Press.

## BIPOLAR DISORDERS AND MANIA

**Description.** Bipolar disorders are a group of cyclical mood disorders characterized by periods of varying degrees of depression/dysthymia or mania/hypomania, separated by periods of normal mood. Mood fluctuations can range on a spectrum of intensity and impairment from mild to severe. Classic euphoric mania involves expansive/elevated mood, decreased need for sleep, impulsive spending, increased libido, grandiosity, and increased physical energy. The symptoms of classic bipolar depression are the same as major depressive disorder with the exception of a higher incidence of atypical symptoms, such as increased sleep, increased appetite, seasonal worsening, and weight gain. *Dysphoric mania* (also known as *mixed states*) refers to symptoms of mania and depression that occur at the same time. The individual will usually have manic symptoms with the euphoria replaced by agitation and irritability. *Hypomania* refers to symptoms of mania that are milder in intensity, impairment, and duration (usually two to four days). *Dysthymia* is the milder version of bipolar depression, but unlike hypomania, it can last for long periods of time.

The bipolar patient cycles between the mood states and periods of normality. The frequency of mood swings can include standard cycling (less than four per year), rapid cycling (more than four per year), and ultrarapid (ultrafine) cycling (more than one per day). *Bipolar type I* refers to mania alternating with major bipolar depression. *Bipolar type II* is hypomania alternating with major depression. *Cyclothymia* describes hypomania alternating with dysthymia.

Patients can develop bipolar symptoms from intoxication or withdrawal from recreational drugs. Medical conditions (thyroid, traumatic brain injury, multiple sclerosis) and medications (steroids) can produce a clinical picture that resembles bipolar disorder.

**Diagnostic Challenges.** Approximately 3% to 4% of Americans have bipolar disorder. However, studies indicate that 69% of these are misdiagnosed and can take up to ten years to get the appropriate diagnosis and treatment. Most (60%) are misdiagnosed as major depressive disorder and are prescribed antidepressants that can worsen the clinical symptoms by exaggerating depression. This is an easy mistake to make because patients spend nearly two thirds of their symptomatic time in some sort of depression. Classic mania or hypomania, which is necessary for the diagnosis, occurs only a small percentage of clients' symptomatic time. In addition, 35% to 60% of first mood episodes in bipolar patients are characterized by depressed mood.

A further complicating factor is the presence of other disorders (comorbidities) that can mask the diagnosis. Substance abuse is present in up to 60% of patients (especially binge drinking). Anxiety is present in 43% of cases. Child and adolescent patients can have cognitive disorganization that can resemble ADHD. In many cases, the medications that are used for these comorbid disorders can also worsen bipolar disorder. Diagnosis is indeed a challenge, but the failure to properly diagnose and treat bipolar disorder can lead to suicide attempts, self-medicating with alcohol or other drugs, reckless sexual and financial behavior, severe relationship damage, severe marriage and family dysfunction, and educational or vocational damage that might be irreversible. Untreated adolescent patients can ruin their lives before the freshman year of high school.

**Assessment.** The initial interview with patients is the first step of assessment. We need longitudinal data about their behavior, not just their current symptoms. I tell my patients, "I need to see the movie of your symptoms, not the snapshot." Collateral information from family and friends is priceless. A bipolar tendency (bipolarity) is suggested by very early onset of symptoms (in puberty and teenage years), severe or recurrent depression, rapid shifts into depression, and agitated responses to antidepressants by a currently depressed individual. Screening tools such as the Mood Disorder Questionnaire (Hirschfeld et al., 2000) can have instructive benefit. Mood charts are very helpful in getting a view of patients' "mood movies."

**Treatment.** Mood stabilizers are drugs that work to stabilize both ends of the mood spectrum—mania and depression. Some of these drugs work quickly to stop acute symptoms and cycling. Others are effective in maintaining improvement (also known as maintenance treatment). Lithium carbonate has been the gold standard for treatment since the early 1960s. Anticonvulsants entered the treatment options in the late 1970s with Tegretol. Since then, Depakote and Lamictal have become the foundational FDA-approved drugs in this category. Neurontin, Topamax, Gabitril, and Keppra have been tried in bipolar disorder with highly variable results. None of this later group is FDA approved for this indication. Atypical neuroleptics have become more prominent since the late 1990s for both acute and maintenance treatment. Examples of these are Zyprexa, Seroquel, Geodon, Risperdal, Saphris, Abilify, and Clozaril. The combination drug Symbyax (prozac/zyprexa) and Seroquel XR are FDA approved as monotherapy for the acute depressed phase of bipolar disorder. In reality, a third to half of patients take more than one drug in their treatment regimen. Antidepressants are used occasionally in combination with mood stabilizers but should not be given alone.

The patient and family need extensive education regarding the management of this disorder; certainly, one must not take a passive stance. Patients need to learn the rhythm of their disorder and the triggers that destabilize them. Psychotherapy is needed to grieve the pain of the past while learning how to come to peace with the relational, spiritual, and financial challenges. Communities of faith become agents of God's acceptance and healing as patients and their families seek to embrace their new normal. They don't have to be held hostage to the emotional terror of untreated bipolar disorder.

Michael R. Lyles

## REFERENCES


El-Mailakh, R. S., & Ghaemi, S. N. (2006). *Bipolar Depression: A Comprehensive Guide.* Washington, DC: American Psychiatric Association.

Hirschfeld, R., Williams, J., Spitzer, R., Calabrese, J., Flynn, L., Keck Jr., P. E.,...Zajecka, J. (2000). Development and validation of a screening instrument for bipolar spectrum disorder: The mood disorder questionnaire. *American Journal of Psychiatry, 157*(11), 1873-1875.

Ketter, T. A. (Ed.). (2010). *Handbook of Diagnosis and Treatment of Bipolar Disorders.* Washington, DC: American Psychiatric Association.

White, R., & Preston, J. (2009). *Bipolar 101: A Practical Guide to Identifying Triggers, Managing Medications, Coping with Symptoms and More.* Oakland, CA: New Harbinger Publications.


## OPPOSITIONAL DEFIANT DISORDER

**Description.** Childhood behavior problems are the most frequent type of referral to counseling practices, comprising a third to half of all outpatient and inpatient referrals. If you see families and children, chances are you have worked with a child with oppositional defiant disorder (ODD).

The *Diagnostic and Statistical Manual of Mental Disorders* (*DSM-IV-TR*) describes the core features of this behavioral problem as a pattern of negativity, hostility, and defiance. Nearly all children experience a few of these symptoms at some point in development, but to meet the criteria for oppositional defiant disorder, children must exhibit a minimum of four of the following eight symptoms for at least six months: temper tantrums, arguing with adults, active noncompliance with adult commands, deliberate attempts to annoy others, blaming others for their own mistakes, being touchy and easily annoyed, anger and resentfulness, spiteful and vindictive behavior.

It is common for ODD to accompany other childhood disorders, such as attention-deficit/hyperactive disorder. Children with ODD may also suffer from learning disorders and anxiety disorders, such as separation anxiety, generalized anxiety, and social phobia. It is not unusual for them to have a depressive disorder characterized by a mixture of psychological and emotional symptoms, such as sad or irritable mood, feelings of hopelessness, pessimism, poor motivation, and even soft suicidal ideation, characterized by thoughts about death and dying with no plan or intent to hurt themselves. Because the depressed mood is often transient (lasting only a day or two) and frequently lacks neurovegetative symptoms (such as changes in appetite and sleep, decreased energy, and decreased concentration), it does not meet full criteria for major depressive disorder or dysthymia and is frequently coded as depressive disorder, not otherwise specified. Children with ODD combined with symptoms of ADHD and depressive symptoms are at particular risk of developing a more serious disruptive behavior disorder known as conduct disorder, which involves the serious violations of societal rules, including running away from home, destruction of property, theft, and various types of aggression.

**Treatment.** A number of different psychosocial treatments have been developed for treating these children. The most common class of treatment is known as parent training (PT) and behavioral family therapy. These approaches focus on altering maladaptive parenting by practicing and building specific parenting skills for managing problematic child behavior. Russell Barkley's (1997) approach is a popular and effective short-term, 10-week behavior management approach. These are the core components:

- teaching parents why children misbehave
- teaching parents how to attend to children's positive behavior and ignore negative behavior during a daily free-play activity known as *special time*
- teaching parents how to give effective commands
- setting up a contingency management program (a *token economy*) that uses chips or points to reward prosocial, compliant behavior. These chips or points can be cashed in for more desirable reinforcers, such as snacks and special privileges
- using time-out procedures to extinguish direct defiant behaviors
- developing skills for handling misbehavior in public settings, such as stores and restaurants
- using a daily report-card system for managing behavior at school
- helping parents to generalize gains to other contexts, such as the school bus, family gatherings, visits with friends, and other places

Other treatment approaches have been developed for children with ODD combined with significant emotional dysregulation, such as anger outbursts and emotional meltdowns. Collaborative problem solving, developed by Ross Greene et al. (2004), is one such approach that is gaining increasing popularity. This approach has four core components:

- helping parents reattribute the cause of explosive behavior and noncompliance to several types of cognitive skill deficits, such as poor emotion regulation skills, low frustration tolerance, poor collaboration skills, cognitive inflexibility, poor internal language skills, inadequate problem-solving skills, and deficient adaptability skills
- teaching parents the relative value of three basic parent strategies for dealing with unmet expectations and compliance interactions (situations that are most likely to lead to explosions and meltdowns)
- teaching parents how to predict which strategies will be most effective in accomplishing important goals, such as (a) addressing parents' unmet expectations, (b) preventing meltdowns, and (c) enhancing the child's cognitive skills used to effectively manage conflict
- developing parent and child proficiency in using collaborative problem-solving skill without compromising parental authority

Both of these approaches have demonstrated efficacy. However, when compared head-to-head, the collaborative problem solving (CPS) approach has been found to be either equal to or superior to the PT approach. Also, these results were maintained at a four-month follow-up. Both these approaches can be effective and can be easily integrated into a biblical perspective on parenting.

Gary Sibcy

## RESOURCES


Barkley, R. A. (1997). *Defiant Children: A Clinician's Manual for Assessment and Parent Training* (2nd ed.). New York, NY: Guilford Press.

Greene, R., Ablon, S., Goring, J. C., Raezer-Blakely, L., Markey, J., Montuteau, M. C.,...Rabbitt, S. (2004). Effectiveness of collaborative problem solving in affectively dysregulated children with oppositional-defiant disorder: Initial findings. *Journal of Consulting and Clinical Psychology, 72,* 1157-1164.

Greene, R., Biederman, J., Zerwas, S., Montuteauz, M. C., Goring, J., & Faraone, S. V. (2002). Psychiatric comorbidity, family dysfunction, and social impairment in referred youth with oppositional defiant disorder. *American Journal of Psychiatry, 159,* 1214-1224.


## DELUSIONAL DISORDER

**Description.** Delusional disorder is a mental-health disorder previously referred to as *paraphrenia* (Late, 1987) and as paranoia (Munro, 2006). By 1987, the term *delusional disorder* was introduced in the third edition of the *Diagnostic and Statistical Manual of Mental Disorders* (*DSM-III*) (American Psychiatric Association [APA], 1987). Delusional disorder is a mental illness characterized by the presence of nonbizarre delusions in the absence of other mood or psychotic symptoms (APA, 2000). The *DSM-IV-TR* (APA, 2000) provides these criteria for diagnosing this disorder:

- Nonbizarre delusions (situations that occur in real life, such as being followed, poisoned, infected, loved at distance, deceived by spouse or lover, or having a disease) occur for at least one month.
- Criterion *A* for schizophrenia has never been met (patients do not have simultaneous hallucinations, disorganized speech, negative symptoms such as affective flattening, or grossly disorganized behavior). However, tactile (touch) and olfactory (smell) hallucinations may be present in delusional disorder if they are related to the delusional theme.
- Apart from the impact of the

delusion or its ramifications, functioning is not markedly impaired, and behavior is not obviously odd or bizarre.

- If mood episodes have occurred concurrently with delusions, they have not lasted as long as the delusional periods.
- The disturbance is not due to the direct physiological effects of a substance (such as a drug or medication) or a general medical condition.

Extensive research has not explored the causes of delusional disorder, but there are some theories. The relatives of those with delusional disorder and paranoid personality disorder appear to report a greater prevalence of delusional disorder (Kendler, Maserson, & Davis, 1985; Winokur, 1985). There may also be a genetic association between schizophrenia and delusional disorder, but it is not well understood (Debnath, Das, Bera, Nayak, & Chaudhuri, 2006).

Delusional disorder may have some foundation in biological factors (Morimoto et al., 2002). Researchers have studied the brain and linked delusions to an imbalance of specific chemicals in the brain, called neurotransmitters. Specifically, when the levels of these neurotransmitters are altered, delusions and the symptoms of delusional disorder may result.

There may also be psychological factors that result in the development of delusional disorder. It has been theorized that a delicate self-esteem in individuals causes them to use paranoia to guard against thoughts that endanger the idealized self (Abdel-Hamid & Brüne, 2008). In an effort to protect the self-esteem, the individual views others and outside forces as the cause of personal difficulties. Over time, the delusional pattern of thought that supports this individual's self-esteem can take root.

Several subtypes of delusional disorder are included in the *DSM-IV-TR*:

- *Erotomanic*. These individuals think that other persons, often important or famous people, are in love with them. There will often be attempts to contact or interact with the object of the delusion. These individuals may exhibit stalking behavior. This tends to be more common in women than men (Kelly, 2005).
- *Grandiose*. These individuals have an exaggerated sense of self, influence, intelligence, or value. They may believe that they have a great gift or skill or that they have made a critical discovery or invention. They may also believe that they have special religious insight.
- *Jealous*. These individuals believe that their spouse or sexual partner is unfaithful. There is the possibility that some degree of infidelity has occurred. However, these individuals defend their accusations by the delusional interpretation of evidence (such as disarrayed clothing or spots on sheets or undergarments). This subtype may even result in violent behaviors, including suicide and homicide (Fennig, Fochtmann, & Bromet, 2005).
- *Persecutory*. These individuals think that they (or people close to them) are being abused or oppressed or that someone is spying on them or planning to harm them. Frequently, individuals with this subtype will make repeated unfounded complaints to legal authorities. This is the most common subtype (de Portugal, Gonzalez, Haro, Autonell, & Cervilla, 2008).
- *Somatic*. These individuals believe

they have a medical problem or physical imperfection.

- *Mixed.* These individuals think they have two or more of the subtypes of delusions listed above.
- *Unspecified.* These individuals have delusions that do not meet the requirements for the other subtypes.

**Treatment.** Treatment for delusional disorder includes medication and psychotherapy. Antipsychotics have been used successfully with this disorder since the 1970s (Munro & Mok, 1995). Antidepressants have been successful in the treatment of the somatic subtype (Hayashi, Oshino, Ishikawa, Kawakatsu, & Otani, 2004). Successful psychotherapy treatment approaches have included cognitive-behavioral therapy (O'Connor et al., 2007), behavioral techniques combined with social-skills training (Liberman, 2008), and insight-oriented therapy (Silva, Kim, Hofmann, & Loula, 2003).

**Karin Dumont**

## REFERENCES


Abdel-Hamid, M., & Brüne, M. (2008). Neuropsychological aspects of delusional disorder. *Current Psychiatry Report, 10*(3), 229-234.

American Psychiatric Association. (1987). *Diagnostic and Statistical Manual of Mental Disorders* (3rd ed., rev.). Washington, DC: Author.

American Psychiatric Association. (2000). *Diagnostic and Statistical Manual of Mental Disorders* (4th ed., text rev.). Washington, DC: Author.

Debnath, M., Das, S. K., Bera, N. K., Nayak, C. R., & Chaudhuri, T. K. (2006). Genetic associations between delusional disorder and paranoid schizophrenia: A novel etiologic approach. *Canadian Journal of Psychiatry, 51*(6), 342-349.

De Portugal, E., Gonzalez, N., Haro, J. M., Autonell, J., & Cervilla, J. A. (2008). A descriptive case-register study of delusional disorder. *European Psychiatry, 23*(2), 125-133.

Fennig, S., Fochtmann, L. J., & Bromet, E. J. (2005). Delusional and shared psychotic disorder. In Kaplan & Sadock (Eds.), *Comprehensive Textbook of Psychiatry* (8th ed., pp 1525-1533). Philadelphia, PA: Lippincott Williams & Wilkins.

Hayashi, H., Oshino, S., Ishikawa, J., Kawakatsu, S., & Otani, K. (2004). Paroxetine treatment of delusional disorder, somatic type. *Human Psychopharmacology, 19*(5), 351-352.

Kelly, B. D. (2005). Erotomania: Epidemiology and management. *CNS Drugs, 19*(8), 657-669.

Kendler, K. S., Maserson, C. C., & Davis, K. L. (1985). Psychiatric illness in first-degree relatives of patients with paranoid psychosis, schizophrenia and medical illness. *British Journal of Psychiatry, 147*, 524-531.

Late, R. M. (1987). Paraphrenia. In N. E. Miller & G. E. Cohen (Eds.), *Schizophrenia and Aging* (pp. 217-234). New York, NY: Guilford Press.

Liberman, R. P. (2008). *Recovery from Disability: Manual of Psychiatric Rehabilitation.* Arlington, VA: American Psychiatric Publishing.

Morimoto, K., Miyatake, R., Nakamura, M., Watanabe, T., Hirao, T., & Suwaki, H. (2002). Delusional disorder: Molecular genetic evidence for dopamine psychosis. *Neuropsychopharmacology, 26*(6), 794-801.

Munro, A. (2006). *Delusional Disorder: Paranoia and Related Illness.* Cambridge, England: Cambridge University Press.

Munro, A., & Mok, H. (1995). An overview of treatment in paranoia/delusional disorder. *Canadian Journal of Psychiatry, 40*(10), 616-622.

O'Connor, K., Stip, E., Pélissier, M. C., Aardema, F., Guay, S., Gaudette, G., & Leblanc, V. (2007). Treating delusional disorder: A comparison of cognitive-behavioural therapy and attention placebo control. *Canadian Journal of Psychiatry, 52*(3), 182-190.

Silva, S. P., Kim, C. K., Hofmann, S. G., & Loula, E. C. (2003). To believe or not to believe: Cognitive and psychodynamic approaches to delusional disorder. *Harvard Review of Psychiatry, 11*(1), 20-29.

Winokur G. (1985). Familial psychopathology in delusional disorder. *Comparative Psychiatry, 26*, 241-248.


## DEMENTIA AND ALZHEIMER'S

**Description.** The report *Losing a Million Minds* (Office of Technology Assessment, 1987) awakened the health-care community to the increase in dementia and Alzheimer's among older adults in America. Twenty years later, more than 5.3 million people were stricken by these diseases, which had become the sixth leading cause of death (Xu, Kochanek, Murphy, & Tejada-Vera, 2010). Additionally, the *Alzheimer's Disease Facts and Figures Report* (Alzheimer's Association, 2010) estimates that there are 10.9 million unpaid (family) caregivers and $172 billion annual related costs. This report also identified older age as the common risk factor for dementia, which is higher among African-Americans and Hispanics than other ethnicities. The higher percentage of women who have dementia is attributed to generally longer lifespan than that of men.

**Types of Dementia.** Alzheimer's is the best known but not the only type of dementia. Other types of irreversible dementia include vascular dementia (formerly known as multi-infarct or stroke-related dementia), Parkinson's disease (dementia can occur in later stage), Pick's disease, Creutzfeldt-Jakob disease, HIV-related dementia, and other instances of chemical poisoning.

Alzheimer's is generally a progressive disease, but vascular dementia can be erratic. "If Alzheimer's is like sliding down a slide unable to stop the forward motion, then vascular dementia is like bouncing off a series of cliff ledges" (Erwin, 1997).

**Identification of the Problem.** To motivate early assessment, the Alzheimer's Association offers the "10 Warning Signs of Alzheimer's," which are easy for home caregivers to understand (Alzheimer's Association, 2009). Those signs include forgetfulness that disrupts normal living, inability to solve basic problems or make plans, confusion over time and place, change in speaking or writing skills, diminished judgment, mood swings, personality changes, and withdrawal from formerly pleasurable activities.

These changes are more than an occasional "off day." They become part of a new pattern of behavior, which is challenging for the family and potentially dangerous to the individual.

An individual with any type of memory impairment gradually loses the ability to transfer information from the short-term memory into the long-term memory. What is "caught" by short-term memory must be "taught" or imprinted in the long-term memory for later retrieval. The memory-impaired person may clearly recall events 60 years ago but not remember eating lunch. This condition continues and progresses, which shows that the cause is not a temporary memory problem caused by such things as a medication reaction, anesthesia, depression, nutritional deficiencies, extreme fatigue, or grief.

**Assessment.** The only accurate diagnosis for Alzheimer's is by autopsy, so the practical approach is to use cognitive assessments to identify a consistent cluster of symptoms. Research centers use PET scans for brain imaging and genetic markers; however, these are not cost effective or open for general diagnostic use.

Initial screening tools include the Short Portable Mental Status Questionnaire (SPMSQ), Mini-Mental State Examination (MMSE), Clinical Dementia Rating Scale (CDR), Global Deterioration Scale (GDS), and Instrumental Activities of Daily Living (IADL). Some tools are suitable for any counselor, but certain cognitive and neuropsychological assessments must be administered by licensed professionals.

With testing and psychosocial review, the assessor or physician can make an estimate of the stage of the disease. The Reisberg Global Deterioration Scale is one commonly used tool to identify status on a 7-stage continuum, from very mild cognitive decline to very severe (Reisberg, Ferris, de Leon, & Crook, 1982).

**Treatment.** Presently, the FDA has approved five drugs to delay disease progression in early stages, but these are not cures. Caregivers must be careful about so-called "undiscovered cures." When there is a real cure, the Alzheimer's Association will happily announce it to the world. Teaching family and paid caregivers to deal with behavioral problems, skill losses, and lack of mobility and to provide loving attention is the realistic "treatment" for dementias.

**Caregiver Burnout.** The average Alzheimer's patient lives eight to twenty years after diagnosis, so the 24/7 demands on family caregivers is extreme. Spouses and adult daughters are the usual caregivers in the home. More than 30% of home care is by the "sandwich generation," or caregivers who also have children to parent. The financial costs, time demands, and loss of one income to provide full-time care are growing burdens on marriages and young families (National Alliance for Caregiving, 2009).

**Spiritual Implications.** Dementia patients are too often kept out of church because of erratic, disruptive behaviors. Yet within their long-term memories is a sweet connection with God, as seen in the calming effect of old hymns, prayers, and Scripture readings. Our churches can provide occasional special services for these patients and can expand their ministries to caregivers. Pastors and counselors need to help connect caregivers with local resources for home health, transportation, adult day care, assisted living with dementia care unit, caregiver support groups, and respite care.

Kathie T. Erwin

## REFERENCES


Alzheimer's Association. (2009). *10 Signs of Alzheimer's.* Retrieved from http://www.alz.org/alzheimers_disease_10_signs_of_alzheimers.asp

Alzheimer's Association. (2010). *Alzheimer's Disease Facts and Figures Report.* Retrieved from http://www.alz.org/alzheimers_disease_facts_and_figures.asp

Erwin, Kathie T. (1997). *Lifeline to Care with Dignity.* St Petersburg, FL: Caremor.

National Alliance for Caregiving and American Association of Retired Persons. (2009). *Caregiving in the United States.* Retrieved from http://www.caregiving.org/data/04finalreport.pdf

Office of Technology Assessment. (1987). *Losing a Million Minds: Confronting the Tragedy of Alzheimer's Disease and Other Dementias.* Honolulu, HI: University Press of the Pacific.

Reisberg, B., Ferris, S. H., de Leon, M. J., & Crook, T. (1982). The Global Deterioration Scale for assessment of primary degenerative dementia. *American Journal of Psychiatry, 139,* 1136-1139.

Xu, J., Kochanek, K. D., Murphy, S. L., & Tejada-Vera, B. (2010). Deaths: final data for 2007. *National Vital Statistics Reports 58*(19), 19, 58. Retrieved from http://www.cdc.gov/NCHS/data/nvsr/nvsr58/nvsr58_19.pdf


## COMPLEX TRAUMA AND DISSOCIATIVE IDENTITY DISORDER

Dissociative identity disorder (DID) and complex traumatic stress disorder (CTSD) are somewhat controversial because of the unusual presentation of DID and because CTSD is not an official diagnostic category in the *Diagnostic and Statistical Manual of Mental Disorders*.

**Description and Assessment.** Complex psychological trauma is almost synonymous with chronic child abuse or neglect. Because children are developmentally vulnerable, such repetitive, prolonged, relational trauma can have ongoing, extremely detrimental effects into adulthood (Courtois & Ford, 2009). Typical symptoms include reexperiencing (including flashbacks, nightmares, intrusive thoughts, and terror), avoidance or numbing (such as avoiding triggers and amnesia), and hyperarousal (including irritability and abnormal startle response), which are characteristic of posttraumatic stress disorder, or PTSD (Wilson & Keane, 2004). However, a PTSD diagnosis does not adequately deal with the additional symptoms of affect dysregulation, impaired self-concept, dissociation, somatic problems, attachment difficulties, and spiritual alienation that lead to intrapsychic and relational disturbances in later life (Courtois & Ford). Therefore, the term CTSDs (Courtois & Ford) has been increasingly used to explain *disorders of extreme stress not otherwise specified* (Herman, 1992).

Dissociative identity disorder can be considered a specific subtype of CTSD, as a history of complex trauma has been strongly associated with DID (Steele & van der Hart, 2009). DID clients exhibit all of the CTSD symptoms, but additional dissociative symptoms are prominent, including amnesia (memory gaps), depersonalization (sense of disconnection from self or body), derealization (surroundings or others seem unfamiliar), identity confusion (greater than usual identity struggles), and identity alteration (two or more personality states recurrently take control of behavior). Identity alteration is the distinguishing factor between DID and other dissociative disorders (American Psychiatric Association, 2000).

**Treatment.** Studies on effective treatments for traumatized individuals have focused almost exclusively on PTSD. However, based on clinical literature from the past 25 years, preliminary treatment recommendations and provisional best practices for CTSD have been developed (Courtois, Ford, & Cloitre, 2009). Differing treatment strategies within various theoretical frameworks exist, and descriptive labels vary, but there has been consensus in the use of Herman's (1992) three-phase model. Treatment for DID follows the same phases, with the addition of some unique interventions.

*Phase I: Safety and stabilization.* In the first phase, careful attention to developing rapport and establishing safety within the therapeutic relationship is crucial, particularly because people have not proven safe in the past. Safety from external danger (such as domestic violence) is also important, as is making sure that clients are safe from themselves (preventing such behaviors as self-mutilation and suicide). Expanding support networks can be valuable.

PTSD symptoms can be reduced through use of cognitive-behavioral techniques. Activities such as spending time with friends, exercising, eating well, journaling, and prayer can reduce other symptoms. With DID clients, obtaining agreement from alter personalities to lessen specific symptoms is helpful. As all CTSD clients dissociate to some extent, similar therapeutic contracts can be negotiated with non-DID clients who have a complex trauma history (Gingrich, 2009).

*Phase II: Processing of traumatic memories.* Counselees may not be psychologically stable enough to face the pain and horror perpetrated against them. In such cases, treatment should end at Phase I. However, in-depth healing requires disclosure of the intimate details of the traumatic events in a self-reflective process that allows them to integrate not only cognitive aspects but also the affective, somatic, and behavioral components of their experiences. Processing feelings of guilt, shame, terror, anxiety, hatred, and so on that are associated with the trauma memories are essential. For those with DID, this process must be repeated with each alter personality.

*Phase III: Reintegration.* Previous therapeutic work must be consolidated and additional preparations made for adaptive living. A focus on issues such as identity, relationships, parenting, self-regulation, and terminating therapy fall in this phase. DID clients have to adjust to life as more fully integrated individuals.

**Spiritual Issues.** Understandably, CTSD clients struggle spiritually. How can someone who was molested or beaten by her father relate to God the Father, especially if the molester or anyone else quotes a Bible passage (such as Ephesians 6:1, which talks about the need for children to obey their parents) to justify the violence? Fortunately, as counselors become the face of Christ to their counselees, clients can begin to internalize a sense of God's unconditional love for them.

Care must be taken not to impose the use of Scripture or prayer in sessions with CTSD clients who have been spiritually damaged. The alter personalities of DID clients are frequently mistaken for demons by well-meaning Christians, making deliverance sessions potentially retraumatizing. Demonization may be an additional issue, but well-informed differential diagnosis is essential. Allowing CTSD clients to process their ambivalent feelings toward God, the church, and other Christians can further promote emotional and spiritual healing, after which judicial use of explicit spiritual interventions may be helpful.

**Conclusion.** Work with CTSD clients, including those with DID, is difficult but extremely rewarding. Christian counselors potentially have much to offer people in such deep pain.

**Heather Davediuk Gingrich**

## REFERENCES

American Psychiatric Association. (2000). *Diagnostic and Statistical Manual of Mental Disorders* (4th ed., text rev.). Washington, DC: Author.

Courtois, C. A., & Ford, J. D. (Eds.). (2009). *Treating Complex Traumatic Stress Disorders: An Evidence-Based Guide.* New York, NY: Guilford Press.

Courtois, C. A., Ford, J. D., & Cloitre, M. (2009). Best practices in psychotherapy for adults. In C. A. Courtois & J. D. Ford (Eds.), *Treating Complex Traumatic Stress Disorders: An Evidenced-Based Guide* (pp. 82-103). New York, NY: Guilford Press.

Gingrich, H. D. (2009). Complex traumatic stress disorders in adults. *Journal of Psychology and Christianity, 28,* 269-274.

Herman, J. L. (1992). Complex PTSD: A syndrome in survivors of prolonged and repeated trauma. *Journal of Traumatic Stress, 5,* 377-391.

Steele, K., & van der Hart, O. (2009). Treating dissociation. In C. A. Courtois & J. D. Ford (Eds.), *Treating Complex Traumatic Stress Disorders: An Evidenced-Based Guide* (pp. 31-58). New York, NY: Guilford Press.

Wilson, J. P., & Keane, T. M. (2004). *Assessing Psychological Trauma and PTSD* (2nd ed.). New York, NY: Guilford Press.

## EATING DISORDERS

The primary categories of eating disorders include anorexia nervosa (AN), bulimia nervosa (BN), and eating disorders not otherwise specified (EDNOS). According to the diagnostic criteria for eating disorders (American Psychiatric Association [APA], 2000), it is evident that these disorders are characterized by severe disturbances in eating and maladaptive efforts to control weight, and they often have associated features of mood fluctuation, anxiety, and a distorted body image (Delinsky, Derenné, & Becker, 2008).

**Description and Prevalence.** Eating disorders involve maladaptive behaviors, including binge-pattern eating, self-induced vomiting or purging, restricting calories, compulsive and excessive exercise, and the use of laxatives, diuretics, and stimulants. Anorexia and bulimia typically result in serious co-occurring medical complications affecting multiple organ systems in the body, such as the heart (cardiac complications), the kidneys (renal disease), and metabolism, which can all have life-threatening results (Becker, Grinspoon, & Herzog, 1999; Delinsky et al., 2008). Eating disorders occur in females in at least 90% of cases (Jacobi, 2005).

More than 30 risk factors, however, have been identified for the development of eating disorders and have led to a modern conceptualization that includes a biological, psychological, and sociocultural framework (Jacobi, Hayward, de Zwann, Kraemer, & Agras, 2004). In recent years, more attention has been given to the critical need for spiritual assessment, intervention, and support for persons with eating disorders (Cumella, Eberly, & Wall, 2008). General risk factors common to both anorexia and bulimia include overconcern with body shape and weight, early dieting, gastrointestinal disorders, sexual abuse and trauma history, negative self-esteem, and psychiatric morbidity (Jacobi et al., 2004).

**Treatment.** Eating disorders are complex problems, typically with multiple co-occurring diagnoses. They are generally viewed conceptually from a bio-psycho-social framework, recognizing the roles of biology, genetics, psychological disturbance in thought, attitudes and beliefs, lack of self-esteem, maturational fears, and social messages that drive people to believe their acceptance in society is based on body shape, weight, and appearance (Cumella et. al., 2008; Yager & Powers, 2007). Therefore, APA treatment guidelines recommend intensive intervention to restore weight and improve cognition, psychotherapy (individual and/or group), and behavioral skill training to enhance coping efforts. It is imperative that body image distortions be treated throughout the counseling process. Psychotropic medications are often utilized under the guidance of a psychiatrist to help with mood stabilization and assist in managing anxiety levels. A team approach is best in managing eating disorders and should include a therapist who specializes in eating disorders, a registered dietician (familiar with eating disorders) to help monitor nutritional gains and educate the person and family about sound nutritional practices, and a primary care physician to monitor physical health complications routine to eating disorders. There are many reasons why an individual may develop an eating disorder; therefore, careful assessment and evaluation must always inform any treatment plan.

**Anorexia Nervosa.** Anorexia is prevalent if not pandemic to industrialized Western societies (Hoek et al., 2005). Even so, it is understood that true prevalence rates are likely underestimated due to the lack of self-reporting, inaccurate assessment, and lack of access to specialized treatment for eating disorders (Delinsky et al., 2008). Anorexia is more prevalent in females than males, with prevalence rates ranging from 0.3% to 3.7% among women (Hoek & van Hoeken, 2003). Anorexia is reported to have a particular effect on younger women, with the peak age of onset for anorexia reported between ages 15 and 19. Estimates vary, but it is reported that 0.5% to 1% of female teens and young female adults develop anorexia (APA, 2000), and up to 3.7% of females experience anorexia in their lifetime (American Psychiatric Work Group on Eating Disorders, 2000). Lifetime prevalence of anorexia and anorexia-related syndromes have been estimated at more than 3% by the Centers for Disease Control and Prevention [CDC] (2006). Males are not exempt from developing eating disorders, but incidence is significantly lower, with the male/female ratio estimated at 1:6 to 1:10 for all eating disorders combined (Hoek & van Hoeken).

Anorexia is a serious mental disorder with significance in morbidity and mortality. Strikingly, it is associated with the highest mortality rate of any mental disorder (Delinsky et al., 2008; Fisher, 2003; Sullivan, 1995). This is because the effects of starvation are so severe they often result in premature and consequential death. Additionally, the suicide rate has been found to be approximately 57 times greater in anorexic women than for women of similar age in the general population (Keel et al., 2003).

The etiology of anorexia is complex, and no one unicausal model can suffice as an explanation for this complicated disorder. Jacobi et al. (2004) identified primary risk factors for anorexia among the eating disorders that include perfectionism and obsessive-compulsive traits. In addition to the psychological markers consistent with a diagnosis of anorexia, biologic research has identified the significance of genetic factors and neurobiological alterations in serotonin levels to play a meaningful role in the vulnerability of developing an eating disorder (Delinsky et al., 2008).

**Multicultural Awareness.** The cultural messages of the thin-body ideal influence the development of eating disorders, not only in Western nations but also in nonindustrialized countries, demonstrating that body image dissatisfaction can have negative effects on one's physical and psychological health in every culture (Becker, 2004; Cash, 1996). Western media exposure and peer influences toward the thin-body ideal have been found to be contributing risk factors in both anorexia and bulimia (Becker, Keel, Anderson-Frye, & Thomas, 2004). Importantly, the Becker et al. (2004) study of population data demonstrates that acculturation, immigration, and the modernization of society have contributed to the vulnerability of developing an eating disorder across cultural groups. Anorexia has been studied across diverse social contexts, with one primary notable difference being that food refusal is primarily related to the cultural context (Keel & Klump, 2003). Variation is particularly apparent in anorexia when Western and Asian populations are compared; the fear of fatness, a marker in anorexia, is prevalent in Western societies and less so in the Asian populations (Lee, 2001). Caucasians were once thought to have the greatest prevalence of eating disorders among the ethnic populations in the United States, but large studies provide evidence that eating disorders may actually be similar among the major ethnic groups (Becker & Fay, 2006).

**Bulimia Nervosa.** Bulimia nervosa is an eating disorder characterized by inappropriate compensatory methods such as self-induced vomiting, enemas, fasting, excessive exercise, and the use of laxatives, emetics, diuretics, or other medications in order to prevent weight gain, in addition to a compulsion to binge-eat larger than usual amounts of food at least twice a week for three months (APA, 2000). Binge eating may initially assuage feelings of anxiety or dysphoria, but the result of these binge episodes, which are typically done in secret, is often shame, depression, and more self-disparagement. Like anorexics, bulimics place a strong emphasis on body shape and weight and overvalue thinness.

The prevalence for bulimia is noted to be higher than anorexia, with estimates of 1.1% to 4.2%, and appears to have increased in the last several decades (American Psychiatric Association Work Group on Eating Disorders, 2000; Hoek & van Hoeken, 2003). According to the 2005 Youth Behavioral Risk Survey, 6.2% of females had engaged in purging or laxative abuse to control weight, and 8.1% admitted to using diet pills, with 17% admitting to fasting for more than a day to manage weight concerns (CDC, 2006).

Additionally, studies have shown that substance abuse disorders co-occur with eating disorders (Cumella et al., 2008), and there is not a statistically significant difference between eating disorder diagnostic groups and substance use disorder. Anorexics, bulimics, and those with EDNOS all tend to use and abuse substances, such as alcohol and marijuana. It is understandable, then, that research in one inpatient treatment center for eating disorders found that nearly 90% of patients had a co-occurring anxiety and depressive disorder (Cumella et al., 2008).

Females are far more likely to develop bulimia than males. Only an estimated 5% to 15% of people with anorexia or bulimia are male (Jacobi, 2005). Research on males with eating disorders has been scarce and is only recently becoming more available. However, of all the eating types and subtypes, eating disorder not otherwise specified (EDNOS) seems to be the most common type among males, not bulimia or anorexia in its strictest form (Striegel-Moore, Garvin, Dohm, & Rosenheck, 1999).

**EDNOS.** Eating disorders not otherwise specified is a category of eating disorders that do not meet the strict clinical severity parameters found in the diagnostic criteria for anorexia and bulimia and is the most common eating disorder category found in outpatient settings (Fairburn & Bohn, 2005). Children and adolescents frequently fall into this category diagnostically.

**Assessment.** Those concerned with early detection of an eating disorder may find a screening toll such as the SCOFF (Luck et al., 2002) to be helpful in detecting dangerous food- and body-related attitudes and behaviors prevalent in persons with eating disorders. A history and physical exam by a medical doctor are essential parts of the evaluation process. A failure to disclose eating disorder thoughts and behaviors is common, but the physical complications can help discover the problem of a hidden eating disorder.

Additional tools used in the evaluation of eating disorders include the Eating Disorder Inventory (Garner, Olmstead, & Polivy, 1983), now in its third revision, which is a self-report questionnaire given by a therapist or psychologist evaluating symptom severity and useful in prognostic evaluation. Psychological testing (such as the Minnesota Multiphasic Personality Inventory-2) can provide in-depth information in regard to personality features and issues common to eating disorders, such as somatization symptoms. The Beck Depression Inventory is useful in evaluating the co-occurrence of depression (Beck, 2006). This is by no means an exhaustive list of favorable testing materials used in the evaluation and treatment of eating disorders.

**Spiritual Considerations.** Shame is a central theme in the treatment and care of those with eating disorders. It wreaks havoc with one's identity in Christ and mars any sense of worth. Addressing the cognitive distortions and helping clients to discern the truth (about God, relationships, their bodies, food, etc.) is the foremost task in the counseling process. The counselor will undoubtedly encounter an opportunity to address issues of control: how control is acted out through resentments and anger, as well as the corrective, healing tools of love and forgiveness. And finally, we must instill hope to the hopeless and fearful person who so struggles to be accepted by man and often by God. This hope is conveyed in Scripture: "Do not be afraid, for I have ransomed you. I have called you by name; you are mine. When you go through deep waters, I will be with you. When you go through rivers of difficulty, you will not drown. When you walk through the fire of oppression, you will not be burned up; the flames will not consume you. For I am the Lord, your God, the Holy One of Israel, your Savior...and I love you" (Is. 43:1-4 NLT).

**Marian C. Eberly**

## REFERENCES


American Psychiatric Association. (2000). *Diagnostic and Statistical Manual of Mental Disorders* (4th ed., text rev.). Washington, DC: Author.

American Psychiatric Work Group on Eating Disorders. (2000). Practice guidelines for the treatment of patients with eating disorders (revision). *American Journal of Psychiatry, 157* (1 Suppl.), 1-39.

Beck, A. T. (2006). *Depression: Causes and Treatment.* Philadelphia: University of Pennsylvania Press.

Becker, A. E. (2004). New global perspectives on eating disorders. *Culture, Medicine and Psychiatry, 28,* 433-437. doi:10.1007/s11013-004-1063-9

Becker, A. E., & Fay, K. (2006). Socio-cultural issues and eating disorders. In S. Wonderlich, M. de Zwaan, H. Steiger, & J. Mitchell (Eds.), *Annual Review of Eating Disorders* (pp. 35-63). Chicago, IL: Academy for Eating Disorders.

Becker, A. E., Grinspoon, S. K., & Herzog, D. B. (1999). Eating disorders. *New England Journal of Medicine, 340,* 1092-1098. Retrieved from http://content.nejm.org/cgi/content/extract/340/14/1092

Becker, A. E., Keel, P., Anderson-Frye, E. P., & Thomas, J. J. (2004). Genes and/or jeans? Genes and socio-cultural contributions to risk for eating disorders. *Journal of Addictive Diseases 23*: 81-103. Retrieved from http://www.ncbi.nlm.nih.gov/pubmed/15256346

Bulik, C. M., Sullivan, P. F., Franz, C. P., Tozzi, F., Furberg, H., Lichenstein, P., & Pedersen, N. L. (2006). Prevalence, heritability and prospective risk factors for anorexia nervosa. *Archives of General Psychiatry, 63,* 305-312. doi:10.1001/archpsyc.63.3.305

Cash, T. (1996). The treatment of body image disturbances. In K. J. Thompson, (Ed.), *Body Image, Eating Disorders and Obesity: An Integrative Guide for Assessment and Treatment* (pp. 83-101). Washington, DC: American Psychological Association.

Centers for Disease Control and Prevention. (2006). Youth risk behavior surveillance system: Adolescent and school health, Atlanta, GA. *Morbidity and Mortality Weekly Report (MMWR), Surveillance Summaries.* Retrieved from http://www.cdc.gov/mmwr/PDF/SS/SS5505.pdf

Cumella, E. J., Eberly M. C., & Wall A. D. (2008). *Eating Disorders: A Handbook of Christian Treatment* (pp.209-245). Nashville, TN: ACW Press.

Delinsky, S. S., Derenne, J., & Becker, A. E. (2008). Specific mental health disorders: Eating disorders. In Quah, S., & Heggenhougen, K. (Eds.), *International Encyclopedia of Public Health* (pp.169-174). Burlington, MA: Academic Press. doi:10.1016/B978-012373960-5.00050-2

Fairburn, C. G., & Bohn, K. (2005). Eating disorder NOS (EDNOS): An example of the troublesome "not otherwise specified" (NOS) category in DSM IV. *Behaviour Research and Therapy, 43,* 691-701. doi:10.1016/j.brat.2004.06.011

Fisher, M. (2003). The course and outcomes of eating disorders in adults and adolescents: A review. *Adolescent Medicine, 14,* 149-158.

Garner, D. M., Olmstead, M., & Polivy, J. (1983). Development and validation of a multidimensional eating disorder inventory for anorexia nervosa and bulimia. *International Journal of Eating Disorders, 2*(2), 15-34. Retrieved from http://www3.interscience.wiley.com/journal/112413209/abstract

Hoek, H. W., & van Hoeken, D. (2003) Review of the prevalence and incidence of eating disorders. *International Journal of Eating Disorders, 34,* 383-396. doi:10.1002/eat.10222

Hoek, H. W., van Harten, P. N., Hermans, K. M., Katzman, M. A., Matroos, G. E., & Susser, E. S. (2005). The incidence of anorexia nervosa on Curacao. *American Journal of Psychiatry, 162,* 748-752. doi:10.1176/appi.ajp.162.4.748

Jacobi, C. (2005). Psychosocial risk factors for eating disorders. In S. Wonderlich, J. E. Mitchell, M. de Zwann, & H. Steiger (Eds.), *Eating Disorders: Review Part I* (pp.59-86). Oxford, UK: Radcliffe.

Jacobi, C., Hayward, C., de Zwann, M., Kraemer, H. C., & Agras, W. S. (2004). Coming to terms with risk factors for eating disorders: Application of risk terminology and suggestions for a general taxonomy. *Psychological Bulletin, 130,*19-65. doi:10.1037/0033-2909.130.1.19

Keel, P. K., Dorer, D. J., Eddy, K. T., Franko, D., Charatan, D. L., & Herzog, D. B. (2003). Predictors of mortality in eating disorders. *Archives of General Psychiatry, 60,* 179-183. doi:10.1001/archpsyc.60.2.179

Keel, P. K., & Klump, K. L. (2003). Are eating disorders culture-bound syndromes? Implications for conceptualizing their etiology. *Psychological Bulletin, 129,* 747-769. doi:10.1037/0033-2909.129.5.747

Lee, S. (2001). Fat phobia in anorexia nervosa: Whose obsession is it? In M. Nasser, M. Katzman, & R. Gordon (Eds.), *Eating Disorders and Cultures in Transition* (pp.40-54). London, England: Routledge.

Luck, A. J., Morgan, J. F., Reid, F., O'Brien, A., Brunton, J., Price, C., Perry, L., & Lacey, J. H. (2002). The SCOFF questionnaire and clinical interview for eating disorders. *British Medical Journal, 325,* 755-756.

Striegel-Moore, R. H., Garvin, V., Dohm, F. A., & Rosenheck, R. A. (1999). Eating disorders in a national sample of hospitalized female and male veterans: Detection rates and psychiatric comorbidity. *International Journal of Eating Disorders, 25,* 405-414. doi:10.1002/(SICI)1098-108X(199905)25:4<405::AID-EAT5>3.0.CO;2-F

Sullivan, P. F. (1995). Mortality in anorexia nervosa. *American Journal of Psychiatry, 152,* 1073-1074. Retrieved from http://ajp.psychiatryonline.org/cgi/content/abstract/152/7/1073

Yager, J., & Powers, P. S. (Eds.). (2007). *Clinical Manual of Eating Disorders.* Arlington, VA: American Psychiatric Publishers.

## PARANOID SCHIZOPHRENIA

**Description.** Schizophrenia presents as a chronic, often debilitating mental disorder distinguished by cognitive, affective, and behavioral alterations (American Psychiatric Association [APA], 2000). A bizarre aspect is common with the alterations in each of these areas. Delusions and hallucinations, frequently auditory, customarily appear with this disorder. The hallucinations could be visual, tactile, or olfactory. This disorder was previously referred to as "dementia praecox" (Walker, Bollini, Hochman, Kestler, & Mittal, 2008). Emil Kraepin, a German psychiatrist in the late nineteenth and early twentieth century, is credited with first differentiating schizophrenia from manic-depressive psychosis and giving it this name.

Paranoid schizophrenia tends to be the most common subtype of schizophrenia and generally has a later onset than the other subtypes (APA, 2000). In order for a diagnosis of paranoid schizophrenia to be given, individuals must first meet the general criteria for schizophrenia (APA). These individuals will commonly experience delusions that are relatively stable and often paranoid. In addition, individuals' ability to perceive things correctly is affected. These are examples of the most common paranoid symptoms (APA):

- Well-organized delusions of persecution, reference, exalted birth, special mission, bodily change, or jealousy.
- Hallucinatory voices that threaten the individuals or give commands, or auditory hallucinations without verbal form, such as whistling, humming, or laughing.
- Hallucinations of smell, taste, sexual, or other bodily sensations. Visual hallucinations may be present, but they are usually not the principal type of hallucination.

Some additional symptoms may be present in paranoid schizophrenia but are not common (APA, 2000). These include the potential for some slight (acute) thought disorder symptoms. However, if these are present, they generally do not prevent the typical delusions or hallucinations from continuing. A blunted affect may be observed but usually will be less blunted than in other subtypes of schizophrenia. Some slight mood disruptions may be present, including sudden anger, irritability, fearfulness, and suspicion. There may be some impairment to volition, but it is not overwhelming. With paranoid schizophrenia, it is not customary for the individual to be excessively distressed by mood problems or problems with thinking, concentration, and attention.

The course of paranoid schizophrenia can be episodic, with partial or complete remissions between episodes, or chronic (APA, 2000). In chronic cases, the more noticeable and disruptive symptoms, such as hallucinations, continue for years. Distinguishing between discrete episodes is not possible. The onset of this subtype is generally later than in the hebephrenic and catatonic forms. In addition, it is also not as debilitating as some of the other subtypes. It generally reacts better to treatment.

**Causality.** Scientists and researchers do not know the specific causes of schizophrenia, but genetics, prenatal development and early environment, neurobiology, and psychological and social processes have all been suggested as sources. The two causes that tend to be the most supported in research are genetics and environmental factors. Some research into the genetic aspects has reported that the potential of developing schizophrenia increases for the biological relatives of patients with schizophrenia but not in adopted relatives (Kety et al., 1994). Specifically, for individuals with schizophrenia, the risk of the disorder in first-degree relatives is 10%. The potential for developing schizophrenia in a child of two parents with the disorder is 40%. The risk of having schizophrenia in the twin of an individual with schizophrenia is 10% for dizygotic twins but increases dramatically to 40% to 50% for monozygotic twins. Gottesman proposed that a vulnerability to the illness may be inherited (Walker et al., 2008). Behavioral genetics has attempted to locate the specific gene or genes that may account for the development into this disorder. Findings from the behavioral genetic research on this disorder have put forth the premise that it arises from the involvement of multiple genes instead of one specific gene (Walker et al.).

There have also been some brain abnormalities noted in individuals with schizophrenia. These include enlarged brain ventricles; decreased frontal, temporal, and whole brain volume; and reductions in the size of the thalamus and hippocampus (Walker et al., 2008). To date, however, no single brain abnormality has been shown to be common among all individuals with schizophrenia.

In the area of neurotransmitters, dopamine appears to be the most influential in schizophrenia, although abnormalities in serotonin, glutamate, or GABA have also been theorized (Walker et al., 2008). Dopamine research has noted both an elevation in dopamine receptors as well as a pronouncement in dopamine synthesis and release in the brain of individuals with schizophrenia.

As for environmental factors, some viral illnesses or malnourishment during a pregnancy have been proposed as potential causes. Research noted that during World War II, Dutch women who were malnourished and gave birth had a higher rate of children with schizophrenia (Susser & Lin, 1992). In addition, women who have the flu during their pregnancy appear to be at greater risk of having a child who develops schizophrenia (Brown et al., 2004). A flu epidemic in 1957 in Japan, Scandinavia, and England seems to be correlated with an increase in schizophrenia in the children born to women who suffered from the flu during their second trimester. Also, between

1959 and 1966, women in California who had the flu during their first trimester of pregnancy tended to have children with a greater potential to develop schizophrenia. One of the labor and delivery complications most often associated with the development of this disorder is oxygen deprivation at birth (Walker et al., 2008).

There could potentially be a single issue that results in the development of schizophrenia, but a more popular proposal is the "stress-vulnerability model" (Ingram & Luxton, 2005). This model proposes that schizophrenia develops out of brain vulnerabilities or a genetic predisposition for the disorder, combined with life events. It is more likely that the combination of genetics and environment triggers schizophrenia. Though genetic and obstetrical factors appear to play a significant role in the development of schizophrenia, as the disorder is often not diagnosed until late adolescence or early adulthood, an individual's developmental path prior to the onset of the disorder needs to be considered (Ingram & Luxton).

**Treatment.** Treatment for paranoid schizophrenia centers on antipsychotic medications (Walker et al., 2008). Some significant and dangerous side effects are associated with these medications, so individuals taking them must be closely monitored. Included in these side effects are tardive dyskinesia, bradykinesia, dystonia, hyperprolactinemia, neuroleptic malignant syndrome, and Parkinsonism (Walker et al.). Due to side effects, individuals forgetting to take the medication, or even individuals stopping the medication once the symptoms decrease or subside, medication noncompliance is common with this disorder.

In addition to medication, psychosocial therapy or counseling is imperative with this population to assist in managing the disorder. The most efficacious treatments for this population appear to be social-skills training, cognitive-behavioral therapy, cognitive remediation, and social-cognition training (Kern, Glynn, Horan, & Marder, 2009).

**Karin Dumont**

## REFERENCES


American Psychiatric Association. (2000). *Diagnostic and Statistical Manual of Mental Disorders* (4th ed., text rev.). Washington, DC: Author.

Brown, A. S., Begg, M. D., Gravenstein, S., Schaefer, C. A., Wyatt, R .J., Bresnahan, M., & Susser, E. S. (2004). Serologic evidence of prenatal influenza in the etiology of schizophrenia. *Archives of General Psychiatry, 61*(8), 774-780.

Ingram, R. E., & Luxton, D. D. (2005). Vulnerability stress models. In B. L. Hankin & J. R. Z. Abela (Eds.), *Development of Psychology* (pp. 32-46). Thousand Oaks, CA: Sage.

Kern, R. S., Glynn, S. M., Horan, W. P., & Marder, S. R. (2009). Psychosocial treatments to promote functional recovery in schizophrenia. *Schizophrenic Bulletin, 35*(2), 347-361.

Kety, S. S., Wender, P. H., Jacobsen, B., Ingraham, L. J., Jansson, L., Faber, B., & Kinney, D. K. (1994). Mental illness in the biological and adoptive relatives of schizophrenic adoptees. Replication of the Copenhagen Study in the rest of Denmark. *Archives of General Psychiatry, 51*(6), 442-455.

Susser, E. S., & Lin, S. P. (1992). Schizophrenia after prenatal exposure to the Dutch hunger winter of 1944–1945. *Archives of General Psychiatry, 49*(12), 983-988.

Walker, E., Bollini, A., Hochman, K., Kestler, L., & Mittal, V.A. (2008). Schizophrenia. In J. E. Maddux & B. A. Winstead (Eds.), *Psychopathology* (pp. 199-222). New York, NY: Routledge.

# COUNSELING PERSONALITY DISORDERS

## PERSONALITY DISORDERS

**Description.** Personality disorders are constructs of psychopathologies centered around varying levels of dysfunction of the personality. They are often found in individuals who "are poorly functioning and/or inefficiently adapting to the requirements of contemporary society" (Magnavita, 2004, p. 3). The American Psychiatric Association (APA) defines a personality disorder as "an enduring pattern of inner experience and behavior that deviates markedly from the expectations of the individual's culture, is pervasive and inflexible, has an onset in adolescence or young adulthood, is stable over time, and leads to distress or impairment" (APA, 2000, p. 685). There has been some disagreement about what these dysfunctions and maladaptations look like, how they should be classified, and what level of dysfunction constitutes a true disorder. But key characteristics the clinician should look for include an enduring (it has been going on a long time, usually since adolescence) and pervasive (it shows up in the majority of the person's interactions with others) pattern of inflexibility (inability to adapt to changes), expressed "in at least *two* of the following areas: cognition, affectivity, interpersonal functioning, and/or impulse control" (APA, p. 686).

Millon, Grossman, Millon, Meaher, & Ramnath (2004) believe the personality is the psychological equivalent of the body's immune system. Average healthy people can fight off most infections, colds, and diseases, but if the personality system consists of maladaptive coping skills, lack of problem-solving abilities, and adaptive inflexibilities, clients will more than likely seem "sick" to others in their psychosocial environment. Another important facet of personality disorders is that those who have them "generally do not perceive that there is anything wrong with *their* behavior and are not motivated to change it" (Strickland, 2001, p. 494). From this information, it can easily be seen why personality disorders tend to cause so much trouble for those who have them and for those who are around them.

**Classification.** The fourth edition of the *Diagnostic and Statistical Manual of Mental Disorders* (*DSM-IV*) records personality disorders (and mental retardation, as well as any prominent maladaptive personality features and defense mechanisms) on Axis II on its multi-axial system of classification. The ten personality disorders are paranoid, schizoid, schizotypal, borderline, histrionic, antisocial, narcissistic, dependent, obsessive-compulsive, and avoidant.

These ten are further grouped together into three sets, or clusters, based on certain shared qualities and characteristics. The "odd or eccentric" group of Cluster A consists of the schizotypal, paranoid, and schizoid personality disorders. Cluster B, called the "dramatic, erratic, and emotional" group, is comprised of the best-known personality disorders: borderline, narcissistic, antisocial, and histrionic. Cluster C, the "anxious and fearful," includes the dependent, avoidant, and obsessive-compulsive personality disorders. There are prominent differences between the three, but clients commonly possess "co-occurring personality disorders from different clusters" (APA, 2000, p. 686).

**Prevalence.** Quite a bit of evidence seems to indicate that the actual numbers of personality disorders in society is undercounted, with some population estimates suggesting that "many more people are affected by these conditions [in the general population] than those who seek treatment" (Lenzenweger & Clarkin, 2005). Two separate comprehensive studies (based on *DSM-III-R* criteria) show that one out of ten meet the criteria for a personality disorder (Weissman, 1983), while more than 50% of those seeking treatment for mental-health issues had a diagnosable personality disorder (Merikangas & Weissman, 1986). Mattia and Zimmerman (2001) reported that clients' complaining of an Axis I disorder also displayed comorbid Axis II personality disorders in from 6.7% to more than 33% of cases. There also seems to be a question of possible gender bias, in which "six disorders (antisocial, narcissistic, obsessive-compulsive, paranoid, schizotypal, schizoid) are more frequently found in men [and] three others (borderline, histrionic, dependent) are presumably more frequent in women" (Jane & Oltmanns, 2007). Johnson and Johnson (2000) feel that church members with diagnosable personality disorders "typically come to the pastor's attention only when they are in trouble, or when others in the church are angry at or concerned about them" (p. 74).

**Diagnostic Considerations.** A diagnosis of a personality disorder should be a carefully planned and well-thought-out procedure, and although one interview may be sufficient for making the diagnosis (APA, 2000), appropriate assessments should always be a part of the process, as well as an extensive gathering of history and familial information. Unlike Axis I clinical disorders, Axis II personality disorders and mental retardation are considered permanent diagnoses. Some of the dysfunctional symptomatology may grow less evident over the course of time (for example, with borderline and antisocial personality disorder), but others (as with schizotypal and obsessive-compulsive personality disorder) tend to stay the same or may get worse (APA, 2000). Because of this, counselors may find it clinically prudent to code a client with a "rule out" or provisional diagnosis until the criteria for a personality disorder can be confirmed and verified over a year of ongoing treatment and/or observation. Because this diagnosis is "permanent" and stays with clients for their entire lives, clinicians should be as confident as possible before assigning someone with a personality disorder.

**Clay Peters**

## REFERENCES


American Psychiatric Association. (2000). *Diagnostic and Statistical Manual of Mental Disorders* (4th ed., text rev.). Washington, DC: Author.

Jane, J. S., & Oltmanns, T. F. (2007). Gender bias in diagnostic criteria for personality disorders: An item response theory analysis. *Journal of Abnormal Psychology, 116*(1), 166-175.

Johnson, W. B., & Johnson, W. L. (2000). *The Pastor's Guide to Psychological Disorders and Treatments.* New York, NY: Haworth Pastoral Press.

Lenzenweger, M. F., & Clarkin, J. F. (2005). The personality disorders: History, classification, and research issues. In M. F. Lenzenweger & J. F. Clarkin (Eds.), *Major Theories of Personality Disorder* (2nd ed.). New York, NY: Guilford Press.

Magnavita, J. (2004). Classification, prevalence, and etiology of personality disorders: Related issues and controversy. In J. Magnavita (Ed.), *Handbook of Personality Disorders: Theory and Practice.* Hoboken, NJ: Wiley & Sons.

Mattia, J. I., & Zimmerman, M. (2001). Epidemiology. In W. J. Livesly (Ed.), *Handbook of Personality Disorders: Theory, Research, and Treatment* (pp. 107-123). New York, NY: Guilford Press.

Merikangas, K. R., & Weissman, M. M. (1986). Epidemiology of DSM-III Axis II personality disorders. In A. J. Francis & R. E. Hales (Eds.), *Psychiatric Update: The American Psychiatric Association Annual Review* (Vol. 5, pp. 258-278). Washington, DC: American Psychiatric Press.

Millon, T., Grossman, S., Millon, C., Meagher, S., & Ramnath, R. (2004). *Personality Disorders in Modern Life* (2nd ed.). Hoboken, NJ: Wiley & Sons.

Strickland, B. R. (Ed.). (2001). *Gale Encyclopedia of Psychology* (2nd ed.). Farmington Hills, MI: The Gale Group.

Weissman, M. M. (1983). The epidemiology of personality disorders: A 1990 update. *Journal of Personality Disorders, 7*(Suppl.), 44-62.

## ANTISOCIAL PERSONALITY DISORDER

**Description and Prevalence.** *Antisocial personality disorder* (ASPD) is a designation for people whose level of disregard for the rights and feelings of others has created significant impairment in their ability to function in society. Typical characteristics of this disorder include deceitfulness, impulsivity, aggressiveness, irresponsibility, disregard for safety, lack of remorse, and failure to obey the law. *Psychopath* and *sociopath* are older terms rooted in the study of criminality still used for this disorder (Millon & Davis, 2000).

In addition to these behaviors, those with ASPD are lacking in conscience and show little ability to empathize with the pain inflicted on others. People with ASPD are often intelligent and charming and use these qualities to manipulate others. The most frequent of the personality disorders, ASPD occurs in about 3% of males and 1% of females. This rate is higher in clinical populations (American Psychiatric Association [APA], 2000).

Antisocial personality disorder has been variously attributed to social-environmental and biological forces. The causes likely lie in complex interactional processes involving biological predispositions (e.g., neuronal failures in transmitting fear responses) and environmental exposure (e.g., to abusive family models) (Millon & Davis, 2000).

**Assessment.** An official diagnosis of ASPD requires long-lasting and "pervasive pattern of disregard for and violation of the rights of others" (at least since the age of 15) that includes at least three of the behaviors listed above (e.g., trouble with the law, deceitfulness, financial irresponsibility, and the like) (APA, 2000, p. 706). It is given only to those over 18, though the characteristic behavioral patterns noted are present before this age. This diagnosis is not given if the noted behaviors comprise a reaction to some environmental threat or are attributed to substance abuse.

Antisocial personality disorder is diagnosed by the presence of certain enduring behaviors rather than discrete symptoms. In addition to the criteria in the *Diagnostic and Statistical Manual of Mental Disorders*, clinicians and researchers sometimes use various scales to help diagnose ASPD, such as Hare's Psychopathy Checklist (Hare, 1991).

All personality disorders, including ASPD, lie along a continuum; not everyone with antisocial tendencies meets the criteria for a formal diagnosis. This means that one should not be quick to label someone an antisocial personality based on intermittent manifestations of some of the above behaviors. However, it also means that one should not be surprised to encounter people who exhibit greater or lesser degrees of such behavior, even in the church.

**Treatment.** For years the prospect of people with ASPD getting better was considered grim, although antisocial characteristics were known to moderate in midlife. Treatment for the more severe manifestations, when it occurs, is often in a correctional facility. Cognitive-behavioral therapy has shown some efficacy in promoting behavioral changes, and empathy-building interventions have shown promise in increasing awareness of others' distress. The overall prognosis remains cautious with more emphasis placed on prevention than treatment (Millon & Davis, 2000; Yarhouse, Butman, & McRay, 2005).

**Spiritual Issues.** Clearly, personality disorders are a distortion of the image of God in humanity. For instance, the lying, irresponsibility, and lack of conscience that characterizes ASPD strike the Christian as obviously sinful. Wayne Oates (1987) has written on how various dimensions of the personality disorders, including ASPD, manifest among those in the church. How does one minister to those who manifest such behaviors? The dimensional nature of personality characteristics means that none are immune from some degree of these undesirable and harmful behaviors. Ministry is therefore from a position of humility that recognizes that all are fallen. Nevertheless, a Christian response to antisocial behavior, though compassionate, must be firm regarding behavior inappropriate to a life in Christ. That all are fallen does not excuse failure to aspire to a life of holiness by God's grace. Several Christians have written on the destructiveness of these kinds of behaviors and have offered help for those who deal with them, either as recipients or perpetrators (McLemore, 2003; Minirth, Meier, & Ratcliff, 1992; Oates, 1987; Yarhouse, et al., 2005).

**Stephen Parker**

## REFERENCES

American Psychiatric Association. (2000). *Diagnostic and Statistical Manual of Mental Disorders* (4th ed., text rev.). Washington, DC: Author.

Hare, R. D. (1991). *The Hare Psychopathy Checklist* (Rev. ed.). Toronto, Canada: Multi-Health Systems.

McLemore, C. W. (2003). *Toxic Relationships and How to Change Them: Health and Holiness in Everyday Life.* San Francisco, CA: Jossey-Bass.

Millon, T., & Davis, R. (2000). *Personality Disorders in Modern Life.* New York, NY: Wiley & Sons.

Minirth, F., Meier, P., & Ratcliff, D. (1992). *Bruised and Broken.* Grand Rapids, MI: Baker Books.

Oates, W. (1987). *Behind the Masks: Personality Disorders in Religious Behavior.* Philadelphia, PA: Westminster Press.

Yarhouse, M. A., Butman, R. E., & McRay, B. W. (2005). *Modern Psychopathologies: A Comprehensive Christian Appraisal.* Downers Grove, IL: InterVarsity Press.

## AVOIDANT PERSONALITY DISORDER

**Description.** The major feature of avoidant personality disorder (APD), as the name suggests, is an instinctive avoidance of social relationships, usually due to the fear of rejection. This disorder also includes low self-esteem, interpersonal withdrawal, sensitivity to and expectation of rejection, discomfort with and restraint within relationships, and an unwillingness to enter new relationships without some kind of guarantee of complete acceptance (Barlow & Durand, 2008).

As with all personality disorders, these dynamics are not restricted to certain people or situations, but are operative across all relationships. People with APD are obsessed with their perceived shortcomings, devalue any accomplishments or their own, and display a marked fear of being rejected, humiliated, teased, or ridiculed in any social setting. This fear becomes a self-fulfilling prophecy as others notice it and can be easily put off by its appearance. The slightest cues of rejection are looked for and often gained by the avoidant, who becomes trapped in a vicious cycle of off-putting behavior that others react to, fulfilling the avoidant person's expectation of rejection (Millon, 1991, as cited in Benner & Hill, 1999).

This vicious cycle of avoidance often fuels bouts of depression, anxiety, and intense self-loathing and anger. The disorder often interferes with the development of meaningful relationships and may block marriage and other intimate relations as well. Job performance is often impaired, especially if it demands any significant social relations (Kantor, 2010).

**History.** Identified in the early 1900s, avoidant personality tendencies were subjects of much discussion and research long before APD was established as a diagnosable disorder. Bleuler (1911) described some patients who "quite consciously shun contact with reality because their affects are so powerful that they must avoid everything which might arouse their emotions" (p. 65). Over the years, such behaviors have been termed hyper aesthetic (Kretschmer, 1925), detached (Horney, 1945), and phobic (MacKinnon & Michels, 1971), to name a few. Fundamentally, individuals with this disorder use "avoidance and inhibition as characterological defenses" (MacKinnon & Michels, p. 149). The system constellation that makes up APD is rooted in biosocial learning theory (Livesley, 1995).

Avoidant disorder may begin in childhood as early as age two or three. The earlier it begins, the more likely it is to become chronic and severe (Sperry, 2003). In children, symptoms often include a lack of assertiveness and a strong impairment in social functioning and making friends. APD may operate very much like separation anxiety in children—proximity to home or a safe parent is calming, but getting out of the home is distressing (Barlow & Durand, 2008). However, etiology is different in that separation anxiety is a fear of being separated from the safe-haven parent, whereas the personality disorder elicits fear at the prospect of interacting with strangers. People with APD are relaxed only in relations with parents or other close family members—people from whom unconditional love is given and is expected. Everyone else becomes an object of fear (American Psychiatric Association [APA], 2000).

**Assessment.** In order to make the diagnosis of APD, the *Diagnostic and Statistical Manual of Mental Disorders* (*DSM-IV-TR*) requires four or more of the following symptoms:

- avoids occupational activities that involve significant interpersonal contact because of fears of criticism, disapproval, or rejection
- is unwilling to get involved with people unless certain of being liked
- shows restraint within intimate relationships because of the fear of being shamed or ridiculed
- is preoccupied with being criticized or rejected in social situations
- is inhibited in new interpersonal situations because of feelings of inadequacy
- views self as socially inept, personally unappealing, or inferior to others
- is unusually reluctant to take personal risks or to engage in any new activities because they may prove embarrassing

This disorder behaves much like schizoid personality disorder. The major difference is that the schizoid does not care about relationships, while the avoidant hungers for acceptance and affection (Barlow & Durand, 2008). The disorder also behaves similarly to a social phobia but is much more generalized than the phobia, fearing all intimate social relations. Likewise, the behavior of APD may be quite similar to the avoidant attachment style. However, these two differ in that the avoidant attachment style also tends toward a higher self-esteem ("I'm OK, you're not"), which contrasts with the self-loathing of APD (Sperry, 2003).

**Treatment.** As with all other personality disorders, successful treatment is labored, and success is often limited (Sperry, 2003). APD treatment is especially difficult because the sufferer must meet and learn to become intimate with the therapist, who is a stranger. However, the blessing in treating APD is that learning to trust the therapist is a process that can be generalized to relations outside of therapy.

Therapy for APD centers on avoidance reduction. Kantor (2010) cites uses of psychodynamic, cognitive-behavioral, and interpersonal therapies to treat APD. When individual therapy is not effective, the treatment of choice is usually family therapy (Yarhouse & Sells, 2009). Clients with APD will come to therapy because trusted family members are coming. The goal is to transfer the trust and ease of relations with family members to people outside of the family. First of course is learning to trust the therapist, but anyone the client sees regularly—a boss, or teacher, or neighbor—can easily become the one toward whom the client works to normalize healthy adult relations.

Group therapy is also a valued treatment modality if clients can be strengthened enough to attend and join a group (Kantor, 2010). The various relationship dynamics that arise in group therapy are grist for the challenge of learning normal adult relations outside of the group. If depression and/or anxiety are significant blocks for clients, they may require an appropriate medication to be able to join some kind of therapy (Sperry, 2003).

**Spiritual Issues.** Any attempt to find complete acceptance and self-esteem apart from addressing underlying spiritual issues will never be successful. Perfect love and unconditional acceptance can ultimately only be found in a relationship with Christ. However, individuals with APD often experience discomfort and restraint at the idea of a relationship with God. Just as they fear rejection and cannot trust people, they often fear God's rejection and judgment. They believe that he, just like everyone else, cannot be trusted. False views of God and oneself can be crippling, further perpetuating the cycle of avoidance.

As Christian therapists focus on avoidance reduction, spiritual issues must be considered. Helping clients understand and live out their true identity in Christ and the spiritual riches available to them (Eph. 2) can be transformative. Failures, mistakes, and other people's opinions do not have to define them anymore. As human beings made in God's image, we are innately relational. Consequently, deep, trustworthy relationships are a critical aspect of the healing process. Safety, love, and acceptance in relationships mediate (and even overcome) the discomfort, restraint, inhibition, and reluctance that are characteristic of APD.

George Ohlschlager

## REFERENCES

American Psychiatric Association. (2000). *Diagnostic and Statistical Manual of Mental Disorders* (4th ed., text rev.). Washington, DC: Author.

Barlow, D. H., & Durand, V. M. (2008). *Abnormal Psychology: An Integrative Approach* (5th ed.). Stamford, CT: Wadsworth.

Benner, D. G., & Hill, P. C. (Eds.). (1999). *Baker Encyclopedia of Psychology and Counseling* (2nd ed.). Grand Rapids, MI: Baker Books.

Bleuler, E. (1911). *Dementia Praecox: Or the Group of Schizophrenias.* New York, NY: International Universities Press.

Horney, K. (1945). *Our Inner Conflicts.* New York, NY: Norton.

Kantor, M. (2010). *The Essential Guide to Overcoming Avoidant Personality Disorder.* Santa Barbara, CA: ABC-CLIO.

Kretschmer, E. (1925). *Physique and Character.* London, England: Kegan Paul.

Livesley, W. J. (1995). *The DSM-IV Personality Disorders.* New York, NY: Guilford Press.

MacKinnon, R. A., & Michels, R. (1971). *The Psychiatric Interview in Clinical Practice.* Philadelphia, PA: Saunders.

Sperry, L. (2003). *Handbook of Diagnosis and Treatment of DSM-IV-TR Personality Disorders* (2nd ed.). London, UK: Routledge.

Yarhouse, M. A., & Sells, J. N. (2009). *Family Therapies: A Comprehensive Christian Appraisal.* Downers Grove, IL: InterVarsity Press.

## BORDERLINE PERSONALITY DISORDER

**Description.** Borderline personality disorder (BPD) is the most frequently seen and difficult to treat personality disorder in clinical practice (Dingfelder, 2004). Even though BPD is an Axis II diagnosis, clients often present Axis I pathology. BPD is also associated with a lifetime pattern of Axis I comorbidity characteristics (Zanarini et al.,1998).

The *Diagnostic and Statistical Manual of Mental Disorders* (*DSM-IV-TR*) defines BPD as "a pervasive pattern of instability of interpersonal relationships, self-image, and affects, as well as marked impulsivity beginning by early adulthood and present in a variety of contexts." The disorder is more common in women than men. The reason for this is unclear (APA, 2000). There does not appear to be one single pathway to BPD, but rather, multiple etiologies—genetic, neurobiological and psychosocial factors (Skodol et al., 2002).

**History.** Historically, the term *borderline* was used to describe symptoms that fell somewhere between *neurotic* and *psychotic* on the psychological continuum. For years, the diagnosis was associated with negative outcomes in psychotherapy and conceptualized through an object-relations or psychoanalytical lens (Kernberg, 1975).

Recovery is often long and difficult, given clients' perpetual crises, intense history of unstable relationships, emotional dysregulation, difficulty trusting, disturbed thoughts and perceptions, and impulsive, suicidal, and parasuicidal behaviors. However, recent advances in treatment have given new hope for successful living.

Since Marsha Linehan published her study in *Archives of General Psychiatry* in 1991, her dialectical behavior therapy (DBT) has become an effective treatment for BPD. Her biosocial theory (emotional vulnerability and an invalidating environment are thought to create BPD) postulates core concepts of acceptance and validation to counter the self-invalidation of clients (Linehan, 1987).

**Assessment.** The *DSM-IV-TR* requires five or more of the following symptoms for a diagnosis of BPD (APA, 2000):

- frantic efforts to avoid real or imagined abandonment
- a pattern of unstable and intense interpersonal relationships, characterized by alternating between extremes of idealization and devaluation
- identity disturbance: markedly and persistently unstable self-image or sense of self
- impulsivity in at least two areas that are potentially self-damaging
- recurrent self-mutilating or suicidal behavior, gestures, or threats
- affective instability due to a marked reactivity of mood
- chronic feelings of emptiness
- inappropriate intense anger or difficulty controlling anger
- transient stress-related paranoia or severe dissociative symptoms

**Treatment.** Once the disorder is identified, comorbidity (such as substance abuse, major depression, etc.) must be identified and treated by way of a strong working alliance between client and therapist. Engaging the client in therapy is a critical therapeutic goal given the propensity for dropout and therapeutic noncompliance. Countertransference and transference issues should be identified and worked through in order to build trust and cooperation.

Effective treatments include dialectical behavior therapy (DBT) and comprehensive validation therapy (CVT). Other promising treatments are interpersonal therapy, cognitive therapy, cognitive analytic therapy (CAT), a fusion of cognitive and psychodynamic therapy, and systems training for emotional predictability and problem solving (STEPPS) (Oldham, 2005).

Because clients have dysfunctional core beliefs about the self, others, and the world, cognitive therapy challenges core beliefs and works to change them. Cognitive therapy also helps clients revisit childhood experiences and reinterpret thoughts and beliefs associated with those experiences. Thinking is often dichotomous, so clients must learn to think on continuous dimensions. This typically results in fewer mood swings and less intense emotional reactions (Beck & Freedman, 1990).

Self-help resources that provide ways of coping with symptoms can be used in conjunction with more traditional forms of treatment. Medication use targets symptoms rather than a cure. Acute hospitalization is appropriate when suicide and psychosis are in play.

Overall goals are to increase self-awareness and break self-harm patterns, control impulsivity and increase tolerance for anxiety, alleviate psychotic and mood disturbances, connect actions to feelings, and learn new behaviors and problem-solving skills that are not mood dependent.

**Spiritual Issues.** Linehan's notion that BPD clients need to cultivate a life worth living is consistent with the Christian belief that life has purpose and should be lived to the fullest. In Christ, there is always hope for a better tomorrow. Effective treatments like DBT that employ a mindfulness component are often based in Eastern religious practices, but mindfulness is also a Christian construct and can be used in DBT treatment. The Christian views mindfulness as an active process between God and man. God is mindful of us (Ps. 8:4; Heb. 2:6), and we are to renew our minds by the power of the Holy Spirit working in us (Rom. 12:2), love God with all our minds (Mt. 22:37), and implant God's laws into our minds (Heb. 8:10). A renewed mind that is filled with God, rather than an emptied one, promotes healing.

Linda Mintle

## REFERENCES

American Psychiatric Association. (2000). *Diagnostic and Statistical Manual of Mental Disorders* (4th ed., text rev.). Washington, DC: Author.

Beck, A. T., & Freedman, A. (1990). *Cognitive Therapy of Personality Disorders*, New York, NY: Guilford Press.

Dingfelder, S. F. (2004, March). Treatment for the "untreatable." *Monitor on Psychology*, 46-49.

Kernberg, O. F. (1975). *Borderline Conditions and Pathological Narcissism*. New York, NY: Aronson.

Linehan, M. M. (1987). Dialectical behavior therapy for borderline personality disorder: Theory and method. *Bulletin of the Menninger Clinic, 51*, 261-276.

Oldham, J. (2005). *Guideline Watch: Practice Guideline for the Treatment of Patients with Borderline Personality Disorder*. Arlington, VA: American Psychiatric Association. Retrieved from http://www.psych.org/psych_pract/treatg/pg/prac_guide.cfm

Skodol, A. E., Siever, L. J., Livesley, W. J., Gunderson, J. G., Pfohl, B., & Widiger, T. A. (2002). The borderline diagnosis II: Biology, genetics, and clinical course. *Biological Psychiatry, 51*, 951-963.

Zanarini, M. C., Frankenburg, F. R., Dubo, E. D., Sickel, A. E., Trikha, A., Levin, A., & Reynolds, V. (1998). Axis I comorbidity of borderline personality disorder. *American Journal of Psychiatry, 155*, 1733-1739.

## DEPENDENT PERSONALITY DISORDER

**Description.** Emotional attachment and dependence on those we love is part of the way mental health is described. For individuals with dependent personality disorder (DPD), this reliance is taken to an extreme. DPD is characterized by an excessive dependence on others, coupled with a lack of self-confidence (American Psychiatric Association [APA], 2000). According to the *Diagnostic and Statistical Manual of Mental Disorders* (*DSM-IV-TR*), DPD is a personality disorder, indicating that the behavior patterns are enduring and involve submissiveness, helplessness, and an exaggerated need to be cared for (APA, 2000). This emotional dependency is typically marked by feelings of pronounced anxiety. Individuals with DPD will go to great lengths to keep the approval of those upon whom they depend, even to the point of sacrificing their own thoughts or feelings in order to maintain important relationships. They fear separation and often feel abandoned when they are not with the people on whom they rely.

Because those with DPD doubt their ability to make decisions and even distrust their own intelligence, they have an extreme need to rely on others for instruction and need constant reassurance on their performance. Not having someone to help them make decisions is frightening. They may even sabotage good quality work in order to retain a significant relationship.

Though the etiology of DPD is unclear, speculations on its origin continue. It is possible that those with DPD experienced separation anxiety in childhood as a result of an anxious attachment style. Another possibility is that some children are easily frightened—an emotion which provokes feelings of protectiveness in caregivers—and the children continue to seek protective relationships well into adulthood. Still another possibility is that severe childhood illnesses resulted in persistent feelings of helplessness (Miller, 2007). Whatever the cause, less than two percent of the population is affected with DPD, with females being diagnosed more often than males (Seligman & Reichenberg, 2007).

**Spiritual Issues.** Those with DPD may have a personal relationship with God but do not draw comfort from him. The conviction that God is not a safe haven stems from the belief that he is unconcerned or is somehow displeased with them and therefore has rejected them (Clinton & Sibcy, 2002). A central spiritual struggle is accepting God as a loving Father who is always present (Ps. 46:1) and whose love is unconditional and everlasting (Jer. 31:3).

**Assessment.** According to the *DSM-IV-TR*, a person would have to meet five of the following criteria in order to be diagnosed with DPD (APA, 2000).

- has difficulty making even simple decisions without the reassurance and advice of others
- avoids assuming responsibility for personal decisions and needs others to shoulder responsibility for most areas of his/her life
- has difficulty disagreeing with others out of fear of alienating significant individuals
- has difficulty starting projects or making decisions on his/her own because of self-doubt
- goes to extreme measures to obtain care from others
- feels distressed or powerless when alone
- when a relationship ends, it will quickly be replaced
- preoccupied with fear of not having someone to care for him/her

Correctly diagnosing DPD may be problematic. It is also important to note that depression and anxiety commonly co-occur with DPD. According to the APA, DPD is not an appropriate diagnosis for children and adolescents because dependent behavior is expected and developmentally appropriate for minors (APA, 2000).

**Treatment.** Psychotherapy is the standard treatment for DPD; those with this disorder tend to respond well to therapy (Miller, 2007). Care should be taken, however, because these individuals are often overly compliant with the therapists' requests. Treatment typically focuses on reducing anxiety, addressing insecurities (especially attachment difficulties), and developing decision-making skills. In addition, spiritual concerns, particularly attachment to God, must be addressed. Termination may be a painful experience for these clients because they may become dependent on the counselor. Finally, those with DPD who initiate counseling commonly do so because of depression, anxiety, or relationship difficulties and not because of the disorder itself.

**Conclusion.** Dependent personality disorder is likely only in Westernized cultures because it is based on the notion of individualism. In contrast, other cultures experience these symptoms as positive traits (Bornstein,

1999). Indeed, due to the multicultural nature of America, therapists must use caution in diagnosing and subsequently treating DPD because the behaviors may very well be appropriate in various families in the United States.

SHANNON WOLF

## REFERENCES


American Psychiatric Association. (2000). *Diagnostic and Statistical Manual of Mental Disorders* (4th ed., text rev.). Washington, DC: Author.

Bornstein, R. F. (1999). Dependent and histrionic personality disorder. In T. Millon, P. H. Blaney, & R. D. Davis (Eds.), *Oxford Textbook of Psychopathology*. New York, NY: Oxford University Press.

Clinton, T., & Sibcy, G. (2002). *Attachments: Why You Love, Feel and Act the Way You Do*. Brentwood, TN: Integrity.

Miller, C. M. (2007). Dependent personality disorder. *Harvard Mental Health Letter, 23*(10), 1-4.

Seligman, L., & Reichenberg, L. W. (2007). Personality Disorders. In L. Seligman & L. W. Reichenberg, *Selecting Effective Treatments: A Comprehensive, Systematic Guide to Treating Mental Disorders* (3rd ed.). San Francisco, CA: Jossey-Bass.


## HISTRIONIC PERSONALITY DISORDER

**DESCRIPTION.** Histrionic personality disorder (HPD), most easily recognized because of its flamboyant presentation, is diagnosed in women more frequently than in men. People with this psychological disorder will most likely be dramatic and reactive in their behavior, sexually seductive and ostentatious in their appearance, and excessively emotional yet shallow in their relationships and communications. They are the center of attention in most situations. Research indicates that those with HPD are generally above average in their physical appearances (American Psychiatric Association [APA], 2000).

The *Diagnostic and Statistical Manual of Mental Disorders* (*DSM-IV-TR*) depicts HPD as a pervasive pattern of excessive emotionality and attention seeking, beginning by early adulthood and present in a variety of contexts, as indicated by five (or more) of the following:

- is uncomfortable in situations in which he or she is not the center of attention
- interaction with others is often characterized by inappropriate sexually seductive or provocative behavior
- displays rapidly shifting and shallow expression of emotions
- consistently uses physical appearance to draw attention to self
- has a style of speech that is excessively impressionistic and lacking in detail
- shows self-dramatization, theatricality, and exaggerated expression of emotion
- is suggestible, i.e., easily influenced by others or circumstances
- considers relationships to be more intimate than they actually are (APA, 2000, p. 711)

**HISTORY.** Although the first edition of the *DSM* did not include histrionic personality disorder, the term *hysteria* refers to a distinguishing feature of what we now consider a conversion disorder or an emotionally unstable personality, descriptors later included (APA, 1952). These two terms were replaced in the *DSM-II* with two separate diagnoses: hysterical neurosis and hysterical personality. Histrionic personality disorder followed in parentheses for the latter (APA, 1968). The first two editions of the *DSM* were written from the psychoanalytic perspective, featuring terms included in Freud's writings such as *hysteria* and *neurosis*, and attributing these hysterical behaviors to the unresolved Oedipus complex. The *DSM-II* included descriptors such as "excitability, emotional instability, overreactivity, and self-dramatization." The self-dramatization is understood to be "self-seeking and often seductive" (APA, 1968, p. 43). In the *DSM-III*, the label *hysterical* was removed from HPD, and references to seductiveness were eliminated (APA, 1980). In the *DSM-III-R*, needed revisions were included, allowing for a clear distinction between HPD and borderline personality disorder. Criterion from former editions related to seductiveness and impressionistic and shallow speech were reinstated (Pfohl, 1991, 1995).

**Assessment.** The diagnosis of HPD is often made after a battery of assessments. This frequently begins with a diagnostic interview, including a psychosocial history, and often follows with a structured interview, such as the Structured Clinical Interview, which is based on the criteria for the *DSM-IV* personality disorders. Also included in the assessment might be a self-report objective assessment such as the Minnesota Multiphasic Personality Inventory-2 or the Millon Clinical Mutiaxial Inventory-III. Some clinicians might include a projective test such as the Rorschach Inkblot Test or the Thematic Appreciation Test, which could offer information related to one's inner state, defenses, and perception of reality. Together, these assessments would provide the clinician with a clearer picture of psychological functioning of the individual.

**Treatment.** Millon, Grossman, Millon, Meagher, and Ramnath (2004) identify the need for HPD treatment to be systematic and goal-directed. The focus of treatment for the individual with HPD in most cases will be the reduction of emotional reactivity, more logical thinking, a greater level of independence, improved self-esteem, more appropriate expression of feelings, and improved reality testing (Seligman & Reichenberg, 2007). In the past it was thought that individuals with HPD would not be good candidates for group therapy, but in recent years, this outlook has changed. In group therapy settings, people with HPD cannot consistently maintain their position as the center of attention if the group is functioning properly, whereas the very nature of individual therapy places the client in the center, which could be counterproductive in light of the targeted behavioral change (Sperry, 2003). Psychodynamic and cognitive-behavioral therapies have been effective treatment approaches for those with HPD (Horowitz, 1997). Because HPD is viewed as one of the milder personality disorders, the prognosis is good for those who commit to treatment. The combination of group and individual therapy is found to be the most effective treatment approach (Seligman & Reichenberg, 2007).

**Carmela O'Hare**

## REFERENCES


American Psychiatric Association. (1952). *Diagnostic and Statistical Manual of Mental Disorders*. Washington, DC: Author.

American Psychiatric Association. (1968). *Diagnostic and Statistical Manual of Mental Disorders* (2nd ed.). Washington, DC: Author.

American Psychiatric Association. (1980). *Diagnostic and Statistical Manual of Mental Disorders* (3rd ed.). Washington, DC: Author.

American Psychiatric Association. (1987). *Diagnostic and Statistical Manual of Mental Disorders* (3rd ed., rev.). Washington, DC: Author.

American Psychiatric Association. (1994). *Diagnostic and Statistical Manual of Mental Disorders* (4th ed.). Washington, DC: Author.

American Psychiatric Association. (2000). *Diagnostic and Statistical Manual of Mental Disorders* (4th ed., text rev.). Washington, DC: Author.

Horowitz, M. J. (1997). Psychotherapy for histrionic personality disorder. *Journal of Psychotherapy Practice and Research, 6*, 93-104.

Millon, T., Grossman, S., Million, C., Meagher, S., & Ramnath, R. (2004). *Personality Disorders in Modern Life* (2nd ed.). Hoboken, NJ: Wiley & Sons.

Pfohl, B. (1991). Histrionic personality disorder: A review of available data and recommendations for DSM-IV. *Journal of Personality Disorders, 5*, 150-166.

Pfohl, B. (1995). Histrionic personality disorder. In W. J. Livesley (Ed.), *The DSM-IV Personality Disorders* (pp. 173-200). New York, NY: Guildford Press.

Seligman, L., & Reichenberg, L. W. (2007). *Selecting Effective Treatments: A Comprehensive, Systematic Guide to Treating Mental Disorders* (3rd ed.). San Francisco, CA: Jossey Bass.

Sperry, L. (2003). *Handbook of Diagnosis and Treatment of DSM-IV-TR Personality Disorders* (2nd ed.). Hove, East Sussex: Brunner-Rutledge.

## NARCISSISTIC PERSONALITY DISORDER

**Description.** Some of the diagnostic classifications in the *Diagnostic and Statistical Manual of Mental Disorders* (*DSM-IV-TR*) most resistant to change are the personality disorders. Narcissistic personality disorder (NPD) is clustered with three other personality disorders (PDs) because they share common themes of dramatic-emotional behaviors and identity disturbance (the other three personality disorders in Cluster B are borderline, histrionic, and antisocial). In making a diagnosis of a PD, several factors must be true: The personality traits must be "inflexible, maladaptive, and persisting and cause significant functional impairment or subjective distress" (American Psychiatric Association [APA], 2000, p. 689). Six specific diagnostic criteria must be met before a clinician may proceed to evaluating whether NPD or any of the other ten PDs are present. Clinicians sometimes fail to make this initial evaluation. For example, one of the six criteria is that symptoms must be consistent, of long duration, and traced back at least to adolescence or early adulthood. Therefore youth should never be diagnosed with a PD. Nor should an adult who develops symptoms later in life.

**Assessment.** As is the case with all PDs, the hallmark of NPD is that the individuals do not learn from the consequences of their behavior. The *DSM-IV-TR* (p. 717) lists nine criteria of which at least five must be present to make the diagnosis:

- has a grandiose sense of self importance
- is preoccupied with fantasies of success, power, brilliance, beauty, or ideal love
- believes that he or she is "special" and can be understood only by (or should associate only with) other special people
- requires excessive admiration
- has a sense of entitlement
- is interpersonally exploitative
- lacks empathy
- is often envious of others or believes others are envious of him or her
- shows arrogant, haughty behaviors or attitudes

There are many other symptoms that can be associated with NPD that are subsets or correlates of the official diagnostic ones. Associated symptoms include these (in random order):

- is moody (perhaps Dr. Jekyll at work and Mr. Hyde in the home)
- is critical and complaining
- requires others to walk on eggshells
- is hard to please
- lectures and pontificates
- has intense emotional responses
- has problems with anger
- sometimes abuses drugs or alcohol
- breaks laws
- has affairs and/or is involved with pornography (or other self-destructive behaviors)
- is a moving target (what upsets them can easily shift)
- is tense inside
- is a black-and-white thinker
- requires others to be loyal to them
- sees difference at times as disloyal
- misperceives reality
- beats a dead horse
- has to prove a point

- physically and verbally abusive
- uses foul language
- feels easily rejected
- insecure and sensitive
- projects blame onto others
- may be ADHD (thereby complicating other symptoms)

**Causes.** The etiology of NPD has not yet been efficiently established. Some theories point to early childhood trauma, and others focus on problems in the parent-child relationship. However, the most promising theory might be that those who suffer with NPD may have a learning disability involving the emotional regulation of the brain—a type of "emotional dyslexia" (DiBlasio, 2001). As with learning disabilities in academic areas, the brain does not seem to learn in certain areas. When it comes to close interpersonal relationships, where expectations are high and emotions are most under stress, the NPD may be particularly symptomatic. The neuroscience is beginning to show that persons with PD may have significant reduction of the hippocampi and amygdala (the brain structure that is critical in emotional processing) (Terbartz van Elst et al., 2003).

**Treatment.** For the most part, clinicians report in the literature that PD is basically "impervious to recovery" (Sadock & Sadock, 2007, p. 791). However, treatment as a brain dysfunction is producing successful clinical outcomes (DiBlasio 2001, 2005). Christian counselors may help NPD clients by engaging them with the love of Christ, emphasizing their strengths, showing admiration for these strengths, advocating that family members do the same, and addressing the "emotional dyslexia" as a brain problem that is usually activated in close interpersonal relationships. (Sometimes when NPD is severe, it is activated also in other relationships). God created all human beings with the capacity not to give way to temptation (1 Cor. 10:13). When tempted, NPD patients can learn not to trust their immediate feelings, but instead to allow other areas of their brains to guide behavior.

**Frederick A. DiBlasio**

## REFERENCES

American Psychiatric Association. (2000). *Diagnostic and Statistical Manual of Mental Disorders* (4th ed., text rev.). Washington, DC: Author.

DiBlasio, F. A. (2001). *Effective Treatment of Personality Disorders*. Geneva Series [DVD]. American Association of Christian Counselors.

DiBlasio, F. A. (2005). Dealing with the hard cases. *Marriage & Family Network, 1*, 1, 6, 8.

Sadock B., & Sadock V. (2007). *Synopsis of Psychiatry* (10th ed.). Philadelphia, PA: Lippincott Williams & Wilkins.

Tebartz van Elst, L., Hesslinger, B., Thiel, T., Geiger, E., Haegele, K., Lemieux, L.,...Ebert, D. (2003). Frontolimbic brain abnormalities in patients with borderline personality disorder: A volumetric magnetic resonance imaging study. *Biological Psychiatry, 54*, 163-171.

## OBSESSIVE-COMPULSIVE PERSONALITY DISORDER

**Description and Prevalence:** Obsessive-compulsive personality disorder (OCPD) is characterized by a need for order, perfection, and control. These qualities manifest in several ways. Such people may be workaholics, overly conscientious (religiously scrupulous), and obsessed with minute details. They often are mercilessly demanding of themselves, feeling guilt or shame at the slightest imperfection. Their inflexibility and expectation that others be as conscientious as they are often cause rifts in their relationships.

According to the *Diagnostic and Statistical Manual of Mental Disorders* (*DSM-IV-TR*), an essential feature of this disorder is a "pervasive preoccupation with orderliness, perfectionism, and...control." Those with OCPD may show excessive devotion to work to the exclusion of leisure activities (even when not economically necessary).

They are reluctant to delegate work for fear it will not be up to their standards. Those with OCPD tend to have an overactive conscience that sees wrongdoing or moral lapse in the tiniest imperfection in self or others. They also tend to express emotion in very controlled ways and are uncomfortable around emotionally expressive people. The prevalence rate for OCPD in the general population is about 1% (American Psychiatric Association [APA], 2000).

Obsessive-compulsive personality disorder should be distinguished from obsessive-compulsive disorder (OCD). Despite the similar sounding names, OCPD is quite distinct from OCD. The latter is characterized by true obsessions and compulsions (e.g., regarding contamination) that create enormous anxiety for those with it. But rarely does OCPD create distress for those with it (though such people can create enormous distress for those having to live and work with them!).

**Assessment.** An official diagnosis of OCPD requires that the "pervasive pattern of preoccupation with orderliness, perfectionism, and...control" includes at least four of the following behaviors:

- preoccupation with details, rules, lists, and such to the extent that the purpose of the activity is lost
- perfectionism that interferes with task completion
- excessive devotion to work that excludes leisure even when not economically necessary
- extreme conscientiousness and inflexibility
- reluctance to delegate work
- financial miserliness
- inability to discard worthless objects devoid of sentimental value
- rigidity and stubbornness (APA, 2000)

Such behaviors must cause significant impairment in social and relational functioning to qualify as OCPD.

Like all personality disorders, OCPD is diagnosed using behaviors rather than symptoms. One must not be too quick to label someone simply because of unpleasant behavior rather than because of a true mental disorder (Millon & Davis, 2000). It is important to remember that personality disorders, including OCPD, lie along a continuum. Not everyone manifesting these behaviors has OCPD. There does not seem to be a biological cause for OCPD; its origin is assumed to be various environmental factors (such as a rigid, critical, perfectionistic, performance-based home life) interacting with personal vulnerabilities (Bixler, 1999; Millon & Davis, 2000; Minirth, Meier, & Ratcliff, 1992; Yarhouse, Butman, & McRay, 2005).

**Treatment.** Treatment of OCPD can be tricky. Because of the person's preoccupation with detail, those trying to help can find themselves bogged down in minutia or in a power struggle to determine how the help is to proceed. Directive help may reinforce tendencies toward self-criticism. Finally, the person's emotional inflexibility makes forming helping relationships difficult. Counselors and pastors who work with this type of person need to be aware of these pitfalls. Nevertheless, cognitive-behavioral techniques, such as thought stopping and relaxation, can decrease the amount of time spent in ruminative worry, and interpersonal therapy helps address emotional rigidity (Millon & Davis, 2000). A chief goal is helping people with these traits learn to relax and enjoy life more.

**Spiritual Issues.** The tendency to bring the preoccupation with orderliness, perfectionism, and control into one's religious life has been noted; this tendency often robs people of joy in the Lord (see Neh. 8:10). Those with these traits may tend toward legalism and be quick to speak the truth but without the love that belongs with it (see Eph. 4:15). From a Christian perspective, helping those with these traits come to understand and appreciate grace, for themselves and others, can bring meaningful change to their lives and preclude inadvertently rewarding a kind of overblown devotion to works (righteousness) that is often a part of these traits (see Eph 2:8).

**Stephen Parker**

## REFERENCES


American Psychiatric Association. (2000). *Diagnostic and Statistical Manual of Mental Disorders* (4th ed., text rev.). Washington, DC: Author.

Bixler, W. G. (1999). Obsessive-compulsive personality disorder. In D. G. Benner & P. C. Hill (Eds.), *Baker Encyclopedia of Psychology and Counseling*. Grand Rapids, MI: Baker Books.

Millon, T., & Davis, R. (2000). *Personality Disorders in Modern Life*. New York, NY: Wiley & Sons.

Minirth, F., Meier, P., & Ratcliff, D. (1992). *Bruised and Broken*. Grand Rapids, MI: Baker Books.

Yarhouse, M. A., Butman, R. E., & McRay, B. W. (2005). *Modern Psychopathologies: A Comprehensive Christian Appraisal*. Downers Grove, IL: InterVarsity Press.


## PARANOID PERSONALITY DISORDER

**Description and Prevalence.** Paranoid personality disorder (PPD) is one of ten Axis II diagnoses classified as personality disorders in the *Diagnostic and Statistical Manual of Mental Disorders* (*DSM-IV-TR*). Personality disorders are characterized by ingrained traits or patterns of behavior, feelings, perceptions, and thinking that make relationships and everyday living difficult. A paranoid person is constantly suspicious and mistrusting of others. Unfounded suspicions lead to blame, hostility, defensiveness, and stubbornness. Minor injustices or slights are perceived to be major (American Psychiatric Association [APA], 2000).

The disorder begins in early adulthood and is seen in multiple contexts. According to the *DSM-IV-TR*, the prevalence of PPD is estimated between 0.5% and 2.5% of the general population of the United States (APA, 2000). The disorder is more common in men than women and appears higher in relatives of clients suffering from delusional disorder of the persecutory type (Webb & Levinson, 1993). Paranoid personality disorder is usually viewed as a lifelong, chronic condition that must be worked on with patience and commitment.

**Assessment.** Diagnosis is made through interview. Therapists look for a pattern of suspicion and distrust of people. Four or more of the following symptoms must be present:

- unfounded suspicion that others are exploiting or harming you
- preoccupation with unjustified doubt regarding loyalty and trust in relationships
- reluctance to confide in others for fear that information will be used against you
- interpretation of benign remarks as demeaning or threatening
- harboring of grudges
- feeling that your character or reputation is being attacked and reacting angrily
- unduc suspicion that your spouse or sexual partner is unfaithful

**Treatment.** People with PPD rarely ask for help due to their suspicious nature. When problems occur, these people often blame others. This makes admitting a need for help difficult and trusting a therapist even more problematic. Motivation for treatment is usually prompted not by diagnosis, but by a life event or developmental crisis that leads to relationship problems, job stress, depression, substance abuse, anxiety, and the like. Therapy usually focuses on the following goals:

1. establishing a relationship and winning the client's trust by being supportive and client directed
2. controlling feelings of paranoia
3. addressing small, not very sensitive issues at the beginning of therapy before moving on to more sensitive and significant issues
4. encouraging behavioral and cognitive change versus self-disclosure
5. challenging the perception of inadequacy rather than challenging the person's paranoia
6. increasing the client's sense of self-efficacy before working on thought modification
7. helping the client see trustworthiness on a continuum (instead of all-or-nothing)
8. improving social skills (such as assertiveness in interpersonal conflicts)
9. becoming aware of other people's points of view
10. understanding and modifying core assumptions (e.g., "people are deceptive" or "they want to attack me").

Medication is contraindicated for this disorder because PPD is primarily a problem of paranoid thinking and ingrained patterns of behavior. In addition, clients are often suspicious of medications, so they may not take them and even drop out of treatment. Group therapy and self-help groups have not been found to be helpful in treatment.

**Spiritual Issues.** Our innate need for meaningful attachments can be fulfilled only with an intimate relationship with God. When our early caretaking experiences are negative, our image of God can be distorted. And because humans are born with a sin nature, our capacity for self-deception is ever present.

Scripture can be used to renew the mind. Passages such as Ephesians 4:22-23 tell believers to be made new in the attitude of their minds. Second Timothy 2:23-25 admonishes us not to be involved in foolish and stupid arguments, but to be kind to everyone, able to teach, and not resentful. James 1:19 encourages believers to be quick to listen, slow to speak, and slow to become angry. We are also commanded by Christ to forgive one another and not bear grudges.

**Conclusion.** The prognosis for change is not encouraging for paranoid personality disorder, but one should never eliminate the power of God to change lives and renew minds. A focus on mind renewal and building trust in order to rethink core assumptions and view the world in a less suspicious lens takes time and patience.

**Linda Mintle**

## REFERENCES

American Psychiatric Association. (2000). *Diagnostic and Statistical Manual of Mental Disorders* (4th ed., text rev.). Washington, DC: Author.

Webb, C. T., & Levinson, D. F. (1993, December). Schizotypal and paranoid personality disorder in the relatives of patients with schizophrenia and affective disorders: A review. *Schizophrenia Research 11*(1), 81-92.

*Part 4*

# Modes and Applications of Christian Counseling

# GROUP COUNSELING

## GROUP COUNSELING

**Definition.** Group counseling is a distinctive helping approach. Small clusters of clients gather with one or more leaders to discuss issues, share experiences, exchange ideas, and join forces to reach goals. Group methods offer distinct advantages over individualized care. Participants not only gain a counselor but also have opportunities to be supported and challenged by a defined community. Interactions occur within a safe society, where interpersonal skills can be honed "as iron sharpens iron" (Pr. 27:17). Observation of fellow counselees coping, stumbling, or growing can prompt vicarious learning. Members gain greater confidence as they serve and contribute to others. The core component of mutuality—members helping members—is critical and unique to this approach.

Irvin Yalom's landmark research identified key curative factors in helping groups (Yalom & Leszcz, 2005). Relationships within defined small groups can spark a resurgence of hope, provide reassurance that one's sensations are not unique, create forums for imparting information, and provide opportunities to display compassion for others. The apostle Paul unapologetically uses the body metaphor to describe relationships between believers in the ministry of the church (1 Cor. 12:12-27; see also Acts 2:42-47). Counseling groups can function as intensive fellowship experiences that prepare members to enter more fully into Christian community (Greggo, 2007).

**Effectiveness.** In today's counseling climate, therapists and clients need to use all available resources. Groups offer an efficient modality because more clients benefit from a counselor's service. Ample empirical evidence is available that a group environment is an effective modality when weighed against individual care (Burlingame, 2010). There is no empirically based substantiation for the negative perception that group therapy is a downgrade or step down from individual therapy. Well-designed groups are constructive treatment options for diverse populations and are viable applications across a broad spectrum of severity and range of difficulties.

The American Group Psychotherapy Association Science to Service Task Force (2008) published a comprehensive set of scientifically credible clinical-practice guidelines. Mounting evidence demonstrates the utility of group counseling in many contexts.

**History and Evangelical Influences.** The modern story line of psychologically oriented group work begins at the outset of the 20th century (Barlow, Fuhriman, & Burlingame, 2004). The creative 1905 initiative of Joseph Henry Pratt, a physician working with tuberculosis patients at Massachusetts General Hospital, was to start an educational clinic at a local church. Besides giving patients the best available information on this deadly disease, conversation between patients was encouraged. Remarkably, this effort to increase knowledge and social support improved survival rates! Jacob Moreno pioneered groups beginning in the 1930s, making extensive inroads in prisons and insane asylums. He suggested people display behaviors in immediate social settings that reveal deep personality issues and entrenched interpersonal patterns. Moreno observed that groups are the ideal tool to leave the past behind in favor of working in the here and now. In 1946, Kurt Lewin researched ways to use small groups to reduce racial tension in communities. After lengthy talk sessions, participants were permitted to overhear the observations of experts who commented on member exchanges, tactics, and nonverbal communication. This expert insight positively impacted subsequent behavior and was granted the label *feedback*. In the 1970s, Carl Rogers promoted encounter groups, where members "let it all hang out." The explosive social bandwagon that flourished for a decade was powered by *cohesion*, an intensive collective experience accompanied by unconditional affirmation.

Christian theologian Thomas C. Oden offers an alternative perspective on the history of intensive small groups (Oden, 1972). He indicates that encounter groups were a secularized version of a style of transparent interpersonal community found in religious communities in the West. The basic prototype is found in pietism, which emphasized here-and-now experience, emotional expression, high levels of trust, honest confession amid a caring community, experimental mysticism, mutual pastoral care, extended conversion marathons, radical accountability to the group, resources for spiritual formation, personal testimony, gut-level self-disclosure, brutally candid feedback, antiestablishment social attitudes, and lay leadership. Essentially, Oden makes the case that the roots of this group methodology are best located in Christian history and not exclusively in modern psychology.

No consideration of Christian perspectives on the history of groups would be complete without recalling the revival in America known as the First Great Awakening during the 1700s. John Wesley (1703–1791) was adamant that new converts from evangelistic meetings should be nurtured in the faith. He was particularly concerned for those with stubborn sins and repetitive struggles. Beyond fostering accurate theology and biblical understanding through teaching Scripture, his discipleship method was built around accountability groups. Wesley's "bands" were intensive group sessions where transparency, accountability, and support were advocated to produce long-term spiritual transformation. Wesley's inspiration came from the epistle of James, known for its practical wisdom in the pursuit of a real-world faith: "Confess your sins to each other and pray for each other so that you may be healed" (Jas. 5:16). The ingredients of mutual confession, individually targeted prayer, and experiences of healing from the effects of sin were carved into the very procedures Wesley authored and circulated to advance such bands (Greggo, 2008).

**Group Types.** The term *group counseling* encompasses a wide assortment of helping endeavors. One framework classifies group types along a continuum, placing structured education, time-limited designs on one end (psychoeducational) and free-flowing, interpersonal, open-style experiences on the other (psychotherapy). In the middle would be a prevalent type of group counseling where a common theme unites membership into a semistructured exchange so that information sharing is merged with interpersonal learning. Examples include groups that deal with life adjustment (including marriage preparation, career transition, parent education, or retirement planning) or contend with a loss (such as bereavement, divorce recovery, or health crises).

This depiction of group types points to the central premise: Benefit is achieved from two layers of communication—content and process. *Content* refers to the subject matter as related through the stories, themes, information, and points of discussion that are evident on the surface. Educational groups offer help through useful content. *Process* refers to the intricate social issues beneath the surface that reflect trust levels, roles, and issues of personal power. Psychotherapy groups that target insight are heavy on process because the major thrust is to grasp not what was said, but who said it, how, and to whom.

**Leadership Role and Function.** Numerous popular efforts closely resemble group counseling but do not technically fit the definition. Self-help groups comprise a vast movement in which people with identified needs assemble to take responsibility to pursue change while assisting others. Self-help groups are versatile and share many characteristics with counseling groups except one—there is no formal leader. Leader-guided groups are identified as counseling because expertise in design, mediated feedback, and group dynamics are utilized to form, direct, and evaluate the experience. The essential core leader competencies have been defined as (a) providing a vision and structure, (b) promoting care, (c) raising awareness of emotions and relational attachments, and (d) forming meaning (Greggo, 2008).

**Christian Applications.** Pastoral-care ministries have a vested interest in small group methods. Churches host such groups to promote hope and healing. The Holy Spirit gave gifts to God's people to fulfill the command of our Lord to love one another (Rom. 12:4-8). The church holds body life and vital fellowship in high regard. The gospel narrative has much to say on the subject of how members function within social groups. Redemption, sanctification, ecclesiology, family life, and the direction/purpose of human development are theological topics that converge by way of the cross on how believers relate to others. Therefore, group counseling taps into a powerful methodology that has been and will continue to be an approach with much promise for gospel ministry application.

**Stephen P. Greggo**

### REFERENCES


American Group Psychotherapy Association Science to Service Task Force. (2008). Clinical practice guidelines for group psychotherapy. *International Journal of Group Psychotherapy, 58*(4), 542-455.

Barlow, S. H., Fuhriman, A. J., & Burlingame, G. M. (2004). The history of group counseling and psychotherapy. In J. L. Delucia-Waack, D. A. Gerrity, C. R. Kalodner, & M. T. Riva (Eds.), *Handbook of Group Counseling and Psychotherapy* (pp. 3-22). Thousand Oaks, CA: Sage.

Burlingame, G. M. (2010). Small group treatments: Introduction to special section. *Psychotherapy Research, 20*(1), 1-7.

Greggo, S. P. (2007). Biblical metaphors for corrective emotional relationships in group work. *Journal of Psychology and Theology, 35*(2), 153-162.

Greggo, S. P. (2008). *Trekking Toward Wholeness: A Resource for Care Group Leaders.* Downers Grove, IL: InterVarsity Press.

Oden, T. C. (1972). *The Intensive Group Experience: The New Pietism.* Philadelphia, PA: Westminster Press.

Yalom, I., & Leszcz, M. (2005). *The Theory and Practice of Group Psychotherapy* (5th ed.). New York, NY: Basic Books.


## SMALL-GROUP DYNAMICS

**Definition.** *Group dynamics* is a term that describes the potent underlying forces enabling small social groups to establish a sense of identity that contributes to the well-being of participants. However, these powerfully positive social ties can also produce undeniable pressure to conform or take previously unacceptable risks. The relational elements that build intricate bonds of trust can contribute to the thrill of unity and solidity, but they may also ignite flames of anger and discouragement when members of the group experience friction, division, and destructive competition. Harnessed for good, group dynamics forge healthy teams that promote closeness and courage. As people gather in groups, an automatic social process is activated, establishing norms or unspoken rules that govern how, when, and to whom individuals relate. Group norms build on individual characteristics to launch patterns for social connection, define expectations, and shape the roles that members assume in relationship with fellow members. Group dynamics contribute to group stability but can also result in stagnation.

The practical wisdom of Scripture assures that human beings made in God's image were not meant to be alone and that "two are better than one" (Gen. 2:18; Eccl. 4:9-12). Human beings are social by design to reflect their relational Creator, the triune God (Gen. 1:26-28). Nonetheless, since the Fall, the intrinsic human desire to join with others is severely hindered by innate sinful tendencies to remain hidden, excuse excesses, and elevate self-interest (Gen. 3; Phil. 2:4; 2 Tim. 3:2-4). The irresistible urge to be socially connected and the ingrained attributes to preserve and protect autonomy merge to form the chemistry that can cohere or explode when small groups come together.

In order to grasp the operating dynamics within a group or between members, look beneath the surface communication and raw content of the topics, themes, and subject matter of the conversation. Look closely to perceive and feel the relational communication (the process) in the tone, tenor, and emotion layered into the discussion (Corey & Corey, 2006).

**Developmental Stages and Trust.** The counseling literature has long described a basic progression of stages that capture the typical progression of the prevailing dynamic in small groups: *forming* (orientation), *storming* (conflict), *norming* (structure), *performing* (work), and *adjourning* (dissolution) (Ward, 2009). These are useful concepts to help us recognize the general movement of a group. These stages appear linear, but in actuality the group can cycle backward or become stuck in a particular stage. An adaptation of this model focuses on the social bonds of trust, or progressive *intimacy pace,* and describes the level of interpersonal closeness in the group: cooperation, competition, collaboration, and consolidation (Greggo, 2008).

*Cooperation* suggests an initial trust level demonstrated by cordial listening with limited interaction, low-risk self-disclosure, acceptance of inconsistencies, and straightforward advice sharing.

*Competition* is an indicator that the parameters of trust are being stretched and strengthened. However, the signs of competition are not always pleasant. In this stage, members may experience one or more people pulling back from engagement, power plays, interpersonal tension, calculated or nonspontaneous sharing, and even the challenge of a group leader, purpose, or procedure.

When cohesion or a sense of group unity is activated, the trust level will reveal an intimate level of *collaboration.* The language of *we* abounds, and expressions of open disagreement are accepted because the members enjoy a pervasive sense of support.

*Consolidation* is marked by group members experiencing the gains of a single participant as an accomplishment of the whole. Ending or leaving a group may be difficult, but when the trust level of consolidation is obtained, members take the voice and unity of the group along with them after departure.

**Christian Applications.** In the relationships and mission of the church, group dynamics may be a useful way of cultivating a deeper sense of fellowship, love, and Christian unity. All types of social groups, families, and even congregations can demonstrate healthy cohesion. This blessing is a sign that the grace of God has broken through human shortcomings and allowed the refreshing movement of the Holy Spirit to be experienced (Greggo, 2007).

Understanding the powerful dynamics of group interaction can help every leader create environments that build trust, provide support for those in need, encourage spiritual growth, and help people know and follow God's calling in their lives.

STEPHEN P. GREGGO

## REFERENCES


American Group Psychotherapy Association Science to Service Task Force (2008). Clinical practice guidelines for group psychotherapy. *International Journal of Group Psychotherapy, 58*(4), 542-455. Retrieved from http://www.agpa.org/guidelines/index.html

Corey, M. S., & Corey, G. (2006). *Groups: Process & Practice* (7th ed.). Belmont, CA: Brooks/Cole.

Greggo, S. P. (2007). Biblical metaphors for corrective emotional relationships in group work. *Journal of Psychology and Theology, 35*(2), 153-162.

Greggo, S. P. (2008). *Trekking Toward Wholeness: A Resource for Care Group Leaders.* Downers Grove, IL: InterVarsity Press.

Ward, D. E. (2009). Group work, developmental stages of. In American Counseling Association, *The ACA Encyclopedia of Counseling* (pp. 227-229). Arlington, VA: Author.


## PSYCHOEDUCATION GROUPS

**DESCRIPTION.** Psychoeducation groups combine teaching with therapeutic interaction (Elliott, Rivera, & Tucker, 2004). Psychoeducation groups have been in use since the early 1900s and can be found in inpatient, outpatient, school, agency, prison, business, church, and other settings (Gladding, 2008). These groups have proven beneficial and effective with multiple groups and populations (Akinsulure-Smith, 2009; Hebert & Tourigny, 2010; Kayler & Sherman, 2009; Lefley, 2010, 2009; Sibitz, Amering, Gossler, Unger, & Katschnig, 2007; Von Ranson, Stevenson, Cannon, & Shah, 2010).

**CHARACTERISTICS.** This widely popular type of group work usually focuses on the acquisition of knowledge and skills regarding a particular topic (Steen, Bryan, & Day-Vines, 2011). Brown (2009) subdivides psychoeducation groups into four categories according to their focus: personal development, support, life transitions, and families and caretakers.

Because psychoeducation groups have both a didactic and therapeutic component, group sessions tend to be longer than that of counseling groups, often lasting 90 minutes to two hours. Additionally, these groups are often larger than counseling groups, with numbers ranging from 20 to 50 participants. Unlike counseling groups, which can last for months or years, psychoeducation groups are often time-limited, lasting one to twelve sessions (Gladding, 2008).

Pychoeducation groups often begin with the group leader disseminating information related to the topic. This is followed by a time of interaction with others who share a similar situation, condition, or purpose for attending group. Because of this format, participants often benefit from the therapeutic factors of universality, imparting of information, and altruism (Yalom & Leszcz, 2005).

**BENEFITS.** There are a number of benefits from psychoeducation groups. They provide information, facilitate a sense of support, reduce feelings of isolation, and normalize uncomfortable feelings, such as guilt and shame (Brown, 2009).

**LEADER QUALIFICATIONS.** The Association for Specialists in Group Work (2000) recommends that counselors wishing to specialize in psychoeducation groups receive 30 to 45 hours of training. Unlike counseling groups, which focus primarily on process, psychoeducation groups focus more on content (Aasheim & Nieman, 2006). Because of this, leadership of these groups is not limited to licensed professionals. However, leaders do need to possess certain leader skills, including group facilitation and instruction.

**USE IN THE CHURCH SETTING.** Psychoeducation groups are widely used within the church to meet the growing needs of the congregation while disseminating biblical truth. A review of literature reveals churches commonly offer groups related to bereavement, forgiveness, disabilities support, cancer survivors, coping with mental illness, and divorce recovery (Bissett, 1990; Goodman & Stone, 2009; Worthingon et al., 2010; Pickett-Schnek, 2002; Stratton, Dean, Nonneman, Bode, & Worthington, 2008).

**Conclusion.** Centered on dissemination of information and social support, psychoeducation groups play an important role in the life of the church. Participation in such groups provides individuals with unique opportunities for healing and health.

**Denise Daniel**

## REFERENCES


Aasheim, L. L., & Nieman, S. H. (2006). Guidance/psychoeducational groups. In D. Capuzzi, D. R. Gross, & M. D. Stauffer (Eds.), *Introduction to Group Work* (4th ed., pp. 269-294). Denver, CO: Love Publishing.

Akinsulure-Smith, A. M. (2009). Brief psychoeducational group treatment with re-traumatized refugees and asylum seekers. *The Journal for Specialists in Group Work, 34*(2), 137-150.

Association for Specialists in Group Work (2000). Professional standards for the training of group workers. *Journal for Specialists in Group Work, 25*(4), 327-342.

Bissett, D. (1990). A church-sponsored divorce recovery through group experience. *Journal of Family Ministry, 4*(2), 45-53.

Brown, N. W. (2009). *Becoming a Group Leader.* Upper Saddle River, NJ: Prentice Hall.

Elliott, T. R., Rivera, P., & Tucker, E. (2004). Groups in behavioral health and medical settings. In J. L. DeLucia-Waack, D. A. Gerrity, C. R. Kalodner, & M. T. Riva (Eds.), *Handbook of Counseling and Psychotherapy* (pp. 338-350). Thousand Oaks, CA: Sage.

Gerrity, D. A., & DeLucia-Waak, J. L. (2007). Effectiveness of groups in the schools. *The Journal for Specialists in Group Work, 32*(1), 97-106.

Gladding, S. T. (2008). *Groups: A Counseling Specialty* (5th ed.). Upper Saddle River, NJ: Prentice Hall.

Goodman, H., Jr., & Stone, M. H. (2009). The efficacy of adult Christian support groups in coping with the death of a significant loved one. *Journal of Religion and Health, 48*(3), 305-316.

Hebert, M., & Tourigny, M. (2010). Effects of a psychoeducational group intervention for child victims of sexual abuse. *Journal of Child & Adolescent Trauma, 3*(2), 143-160.

Kayler, H., & Sherman, J. (2009). At-risk ninth-grade students: A psychoeducational group approach to increase study skills and grade point averages. *Professional School Counseling, 12*(6), 434-439.

Lefley, H. P. (2009). A psychoeducational support group for serious mental illness. *The Journal for Specialists in Group Work, 34*(4), 369-381.

Lefley, H. P. (2010). Treating difficult cases in a psychoeducational family support group for serious mental illness. *Journal of Family Psychotherapy, 21*(4), 253-268.

Pickett-Schnek, S. A. (2002). Church based support groups for African American families coping with mental illness: Outreach and outcomes. *Psychiatric Rehabilitation Journal, 26*(2), 173-180.

Sibitz, I., Amering, M., Gossler, R., Unger, A., & Katschnig, H. (2007). Patients' perspectives of what works in psychoeducational groups for schizophrenia. *Social Psychiatry and Psychiatric Epidemiology, 42*(11), 909-915.

Steen, S., Bryan, J., & Day-Vines, N. L. (2011). Leading psychoeducational groups. In B. T. Erford (Ed.), *Group Work: Processes and Applications* (pp. 187-201). Upper Saddle River, NJ: Prentice Hall.

Stratton, S. P., Dean, J. B., Nonneman, A. J., Bode, R. A., & Worthington, E. L., Jr. (2008). Forgiveness interventions as spiritual development strategies: Comparing forgiveness workshop training, expressive writing about forgiveness, and retested controls. *Journal of Psychology and Christianity, 27*(4), 347-357.

Von Ranson, K. M., Stevenson, A. S., Cannon, C. K., & Shah, W. (2010). Changes in eating pathology and associated symptoms among chronically ill adults attending a brief psychoeducational group. *Eating Behaviors, 11*(3), 186-189.

Worthington, E. L., Jr., Hunter, J. L., Sharp, C. B., Hook, J. N., van Tongeren, D. R., Davis, D. E.,...Monforte-Milton, M. (2010). A psychoeducational intervention to promote forgiveness in Christians in the Philippines. *Journal of Mental Health Counseling, 32*(1), 75-93.

Yalom, I. D., & Leszcz, M. (2005). *The Theory and Practice of Group Psychotherapy* (5th ed.). New York, NY: Basic Books.


## SMALL-GROUP FELLOWSHIPS

**Definition.** Small fellowship gatherings with an emphasis on pastoral care have been a primary means of discipleship since Jesus announced the coming of his kingdom along the Sea of Galilee. His initial ministry strategy included inviting a ragged group of tired fishermen to leave their nets to follow him (Mk. 1:14-19). Here Jesus Christ modeled the critical importance of small groups by conducting his ministry in the presence of select disciples.

Most versions translate the New Testament term *koinonia* as "fellowship" (2 Cor.

6:14; 1 Jn. 1:3). Contemporary usage may tend to reduce these essential mutual bonds to companionship, social affinity, and camaraderie. However, the key notion in the biblical sense of the word is that of partnership and common belonging. Consider the ordinance of the Lord's Supper, or *Communion* (a word that also refers to close fellowship). This is an ideal way to maintain awareness that Christian fellowship is the loving expression of unity and oneness in Jesus Christ.

Fellowship is not merely a superficial opportunity to add a friend or increase affiliations. The bonds that connect us in Christ are miracles of grace, made possible through the cross and resurrection of our Lord. Pastoral caregivers and people helpers foster diverse small-group experiences, empowering Christians to enjoy rewarding relationships that have both horizontal and vertical dimensions.

**Word-Focused Fellowship Groups.** Extraordinary numbers of people gather in small groups to pursue the cultivation of their faith and to explore true Christian spirituality (Crabb, 2004; Wuthnow, 1994). Small groups, the size of large or extended families, are superb means to build a faith-based foundation for life, ease suffering, or create a supportive team with exceptional evangelistic potential. Following the outpouring of the Holy Spirit as recorded in the book of Acts, believers gathered together in homes to submit to biblical teaching, share meals, pour out their hearts in prayer, and share resources (Acts 2:42-46). The Holy Spirit touches hearts in unique ways when meaningful relational encounters are built around the process of internalizing the Word of God together. The tangible experience of love between early believers launched the movement of Christianity around the world. Bonds of love in fellowship groups have timeless and cross-cultural appeal.

Contemporary ministry-oriented small groups still follow the model portrayed in the early church. Four components of healthy Christian fellowship groups are based on Acts 2: nurture (teaching the Word), worship (honoring God), community (caring, giving, and praying for each other) and mission (tasks, service, and outreach) (Barker, Johnson, Malone, & Nicholas, 1985). A prototypical discipleship group—whether in a college dorm, coffee shop, church courtyard, or family room—dedicates time in approximately equal proportions to activities within each of these four areas. The ratio can be adjusted to fit specialized groups that are dedicated to a unique purpose (Greggo, 2008).

Fellowship groups that have a core purpose to increase the powerful application of the Word of God in the lives of its members may dedicate additional time to teaching. Or, such groups may be designed to supplement a large assembly, where the emphasis is on proclamation of the Word. Comprehension of the text and appropriation into routines and relationships is accelerated in these fellowship settings.

**Walk-Targeted Fellowship Groups.** In an era when isolation abounds, small groups with a sanctification orientation offer an incredible means of ongoing support to those struggling with painful separations, addictions, economic setbacks, or fractured relationships. For example, the Celebrate Recovery (CR) phenomenon started by Saddleback Church in Lake Forest, California, began as a Christ-centered local alternative to the traditional, self-help, 12-step approach of Alcoholics Anonymous (AA). This CR movement has spawned hundreds of other host ministries worldwide, where multiple groups undertake specific recovery expeditions using the step format to foster support and accountability.

There are also small helping groups that aid in grief recovery, financial stewardship, employment transitions, marital disruption, sexual purity, and healthy living. When the human support dimension of these groups is fused with the bonds of fellowship, the potential to spread the good news of the gospel is significant. It is true that small groups offer encouragement through mutual partnership. Just as critical is the conversational climate, where it is safe to be transparent, share defeat, confess sin, and earnestly pursue holy living that honors Christ (Jas. 5:16). (*See also* Group Counseling and Small-Group Dynamics).

**Stephen P. Greggo**

## REFERENCES


Barker, S., Johnson, J., Malone, R., & Nicholas, R. (1985). *Good Things Come in Small Groups: The Dynamics of Good Group Life.* Downers Grove, IL: InterVarsity Press.

Crabb, L. (2004). *Connecting: Healing Ourselves and Our Relationships.* Nashville, TN: Thomas Nelson.

Greggo, S. P. (2008). *Trekking Toward Wholeness: A Resource for Care Group Leaders.* Downers Grove, IL: InterVarsity Press.

Wuest, K. S. (1984). *Wuest's Word Studies from the Greek New Testament: For the English Reader.* Grand Rapids, MI: Eerdmans.

Wuthnow, R. (Ed.). (1994). *I Come Away Stronger: How Small Groups Are Shaping American Religion.* Grand Rapids, MI: Eerdmans.

13

# PREMARITAL, MARRIAGE, AND FAMILY COUNSELING

## PREPARE-ENRICH

**Description.** Preparing couples for marriage and enriching their marriage are the major goals of the PREPARE-ENRICH Program. It is referred to as a program because it contains two components: an online couple assessment and feedback using skills-building exercises selected and driven by the assessment.

The defining feature of the online customized version of PREPARE-ENRICH is that it customizes the assessment for each couple based on their answers to background questions. The program is designed for couples who are dating, engaged, or married, and it automatically tailors the content for a couple's relationship stage and family structure.

**Popularity and Rigor of the Program.** PREPARE-ENRICH was created more than 30 years ago and is now in its sixth edition. More than 3 million couples have benefited from the program, which is offered by more than 80,000 trained professionals in the United States and 30,000 professionals in other countries. The assessments have been translated into six languages (Chinese, French, German, Japanese, Korean, and Spanish), and there are international offices in several other countries, including Australia, Canada, China, England, Germany, Japan, Korea, New Zealand, Singapore, and Taiwan.

The program is used by counselors, clergy, relationship educators, and mentor couples. Most people are trained to use PREPARE-ENRICH in a one-day workshop, but professional counselors can purchase a DVD-based home-study and earn continuing education units as well. The workshop trains professionals to administer and interpret the assessment and to provide feedback to couples. A schedule of certification workshops is listed online at www.prepare-enrich.com.

The couple assessment has high levels of reliability, validity, and scientific rigor. Scale reliability is consistently high (average r = .80), and it also has very good content validity, construct validity, discriminant validity, and predictive validity. In terms of discriminant validity, PREPARE scores can discriminate between premarital couples who end up happily married versus those who divorced with 85% accuracy. For more details on more than 15 studies on PREPARE-ENRICH, go to the research section of the website.

**Major Couple Areas Assessed.** The assessment focuses on more than 25 aspects of the couple relationship. The figure below illustrates the major areas, including ten core areas, personality, relationship dynamics, couple and family system, and cultural context. The ten core areas include communication, conflict resolution, partner style and habits, finances, relationship roles, family and friends, parenting, sexual relationship, leisure activities, and spiritual beliefs. The SCOPE personality assessment is based on five key areas from the Five Factor theory of personality. SCOPE is an acronym for Social, Change, Organized, Pleasing, and Emotionally steady.

The four areas included in the relationship dynamics section are assertiveness,

## Systemic Components of PREPARE-ENRICH

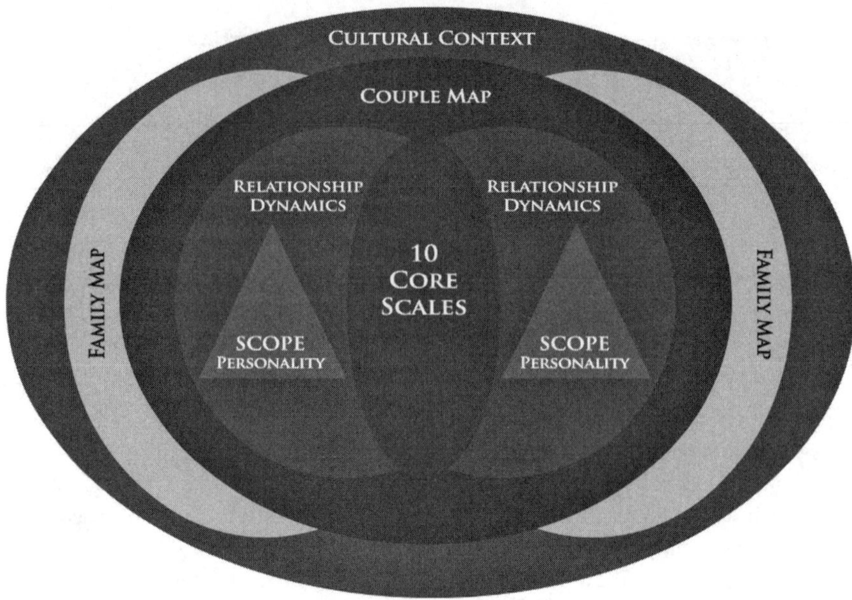


self-confidence, avoidance, and partner dominance. For the couple and family system, the assessment includes both cohesion and flexibility scales for the couple and their families of origin. To address issues related to culture, content has been added to assess rapidly changing trends, such as cohabitation and stepfamily formation. Lastly, the scales are translated and adapted for international cultures whenever appropriate.

**Materials for Counseling Couples.** Once couples complete the online assessment, facilitators are notified that the Facilitator's Report is ready to view, save, or print. Facilitators can also print a Couple's Report, which summarizes results in a format for couples to keep.

Couples also receive a Couple's Workbook, which contains more than 20 exercises designed to increase understanding and build relationship skills. The six core exercises include

- identifying strengths and growth areas
- communication—assertiveness and active listening
- stress—identifying critical issues
- conflict resolution—a 10-step model
- couple and family map
- SCOPE personality compatibility

There are approximately 15 additional couple exercises that can be used as needed or assigned as homework.

**Counseling Using PREPARE-ENRICH.** In working with couples, the first step is to study the Facilitator's Report, noting the strength and growth areas. Second, select which topics and exercises to use. The six core exercises are always recommended and can be supplemented by additional exercises as needed.

**Spiritual Beliefs.** PREPARE-ENRICH has historically contained a category called Spiritual Beliefs, which was created and endorsed by clergy from various denominations. The ten items in the scale measure the couple's agreement regarding their beliefs. This scale has been used in a variety of studies, including one where we compared married couples with high agreement versus married couples with low agreement on spiritual beliefs. Our study entitled "Spiritual Beliefs and Marital Success" found that couples with high agreement on spiritual beliefs had significantly more strengths in most areas of their marriage than those with low agreement (Larson & Olson, 1995). For more details, go to the website and click on Research Studies.

In addition to the standardized spiritual beliefs scale, the customized version contains several faith-based scales for different groups, including Catholic, Protestant, and Jewish versions. Every married couple receives a forgiveness scale, and there is also an interfaith/interchurch scale if the couple has different religious backgrounds.

Because clergy have expressed interest in integrating spiritual beliefs into the counseling process, we have created a Couple's Workbook with scriptural references for each major category of PREPARE-ENRICH.

David H. Olson
Peter J. Larson

## REFERENCES

Larson, P. J. & Olson D. H. (1995). *Spiritual Beliefs and Marriage: A National Survey Based on ENRICH.* https://www.prepare-enrich.com/pe_main_site_content/pdf/research/beliefsandmarriage.pdf

Olson, D. H. (1988). *Prepare/Enrich: Counselor's Manual.* Life Innovations, Inc.

## PREMARITAL COUNSELING

Divorce rates today are hovering around 50% for churchgoers and nonchurchgoers alike. In response to this crisis, we need to build a guardrail at the top of the cliff instead of sending an ambulance to the bottom. The guardrail is premarital counseling.

Preparing couples for marriage can be a daunting task. Many professional counselors and pastors did not receive the wisdom and experience offered by insightful counselors, pastors, or mentor couples, but they would have greatly benefited from these things. In fact, less than 20% of all marriages in America begin with premarital training (Parrott & Parrott, 2006). Research shows that the average cost of weddings today is $22,000. Most of a couple's preparation and resources go into the wedding day, and only a fraction is invested in the rest of their lives. Participating in premarital training can reduce the risk of divorce by as much as 30% (Stanley, Amato, Johnson, & Markham, 2006) and prevent many sleepless nights.

**Description.** Training young couples for marriage can be a difficult and sometimes confusing endeavor. Preparing couples for marriage may sometimes seem like teaching swimming lessons on the shore. Some skills simply cannot be learned until people dive in. Before a couple gets married, they tend to be naive about what it takes to live, work, and function as a married couple. Only afterward, within the first year or two, do they begin to learn what a marriage relationship is really like. Premarital counseling gives couples an important head start by helping them learn the basics of sharing their lives with one another.

**Purpose.** The purpose of premarital counseling is to prepare the couple for marriage by anticipating problems, facilitating communication about a wide range of important topics, and providing hope for the future. It can help ensure a strong, healthy, and lasting relationship. Carpenters have many types of tools to use for the many different jobs they perform. Premarital counseling provides couples with the tools they will need to perform important tasks when they are married. For mentors, pastors, and counselors, working with premarital couples involves a great deal of transparency regarding their own victories and struggles in marriage.

**Core Components.** The many components of a successful premarital ministry address conflict resolution, expectations, communication, gender differences, marriage myths, marital roles, finances, and the big three: money, sex, and power (Markman, Stanley, & Blumberg, 2001; Parrott & Parrott, 2005). Many successful curricula are video-based, providing ample time for questions and answers. Meeting in a large group can also be very powerful and productive for couples because some of the problems they will face can be normalized in the group setting.

**Resources.** Many different resources are available for those who minister to premarital couples, and a few of them are especially noteworthy. *Genesis 2:24* is a 12-week video-based curriculum featuring a world-class faculty and produced by the American Association of Christian Counselors (AACC). The lessons focus on many topics, including faith, conflict, love languages, finances, sex, and communication. *Saving Your Marriage Before It Starts* by marriage experts Les and Leslie Parrott is an eight-week video-based curriculum that features seven key questions every couple needs to ask before they tie the knot. *PREP*, the Prevention and Relationship Enhancement Program, was developed by marriage researchers Scott Stanley and Howard Markman. *PREP* is a research-based, skills-building curriculum designed to get at the heart of marital problems. Finally, the PREPARE-ENRICH program starts with a couple assessment followed by six to ten skills-building feedback sessions designed to help couples learn proven relationship skills to deal with current and future issues.

Many counselors will also utilize a premarital inventory, which assesses a couple's relational strengths and weaknesses. Among the most widely used inventories are PREPARE-ENRICH, Foccus, and Relate. Each of these inventories provides a report for the counselor to review with each couple, and each supplies the same amount of information that four sessions of counseling would deliver.

**Conclusion.** Beginning a premarital ministry is an exciting and incredibly worthwhile endeavor. You will have the opportunity to speak into young couples' lives and prepare them to start their marriage on the right foot. Premarital counseling is also an excellent way for professional counselors to get involved in a local congregation. It helps counselors build the guardrail and save marriages for generations to come.

Ryan Carboneau
Scott Hawkins

## REFERENCES


Markman, H. J., Stanley, S. M., & Blumberg, S. L. (2001). *Fighting for Your Marriage.* San Francisco, CA: Jossey-Bass.

Parrott, L., & Parrott, L. L. (2005). *The Complete Guide to Marriage Mentoring.* Grand Rapids, MI: Zondervan.

Parrott, L., & Parrott, L. L. (2006). *Saving Your Marriage Before It Starts.* Grand Rapids, MI: Zondervan.

Stanley, S., Amato, P. R., Johnson, C. A., & Markman, H. J. (2006). Premarital education, marital quality, and marital stability: Findings from a large, random household survey. *Journal of Family Psychology, 20*(1), 117-126.


## LOVE LANGUAGES

One of man's deepest emotional needs is to feel loved. When children feel loved, they are far more receptive to their parents' teaching and discipline. When teenagers feel loved, they more successfully navigate the physical, emotional, and intellectual changes pushing them toward adulthood. When single adults feel loved, they are far more likely to build meaningful, supportive relationships. When married individuals feel loved by their spouses, they are much better equipped to solve the conflicts that come in the normal flow of life.

When people do not feel loved, the unmet need is reflected in their behavior.

Children will grow up with many internal struggles, expressing themselves in attention-getting behavior. Teenagers will go looking for love, often in drugs, alcohol, and sexual activity. Single adults are likely to be estranged from their parents and have difficulty building positive relationships. Married couples often evidence pain by arguing or withdrawing and are far more tempted by extramarital relationships. These behavioral problems surface in the offices of Christian counselors on a regular basis.

The concept of love languages provides counselors with a tool that can help individuals learn to give and receive love effectively. The thesis is that there are five fundamental ways of expressing love emotionally: by means of words of affirmation, acts of service, quality time, gifts, and physical touch. These five were first discovered in the context of marital counseling (Chapman, 2010a) and were later applied to children (Chapman & Campbell, 2005), teenagers (Chapman, 2010b), and single adults (Chapman, 2009a). The basic concept is that each individual has a primary love language. If you do not speak his or her primary love language, that person will not feel loved even though you are expressing love in some of the other languages.

As adults, we tend to speak our own language. If "words of affirmation" is our primary love language, we will speak that language to the significant people in our lives. Our intentions are likely good, but we may well miss the other person emotionally. The husband may be giving words of affirmation while the wife is wondering, "If you really love me, why don't you help me? How can you sit on the couch and watch me do all the work?" Many couples sincerely love each other but do not feel loved because they are not speaking each other's primary love language.

Most parents love their young children and teenagers, but many children and teenagers do not feel loved. Helping kids feel loved takes more than sincerity. We must learn to speak the primary language of the child and teenager. Applying the concept to children means that parents will give heavy doses of the child's primary love language while speaking the other four languages as often as possible. The ideal is that the child will learn how to receive and give love in all five languages. That is the best prospect for a healthy adult.

If you are a parent with teenagers, you must understand that although the teenagers' primary love language does not change, you must learn to speak new dialects of that language. Whatever you have been speaking to them when they were children is now childish. You must give more adult expressions of their love language. If "physical touch" is their language, you no longer hug and kiss the same way you did when they were six. You give them elbows, you wrestle them to the floor. They still need physical touch, but they need it in a more adult manner.

Single adults can come to experience parental love in two ways. Often, when single adults understand the concept that people have different languages, they can look back on their childhood and realize intellectually that their parents did indeed love them. Their parents were speaking one or more of these languages. The children did not feel loved because the parents were not speaking their primary language. Now as adults, they can give their parents emotional credit for expressing love in another language. A second approach is to encourage single adults to discuss the concept of love languages with their parents. In such discussions, the goal is for them to honestly share their feelings and for parents to understand. And the two will be able to forge a more meaningful emotional relationship in the future.

For married couples, the key is learning each other's primary love language and choosing to speak it on a regular basis while sprinkling in the other four languages for extra credit. Thousands of couples have given testimony that understanding and applying the concept of love languages has saved their marriages.

How then do you discover one's primary love language? Each of the books in the reference list have profiles of love languages that will aid in the process. But here are three additional ways:

1. Observe how people express love to other people. If they are always giving people hugs or pats on the back, "physical touch" is probably their language. If they are commonly giving words of encouragement to other people, then "words of affirmation" is likely their language. People tend to speak their own language.
2. What do they complain about? When wives say, "We don't ever spend any time together. We're like two ships passing in the night," they are loudly proclaiming that their primary love language is "quality time." Husbands who say, "I don't think you would ever touch me if I did not initiate it," reveal that their love language is "physical touch." Teenagers who say, "I don't ever do anything right," indicate that their primary language is "words of affirmation."
3. What does the other person request of you most often? The child who says, "Come into my room—I want to show you something," is asking for "quality time." The child who says to you when you leave on a business trip, "Be sure and bring me a surprise," is telling you that "receiving gifts" is her love language. The wife who says, "Would you be able to take the recycles out on the way to the car this morning?" is revealing that "acts of service" is her love language.

Ask those three questions—How do they most often express love to others? What do they complain about? What do they request most often?—and you will likely discover their love language.

All of these love languages are rooted in Scripture and are reflections of God's love (Chapman, 2009b). As Christian counselors, we take seriously the words of Jesus: "A new commandment I give to you: Love one another. As I have loved you, so you must love one another. By this everyone will know that you are my disciples, if you love one another" (Jn. 13:34-35). In Titus 2:4, the older women in the church are admonished to teach the young women to love their husbands and children. What must be taught and learned about loving husbands and children? I believe it is how to love them in a language that will be meaningful to the individuals; in short, learning to speak their love language.

GARY CHAPMAN

### REFERENCES


Chapman, G. D. (2009a). *The Five Love Languages: Singles Edition* (2nd ed.). Chicago, IL: Northfield.

Chapman, G. D. (2009b). *God Speaks Your Love Language: How to Feel and Reflect God's Love* (2nd ed.). Chicago, IL: Northfield.

Chapman, G. D. (2010a). *The Five Love Languages: The Secret to Love That Lasts* (4th ed.). Chicago, IL: Northfield.

Chapman, G. D. (2010b). *The Five Love Languages of Teenagers: The Secret to Loving Teens Effectively* (3rd ed.). Chicago, IL: Northfield.

Chapman, G. D., & Campbell, R. (2005). *The Five Love Languages of Children* (2nd ed.). Chicago, IL: Northfield.


## MARRIAGE ENRICHMENT AND INTIMACY

**DESCRIPTION.** Marriage is our most treasured human relationship. This relationship is important to God—so important, in fact, that he gave marriage a central role throughout the Scriptures. The Bible begins with a wedding (Gen. 2:18) and ends with a wedding (Rev. 21:9). In the Gospel of John, Jesus performs his first miracle at a wedding in Cana (Jn. 2:1-11). The metaphor of a bride and groom is used to describe the relationship between God and the children of Israel and between Christ and the church. This is why the writer of Hebrews proclaimed, "Give honor to marriage, and remain faithful to one another in marriage" (Heb. 13:4 NLT).

**The Wholehearted Marriage.** One way to honor and strengthen marriages is by helping couples live out a *wholehearted* marriage. God calls us to live wholeheartedly in the greatest commandment, directing us to love him and others with all our hearts (Mk. 12:30-31). We are also told that the very reason Jesus came was so that we could experience the fullness and abundance of life (Jn. 10:10). Living wholeheartedly means fully engaging your heart in whatever is before you.

The heart is the key to a fully engaged life. Client after client sitting across from me in my counseling office attest to the fact that living a life without the heart engaged is less than fulfilling. Money, fame, success, possessions, and even relationships are meaningless if our hearts are not fully engaged. The apostle Paul made this clear when he challenged early Christians: "We have spoken freely to you, Corinthians, and opened wide our hearts to you. We are not withholding our affection from you, but you are withholding yours from us. As a fair exchange—I speak as to my children—open wide your hearts also" (2 Cor. 6:11-13). In the same way, a marriage without heart is not really a marriage at all. Without heart, spouses are left in empty, disconnected, coexisting relationships. Many of their complaints sound similar:

"We just don't connect anymore."

"Our marriage has no passion."

"My spouse doesn't really want me."

"I feel alone in my own house."

"I'm not in love anymore."

These statements are the result of closed, disengaged hearts. These couples may go their separate ways, or they may stay in empty marriages to honor their covenant commitments. This is why Jesus replied, "Moses permitted you to divorce your wives because your hearts were hard" (Mt. 19:8).

Couples can get the help they need to reenergize their marriage by fully engaging their hearts, just as 1 Peter 1:22 says: "Love one another deeply, from the heart." Two spouses wholeheartedly engaged can enjoy a great marriage. With their hearts open and engaged, people are free to love without reservations. Spouses are interested in fully pursuing each other, which communicates desire and makes them both feel wanted. Passion energizes the marriage, allowing couples to connect deeply. Openness characterizes the marriage so that true intimacy can occur. You hear statements like these:

"I am so in love with my spouse!"

"I feel more connected than ever."

"My home is the safest place on earth."

"My spouse is so passionate and romantic."

In short, hearts that are open and fully engaged lead to thriving marriages. So what's the problem? God created us to fully engage life, and marriages reach their full potential when hearts are open and engaged, yet many couples are not living wholeheartedly. Why?

We are not fully engaging life and marriage because we have an enemy that will not stop in his relentless effort to separate us from our hearts or shut our hearts down. When Jesus tells us that he came to give us life to the fullest, he also warns us that the thief (enemy) comes to rob, kill, and destroy. What do you think he's trying to kill, steal and destroy? Our hearts! The enemy robs us of abundant life by cutting us off from our hearts. He delights in seeing us close or disengage our hearts in our marriages so that we end up settling, compromising, surviving, or simply giving up. In his excellent book *Waking the Dead*, John Eldridge (2003) explains why Satan goes after our hearts.

> The enemy knows how vital the heart is, even if we do not, and all his forces are fixed upon its destruction. For if he

> can disable or deaden your heart, then he has effectively foiled the plan of God, which was to create a world where love reigns. By taking out your heart, the Enemy takes you out, and you are essential to the Story.

If the heart is as important as the Bible says it is (the wellspring of life, the dwelling place of the Lord, the essence of who we are, and our connection point with others), it makes sense that the enemy would level his greatest attacks there. King Solomon (the wisest man who ever lived) recognized this threat when he warned, "Above all else, guard your heart, for everything you do flows from it" (Pr. 4:23). The 1984 edition of the NIV says, "It is the wellspring of life." In earlier times, the easiest way to take out a village was to poison its water supply at the well. Similarly, taking out our wellspring (the heart) means certain defeat for us. When this happens, life is survived, not enjoyed; work is routine, not fulfilling. Sadly, a disengaged or closed heart makes it impossible to experience an intimate, connected marriage. Couples drift apart. They endure marriage instead of appreciating and nurturing it. Ultimately many give up and go looking for love somewhere else.

In order to recapture a vision for a wholehearted marriage, encourage couples to recite the words they used on their wedding day to pledge their hearts to each another. Perhaps it sounded something like this:

> I love you. You are my best friend.
> Today I give myself to you in marriage.
> I promise to encourage and inspire you, to laugh with you,
> and to comfort you in times of sorrow and struggle.
> I promise to love you in good times and in bad,
> when life seems easy and when it seems hard,
> when our love is simple, and when it is an effort.
> I promise to cherish you and to always hold you in highest regard.
> These things I give to you today and all the days of our life.

This is the type of relationship God envisioned for us to enjoy—a wholehearted marriage.

**Application.** The best strategy for helping couples to live with open and fully engaged hearts is to empower them to focus significant time, attention, and energy into creating a marriage that feels like the safest place on earth. This is critical because when people feel unsafe, their hearts close and they disconnect relationally. On the other hand, when people feel safe, they naturally open their hearts. Intimacy, then, occurs effortlessly and naturally when hearts are open to one another. It does not require effort or conscious attention. This is because openness is the default setting of our hearts. Our hearts were designed to be open. King David recognized this attribute in our heavenly Father when he wrote, "Keep me safe, my God, for in you I take refuge" (Ps. 16:1).

Encourage couples to make creating safety in their marriage a top priority—it must be the foundation. People can intertwine their hearts together and become one only when they feel safe. Here are some basic questions to ask couples.

- On a scale of 0 to 10 (with ten being the safest), how safe is your marriage for you and for your spouse?
- How do you react when you feel unsafe?
- How have you made it unsafe for your spouse?
- What does your spouse do that helps you to feel safe?
- What can you do to help your spouse feel safe?

The best way to enjoy a close, open, intimate marriage is to create an environment where two people who want to stay in love and harmony feel safe with each other. Emotional safety will help couples create a climate in which they can build open relationships that will grow and flourish. It will help them build a relationship in which they will feel cherished, honored, and alive. It will help them create a wholehearted marriage.

Greg Smalley

### RESOURCES

Eldredge, J. (2003). *Waking the Dead: The Glory of a Heart Fully Alive.* Nashville, TN: Thomas Nelson.

For more information, see Smalley, G., & Stoever, S. (2009). *The Wholehearted Marriage.* Brentwood, TN: Howard Books.

## HOPE-FOCUSED MARITAL THERAPY

**Description.** The hope-focused couples approach (HFCA) (Worthington, 2005) is an approach to helping couples reach their relationship goals. It is *religiously accommodative* in that it was designed with religious themes as part of the theory, it has religious intervention options, and it is utilized by ministers as well as therapists to help couples. HFCA is also *empirically supported.* A program of research has been ongoing since 1995, with more than a dozen published articles supporting the components and general approach (Jakubowski, Milne, Brunner & Miller, 2004; Ripley et al., 2008; Ripley et al., 2010). Books (Worthington, 2005) and an online training certificate to standardize training (www.hopecouples.com) are available. Finally, HFCA is rooted in *hope theory* (Snyder, 1994). This approach uses strategies for quick, observable change in a short-term format with the goal of increasing a sense of agency, increasing pathways for change, and willingness to patiently wait for the effects of change to be experienced.

**Religious Accommodation.** Many couples see their marriage relationships as sacred (Mahoney, Rye, & Pargament, 2005). If couples view their marriages as sacred and believe that God has a role in their relationships, they usually value the honoring of these beliefs in therapeutic interventions. There is evidence that religious couples prefer a religious therapist (Ripley & Worthington, 2001). Research has demonstrated that prayer has been effective in couples intervention (Fincham, Lambert, & Beach, 2010). HFCA accommodates religion in the following ways.

- It assesses the importance and practice of religion in the family.
- It assesses the contribution of religion or faith as a resource for growth and as a potential roadblock to improvement.
- It includes advanced informed consent to include religious therapy or enrichment.
- It uses nonsectarian terminology in communicating with couples about the problems in their relationship and how they can be improved. For example, a possible frame for treatment includes faith in each other, the therapy situation, and God to motivate for change.
- It uses Scripture to reinforce principles, such as "speak the truth in love" as a principle for good communication.
- It includes discussing not only relationship health but also spiritual growth and virtues as goals for treatment.
- It encourages collaboration or consultation with spiritual leaders.
- It promotes use of a prayer journal as homework to encourage couples to pray for each other effectively without blaming or criticizing each other.
- It encourages blessings and prayers in sessions when ethical.

**Course of Treatment.** First, an assessment phase of treatment provides couples with information about the approach and screens for factors that would contraindicate the HFCA for couples. Therapists would not use the HFCA with couples if the assessment revealed (a) untreated active substance abuse, (b) a current or recent extramarital affair, (c) one partner intent on divorce or already separated, (d) psychopathology that would need to be addressed before couples treatment could be effective, or (e) violence beyond "common couples violence."

Assessment of the couple would continue with questionnaires and a dyadic interview. These are typical questions asked in the dyadic interview:

- What brought you to seek counseling?
- How did you become a couple?
- If a miracle happened tonight and your relationship was just the way you wanted it to be, what would that look like for each of you?
- What can you tell me about your gender, ethnicity, religion, or other important parts of who you are that would help me understand you?
- Are there any hurts in your relationship that you struggle to apologize and forgive each other for?

The counselor then writes a two- or three-page report summarizing the assessments and establishing goals for counseling. The report is written for the couple in a conversational tone they can understand. This report is given to the couple in a session, and goals are discussed and created with the counselor and couple. This assessment is crucial because the established goals are used to strategically select interventions that will be useful in the couple reaching their relationship goals.

The interventions that are selected should match the couple's goals for treatment. Hope is established for the couple by beginning treatment with interventions that establish safety, promote trust in the therapy process, and demonstrate noticeable change. For example, the TANGO intervention is commonly used for couples' communication problems. The speakers...

- *tell* what happened, briefly and using "I" statements
- describe how the experience *affected* them emotionally
- use *nurturing* words, even during difficult conversations

The listeners respond by...

- using informal reflection skills to see if they "*got* it"
- *observing* the effects of the conversation

I believe that if a couple were offered a million dollars to communicate effectively for an hour, they could. But couples lose hope and don't put effort into their communication. Couples give up, stretch their attachment bonds, become self-protective, and give in to habits of ineffective communication and conflicts. The goal of TANGO and other communication interventions is to help couples experience hope through effective times of communication. The principles behind the technique are for couples to learn how to

- break up negative communication patterns,
- communicate clearly and briefly about the topic and their feelings,
- slow down the conversation by checking that they understand,
- communicate understanding to each other,
- use valuing and a nurturing style in difficult communication, and

- observe nonverbal and other cues to determine whether the conversation is going well.

**Conclusion.** The HFCA is a religious accommodative, empirically supported, and strategic hope-focused approach that helps couples reach their goals for their relationship. The approach is flexible, it is effective for novice therapists who are learning how to help couples, and it has been developed into a training program to standardize the approach.

**Jennifer Ripley**

### REFERENCES

Fincham, F. D., Lambert, N. M., & Beach, S. R. H. (2010). Faith and unfaithfulness: Can praying for your partner reduce infidelity? *Journal of Personality and Social Psychology, 99*, 594.

Jakubowski, S. F., Milne, E. P., Brunner, H., & Miller, R. B. (2004). A review of empirically supported marital enrichment programs. *Family Relations, 53*, 528-536.

Mahoney, A., Rye, M. S., & Pargament, K. I. (2005). When the sacred is violated: Desecration as a unique challenge to forgiveness. In E. L. Worthington, Jr. (Ed.), *Handbook of Forgiveness* (pp. 57-72). New York, NY: Brunner-Routledge.

Ripley, J. S., Leon, C., Davis, E., Smith, A., Mazzio, L., Worthington, E. L., Jr., & Atkinson, A. (2008, August). Hope focused couple therapy clinical trial: Implicitly and explicitly religious. American Psychological Association National Conference, Division 36. Boston, MA.

Ripley, J. S, Maclin, V. L., Pearce, E., Tomasulo, A., Smith, A., Rainwater, S.,...Davis, E. (2010, August). Religion-accommodative couples therapy: Process and outcome research. American Psychological Association National Conference, Division 36. San Diego, CA.

Ripley, J. S., & Worthington, E. L., Jr. (2001). Married Christians' preferences for and expectations of Christian and non-Christian marital therapists and interventions. *American Journal of Family Therapy, 29*, 39-58.

Snyder, C. R. (1994). *The Psychology of Hope: You Can Get There from Here.* New York, NY: Free Press.

Worthington, E. L., Jr. (2005). *Hope-Focused Marriage Counseling: A Guide to Brief Therapy* (Rev. ed.). Downers Grove, IL: InterVarsity Press.

## CONFLICT RESOLUTION

**Description.** When a normal disagreement escalates to the point that the safety, interests, or well-being of others is at risk, conflict resolution is needed. Whether the dispute began with a misunderstanding, manipulation, or exaggeration, the dispute must either be resolved or reach a danger point. Left unresolved, the conflict can intensify from shouting and property damage to the worst-case scenario of "going postal" as a disgruntled individual unleashes anger with a weapon, leaving a trail of death and destruction.

A popular misconception is that conflict resolution is a way to avoid conflict. Actually, conflicts among people of differing interests, perceptions, needs, and interests can be healthy as long as there is a constructive resolution. In Philippians 4:2, Paul seemed to be in the middle of a conflict resolution: "I plead with Euodia and I plead with Syntyche to be of the same mind in the Lord."

**Process and Benefits.** Conflict can provide opportunities for individuals in a relationship or coworkers in a business to see beyond the current reality and negotiate new options that may not have been attempted without challenging the status quo. When individuals become locked into verbal combat without focusing on a common objective, the conflict becomes an end rather than a means of reaching a solution. As tensions rise, disputants are less able to open their minds to other opinions, options, or recommendations. Without effective resolution, the conflict may be delayed, only to erupt at a future time.

Hidden agendas abound in unrestrained conflict. Competition can become a disguise for pressing one person's views on the group. The "winner take all" game is about control, not honest competition. The "losers" who accommodate by yielding may hold resentments that boil and erupt later in a seemingly unrelated situation. A collaborative approach works as long as all parties have respect, voice, and equal opportunity for their recommendations to be considered. When those conditions are not met, the collaboration can divide the group or couple. Competition, accommodation, and collaboration can be incorporated into effective conflict resolution or twisted into further conflict.

Individuals tend to respond to conflict according to the values, beliefs, and experiences of their cultural heritage, gender, and socioeconomic status. The cultural traits represent degrees of individualism versus collectivism, the knowledge of which is important in choosing a conflict-resolution approach (Morris & Fu, 2000). Cultural context is also important to consider when determining whether the customs for behavior in negotiation favor compromise or conformity (Morris & Fu).

The conflict response is a combination of cognitive, emotional, and physical responses that the disputants may not observe accurately in themselves or others. The thought process during conflict can become so loud inside one's head that little is heard from the other person. The same inattention occurs while thinking about how to fire back an accusation or defense. The disputant's cognitive processes are self-centered. As a conflict increases, the emotions may range from frustration and confusion to anger or rage. Each person may inaccurately assume that the other person holds the same feelings and may respond accordingly. Physically, conflict is hard on the body. Under such duress, an individual experiences tension, interrupted breathing, racing heartbeat, and adrenaline rush. These physical stressors further complicate focus on the real subject of conflict.

**Intervention and Mediation.** When the conflicting parties are unable or unwilling to find a resolution, outside intervention by a counselor or a professional skilled in conflict resolution can diffuse a volatile situation and reduce the likelihood of further emotional or physical harm. The Peacemaker Ministries program offers training for professional and pastoral counselors with a biblically based approach to identifying and resolving conflict. Its Slippery Slope chart identifies the differences between peacemaking responses and escape or attack responses. The Peacemaker's PAUSE Principle (Peacemaker Ministries, 2010) recommends five steps to Christian conflict resolution.

1. *Pause* for prayer and fact-finding.
2. *Affirm* respect of the relationship.
3. *Understand* the interests of all parties.
4. *Search* prayerfully and brainstorm for creative solutions.
5. *Evaluate* all the options objectively and openly.

This biblical approach to conflict resolution is suitable (except for the prayer) for dealing with conflict in any situation at work or home.

**Training.** Counselors and pastors who want to be trained in conflict resolution will need to understand the dynamics of conflict and be capable of managing, never suppressing, the emotions that will surface during mediation. Working from a specific, validated conflict-resolution model gives a framework to a situation that desperately needs structure. Ethically, the mediator must enter the conflict with an open mind and heart, focused on respecting and empowering all parties. An effective mediator is open to options and does not impose his or her opinions on the disputants. When managed properly, conflict resolution can demonstrate to the disputants the value of their differences through constructive expression.

Kathie T. Erwin

## RESOURCES

Morris, M., & Fu, H. Y. (2000). *How Does Culture Influence Conflict Resolution? A Dynamic Constructive Analysis* (Research Paper No. 1649). Stanford University, Graduate School of Business. Retrieved from http://ideas.repec.org/p/ecl/stabus/1649.html

Peacemaker Ministries. (2010). *PAUSE Principle.* Retrieved from www.peacemaker.net

Webne-Behrman, H. (1998). *Academic Leadership Support for University of Wisconsin–Madison.* Retrieved from www.ohrd.wisc.edu/onlinetraining/resolution

## FIDELITY AND INFIDELITY

**Description.** The terms *adultery* and *infidelity* have often been used interchangeably, but recent developments are requiring more specific definitions. *Adultery* is used almost exclusively of sexual betrayal. *Infidelity* is much broader and can be applied to any betrayal of a commitment to beliefs, religious values, marital vows, and so on. Sexual betrayal in marriage is commonly considered to have three levels: sexual infidelity (adultery), emotional infidelity (emotional affairs), and visual infidelity (pornography). All three are kept hidden from the spouse, have similar impacts upon the spouse at disclosure, destroy trust and respect, require a forgiveness process, and in recovery, provoke distinct changes within the marital relationship (Carder & Jaenicke, 2008; Glass & Staeheli, 2003; Laaser, 2004; Shriver et al., 2009).

**History.** Adultery has long been a part of the human story. It is forbidden in the Ten Commandments, condemned throughout Scripture, and warned about in the book of Proverbs. Jesus taught that adultery breaks the marriage commitment, and Paul admonished that adulterous believers who refuse to repent should be shunned. The early church fathers continued in the same vein and actually declared the marriage void in proven cases of adultery. Traditionally, adulterers have been scorned, punished, and considered dire threats to the institution of marriage. Recently, however, adultery has come to be viewed as a treatable offense, and in the last decade, research-based strategies of treating marital infidelity have been developed (Carder & Jaenicke, 2008).

**Assessment.** All three levels of infidelity initially produce infatuation and lust, can become addictive (compulsive), calm anxiety, lower depression levels, and provoke major mood elevations (Carder & Jaenicke, 2008; Peluso, 2007).

First-time emotional and sexual infidels most commonly find their partners from one of three sources: a platonic friendship growing out of a shared endeavor; an individual whose profile powerfully matches the needs, wants, or preferences of the other; and the reconnection with former dating partners (Carder, 2008a; Glass & Staeheli, 2003; Peluso, 2007; Shriver et al., 2009). The loosening of cultural morals, the intermingling of men and women (not only in the workforce but also for exercise, ministry, recreation, and the like), and recent Internet developments have all contributed to high levels of infidelity, which are assumed to be underreported. Most frequency studies indicate that about 65% of men and 50% of women report committing adultery. Studies within the Christian population indicate approximately 40% of spouses will acknowledge such behavior (Carder; Glass & Staeheli; Peluso; Shriver et al.).

Visual infidelity has become even more sinister. Pornography not only enslaves its participants, but its mobile availability and secrecy make it pervasive. In the last decade, treatment specialists have recognized that the age at onset of the use of pornography has become critical to the development of the best treatment plan (Earle & Laaser, 2002). The start of regular *adult* use of pornography usually requires treatment similar to that of any other addiction—in other words, a stable sobriety prior to starting marital therapy. Regular exposure to and use of pornography in childhood and through adolescence often requires the addition of individual therapy while developing abstinence (Carder, 2008b; Earle & Laaser; Laaser, 2004).

**Treatment.** The field of adultery recovery is too new to have produced accepted, evidence-based treatment strategies. However, several constructs of couple treatment appear to be commonly accepted (Carder,

2008b; Gaither, 2008; Laaser, 2004; Peluso, 2007; Shriver et al., 2009):

- The goal of the initial therapy is to stabilize the relationship so the couple can make appropriate decisions for the family.
- Therapy appears most effective when a contract is used to keep the couple in the therapy process.
- The therapist must be sensitive to the posttraumatic stress symptoms of the betrayed spouse (PTSD).
- A good marital history prior to the betrayal is the best predictor of a positive outcome.
- Therapy needs to be highly structured to enable the couple to walk through the trauma.
- The marital issues that contributed to the vulnerability of the spouse might need to be addressed after the trauma has been processed.

Any form of sexual compulsivity, whether visual (pornography) or sexual (multiple infidelities), requires personal sobriety prior to the onset of marital counseling. It is important that this sobriety be stable over time (for six to nine months) and free from relapse prior to starting couple counseling. Otherwise, as the spouses draw closer in therapy, the infidel will become increasingly dissatisfied with the level of emotional and sexual excitement, relapse, and act out again (Carder, 2008b; Gaither, 2008; Laaser, 2004; Peluso, 2007; Shriver et al., 2009).

Most of those who work in the field of adultery recovery practice the following components (Carder; Gaither; Laaser; Shriver et al.):

*Marital history.* Similar perceptions, high satisfaction levels, shared recovery from difficult experiences, and agreed upon highlights in the marriage all contribute to positive outcomes. Some practitioners like to chart this history in a form commonly referred to as a marital satisfaction time line (MSTL).

*Truth telling.* Betrayed spouses have the right to know as much as they want to know about the betrayal. To discount their need to know or to refuse to respond to their questions feels very much as if the inappropriate relationship is still being protected.

*Affair classification and severity.* Some kinds of infidelity are more damaging to the relationship and harder to forgive than others.

*Forgiveness process.* Most couples recognize the need for two levels of forgiveness: the first having to do with how each spouse has hurt the relationship apart from the affair, and secondly, the affair itself. The infidel must be encouraged to be specific in the request for forgiveness. Detailed requests are necessary for both spouses to be cleansed.

*Respect and trust rebuilt.* Healing is commonly viewed as working through forgiveness to respect, then to trust, and finally to love. If the couple has children, this stage is a necessary process regardless of whether the couple stays married.

*Final project.* In some form, the couple has to come to agreement about *how* and *why* infidelity occurred in their marriage. This agreement will probably include some family-of-origin predispositions that each brought into the marriage and a review of some of their marital patterns that contributed to the infidelity, and it certainly will take a look at the circumstances that triggered the affair. Finally, spouses will have to agree on the changes that they want to make in their future relationship. These changes might require ongoing training and skill building in communication, conflict management, sexual therapy, financial planning, and so on.

**David Carder**

## REFERENCES

Bercht, A., Bercht, B., & Bercht, D. (2004). *My Husband's Affair Became the Best Thing That Ever*

*Happened to Me: An Inspiring True Story.* Victoria, Canada: Trafford.

Carder, D. (2008a). *Close Calls: What Adulterers Want You to Know About Protecting Your Marriage.* Chicago, IL: Northfield.

Carder, D. (2008b). *Torn Asunder Workbook: Recovering from Extramarital Affairs.* Chicago, IL: Moody.

Carder, D., & Jaenicke, D. (1992/2008). *Torn Asunder: Recovering from Extramarital Affairs.* Chicago, IL: Moody.

Earle, R. H., & Laaser, M. R. (2002). *The Pornography Trap: Setting Pastors and Laypersons Free from Sexual Addiction.* Kansas City, MO: Beacon Hill Press.

Gaither, M. W. (2008). *Redemptive Divorce: A Biblical Process that Offers Guidance for the Suffering Partner, Healing for the Offending Spouse, and the Best Catalyst for Restoration.* Nashville, TN: Nelson.

Glass, S. P., & Staeheli, J. C. (2003). *Not "Just Friends": Protect Your Relationship from Infidelity and Heal the Trauma of Betrayal.* New York, NY: Free Press.

Laaser, M. R. (2004). *Healing the Wounds of Sexual Addiction.* Grand Rapids, MI: Zondervan.

Peluso, P. R. (2007). *Infidelity: A Practitioner's Guide to Working with Couples in Crisis.* New York, NY: Routledge.

Shriver, G., Shriver, M., Dillow, J. C., Dillow, L., Pintus, P., & Pintus, L. (2009). *Unfaithful: Hope and Healing After Infidelity* (2nd ed.). Colorado Springs, CO: Cook.

## EMOTIONAL ABUSE

**Description.** Emotional and psychological abuse systematically degrade and diminish and can eventually destroy the personhood of the victim. Most victims report that emotional abuse is more painful and traumatic than physical abuse.

**Assessment.** An emotionally abusive relationship isn't defined by one single incident of sinful or abusive behavior, but rather by repetitive actions and attitudes that result in either tearing someone down or inhibiting his or her growth (Vernick, 2007).

Emotionally abusive behaviors and attitudes include yelling, criticizing, ridiculing, demeaning, belittling, withholding (money, sex, attention, or other necessities), restricting (freedom of movement, choices, or another's emotional expression), isolating (from family, friends, or peers), threatening (to harm self, others, or objects of affection, such as a child, a pet, or property), abandonment, coercing, accusing, and ordering. These overt actions communicate over time that the personhood of the other is not valued or important, even if declarations of love are made.

Emotional abuse can also be covert. Ignoring someone over time conveys the message "you don't exist" and may be one of the most unrecognized yet serious forms of emotional abuse (Sackett & Saunders, 1999). Regularly minimizing someone's feelings, thoughts, desires, or needs as well as other subtle nonverbal cues of disgust, disapproval, or disdain diminish the personhood of the other. Denial of reality ("That didn't happen," or "You took it the wrong way"), denial of the abuse ("I didn't do that! You're crazy"), negative labeling, and chronic deceit can also be part of the abusive repertoire and can make someone feel confused, uncertain of what's real, and open to the thought that he or she is going crazy.

Individuals or couples rarely present themselves for treatment as victims of emotional battering. Instead, they seek help for symptoms like depression, low self-esteem, relationship struggles, suicidal ideation, intrusive thoughts, and anxiety and confusion (Sackett & Saunders, 1999). If emotional abuse is suspected or witnessed in marital interaction, a more careful assessment must be made. This can best be accomplished by interviewing each spouse separately.

In all forms of domestic abuse, it is crucial to identify any imbalance of power and control in high-conflict marriages and assess whether abusive tactics are part of the abusers' strategy to gain or keep control over the partners. If so, marital therapy is contraindicated until the abusive behavior has stopped and a safety plan is implemented.

**Treatment.** Psychological and emotional abuse is reported to be more painful and harder to heal than injuries due to physical abuse (Follingstad, Rutlege, Berg, Hause, & Polek, 1990; Tolman & Bhosley, 1991). The lingering damage to one's sense of self remains even when the relationship with the abuser has long ended (Briere, 2002).

Traditional treatments for emotional abuse have focused on anger validation, assertiveness training, and increasing one's interpersonal skills (Reed & Enright, 2006). Reed and Enright's forgiveness therapy (FT) shows promise in reducing depression and anxiety as well as increasing self-esteem and healthy decision making for victims of emotional abuse (Reed & Enright).

Reed and Enright postulate that the capacity to successfully choose good for one's self and others is crucial to healing a person's sense of self. In FT, clients are taught to mourn their losses and set specific goals to relinquish resentment and revenge, choose to forgive instead of holding onto resentment, and choose to develop goodwill toward their abusers. Forgiveness therapy strongly emphasizes that these choices do not correlate with reconciliation with abusers. The study on the efficacy of FT was done with post-relationship, post-crisis women who had been divorced or separated from their abusers for at least two years.

**Biblical and Spiritual Implications.** Christian counseling has been woefully inadequate in identifying and treating emotional abuse, especially within a marriage and family. Yet God's Word is very clear that words have the power to heal or destroy (see for example Ps. 52:2-4; Pr. 10:11; 11:9; 12:18; Mt. 5:21-22).

Reed and Enright's forgiveness therapy model is compatible with Christian values because it empowers victims not to be overcome by evil, but rather to overcome evil's internal influence with good through choosing forgiveness and goodwill toward enemies (Rom. 12:21). God calls believers to unconditional love, but we must understand that he does not call people to have unconditional relationships. We need to draw a clear distinction between forgiveness and reconciliation. One is unilateral, but the other requires both parties to prove trustworthiness. This distinction empowers victims to forgive and have goodwill and yet maintain appropriate boundaries with abusers.

**Conclusion.** A person's sense of self is formed in relationships. When a significant caregiver or intimate partner damages another person's sense of self, healing is found by restoring one's capacity to make good choices and let go of hurts, and also by building a more loving and trusting relationship with God (Vernick, 2007).

**Leslie Vernick**

### REFERENCES

Briere, J. (2002). Treating adult survivors of severe childhood abuse and neglect: Further development of an integrative model. In J. E. B. Myers, L. Berliner, J. Briere, C. T. Hendrix, T. Reid, & C. Jenny (Eds.), *The APSAC Handbook on Child Maltreatment* (2nd ed.). Newbury Park, CA: Sage.

Follingstad, D., Rutlege, L., Berg, B., Hause, E., & Polek, D. (1990). The role of emotional abuse in physically abusive relationships. *Journal of Family Violence, 5,* 107-119.

Reed, G. L., & Enright, R. D. (2006). The effects of forgiveness therapy on depression, anxiety, and posttraumatic stress for women after spousal emotional abuse. *Journal of Consulting and Clinical Psychology, 74*(5), 920-929.

Sackett, L., & Saunders, D. (1999). The impact of different forms of psychological abuse on battered women. *Violence and Victims, 14*(1), 10-12.

Tolman, R. M., & Bhosley, G. (1991). The outcome of participation in a shelter-sponsored program for men who batter. In D. Knudsen & J. Miller (Eds.), *Abused and Battered: Social and Legal Responses.* New York, NY: Aldine de Gruyter.

Vernick, L. (2007). *The Emotionally Destructive Relationship: Seeing It, Stopping It, Surviving It.* Eugene, OR: Harvest House.

## DOMESTIC VIOLENCE

**Description.** Most states define *domestic abuse* as physical, verbal, or sexual violence occurring between people who are related by law, who were once related by law, who have lived together, or who have had a child together. No socioeconomic groups are exempt. Domestic abuse causes physical harm, psychological trauma, and sometimes death. Women account for 85% of the victims of partner violence (Rennison, 2003).

Estimates indicate that one in every four women experience domestic abuse during their lifetime (Tjaden & Thoennes, 2000), although these figures may not be accurate due to underreporting (U.S. Department of Justice, 2003).

**Assessment or Awareness.** Domestic violence appeared shortly after sin entered the world, when Cain murdered Abel (Gen. 4:8). However, until the mid-1980s and early 1990s, mental-health professionals and marital therapists by and large ignored the problem of domestic abuse (O'Leary, 2008). Fear, shame, guilt, denial, and wanting to maintain the existing relationship often keep victims silent.

When someone seeks counseling, domestic violence is usually not the presenting problem. The issue is often identified as relationship problems, depression, posttraumatic stress symptoms, anxiety, or substance abuse. It is important that the clinician assess for partner abuse with questions like these:

1. Have you ever been threatened or physically hurt in this relationship?
2. Have you ever been an unwilling participant in a sexual act?
3. Do you ever feel fearful around your partner?

A positive response to any of these questions would elicit a more detailed assessment. Not all domestic abuse looks the same. When domestic violence is indicated, evaluate these five areas.

1. *Frequency.* How often does abuse happen, and is it increasing in frequency?
2. *Intensity.* What do the abusive incidents look like? How severe are they? Are incidents escalating in intensity? Has a push become a shove, a slap become a beating?
3. *Danger.* What is the level of danger to the victim? Abusive behavior may be infrequent but can still be extremely dangerous.
4. *Substance abuse.* Assess for alcohol abuse. Studies show that excessive alcohol use is greater than 50% for male batterers (American Psychological Association [APA], 1996).
5. *Power and control.* Is one partner trying to exercise power and control over another through the use of physical aggression, verbal threats or put-downs, economic control, twisting of Scripture, or isolation? Or are the abusive patterns less severe and mutually expressed out of immaturity, stress, and poor coping skills?

**Treatment.** Firm conclusions about best treatment programs for offenders are still uncertain, and research outcomes on various approaches don't show significant positive change on reducing recidivism (other than being arrested) (Babcock, Green, & Robies, 2004). Individual variables, such as severity and generality of violence, personality characteristics, and childhood trauma, need to be factored into treatment models (Saunders, 2001). Marital therapy is contraindicated when there is a pattern of intimidation, fear, or injury (O'Leary, 2008).

Treatment for victims involves helping them find safety, validating their concerns, providing education and resources, and helping them learn to make decisions and to think for themselves (Walker, 1995).

**Biblical and Spiritual Application and Treatment.** The Scriptures teach us God's view on domestic abuse.

1. Domestic violence is sin (Ps. 11:5; Mal. 2:16-17; Col. 3:19). Abusive speech is never an acceptable way to communicate (1 Cor. 5:11; Col. 3:8).

2. Violence is never justified, even when

provoked. People provoke us all the time, but we are still responsible to respond with wisdom, clarity, and restraint (Lk. 6:45; Eph. 4:26).

3. Biblical headship does not entitle a husband unlimited power over his wife, the right to remove her choices from her, or the right to have his own way all the time (Mk. 10:42-45; Eph. 5:1-2,21-29). The proper lens to view biblical headship is servanthood rather than ruling authority or power over someone.

4. Safety is prioritized and validated (Pr. 11:9; 27:12). For example, David fled King Saul when Saul was violent, even though Saul was in authority over David. The angel of the Lord warned Joseph to flee to Egypt with Mary and Jesus because Herod was trying to kill Jesus. Paul escaped from those who sought to stone him. Help a victim to get safe and stay safe. However, recognize that the highest risk for serious injury or death for a person in a violent relationship is often when the decision to separate is made (APA, 1996).

5. Outside authority may be necessary (Mt. 18:15-17). When someone grievously sins against us and will not listen, it is good to bring the matter before the church for additional support and authority. Church leaders need to respond in a timely and competent manner when people ask for help.

6. Violent persons must experience the consequences of their sinful behavior. Consequences are some of life's greatest teachers. God says what we sow, we reap (Gal. 6:7). Quite often, people continue to use violence at home because they get away with it (Pr. 19:19). God has put civil authorities in place to protect victims of abuse. The apostle Paul appealed to the Roman government when he was being mistreated (Acts 22:24-29). Legal means and church discipline may be necessary for victims' safety and may help bring perpetrators to repentance.

To combat domestic violence, churches can...

- educate teens on healthy dating relationships
- teach the proper relationship between husbands and wives as well as the misuse of authority
- create a healing environment in the church
- have a zero tolerance for abuse of any kind
- become familiar with community resources to help women and families in crisis

**Additional Issues.** The consequences of domestic abuse are long-term and devastating, not only directly to victims but also to children who witness the abuse. Counselors who see couples or individuals should consult with professionals who can advise them about safety issues and treatment protocols if domestic violence is reported. For information on the domestic violence laws in your state, visit www.womenslaw.org or call the National Domestic Violence Hotline at 1-800-799-7233.

**Leslie Vernick**

## REFERENCES


American Psychological Association. (1996). *Violence and the Family: Report of the APA Presidential Task Force on Violence and the Family.* Washington, DC: Author.

Babcock, J. C., Green, C. E., & Robies, C. (2004). Domestic Violence Treatment. *Clinical Psychology Review, 23,* 1023-1053.

O'Leary, K. D. (2008). Couple therapy and physical aggression. In A. S. Gurman (Ed.), *Clinical Handbook of Couples Therapy* (4th ed.). New York, NY: Guilford Press.

Rennison, C. M. (2003, February). *Intimate Partner Violence, 1993–2001: Crime Date Brief* (NCJ 197838). U.S. Department of Justice, Office of Justice Programs, Bureau of Justice Statistics. Retrieved from http://bjs.ojp.usdoj.gov/content/pub/pdf/ipv01.pdf

Saunders, D. G. (2001). Developing guidelines for domestic violence offender programs. *Journal of Aggression, Maltreatment & Trauma.* New York, NY: Routledge.

Tjaden, P., & Thoennes, N. (2000). *Extent, Nature and Consequences of Intimate Partner Violence: Findings from the National Violence Against Women Survey* (NCJ 181867). Washington, DC: National Institute of Justice and the Centers for Disease Control and Prevention. Retrieved from http://www.ncjrs.gov/pdf files1/nij/181867.pdf

U.S. Department of Justice, Office of Justice Programs, Bureau of Justice Statistics. (2003). *Criminal Victimization in the United States, 2003 Statistical Tables* (NCJ 207811). Retrieved from http://bjs.ojp.usdoj.gov/content/pub/pdf/cvus0302.pdf

Vernick, L. (2007). *The Emotionally Destructive Relationship: Seeing It, Stopping It, Surviving It* (pp. 233-235). Eugene, OR: Harvest House.

Walker, L. E. A. (1995). *Abused Women and Survivor Therapy*. Washington, DC: American Psychological Association.

## VICTIMIZATION

**Description.** Marriage is meant to represent Christ's relationship with the church—respectful, loving, and enduring. But many husband-wife relationships involve emotionally charged, volatile, or withdrawn patterns. These marriages spawn a vicious cycle of perpetrators, victims, and pain. They also present significant challenges for the Christian counselor.

**Assessment.** It doesn't take long to recognize a high-conflict relationship. Standard counseling interventions, such as teaching communication skills and encouraging date nights, don't generate improvement. In fact, episodes of conflict often escalate, even during counseling sessions. Simple disagreements and differing points of view become fights to the finish. Trust and goodwill are absent. Both partners exhibit significant distress, though one is usually more vocal or aggressive than the other.

When presented with this kind of distress in a marriage, the Christian counselor must keep several premises in mind. Despite what the couple may believe, their difficulty wasn't created by the current relationship. The pattern of attack and withdrawal is usually historical and enduring though often unconscious. One or both spouses probably grew up in a reactive home. Frequently, both partners are unaware victims of attachment injuries and unresolved trauma (whether the "big *T*" trauma of specific abuse or the "little *t*" trauma of various kinds of dysfunctional dynamics). One or both mates may be suffering from a personality disorder or at least significant traits related to these disorders.

**Treatment.** Repeated victimization characterizes this dysfunctional dance, and the Christian counselor must be able to step boldly into the center of the conflict. A primary challenge is to recognize the patterns of victimization in order to identify the victims and the victimizers, which isn't always as easy as the counselor may think. Karpman (1968) provides a helpful model known as Karpman's Triangle, which outlines the changing movement of victim, perpetrator, and rescuer.

Children are clearly victims of these volatile relationships and deserve protection and clinical attention. Children often act out the tension in the family and take on the role of rescuers, peacemakers, mediators, or secret keepers. Sometimes children lash out against the perceived aggressors or victims. Most counselors are familiar with these dynamics and can treat or refer children appropriately. Legally, counselors are required to report cases of "a child in need of protection," which includes exposure to interpartner violence (Tufford, Mishna, & Black, 2010).

Equally obvious is the victimization of a spouse who suffers domestic violence. Wives and husbands alike are victims of partner relational violence, which is never acceptable. However, especially in Christian settings, many women who are being abused will not seek help because of the convictions they hold to regarding marital submission (Nash, 2006). Christian counselors must be intentional to identify these kinds of situations and respond properly, including reporting the violence as required by law.

It is harder to address less obvious forms of victimization in high-conflict marriages.

Often, one spouse presents as the aggressive victimizer and the other spouse as the passive victim. This pattern may be accurate on the surface, but the Christian counselor must refuse to be a referee or judge for the relationship. Solving the specific conflict *du jour* will not generate long-term improvement. Victimizers are almost always unhealed victims of some kind, and they must address the injuries that prompted this defensive, protective stance. Victims are equally living out an earlier dynamic, and they must be empowered to stop "volunteering" for that role.

Several steps are crucial in stopping victimization in high-conflict couples:

1. Create a safe container. The counselor must be self-confident and resistant to countertransference, enforcing boundaries during the session that prohibit violence of any kind. This task requires the counselor to be assertive and directive.

2. Build goodwill to generate hope. If partners can view each other as wounded mates instead of bad persons, they can develop empathy. Then the partners will have a growing sense of hope that addressing underlying wounds will ease the relationship challenges.

3. Teach communication skills to address here-and-now discord. High-conflict couples must learn to take a time-out when emotions escalate. Each spouse must communicate with "I" statements instead of blaming, "you" statements.

4. Address underlying issues in each spouse. It takes two healthy people to have a healthy relationship. Both spouses must resolve underlying core issues that generate the harmful dynamics. Without this deeper work, the victimization and distress are destined to continue.

Every marriage experiences conflict, and conflict levels may fluctuate based on current levels of stress as well as personal issues. Surprisingly, Fincham (2003) found that at times, conflict can predict a high level of marital satisfaction. This sounds like a contradiction in terms, but it gives therapists and couples hope that high-conflict relationships are not doomed. The cycle of marital conflict can be difficult to break, but if help and healing are sought out, conflict can lead to a greater level of intimacy and satisfaction (Worthington, 2005).

**Biblical and Spiritual Issues.** Scripture rightly exhorts, "A gentle answer turns away wrath" (Pr. 15:1). Unfortunately, well-meaning but uninformed Christians sometimes cite passages about a wife's submission to her husband's leadership, essentially condoning victimization. No one wins—and more important, no one honors God—in high-conflict marriages and the victimization they harbor. With time, persistence, patience, and support, the healing of individuals by the grace and power of God is the pathway to healing a high-conflict marriage.

**Marnie C. Ferree**

### REFERENCES


Fincham, F. D. (2003). Marital conflicts: Correlates, structure, and context. *Current Directions in Psychological Science, 12*, 23-27.

Karpman, S. (1968). Fairy tales and script drama analysis. *Transactional Analysis Bulletin, 7*(26), 39-43.

Nash, S. (2006). The changing of the gods: Abused Christian wives and their hermeneutic revision of gender, power, and spousal conduct. *Qualitative Sociology, 29*, 195-209.

Tufford, L., Mishna, F., & Black. T. (2010). Mandatory reporting and child exposure to domestic violence: Issues regarding the therapeutic alliance with couples. *Clinical Social Work Journal 38*, 426-434.

Worthington, E. L., Jr. (2005). *Hope-Focused Marriage Counseling: A Guide to Brief Therapy.* Downers Grove, IL: InterVarsity Press.


## AGING

In a culture that values youthful vitality and appearance, the thought of aging can generate fear and anxiety. The anti-aging industry (cosmetics and cosmeceuticals) generates more than $230 billion each year worldwide in an effort to thwart the effects of aging (Briney, 2005). Distinguishing myth from reality can be an important component of aging successfully.

**Description.** The aging population is growing. In the U.S., persons age 65 and older made up only 4% of the population in 1900, but they now comprise 12.7%, and by 2050, they are expected to constitute 20% (U.S. Census Bureau, 2009). Similarly, life expectancy has increased from 47 years in 1900 to 78.1 years in 2006 and is projected to rise to 82.6 by 2050 (U.S. Census Bureau). Although gender differences in life expectancy have recently declined, females born in 2006 can still expect to live 5.3 years longer than males—80.7 years versus 75.4 years, respectively (U.S. Census Bureau).

Aging is typically divided into two forms (Anstey, Stankov, & Lord, 1993). *Primary aging* is normal, intrinsic aging that is genetically programmed. For example, changes are observed over time in the skin, hair, senses, and organ systems. This type of aging is irreversible, universal (it happens to everyone), and inevitable. *Secondary aging* is pathological, extrinsic aging that results from environmental factors. For example, sun exposure and smoking can both lead to cancer. Thus, secondary aging (disease) is largely preventable. Due to the interaction between biological and environmental influences, there is some variability in how people age.

One particular aging-related concern is memory. Although it is true that cognitive processing speed declines after the age of 25 (Salthouse, 1985), the impact of the slowdown is not the same for all areas of thinking (MacDonald, Hultsch, & Dixon, 2003). Areas involving quick problem-solving, focus of attention, and use of new information decline first. Other areas, such as remembering well-practiced procedures or general cultural information, remain relatively stable over time. In fact, some components of intelligence and creativity grow throughout the lifespan.

An important aspect of memory is one's memory self-efficacy, or one's positive evaluation of his or her memory. Those who lack confidence in their memory, or who believe their memory will inevitably decline, perform worse on memory tasks than those who believe they have a good memory (Zelinski & Gilewski, 2004). In other words, one's attitude about memory actually predicts how well one will remember.

**Application.** Due to the rising population of older adults, a particular concern of gerontologists is a shortage of workers in the helping professions (medicine, counseling, church ministry, etc.) who are trained to help older adults (Lun, 2011). Older adults have different developmental needs than do adults at earlier points in the lifespan, and a basic knowledge of these needs is essential in providing good care for this population. People helpers must confront their stereotypes of aging and learn how to engage older adults in processes that facilitate successful aging. Examples of these processes include diet, exercise, and active life engagement.

**Biblical Issues.** It is easy to internalize the Western idea that one's worth or value is defined by one's youth or productivity. Scripture, however, paints a different picture. According to Genesis 1:26-27, all human beings are created in God's image. As such, every person, whether young or old, able-bodied or bedridden, has inherent and inestimable value. Furthermore, Abraham, Moses, Aaron, Zechariah, and Elizabeth are biblical examples of older adults whom God used in various ways. Scripture is clear that God plans to use older adults, whether through dreams (Acts 2:17) or through serving as mentors for younger adults (Tit. 2:2-5). From a biblical perspective, older adults are not simply "benchwarmers" in the body of Christ. Instead, Christian leaders should seek to engage older adults and equip them for ministry (Eph. 4:11-13).

**Chad M. Magnuson**

## REFERENCES

Anstey, K., Stankov, L., & Lord, S. (1993). Primary aging, secondary aging, and intelligence. *Psychology and Aging, 8*(4), 562-570.

Briney, C. (2005). Industry growth on the horizon. *Global Cosmetic Industry, 173*(6), 41-42.

Lun, M. W. A. (2011). Student knowledge and attitudes toward older people and their impact on pursuing aging careers. *Educational Gerontology, 37*(1), 1-11.

MacDonald, S. W., Hultsch, D. F., & Dixon, R. A. (2003). Performance variability is related to change in cognition: Evidence from the Victoria Longitudinal Study. *Psychology and Aging, 18,* 510-523.

Salthouse, T. A. (1985). Speed of behavior and its implications for cognition. In J. E. Birren & K. W. Schaie (Eds.), *Handbook of the Psychology of Aging* (2nd ed., pp. 400-426). New York, NY: Van Nostrand Reinhold.

U.S. Census Bureau. (2009). *Statistical Abstract of the United States: 2009* (128th ed.). Retrieved from http://www.census.gov/compendia/statab/2009/2009edition.html

Zelinksi, E. M., & Gilewski, M. J. (2004). 10-item Rasch modeled memory self-efficacy scale. *Aging and Mental Health, 8,* 293-306.

## EMPTY-NEST ISSUES

Families experience unique dynamics in each stage of family development. From the early years of marriage to the retirement years, adults face varied challenges. The challenges faced by couples who are "launching" their children often result in what is known as the empty-nest syndrome. As children move away from home into college, military service, adult independence, or marriage, parents experience changes that often negatively impact them.

**Definition.** The empty-nest syndrome is the period in family life stage theory when children leave the home. It may be characterized by sadness, depression, emptiness, purposeless, and sometimes divorce. It is most often seen in women (Olson, DeFrain, & Skogrand, 2008; Gladding, 2011). The main issues in therapy revolve around creating a partner-focused marriage as opposed to one that is child focused (Arp & Arp, 1996). Parents who have launched children are often left with painful and empty feelings because much of their lives has been child-centric. Mothers report these symptoms more often than fathers because of mothers' role as caregivers through the child-rearing years. During the empty-nest stage of family life, the developmental task of adult-to-adult relationship is central. Children are now young adults. If these adult children have married, empty-nesters must develop relationships with in-laws (Goldenberg & Goldenberg, 2008).

This time can be especially difficult if couples have not prepared for it. With the advent of modern medical technology, this stage of life can be the longest (Clinton & Ohlschlager, 2002). Because of the lack of preparation for refocusing on the marital dyad, divorce rates have increased (Olson et al., 2008). In one study by Enright (2004), 66% of wives asked for divorce compared to 41% of men after the children left home. Many of the men reported being surprised by their wives' request for divorce. Some have suggested that these adults may hang on until their children leave home and then feel freedom to consider divorce (Yarhouse & Sells, 2008). For various reasons, this time can be filled with insecurities.

Not all empty nests are truly empty; many have variations that keep the nest filled. Some adult children return home after college, military service, or a divorce. These "boomerang" adult children return to the nest to become reestablished or to use their homes as a second launching pad for new careers (Gladding, 2011; Olson et al., 2008). If the empty-nest parents have aging parents themselves, they may find that they have joined the "sandwich generation" as they care for their elderly parents while seeking to help their adult children relaunch (Olson et al.; Clinton & Ohlschlager, 2002).

**Successfully Navigating the Empty-Nest Years.** It may seem obvious to some that these obstacles can be avoided. Some basic and practical steps will help make this stage a smooth and enjoyable experience. Wallerstein and Blakeslee (1995) researched successful and happily married couples and found that during this stage they reported a high degree of humor and interest. These couples committed to revisiting their relationship after years of being child centered. Success is largely determined by the level of flexibility in the family boundaries and how easily the family allows exits and entries (Yarhouse & Sells, 2008). Couples who place high priority on their own relationship before, during, and after child-rearing years are better able to cope with the pressures of the empty nest.

VICTOR HINSON

## REFERENCES


Arp, D., & Arp, C. (1996). *The Second Half of Marriage.* Grand Rapids, MI: Zondervan.

Clinton, T., & Ohlschlager, G. (2002). *Competent Christian Counseling: Foundations and Practice of Compassionate Soul Care.* Colorado Springs, CO: WaterBrook Press.

Enright, E. (2004, July/August). A house divided. *American Association of Retired Persons Magazine,* pp. 60, 64-66, 68, 81.

Gladding, S. (2011). *Family Therapy: History, Theory, and Practice.* (5th ed.). Upper Saddle River, NJ: Prentice Hall.

Goldenberg, H., & Goldenberg, I. (2008). *Family Therapy: An Overview* (7th ed.). Belmont, CA: Thomson Brooks/Cole.

Olson, D. H., DeFrain, J., & Skogrand, L. (2008). *Marriage and Families: Intimacy, Diversity, and Strengths* (6th ed.). New York, NY: McGraw-Hill.

Wallerstein, J. S., & Blakeslee, S. (1995). *The Good Marriage: How and Why Love Lasts.* New York, NY: Houghton Mifflin Company.

Yarhouse, M. A., & Sells, J. N. (2008). *Family Therapies: A Comprehensive Christian Appraisal.* Downers Grove, IL: InterVarsity Press.


## RETIREMENT PLANNING

As retirement approaches, aging adults need to ask the classic reporter's questions: Who, what, when, where, and why? The answers to these questions can make transition from working adult to retiree less emotionally and financially stressful.

- *Whom* do you want to surround yourself with in retirement? Is it critical to live near children and grandchildren, or it is time to explore new places?
- *What* delayed opportunities will you enjoy with more free time?
- *When* will you be ready to retire?
- *Where* will you live—in the family home, in a condo, or in a retirement village?
- *Why* are you retiring? Is it because of health, age, illness, choice, or to meet others' expectations?

Retirement planning is often focused on financial issues. The average 65-year-old American may live an additional 18 years after retirement (Arias, 2010). With longer life spans and fewer people who have employment-based pensions to supplement Social Security, the risks of outliving income and assets are major concerns for many retirees. Even among those who have pension income, there is gender inequality. Less than half of women retirees receive pensions, and their benefits are typically 50% or less of what men receive (Burnes & Schulz, 2000). Younger retirees (ages 59–64) who are healthy but not wealthy have a similar risk of outliving assets, as do those who retire due to illness or disability.

Extreme medical expenses can erode retirement. As a result, home care is increasing. More than 65 million family caregivers (29% of the U.S. population) attend to aging relatives with chronic illness, memory impairment, or disability (National Family Caregiving, 2009). Few retirees have long-term care insurance, and even among those who do, the costs of lengthy illness, caregiving, or nursing-home care result in reduced assets for the surviving spouse's remaining retirement years.

Financial planning is needed, but retirees often neglect preparation for the emotional challenges noted in Blau's role exit theory (1973). Moving from the work-centered pace to having no schedule may sound idyllic, yet when the novelty wears off, some people find their golden years tarnished with depression, substance abuse, and social isolation (Simoni-Wastila & Yang 2006; Steffens, Fisher, Langa, Potter, & Plassman, 2009). Anxiety is another emotional problem among older adults. The National Council of Aging listed what retirees perceive as their greatest problems (in order of severity): health, money, crime, and loneliness (National Council on Aging, 2000).

No longer packing up for senior communities in Florida or Arizona, retirees today increasingly favor "aging in place"—remaining in their homes, neighborhoods, and social support networks. According to the National Aging in Place Council, record numbers of older homeowners are modifying their homes with safety features, wheelchair ramps, and functional improvements in kitchens and bathrooms (National Aging in Place Council, 2010). Adding remodeling costs to the retirement budget and completing these projects during the preretirement phase gives the homeowners time to adjust to the changes and reduce the risk of being unable to remain at home as care needs change.

Retirement planning needs to include coaching or counseling to help the preretiree find a new life purpose. With time available to serve in short-term missions, travel, volunteer locally, fill a part-time place in ministry, or assist in the children's ministry, the new Baby Boomer retirees are likely to see retirement as a second chance to make aspirational goals a reality. The National Council on Aging identified an "emerging trend of civic engagement" among adults over 55 and actively seeks these new retirees for community volunteer service. Imagine how much could be achieved in ministry if the Christian community recognized and tapped the potential of this volunteer retiree group. This new retiree cohort group widely believes in what trend analyst Faith Popcorn termed "down aging," which is the intent to remain vital, active, and involved in the community, consistent with the Christian worldview to continually be about the Lord's work.

**Kathie T. Erwin**

## REFERENCES


Arias, E. (2010, June 28). *National Vital Statistics Reports, 58*(21), 2-3. Retrieved from http://www.cdc.gov/nchs/data/nvsr/nvsr58/nvsr58_21.pdf

Blau, Z. S. (1973). *Old Age in a Changing Society*. New York, NY: New Viewpoints.

Burnes, J., & Schulz, J. H. (2000). *Older Women and Private Pensions in the United States*. Waltham, MA. Retrieved from http://iasp.brandeis.edu/womenandaging

National Aging in Place Council. (2010). *Interior Design and Home Remodeling*. Retrieved from http://www.ageinplace.org

National Council on Aging. (2000). *American Perceptions on Aging: Myths and Realities of Aging*. Retrieved from www.ncoa.org

National Family Caregiving. (2009, November). *Caregiving in the United States*. Retrieved from http://www.nfcacares.org/who_are_family_caregivers/care_giving_statstics.cfm#2

Simoni-Wastila, L., & Yang, H. K. (Dec, 2006). Psychoactive drug abuse in older adults. *American Journal of Geriatric Pharmacotherapy, 12*(4), 380-394. Retrieved from http://www.ncbi.nlm.nih.gov/pubmed/17296542

Steffens, D. C., Fisher, G. G., Langa, K. M., Potter, G. G., & Plassman, B. L. (2009). Prevalence of depression among older Americans: The aging, demographics and memory study. *International Psychogeriatrics, 21*(5), 2009.

# SEPARATION, DIVORCE, AND DIVORCE MEDIATION

## SEPARATION

**When Couples Are Separated.** Many times, the counselor is introduced to a failing marriage—or an impending divorce—after one of the partners has left it and the forsaken and devastated spouse comes in for counseling. In these cases, a couple must risk losing their marriage by separation in order to save it (Mk. 8:34-36; Lk. 17:33).

According to 2009 census data, 2.3% of the population claimed to be separated from their spouses. More than 9% of the people claimed to be divorced from their spouses, and 30% of the people over the age of 15 have never been married. The census further categorized these statistics on separated U.S. residents:

- More females than males claimed to be separated.
- The lowest number of separations reported for both genders was within the age bracket of 65 and older.
- The highest number of women claiming to be separated from their spouses were 35 to 44 years old.
- Women with income are more likely than women without income to separate, with the exception of women who earn $75,000 or more annually, who are less likely to separate.
- Men with higher incomes were less likely to be separated than men with lower incomes (U.S. Census, 2010).

Separation is risky. Some research shows that it leads to divorce in 75% to 80% of all cases where sexual infidelity is involved (*What Are the Causes?*, 2011). However, there are many other reasons why couples separate, including separation to save the marriage. Five of the most common reasons given for separation include: infidelity, sexual issues other than cheating, money conflicts, communications breakdown, and addictions of all kinds (*What Are the Causes?*, 2011).

For many others, separation can be a blessing in disguise because it sometimes breaks powerful interaction patterns that are harming or destroying the marriage. This is especially true if abuse and violence have become the norm for marriages or family life. Sometimes an abused spouse must leave the home and find protective shelter for herself and her children (Kressell, 1985).

As an alternative to divorce—as a last-step intervention—we suggest separation with an intent and effort at marital reconciliation. This may serve God's interest in saving marriages, and it fulfills the policy behind state law to give couples time to resolve their marital disputes and avoid divorce. California, in fact, has for years offered a legal action of marital separation (a wholly separate action from divorce) that was legislated to fulfill this wise policy.

Why should any couple separate at all? Won't that lead inevitably to divorce? Doesn't that violate God's intent for marriage and his prohibitions against divorce? These are good and common questions asked by Christian couples with marital conflicts. It is true that some couples should not separate, as doing so will only increase the risk of divorce. For some marriages, however, the level of conflict and destructive interaction has become so powerful and reached such a high level of harm that these patterns must be broken or they will destroy the marriage. Sometimes these harmful and powerful patterns are broken only by a time of marital separation. Living together becomes so toxic that continuing to live under the same roof leads to violence or irreparable harm.

There are numerous circumstances—situations where the problems are not stopping, but are continuing or escalating—in which counselors can work with separated couples. Some of the more common are marital infidelity, physical or sexual abuse, verbal or emotional abuse, unrelenting domination or control, abandonment of basic marital responsibilities, harmful addiction patterns, and unresolved financial, legal, or relational crises. We do caution that there is no legalistic list of things that demand or suggest separation. It is primarily a judgment by one or both members of the marriage that marital love is dead, that life together has become harmful or dangerous, and that it hasn't changed after many efforts, including counseling.

Be very clear that separation is a last-ditch effort at marital salvation. We encourage this action only when continuing to live together is likely to be dangerous or produce destructive fruits, or when divorce is strongly desired or being actively pursued by one of the marital partners.

Structured and mutually agreed-upon separations can save marriages. For those couples for whom this program has worked we have witnessed these dynamics:

- Powerful and destructive patterns of conflict, abuse, addiction, and control are broken as a result of or concurrently with the separation.
- The separation is respected and structured to reduce harmful behavior and strengthen positive marital actions. There is a mutual and detailed agreement to work at reconciliation, even if the degree of commitment to it is not equal.
- The threatened or endangered partner begins to feel safe and willing to interact again and take new risks of interacting with the feared partner.
- Addicted, abusive, or controlling partners admit and own their trouble, become more humble, and consider real (not feigned or minimal) help and change.
- Partners engage in individual treatment to resolve serious personal problems they had not overcome and had previously blamed on their spouse.
- Neither partner gets involved romantically or emotionally with someone else.
- Partners experience a renewal of intimacy and power in their relationship with God.

Matthew 19 and 1 Corinthians 7 are clear about avoiding other sexual relations while one is married. They confirm that any separation is to eventually lead to a reconciliation between husband and wife with the aid of prayer and fasting.

Structured separation agreements can be found at various Internet sites. The best agreements should...

- Set a clear time frame for the separation—usually 3 to 6 months.
- Define any lawyer's involvement, including whether the separation will be supervised by lawyers.
- Define exact living arrangements and costs—who moves out, what is taken, what are budgets for both, and how money is accessed (no draining

accounts or setting up secret slush funds).

- Define time together in counseling, in dating, in negotiations (or whether mediation is needed due to inevitable fighting).
- Define time seeing children and being together as a family.
- Avoid dating or seeing others—critical to separation success.
- Define limits on gossip and involvement of grandparents and other close family and friends.
- Define counseling and behavioral goals.
- Write down the agreement, with terms of modification spelled out.
- Define deal breakers and contract spoilers (*What Is a Separation Agreement?*, 2011).

**Conclusion.** At the core of successful reconciliation is an individual and marital surrender to God that ushers in the transforming experience of his loving, gracious power—God changing the couple and accomplishing that which was impossible for them to do in their own strength (Sande, 1989).

The church provides the reason, and should provide the resources, for couples to avoid divorce and, if they are divorced, to be surrounded with love and grace and support in a separation. Christian counselors should do all they can to support both objectives and become the best helpers possible for both parties. Like the poor, those who divorce will always be with us, and we cannot turn our backs on them. And because it may be a "special call" to work primarily in this field, we must do all we can to assist those who labor here, for their sakes and for the sake of those they serve.

God knows the pain and brokenness of those touched by the suffering of divorce. However, he loves divorcing people and reaches out to them with a special care and tenderness. Can those in Christian counseling and church ministry do any less?

George Ohlschlager
Ron Hawkins
Tim Clinton

## REFERENCES


Buzzard, L., & Eck, L. (1982). *Tell It to the Church: A Biblical Approach to Resolving Conflict Out of Court.* Elgin, IL: Cook.

Ellison, S. (1977). *Divorce and Remarriage in the Church.* Grand Rapids, MI: Zondervan.

Kressel, K. (1985). *The Process of Divorce: How Professionals and Couples Negotiate Settlements.* New York, NY: Basic Books.

Lewis, J., & Blakeslee, S., (2000). *The Unexpected Legacy of Divorce.* New York: Hyperion.

Sande, C. K. (1989). *Christian Conciliation: A Better Way to Settle Conflicts.* Billings, MT: Association of Christian Conciliation Services.

U.S. Census Bureau. (2010). *America's Families and Living Arrangements: 2009.* Retrieved from http://www.census.gov/population/www/socdemo/hh-fam/cps2009.html

*What Are the Causes of Marriage Separation?* (2011). Retrieved from http://www.ehow.com/about_5368317_causes-marriage-separation.html

*What Is a Separation Agreement?* (2011). Retrieved from http://www.ehow.com/facts_6182344_separation-agreement.html


## DIVORCE

Divorce is a legal act that permanently ends a marriage. For petitioners, it is usually the last act of ending a relationship they've already forsaken morally, emotionally, physically, or sexually. For respondents, it is often the beginning of the end, with the trauma continuing for many years. For both, and especially for children and extended family, it is a costly and painful journey beyond most expectations.

Divorce experience is very much like experiencing death—it is, in fact, the death of a marriage. Recovery from divorce is a multiyear process of adjustment and healing through the grief process. In fact, the effects of divorce are often traumatic at numerous levels and may well last a lifetime. Divorce reverberates through many lives and families, and its long-term effects are tinged with an impact upon generations of families (see Wallerstein, 2000; Lewis & Blakeslee, 2000; Wallerstein & Blakeslee, 1989; Dronkers & Härkönen, 2008).

**No-Fault Divorce in America.** Since its inception in California in 1970, no-fault divorce has become the American standard (Family Law Act of 1970). The advent of the "easy" divorce—banishing the requirement of one finding fault against the other and creating a presumption for joint custody of children—has led to a mushrooming divorce rate in the United States. From 1960 to 1990, the divorce rate in America tripled from 400,000 to more than 1.2 million divorces annually. For more than 20 years, more than a million divorces have happened annually in the United States, with a fairly steady rate of nearly one divorce for every two marriages. In contrast to America's 2 to 1 rate of marriages to divorces, Mexico has a 12 to 1 rate, Guatemala is at 25 to 1, Japan is at 5 to 1, and Jordan has an 8 to 1 rate. European divorce rates are also high, with rates very close to the United States: Sweden's rate is 2.5 to 1, and Denmark's is 2 to 1 (Gallup & Jones, 2000).

**The Effects of Divorce.** The negative effects of divorce on all family members is pervasive and long-lasting. Men and women are affected by divorce across many arenas of their lives and for long after the divorce is finalized. A summary of more than 40 years of research on the effects of divorce reveal these findings:

- Both spouses suffer financial loss in the divorce. The divorce costs from $20,000 to more than $100,000, and both parties are left poorer for many years (Stroup & Pollock, 1994).
- Life expectancies for the divorced are significantly lower than for married people, who have the longest life expectancies (Joung, van de Mheen, Stronks, van Poppel, & Mackenbach, 1994; Kaplan & Kronick, 2006).
- A recent study found that those who were unhappy but stayed married were more likely to be happy five years later than those who divorced (Waite & Gallager, 2000, p. 148).
- The emotional trauma of divorce has a long-term effect on one's physical health. One study showed that after a diagnosis of cancer, married people are most likely to recover, but the divorced are least likely to recover (Goodwin, Hunt, Key, & Sarmet, 1987; Pruthi, Lentz, Sand, Kouba, & Wallen, 2009).
- Men and women both suffer a decline in mental health following divorce, with some of the more common mental-health indicators including depression, hostility, self-acceptance, personal growth, and positive relations with others. Researchers have found that women are more greatly affected than men (Marks & Lambert, 1998; Gray, de Vaus, Qu, & Stanton, 2011).
- Fighting and hostility often remain after divorce. Anger usually increases when a divorce occurs. Second marriages have a higher rate of divorce than first marriages, and third marriages suffer divorce at higher rates than second marriages.

Divorced parents also suffer harm in their relationships with their children. In most cases, noncustodial fathers are unable to maintain the level of involvement with their children, and the damage does not always heal when the child grows up. Researchers found that nearly two thirds of young adults from disrupted families had poor relationships with their fathers. And a substantial minority of these young adults had poor relationships with *both* parents (Zill, Morrison, & Coiro, 1993). (For more information on the effects of divorce on kids, please see article "Children of Divorce.")

**Divorce in the Bible.** Divorce and its controversies wind their way throughout both Testaments of Scripture and throughout the history of the church (see Ellison, 1977; Adams, 1980; Richmond, 1988). Like today, a key dynamic throughout biblical history has been the tension between strict and permissive views on divorce.

*Old Testament revelation.* The most significant passage on divorce in the Old Testament is found in Deuteronomy 24:1-4, set in the Covenant Law. "If a man marries a woman who becomes displeasing to him because he finds something indecent about her, and he writes her a certificate of divorce, gives it to her and sends her from his house..."

Three things stand out in this text. First, divorce was permitted. Second, a standard for divorce was revealed—the grounds of "indecency"—an attempted objective, legal check to the otherwise purely subjective judgment of a man's displeasure with his wife. Third, there was prescribed a formal procedure: a divorce certificate writing, a giving of the certificate to the wife, and a removal of the wife from one's house.

The meaning of indecency and the limits to the grounds given for divorce were hotly disputed by the ancients, just as they are today. Some tried to define the content of indecent behavior, but this was found to be so controversial that most succumbed to the patriarchal double-standard that a man was allowed to divorce a woman for any reason.

*New Testament teaching.* By Jesus' day, the question of divorce had become polarized and politicized as two major schools of thought contended for influence. The liberal Hillel school—urbane, sophisticated, worldly, and influential in Jewish-Roman affairs at the birth of Christ—had adopted the view that a man could divorce his wife for any reason. The Shammai group—conservative, orthodox, separatist, and suspicious of Roman rule and worldly corruption—held that divorce was allowed only in the case of adultery (Köstenberger & Jones, 2004).

Jesus could not escape these controversies in his public ministry. Matthew 19:3-9 recounts the Pharisees' attempts to test Jesus:

> "Is it lawful for a man to divorce his wife for any and every reason?"
>
> "Haven't you read," [Jesus] replied, "that at the beginning the Creator 'made them male and female,' and said, 'For this reason a man will leave his father and mother and be united to his wife, and the two will become one flesh'? So they are no longer two, but one flesh. Therefore what God has joined together, let no one separate."
>
> "Why then," they asked, "did Moses command that a man give his wife a certificate of divorce and send her away?"
>
> Jesus replied, "Moses permitted you to divorce your wives because your hearts were hard. But it was not this way from the beginning. I tell you that anyone who divorces his wife, except for marital unfaithfulness, and marries another woman commits adultery."

One thing is clear from Jesus' views about divorce: He aligned more closely with the stricter Shammai view (infidelity only) than the permissive Hillel school (divorce for any reason). However, it is significant that the parallel passages on these incidents in Mark (10:2-9) and Luke (16:18) do not contain the exception of marital unfaithfulness as a cause for divorce. Throughout history, this has bolstered both the permissive and restrictive arguments regarding divorce.

Paul's teaching about divorce is contained

in 1 Corinthians 7. Like Jesus, Paul sets his teaching in the context of marital advocacy to a church that struggled with immorality, dissension, and worldly influence. Understandably, many parallels between Corinth and modern America have been recognized. Paul wrote to the church to apply the teachings of Christ—a church struggling with unsettling numbers of marital problems and divorces.

**Five Positions in the Modern Church.** Unfortunately, the church today is as divided as it has been at any historical period. These are the five major views on divorce in the church today:

1. *No divorce is allowed.* At one end of the spectrum is the position that no divorce is ever allowed. This is the official position of the Catholic Church, but the American Catholic Church has so liberalized its canon law on annulment (which takes the view that no marriage existed if it was not legitimized at some point) that it may be considered civil divorce by other means.

2. *Any divorce is allowed.* At the other extreme are various churches that have, in effect, capitulated to modern culture and now accept any divorce that its parishioners arrange. Regardless of the official doctrinal position of the church, in practice nearly any divorce is acceptable.

3. *Adultery only.* Some churches allow for divorce only in the case of sexual infidelity—sexual intercourse with another, which breaks the marital union. Some churches define infidelity more broadly than sexual intercourse outside marriage, including such things as incestuous relations with one's child or a pornography addiction, as grounds for divorce.

4. *Infidelity or abandonment, strictly construed.* Other churches wrap in Paul's Corinthian instructions on abandonment and, adhering to a strict reading of the Scriptures, also allow divorce when an unbelieving spouse abandons the marriage and divorces the believing spouse.

5. *Infidelity or abandonment, broadly construed.* Some churches make an expansive application to the understanding of infidelity and abandonment to affirm a broader set of grounds for divorce. "Constructive" abandonment may include a believer who refuses to materially support his family (wrapping 1 Timothy 5:8 into Paul's Corinthian equation). This position generally allows divorce in cases of serial sexual affairs, sex addiction, drug addiction, and other addictions that are not forsaken; spousal or child abuse; or abandonment of financial and other primary care-taking responsibilities.

God "hates divorce" and prefers reconciliation. In no case, no matter how egregious, is divorce commanded by God. He permits divorce owing to his own merciful nature and the exceeding sinfulness of humanity. In any case, however, God would prefer that couples be reconciled and made whole (Parrott & Parrott, 1995).

**Divorce Process and Counseling.** The divorce counselor must honestly confront these conflicted realities: Divorce happens, it happens frequently, and it happens in the church. Divorce always hurts, and it is better in most cases to avoid divorce and rebuild a marriage if at all possible. This does not mean that counselors should abandon those who do divorce in order to show their unerring support for marriage. This also does not mean that one support divorce contrary to one's beliefs when it is inevitable or confuse support for the client with support for divorce action.

Rather, it means to ethically engage in divorce work with the hope and prayer for reconciliation and with an eye to advocate for and offer marital renewal whenever possible. This entails an artful and difficult balance in practice. It means being there for the clients and being committed enough to their goals to maintain their trust and working alliance while also looking for opportunities to advocate for reconciliation and individual healing. This can be done by recognizing that when divorce is inevitable, intervention for the purposes of quelling hate and bitterness—to create the least toxic divorce settlement for the family—is preferred over the violent or uglier alternative (Kressel, 1985).

Rich (2002) cogently argued that all couples face four stages in divorce: (a) shock and disbelief, (b) initial adjustment, (c) active reorganization, and (d) life reformation. Crisis intervention process, reality testing, and verbalizing events and emotions are the best responses to shock and disbelief. Legal representation, moving, adjusting finances, and helping family members adjust are all parts of initial adjustments. The conclusion of divorce and end of the legal process is usually the beginning of the active reorganization stage—assisting the process of new relationships is most helpful here. The life reformation stage, like the acceptance phase in grief counseling, solidifies new values and new directions for the divorced person.

Overall, we look to God himself for direction and power. In the same way that God hates divorce but allows it, the church should acknowledge its loathing of divorce but be dedicated to serve those going through it, always offering a loving, caring hand. This may seem contradictory, but it is not. It is biblical, paradoxical, and heuristic, reflecting the balance of God's character rather than adhering to a rigid theological norm that looks godly but ultimately is hurtful to God's way.

George Ohlschlager
Tim Clinton

## REFERENCES


Adams, J. (1980). *Marriage, Divorce, and Remarriage.* Grand Rapids, MI: Baker.

Astone, N., & McLanahan, S.S. (1991). Family structure, parental practices and high school completion. *American Sociological Review, 56,* 309-320.

Chase-Lansdale, P., Cherlin, A., & Kiernan, K. (1995). The long-term effects of parental divorce on the mental health of young adults: A developmental perspective. *Child Development, 66,* 1614-1634.

Coombs, R., (1991). Marital status and personal wellbeing: A literature review, *Family Relations* 40:97-102.

Dronkers, J. & Härkönen, J. (2008). The intergenerational transmission of divorce in cross-national perspective: Results from the fertility and family surveys. *Population Studies, 62*(3), 273-288.

Ellison, S. (1977). *Divorce and Remarriage in the Church.* Grand Rapids, MI: Zondervan.

Family Law Act of 1970, California Civil Code, §§ 4000-5138 (West Supp. 2001).

Flewelling, R., & Bauman, K. (1990). Family structure as a predictor of initial substance use and sexual intercourse in early adolescence. *Journal of Marriage and the Family, 52,* 171-181.

Gallup, G., & Jones, T. (2000). *The Next American Spirituality: Finding God in the Twenty-First Century.* Colorado Springs, CO: Victor/Cook Communications.

Goodwin, J. S., Hunt, W. C., Key, C. R., & Sarmet, J. (1987). The effect of marital status on stage, treatment, and survival of cancer patients. *Journal of the American Medical Association, 258,* 3125-3130.

Gray, M., De Vaus, D., Qu, L., & Stanton, D. (2011). Divorce and the wellbeing of older Australians. *Ageing & Society, 31,* 475-498.

Harper, C., & McLanahan, S. S. (2004). Father absence and youth incarceration. *Center for Research on Child Wellbeing* (Working Paper #99-03). Retrieved from http://crcw.princeton.edu/publications/articles/2004/WP99-03-pub.pdf

Joung, I. M., van de Mheen, H., Stronks, K., van Poppel, F. W., & Mackenbach, J. P. (1994). Differences in self-reported morbidity by marital status and by living arrangement. *International Journal of Epidemiology, 23,* 91-97.

Kaplan, R. M., & Kronick, R. G. (2006). Marital status and longevity in the United States population. *Journal of Epidemiology and Community Health, 60,* 760-765.

Köstenberger, A. J., & Jones, D. W. (2004). *God, Marriage, and Family: Rebuilding the Biblical Foundation.* Wheaton, IL: Crossway Books.

Kressel, K. (1985). *The Process of Divorce: How Professionals and Couples Negotiate Settlements.* New York, NY: Basic Books.

Lewis, J., & Blakeslee, S. (2000). *The Unexpected Legacy of Divorce.* New York, NY: Hyperion.

Lundberg, O. (1993). The impact of childhood living conditions on illness and mortality in adulthood. *Social Science and Medicine, 36,* 1047-1052.

Margolin, L. (1992). Child abuse and mother's boyfriends: Why the overrepresentation? *Child Abuse and Neglect, 16,* 541-551.

Marks, N. F., & Lambert, J. D. (1998). Marital status continuity and change among young and midlife adults: Longitudinal effects on psychological well-being. *Journal of Family Issues, 19,* 652-686.

McLanahan, S. S., & Sandefur, G. (1994). *Growing Up with a Single Parent: What Hurts, What Helps.* Cambridge, MA: Harvard University Press.

Parrott, L., & Parrott, L. (1995). *Saving Your Marriage Before It Starts.* Grand Rapids, MI: Zondervan.

Pruthi, R., Lentz, A., Sand, M., Kouba, E., & Wallen, E. (2009). Impact of marital status in patients undergoing radical cystectomy for bladder cancer. *World Journal of Urology, 27*(4), 573-576.

Rich, P. (2002). *Divorce Counseling Homework Planner.* New York, NY: Wiley.

Richmond, G. (1988). *The Divorce Decision: What It Can Mean for Your Children, Your Finances, Your Emotions, Your Relationships, Your Future.* Waco, TX: Word.

Ross, C., & Mirowsky, J. (1999). Parental divorce, life-course disruption, and adult depression. *Journal of Marriage and the Family, 61,* 1034-1045.

Stroup, A. L., & Pollock, G. E. (1994). Economic consequences of marital dissolution. *Journal of Divorce and Remarriage, 22,* 7-54.

Taylor, R., & Andrews, B. (2009). Parental depression in the context of divorce and the impact on children. *Journal of Divorce and Remarriage, 50,* 472-480.

Troxel, W. M., & Matthews, K. A. (2004). What are the costs of marital conflict and dissolution to children's physical health? *Clinical Child and Family Psychology Review, 7,* 29-57.

U.S. Census Bureau. (2009). *Living Arrangements of Children Under 18 Years and Marital Status of Parents, by Age Sex, Race, and Hispanic Origin and Selected Characteristics of the Child for All Children.* Retrieved April 20, 2011, from http://www.census.gov/population/www/socdemo/hh-fam/cps2009.html

Waite, L., & Gallagher, M. (2000). *The Case for Marriage.* New York, NY: Doubleday.

Wallerstein, J., & Blakeslee, S. (1989). *Second Chances.* New York, NY: Ticknor and Fields.

Wolfinger, N. H. (2005). *Understanding the Divorce Cycle: The Children of Divorce in Their Own Marriages.* New York, NY: Cambridge University Press.

Zill, N., Morrison, D. R., & Coiro, M. J. (1993). Long-term effects of parental divorce on parent-child relationships, adjustment, and achievement in young adulthood. *Journal of Family Psychology, 7,* 91-103.

## CHILDREN OF DIVORCE

**Description.** Every year nearly one million children experience their parents' divorce. Approximately 40% of American kids woke up in a home this morning where their biological father does not live (Blankenhorn, 1996). Nearly half of these children haven't seen their fathers in the last 12 months (National Center for Fathering, 2007). Psychologists and child therapists all say divorce hurts kids—period. Numerous studies are providing insights and direction on how to help, encourage, and counsel.

**Effects of Divorce on Children.** When divorce tears a family apart, the children are among those most negatively affected. Even if parents deal openly with the divorce, any number of variables influences their children's reactions:

- the children's ages at the time of the divorce
- how mature the children are emotionally
- how resilient or susceptible the kids are to ongoing stressors
- the children's relationship with both parents
- the degree of hostility and fighting that took place
- other people's reactions to the divorce
- the children's psychological problems before the divorce
- friends and other family who are willing to help, especially grandparents (Wallerstein & Kelly, 1980).

*Short-term effects.* Research indicates that all children are negatively affected by the trauma of a divorce. They often experience emotional turmoil and show classic symptoms of grieving and heightened insecurity. Boys experience a great deal of anger and aggressive behavior. Girls more readily verbalize their anxieties, but they may also show signs of depression and emotional withdrawal (Chase-Lansdale, Cherlin, & Kiernan, 1995; Portnoy, 2008; Potter, 2009; Woosley, Dennis, & Goldstein, 2009).

Nearly all children go through a period of regression. School grades drop, toilet-trained children have accidents, and whining and clinging behaviors increase. These are all signs of an underlying insecurity and anxiety. Children naturally regress back to an earlier, safer stage of development when they feel threatened at home (Astone & McLanahan, 1991; Ebling, Pruett, & Pruett, 2009; Potter, 2009).

Teens of divorced parents are much more likely to engage in drug and alcohol use and sexual intercourse than are those from intact families. They look for excuses to get away from home to spend more time at friends' houses or with their peers at other locations. Their insecurity may drive them into relationships with others—even premature sexual relationships—or toward other support, such as a youth group or even a gang (Flewelling & Bauman, 1990).

*Effects in the two years after divorce.* After the initial break-up and turmoil has passed, anxiety and anger may be replaced with depression that can last for months or even years. In children, this is often referred to as *masked depression* because it may not look at all like what we see in adults. One might expect a depressed child to mope around or lock herself in her room to escape the world. This might in fact be the case, especially for teens. But younger children might be quite active and engaging even though they have an underlying depressed mood (Chase-Lansdale, Cherlin, & Kiernan, 1995).

Teens are even more likely to engage in drug and alcohol use as well as sexual intercourse than are those from intact families (Flewelling & Bauman, 1990). Children of divorce suffer illness more frequently and recover from sickness more slowly (Lundberg, 1993). They are also more likely to suffer child abuse, especially if their mother has a new live-in boyfriend (Margolin, 1992).

*Five years after divorce.* The emotional roller coaster and grieving process can last up to five years—and even longer if there are complicating factors, such as alcoholism, abuse, extended court battles, or a remarriage with blended-family conflict (Wallerstein & Kelly, 1980). Wallerstein's research indicates that five years after the initial breakup, the children of divorce tend to experience three levels of severity. Thirty-four percent of the children appear to be fully recovered and emotionally well adjusted. The next 29% fall into a middle range of emotional adjustment. More specifically, they have worked through the initial grief reactions but continue to struggle emotionally even though they may appear to be stable and secure (Wallerstein & Kelly, 1980).

Girls often have an ongoing struggle with insecurity and low self-image. This can last so long that it seems to become part of their personality. They might seek acceptance by getting too involved in dating relationships. Or they may go to the other extreme by avoiding marriage or commitment altogether, expressing deep-seated doubts about the viability of lasting relationships.

Boys or young men have the same insecurities, but they tend to show it by chronic underachievement in school or chronic underemployment. They may have high intelligence and great potential, but for many years after the divorce, they underachieve. They might have difficulty choosing a major in college and then drift from class to class and from major to major. After graduation they might avoid anything challenging and then settle for a job that they could have gotten without a degree. These are examples of an underlying insecurity about themselves and the future (Wallerstein & Kelly, 1980).

The other 37% of the children of divorce are those who never seem to quite get over the emotional trauma. They continue to be intensely unhappy and dissatisfied with their lives and their postdivorce families. These children tend to be the ones we see in our counseling centers when they get into trouble with the law, develop addiction problems, or get into their own bad relationships. Even though they have made enough of their own bad choices, they frequently blame their parents' divorce for their unhealthy lifestyle long into their own adult lives (Wallerstein & Kelly, 1980).

*Long-term effects—25 years after.* Wallerstein followed this same group of children over 25 years in the best longitudinal study of its kind in the literature. Expecting to find well-recovered kids, she found quite the opposite. Even 25 years after the divorce, these now-adult children continued to experience substantial levels of fear of loss, fear of change, fear of conflict, and expectations of failure, especially in their own romantic relationships (Crowell, Treboux, & Brockmeyer, 2009; Lewis & Blakeslee, 2000; see Ross & Mirowsky, 1999).

Wallerstein described the difficulty in the formation of adult relationships by these divorced children: "Contrary to what we have long thought, the major impact of divorce does not occur during childhood or adolescence. Rather, it rises in adulthood as serious romantic relationships move center stage.... Anxiety leads many [adult children of divorce] into making bad choices in relationships, giving up hastily when problems arise, or avoiding relationships altogether" (Lewis & Blakeslee, 2000, p. xxvii). She stated conclusively, "The kids [in my study] had a hard time remembering the pre-divorce family...but what they remembered about the post-divorce years was their sense that they had indeed been abandoned by both parents, that their nightmare [of abandonment] had come true" (Lewis & Blakeslee, 2000, p. xxix; see also Crowell, Treboux, & Brockmeyer, 2009).

**Modalities for Treating Children.** Several types of therapeutic intervention are applied to help children of divorced couples (Deal, 2002).

*Individual counseling.* This mode is appropriate when pronounced anger and sadness are present. All children must understand why the divorce happened and that it wasn't their fault. Most children hold on to fantasies that Mom and Dad will eventually get back together. If this is not likely, the counselor should gently help them face reality. They also need to talk through their emotions. Play therapy with young children, using dolls or drawings to represent the family members, may be the best way to elicit true feelings (Ebling, Pruett, & Pruett, 2009). Older kids, especially teenagers, are much more likely to benefit from talk therapy and journaling their feelings. Anger, disinterest, and disillusionment with God are also prevalent; working through this will take time.

*Family counseling.* Sometimes it is beneficial to include both parents in some of the counseling with their children. This should be done only when they have joint custody or when you have permission from both parents. Sometimes these sessions do not include the mother and father coming in together. Instead, try to meet with Mom and the kids one week and then Dad and the kids another week. In this way counselors get a more balanced perspective on things that need to change and on ways they all might work together better for the sake of the children (Gladding, 2007).

*Group therapy.* Group counseling with children of divorce can be very practical. First of all, it can make therapy much more affordable at a time when parents are financially stretched. Secondly, kids love to hear what other kids are feeling and how they cope. Young children will need more structure in their group, such as an activity each week that addresses an issue they face (e.g., write a letter to God, draw your family, role play your feelings, etc.). Teenagers respond well to open discussions based on issues they face. Be prepared to listen to them complain about their parents, school, church, and just about everything else in their lives. Let it go for the first half of the group and then help them find solutions to the situations.

**Helping Children of Divorce.** Apart from trying to keep families together, our highest goal is to lessen the impact of divorce on the children—to see if we can help them fall into the mildest third on the scale of severity. Research indicates that there is a lot we can do to make a difference for the children (Gladding, 2007; Hart, 1996; Levy, 1993).

*Help the parents.* Perhaps the best indicator of children's adjustment is the progress of the custodial parent; almost as important is the adjustment of the noncustodial parent. In other words, the best way to help the children is to help their parents. If parents don't learn to work through their own emotions and reach a point of forgiveness and peace, the children are very unlikely to fully recover. Kids do best when they have loving relationships with both parents.

*Avoid needless conflict.* Most counselors understand that they need to help minimize the conflict kids are exposed to with divorce. Though not advisable for some clients, it may be profitable to encourage your clients to seek mediation rather than using attorneys. Some folks have a hard time with amicable divorces—they'd rather see blood spilled to assure themselves that this really is an irreconcilable relationship. But if we take seriously the command to love our enemies, we need to do all we can to help clients forgive each other and reduce the rancor.

*Help parents speak the truth in love.* Many parents either sugarcoat the truth or are caustic in the way they communicate with their children about divorce. "Daddy's on vacation for a while" might be used to explain away a parent's departure. Or "Your mom's a vicious monster" to describe a mom who disagrees with the way Dad wants to run things. Help the parents "write scripts," explaining difficult situations, emphasizing Ephesians 4:15 to balance telling the kids the truth in a loving way. You may be called upon to help a mom explain to her children that their father had an affair or that their mom really loves them but can't see them for now. Children need to hear and deal with the truth of their situation, but you need to help frame it as lovingly as possible.

*Allow children to grieve.* Help children understand the grieving process, how long it takes, and God's purpose in allowing this kind of pain to enter our lives. It is unfortunate that children need to learn these lessons at such a young age, but it certainly prepares them for a future that we all face—one of disappointments and difficulties.

*Let children remain children.* All children of divorce end up taking on more responsibilities, and too often, they have to deal with adult issues, such as adultery, financial stress, and broken trust. This is not necessarily all bad because many of these kids become quite mature for their ages. Yet it is important that parents and others do not succumb to the temptation to treat them as adults. A little boy should not be told that he is now the man of the house, and teens should not be parentified, assuming parental roles and responsibilities for regressed and needy adults.

*Foster relationships that are good for the children.* Some parents mistakenly think that a good role model for their children might be a series of people whom they happen to date. However, that's not true. Help parents find healthy role models for their children. These usually include grandparents, extended family members, youth workers, or Sunday school teachers.

Help single parent families identify happily married couples in their church or community that might provide examples of a good relationship. If parents come from a dysfunctional family or find their own family too distant, they need to find a substitute. Sometimes an older couple that also has distant family can be a good option. Getting together for meals, holidays, or camping trips can be encouraging for them and a big help to a single mom or dad. One caution though: Make sure this is a stable and healthy family who will provide a positive role model.

God sees the tears of each and every child and welcomes each one into his home as his own. "Deep calls to deep in the roar of your waterfalls; all your waves and breakers have swept over me" (Ps. 42:7). The love of God reaches through the destruction and the waves and into the hearts of his children. The adopted child can rest safely and securely in the love of the Father.

**Tim Clinton**
**George Ohlschlager**

## REFERENCES


Astone, N. M., & McLanahan, S. S. (1991). Family structure, parental practices and high school completion. *American Sociological Review, 56,* 309-320.

Amato, P., & Booth, A. (1997). *A Generation at Risk.* Cambridge, MA: Harvard University Press.

Blankenhorn, D. (1996). *Fatherless America: Confronting Our Most Urgent Social Problem.* New York, NY: Harper Perennial.

Chase-Lansdale, L., Cherlin, A. J., & Kiernan, K. E. (1995). Parental divorce in childhood and demographic outcomes in young adulthood. *Demography, 32*(3), 299-316.

Crowell, J. A., Treboux, D., & Brockmeyer, S. (2009). Parental divorce and adult children's attachment representations and marital status. *Attachment & Human Development, 11*(1), 87-101. doi:10.1080/14616730802500867

Deal, R. (2002). *Smart Stepfamily: The Seven Steps to a Healthy Family.* Bloomington, MN: Bethany House.

Ebling, R., Pruett, K. D., & Pruett, M. (2009). "Get over it": Perspectives on divorce from young children. *Family Court Review, 47*(4), 665-681. doi:10.1111/j.1744-1617.2009.01280.x

Fagan, P., & Rector, R. (2000, June). The effects of divorce on America. *Heritage Foundation Backgrounder,* article #1373.

Flewelling, R. L., & Bauman, K. E. (1990). Family structure as a predictor of initial substance use and sexual intercourse in early adolescence. *Journal of Marriage and the Family, 52,* 171-181.

Gladding, S. (2007). *Family Therapy: History, Theory, and Practice* (4th ed). Upper Saddle River, NJ: Merrill Prentice Hall.

Gottman, J. (1994). *Why Marriages Succeed or Fail... and How You Can Make Yours Last.* New York, NY: Simon & Schuster.

Hart, A. (1996). *Helping Children Survive Divorce.* Dallas, TX: Word Books.

Levy, D. (1993). *The Best Parent Is Both Parents: A Guide to Shared Parenting in the 21st Century.* Norfolk, VA: Hampton Roads.

Lewis, J. M., & Blakeslee, S. (2000). *The Unexpected Legacy of Divorce: A 25 Year Landmark Study.* New York, NY: Hyperion.

Margolin, L. (1992). Child abuse by mother's boyfriends: Why the overrepresentation? *Child Abuse & Neglect, 16,* 541-551.

National Center for Fathering (2007). *Trends in Fathering.* Retrieved from http://www.fathers.com/content/index.php?option=com_content&task=view&id=412

Portnoy, S. M. (2008). The psychology of divorce: A lawyer's primer, part 2: The effects of divorce on children. *American Journal of Family Law, 21*(4), 126-134.

Potter, D. J., (2009) Childhood interrupted: The unique role of distress in understanding the effects of divorce on children's schooling. Paper presented at the annual meeting of the American Sociological Association Annual Meeting, San Francisco, CA. Retrieved from http://www.allacademic.com/meta/p306620_index.html

Richmond, G. (1988). *The Divorce Decision: What It Can Mean for Your Children, Your Finances, Your Emotions, Your Relationships, Your Future.* Waco, TX: Word.

Ross, C. E., & Mirowsky, J. (1999). Parental divorce, life course disruption, and adult depression. *Journal of Marriage and Family, 61*(4), 1034-1045.

Wallerstein, J. (2000). *The Unexpected Legacy of Divorce.* New York, NY: Hyperion.

Wallerstein, J., & Blakeslee, S. (1989). *Second Chances: Men, Women and Children a Decade After Divorce.* New York, NY: Ticknor and Fields.

Wallerstein, J., & Kelly, J. (1980). *Surviving the Breakup: How Children Cope with Divorce.* New York, NY: Basic Books.

Woosley, J., Dennis, C., Robertson, K., & Goldstein, J. (2009). Perceived psychological well-being of children from divorced and nondivorced families. *Psi Chi Journal of Undergraduate Research, 14*(1), 34-39.


## RECONCILIATION

**Description.** When something is broken, one is faced with several options:

- Ignore it and continue as if it never existed, relegating it to a quasi-invisible status. It's there, but it has little or no effect on daily life.
- Discard it and don't replace it. Live without it.
- Discard it and replace it with something similar—either a new and untried version or one that is as much like the discarded object as possible.
- Try to repair it, which leads to failure, necessitating the above process again, or success, leading to either permanent or temporary restoration of its earlier state.

These options apply when a computer or

television is broken, and they also apply to a marriage relationship when the repairing and reinitiation of the relationship is termed *reconciliation.*

An excellent definition of reconciliation is provided by Virginia Holeman (2004), who states that it is "the active commitment to the restoration of love and trustworthiness by both injured party and transgressor so that their relationship may be transformed."

Christian counselors must take into consideration God's authority as well as civil laws. Consult an attorney regarding all legal aspects. Based upon the entire Bible, it is clear that God never intends for two people joined in marriage to end that relationship and go their separate ways. Olshewsky (2001) writes, "Christian divorce is construed as letting go of past sin in repentance and seeking a new life in faithfulness and forgiveness. This painful crisis is seen as a confrontation with God's judgment and as an opening up to God's grace; one is urged to maintain an awareness of temptations to continue in sin and of opportunities for reconciliation and cooperation." Christian author Gary Chapman (2005) says that there are three primary reasons that marriages end.

- lack of an intimate relationship with God
- lack of an intimate relationship with your mate
- lack of an intimate understanding and acceptance of yourself

These need to be addressed prior to attempting reconciliation to avoid repetition of the presenting problem.

**Practice.** From a Christian perspective, the parties involved are to always do their utmost to reconcile, to save the marriage if at all possible, whatever the cause. As counselors, we must take into consideration additional factors when reconciliation is attempted, especially the link between forgiveness and reconciliation. Dr. Everett Worthington (2003), arguably the world's leading authority on forgiveness, states this plainly when he says that "damage can be repaired in many ways, but complete healing and restoration can come only through forgiveness and reconciliation" (p. 13).

The reconciliation process must also include all factors pertaining to the safety of the parties involved. If domestic violence, child abuse, or another major destructive behavior is contributing to the separation or divorce, this problem must be completely and satisfactorily dealt with prior to attempting reconciliation. Putting a clean dressing over a suppurating and gangrenous wound will temporarily hide the deterioration and destruction of tissue, but it won't bring about healing.

The reconciliation process itself should include an examination of the reasons for the situation, steps to address all issues, apologies and forgiveness, putting together a plan to prevent a reoccurrence due to similar reasons, selection of accountability partners for one or both parties as needed, utilization of professionals (counselors, pastors, lawyers, etc.) as needed, and careful attention to the needs of all children and immediate family members. All parties involved must be honest, accept responsibility for their actions, work on understanding the other person's perspective, avoid pride, and keep God in the center.

Of the positive factors affecting the likelihood of successful reconciliation, religion has been shown to have the strongest relationship with a positive outcome (Wineberg, 1994).

**Edgar E. Barker**

## REFERENCES


Chapman, G. (2005). *Hope for the Separated: Wounded Marriages Can Be Healed.* Chicago, IL: Moody.

Holeman, V. T. (2004). *Reconcilable Differences: Hope and Healing for Troubled Marriages.* Downers Grove, IL: InterVarsity Press.

Olshewsky, T. M. (2001). A Christian understanding of divorce. *The Journal of Religious Ethics, 7*(1), 118-138.

Wineberg, H. (1994). Marital reconciliation in the United States: Which couples are successful? *Journal of Marriage and the Family, 56,* 80-88.

Worthington, E. L., Jr. (2003). *Forgiving and Reconciling: Bridges to Wholeness and Hope.* Downers Grove, IL: InterVarsity Press.

## MEDIATION

**Description.** Mediation is a process in which an impartial person (the mediator) works with disputing parties to help them explore a settlement, reconciliation, and understanding among them. In mediation, the primary responsibility for the resolution of a dispute rests with the parties.

In Christian mediation, the goal and process are the same; however, it offers a faith-based approach for resolving disputes utilizing biblical principles, prayer, discernment, and creative problem solving. The Christian mediation process embodies this effort by providing a nonadversarial process to openly communicate issues and assist in structuring an equitable settlement and provisions privately and confidentially. The Bible discourages Christians from bringing lawsuits against other Christians in secular courts of law (1 Cor. 6:1-8) and instructs them to be reconciled to one another when disputes of any nature arise between them (Mt. 5:21-24; 6:9-15; 18:15-20).

Christian mediation helps people resolve their issues without losing their wallets, their sanity, or their faith. It is an empowering forum in which the parties make the decisions, ultimately holding the responsibility to decide the outcome of their disputes and determine the terms of their agreements.

**History of Mediation.** In England around 1066 AD, Norman kings introduced law judges, which emerged into common law. This approach evolved into parties hiring the best "fighters" (attorneys) to take their disputes in front of a judge and/or a jury trial in a law court. Over the past 20 years, mediation has gained recognition as the first approach to solving conflicts. In fact, mediation and mediators are featured in the news almost daily. Mediators are dispatched to the Middle East and other troubled spots around the world to assist battling nations, and they are called in to help negotiate business disputes between management and labor. Family mediations are becoming the first choice of resolution in divorces (facilitating healing and health for parents and children). We are seeing an increasing need for mediators in church disputes between congregations and church staffs. Mediators are even being used in schools to assist students in working out personal differences (this is called *peer mediation*).

**Benefits of Christian Mediation.** People who are in the midst of conflict often lack structure for resolution. Mediation provides the framework for this structure while the Holy Spirit works through and with the parties. This approach gives parties greater control over the outcome of their disputes and provides an effective setting for resolving difficult issues. Furthermore, the process of peacemaking glorifies God and demonstrates our commitment to protecting the Christian body as a whole.

Mediation offers significant benefits because it is...

- *Confidential.* Unlike the court system, your personal information will not be made available to the public. Many consumers fail to realize that once you file a lawsuit, your personal information becomes public record.
- *Affordable.* Mediation usually costs considerably less than litigation.
- *Convenient.* Sessions can be scheduled quickly and conveniently.
- *Amicable.* Mediation is a fair and impartial process. The goal of mediation is not to defeat the other party, but to find a solution with the

assistance of a trained professional. By utilizing this method to resolve disputes, parties are choosing to address problems in a healthy and mature way that opens lines of communication. This helps to preserve personal and professional relationships.

- *Successful.* Mediation resolves more than 85% of disputes. The overwhelming majority of mediation cases settle before going to trial.

**The Mediator's Role.** The mediator is a facilitator, helping the disputants to voluntarily reach their own mutually acceptable resolution of the issues. The mediator facilitates communications and negotiations between the parties by helping them identify and clarify the key issues surrounding their conflicts. Mediators can help people step back, examine the context, and find an acceptable way toward resolution.

Often parties become embroiled in an unnecessary and embittered tussle over entrenched positions. Many deals collapse because the participants cannot see the forest for the trees. In other words, they fail to see the bigger picture, and they focus too much on winning instead of finding a mutually profitable solution (Fisher & Ury, 2006). If the parties are too adversarial to talk to each other, the mediator can talk to each side without the emotional language of anger and frustration. The mediator is the "keeper of the process" and controls the structure rather than the content of the mediation.

Another role of the mediator is to help the disputing parties focus on the steps of problem solving. The following elements are essential in any mediation, regardless of the conflicting issues or confrontation level: (a) identify the problem; (b) summarize, restate, and prioritize issues in a nonjudgmental way; (c) brainstorm; and (d) evaluate the viability of the options and obstacles. To fulfill these elements, the mediator must

- show genuine interest in disputants,
- be a good listener,
- encourage the disputants to talk in terms of interests, and
- allow some discussion of the conflict history.

**Divorce Mediation.** Few areas of conflict inflict more damage than divorce. Litigation only increases the damage to the family emotionally, financially, and spiritually. For that reason, mediation should be preferred as the first step in resolving problems associated with the dissolution of the marriage. This negotiation process helps focus couples on the future for themselves and their children. For both parties, as well as their children, finding a compatible resolution is invaluable for ongoing relationships.

**Spiritual Issues.** Conflict is a part of life. It comes in many shapes and sizes, but it shows up in everyone's life from time to time. When hearts are conflicted with each other, disputes can become breeding grounds for hardened hearts and bitterness.

Taking a conflict directly to the other party should be the first approach to resolution, but when that is not successful, mediation is the best hope for maintaining the peace and relational healing. Jesus' greatest mission was reconciliation—to reconcile us sinners to God because he loves and values each one of us. Our job is to pursue peace with one another (Rom. 12:9-21).

Sandra Dopf

## REFERENCES

Fisher, R., & Ury, W. (2006). *Getting to Yes: Negotiating Agreement Without Giving In* (2nd ed.). New York, NY: Penguin Books.

Clinton, T. (2001). *The Bible of Hope: Caring for People God's Way: Personal and Emotional Issues, Addictions, Grief, and Traumas.* Nashville, TN: Thomas Nelson.

## DIVORCE RECOVERY

**Description.** Those experiencing divorce need forgiving love, understanding, and guidance. Morphis (1994) states divorce recovery entails learning to live single again, grief resolution, rediscovering self without the spouse, and setting new goals. He suggests that regardless of the reasons for divorce, one must come to an acceptance of the divorce. Divorce recovery, then, involves grieving the loss, forgiving oneself, and forgiving the other. In doing so, one can heal and move on into healthy relationships; failure to grieve and forgive leaves one vulnerable to creating another unhealthy relationship that can turn into another divorce (Powers, 2009).

**History and Assessment.** Approximately 50% of today's marriages end in divorce. On the stress scale, divorce is ranked second after the loss of a loved one (Carter & McGoldrick, 2005). Over a million U.S. children are affected annually by divorce. Garrity & Baris (1994) report that children continue to feel sad and resentful ten years after the divorce of their parents. They state children report the breakup of their parents as the most significant event in their lives. Sixty-seven percent of second marriages end in divorce (Carter & McGoldrick). Given these staggering facts, the need for guidance for those affected by divorce is evident.

The effects of a marital breakup change all aspects of a person's life, leading to many issues associated with grief, change, loss, and actual or perceived wrongs. Carter and McGoldrick (2005) suggest the adjustment after the legal issues are resolved is the key to whether the crisis of divorce is relatively brief or long lasting. The adjustment to divorce occurs during both the postdivorce phase (adapting to singleness) and remarriage phase (adjusting to a new family system). During the postdivorce phase, individuals must resolve grief and forgiveness issues; during the remarriage phase, the new blended family must find a new definition of family.

Powers (2009) defines the divorce and postdivorce phase as the crisis stage in which individuals experience many emotions that are associated with grief, such as shock, denial, withdrawal, self-pity, and depression. Research has shown that divorce recovery workshops that focus on forgiveness, grief, and acceptance are effective in the healing process (Boney, 2002; Rye, Folck, Heim, Olszewski, & Traina, 2004; Quinney & Fouts, 2003). Powers warns that if one does not come to a place of forgiveness and acceptance (or healing), the vulnerability of continued woundedness increases the risk of becoming involved in another unhealthy relationship.

Carter and McGoldrick (2005) suggest that counselors are needed at the remarriage phase because society currently offers only two models of family—an intact family model (first marriage) or the wicked stepfamily model. Redefining family after blending can be stressful. In addition, higher divorce rates for second marriages strongly indicate individuals making similar mistakes in the second marriage as the first. Guidance is needed for couples and families to adjust during this critical period.

**Treatment.** Divorce recovery programs are designed to help people come to a place of acceptance and healing. The emotions associated with divorce, if left unmended, can build resentments, irrational beliefs, fears, and emotional instability. Carter and McGoldrick (2005) state that a bad divorce is one in which the individuals refuse to resolve predivorce conflict and are unwilling to minimize the effects of divorce on the children and integrate the new multidimensional family system. Divorce recovery addresses all the emotions associated with the loss and perceived injustices, and it prepares individuals for the inevitable changes that occur. Emotional responses to divorce include anger, fear, denial, rejection, and guilt, and the changes include preparing for singleness and possibly remarriage. The goal of divorce recovery is to come to a place of acceptance and peace when accepting this new redefined life.

Processing the emotional baggage and cleaning it out is paramount to healing from a divorce. Part of the process is to forgive and let go of the anger, resentment, and rejection. Worthington (2006) suggests that forgiveness changes individuals and the way they respond to others; therefore, it changes their relationships and the feedback they receive in relationships. This allows people to heal the woundedness and enhances their ability to establish healthy relationships.

In addition to forgiveness, people need to address feelings of guilt associated with their behavior in the marriage or predivorce stage. Steere (2009) suggests that nowhere else is the blame game more evident than in marital discord and divorce. For personal growth to occur, individuals must be willing to gain insight into their own destructive attitudes and behaviors that are hurtful to relationships. This helps them learn to embrace a new life rich with possibilities, decreases their chances of falling into unhealthy relationship patterns, and therefore increases their chances for a healthy second marriage.

**Biblical and Spiritual Issues.** The Bible clearly states in Malachi 2:16 that God hates divorce, but he dearly loves broken, divorced people. God hates sin of any kind, yet "since we have been justified through faith, we have peace with God through our Lord Jesus Christ" (Rom. 5:1). Christian counselors can help individuals experience the same forgiveness Jesus gave the Samaritan woman at the well (Jn. 4). Divorce recovery offers people an opportunity to heed Jesus' warning: "If you forgive other people when they sin against you, your heavenly Father will also forgive you. But if you do not forgive others their sins, your Father will not forgive your sins" (Mt. 6:14-15). As forgiveness is given and insights are gained, individuals can realize that "those who walk uprightly enter into peace" (Is. 57:2). Finally, even those whose lives have been devastated by divorce can learn how to love the way Christ loved the church and rejoice that love keeps no record of wrongs (1 Cor. 13:5).

Starting a new life after divorce can be difficult, but many programs are available to help those getting back on their feet. Divorce Care is the best-known program offering expert advice, video presentations, and support groups to help make the process easier. Helping others begin the process is often the biggest hurdle, and referring to outside groups is a great way to help clients move on toward health and healing (Morphis, 1994).

**Jeanne Brooks**

## REFERENCES


Boney, V. M. (2002). Divorced mothers' guilt: Exploration and intervention through a postmodern lens. *Journal of Divorce & Remarriage, 37*(3/4), 61-83.

Carter, B., & McGoldrick, M. (2005). *The Expanded Family Life Cycle.* Boston, MA: Prentice Hall.

Garrity, C. B., & Baris, M. A. (1994). *Caught in the Middle: Protecting the Children of High-Conflict Divorce.* New York, NY: Lexington Books.

Morphis, D. (1994). *Divorce Recovery Workshop.* Nashville, TN: Discipleship Resources Editorial Offices.

Powers, W. (2009). *The Covenant Divorce Recovery Leader's Handbook.* Longwood, FL: Xulon Press.

Quinney, D. M., & Fouts, G. T. (2003). Resilience and divorce adjustment in adults participating in divorce recovery workshops. *Journal of Divorce & Remarriage, 40,* 55-68. doi:13.1300/J087v40n01_04

Rye, M. S., Folck, C. D., Heim, T. A, Olszewski, B. T., & Traina, E. (2004). Forgiveness of an ex-spouse: How does it relate to mental health following a divorce? *Journal of Divorce & Remarriage, 41,* 31-51. doi:10.1300/J087v41n03_02

Steere, D. A. (2009). *Rediscovering Confession.* New York, NY: Routledge.

Worthington, E. (2006). *Forgiveness and Reconciliation: Theory and Application.* New York, NY: Routledge.

# SEXUALITY AND SEXUAL THERAPY

## SEX AFTER 50

**Description.** Beginning January 1, 2011, it is estimated that every day for the next 19 years, 10,000 people in America will turn 65 (Attkisson, 2010). This huge population of Baby Boomers is aging with dramatic sexual changes. Our belief is that the after-60 years can be some of the richest and most meaningful—personally, relationally, and sexually. Unfortunately, many Boomers are not aging very gracefully.

Let's be honest—frustrating and difficult situations assault all of us. Our bodies are sagging and don't seem as erotic, cancer and other diseases are more prevalent, getting beyond menopause is not easy, and the penis and vagina have changed, as have orgasms (Bancroft, 2009). But we all have the opportunity to make choices around these changes. Boomers can take the low road, get bitter, and spend billions on plastic surgery as they fight aging, or they can find creative solutions that create a new normal for their lovemaking (Butler & Lewis, 2002).

**Challenges and Changes.** A great place to start in creating a new normal is to understand the common changes that take place with men and women physically and sexually as they age. This diagram shows the difficulties and two different courses of action:

Changes ➔ Challenges ➔ Choices ➚ Creative Solutions / ➘ Negative Existence

Let's examine some common challenges and creative solutions.

*Arousal and lubrication.* Men need to have more direct stimulation of the penis to become aroused, erections may be less firm and disappear rapidly after a climax, orgasms can diminish in explosive intensity with less ejaculate, and the time between being able to climax may increase to several days or even a week. Also, as testosterone decreases, men's desire decreases, and they put on weight more easily. A fascinating observation is that male sexuality becomes more like female sexuality as men age. They are more subject to distractions and have to be more intentional about choosing to make love and reaching a climax, with orgasms more of a surge or a wave of pleasurable feeling rather than an explosion.

Women's vaginas can shrink and lose elasticity, and lubrication declines, which can make intercourse painful, especially if too vigorous. Some urinary incontinence is common, hair loss can be damaging to self-esteem, fatigue and memory loss can also occur, along with mood swings, lower metabolism, and weight gains. Libido may lessen, and orgasms become less intense. Here are some creative solutions:

- Find and utilize a good lubrication (Wet Platinum with silicon, Eros).

These can now be easily purchased at stores and on the Internet at Amazon .com.

- Choose those optimal times and take advantage of slower arousal to extend pleasuring.
- Work closely with medical professionals and physical therapists for possible hormone replacement therapy, symptom relief, help with erectile functioning, and Kegel exercises for bladder control.

*Body image.* Body image can become a challenge for both men and women. As we age we will need to identify old fears, cultural myths, and irrational beliefs. Some of these falsehoods are that great lovemaking depends on healthy, youthful bodies with stamina, flexibility, and exuberant orgasms; sexual desire and a longing for erotic connection fade rapidly in our fifties and sixties; or that less-than-perfect conditions destroy any possibility of sexual contentment and fulfillment.

Scripture says wisely, "No, your beauty should come from within you—the beauty of a gentle and quiet spirit that will never be destroyed" (1 Peter 3:4 NCV). Body image at any stage of life, but especially as we age, comes down to our mental perceptions and our cognitive attitudes (see Ps. 139:14; Rom. 12:2; 2 Cor. 4:16). Beauty is indeed in the eye of the beholder, and great lovers have become comfortable and confident with their bodies and sexuality. Here are some creative solutions:

- Lose the word *sexy* and learn to be sensual and erotic in new ways. Touch is more important than firm flesh or body parts.
- Value your partner's masculinity or femininity on a deeper soul level as you affirm qualities you deeply appreciate (e.g., your husband's pursuing you, or your wife's nurturing spirit).
- Take care of things you can control, such as grooming, diet, and exercise.

*Health concerns.* Health issues with diseases, such as heart attacks, high blood pressure, cancers, hysterectomies, and arthritis, can have dramatic effects on lovemaking and sexual functioning. For some couples, these challenges become the kiss of death to their sex lives. But it doesn't have to be this way. Even with these difficult and even life-threatening situations, lovers can work through to affirming their love and meaningfully connecting sexually. Here are some creative solutions:

- Take advantages of greater medical opportunities as you maximize medical advice and medications.
- Learn new moves and positions as you develop flexibility and expand your senses and knowledge of sexuality for meaningful lovemaking.
- Learn to enjoy a different orgasmic pleasure after a hysterectomy, prostate surgery, or general aging. Focus more on the arousal and sensual pleasure, and with your climax, exaggerate and stay with the pleasurable feelings.

*Major changes.* Both men and women will have to create new attitudes and ways of responding around environmental and relational issues that affect sexuality in direct and indirect ways (Lee & Prather, 2002). Retirement, an empty nest, or moving to new locations can create psychological and marital distress as roles change.

Will we fight aging or work through new mind-sets and roles as our bodies change, our energy diminishes, and the ways we receive identity and affirmation change? Men and women have to work through the big existential questions: Who am I now, what is sensual and erotic, how does God keep loving me, and how do I keep loving those around me? Here are two creative solutions:

- Enjoy being a grandparent to your own or others' children. Mentor young people who need your wisdom and attention.
- Take greater leisure time to enjoy each other as companions and lovers. Be intentional with dates and extended sensual touching and pleasuring times.

**Conclusion.** How do we ensure great lovemaking in our sixties, seventies, and eighties? Communicate openly and often, grieve the losses, and above all, choose positive solutions for those inevitable challenges.

**Doug Rosenau**
**Jim Childerston**
**Carolyn Childerston**

## REFERENCE


Attkisson, S. (2010, December 30). Medicare bound to bust as first Boomers hit 65. *CBS Evening News.* Retrieved from http://www.cbsnews.com/stories/2010/12/30/eveningnews/main7199116.shtml

Bancroft, J. (2009). *Human Sexuality and Its Problems* (3rd ed.). New York, NY: Churchill Livingstone.

Butler, R. N., & Lewis, M. I. (2002). *The New Love and Sex After 60.* New York, NY: Random House.

Lee, V., & Prather, G. (2002). *Ecstatic Lovemaking: An Intimate Guide to Soulful Sex.* Berkley, CA: Conari Press Books.


## SEXUAL INTIMACY AND DELIGHT

**Definition and Biblical Foundation.** Life is all about relationships—particularly with God and with those we love. You don't have to go very far in the Bible to be reminded that God desires to be in a relationship with each and every one of us. Even more, the Bible says that he is a pursuer God and that he works to win our hearts. His desire and his love are for us.

The apostle Paul knew of the great love of God and concluded that to know him and be found in him was the greatest joy in the world. John the beloved talked often of the great love of God—"not that we loved God but that he loved us" (1 Jn. 4:10). The Father expressed his deep love for his Son: "You are my Son, whom I love; with you I am well pleased" (Lk. 3:22). Paul said in Romans 8:35, "Who shall separate us from the love of Christ?" It really is a sacred romance. When a man or woman understands that love, it changes everything.

God placed that same relational impetus in the hearts of men and women. After all of creation was completed, before the Fall, God looked around the garden and realized something wasn't good. Even though God walked with Adam, he knew that man should not be alone. So out of the rib of Adam he created an *ezer*, a helpmate, to come alongside and complement Adam—bone of his bone and flesh of his flesh. God gave him Eve. He designed them for the deepest of all intimacy—united as one flesh. Their intimacy was characterized by innocence, beauty, and freedom. They were naked together, unashamed, and safe.

Sexual intimacy and expression are intended to bring deep joy and oneness to the marriage relationship. The act of sex expresses love between married couples, and it is God's desire that couples have a full and free expression of sexual intimacy in their relationship. Many Christian authors believe that human sexuality is a portrait of God's divine love (Akin, 2003; Cutrer & Glahn, 2007; McCluskey & McCluskey, 2004; Penner & Penner, 2003). According to Clinton and Laaser (2010), God's creation of sexuality reminds us of the intimate relationship that exists between the Father, Son, and the Holy Spirit. Rosenau (2002a, 2002b) believes that sexual intimacy, therefore, is an act of worship before God. It is a picture of his unconditional, pure, and holy love.

**The Bible and Sexual Expression.** Sexual expression has been studied and reported through the years by researchers such as Kinsey, Pomeroy, & Martin (1948), Masters & Johnson (1970), and the Chicago study by Laumann, Gagnon, Michael, & Michaels (1994). There has also been much study on sex and sexual expression from a Christian perspective (Leman, 2003; McCluskey & McCluskey, 2004; Penner & Penner, 2003; Rosenau, 2002a). In the most provocative book of the Bible, Song of Solomon, we see God's design for sexuality. This book teaches that couples are designed to have holiness, fun, and freedom in their sexuality, to become one in both flesh and spirit (Clinton & Laaser, 2010; Cutrer & Glahn, 2007). In addition, Hebrews 13:4 specifically states that "Marriage should be honored by all, and the marriage bed kept pure, for God will judge the adulterer and all the sexually immoral." Proverbs also teaches a man is to keep God's commands on his heart so that he "keeps from his neighbor's wife and the lips of a wayward woman [so that] she does not captivate him with her eyes" (Pr. 6:24-25). Paul goes on to warn against sexual immorality and offer further insight and understanding into what it means to glorify God with our bodies.

> Do you not know that your bodies are members of Christ himself? Shall I then take the members of Christ and unite them with a prostitute? Never! Do you not know that he who unites himself with a prostitute is one with her in body? For it is said, "The two will become one flesh." But whoever is united with the Lord is one with him in spirit.
>
> Flee from sexual immorality. All other sins a person commits are outside the body, but whoever sins sexually, sins against their own body. Do you not know that your bodies are temples of the Holy Spirit, who is in you, whom you have received from God? You are not your own; you were bought at a price. Therefore honor God with your bodies (1 Cor. 6:15-20).

The Bible is very clear that husbands are to love their wives (Eph. 5:25; 1 Pet. 3:7) and that wives are to respect and honor their husbands (Eph. 5:33; 1 Pet. 3:1). When a mutual love and respect is lived out in the marital relationship with both spouses glorifying and adorning the other, sexual intimacy that is pure and undefiled is the result. It is within the context of this marital safety and freedom that we glorify God with our bodies.

**Tim Clinton**
**Ryan Carboneau**
**Joshua Straub**

## REFERENCES


Akin, D. (2003). *God on Sex: The Creator's Ideas About Love, Intimacy, and Marriage.* Nashville, TN: Broadman & Holman.

Clinton, T., & Laaser, M. (2010). *The Quick-Reference Guide to Sexuality and Relationships Counseling.* Grand Rapids, MI: Baker Books.

Cutrer, W., & Glahn, S. (2007). *Sexual Intimacy in Marriage* (3rd ed.). Grand Rapids; MI: Kregel.

Hart, A. D. (1994). *The Sexual Man: Masculinity Without Guilt.* Dallas, TX: Word.

Kinsey, A. C., Pomeroy, W. B., & Martin, C. E. (1948). *Sexual Behaviour in the Human Male.* Philadelphia, PA: WB Saunders.

Laumann, E. O., Gagnon, J. H., Michael, R. T., & Michaels, S. (1994). *The Social Organization of Sexuality: Sexual Practice in the United States.* Chicago, IL: University of Chicago Press.

Leman, K. (2003). *Sheet Music: Uncovering the Secrets of Sexual Intimacy in Marriage.* Carol Stream, IL: Tyndale House.

Masters, W. H., & Johnson, V. E. (1970). *Human Sexual Inadequacy.* Boston, MA: Little Brown.

McCluskey, C. & McCluskey, R. (2004). *When Two Become One: Enhancing Sexual Intimacy in Marriage.* Grand Rapids, MI: Revell.

Penner, C., & Penner, J. (2003). *The Gift of Sex: A Guide to Sexual Fulfillment* (Rev. ed.). Nashville, TN: Nelson.

Rosenau, D. E. (2002a). *A Celebration of Sex.* Nashville, TN: Thomas Nelson.

Rosenau, D. E. (2002b). Sexuality and sexual therapy: Learning and practicing the DEC-R model. In T. Clinton & G. Ohlschlager (Eds.), *Competent Christian Counseling: Foundations and Practice of Compassionate Soul Care.* Colorado Springs, CO: WaterBrook Press.

Sullivan, C. (2006). *Rescuing Sex from the Christians.* New York, NY: Continuum.

## SEXUAL ABUSE

**Description.** Sexual abuse is one person's misuse of power over another person in a sexual manner. Abusers likely use some means of force or intimidation or the threat of force to achieve their goal. Sexual activity is any activity involving private parts of the body. The legal terms vary depending on the state, but generally, penetration is referred to as rape; otherwise, the term used is *sexual assault* (National Institute of Justice, 2010).

When both the victim and the perpetrator are minors, the sexual activity is considered abusive if the perpetrator is somewhat older, larger, or even developmentally more advanced. When the victim is a child and the perpetrator is an adult, consent is not an issue—any sexual activity is considered sexual abuse (Myers, 2002).

Persons who have experienced sexual abuse were initially referred to as victims, and those who abused them as perpetrators. However, in counseling, victims are now referred to as survivors.

**Prevalence.** Because sexual abuse is usually committed in private and often not reported, it is difficult to determine the rates of abuse in the United States. Researchers vary on how they define sexual abuse, including rape, assault, attempts, exhibitionism, and the like.

Early research on sexual abuse found that between "15 percent and 45 percent of women were sexually traumatized as children" (Everstine & Everstine, 1989, pp. 2-3). Collaborative research over the past 20 years estimates that one in four women have experienced sexual abuse (Duncan, 2004). Using several data sets, the Rape, Abuse and Incest National Network (RAINN) (2009) reports that every two minutes someone in the United States is sexually assaulted, and 44% of the victims of sexual assault are minors. The perpetrator is someone known to the victim in two thirds of all cases; in more than a third, it is a close friend or family member. The most vulnerable group is that of females between age 16 and 19, who are four times more likely to be victims of rape, attempted rape, or sexual assault than the general population.

As a result of sexual abuse, individuals may initially experience physical pain, nausea, and headaches, and they may react by either withdrawing from others or desperately clinging. Later symptoms may include displays of irrational anger, anxiety, panic, flat affect, thoughts of death and/or suicide, eating disorders, low self-esteem, concentration issues, nightmares, flashbacks, shame, guilt, embarrassment, insomnia, exaggerated startle response, and hypervigilance (RAINN, 2009).

Parents of child victims of sexual abuse often note that there is a dramatic change in the child's behavior—so much so that she or he appears to be a "different person." Children may regress (e.g., a return to thumb sucking or potty accidents) and act out sexually (such as a female child inserting objects into her vagina), engaging in behaviors that may be similar to the traumatic experience.

The negative effects of sexual abuse are pervasive. Compared to those who have not experienced sexual abuse, survivors are three to four times more likely to experience depression, even to the point of considering suicide, six times more likely to experience posttraumatic stress disorder, thirteen times more likely to abuse alcohol, and twenty-six times more likely to abuse drugs (RAINN, 2006). Research has also shown that sexual abuse survivors are much more likely to engage in high-risk sexual behaviors and to use avoidant coping mechanisms (Batten, Follette, & Aban, 2001).

**Biblical and Spiritual Issues.** More than just a physical issue, sexual abuse affects every aspect of the self.

> The body is infringed upon; the mind and emotions are chaotic and confused,

> and the spirit is desecrated. There is the sense of a loss of self. The life and the person feel littered with the trash of another. The mind cannot grasp what has happened and is full of confusing thoughts and questions: Was it my fault? Did I deserve it? Could I have prevented it? Am I ruined, tarnished, and unredeemable? Lies and misbeliefs take hold, often tenaciously: I cannot get clean. I am of no value. What has been done says who I am. Shame seeps into the identity and lodges there. God has forgotten me, or worse, discarded me. I deserve to be thrown away (Langberg, 2007, pp. 50-51).

The sexual abuse victim may have difficulty with faith for several reasons. If we think of the marital union of man and woman as a symbol of the unity and oneness that God desires for us to have with him, and of sex as a physical expression of love and unity, then anything that damages the ability of an individual to express love sexually is spiritually damaging. The preponderance of sexual abuse involves a male predator, often a father or a father figure, who almost always has power or authority over the victim. To a victim of sexual abuse, God may seem to be a frightening person to avoid due to his title as Father, the image of him as male, and his authority. A counselor may wish to avoid the use of the title *Father* until the victim has made progress and is ready to deal with that issue.

Child sexual abuse is particularly abhorrent because of the innocence of children, the damage it causes to children's development, and children's inability to protect themselves. Additionally, the perpetrator of child abuse is often a close family member. This may damage children's very foundations for trust and attachment (Batten et al., 2001), which is a core aspect of all other relationships, including their relationship with and understanding of God.

Another problem for victims is their difficulty of seeing God as loving, all-powerful, and all-knowing. "If God has these attributes," the victim asks, "why didn't he prevent the abuse from happening?" All good parents, and in fact, all good people would do all within their power to prevent sexual abuse, especially the sexual abuse of children. The question of why God allows evil is one that counselors must answer for themselves before trying to help abused people. Any response to this question that even hints that the victim caused the abuse is likely to do deep and lasting damage.

Unfortunately, church leaders are at times abusers themselves. In such cases, counselors must carefully help victims recognize that leaders in the church who are perpetrators are not indicators that God condones such sin. It will be therapeutic to help victims see that destroying the church through any and all means is one of Satan's favorite goals. Then, recognizing that Satan wants to devour these victims, just as he tried to devour Job, counselors can encourage victims of sexual abuse to face their fears and find a supportive church home.

**Kathryn Scott-Young**

## REFERENCES

Batten, S. V., Follette, V. M., & Aban, I. B. (2001). Experiential avoidance and high-risk sexual behavior in survivors of child sexual abuse. *Journal of Child Sexual Abuse, 10*(2), 101-120.

Duncan, K. A. (2004). *Healing from the Trauma of Childhood Sexual Abuse: The Journey for Women.* Westport, CT: Praeger.

Everstine, D. S., & Everstine, L. (1989). *Sexual Trauma in Children and Adolescents: Dynamics and Treatment.* New York, NY: Brunner/Mazel.

Langberg, D. (2007). Violence, violation, and godly responses to vile acts. *Christian Counseling Today, 15*(3), 50-52.

Myers, J. E. B. (Ed.). (2002). *The APSAC Handbook on Child Maltreatment* (2nd ed.). Thousand Oaks, CA: Sage.

National Institute of Justice. (2010). *Rape and Sexual Violence.* Retrieved from http://www.nij.gov/nij/topics/crime/rape-sexual-violence/welcome.htm

Rape, Abuse and Incest National Network. (2009). *Statistics.* Retrieved from http://www.rainn.org/statistics

## SEXUAL DESIRE DISORDERS

Sexual desire issues are the most common presenting problem for couples frustrated with their sex lives. Low or absent libido creates significant distress within the relationship, causing an emotional gridlock that couples struggle to work through on their own. Sexual issues often have five or six contributing factors, and all must be taken into consideration. Often, both partners are contributing to the multilayered causes, and the complexity makes resolving problems of low sexual desire delicate and challenging (Rosenau, Sytsma, & Taylor, 2002).

**Description.** One of the revolving disputes among clinicians is how exactly to define *desire*. The *Diagnostic and Statistical Manual of Mental Disorders* offers the diagnostic criteria as "persistently or recurrently deficient (or absent) sexual fantasies and desire for sexual activity" (American Psychiatric Association [APA], 2000). The judgment of deficiency or absence is made by the clinician, taking into account factors that affect sexual functioning, such as age and the context of a person's life. The disturbance must cause marked distress or interpersonal difficulty, and the sexual dysfunction must not be accounted for by some other disorder, the effects of a substance, or a general medical condition.

Some researchers have argued that this model is too linear, challenging the measures of desire. One suggests that the wellsprings of desire in women are quite different from those in men and arise not so much from hormonal or genital stirrings as from feelings that are not specifically sexual (Basson, 2007). In light of the vast distinctions between what drives male and female sexual desire, clinical intervention must expand beyond libido.

**Assessment.** The focus in the timely and complex assessment of sexual difficulties ideally encompasses not only the sexual content itself but also the broader context of sexual motivation and arousability. This multifaceted approach is best initiated with a broad understanding of the individuals' and couple's dynamics.

Assessing the emotional health of the couple typically includes questioning about their ability to trust, to be vulnerable and not judgmental or highly critical, and to have a balance of power and assertiveness in the relationship. An understanding of the overall mental health of both partners is critical. Assessment, including mood stability, energy levels, self-esteem, body image, and concurrent life stressors and distractions gives a necessary foundation upon which to evaluate the sexual contexts (Basson, 2007). Additionally, a history of medical issues, drugs prescribed, and nutritional intake are helpful for diagnosis and treatment.

Only when the previous realms have been examined can a clinical assessment progress accurately into the sexual content of the relationship. The first step is delineating a sexual history for each partner in individual sessions. Topics essential to this process will generally include (a) developmental issues and beliefs about sex, (b) mental or psychological habits (fantasies and dreams, as well as thoughts during sexual interaction), (c) behavior that involves oneself (masturbation), and (d) behavior that involves the partner (Maurice, 2005). A structured interview using an intake, such as the sexual history form found in *Counseling for Sexual Disorders,* is both thorough and effective in gaining the necessary information, particularly with vulnerable and exposing issues (Penner & Penner, 1990). Additionally, it will be necessary to examine the pattern of the problem to determine whether the onset is lifelong or acquired and whether the context is generalized or situational (APA, 2000).

**Treatment.** If any relationship or mental-health therapy is needed, it should always precede recommendations regarding sexual interaction (Basson, 2007). With libido differences, it is important for partners to understand how the other is interpreting *desire*. When a desire discrepancy occurs, one partner might have a higher normal level of desire while the other has a lower normal level of desire, or desire might not be present at all (Rosenau et al., 2002). It is critical to dialogue with partners as to what has shaped their expectations of a normal sex life. If media and popular culture images have defined what they think should be going on in their bedroom, they will need to process what is realistic and what is not and have the courage and commitment to invest in creating their own unique culture.

More than anything else in treatment, couples need education. Gender differences hold their own unique types of sexual desire. When couples understand this, they can get beyond false expectations and relax with the way their bodies and minds naturally respond. Sexual desire can be assertive, receptive, or blocked. Assertive desire is more typical in men because of their testosterone levels. They often think about sex and come to the time of intimacy ready to initiate and seek out sexual connection with more of a physical drive (Rosenau et al., 2002). Receptive desire (which is just as important) is more typical of women. They may not feel the main focus on sex initially, but being open to sex, enjoying the closeness it can bring, and getting involved after initiation often brings them to a place of enjoyment. Blocked desire is often the result of childhood sexual abuse or trauma, and healing should be pursued before any new sexual strategies are put into practice.

Partners must learn how to develop a language for their sexual lives. Treatment, then, involves teaching them how to communicate their ideal script for a sexual encounter. It is critical for them to learn how to express likes and dislikes without a fear of defensiveness or rejection from the other person. How partners engage in sexual activity with regard to sights, sounds, smells, words that are said or not said, location, time of day, and fatigue level all contribute to their interpretation of the connection taking place. Looking at the sexual process broken down into stages can provide the structure for discussion on internal and external inhibitors and enhancers of sexual desire (Rosenau et al., 2002).

**Biblical and Spiritual Issues.** God speaks in magnitude to his people through the scriptural grand metaphors of Christ being the bridegroom and the church being his bride. Christians, then, must be invited into the glorious spiritual potential that their sexual relationships hold to reflect the seduction of God's heart in worship to him, and on a reflective level, to one another as husband and wife. In treating these disorders and any other sexual complications, counselors would think too simply if they merely focused on desire or enlivened communication. The joy of having God's story as the backdrop for the reality of the lives encountered adds a richness to the meaning of oneness, the depth of hope offered, and a higher calling to the personal ecstasy found in nurture and sacrifice. To empower couples to experience anticipatory pleasure at the thought of connection in intimacy together is merely a slice of what it is to live in the delight of expectation for moments of oneness with God.

**Conclusion.** Complexities surrounding sexual desire demand thorough assessment. Treatment, heavily focused on the examination and alteration of expectation, assumption, and language development, can bring hope and perspective toward a more satisfying sexual union.

Dan Seaborn
Sarah Young

## REFERENCES

American Psychiatric Association. (2000). *Diagnostic and Statistical Manual of Mental Disorders* (4th ed., text rev.). Washington, DC: Author.

Basson, R. (2007). Sexual desire and arousal disorders in women. In S. Lieblum (Ed.), *Principles and Practice of Sex Therapy* (pp. 25-53). New York, NY: Guilford Press.

Maurice, W. L. (2005). Male hypoactive sexual desire disorder. In R. Balon & R. T. Segraves (Eds.), *Handbook of Sexual Dysfunction* (pp. 67-109). Boca Raton, FL: Taylor & Francis.

Penner, J. J., & Penner, C. L. (1990). *Counseling for Sexual Disorders.* Dallas, TX: Word.

Rosenau, D., Sytsma, M., & Taylor, D. (2002). *A Celebration of Sex.* Nashville, TN: Nelson.

## ORGASMIC DISORDER

**Definition.** An orgasm is a reflex response to the buildup of vasocongestion and sexual tension (Penner & Penner, 2005). The orgasm consists of a series of involuntary muscle contractions in the anus, lower pelvic muscles, and sexual organs, accompanied by a sudden release of endorphins, providing a feeling of euphoria (MedicineNet.com). It is controlled by the autonomic/involuntary nervous system, which is part of our limbic system, which is subdivided into the parasympathetic (PNS) and the sympathetic (SNS). The PNS is the relaxed, energy-conserving branch. It slows the heart, helps us fall asleep, and allows us to soak in pleasure that encourages arousal. It is dominant when we are passive. The SNS is the active, go-after branch that prepares us for emergencies. The body has to shift from PNS dominance to SNS in order to move from arousal to release (Penner & Penner, 2010).

**Male-Female Orgasmic Differences.** "Women have described the sensations of orgasm as beginning with a sense of suspension, quickly followed by an intensely pleasurable feeling that usually begins at the clitoris and spreads throughout the pelvis...[and] some portion of the body. Most women also feel muscle contractions in their vagina or lower pelvis, often described as 'pelvic throbbing'....

"Orgasm in men has been described... as beginning with the sensation of deep warmth or pressure that corresponds to ejaculatory inevitability, the point when ejaculation cannot be stopped. It is then felt as sharp, intensely pleasurable contractions involving the pelvic muscles, anal sphincter, rectum, perineum, and genitals. Finally, a warm rush of fluid or a shooting sensation describes the actual process of semen traveling through the urethra during ejaculation.

"A major difference between the female and the male orgasmic phase is that far more women than men have the physical capability to have one or more additional orgasms within a short time without dropping below the plateau of sexual arousal.

"On the other hand, upon ejaculation, men enter a recovery phase called the refractory period. During this time, further orgasm or ejaculation is physiologically impossible. However, some men can learn to have an orgasm without ejaculating, thereby making it possible to experience multiple orgasms" (Sinclair Intimacy Institute, 2002).

Men and women tend to struggle in opposite directions with orgasmic phase disorders. Men often respond too quickly, whereas women may have difficulty allowing a release.

**Orgasmic Inhibition for Women.** Even though the reflex of orgasm is as natural as the foot jerk in response to the doctor's tap on the knee, many women have never experienced, rarely experienced, do not know if they have experienced, or believe they have to work to experience release. Women have difficulty making the shift from arousal to release—from the passive to the active—because they tend to be passive in the sexual experience and often don't give themselves permission to go after sexual intensity. However, women whose physical arousal and subjective arousal are in sync are more likely to be able to make that shift from PNS to SNS and be orgasmic during sex (Elton, 2010). As they experience the sensations of their bodies, they get active and pursue the stimulation they need.

Another factor affects a woman's ability to orgasm: the fear and anxiety center of the brain, the amygdala, has to be turned off in order for a woman's pleasure center to be able to trigger an orgasm. This extra step of brain turn-off may be why she requires more time to reach orgasm. "It's a delicate system.... Nerves in the tip of the clitoris communicate straight to the sexual pleasure center of the female brain. When those nerves are stimulated, they boost electrochemical activity until it hits a threshold, triggers a burst of impulses, and releases bonding, feel-good petrochemicals such as dopamine, oxytocin and endorphins. Ah, climax!" (Brizendine, 2006, p. 78).

This information is critical to helping women transition from arousal to orgasm. They require adequate stimulation and lack of interference of fear, stress, guilt, evaluation, or pressure to be orgasmic. According to Brizendine, women are more likely to have orgasms if they are warm, particularly their feet, are deeply in love, and feel their spouses desire and adore them.

**Treatment of Orgasmic Inhibition for Women.** Orgasmic response is not a skill to be learned—the ability to release is already inside the woman. She may have to address barriers from her past, give herself permission to be intensely sexual, and get out of the spectator role. The sexual therapy guidelines and tools will help her to...

- stop trying (stop focusing on the goal)
- focus on pleasurable sensations—learning to give and receive pleasure
- reduce self-consciousness by practicing the breathing and sounds of a sexual response (see sexual therapy exercises in Penner & Penner, 2005)
- take responsibility for her own sexuality by listening to her body and pursuing her desires
- possibly, let go of female ejaculation

(A small percentage of intensely sexual women have the feeling of a need to urinate when they are about to orgasm. If the woman empties her bladder before sex, protects the bed, informs her husband, and lets go, she may experience an intense orgasm with a flooding response of fluid that is not urine.)

When a woman can't let go in a way that she desires, a bridging technique with successive approximation is used. For example, if a woman can be orgasmic with self-stimulation but not with her husband, she gradually brings her husband into her experience until he participates and then takes over the stimulation. If she can be orgasmic with manual stimulation but not during intercourse, including the self- or manual-stimulation during intercourse is helpful.

**Premature Ejaculation for Men.** "[This is] persistent or recurrent ejaculation with minimal sexual stimulation before, on, or shortly after penetration and before the person wishes it. The clinician must take into account factors that affect duration of the excitement phase, such as age, novelty of the sexual partner or situation, and recent frequency of sexual activity" (Raymond & Grant, 2008, p. 268).

Men are more likely to have difficulty with delaying the shift from the PNS to the SNS because they tend to be active in the sexual experience. Treatment is highly effective if the steps are followed correctly. It works by weakening the habituated reflex response. The man must learn to be passive and soak in the pleasure of touch without going for the release. The man can learn control through self-stimulation or with his wife. These are some of the techniques:

- scrotal tug (the scrotum is kept from elevating toward the body)
- stop-start method (Kaplan, 1989)
- squeeze technique (Penner & Penner, 2005)

**Inhibited Ejaculation for Men.** Inhibited ejaculation is the inability of a man to ejaculate or the inability to ejaculate in some way that he desires. The ejaculatory reflex in inhibited. The man may have sexual desire and be able to become aroused with a full erection, but even with intense arousal, the felt need for release, and more than sufficient stimulation, he can't let go. Treatment begins with the talking, touching, and teaching exercises of the sexual therapy process. Intercourse, attempts at intercourse, or pursuit of ejaculation are ruled out. All demands are removed and anxiety-triggering behaviors eliminated. Gradual, small steps toward release are assigned by the therapist for the couple (Penner & Penner, 2005).

**Conclusion.** Orgasmic disorders are highly responsive to the prescribed sexual therapy process. When the tools are taught and applied effectively, the release is possible unless physiological issues need to be evaluated and addressed. With an orgasm comes a surge of the neurochemical dopamine, which is the biggest reward we ever experience. Dopamine is a major motivator and the reason why getting release is important to keep desire for sex alive (Brizendine, 2006).

Clifford Penner
Joyce Penner

## REFERENCES

Brizendine, L. (2006). *The Female Brain.* New York, NY: Morgan Road Books.

Elton, C. (2010, May 1). Learning to lust. *Psychology Today.* Retrieved from http://www.psychologytoday.com/articles/201005/learning-lust

Kaplan, H. S. (1989). *How to Overcome Premature Ejaculation.* New York, NY: Brunner/Mazel.

MedicineNet.com. (n.d.) Orgasm. Retrieved from http://www.medterms.com/script/main/art.asp?articlekey=11783#

Penner, C., & Penner, J. (2005). *Counseling for Sexual Disorders.* Dallas, TX: Word.

Penner, C., & Penner, J. (2010, November 16). Sex in the brain. *CounselTalk.* Lecture conducted from American Association of Christian Counselors. Forest, VA.

Raymond, N. C., & Grant, J. E. (2008). Sexual disorders: Dysfunction, gender identity, and paraphilias. In S. H. Fatemi & P. J. Clayton (Eds.), *The Medical Basis of Psychiatry* (pp. 267-284). Totowa, NJ: Humana Press.

Sinclair Intimacy Institute. (2002). Orgasm. *Discovery health.com.* Retrieved from http://healthguide.howstuffworks.com/orgasm-dictionary.htm

## SEXUAL PAIN DISORDER

**Definition.** *Dyspareunia,* the medical term for sexual pain, is "genital pain that is associated with sexual intercourse" (American Psychiatric Association, 2000, p. 511). Or more encompassing, it is any pain associated with the genitals and sexual function. Sexual pain is experienced more frequently by women than by men.

**Assessment.** Sex is for pleasure; painful sex ought not to be allowed to continue. The pain must be taken seriously and identified carefully by a pelvic-floor physical therapist or a physician who specializes in diagnosing and treating dyspareunia—usually a uro-gynecologist. (To find a dyspareunia specialist, go to www.pelvicpain.org and click on "Find a Provider." Other helpful resources include the National Vulvodynia Association [www.nva.com] and the Vulvar Pain Foundation [www.vulvarpainfoundation.org].)

Before seeking diagnosis, the person experiencing the pain should identify precisely where the pain is, when in the process it gets triggered, what sexual activity starts or exaggerates the pain, and the type of pain.

**Sexual and Pelvic Pain in Females.**

*Vulvodynia.* This generalized vulvar pain is characterized by itching, burning, shooting pain, hypersensitivity, or sensations of dryness, swelling, or tightening of the vulvar skin in the genital and anal areas. Urinary urgency, frequency, and burning, as well as rectal itching and burning, may also be reported. Women suffering with vulvodynia may have difficulty walking or experience discomfort from touching or rubbing the pubic hair or wearing tight pants or pantyhose. This condition can be debilitating. These are some types of vulvodynia:

- *Vulvar vestibulitis* or *vestibulodynia* is an "inflammation, whether visible to the eye or not, in the tissue of the vestibule"—the oval-shaped area surrounding the vaginal opening and extending to the urethral opening, particularly the lower part, where the vestibular glands enter the pelvic floor (Willems, 1994). Thus, tapping a Q-tip around the opening of the vagina will elicit a sharp pain at four and/or eight o'clock. "The most common causes...are hormonal changes, tight pelvic floor muscles, and an increased number of nerve endings in the vestibule" (Goldstein, Klingman, Christopher, Johnson, & Marinoff, 2006).
- *Dysesthetic vulvodynia* is "connected with pelvic floor muscle weakness" (Goldstein, Pukall, & Goldstein, 2011, p. 39) rather than tightness.
- *Vulvar or vaginal skin disorders*, most commonly *lichen sclerosus* and *erosive lichen planus*, are inflammations that cause ulcers, erosions, and scarring (Goldstein et al., 2011, p. 15).
- *Pudendal neuralgia* is pain in the areas innervated by the pudendal nerve—a sensory, autonomic, and motor nerve that carries signals to and from the genitals, anal area, and urethra.
- *Persistent genital arousal disorder* (PGAD) involves pudendal nerve triggers and brain chemicals. The inhibiting brain chemicals, such as serotonin, need to be activated (Leiblum & Nathan, 2001).
- *Urethritis* or *urethral syndrome* is due to an irritation of the urethra. The woman will experience a sharp pain at the 12 o'clock position in response to tapping around the opening of the vagina with a Q-tip.

Unfortunately, physicians, nurse practitioners, or other professionals not trained in these diagnoses may find that the vulvar skin looks completely normal.

*Pain of the vaginal barrel.* This includes three varieties:

- *Vaginitis* is a stinging pain due to vaginal wall irritation/inflammation with or without infection.
- *Vaginismus* is an involuntary spastic or rigid contraction of the muscles controlling the opening of the vagina causing painful intercourse (dyspareunia) or no intercourse (apareunia). "[It] is probably the most common cause of entry dyspareunia, affecting about 1% of women. Vaginismus can be primary (the woman has never been able to have intercourse) or secondary" (the woman was previously able to have intercourse and now isn't due to a trauma, injury, or painful intercourse) (Howard, Perry, Carter, & El-Minawi, 2000, p. 114). It can be situational (only in response to attempted entry) or generalized (the muscles are always clamped). "Many women with vaginismus have normal sexual desire, experience normal vaginal lubrication, and are orgasmic, but cannot have intercourse" (Howard et al., p. 114). The couple may have a full sexual life but without entry.
- *Tears or fissures in the wall of the vagina* cause sharp pain at the specific location of the injury.

*Pain of the pelvic cavity and structures.*

- *Endometriosis* "is a condition in which uterine tissue grows outside the uterus.... In addition to chronic pelvic pain, these women may also suffer from deep dyspareunia" (pain upon deep thrusting or with an orgasm) (Goldstein et al., 2011, p. 15).

- *Trauma* that leads to dyspareunia may occur because of childbirth, a fall, bicycle riding, and other injuries.
- *Pain due to lack of release* following the buildup of vasocongestion during sexual arousal is experienced as a dull aching pain in the lower back or abdomen and can last for hours after sexual arousal without release.
- *Deep dyspareunia* is sharp, stabbing pain upon deep thrusting caused by a retroflexed (tipped) uterus. The uterus doesn't pull up and out of the way, so the penis thrusts against the cervix (the lower, narrow portion of the uterus where it joins with the top end of the vagina).

**Sexual and Pelvic Pain in Males.**

- *Prostatitis* due to muscle tightness may have been caused by bicycle riding on a narrow saddle or by an infection. "Nonbacterial prostatitis is a condition that produces much suffering. There are no curative drugs or effective surgical procedures" (Wise & Anderson, 2003, p. 10).
- *Orchalgia* is a deep aching or sometimes burning pain in the testicles that may exhibit a pressure-like quality as though the testicle were being squeezed in a vise.
- *Chronic sterile epididymitis* is a rare condition causing mild to severe pain due to inflammation of the epididymis (a curved structure at the back of each testicle).
- *Peyronie's disease* is a curvature of the penis due to scar tissue inside the penis causing pain and making intercourse impossible or difficult. Treatment is available (see www.mayoclinic.com/health/peyronies-disease).

**Treatment of Sexual and Pelvic Pain.** Whatever the type of pain, the goal of the counselor is to support and advocate for the client until the source of pain is identified and relieved and the couple is able to enjoy pleasurable intercourse without pain. Until that goal is reached, the counselor is to emphasize the importance of not engaging in any activity that triggers pain. Pain perpetuates more pain, so the cycle of pain must be interrupted. In this context, the presentation will be general to all sexual/pelvic pain with a few identified specifics as indicated.

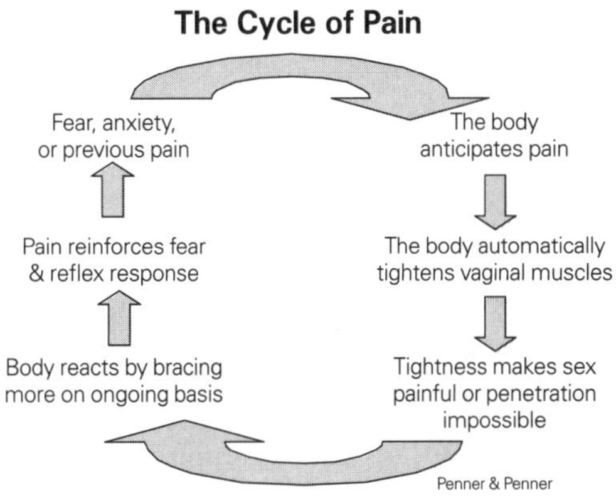

**The Cycle of Pain**

Fear, anxiety, or previous pain
The body anticipates pain
The body automatically tightens vaginal muscles
Tightness makes sex painful or penetration impossible
Body reacts by bracing more on ongoing basis
Pain reinforces fear & reflex response

Penner & Penner

*Biochemical and nutritional balance.* Keeping the pH balanced will reduce most sexual/pelvic pain. The vaginal secretions should run between 4.5 and 5. "In terms of body pH balance, there is no one 'correct' reading for the entire body. For instance, healthy human skin has an approximate pH of 5.5 (slightly acid). Saliva, on the other hand, has a pH of around 6.5–7.4 (teetering on either side of neutral). The lower the pH reading, the more acidic the solution. Readings from 0–7 are considered acidic, and numbers from 7–14 are considered basic, or alkaline.... The vagina maintains an acidic environment to protect itself"

(Pick, 2011). Change in diet can positively affect body pH.

- Eliminate foods that trigger allergic reactions.
- Eliminate chemically reactive foods, such as caffeine and citrus, and refined carbohydrates, such as sugar, white flour, and white rice.
- The literature reports conflicting results regarding the benefits of a low-oxalate diet.
- Eat small meals frequently and chew food well and slowly.
- Eat foods that calm the gut, including fresh cooked vegetables with lemon.
- Take a vitamin-mineral supplement that is high in the B vitamins, magnesium, and calcium.
- Take additional 1200 mg of calcium citrate (helps sleep if taken at bedtime).
- Take a probiotic and eat plain yogurt.
- Drink a full glass of water before and between meals.

(Visit www.Vulvodynia-Treatment.com for a "One-Page Daily V-Health Guide & Suggested Supplement Dosage.")

Hormonal intervention has also proved beneficial. Stop or change hormonal birth control to one that is low in progestin activity and high in androgen activity (Dickey, 2010). (Visit www.emispub.com for hormonal activity in birth control products.) Hormone creams, prescribed by a physician or nurse practitioner, are also effective. "I tried the combination of estrogen and testosterone on my patients, and I was amazed with the results. About two-thirds got completely better!" (Goldstein et al., 2011, pp. 98-99). Estrogen cream (estradiol vaginal cream 0.001%) is applied intravaginally at bedtime. One or two percent testosterone cream is applied in the vulvar and clitoral area daily in the morning (Penner & Penner, 2005, p. 253.)

*Pelvic floor physical therapy.* Techniques such as these are key to treating dyspareunia.

- Biofeedback for neuromuscular re-education. A sensor is inserted into the vagina to test the strength of the pelvic floor muscles and help the client get greater control (Glazer, 1997).
- progressive muscle relaxation (PMR) technique
- identifying and treating involved external and internal muscles
- use of graduated dilators
- pelvic floor exercises (Stein, 2009)

*Medical/surgical interventions.*

- antibiotics if infections are present
- injection of cortisone or botox into the pelvic floor
- pudendal and caudal nerve blocks (by an anesthesiologist)
- vestibulectomy (Goldstein et al., 2006). (Surgery should only be done with recommendation of a highly regarded MD who specializes in treatment of pelvic pain and after securing a second opinion.)
- acupuncture

*Specific recommendations for deep dyspareunia.*

- gynecological exam to confirm retroflexed uterus
- knee-chest exercises (unless pregnant)
- pubococcygeus (PC) muscle exercises
- adapt position for intercourse to avoid thrusting against the cervix

*Specific approach to vaginismus and unconsummated marriages.* Four tracks are recommended:

- Resolve medical issues and/or emotional conflicts interfering with entry of the penis into the vagina.
- Learn to give and receive pleasure and enjoy each other sexually (sexual therapy).
- Accept your God-given sexuality and God-designed genitals.
- Gain control of vaginal muscles through pelvic-floor physical therapy and/or use of kit from www.vaginismus.com, including graduated dilators inserted daily for 20 to 30 minutes.
- Transition to intercourse by using the penis as a paintbrush around the opening of the vagina, poking the penis into the vagina in tiny increments, switching from largest dilator to penis (Penner & Penner, 1993, pp. 197, 202, 307-308).
- Do not use surgery. This is a muscle problem and is not cured by surgical intervention (Penner & Penner, 2005, pp. 262-272).

**Conclusion.** The counselor is a critical part of the team for the person with sexual pain. The discouragement that comes until a solution is found can be devastating. Help and relief are available, but the hard road to success can be wearisome. Sexual therapy is often necessary as part of the process to help the couple establish mutually satisfying patterns of relating sexually.

Clifford Penner
Joyce Penner

## REFERENCES

American Psychiatric Association. (2000). *Diagnostic and Statistical Manual of Mental Disorders* (4th ed., text rev.). Washington, DC: Author.

Dickey, R. P. (2010). *Managing Contraceptive Pill Patients* (14th ed.). Dallas, TX: EMIS Medical.

Glazer, H. I. (1997). Biofeedback and vulvovaginal pain. *NVA News, 3*(3). Retrieved from http://www.vulvodynia.com/bio_vvpn.htm

Goldstein, A., Klingman, D., Christopher, K., Johnson. C., & Marinoff, S. C. (2006). Surgical treatment of vulvar vestibulitis syndrome: Outcome assessment derived from a postoperative questionnaire. *International Society for Sexual Medicine, 3*, 923-931.

Goldstein, A., Pukall, C., & Goldstein, I. (2011). *When Sex Hurts: A Woman's Guide to Banishing Sexual Pain.* Cambridge, MA: Da Capo Lifelong Books.

Howard, F. M., Perry, C. P., Carter, J. E., & El-Minawi, A. M. (Eds.). (2000). *Pelvic Pain Diagnosis & Management.* Philadelphia, PA: Lippincott Williams & Wilkins.

Leiblum, S. R., & Nathan, S. G. (2001, July 1). Persistent sexual arousal syndrome. *Journal of Sex & Marital Therapy, 27*(4), 365-380.

Penner, C., & Penner, J. (1993). *Restoring the Pleasure: Complete Step-by-Step Programs to Help Couples Overcome the Most Common Sexual Barriers.* Nashville, TN: Word.

Penner, C., & Penner, J. (2005). *Counseling for Sexual Disorders.* Dallas, TX: Word.

Pick, M. (2011). *The Truth About pH Balance.* Retrieved from http://www.womentowomen.com/digestionandgihealth/phbalance.aspx

Stein, A. (2009). *Heal Pelvic Pain: Proven Stretching, Strengthening, and Nutrition Program for Relieving Pain, Incontinence, IBS and Other Symptoms Without Surgery.* New York, NY: McGraw-Hill.

Willems, J. (1994). New direction in medical management of vulvar vestibulitis. *The Vulvar Pain Newsletter, 5.*

Wise, D., & Anderson, R. (2003). *A Headache in the Pelvis.* Occidental, CA: National Center for Pelvic Pain.

## PARAPHILIAS AND SEXUAL DEVIANCE

**History.** First coined by Wilhelm Stekel in the 1920s, the term *paraphilia* is derived from two Greek words—*para*, meaning "beside," and *philia*, meaning "friendship" or "love." In psychological and medical fields, the term has been used to describe sexual practices that are beside or outside the norm for sexuality. The sexologist John Money was the first to list various types of paraphilias (Money, 1986). Dr. Money sought to normalize them, or create nonjudgmental ways of talking about them.

A significant divide exists between Christian and secular counselors regarding what is sexually normal. Christians, based on their understanding of biblical sexuality, consider any sexual activity outside of God's commandments, including paraphilias, to be deviant. For example, until 1973, homosexuality was considered to be a paraphilia.

Even within the secular scientific community, there is disagreement about what is normal sexually. In general, paraphilias are considered to be sexual behaviors that involve

- non-human objects,
- the suffering or humiliation of oneself or one's partner,
- children, or
- nonconsenting persons.

In the current version of the *Diagnostic and Statistical Manual of Mental Disorders* (*DSM*), a paraphilia is not diagnosable as a disorder unless it causes distress to the individual or harm to others. The draft of the 5th edition of the *DSM* adds a terminology distinction between the two cases, stating, "Paraphilias are not *ipso facto* psychiatric disorders," and defining *paraphilia disorder* as "a paraphilia that causes distress or impairment to the individual or harm to others."

**Assessment.** The *DSM* includes these categories of behaviors as paraphilias:

- Exhibitionism: the recurrent urge or behavior to expose one's genitals to an unsuspecting person or to perform sexual acts that can be watched by others.
- Fetishism: the use of inanimate objects to gain sexual excitement. *Partialism* refers to fetishes specifically involving nonsexual parts of the body.
- Frotteurism: recurrent urges of behavior of touching or rubbing against a nonconsenting person.
- Pedophilia: strong sexual attraction to prepubescent children.
- Sexual masochism: the recurrent urge or behavior of wanting to be humiliated, beaten, bound, or otherwise made to suffer for sexual pleasure.
- Sexual sadism: the recurrent urge or behavior involving acts in which the pain or humiliation of a person is sexually exciting.
- Transvestic fetishism: arousal from wearing clothing associated with members of the opposite sex.
- Voyeurism: the recurrent urge or behavior to observe an unsuspecting person who is naked, disrobing, or engaging in sexual activities, or who is engaging in activities usually considered being of a private nature.

Under *Paraphilia NOS*, the *DSM* mentions telephone scatalogia (obscene phone calls), necrophilia (corpses), partialism (exclusive focus on one part of the body), zoophilia (animals), coprophilia (feces), klismaphilia (enemas), urophilia (urine), and emetophilia (vomit). *Paraphilia NOS* in the *DSM* is equivalent to *sexual disorder NOS* in the *International Classification of Diseases*. Sexual arousal in association with objects that were designed for sexual purposes is not diagnosable in the *DSM*.

In order to diagnosis any of these conditions, a counselor must feel comfortable taking a complete sexual history from birth to the present. Many paraphilic behaviors originate in erotically charged experiences in childhood. Carnes (2001), for example, has called this dynamic the "arousal template." These early associations are symbolic representations of universal longings that we all have for love, nurture, and attention (Laaser, 2011).

These behaviors are erotically charged, so they produce powerful chemicals in the brain, which can then become tolerant to their production. A feeling of unmanageability, escalation, and need for medication is often the result. All of these are the symptoms of addiction, which must also be considered in the assessment process.

**Treatment.** It is vitally important for a Christian counselor to be nonreactive to the presentation of paraphilic behaviors. Hearing a client describe these behaviors can evoke feelings of revulsion and disgust. The counselor needs to remember that God's grace covers all sins. We must be nonshaming instruments of God's love. On the other hand, we must not be lulled into being tolerant or accepting of these behaviors by the secular and medical/psychological communities. The following treatment approaches are recommended:

- Accurate assessment of the etiology of the behavior in childhood or adolescence. Current or recent behaviors are always symbolic of associations made in the past.
- Trauma resolution: Many of these behaviors are the result of wounds inflicted by others.
- Group accountability encourages a person to abstain completely from the behavior.
- Inpatient or outpatient treatment for sexual addiction (Laaser, 2004).
- Sex therapy that includes behavioral exercises to reorient a person to normal sexual behaviors.
- Relationship therapy or couples' counseling to reconcile the difficulties created by these behaviors.
- Psychiatric treatment of any comorbid mental-health issues. However, aberrant behaviors should not be treated by "chemically castrating" the client with medication.
- Spiritual direction to point people to the truth of how to get deep needs for love, nurture, and attention met through a relationship with God.

**Spiritual Issues.** The Bible contains references that show how much God deplores sexual behaviors that are outside his commandments for marital sexuality. For example, Deuteronomy 22:5 tells us, "A woman must not wear men's clothing, nor a man wear women's clothing, for the Lord your God detests anyone who does this." Paul describes the sexual immorality of the Roman world in Romans 1, and in Romans 12:2 he says we are not to be conformed to the ways of this world, but to be transformed by the renewing of our mind. As John Money and many others have said, paraphilic behaviors are "mapped" or "wired" into the chemistry of the brain. A new wiring can take place with the right accountability and new conditioning.

People who practice paraphilias can feel extremely ashamed, but these practices may present as a certain defiance as people insist that their behaviors are normal and that they should be entitled to do them. Increasingly, the secular world is supporting this sense of entitlement. Christian counselors are walking a tightrope to avoid running afoul of the world's judgment and be accused of malpractice. We must all be spiritually strong and rooted in our faith and biblical understanding. We must understand the pain and shame that creates these behaviors, but at the same time, we must be able to confront their immorality. God's law will always point us to his design for the healthiest kind of sexuality, the expression of it in a one-flesh union.

**Mark R. Laaser**

## REFERENCES


Carnes, P. (2001). *Out of the Shadows*. Center City, MN: Hazelden.

Laaser, M. (2004). *Healing the Wounds of Sexual Addiction*. Grand Rapids, MI: Zondervan.

Laaser, M. (2011). *Taking Every Thought Captive*. Kansas City, MO: Beacon Hill.

Money, J. (1986). *Love Maps*. New York, NY: Irvington.

## PEDOPHILIA

**Description.** When a natural disaster affects hundreds of thousands of people, the world is shocked and turns the media spotlight on the location, with the cameras often highlighting lost and crying children in order to appeal to the deepest sensibilities of their audience. However, it has become apparent that there is a worldwide but little-known epidemic of child molestation, and its numbers eclipse any but the most cataclysmic natural disaster. Statistics on the exact numbers of victims of child molestation vary widely based on the definitions and methodology utilized in research. However, in the United States, it has been estimated that up to one in three females and one in six males (Finkelhor, 1994) have been abused as minors, which amounts to more than 320,000 per year (Finkelhor, Hammer, & Sedlak, 2008). The youngest and most innocent of these are targeted by a number of abusers, the most prominent of which are those classified as pedophiles.

**Assessment.** A clinical diagnosis of pedophilia is normally made following a formal evaluation by a psychiatrist or clinical psychologist of an individual whose sexual preference is prepubescent children, classified as 13 years of age or younger. A related term, *ephebophilia,* refers to those who are attracted sexually to adolescents (14 to 19). The legal or criminal classification of *child molester* is applied to individuals who act upon these desires with underage victims. One may say that all active pedophiles are child molesters, but not all child molesters are pedophiles. Feelgood and Hoyer (2008) point out that the term *child molester* is sociolegal and relates to behavior, whereas the term *pedophile* is psychopathological and relates to mental disorders. Pedophilia is one of a number of sexual behaviors classified as *paraphilias,* which involve sexual fantasies, urges, or behaviors deemed by society as deviant or aberrant. Recently, some researchers have claimed that pedophilia should not be classified as a paraphilia but rather as a sexual orientation ("Pessimism About Pedophilia," 2010) and is therefore unlikely to change or be affected by treatment. Pedophilia has traditionally been viewed as extremely difficult to "cure," so Hall and Hall (2007) have stated, "Currently, much of the focus of pedophilic treatment is on stopping further offenses against children rather than altering the pedophile's sexual orientation toward children."

The *Diagnostic and Statistical Manual of Mental Disorders* (*DSM-IV-TR*) adds that to be diagnosed as a pedophile, the individual must be at least 16 years old and a minimum of 5 years older than the minor victimized, and that these aberrant sexual urges must occur for a period of at least six months.

Although most pedophiles are male, research has indicated that approximately 5% may be female. Additional female involvement may occur when coerced or accompanied by a male, who is usually the initiator of the assault. There are different types of pedophiles, with the basic dichotomous factors centered on exclusivity/nonexclusivity (regarding age and gender of victims), homosexual/heterosexual/bisexual (referring primarily to perpetrator/victim), and opportunistic/hunter. Incest and caretaker assaults are most common due to ease of access to victims; the media-focused "dirty old man in a raincoat" is responsible for a minority of the assaults. Homosexual pedophiles are represented at a rate up to 20 times the rate of adult men attracted to other adult men, with a staggering average of 150.2 children victimized and an average of 281.7 acts (Abel et al., 1987).

**Biblical and Spiritual Issues.** The Bible makes it clear that sexual activity between adults and children is forbidden. First Corinthians 6:9-10 says all sexual impurity is forbidden and that it leads to eternal separation from God. Ephesians 5:3-5 also emphasizes the wrongness of such sexual contact. Matthew 18 is also often quoted in this context—in no uncertain terms, Jesus warns those who hurt children of the terrible fate that awaits them. Some may argue the particulars here, but taken in the context of Jesus' teaching, the meaning is clear. Those who harm the innocent will be severely punished.

In addition, research from numerous sources, including Dr. Jay Giedd of the National Institute of Mental Health, has shown that the portion of the brain responsible for reasoning and rational thought may not fully mature until young adulthood (Giedd et al., 1999). With this in mind, it is clear that a prepubescent child is not able to rationally make a decision regarding sexual activity. This is one reason why the concept of the age of consent exists—to protect children from sexual predators, such as practicing pedophiles.

Edgar E. Barker

## REFERENCES


Abel, G. G., Becker, J. V., Mittelman, M., Cunningham-Rathner, J., Rouleau, J. L., & Murphy, W. D. (1987). Self-reported sex crimes of nonincarcerated paraphiliacs. *Journal of Interpersonal Violence, 2,* 3-25.

American Psychiatric Association. (2000). *Diagnostic and Statistical Manual of Mental Disorders* (4th ed., text rev.). Washington, DC: Author.

Feelgood, S., & Hoyer, J. (2008). Child molester or paedophile? Sociolegal versus psychopathological classification of sexual offenders against children. *Journal of Sexual Aggression, 14*(1), 33-43.

Finkelhor, D. (1994). The international epidemiology of child sexual abuse. *Child Abuse & Neglect 18*(5), 409-417.

Finkelhor, D., Hammer, H., and Sedlak, A. J. (2008). Sexually assaulted children: National estimates and characteristics. *National Incidence Studies of Missing, Abducted, Runaway, and Thrownaway Children.* U.S. Department of Justice, Office of Justice Programs, Office of Juvenile Justice and Delinquency Prevention.

Giedd, J., Blumenthal, J., Jeffries, N., Castellanos, F., Liu, H., Zijdenbos, A.,...Rapoport, J. (1999). Brain development during childhood and adolescence: A longitudinal MRI study. *Nature Neuroscience, 2*(10), 861-863.

Hall, Ryan C. W., & Hall, Richard C. W. (2007). A profile of pedophilia: Definition, characteristics of offenders, recidivism, treatment outcomes and forensic issues. *Mayo Clinic Proceedings, 82*(4), 457-471.

Pessimism about pedophilia. (2010, July). *Harvard Mental Health Letter.* Retrieved from http://www.health.harvard.edu/newsletters/Harvard_Mental_Health_Letter/2010/July/pessimism-about-pedophilia


## SEXUALLY TRANSMITTED DISEASES

**Description.** Sexually transmitted diseases (STDs; or sexually transmitted infections, STIs) have become increasingly common in our society, affecting more than 70 million Americans (U.S. Dept. of Health and Human Services, Centers for Disease Control and Prevention [CDC] 2009). According to the Centers for Disease Control and Prevention, STDs are a set of infectious diseases transmitted "from person to person by close, intimate contact" (Nelson & Woodward, 2006, p.1).

STDs are caused by various bacteria (chlamydia, gonorrhea, syphilis), viruses (HIV/AIDS, hepatitis, herpes, human hapillomavirus [HPV]), or parasites (trichomoniasis) (Nelson & Woodward, 2006). Most STDs are transmitted by sexual activities, including oral, vaginal, and anal sex. Some viruses, such as HPV and herpes, can be transmitted by skin contact. HIV and hepatitis are spread through contact of infected blood through needle sharing (CDC, 2009).

**History.** In the 1490s, one of the first STDs was recognized and named the *French disease* (mobus gallicus) because it broke out in the French invasion of Naples, Italy, in 1495. It spread rapidly through Europe and infected a large number of people. The infection was eventually named *syphilis* after a poem by an Italian pathologist. Prior to the discovery of antibiotics, STDs were incurable diseases. Currently, more than 20 different STDs have been identified. Especially widespread among adolescents, these infections have become a significant social problem (CDC, 2009). Coupled with the emergence and rapid spread of HIV/AIDS in the 1980s, STDs have become a staggering worldwide problem.

In most cases, people with STDs do not show symptoms immediately after infection. Sometimes, individuals do not develop any symptoms at all; however, infected individuals can still transmit the disease to their sexual partners (CDC, 2009). Common signs of STDs include abnormal discharge from the penis or vagina; blisters, warts, rashes, sores around genitals or other parts of the body; painful intercourse, painful urination, and lower abdominal pain (CDC; Nelson & Woodward, 2006). When symptoms are unrecognized and therefore untreated, consequences may be severe, leading to infertility (from gonorrhea or chlamydia), cancer (from HPV or HIV), permanent damage to various organs (e.g., uterus, brain, nerve, eye, liver, or joints), and other life-threatening illnesses (CDC; Nelson & Woodward).

STDs can affect pregnant women and their infants. Transmission can occur before, during, or after the birth of the child and may cause miscarriage, stillbirth, and preterm delivery. Infections can lead to serious conditions among infants. For example, gonorrhea can affect infants through the birth canal and can lead to blindness or life-threatening blood diseases. Syphilis may cause the child's developmental delay, seizures, or death (CDC, 2009).

Many individuals infected with STDs suffer not only physical symptoms but also emotional, relational, and spiritual problems (Clinton & Laaser, 2010). For example, adjustment disorders, depression, and anxiety are common (Sadeghi-Nejad, Wasserman, Weidner, Richardson, & Goldmeier, 2010). Infertility caused by STDs can lead to distress, depression, anxiety, and relational problems. Violence and substance abuse are also problematic among individuals with STDs, especially among low-income minorities (Senn, Carey, & Vanable, 2010). Drug abuse and addictions can be serious co-occurring problems, especially with HIV/AIDS, because they can facilitate the sexual transmission of the disease from sharing needles and decreased inhibitions that can lead to unprotected sex (Mamuella, 2006).

**Treatment.** STDs are serious medical problems. Most bacterial STDs are treated with antibiotics, while other conditions such as HIV/AIDS can be treated but not cured (Clinton & Laaser, 2010). Counselors must work together with physicians who provide assessment and treatment of infections. The major role of counselors is to help clients process the initial shock, fear, anger, guilt, shame, and confusion (Clinton & Laaser, 2010; Shoquist & Stafford, 2004). Clients should be also empowered to take steps to prevent their spouses from becoming infected. If sexual partners other than spouses are involved, clients must notify those partners. Various prevention programs have been developed—especially for adolescents because nearly half of the new infections occur in those 15 to 24 years of age (CDC, 2009). These programs address abstinence, sexual health, emotional and relational needs, peer pressure, and life skills. In addition, parental involvement is critical (Dubios-Arber & Carael, 2002).

Helping those with STDs and associated difficulties is challenging and calls for God's deep forgiveness and redemptive grace. Couples will need honesty and a special focus on shame, forgiveness, and the rebuilding of broken trust.

Tim Clinton
Scott Hawkins

## REFERENCES

Clinton, T., & Laaser, M. (2010). *The Quick-Reference Guide to Sexuality & Relationships Counseling.* Grand Rapids, MI: Baker Books.

Dubios-Arber, F., & Carael, M. (2002). Behavior change for STD prevention and sexual health. In J. Green & D. Miller (Eds.), *The Psychology of Sexual Health* (pp. 38-52). Malden, MA: Balckwell Science.

Mamuella, A. (2006). Addiction and sexually transmitted disease (STD), human immunodeficiency virus (HIV), and acquired immune deficiency syndrome (AIDS):

Their mutual interactions. *Substance Use & Misuse, 41*, 1337-1348. doi:10.1080/10826080600837978

Nelson, A. L., & Woodward, J. (2006). *Sexually Transmitted Diseases: A Practical Guide for Primary Care.* Norwalk, CT: Crown House.

Sadeghi-Nejad, H., Wasserman, M., Weidner, W., Richardson, D., & Goldmeier, D. (2010). Sexually transmitted diseases and sexual function. *Journal of Sexual Medicine, 7*(1), 389-413. doi:10.1111/j.1743-6109.2009.01622.x

Senn, T. E., Carey, M. P., & Vanable, P. A. (2010). The intersection of violence, substance use, depression, and STDs: Testing of a syndemic pattern among patients attending an urban STD clinic. *Journal of the National Medical Association, 102*(7), 614-620.

Shoquist, J., & Stafford, D. (2004). *The Encyclopedia of Sexually Transmitted Diseases.* New York, NY: Facts on File.

U.S. Department of Health and Human Services, Centers for Disease Control and Prevention, National Center for HIV/AIDS, Viral Hepatitis, STD, and TB Prevention, Division of STD Prevention. (2009). *Sexually Transmitted Disease Surveillance.* Retrieved from http://www.cdc.gov/std/stats09/surv2009-Complete.pdf

## SEXUAL THERAPY

**Definition.** Sexual therapy is a systematic approach to treating sexual dysfunctions and a tool for building intimacy in marriage. The couple who reports unsatisfactory sexual experiences is retrained to behave and communicate with each other in ways that reduce demand, enhance pleasure, and facilitate the natural physiological sexual responses. Sexual therapy is usually short-term therapy (10 to 20 sessions) that combines a cognitive-behavioral approach of sensate focus exercises, communication training, and education with psychotherapy (Penner & Penner, 2003).

**History.** "From the start of the twentieth century until the late 1960s, sexual dysfunction was typically treated within a psychoanalytic framework" (Wiederman, 1998, p. 88). Two publications in the late 1950s (Semans, 1956; Wolpe, 1958) began to change therapeutic approaches to sexual dysfunction. Masters and Johnson's *Human Sexual Inadequacy* (1970) expanded these direct approaches into a comprehensive therapy program for sexual dysfunctions. Masters and Johnson, known as the founders of sex therapy, formulated the short-term, directive, cognitive-behavioral approach to sexual dysfunction that has been subsequently used and adapted by many. The prescribed behavioral, sensate-focused exercises were designed to reduce performance anxiety ("spectatoring") and increase pleasure. Therapists worked as a male-female pair with couples (conjoint therapy); the therapy room included four individuals—the cotherapists and the client couple.

In 1974, Helen Singer Kaplan's *The New Sex Therapy* integrated psychoanalytic therapy with the behavioral approach to treatment of sexual dysfunctions. She noted that although sex therapy improved sexual functioning, "in the course of sex therapy intrapsychic and transactional conflicts are almost invariably dealt with to some extent" (Kaplan, 1974, p. xii).

The issues presenting for sex therapy have become more complex. There is greater awareness of physiological factors contributing to sexual dysfunction. Knowledge of the brain and its impact on sexual functioning is growing significantly. What is now known about neurological triggers, brain chemicals/hormones, and male-female differences validates clinical observations and guides therapeutic techniques in working with individuals and couples seeking sexual therapy (Meston & Frohlich, 2000; Pfaus, 1999). The findings are fascinating, exciting, complex, and continually expanding. Currently, sex therapists find it necessary to employ a range of treatment modalities and to coordinate on behalf of the client with medical and other professionals.

**Assessment.** Precise assessment is an essential ingredient to effective diagnosis and treatment of sexual disorders. Accurate gathering of an individual's or couple's personal sexual data requires a comfortable, qualified therapist and a well-defined system of assessment.

Structure provides safety for the intense

emotions of clients' sexual histories and is necessary to be able to acquire an explicit behavioral picture. If new behaviors are to be learned, the old behaviors have to be clearly defined and understood. Forms to gather the necessary content during the sexual assessment are available (Kaplan, 1983). Content to gather during the assessment with each spouse separately includes these items:

- physical history or symptom survey, including medications and medical reports
- history of family members, clients' relationship with each, and relationship between mother and father
- history of sexual education and development, exploratory play, self-stimulation, dating and sexual behavior, and abuse
- description of the difficulty the couple is experiencing, its history, and its impact
- options for help the couple has pursued
- frequency of sexual activity and who initiates; role of kissing and various form of bodily stimulation; comfort with bodies, entry, and orgasm; and feelings and interaction after sex
- additional factors might include personality inventories, MMPI-2 or other diagnostic tools, pelvic-floor physical therapy assessment, urogyn for women with pain, hormonal panel, and urologist examination for male sexual dysfunction

After gathering the data from each spouse, meet with the couple to clarify differences, offer your picture of the problem, and describe the patterns that have perpetuated their negative system. Define the goals and the recommended therapy approach for their situation (Penner & Penner, 2005).

**Treatment.** The process of sexual therapy begins the same regardless of the problem and becomes individualized as the process progresses. These are the primary goals of sexual therapy:

- distract from anxiety
- remove demands
- eliminate negative or failure experiences
- build new patterns of sexual relating
- gain new and positive attitudes about sexuality and positive anticipation of sexual times

Sexual therapy techniques often include talking, teaching, and touching exercises, and they are quite similar from one sexual therapist to another (Penner & Penner, 2005).

- *Talking.* In these communication exercises, each spouse completes the forms individually and then shares the responses with the other using active listening skills.
- *Teaching.* Spouses learn about themselves, each other, the physical sexual responses, the emotional-relational process, and the scriptural affirmation of sexuality and sex in marriage.
- *Touching.* Sensate-focus exercises help the couple change from arousal, release, intercourse goals to learning to give and receive pleasure without demand.

Clearly defined, small, incremental steps also help the therapist and couple identify when in the sexual process sexual barriers surface. These are the keys to therapeutic success:

- clear guidelines
- an in-charge therapist who prescribes and decides with the couple every detail of their homework

- gathering data of the couple's experience of their homework
- recognition and effective management of emotional and/or relational barriers that interfere with progress

A skilled sexual therapist will assess the need for and make necessary adjustments to the prescribed exercises, using creativity and taking into consideration each partner's desires and needs.

**Conclusion.** Sexual therapy has brought hope and healing to many individuals and couples. The sexual therapy process can relieve specific sexual dysfunction, diagnose sexual and other issues, open the world of sexuality between spouses, break down inhibitions and shame, build intimacy, elicit awareness of and work past the consequences of sexual abuse, deal with body image, identify addictive patterns, manage resistance, and help couples develop the passion and get the love they are longing for with each other.

Clifford Penner
Joyce Penner

## REFERENCES

Kaplan, H. S. (1974). *The New Sex Therapy: Active Treatment of Sexual Dysfunctions.* New York, NY: Brunner/Mazel.

Kaplan, H. S. (1983). *The Evaluation of Sexual Disorders: Psychological and Medical Aspects.* New York, NY: Brunner/Mazel.

Masters, W. H., & Johnson, V. E. (1970). *Human Sexual Inadequacy.* Boston, MA: Little, Brown.

Meston, C. M., & Frohlich, P. F. (2000). *Archives of General Psychiatry, 57,* 1012-1030.

Penner, C., & Penner, J. (2003). *The Gift of Sex: A Guide to Sexual Fulfillment.* Nashville, TN: Thomas Nelson.

Penner, C., & Penner, J. (2005). *Counseling for Sexual Disorders.* Nashville, TN: Word.

Pfaus, J. G. (1999). Neurobiology of sexual behavior. *Current Opinion in Neurobiology, 9*(6), 751-758.

Semans, J. H. (1956). Premature ejaculation: A new approach. *Southern Medical Journal, 49,* 353-357.

Wiederman, M. W. (1998). The state of theory in sex therapy. *Journal of Sex Research, 35*(1), 88-100.

Wolpe, J. (1958). *Psychotherapy by Reciprocal Inhibition.* Stanford, CA: Stanford University Press.

## SENSATE FOCUS

**Definition.** Sensate focus, or sensual touching, was popularized through Masters and Johnson's bestseller *Human Sexual Inadequacy* (1970). I (Doug) remember what a phenomenon our culture experienced at that time. A technical, medical book on sexual dysfunction, though often difficult to understand, hit the *New York Times* bestseller list. As introduced in the book, sensate focus was simply sensual massage, structured as an exercise to help overcome sexual difficulties in a relationship.

In sensate focus, both partners set aside an agreed on amount of time (from 30 minutes to more than an hour) to be in a relaxed, comfortable atmosphere, to be naked together, and to explore each other's bodies. They do this through alternating the roles of giver/toucher/pleasurer and receiver/touchee/pleasuree.

*The active toucher (or giver).* The giver touches the receiver in ways intended to feel good to the receiver. The primary goal of the giver is to enjoy giving pleasure to the receiver with no demands or expectations for performance. The giver experiments with a variety of touches and strokes on all areas of the partner's body—other than genitals and breasts. It is often helpful to start with the receiver lying facedown. The giver begins at the top of the receiver's head and slowly pleasures the partner down to the feet. The receiver rolls over, and the giver pleasures from the feet to the head.

*The passive touchee (or receiver).* The receiver focuses on feeling the touches and enjoying the sensations. Often the touches that pleasure the receiver give stimulation and pleasure to the giver as well. The receiver can increase self-awareness by noticing which areas and types of touching give the greatest pleasure. The receiver can also learn about the giver—what kinds of touching and strokes the giver enjoys giving and perhaps receiving.

**How Does Sensate Focus Work?** The

external or internal demands to perform sexually, and anxiety about the possible inability to perform and enjoy sex, can be major culprits in many sexual problems. For example, a husband may have difficulty getting an erection because he just returned from a rigorous business trip and is trying to make love after a huge dinner with two margaritas. He can't "perform" to his (or possibly his wife's) expectations. Both mates then get nervous and try anxiously the next day to make love. His performance anxiety short-circuits both his desire and the ability to get or maintain an erection or to climax. In another common scenario, the wife fears she is taking too long to reach orgasm. She becomes anxious, sabotaging her ability to relax and climax. There are many variations of these two common scenarios. Sensate focus can take the emphasis off the goal of performance or the inability to perform. It emphasizes exploring and enjoying sensuality together.

> For most women, and for many men, the sensate focus sessions represent the first opportunity they have ever had to "think and feel" sensuously and at leisure without intrusion upon the experience by the demand for end-point release (own or partner's)...or without a sense of need to rush to "return the favor." The partner who is pleasuring is committed first to do just that: give pleasure (Masters & Johnson, 1970, p. 73).

Beyond taking the focus off the problem and performance, sensuous massage and the sensate focus exercises can express loving and sensual connection. These exercises help couples tune into deeper sensuality and can be modified to suit each couple's needs. "Sensate focus, when explored without overt performance pressures, becomes something which marital partners can shape and structure as they mutually desire" (Masters & Johnson, 1970, p. 74).

**Therapeutic Uses.** Christian counselors can see how these exercises fit with our belief system and desires for deeply intimate marital relationships. Yarhouse and Sells (2009) report that sensate focus exercises have been used "to facilitate self-awareness of what [each partner] found arousing and to facilitate feedback-rich communication about what each experienced as pleasurable" (p. 255). Following are four benefits of sensate focus to marriage enrichment and sex therapy.

1. Scripture exhorts us, "Do not be anxious about anything" (Phil. 4:6). Overcoming performance demands and anxiety follows God's plan for our lives and relationships. Relaxing and reducing anxiety or expectations, sensuously enjoying pleasure, and choosing to focus in the moment on each other are all crucial for connecting and lovemaking. They provide a way to begin overcoming performance goals and the crippling effects of performance anxiety.

2. Most couples are too busy and are therefore intimately disconnected. Scripture says to the lover, "May you ever be intoxicated with [the bride's] love" (Pr. 5:19). Inertia can set in, causing a sex life at rest to dig a deeper rut. This contrasts sharply with the way a love life in motion gathers steam. Sensual touch and increasing nonsexual physical affection jumpstart a couple's feelings of being in love and increase intimacy. Sensate focus can be an antidote not only to performance demands but also to inertia and waning intimacy.

3. Great lovemaking in marriage is complex and multidimensional. The goal must extend beyond intercourse and orgasm to intimately connecting with the mate we love. The Old Testament uses the word *know* (*yada*) for sexual interaction and lovemaking. Sensual massage and structured sensate focus provide a great way to really know your mate and to enrich love-making.

4. Tuning in to sensual touch becomes a vital way those Boomers in their fifties and sixties can keep romance alive. Lack of

muscle tone and sagging skin don't matter. Loving and touching the aging body of our beloved partner nurtures, encourages, comforts, and affirms our lover and ourselves.

**Conclusion.** In their sexual relationship, many couples "know all about the so-called erogenous zones, but many ignore the remaining 95 percent of the body" (McGinnis, 2004, p. 91). Sensual touching can be an exercise, but it is so much more! Sensate focus goes beyond performance and anxiety to connecting lovers three-dimensionally—in body, mind, and spirit. Marital partners can "know" each other and fall deeper in love as they focus on each other through relaxed, intentional, meaningful touching.

Doug Rosenau
Debra Taylor

### REFERENCES

Masters, W. H., & Johnson, V. E. (1970). *Human Sexual Inadequacy.* Bronx, NY: Ishi Press.

McGinnis, A. L. (2004). *The Friendship Factor: How to Get Closer to the People You Care For.* Minneapolis, MN: Augsburg Press.

Yarhouse, M. A., & Sells, J. N. (2009). *Family Therapies: A Comprehensive Christian Appraisal.* Downers Grove, IL: InterVarsity Press.

## DEC-R SEXUAL COACHING

**Description.** Most counselors have seen clients like Tim and Jane, who were in my office sobbing. Jane struggled to speak through her tears: "Tim wants so much more sex than I do. I wonder if something is terribly wrong with me. We can't reach a compromise." I reassured Tim and Jane during that first session that an inconsistent or unsatisfying sex life plagues most marriages at some point (Clinton & Laaser, 2010; Long, Burnett, & Thomas, 2005). I realized once again that the keys for helping them heal were creating sexual dialogue, educating them on certain critical concepts, and providing some specific coaching. I referred Jane for some individual counseling with a female colleague.

The DEC-R model (pronounced Deck-Are) is a four-step process for helping clients start to deal with their sexual issues (Sells & Yarhouse, 2011). The four steps are dialogue, education, coaching, and referral. Although the DEC-R model is taught sequentially, in reality you will find yourself jumping from one step to another throughout the therapy process. Everyone who desires to do marriage counseling can learn the basic skills of the DEC-R model and, with a little reading and practice, become comfortable in each of the four areas.

**Dialogue.** I asked Jane why she had never talked about her sexual concerns with her former therapist or Christian girlfriends. Her reply was typical: "My therapist never asked me about anything sexual. I mentioned it once to my friends, but they never picked up on it. I didn't bring it up again."

In marriage counseling as in therapy in general, counselors must give clients permission to talk about the sexual aspect of their lives and relationships (Worthington, 1989). Counselors are responsible to directly initiate comfortable sexual dialogue. The dialogue can begin very simply: "How is the sexual part of your life?" Counselors who want to create sexual dialogue may need to take a few steps.

- Accept and make peace with your own sexuality. This might involve getting some counseling or supervision to heal and grow.
- Desensitize yourself to talking about sexual topics. Take a human sexuality class. Read out loud from sexual books and engage in conversations with your mate or an appropriate friend.
- Remember that sexual responses can be reflexive. When you dialogue about sexual topics, you may experience some arousal. This is normal. It

should be noted and then ignored as you choose not to feed this sexual surge and focus instead on your client's needs. If countertransference continues with a particular client, be sure to discuss this with a supervisor or therapist and refer.

As clients learn to communicate in general but especially around sexual topics, therapy becomes meaningful and exciting. Remember that the counselor is responsible for creating dialogue. It usually will not occur without our initiation.

**Education.** A second critical aspect of sexual counseling is educating couples. We must counter myths that are learned in the locker room, from popular culture, and sadly, in the church. According to common but inaccurate cultural stereotypes, men know all about and are always ready for sex, and the size of one's anatomy is important (Good & Brooks, 2005). Television and movies teach that everyone is having affairs with few if any consequences and that lovemaking comes naturally and must be spontaneous to be fun. Magazines tell women that they must have a certain body type to be sexy and that their desire should look more like a man's desire.

Clients are yearning for sexual education. Concise, practical teaching works wonders. You'll be surprised how reading several chapters in a good sexual manual will increase your teaching skills and help your clients. Education can thrive on prescribing pertinent reading, and Christian books are increasingly available. Here are some concepts you will find yourself teaching over and over:

- Sexiness is in our minds and attitudes, not our body shape and size.
- Sex is subject to inertia. Romance and erotic passion must be kept in motion. Busy couples must intentionally structure time for lovemaking.
- Great sex does not always make intercourse and orgasms the final destination.
- The backbone of a great sex life is a committed and playful companionship—a satisfying sex life is a realistic expectation for every marriage.
- Marital conversations about sex foster fulfillment, arousal, and healing.

Strategic education is the backbone of successful sex therapy and counseling and will also be an important part of our next skill—coaching.

**Coaching.** The metaphor of coaching is appropriate for sex therapy. We aren't on the playing field with our clients. In fact, we are not even on the sidelines. We are in the locker room with dialogue, education, and helpful instructions. We then respectfully send the couple back to the privacy of their own homes and lives to play the game.

In our DEC-R model for beginning sex counseling, coaching refers especially to guiding couples beyond education into growing and healing their sexual intimacy by assigning strategic self-help exercises (Sells & Yarhouse, 2011). Of course, some couples' problems require intensive therapy, and you may need to make a referral to a more experienced sex therapist.

Many times clients have already bought self-help books and read about their problems. They may even have begun trying some exercises. Most will still need a coach/therapist to explain the exercises, guide them through them, and provide accountability.

An initial step in coaching for those learning to deal with sexual issues is finding a helpful layman's book, such as *A Celebration of Sex* (Rosenau, 2002), *Secrets of Eve* (Hart, Weber, & Taylor, 2004), and *Restoring the Pleasure* (Penner & Penner, 1993). Then, utilize exercises from the books with couples as they work toward changes.

**Referral.** We have made referral a separate part of the DEC-R model for a purpose (Sells & Yarhouse, 2011). Referral should take place strategically within all three parts of dialogue, education, and coaching. As you begin the dialogue, you may discover severe sexual abuse or a medical condition that needs immediate referral to an appropriate specialist. As you educate a couple or help them work through self-help exercises, you may realize you have exhausted your skills and need further resources. Skillful referral is crucial in sex therapy.

There are several factors to keep in mind in knowing when to make a referral. It is important to know when we are beyond our training and experience, but there are other considerations also.

- Access medical or other professional help to assist therapy. Always begin with eliminating the physical and medical issues.
- Refer when additional training and skill level is warranted. We need to know when we've reached the limit of our training and experience. Keep yourself safe and within ethical bounds.
- Know where to refer. Several important types of resources must be considered in making a sex-therapy referral. Create a list of these in your community and geographic area, including physicians, adjunct professionals, and physical therapists.

This is an exciting time in the history of the church. We are poised to tackle issues that have never been dealt with comfortably before, such as sex. Christian counselors can help by learning the skills of dialogue, education, coaching, and referral as they make a profound difference in their clients' sex lives.

**Douglas E. Rosenau**
**Michael Sytsma**
**Debra L. Taylor**

## REFERENCES


Clinton, T., & Laaser, M. (2010). *The Quick-Reference Guide to Sexuality and Relationships Counseling.* Grand Rapids, MI: Baker Books.

Good, G. E., & Brooks, G. R. (Eds.). (2005). *The New Handbook of Psychotherapy and Counseling with Men: A Comprehensive Guide to Settings, Problems, and Treatment Approaches.* San Francisco, CA: Wiley & Sons.

Hart, A. D., Weber, C. H., & Taylor, D. L. (2004). *Secrets of Eve.* Nashville, TN: Thomas Nelson.

Long, L. L., Burnett, J. A., & Thomas, V. (2005). *Sexuality Counseling: An Integrative Approach.* Saddle River, NJ: Prentice Hall.

Penner, C. L., & Penner, J. J. (1993). *Restoring the Pleasure: Complete Step-by-Step Programs to Help Couples Overcome the Most Common Sexual Barriers.* Nashville, TN: Thomas Nelson.

Rosenau, D. E. (2002). *A Celebration of Sex.* Nashville, TN: Thomas Nelson.

Sells, J. N., & Yarhouse, M. A. (2011). *Counseling Couples in Conflict: A Relational Restoration Model.* Downers Grove, IL: InterVarsity Press.

Worthington, E. L., Jr. (1989). *Marriage Counseling: A Christian Approach to Counseling Couples.* Downers Grove, IL: InterVarsity Press.


## SEXUAL AND GENDER IDENTITY

**Description.** Sexual identity constitutes the way in which individuals label or identify themselves in terms of their sexual preferences. Common labels include *gay*, *lesbian*, *bisexual*, and *heterosexual*, or *straight*. Sexual identity is different from sexual attraction and sexual orientation (which refers to a stable pattern of one's sexual attractions).

Gender identity refers to a person's sense of being male or female. It can be thought of in terms of how masculine or feminine a person feels, which is often tied to social and cultural messages concerning what it means to be male or female in that specific cultural context.

**History.** The terms for sexual orientation emerged in the mental-health literature in the late 19th century, and the language for sexual identity emerged in the 20th century. The development of language for sexual identity is due in part to the fact that language for identifying oneself as gay, lesbian, or otherwise was nonexistent until the advent of modern Western sociopolitical movements (Greenberg, 1980). Until recently, sexual identity was not differentiated from sexual orientation, but treated as synonymous.

Sexual identity is believed to develop gradually. Theories of heterosexual identity have been somewhat sparse (see Mohr, 2002; Worthington, Savoy, Dillon, & Vernaglia, 2002), but many models of nonheterosexual identity development exist (e.g., Cass, 1979; Sophie, 1986; Troiden, 1989; Yarhouse, 2001). The general trend in these latter models is from awareness of same-sex attraction, to same-sex behavior and questioning of one's identity, to identity labeling and the initiation of a same-sex relationship. Current data on young people suggest that between 1% and 2% of females identify as lesbian, and 2% to 5% identify as bisexual. In males, 2% to 4% identify as gay, and 1% to 3% identify as bisexual (Chandra, Mosher, Copen, & Sionean, 2011). A slightly greater percentage may experience attraction to the same sex but not take on a nonheterosexual identity.

Children begin sensing themselves as male or female between 18 months and 3 years of age. This gender identity most often corresponds with biological sex. However, in some cases gender identity is experienced as a conflict with one's biological sex. This is often first understood through gender nonconforming behaviors observed by parents or caregivers, and then it can be noted through comparisons with one's peers in terms of gender atypical interests and activities.

**Assessment.** When clients present with sexual identity questions or concerns, it is imperative that their motivation for treatment be assessed, primarily through a clinical interview. Some individuals may have been coerced into therapy by parents or spouses, and others' goals may be unrealistic, given the current findings of research. Assessment of motivation, therefore, will often guide treatment as well as give direction to possible points of psychoeducation that would assist clients in making informed decisions.

Gender identity questions or concerns are often assessed through parent interviews, observation of the child, and additional clinical interviews or play-therapy activities.

**Treatment.** Historically, there have been two approaches to treatment available for clients presenting with sexual identity concerns. These involve attempts to change orientation (reorientation or conversion therapy) or steps to affirm a gay identity (gay affirmative treatment). However, mental-health professionals are trending toward a third model, which is more client-centered and avoids a predefined treatment goal (APA Task Force on Appropriate Therapeutic Responses to Sexual Orientation, 2009). This approach focuses on acceptance of clients, support, and facilitating a sexual identity that is aligned with personal values.

Gender identity concerns have often been addressed by accurate assessment of gender identity disorder, if that is the case. In such cases, enhancing self-understanding and identifying ways of managing or resolving dysphoria is important (Carroll, 2007). Parents sometimes choose to ignore their children's gender atypicality while implementing interventions that reinforce alignment with a child's biological sex. Those who endorse transitioning to the preferred gender identity have introduced the controversial practice of blocking puberty and introducing hormones of the preferred gender later in adolescence once a decision is made to transition.

**Biblical and Spiritual Issues.** Many of those who seek mental-health treatment for sexual identity concerns experience conflict due to their religious beliefs and values. Those who hold to a traditional Christian sexual ethic may be particularly distressed because they believe that acting on attractions to the same sex does not correspond with God's intentions for the healthy expression of sexuality. A traditional understanding would hold that sexual expression belongs only within the bounds of heterosexual marriage. Many individuals may experience great emotional pain if they wish to eventually identify as heterosexual, marry, and have children through traditional means but are unable to experience change in their sexual attractions. They may need significant support to live in a manner they deem to be faithful to biblical standards, which may include celibacy, as well as to find a place in church communities whose activities and teachings are designed primarily for the heterosexuals and their families. Indeed, they may choose to form their identity chiefly around their faith. Notably, not all individuals identifying as Christian hold to a traditional sexual ethic; they may interpret Scripture in a manner that does not conflict with same-sex behavior.

Gender identity concerns raise similar questions and conflicts, although the behavioral component is less clear and less of a focus for many who experience dysphoria. Typically, their primary interest is managing the dysphoria itself, and the experience of conflict is often understood as a reflection of the fallen human condition rather than an experience that is volitional.

Mark A. Yarhouse
Heidi J. Erickson

## REFERENCES

APA Task Force on Appropriate Therapeutic Responses to Sexual Orientation. (2009). *Report of the Task Force on Appropriate Therapeutic Response to Sexual Orientation.* Washington, DC: American Psychological Association.

Carroll, R. A. (2007). Gender Dyshphoria and Transgender Experiences. In S. R. Leublum (Ed.). *Principles and Practices of Sex Therapy* (pp. 477-508). New York, NY: Guilford.

Cass, V. C. (1979). Homosexual identity formation: A theoretical model. *Journal of Homosexuality, 4,* 219-235.

Chandra, A., Mosher, W. D., Copen, C., & Sionean, C. (2011, March). Sexual behavior, sexual attraction, and sexual identity in the United States: Data from the 2006-2008 National Survey of Family Growth. *National Health Statistics Reports, 36,* 1-47.

Greenberg, D. G. (1980). *The Construction of Homosexuality.* Chicago, IL: University of Chicago Press.

Mohr, J. J. (2002). Heterosexual identity and the heterosexual therapist: Using identity as a framework for understanding sexual orientation issues in psychotherapy. *The Counseling Psychologist, 30,* 532-566. doi:10.1177/00100002030004003

Sophie, J. (1986). A critical examination of stage theories of lesbian identity development. *Journal of Homosexuality, 12*(2), 39-51.

Troiden, R. R. (1989). The formation of homosexual identities. *Journal of Homosexuality, 17,* 43-73.

Worthington, R. L., Savoy, H. B., Dillon, F. R., & Vernaglia, E. R. (2002). Heterosexual identity development: A multidimensional model of individual and social identity. *The Counseling Psychologist, 30*(4), 496-531. doi:10.1177/001000020 30004002

Yarhouse, M. A. (2001). Sexual identity development: The influence of valuative frameworks on identity synthesis. *Psychotherapy, 38*(3), 331-341.

## HOMOSEXUALITY

**Description and Prevalence.** Although the term *homosexuality* did not exist until the early to mid-19th century, homosexuality or a homosexual orientation has been described in literature from ancient times. It refers to an enduring and persistent sexual and emotional attraction toward the same sex. About 2% to 3% of the adult population in the United States reports having a homosexual orientation (Yarhouse, Butman, & McRay, 2005). It can be helpful to distinguish between same-sex attraction, a homosexual orientation, and a gay (or lesbian) identity. *Same-sex attraction* refers to an individual's experience of erotic attraction toward someone of the same sex. *Homosexual orientation* is a consistent attraction for members of the same sex. *Gay* and *lesbian* are contemporary sociocultural labels meant to convey something about one's sexual attractions or orientation. The term *gay* has been preferred by some sexual minorities as a result of a potentially negative stigma associated with the term *homosexual.*

**Relevant History.** Although same-sex sexual behaviors have been reported for centuries, the modern gay-rights movement has been the recipient of increased focus in society and the church community. This movement was made possible by a number of historic factors, not the least of which was the removal of homosexuality from the *Diagnostic and Statistical Manual of Mental Disorders* (*DSM*) in 1973. Following the removal of homosexuality in the *DSM*, many other relevant legal challenges have continued the momentum to reduce stigma associated with homosexuality and increase the visibility of sexual minorities in society through various media and entertainment outlets.

The relevant history concerning causation includes several different views regarding the etiology of homosexuality. Research has not established one particular cause of a homosexual orientation. Some scientists suggest that a homosexual orientation is largely the result of "nature" and reference studies of direct genetic evidence or exposure to prenatal hormones. Others prefer to look to "nurture," or the idea that homosexuality is caused by environmental variables, citing most often theories about parent-child relationships or childhood sexual abuse. The emerging consensus among professionals is that both nature and nurture probably contribute to differing degrees in the development of same-sex attractions, though these contributions may be weighted differently for different people (Jones & Yarhouse, 2000).

**Assessment.** A person's sexual identity and/or attractions can be assessed through a clinical interview in which past history and current functioning is explored. It is generally recommended that mental-health providers approach clients respectfully and create an environment in which the people feel safe to share their experiences. Open questions about individuals' experience of same-sex attractions, reasons for seeking treatment, relationship history, and perspective of their sexuality are often relevant as well. Although assessment measures exploring homosexuality are limited, counselors and therapists may find it helpful to use the Kinsey scale or the Shively and DeCecco measure of sexual attraction. At times and depending on the clients' age and situation, it may also be appropriate to include parents, other family members, or romantic partners in portions of the assessment and treatment process.

**Treatment.** Just as there are differing views on the etiology of homosexuality, there are some who suggest that one's sexual orientation can be changed, and others see this as impossible and unwarranted. In the treatment for homosexuality, two polarized models are often noted in the literature. Gay-affirmative therapy has emerged less as a specific model of treatment and more as a posture clinicians take toward those who experience same-sex attraction. The assumption in this approach is that the person is discovering a gay or lesbian identity, and this identity is essentially being affirmed as a preexisting reality with which the client is coming to terms. Such a posture supports "coming out" as gay or lesbian and finding resources within the gay, lesbian, and bisexual (GLB) community for support as a gay person.

In contrast to gay-affirmative therapy, reorientation therapy (sometimes referred to as conversion therapy) focuses on changing orientation from homosexual to heterosexual. Treatment approaches have ranged from behavioral and aversive approaches to psychoanalytic models. More recently, reparative therapy has emerged as a subtype of reorientation therapy and focused on addressing normal emotional needs that have gone unmet and are being expressed through same-sex attraction and behavior (APA Task Force on Appropriate Therapeutic Responses to Sexual Orientation, 2009).

In addition to these models, several "third way" approaches for those who are conflicted by their experiences of same-sex attraction have emerged. One such approach is referred to as sexual-identity therapy (see sitframework.com), which focuses more on labeling sexual identity rather than changing orientation. This form of therapy is designed to help individuals make meaning of their attractions and live and identify themselves in ways that are consistent with their beliefs and values.

The method and style of treatment will vary depending on clients' personal wishes and perspective on their sexuality. Both individual and group psychotherapy has been shown to be beneficial in assisting members of the GLB community, and treatment goals will likely vary, depending on one's wishes to affirm either a homosexual or a heterosexual identity (Yarhouse, 2010).

**Biblical and Spiritual Issues.** The traditional Christian sexual ethic is that genital sexual expression was intended by God to occur in the context of a union between one man and one woman in marriage (Yarhouse, 2010). The book of Genesis displays God's design for sexual intimacy within a heterosexual relationship. The Genesis story is also understood to introduce the effect of the Fall on all of creation, including human sexuality. The traditional Christian sexual ethic, then, considers homosexuality to be the result of the Fall, and same-sex behavior is viewed as sin. Other biblical texts are often cited regarding homosexuality, including Genesis 19:1-26; Leviticus 20:13; Romans 1:24-32; 1 Corinthians 6:9-11; and 1 Timothy 1:8-11. In recent years, some theologians have provided alternative interpretations to some of these passages, lending support for gay-affirmative churches and splits in some mainstream Christian denominations in the United States. Even as church groups and congregations struggle with how to respond to those who experience same-sex attraction, the research has also been clear that Christians who experience same-sex attraction often experience an internal struggle with issues of religious identity and faith (Yarhouse & Tan, 2005).

Mark A. Yarhouse
Tiffany C. Erspamer

### REFERENCES

APA Task Force on Appropriate Therapeutic Responses to Sexual Orientation. (2009). *Report of the Task Force on Appropriate Therapeutic Responses to Sexual Orientation.* Washington, DC: American Psychological Association.

Jones, S. L., & Yarhouse, M. A. (2000). *Homosexuality: The use of Scientific Research in the Church's Moral Debate.* Downers Grove, IL: InterVarsity Press.

Yarhouse, M. A. (2010). *Homosexuality and the Christian.* Minneapolis, MN: Bethany House.

Yarhouse, M. A., Butman, R. E., & McRay, B. W. (2005). *Modern Psychopathologies: A Comprehensive Christian Appraisal.* Downers Grove, IL: InterVarsity Press.

Yarhouse, M. A., & Tan, E. S. N. (2005). Addressing religious conflicts in adolescents who experience sexual identity confusion. *Professional Psychology: Research and Practice, 26*(5), 530-536.

## HOMOSEXUALS SEEKING CHANGE

**Describing Change.** CNN announced with a flourish, both on television and their website, "An explosive new study says some gay people can turn straight if they really want to" (see Spitzer, 2003). Famed psychiatrist Robert Spitzer of Columbia University—ironically, one of the key advocates for dropping homosexuality from *Diagnostic and Statistical Manual of Mental Disorders* (*DSM-III*) in 1973—completed a study of 200 "ex-gays" (143 males and 57 females with an average age of 43) to determine whether and how some people can change their sexual orientation.

Based on phone interviews running about 45 to 60 minutes with each participant, the study asked 60 questions about sexual behavior, feelings, history, change attempts, relapse and success, and other related topics. Spitzer announced his findings at a meeting of the American Psychiatric Association, which, through an official spokesperson, made it clear that selecting a presentation does not imply associational endorsement of its findings.

Spitzer, who does not offer or practice same-sex change therapy and began the study as a change skeptic, indicated that 66% of the men and 44% of the women had genuinely changed, arriving at "good heterosexual functioning." This was defined as "being in a sustained, loving, heterosexual relationship" for the past year, deriving emotional satisfaction from it, having satisfying sexual relations at least once monthly without (or rarely) thinking about homosexual fantasies while having heterosexual sex. Furthermore, fully 89% of the men and 95% of the women were not bothered, or were bothered only slightly, by unwanted homosexual feelings at any time (see also Koblin et al., 2003).

Stan Jones and Mark Yarhouse (2007) tested the two primary assertions behind the embrace of homosexuality by the American Psychological Association: (a) Change therapies do not work in changing gays to heterosexuals, and therefore, (b) such therapy is inherently harmful and unethical and should be condemned—not condoned—by anyone in the profession. What these two scientists found refuted both of these ideological assertions. Though not in every case, they found that some people struggling with homosexuality do change and that many others work at change in the hope that change or control of unwanted behavior and feelings is possible. They also found that attempts at change, though not always successful, were not dangerous or harmful in any way.

These are just two studies in the growing body of empirical literature showing that change away from homosexual behavior and feelings is possible and that it is not harmful to those who attempt such change (see also Kronemeyer, 1980; Nicolosi, 1991; Rosik, 2003; Satinover, 1996). Both of these studies include the entire corpus of change research, and they are essentially ignored by gay activists in the counseling professions because they challenge the core ideology of homosexuality and gay living as an immutable condition—especially as a desirable and preferable way of living.

**Dilemma.** The person who professes a belief in Christ and who seeks to change or control his unwanted homosexual behavior and attractions is in a mental-health quandary. He or she is caught in the intense debate about differing sexual and human values, client self-determination, therapeutic choice, and doing difficult and responsible therapy with excellence around the many dilemmas of sexual behavior and orientation.

On one hand, the secular mental-health professions argue that the only legitimate goal is to help struggling individuals accept and assimilate their homosexual feelings and attractions—"once gay, always gay" is a central belief of this unscientific ideology. This worldview also believes that homosexual feelings are a sign of a gay nature just waiting to break out and become the core identity of the person. Many people are challenged to embrace a gay lifestyle and culture as a superior way of living. Same-sex behavior and all that goes with it are seen by most of our secular colleagues as a normal variant of human sexuality.

Many Christian professionals, on the other hand, believe that homosexual feelings and actions are chosen values and behavior and that all that clients need to do is choose to forsake this way of living and walk in the sexual purity that God will give them if they ask. Sadly, some have declined to work in this arena because they do not want to put their licenses at risk or alienate colleagues who—because they view homosexuality as an immutable condition, akin to race or ethnicity—believe that offering any type of change therapy is ineffective, harmful, and unethical.

For all of these conflicted reasons, the struggling believer is faced with a shrinking population of mental-health change agents. Fewer and fewer therapists are willing to deliver the change effort necessary to help struggling clients live lives that are consistent with their religious and spiritual values.

**A Principled Third Way Exists.** We believe a third way exists that avoids these extremes—that honors God's revelation in the Bible and accepts certain factual realities about homosexuality. We believe in and will advocate for a protected "carve-out" for this third way—for an effective and ethically sensitive same-sex change therapy (Ohlschlager, 2011; Hamilton & Henry, 2009). We argue for the fundamental right of competent therapeutic change services (see Corey, Corey, & Callanan, 2009) to be delivered by professionals in every mental-health discipline in granting all struggling clients who want to leave the gay lifestyle and live according to their understanding of God's revelation in the Bible. To offer only gay-affirming therapy is ethically insensitive and scientifically indefinable. For our professions to recognize and respect those who don't want it even in the face of the most torrid advocacy, client choice should rule here as in every other arena of psychotherapy delivery (for example, even with other behaviors that pose biological roots such as quitting smoking, alcoholism, sexual addiction, or obesity).

We also believe that Christian counseling should be in the vanguard of defining and defending this third way—arguing for these rights and for creating therapies that genuinely work for people in need (American Association of Christian Counselors, 2004). We argue in the affirmative, then, that the right to professional practice and, as a client or patient, to receive consent-based same-sex change therapy is grounded on these things:

*Clinical ethics.* Grounded on client self-determination, respect for religious diversity and multicultural values, and informed consent, all of which support the cardinal clinical ethic that a client who wants to change or control his or her sexual behavior will not be denied the opportunity to do so.

*Clinical etiology.* We recognize that homosexual feelings and attractions involve a complex interplay of bio-psycho-social-spiritual dynamics and that homosexual etiology is a challenging and multifactored phenomenon that is not completely understood by the best science we have today. We also believe that, unlike sexual feelings, gay identity is a volitional process and that competent adults can also decide to leave the gay lifestyle and mature in their identity in Christ.

*Bio-psycho-social science.* There is a need to develop an honest (rather than an ideological and politically correct) science of human sexuality, which does not support the assertion that a gay orientation is an unchanging and immutable condition. This includes the incremental development and pursuit of an evidence-based determination of how and under what conditions it is possible to change homosexual behavior, feelings, and orientation (see Hamilton & Henry, 2009).

*American law.* The speech, association, due process, and religious freedom rights contained in the 1st and 14th Amendments to the United States Constitution and in every state constitution in America uphold the right of citizens to receive religious-based change therapy and of professional counselors and ministers to offer and deliver it.

*The Bible and the church.* Grounded on the revelation of God in the Bible and historic orthodox Christian ethics, which reveals that homosexual practice and advocacy is not a biblical practice, but is counter to God's prescribed design for heterosexual marriage and family life.

**Conclusion.** Same-sex change therapy is, admittedly, a difficult and often unsuccessful intervention. It succeeds in only one-third to one-half of all cases, a fact that competent counselors should disclose to their clients seeking change (Ohlschlager, 2011). Further ongoing research needs to be conducted to determine the most effective protocols and treatment strategies for intervention. In a professional counseling relationship, there should be no discrimination toward those seeking to affirm or change their behavior. It requires expertise and experience beyond that of most professional counselors. We encourage pastors and lay helpers to work with professional therapists in serving the same-sex struggler who, because of Christ, desires to walk away from gay behavior and lifestyles. And it is in Christ's power, by invitation to the Holy Spirit to daily come inside and transform that which is renounced and unwanted and to live instead in new life and new hope that is embraced and delighted in. What is impossible for man is possible with God.

TIM CLINTON
GEORGE OHLSCHLAGER

## REFERENCES

American Association of Christian Counselors. (2004). *AACC Christian Counseling Code of Ethics*. Forest, VA: Author.

Corey, G., Corey, M., & Callanan, P. (2009). *Issues and Ethics in the Helping Professions* (7th Ed.). Pacific Grove, CA: Brooks/Cole.

Hamilton, J., & Henry, P. (Eds.). (2009). *Handbook of Therapy for Unwanted Homosexual Attractions: A Guide to Treatment*. Xulon Press.

Jones, S., & Yarhouse, M. (2007). *Ex-Gays: A Longitudinal Study of Religiously Mediated Change in Sexual Orientation*. Downers Grove, IL: IVP Academic.

Koblin, B. A., Chesney, M. A., Husnik, M. J., Boseman, S., Celum, C. L., Buchbinder, S.,...Coates, T. J. (2003). High-risk behaviors among men who have sex with men in 6 U.S. cities: Baseline data from the EXPLORE study. *American Journal of Public Health, 93*, 926-932.

Kronemeyer, R. (1980). *Overcoming Homosexuality*. New York, NY: Macmillan.

Nicolosi, J. (1991). *Reparative Therapy of Male Homosexuality: A New Clinical Approach*. Northvale, NJ: Aronson.

Ohlshlager, G. (2011). *Advanced Consent Practice with Change-Seeking, Ego-Dystonic Homosexuals* (Presentation at the AACC World Conference). Nashville, TN.

Rosik, C. H. (2003). Motivational, ethical, and epistemological foundations in the clinical treatment of unwanted homoerotic attraction. *Journal of Marital and Family Therapy, 29*, 29-38.

Satinover, J. (1996). *Homosexuality and the Politics of Truth*. Grand Rapids, MI: Baker Books.

Spitzer, R. L. (2003), Can some gay men and lesbians change their sexual orientation? Two hundred participants reporting a change from homosexual to heterosexual orientation. *Archives of Sexual Behavior, 32*(5), 403-417.

## SEXUAL-IDENTITY THERAPY

Professional codes of conduct for the state-licensed professional provider require that the highest ethical codes be maintained in terms of providing unbiased treatment to all clients. The unlicensed Christian counselor or helper may provide soul care or lay counseling to those struggling with sexual-orientation issues without professional repercussions.

**DESCRIPTION.** Sexual-identity therapy (SIT) is a framework to "aid mental-health practitioners in helping people arrive at a healthy and personally acceptable resolution of sexual identity and value conflicts" (Throckmorton & Yarhouse, 2006). The framework was developed by Warren Throckmorton and Mark Yarhouse and endorsed by former American Psychological Association president Nick Cummings, psychiatrist Robert Spitzer, and the provost of Wheaton College, Stanton Jones.

Sexual-identity therapy places emphasis on helping clients identify and live according to their core beliefs and values about sexuality. Throckmorton and Yarhouse (2006) state that their recommendations "are not sexual reorientation therapy protocols in disguise," but a framework to help therapists work with clients to pursue lives they value.

**RELEVANT HISTORY.** The framework was first conceptualized in 2005 by Warren Throckmorton and Mark Yarhouse and built on Yarhouse's research into sexual identity (Yarhouse, 2001; Yarhouse & Tan, 2004; Yarhouse, Tan, & Pawlowski, 2005). The SIT framework was published on a website dedicated to the approach in 2006 and then presented at the American Psychological Association convention in San Francisco in 2007. The SIT framework is intended to be under continual revision due to the need to incorporate ongoing research regarding sexual orientation. The current website dedicated to the approach is sitframework.com.

The framework for SIT is presented in four steps: assessment, advanced informed consent, psychotherapy, and sexual identity synthesis. At any point during the therapy, a previous step may be revisited for further investigation or to explore a new direction in the therapy.

**Assessment.** In addition to standard mental-health assessment, the first step in SIT is to explore the reasons clients request therapy and what they hope to accomplish. This includes an assessment of sexuality and beliefs regarding sexuality. Furthermore, therapists should assist clients to clarify their values in order to determine their preferred course of action. Because therapists practicing in this manner do not prescribe a particular value or behavioral course of action, the assessment process must be individualized.

**Advanced Informed Consent.** Therapists inform clients about current practice and information regarding sexual orientation. One of the more recent documents informs clients that no consensus currently exists about the causal factors that drive sexual orientation (APA Task Force on Therapeutic Responses to Sexual Orientation, 2009). Therapists practicing within the SIT framework inform clients that the major mental-health associations do not consider homosexuality to be a mental illness. Sexual reorientation remains a controversial issue, but therapists inform clients that sexual identity may change in the pursuit of congruence with traditional religious beliefs, but sexual orientation is thought to be more durable for many if not most people. In short, clients are provided state-of-the-art scientific findings on sexual orientation.

**Psychotherapy.** SIT provides a framework for existing techniques rather than a specific method of psychotherapy. Presumably, any number of therapeutic models could be used to facilitate congruence in keeping with SIT. Indeed, Yarhouse (2008) published one such variation on SIT for a narrative approach. Tan and Yarhouse (2010) provided several case studies of the use of mindfulness techniques in facilitating the SIT goal of congruence.

If a therapist's value position is in conflict with the client's preferred direction, a referral to a more suitable mental professional may be indicated. The goal of therapy is to help the person explore and eventually live more comfortably within a sexual identity that is congruent with personal values and beliefs. Therapists should continually assess for the mental-health effects of interventions and be prepared to move to clinical interventions that directly address mental-health sequelae often associated with sexual identity conflict (e.g., depression, anxiety).

**Sexual-Identity Synthesis.** As clients settle on a course of action, therapists can assist them by making plans to pursue actions and decisions congruent with their values and beliefs. The decision is the clients', but they are advised against making abrupt changes in sexual behavior until they are comfortable with their new identity. Many clients find it helpful to attend support groups and avoid social situations that do not support the new identity.

Warren Throckmorton
Mark A. Yarhouse

## REFERENCES

APA Task Force on Appropriate Therapeutic Responses to Sexual Orientation. (2009). *Report of the Task Force on Appropriate Therapeutic Response to Sexual Orientation.* Washington, DC: American Psychological Association.

Tan, E. S. N., & Yarhouse, M. A. (2010). Facilitating congruence between religious beliefs and sexual identity with mindfulness. *Psychotherapy, 47*(4), 500-511.

Throckmorton, W., & Yarhouse, M. A. (2006). Sexual identity therapy: Practice guidelines for managing sexual identity conflicts. Unpublished paper. Retrieved February 1, 2011, from http://sitframework.com/wp-content/uploads/2009/07/sexualidentitytherapyframeworkfinal.pdf

Yarhouse, M. A. (2001). Sexual identity development: The influence of valuative frameworks on identity synthesis. *Psychotherapy, 38*(3), 331-341.

Yarhouse, M. A. (2008). Narrative sexual identity therapy. *American Journal of Family Therapy, 36,*1-15.

Yarhouse, M. A., & Tan, E. S. N. (2004). *Sexual Identity Synthesis: Attributions, Meaning-Making, and the Search for Congruence.* Lanham, MD: University Press of America.

Yarhouse, M. A., Tan, E. S. N., & Pawlowski, L. M. (2005). Sexual identity development and synthesis among LGB-identified and LGB dis-identified persons. *Journal of Psychology and Theology, 33*(1), 3-16.

## HIV/AIDS COUNSELING

**Description.** The AIDS pandemic, which began almost 30 years ago, has spread and continues to spread through sexual intercourse, IV drug use, transfusions, breastfeeding, and other contact with such bodily secretions as semen, vaginal secretions, blood, and breast milk. The estimated number of people worldwide currently infected with HIV/AIDS is 33 million, with 2.6 million new cases and 1.8 million deaths per year (Kalling, 2008). The total number of 30 years of infections is approximately 70 million men, women, and children. This number compares to the loss of 66 million souls in World War II, 15 million deaths in World War I, and the mass executions under Stalin's regime of 20 million people. Not through bullets or bombs, but through intimate human contact, almost 2 million persons are dying each year.

How can we respond? What can we say that brings hope and healing to those who are suffering from this viral destruction of their immune system?

**Current Counseling of HIV-Positive Patients.** The secular standard of care for HIV-positive individuals is education (Volberding, 2008; Padian, van de Wijgert, & O'Brien, 1994). Patients who test positive are taught how the virus is spread by risky behaviors. They are also taught how the infection is not spread, attempting to dispel some of the myths and disinformation. Infected individuals need to know the differences between exposure, testing positive to HIV, infections, AIDS, and how this information is related to the "viral load" that clients carry. Compliance with difficult regimes of medications and follow-up blood testing are essential to keep the HIV/AIDS patient healthy (Albers, 1990, 1998).

There is so much more that we can do as professional counselors, as caring individuals, and as followers of the Great Physician. We can educate our colleagues, and we can show what real caring does in a counseling relationship, how prayer fosters hope and strength, and how Christ can transform and heal broken, grief-stricken people with HIV into growing, hope-filled new creations on life-support from the Holy Spirit—people who can share their faith and journey with those they love (Albers, 1987).

**Preparing for HIV/AIDS Counseling and Ministry.** HIV/AIDS is not a complex disease, so therapists should become familiar with how the virus is spread, how it is not spread, the different stages of the disease, antiviral medications to control the disease, and varying ways the disease affects people (Albers, 1990).

The counseling process begins when we help clients deal with their grief, empower them to push through their denial, and walk with them as they accept their infection and then move on. Our goal is to help them to grow, embrace the trial they face, and mature spiritually, accepting God's gift of grace and maturing to be more like Jesus. Together, we will go through the peaks and valleys of their other emotional needs and previous emotional damage, helping them to love others as Christ loves us and sharing their journey openly and confidently (Albers, 1990, 1998).

Antiviral research has given HIV/AIDS patients temporary hope, longer lives, better health, and fewer infections. Our counseling will offer them eternal hope, improved relationships, growth in their spiritual lives, and true compassion and love for others (Albers, 1990).

**Gregg R. Albers**

## REFERENCES


Albers, G. (1987). *Plague in Our Midst.* Lafayette, LA: Huntington House.

Albers, G. (1990). *Counseling and AIDS.* Dallas, TX: Word.

Albers, G. (1998). *Counseling the Sick and Terminally Ill.* Dallas, TX: Word.

Kallings, L. O. (2008). The first postmodern pandemic: 25 years of HIV/AIDS. *Journal of Internal Medicine.* doi:10.1111/j.1365-2796.2007.01910.x

Padian, N. S., van de Wijgert, J. H. H., & O'Brien, T. R. (1994). Interventions for sexual partners of HIV-infected or high-risk individuals. In R. J. DiClemente & J. L. Peterson (Eds.), *Preventing AIDS: Theories and Interventions* (pp. 223-242). New York, NY: Plenum Press.

Volberding, P. (2008). *Global HIV/AIDS Medicine.* Philadelphia, PA: Elsevier.

# 16

# FAMILIES AND FAMILY THERAPY

## FAMILY-OF-ORIGIN ISSUES IN BLENDED FAMILIES

**Description.** The family in which one grows and develops is referred to as the *family of origin.* In our original families, we learn patterns of behavior that are played out in current and future relationships. These learned relationship patterns are then reenacted in the creation of new families.

During the 1950s, the idea that psychological problems could be explained in terms of circular, repetitive events in interpersonal relationships took hold in the field of family therapy (Nichols, 2009). Couple work focused on each spouse's family of origin as a major influence in a marriage. When two people marry, they bring to the marriage their ideas and beliefs as well as their experiences with parents, siblings, and extended family. Unresolved issues related to the family of origin are carried to the newly formed couple relationship. Couples are then faced with the task of renegotiating issues that previously defined them individually and in past relationships.

Treatment with blended families is complex because there are a number of behavior patterns operating in any given family system that must be identified and addressed. Unresolved issues ("baggage") related to interpersonal patterns of behavior accumulate if untreated. In remarriage, a spouse may bring emotional baggage from the family of origin as well as from the first marriage, the separation and divorce, and the period between marriages.

Trouble arises when one or both members of a blended family expect the other to "fix" their baggage. This expectation is unrealistic and inevitably leads to disappointment and conflict. Spouses must sort out their own baggage and work to resolve it. Doing so frees the remarried couple to begin afresh and focus on issues unique to the blended family.

**Assessment.** Three generational genograms are used to identify couples' learned interactional patterns and serve as a visual map for the therapist. Genograms help the therapist to track family patterns (McGoldrick, Gerson, & Petry, 2008) and outline previous marriages and history. Multigenerational genograms also highlight areas of loss, which are important to the histories of blended families (Paul & Paul, 1986).

Other areas of assessment include each family's life-cycle stage, expectations for the blended family, child adjustment issues, and the couple's ability to tolerate ambiguity and work to resolve differences from the past with former partners.

**Treatment.** In treatment, blended families must become open, flexible systems in which a new group identity is created and maintained. A couple must develop a new model of operating and form a family in which rigid patterns give way to a more flexible style that accommodates change and the needs of many (Walters, Carter, Papp, & Silverstein, 1988). Given the influence of family of origin and past marriages, challenges include how the couple communicates, how they deal with emotions, and coming to agreement on values, beliefs, and parenting.

Family therapists who use a Bowenian systems approach use the genogram not only for family assessment but also to design intervention strategies (Bowen, 1994). Goals include achieving family harmony, reducing couple conflict, negotiating marital and parental roles, improving communication, and managing conflict and stress. Role conflicts must be addressed between members of the original families and the parent-child bonds operating in the newly formed family. Couples must sort out their interpersonal baggage, or problems will continue. Therapy with blended families identifies past and current patterns of interaction influencing the newly formed family, helps develop open coparent relationships with former spouses, establishes parental boundaries and responsibilities in a clear fashion, and works with children regarding divided loyalties and bonding (Nichols, 2009).

When a child is the focus of treatment, the family therapist may request that all parents participate in the therapy. This may include joint sessions in which current spouses work with biological parents. However, the therapist must assess the biological parents' and stepparents' ability to work together to resolve issues for the sake of children.

Family therapy with blended families often includes parents and stepparents, stepsiblings, and half siblings. The decision regarding who will be included in the family work depends on the divorced parents' willingness and ability to work together to help their children with adjustment issues and/or psychological problems. Approaches include various family-systems models, individual therapy targeting family of origin work, psychodrama and psychodynamic therapies, as well as specific couples models, such as the Gottman Method couple therapy.

**Spiritual Issues.** The key to building a strong and healthy family is to model all relationships after Christ. Families who pray together and follow biblical directives regarding the treatment of others have a spiritual basis for resolving conflict and relating. Family members who evidence the fruit of the Spirit—love, joy, peace, patience, kindness, goodness, faithfulness, gentleness, and self-control—will fare best at meeting the challenges of blending families. In addition, mistakes from the past should be confronted, not avoided, with the goal of change. Finally, forgiveness and grace are two healing forces needed to work through family of origin hurts and losses.

**Linda Mintle**

### REFERENCES

Bowen, M. (1994). *Family Therapy in Clinical Practice.* New York, NY: Aronson.

McGoldrick, M., & Carter, B. (1988). Forming a remarried family. In B. Carter & M. McGoldrick (Eds.), *The Changing Family Life Cycle* (pp. 399-429). New York, NY: Gardner Press.

McGoldrick, M., Gerson, R., & Petry, S. (2008). *Genograms: Assessment and Intervention* (3rd ed.). New York, NY: Norton.

Nichols, M. P. (2009). *Family Therapy: Concepts and Methods.* Boston, MA: Allyn & Bacon.

Paul, N., & Paul, B. (1986). *A Marital Puzzle.* New York, NY: Gardner Press.

Walters, M., Carter, B., Papp, P., & Silverstein, O. (1988). *The Invisible Web: Gender Patterns in Family Relationships.* New York, NY: Guilford Press.

## BLENDED FAMILIES

Nearly 100 million Americans have a step-relationship of some kind, and it is projected that half of Americans will have blended families at some point in their lifetime (Parker, 2011; Larson, 1992). Because blended-family dynamics underlie many of the individual, couple, and family presenting problems of modern-day Christian counseling, counselors need to understand stepfamily relationships, systemic dynamics, and integration processes.

**Description.** A blended family or stepfamily is formed when an adult with at least one child marries an adult who is not the child's parent. There are multiple avenues into the blended family experience. The new family relationship may have been preceded by the death of a parent, divorce, or a nonmarital birth and subsequent marriage. Blended family composition varies widely. For example, there are many different marital combinations in blended families. The couple's marriage may be a second for a spouse following divorce but the first marriage for the other, or a third marriage for one after being widowed twice and a second marriage for the other following divorce, or many other combinations. In addition, blended families may include children from only one adult (*simple* stepfamilies) or both (*complex* stepfamilies), children born to the new couple, and/or adoptive or stepchildren from previous relationships. Stepfamilies, then, are not homogeneous in their composition, but quite diverse and complex. In fact, researchers have identified 67 different types of stepfamilies. Therapy with remarried couples and blended families must consider the specific family composition and adapt accordingly.

**History.** Christian counselors should realize that the blended family is not a recent phenomenon. Many Old Testament families could be classified as blended families. However, instead of being born out of second or subsequent marriages resulting from divorce, as is generally the case in modern society, biblical blended families were born from multiple marriages. The dynamics of families like Abraham, Sarah, and Hagar's (Gen. 16; 21) or Jacob, Leah, Rachel, Zilpah, and Bilhah's (Gen. 29–37) still closely mirror those of modern-day stepfamilies.

**Assessment.** Blended families often present for treatment with similar complaints to first-marriage families, such as parenting issues, marital strife, and depression (Browning & Bray, 2007), but in addition, they also complain of frustrations with ex-spouses, multiple-home complexities, boundary ambiguities, and matters related to a lack of family identity. It is important that counselors not make the mistake of assessing blended family dilemmas through the lens of the biological family. Stepfamily functioning is different on many levels, and counselors should familiarize themselves with the differences, such as remarriage instability, stepparent roles, coparenting with the other home, loss, biological family loyalty, and emotional triangles involving biological parents, their children, and stepparents before beginning treatment.

Starting with the first phone call, explore who is connected to the family and the nature of the initial complaint, and then determine who should attend the first session. Frequently, this should be the couple. This strategy supports the dyad, avoids unforeseen first-session aggression between stepfamily members, and allows the counselor time to explore subsystem dynamics. Using genograms to map family structure and understand family process is recommended (McGoldrick, Gerson, & Shellenberger, 1999).

Early sessions should include primary subsystems: marital or biological parent and child. Then, if appropriate to the presenting problem, see another subsystem at the second or third session. Alternating sessions with the couple and other primary subsystems (e.g., sibling subsystem, biological children or stepchildren, or the stepparent-stepchildren subsystem) are advisable. The goal is to listen to everyone's concerns and form a therapeutic alliance with each subsystem. Eventually, various subsystems may be brought together for intervention, but only when the therapist deems it productive.

**Treatment.** One goal of treatment, of course, is to resolve immediate conflicts and presenting problems. However, a vital long-term goal is to make pathways so the not-so-blended family can move toward family integration. Relationship building and identity formulation is crucial to family stability. One key intervention to help facilitate this process includes psychoeducation to help family members make sense of what is happening among them. For example, stepparents need to depersonalize a child's emotional distance and view it for what it usually is—loyalty to biological parents (living or deceased), not a personal rejection of them (Deal, 2006). Psychoeducational interventions that normalize stepfamily development as well as between-home conflicts, stepparent quandaries, and children's loyalty issues help individuals relax and begin to view their family as a work in progress rather than a failure. This engenders hope and fosters a cooperative attitude.

In addition, couples in blended families frequently have unresolved attachment injuries from previous relationships (dating or a first marriage). The ghost of marriage past, as I like to refer to it, increases fear of another breakup, resulting in guardedness and quick retreats when feeling insecure (Deal & Olson, 2010). This also adds to a common triangle in blended families: biological parents who align themselves with children to the exclusion of the stepparents. This fear-based dynamic sabotages couple solidarity, parenting, and family integration.

In addition to addressing couple attachment injuries, common interventions include helping to define stepparent roles (especially regarding discipline and affection), helping children with loss and grief issues, teaching adults to allow relationship bonds to develop at their own pace (not demanding love), and actively encouraging empathy and emotional attachment between family members (Browning & Bray, 2007).

**Biblical and Spiritual Issues.** Blended families often experience spiritual shame and unworthiness stemming from divorce and social judgment from people in the church (Deal, 2006). Stepfamilies frequently feel like second-class citizens in God's kingdom. Therapy should remind them that one's family structure does not determine one's acceptance before God. Just as Old Testament faithful men and women who had less-than-perfect families received God's grace, so can people in blended families today.

**Conclusion.** Therapy with blended families requires a working knowledge of stepfamily complexities and systemic dynamics. Due to the inherent difficulties and stresses, the blended family divorce rate hovers around two-thirds. But with competent guidance, blended families can beat the odds. Preventing redivorce and strengthening the stepfamily prevents further family dissolution, gives children a healthier environment in which to grow, and strengthens the institution of marriage for the next generation.

**Ron L. Deal**

## REFERENCES


Browning, S., & Bray, J. H. (2007). Treating stepfamilies: A subsystems-based approach. In J. H. Bray & M. Stanton (Eds.), *The Wiley-Blackwell Handbook of Family Psychology* (pp. 487-496). Chichester, West Susex, United Kingdom: Blackwell.

Deal, R. L. (2006). *The Smart Stepfamily: Seven Steps to a Healthy Family.* Minneapolis, MN: Bethany House.

Deal, R. L., & Olson, D. H. (2010). *The Remarriage Checkup: Tools to Help Your Marriage Last a Lifetime.* Minneapolis, MN: Bethany House.

Larson, J. (1992). Understanding stepfamilies. *American Demographics, 14,* 360.

McGoldrick, M., Gerson, R., & Shellenberger, S. (1999). *Genograms: Assessment and Intervention.* New York, NY: Norton.

Parker, K. (2011). *Pew Research Center Report: A Portrait of Stepfamilies.* Retrieved from http://pewsocialtrends.org/2011/01/13/a-portrait-of-stepfamilies/


## GENERATIONAL TRANSMISSION

**Description.** I was listening to Jennie as she poured out her expressions of pain over the unfaithfulness of her husband, Ron. He had left her and their children and moved in with his father while carrying on the affair.

"There is so much I don't understand," she

explained. "But the one thing I really can't get over is that since Ron was 13, he has had absolutely no relationship with his father. They never spoke and never saw each other."

"What happened when he was 13?" I asked.

"His father had an affair and left the family. Ron refused to ever see him again after that."

I turned over my intake sheet and noticed the ages of their children. I said to Jennie, "That's interesting. Your oldest son is 13. Ron is acting out the very thing he has hated in his father all these years, and at the time when his son is the exact same age he was when his father left."

Jennie just looked stunned—this connection hadn't even entered her mind. I reminded her that as part of the second commandment, God said, "I, the LORD your God, am a jealous God, punishing the children for the sin of the parents to the third and fourth generation" (Ex. 20:5). I quickly added that I didn't believe all generational patterns are God's punishment—they are just the consequence of sin modeled by parents as their children watched. The research in family systems points out that these dysfunctional generational patterns usually continue in a family for three to four generations. Observation of families by researchers confirmed the pattern set out by God.

**BIBLICAL PATTERNS.** One can also see this pattern in the biblical family of Abraham. For three generations, beginning with Abraham and Sarah, there was a repetitive pattern of favoritism shown by the parents to the children. Both Abraham and Sarah favored Isaac, and the consequence was that the other son Ishmael was sent away. When Isaac married Rebekah, they had twins. In this case, the pattern of favoritism changed as each parent favored one child and rejected the other. The consequence was that one son, Jacob, fled from the home after stealing his elder brother's birthright. When Jacob married, the pattern of favoritism changed again. He had two wives and favored one wife, Rachel, over the other, Leah. As a result, Jacob favored the children of Rachel and had very limited relationships with his other children. Again, the consequence was that one of the children, in this case Joseph, was betrayed by his brothers and sent away into slavery in Egypt.

In each of the three generations, the dysfunctional pattern intensified. First, Ishmael was sent away because of Sarah's jealousy. Second, when Jacob was sent away, his mother, Rebekah, feared for his life. Then in the third generation, when Joseph was sent away, his brothers had fully intended to kill him but sold him instead. Finally, Joseph became the transitional person to stop the dysfunctional pattern.

**RESEARCH.** Current research, particularly that being done by molecular biologist Michael K. Skinner and his associates at Washington State University, is looking deeper to reveal a molecular basis to these generational patterns. They are finding that the life experiences of one generation cause changes in the structure of the DNA in either the sperm or the egg. Their theory is that there are on/off switches in our DNA. A life experience of a grandfather or grandmother could turn one of these off switches to on, and the effect would be passed on for several generations. For example, a grandfather starts drinking at age 11. He turns on the alcoholism switch, and it affects his sons and his grandsons.

Larry Feig, director of the Sackler Graduate School at Tufts University in Boston, has researched the same connections. In an article in *The Journal of Neuroscience,* he points out that qualities in our own lives can be influenced by the environment our grandmothers experienced when they were children or adolescents. In a 2006 study done in Overkalix, Sweden, researchers found a number of intriguing generational connections, such as the correlation between a father having a poor food supply as a child and a lower risk of cardiovascular death in his grandchildren.

As counselors, we cannot look at the on/off switches in our clients' DNA, but we can invite them to talk about the generational patterns in their families. When secret patterns come into the light, God can work to break the dysfunctional patterns.

**David Stoop**

## BLESSINGS

"Esau said to his father, 'Do you have only one blessing, my father? Bless me too, my Father!' Then Esau wept aloud" (Gen. 27:38). This cry from a grown son is one of the most heartfelt in all of Scripture. It also pictures for us a biblical gift that was given or withheld in families in biblical times. Still today, receiving or missing a parent's blessing remains an incredibly important aspect of emotional and spiritual health and a key picture on earth of God's blessing on his people.

**Description and Prevalence.** The term *the blessing* has been used for almost 30 years to describe one of the deepest needs for love and acceptance that children of all ages long for in relation to their parents and significant others (Trent & Smalley, 2011). Indeed, the blessing in our personal, familial, and spiritual relationships is now the focus of the Institute for the Blessing at Barclay College and has been used in both secular and Christian healthy-family research and writing for two decades (Stinnett, 1986).

**History.** An extraordinary event in the history of God's people is recorded in Deuteronomy 30:19 and illustrates the meaning behind the word *blessing*. As the nation of Israel is about to enter into the Promised Land, the Lord lays before them a dramatic choice. "I call the heavens and the earth as witnesses against you that I have set before you life and death, blessings and curses. Now choose life, so that you and your children may live."

In God's Word, *life* means "to move toward" someone or something (Brown, Driver, & Briggs, 1974, p. 311). The word *death* literally means "to step away" into isolation or separation (Brown et al., p. 559). That "life or death" choice to move toward others or to step away is then linked with the second choice, blessing or curse. The word *blessing* in Hebrew means literally "to bow the knee" (Brown et al., p. 457). It's a picture of extending great value to someone, as you would in bowing before a person of great importance.

Linked with this idea of bowing the knee is the cognate word *honor*, which links the picture of adding a coin to a scale. In biblical times, the greater the weight, the more the value. In contrast (and in the choice set before us), the word *curse* literally means "to dam up the stream" (Brown et al., 1974, p. 886). In contrast to the *blessing*, which is a picture of adding great value, a curse is a graphic picture of subtraction—in this case withholding life-giving water from a desert dweller.

This idea then of choosing life (stepping toward) and blessing can be seen as it was applied in a family context most clearly in Genesis 27. In that chapter, Jacob and Esau, twin brothers, vie over the same gift—their father's blessing. Jacob tricks his father into giving him his blessing. These brothers are not arguing or fighting for property rights. The inheritance in Scripture was linked to the birthright, not the blessing. Here, two brothers battle over that deeply personal blessing from their father. And when Esau hears that he will never receive it, we hear his first terrible cry, "Bless me—me too, my father!" (Gen. 27:34,38).

**Assessment.** Receiving or missing a parent's blessing can usher in positive or negative short- and long-term behavioral, emotional, and spiritual health patterns. Being given the blessing or having it withheld can also directly impact the faith formation of a child or young adult. When children receive the blessing at home, they also receive a deep sense of acceptance, love, value, and optimism about the future. All these things are keys to forming faith and to establishing positive personal relationships. On the negative side, homes that withhold the blessing can cause deep-seated anger, fear of failure, and elements of attachment disorder, both in personal relationships and in our relationship with our heavenly Father (Trent & Smalley, 2011; Clinton and Straub, 2010). The Institute for the Blessing at Barclay College continues to conduct clinical studies and collect personal stories documenting the effects of gaining or missing the blessing.

**Application.** Five specific things were done when giving the blessing to children (Trent & Smalley, 2011). Scripture provides examples of parents, grandparents, husbands, and friends giving their blessing. Jesus blesses children who are not his own as well. These are the five elements of the blessing:

- *Appropriate meaningful touch.* This ranges from the laying on of hands to a kiss or hug.
- *The spoken message.* The blessing was always verbalized. Today, it is often written as well.
- *The attachment of high value.* Each child received a unique blessing, attaching high value to him or her (see Genesis 49).
- *The anticipation of a special future.* Parents today do not have the prophetic certainty of a biblical patriarch. Still, the blessing of children includes a parent or loved one picturing a trait or experience that God could value and use in future days.
- *Genuine commitment.* The blessing was irrevocable. It pictures as well the commitment on behalf of the giver to continue to add to that person's life.

**Additional Issues.** The blessing of children is such a seemingly simple act that one would assume that parents, grandparents, or loved ones would almost automatically provide this gift to children. However, personal and societal factors keep people from understanding the blessing or choosing to give it to children. Many people today have grown up with fractured relationships and without a deep sense of personal acceptance, and as a result of their own needs, fears, and ignorance, they may withhold the blessing from (i.e., curse) a child. Thankfully, both secular and religious school employees and social workers are adopting the blessing as a foundational tool for adding health and love to children. People in ministry and faith@home adherents are using the blessing to help children build a healthy faith. The Blessing Challenge, a seven-year project by StrongFamilies.com and Focus on the Family, seeks to help one million people choose to take a first step in blessing a child. (See www.TheBlessing.com.)

**John Trent**

## REFERENCES


Beam, J., & Stinnett, N. (2008). *Fantastic Families: 6 Proven Steps to Building a Strong Family.* Peabody, MA: Howard Books.

Brown, F., Driver, S. R., & Briggs, C. A. (1974). *A Hebrew and English Lexicon of the Old Testament* (p. 311). Oxford, MA: Clarendon Press.

Clinton, T., & Straub, J. (2010). *God Attachment: Why You Believe, Act, and Feel the Way You Do About God.* Brentwood, TN: Howard Books.

Stinnett, N. (1986). *Secrets of Strong Families.* New York, NY: Berkley Books.

Trent, J., & Smalley, G. (2011). *The Blessing* (Rev. ed.). Nashville, TN: Thomas Nelson.


## INDIVIDUATION

**Description.** In family therapy, the term *individuation* refers to the process of becoming an individual self while maintaining relationships with family and others. Individuation requires a person to negotiate a balance between closeness and distance in one's family of origin. During this developmental process, the self emerges as a distinct entity from the family mass. Autonomy is difficult to achieve when family members become emotionally fused or too distant and cut off (Bowen, 1978).

The construct of individuation is taken from family-systems theory and individual personality development (Bray, Harvey, & Williamson, 1987). Carl Jung used the term to denote a person who has become an integrated personality (Jung, Adler, & Hull, 1977). According to Jung, individuation is a lifelong process in which a person acknowledges unconscious tendencies of the self and yet does not yield to those tendencies through possession or projection. In family therapy, the construct is broadened to include the family system in which a person grows and develops. Murray Bowen's definition of individuation works alongside his key theoretical concept of differentiation (Bowen, 1978). Bowen theorized that in order to become an autonomous self or differentiate from the family of origin, one must balance too much togetherness (fusion) with too much distance (cutoff) in families. Minuchin (1974) similarly talked about families that were enmeshed on the one extreme and disengaged on the other. His work often included helping individuals find a balance between the two extremes. Boszormenyi-Nagy and Ulrich (1991), of the contextual family-therapy movement, conceptualized individuation as a balance between individual freedom and mandatory family obligations. Successful individuation is seen when a person becomes satisfied with levels of connectedness and knows how to balance family loyalty with personal beliefs.

Feminist therapists refer to the psychological process of individuation as a maturation issue in which one learns to be separate but attached to the family of origin. Autonomy is often misunderstood as independence without attachment, but through our attachments we find our voices and define who we are. According to Carter and McGoldrick (2004), therapists should also be aware that individuation and family process are sensitive to ethnicity, race, class, and gender. For example, women and men may differ in the way they express fusion due to the socialization of women to be dependent and approval seeking. Furthermore, different cultures value collectiveness over individualism, thus influencing fusion and distance issues.

**Assessment and Treatment.** Helping people define who they are in the context of others is foundational work in couple and family therapy. Negotiating separateness from their families of origin is a key issue for spouses to attain a successful marriage. Other family goals include helping children launch and navigate their independence without cutoff or enmeshment from their families of origin, making sure growing children are not caught in emotional overinvolvement with parents, and assisting parents to allow their children to develop into autonomous adults. In all these cases, the goal of therapy is to help family members negotiate needed autonomy while staying connected to one another. Individuation is not achieved when a false sense of autonomy is reached through distancing or excessive closeness. Family therapists work on helping family members find their voices, define their beliefs, and take positions on emotionally charged issues without becoming angry or defensive. Through structural work, family members are encouraged to communicate directly and stay connected during disagreements and conflicts.

**Spiritual Issues.** God sees each of us as unique individuals whom he calls into relationship. It is through our relationship with God that we find our true self. Our individual selves are held accountable for our actions, regardless of our family influences and attachments. However, family attachments influence our relationship with God and others. Therefore, our ability to be ourselves while serving God is influenced by family process, and God influences our individual selves while in relationship with others.

**Linda Mintle**

## REFERENCES


Boszormenyi-Nagy, I., & Ulrich, D. N. (1991). Contextual family therapy. In A. S. Gurman & D. P. Kniskern (Eds.), *Handbook of Family Therapy* (pp. 159-186). New York, NY: Brunner/Mazel.

Bowen, M. (1976). Theory in the practice of psychotherapy. In P. J. Guerin (Ed.), *Family Therapy*. New York, NY: Gardner.

Bowen, M. (1978). *Family Therapy in Clinical Practice*. New York, NY: Aronson.

Bray, J. H., Harvey, D. M., & Williamson, D. S. (1987). Intergenerational family relationships: An evaluation of theory and measurement. *Psychotherapy: Theory, Research, and Practice, 24*, 516-528.

Carter, B., & McGoldrick, M. (2004). *The Expanded Family Life Cycle: Individual, Family, and Social Perspectives* (3rd ed.). Boston, MA: Allyn & Bacon.

Jung, C. G., Adler, G., & Hull, R. F. C. (Eds.). (1977). *Collected Works of C. G. Jung* (Vol. 18, *The Symbolic Life: Miscellaneous Writings*). Princeton, NJ: Princeton University Press.

Minuchin, S. (1974). *Families and Family Therapy*. Boston, MA: Harvard University Press.


## IDENTIFIED PATIENT

**Description.** In family therapy, the term *identified patient* (IP) refers to a family member who is blamed for problems or becomes symptomatic as a result of dealing with dysfunctional family patterns. The IP becomes a scapegoat for a problem even though symptoms are believed to be a reflection of larger family system issues.

**History.** In the 1920s, interpersonal theorist Harry Stack Sullivan, social psychologist Kurt Lewin, family therapy pioneer Don Jackson, and others focused on communication patterns between people and noted that people function in interpersonal systems that influence behavior. General-systems theory was adapted to living systems and applied to family systems. Inspired by the work and research of social scientist Gregory Bateson, mental-health treatment began to include families instead of focusing solely on individuals (Nichols, 2009). Shortly after WWII, doctors treating schizophrenic patients began to notice that their patients often lived in families with distinct communication patterns. The tension between the parents and patients played a role in the patients' functioning. Even though family systems did not cause schizophrenia, patterns of communication and interaction could exacerbate or minimize schizophrenic behavior. The idea of involving family members in treatment gained momentum, and patients were viewed in the context of family systems. Therapists began to include family members in the treatment of numerous mental disorders, shifting the focus from treating only the individual to treating the larger system.

**Assessment.** Family therapists are aware of intrapsychic processes at work in people, but they are more focused on the interpersonal dynamics operating in a family system. Consequently, family members are included in evaluation and assessment of mental disorders.

For example, a teen is referred for treatment because she is evidencing symptoms of anorexia. The family therapist would ask the family of origin to attend the assessment in order for the therapist to observe the interpersonal processes that unfold between the teen (IP) and the family system. The therapist looks for patterns of behavior that maintain or exacerbate symptomatic behavior. As an example, the therapist may observe conflict between the teen and parents. However, the therapist notices that the conflict is not addressed and that the teen passively accepts the avoidance.

The therapist may begin to conceptualize the tension between the teen (IP) and her parents as part of the reason why the teen does not eat. Perhaps she is swallowing her negative feelings, leaving no room for food, rather than addressing the tension and working toward resolution. Further questioning of the parents may reveal patterns that make conflict resolution difficult between teen and parents. Do parents welcome conflict, avoid it, or refuse to acknowledge it? The interpersonal pattern of conflict resolution may factor into the teen's eating symptoms.

**Treatment.** Family therapists have many different treatment approaches but usually agree that individuals must be treated in the context of the systems that influence them. For this reason, treatment extends beyond the individual and inner psychic processes to include the family system and larger context. The therapist's goal is to help families operate in healthy ways as a system rather than scapegoat individual family members. Therefore, when a person is symptomatic, the focus of treatment is the family system, not the internal world of the patient. Presenting problems are treated as problems that develop and are maintained by the interpersonal patterns operating in families.

**Spiritual Issues.** We are all individuals accountable before God but also part of a spiritual family. The health of that spiritual family influences the health of individual believers. Each member is important to the functioning of the entire body. When one hurts, all are impacted. Thus, the health of individual believers is mutually influenced and must be addressed.

**Conclusion.** Individuals suffer or grow in context. Individuals with mental disorders are influenced by family of origin and other systems in which they live and operate. Therefore, the notion of identified patient is expanded to include the larger system.

Linda Mintle

### REFERENCES

Nichols, M. P. (2009). *Family Therapy: Concepts and Methods* (9th ed.). Englewood Cliffs, NJ: Prentice Hall.

## TRIANGULATION

**Description.** *Triangulation* is a family-systems theory term used to describe family processes that include three people. Triangles are basic units of systems that operate in all families and social groups. They develop when dyads are unstable and a third party is engaged in order to reduce tension or stabilize the unit. Triangles can be fluid or static and usually come in to play when two people vacillate between cycles of closeness and distance. Rather than resolve an issue, two people engage a third party, who functions to relieve anxiety. Triangles can occur in cross-generational coalitions as well as family subsystems.

The theoretical concept works like this: Think of the three sides of a triangle. Imagine one side being person *A* and another side, person *B*. Let's say that person *A* has a conflict with person *B*. But persons *A* and *B* refuse to talk to each other about the conflict and instead engage person *C* in their emotional upset. Person *C* is *triangulated* into the conflict between persons *A* and *B*. Person *C* temporarily stabilizes the interactions of *A* and *B* by diverting attention away from the direct conflict. However, persons *A* and *B* do not solve their disagreement, and person *C* is now in the middle of their conflict. When unhealthy triangles form under distress or intense emotions, problems erupt.

For example, John and Mary have an unresolved marital fight. Mary is upset with John and calls her mother to complain about how stubborn John seems to be. John also calls Mary's mom to ask her to calm down her daughter and tell her to be more reasonable. Mary's mom was not part of the marital disagreement but is now triangulated into the marital conflict.

According to Kerr and Bowen (1988), triangulation occurs four ways:

- A stabilized twosome can become destabilized by adding a third person (e.g, a mother-in-law).
- A stabilized twosome can become destabilized by the removal of a third person (e.g., a child leaves home).
- An unstable twosome becomes stabilized by the addition of a third party (e.g., the birth of a child).
- An unstable twosome becomes stabilized by the removal of a third party (e.g., a boss who has been causing problems is fired).

The term *triangulation* became popular in the mid-1960s family-therapy movement as the importance of the family environment was studied in normative child development. American psychiatrist Murray Bowen and the founder of the structural school of family therapy, Salvador Minuchin, used the construct in their work with maladjusted children (Bowen, 1978; Minuchin, 1974). They observed that parents who were unable to solve problems between themselves often directed attention away from the marital dyad and onto a child in order to lower the tension of the marriage.

**Assessment.** Assessment is based on the observation or description of an operating triangle in a family system. To identify a triangle, look for these indicators:

- overinvolvement of a third party playing a role in the tension of a dyad
- someone who plays the role of confidante or sides with one person in the dyad
- a person in the dyad who is unable to get a need met looking outside the relationship to get the need met
- a relationship that seems stuck despite intervention

**Treatment.** The goal of treatment is to *detriangulate* by moving the third party out of the conflict in order for the dyad to deal directly with each other. The dyad must learn to resolve issues person to person. When a cross-generational triangle is at work, the therapist realigns the subsystem boundaries. This is often done by making physical changes in seating arrangements and having people speak directly to each other. Furthermore, therapists often form healthy triangles with distressed marital couples in order to lower emotional arousal so the couple can resolve issues.

**Spiritual Issues.** Matthew 18:15 instructs us to face conflict directly with the person involved. Others are brought into disputes when we cannot resolve an issue and need a witness (verse 16). The role of the witness is like that of a therapist—a neutral party that is not siding with one person, but instead is helping toward conflict resolution. Once the conflict is settled, we are to forgive, move on, and live in peace and harmony with each other.

**Linda Mintle**

### REFERENCES


Bowen, M. (1978). *Family Therapy in Clinical Practice.* Northvale, NJ: Aronson.

Kerr, M., & Bowen, M. (1988). *Family Evaluation.* New York, NY: Norton.

Minuchin, S. (1974). *Families and Family Therapy.* Boston, MA: Harvard University Press.


## DOUBLE BIND

**Description.** In 1956, the term *double bind* was coined by a group of researchers headed by Gregory Bateson (Bateson, Jackson, Haley, & Weakland, 1956) exploring the way disordered thought patterns of schizophrenics could stem from "exposure to, and participation in, dysfunctional communication patterns in the family" (Koopmans, 1997). The double bind was defined as a pattern of communication in which a person receives two sets of instructions, one effectively canceling out the other. The double bind has also come to be known as a lose-lose situation. Here are two examples:

*Double bind in marriage.* When a wife asks her husband how to handle situations, he constantly yells at her, "Stop bothering me with all these details!" However, the husband consistently belittles his wife for the decisions she makes, large and small.

*Double bind in parenting.* A parent holds unreachable expectations for a child regarding school, chores, family duties, and the like, but the parent also berates the child for always failing to get to bed on time.

**Assessment.** A double bind has the following components: (a) There is a disparity in position, with the person considered higher having the ability to punish the person who is lower; (b) the contradictory messages are ongoing and persistent; (c) the contradictory messages are not always verbal but are often nonverbal and implied through actions and attitudes; (d) withdrawal from the relationship is not seen as an option; and (e) talking through the contradiction is not seen as an option.

**Treatment.** Double binds are based on a series of assumptions. Ideally, treatment would include all family members so each person's underlying assumptions could be brought into the open, examined, and evaluated for truth. Sadly, by the time treatment is sought for this type of family dysfunction, the relationship has often been severed, and family counseling is not a current, viable option. Significant progress can still be made with the individual even if all affected parties do not participate. One of the primary conditions leading to a double bind is a belief it cannot be talked through and resolved. This is the strength and benefit of counseling: Even if the one person refuses to discuss it, a counselor can help the other person come to an understanding and resolution.

A double bind is not a presentation of truth; rather, it is one person's willful manipulation of another in order to gain compliance or control. It is vital for clients to begin to unhook feelings of self-worth, value, and competence from the shackles of this false and contradictory pattern. Once the double-bind strategy has been uncovered and the underlying false assumptions debunked and countered with the truth, it is important to give the person tools to recognize these situations in the future and refrain from participating.

**Spiritual Issues.** People who perpetrate double binds seek to control and manipulate those perceived as weaker or vulnerable. Double binds exist in part because the imprisoned people have the false belief that they lack the power to escape, whether physically by leaving the situation or mentally by understanding the truth and establishing boundaries. Truth provides the path to freedom. In John 8:31-32, Jesus says that when people understand God's truth—not man's truth, but God's truth—his truth results in freedom. As the false assumptions of double binds are jettisoned, God's truth can fill the void, expanding an understanding of love, value, worth, and redemption.

Gregory L. Jantz

## REFERENCES

Bateson, G., Jackson, D., Haley, J., & Weakland, J. (1956). Toward a theory of schizophrenia. *Behavioral Science, 1,* 251-254.

Koopmans, M. (1997). Schizophrenia and the family: Double bind theory revisited. *Dynamical Psychology.* Retrieved from http://www.goertzel.org/dynapsyc/1997/Koopmans.html

# CHILD AND ADOLESCENT ISSUES

## CHILDHOOD DEVELOPMENT

The highest acclamation or heaviest indictment that any society receives may involve its response to the call and trust to care for its children. Children, as the next generation and as our legacy, deserve the priority that God intended. Children are indeed a "heritage from the LORD" (Ps. 127:3) and should not be hindered, "for the kingdom of heaven belongs to such as these" (Mt. 19:14). Without doubt, the Creator holds children in high esteem.

These are basic truths that few would deny. However, actions speak louder than words, and it appears that we do not always place a priority on children's issues. Seeing this lack of priority reflected even among believers and particularly in the Christian counseling world is particularly disappointing and frustrating. There are simply too few therapists at any level who specialize in or are devoted to child counseling. This observation is not intended to harangue the Christian therapist or indict the Christian counseling world. Rather, it is an opportunity to inform and encourage about a crucial need—the need to work with children and the need for more Christian therapists to take up this calling.

**THE CHILD'S WORLD.** The world of children is different than it used to be. It is more dangerous, less secure. Christian professionals and nonprofessionals can attest to the importance of attachment. This process is often disrupted or nonexistent, which can result in a myriad of challenges. The U.S. Surgeon General estimates that almost 21% of U.S. children ages 9 to 17 have a diagnosable mental or addictive disorder, and up to 70% of these do not receive adequate services (U.S. Public Health Service, 2000).

The Children's Defense Fund provides data about the state of our nation's youth, detailing some of the heartbreaking challenges and crises that children in the United States regularly face.

- Every 32 seconds a baby is born into poverty.
- Every 41 seconds a child is confirmed as abused or neglected.
- Every minute a baby is born to a teen mother.
- Every 4 minutes a child is arrested for a drug offense.
- Every 7 minutes a child is arrested for a violent crime.
- Every 45 minutes a child or teen dies from an accident.
- Every 3 hours a child or teen is killed by a firearm.
- Every 5 hours a child or teen commits suicide.
- Every 6 hours a child is killed by abuse or neglect (Children's Defense Fund, 2011).

Children live in a frightening world, and mental-health challenges are devastating consequences. Fortunately, the situation is not beyond hope. Although too few mental-health professionals are focused on children, the numbers appear to be growing. Additionally, there is greater recognition of the importance of families, communities, and faith communities to step into the gap for hurting children.

**Childhood Problems.** Perhaps the most important issues to consider regarding childhood and child counseling are the basic developmental differences between children and adults. The etiology of childhood problems is similar to that for adult psychopathology, but there is considerable evidence of developmentally different neurobiological, psychological, and psychosocial factors that influence the development and perpetuation of childhood disorders.

The apostle Paul provides a point of reference when considering these developmental differences. "When I was a child, I talked like a child, I thought like a child, I reasoned like a child. When I became a man, I put the ways of childhood behind me" (1 Cor. 13:11). Although adult counselors may have indeed put the ways of childhood behind them, child clients have not. They still speak, think, and reason as children. Counseling interventions need to reflect these developmental differences.

Some other distinct differences when working with children should also be noted. One forgotten factor is that children are fundamentally mandated clients; they simply do not self-refer. Adults thus commission counseling, and the underlying message may simply be "fix my child," so treatment planning is an essential consideration. Adults may not be accurate reporters for several reasons. They may be dealing with their own stress, concealing their own problems or perceived failure as caretakers, or perhaps covering for abuse (systemic and cultural issues *must* be considered).

Many referrals for intervention relate to noncompliance; the child is engaged in something the parent does not want to occur, or the child is not engaged in something the parent does want to occur. There may a possible diagnosis, but this may well be considered a parent-child problem as opposed to child psychopathology. Interventions would seem most appropriately focused on parenting and parent-child relationships as opposed to "fixing" the child.

A significant challenge in this process involves knowing when children and parents are in need of intervention. Christian counselors can educate their clients, churches, and communities about the importance of and need for child intervention. Adults' and children's psychological health may be measured by changes in emotional and behavioral presentation, school or work performance, sleep patterns, diet, etc. Adults who are concerned about children should focus on the intensity, frequency, and duration of these changes in the children, recognizing that childhood is itself a dynamic process.

**Conclusion.** The dynamic process of childhood may be challenging to navigate for both children and the adults in their lives. It is nevertheless an important psychological, physiological, and spiritual journey. Christian helpers must be supportive and instructive lenders of hope. Parents and children faced with challenges are desperately looking for hope, and it must be available inside and outside the Christian counseling community.

Finally, working with children is both a calling and a lifestyle. Sweeney and Landreth (2009) suggest that "child...therapy is not a cloak the...therapist puts on when entering the (therapy) room and takes off when leaving; rather, it is a philosophy resulting in attitudes and behaviors for living one's life in relationships with children" (p. 123). This calling and lifestyle is a crucial one that too few have answered. Therapists, pastors, and other caregivers need to see God's priority in working with his little ones, for the benefit of current and future generations.

Daniel S. Sweeney

## REFERENCES

Children's Defense Fund. (2011). *Moments in America for Children*. Washington, DC: Author. Retrieved from http://www.childrensdefense.org/child-research-data-publications/moments-in-america-for-children.html

Sweeney, D., & Landreth, G. (2009). Child-centered play therapy. In K. O'Connor & L. Braverman (Eds.), *Play Therapy Theory and Practice: Comparing Theories and Techniques* (pp. 123-162). Hoboken, NJ: Wiley & Sons.

U.S. Public Health Service. (2000). *Report of the Surgeon General's Conference on Children's Mental Health: A National Action Agenda*. Washington, DC: Department of Health and Human Services.

## CHILDHOOD MATURATION

An understanding of normal child development is essential to developing an effective counseling approach when working with children or adolescents. Typically, children proceed, or mature, through certain developmental stages in physical, cognitive, and emotional skills. The stage of cognitive and/or emotional development has a direct impact on children's behavior, and if understood, will guide Christian counselors' therapy approaches.

**History.** A developmental approach has been intrinsic to the fields of counseling and psychology since the 1950s. Prior to this time, little attention was paid to the differences in the thought processes of children when compared with adults. Several prominent psychologists during this era contributed to our understanding of child maturation, including Piaget, Erikson, Kohlberg, and Gesell. Their groundbreaking work is still widely applied today and serves as the basis for many standardized cognitive and behavioral assessments (Accardo, Accardo, & Capute, 2008).

**Gesell's Stages of Development.** Arnold Gesell compiled structured observations of children to determine the usual ages at which developmental tasks are learned. He observed that typical child development occurs in a sequential manner in five areas of development: gross motor, visual-motor, language, adaptive, and social skills. His work emphasized the importance of both genetic influences (nature) and environmental influences (nurture) on child development. His work formed the basis of determining the definitions of *developmental delay* and *developmental deviance* (Gesell, 1940).

*Developmental delay* is defined as meeting milestones at a later age than expected. If persistent, developmental delay may progress to a diagnosis of *intellectual disability* in an older child. *Developmental deviance* occurs when a child does not meet milestones in a typical manner. For instance, a child with autism may know many words but not be able to use them conversationally.

**Piaget's Stages of Development.** Piaget's work focused more on cognitive and emotional development. The primary assumption behind Piaget's *cognitive developmental theory* is that reasoning and behavior are related to cognitive complexity, which increases with age. Progression through developmental stages is linear, and at a higher level of stage development, there is better adaptability to environmental changes (Piaget, 1952). These are the stages:

1. *Sensorimotor stage* (age 0 to 2 years). At this stage children use their senses and body movement to learn more about themselves and the surrounding environment. This is the stage in which object permanence is learned.

2. *Preoperational stage* (age 2 to 7 years). At this stage a child learns symbolic representation with language but still is egocentric and unable to see the perspective of others.

3. *Concrete operational stage* (age 7 to 11 years). At this stage children can

engage in logical thought, but only for situations that are concrete or observable. They can begin to see the perspective of others.

4. *Formal operational stage* (age 11 to adulthood). At this stage people can engage in logical thought about abstract or theoretical situations. They can begin to see situations from multiple perspectives and see multiple potential solutions to a problem. Most counseling approaches for adults assume that the client is at a formal operational stage of development.

**The DIR Model.** The developmental, individual-difference, relationship-based (or DIR) model by Wieder and Greenspan (2001) was created to bring new insights that have become cornerstones of a new way of working with children. There are three major insights to this model:

1. Language, cognition (including math and quantity concepts), and emotional and social skills are learned through interactive relationships that involve affective exchanges.
2. Variations exist in underlying motor and sensory processing (i.e., regulatory capacities).
3. The model provides a new roadmap of functional emotional developmental capacities. There are six levels of functional development:
   - ability for regulation and shared attention
   - engagement with warmth and trust and intimacy
   - two-way purposeful communication
   - interactive problem solving and use of gestures in a continuous flow
   - functional use of ideas
   - building bridges between areas

**Psychotherapy Approaches in Childhood.** Psychotherapy approaches in children often focus on environmental changes around the child because children may not be developmentally ready for the abstract thinking required for inner personal change. The American Academy of Child and Adolescent Psychiatry (2008) notes these common approaches for pediatric therapy:

1. *Parent-child interaction therapy* focuses on guiding a parent in appropriate interactions and responses to a child's negative behaviors. This may be effective in younger children with behavior problems.
2. *Family therapy* includes parents, the child, and siblings, and it assists in identifying and changing patterns of relating that are affecting family functioning.
3. *Play therapy* engages the child in the use of toys, games, and the like in role play to identify feelings or thought patterns that are affecting behavior and emotional development.
4. *Cognitive behavior therapy* (CBT) helps the child identify and replace erroneous thought patterns that can cause feelings and behaviors. This may be particularly effective in anxiety and depression, and it is more applicable to children in the formal operational developmental stage.

**Spiritual Issues.** Caution should be exercised when applying secular psychological theories to the spiritual growth of children. However, just as God has provided laws of order in the physical universe, he provided sequential order in the physical, emotional, and cognitive development of children. For instance, the spiritual concept of an "age of accountability" is related to the ability of the child to fully comprehend the law, sin, forgiveness, and grace. This is a subject of great debate, but in the Catholic Church and some Protestant denominations, this age is set between 7 and 10 years—the same time frame as Piaget's concrete operational stage, when a child can engage in logical thought processes.

**Conclusion.** By accurately understanding the maturation of children, the Christian counselor can provide the most effective therapy for children and adolescents. These concepts can also be applied to counseling parents of typically developing children and children with developmental disabilities regarding normal and abnormal childhood behaviors (Collins, 2007).

Amy J. Newmeyer
Mark D. Newmeyer

## REFERENCES


Accardo, P., Accardo, J., & Capute, A. (2008). A neurodevelopmental perspective on the continuum of developmental disabilities. In P. Accardo (Ed.), *Capute and Accardo's Neurodevelopmental Disabilities in Infancy and Childhood* (3rd ed.). Baltimore, MD: Brookes.

American Academy of Child and Adolescent Psychiatry. (2008). Psychotherapies for children and adolescents. *Facts for Families, 86*. Retrieved February 6, 2011, from http://www.aacap.org/galleries/FactsForFamilies/86_psychotherapies_for_children_and_adolescents.pdf

Collins, G. R. (2007). *Christian Counseling: A Comprehensive Guide* (3rd ed). Nashville, TN: Thomas Nelson.

Gesell, A. (1940). *The First Five Years of Life*. New York, NY: Harper & Brothers.

Piaget, J. (1952). *The Origins of Intelligence in Children*. New York, NY: International University Press.

Wieder, S., & Greenspan, S. (2001). The DIR (developmental, individual-difference, relationship-based) approach to assessment and intervention planning. *Zero to Three, 21*(4), 11-19.


## MORAL DEVELOPMENT

**Description.** Primarily, the term *moral development* denotes the change process all people experience in both their "sense of justice and of what is right and wrong, and in their behavior [in] moral issues" (Feldman, 2011, p. 308). The term also can refer to a subfield in the academic discipline of developmental psychology dedicated to the exploration and understanding of morality, moral reasoning, moral lapses, and moral behavior (Broderick, 2009; Feldman).

**History.** The topic of moral behavior is emphasized in a variety of disciplines, including philosophy, theology, and education (Dewey, 1975; Hawkins, 2005), but the study of moral development belongs almost exclusively to the field of psychology and began with the work of child psychologist Jean Piaget (Feldman, 2011). Piaget focused largely on the realm of moral reasoning and moral judgment and believed that moral development, much like cognitive development, occurs in stages (Feldman, p. 308). Piaget (1932) argued that children in the initial stage of moral development (up to age 10) regard rules as fixed, absolute, and unchanging. After age 10, he claimed, children's moral thinking undergoes a sophisticated shift in which they understand that rules are "created by people and subject to change according to the will of people" (Feldman, p. 309). Now, rather than making moral judgments based on the obedience (or disobedience) to rules, the older child is more likely to judge moral decisions in terms of the motives and intentions underlying the act.

Lawrence Kohlberg built on Piaget's work by conducting cross-cultural studies that also looked at children's moral reasoning. Kohlberg (1981) identified "universal levels of development in moral thought" (p. 17), which he believed all people invariantly move through in fixed order. These are the levels or stages (adapted from Kohlberg):

*Level I: Preconventional morality.* This is based on cultural rules and labels.

Stage 1: obedience and punishment orientation

Stage 2: reward orientation

*Level II: Conventional morality.* This is based on role as member of society.

Stage 3: good boy–nice girl orientation

Stage 4: maintaining social order orientation

*Level III: Postconventional morality.* This is based on universal values/principles.

Stage 5: Social contract orientation

Stage 6: Universal ethical principles orientation

However, as his critics point out, "although Kohlberg's theory provides a good account of the development of moral *judgments,* the links with moral *behavior* are less strong" (Feldman, 2011, p. 313). For this reason, moral-development researchers have recently shifted their attention in a more practical direction, from examining these cognitive, moral reasoning approaches toward those variables thought to influence moral/immoral actions and behavior (Broderick, 2009). These include the influence of the social context/environment (Bandura, 1991), moral emotions, such as empathy (Hoffman, 2000), and the role of moral self-identity (Blasi, 1984) to name but a few.

**Biblical and Spiritual Issues.** The Bible's focus on this topic is similar to that currently seen in the moral-development literature—less on moral reasoning and more on factors that influence moral actions and behavior. Scripture makes it clear that all people are born with a sinful nature (Ps. 51:5). This in turn has a direct bearing on people's thoughts, which according to Jesus are basically evil (Mt. 15:18-19). Not surprisingly, this combination of an innate sinful nature and propensity toward evil thinking has a detrimental effect on moral actions/behavior (Pr. 23:7). It also helps explain why all human beings find themselves in a moral dilemma similar to that experienced by the apostle Paul, struggling between the desire to do good and yet being unable to carry out those good intentions—a struggle that leads to feelings of guilt and frustration (Rom. 7:15-24).

Thankfully, the Bible also offers a solution to this moral dilemma in the person and work of Jesus Christ (Rom. 7:25–8:8). He makes it possible for people's innate sin nature to be replaced by a new, godly (moral) nature that includes a renewed mind (Eph. 4:20-24) capable of thinking moral, godly thoughts (Phil. 4:6-8). These factors, along with regular contact with the Word of God (Ps. 119:11), empower the Christian to think, behave, and act morally.

**Fred Milacci**

## REFERENCES


Bandura, A. (1991). Social cognitive theory of moral thought and action. In W. M. Kurtines & J. L. Gewirtz (Eds.), *Handbook of Moral Behavior and Development.* Hillsdale, NJ: Erlbaum.

Blasi, A. (1984). Moral identity: Its role in moral functioning. In J. Gewirtz & W. Kurines (Eds.), *Morality, Moral Behavior, and Moral Development* (pp. 128-139). New York, NY: Wiley & Sons.

Broderick, P. M. (2009). *To Thine Own Self Be True: A Phenomenological Investigation into the Role of Self in a Moral Dilemma.* (Unpublished doctoral dissertation). Liberty University, Lynchburg, VA.

Dewey, J. (1975). *Moral Principles in Education.* Carbondale, IL: Southern Illinois University Press.

Feldman, R. S. (2011). *Lifespan Development: A Topical Approach.* Upper Saddle River, NJ: Prentice Hall.

Hawkins, S. (2005). *The Influence of Parenting Styles on the Development of Moral Judgment in College-Level Adolescents.* (Unpublished doctoral dissertation). Liberty University, Lynchburg, VA.

Hoffman, M. (2000). *Empathy and Moral Development.* New York, NY: Cambridge University Press.

Kohlberg, L. (1981). *The Philosophy of Moral Development: Moral Stages and the Idea of Justice* (Vol. 1). San Francisco, CA: Harper and Row.

Piaget, J. (1932). *The Moral Judgment of the Child.* New York, NY: Harcourt, Brace & World.


## IDENTITY FORMATION

**Description.** The term *identity formation* refers to the process by which individuals develop a sense of themselves, a sense of continuity in who they are, including their values, goals, and purpose (Schwartz, 2001). As Schwartz put it, "Identity helps one to make sense of, and to find one's place in, an almost limitless world with a vast set of possibilities" (p. 294). Identity formation has been looked at across the life span with special attention to the transitions from childhood through adolescence and into young adulthood.

**History.** Sigmund Freud (1933/1965) introduced the idea of establishing an identity or self-concept when he described a unique stage of development, the Oedipal conflict, which resulted in a child identifying himself or herself with a parent. Building on Freud's theories, Erik Erickson (1950) explored identity formation across the life span. Erickson suggested that potential identity states existed on a continuum ranging from synthesis (a sense of purpose and stability) to confusion (a sense of uncertainty and hopelessness) (Schwartz, 2001). In his later work, Erikson (1974) proposed three levels of identity: ego, personal, and social. *Ego identity* can be conceptualized as the rigid and largely unconscious core beliefs one holds about himself or herself. *Personal identity* refers to the distinguishing qualities or characteristics that can be easily perceived by others. *Social identity* is comprised of factors such as race or ethnicity that contribute to group belonging.

Though Erikson's theory appeared to be sound, it provided a broad definition of identity that had not been tested. James Marcia (1966) produced the first empirical research based on Eriksonian theory. As a result, Marcia (1980) proposed four identity statuses: diffusion, foreclosure, moratorium, and achievement, characterized by varying levels of exploration and commitment. Current researchers continue to expand on Marcia's work by focusing on other factors, such as genetics, cognition, and responsibility (Schwartz, 2001).

**Assessment.** Formal psychological measures have been developed based on both Erikson's and Marcia's theories of identity formation. One of the earliest assessments, the Ego-Identity Scale, was designed to measure the ego development of adolescents (Dignan, 1965). Another test for adolescents, the Ego Identity Process Questionnaire, was developed to assess levels of exploration and commitment (Balistreri, Busch-Rossnagel, & Geisinger, 1995). The Extended Objective Measure of Ego Identity Status II (Bennion & Adams, 1986) is one of the most popular adolescent assessments because it provides an identity status within ideological and interpersonal domains. Since adolescence is typically a time of identity crisis, exploration, and formation, it is important for clinicians to attend to the process of ego identity development. Studies have demonstrated correlations between adolescent identity status and self-esteem, coping skills, and general psychological adjustment (Markstrom & Marshall, 2007; Crawford, Cohen, Johnson, Sneed, & Brook, 2004; Luyckx, Goossens, Soenens, Beyers, & Vansteenkiste, 2005; Vleioras & Bosma, 2005).

Identity formation can also be assessed in adulthood by using the Loyola Generativity Scale, a self-report inventory based on Erickson's developmental stages (McAdams & de St. Aubin, 1992). As a cautionary note, practitioners should be aware that many assessments measuring identity development rely on self-report data from questionnaires and structured interviews, which can be biased or inaccurate.

**Application.** The praxis or applied dimension of identity development is focused primarily on how to facilitate various identity processes in adolescence and young adulthood. Early work in this area centered on fostering perspective-taking skills and problem-solving tasks. This has continued with more emphasis on anchoring specific interventions in theory and tying them more explicitly to specific identity processes (Schwartz, 2001). For example, it has been argued that the foreclosed individuals might benefit from a softening of existing beliefs, whereas diffused individuals, who may have a diminished motivation, may benefit from more "guided exploration of identity choices" (p. 47). In any case, more recent contributions to the applied discussion of identity development, such as discovery-based and co-constructivist approaches, are often provided in group format and foster critical skills for exploration and thoughtful reflection and discussion of various real-life scenarios (Schwartz, 2001; see also Archer, 1994; Waterman, 1990).

**Biblical and Spiritual Issues.** The identity-formation literature has seen recent interesting research on religious and spiritual identity development. For example, theoretical models of spiritual identity development in relation to cognitive, psychodynamic, systems, and narrative theories have been offered (e.g., Poll & Smith, 2003), as have empirical studies on specific religious experiences, such as religious doubt. Indeed, Puffer et al. (2008) examined the place of doubt in religious identity formation and suggest that doubt may be a meaningful experience, particularly depending on the identity status of the person. Still others have looked at Erikson's published and unpublished papers and provided insight into how Erikson understood the relationship between spirituality and identity development.

**Additional Issues.** There is a growing field of research with regard to ethnic identity. In recent years, the research has progressed from theory to empiricism with the development of formal measures, such as the Multigroup Ethnic Identity Measure (Phinney, 1992). A goal for future researchers is to use data from individual assessments to develop a broad theory of ethnic identity with principles that can be generalized across individuals and groups (Ong, Fuller-Rowell, & Phinney, 2010).

**Mark A. Yarhouse**
**Kristina High**

## REFERENCES


Adams, G. R., Bennion, L. D., & Huh, K. (1989). *Extended Objective Measure of Ego Identity Status: A Reference Manual* (Unpublished manuscript). Utah State University, Logan, UT.

Archer, S. L. (Ed.). (1994). *Interventions for Adolescent Identity Development.* Thousand Oaks, CA: Sage.

Balistreri, E., Busch-Rossnagel, N. A., & Geisinger, K. F. (1995). Development and preliminary validation of the Ego Identity Process Questionnaire. *Journal of Adolescence, 18,* 179-190 .

Bennion, L., & Adams, G. (1986). A revision of the extended version of the objective measure of ego-identity status: An identity instrument for use with late adolescents. *Journal of Adolescent Research, 1,* 183-198.

Crawford, T. N., Cohen, P., Johnson, J. G., Sneed, J. R., & Brook, J. S. (2004). The course and psychosocial correlates of personality disorder symptoms in adolescence: Erikson's developmental theory revisited. *Journal of Youth and Adolescence, 33,* 373-387.

Dignan, M. H. (1965). Ego identity and maternal identification. *Journal of Personality and Social Psychology, 1,* 476-483.

Erikson, E. H. (1950). *Childhood and Society.* New York, NY: Norton.

Erikson, E. H. (1974). *Dimensions of a New Identity.* New York, NY: Norton.

Freud, S. (1933/1965). *New Introductory Lectures on Psychoanalysis.* (J. Stachey, Trans.). New York, NY: Norton.

Luyckx, K., Goossens, L., Soenens, B., Beyers, W., & Vansteenkiste, M. (2005). Identity statuses based upon four rather than two identity dimensions: Extending and refining Marcia's paradigm. *Journal of Youth and Adolescence, 34,* 605-618.

Marcia, J. E. (1966). Development and validation of ego identity status. *Journal of Personality and Social Psychology, 5,* 551-558.

Marcia, J. E. (1980). Identity in adolescence. In J. Adelson (Ed.), *Handbook of Adolescent Psychology* (pp. 159-187). New York, NY: Wiley & Sons.

Markstrom, C., & Marshall, S. (2007). The psychosocial inventory of ego-strengths: Examination of theory and psychometric properties. *Journal of Adolescence, 30,* 63-79.

McAdams, D. P., & de St. Aubin, E. (1992). A theory of generativity and its assessment through self-report, behavioral acts, and narrative themes in autobiography. *Journal of Personality and Social Psychology, 62,* 1003-1015.

Ong, A. D., Fuller-Rowell, T. E., & Phinney, J. S. (2010). Measurement of ethnic identity: Recurrent and emergent issues. *Identity: An International Journal of Theory and Research, 10*, 39-49.

Phinney, J. S. (1992). The multigroup ethnic identity measure: A new scale for use with diverse groups. *Journal of Adolescent Research, 7*, 156-176.

Poll, J. B., & Smith, T. B. (2003). The spiritual self: Toward a conceptualization of spiritual identity development. *Journal of Psychology and Theology, 31*(2), 129-142.

Puffer, K. A., Pence, K. G., Graverson, T. M., Wolfe, M., Pate, E., & Clegg, S. (2008). Religious doubt and identity formation: Salient predictors of adolescent religious doubt. *Journal of Psychology and Theology, 36*(4), 270-284.

Schwartz, S. J. (2001). The evolution of Eriksonian and neo-Eriksonian identity theory and research: A review and integration. *Identity: An International Journal of Theory and Research, 1*(1), 7-58.

Vleioras, G., & Bosma, H. A. (2005). Are identity styles important for psychological well-being? *Journal of Adolescence, 28*(3), 397-409.

Waterman, A. S. (1990). Personal expressiveness: Philosophical and psychological foundations. *Journal of Mind and Behavior, 11*, 47-74.

## DEVELOPMENTAL DISORDERS

The topic of developmental disorders frequents the daily conversations of many families and professionals. For some, the term suggests any disorder that emerges early in the life span and impacts one's typical developmental trajectory (Odom, Horner, Snell, & Blacher, 2007). For others, however, the topic is limited to the subset of pervasive developmental disorders that are listed in the *Diagnostic and Statistical Manual of Mental Disorders* (*DSM-IV-TR*) (American Psychiatric Association [APA], 2000). The topic is further complicated by its ever-evolving nature. The definition of the umbrella term *developmental disorder* is often subject to changes in both scientific knowledge and cultural perspectives. Pragmatically, the term is frequently employed by professionals and families to describe a variety of individuals with a diverse set of abilities and characteristics (Odom et al.).

**Description and Prevalence.** Odom et al. (2007) created a working definition that identified developmental disabilities as "a set of abilities and characteristics that vary from the norm in the limitations they impose on independent participation and acceptance in society...[and] exist within traditionally conceived developmental domains such as cognitive, communication, social, or motor abilities...appear[ing] in the 'developmental period,' which is usually characterized as before 22 years of age" (p. 4). Similarly, the Administration on Developmental Disabilities qualified that developmental disabilities result in substantial limitations in three or more of the following areas:

- self-care
- comprehension and language
- skills (receptive and expressive language)
- learning
- mobility
- self-direction
- capacity for independent living
- economic self-sufficiency
- ability to function independently without coordinated services (continuous need for individually planned and coordinated services) (U.S. Department of Health and Human Services, 2010, paragraph 2)

An overarching, general category of developmental disorders was not classified in the *DSM-IV-TR*; however, a more specific diagnosis of pervasive developmental disorders was included on Axis I. Specifically, these disorders include the autism spectrum disorders (autistic disorder; Asperger's disorder; pervasive developmental disorder, not otherwise specified [PDD-NOS]; Rett's disorder; childhood disintegrative disorder). This subgroup of developmental disabilities is characterized by early-emerging impairments in social functioning, language, and communication, as well as unusual behaviors or interests and a resistance to change (Koenig, Rubin, Klin,

& Volkmar, 2000; see APA, 2000, for a full review of criteria).

Utilizing these definitions, research has suggested that approximately 13% of children have a developmental disability, and as many as 1.3% have three or more developmental disabilities (Boulet, Boyle, & Schieve, 2009). In general, prevalence rates for developmental disabilities did not differ based on race/ethnicity, age, or sex. However, Hartung and Widiger (1998) reported that boys were more frequently diagnosed with attention-deficit hyperactivity disorder, childhood conduct disorder, intellectual disability, autistic disorder, language disorder, reading disorder, and enuresis, whereas girls were more frequently identified as having anxiety disorders, adolescent depression, and eating disorders. When specifically exploring rates of autism spectrum disorders (ASD), the Centers for Disease Control estimated that between 1 in 80 and 1 in 240 children in the United States have an ASD (U.S. Department of Health and Human Services, 2010). Moreover, boys were four to five times more likely to receive an ASD diagnosis.

**Assessment.** Given the wide array of developmental disorders, assessments typically begin with developmentally appropriate measures that assess whole-child development. Meisels and Fenichel (1996) underscored the role of assessment for screening and identifying children, confirming or diagnosing, planning intervention programming, ascertaining skill readiness, or demonstrating competence/achievement levels. Consistent with the Division of Exceptional Children's (DEC) recommended practices, these authors identified several key principles:

- Assessment includes multiple sources of information and is a collaborative process.
- Assessment builds on child and family strengths.
- Assessment occurs in natural environments and daily routines.
- Assessment follows a sequence of establishing rapport with parents, obtaining a developmental history, observing the child, assessing child functioning, and synthesizing information.
- The child-caregiver relationship serves as a foundation for assessment.
- An understanding of typical developmental milestones and trajectories is essential.
- Assessment is viewed as an initial step in the intervention process (Meisels & Fenichel).

In general, assessments utilized for diagnosing developmental disorders can be grouped into three primary areas: norm-referenced, criterion-referenced (or curriculum-based), and performance assessments (see Gilliam & Mayes, 2000, for a full review of developmental assessments). For screening and diagnosing ASDs, most assessments are criterion-referenced, with the most common tool being the Childhood Autism Rating Scale (CARS; see txautism.net for a full review of ASD assessments). In contrast to norm- and criterion-referenced assessments, performance assessments are formative assessments that allow children to demonstrate their abilities through a variety of naturally occurring routines and activities. These functional assessments are often closely linked to intervention, allowing for a transactional interaction between the assessment and intervention that is informed by multiple sources of information in a variety of contexts. Performance assessments are considered the "best practice" of assessment within the field of developmental disorders because they allow for assessment of intervention-related and incremental changes; however, they can be costly and time-consuming (Meisels & Fenichel, 1996).

**Treatment.** The general consensus in the field of developmental disorders is to intervene early and often (Koenig et al., 2000). There have been some concerns, however, about whether "less is more" or "more is less," with some research suggesting that more intense programs are not necessarily more effective (Innocenti & White, 1993). As a whole, treatment plans should be individualized and family-centered, and they should promote competence within naturally occurring routines that are developmentally appropriate and age-appropriate (Carta & Kong, 2007). In general, interventions begin in home- or center-based programs, transitioning into schools and later the community.

Specifically addressing ASD, Koenig et al. (2000) highlighted interventions targeting social, cognitive, and communication goals. Many families choose intensive Applied Behavioral Analysis (ABA) intervention programs; however, the literature is mixed as to the actual effectiveness of these programs. Many professionals recommend balancing ABA therapy with other developmentally appropriate interventions that focus on development within natural environments (see Odom, Rogers, McDougle, Hume, & McGee, 2007, for a full review of treatments). Other predictors of success include the inclusion of the family, consistency, and predictability (Koenig et al.).

**Spiritual Issues.** The Bible reveals many truths that are particularly salient for individuals who have developmental disabilities and for the professionals, family members, and others who work with them. First, the Bible clearly states that all people were made in the image of God (Gen. 9:6), being carefully designed by God (Ex. 4:11; Ps. 139:13). Moreover, believers are repeatedly reminded that God judges man not by outward appearance, but by one's heart (1 Sam. 16:7). Second, Jesus reminds us that disability may be used to bring glory to God (Jn. 9). Third, as the body of Christ, we are advised that "those parts of the body that seem to be weaker are indispensable" (1 Cor. 12:22). Fourth, as Christ followers, we are called to administer justice and serve with mercy and compassion (Mic. 6:8; Zech. 7:9), traits which serve as practical means of fulfilling the greatest commandment (Mt. 22:37-40). Finally, it is important to note that many theologians address disability through a "theology of suffering"; however, some parents of individuals with disabilities, as well as those who have disabilities themselves, see disability not as suffering, but rather as a gift.

Research has found that families with children with disabilities are at risk for decreased family well-being compared to families with typically developing children (Blacher & Hatton, 2007). However, Tarakeshwar and Pargament (2001) revealed that positive religious coping (e.g., perceiving God's will or the child as a gift from God, spiritual support, and collaborative religious coping) in families of children with autism was significantly associated with a positive religious outcome (i.e., spiritual growth and elevated closeness to God or the church), and higher stress-related growth. Family interviews also noted the church as a protective factor associated with higher well-being, which is consistent with other research on the role of religiosity in coping and as a form of social support (Blacher & Hatton).

**Conclusion.** After examining the research, the summary message is that "difference is not deviance" in the field of developmental disorders. By adopting a person-first ideology (i.e., a child with autism, as opposed to an autistic child) that acknowledges each individual as a beautiful work of God, professionals, families, and the church can set individuals with developmental disorders on a positive developmental trajectory that promotes competence across the life span.

**Brianne L. Friberg**

## REFERENCES

American Psychiatric Association. (2000). *Diagnostic and Statistical Manual of Mental Disorders* (4th ed., text rev.). Washington, DC: Author.

Blacher, J., & Hatton, C. (2007). Families in context: Influences on coping and adaptation. In S. L. Odom, R. H. Horner, M. E. Snell, & J. Blacher (Eds.), *Handbook of Developmental Disabilities* (pp. 469-482). New York, NY: Guilford Press.

Boulet, S. L., Boyle, C. A., & Schieve, L. A. (2009). Health care use and health and functional impact of developmental disabilities among U.S. children, 1997-2005. *Archives of Pediatrics and Adolescent Medicine, 163*(1), 19-26.

Carta, J. J., & Kong, N. Y. (2007). Trends and issues in interventions for preschoolers with developmental disabilities. In S. L. Odom, R. H. Horner, M. Snell, & J. Blacher (Eds.), *Handbook on Developmental Disabilities* (pp. 181-198). New York, NY: Guilford Press.

Centers for Disease Control. (2010). *Autism Spectrum Disorders (ASDs)*. Retrieved from http://www.cdc.gov/ncbddd/autism/data.html#prevalence

Gilliam, W. S., & Mayes, L. C. (2000). Developmental assessment of infants and toddlers. In C. H. Zeanah, Jr. (Ed.), *Handbook of Infant Mental Health* (2nd ed., pp. 236-248). New York, NY: Guilford.

Hartung, C. M., & Widiger, T. A. (1998). Gender differences in diagnosis of mental disorders. *Psychological Bulletin, 123*, 260-278.

Innocenti, M. S., & White, K. R. (1993). Are more intensive early intervention programs more effective? A literature review. *Exceptionality 4*(1), 31-50.

Koenig, K., Rubin, E., Klin, A., & Volkmar, F. R. (2000). Autism and the pervasive developmental disorders. In C. H. Zeanah, Jr. (Ed.), *Handbook of Infant Mental Health* (2nd ed., pp. 298-320). New York, NY: Guilford Press.

Meisels, S. J., & Fenichel, E. (Eds.). (1996). *New Visions for the Developmental Assessment of Infants and Young Children*. Washington, DC: Zero to Three.

Odom, S. L., Horner, R. H., Snell, M. E., & Blacher, J. (2007). The construct of developmental disabilities. In S. L. Odom, R. H. Horner, M. E. Snell, & J. Blacher (Eds.), *Handbook of Developmental Disabilities* (pp. 3-14). New York, NY: Guilford Press.

Odom, S. L., Rogers, S., McDougle, C. J., Hume, K., & McGee, G. (2007). Early intervention for children with autism spectrum disorders. In S. L. Odom, R. H. Horner, M. E. Snell, & J. Blacher (Eds.), *Handbook of Developmental Disabilities* (pp. 199-223). New York, NY: Guilford Press.

Tarakeshwar N., & Pargament, K. I. (2001). Religious coping in families of children with autism. *Focus on Autism and Other Developmental Disabilities, 16*(4), 247-260.

Texas Statewide Leadership for Autism Training. (2010). Autism screening and assessment. *Texas Autism Resource Guide for Effective Teaching*. Retrieved from http://www.txautism.net/docs/Guide/Evaluation/AutismScreen_Assess.pdf

U.S. Department of Health and Human Services, Administration for Children and Families, Office of Public Affairs. (2010). *Administration on Developmental Disabilities (ADD)*. Retrieved from http://www.acf.hhs.gov/opa/fact_sheets/add_factsheet.html

## INTELLECTUAL DISABILITIES

**Terminology.** Throughout history, the terminology of special education has undergone continuous changes. For many years, the vocabulary most often chosen to describe people with cognitive limitations has been *mental retardation*, but more recently, *intellectual disabilities* has become a popular term. The Individuals with Disabilities Education Act (IDEA) used the term *disability*, which is "probably an unfortunate choice of terms because it conflicts with current philosophy in special education and with the intent of the *IDEA* by focusing on a person's lack of ability" (Thomas, 1996, p. 5). This term for those who are precious in God's sight has slowly begun to be viewed as unacceptable, just as its predecessor terms are no longer used: *mental deficient*, *idiot*, *imbecile*, and *moron*. The National Association for Retarded Children chose to change its name to the Arc, eliminating any reference to intellectual disabilities. Likewise, in 2002 the Council for Exceptional Children's Division on Mental Retardation voted to change the name to The Division on Developmental Disabilities.

**Identification.** Two concepts are essential to understanding the identification of people with intellectual disabilities: intelligence and adaptive behavior. The construct of intelligence refers to general mental capabilities. According to the 9th edition of *Mental Retardation: Definition, Classification, and Systems of Supports*, significantly subaverage intellectual functioning was "defined as an IQ of approximately 70 to 75 or below" (Cuskelly, 2004, p. 118).

The second essential concept to be aware of was adaptive behavior. "It now consists of three areas, as resulting from factor analytical research studies" (de Bildt et al., 2005, p. 318). These areas were conceptual, social, and practical skills that enable those with an intellectual disability to function independently. These conceptual skills include reading and expressive language, reading and writing, money concepts, and self-directions. Social skills include interpersonal relationships, responsibility, self-esteem, and following rules and laws. Finally, the practical skills were defined as personal hygiene and grooming, daily living activities, and occupational skills (American Association on Mental Retardation, 2002).

The awareness of these two concepts enables those who work with people with disabilities to have a thorough understanding of intellectual disabilities. In order to meet the needs of this population, specific skills in these deficit areas must be taught.

**Legislation.** The most notable legislative action regarding intellectual disabilities was Section 504 of the Rehabilitation Act of 1973. Section 504 prohibited the discrimination against individuals who meet the definitions of a disability. According to Wegner (1988), the primary objective of Congress was to "honor the requirements of 'simple justice' by ensuring that federal funds not be expended in a discriminatory fashion" (Smith, 2001, p. 336). This civil rights law served as a protection of rights entitled to people with disabilities. "Section 504 requires entities receiving federal funds (e.g., schools, colleges) to make 'reasonable accommodations to known physical or mental limitations of an otherwise qualified handicapped (person)'" (Shriner, 2000, p. 234).

The first trend of integration stems from the concept of normalization. "Normalization dictates that both the means and the ends of education for people with disabilities should be as normal as possible" (Hallahan & Kauffman, 2000, p. 44). The drive toward integration has been instigated by the deinstitutionalization movement and the push for full inclusion. During the 1960s, people with disabilities were slowly moved out of institutional settings into community placements. Likewise, inclusion advocates fought for the rights for people with disabilities to attend their neighborhood school, placing the responsibility of education on the local educational systems.

**Treatment.** It is important to recognize the need for those with intellectual disabilities to be exposed to a curriculum that is both academic and functional in order for them to learn essential social skills. This is accomplished by reviewing the historical developments, legislative progress, and curriculum developments. In addition, the significance of social skills and ethical issues must be considered when working with people with intellectual disabilities.

Beth Ackerman
M. Katherine Quigley

## REFERENCES

American Association on Mental Retardation. (2002). *The Definition of Mental Retardation.* Retrieved from http://www.aamr.org

Council for Exceptional Children (CEC). (2003). *No Child Left Behind Act of 2001: Implications for Special Education Policy and Practice.* Retrieved from http://www.ksde.org

Cuskelly, M. (2004). The evolving construct of intellectual disability: Is everything old new again? *International Journal of Disability, Development and Education, 51,* 1.

De Bildt, A., Serra, M., Luteijn, E., Kraijer, D., Sytema, S., & Minderaa, R. (2005). Social skills in children with intellectual disabilities with and without autism. *Journal of Intellectual Disability Research, 49*(5), 317-328.

Hallahan, D., & Kauffman, J. (2000). *Exceptional Learners: Introduction to Special Education.* Boston, MA: Allyn & Bacon.

Shriner, J. G. (2000). Legal perspectives on school outcome assessment for students with disabilities. *Journal of Special Education, 33*(4), 232-240.

Smith, T. (2001). Section 504, the ADA, and Public Schools. *Remedial & Special Education, 6,* 335-344.

Thomas, G. (1996). *Teaching Students with Mental Retardation: A Life Goal Curriculum Approach.* Englewood Cliffs, NJ: Prentice-Hall.

Wegner, J. H. (1988). Educational rights of handicapped children: Three federal statutes and an evolving jurisprudence. Part 1: The statutory maze. *Journal of Law and Education, 17*(3), 387-457.

## CONDUCT DISORDER

An impulsive, aggressive, behaviorally disordered, or even violent minor is not new, and this phenomenon can be found in almost any culture or society. Frequently classified as juvenile delinquency or antisocial behavior, conduct disorder is a diagnosis that continues to present challenges for mental-health professionals. Left unchecked and untreated, impacted adolescents can develop into sociopathic and/or psychopathic adults. The events at Columbine High School in Colorado and Virginia Tech are grim reminders for anyone working with this volatile population. Nevertheless, it remains difficult to pinpoint a singular or absolute causal factor (Burke, Loeber, & Birmaher, 2002).

According to the *Diagnostic and Statistical Manual of Mental Disorders* (*DSM-IV-TR*), conduct disorder is a "repetitive and persistent pattern of behavior in which the basic rights of others or major age-appropriate societal norms or rules are violated" (American Psychiatric Association [APA], 2000, p. 93). The onset of the disorder, which is estimated to affect between 1% and 10% of the general population, can occur in either childhood or adolescence, with a higher prevalence among males. Other features include aggression toward people and/or animals, property destruction, truancy, vandalism, deceitfulness, and theft—all of which are usually accompanied by a general lack of guilt, shame, or remorse. Typically, the diagnosis is given if there are multiple symptoms over a 12-month period. Comorbidity with certain mood disorders (Rohde, Clarke, Mace, Jorgensen, & Seeley, 2004) or substance use disorders (Elkins, McGue, & Iacono, 2007) is also common. One study (Herpertz, Mueller, Qunaibi, Lichterfeld, & Konrad, 2005) has linked childhood ADHD with a higher risk of developing conduct disorder due to autonomic hyporesponsiveness (an inability to appropriately process information that produces adaptive cognitive-emotional reactions).

The fastest-growing segment of the nation's criminal population is young people. Statistics from the U.S. Department of Justice reveal an alarming trend:

- In the last two decades, the arrest rate for juveniles committing murder increased 93% (72% for aggravated assault and 24% for forcible rape).
- About 3 million thefts and violent crimes occur on or near a school campus each year (nearly 16,000 incidents per day).
- 20% of high school students now carry a firearm, knife, razor, club, or some other weapon on a regular basis.
- 75% of all juvenile delinquents have at least one alcoholic parent.

According to the Centers for Disease Control, more than 150,000 teens use cocaine and 500,000 use marijuana once or more per week; nearly half a million junior and senior high students are weekly binge drinkers; and an estimated 10 million to 15 million teens need treatment for abuse each year. To say that "at risk" adolescents represent a growing problem would be a significant understatement. The primary determinants and etiology of this disorder need ongoing research (both biological and environmental), as do the factors that promote and enhance resiliency and empowerment among young people (Capuzzi & Gross, 2004).

Conduct disorder is more severe than what is considered as simple adolescent rebellion or the testing of limits, and it presents a more complex clinical picture. The lack of empathy or empathic concern—defined as a callous disregard for the welfare of others—is an identified risk factor. This is an important dynamic because empathy plays a central role in the inhibition of unwarranted aggression toward others. The feelings of powerlessness, especially those associated with childhood trauma, abuse, and a lower socioeconomic status, can also be critical when assessing a client's behavior. More recent research has further identified a disruption of normal developmental pathways leading to callous-unemotional traits that may eventually result in antisocial, aggressive, or delinquent tendencies (Frick, 2006).

Successful treatment often incorporates the close involvement of the child's family and includes a strong psychoeducational component. Early and comprehensive care is critical in stemming the likelihood of continuing destructive behaviors into adulthood. Due to conduct-disordered clients' inherent distrust of most adults and an underlying aggressive nature, working effectively with them can be challenging, is rarely brief, and may require a team approach. Proactive and intentional methods, especially those having a high degree of structure, are often helpful. In the first randomized and controlled study of its kind, Rohde et al. (2004) found that cognitive-behavioral interventions significantly influenced positive treatment results. It is also vital for parents and other family members to receive appropriate support.

Beyond the valid clinical concerns that must be addressed within a Christian framework, it is equally important to note the active role that parents play in the development of their children. The Greek word for discipline is *paideia*, which is a much broader construct than mere corporal punishment or penal retribution because it includes the notion of instructing and guiding with the purpose of correction, education, and spiritual growth. Godly and grace-oriented discipline communicates love (Pr. 3:12), teaches wisdom and understanding (Pr. 9:9), teaches a proper lifestyle (Pr. 6:23), protects against destruction (Pr. 23:12-14), and brings the peaceable fruit of righteousness (Heb. 12:11).

Eric Scalise

## REFERENCES


American Psychiatric Association. (2000). *Diagnostic and Statistical Manual of Mental Disorders* (4th ed., text rev.). Washington, DC: Author.

Burke, J. D., Loeber, R., & Birmaher, B. (2002). Oppositional defiant disorder and conduct disorder: A review of the past 10 years. *Journal of the American Academy of Child & Adolescent Psychiatry, 41*(11), 1275-1293.

Capuzzi, D., & Gross, D. (Eds.). (2004). *Youth at Risk* (4th ed.). Alexandria, VA: American Counseling Association.

Elkins, I. J., McGue, M., & Iacono, W. G. (2007). Prospective effects of attention-deficit/hyperactivity disorder, conduct disorder, and sex on adolescent substance use and abuse. *Archives of General Psychiatry, 64*(10), 1145-1152.

Frick, P. J. (2006). Developmental pathways to conduct disorder. *Child and Adolescent Psychiatric Clinics of North America, 15*(2), 311-331.

Herpertz, S. C., Mueller, B., Qunaibi, M., Lichterfeld, C., & Konrad, K. (2005). Response to emotional stimuli in boys with conduct disorder. *American Journal of Psychiatry, 162*(6), 1100-1107.

Rohde, P., Clarke, G. N., Mace, D. E., Jorgensen, J. S., & Seeley, J. R. (2004). An efficacy/effectiveness study of cognitive-behavioral treatment for adolescents with comorbid major depression and conduct disorder. *Journal of the American Academy of Child & Adolescent Psychiatry, 43*(6), 660-668.


## IMPULSE CONTROL DISORDERS

Impulse control disorders are a broad group of diagnoses in the *Diagnostic and Statistical Manual of Mental Disorders* (*DSM-IV-TR*) surrounding a core concept of difficulty with controlling impulsive acts (American Psychiatric Association [APA], 2000). Most of these disorders are first diagnosed in childhood or adolescence and encompass the common diagnoses of attention-deficit/hyperactivity disorder (ADHD), oppositional defiant disorder (ODD), and conduct disorder (CD). Impulse control disorders not elsewhere classified often have onset in the young adult years and include the diagnoses of intermittent explosive disorder, kleptomania, pyromania, pathological gambling, trichotillomania, and impulse control disorder NOS. Impulse control disorders may co-occur with each other (such as ADHD and ODD) or with other mental-health diagnoses, such as anxiety disorder, obsessive-compulsive disorder, or depression (APA; Kessler et al., 2007).

**Description and Prevalence.** ADHD was originally described as minimal brain dysfunction in the 1950s because the symptoms mirrored those seen in individuals with traumatic brain injury (Accardo, Shapiro, & Capute, 1997). All of the impulse disorders are more common in individuals with a known family history of these disorders (Elia & Devotto, 2007), and more recent genetic and neuroimaging studies also lend support to the neurological basis of these behaviors (Castellanos et al., 2002).

A recent national study in the United States suggests a projective lifetime risk of approximately 25% for a diagnosis of one or more impulse control disorders, with a fairly even distribution between ADHD, ODD and CD (Kessler et al., 2005). The age of onset for this group of mental-health diagnoses is quite young, with 99% of patients being diagnosed by age 18. Intermittent explosive disorder is an exception to this pattern, with onset in young adult years (Kessler et al.). These disorders are all more common in boys than girls. The most common impulse control disorders in adolescents are described below.

*Attention-deficit/hyperactivity disorder* (ADHD). There are three subtypes of ADHD: predominately inattentive subtype, predominately hyperactive-impulsive subtype, and the combined subtype, which is most common. Presenting symptoms often include distractibility, hyperactivity, and poor attention to task. In the school years, there may be reports of poor school performance and poor organizational skills. However, these individuals are often able to focus on tasks they enjoy, such as TV or video games. Symptoms must be present before age 7, although diagnosis can be made even in adulthood. There must also be impairment in at least two life areas, such as home, school, or other social settings (APA, 2000).

*Oppositional defiant disorder* (ODD). This disorder is characterized by purposefully noncompliant, argumentative, and hostile behavior. It must be differentiated from both ADHD and normal developmental oppositional behavior in children of a comparative age and developmental level. Symptoms must also cause impairment in functioning in home, school, or social settings and be present for more than 6 months (APA, 2000).

*Conduct disorder.* Conduct disorder is usually diagnosed in older children and adolescents. It is a repetitive pattern of behavior that violates the rights of others or societal norms. Behaviors associated with conduct disorder include aggression to people or animals, deliberate destruction of property, theft, or school truancy. Children with conduct disorder may have involvement with law enforcement as a result of their behaviors (APA, 2000).

**Diagnosis.** A thorough history is essential to accurately diagnose impulse control disorders. If needed, the adolescent should be referred to a physician to rule out organic causes of behavior problems, such as thyroid disorders or sleep disturbance. Standardized screening tools can be helpful in differential diagnosis and evaluating for comorbid conditions. Several reliable screening tools for ADHD are readily available, including the Vanderbilt ADHD Diagnostic Rating Scales (Wolraich et al., 2003), the Conners Rating Scales—Revised (CRS-R) (Conners, 2008), and the Achenbach Child Behavior Checklist (CBCL) (Achenbach & Rescorla, 2001).

All of these screening tools offer parent and teacher versions, which include the core *DSM-IV-TR* criteria for ADHD as well as screening for comorbid conditions of ODD, conduct disorder, anxiety, depression, and learning disability. There are also CBCL and Conner's self-report measures for adolescents.

**Treatment.** The most common pharmacologic treatments for ADHD are stimulant medications, and approximately 80% of patients will respond to the first stimulant medication trial. The other impulse control disorders may be treated with medications, but response rate is not as high as for ADHD. The best treatments for all impulse control disorders is a combination of pharmacotherapy with behavioral interventions, including intensive family therapy, parent management training, and involvement of community services (Jensen et al., 2001a; Jensen et al., 2001b). Adolescents with impulse control disorders may benefit from involvement of school personnel to develop structured behavior plans and/or individualized education plans.

**Spiritual Issues.** It is tempting to view the adolescent with an impulse control disorder in isolation and label the presenting problems at the individual level. However, a robust literature exists in both secular (e.g., Bronfenbrenner, 1979; Minuchin, 1974) and Christian (e.g., Collins, 2007; Cloud & Townsend, 2003) arenas calling for analysis to occur at the systems level, taking into account both personal and environmental factors as they are related to an individual's behavior. For example, parents of children with impulse disorders have a higher probability of having a mental-health diagnosis, which may result in an even greater level of parenting stress and affect the adolescent's home environment.

Because adolescents with impulse control disorders may experience a strong sense of failing in key areas (e.g., schooling, family, and establishing and maintaining friendships), they may struggle to see themselves as gifts from God with intrinsic value. Instead, they may feel isolated, frustrated, misfits, or even a burden to society and others (Collins, 2007).

Thus, parenting an adolescent with an impulse control disorder often causes a high level of parenting stress. Under these conditions a parental tendency emerges to overgeneralize or mislabel, particularly as the adolescent's behavior may often be interpreted as a reflection of poor parenting skills. Short-circuiting this negative feedback loop is critical for the parent and adolescent and is expressed in Paul's instructions to parents in Ephesians 6:4 concerning not exasperating your child.

**Conclusion.** Effective Christian counseling approaches concerning adolescents with impulse control disorders entail a bio-psycho-social-spiritual perspective. In this model, diagnosis requires use of well-established diagnostic instruments as well as collaboration with other key stakeholders (including parents, teachers, and allied health-care professionals). Likewise, efficacious treatment typically requires a multisystem approach—some combination of counseling, family support, pharmacotherapy, and a careful, nonlegalistic integration of biblical Christianity.

Mark D. Newmeyer
Amy J. Newmeyer

## REFERENCES


Accardo, P. J., Shapiro, B. K., & Capute, A. J. (Eds.). (1997). *Behavior Belongs in the Brain: Neurobehavioral Syndromes*. Baltimore, MD: York Press.

Achenbach, T. M., & Rescorla, L. A. (2001). *Manual for the ASEBA School-Age Forms & Profiles*. Burlington, VT: University of Vermont Research Center for Children, Youth, & Families.

American Psychiatric Association. (2000). *Diagnostic and Statistical Manual of Mental Disorders* (4th ed., text rev.). Washington, DC: Author.

Bronfenbrenner, U. (1979). *The Ecology of Human Development: Experiments by Nature and Design*. Cambridge, MA: Harvard University Press.

Castellanos, F. X., Lee, P. P., Sharp, W., Jeffries, N. O., Greenstein, D. K., & Clasen, L. S. (2002). Developmental trajectories of brain volume abnormalities in children and adolescents with attention-deficit hyperactivity disorder. *Journal of the American Medical Association, 288,* 1740-1748.

Cloud, H., & Townsend, J. (2003). *Making Small Groups Work.* Grand Rapids, MI: Zondervan.

Collins, G. R. (2007). *Christian Counseling: A Comprehensive Guide* (3rd ed.). Nashville, TN: Thomas Nelson.

Conners, C. K. (2008). *Conners' Rating Scale Technical Manual* (3rd ed.). New York, NY: Multi-Health Systems.

Elia, J., & Devotto, M. (2007). ADHD genetics: 2007 update. *Current Psychiatry Reports 9,* 434-439.

Jensen, P. S., Hinshaw, S., Kraemer, H. C., Lenora, N., Newcorn, J. H., Abikoff, H. B.,...Vitiello, B. (2001). ADHD comorbidity findings from the MTA study: Comparing subgroups. *Journal of the American Academy of Child and Adolescent Psychiatry, 40,* 147-158.

Jensen, P. S., Hinshaw, S. P., Swanson, J. M., Greenhill, L. L., Conners, C. K. Arnold, L. E.,...Wigal, T. (2001). Findings from the NIMH multimodal treatment study of ADHD (MTA): Implications and applications for primary care providers. *Journal of Developmental & Behavioral Pediatrics, 22,* 60-73.

Kessler, R. C., Amminger, G. P., Aguilar-Gaxiola, S., Alonso, J., Lee, S., & Ustun, T. B. (2007). Age of onset of mental disorders: A review of recent literature. *Current Opinion in Psychiatry, 20,* 359-364.

Kessler, R. C., Berglund, P., Demler, O., Jin, R., Merikangas, K. R., & Walters, E. (2005). Lifetime prevalence and age-of-onset distributions of DSM-IV disorders in the national comorbidity survey replication. *Archives of General Psychiatry, 62,* 593-602.

Minuchin, S. (1974). *Families and Family Therapy.* Boston, MA: Harvard University Press.

Wolraich, M. L., Lambert, W., Doffing, M. A., Bickman, L., Simmons, T., & Worley, K. (2003). Psychometric properties of the Vanderbilt ADHD Diagnostic Parent Rating Scale in a referred population. *Journal of Pediatric Psychology, 28,* 559-568.

## ATTENTION-DEFICIT/HYPERACTIVITY DISORDER (ADHD)

**Description.** Attention-deficit/hyperactivity disorder (ADHD) is the most commonly diagnosed childhood mental-health disorder (Barlow & Durand, 2009; Mash & Wolfe, 2010). ADHD often continues through adolescence and adulthood and is essentially characterized by difficulty paying attention and staying focused, difficulty controlling behavior, and hyperactivity. This hyperactivity is sometimes referred to as overactivity.

One of the challenges in diagnosing ADHD is that these symptoms are fundamentally common characteristics of childhood. The distinguishing factor is that these symptoms must cause significant impairment and *not* be developmentally consistent.

Affecting about 3% to 8% of school-age children, ADHD describes children who struggle with persistent, age-inappropriate symptoms of distractibility, impulsivity, and hyperactivity. These symptoms cause substantial challenges in day-to-day activities. Specific criteria for diagnosis exist, but the presentation can vary considerably between children. ADHD is two to three times more common in boys than girls.

According to the *Diagnostic and Statistical Manual of Mental Disorders* (*DSM-IV-TR*), a diagnosis of ADHD can be given for hyperactive-impulsive or inattentive symptoms that cause impairment if the impairment was present before the age of seven and the impairment is present in two or more settings. Specific diagnostic criteria include six or more symptoms of inattention or six or more symptoms of hyperactivity-impulsivity. The symptoms (listed below) must have persisted for at least six months to a degree that is maladaptive and inconsistent with developmental level (American Psychiatric Association [APA], 2000, p. 92).

*Inattention.*

- often fails to give close attention to details or makes careless mistakes in schoolwork, work, or other activities
- often has difficulty sustaining attention in tasks or play activities
- often does not seem to listen when spoken to directly
- often does not follow through on instructions and fails to finish schoolwork, chores, or duties in the workplace (not due to oppositional behavior or failure to understand instructions)
- often has difficulty organizing tasks and activities

- often avoids, dislikes, or is reluctant to engage in tasks that require sustained mental effort (such as schoolwork or homework)
- often loses things necessary for tasks or activities (e.g., toys, school assignments, pencils, books, or tools)
- is often easily distracted by extraneous stimuli
- is often forgetful in daily activities

*Hyperactivity.*

- often fidgets with hands or feet or squirms in seat
- often leaves seat in classroom or in other situations in which remaining seated is expected
- often runs about or climbs excessively in situations in which it is inappropriate (in adolescents or adults, may be limited to subjective feelings of restlessness)
- often has difficulty playing or engaging in leisure activities quietly
- is often "on the go" or often acts as if "driven by a motor"
- often talks excessively

*Impulsivity.*

- often blurts out answers before questions have been completed
- often has difficulty awaiting turn
- often interrupts or intrudes on others

**Causes.** There are multiple theories about the causes of ADHD. There is evidence that ADHD is a neurobiological disorder (Barlow & Durand, 2009; Mash & Wolfe, 2010), including genetic and environmental issues. There are theories about motivational deficits, self-regulation, response inhibition, and arousal levels—all of which need to be considered within the context of biology and environment.

Prenatal and perinatal factors may compromise neurobiological development (e.g., maternal substance use during pregnancy, malnutrition, trauma) and lead to ADHD symptoms. Children with ADHD often demonstrate brain anomalies, but this cannot explain causation. Psychosocial factors are not considered causal but can affect symptom severity and treatment response. Diets and food allergies have been hypothesized to be causes for ADHD, but the research does not support this.

**Assessment.** The *DSM-IV-TR* (APA, 2000) provides the diagnostic criteria for the identification and classification of ADHD. Unfortunately, a diagnosis of ADHD may be given simply following a phone call from the school to the parents and a brief trip to the pediatrician. This oversimplified process may or may not lead to an accurate diagnosis and is inadequate.

Erk (2008, p. 123) suggests that an ADHD evaluation should include the following foundational elements:

- an interview with the suspected child or adolescent
- the use of parent and teacher interviews or reports
- the administration of ADHD checklists to parents and key teachers
- observations from across multiple settings that describe the degree of impairment that might exist in each setting
- a written report from the examining counselor

It is recommended and appropriate that mental-health professionals involved with ADHD clients have appropriate training and supervised experience to assess, evaluate, and diagnose ADHD. Some assert that

ADHD is overdiagnosed, but it can certainly be argued that ADHD is inadequately assessed before treatment is implemented.

Additionally, in the assessment of ADHD, the issue of differential diagnosis is crucial. Other psychological conditions and disorders should be ruled out, including pervasive developmental disorders, trauma, or substance abuse. It is also possible for the diagnosis of ADHD to coexist with other diagnoses.

**Treatment.** Treatment for ADHD is generally focused on two fronts: biological and psychosocial interventions (Barlow & Durand, 2009). Biological interventions involve medications that are intended to improve attention and reduce hyperactivity and impulsivity. Psychosocial treatment involves parent training and school interventions focused on decreasing disruptive behaviors, improving academic performance, and working on social skills.

Some parents are reluctant to see their children medicated for ADHD, but if the diagnosis is accurate, medications are almost always needed. Parents may worry that prescribing medications for children may predispose them to later substance abuse. On the contrary, the unmedicated ADHD child is at greater risk of adolescent drug use, delinquency, and dropping out of school. Child counselors should encourage medication evaluations and support continued compliance with prescribed medications.

The most common class of medications prescribed for children with ADHD are the psychostimulants, such as methylphenidate (Ritalin, Metadate, Concerta). Stimulants come in various forms—pills, capsules, liquid, or skin patches. Using a stimulant medication to treat hyperactivity may seem paradoxical; however, low doses are effective for children, adolescents, and adults. Methylphenidate is the most commonly prescribed ADHD medication, but there are other stimulant and nonstimulant medications used in the medical treatment process.

A treatment focus that may be overlooked for ADHD children includes the issue of self-image or self-esteem. Often due to the behavioral disruptions related to ADHD, these children may have peer and sibling relational challenges as well as conflicts with parents and teachers. The potential damage to self-esteem and the need for commensurate intervention is crucial. Medications are effective in symptom reduction but do not heal wounded self-images.

**Spiritual Issues.** The primary spiritual issue related to ADHD may be the loneliness and alienation felt by children and families struggling with this diagnosis. Children and families may feel abandoned (or even punished) by God in and through this struggle. The treatment for ADHD may include a combination of medical and mental-health interventions, but these children and families also benefit from the support of loving communities. This should, of course, occur in Christian churches. Some churches sponsor or host support groups for parents who have children struggling with ADHD. Additionally, children's ministry staff and youth pastors should be educated on the fundamental information about ADHD.

**Conclusion.** ADHD is considered a chronic condition and is not viewed as curable. Most ADHD children carry the symptoms into adolescence and adulthood, but the symptoms can become more manageable. Assuming compliance with treatment, symptom relief is probable. Treatment is very effective, and research continues in the understanding of ADHD as well as the development of more effective treatments and interventions. As effective as treatment may be, however, ADHD children need the support of family, friends, school personnel, and the Christian community.

Daniel S. Sweeney

## REFERENCES

American Psychiatric Association. (2000). *Diagnostic and Statistical Manual of Mental Disorders* (4th ed., text rev.). Washington, DC: Author.

Barlow, M., & Durand, M. (2009). *Abnormal Psychology: An Integrative Approach* (5th ed.). Belmont, CA: Wads worth Cengage Learning.

Erk, R. (2008). *Counseling Treatment for Children and Adolescents with DSM-IV-TR Disorders* (2nd ed.). Upper Saddle River, NJ: Prentice Hall.

Mash, E., & Wolfe, D. (2010). *Abnormal Child Psychology* (4th ed.). Belmont, CA: Wadsworth Cengage Learning.

National Institute of Mental Health. (2011). *Attention Deficit Hyperactivity Disorder.* Retrieved from http://www.nimh.nih.gov/health/publications/attention-deficit-hyperactivity-disorder/complete-index.shtml

## CHILD ABUSE

Reports of the maltreatment of children and adolescents date back thousands of years. Yet it was not until "The Battered Child Syndrome" was published in the *Journal of the American Medical Association* in 1962 that maltreatment of children gained the attention of the medical community and the public (Kempe, Silverman, Steele, Droegemueller, & Silver, 1962). A decade later, the Child Abuse Prevention and Treatment Act of 1974 was signed into law. Since that time, interest in this issue has become widespread.

**Description.** The maltreatment of children is a major concern not only in America but also around the world. The Centers for Disease Control and Prevention estimates that almost 9 million children in this country have experienced maltreatment at some point in their lives (Wulczyn, 2009), and the World Health Organization (WHO) estimates that worldwide, nearly 60,000 children die annually as a result of abuse. However, these numbers fail to reflect the true scope of the problem (WHO, 2006).

Maltreatment can be divided into four categories: neglect, physical abuse, sexual abuse, and psychological abuse (Lawson, 2009) and is generally defined as

> any act or failure to act on the part of a parent or caretaker which results in death, serious physical or emotional harm, sexual abuse or exploitation; or an act or failure to act which presents an imminent risk of serious harm (U.S. Department of Health and Human Services, 2004).

*Physical maltreatment* is any act that causes physical injury or has the potential to harm a child. *Emotional abuse* includes nonphysical forms of hostile treatment, typically including ridicule, intimidation, rejection, and denigration. *Neglect* has recently been recognized to include both physical and emotional types (Music, 2009). Physical neglect refers to the failure of a caregiver to provide basic life necessities when the caregiver is able to do so. It is important to distinguish situations of poverty from cases where resources are available to the caregiver. Emotional neglect transpires when a caregiver ignores the child and withholds love even though physical needs are met (Music). *Sexual abuse* occurs when a child is used for the sexual gratification of an adult or is purposefully exposed to developmentally inappropriate sexual material.

Children's reactions to maltreatment vary, although the consequences frequently have a destructive impact on their physical well-being and their behavioral, emotional, and neurological functioning. Psychological maladies include somatic complaints, depression, anxiety, panic, impulsivity, suicidal ideation, and PTSD symptoms (Lawson, 2009). Children experiencing various forms of abuse from attachment figures may develop complex trauma symptoms (Sibcy, 2007). In addition, these children often have inadequate coping skills, poor school performance, and difficulty maintaining relationships—problems that may follow them well into adulthood (Wulczyn, 2009).

**Spiritual Issues.** Maltreatment profoundly impacts children's basic assumptions about God and the world. Early relationships are foundational to the development of self-worth and the ability to relate to others, especially God (Clinton & Sibcy, 2002). When the abusers are the parents, the children may experience an intense fear of God stemming from the belief that God is angry with or does not love them, which often keeps children from turning to God for comfort (Jones, 2002).

**Assessment.** At-risk families tend to be isolated and impoverished and to be experiencing multiple stressors (Lawson, 2009; Wulczyn, 2009). Therefore, a thorough assessment of the family system and the events surrounding the abuse are vital in determining the course of treatment. Subjective and objective assessment techniques are necessary in the assessment process. Objective evaluations determine the presence of symptoms, and subjective factors help predict the severity and intensity of symptoms. Assessments include attention to these issues:

- family history
- separation, illnesses, or abandonment by parents
- relationship with attachment figures
- family stressors
- Child Protective Services involvement
- legal history

These are some of the available assessment instruments:

- The Child Behavior Checklist (Achenbach, 1991)
- The Trauma Symptom Checklist for Children (Briere, 1996)
- The Trauma Symptom Checklist for Young Children—Caretaker Report (Briere et al., 2001)
- The UCLA PTSD Index for DSM-IV (Pynoos, Rodriguez, Steinberg, Stuber, & Frederick, 1998)

**Treatment.** Interventions must adapt to the unique needs of the child (Wulczyn, 2009). Typically, the more intense and extensive the maltreatment, the younger the child, and the less support from the caregiver, the more time is necessary in therapy. According to Zonnebelt-Smeenge and Devries (2007), "What is crucial in treatment is the retelling of the traumatic experience and working toward changing thoughts and behaviors that interfere with a healthy emotional and functional state of being" (p. 21).

**Conclusion.** When proven counseling techniques are coupled with deepening the individual's relationship with Christ, survivors of abuse are offered hope for a life beyond the scars. For this, Langberg (2007) asserts, "You can sit with hope, no matter the darkness, the silence, or the assault, for the God we serve is in the darkness with you preparing glory yet unseen" (p. 52).

**Shannon Wolf**

## REFERENCES


Achenbach, T. M. (1991). *Manual for the Child: Behavior Checklist 4-18, 1991 Profile.* Burlington, VT: Department of Psychiatry, University of Vermont.

Briere, J. (1996). *Trauma Symptom Checklist for Children (TSCC) Professional Manual.* Odessa, TX: Psychological Assessment Resources.

Briere, J., Johnson, K., Bissada, A., Damon, L., Crouch, J., Gift, E.,...Ernst, V. (2001). The trauma symptom checklist for young children. *Child Abuse & Neglect, 25*(8), 1001-1014.

Clinton, T., & Sibcy, G. (2002). *Attachments: Why You Love and Feel and Act the Way You Do.* Brentwood, TN: Integrity.

Jones, I. (2002). *Counsel of Heaven on Earth.* Nashville, TN: Broadman & Holman.

Kempe C. H., Silverman, F. N., Steele, B. F., Droegemueller, W., & Silver, H. K. (1962). The battered child syndrome. *Journal of the American Medical Association, 191,* 17-24.

Langberg, D. (2007). Violence, violation, and godly responses to vile acts. *Christian Counseling Today, 15*(3), 50-52.

Lawson, D. M. (2009). Understanding and treating children who experience interpersonal maltreatment: Empirical findings. *Journal of Counseling & Development, 87,* 204-215.

Music, G. (2009). Neglecting neglect: Some thoughts about children who have lacked good input, and are "undrawn" and "unenjoyed." *Journal of Child Psychotherapy, 35*(2), 142-156.

Pynoos, R., Rodriguez, N., Steinberg, A., Stuber, M., & Frederick, C. (1998). *UCLA PTSD Index for DSM-IV.* Los Angeles, CA: UCLA Trauma Psychiatry Service.

Sibcy, G. (2007). Attachment therapy for complex trauma. *Christian Counseling Today, 15*(3), 24-27.

U.S. Department of Health and Human Services; Administration for Children and Families; Administration on Children, Youth, and Families; Children's Bureau. (2004). *Long-Term Consequences of Child Abuse and Neglect.* Retrieved from the National Clearinghouse on Child Abuse and Neglect Information at http://www.childprotectionoffice.org/pdf/long_term_consequences.pdf

World Health Organization. (2006). *World Report on Violence and Health: Child Abuse and Neglect by Parents and Caregivers.* Retrieved from http://www.who.int/violence_injury_prevention/violence/global_campaign/en/chap3.pdf

Wulczyn, F. (2009). Epidemiological perspectives on maltreatment prevention. *Future of Children, 19*(2), 39-66.

Zonnebelt-Smeenge, S. J., & Devries, R. C. (2007). Kids traumatized by a crisis. *Christian Counseling Today, 15*(3), 20-22.

## PLAY THERAPY

Tragically, we live in a world where children experience pain and trauma all too often. As counselors, we want to provide places of safety, knowing that people don't grow when and where they don't feel safe. But how is this done?

Many counselors would say that hurting children need to talk about what happened to them and that they must verbalize their pain as part of the healing process. After all, people need to talk about their problems, don't they? Perhaps, but counseling with any client clearly needs to be developmentally appropriate. To expect children to engage in adult "talk therapy" does not honor their developmental level. Play therapy does.

**Introduction.** Children simply do not communicate the same way adults do. Adult communication requires verbal, cognitive, and abstract thinking skills. Children do not communicate this way. Children communicate though play. It is their natural medium of communication. Therefore, the basis for doing play therapy is to honor children by entering their world of communication rather than forcing children to enter our adult world of verbalization. This is empathy in action. The greatest act of empathy in the history of the world was modeled for us by the Creator himself through the Incarnation. If it was not below God to humble himself and enter our world of humanity through Christ, perhaps it should not be below those of us who work with children to enter their world.

Play therapy focuses on entering the child's world, creating a shift in approaching presenting problems. The play therapist is a facilitator and fellow explorer on a journey with a child on a mission of self-discovery. "Play therapy is not a cloak the play therapist puts on when entering the playroom and takes off when leaving; rather, it is a philosophy resulting in attitudes and behaviors for living one's life in relationships with children" (Sweeney and Landreth, 2009, p. 123).

The therapist who insists on using traditional talk therapy with children communicates a negative message. "I'm unwilling to enter your world. I am an expert, and I know best. You must leave your world of play and come up to my level of communication and interaction. The responsibility is yours." The responsibility to meet the other in a therapeutic relationship belongs, however, to the therapist.

**Play and Play Therapy.** Play is the most important and natural activity of childhood. Children have played through history, and children in all cultures play. Scripture recognizes play as a natural activity for children. "The city streets will be filled with boys and girls playing there" (Zech. 8:5). For children, play is not only what they do but also an expression of who they are. Play is instinctive, voluntary, and spontaneous. It helps children develop physically, mentally, emotionally, socially, and spiritually. Children express themselves more fully and directly through play, and for children to "play out" their experiences and feelings is a natural, dynamic, and self-healing process (Landreth, 2002). So, what is play therapy?

> A dynamic interpersonal relationship between a child (or person of any age) and a therapist trained in play therapy procedures who provides selected play materials and facilitates the development of a safe relationship for the child (or person of any age) to fully express and explore self (feelings, thoughts, experiences, and behaviors) through play, the child's natural medium of communication, for optimal growth and development (Landreth, 2002, p. 16).

This definition contains some crucial elements. Play therapy involves a *dynamic interpersonal relationship*. Relationship with Christ brings us spiritual healing, and relationship is also the basis for therapeutic healing. It seems fundamental that all therapeutic relationships should be dynamic and interpersonal. The play therapist should be *trained in play therapy procedures*. Providing play media and using talk therapy does turn the process into play therapy. Attending a brief workshop or reading a book about play therapy does not make a play therapist. Training is essential. *Selected play materials* should be provided, not a random collection of toys. In play therapy, the play is the child's language, and the toys are the child's words. The *development of a safe relationship* is facilitated by the play therapist. This does not involve following the agenda of the therapist. Most referred children already feel disempowered and out of control. When empowered, children are given the opportunity to *fully express and explore self*. Healthy self-exploration enables any client to discover a proper self-image, which is a process that arguably should lead a person to the Creator. Play therapy then allows the children to use their *natural medium of communication*—play.

**Play Therapy and Trauma.** The use of play therapy becomes even more important in cases of trauma. Children who have been traumatized need a therapeutic experience that is safe and empowering. Therapy must touch their senses and provide them with the mastery and control that have been stripped away by the traumatizing event. The sensory and kinesthetic quality of play is key in this regard.

Placing traumatized children in a room with strange adults who ask questions about the trauma is yet another disempowering experience. Questions inherently cause people to think and thus remain in a cognitive realm. Could it be that the issues of the heart—out of which flow "the springs of life" (Pr. 4:23) —might not be adequately dealt with in traditional therapeutic settings? Allowing children to communicate on their terms and at their level provides a forum for the issues of the heart to be safely addressed. Through play, traumatized children can process intrapsychic pain in a safe and therapeutically distant way.

There are neurobiological reasons for using play therapy with traumatized clients. The neurobiological effects of trauma can affect the brain's limbic system—the part of the central nervous system that guides emotion and memory. Specifically, trauma may cause abnormalities in the amygdala and hippocampus. The amygdala, which readies the body for action, may get "hijacked" by these neurobiological changes, and the trauma victim responds before the "thinking" part of the brain (the cerebral cortex) can weigh threats. This can cause trauma victims to go immediately from a stimulus to an arousal response without being able to make the intervening assessment of the cause of their arousal.

"Trauma by definition involves *speechless terror*: Patients often are simply unable to put what they feel into words and are left with intense emotions simply without being able to articulate what is going on" (van der Kolk, 2002, p. 150). This has been demonstrated through brain research, which shows that when people with PTSD relive their traumatic experiences (which is often required of them in therapy), there is decreased activity in the Broca's area of the brain, which is related to language. At the same time, there is increased activity in the limbic system. When traumatized people relive their trauma, they have great difficulty verbalizing (van der Kolk).

This observation is echoed by child trauma researchers, who note that regardless of the words used in therapy, there is little change in the midbrain or brain stem (Perry & Pate, 1994). Perry (2006) further states, "Simply stated, traumatic & neglectful experiences...cause abnormal organization and function of important neural systems in the brain, compromising the functional capacities mediated by these systems.... Matching the correct therapeutic activities to the specific developmental stage and physiological needs of a maltreated or traumatized child is the key to success" (p. 34). Play therapy recognizes both the specific developmental stage and the physiological needs of the traumatized child.

**Conclusion.** Play is necessary for normal childhood development and for the healing of childhood pain. Providing children with the opportunity to communicate through their own medium of communication and to process pain through the safety of play therapy is crucial.

Hurting children need to work through their pain through play. If lonely, hurting, and traumatized children do not have the opportunity to experience the healing power of play, the emotional wounds might never close. Christian counselors must work against leaving a generation of hurting children to live out lives of fear and anxiety. Their survival may depend on it. Despite the well-known adage, time does *not* heal wounds. Rather, the power of relationship heals wounds—a relationship with God and relationships with his children.

**Daniel S. Sweeney**

## REFERENCES


Landreth, G. (2002). *Play Therapy: The Art of the Relationship* (2nd ed.). New York, NY: Brunner-Routledge.

Perry, B. (2006). Applying principles of neurodevelopment to clinical work with maltreated children. In N. B. Webb (Ed.), *Traumatized Youth in Child Welfare* (pp. 27-52). New York, NY: Guilford Press.

Perry, B., & Pate, J. (1994). Neurodevelopment and the psychobiological roots of posttraumatic stress disorder. In L. Koziol & C. Stout (Eds.), *The Neuropsychology of Mental Disorders: A Practical Guide* (pp. 129-146). Springfield, IL: Thomas.

Sweeney, D., & Landreth, G. (2009). Child-centered play therapy. In K. O'Connor & L. Braverman (Eds.), *Play Therapy Theory and Practice: Comparing Theories and Techniques* (pp. 123-162). Hoboken, NJ: Wiley & Sons.

Van der Kolk, B. (2002). Assessment and treatment of complex PTSD. In R. Yehuda (Ed.), *Treating Trauma Survivors with PTSD* (pp. 127-156). Washington, DC: American Psychiatric Publishing.

# SUBSTANCE ABUSE AND BEHAVIORAL ADDICTIONS

## ADDICTION

**Description and Prevalence.** Substance abuse and other addictive problems are prevalent in almost every segment of society today. These problems cross all ethnic, cultural, educational, socioeconomic, gender, and age barriers. There has been an upward trend in elder substance abuse and prescription abuse over the past decade, but adolescent rates have stabilized somewhat. Yet the statistics are staggering (sources include the U.S. Department of Health and Human Services, the U.S. Department of Justice, the National Center for Health Statistics, the Centers for Disease Control and Prevention, and the U.S. Bureau of Labor Statistics):

- There are an estimated 15 million alcoholics and 10 million drug addicts in the United States, 40% of all family problems brought to domestic court are alcohol related, and 75% of all juvenile delinquents have at least one alcoholic parent. More than 150,000 teens use cocaine, and 500,000 use marijuana once a week or more. In addition, nearly half a million junior and senior high students are weekly binge drinkers. An estimated 10 million to 15 million adolescents need treatment for substance abuse each year.
- An estimated 5 million to 7 million people are addicted to prescription drugs.
- Every addict directly affects at least 5 other people. In a recent Gallup poll, 41% of those polled indicated that they had suffered physical, psychological, or social harm as a result of someone else's drinking or drugging (this is double the level reported in 1974).
- 40 million to 80 million Americans suffer from compulsive overeating, and 5% to 15% will die from its consequences each year. Some $20 billion is spent yearly by Americans seeking to lose weight.
- 1% to 2% of adolescent girls (close to 100,000 people) and 4% to 5% of college-age women struggle with anorexia and/or bulimia.
- There are 2.5 million pathological gamblers and another 3 million compulsive gamblers in the United States. Gambling has become a $500 billion industry. The suicide rate for this population is 20 times higher than the national average. Some 50 million family members are said to be adversely affected.
- There are currently more than 300 million pornographic websites with an estimated 6% to 8% of the population diagnosed with some level of sexual addiction.
- No one really knows how many workaholics there are because this addiction has received comparatively little attention. One study indicated that more than 10 million adults average 65 to 70 hours of work each week.

**Causes.** The most prevalent debate centers on whether addictive problems are disease-based (primarily genetic/biological) or choice-based (primarily habits/social environment). Major theoretical orientations include moral theory, disease theory, behavioral theory, social-learning theory, and systems theory. People of faith often incorporate the sinful nature of fallen man into the equation. Romans 7:15-25 is a poignant reminder of this. Paul wrote, "But I see another law at work in me, waging war against the law of my mind and making me a prisoner of the law of sin at work within me" (v. 23).

Even though children of alcoholics are four times as likely to become alcoholics as are children of nondrinkers, initial theories of a single alcoholism gene have been disproven. Nevertheless, biological determinants cannot simply be ignored or discarded. Years of qualified research have now clearly demonstrated that addiction is influenced both by multiple genetic traits, called *polygenic* or addictive inheritance, and by a complex array of psychosocial dynamics. However, it is important to keep in mind that susceptibility does not necessarily imply inevitability. If genetics and biology were all-encompassing and determinative, no one would freely choose to move toward recovery. Alcoholics Anonymous and other 12-step approaches have consistently demonstrated this power of choice.

Recent research continues to explore the neurobiology of addiction. In all brain functioning, neurotransmitters (chemical messengers) are released by the electrical impulses of a neuron and record sensory experiences called imprints. These imprints are encoded, passed along appropriate pathways (across a synapse), and stored (usually at the unconscious level). Dopamine is one of the major agents related to the "pleasure pathway" to/through the limbic system (where the feeling of pleasure is produced and regulated) and plays an important role in the development of addiction. Studies have shown that addictive substances (as well as behaviors) can adversely affect the nucleus accumbens, a circuit of specialized nerve cells within the limbic system. The amygdala—an almond-shaped mass of nuclei that is located deep within the temporal lobe of the brain and that plays a primary role in the processing and memory of emotional reactions—in essence hijacks normal messaging that passes through the neocortex, where cognition is managed and creates new neural pathways that enhance the addictive process. The brain has a natural blood-brain barrier, which normally does not allow water-soluble molecules to pass through capillary walls. A substance is considered to be psychoactive when it can penetrate that barrier and create changes in neurochemistry and subsequent brain functioning.

**Assessment.** Most practitioners who work in this field also understand and consider the needs-based aspect of addictive behavior that seems to fuel the dynamic. This can include the need to be insulated from worry and anxiety, the need to reduce manipulative guilt feelings, the need for approval and acceptance, the need to maintain a sense of control and power in one's environment, the need to avoid pain (physical, emotional, and psychological), and the need to be a perfect person and measure up to the expectations of others. As such, all addictions typically fit into four basic categories:

- addictions that stimulate—activities or substances that provide arousal and ecstasy, usually resulting in a release of adrenaline
- addictions that tranquilize—activities or substances that calm, comfort, or reduce tension and anxiety, usually resulting in a release of endorphins
- addictions that serve some psychological need, such as self-punishment, codependency, and workaholism

- addictions that satisfy unique appetites, involving both psychological and physiological components, such as pornography and some fetishes

All addictions share several common identifiers.

- They remove people from their true feelings in order to provide a form of escape.
- They control people, and the control transcends all logic or reason.
- They always involve pleasure.
- They involve psychological dependence.
- They are ultimately destructive and unhealthy.
- They eventually take priority over all of life's other issues.
- All addicts minimize or deny their addiction.

The *Diagnostic and Statistical Manual of Mental Disorders* (*DSM-IV-TR*) quantifies the difference between substance abuse and dependency. The latter can be characterized as a maladaptive pattern of substance use leading to clinically significant impairment or distress that can include tolerance, withdrawal symptoms, and increased usage in spite of the fact that doing so is ultimately destructive. Addicts usually do not become dependent on a substance or activity immediately, but only after progressing through a number of distinct stages:

*Experimentation*. People are motivated by curiosity or a desire for acceptance or escape, they do not go overboard, they learn that the effects are controlled by the level of intake, and they suffer few if any consequences.

*Occasional use or doing*. People experience periodic disruptions at work/school/home, need more of the substance or activity to get the same effect, have more actual seeking behavior, and are frequently guided by more experienced "users."

*Regular use or doing*. People begin obsessing more and are preoccupied with using or doing, begin to do it more on their own, may experience a periodic loss of control, begin to break their own self-imposed rules that regulate the behavior, experience increased shame and guilt, and look for ways to hide the behavior.

*Addiction and dependence*. These people need the substance or behavior to survive, cope, and get by in daily living/functioning, and they experience a deterioration in mental, emotional, physical, moral, and spiritual health.

However otherwise unique, all addictive behaviors throughout these stages provide short-term gain but lead to long-term pain.

Eric Scalise

## REFERENCES

American Psychiatric Association. (2000). *Diagnostic and Statistical Manual of Mental Disorders* (4th ed., text rev., pp. 181-183). Washington, DC: Author.

McNeece, C. A., & DiNitto, D. M. (2005). *Chemical Dependency: A Systems Approach* (3rd ed.). Boston, MA: Prentice Hall.

Stevens, P., & Smith, R. L. (2005). *Substance Abuse Counseling: Theory and Practice* (3rd ed.). Upper Saddle River, NJ: Prentice Hall.

## ADDICTIONS COUNSELING

**Description.** Webster's defines the word *addiction* as a "compulsive need for and use of a habit-forming substance (as heroin, nicotine, or alcohol) characterized by tolerance and by well-defined physiological symptoms upon withdrawal; broadly: persistent compulsive use of a substance known by the user to be harmful." Many use the term to imply a form of servitude or compulsion: "An obsession of the mind coupled with an allergy of the body" (Alcoholics Anonymous, 2001).

In the *Diagnostic and Statistical Manual of Mental Disorders* (*DSM-IV-TR*), the American Psychiatric Association (APA) uses the terms *abuse* and *dependence* to describe a maladaptive pattern of substance use. This condition is characterized by tolerance, withdrawal, repeated attempts at abstinence or control, continued use despite negative consequences, and a preoccupation with use. Addiction counselors specialize in helping people overcome this debilitating condition.

**Assessment.** Several attempts have been made to develop a framework for the development of addictions. Addiction counseling makes use of four models: medical, psychosocial, spiritual, and integrated bio-psycho-social-spiritual.

*The medical model.* In 1956 the American Medical Association classified alcoholism as a disease because much of an addict's behavior is based on biological predisposition. This model perceives addiction as a biophysical dysfunction or a genetic disorder, possibly impacted by acquired trauma (Doweiko, 2009).

*The psychosocial model.* Some researchers view addiction as being rooted in abnormalities of personality or character. This model is based on the assumption that there exists an addictive personality. Traits associated with the addictive personality include poor impulse control; low self-esteem; an inability to cope with stressors; egocentricity; manipulative traits; and a need for control and power, while feeling impotent and powerless (Doweiko, 2009).

*The spiritual model.* Some believe that addiction has a spiritual origin and that recovery requires a restored relationship with God. Most addicts struggle with feeling alienated from God, so at its core, addiction is a spiritual malady. They often believe "God has abandoned them for all time, and hell is inevitable" (see Clinton & Ohlschlager, 2002). Recovery is contingent on a spiritual awaking (Edmeades, 1987). Alcoholics Anonymous is one of the most popular of the spiritual treatment models and is based on a 12-step spiritual model of recovery. However, there are also several other Christian spiritual recovery models, such as Freedom Ministry and Celebrate Recovery.

*The integrated bio-psycho-social-spiritual model.* This model conceptualizes addiction as having several multidimensional factors that contribute to the disorder. It views addiction as having a myriad of causation factors, which require multiple pathways to recovery (Clinton & Jenkins, 2011). This model combines many of the aspects of the other models and focuses on the recovery of multiple dimensions of the person struggling with addiction.

During the past three decades, the addiction field has experienced substantial change in the way addictive problems are addressed. An increased influence of mental-health theory instilled a different paradigm into traditional addiction treatment philosophy. More recently, addictions strategists have placed an increased emphasis on outcome-driven therapy, positive psychology, Christian-based step programs, whole-life treatment, and biological interventions.

Some of the more recent therapeutic approaches, such as motivational enrichment therapy, whole-life counseling, and psychopharmacological interventions have been showing promising results. However, there is still an ever-enduring debate about what constitutes the most effective treatment for addiction (Doweiko, 2009).

**Application.** Addiction counseling can be both a highly rewarding and significantly challenging endeavor. Addiction counselors traditionally work with people who have problems with alcohol or drugs. However, many now accept an expanded definition of addiction and work with those who are struggling with impulse control and obsessional and compulsive disorders. Many addiction counselors find themselves working with clients struggling with addictions to substances, food, sex, gambling, work, video games...the list is ever expanding.

Addiction counselors help individuals identify behaviors and problems related to their addiction and recover from the effects of the disorder. The counseling process can be completed individually or in group settings in churches, small groups, and/or intensive outpatient or inpatient facilities. Addiction counselors may also work with family members who have been affected by addiction. Some counselors focus more on the preventive aspect of addiction and may work in community outreach or education programs. Addiction counselors should have a strong conceptualization and theoretical understanding of addiction so they can competently assess, diagnose, and treat individuals with addiction-related problems.

Another important aspect of addiction counseling involves working with clients to counteract relapse. Relapse prevention involves developing skills to decrease the probability of the return to maladaptive coping strategies and to minimize the impact and length of relapse episodes.

**Key Elements.** Addiction counselors typically acquire certifications from state and national boards. Most professional therapists acknowledge that working in the addiction field is often perplexing. People who struggle with addiction are in the grips of progressive disorders. "Many pursue it into the gates of insanity or death" (Alcoholics Anonymous, 2001). It takes a resilient therapist to work with addicts. A counselor who works with addictions should "possess genuineness, empathy, modeling the desired behavior, and an appropriately humorous outlook" (Shea, 2006, p. 13). They should be supportive guides who can lead clients to recovery rather than tell them what to do (Shea). Effective addiction therapists empower their clients and involve them in the change process (Miller, 2003). But helping clients stay clean and sober requires ongoing vigilance, and recidivism among substance abusers is a painful reality that can be a source of depression for counselors as well as the abusers themselves ("Substance Abuse Counselor," 2011).

Working with addicts is often challenging and frustrating. A competent Christian counselor will often guide an addict through a variety of resources and network of people. "Sometimes, therapists are team leaders, shepherding others working with the addict, his or her spouse, and children, and addressing other aspects of the problem" (Clinton & Ohlschlager, 2002). Successful long-term recovery is contingent on a reunion with God and restoration of body, soul, mind, and relationships. Counselors have the privilege and responsibility to become agents of change. "To help our clients stay the journey and bring real change, we need three elements: vision, courage, and competence" (Clinton, n.d.). To be successful Christian addictions counselors, we must be able to integrate what we have learned about the multidimensional nature of addiction while preserving the priority in our own lives of establishing, strengthening, and maintaining a vital relationship with God in Christ.

**Steve Baker**

## REFERENCES


Alcoholics Anonymous. (2001). *Alcoholics Anonymous* (4th ed.). New York, NY: A. A. World Services.

Clinton, T. (n.d.). Change: Breaking through the barriers. *TimClinton.com.* Retrieved April 26, 2011, from http://www.timclinton.com/general-articles/change-breaking-through-the-barriers/

Clinton, T. (Producer), & Jenkins, D. (Presentor). (2011). *Addiction & Recovery, Models of Addiction* [Video presentation]. Liberty, VA: Liberty University.

Clinton, T., & Ohlschlager, G. (2002). *Competent Christian Counseling: Foundations and Practice of Compassionate Soul Care.* Colorado Springs, CO: WaterBrook Press.

Doweiko, H.E. (2009). *Concepts of Chemical Dependency* (7th ed.). Belmont, CA: Brooks/Cole.

Edmeades, B. (1987). Alcoholics Anonymous celebrates its 50th year. In W. B. Rucker & M. E. Rucker (Eds.), *Drugs, Society, and Behavior.* Guilford, CT: Dashkin.

Miller, W. R. (2003). What really motivates change? Reflections on 20 years of motivational interviewing.

Symposium presented to the Department of Psychiatry at the Cambridge Hospital, Boston, MA.

Shea, C. W. (2006). Alcohol dependence treatment. *Advances in Addiction Treatment, 1*(1), 12-14.

Substance abuse counselor. (2011). *The Princeton Review.* Retrieved from http:// www.princetonreview .com/Careers.aspx?cid=172

## 12-STEP PROGRAMS

**History.** Twelve-step programs have a long connection to evangelical Christianity. As rector of Calvary Episcopal Church in New York City, Rev. Sam Shoemaker started two ministries, both of which contributed to the genesis of Alcoholics Anonymous. In that rescue mission, Bill W. found Christ in 1935. To stay sober, he joined that chapter of the Oxford Group. Later that same year, while on a business trip to Akron, Ohio, and barely sober, Bill W. met Dr. Bob, a surgeon struggling with alcoholism. June 10, 1935, the day Bill W. took care of Dr. Bob (after another of his drinking binges), is considered the day that Alcoholics Anonymous was formed (Dick, 2006).

The Oxford Group, originally called "A First Century Christian Fellowship," held revivals on most of the Ivy League campuses, but in 1941, due to growing differences, Sam Shoemaker resigned from the group's leadership (Dick, 1998; John, 2003). The concepts of the group's original practices, though, are still found in the 12 steps and the small group structure of A.A. In 1939 Bill W. wrote the text of *The Big Book*, which still sells over a million copies a year. In those early years, the term *Higher Power* came into use to ward off religious debates in the A.A. meetings (a distraction to the goal of sobriety). Even earlier, directly from the Oxford Group, came the references to God as "a Power greater than ourselves" and "God as we understood Him" (A.A. World Services, 2001, pp. 45, 59).

In the 1970s, as the references to God became even less precise, evangelical Christians in A.A. began to gather in additional meetings which they viewed as a "bridge" to their regular A.A. attendance. Overcomer's Outreach and Liontamers were two such organizations that were specifically Christian and looked to the God of the Bible as their higher power (White & Kurtz, 2008). Following publication of several books on codependency and alcoholic family systems, a 12-step group called New Hope was formed in 1982 at the First Evangelical Free Church in Fullerton, California, for adult children who grew up in alcoholic families. From there, multiple applications of the 12 steps developed, and by the early 90s, more than 15 million individuals identified themselves as attending a group. Today, similar activity continues under the banner of Celebrate Recovery, an international organization focused on Christian healing from compulsive behavior (Baker & Warren, 1998).

**Practices.** Each 12-step group has a unique personality, but there are practices common to most meetings.

- There is no teacher or leader. Most groups operate with a rotational leadership, moving around the circle. A facilitator one week asks the person on the right to lead the discussion next week. Everyone is equal. Everyone is trying to recover (Laudet, 2008).

- A core value is both having and being a sponsor to someone else. Individuals look for and request sponsors who are further along in their individual recovery. Sponsors are readily available and will often meet outside regular meetings with the people they are sponsoring (Hamilton, 1996).

- Depending on the size of the group, many 12-step groups start with a Big Meeting, where testimonies are shared; the Problem, the Solution, and the Rules are read; and an offering is taken. Announcements are made for newcomers and upcoming closed groups, and sometimes a brief talk might be shared, especially around difficult themes or seasons for those in recovery (Borkman, 2008).

- Most groups offer several layers of opportunities for participants: newcomers (often for six to eight weeks), open groups (people come and go as they feel necessary), and closed Step Studies (where intimacy, vulnerability, and support are at their highest levels). Once closed, no new individuals can enter (A.A. World Services, 2001).

It is common for groups to have rules that help manage behavior, provide safety, and establish predictability. The following is a typical set of group rules:

1. While others are talking, please let them finish without interruption.
2. No fixing (cross talk). We are here to listen, to support, and be supported by each other in the group, not to give advice. Please save any questions you might have until after the group is dismissed.
3. Speak in the *I* form instead of *we, they,* or *you.* This helps us take responsibility for our feelings and to accept them as being valid. For example: *I believe* rather than *They say, I felt angry* rather than *She made me angry, I think* rather than *Don't you think,* and *I felt hurt* rather than *He hurt my feelings.*
4. Keep sharing to no more than five minutes so that others in the group will have time to share. It is common to have timers.
5. Try to share from the heart and as honestly as you can. It is okay to cry, laugh, and be angry in the group; there will be no condemnation from others.
6. What is shared and who you see in the group is to stay in the group and not be shared with anyone else.

Today, one can find 12-step groups in just about every country of the world for just about every behavior known to man.

**Dave Carder**

## REFERENCES


A. A. World Services. (2001). *Alcoholics Anonymous: The Big Book.* New York, NY: Author.

Baker, J., & Warren, R. (1998). *Celebrate Recovery: A Program for Implementing a Christ-Centered Recovery Ministry in Your Church* (Updated ed.). Grand Rapids, MI: Zondervan.

Borkman, T. (2008). The twelve-step recovery model of AA: A voluntary mutual help association. In M. Galanter & L. A. Kaskutas (Eds.), *Research on Alcoholics Anonymous and Spirituality in Addiction Recovery* (pp. 9-30). Totowa, NJ: Science+Business Media.

Dick, B. (1998). *The Oxford Group & Alcoholics Anonymous: A Design for Living That Works.* Maui, HI: Good Book.

Dick, B. (2006). *The Conversion of Bill W.: More on the Creator's Role in Early A.A.* Kihei, HI: Paradise Research.

Hamilton, B. (1996). *Twelve Step Sponsorship: How It Works.* Center City, MN: Hazelden.

John, R. (2003). *Big Book Unplugged: A Young Person's Guide to Alcoholics Anonymous.* Center City, MN: Hazelden.

Laudet, A. B. (2008). The impact of Alcoholics Anonymous on other substance abuse related twelve-step programs. In M. Galanter & L. A. Kaskutas (Eds.), *Research on Alcoholics Anonymous and Spirituality in Addiction Recovery* (pp. 71-85). Totowa, NJ: Science+Business Media.

White, L., & Kurtz, E. (2008). Twelve defining moments in the history of Alcoholics Anonymous. In M. Galanter & L. A. Kaskutas (Eds.), *Research on Alcoholics Anonymous and Spirituality in Addiction Recovery* (pp. 37-53). Totowa, NJ: Science+Business Media.


## DUAL DIAGNOSIS

**Introduction and Definition.** Dual diagnosis is one type of disorder co-occurring and interacting with another disorder (Hyrb, Kirkhart, & Talbert, 2007; Handmaker, Packard, & Comforti, 2002). The term does not imply one diagnosis is primary and another secondary or causal to the other. The term *dual* is somewhat misleading. The patient typically has several substance and mental-health disorders and might have serious medical problems as well. Due to this complexity and the fact that the *Diagnostic and Statistical Manual of Mental Disorders* (*DSM*) does not discuss concurrent problems, Hyrb et al. advocate for a standardized definition of dual diagnosis.

**Description and Prevalence.** The dual nature of the diagnosis can be considered as a single substance and mental-health diagnosis. Yet the diagnosis can also be a group of substance disorders and a group of mental-health disorders, including Axis II disorders. It is likely that medical disorders, such as chronic pain, may be coded on Axis III. Due to chronic addiction and mental-health problems, cognitive impairment is a frequent obstacle to recovery. Judgment problems due to mental illness are accentuated by chronic substance abuse or dependence. Social stressors such as family dysfunction and negative peer influences add to the mental chaos of the dually diagnosed. Frequently, these clients can present well and are successful, but the counselor should assess for substance use. The clinical picture is complicated—either addiction or mental illness can mimic or mask each other, the client may be self-medicating due to a medical or mental illness, and the client might admit to one disorder and be in denial of the other.

Prevalence of antisocial behavior is highly associated with dual diagnosis (Lukasiewicz, 2009). This means that initial contact with treatment could be within the criminal justice system, which can add to client treatment resistance. Substance abuse is three times higher with mental-health patients compared to the general population (Handmaker et al., 2002). Those with severe and chronic problems such as bipolar affective disorders or schizophrenia are especially vulnerable.

**Diagnostic Criteria.** There are two basic forms of substance disorders, regardless of the intoxicant. One pattern is of excessive use known as substance "abuse." Abuse is characterized by seeking a sense of intoxication, reduced inhibition, and/or self-medication of emotional or physical pain. It is a precursor to dependency. The second pattern is typically a chronic pattern of use that can be of any time frame, but is often a period of days and can include binge patterns of use. However, the psychological and/or physical dependency exists. The user seeks to feel or function normally instead of seeking intoxication. Unfortunately, it takes more of the substance to achieve this goal. Concurrently, diagnosable psychiatric disorders coexist with the substance disorders. Each diagnosis meets the standard symptom criteria in the *DSM*.

**Assessment.** Therapists' assessments should include thorough bio-psycho-social histories that examine both the psychiatric behavior and substance use in clients and their generational systems. A tool for assessing dual diagnosis is *The Screening Tool for Identifying Dual Diagnosis* (Gulledge, 2004). The STIDD examines patient responses to 14 questions that determine whether the respondent has a dual diagnosis or only a substance disorder. Any history of cognitive impairment should be inquired about due to the impairments from chronic substance disorders, head injury, learning disabilities, and affective disorders that affect emotional control, concentration, and judgment.

Assessment should also focus on treatment adherence issues. Often the transition from inpatient to outpatient is where dropping out or relapse occurs (Handmaker et al., 2002). Assessing the patient's attitude toward medication compliance, attending appointments, and recovery will be necessary to predict the client's level of treatment adherence, facilitation, and motivation for change.

**Treatment.** Treatment needs a multimodal and disciplinary approach to help with the myriad and interwoven problems of the client. Stages of treatment should follow a motivational-interviewing paradigm (Miller & Rollnick, 1991). Usually treatment will begin with inpatient care that moves to some form of outpatient care. Treatment is long-term and highly challenging for both the professional and the client. Focus of treatment will need to be flexible and to address a variety of problems. Abstinence is difficult to maintain for this population. Initially, goals need to be simple and short-term, including making therapy appointments, stabilizing symptoms, working toward abstinence, and learning about recovery and mental illness. A hierarchy of needs and list of goals are initially established to help stabilize the patient's chaotic life (Handmaker et al., 2002).

Dually diagnosed patients are best served in integrated dual diagnosis programs (Surface, 2008; Minkoff, 1989), which have guidelines for the multifaceted services and professionals needed to serve this population. Clinical treatments are also multimodel, including cognitive-behavioral, family therapy, and motivational techniques (Haddock, Barrowclough, Tarrier, & Moring, 2003; Barrowclough et al., 2001). Group counseling that (a) focuses on discussions of change and (b) uses motivational interviewing interventions are advocated to develop client recovery adherence (Handmaker et al., 2002). Relapse prevention interventions are important to help reduce the high relapse rate (Marlatt & Donovan, 2005). Integrated treatment combines these other areas:

- home-based intensive case management to help access multiple services
- counseling social skills and stress-management therapies
- education for client and significant others regarding the recovery process from addiction and mental illness
- psychopharmacology services
- life-skills education, such as money management, job interviewing, home management, and friendship building
- discipleship training, church support, and/or recovery groups
- spiritual care that utilizes disciplines, such as Christian meditation, contemplative prayer, and use of Christian imagery

**Spiritual Issues.** People who have a dual diagnosis are spiritually fragile clients with deep feelings of spiritual shame and guilt. These emotions surface and start an addictive cycle that reinforces distance from God and rejection of his grace and forgiveness. They suffer from a belief that God has abandoned them due to their mental illness. In turn, fellowship is often affected by their moods, their tendency toward isolation, and their lack of social judgment. Helping them to accept God's forgiveness and work through the underlying trauma of their shame and guilt will reduce the addiction cycle.

If there were ever a need for a Savior, these clients cry out for one. Counselors of these clients must have strong patience, mercy, and exhortation. They must also be willing to maintain tough client accountability. In many ways, these clients are our social and spiritual "down and outs." The love and acceptance of a grace-oriented fellowship of believers is crucial to the lifestyle changes and needed social affiliation of the dually diagnosed.

These clients are highly resistant to change, accountability, and admitting their problems. They are clinically, spiritually, and personally the most challenging and stressful people to counsel. The love of Christ must act as a foundation and motivation for the counselor. The basic spiritual need of these clients is to learn to love God with all their heart, soul, and mind, and to love themselves as they love others. From the counselor they need a powerful love that resists self-doubt and holds to a task regardless of the success ratio. These clients also need to learn to be spiritually controlled and take charge of their lives to the degree of functioning they can maintain successfully. This leads to learning to take care of their "temple." They need the kind of counselor who can model spiritually controlled behavior in the face of a challenging client; who can speak truth in love and not give up on them.

**Conclusion.** Dual diagnosis is a set of disorders that are grouped under substance use disorders and mental-health disorders, and there may be more than one diagnosis in each category. Furthermore, medical conditions, social stressors, and difficulty coping with God will likely underlie their diagnoses. Medicine and counseling alone often aren't enough; issues of concrete problems from housing to health-care are common. All of these must be addressed, with the ultimate healing love of God expressed and imparted by a counselor able to remain in a difficult and challenging clinical role.

Mark Shadoan
Lynnette Shadoan

## REFERENCES

Barrowclough, C., Haddock, G., Tarrier, N., Lewis, S. W., Moring, J., O'Brien, R.,...McGovern, J. (2001). Randomized trial of motivational interviewing, cognitive behavioral therapy and family interventions for patients with comorbid schizophrenia and substance use disorders. *American Journal of Psychiatry, 10*(158), 1706-1713.

Gulledge, J. B. (2004). Predicting the dual diagnosis client among substance abusers using the demographic and substance-related variables. Lincoln, NE: University of Nebraska–Lincoln. Retrieved from http://digitalcommons.unl.edu/dissertations/AAI3147139/

Haddock., G., Barrowclough, C., Tarrier, N., & Moring, J. (2003). Cognitive behavioral therapy and motivational interviewing interventions for schizophrenia and substance abuse. *The British Journal of Psychiatry, 183*, 416-426.

Handmaker, N., Packard, M., & Comforti, K. (2002). Motivational interviewing in the treatment of dual disorders. In W. R. Miller & S. Rollnick (Eds.), *Motivational Interviewing: Preparing People for Change of Addictive Behavior* (2nd ed., pp. 377-391). New York, NY: Guilford Press.

Hyrb, K., Kirkhart, R., & Talbert, R. (2007). A call for standardized definition of dual diagnosis. *Psychiatry, 4*(9), 15-17.

Lukasiewicz, M. (2009). Dual diagnosis: Prevalence and relationship with suicide risk in a nationwide sample of French prisoners. *Alcohol Clinical Experimental Research, 33*(1), 160-168.

Marlatt, G. A., & Donovan, D. (Eds.). (2005). *Relapse Prevention: Maintenance Strategies in the Treatment of Addictive Behaviors* (2nd ed.). New York, NY: Guilford Press.

Miller, W. R., & Rollnick, S. (Eds.). (1991). *Motivational Interviewing: Preparing People to Change Addictive Behavior.* New York, NY: Guilford Press.

Minkoff, K. (1989). Integrated treatment model for dual diagnosis of psychosis and addiction. *Hospital Community Psychiatry, 10*(40), 1031-1036.

Surface, D. (2008). Integrational dual disorders treatment: New wave in recovery. *Social Work Today, 8*(6).

## GAMBLING

Addictions rarely walk alone. They tend to cluster in groups, and when they do, they are often called *co-occurring disorders.* Gambling addiction, also known as problem gambling or pathological gambling, can exist on its own but often comes with complicating companions.

**Description.** The *Diagnostic and Statistical Manual of Mental Disorders* (*DSM-IV-TR*) says pathological gambling "is characterized by recurrent and maladaptive gambling behavior that disrupts personal, family or vocational pursuits" (American Psychiatric Association, 2000). It can be present along with a variety of co-occurring disorders, such as alcohol use disorder (73.2%), drug use disorder (38.1%), nicotine dependence (60.4%), mood disorders (49.6%), anxiety disorders (41.3%), and personality disorders (60.8%) (Petry, Stinson, & Grant, 2005).

**Assessment.** Addiction can be determined by a variety of assessment tools, including the South Oaks Gambling Screen or a self-assessment called "20 Questions" by Gamblers Anonymous. However, the following criteria from the *DSM-IV-TR* can also be used, as determined by the presence of five or more of the following consequences:

preoccupation with gambling (reliving past gambling experiences, planning the next, devising ways to come up with money in order to gamble); the need to gamble with higher amounts of money; repeated, unsuccessful attempts to control, cut back, or stop gambling; becoming restless or irritable when trying to cut back or stop gambling; using gambling as a way to escape from problems or unpleasant or uncomfortable feelings; chasing losses by continuing to gamble even after losing money; lying to others about the extent of the gambling; committing illegal acts in order to finance continued gambling; jeopardizing or losing a significant relationship or personal, educational, or career opportunity because of gambling; relying on other people for money to address financial challenges brought on by gambling; and to continue gambling.

Because of the high prevalence of gambling with other disorders (Petry et al., 2005), it is important that each of these be evaluated in conjunction with the assessment for a gambling addiction. The *DSM-IV-TR* also links the following with pathological gambling: mood disorders, attention-deficit/hyperactivity disorder, substance abuse or dependence, other impulse-control disorders, and antisocial, narcissistic, and borderline personality disorders.

**Treatment.** Once a clearer picture emerges of the conditions occurring in conjunction with the gambling addiction, a treatment plan should be created that includes professionals trained in mental health, chemical dependency, and medicine. The substance abuse issue should initially take precedence in order to promote and enhance the person's ability to engage in the cognitive work necessary for recovery. Once sobriety/abstinence has been stabilized, a secondary track of mental-health counseling should be implemented, along with a comprehensive medical assessment and, if necessary, pharmaceutical intervention.

Whenever possible, family/community support and accountability should be specifically factored into the overall treatment plan. In addition, financial counseling should be recommended due to the devastation that occurs to personal and family finances with a gambling addiction. If applicable, cultural and ethnic views of gambling should be acknowledged and factored.

It is imperative to have a cohesive team of therapists, physicians, and financial counselors communicating regularly and treating the individual as a whole person with multiple but integrally connected disorders. This whole-person approach integrates not only the medical, mental-health, and chemical dependency issues, but also factors in the emotional, relational, physical, financial, and spiritual aspects of the person.

**Spiritual Issues.** Jesus tells the parable of the man with an unclean spirit. He warns that once that unclean spirit departs, it can gather up others worse than itself and take up residence again. Too often, when a compulsive gambler stops that particular habit, he gravitates to other addictions and compulsive behaviors. After a while, he may take up his gambling again, "and the final condition of that person is worse than the first" (Lk. 11:26). For long-term recovery to take hold, it is important for any treatment plan to include a personal rediscovery and reconnection with God and faith in the context of a supportive, honest faith community.

Gregory L. Jantz

## REFERENCES

American Psychiatric Association. (2000). *Diagnostic and Statistical Manual of Mental Disorders* (4th ed., text rev.). Washington, DC: Author.

Gamblers Anonymous. *Twenty Questions.* Retrieved from http://gamblersanonymous.org/20questions.html

Petry, N. M., Stinson, F. S., & Grant, B. F. (2005). Comorbidity of DSM-IV pathological gambling and other psychiatric disorders: Results from the national epidemiologic survey on alcohol and related condition. *Journal of Clinical Psychiatry, 66,* 564-574.

*South Oaks Gambling Screen.* Retrieved from http://www.in.gov/judiciary/ijlap/docs/south-oaks-gambling-screen.pdf

## PORNOGRAPHY AND SEX ADDICTION

**Description and History.** Sex addiction was first described by Patrick Carnes in 1981 in his groundbreaking book *Out of the Shadows* (Carnes, 1981/2001). Dr. Carnes had been instrumental in establishing Sex Addicts Anonymous, the first 12-step program for people who struggle with this problem, in 1976 in Minneapolis. He and a group of other therapists adopted and adapted the principles of Alcoholics Anonymous and found them useful in helping sex addicts get "sober." Parallel developments in California and New England led to similar 12-step fellowships there. Since their inception, these groups have spread across the country. Carnes also established the first inpatient treatment program for sex addiction in 1985 in Minneapolis.

To date, the diagnosis of sex addiction has not been fully accepted by the medical and psychological communities. The most recent edition of the *Diagnostic and Statistical Manual of Mental Disorders (DSM-IV-TR)* does not include a category for it. The diagnosis, however, enjoys a wide acceptance among therapists and counselors at all levels. Most clinicians use the code for sexual disorder NOS (302.9) as an alternative for insurance purposes. Certain types of sexual behavior can be classified, such as the paraphilias.

Pornography addiction is also widely accepted as a subcategory of sexual addiction. The widespread use of the Internet has greatly increased the number of sex addicts. In fact, Internet pornography has been called the crack cocaine of sex addiction. A recent report of a case of pornography addiction described a whole tribe of aboriginal men in New Guinea who could not stop looking at pornography on their Internet connection in the jungle. Certain interventions might be unique to certain sexual behaviors, but pornography addiction can generally be treated as a subset of sexual addiction. For some, pornography is the portal that leads to other forms of deviant and addictive sexual behaviors.

Sexual addiction was first described from an evangelical Christian perspective in 1992 (Laaser, 2004). Other books have followed, such as Schaumberg's (1997). Today many authors have treated this subject from a Christian perspective, and some offer workbooks for use in churches providing support groups for sex addicts.

**Assessment.** These are the key criteria for the diagnosis of sex addiction:

1. *Unmanageability.* This means that a sex addict will have made attempts to stop but can't, leaving the addict feeling out of control. This unmanageability is also the result of the addict's inability to completely surrender the addiction to God, which results in "double-mindedness" (Laaser, 2004).
2. *Neurochemical tolerance.* Like alcoholics or drug addicts, sex addicts become tolerant to the powerful chemicals produced in the brain during sexual arousal and orgasm.
3. *Acting out.* This tolerance leads to an escalating pattern of behaviors. An addict may need more and more of the same kind of activity or may need to move on to different kinds of sexual behaviors.
4. *Avoidance of negative feelings.* Sex addicts use sexual arousal and activity to alter their brain chemistry and thus avoid feelings of sadness, fear, anxiety, anger, and the like.

Some people commit sexual sin but are not addicted. The same distinctions that we apply to drinking behaviors apply to sexual behaviors. Some can sin by abusing sex, others can go through periods of life in which they become dependent on sinful sexual activity, and finally, some can become fully addicted. Today, more and more females are becoming addicted to sex and are quickly catching up to men in terms of prevalence. The same assessment dynamics apply to women as to men. But the prevalence of shame that is culturally attached to sexual sin is different for women than for men.

Every form of sexual activity can become addictive. Even marital sexuality can be addictive if it meets the assessment criteria. Marital sexuality, regardless of frequency, is addictive if it is used to avoid intimacy and the expression of a spiritual and emotional connection. Fantasy is the cornerstone of sex addiction and can be addictive in itself as it produces sexual arousal and the resulting neurochemical high. Masturbation and pornography are the most frequent types of acting-out behavior.

**Treatment Issues.** Successful treatment of sexual addiction achieves total and complete sobriety or purity. Sobriety should be defined by Christians as the abstinence of any kind of sexual activity with self or others outside of the marriage of a man and woman. Treatment is multi-factored and should include the following:

1. *Accountability.* This is most successfully accomplished through support groups, either 12-step or specifically Christian. The principles of accountability are essential to recovery (Laaser, 2011b).
2. *Neurochemical detoxification.* This includes complete abstinence from any form of sex, even marital, for 90 days. The spouse must agree to this program (1 Cor. 7:5).
3. *Evaluation and treatment of comorbid mental-health issues.* Special attention should be given to attention-deficit disorder (there is a strong correlation between ADD and all addictions).
4. *Personal therapy.* The emotional roots of addiction must be healed. Group therapy has been shown to be especially valuable in this regard.
5. *Reestablishment of control.* Thoughts and fantasies must be disciplined (Laaser, 2011c).
6. *Spiritual direction.* Surrender to Christ is essential in the complete recovery of a sex addict.
7. *Marital or relationship counseling.* The spouse of an addict will also need individual counseling (Laaser, 2009).

The American Association of Christian Counseling has established a certification program for those who need more training or who wish to specialize in it.

**Spiritual Issues.** Special attention must be paid to the following spiritual issues, which are extensively covered in *Becoming a Man of Valor* (Laaser, 2011a):

1. Unmanageability and the need for surrender (Rom. 7:15).
2. Personal willingness to get well (Jn. 5:1-11).
3. The double-minded thinking processes inherent in addiction (Jas. 1:8).
4. Understanding of how sex is a false substitute for the desires of every heart (Jn. 4).
5. Conviction of God's grace (1 Jn. 1:8-9).
6. The meaning of suffering in the pain and consequences of addiction (Jas. 1:2).

People who struggle with sexual addiction need the hope and assurance that complete purity or sobriety is possible for those who are completely willing.

**Mark R. Laaser**

## REFERENCES


Carnes, P. (2001). *Out of the Shadows.* Center City, MN: Hazelden.

Laaser, D. (2009). *Shattered Vows.* Grand Rapids, MI: Zondervan.

Laaser, M. (2011a). *The 7 Principles of Accountability for Men.* Kansas City, MO: Beacon Hill.

Laaser, M. (2004b). *Healing the Wounds of Sexual Addiction.* Grand Rapids, MI: Zondervan.

Laaser, M. (2011c). *Becoming a Man of Valor.* Kansas City, MO: Beacon Hill.

Laaser, M. (2011). *Taking Every Thought Captive.* Kansas City, MO: Beacon Hill.

Schaumberg, H. (1997). *False Intimacy.* Colorado Springs, CO: NavPress.


## SUBSTANCE ABUSE

Substance abuse is the overindulgence in and ensuing potential dependence on an addictive substance, especially alcohol or a narcotic drug. The causes of and treatments for substance abuse and dependence vary, but most treatment models include a multifaceted program of biological, psychological, social, and spiritual interventions.

**Description.** Substance abuse is defined in the *Diagnostic and Statistical Manual of Mental Disorders* (*DSM-IV-TR*) as a maladaptive pattern of substance use leading to clinically significant impairment or distress as manifested by one (or more) of the following, occurring within a 12-month period:

- Recurrent substance use resulting in a failure to fulfill major role obligations at work, school, or home (such as repeated absences or poor work performance related to substance use; substance-related absences, suspensions, or expulsions from school; or neglect of children or household).
- Recurrent substance use in situations in which it is physically hazardous (such as driving an automobile or operating a machine when impaired by substance use).
- Recurrent substance-related legal problems (such as arrests for substance-related disorderly conduct).
- Continued substance use despite having persistent or recurrent social or interpersonal problems caused or exacerbated by the effects of the substance (for example, arguments and physical fights with spouse about consequences of intoxication).

The symptoms for abuse do not necessarily meet the criteria for dependence. Continued use can result in what the *DSM-IV-TR* describes as substance dependence, defined as a maladaptive pattern of a substance use leading to clinically significant impairment or distress, as manifested by three or more of the following, occurring anytime in the same 12-month period:

- Tolerance, as defined by either of the following: (a) a need for markedly increased amounts of the substance to achieve intoxication or the desired effect or (b) markedly diminished effect with continued use of the same amount of the substance.
- Withdrawal, as manifested by either of the following: (a) the characteristic withdrawal syndrome for the substance or (b) the same (or closely related) substance is taken to relieve or avoid withdrawal symptoms.
- The substance is often taken in larger amounts or over a longer period than intended.
- There is a persistent desire or unsuccessful effort to cut down or control substance use.
- A great deal of time is spent in activities necessary to obtain the substance,

use the substance, or recover from its effects.

- Important social, occupational, or recreational activities are given up or reduced because of substance use.
- The substance use is continued despite knowledge of having a persistent physical or psychological problem that is likely to have been caused or exacerbated by the substance (for example, current cocaine use despite recognition of cocaine-induced depression or continued drinking despite recognition that an ulcer was made worse by alcohol consumption).

The problem of substance abuse, especially among teens, is far more widespread in the United States than many realize. According to a study published in *The Archives of Pediatric and Adolescent Medicine*, addiction often begins during adolescence and can predict future addictive disorders. Roughly 80 percent of teens have begun to drink, and half have used an illegal drug by their senior year in high school. Depression, conduct disorder, and unplanned sexual activity were also associated with substance use.

**Assessment.** A variety of substance-abuse screening tools are available through the National Institute of Drug Abuse (NIDA), an arm of the National Institute of Health (NIH). They include short questionnaires that can be self-administered or given by a treatment professional. Most substance-abuse screening tools contain questions like these to be answered by the patient/client:

- Have you used drugs other than those required for medical reasons?
- Have you abused prescription drugs?
- Do you abuse more than one drug at a time?
- Can you get through the week without using drugs?
- Are you unable to stop using drugs when you want to?
- Have you had "blackouts" or "flashbacks" as a result of drug use?
- Do you ever feel bad or guilty about your drug use?
- Does your spouse (or do your parents) ever complain about your involvement with drugs?
- Has drug abuse created problems between you and your spouse or your parents?
- Have you lost friends because of your use of drugs?
- Have you neglected your family because of your use of drugs?
- Have you been in trouble at work because of your use of drugs?
- Have you lost a job because of drug abuse?
- Have you gotten into fights when under the influence of drugs?
- Have you engaged in illegal activities in order to obtain drugs?
- Have you been arrested for possession of illegal drugs?
- Have you ever experienced withdrawal symptoms (felt sick) when you stopped taking drugs?
- Have you had medical problems as a result of your drug use (e.g., memory loss, hepatitis, convulsions, bleeding, etc.)?
- Have you sought help for a drug problem?
- Have you been involved in a treatment program especially related to drug use?

A "yes" answer to five or more of these questions would indicate that substance abuse and possible dependence is likely.

**Treatment.** A variety of treatment models exist, most of which center on the biological, psychological, social, and spiritual components of recovery. Even treatment programs that are not Christian faith-based generally acknowledge the role of a higher power in resolving the internal conflict that drives the abuse and addictive cycles.

From a biological perspective, if the addiction has manifested in physical dependence, it is generally accepted that a physical detoxification must occur before effective subsequent treatment can begin. Alcohol and drug use affect brain function and impair the user's thoughts, social interactions, impulse control, and decision making. There is also supporting evidence that alcohol and drug abuse can be related to a genetic predisposition. Whether genetic or a learned pattern of behavior, substance abuse and dependence tend to run in families. People who have family members who are alcohol or drug dependent are at greater risk of becoming so as well.

From a psychological perspective, recovery involves examining the inaccurate thinking that is part of the addictive cycle. With the help of a grounded community of support, users can begin to challenge their existing thought patterns and move toward more accurate thinking. Many addicts have been ingrained with false or inaccurate thought patterns by their family of origin or others in their social circle.

From a social perspective, the role of a healthy, supportive community in recovery is essential. Wise King Solomon, one of the early Scripture writers, spoke nearly 3,000 years ago about the value of a supportive community: "Two are better than one, because they have a good return for their labor: If either of them falls down, one can help the other up. But pity anyone who falls and has no one to help them up." (Eccl. 4:9-10). Those within the Alcoholics Anonymous community who have good relationships with their sponsors have a much higher recovery and long-term sobriety rate than those who don't. As the addictive process unfolds, those struggling with substance abuse tend to damage their helpful relationships and isolate themselves, leaving them without healthy support at a time when they need it most. Many churches offer clinically and scripturally sound programs to assist in recovery. The largest national Christian program used in churches is called Celebrate Recovery. Several Christian inpatient treatment centers are scattered across America.

From a spiritual perspective, beginning a journey of recovery is an excellent time to explore one's core beliefs. Many struggling with abuse and addiction feel shame about their drug and alcohol use and see themselves as unworthy of God's care. Their concept of a loving and helpful God has often been clouded by their shame, either self-imposed or (unfortunately) from those in the spiritual community. However, Scripture clearly refutes their belief that God is unwilling to help. Like the father of the prodigal son, he waits with open arms. Just a few of many examples of God's love and grace are found in the following verses:

- "For God did not send his Son into the world to condemn the world, but to save the world through him" (Jn. 3:17).
- "Therefore, there is now no condemnation for those who are in Christ Jesus" (Rom. 8:1).
- "But God demonstrates his own love for us in this: While we were still sinners, Christ died for us" (Rom. 5:8).

Examining one's personal beliefs and determining their origin is a major step in deciding to embrace God's involvement in the recovery process. Again, the importance of healthy support from a spiritual community is vital.

**Conclusion.** Substance abuse and dependence is a widespread and destructive condition that destroys many lives and families around the world. It is treatable, and long-term recovery and sobriety are possible, but progress is best accomplished within the context of a safe community and with a structured program addressing biological, psychological, social, and spiritual factors.

**Todd Clements**

## REFERENCES

American Psychiatric Association. (2000). *Diagnostic and Statistical Manual of Mental Disorders* (4th ed., text rev.). Washington, DC: Author.

Knight, J. R., Harris, S. K., Sherritt, L., Van Hook, S., Lawrence, N., Brooks, T.,...Kulig, J. (2007). *Archives of Pediatric and Adolescent Medicine. 161*(11), 1035-1041.

# GRIEF, CRISIS, AND TRAUMA INTERVENTION

## GRIEF

"The Lord is close to the brokenhearted and saves those who are crushed in spirit" (Ps. 34:18).

**Description.** Loss is an inevitable part of the human experience, and grief is a natural response to loss (Shear et al., 2011; Humphrey, 2009). Grief is a transformational, multidimensional, and unique experience; no two people experience grief in exactly the same way. Although grief is often conceptualized as a response to death or dying, persons may also struggle with grief in the wake of divorce, termination from work, lost expectations, and lost dreams.

The symptoms of acute grief are natural responses to significant loss and should not be pathologized. However, grief can become pathological. Bereavement may progress to a condition known as complicated grief (Shear et al., 2011), which is distinguished from acute grief by intensity and duration. Although complicated grief was not included in the fourth edition of the *Diagnostic and Statistical Manual of the American Psychiatric Association* (*DSM-IV-TR*), Shear and colleagues (2011) proposed that complicated grief should be added to the *DSM-V*. In cases where acute grief is experienced, symptoms tend to diminish in intensity across time. However, the grieving period varies based on the magnitude of the loss. Complicated grief occurs in approximately ten percent of bereaved individuals (Shear et al., 2011) and is more likely to occur in women. Risk factors for developing complicated grief include losing a child, suffering a loss due to natural disaster, or suffering a loss due to violence. It is also important to note that children grieve differently than adults and do not have the ego strength to endure grief in the same intensity and duration. Grief counselors need to look for opportunities when children are open to expressing grief and capitalize on those opportunities by inviting expression of loss.

**Assessment.** Counselors should assess the severity of grief and distinguish between those who have *acute grief* and those who have *complicated grief*. The primary feature of complicated grief is a sadness and yearning, which is severe and prolonged. Complicated grief is often misdiagnosed, partially due to omission from the *DSM-IV-TR* and lack of awareness (Shear et al., 2011). Shear and colleagues (2011) performed a factor analysis and identified six different criteria that they are proposing for complicated grief in the *DSM-V*:

1. yearning and preoccupation with the deceased
2. shock and disbelief
3. anger and bitterness
4. estrangement from others
5. hallucinations of the deceased
6. behavior change, including avoidance and proximity seeking

**Treatment.** Often, the bereaved are resilient and have developed life skills that help them integrate the loss in a meaningful way.

For this reason they may not need treatment (Humphrey, 2009). However, through the therapeutic interview counselors can assess severity and duration of symptoms and the presence of risk factors that may predispose individuals to complicated grief. Care should be taken to prevent complications and address risk factors. Counselor characteristics including caring and empathic listening are important in facilitating the grief process (Kübler-Ross, 1969). More recent approaches to grief and loss include art therapy and eye movement desensitization and reprocessing (EMDR) for cases of traumatic loss, such as in the case of sexual trauma (Underwood, Stewart, & Castellanos, 2007). Complicated grief treatment includes in vivo and imagined exposure that emphasizes processing traumatic symptoms and establishing a sense of connection with the lost loved one (Shear et al., 2005), cognitive-stress theory (Folkman, 2001), and family-focused grief therapy.

**Spiritual Implications.** The Wonderful Counselor (Is. 9:6) provides guidance for Christians on how to grieve—with hope and in the awareness of life after death. Paul wrote, "And now, dear brothers and sisters, we want you to know what will happen to the believers who have died so you will not grieve like people who have no hope" (1 Th. 4:13 NLT). The passage discusses the reunion between the deceased and the Lord. This vision of resurrection and reunion provides hope to those grieving a lost loved one.

Romans 12:15 provides guidance for pastoral counselors: "Rejoice with those who rejoice; mourn with those who mourn." A Swedish proverb captures the same sentiment and states, "Shared joy is double joy and shared sorrow is half-sorrow." There is comfort and relief in the process of sharing grief with others. Christian counselors can extend this comfort to those who need their care, wisdom, and support.

Anita M. Knight

## REFERENCES


Bowlby, J. (1980). *Loss: Sadness and Depression.* New York, NY: Basic Books.

Crenshaw, D. (1990). *Bereavement: Counseling the Grieving Throughout the Life Cycle.* New York, NY: Continuum.

Engel, G. L. (1961). Is grief a disease? A challenge for medical research. *Psychosomatic Medicine, 23,*18-22.

Folkman, S. (2001). Revised coping theory and the process of bereavement. In M. S. Stroebe, R. O. Hansson, & H. A. W. Schut (Eds.), *Handbook of Bereavement Research: Consequences, Coping and Care* (pp. 563-84). Washington, DC: American Psychological Association Press.

Humphrey, K. M. (2009). *Counseling Strategies for Grief and Loss.* Alexandria, VA: American Counseling Association.

Kissane, D. W., & Bloch, S. (1994). Family grief. *British Journal of Psychiatry, 164*(6), 720-740.

Kübler-Ross, E. (1969). *On Death and Dying.* Scribner: New York, NY.

Love, A. (2007). Progress in understanding grief, complicated grief, and caring for the bereaved. *Contemporary Nurse: A Journal for the Australian Nursing Profession, 27*(1), 73-83.

Parkes, C. M. (1998). Bereavement in adult life. *BMJ, 316,* 856-859.

Shear, K., Frank, E., Houck, P. R., & Reynolds, C. F. (2005). Treatment of complicated grief: A randomized controlled trial. *Journal of the American Medical Association, 293*(21), 2601-2608.

Shear, M. K., Simon, N., Wall, M., Zisook, S., Neimeyer, R., Duan, N.,…Keshaviah, A. (2011). Complicated grief and related bereavement issues for DSM-V. *Depression & Anxiety, 28,* 103-117.

Underwood, L., Stewart, S., & Castellanos, A. (2007). Effective practices for sexually traumatized girls: Implications for counseling and education. *International Journal of Behavioral Consultation and Therapy, 3*(3).

Worden, L. (1982). *Grief Counseling and Grief Therapy* (p. 41). New York, NY: Springer.


## DISABILITY

**Description.** A disability is any physical, emotional, or mental impairment that significantly impacts one or more major life activities, such as walking, seeing, hearing, thinking clearly, or relating appropriately. A handicap is any societal encumbrance that makes success in life more difficult to achieve. In other words, our bodies disable us, but barriers in society often handicap us.

**History.** In the past few decades, tremendous advancements in cure and rehabilitation have been made for people with disabilities. The Rehabilitation Act of 1973 established federally funded networks of rehabilitation techniques and therapies for people suffering from disabling conditions. The Americans with Disabilities Act of 1990 has opened doors of opportunity in employment and provided access to public accommodations and transportation. Advances in medical technology are making it possible for many more people to survive catastrophic injuries or illnesses. Regrettably, the support systems in churches and in our society have not been able to keep pace.

**Assessment.** Limitations in insurance coverage unfortunately rush many people through trauma care and rehabilitation, leaving the family to deal with a new disability without proper emotional and practical resources.

**Treatment.** Counselors must remember that people need time to work through stages of trauma, grief, and anger. For some time, a person with a disability will be emotionally numb and unable to process the reality of a life-altering condition. Invariably, grief will arise over what was lost, including normal physical or mental functions. Anger and depression may set in as people grasp the permanence of their disability and its impact on life.

*Anger.* It is understandable for people to feel angry when the reality of a permanent disability sinks in. When Ephesians 4:26 states, "In your anger do not sin," it's clear that hostility is not always synonymous with sin. Not all anger is wrong. A disability can push people to extremes. Affliction either warms people toward spiritual things or turns them cold. Jesus said in Revelation 3:15-16, "I know your deeds, that you are neither cold nor hot. I wish you were either one or the other! So, because you are lukewarm—neither hot nor cold—I am about to spit you out of my mouth." Hate is infinitely closer to love than is indifference. And being lukewarm is the only road that never gets to God.

*Strong emotions.* These open the door to asking the really hard questions: Does life make sense? Is God good? Deep emotions reveal the spiritual direction in which people with disabilities are moving. Are we moving toward God, or are we moving away from him? Anger that is turned toward God makes Some*one* the issue of our suffering rather than some*thing*—and that's moving in the right direction.

*Acceptance.* What people think about their disabilities reflects what they think about God. A right orientation toward their new circumstances requires a right orientation toward God and his Word. First Thessalonians 5:18 (NKJV) says, "In everything give thanks, for this is the will of God in Christ Jesus concerning you." Trusting God with a disability has nothing to do with trustful feelings. Trusting God is a step of faith in which people with disabilities recognize the trustworthiness of the One who permitted their accident or illness to occur.

*Resignation.* To resign oneself to a disability can produce feelings of stoicism, but to submit may only cover up feelings of submerged rebellion. To trust God involves something deeper than resignation or submission to a disability; it's an *embrace* of difficult circumstances that necessitates the supernatural grace of God.

**Additional Issues.** People who suddenly face the world of disability must never suffer alone—that's why God created spiritual community. Counselors will serve their counselees well if they can introduce them to other Christians who are dealing successfully with their disabling conditions. However, counselors must not assume that their counselees will automatically feel comfortable around other people with wheelchairs, walkers, or white canes. It takes time to recognize that this, indeed, is the world in which people with disabilities can find empathy, understanding, advice, and most importantly, a support network.

**Terminology.** Avoid terms such as *cripple* or *invalid.* Contemporary euphemisms such as *physically challenged* or *differently-abled* also can connote a reluctance to accept the hard-hitting realities of a significant disability. It's wise to choose "person first" language.

A person with a disability is not a victim. He is a survivor—a polio survivor, a stroke survivor, a burn survivor, and so on.

Avoid using *normal* to describe people or families without disabilities. They are *typical,* such as, "My child with spina bifida is progressing in school as well as his typical classmates."

**Support and Resources.** Joni and Friends exists to serve families affected by disability with programs of practical and spiritual support. The organization also works with churches to help them become disability friendly. The ministry holds family retreats across the United States every summer, providing five days of spiritual refreshment, recreational activities, and networking opportunities for the entire family. For more information, contact joniandfriends.org.

Joni Eareckson Tada

## END-OF-LIFE ISSUES AND DEATH

The moment we are born, we take our first step toward death. Embracing the God-given gift of life means accepting death as a part of life. For some, the thought of death hovers like a dark cloud, diminishing all hope. For others, death is the doorway to eternity and a hope-filled future.

In truth, both life and death can be affirmed and embraced by Christians because of the hope stored up for them in heaven (Col. 1:5). As ironic as it sounds, many experience some of life's richest and most meaningful moments when traveling down the road of a terminal illness (Stevens, 1997).

During this critical time, as the terminally ill are contemplating their own mortality and facing eternity, they often major on the majors, setting aside minor issues that once seemed so important. People facing death have specific needs—even if unspoken. When counseling seriously ill people, a counselor can help them clarify issues they are facing, learn coping techniques, and evaluate their end-of-life options (Stevens, 1997).

Realize that those with a "deeper or more genuine religious commitment" experience less fear than those whose faith is "superficial" (Neimeyer, Wittkowski, & Moser, 2004). When facing death, this verse gives great peace of mind: "The Lord himself goes before you and will be with you; he will never leave you nor forsake you. Do not be afraid; do not be discouraged" (Dt. 31:8).

Those facing death often wrestle with anxiety, which can be addressed through wise counsel. Therefore ask, "What are your specific fears?" Then, consider following these action plans.

| The Client's Fear | The Counselor's Action Plan |
|---|---|
| death | Explain how to enter into a personal relationship with Jesus Christ. |
| pain | Manage pain through properly administered medication. |
| loneliness | Affirm that God will never leave or forsake his children. |
| control | Affirm that God is in control and will be faithful to handle all end-of-life affairs entrusted to his care. |
| responsibility | Affirm that God will provide for the bereaved family as they lean on him. |

The Lord promises his direct involvement: "I know the plans I have for you...plans to give you a hope and a future" (Jer. 29:11).

The rights of the dying should be discussed and respected. Bailey (1976) notes that those with a terminal illness need to...

- be told they have a terminal condition
- decide how they will live out their final days—what they will do, whom they will see
- prepare to sever their ties with this life
- express their desires for their funeral or memorial service
- die with dignity

The terminally ill are wise to consider what they can do to ease their family's transition. Compassionately give this counsel: "Many decisions can be made to lighten the load of your loved ones." The Lord says, "Put your house in order, because you are going to die" (2 Ki. 20:1). Counselors can help them with these important tasks:

*Record a will.*

- Be sure it is legally documented.
- List specific items to leave to special family and friends.
- Consider any bequests for church or respected ministries.
- Pray about becoming an organ donor.
- Consider making a "living will," stating medical decisions.

*Express their desires for the funeral service.*

- Choose a person to conduct the service.
- Select meaningful music, poems, and Scripture.
- Designate pallbearers and musicians.
- Name organizations to be honored.
- Choose a location for the funeral.

*Arrange their personal affairs.*

- Select a person to have power of attorney.
- Gather important documents and items in one place (insurance, investments, safety deposit box keys, and the like).
- Secure legal guardianship for dependents.
- List persons to be contacted upon death (including lawyers, family, and friends).
- Communicate their decisions to their dependents.

*Consider how to leave a legacy of love.*

- Explain the significance of sharing their Christian testimony with others.
- Communicate love, appreciation, and words they've always wanted to say.
- Write or record their thoughts for the benefit of family members.
- Write, phone, or visit dear friends—now.
- Mend broken relationships by saying, "I'm sorry" or "Please forgive me."

**Hospice.** Explain the critical and beneficial option of hospice care—a cost-effective, compassionate bridge between expensive hospitals and the risk of medically insufficient care at home. The main goal of hospice care is to allow patients to die with dignity in a worry-free, loving environment. With an emphasis on quality of life, hospice assists with multiple services (Kolf, 1993).

**Eternal Life.** Leading a dying person to the Lord is a job not just for pastors and ministers. Be sensitive to opportunities to speak about eternal matters. Those close to death are often more receptive to spiritual truth, potentially opening the door for counselors to fulfill one of their most impactful roles—ministers of reconciliation through Christ, our Lord.

June Hunt

## REFERENCES

Bailey, R. (1976). *Ministering to the Grieving.* Grand Rapids, MI: Zondervan.

Kolf, J. C. (1993). *Comfort and Care for the Critically Ill.* Grand Rapids, MI: Baker.

Neimeyer, R., Wittkowski, J., & Moser, R. P. (2004). Psychological research on death attitudes: An overview and evaluation. *Death Studies, 28,* 325.

Stevens, D. (1997). When healing isn't possible. *Christian Counseling Today, 5*(3), 40-41.


## DEATH OF A CHILD

Of the possible losses one might experience, the death of a child is among the most intense and devastating. For a parent to bury a child screams against the order of the universe, beginning a journey of bereavement that may linger in varying degrees and manifestations throughout a parent's lifetime (Moules, 2008). Specific circumstances prior to and surrounding the death of a child—such as the manner of death (e.g., sudden accident, suicide, or prolonged illness) or preexisting family stress—may complicate the grieving process for both relatives and friends.

**Description.** Though the experience of parental grief is an idiosyncratic process, certain commonalities can assist the counselor in understanding and ministering to the bereaved (Talbot, 2002). A parent's initial reaction, especially the mother's, may be profoundly disorienting as she begins to sense a displacement of her role. Mothers commonly find their greatest solace with others who have experienced a similar type of loss; they may feel misunderstood by and isolated from those who appear to minimize their grief. A father's grief, though manifested in a markedly different manner, can be just as intense as the mother's (Nelson, 2004). He may sense a feeling of loss of control because of his inability to have prevented the death and now to alleviate the mother's grief. Both parents commonly struggle with remorse for neglecting to express sufficient love to the child or with guilt that they might have actually done something to cause the death. In some situations, such as sudden infant death syndrome (SIDS), this can be compounded, especially by suspicions conveyed by medical staff and law enforcement (Silverman & Kelly, 2009).

**Treatment.** As bereaved parents learn to live without their child, they require a support system of individuals who will acknowledge the extent of their sorrow without directing them in supposedly "proper ways" of grieving. Too often church and family members administer initial care immediately after the loss but soon begin to avoid contact. This withdrawal may be due to a feeling of inadequacy to minister effectively rather than a disregard for the loss. Nevertheless, the result may be that the parents feel neglected and betrayed.

In addition to grief counseling, parents may find it helpful to attend support meetings of groups such as the Compassionate Friends, a national organization of bereaved parents that provides resources such as books, newsletters, and online support communities. Parents should be encouraged to reflect on experiences by talking to others, journaling, scrapbooking, blogging, and honoring the child's memory through meaningful acts of service or rituals.

Counselors should intentionally speak the child's name and not be concerned if doing so elicits tears or other signs of grief. Though the name represents painful loss, it is a precious sound to the parents' ears and can serve as a powerful gesture that can bring healing. Counselors can express interest in the child by asking questions about and commenting on pictures of him or her. Refrain from using language that directs parents to move on or get over their grief. They will resent the insensitivity of such a suggestion.

The goal of recovery, or the complete absence of grief, may not be the best model for bereaved parents. Rather than looking for indicators of grief's absence, counselors should be encouraged by signs that parents are learning to live with a healthy connection to their child's memory. Barrera et al. (2007) refer to this as *integrated grief*—the ability to positively reframe reality and to exercise some control over grief reactions while focusing on life being back to normal.

**Spiritual Issues.** Though many bereaved families find solace in faith, it is just as typical for some to experience a profound spiritual crisis and question their spiritual beliefs (Talbot, 2002). Those who blame themselves for their child's death may find it difficult to believe God would ever forgive them, and those who blame God struggle with relating to him as they had prior to the loss. Resolving this spiritual crisis, however, is instrumental in their healing. Later, parents who claim that their faith had sustained them describe a point at which they consciously chose to believe despite their doubts. They begin to identify with God the Father as a bereaved parent, with the suffering of Job, and with David in the loss of both his infant son and adult son Absalom. They find hope in the assurance that their child is safe in eternity and that they will one day be reunited.

**Conclusion.** Though bereaved parents report a sense of enduring loss, they also commonly report a transformed approach to life and relationships (Talbot, 2002). Their values often become more family oriented, and they develop a heightened compassion toward others, evidenced by acts of kindness and service. With a strong support system, especially of others who can empathize with the loss of a child, bereaved parents can achieve a healthy measure of integrated grief as they learn to live differently.

**Samuel J. Smith**

## REFERENCES

Barrera, M., D'Agostino, N. M., Schneiderman, G., Tallett, S., Spencer, L., & Jovcevska, V. (2007). Patterns of parental bereavement following the loss of a child and related factors. *Omega: Journal of Death & Dying, 55*(2), 145-167. doi:10.2190/OM.55.2.d

Moules, N. (2008). A parent's worst nightmare: Grief, families, and the death of a child. *Relational Child & Youth Care Practice, 21*(4), 63-69.

Nelson, T. (2004). *A Guide for Fathers: When a Baby Dies.* St. Paul, MN: A Place to Remember.

Silverman, P. R., & Kelly, M. (2009). *A Parent's Guide to Raising Grieving Children: Rebuilding Your Family After the Death of a Loved One.* New York, NY: Oxford University Press.

Talbot, K. (2002). *What Forever Means After the Death of a Child.* New York, NY: Brunner-Routledge.

## CRISIS INTERVENTION

**Description.** Crisis intervention, or early psychological intervention, is a form of helping that brings brief, immediate, and practical assistance to individuals and groups that have experienced a crisis event or critical incident. In the field of crisis intervention, critical incidents are defined as unusually challenging events that have the potential to create significant human distress and overwhelm a person's usual coping mechanisms. The human psychological response to such incidents is called a psychological crisis (Everly & Mitchell, 1999, 2003). Critical incidents can include natural disasters (such as hurricanes and tornados), acts of violence or terrorism, or more ordinary events, such as automobile or workplace accidents or other emergencies. The goal of crisis intervention is to mitigate the response to a psychological crisis experienced by individuals or groups following a crisis event. When a psychological crisis disrupts one's psychological balance and creates increased levels of stress, coping mechanisms can be overwhelmed, and evidence of significant impairment or dysfunction can be present (Everly and Mitchell, 1999). Crisis intervention attempts to provide psychological stabilization, reduction of the symptoms of traumatic stress, and a return to adaptive functioning (Roberts, 2005). Another goal of crisis intervention is to facilitate access to continued levels of care, including mental-health assistance, when needed.

It is important to understand that crisis intervention is a distinct field and is not a form of counseling. It is widely recognized that specialized training in emergency mental health and early psychological intervention is necessary. This is consistent with guidelines offered by the National Institutes of Mental Health and by the National Volunteer Organizations Active in Disaster (Mitchell, 2006).

**History of Crisis Response.** People have been responding to their brothers and sisters in crisis since biblical times, but the formal field of crisis intervention is relatively new. The roots of modern crisis intervention date back to the turn of the century. In 1906, the National Save-A-Life League was established for suicide prevention. Soon, World War I revealed a clear need for early psychological intervention for troops experiencing the trauma of war. In fact, the first empirical evidence that early psychological intervention is helpful in reducing chronic problems comes from military psychiatry in World War I (Mitchell, 2006). However, it would be decades before posttraumatic stress disorder, now a commonly recognized problem in military personnel and others, would be recognized as a psychiatric diagnosis.

During World War II, the processes that are a part of our current models of crisis response—immediacy, proximity, and expectancy—became recognized as active ingredients in effective emergency psychological response (Everly & Mitchell, 1999). These factors are key components of all models of crisis intervention and psychological first aid that are used today. Crisis intervention should be *immediate*—offered within the first 24 to 72 hours following the crisis. Crisis responders should go to the place where survivors are located rather than waiting for them to come to an office or center to receive services, meaning we should have close *proximity* to the event. And we must offer an *expectation* of the symptoms those in crisis will experience, as well as offer the expectation that they will recover from those symptoms over a course of days and weeks following the event (Cisney & Ellers, 2009).

Beginning in the 1970s, modern models of crisis intervention were created for application with emergency services personnel. It was clear that firefighters, law enforcement officers, and paramedics/EMTs were exposed to traumatic events with much greater frequency and intensity and much closer proximity than the general population. These groups also experienced higher rates of addictions, divorce, suicide, and other trauma related issues. However, major developments did not occur for the field until the 1980s.

In 1980, the *Diagnostic and Statistical Manual of Mental Disorders* (*DSM-III*), which served as the textbook for diagnosis in the field of psychiatry, recognized posttraumatic stress disorder (PTSD) as a legitimate mental illness under the category of anxiety disorders. This legitimized crisis and traumatic events as viable threats to long-term mental health and validated crisis intervention to mitigate the symptoms of critical incident stress and to facilitate access to mental health care for those with risk factors for PTSD (Cisney & Ellers, 2009).

**Assessment.** The first order of assessment for those doing crisis intervention is to address the response of the survivor(s) rather than addressing the incident. For example, novice crisis responders can make assumptions based on the magnitude of the incident or event about how individuals will be affected. In cases of a major or catastrophic event, it may be assumed that people will be severely affected and show major symptoms of distress. On the other hand, if the event is not a large-scale event or does not involve serious injuries or fatalities, some responders may assume that individuals will not experience symptoms of posttraumatic stress or that those symptoms will be less severe or enduring (Roberts, 2005). This can be a critical mistake because many factors must be considered regarding the impact of an event on an individual or group (Cisney & Ellers, 2009).

**Application.** Current application for crisis intervention is wide and varied. It can be practiced by anyone with specialized training in the field. It is no longer the domain of mental-health professionals, though mental-health practitioners still play a vital role in supervision and oversight of crisis intervention teams (Mitchell, 2006). Pastors, chaplains, emergency service personnel, and trained lay volunteers do much of the crisis intervention offered through nonprofit, faith-based, and governmental organizations.

In the last two decades, there has been a significant increase in crisis intervention in response to crises, disasters, or acts of violence in the workplace. Most of this crisis intervention is done by mental-health professionals through employee assistance programs. In October of 2002, the Employee Assistance Professional Association related a report from its Disaster Preparedness Task Force with recommendations for crisis intervention in the business and industrial sectors (Everly & Mitchell, 2008). Similarly, in January 2003, National Organizations Active in Disaster organized a task force made up of representatives from major organizations that provide training in crisis intervention and disaster mental health. Representatives from the American Red Cross, the International Critical Incident Stress Foundation, National Organization for Victims Assistance, and the Salvation Army came together to discuss practices and increase collaboration and partnership across their organizations. The result was a consensus report released in May 2005 outlining points of consensus about crisis intervention, referred to as Early Psychological Intervention (Everly & Mitchell, 2008). It is recommended that these extensive consensus points be reviewed for an understanding of current recommendations and guidelines for training and practice of early psychological intervention.

**Biblical and Spiritual Issues.** In reaching out to those whose lives have been touched by trauma and crisis, we have a beautiful example in Scripture. The parable of the Good Samaritan clearly demonstrates the compassion as well as the practical assistance we are to offer victims of crisis and traumatic events. In Luke 10:25-38, Jesus is speaking to a lawyer who is inquiring how he can inherit eternal life. Christ answers, "You shall love the Lord your God with all your heart, and with all your soul, and with all your strength, and with all your mind; and your neighbor as yourself."

His response inspires the lawyer to ask, "And who is my neighbor?"

To illustrate his point, Jesus tells a story about a Jewish man who was attacked by thieves, robbed, wounded, and left for dead at the side of the road. Two Jewish religious leaders walked by without stopping to assist the man. Jews despised Samaritans as a half-breed race, but a Samaritan traveling on the road felt compassion for the man in crisis and stopped to help him. This brief parable demonstrates the heart we are to have toward those in crisis and the interventions we are to offer as Christians (Cisney & Ellers, 2009). The Samaritan stopped to help the man in his hour of greatest need. He offered practical assistance and made sure the man got to safety and received the care he needed. Later, the Samaritan followed up to make sure the man's ongoing needs were met. And he did this for a stranger. May this parable serve as a calling to the body of Christ to care for others who are in crisis.

**Conclusion.** Crisis intervention is a new and rapidly evolving field. It is critical for Christian caregivers (mental-health professionals, pastors, chaplains, and lay caregivers) to be adequately trained in crisis intervention so that the church and parachurch organizations can be at the forefront of caring for people and leading the developing fields of crisis intervention and emergency and disaster mental health.

**Jennifer Cisney**

## REFERENCES


Cisney, J. S., & Ellers, K. L. (2009). *The First 48 Hours: Spiritual Caregivers as First Responders.* Nashville: Abingdon Press.

Everly, G. S., Jr., & Mitchell, J. T. (1999). *Critical Incident Stress Management* (2nd ed.). Ellicott City, MD: Chevron.

Everly, G. S., Jr., & Mitchell, J. T. (2003). Critical incident stress management and critical incident stress debriefing: Evolution, effects, and outcomes. In B. Raphael & P. J. Wilson (Eds.), *Psychological Debriefing: Theory, Practice, and Evidence* (pp. 72-90). New York, NY: Cambridge University Press.

Everly, G. S., Jr., & Mitchell, J. T. (2008). *Integrative Crisis Intervention and Disaster Mental Health.* Ellicott City, MD: Chevron.

Mitchell, J. T. (2006). *Critical Incident Stress Management (CISM) Group Crisis Intervention* (4th ed.). Ellicott City, MD: Chevron.

Roberts, A. R. (2005). *Crisis Intervention Handbook: Assessment, Treatment, and Research* (3rd ed.). Oxford, NY: Oxford University Press.


## COMBAT TRAUMA

**Description.** Many would say that trauma is a natural response to abnormal events in one's life. In the case of *combat trauma*, the abnormal events result from a brutal assault on the collective senses by means of combat-related violence, violation of core values, and loss of physical, emotional, mental, and spiritual identity. The severity of the response to combat trauma ranges from simple reintegration issues to diagnosable posttraumatic stress disorder (PTSD) and other serious mental disorders described in the *Diagnostic and Statistical Manual of Mental Disorders* (*DSM-IV-TR*). A related issue is secondary trauma in the lives of spouses, children, and other caregivers who maintain relationship with combat trauma sufferers.

The diagram below illustrates the spectrum of combat trauma (U.S. Army, 2006). The normalization and proper characterization of reactions to the stressors of military life, and particularly combat trauma, are important first steps in helping sufferers and deriving institutional solutions. This is especially critical in a military culture, which, in a real or perceived manner, stigmatizes admission of weakness.

**The Spectrum of Combat Trauma**

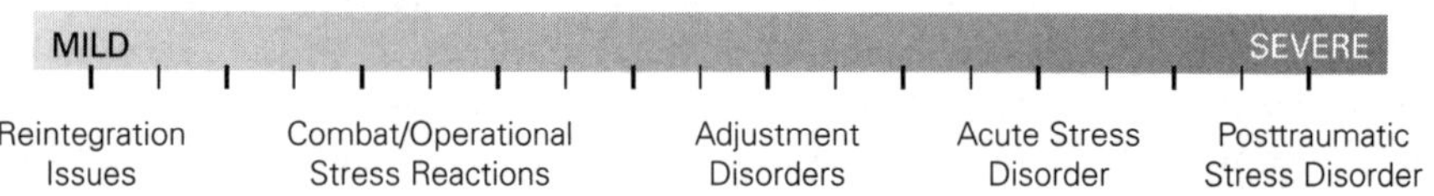


**History.** At the far end of the trauma spectrum, PTSD was defined by the American Psychiatric Association in 1980 in the *DSM III* but has existed over the course of warfare. In former conflicts it was called soldier's heart, battle fatigue, and shell shock.

The reality and scope of PTSD and related trauma issues was vigorously debated just a few years ago, but the discussion has now shifted to how to respond to the "clear and present danger" of the mental health of this generation of returning warriors. As this long war (the global war on terror) grinds on, second- and third-order effects are also becoming more evident and persistent, most graphically punctuated by historically high suicide statistics in the Army and Marines. The Department of Defense's (DOD) recent Mental Health Task Force's report (2007) found that programs within the DOD are not adequately addressing the increasing demand for mental-health services by recent veterans of Iraq and Afghanistan and their families. These shortcomings are caused partly by a lack of mental-health treatment capacity and partly by an overly cautious approach toward integration of faith-based elements of treatment.

Our national institutions are working hard to expand capacity to help wounded warriors from past battlefields, but this military mental-health bow wave will persist for years to come, and much remains to be done to stem this tide. Timely opportunities (and responsibilities) exist for the nationwide community of Christian counselors to play a significant role in the effective prevention and treatment of mental disorders among our nation's troops and veterans and their families.

**Assessment.** Combat trauma behaviors generally fall into three symptom categories: intrusive (flashbacks and somatic flashbacks, sleep walking and sleep fighting, nightmares, panic attacks), avoidance (reactions to triggers, emotional numbness, anxiety in crowds, self-neglect, inability to trust, and depression, sadness, and emptiness), and hyperarousal (anger, outbursts, rage, a short fuse, reduced cognitive ability, fear of becoming violent, always being on guard, easily startled, self-medicating, night sweats). Furthermore, spiritual symptoms (extreme bitterness and guilt, feeling abandoned by God and others, inability to forgive, seeking isolation, finding it hard to pray, no yearning for righteousness, inability to be thankful, loss of hope) lend themselves to best practices from the Christian faith realm (prayer, community, biblical instruction, forgiveness, and hope).

**Treatment.** Treatment follows traditional paths of counseling, with keen understanding of military experience and culture being an asset. Given the emerging nature and scope of military trauma issues, the field is characterized by widespread experimentation to find new and effective protocols. There are no "silver bullets" in treatment, but a counselor who is clinically sound, abreast of emerging research, consistent and persistent over time, and encouraging and hopeful will be able to do a good work in the life of a combat trauma sufferer. For further study, consult the *Care & Counsel for Trauma* video series (American Association of Christian Counselors, 2009).

**Biblical Relevance.** David's psalms indicate he was a serious PTSD sufferer. Consider this lament: "My heart is in anguish within me, and the terrors of death have fallen upon me. Fear and trembling come upon me, and horror has overwhelmed me" (Ps. 55:4-5 NASB).

But David trusted God for his ultimate healing: "He will redeem my soul in peace from the battle which is against me" (Ps. 55:18 NASB).

Faith is absolutely a critical factor in resilient recovery from combat trauma, every bit as relevant today as in David's age. For further biblical foundations regarding resilience, see 2 Corinthians 4.

**Summary.** Our nation's military is truly the exoderm—the outer skin—of our country. It protects the internal organs by ensuring the freedoms and way of life that make us America. At best, our soldiers' lives in the military are significantly challenged: They are called to hardship, separation, and selfless service around the world. As warriors, ambassadors, and on-the-ground statesmen for our nation, they often get bruised and cut, and they bleed. And yes, many of them pay the ultimate price. Their families and loved ones also sacrifice greatly.

Our military and their families certainly deserve our utmost respect and appreciation, but can we do more? For Christian counselors across our nation, the answer is a resounding yes!

**Bob Dees**

REFERENCES

American Association of Christian Counselors. (2009). *Stress & Trauma Care with Military Application.* [DVD series for counselors and military caregivers]. Forest, VA: Author.

U.S. Army Public Health Command. (2006). *Redeployment Health Guide: A Service Member's Guide to Deployment-Related Stress Problems.* Retrieved from http://usaphcapps.amedd.army.mil/HIOShoppingCart/ViewItem.aspx?id=72

U.S. Defense Health Board Task Force on Mental Health. (2007). *An Achievable Vision: Report of the Department of Defense Mental Health Task Force.* Retrieved from: http:// www.health.mil/dhb/mhtf/mhtf-report-final.pdf

## POSTTRAUMATIC STRESS DISORDER

**Description.** Posttraumatic stress disorder (PTSD) is a multifaceted syndrome that involves three primary constellations of responses to extreme stress following a traumatic event involving actual or perceived death, serious injury, or threat to self or others (Vermetten & Bremner, 2002; Vieweg et al., 2006; American Psychiatric Association, 2000). The primary symptom clusters include *re-experiencing* (e.g., recollections, flashbacks, dreams, physiological/psychological reactivity), *avoidance* and *numbing* (e.g., avoiding thoughts and feelings related to a traumatic experience, inability to recall key aspects of the event, detachment, restricted affect), and *hyperarousal* and *hypervigilance* (e.g., sleep disturbance, exaggerated startle response, concentration difficulty, irritability). Overall, lifetime prevalence in the U.S. population is estimated to be 7.8%, although nearly 85% of the population will experience a traumatic event at some point. Although PTSD resulting from combat exposure accounts for much of the disorder's prevalence in men, most PTSD results from much more common events, such as criminal victimization, motor vehicle accidents, and childhood maltreatment (physical, emotional, and sexual abuse). A significant proportion of the burden of PTSD in women results from domestic violence, particularly when sexual violence is also involved (Nemeroff et al., 2006).

Nearly 80% of those with PTSD have at least one other psychiatric disorder (Allen, 1996). Other disorders frequently co-occurring with PTSD include other anxiety disorders, depressive disorders, and substance-use disorders. For example, between 25% and 42% of those seeking substance use treatment meet criteria for PTSD (Henslee & Coffey, 2010). Childhood maltreatment may increase the risk of substance abuse, and prior substance use increases the risk of trauma exposure and PTSD (Nemeroff et al., 2006).

**Assessment.** Competent understanding of PTSD helps guide the assessment process. The nature of the traumatic event or situation is often obvious in cases of natural disaster and acts of terrorism; however, other traumatic experiences may be subtle and have a cumulative effect over the course of a lifetime. Adequate assessment of the three symptom clusters needs to occur. Cognitive, affective, behavioral, social, and spiritual modalities should be considered because all of these areas may be involved. Assessment should also consider the presence of co-occurring disorders because the majority of individuals with PTSD have at least one additional condition that meets diagnostic criteria. The National Center for PTSD of the United States Department of Veterans Affairs is a valuable resource for locating PTSD screening and assessment information.

In order for PTSD to be formally diagnosed, the *Diagnostic and Statistical Manual of Mental Disorders* (*DSM-IV-TR*) (American Psychiatric Association, 2000) criteria must be met. The person must have had exposure to a traumatic event that involved actual or threatened death, serious injury, or threat to physical integrity, and the response must involve intense fear, hopelessness, or horror. The traumatic event must be persistently reexperienced in at least one of several ways, including intrusive distressing recollections, recurrent distressing dreams, acting or feeling as if the event is occurring, or intense psychological or physiological distress at internal or external cues related to an aspect of the traumatic event. Persistent avoidance of associated stimuli and numbing of general responsiveness that was not present prior to experiencing the trauma must also be occurring. Indications of avoidance and numbing include the following: efforts to avoid thoughts, feelings, or conversations associated with the traumatic event; efforts to avoid activities, places, or persons that are reminders of the trauma; inability to recall an important aspect of the trauma; feelings of detachment or estrangement from others; restricted range of affect; sense of a foreshortened future; and diminished interest or participation in significant activities. There must also be persistent symptoms of increased arousal not present prior to the trauma. Symptoms of arousal include difficulty staying or falling asleep, irritability or outbursts of anger, difficulty concentrating, hypervigilance, and an exaggerated startle response. The duration of the symptoms in the three clusters must be more than one month and must cause clinically significant distress or impairment in social, occupational, or other important areas of functioning. As diagnostic criteria are being assessed, key terms to consider in diagnosing PTSD are *persistent*, *recurrent*, *intrusive*, and *distressing*. The frequency and intensity of symptoms from each of the three clusters are important considerations that can help direct the treatment process.

**Treatment.** There are three primary treatment principles to keep in mind when working with those struggling with PTSD: (a) address symptoms and co-occurring conditions, (b) improve adaptive functioning and return person to a state of safety and trust, and (c) limit generalization of initial trauma and protect against relapse (Allen 1996; Baschnagel, Coffey, & Rash, 2006; Henslee & Coffey, 2010; Nemeroff et al., 2006; Vermetten & Bremner, 2002; Vieweg et al., 2006; Yehuda, 2002).

Three treatment domains can be considered: exposure, cognitive-behavioral, and medical therapies. Exposure therapy helps facilitate confrontation of feared objects, situations, and images and can involve imaginal or in vivo and repeated or prolonged exposure. Systematic desensitization can also be helpful. There is some evidence that exposure may be more effective with intrusive symptoms. Cognitive-behavioral approaches modify maladaptive thoughts, beliefs, and assumptions. Key cognitions include thoughts such as these: "Protection from risk and harm is not under my control," "The world is dangerous and unpredictable," and "I am inadequate and incapable." Key assumptions include belief in personal vulnerability and the perception of the world as meaningfulness and unfair. Cognitive-behavioral approaches may be more helpful with avoidance and numbing. Medical approaches include the use of selective serotonin reuptake inhibitors (SSRIs), anxiolytics, mood stabilizers, and antipsychotics. These medications can help with disturbances in mood, anxiety, and thought. Generally, effective treatment addresses two core domains (memory and emotional regulation) involving two key elements (exposure to traumatic information and modification of maladaptive beliefs about events, symptoms, and behaviors). Development of healthy social support is a critical component of recovery from PTSD. It is important to note that most people who experience traumatic events do not develop PTSD. Most who do develop PTSD recover successfully. Resilience is the norm, not the exception, and posttraumatic growth is possible.

**Biblical and Spiritual Issues.** The complexity of PTSD reminds us of how we are "fearfully and wonderfully made" (cf. Ps. 139:7-14). Often in the face of traumatic events, questions of God's presence, purposes, and goodness arise. The Bible is replete with godly people who experienced traumatic events. Particularly, though, skillful Christian counselors will keep Jesus Christ in mind. Hebrews 12:1-3 (NASB) is one key passage that serves as a foundation for our response to life's traumas: "Therefore, since we have so great a cloud of witnesses surrounding us, let us also lay aside every encumbrance and the sin which so easily entangles us, and let us run with endurance the race that is set before us, fixing our eyes on Jesus, the author and perfecter of faith, who for the joy set before Him endured the cross, despising the shame, and has sat down at the right hand of the throne of God. For consider Him who has endured such hostility by sinners against Himself, so that you will not grow weary and lose heart."

**David E. Jenkins**

## REFERENCES


Allen, J. G. (1996, Summer). Neurobiological basis of posttraumatic stress disorder: Implications for patient education and treatment. *Bulletin of the Menninger Clinic, 60*(3), 377-395.

American Psychiatric Association. (2000). *Diagnostic and Statistical Manual of Mental Disorders* (4th ed., text rev.). Washington, DC: Author.

Baschnagel, J. S., Coffey, S. F., & Rash, C. J. (2006). Treatment of co-occurring PTSD and substance use disorders using trauma-focused exposure therapy. *International Journal of Behavioral and Consultation Therapy, 2*(4), 498-508. Retrieved from http://www.baojournal.com/IJBCT/IJBCT-index.html

Henslee, A. M., & Coffey, S. F. (2010). Exposure therapy for posttraumatic stress disorder in a residential substance use treatment facility. *Professional Psychology: Research and Practice, 41*,34-40. doi: 10.1037/a0018235

Nemeroff, C. B., Bremner, J. D., Foa, E. B., Mayberg, H. S., North, C. S., & Stein, M. B. (2006). Posttraumatic stress disorder: A state-of-the-science review. *Journal of Psychiatric Research, 40*,1-21. doi:10.1016/j.jpsychires.2005.07.005

Vermetten, E., & Bremner, J. D. (2002). Circuits and systems in stress. II. Applications to neurobiology and treatment in posttraumatic stress disorder. *Depression and Anxiety, 16*, 14-38. doi: 10.1002/da.10017

Vieweg, W. V. R., Julius, D. A., Fernandez, A., Beatty-Brooks, M., Hettema, J. M., & Pandurangi, A. K. (2006). Posttraumatic stress disorder: Clinical features, pathophysiology, and treatment. *American Journal of Medicine, 119*, 383-390. doi: 10.1016/j.amjmed.2005.09.027

Yehuda, R. (2002). Clinical relevance of biologic findings in PTSD. *Psychiatric Quarterly, 73*, 123-133. doi: 10.1023/A:1015055711424


## TRAUMATIC MEMORY

A trauma is an inescapably stressful event that overwhelms existing coping mechanisms.

**Paralyzed by Memory.** I'll never forget the words of a Liberian student in my class: "Let me tell you what it is like for my people. I have a friend who lost his parents, his wife, and his children. He does not speak anymore. He stays alone in his house and will not come out. He shrugs his shoulders in response to any suggestion, for what does it matter?"

Every experience produces memories. For those who experience trauma, these memories can be unforgettable, retraumatizing, and crippling. As people helpers, we must understand what to do with the memories of traumatic events. A trauma, unlike a more common misfortune, involves a threat to life or bodily integrity. It is often a close personal encounter with violence or death.

The common denominator of psychological trauma is a set of feelings including intense fear, helplessness, loss of control, and anticipation of annihilation. Certain aspects of the experience increase the likelihood of harm to those involved. These include being taken by surprise, being trapped or exposed to the point of exhaustion, physical violation or injury, exposure to extreme violence, or witnessing grotesque death. Sexual abuse, war, rape, and natural or man-made disasters carry within them all of those factors that threaten harm.

> Psychological trauma is an affliction of the powerless. At the moment of trauma, the victim is rendered helpless by overwhelming force. When the force is that of nature, we speak of disasters. When the force is that of other human beings, we speak of atrocities. Traumatic events overwhelm the ordinary systems of care that give people a sense of control, connection, and meaning (Herman, 1997, p. 32).

Research shows that trauma results in silence, isolation, and helplessness (Briere

& Scott, 2006)—silence because words are inadequate for communicating the unspeakable; isolation because either no one knows, no one understands, or no one can help; and helplessness because every attempt to stop the tragedy was ineffective.

**Responses to Trauma.** The ordinary human response to danger is quite complex and involves both body and mind (Scaer, 2005). When action seems pointless, the human system of self-defense becomes overwhelmed and disorganized. Coping responses to danger often persist in an exaggerated way long after the danger is over. Trauma produces lasting changes in physiological arousal, emotion, cognition, and memory. Sometimes traumatic events separate these normally integrated functions from one another so that what usually functions as a unit becomes disjointed. For example, a traumatized person may demonstrate strong feeling with no clear memory of the events, or very clear memory without emotion. Trauma often results in disrupted cognitive and emotional processes.

After an experience of overwhelming danger, two contradictory responses or two opposing psychological states often occur: intrusion and constriction. The victim is caught between amnesia and reliving the trauma, intense overwhelming emotion and numbness, impulsivity and inhibition or passivity. These alternating states continue the feelings of chaos and unpredictability that the trauma caused, creating the impression that the trauma is continuing. Often, people continue functioning as if it just happened. Flashbacks, recurrent nightmares, and intrusive memories keep the feelings of unpredictability and chaos ever present. People cannot get better because it is still happening in their minds.

Initially, the victim has ongoing, intrusive recollection of the event both as flashbacks and nightmares. The victim stays highly agitated and on alert for new danger. The intrusive symptoms often decrease after three to six months, though if the threat of recurrence were still present, obviously the symptoms would continue for a longer period. As intrusive symptoms decrease over time, numbing and constrictive symptoms remain.

This is a very important point. Unfortunately, because survivors *seem* to have resumed their former life to a great extent, many people think they have recovered from the trauma. Sadly, the survivors function but feel dead inside and disconnected from life and relationships. Many people who have been traumatized by something like childhood sexual abuse live the majority of their lives in this constrictive state. Obviously, we want to respond to trauma in a way that helps people deal with their memories, their emotions, and their reactions in ways that return them to a place of care, connection, and meaning.

Trauma leads to extremes of retention and forgetting. Terrifying experiences may be remembered with extreme vividness, or they may completely resist integration. Many traumatized individuals report a combination of both (Read & Lindsay, 1997). Those who have experienced trauma consistently report that the emotional and perceptual elements of memory tend to be more prominent than what is known as the declarative component (conscious awareness of facts or events). In other words, survivors would be more likely to recall what they felt and experienced perceptually than they would be able to give a clear accounting of what happened and in what order.

Memories of trauma tend to be experienced as fragments of the sensory components of the event—visual ("I saw the color of their ties" or "I can still see their faces"), olfactory (the smells of that day), auditory (the sound of buildings collapsing, the sound of the water), kinesthetic (the push of the crowds, the feeling of the water swirling around them, the ground moving), or intense waves of emotion that are used to describe the event (fear, panic, terror, etc.).

Survivors see such perceptions as exact representations of sensations at the time of the trauma, so when they talk about their fear, they mean they are feeling the same fear that they felt during the trauma. It is not diluted. It is just as potent as when it first occurred. It is *not* a memory of the feeling, but a re-experiencing of the feeling.

Normal memory is given in narrative form. Feelings are recalled. But traumatic memory is not initially narrative. A victim cannot tell a story about a trauma. Rather, there is some kind of sensory experience. Researchers believe this indicates that traumatic memory is stored in the brain differently than is narrative memory (Stien & Kendall, 2004). Traumatic memory is more disconnected, seems to be stored as sensory fragments, and has little to no linguistic components. That is why those who have just been traumatized use a very small vocabulary, if they speak at all.

**Types of Trauma Memory.** Some people who have experienced trauma seem to go back to normal after months or years, but a large group continue to live with traumatic memories. For them, life will never be the same. Langer (1993) demonstrates how trauma divides the self and keeps it from being whole. It divides into "me and not-me" or "my life and not-my-life." There is a very basic split that occurs due to the trauma.

*Deep memory (buried self)* occurs when efforts to leave the memory behind prove ultimately futile. Those who survive a trauma will find themselves in a business meeting or at a dinner party and suddenly experience that double existence, desperately wanting the images of crushed bodies, death, and tragedy to go away, trying to make sure the skin that holds the trauma separate will prove strong enough because they are supposed to be having a dinner conversation. Survivors of chronic childhood abuse will see an image on television and suddenly find themselves physically reacting as if they are being abused.

*Anguished memory (divided self)* refers to memory that assaults and finally divides the self. Survivors talk about the inability to link the past and the future: "I split myself. It wasn't me there. I was somebody else." And from another survivor, "My head is filled with garbage, all these images you know, and sounds, and my nostrils filled with smells... you can't excise it...it's like another skin beneath this skin and you cannot shed it...I am not like you. You have one vision of life and I have two...I have a double life." You will hear survivors of the World Trade Center trauma in 2001 or the Indian Ocean tsunami in 2004 or Hurricane Katrina in 2005 or the earthquake in Haiti in 2010 speak about "before the event" or "after the event." The event divides their lives in two.

*Humiliated memory (besieged self)* recalls an utter distress that shatters all molds designed to contain a unified and irreproachable image of the self. It is the memory of things that makes death preferable to life. People who acted during the trauma in ways that are diametrically opposed to their views of themselves will experience humiliated memory. Those present on 9/11 or in Haiti or during Katrina who acted less than heroically or altruistically will experience this kind of memory. Survivors may tend to judge themselves harshly when they reflect back on their choices and behavior: "I should have...I could have...why didn't I?"

**Trauma and Faith.** Trauma freezes thinking. People who have experienced trauma think about themselves, their lives, their relationships, and their futures through the grid of the trauma. Trauma stops growth because it shuts everything down. It is of the nature of death. The thinking that grows out of the traumatic experience controls the input from new experiences. The trauma will serve as the grid for future decisions and interactions. The more aspects of a person involved in the trauma, the greater the likelihood of traumatic memories. In the trauma of sexual abuse, every sense is involved (touch, taste, smell, sound, and sight), and it was involved during a state of hyperalertness. The lessons learned (such as being vulnerable is always stupid or all men are predators), right or wrong, will not be forgotten.

Humans learn about the unseen through the seen. For many survivors, God is viewed through the lens of the trauma. Often, the truths of Scripture, which victims so desperately need, have virtually no impact. They do not go *in*. Intellectually, truth is rooted in the Word of God, but experientially, it is rooted in the trauma. Often, trauma survivors can hold on to their belief in God because they are living in self-deceit.

Weisel (1982), a holocaust survivor, found that it is not necessarily a consolation to believe that God is still alive. Rather than being the solution, saying God is alive merely states the problem. Many who suffered the experience of trauma will struggle with two seemingly irreconcilable realities: God, who is a refuge, and the trauma. Each seems to cancel out the other, yet both exist. The human mind can manage either alternative—trauma and no God, or God and no trauma. What is one to do with trauma *and* God?

The only answer to this dilemma is the cross of Jesus Christ. It is there that trauma and God come together. Christ has endured all fears, powerlessness, helplessness, destruction, alienation, silence, loss, and hell. He understands trauma. He endured trauma and was abandoned by the Father so that his children never have to be traumatized without the presence of the Father. How will such precious truths be communicated effectively to those who have been traumatized?

By you. Christian counselors and caregivers are representatives of this crucified God to the traumatized. It is your work to teach and to live out that which is true of the Father. Your words, your tone of voice, your actions, and your responses to rage, fear, and failure all become ways that the traumatized person learns about this God. Even when you cannot openly speak of him, you bring his presence with you wherever you go.

**Listening Well.** Working with trauma requires us to listen. I fear we are much better at talking, but this will require us to sit with. We are better at instituting programs, but this will mean learning how to weep with. We would rather organize, but if we will let it, this work can change us and change the church of Jesus Christ, for it will teach us how to suffer with the suffering. That is, of course, in part what our Lord did for us.

Traumatic memories are far more complex than something that can be remedied by the push of a mental button. As we listen, we must acknowledge our limitations. Words must be used, but they cannot convey all. A vast chasm separates what was endured from our capacity to absorb it. The survivor is remembering what was. The hearer is imagining what was. That calls for ongoing humility in the listener. As we listen to memories of trauma from others, we must do so with respect and humility, knowing that no vocabulary is sufficient for communicating the whole of the experience.

**Diane Langberg**

## REFERENCES

Briere, J., & Scott, C. (2006). *Principles of Trauma Therapy: A Guide to Symptoms, Evaluation and Treatment.* Thousand Oaks, CA: Sage Publications.

Herman, J. (1997). *Trauma and Recovery.* New York, NY: Basic Books.

Langer, L. (1993). *Holocaust Testimonies: The Ruins of Memory.* New Haven, Connecticut: Yale University Press.

Read, J. D., & Lindsay, D. S. (1997). *Recollections of Trauma: Scientific Evidence and Clinical Practice.* New York, NY: Springer.

Scaer, R. C. (2005). *The Trauma Spectrum: Hidden Wounds and Human Resiliency.* New York, NY: Norton.

Stien, P. T., & Kendall, J. C. (2004). *Psychological Trauma and the Developing Brain.* Binghamton, NY: Haworth Press.

Wiesel, E. (1982). *Night.* New York City: Bantam Books.

*Part 5*

# Counselor Skills, Theories, and Therapies

# CORE SKILLS AND CONCEPTS FOR CHRISTIAN HELPERS

## HELPING RELATIONSHIPS

**Description.** The goal of a helping relationship is to promote growth. More specifically, the goal of the helping relationship in Christian counseling is to help people enter into a richer experience with God and others (Crabb, 1977). David Brandon (1982, pp. 8-9) encapsulates the true nature of any helping relationship:

> The foundation of genuine helping lies in being ordinary. Nothing special. We can offer only ourselves, neither more nor less, to others—we have in fact nothing else to give. Anything more is conceit; anything less is robbing those in distress. Helping demands wholeheartedness, but people find it hard to give themselves to others.... In essence, we are afraid to offer ourselves for fear we will prove insufficient, and if all that we have and are is not enough, what then? We are afraid to risk using simply our own warmth and caring.

**History.** Carl Rogers' client-centered approach concentrates on therapists' ability to be genuine, trustworthy, caring, and transparent. Corey & Corey (2010) describe these helpers as people who commit to an honest assessment of self, are open to learning, have good interpersonal skills, are genuine, and realize change is hard work. In addition, they stress the importance of counselors' willingness for self-examination, insight, and growth. Finally, Corey (2009) stresses the importance of counselors' intimate awareness of the ethical guidelines to helping relationships. Corey, Corey, & Callahan (2006) state that ethical codes are developed to safeguard clients, offer accountability for counselors, and protect the integrity of helping relationships.

**Assessment and Treatment.** Ribner & Knei-Paz (2002) reported that the principal factors clients report as effective in the helping relationship are warmth, empathy, understanding, acceptance, and involvement. They suggest that clients look for a sense of equality in the helping relationship, and they gauge the presence of this trait by love, friendship, and a nonjudgmental stance. Borg & Kristiansen (2004) report that clients desire a collaborative approach and need to know that professionals are willing to be flexible in the approach taken. De Boer & Coady (2006) state that clients need to sense the helper is taking a soft, judicious stance of power and is mindful of the needs of the individual.

In addition, Corey & Corey (2010) strongly emphasize that effective helpers must explore their own family-of-origin issues. They state if these issues are left unexplored, counselors will not be self-giving in the helping relationship. It is the act of self-exploration and healing that produces an even greater depth of understanding and compassion for other wounded people. The helping relationship requires a genuineness that can come only from men and women who have walked through the valley, faced their own wounds, risen above the pain and suffering, and come through it changed individuals.

**Biblical Issues.** God offers the best handbook on developing helping relationships—the Bible. Charles Allen (1953) writes, "The very essence of religion is to adjust the mind and soul of man. [Quoting] Augustine, 'My soul is restless until it finds its rest in Thee, O God.' Healing means bringing the person into a right relationship with the physical, mental, and spiritual laws of God" (p. 7). The helping relationship is one that brings a person to this place. Philippians 2:3-4 reminds us, "Do nothing out of selfish ambition or vain conceit, but in humility consider others better than yourselves. Each of you should look not only to your own interests, but also to the interest of others."

As helpers, Christian counselors need to be genuine, transparent, and compassionate. In addition, in the helping relationship, Christians are called to serve. Jesus said that his followers would be known by their selfless care for those in need. Caring for others, he suggested, was the same as caring for him: "I was hungry and you gave me something to eat, I was thirsty and you gave me something to drink, I was a stranger and you invited me in, I needed clothes and you clothed me, I was sick and you looked after me, I was in prison and you came to visit me" (Mt. 25:35-36). Finally, as helpers, Christian counselors must first become healed, and then, "we who are strong ought to bear with the failings of the weak and not please ourselves. Each of us should please his neighbor for his good, to build him up" (Rom. 15:1-2).

**Jeanne Brooks**

## REFERENCES


Allen, C. (1953). *God's Psychiatry.* Grand Rapids, MI: Spire.

Borg, M., & Kristiansen, K. (2004). Recovery-oriented professionals: Helping relationships in mental health services. *Journal of Mental Health, 13*(5), 493-505. doi:10.1080/09638230400006809

Brandon, D. (1982). *The Trick of Being Ordinary: Notes for Volunteers & Students.* London, England: Mind.

Corey, G. (2009). *Theory and Practice of Counseling and Psychotherapy.* Belmont, CA: Thomson Higher Education.

Corey, M. S., & Corey, G. (2010). *Becoming a Helper.* Belmont, CA: Brooks/Cole.

Corey, G., Corey, M. S., & Callanan, P. (2006). *Issues & Ethics in the Helping Professions.* Pacific Grove, CA: Brooks/Cole.

Crabb, L. (1977). *Effective Biblical Counseling.* Grand Rapids, MI: Zondervan.

De Boer, C., & Coady, N. (2006). Good helping relationships in child welfare: Learning from stories of success. *Child and Family Social Work, 12,* 32-42. doi:10.1111/j.1365-2206.2006.00438.x

Ribner, D. S., & Knei-Paz, C. (2002). Client's view of a successful helping relationship. *Social Work, 47*(4), 379-387.

Ruelas, S. R., Atkinson, D. R., & Ramos-Sanchez, L. (1998). Counselor helping model, participant ethnicity and acculturation level, and perceived counselor credibility. *Journal of Counseling Psychology, 45*(1), 98-103.

Smith, M. K. (2008). Helping relationships—principles, theory and practice. *The Encyclopedia of Informal Education.* Retrieved from http://www.infed.org/helping/helping_relationships.htm


## THERAPEUTIC ALLIANCE

**Description.** *Therapeutic alliance* refers to the relationship between the therapist (e.g., a psychiatrist, psychologist, mental health counselor, or social worker) and the client. Martin, Garske, and Davis (2000) define the therapeutic alliance as "the collaborative and affective bond between therapist and patient—[that] is an essential element of the therapeutic process" (p. 438). It is the means by which the therapist and the client "become allies against mental illness and distress" (Michel, 2011). It is considered the common curative factor among all treatment approaches (Horvath & Symonds, 1991). Both the therapist's presentation and the client's perception of the therapist affect the therapeutic alliance (Marshall, 2011). The client and the therapist need to have similar expectations of the therapy process for a collaborative relationship to develop (Michel). The development of this therapeutic alliance occurs in the early phase of effective therapy (Michel).

Trust is a critical ingredient to the therapeutic alliance—the ability to achieve any real progress in counseling depends on a trusting relationship (Marshall, 2011). It is an act of vulnerability or dependency that can build a strong connection, or if violated, expose the trusting person to hurt or shame (Springle, 1995). Craig Ellison (1999) stated the "trust equation" very well: "Trust is not usually an all or none phenomenon. There are degrees of trust, which can be assessed by the level of positive expectancy about someone's trustworthiness together with the magnitude of the damage if betrayal occurs" (p. 1232).

**History.** This idea of a therapeutic alliance can be traced to the genesis of talk therapy—psychoanalysis. Freud believed that a positive transference leads to a successful alliance, thereby associating the therapist with pleasing relationships from the client's early years (Freud, 1913/1995). One of Freud's successors, Winicott, an object-relations therapist, describes this same therapeutic relationship as the holding environment. This holding environment is characterized by empathy, listening, understanding, respect, and patience (Stone, 1981). Carl Rogers, in his client-centered therapy, identified the empathic bond between the patient and therapist as the key therapeutic factor in treatment (Rogers, 1965).

**Therapist Characteristics.** By synthesizing research spanning three decades, Marshall (2011) developed a list of therapist qualities that promote client change: "empathy, warmth, genuineness, respectfulness, support, confidence, emotional responsivity/expressiveness, self-disclosure, asks open-ended questions, directiveness, flexibility, encourages active participation, is rewarding/encouraging, uses humor, supportively challenging, sincerity, honest, interest" (p. 66). Paivo & Pascual-Leone (2010) identify intervention principles needed for developing a productive alliance: "empathize and communicate compassion, understanding, and nonjudgmental acceptance; validate client perceptions and experience; provide information…; define therapist and client roles; make process observations; provide reassurance and hope; and foster realistic expectations" (p. 104).

**Research.** Various research studies spanning decades have demonstrated the importance of the therapeutic alliance on counseling outcomes. Research has demonstrated that the therapeutic alliance is the best predictor of treatment outcome (Horvath & Symonds, 1991). In a meta-analysis reviewing 24 studies considering the relationship between alliance and therapy outcomes, findings suggested a consistent relationship between a strong therapeutic alliance and better psychotherapy treatment outcomes for all psychotherapy modalities included in this meta-analysis (Horvath & Symonds). A more recent meta-analysis of 11 studies including 1301 participants focused on the relationship between dropout rate and therapeutic alliance. It indicated weaker therapeutic alliance is associated with higher psychotherapy dropout (Sharf, Primavera, & Diener, 2010).

**Spiritual Implications.** Clients who consider their spiritual beliefs of significance bring this value with them into counseling, yet in the past, spiritual or religious involvement was regarded in a negative manner with the therapist often considering the individual who valued spirituality, religion, or any type of faith commitment as problematic or even clearly pathological (Young, Dowdle, & Flowers, 2009). Given this historic view, spiritually oriented clients are more likely to be tentative in establishing a trusting relationship with a secular therapist, possibly disrupting or delaying the development of a positive therapeutic alliance. Young, Dowdle, and Flowers suggest a therapist should possess an openness when working with a spiritually oriented client, supporting clients in their spiritual interests, thereby allowing clients to benefit from their spiritual practices. Cultivating a positive and supportive approach when working with the religious client has become increasingly significant given the counseling profession's recently renewed focus on the relationship between spirituality and psychological adjustment.

It would be difficult for a Christian to miss the similarity between the list of characteristics contributing to a positive therapeutic alliance and personal traits encouraged throughout the Bible. The concept of a therapeutic alliance relates strongly in many ways to the quality of relationship believers are encouraged to develop with one another throughout Scripture. "Clothe yourselves with compassion, kindness, humility, gentleness and patience" (Col. 3:12). Passages such as this echo what research reflects are the qualities of a healing relationship.

Carmela O'Hare

## REFERENCES


Ellison, C. (1999). Trust. In D. Benner & P. Hill (Eds.), *Baker Encyclopedia of Psychology and Counseling* (2nd ed.). Grand Rapids, MI: Baker Books.

Freud, S. (1913/1995). On the beginning of treatment: Further recommendations on the technique of psychoanalysis. In P. Gays (Ed.), *The Freud Reader* (pp. 363-378). New York, NY: Norton.

Horvath, A. O., & Symonds, B. D. (1991). Relation between working alliance and outcome in psychotherapy: A meta-analysis. *Journal of Consulting and Clinical Psychology, 38*, 139-149.

Marshall, W. L., & American Psychological Association. (2011). *Rehabilitating Sexual Offenders: A Strength-Based Approach.* Washington, DC: American Psychological Association.

Martin, D. J., Garske, J. P., & Davis, M. K. (2000, January 1). Relation of the therapeutic alliance with outcome and other variables: A meta-analytic review. *Journal of Consulting and Clinical Psychology, 68*(3), 438-50.

Michel, K. (2011). General aspects of therapeutic alliance. In K. Michel & K. A. Jobes (Eds.), *Building a Therapeutic Alliance with the Suicidal Patient* (pp. 13-28). Washington, DC: American Psychological Association. doi:10.1037/12303-001

Paivio, S. C., Pascual-Leone, A., & American Psychological Association. (2010). *Emotion-Focused Therapy for Complex Trauma: An Integrative Approach.* Washington, DC: American Psychological Association. doi:10.1037/12077-005

Rogers, C. R. (1965). *Client-Centered Therapy.* Boston, MA: Houghton Mifflin.

Sharf, J., Primavera, L. H., Diener, M. J. (2010). Dropout and therapeutic alliance: A meta-analysis of adult individual psychotherapy. *Psychotherapy Theory, Research Practice, Training, 47*(4), 637-645. doi: 10.1037/a0021175

Springle, P. (1995). *Trusting: The Issue at the Heart of Every Relationship.* Nashville, TN: Highland Books.

Stone, L. (1981). Notes on the noninterpretive elements in the psychoanalytic situation and process. *Journal of the American Psychoanalytic Association,* 29(1), 89-118.

Young, J. S., Dowdle, S., & Flowers, L. (2009). How spirituality can affect the therapeutic alliance. In J. D. Aten & M. M. Leach (Eds.), *Spirituality and the Therapeutic Process: A Comprehensive Resource from Intake to Termination* (pp. 167-192). Washington, DC: American Psychological Association. doi:10.1037/11853-008


## COUNSELING SKILLS

**Description.** The term *counseling skills* refers to a variety of techniques and competencies helpers utilize to (a) establish a therapeutic relationship with clients and (b) facilitate a process of healing, growth, and change in clients' lives and relationships. Although counseling techniques and implementation vary according to the therapists' theoretical background, a set of core counseling skills is generally common to all helping approaches.

The term *counseling* applies to a broad range of helping professions. Professional counselors, lay counselors, and pastoral counselors, depending on their experience, education, and specialty, have varying definitions for counseling and varying ideas of how counseling should be conducted. Approaches to counseling are guided by different worldviews and theories of human nature, some of which may be grounded in Scripture, while other aspects may be born out of psychological theory and empirical research. These differences notwithstanding, a wide variety of counseling approaches have been shown to be equally effective (Wampold, 2001). A common explanation for this phenomenon is that all approaches share a set of common therapeutic factors that are associated with successful outcomes.

**History.** Counseling, as a distinct profession from traditional psychotherapy, began to emerge around the turn of the 20th century. In its early years, it was largely associated with vocational guidance and was conducted mostly in schools and career centers (Gladding, 2008). Over time, counseling evolved into a process of not only offering guidance on school and career decisions but also helping people change significant aspects of their lives and relationships. Today, counseling can include working with a wide variety of presenting issues, ranging from relationship concerns to more serious pathologies, and the line between counseling and psychotherapy is less distinct.

Due to the broadening of counseling's application and the common factors theory, a core set of general counseling skills is often taught in helping-profession training programs, and they apply to a wide range of client problems and counseling approaches. These skills are fundamental to facilitating the process of counseling whereby the helper assists the client to explore the nature of the problem, establish goals, and make self-sustaining changes. Current models for teaching basic counseling skills frequently contextualize them within stages of the helping process. Although the identified stages of helping may differ somewhat by author, the counseling process typically includes the establishment of the therapeutic relationship, exploration and identification of the problem, development of goals and implementation strategies, and evaluation and termination (Cormier, Nurius, & Osborn, 2009; Egan, 2010; Hill, 2009).

**Core Skills.** The counselor's ability to establish a therapeutic relationship, or working alliance, with the client is essential for the counseling process to continue and for successful outcomes (Horvath & Bedi, 2002). Fundamental to establishing therapeutic rapport are the skills of attending, observing, and listening.

*Attending* refers to physically and mentally orienting oneself toward the client (Hill, 2009). It involves aspects of body posture, such as facing the client, leaning slightly forward and in an open manner (i.e., legs and arms uncrossed), making appropriate amounts of eye contact, using a moderate amount of head nods and acknowledgments (i.e., "Um-hmm"), using space appropriately (i.e., positioning yourself three to four feet from the client), matching the client's facial expression, and giving the client your undivided attention. All of these skills are intended to show that you are paying close attention to what your clients are saying and that you genuinely care about their concerns.

*Observing* involves paying attention to the client's (and your own) nonverbal communication for additional understanding. This includes such things as body language and paralanguage (i.e., speech volume, tone, and speed).

Finally, *listening* involves hearing clients' verbal and nonverbal communication to fully understand their narrative and experience. The ability to convey empathy while using each of these skills is critical for building trust and openness in the therapeutic relationship.

Several core skills are involved in the process of exploring the client's presenting issue and identifying the problem. These include restating the content of the client's speech, reflecting the client's expressed and underlying feelings, summarizing themes and patterns in the client's narrative, challenging blind spots and discrepancies between the client's words, actions, and values, offering interpretations for how the problem originated and how it is being maintained, asking questions for furthering insight, and probing for deeper meaning. Again, counselors should implement these skills empathically and with respect for clients' needs and desires.

When developing goals and implementation strategies, counselors work collaboratively with clients to establish goals that are consistent with clients' values. Skills in this stage include exploring previous attempts and obstacles to change, giving clients specific information on change strategies, offering feedback on their progress, confronting resistance to change, assisting them in developing strategies for accomplishing their goals, and helping them to evaluate these strategies and revise them as needed. The degree of involvement in this process will likely vary according to the counselors' personality and theoretical approach, but most people in the helping profession agree that it is not the counselors' role to direct the clients' behavior.

**Spiritual Issues.** From the Christian viewpoint, Jesus is the Wonderful Counselor (Is. 9:6) and exemplar of skills fundamental to promoting hope, healing, and change. Compassion and love were the hallmarks of Christ's ministry to those who were hurting. More important than the rote implementation of skills is the need for the Christian counselor to be guided by the Holy Spirit and motivated by a genuine love and concern for the well-being of others. Additionally, Christians recognize that the Holy Spirit is the agent of change, and as counselors, we are merely facilitators of change.

**David J. Jennings II**
**Joshua N. Hook**

## REFERENCES

Cormier, S., Nurius, P. S., & Osborn, C. J. (2009). *Interviewing and Change Strategies for Helpers: Fundamental Skills and Cognitive-Behavioral Interventions* (6th ed.). Belmont, CA: Brooks/Cole.

Egan, G. (2010). *The Skilled Helper: A Problem-Management and Opportunity-Development Approach to Helping* (9th ed.). Belmont, CA: Brooks/Cole.

Gladding, S. T. (2008). *Counseling: A Comprehensive Profession* (6th ed.). Upper Saddle River, NJ: Merrill.

Hill, C. E. (2009). *Helping Skills: Facilitating Exploration, Insight, and Action* (3rd ed.). Washington, DC: American Psychological Association.

Horvath, A. O., & Bedi, R. P. (2002). The alliance. In J. C. Norcross (Ed.), *Psychotherapy Relationships That Work: Therapist Contributions and Responsiveness to Patients* (pp. 37-70). New York, NY: Oxford University Press.

Wampold, B. E. (2001). *The Great Psychotherapy Debate: Models, Methods, and Findings.* Mahwah, NJ: Erlbaum.

## CORE SKILLS

### COMPASSION AND EMPATHY

In an article in the *New York Journal-American*, Abraham Joshua Heschel wrote, "A religious man is a person who holds God and man in one thought at one time, who suffers when harm is done to others, whose greatest strength is love and defiance of despair, whose greatest passion is compassion."

**Description.** Webster's defines the term *compassion* as a "sympathetic consciousness of another's distress, together with a desire to alleviate it." The word is derived from the Latin *pati* (to suffer) and the prefix *cum* (to bear alongside). Much of the research on this subject underscores the critical importance of the helping relationship with caregivers who are frequently in close proximity to the emotional suffering and resulting grief of those they minister to and counsel. Lilius et al. (2003) expanded the definition further in their statement that compassion is an "empathetic emotional response to another person's pain or suffering that moves people to act in a way that will either ease the person's condition or make it more bearable" (p. 4). This is the essence of the therapeutic alliance.

*Empathy*, on the other hand, is often referred to as the ability to "put oneself into another's shoes." Titchener (1909) was one of the first to use the term, which he defined as a "process of humanizing objects, of reading or feeling ourselves into them" (p. 417). His conceptualization of empathy came from an even earlier construct originating in German aesthetics called *einfühlung*, described as a person's spontaneous projection of intuitive feelings toward another (Vischer, 1883 as cited in Hare, 1934). *Sympathy* focuses on one's own thoughts and feelings, but *empathy* shifts the focus to the other person. In a review of Norman Levine's book *A Passion for Compassion*, Ohrman (2002) commented that "other-centeredness" can become a meaningful guide to life, taking place through what is described as the exchange of genuine and authentic relationships. This is at the core of the client-therapist paradigm.

**Application.** Indeed, the interplay between compassion and empathy—defined by this author as a *compathic* response—has significance to the counselor. For Young-Mason (2001), compassion is "born of wisdom and courage." To fully comprehend the construct, it "means to study the nature of suffering—the intertwining of moral, spiritual, psychological, and physical suffering" and "like freedom, is a word whose meaning becomes clearer and finally clarified in practice" (p. 347). According to Ruiz and Vallejos (1999), compassion is a feeling, "but it is a feeling mediated by reason: that the other person is worthy of compassion, is not a mere suffering object, but a subject with a wounded, abused, or frustrated dignity who demands a response" (p. 6). They go on to describe compassion as a developmental construct where moral engagement requires compassion, acquired by guidance and learning for the commitment to be effective, so that one can move from understanding people at a deeper level (empathy) to responsible action (compassion).

**Biblical and Spiritual Issues.** From a biblical perspective, compassion can be viewed as one of the distinguishing characteristics of Christ and his own relational style. Numerous Old and New Testament passages give insight into this model (Ps. 103:4; 135:14; Is. 49:13; 54:8; Jer. 42:12; Mic. 7:19; Mt. 15:32; 20:34; Jas. 5:11). Christ himself, rebuking the Pharisees because their religious form took precedence over their concern for others, said, "I desire compassion and not a sacrifice" (Mt. 12:7). The Greek term used here is *splagchon,* and the connotation is "tender affection from the inward parts." In the Hebrew text, the word *compassion* is rendered as *racham* and literally means "deep mercies." Ramsay (1998) regarded compassion as "redemptive empowerment," which is the "exercise of love that honors the integrity and dignity of each life" (p. 219).

The closest analogy in understanding this phenomenon would be the principle of acoustic resonance, which occurs when two violins are located in the same room. As a string is plucked on one, it causes the string tuned to the same frequency on the second violin to begin to vibrate as well. This is a beautiful picture of Christ-centered counselors being attuned not only to their client but also to the Spirit of the living God—in unison moving together to accomplish his will.

**Eric Scalise**

### REFERENCES

Hare, W. F. (1934). *Critical History of Modern Aesthetics.* London, England: G. Allen & Unwin.

Lilius, J. M., Worline, M. C., Dutton, J. E., Kanov, J., Frost, P. J., & Maitlis, S. (2003, August). What good is compassion at work? (Paper presented at the meeting of the National Academy of Management Meetings.) Seattle, WA.

Ohrman, K. J. (2002). A passion for compassion. *Advisor Today, 97*(1), 72-75.

Ramsay, N. J. (1998). Compassionate resistance: An ethic for pastoral care and counseling. *The Journal of Pastoral Care, 52*(3), 217-226.

Ruiz, P. O., & Vallejos, R. M. (1999). The role of compassion in moral education. *Journal of Moral Education, 28*(1), 5-17.

Titchener, E. (1909). *Experimental Psychology of the Thought Processes.* New York, NY: Macmillan.

Titcher, E. (1924). *A Textbook of Psychology.* New York, NY: Macmillan.

Young-Mason, J. (2001). Understanding suffering and compassion. *Cross Currents, 51*(3), 347-356.

## GENUINENESS

**Description and Prevalence.** In the 1940s and 1950s, Carl Rogers, founder of client-centered psychotherapy, outlined three essential ingredients of a successful healing therapeutic relationship: unconditional positive regard, genuineness (or congruence), and accurate empathy. Neither empathy nor positive regard can be conveyed in the therapeutic relationship unless the therapist comes across as genuine, so genuineness is essential to the healing counseling relationship. Being genuine—authentic and real—is one of the six core conditions for therapeutic change and growth (Tan, 2011). "It's the relationship that heals, the relationship that heals, the relationship that heals—my professional rosary," says Irv Yalom (1989, p. 91).

**Therapeutic Genuineness.** Client-centered therapists who are genuine practice the art of being themselves without playing a role or being a false self. They are authentic, real, honest, and open when relating to clients in the therapeutic relationship. Being a genuine therapist requires being aware of who you are and what is going on inside you. It means not shutting off your own experience, but being present and open to it in a way that benefits the client. When we are fully human and fully alive, or "fully-functioning" people as Rogers would say, we can be totally genuine.

Genuineness requires therapists to be self-aware and comfortable with being themselves, not adapting or changing roles in order to be acceptable to clients (Norcross, 2002). Therapists may share experiences or engage in appropriate self-disclosure with clients, as well as express both positive and what may be perceived as negative feelings that would be beneficial to clients. For example, if the therapist feels disconnected from how the client is reporting events of the week, the therapist may express that to the client in a genuine statement that helps the client be aware of his or her distance and lack of connection in other relationships. This means that both therapist and client are able to be real and more truly in touch with their real selves (Tan, 2011). This reduces the emotional distance in the relationship and helps the client identify with the therapist. It also encourages collaboration between the therapist and the client.

However, some discernment and self-regulation is necessary. Therapists don't say everything they think in the name of honesty, but only what is appropriate and most therapeutically helpful for clients. Self-disclosure needs to be applicable to clients' experience and is not intended for the therapists' gratification. Some thoughts and feelings should not be shared with clients directly but with supervisors, such as times of sexual attraction, negative feelings, or strong countertransference.

Genuineness has at least four components: supportive nonverbal behaviors, role behavior, consistency, and spontaneity. Rogers also suggested that if techniques were ever used, they should be used in a genuine and spontaneous way, and only when they are appropriate to the particular needs of the client (Tan, 2011).

**Genuineness Criteria.** More than 30 years of clinical research verify the direct correlation of therapeutic effectiveness to the quality of the relationship between the therapist and the client. The conclusion is that a genuine, authentic connection between the client and therapist is crucial for therapeutic success. Lambert and Ogles (1986) state that "at least from the patient's point of view, effective treatment is due to factors associated with relationship variables and the personal qualities of the therapist" (p. 189).

**Spiritual Issues.** God calls us to powerful, life-changing interactions through genuineness in love. Love changes everything. When we are "real," living out our most authentic self that God has created us to be, we become agents of change and transformation (Hart Weber, 2010). God calls us to truth, sincerity, and authenticity in our interactions with one another. Being "real," genuine, and authentic, and developing this kind of relationship with clients, require being self-aware and intentional. Here are some suggestions for reflection and affirmation in being authentically genuine in a therapeutic setting:

- In my professional role, I don't use a facade to be guarded or protect myself.
- I aim to reflect the genuine love of God through me as an authentic person.
- I work in collaboration with my client, viewing us both as experts in the relationship.
- I aim to practice the art of being genuine, real, and authentic as a therapist.
- I am not hiding behind a role or a false front, but focus on the genuine relationship.
- I am nondefensive. I am comfortable with myself, open to hearing and responding to negative feedback and criticism honestly.
- I validate my client's insights, strengths, and self-discovered decisions about change.
- I am able to share genuine facial expressions.
- I am spontaneous and provide freedom, yet I'm not impulsive.
- I am not bound to rules or techniques; instead, I am relationship centered.
- I am consistent in my thoughts, feeling, and behavior. I have few discrepancies, not having different values for each situation I am faced with.
- I show consistency in my value statements and behavior.
- I am capable of deep self-disclosure, able to share genuinely both verbally and nonverbally when appropriate to help the client achieve goals in the counseling process and also to build authenticity in life.
- I don't simply rely on techniques or intellectual interventions to help my clients reach their goals, but focus primarily on the genuine relationship connection.
- I can openly express my feelings, thoughts, and reactions that are present in relationships with my clients.

**Conclusion.** Regardless of the therapeutic model you may follow, the degree to which you are able to be genuine and congruent in relationships with your clients will determine the quality and effectiveness of the healing relationship.

**Catherine Hart Weber**

## REFERENCES


Hart Weber, C. (2010). *Flourish: Discover the Daily Joy of Abundant Vibrant Living.* Minneapolis, MN: Bethany House.

Lambert, M. J., & Ogles, B. M. (1986). The efficacy and effectiveness of psychotherapy. In Garfield & Bergin (Eds.), *Handbook of Psychotherapy and Behavior Change* (3rd ed.), pp. 157-211. New York, NY: Wiley & Sons.

Norcross, J. (2002). *Psychotherapy Relationships That Work.* New York, NY: Oxford University Press.

Tan, S.-Y. (2011). *Counseling and Psychotherapy: A Christian Perspective.* Grand Rapids, MI: Baker Academic.

Yalom, I. (1989). *Love's Executioner and Other Tales of Psychotherapy.* Palo Alto, CA: Stanford Alumni Association.


## RESPECT

Communicating authentic respect is a core skill of the professional counselor. Respect corresponds to "unconditional positive regard," one of Rogers' (1958) three core conditions. It is one of the most basic tenets of the therapeutic relationship (Hill, 2009). Giving respect to the client means having the ability to prize or value the client as a person of worth and dignity (Rogers, 1957). It is a way of giving unconditional acceptance and support to the client regardless of what he or she says or does. In Christian terms, respect and unconditional positive regard might be referred to as an expression from one person to another of God's amazing grace.

**Description.** Respect, within the confines of the counseling relationship, is a mutual liking that takes place between the counselor and the client. Young (2009) says that it resides at the base of the therapeutic relationship. Counselors must respect the autonomy, decisions, values, attitudes, and beliefs of their clients. Respect, when given along with empathy and warmth in the context of counseling, is a powerful force that helps bring healing to the client through a healthy relationship with the therapist.

**Purpose.** The purpose of giving respect to clients is to create an alliance in order to bring a resolution to the issues that brought them to counseling (Hill, 2009). Safety and trust are therefore foundational to develop mutual respect in the counseling relationship.

**Core Components.** Four core components have been identified regarding respect and positive regard (Cormier, Nurius, & Osborn, 2009). The first component is commitment. Commitment is the counselor's willingness to make the client feel safe and to communicate the importance of the relationship. Cultivating a general concern for the client, practicing confidentiality and privacy, and reserving time are building blocks to help ensure commitment to the therapeutic relationship.

The second core component is understanding. Clients intuitively sense whether counselors are attempting to understand them and treat their problems with care or simply trying to get them out of the office. Understanding clients' struggles and helping them feel understood is a vital part of the counseling process.

The third core component is having a nonjudgmental attitude. This is the counselor's capacity to suspend judgment in order to avoid condemning or condoning a client's words, thoughts, feelings, and actions. Displaying a nonjudgmental attitude can be most difficult for the counselor because it involves overcoming personal and cultural biases. Implementing a nonjudgmental attitude reduces a client's feelings of perceived worthlessness while improving the counselor-client relationship.

The last core component of respect and positive regard is an expression of warmth. A counselor exuding warmth has the capacity to reduce the impersonal nature of the counseling relationship. It can be imparted through verbal and nonverbal means by tone of voice, eye contact, facial expressions, and touch. Warmth can also help dismiss feelings of anger and hostility in the client (Young, 2009).

**Conclusion.** Respect is nonnegotiable in counseling and therapeutic relationships. It is also what Jesus treated everyone with, regardless of race, creed, or religious affiliation. Mutual respect is what we as Christians are called to give (see Eph. 5:21). The presence of respect can add incredible value to the relationship, but its absence can tear it down. Combining the four core components of respect is especially helpful in building successful and lasting bonds with counselees. Respect is truly one of the greatest tools in a counselor's arsenal.

**Ryan A. Carboneau**

## REFERENCES

Cormier, S., Nurius, P. S., & Osborn, C. J. (2009). *Interviewing and Change Strategies for Helpers: Fundamental Skills and Cognitive-Behavioral Interventions* (6th ed.). Belmont, CA: Brooks/Cole.

Hill, C. E. (2009). *Helping Skills: Facilitating Exploration, Insight, and Action* (3rd ed.). Washington, DC: American Psychological Association.

Rogers, C. (1957). The necessary and sufficient conditions of therapeutic personality change. *Journal of Consulting Psychology, 21,* 95-103.

Rogers, C. (1958). Characteristics of a helping relationship. *The Personnel and Guidance Journal, 37*(1), 6-10.

Young, M. E. (2009). *Learning the Art of Helping: Building Blocks and Techniques* (4th ed.). Upper Saddle River, NJ: Merrill.

INTERMEDIATE SKILLS

## NONVERBAL COMMUNICATION

Research has found that up to 90% of communication is based on nonverbal cues. Wright (2000) said that communication is "the link that creates a relationship between people" (p. 61). Counselors are trained to discern nonverbal communication in clients. There is more than what the counselee is saying, and this information often lies beneath the surface and remains undetected (Clinton & Ohlschlager, 2002). Counselors must learn to distinguish between what clients say and how they act (Cormier & Cormier, 1991). Bringing those two worlds together and attempting to read between the lines will help bring congruence to clients' lives and help them see the discontinuity between their words and actions.

**Description.** Nonverbal communication may include a number of different gestures or movements by the client. These are also known as *mixed messages.* Kinesics is the study of the nonverbal cues expressed by the client's body language (Clinton & Ohlschlager, 2002), including a wide range of behaviors, such as eye movements, fidgeting, tone of voice, or sitting with arms folded and legs crossed. Every day, counselors interpret hundreds of nonverbal communications in personal and professional relationships. To help clients change, counselors make mental notes of behaviors and decipher what they mean.

**Understanding Nonverbal Communication.** "It is mutual understanding that leads to good communication" (Eggerichs, 2007). Due to the nature of therapeutic relationships, clients often lie in order to protect themselves from perceived or potential harm. Fortunately for the counselor, however, nonverbal cues speak volumes of truth. The eyes are the windows to the soul. They give us a glimpse into the internal world of our clients. Clients may look away, stare blankly, look up and down, be unfocused, or look intensely at something, and their eyes often express unspoken feelings and perceptions. The head and face also communicate clearly with a move of the eyebrow, a grimace of the lips, a smile, or a look away to let the counselor know what is being internalized. Body is also important. People can turn away, appear relaxed or tense, fidget or tap their foot, or any number of other actions. When counselors study the meaning of these nonverbal cues, they get a clearer picture of their clients' hearts and minds.

**Conclusion.** God gives many counselors the gift of discernment to reveal hidden issues that clients attempt to conceal from God and others. Congruence is one of Rogers' three necessary conditions, and it is one of the most important tasks of the counselor (Rogers, 1957; Cormier & Cormier, 1991). By accurately reading and interpreting nonverbal communication, we take steps to bring together the spoken and unspoken truths in a client's life to facilitate real growth.

**Ryan A. Carboneau**

REFERENCES

Clinton, T., & Ohlschlager, G. (2002). *Competent Christian Counseling: Foundations and Practice of Compassionate Soul Care* (Vol. 1). New York, NY: WaterBrook.

Cormier, W. H., & Cormier, L. S. (1991). *Interviewing Strategies for Helpers: Fundamental Skills and Cognitive-Behavioral Interventions* (3rd ed.). Pacific Grove, CA: Brooks/Cole.

Eggerichs, E. (2007). *Cracking the Communication Code: The Secret to Speaking Your Mate's Language.* Nashville, TN: Nelson.

Rogers, C. (1957). The necessary and sufficient conditions of therapeutic personality change. *Journal of Consulting Psychology, 21,* 95-103.

Wright, H. N. (2000). *Communication: Key to Your Marriage.* Ventura, CA: Regal Books.

## ATTENDING SKILLS

Of the numerous character traits and skills professional counselors must practice in order to become more effective in their work, one of the most important is *attending*. It is foundational in building trust in the therapeutic relationship (Hill, 2009). Attending to clients means physically orienting oneself toward them and giving them full and complete attention without giving way to distractions (Hill; Cormier, Nurius, & Osborn, 2009).

**Description.** An elementary term for attending is simply *paying attention*. Counselors use all available resources, including time, space, and their bodies to indicate that their full concentration is focused on the client (Egan, 2010; Cormier et al., 2009). The skills involved include nonverbal listening as well as physical, emotional, and psychological attending (Hill, 2009).

**Purpose.** Attending skills can greatly increase the amount of trust and respect in the therapeutic relationship. It also helps build rapport and convey warmth, empathy, and concern for clients' overall well-being (Clinton & Ohlschlager, 2002). A therapist's awareness of the physical, emotional, and psychological aspects of a client's life helps to equalize the balance of power in the counseling relationship.

**Core Components.** Egan (2010) identified five core components to help professional therapists attend to clients. The acronym SOLER can help counselors focus on their clients in an intentional way.

*Squarely facing the client.* When the therapist faces the client directly in a face-to-face manner, it makes the client the center of attention.

*Open posture.* The posture of the therapist should stay open and appear receptive to what the client has to say. The counselor must be careful to remain neutral because certain gestures or postures may indicate an attitude of being detached or disconnected from the counseling relationship.

*Leaning forward.* When the counselor leans forward, he sends the client the message that he is interested in what the client is saying and feeling. Leaning in to the client can create a sense of closeness and intimacy, which can raise the level of trust and commitment in the relationship.

*Eye contact.* The amount, degree, and intensity of eye contact can add a great deal to the closeness of the therapeutic relationship. Maintaining steady eye contact indicates interest in what is being said. Be aware, however, that too much or too little eye contact for people of other cultures may send them the wrong message.

*Relax.* Preserving a relaxed posture and attitude is essential to effectively attending to clients. Relaxing is the key that brings all the other four elements together.

**Conclusion.** Beginning and seasoned counselors alike must master the art of attending skills if they hope to be successful in their practice. As with all skills, we can continue to learn and grow more proficient in this area of counseling. To meet your clients' needs and build trust, be aware of the physical, emotional, and psychological needs that arise while attending to them.

**Ryan A. Carboneau**

### REFERENCES

Clinton, T., & Ohlschlager, G. (2002). *Competent Christian Counseling: Foundations and Practice of Compassionate Soul Care* (Vol. 1). New York, NY: WaterBrook.

Cormier, S., Nurius, P. S., & Osborn, C. J. (2009). *Interviewing and Change Strategies for Helpers: Fundamental Skills and Cognitive-Behavioral Interventions* (6th ed.). Belmont, CA: Brooks/Cole.

Egan, G. (2010). *The Skilled Helper: A Problem Management Approach to Helping* (9th ed.). Pacific Grove, CA: Brooks/Cole.

Hill, C. E. (2009). *Helping Skills: Facilitating Exploration, Insight, and Action* (3rd ed.). Washington, DC: American Psychological Association.

## REFLECTING SKILLS

Research shows reflective listening is quite effective in the therapeutic process.

When this technique is employed, people not only feel more comfortable in revealing their feelings but also report having a better relationships with their therapists (Rautalinko, Lisper, & Ekehammar, 2007).

**Description.** Reflective listening is a therapeutic skill in which counselors closely listen to what is being said and reflect back the content as well as the underlying feelings clients are communicating. With this method, therapists can clarify what thoughts and emotions are being expressed and show a willingness to understand how clients view their circumstances.

**History.** The beginnings of reflective listening originated with Carl Rogers' client-centered therapy (Rogers, 1951). Rogers and others stressed the importance of empathy and acceptance. An empathic counselor strives to understand what clients are feeling about themselves and the situations they are discussing. Acceptance means respecting people without judging who they are, what they say, or how they feel. Rogers believed that when therapists respond with empathy and acceptance, clients will be more open to disclosing their feelings and eventually get to the root of their problems.

**Application.** When employing this method, counselors must resist the tendency to offer solutions, challenge opinions, or direct their clients to see their situations differently. It's important to be attentive not only to the feelings but also the level of intensity being expressed both verbally and nonverbally. A great deal of information regarding clients' emotions can be picked up through facial expressions, eye contact (or lack of eye contact), tone of voice, and body language. Responding with a simple sentence that acknowledges clients' feelings and concerns reassures them they have been heard and are free to continue (Summers, 2009).

A client may say, "It seems as if every week at work someone gets the ax. I wonder if I'll be next." In this example the primary feelings appear to be worry and fear. An empathic response restating what was said could be, "It sounds like you're worried about keeping your job." Another statement that focuses on the emotions and content might be, "It must be frightening to see your coworkers lose their jobs."

Although counselors can ask simple questions, they should avoid giving advice or detailed explanations. To say, "Well, I'm sure you have nothing to worry about," would discount the client's concern and leave him wondering if the counselor really understands or cares. This type of response also tends to shut the door to further exploration of the client's feelings.

Reflective listening is only one tool counselors can use. For instance, if clients are dangerous to themselves or others, a more direct approach might be necessary. Nonetheless, "clients who are supported through this process by skilled listeners heal better than clients who have been forced to shut down their feelings in front of the worker and deal with them alone" (Summers, 2009, p. 158).

**Biblical and Spiritual Issues.** In Romans 15:7 we are encouraged to "accept one another, then, just as Christ accepted you, in order to bring praise to God." Communicating unconditional acceptance, just as Jesus does, is far from easy. Counselors who genuinely display this attitude of acceptance without judgment or immediately giving advice are able to build rapport with their clients and facilitate the healing process.

Georgia Shaffer

## REFERENCES

Rautalinko, E., Lisper, H., & Ekehammar, B. (2007). Reflective listening in counseling: Effects of training time and evaluator social skills. *American Journal of Psychotherapy, 61*(2), 191-209.

Rogers, C. (1951). *Client-Centered Therapy: Its Current*

*Practice, Implications, and Theory.* Boston, MA: Houghton Mifflin.

Summers, N. (2009). *Fundamentals of Case Management Practice: Skills for the Human Services.* Belmont, CA: Brooks/Cole.

## MODELING

**Description.** *Modeling* is a treatment procedure in which the counselor demonstrates behaviors and the client observes and rehearses them in order to gain skill in using them. The technique is used in behaviorally oriented psychotherapies, but it can be used in any therapy modality. There are two kinds of modeling: overt and covert.

*Overt modeling* is a live model or media demonstration of structured behaviors. The live modeling is typically done by a therapist but can include anyone who is a good demonstrator. Media demonstrations are called *symbolic* models. This includes film demonstrations, comic strips, puppets, and pictorial media. Models are most effective when they are culturally meaningful and the client values and respects them. Models similar to the client are most effective in helping him learn the skill and develop the confidence to use it. In overt modeling, a live or symbolic model demonstrates a behavior that is then reinforced (Bellack & Hersen, 1985).

*Covert modeling* is the client's use of imaginary models or reduction of physical sensations related to a stressor. The client imagines the demonstrated response to a stressful situation.

**Purposes, Procedures, and Therapeutic Uses of Modeling.** A variety of modeling strategies exist. All consist of a skill demonstration and a participant observing and practicing the skill. The therapist's goal is to integrate a new way of coping into the client's repertoire and to extinguishing the old coping pattern. Covert modeling is helpful for children learning self-control skills. A rationale for the procedure is made to the client. Stressful scenes and proactive responses are first discussed, and these are later imagined and rehearsed by the client. Before the trials begin, a counselor will model the proper skill response. Self-instructional training is a covert modeling procedure developed by Meichenbaum (1977) to teach children how to coach themselves to avoid impulsiveness. The counselor verbally states a script of self-instruction in increasingly lower tones of voice. The child rehearses this to a point where he is whispering the script and then internalizing it by means of self-talk. The client is instructed to rehearse this skill 20 to 30 times a day in a relaxed setting.

Several considerations of the participant's ability to use modeling procedures include attention skills, retention ability, rehearsal competency and motor ability, and motivation (self-evaluation and social reinforcement) (Bandura, 1969). The counselor should consider adjustments to the procedure based on the evaluation of these considerations. The modeling paradigm includes these brief therapy procedures:

*Graduated modeling.* Progressively difficult skills are presented.

*Guided modeling.* Gradual verbal prompting is used.

*Induction.* The client is motivated to do something he naturally wants to resist. Inducing the client is difficult to do by just saying, "Let's try this skill that helps people with your kind of stress." An induction might have the client observe people in a setting he wants to join. Or to help him learn to be assertive, the counselor might lead a discussion about what acting assertive might be like for a nonassertive person. Perhaps having him interview an assertive person he knows about being assertive could increase induction. Utilizing motivational interviewing questions can help assess client readiness to learn a new skill—even if he is simply considering it. Helping clients develop a belief system or a positive attitude toward a new skill may encourage them to take the risk of learning the new skill (Kanfer, 1996).

*Education.* The rationale for the procedures must be taught. This also involves learning what triggers the client's negative reactions. He can monitor for these triggers and the personal reactions of the stressors. Generalizable principles of behavior change are explained. Goals are discussed and structured in gradual and achievable steps. Behaviors are explained and modeled.

The client observes and rehearses direct coping responses (e.g., deep breathing), escape plans, and coping self-statements. Rehearsal is guided by continued coaching, instruction, encouragement, and feedback on the effort.

*Application.* The skills are practiced in therapy sessions with increasingly stressful levels. This includes home assignments for daily practice. As assistance from the therapist is not needed, the client is asked to test this in real-life scenarios.

*Evaluation.* The skill and its effectiveness in reducing stress are discussed. What did the client learn to do differently? What was difficult? What was easy? Was this skill as helpful as another skill?

*Identification of obstacles.* In each step, attention is given to environmental or cognitive performance obstacles. Being able to identify these in the session will give the client confidence, added induction, and motivation to keep practicing. Predicting problems gives the client the opportunity to discuss, observe, and rehearse a wider range of skills to meet any potential problems.

*Relapse prevention.* What factors might cause clients to revert to old behaviors? What do they need to do to maintain their gains?

**Uses of Modeling.** Modeling is used primarily to reduce anxiety, anger, or impulsive reactions. It is used with stress reduction, social-skill training, communication training in marriages, problem-solving training, and assertiveness training (Cormier & Cormier, 2008). It has also been used with obsessional disorders (Salkovskis & Kirk, 1993) and teaching schizophrenics to engage in healthy self-talk (Meichenbaum, 1977).

**Spiritual Considerations.** As Christians, we are exhorted to be imitators of Christ. Part of Jesus' discipleship of the Twelve was showing them how to live. For more than three years, they watched him heal the sick, confront legalistic leaders, teach truth, and model a life of grace and truth. He was the Christ, and those who paid attention saw a person quite different from the rigid, judgmental leaders of the religious sects. In part, the Word of God is the recorded "modeling" of how to live for God, as demonstrated by his Son, Jesus, and later by his apostles. In counseling, it is important to remember the actual work of changing a life is done by the third person in the room—the Spirit of God. Our role is to help our clients understand and apply the example of Christ to the problems they face. Christian imagery of visualizing the behavior of Jesus gives insight beyond their faculties and experiences.

Clients can fellowship with mature believers who can help them with areas of marriage, parenting, business, being a friend, or dealing with a stressful event. Mature believers can aid those who suffer or need direction. Many examples come from the Old Testament. We read the lives of imperfect men and women who model what to do and what not to do. Powerful biblical models empower us and exhort us to be Christlike, to face our problems, and to make good and godly choices. Their example confronts our ambivalence to change (our focus on what we want versus what God commands), and they give us hope that we can change (Adams, 1982).

**Conclusion.** Modeling is not simply the observation and imitation of a skill; it is the competent use of the skill. Modeling is more than simply showing how to do a skill; it is inducing reluctant clients to do something uncomfortable, integrating this skill into their lives, increasing their self-efficacy, and helping them apply the skill to life. Lastly, it is reminding clients that the ultimate modeling agent exists in their hearts, in their Bible, and in the lives of many wise and loving fellow believers.

MARK SHADOAN

## REFERENCES


Adams, J. E. (1982). *The Christian Counselor's Manual.* Phillipsburg, NJ: Presbyterian and Reformed.

Bandura, A. (1969). *Principles of Behavior Modification.* New York, NY: Holt, Rhinehart and Winston.

Bellack, A., & Hersen, M. (Eds.). (1985). *The Dictionary of Behavior Therapy Techniques.* Elmsford, NY: Pergamon Press.

Cormier, S., & Cormier, B. (2008). *Interviewing Skills for Helpers: Fundamentals of Cognitive Behavior Interventions.* Pacific Grove, CA: Brooks/Cole.

Kanfer, F. (1996). Motivation and emotion in behavior therapy. In K. S. Dobson & K. C. Craig (Eds.), *Advances in Cognitive Behavioral Therapy.* Thousand Oaks, CA: Sage Publications.

Meichenbaum, D. (1977). *Cognitive Behavioral Modification: An Integrated Approach.* New York, NY: Plenum.

Salkovskis, P., & Kirk, J. (1993). Obsessional disorders. In K. Hawthorne, P. M. Salkovskis, J. Kirk, & D. Clark (Eds.), *Cognitive Behaviour Therapy for Psychiatric Problems.* Oxford, England: Oxford University Press.


## OPEN-ENDED QUESTIONS

**DESCRIPTION.** Whether you are a practicum student or a seasoned professional, one of the most important tools in your toolkit is the ability to ask good questions—to know what kind of questions to ask and when to ask them (Berman & Shopland, 2009). There are two primary kinds of questions: closed and open-ended. Both can be valuable, but one of them will yield a lot more information than the other.

**CLOSED QUESTIONS.** Closed questions are the easiest ones to ask, and they can usually be answered with one word or a short phrase—often with a simple yes or no. "How old are you?" and "Where do you work?" are examples of closed questions. They are a valuable source of facts and give you more specific and sometimes essential information. They also involve less engagement with the client, are usually easier for the client to answer, take less thought, and involve less risk. With closed questions, clients don't have to reveal as much about themselves. Closed questions tend to produce less information, but they can be valuable when you need more specific information (Berman & Shopland, 2009; Eagan, 2007). They can also help you bring focus to a talkative client who is just rambling and sharing information that isn't relevant to the session.

These are also examples of closed questions: "Are you happy?" "Do you like your boss?" "What is your favorite song?" Because of their simplicity and specificity, closed questions may not give clients the options they may need in order to communicate the complexity of their feelings or their reasons for seeking help, and therefore, we see the need for open-ended questions.

**OPEN-ENDED QUESTIONS.** Open-ended questions can't be answered with a single word or a short phrase. "How did that make you feel?" and "Tell me about your relationship with your parents" are classic examples of open-ended questions. Sometimes a closed question can cause a person to feel as if he is being interrogated, whereas an open-ended question can help him feel more comfortable. Open-ended questions are less leading than closed questions (Nelson-Jones, 2005) and can be especially helpful in the information-gathering stage of counseling (Borck & Fawcett, 1982) because they help build rapport and provide more information (Eagan, 2007). They encourage clients to share their feelings, opinions, and experiences, and they suggest that what they bring to the session may be an important part of the change and growth process.

Open-ended questions are great discussion starters because they don't necessarily have a correct answer. They are more likely to lead the client to open up and share the feelings and emotions essential to relationships and human behavior (Teyber & McClure, 2006). They also can provide insight into how clients think, how they process information, how well they organize their thoughts, and other things that could be essential if they are to be helped. They are a great way to get a better sense of what is important to them and allow them to tell their story in their own words.

In addition, open-ended questions empower clients to generate their own solutions and take ownership for their choices. These are some additional examples of open-ended questions: "What do you think about your boss?" "What are some of the things that make you angry?" "What led you to come in for counseling?" "How are you hoping I might be helpful?"

**Gary J. Oliver**

## REFERENCES


Berman, P. S., & Shopland, S. N. (2009). *Interviewing and Diagnostic Exercises for Clinical and Counseling Skills Building.* Mahwah, NJ: Erlbaum.

Borck, L. E., & Fawcett, S. B. (1982). *Learning Counseling and Problem-Solving Skill.* New York, NY: Haworth Press.

Eagan, G. (2007). *The Skilled Helper: A Problem-Management and Opportunity-Development Approach to Helping* (9th ed.). Belmont, CA: Brooks/Cole.

Nelson-Jones, R. (2005). *Introduction to Counseling Skills: Texts and Activities* (2nd ed.). Thousand Oaks, CA: Sage Publications.

Teyber, E., & McClure, F. H. (2006). *Interpersonal Process in Therapy: An Integrative Model* (6th ed.). Belmont, CA: Brooks/Cole.


## VISUALIZATION

*Visualization* is defined by Webster as "to recall or form mental images or pictures, or to make perceptible to the mind or imagination." As a therapeutic technique, visualization fosters healing and aids in changing distorted and deceptive perceptions. The process of visualizing a traumatic event, combined with eye movement desensitization and reprocessing (EMDR), enables survivors to release fear and anxiety associated with the event. Spiritual truths that are visualized can bring healing and comfort that words alone cannot. For example, visualizing the Lord's presence as described in Hebrews 13:5-6 can eliminate overwhelming feelings of aloneness and abandonment: "He [God] Himself, has said, '...I will not leave you without support...leave you helpless, nor forsake, nor let you down, (relax my hold on you)! Assuredly not!'" (AMP).

Current research and brain scans help us understand the power and value of visualization in contrast to talk therapy or cognitive-behavioral therapy. Visual pictures are processed by the right frontal lobe of the brain, which is where traumatic memories are stored. Visualization has been utilized by coaches for years. According to the bio-informational theory, visualizing used to enhance performance activates the same brain regions as if it were the actual situation (Lang, 1979; Murphy, Nordin, & Cumming, 2008). Neuroimaging studies show that similar processes occur in the brain with imagery and that they are equivalent to interpreting real situations (O'Craven & Kanwisher, 2000). Visualization affects the encoding and retrieval of memory, influencing recall and concreteness (Arbuthnott, Arbuthnott, & Rossiter, 2001). It also activates the fear network, allowing individuals to incorporate corrective information to enhance coping (Rothbaum & Mellman, 2001).

**Treatment.** Visualization may be the safest method of evaluating the truth of traumatic memories (McDonald, 1995). Clients retain full consciousness and control at all times (unlike drugs or hypnosis), creating less opportunity for suggestibility from leading questions from the therapist. Guided visualization can create false memories, especially for young children and suggestible clients (McDonald; Loftus, Doyle, & Dysert, 2008; Bruck, Ceci, Kulkofsky, Klemfuss, & Sweeney, 2010). It is important for counselors to encourage clients to later sort out facts from fears and fantasies. Visualizations may be accurate, but they may also be partially false, based on the client's perceptions at the time rather than the reality of the situation. Visualizations can also reveal fears or fantasies, similar to dreams, and therefore are not strong enough evidence to convict the accused.

**Spiritual Issues.** When using visualization, clients and counselors should pray for truth and wisdom, seek God's answers, and follow the Lord's healing direction. No one follows God perfectly, so it is important to understand that clients and counselors have their own thoughts and pictures in combination with God's wisdom. When ideas are from God, they will never go against biblical truth because God does not contradict himself. Prayer is not a one-time event and needs to continue throughout the counseling process. Avoid praying for clients' truth and then informing them about your insights, as if God had spoken through you. In some cases, the information may be false, but it can nonetheless traumatize the client if the client visualizes it as if it were true. In other cases, the information may be accurate but traumatic because the client is incapable of coping with it at that time.

**Conclusion.** Visualization is a powerful tool to release people from the anxiety of trauma. It gives peace about truth and creates hope and direction for the next step of recovery (Ps. 40:1,3; Is. 40:31). People who picture God as strong, trusting, rescuing, and loving will shorten their healing period. The road to recovery is unique for each person.

**Arlys McDonald**
**Paula Johnston**

## REFERENCES


Arbuthnott, K. D., Arbuthnott, D. W., & Rossiter, L. (2001). Guided imagery and memory: Implications for psychotherapists. *Journal of Counseling Psychology, 48*(2), 123-132.

Bruck, M., Ceci, S., Kulkofsky, S., Klemfuss, Z., & Sweeney, C. (2008). Children's testimony. In M. Rutter, D. Bishop, D. Pine, S. Scott, J. Stevenson, E. Taylor, & A. Thapar (Eds.), *Rutter's Child and Adolescent Psychiatry* (5th ed., pp. 81-94). Hoboken, NJ: Wiley-Blackwell.

Lang, P. J. (1979). A bio-informational theory of emotional imagery. *Psychophysiology, 16*, 495-512.

Loftus, E., Doyle, J. M., & Dysert, J. (2008). *Eyewitness Testimony: Civil and Criminal 2008 Cumulative Supplement.* Charlottesville, VA: Law Publishing.

McDonald, A. N. (1995). *Repressed Memories: Can You Trust Them?* Grand Rapids, MI: Revell.

Murphy, S., Nordin, S. M., & Cumming, J. (2008). Imagery in sport, exercise and dance. In T. Horn (Ed.), *Advances in Sport and Exercise Psychology* (3rd ed., pp. 297-324). Champagne, IL: Human Kinetics.

O'Craven, K. M., & Kanwisher, N. N. (2000). Mental imagery of faces and places activates corresponding stimulus-specific brain regions. *Journal of Cognitive Neuroscience, 12*(6), 1023.

Rothbaum, B., & Mellman, T. (2001). Dreams and exposure therapy in PTSD. *Journal of Traumatic Stress, 14*(3), 481.


## ROLE PLAYING

**Description.** Shakespeare says, "All the world's a stage, and all the men and women merely players; they have their exits and their entrances, and one man in his time plays many parts, his acts being seven ages" (*As You Like It,* Act 2, scene 7, 139-143). Whether the bard got it right all the time remains to be seen, but in this case his observation is a valid one. Each of us plays various roles in different stages of life. Sometimes we are someone's child, sometimes a spouse, sometimes a parent, an employer or employee, or a friend.

Counselors push that reality a bit further. We've observed that having our clients act out a certain role provides a different perspective for both the client and us than if we just talk about a role. These *action methods* (Weiner & Pels-Roulier, 2005) are traditionally expressed through a number of therapist-initiated tasks in such psychotherapies as psychodrama, play therapy, and drama therapy in individual therapy. Often viewed as supplemental in marriage and family therapy, role play is actually helpful in dramatizing familial role relationships, projecting what changes in family relationships might look like, and offering a safe way to explore and practice new behavior patterns (Weiner & Pels-Roulier).

**Role Play with Couples and Families.** Counseling with couples is generally considered to be more complicated than counseling individuals because of the ever-shifting dynamics within the session. Ideally, marriage therapy would be done with people who are motivated to see their relationship improve. Sometimes both clients cannot or will not participate in counseling. As a result, therapists sometimes find themselves doing marriage counseling with only one person in the room. In such situations, role playing can be particularly effective because the therapist may actively play the role of either the absent or present partner in the counseling session (Sharf, 2004). Often, this technique is used to help clients build the skills that will help them interact with others in a successful way by increasing insight, desensitizing, and improving coping strategies (Mullen, 1996). However, there are certain criticisms of the therapist taking this role in the therapeutic process that center around therapeutic boundaries, complications with transference, creating dependency, and the chance that the client may see the counselor as taking a side (Leveton, 2005).

The empty chair in Gestalt theory is a technique that can be adapted to marriage and family therapy (Nichols & Schwartz, 2001). It can be used in both interpersonal and intrapersonal work. In this technique, absent partners can be addressed and thoughts and feelings expressed. Multiple family roles can be played by the client, allowing the client to experience the complexities of the relationship more fully. Rather than simply talking about the conflict, these action methods may intensify feelings and enable the client to experience emotions more fully, helping him get in touch with a long-repressed feeling or gain an insight that would normally be denied (Jacobs, Masson, & Harvill, 2009). The empty chair technique can also be used for intrapersonal work as the client is given the opportunity to address various intrapsychic elements.

**Conclusion.** Role playing, when skillfully applied, can help promote rapid change in clients who would not normally respond to only verbal counseling. In the current climate of the mental-health field, where shorter treatment times are preferred, the employment of action methods may become more widely accepted (Weiner & Pels-Roulier, 2005).

Matthew E. Appleby
David W. Appleby

## REFERENCES

Jacobs, E. E., Masson, R. L., & Harvill, R. L. (2009). *Group Counseling: Skills and Strategies* (6th ed.). Belmont, CA: Thompson.

Leveton, E. (2005). Escaping the blame frame: Experiential techniques with couples. *Journal of Group Psychotherapy, Psychodrama, & Sociometry, 58*(2), 55-69.

Mullen. P. E. (1996). The clinical management of jealousy. In J. Lonsdale, S. Powell, & L. Soloman (Eds.), *The Hatherleigh Guide to Marriage and Family Therapy* (pp.241-266). New York, NY: Hatherleigh.

Nichols, M. P., & Schwartz, R. C. (2001). *The Essentials of Family Therapy.* Boston, MA: Pearson.

Sharf, R. S. (2004). *Theories of Psychotherapy and Counseling: Concepts and Cases* (3rd ed.). Pacific Grove, CA: Thompson.

Weiner, D, & Pels-Roulier, L. (2005). Action methods in marriage and family therapy: A review. *Journal of Group Psychotherapy, Psychodrama, & Sociometry, 58*(2), 86-101.

## ADVANCED SKILLS

### IMMEDIACY

Immediacy is a crucial and foundational skill of the professional therapist. Those who are beginning the practice of counseling often find immediacy difficult to master because it is one of the more complex skills. Carkhuff and Pierce (1977) place this skill at the highest level of helping because it focuses on "the here and now" in the counseling relationship. Immediacy is also described as the ability to be "emotionally present." Crabb (2009) has used the words "relational holiness" to describe authentic and emotionally present relationships. Immediacy can also refer to biblical concepts, such as "speaking the truth in love," which brings honesty and altruism together in a conversation (Eph. 4:15).

**Description.** Most people do not practice immediacy in their relationships with family, friends, or career. When they experience relational tension or conflict, many individuals try to avoid making waves by swallowing their feelings and becoming increasingly distant over time. In contrast, immediacy involves being emotionally open with clients, and it incorporates some self-disclosure. It may also encompass exposing a hunch about a perceived discrepancy between what the client feels and says. Appropriate self-disclosure makes a connection, communicates understanding, and helps clients disclose their own feelings (Clinton & Ohlschlager, 2002).

**Purpose.** Immediacy in the therapeutic environment enables the counselor to access some of the hidden undercurrent of what the client is really trying to say. It is rare when individuals—especially those in the early stages of counseling—are truly in tune with their emotions and have the ability to self-assess their internal world. As counselors provide immediate feedback throughout the session, their self-disclosures will be much more challenging and powerful for their clients. Immediacy helps clients understand the feelings buried underneath the dialogue.

**Types of Immediacy.** There are three types of immediacy in counseling: counselor, client, and relationship (Cormier, Nurius, & Osborn, 2009). *Counselor immediacy* occurs when counselors are able to interject their thoughts and feelings throughout the counseling process as they occur "in the moment." *Client immediacy* happens when the counselor provides feedback to the counselee about a behavior or feeling as it develops. In *relationship immediacy*, the counselor discloses thoughts or feelings about how he experiences the therapeutic relationship.

**Conclusion.** The use of immediacy is vital to the counselor because it helps to heal the emotional world of the client, which is one of the main goals of therapy. Counselors who tend to ignore the skill of immediacy may contribute to a somewhat stagnant counseling relationship and environment. Immediacy involves a delicate boldness on the counselor's part to gently extract the concealed meaning of what the client is saying. Immediacy helps the counselor discover what lies beneath the surface and exposes the root of the problem in the client's life.

**Ryan A. Carboneau**

### REFERENCES

Carkhuff, R. R., & Pierce, R. (1977). *The Art of Helping III: Trainer's Guide*. Amherst, MA: Human Resource Development Press.

Clinton, T., & Ohlschlager, G. (2002). *Competent Christian Counseling: Foundations and Practice of Compassionate Soul Care* (Vol. 1). New York, NY: WaterBrook.

Cormier, S., Nurius, P. S., & Osborn, C. J. (2009). *Interviewing and Change Strategies for Helpers: Fundamental Skills and Cognitive-Behavioral Interventions* (6th ed.). Belmont, CA: Brooks/Cole.

Crabb, L. J. (2009). *Real Church: Does It Exist? Can I Find It?* Nashville, TN: Thomas Nelson.

## SELF-DISCLOSURE

**Description.** Self-disclosure is the communication of personal revelations or information about the self to another. It is the basis upon which relationships develop mutuality and intimacy. All counseling is built around relationships. Self-disclosure is, therefore, essential to the counseling process because "it is the most direct means by which an individual makes him- or herself known to another" (Sue & Sue, 2008,

p. 83). Self-disclosure by the client is a core value and expectation in any type of therapy. However, counselor self-disclosure, when the counselor shares personal information about the self with the client, is a complex skill requiring intentionality as well as genuineness.

Counselor self-disclosure has been differentiated between *self-disclosing statements*, which focus on counselor cognitions and emotions related to the immediate therapeutic endeavor, and *self-involving statements*, in which the counselor discloses personal factual information (Cashwell, Shcherbakova, & Cashwell, 2003).

**History and Rationale.** Counselor self-disclosure has historically been a controversial issue tied to concerns about transference and countertransference. At one time it was considered to be detrimental to clients in all cases and unethical for counselors to bring themselves into the therapeutic frame in any way. This was driven largely by psychoanalytic modalities in which the therapist facilitated essential transference by remaining aloof in order to provide the necessary "blank slate" upon which clients could project their image of past significant individuals (Kottler & Shepard, 2011, p. 90). With the advent of Rogers' focus on genuineness and mutuality in the counseling relationship, counselor self-disclosure became more widely practiced as a form of immediacy designed to enhance the relationship (i.e., *self-disclosing statements*). In the latter part of the 20th century, the consumer-rights movement began to dictate certain aspects of therapist self-disclosure through informed consent requirements (i.e., *self-involving statements*). It is now unethical not to disclose a certain level of therapist information minimally including qualifications, credentials, and relevant experience. (For more information, see American Counseling Association [2005] and American Association of Christian Counselors [2004].)

**Application.** Both types of self-disclosure by the counselor have now become accepted parts of the minimal skill set required for effective therapy (Ivey, Ivey, & Zalaquett, 2010, p. 331). Research has consistently shown that self-disclosure generally enhances counselor attractiveness, which facilitates client trust and openness (Cashwell et al., 2003). However, it is a skill that requires intentionality and significant care in its use.

The guiding principle for appropriate self-disclosure is that it should always be for the client's benefit. Careful reflection on one's motives for the disclosure, the potential effect on the client and the therapeutic relationship, the genuineness of the data, and the timing of the disclosure is essential. Self-disclosure does not burden the client with the counselor's material but facilitates the client's exploration and trust, and it models openness.

Formal self-disclosure as part of informed-consent procedures is now mandated ethically and legally, but spontaneous forms of therapeutic self-disclosure are largely driven by theoretical orientation, client need, and counselor personality. Some theoretical modalities would not advocate for or be enhanced by the use of the counselor's self-disclosure (e.g., psychodynamic), whereas others would essentially require some form of self-disclosure (e.g., immediacy reflections).

The timing, content, and comprehensiveness of self-disclosing or self-involving statements require careful attention. Recognizing when a self-disclosure may assist a client is a skill that develops with experience and practice. Learning how to keep self-referencing content appropriate, brief, and client-focused is part of the art of therapy. This involves learning to use one's self appropriately in many varied counselor-client relationships. Too much time spent on a self-disclosure may take away from its effectiveness by reducing the focus on the client. The goal is to provide just enough information to enhance the client's understanding or facilitate client disclosure. Recognizing client need and structuring the self-disclosure to meet that need is a complex task but one that can be used productively and powerfully.

**Related Issues.** Cultural and social variables must also be carefully considered in any self-disclosure. Research generally shows positive results for increased counselor disclosure when working with culturally diverse clients (Cashwell et. al., 2003). With some culturally diverse clients, the use of direct, active interventions are more likely to be beneficial because they provide more personal information (self-disclosure) about the therapist. Likewise, self-disclosure may need to be modeled for a culturally diverse client in order to facilitate the necessary trust and experience (Sue & Sue, 2008).

Appropriate use of self-disclosure in counseling requires self-awareness and integrity. Honestly assessing motivation and creating authentic boundaries around interactions are parts of developing therapeutic skill. Therapy is an intimate endeavor, yet one with explicit boundaries that need to be carefully maintained and facilitated. How and what we share of ourselves is critical to the process.

Scripture has much to say about our speech. It should be used for building others up (Eph. 4:29), it is never perfect (Jas. 3:2), and it should be guided by the heart and promote instruction (Pr. 16:23). Proverbs 17:27-28 stands out: Silence and restraint of words is valued. When it comes to counselor self-disclosure, this principle may be of significant assistance. When in doubt, refrain from disclosure. Consider carefully before sharing, and be willing to err on the side of self-silence rather than self-disclosure.

**Miriam Stark Parent**

## REFERENCES

American Counseling Association. (2005). *ACA Code of Ethics.* Alexandria, VA: Author.

American Association of Christian Counselors. (2004). *AACC Christian Counseling Code of Ethics* (5th ed.). Forest, VA: Author

Cashwell, C., Shcherbakova, J., & Cashwell, T. (2003). Effect of client and counselor ethnicity on preference for counselor disclosure. *Journal of Counseling and Development, 81,* 196-201.

Ivey, A., Ivey, M., & Zalaquett, C. (2010). *Intentional Interviewing and Counseling: Facilitating Client Development in a Multicultural Society* (7th ed.). Belmont, CA: Brooks/Cole.

Kottler, J., & Shepard, D. (2011). *Introduction to Counseling: Voices from the Field* (7th ed.). Belmont, CA: Brooks/Cole.

Sue, D. W., & Sue, D. (2008). *Counseling the Culturally Diverse: Theory and Practice* (5th ed.). Wiley & Sons.

## TRANSFERENCE AND COUNTERTRANSFERENCE

**Description and Definition.** Transference is defined as "the way in which the patients' view of and relationships with childhood objects are expressed in current feelings, attitudes, and behaviors in regard to the therapist" (Mills, Bauer, & Russell, 1989, p. 112). Countertransference operates in the opposite direction and is defined as "the therapist's internal or external reactions that are shaped by the therapist's past or present emotional conflicts and vulnerabilities" (Gelso, 2011, p. 5). Originated in psychoanalysis traditions, however, it is acknowledged that transference and countertransference are present in all types of treatments (Gladding, 2009; Gelso).

Gladding (2009) discusses that transference can be direct (e.g., a client says, "You remind me of my mother") or indirect (e.g., a client says, "This therapy is ineffective"). It can be positive (e.g., a client admires the counselor) or negative (e.g., a client accuses the counselor). Countertransference can take several forms: a constant urge to please the client, overidentification with the client's feelings and problems, compulsive advice giving, and a desire for a social relationship with the client (Corey, Corey, & Callanan, 2007). It is critical for therapists to become aware of such feelings and work through their own conflicts as part of ongoing training and supervision. Therapists' unresolved conflicts may lead not only to unproductive services but also harmful relationships to the clients (Gladding).

**History.** Freud constructed the concepts of transference and countertransference based on his observation that clients' unconscious conflicts that originate in early relationships become repeated in the relationship between the patient and the therapist (Gabbard & Westen, 2003). Conceptualizations and uses of transference and countertransference have changed over the years. In classical psychoanalysis, the therapist's role was viewed as neutral and passive. It was believed that the client's unresolved conflicts were projected onto the therapist's neutral state. In modern psychodynamic theory, the therapist's contribution to this experience is acknowledged and is now considered as an intersubjective process cocreated by client and therapist (Gelso, 2011). The focus of the relationship has shifted from the relationship with childhood objects to the here-and-now relationship with the therapist. Therapists use this here-and-now relationship to clarify, examine, and modify maladaptive interpersonal conflicts rather than merely observe and provide interpretations of the client's past relationships (Mills et al., 1989). As transference has been accepted as coconstruction, several views were presented as to what extent the client contributes to the therapist's countertransference. Gelso argues that while clients may stimulate the therapist's issues, countertransference is fundamentally rooted in the therapist's emotional conflict and must be dealt with appropriately.

**Treatment and Application.** Transference/countertransference relationship is one of the chief transformative interventions to reconstruct the client's relational pattern (Parlow & Goodman, 2010; Jones & Butman, 1991). The goal of this intervention is to bring unconscious conflict into consciousness and to obtain deeper insights about how such past experiences still influence current relationships. Furthermore, it is used to facilitate more flexible and mature relational patterns. Working through transference is also considered a prerequisite for the establishment of a good working alliance with a client (Mills et al., 1989).

**Christianity and Spirituality.** How do we, as Christian therapists, respond to clients who complain, "You are not helping me!" or clients' cold and disrespectful attitude toward us? Our tendency is either to fight back or withdraw from these attacks. They might remind us of prior painful and personal relational conflicts (countertransference). Clients come to therapy after repeatedly experiencing hurtful relationships that, in part, they have created. Underneath their negative behaviors, clients hide their inner cries to be understood, trusted, respected, and loved. Parlow and Goodman (2010) remind us to serve our clients by believing they are made in God's image (*imago Dei*). One of the implications of the *imago Dei* is that God creates each person to fully receive love and openly love others and God, for God is love (1 Jn. 4:8). Yet due to the Fall and our sins (i.e., apart from perfect love), each person falls short of such full potential. Psychoanalysis is founded on the premise that in early attachment relationships, individuals' needs and love are deprived and their personalities developed around "protecting the heart rather than opening it" (Parlow & Goodman, p. 119). The hope is that such damaged bonds can be reworked in a new light or in new relationships, ones where the clients' distorted ways of loving are reengaged and reworked from within (working through transference). Parlow and Goodman say, "Transference is the set of unconscious, organizing principles from past relationships where love has gotten frozen in the person through the tension of damaging events that are repeated" (p. 119). They add, "Love in the present is blocked by lack of love in the past." The goal of therapy is to unlock this frozen love in a safe and authentic therapeutic relationship so the clients become free to receive love and love others in the way God originally designed.

**Hitomi Makino**

## REFERENCE


Corey, G., Corey, M. S., Callanan, P. (2007). *Issues and Ethics in the Helping Professions* (7th ed.). Belmont, CA: Thomson Brooks/Cole.

Gabbard, G. O., & Westen, D. (2003). Rethinking therapeutic action. *International Journal of Psychoanalysis, 84*, 823-841.

Gelso, C. J. (2011). Contextualizing the real relationship in psychotherapy and psychoanalysis. In C. J. Gelso (Ed.), *The Real Relationship in Psychotherapy: The Hidden Foundation of Change* (pp. 3-23). doi:10.1037/12349-001

Gladding, S. T. (2009). *Counseling: A Comprehensive Profession* (6th ed.). Upper Saddle River, NJ: Person.

Jones, S. L., & Butman, R. E. (1991). *Modern Psychotherapies: A Comprehensive Christian Appraisal.* Downers Grove, IL: InterVarsity Press.

Mills, J. A., Bauer, G. P., & Russell, M. D. (1989). Use of transference in short-term dynamic psychotherapy. *Psychotherapy: Theory, Research, Practice, Training, 26*, 338-343. doi:10.1037/h0085444

Parlow, S., & Goodman, D. M. (2010). The transformative action of the transference/countertransference relationship: A case example. *Journal of Psychology and Christianity, 29*(2), 116-120.


## SILENCE

**An Illustration.** When I was a fairly new counselor, one of my early clients was a woman named Sandy. I'd been working with her for several months on issues of grieving because she'd lost her husband a year before. He had been on a business trip and was in a horrible car crash. His body was burned almost beyond recognition. When his body was shipped home, Sandy's father kept her from viewing it, saying that having her husband's watch and ring were all she needed to know that he was gone.

Sandy was stuck in her grieving process. We worked hard together to address her hurt, fear, and anger, but each topic proved to be a dead end. We looked at what would have been different if she could have seen his body...and just about everything else we could think of. Nothing unlocked the healing process for Sandy.

Finally, in one session, I reached the point where I didn't know where to go or what to say, so I sat in silence for what seemed like an eternity. Suddenly Sandy blurted, "I didn't tell him I loved him!" The floodgate of tears opened.

When she was able to regain her composure, I asked what she meant. She told me that just before her husband got into his rental car, they talked on the telephone and had an argument. He'd tried to smooth things over and told her he loved her, but she was too upset to respond. She hung up without telling him she loved him. Neither one of them knew it would be their last conversation.

What seemed to me to be awkward silence was actually the perfect environment for Sandy to gain insight about her pain. Finally she had the courage to tell someone her secret memory of that horrible day. It wasn't long after that session that she finished counseling and felt confident enough to move forward in her life.

**Description.** Using silence appropriately is often one of the last counseling skills we learn. The difficulty of mastering the use of silence is compounded by our discomfort with it (Guindon, 2011). We all know the adage "Silence is golden," but we also know the pain of experiencing the silent treatment. Even an introverted person can be uncomfortable with too much silence. For most counselors, silence feels very unproductive. After all, aren't we supposed to be doing something in the session? (See Ivey, Ivey, & Zalaquett, 2010.) Also, silence can be used as a power play. We must learn when to use silence effectively and when not to.

**In Treatment.** We've all had the experience of counseling adolescents who don't want to be in the sessions and use silence as a power tactic (Grunwald & McAbee, 1999). Why wouldn't they be silent when they feel powerless because they are being forced by a parent to come to the counseling appointment? What do we do when we run out of questions—especially when adolescents are so adept at giving one-word answers? Or what do we do when no one wants to talk in a group counseling session?

Learning to tolerate—and effectively use—silence in a session should be one of the first skills we learn. To master this skill, we need to know when silence is helpful. For many people who come to counseling, silence in a session may be the only time they have to experience quietness and reflect on what they have heard or felt. It may be the only time and the only place where they can listen to their own thoughts, discover alternatives, and reach solutions (Meier & Davis, 2011; Cormier, Nurius, & Osborn, 2009).

For silence to be helpful, it must have meaning. Jesus took the time to write in the sand when dealing with a difficult situation (Jn. 8:6,8). Silence oftentimes allows the Spirit of God to do his most deep and profound work. When you are in a time of silence, ask the Holy Spirit to offer counsel. Also ask yourself or, maybe even better, ask your client, "What does this silence mean to you right now?" The answer may open up new avenues that lead to a new and deeper level of healing for your client.

David Stoop

## REFERENCE


Cormier, S., Nurius, P., & Osborn, C. J. (2009). *Interviewing and Change Strategies for Helpers: Foundational Skills and Cognitive Behavioral Interventions* (6th ed.). Belmont, CA: Books/Cole.

Grunwald, B. B., & McAbee, H. V. (1999). *Guiding the Family: Practical Counseling Techniques.* New York, NY: Taylor & Francis.

Guindon, M. H. (2011). *A Counseling Primer: An Introduction to the Profession.* New York, NY: Taylor & Francis.

Ivey, A. E., Ivey, M. B., & Zalaquett, C. P. (2010). *Intentional Interviewing: Facilitating Client Development in a Multicultural Society.* Belmont, CA: Books/Cole.

Meier, S. T., & Davis, S. R. (2011). *The Element of Counseling.* Belmont, CA: Books/Cole.


## MOTIVATIONAL INTERVIEWING

**Description.** Motivational interviewing (MI) is defined as "a client-centered directive method for enhancing intrinsic motivation to change by exploring and resolving ambivalence" (Miller & Rollnick, 2002, p. 25). MI stresses the importance of the counselor's relational style in initiating, enhancing, and maintaining the counselee's motivation for change. A primary emphasis is on the counselor relating in such a way that the counselee becomes the advocate for change. Particular attention is given to eliciting and reinforcing counselees' statements reflecting their commitment to change (Arkowitz & Westra, 2009).

**Key Issues.** Understanding assumptions regarding the nature of motivation is foundational to MI. Motivation is assumed to be: (a) a key to change, (b) multidimensional, (c) a dynamic and fluctuating state, (d) interactive, (e) able to be modified, and (f) influenced by the counselor's style (Substance Abuse and Mental Health Services Administration [SAMHSA], 1999).

Miller and Rollnick (2002) identify four basic principles of MI: expressing empathy, developing discrepancy, rolling with resistance, and supporting self-efficacy. Counselor skills important in MI include using open-ended questions, reflective listening, affirmation, summarizing, and eliciting and reinforcing change talk. The spirit with which MI is best conducted has been described as (a) collaborative and conducive rather than confrontational and coercive, (b) evocative and enhancing rather than educative and imposing, and (c) honoring autonomy and facilitative rather than authoritative and restrictive (Miller & Rollnick; Miller & Rose, 2009). The transtheoretical stages-of-change model is a helpful conceptual framework for understanding how people change and how MI can facilitate the change process (Miller & Rollnick; SAMHSA, 1999).

**Effectiveness.** MI has been shown to influence change talk within sessions, leading to improved outcomes for counselees (Miller & Rose, 2009). "Research has shown that simple motivation-enhancing interventions are effective for encouraging clients to return for another clinical consultation, return to treatment following a missed appointment, stay involved in treatment, and be more compliant" (SAMHSA, 1999, Motivational Interventions section, paragraph 2). MI is demonstrating efficacy in a variety of settings with a number of conditions, including cardiovascular rehabilitation, diabetes management, dietary change, hypertension, illicit drug use, infection risk reduction, management of chronic mental disorders, problem drinking, problem gambling, smoking, and concomitant mental and substance use disorders (Miller & Rose). Recent evidence suggests that MI is effective when integrated with other treatment approaches (Miller & Rollnick, 2002; Miller & Rose; Arkowitz & Westra, 2009).

**Application.** The forms of MI and the types of settings in which it occurs have expanded significantly (Arkowitz & Westra, 2009; Miller & Rose, 2009; SAMHSA, 1999). Interventions consistent with MI include the FRAMES approach, decisional balance exercises, developing discrepancy, flexible pacing, and personal contact with those not currently in treatment. Training in MI for counselors is available through the Motivational Interviewing Network of Trainers (MINT).

**Biblical and Spiritual Issues.** MI has a number of assumptions, principles, and components that are consistent with biblical teaching. There is a clear emphasis on the responsibility and freedom of individuals to choose for themselves which behaviors and attitudes, if any, are the focus of change. The counseling style required to be effective with MI is inherently honoring of counselees, yet directive regarding the facilitation of change. MI emphasizes the importance of deeply held values and beliefs and how counselee behavior is or isn't consistent with those. A fascinating study would be to think of the key principles and components of MI when reading how Jesus interacted with the Samaritan woman at the well (cf. Jn 4:7-31,39-42). Not only did she change, but she was instrumental in bringing change to her entire community!

**David E. Jenkins**

### REFERENCES

Arkowitz, H., & Westra, H. A. (2009). Introduction to the special series on motivational interviewing and psychotherapy. *Journal of Clinical Psychology: In Session, 65*, 1149-1155. doi:10.1002/jclp.20640

Miller, W. R., & Rollnick, S. (2002). *Motivational Interviewing: Preparing People for Change* (2nd ed.). New York, NY: Guilford Press.

Miller, W. R., & Rose, G. S. (2009). Toward a theory of motivational interviewing. *American Psychologist, 64*, 527-537. doi:10.1037/a0016830

Substance Abuse and Mental Health Services Administration, Center for Substance Abuse Treatment. (1999). *Enhancing Motivation for Change in Substance Abuse Treatment: (TIP) Series 35* (DHHS Publication No. SMA 99-3354). Rockville, MD: Author.

## EXPERTNESS

**What Is Expertness?** *Expertness* refers to the client's perception of whether the counselor is competent enough to help him or her successfully work through the presenting problem(s). Factors that can play a role in this perception include the age, physical appearance, and professionalism of the counselor; the counseling office environment; the counselor's educational level; licenses, certifications, and credentials; experience or training in a specialized area of counseling; apparent skill level; status; job title or seniority; a proven track record of success; level of religious commitment; and the counselor's assigned role as helper (Cormier & Cormier, 2008; Egan, 2009).

**Why Is Expertness Important?** Expertness is especially vital in the early stages of counseling because it contributes to the rapport between the counselor and client. A reputable environment and waiting room, diplomas and certificates framed on the wall, and a professional presentation of oneself can help enhance the perception that you are able to handle the presenting issues of the client (Cormier & Cormier, 2008; Cormier, Nurius, & Osborn, 2009). In a recent study on perceived counselor effectiveness, researchers found that the presence of diplomas and credentials hanging on the wall positively affected counselor quality and energy for clients (Devlin et al., 2009). In addition, the reputation of the counselor as effective can also be foundational to the level of influence the counselor eventually has in a client's life (Cormier & Cormier).

Consider the first day of class in a school setting. If a teacher is too lenient early on and the class becomes rowdy, building the respect of the students and becoming stricter later will be an uphill battle. Similarly, if the client perceives the counselor with little expertness, building rapport could be equally as difficult.

**Increasing Expertness.** Expertness is not always equivalent to the true competency of the counselor. Nonverbal and verbal factors play roles in increasing perceived expertness. Nonverbal behaviors include good eye contact, having good posture while leaning forward, attentiveness, and confident and direct speech delivery. Verbal behaviors that enhance perceived expertness include effective two-way communication, the ability to ask insightful questions, good reflective listening skills, direct and confident interpretations, and concrete responses (Cormier & Cormier, 2008; Cormier et al., 2009). One recent study found that when counselors use informal language to respond to a client's formal expressions, those counselors were perceived as having decreased expertise. On the other hand, when counselors mirror a client's expressions, either informal–informal or formal–formal, perceptions of expertise increased (Haberstroh, 2010).

**Expertness Throughout the Counseling Relationship.** *Early stages.* The mere role of the counselor as an educated helper provides a sense of expertness and brings with it relational power. Whether the counselor in that position is competent or not makes no difference. The power is in the position. In fact, Cormier and Cormier state, "The legitimate power of our role is, in fact, so strong that demonstrated or behavioral cues of counselor expertness are masked in the initial stage of counseling because sufficient inherent power is ascribed to the role of a helper" (2008, p. 44). In addition to the aforementioned power are the demonstrated, or exhibited, cues of counselor expertness in the early stages (i.e., a diploma hanging on the wall, the reputation of the counselor). Together, these factors increase expertness perception.

*Middle and later stages.* To maintain a high level of expertness, behavioral cues must be present. Education level, license, and office setting are not enough to maintain rapport for the client with the counselor beyond the early stages. The ability of the counselor to effectively assess client issues, set realistic goals for the client to achieve, and develop helpful strategies for the client to work through the issues are vital to maintaining expertness (Cormier et al., 2009). As it relates to Christian counseling, many clients may also be looking for spiritual maturity in the life of the counselor to help them through difficult times. If the counselor does not display biblical knowledge, discipline, or prayer in the counseling setting, it could seriously hinder perceived expertness for clients looking for faith-based care.

Joshua Straub

## REFERENCES

Cormier, W. H., & Cormier, L. S. (2008). *Interviewing*

*Strategies for Helpers: Fundamental Skills and Cognitive Behavioral Interventions* (6th ed.). Pacific Grove, CA: Brooks/Cole.

Cormier, S., Nurius, P. S., & Osborn, C. J. (2009). *Interviewing and Change Strategies for Helpers: Fundamental Skills and Cognitive Behavioral Interventions* (6th ed.). Belmont, CA: Brooks/ Cole.

Devlin, A. S., Donovan, S., Nicolov, A., Nold, O., Packard, A., & Zanden, G. (2009, December). "Impressive?" Credentials, family photographs, and the perception of therapist qualities. *Journal of Environmental Psychology, 29*(4), 503-512.

Egan, G. (2009). *The Skilled Helper: A Problem Management Approach to Helping* (9th edition). Pacific Grove, CA: Brooks/Cole.

Haberstroh, S. (2010, August). College counselors' use of informal language online: Student perceptions of expertness, trustworthiness, and attractiveness. *Cyberpsychology, Behavior and Social Networking, 13*(4), 455-459.

## PSYCHODRAMA

**Description.** Psychodrama is an experiential form of group therapy that utilizes the reenactment of significant events in one's life, thereby allowing the individual to examine, re-experience, and amend the situation in a curative manner within a safe therapeutic environment (Dayton, 1994). Using the group therapist as the director of this drama, group members participate by either acting as characters in the drama or as part of the audience. The drama has no script; rather, the event is initially performed in the manner the individual remembers it (Djurić, Veljković, & Tomić, 2006).

**History.** Jacob Levy Moreno, a Venetian psychiatrist, introduced his experiential therapy, psychodrama, in 1921. Inspired by watching children play-acting poignant situations from their lives, Moreno recognized the therapeutic potential such activities possessed (Dayton, 1994). After migrating to United States in the late 1920s, Moreno established the Moreno Institute in New York City (Dayton).

**The Therapeutic Process.** The therapeutic process of psychodrama includes three phases: warm-up, action or enactment, and sharing. The warm-up process allows for an increased level of trust and cohesion within the group and a waning of inner defensiveness (Blatner, 2007). These changes are fostered by activities requiring interaction among the group members and drawing upon members' intuitive natures (Blatner).

Following the warm-up, the protagonist is chosen. Whether chosen by the group or the director, an important consideration is the individual's readiness and willingness to do the work needed in this role (Dayton, 1994). Once the protagonist is chosen, the action or enactment phase commences. The protagonist, now on stage, describes the situation for the psychodrama. This could include a relationship, a past event, a dream, or a missed opportunity.

> Experiencing the self in all of its complexity, giving voice to the rumblings, wishes and concerns of the inner person, answering questions in a way that reveals what is living inside the protagonist, standing in the shoes of others, and experiencing them and staring back at the self through their eyes make this method unique among all others (Dayton, 2005, p. 24).

Various roles and techniques are often employed during the action phase, depending on the needs of the protagonist. Roles would include the director (the therapist), the protagonist (the person whose story is being enacted), and the audience (the group members), as well as the auxiliary ego (a group member who plays an important person in relationship to the enactment) (Dayton, 1994; Djurić et al., 2006; Blatner, 2007). Some techniques used include *doubling*, which occurs when a member of the group stands in for the protagonist; *mirroring*, when a group member sees an aspect of himself or herself, usually a repressed aspect, through the actions or behavior of another member; *soliloquy*, when a monologue is presented by the protagonist verbalizing his thoughts and feelings (Djurić et al.); and *role reversal*, when the protagonist stands in for one of the alter egos, allowing the protagonist to actually experience what it is like to be that person (Dayton, 2005)—e.g., the son experiences what his father suffers when he argues with his son.

The last phase in the psychodrama process is the sharing phase. During this phase, group members face the protagonist and share their own experiences of the drama and how it relates to their particular life situations. They speak of their emotions and their lives (Djurić et al., 2006).

**Spiritual Issues.** Moreno acknowledged a Godlikeness in each person and the ability for each person to elicit the Creator in others (Centore, 2010). He sees it fitting that healing comes from relationships, especially when the wounding originated from relational problems (Centore). The restoration generated from the therapeutic process found in psychodrama, aided by the safety and support provided by the group, mirrors the healing that Moreno acknowledges belongs to the body of Christ (Centore).

**Empirical Support.** In spite of the fact that psychodrama is one of the oldest forms of therapy, as well as the large number of published journal articles describing its procedures and usefulness, there is little research completed to support its therapeutic efficacy (Blatner, 1995). Several factors, such as its unconventional methods and that it is rarely used as a sole treatment modality, make it difficult to scientifically evaluate its effects. In an attempt to offer some empirical support, Kellermann (1987) reviewed numerous research studies and concluded that the limited scope of these studies prevents generalization of the findings. Yet psychodrama is viewed as "a valid alternative to other therapeutic approaches, primarily in promoting behavior change with adjustment, antisocial, and related disorders" (Blatner, 1995, p. 466).

**Carmela O'Hare**

## REFERENCES

Blatner, A. (1995). Psychodramatic methods in psychotherapy. *Psychiatric Times, 12*(5), 20-23.

Blatner, A. (2007). Morenean approaches: Recognizing psychodrama's many facets. *Journal of Group Psychotherapy, Psychodrama & Sociometry, 59*, 159-170.

Centore, A. (2010, June 10). *Psychodrama and Christian Counseling—Christian User-Friendly Psychodrama.* Retrieved March 7, 2011 from http://EzineArticles.com/?expert=Anthony_Centore

Dayton, T. (1994). *The Drama Within: Psychodrama and Experiential Therapy.* Deerfield Beach, FL: Health Communications.

Dayton, T. (2005). *The Living Stage: A Step-by-step Guide to Psychodrama, Sociometry and Experiental Group Therapy.* Deerfield Beach, FL: Health Communications.

Djuric, Z., Veljkovic, J., & Tomic, M. (2006). *Psychodrama: A Beginner's Guide.* Philadelphia, PA: Kingsley.

Kellerman, P. F. (1987). A proposed definition of psychodrama. *Journal of Group Psychotherapy, Psychodrama, & Sociometry, 40*(2), 76-80.

# COUNSELING THEORIES AND THERAPIES

## PSYCHODYNAMIC THEORY

**Description.** *Psychodynamic theory* refers to an array of psychological and personality theories that share a common understanding that unconscious forces (dynamics) are the chief motivators of human behavior. Although influenced by Freudian or psychoanalytic concepts, especially the unconscious, psychodynamic theory is usually considered a more inclusive term than psychoanalytic theory. Psychodynamic theory includes the works of Carl Jung, ego psychology, neo-analytic theories, object-relations theory, and relational analysis. Even aspects of Adler's work have been subsumed under this umbrella (Hall, Lindzey, & Campbell, 1998; Ryckman, 2004).

**History.** Because psychodynamic theory includes such a broad group, it is difficult to circumscribe common characteristics without some distortion. Nevertheless, we can note the following common themes. First, it emphasizes the role of the social environment (relationships with others) in shaping personality rather than attributing the dominant influence to biological drives (cf. Greenberg & Mitchell, 1983). Second, it focuses on social-constructivist interpretations of reality in contrast with Freud's logical positivism. For the social constructivist, reality is not so easily distinguished from the one(s) who created it. What is considered abnormal in one social context may be acceptable in another (Murdock, 2009). (The recognition of unconscious motives has already been noted.)

Some of those who modified Freud's model to be more inclusive of the sociocultural environment in shaping personality are the so-called *neo-analytic theorists*. This designation is given to the theories of Karen Horney, Harry Stack Sullivan, and Erich Fromm. Sometimes it is extended to take in the "ego psychologies" of Anna Freud and Erik Erikson. Probably the best known of this group is Erikson, who illustrates a tendency to modify Freud's early description of developmental stages (the psychosexual stages) to be more inclusive of social and cultural factors. He notes a series of crises between biological maturation and social constraint that allows him to outline eight psychosocial stages that take in the life span rather than only the early years of development (Ryckman, 2004).

A second group of personality theorists who modified Freud's work to focus more on the role of early relationships is the group of *object-relations theorists*. Emerging primarily from Britain, this group includes Melanie Klein, Donald Winnicott, and Ronald Fairbairn, although the roots of both object-relations theory and contemporary relational analysis draw common threads from the work of Sandor Ferenzi (Hoffman, 2011). *Object relations* derives its name from Freud's notion that in seeking early instinctual gratification (e.g., hunger), the child gravitated toward "objects" (in this case the mother or mother figure) who could satisfy such needs. Thus, *object relations* refers to the special relationship a person has with such "objects"—generally the people in someone's environment (Parker, 2009). However, these relationships also are "object" relationships in that these interactions with early primary figures are carried around as mental images with which one interacts. When relating to figures from an early environment, a person does not interact with them simply as objective persons whom others might meet and describe, but in terms of his or her personal subjective reality that was constructed in early interactions with them.

Carl Jung's approach to the unconscious, known as *analytic psychology*, focuses primarily on the influence of deep memory traces in the human race, what he called the *collective unconscious*. In addition to a personal unconscious as Freud taught, Jung posits a deeper sociocultural layer of the unconscious that was accessible through *archetypes*, a concept denoting inherited patterns that help humans organize experiences. The archetypes influence the *psyche* (the whole of our personality for Jung) by giving shape to our experiences of femininity, masculinity, heroism, wisdom, and a dark or "shadow" side of our personality, among other experiences (Tan, 2010). Jung also articulated various individual differences in personality through his description of personality types. These various types have been popularized through the Myers-Briggs Type Indicator (MBTI). This instrument sorts personality types along the dimensions of introversion/extraversion, thinking/feeling, sensing/intuiting, and the dominance in each of these (the judging/perceiving score) (Ryckman, 2004). Jung also saw spirituality as a deep wellspring of human desire and creativity; he took a more positive stance toward its presence than did Freud (Jones & Butman, 1991; Tan).

**Application.** Psychodynamic theory continues to have significant influence on the field of counseling and therapy. Concepts such as the unconscious permeate Western culture. In a survey of American psychotherapists conducted by Prochaska and Norcross (1999), a third of psychiatrists and social workers identified themselves as psychoanalytic or psychodynamic in orientation, while approximately 20% of clinical psychologists and 10% of counselors and counseling psychologists also claimed this identification. Many practitioners of this approach have adapted it to provide "brief psychodynamic therapy" in a market geared toward brief, solution-focused therapies. There is a growing literature on the efficacy of psychodynamic therapy, although research support historically has not been the strength of this approach (Hall et al., 1998; Seligman & Reichenberg, 2010). Some Christian counselors and therapists identify with and have adapted various psychodynamic approaches to their methods (Hoffman, 2011; Jones and Butman, 1991; Tan, 2010).

**Biblical and Spiritual Issues.** Certainly for the Christian, there are ideas to appreciate from this cluster of theories. The idea of the unconscious has echoes in the Old Testament. The prophet Jeremiah wrote, "The heart is deceitful above all things and beyond cure. Who can understand it?" (Jer. 17:9). Psychodynamic notions of the deceitfulness and defensiveness of the human heart accord with our fallen nature (cf. Gen. 3; Jones & Butman, 1991; Tan, 2010). The influence of a person's early caregiving environment also accords with the role of the family in shaping personality and values (cf. Deut. 6:4-9).

Nevertheless, there are concerns for Christians to discern regarding this cluster of theories. For instance, Jung's openness to spirituality and its creativeness is inclusive of all spirituality, not just Christianity. The social constructivism of these theories can mire someone in moral relativism. Discernment is needed, but with it, we can find some golden wheat among the chaff.

**Stephen Parker**

## REFERENCES

Greenberg, J. R., & Mitchell, S. A. (1983). *Object Relations in Psychoanalytic Theory.* Cambridge, MA: Harvard University Press.

Hall, C. S., Lindzey, G., & Campbell, J. B. (1998). *Theories of Personality* (4th ed.). New York, NY: Wiley & Sons.

Hoffman, M.T. (2011). *Toward Mutual Recognition: Relational Psychoanalysis and the Christian Narrative.* New York, NY: Routledge.

Jones, S. L., & Butman, R. E. (1991). *Modern Psychotherapies: A Comprehensive Christian Appraisal.* Downers Grove, IL: InterVarsity Press.

Murdock, N. L. (2009). *Theories of Counseling and Psychotherapy* (2nd ed.). Upper Saddle River, NJ: Prentice Hall.

Parker, S. (2009). Object relations. *ACA Encyclopedia of Counseling* (pp. 373-374). Washington, DC: American Counseling Association.

Prochaska, J. O., & Norcross, J. C. (1999). *Systems of Psychotherapy: A Transtheoretical Analysis* (4th ed.). Pacific Grove, CA: Brooks/Cole.

Ryckman, R. M. (2004). *Theories of Personality* (8th ed.). Belmont, CA: Wadsworth/Thomson.

Seligman, L., & Reichenberg, L. W. (2010). *Theories of Counseling and Psychotherapy* (3rd ed.). Upper Saddle River, NJ: Prentice Hall.

Tan, S.-Y. (2010). *Counseling and Psychotherapy: A Christian Perspective.* Grand Rapids, MI: Baker Academic.

## ADLERIAN THERAPY

**Description.** Alfred Adler (1870–1937) is considered by many to be the father of present-day cognitively oriented therapies. Early in his career he had a nine-year association with Sigmund Freud through the Vienna Psychoanalytical Society, but he broke this connection in 1911 and developed his *individual psychology* (IP) approach to emphasize the indivisibility and holistic nature of man. According to Abraham Maslow (1962), Adler was a contemporary of Freud, but he was never a disciple of Freud. Freud believed that man is motivated by biological instinctual drives that are largely unconscious, but Adler believed that man innately strives holistically to overcome real and perceived feelings of *inferiority* in order to gain a sense of *superiority*, a sense of completion, mastery, or perfection, and to find a place of significance in his social world (Murdock, 2009).

Man's behavior is thus purposive and goal directed. Rather than being driven by biological factors, man is pulled by his future as he anticipates it and as he purposes to gain a place in society. This *striving for superiority* can be done in a way that benefits others (*social interest*), or the striving can be done in a self-centered way with little social interest. Adler believed that psychologically healthy people have high social interest.

**Lifestyle.** According to individual psychology, by about the fifth year of life, a child develops a unique style of acting, thinking, and perceiving, which Adler called the person's *lifestyle.* One's lifestyle is the person's cognitive and behavioral blueprint through which the individual functions in the world to gain a sense of significance (or superiority). It develops from the child's *private logic,* which is made up of early subjective perceptions of himself, others, and the world around him, as well as the meaning that he gives to those perceptions. It is gained primarily through his interactions with his parents. The individual moves through life being influenced by an imagined life goal that Adler called a *guiding self-ideal.* Though Adler believed the environment, especially the early family environment, had a very significant influence on how an individual perceives life, he did not believe it determined who the person became. He didn't think heredity did either (Gladding, 2009). Adler believed that every person has a creative power, or creative self, that plays a major role in the development of the individual's lifestyle and gives the person the possibility of developing in ways that go against his or her environmental and hereditary influences.

Once formed, one's lifestyle tends to remain fairly consistent throughout life. However, because of this creative power, a person has the ability to make choices that go against his lifestyle tendencies. Since one's lifestyle is based on the person's belief system, it can be overridden and, to some degree, changed as the person becomes aware of his goals and the underlying beliefs that support his goals (Gladding, 2009). Adler identified four basic lifestyle types: the *socially useful type,* where a person has high *social interest*;

the *ruling type,* where a person gains his significance by controlling others; the *getting type,* where a person gains significance by putting others in his service; and the *withdrawing type,* where the person retreats from life's tasks to avoid anticipated failure (Murdock, 2009). Present-day Adlerians have expanded on Adler's four lifestyle types.

**Goals of Therapy.** The primary goal for Adlerian therapists is to increase the client's social interest by identifying and changing faulty beliefs and goals, as well as faulty behaviors, thereby overriding the individual's lifestyle tendencies (Murdock, 2009). Since Adler believed that clients are basically discouraged, another primary goal would be to encourage them to take courage and change their faulty beliefs and behaviors, thus altering their lifestyles.

**Counseling Process and Primary Techniques.** *Assessment.* An Adlerian therapist seeks to establish a warm, empathic, encouraging, and collaborative relationship with the client throughout the counseling process. The first task would be to assess the client's lifestyle to uncover the purpose of his or her behaviors and the maladaptive goals that pull the individual toward his or her imagined goal of superiority or completion. The therapist would assess the lifestyle by exploring the client's *family constellation* in order to gain insights into the client's perceptions of self, others, and the world, particularly in context of his or her family. Included in the assessment process is exploring a client's *early recollections* by having the person recall his or her earliest memories. Adler believed that of the thousands of experiences we have in early life, we tend to remember those that fit with the way we see ourselves and others and that support our lifestyle tendencies. Adler would also look at the client's *birth order.* It's important to note that Adlerians believe it is not the actual order of birth that affects the person's personality, but the social setting and the perceived psychological place that a person experiences in early childhood that influences the lifestyle beliefs and tendencies that are developed. Adlerians would also assess the client's *basic mistakes,* which are the negative, self-defeating aspects of a client's private logic and thus lifestyle (Oberst & Stewart, 2003).

*Interpretation and encouraging insight.* Interpretation of the material gained during the assessment phase is provided to create awareness of the client's goals and purposes of behavior, the mistakes in private logic, and how the client tends to operate in the world to overcome inferiority. This phase of therapy would help the client understand his or her faulty beliefs and maladaptive behaviors. Interpretation is typically done in a very gentle way, often as a tentative suggestion or possibility, using statements such as "I'm wondering, though I could be wrong, if you choose this action in order to..."

*Facilitating reorientation and reeducation.* The last phase of therapy would be to put insight into action. One key aspect in this phase is to help the client overcome his or her discouragement and to encourage the taking of courageous steps to bring about constructive changes that increase social interest. Adlerians help clients identify and capitalize on the strengths and internal resources available to them. Though Adlerians have many additional techniques available to help bring about change, a key variable in addition to insight is the therapist's ability to encourage the client to be courageous and to gain internal motivation to make difficult choices that would not have been made previously (Oberst & Stewart, 2003).

**Biblical Critique.** Adler's belief that the behavior of humans is purposive and directs them toward the broad goal of overcoming inferiority to gain a sense of superiority fits with the biblical view that man is goal-directed and that he is ultimately striving to overcome the effects of the fall of mankind.

Adler's assertion that a person's beliefs largely determine his behaviors, his emphasis on early childhood influences, his desire that people develop a primary interest in the welfare of others, and his use of encouragement in therapy are all consistent with a biblical view (Jones & Butman, 1991).

For Adler, however, inferiority is largely the result of human inability due to a lack of maturation or the result of discouragement because of a faulty view of self. Adler's simplistic view—that what people need is the courage to challenge their faulty beliefs and behaviors (their lifestyle tendencies) and to gain social interest—falls far short of the biblical view that man is indeed inferior in every way because of the fall of man and the resulting sin nature that infects every human (Jones & Butman, 1991). The belief that man can get back to the Garden of Eden (reach human perfection, happiness, etc.) if only he would enlist his own ability to change himself from self-interest to social interest is the essence of humanistic psychology.

Though changing what one believes in order to change outlook and behavior is biblical, Adler's view misses the fact that change is not a simple change of mind and behavior through self-effort, but rather a spiritual battle involving the fallen human heart, which includes God's work in the process of redemption as well as man's part (Eph. 2:8; 6:12).

LARRY ANDERSON

## REFERENCES


Gladding, S. T. (2009). *Counseling: A Comprehensive Profession.* Upper Saddle River, NJ: Prentice Hall.

Jones, S., & Butman, R. (1991). *Modern Psychotherapies: A Comprehensive Christian Appraisal.* Downers Grove, IL: IVP Academic.

Maslow, A. H. (1962). *Toward a Psychology of Being.* Princeton, NJ: Van Nostrand.

Murdock, N. (2009). *Theories of Counseling and Psychotherapy: A Case Approach.* Upper Saddle River, NJ: Prentice Hall.

Oberst, U. E., & Stewart, A. E. (2003). *Adlerian Psychotherapy: An Advanced Approach to Individual Psychology.* New York, NY: Brunner-Routledge.


## EXISTENTIAL COUNSELING

**DEFINITION.** In the broad study of human existence, *existentialism* focuses on four major issues: freedom, death, isolation, and meaninglessness. Compared to the other theoretical constructs central to psychology and psychotherapy, no other framework focuses on the human capacity to address life's deepest questions as much as does existentialism. This bodes well for the therapist looking to integrate the Christian faith with existential therapy (Jones & Butman, 1991).

**KEY PROPONENTS OF EXISTENTIAL COUNSELING.** Though existentialism was not a term used while he was alive, Søren Kierkegaard (1813–1855) is generally regarded as the father of existentialism (Marino, 2004). Another pioneer in existential philosophy was Friedrich Nietzsche (1844–1900). Unlike Kierkegaard, who based his philosophical thought on his Christian faith, Nietzsche believed that a person's value system and conditions for living were decided solely by the individual. Pioneering philosophers also include Martin Hiedegger (1889–1976), Jean-Paul Sartre (1905–1980), and Martin Buber (1878–1965), a theological proponent of existentialism who believed in an "I–Thou" relationship, whereby two people are connected in genuine relationship (Corey, 2009; Tan, 2011). The move from philosophy to a developmental method of existential therapy was led by pioneers such as Ludwig Binswanger (1881–1966), Medard Boss (1903–1991), Rollo May (1909–1994), Viktor Frankl (1905–1997), and Irvin Yalom (Corey; Tan).

**THEORETICAL CONSTRUCTS OF EXISTENTIALIST PSYCHOTHERAPY.** Kierkegaard famously observed, "Life is not a problem to be solved, but a reality to be experienced." This statement accurately contrasts the philosophical nature of existentialism to other approaches of psychotherapy. For instance, psychoanalysis and behaviorism are based on empirical, objective techniques that tend to minimize human freedom and responsibility and espouse a deterministic view of human nature. Psychoanalysis limits the human condition based on past experience and irrational and unconscious forces. Behaviorism constrains human potential to the conditioning of societal and cultural mores and, as a result, human freedom is controlled and determined (Corey, 2009; Jones & Butman, 1991).

Existential psychotherapy began in Europe in the 1940s by psychologists and psychiatrists who were unhappy with the state of psychiatry and the deterministic models prevalent at the time (Mendelowitz & Schneider, 2008). Rather than being restricted by intrinsic and extrinsic forces, they believed humans are genuinely free and responsible for their choices. As a result, humans control their own lives; therefore, they must deal with the deepest questions of life—that is, the questions specifically pertaining to freedom, death, isolation, and meaninglessness (Corey, 2009). People's ability to effectively become aware of and work through these core life issues is characteristic of their level of psychopathology (Yalom, 1980). When viewing the human condition from this standpoint, the existential psychotherapist can allow the client to reveal his inner experience without projecting distortions or becoming objective in an attempt to theorize or diagnose pathology. Therefore, existential psychotherapy does not concern itself with a set of rules or techniques. Instead, it focuses on recognizing and appreciating the client's awareness of the core issues facing humanity and helping him discover his own answers to life's deepest questions (Mendelowitz & Schneider).

**The Purpose of Existential Psychotherapy.** Viewing life as a reality to be experienced instead of a problem to solve is what differentiates the process of therapy for the existentialist from the psychoanalyst or behaviorist (Tan, 2011). As a result of this polarity, the existential counselor, instead of objectifying the client's problems and viewing the client as an ill patient in need of being healed or fixed, appreciates the subjectivity of the client's worldview. The goal of the therapist is to seek the client's answers to the core issues addressed by existentialism, and also to examine the way he answers these existential questions to help him choose his own values and meaning in life (Tan). Helping a client modify the way he answers these questions provides the opportunity for more authenticity in life as he gains awareness of his potential to become more of who he is in the present (Corey, 2009).

**The Purpose of Existential Group Therapy.** Existential group therapy helps members discover who they are based on their solutions or answers to the existential questions (Corey, 2009). This is accomplished when the group is free enough to create a microcosm of the world in which they live. Over time they begin interacting and behaving within the group the same way they do outside the group. As this occurs, group members will eventually reveal their dysfunctional interpersonal styles of communication in the presence of the group (Yalom, 1995). As group members are encouraged to openly share their beliefs and values to life's deepest questions, a sense of universality and mutuality is discovered (Yalom). As cohesion develops, group members can intrinsically search for and listen to their subjective experience, coming to realize the *how* by which they live (Corey).

**The Role of God in Existentialism.** Since the time of Kierkegaard's Christian approach to finding meaning in life, existentialism has assumed various philosophical methodologies that include theological, atheistic, and antireligious views (Tan, 2011). Existential psychotherapy deals with deep questions such as "Where have I come from?" "What do I value?" and "What happens to me when I die?" (Mendelowitz & Schneider, 2008). Depending on the view of the counselor, the answers to these life questions can be fatalistic—characterized by meaningless, nothingness, loneliness, and despair—or they can be answered with encouraging hope and optimism. The questions and issues raised by existentialism align with the Bible, especially Solomon's writings in Ecclesiastes. Though much of contemporary existential psychotherapy asserts that the existence of God is up to the individual to discover and holds no value, the theoretical framework of existentialism lends itself to an incredible opportunity for the Christian counselor because Jesus Christ fulfilled each of the existential issues of freedom (Gal. 5:1), death (1 Cor. 15:3-26), isolation (Jn. 17:24), and meaninglessness (Rom. 15:5-6) with his sacrificial death and resurrection (Tan).

**Self-Awareness and Anxiety.** A primary goal of existential counseling is to assist clients in breaking free from victimized thinking and help them understand that their choices enable them to sculpt their lives. Such recognition is not easy to attain, but it represents the beginning stages of growth and change. As clients realize their freedom, they can grasp their responsibility to act and choose (Corey, 2009). These choices create anxiety, but when the anxiety is resolved appropriately, self-awareness manifests. Therefore, self-awareness and anxiety lay the foundation for counseling individuals who are trying to resolve the four major existential issues in life. When people choose, instead, to ignore the anxiety and further repress it, they restrict their freedom, ignore their responsibility, and further limit their ability to choose (Corey). It is important that Christian counselors allow clients to wrestle with these life issues rather than merely have them naively accept them without understanding why (Tan, 2011). Existentialism honors clients' processes of answering these questions for themselves (Jones & Butman, 1991).

JOSHUA STRAUB
LAURA FAIDLEY

## REFERENCES

Corey, G. (2009). *Theory and Practice of Counseling and Psychotherapy* (8th ed.). Belmont, CA: Brooks/Cole.

Jones, S. L., & Butman, R. E. (1991). *Modern Psychotherapies.* Downers Grove, IL: InterVarsity Press.

Kierkegaard, S. (1962). *Works of Love.* New York, NY: Harper & Row.

Marino, G. (2004). *Basic Writings of Existentialism* (pp. ix, 3). New York, NY: Modern Library.

Mendelowitz, E., & Schneider, K. (2008). Existential psychotherapy. In R. J. Corsini & D. Wedding (Eds.), *Current Psychotherapies* (8th ed., pp. 295-327). Belmont, CA: Brooks/Cole.

Perkins, R. L. (Ed.). (1997). *Concluding Unscientific Postscript to "Philosophical Fragments" (International Kierkegaard Commentary).* Macon, GA: Mercer University Press.

Tan, S.-Y. (2011). *Counseling and Psychotherapy: A Christian Perspective.* Grand Rapids, MI: Baker.

Yalom, I. D. (1980). *Existential Psychotherapy.* New York, NY: Basic Books.

Yalom, I. D. (1995). *The Theory and Practice of Group Psychotherapy* (4th ed.). New York, NY: Basic Books.

## LOGOTHERAPY

**Description.** *Logotherapy* is a humanistic and existential counseling theory that was developed by Viktor Frankl, a practicing physician prior to World War II. Between 1942 and 1945, Frankl was imprisoned in the Nazi concentration camps of Auschwitz and Dachau. Frankl's mother, father, brother, first wife, and all of his children died in the camps. Through his experiences, he developed logotherapy, which is detailed in his major work *Man's Search for Meaning* (1963).

Logotherapy is a therapy of meaning: All circumstances hold meaning, the basic human motivation is the will to meaning, each person has the freedom to find meaning in everything, and each person is an integration of body, mind, and spirit. Human beings are not by-products of internal drives and external factors such as the environment. Rather, each person possesses a spiritual dimension that allows for the ability to make autonomous decisions.

Frankl believed that many people have the means to live but often live without meaning. Humans are not only free, they are free to obtain self-chosen goals. Frankl was influenced by Nietzsche, who said, "He who has a *why* to live for can bear with almost any how" (cited in Frankl, 1963, pp. 121, 164). Frankl was convinced that every situation contains the seed of meaning (Frankl, 2000). Upon this conviction he based logotherapy; a term derived from the Greek word "logos," which means "that which gives reason for being" or simply "meaning." Rather than the counselor providing specific meaning to the client's situation, the client is oriented to all the possibilities of meaning and encouraged to pursue them.

Frankl also believed that each person had an inherent responsibility to find *ultimate meaning* and *meaning in the moment.* Ultimate meaning relates to the human search for God. For the atheist it could be found in science or simply the search for truth. People must also find meaning in each moment. Since life, not the person, is the real questioner, people must respond to the questions that life brings by searching for meaning and then making responsible decisions within one's available area of freedom.

Meaning can be found by three means:

- *creativity* of giving something to the world through self-expression, such as the work we do and the gifts we give to life
- *experiencing* the world through nature, culture, relationships, interactions with others and with the environment
- *changing one's attitude.* Perhaps Frankl's best idea is that no one can take away a person's attitude: It is "the last human freedom"

Every day we have many possibilities from which to choose within our areas of freedom. We must choose the most responsible option—make the best choice not only for ourselves, but also for the people around us so happiness and meaning fulfillment will ensue.

**Treatment.** The logotherapist's tasks are to help clients (a) discover and notice where they possess freedom and the potential for meaning, (b) actualize those potentials to transform and make meaning in their lives, and (c) honor meanings realized in the past (Lantz, 2000). Clients identify and eliminate those factors that hinder them from moving toward and finding self-fulfillment. Since meaning can be found in every circumstance, counseling is aimed at helping people develop meaning and purpose through such things as work, love, and suffering. Rather than searching for a client's pathology, logotherapy looks to the person's spiritual core to find resources of healing.

Logotherapists use techniques such as *Socratic dialogue*, in which the counselor and client search for meaning. Clients are helped to realize they are not victims of circumstances. They might have symptoms, but they are not defined by their symptoms. Another technique is *paradox*—helping clients overcome their problems through self-exaggeration and contradiction. Clients are encouraged to do or wish for the very thing they fear the most. Another technique, called *dereflection,* is a form of paradox. Unlike hyperreflection, in which a person becomes self-absorbed in thoughts, dereflection shifts the focus to other people or meaningful goals.

**Biblical and Spiritual Issues.** Logotherapy advocates much that a Christian counselor can appreciate, but Frankl did not believe that meaning was rooted in a transcendent God. Instead, he saw mankind as central to the universe and advocated subjective truth over objective or absolute truth.

Logotherapy holds that meaning is subjectively determined. Christianity believes meaning is rooted in a relationship with our creator through the person of Jesus Christ.

John C. Thomas

## REFERENCES


Frankl, V. E. (1963). *Man's Search for Meaning*. Boston, MA: Beacon.

Frankl, V. E. (2000). *Man's Search for Ultimate Meaning*. New York, NY: Perseus.

Lantz, J. (2000). Phenomenological reflection and time in Viktor Frankl's existential psychotherapy. *Journal of Phenomenological Psychology, 3*, 220-228.


## ROGERIAN THERAPY

"The curious paradox is that when I accept myself just as I am, then I can change" (Carl Rogers).

**Description.** The early 20th century was an era of Freudian psychotherapy, but midcentury, Carl Rogers emerged with the revolutionary idea of a client-centered approach. He emphasized the supremacy of the client's personal experience in the therapeutic process, and he viewed the client (rather than the therapist) as the expert on his own experience. Rogers' approach has been described as "the most widely adapted approach to people-helping that has ever been developed" (Corey, 1986, p. 272).

Rogerian therapy (also known as client-centered therapy) is a nondirective approach in which the therapist displays an unconditional positive regard, an ability to listen empathically, and a belief that the client has a drive toward self-actualization (Rogers, 1951). Forsaking the role of the expert in favor of serving as one who walks alongside the client, the therapist sets the stage for transformation through "non-possessive love," or prizing the client. Only at this point, when there is full acceptance, does change occur.

Rogers found that some of the theories of his time followed divergent paths. He described the discrepancy by quoting Rudyard Kipling: "Never the twain shall meet." His experiences led him to question the status quo of the 1940s and develop his own ideas about the conditions necessary for effective psychotherapy. His encounters, both in the Orient following World War I and later in seminary, challenged his philosophical beliefs and shaped his approach. After witnessing the attitudes of the French and Germans in 1922, he concluded that good people could have different belief systems. Rogers subsequently departed from his previously held beliefs (Rogers, 1951; Jones & Butman, 1991). Other experiences during seminary and while practicing counseling led him to challenge dominant counseling ideas of the time.

**In Practice.** The therapeutic conditions championed by Rogers, such as unconditional positive regard, require a suspension of judgment (assessment) in favor of full acceptance of the client. If the therapist is successful, "he has been able to enter into an intensely personal and subjective relationship with the client, relating not as a scientist to an object of study, not as a physician expecting to diagnose and cure, but as a person to a person." Since a prerequisite to change is self-acceptance, it is also crucial for the therapist to extend "non-judgmental acceptance" (Rogers, 1961, pp. 183-196). The practice of being present with the client and reflecting without judgment what the client presents can facilitate conditions under which the client could accept the self and behaviors, then self-assess, and eventually make desired changes.

Rogers identified several conditions he deemed necessary and sufficient for the practice of therapy (Rogers, 1946).

1. Holding to the underlying belief that the client is responsible for self, and allowing the client to maintain responsibility.

2. The client has an internal force moving toward self-actualization, and the therapist relies on that force rather than his or her skills.
3. The therapist creates a safe atmosphere allowing freedom for the client to share what he or she desires.
4. Boundaries are established for behaviors but not for attitudes.
5. The therapist implements skills that communicate acceptance, not evaluation.
6. The therapist refrains from "fixing" behaviors such as advice giving, interrogating, and blaming.

Each of these treatment conditions has a corresponding positive outcome (Rogers, 1946), and they have been adapted to other disciplines, such as business, with success (see Covey, 1989).

**Spiritual Issues.** For the Christian counselor, the Rogerian model requires some modifications. Rogers was raised in a Christian household, but he later departed from some of the beliefs of his childhood. Jones and Butman (1991) have critically examined his work and its adaptability to a Christian worldview. Some of Rogers' concepts are inconsistent with Christian teaching. For instance, he taught that authority comes from within the client rather than from God. However, Jones and Butman also observed, "Perhaps the enduring legacy of person-centered therapy for Christians will be the respect this tradition has for persons" (p. 274). In practicing the Rogerian approach, the therapist is fully present with another person and genuinely listens—traits that are consistent with treating others as people who have been created in the image of God (*imago Dei*). Christians must carefully reconstruct underlying philosophies to be consistent with a Christian worldview; however, developing skills such as empathic listening and the ability to hear confessions is certainly of value to the Christian counselor (Jas. 5:16).

Anita M. Knight

## REFERENCES


Corey, G. (1986). *Theory and Practice of Counseling and Psychotherapy* (3rd ed.). Monterey, CA: Brooks/Cole.

Covey, S. (1989). *The 7 Habits of Highly Effective People.* New York, NY: Simon & Schuster.

Ellis, A., Abrams, M., & Abrams, L. D. (2008). *Personality Theories: Critical Perspectives.* Thousand Oaks, CA: Sage.

Jones, S. L., & Butman, R. E. (1991). *Modern Psychotherapies: A Comprehensive Christian Appraisal.* Downers Grove, IL: InterVarsity Press.

Rogers, C. R. (1946). Significant aspects of client-centered therapy. *American Psychologist, 1,* 415-422.

Rogers, C.R. (1951). *Client-Centered Therapy: Its Current Practice, Implications, and Theory.* Boston, MA: Houghton Mifflin.

Rogers, C. R. (1961). *On Becoming a Person: A Therapist's View of Psychology.* New York, NY: Houghton Mifflin Harcourt.

Rogers, C. R. (1995). *Client-Centered Therapy: Its Current Practice, Implications and Theory.* London, England: Constable.


## REALITY THERAPY

**Description.** Reality therapy is an approach to counseling that focuses on helping people learn to change their behavior to maximize achievement of their wants and needs. It was developed originally by William Glasser as a therapeutic intervention in his work with juvenile delinquents; in recent years Glasser has sought to give his therapeutic approach a more solid theoretical foundation with his articulation of choice theory (Glasser, 1965, 1998). Glasser argues that all people have certain needs (such as for survival, love and belonging, independence, power or achievement, and fun) and a variety of other things we want (Corey, 2009). Glasser is quick to point out that we choose a variety of behaviors in attempts to meet our needs and wants, but the behaviors chosen (e.g., being angry, depressed, anxious) do not always serve us best in achieving these ends. Although people often resist the idea that they have chosen their anger or anxiety or depression, Glasser points out that while such painful experiences may not have been chosen directly, what lies behind these behaviors are ineffective attempts to achieve one's needs and wants.

**Application.** In reality therapy, counselors help clients articulate what it is they need or want (generally some type of better relationship or a better sense of control or choice in matters) and then help them assess how their behavior is helping or hindering achievement of this need or want. A series of questions often sets up this process: What do you want? What are you doing? Is what you are doing getting you what you want? A negative answer to the last question puts the person in a position to explore other behavioral options. In approaching problems in this manner, counselors are able to cast themselves as "in the person's corner." Counselors are mentors or guides who coach or teach their clients better behavior to more effectively achieve their wants and needs. Thus, it is a much more directive and educative therapy than client-centered or psychodynamic therapy (Corey, 2009).

In contrast to other approaches to counseling, reality therapy rejects notions of the unconscious and thus of transference and countertransference, the power of the past, including early childhood experience or trauma, and the therapeutic value of dreams. In recent years Glasser has drawn criticism for his rejection of the medical model for understanding or treating psychological problems or mental disorders. His approach is seen as too radical and dismissive of legitimate biological aspects of such problems (Corey, 2009; Tan, 2010).

Reality therapy continues to be widely used in school settings and other contexts that involve adolescents, though it has been expanded to work with a variety of problems and populations. Training in reality therapy can be obtained through the William Glasser Institute in Chatsworth, California, or the Center for Reality Therapy in Cincinnati, Ohio. Two journals focus on the dissemination of reality therapy and research associated with it: *The International Journal of Reality Therapy* and the *International Journal of Choice Theory* (Corey, 2009).

**Biblical and Spiritual Issues.** A Christian appraisal of this theory finds much to appreciate in Glasser's affirmation of the role of choice and responsibility for one's actions. Some Christians appreciate his rejection of the medical model as a guard against turning every problem, including sinfulness, into a medical illness (cf. Tan, 2010). An early influence on Glasser, O. Hobart Mowrer, also worried about the overmedicalization of psychological disorders (Glasser, 1965) and was also an early influence on Jay Adams, a pioneer of nouthetic counseling (Adams, 1970). The focus on changing one's behavior fits with a Christian emphasis on behavioral change (cf. Eph. 4: 22-32, with its list of behaviors to "put off" and "put on").

Nevertheless, choice theory and reality therapy are overly optimistic about human goodness and suffer from relativism in their ethic (e.g., who decides what is and is not good for a person?) (Jones & Butman, 1991; Tan, 2010). One also might note that changes in behavior do not necessarily mean changes in the heart (cf. McMinn, 1996).

**Stephen Parker**

## REFERENCES

Adams, J. (1970). *Competent to Counsel*. Grand Rapids, MI: Zondervan Reprint.

Corey, G. (2009). *Theory and Practice of Counseling and Psychotherapy* (8th ed.). Belmont, CA: Thomson Higher Education.

Glasser, W. (1965). *Reality Therapy: A New Approach to Psychiatry*. New York, NY: Harper & Row.

Glasser, W. (1998). *Choice Theory: A New Psychology of Personal Freedom*. New York, NY: HarperCollins.

Jones, S. L., & Butman, R. E. (1991). *Modern Psychotherapies: A Comprehensive Christian Appraisal.* Downers Grove, IL: InterVarsity Press.

McMinn, M. R. (1996). *Psychology, Theology, and Spirituality in Christian Counseling.* Wheaton, IL: Tyndale House.

Tan, S.-Y. (2010). *Counseling and Psychotherapy: A Christian Perspective.* Grand Rapids, MI: Baker Academic.

## INTEGRATIONIST PERSPECTIVE

**Description.** Christian integration encompasses integration of the Christian faith and the discipline of psychology. Christian integration is sometimes a difficult subject to understand due to the lack of a clear definition for the term. Many well-meaning Christian counselors have very different ideas about what integration is and what a Christian integrationist perspective looks like (Carter & Narramore, 1979; Crabb, 1986; Entwistle, 2010; Jones & Butman, 1991; McMinn, 1996; Tan, 2001). What are we seeking to integrate? Various combinations may include faith beliefs and spiritual or biblical principles (Crabb; McMinn); a unique worldview (Entwistle); psychology and psychological research findings (McMinn; Tan); theology and Christianity or psychotherapy (Entwistle; Tan). This complexity shows the difficulty in defining Christian integration—which provides a constant topic of discussion.

Thoughtful Christian counselors need to address a number of critical components that will bring clarity to this important topic. Numerous committed Christian authors have written great scholarly works on the topic, yet there is not a single definition that all agree upon. Jones and Butman (1991) encapsulate this argument when they write, "We do not have a definitive model to propose.... In fact, we do not believe that a definitive model exists and think it unlikely that it will ever exist" (p. 380).

**Personal Integration.** To have a Christian integrationist perspective, you must be an integrative person who has a desire for personal wholeness. Some, including Tan (2001), argue that this personal integration affects everything the Christian counselor does. Without this personal integration, the motivation to become an integrationist on other levels may be impossible. Before we can do counseling ministry or Christian psychotherapy with others, we must examine the bio-psycho-social-spiritual areas of our own lives. As mature followers of Christ, we are motivated when we realize that God desires to use us in powerful ways as we yield our talents, abilities, and passions to him (Entwistle, 2010).

**Christian Worldview.** The way we view humanity, purpose, sin, creation, the world, and God, to name a few crucial worldview areas, is very important for a Christian integrationist's perspective. As we increasingly understand these areas as revealed through God's Word, we are able to see humanity the way God sees us: created in his image (*imago Dei*), now fallen and living in a broken world, but still central in God's redemptive plan (Entwistle, 2010). Gary Collins describes these distinctions as "unique assumptions" (Collins, 1988). All Christians who seek to be integrationists should have a worldview that reflects biblical understandings of these foundational principles. Everett Worthington (2010) suggests that Christian counselors can actually understand God more accurately through the study of psychological science. In doing so, we learn about humanity, God's workmanship, and what it means to be the bearers of his image.

**Responsible Eclecticism.** Borrowing from Jones and Butman (1991), this term purposes that through our acknowledgment of the supremacy of biblical faith and truth, we also need a psychology that aids in our understanding of persons. The integrationist uses various resources, biblical knowledge, theoretical orientations, and techniques that are designed to help clients develop and nurture a healthy relationship with God and others. Clinton and Ohlschlager (2002) argue that a Christian counselor "does not use counseling techniques that would be considered immoral or inconsistent with biblical teachings.... Other techniques are distinctly Christian and would be used in Christian counseling" (p. 43). Thus, responsible eclectic Christian counselors will draw on their faith beliefs for foundational conceptions of persons and then incorporate psychological findings in a way that is systematic and logical and does not violate who they are as counselors and who their clients are. Responsible eclecticism can create avenues of intervention to confront personal and social issues, promote a message of "hope and reconciliation, and...minister grace and healing to the world" (Entwistle, 2010, p. 219). In many situations, this kind of responsible eclecticism will use one orientation as a road map while pulling from another to expand or enrich that road map (Jones & Butman, 1991).

**Spirit Influenced and Directed.** One of the core characteristics of integrationist counselors is their reliance on the leading and work of Jesus Christ through the Holy Spirit. For the Christian integrationist, there is always a third person in the counseling room: Christ. His presence not only makes Christian counseling unique but also shapes the character of the counselor. "It is He who gives the most effective counselor characteristics: love, joy, peace.... He is the comforter or helper who teaches 'all things,' reminds us of Christ's sayings, convicts people of sin, and guides into all truth" (Clinton & Ohlschlager, 2002, p. 43).

**Unique goals.** Although it is common for a therapist and a client to develop goals within the therapeutic process, the Christian integrationist goes a step further. A divine perspective is at the center for the client and determines the client's purpose. Goals such as confession of sin; forgiveness; developing Christian beliefs, values, and lifestyle; and even encouragement for clients to commit their lives to Christ are goals that reflect eternal values (Clinton & Ohlschlager, 2002). In development research performed by Dan McAdams (1998), adults were found to see their lives in terms of redemption or hope of redemption. Often, people see their lives as having been "contaminated" and in need of redemption. These two themes—*contamination* and *redemption*, and moving from the former to the latter—are central to the goals of a Christian integrationist perspective.

Victor Hinson

## REFERENCES


Carter, J. D., & Narramore, B. (1979). *The Integration of Psychology and Theology: An Introduction.* Grand Rapids, MI: Zondervan.

Clinton, T., & Ohlschlager, G. (2002). *Competent Christian Counseling: Foundations and Practice of Compassionate Soul Care.* Colorado Springs, CO: WaterBrook Press.

Collins, G. R. (1988). *Can You Trust Psychology?* Downers Grove, IL: InterVarsity Press.

Crabb, L. (1986). *Effective Biblical Counseling.* Winona Lake, IN: BMH Books.

Entwistle, D. N. (2010). *Integrative Approaches to Psychology and Christianity: An Introduction to Worldview Issues, Philosophical Foundations, and Models of Integration.* (2nd ed.) Eugene, OR: Cascade Books.

Jones, J. L., & Butman, R. E. (1991). *Modern Psychotherapies: A Comprehensive Christian Appraisal.* Downers Grove, IL: InterVarsity Press.

McAdams, D. P., & de St. Aubin, E. (Eds.). (1998). *Generativity and Adult Development: How and Why We Care for the Next Generation.* Washington, DC: American Psychological Association.

McMinn, M. (1996). *Psychology, Theology and Spirituality in Christian Counseling.* Wheaton, IL: Tyndale House.

Tan, S.-Y. (2001). Integration and beyond: Principled, professional, and personal. *Journal of Psychology and Christianity, 20,* 18-28.

Worthington, E. L., Jr. (2010). *Coming to Peace with Psychology: What Christians Can Learn from Psychological Science.* Downers Grove, IL: InterVarsity Press.


## COGNITIVE-BEHAVIORAL THERAPY

**Description.** Cognitive-behavioral therapy (CBT) combines principles originating from

B. F. Skinner and Albert Bandura (behavioral therapy) with Aaron Beck's cognitive therapy and Albert Ellis' rational emotive therapy. CBT is one of the most empirically researched therapeutic approaches, partially due to the structured model, which includes a number of observable and quantifiable behavioral strategies. CBT is a collaborative approach with the underlying therapeutic assumptions that psychological distress is a result of disturbances in cognitive processes and that changing the way one thinks results in a positive healthy change in behavior and affect. It combines a psychoeducational model, which incorporates the importance of homework assignments, with the belief that clients must play active roles in their own change both during and outside of therapy sessions. The purpose of the homework assignments is to elicit insight into the positive results of changing one's self-thoughts and how that leads to changing one's responses and behavior. In essence, CBT results in positive behavioral changes due to the collaborative therapeutic relationship between therapist and client with the focus predominantly on the recognition of unhealthy thought patterns and the client's commitment to changing these thought patterns, leading to a healthier perspective of relationships and more positive interactions.

**History and Prevalence.** Freud, often considered the father of psychology, introduced the two concepts of unconscious processes/motivation and developmental antecedents of behavior. These concepts were quite a break from the perspective of the Enlightenment, which was popular at the time. It was considered revolutionary to consider the way past events influence current emotional and behavioral responses. As the field grew and theorists such as Watson, Skinner, Pavlov, and Thorndike influenced the field, more attention was drawn to the antecedents that motivate behavior. A pure form of behaviorism was established, suggesting behavior is a direct function of reward and punishment. Albert Bandura was influential in the shift from the purest form of behaviorism by suggesting that human behavior was not simply reinforced by external stimuli, but in fact, there were unseen internal reinforcers (cognitions, or thought) to behavior. Aaron Beck and Albert Ellis are considered the most influential in the movement from behaviorism to cognitive behaviorism.

Aaron Beck developed the therapeutic approach known as *cognitive therapy*, with the primary focus on faulty thinking and the effects it has on the emotional well-being of an individual. Beck's theory evolved from his work with depressed patients. He found their depression often arose from faulty thinking patterns. Although Beck's studies had a Freudian base, he began questioning the purely psychoanalytical approach when his research suggested that depression appeared to be a result of errors in logic. The primary focus of cognitive therapy is to help clients change their distorted and faulty thinking. Once individuals are able to recognize their own faulty thinking, the therapist helps them learn how to challenge faulty belief systems against reality. This brief therapeutic approach focuses primarily on providing immediate symptom relief of current problems.

Albert Ellis, one of the first cognitive behaviorists, became disillusioned by the psychoanalytic approach because of its slow progress. He began to observe that clients progressed faster as they began changing their thought processes. From his work with clients, he developed *rational emotive behavior therapy* (REBT). The basic premise is that people respond to certain events due to their perception of that event. Therefore, changing a person's perception will help change the response. Ellis believed that individuals are born with the innate ability to think, rationally as well as irrationally, and to be constructive or destructive in their responses. His approach is to help individuals accept the inevitability of their mistakes while embracing the ability to learn to grow and adjust from these mistakes. They in turn learn healthier emotional and behavioral responses.

Ellis proposes an ABC approach to gain insight into cognitions, behavior, and change. Ellis proposes that *A* (an activating event) happens, and *B* (the person's belief, or perception) is formulated, and *C* (the emotional and behavioral consequences) occurs. The REBT approach is to *D* (dispute) the belief, changing *E* (the effect), and therefore establishing *F* (a new feeling). He emphasizes that a person's belief about an event stimulates an emotional and behavioral response; therefore, changing the perception of the event will lead to an emotional and behavioral change. The *D* is the therapeutic intervention that in turn leads to *E* and *F*.

Ellis (Corey, 2009) purports that individuals define themselves by their behavior, rating it as good or bad, worthy or unworthy. Helping individuals to understand their behavioral responses to events and to reframe environmental events empowers them to positively evaluate their internal worthiness separate from their external behavior. Emotional and behavioral responses will continue to improve as the individual continues to challenge the irrational belief system of unworthiness. Corey describes REBT as a collaborative effort between the therapist and client in choosing self-enhancing cognitive restructuring while disputing self-defeating irrational beliefs that lead to self-deprecating emotional and behavioral responses. Since the conception of REBT, other forms of CBT have evolved, such as Meichenbaum's cognitive behavior modification and a plethora of ever-evolving coping skill programs.

**Assessment and Treatment.** As stated earlier, CBT is one of the most researched therapeutic approaches. Therapists considering this technique must first fully understand the need to properly prepare the client for this highly structured interactive psychoeducational approach. The most common mistake with CBT is that a therapist is not properly trained. Corey (2009) reports that the use of CBT requires extensive training in the theoretical concepts, skills required, techniques used, and interventions needed. With these requirements, CBT is effective in working with families, adolescents, children, groups, couples, and individuals with depression and anxiety disorders. However, consideration must be given to the cognitive functioning of the individual in addition to the cultural adaptations needed (Wood, Chiu, Hwang, Jacobs, & Ifekwunigwe, 2008; Joyce, Globe, & Moody, 2006).

**Biblical and Spiritual Application.** Ellis' primary premise in REBT is that individuals define their worth by means of their behavior. Paul writes, "I know that nothing good lives in me, that is, in my sinful nature. I want to do what is right, but I can't. I want to do what is good, but I don't. I don't want to do what is wrong, but I do it anyway. But if I do what I don't want to do, I am not really the one doing wrong; it is sin in me that does it" (Rom. 7:18-20 NLT). Christian counselors can establish biblically based CBT with clients and be in complete alliance with the premise of CBT. Understanding clients' sin nature gives the Christian counselor a deeper understanding of behavior and helps clients embrace a deeper understanding of God's purpose for them. Paul wrote, "You were taught, with regard to your former way of life, to put off your old self, which is being corrupted by its deceitful desires; to be made new in the attitude of your minds; and to put on the new self, created to be like God in true righteousness and holiness" (Eph. 4:22-24). The prophet Isaiah addressed God and observed the positive impact of right thinking: "You will keep in perfect peace all who trust in you, all whose thoughts are fixed on you! Trust in the Lord always, for the Lord God, is the eternal Rock" (Isa. 26:3-4 NLT).

**Jeanne Brooks**

## REFERENCES


Corey, G. (2009). *Theory and Practice of Counseling and Psychotherapy.* Belmont, CA: Thomson Higher Education.

Joyce, T., Globe, A., & Moody, C. (2006). Assessment of the component skills for cognitive therapy in adults with intellectual disability. *Journal of Applied Research Intellectual Disabilities, 19,*17-23. doi:10.1111/j.1468-3148.2005.00287.x

Wood, J. J., Chiu, A. W., Hwang, W., Jacobs, J., & Ifekwunigwe, M. (2008). Adapting cognitive-behavioral therapy for Mexican American students with anxiety disorders: Recommendations for school psychologists. *School Psychology Quarterly, 23*(4), 515-532. doi:10.1037/1045-3830.23.4.515


## DIALECTICAL BEHAVIORAL THERAPY

**Description.** Dialectical behavior therapy (DBT) is a comprehensive cognitive-behavioral form of psychotherapy that is based on a central dialectic of change (extreme difficulty with change) and acceptance (the acceptance of circumstances, self, and others as they are) (Linehan, 1993a, 1993b). This dialectic is expanded to include the extremes of the rational mind-set vs. the emotional mind-set. The tension that exists between the two opposing forces of change and acceptance is characterized by chaotic interpersonal relationships and emotional dysregulation that can lead predisposed individuals into self-destructive and self-sabotaging behaviors.

Treatment is generally delivered in a team approach that involves four modalities: (a) individual therapy, (b) group skills training, (c) telephone consultation between sessions, and (d) DBT team consultation, all designed to establish a harmonious state of being (Linehan, 1993a). DBT has an extensive research history documenting its efficacy in several clinical trials (Linehan, Heard, & Armstrong, 1993; Linehan et al., 1999; Linehan et al., 2006).

**History.** DBT was developed and introduced as a treatment for chronically parasuicidal women by Marsha Linehan and was later published as a treatment for borderline personality disorder (Linehan, 1993a, 1993b).

**Application.** DBT addresses five core areas: (a) enhancing individual capabilities (skills training in mindfulness, emotion regulation, interpersonal effectiveness, and distress tolerance), (b) increasing motivation (individual therapy targeting and treating hindrances to motivation), (c) generalization of acquired skills (phone-contact coaching between sessions), (d) environment restructuring (therapy that involves family members who focus on modifying behavioral patterns that feed into symptoms), and (e) improvement of therapist capabilities (team meetings, case consultation, etc.) (Linehan, 1993a). The majority of research on DBT has centered on the effects of skills training (Robins & Chapman, 2004). Teaching and rehearsing new skills that enable an individual to regulate emotions can increase that individual's ability to tolerate distress without reacting on the extreme ends of the emotional spectrum (Telch, Agras, & Linehan, 2001).

Skills training includes behavioral strategies and mindful awareness (or meditation). The development of mindfulness is the core of acceptance and is an essential practice for the patient and therapist alike. This form of mindfulness is taken from Zen principles and simply teaches individuals the "awareness that emerges through paying attention on purpose, in the present moment and nonjudgmentally to the unfolding of experience moment by moment" (Kabat-Zinn, 2003, pp. 145-146).

Mindfulness in DBT teaches individuals to *observe, describe,* and *participate. Observation* requires the individual to pay attention to what is unfolding in the moment, be it a thought or feeling. Observation means to simply watch the mind in action. Individuals are taught to not push the thought or feeling away because this leads to avoiding, which triggers the visceral emotional and behavioral reactions. As clients observe what is taking place in the mind and other senses, they also *describe* or label the thought or feeling accordingly. Once they are able to observe and describe without judgment, they can allow themselves to *participate* in the action of the mind, but without emotionality. They are instructed and taught how to participate from a rational perspective, which opens the door for the brain to utilize active problem-solving strategies.

Given its utility, DBT has been modified and used in a variety of settings to treat different populations, including those with binge eating disorder (BED) and bulimia (Telch et al., 2001), depression (Lynch, Morse, Mendelson, & Robins, 2003), and attention-deficit/hyperactivity disorder (ADHD) (Hesslinger et al., 2002), as well as clients in couples counseling (Fruzzetti & Fruzzetti, 2003), to name but a few.

**Biblical and Spiritual Issues.** Many in Christian circles look upon mindfulness with suspicion. However, their apprehensions are primarily based on misunderstandings of mindfulness. Although the practice of mindfulness has been made popular by Eastern philosophy, it is not a religion, as some may think. It is also not emptying one's mind, which is a neurological impossibility. Rather, it is a tool to teach someone how to harness the power of the mind and keep it from wandering and generating thoughts and feelings that so often lead to worldliness and materialism. Being mindful is a state of being.

If we bring this concept into the context of Christianity, we understand that being a Christian is not something we do; it is who we are. Scripture uses various forms of the word *meditate* throughout the Old and New Testaments. This word means to ponder, muse, attend to. It speaks of attending to our mind and its content. In Romans 8:6, Paul explains that the mind of sinful man leads to death, but the mind controlled by the Spirit is life and peace. It is the nature of the human mind to wander and become captivated by the world. However, it takes practice to train the mind to focus on things that are true, noble, right, pure, lovely, and admirable (Phil. 4:8). Then too, Jesus tells us in Matthew 6 and 10, Mark 13, and Luke 12 that while it is the nature of the mind to worry, his followers are not to worry or fret. One might ask, how can we do this? Peace and trust don't just happen because we are believers. Rather, the peace God promises requires believers to cultivate the proper state of mind and possess the ability to stand in the midst of unpleasant events with the mind-set of hope in God's goodness, greatness, and purposes. Ultimately then, our trust in God's sovereignty and grace rests on our state of mind.

**Timothy H. Barclay**

## REFERENCES


Fruzzetti, A. E., & Fruzzetti, A. R. (2003). Dialectical behavior therapy for domestic violence: Rationale and procedures. *Cognitive and Behavioral Practice, 7*, 435-447.

Hesslinger, B., Tebartz van Elst, L., Nyberg, E., Dykierek, P., Richter, H., Berner, M., & Ebert, D. (2002). Psychotherapy of attention deficit hyperactivity disorder in adults: A pilot study using a structured skills training program. *European Archives of Psychiatry and Clinical Neuroscience, 252*, 117-184.

Kabat-Zinn, J. (2003). Mindfulness-based interventions in context: Past, present, and future. *Clinical Psychology: Science and Practice, 10*(2), 144-156.

Linehan, M. M. (1993a). *Cognitive-Behavioral Treatment of Borderline Personality Disorder.* New York, NY: Guilford.

Linehan, M. M. (1993b). *Skills Training Manual for Treating Borderline Personality Disorder.* New York, NY: Guilford.

Linehan, M. M., Comtois, K. A., Murray, A. M., Brown, M. Z., Gallop, R. J., Heard, H. L.,...Lindenboim, N. (2006). Two-year randomized controlled trial and follow-up of dialectical behavior therapy vs. therapy by experts for suicidal behaviors and borderline personality disorder. *Archives of General Psychiatry, 63*, 757-766.

Linehan, M. M., Heard, H. L., & Armstrong, H. E. (1993). Naturalistic follow-up of a behavioral treatment for chronically parasuicidal borderline patients. *Archives of General Psychiatry, 60*, 971-974.

Linehan, M. M., Schmidt, H., Dimeff, L. A., Craft, J. C., Kanter, J., & Comtois, K. A. (1999). *American Journal on Addictions, 8*(4), 279-292.

Lynch, T. R., Morse, J. O., Mendelson, T., & Robins, C. J. (2003). Dialectical behavior therapy for depressed older adults: A randomized pilot study. *American Journal of Geriatric Psychiatry, 11*, 33-46.

Robins, C. J., & Chapman, A. L. (2004). Dialectical behavior therapy: Current status, recent developments, and future directions. *Journal of Personality Disorders, 18*, 73-89.

Telch, C. F., Agras, W. S., & Linehan, M. M. (2001). Dialectical behavior therapy for binge eating disorder. *Journal of Consulting and Clinical Psychology, 69*, 1061-1065.

## NARRATIVE THERAPY

**Description.** Narrative therapy holds that human identities are shaped by the accounts of their lives found in personal stories. Most people do not understand their lives to be a series of unrelated and isolated events, but believe those events to be linked in sequence across time according to a plot. Story is a primary way in which humans organize experience, but human stories are anything but simple. They are most complicated, involving major and secondary plotlines. Narrative therapy developed in the 1970s and 1980s as a way to help clients who view their stories as problematic. Such stories are often referred to as *problem-saturated*.

Central to narrative therapy is the philosophical belief that reality is socially constructed. There is no objective, direct access to reality; therefore, reality always comes filtered through cultural realities such as family, economics, religion, and so on. These factors profoundly affect how people understand their life story (Lee, 1999; France & Uhlin, 2006). Many narrative therapists have also been influenced by the work of Michel Foucault, who linked these cultural realities with systems of power (Lee). According to Foucault, a truth claim always involves a power play, and he critiqued psychiatry in this light. By applying clinical labels, psychiatry reduces people to problems to be treated, and a diagnosis profoundly changes a person's story.

**Application.** The first step in treatment is to help a person deconstruct their problem-saturated narrative. This is accomplished by having the client pay attention to alternate plotlines in their story and to *name* the problem as they see it. Significantly, the client, rather than the therapist, must name the problem (Payne, 2006). Naming exerts power and deeply influences the story.

After the problem is named, the important work of *externalization* occurs. Externalization creates space between the person and the problem. This process achieves several things (Drewery & Winslade, 1997). First, clients begin to understand the power of dominant discourses. In this way, the clients may begin to see that their story is being authored by others. Second, clients gain greater dignity through the realization that they can be the primary agents and authors of their story. Finally, externalization deprofessionalizes problems. Clients are empowered to discuss problems in their own terms and thus take greater control of authoring their story. At this point, narrative therapy's central insight emerges: The "problem becomes the problem," and thus ends the idea that the "person is the problem" (White & Epston, 1990).

Clients can next focus on constructing *unique outcomes*. These are exceptions to the main plotline. Other, formerly unobserved parts of personal stories are brought to the foreground. Just as clients have authority to name the plot, they now may name a counterplot, that is, an alternative way to read their lives and live them. The problem is recognized but is not given power to dominate the main life plot (White & Epston, 1990).

**Spiritual issues.** Story is a primary way in which the Bible imparts God's truth. In the Old Testament, God's redemptive work is told through the stories of the patriarchs, the exodus, the prophets, and the kings. In the New Testament, the primary way that Jesus reveals God's kingdom is through the telling of stories (parables). Christians invite unbelievers to allow their stories to be formed by the story of Jesus Christ (Alexander, Silver, & Brown, 2008). Therefore, story should have immediate attraction to Christian counselors. Particular insights of narrative therapy are also in harmony with Christian concerns. The externalization of problems recognizes the broken places in clients' lives, while at the same time acknowledging that they bear God's very image. Removing the therapist from the central role can also be an important Christian insight. A more humble role helps the therapist recall that Christ alone has the power to heal broken lives. In narrative therapy, therapists are not change agents as much as they are facilitators of God's work.

In spite of these positive features, significant problems exist. Most prominent is the philosophical presupposition that all reality is socially constructed, and by implication, that any metanarrative (a narrative that seeks to interpret all reality), such as the Bible, is oppressive by its very nature. Related to this is the primary belief that clients alone can and must author their lives. Christians believe that God is ultimately the author of one's story and that healing and hope are found as that story is embraced.

In conclusion, narrative therapy offers some very helpful insights for Christian counselors, and when properly modified, can be a very fruitful way in which God's healing power is facilitated.

**Philip Jamieson**

## REFERENCES

Alexander, I., Silver, J., & Brown, J. (2008). Narrative ideas & practices in pastoral care and counseling. In R. Cook & I. Alexander (Eds.), *Interweavings: Conversations Between Narrative Therapy and Christian Faith* (pp. 194-226). North Charleston, SC: CreateSpace Books.

Drewery, W., & Winslade, J. (1997). The theoretical story of narrative therapy. In G. Monk, J. Winslade, K. Crocket, & D. Epston (Eds.), *Narrative Therapy in Practice*. San Francisco, CA: Jossey-Bass.

France, C. M., & Uhlin, B. D. (2006). Narrative as an outcome domain in psychosis. *Psychology and Psychotherapy: Theory, Research and Practice, 79*, 53-67. doi:10.1348/147608305X41001

Lee, S. (1999). Postmodernism and narrative therapy: A Christian response. *Jian Dao: A Journal of Bible and Theology, 13*, 275-296.

Payne, M. (2006). *Narrative Therapy: An Introduction for Counselors* (2nd ed.). Thousand Oaks, CA: Sage.

White, M., & Epston, D. (1990). *Narrative Means to Therapeutic Ends*. New York, NY: Norton.

## GENERAL-SYSTEMS THEORY

General-systems theory (GST) was developed in 1928 by Ludwig von Bertalanffy (1901–1972), a Hungarian biologist who proposed that the world is a holistic system of interdependent and interconnected components (Bertalanffy, 1968). GST gave counselors a radically new model for understanding families. Historically, counseling was dominated by theories that explained individual behavior in ways that failed to provide a functional framework for conceptualizing families.

A *system* is a complex organism of interacting components. Bertalanffy believed that living organisms are organized wholes; that is, no system can be explained in isolation or by the study of its individual parts. In short, the whole is greater than the sum of its parts. Like any organism, a family is a system of interacting members. Uncovering the dynamics of these interactions provides understanding for the client. The relationships among spouses, parent and child, and siblings are considered subsystems of the family system. In the same way, a family may be considered a subsystem of a church. One can also view an individual as a representation of a larger system (e.g., family), but to truly conceptualize the person, the counselor must understand the interpersonal dynamics of the family. To change one member of a family is to impact the whole system. Subsequently, GST replaced the idea of working with only one individual in counseling.

**Open or Closed.** Systems can be open or closed. An open system maintains itself with continuous inputs from and outputs to the environment. For example, a family interacts with other systems, such as the extended family, schools, and churches, receiving from and giving to the others. As a dynamic organism, the family has a symbiotic relationship with the world. Bertalanffy believed that people are not passive but active and creative, exerting control over their lives and surroundings. A closed system, however, is one in which there is no influx of energy into it. A dysfunctional family, for instance, might isolate itself from the outside world and create rigid boundaries that protect it from outside influence.

**Feedback.** The individual components of a system communicate with each other, a process referred to as "feedback" (Bateson, 1971). Systems are regulated by feedback in a circular rather than linear fashion. Linear thinking posits that *A* produces change in *B*, which produces change in *C*. In contrast, a circular system believes that *A* interacts with *B*, which interacts with *C*, which interacts with *A*. Consider the functioning of a thermostat, a device that regulates the operation of heating and cooling in a home. Once the thermostat is set to a desired temperature, the thermostat automatically turns on and off to maintain the selected temperature. This is an example of circular functioning. Feedback that reflects change or growth is known as *positive feedback*, whereas feedback that reinforces state stability is known as *negative feedback*. For example, a family engages in negative feedback when it labels a teenager's movement toward independence as bad. Therefore, counselors must carefully consider the feedback mechanisms of a family.

**Balance.** All systems seek stability or equilibrium, known as *homeostasis* (balance). Once a family has established a dynamic, the members of the system regulate their behavior in order to maintain it. This is one reason families can be so resistant to change. No matter how dysfunctional a system may be, it will work to restore its preexisting state. For example, family members may identify one member as the *identified patient* or *scapegoat* to take attention off the real problem. Though the scapegoat is identified as the problem, GST understands that the role of the scapegoat is to stabilize the system and maintain the preexisting state of balance.

**Equifinality.** Finally, according to the principle of *equifinality*, more than one set of events can lead to a certain end state. That is, many paths can achieve the same outcome. Families develop characteristically repetitive patterns of communication so that regardless of how a situation starts, it will end with the same outcome. For example, different parenting approaches can produce children who all behave in an appropriate manner. In essence, there is no single way or path to becoming a functional or dysfunctional family (the outcome).

**Conclusion.** GST revolutionized the field of counseling in general and influenced family counseling in two ways. It provided a conceptual framework that can be used to understand and explain family functioning, and it birthed many methods that can be used to alter family dynamics.

John C. Thomas

### REFERENCES

Bateson, G. (1971). A systems approach. *International Journal of Psychiatry, 9*, 242-244.

Von Bertalanffy, L. (1968). *General Systems Theory*. New York, NY: Braziller.

## EMOTION-FOCUSED THERAPY

What should a counselor focus on to bring about meaningful and lasting change in a client's life? Counselors' theories and therapeutic models guide their assumptions regarding what determines unhealthiness and what fosters wholeness and change. For example, cognitive therapists propose that faulty cognitions and beliefs fuel unhealthy ways of reacting and being, so therapy should aim to change beliefs and identify distorted thinking. Behaviorists, guided by learning theory, aim to change the unproductive behaviors while increasing more adaptive and productive behaviors.

**History.** In the 1980s, South African–born Les Greenberg and Canadian Susan Johnson (both trained in client-centered and Gestalt therapy) began to realize that the role of emotion was vitally important in the process of change but was missing in most therapeutic models. In contrast to cognitive therapy, Greenberg and Johnson named their emerging model *emotion-focused therapy* (EFT). During the past 20 years, emotion-focused therapy has brought a profound shift by highlighting the importance of emotions in bringing about change. EFT is modified to work with both individuals (Greenberg, 2002) and couples (Johnson, 2004). The safe-haven model, conceptualized by Sharon May, is the integration of EFT and Christian principles.

**Application.** The theory of emotions states that emotions are God-given and serve a powerful purpose. Emotions provide information regarding ourselves and our world, priming us to move to action. For example, when we are afraid, we are primed to flee the perceived danger; when we are sad, we are primed to cry for what is lost; and when we are angry, we are primed to attack to protect a violated boundary (Johnson & Greenberg, 1994).

Of the different kinds of emotions, primary emotions are said to be our core heart emotions—the first emotions we feel in a situation. Secondary emotions are protective emotions—they are what we feel when a primary emotion arises. For example, instead of feeling vulnerable and sad when your friend ignores you, you feel angry. Your anger helps you manage and protect yourself from the vulnerable state of sadness. All emotions can serve an adaptive or maladaptive role. Adaptive emotions help orient and guide you through the maze of life, relationships, and the world around you. According to Les Greenberg, if you are unaware of and don't have access to your primary emotions, you are left disoriented, missing a very important piece of information that can provide wisdom as well as direction for your life.

Emotion-focused couples therapy (EFCT), as conceptualized by Susan Johnson, is rooted in attachment theory and states that when a couple's relational bond is threatened, powerful emotions fuel negative interactional patterns that hinder a secure attachment bond. For example, if a wife feels ignored by her husband, strong primary emotions arise, causing her to feel sad, rejected, and alone. In a securely attached couple, a wife is able to share the sadness of feeling rejected in a clear and congruent manner. Her husband is able to hear her cry and move toward her to comfort and repair the rupture. But in a distressed couple, a wife often shares her secondary emotion, as found in the research of John Gottman (2011), in a form of a criticism with a harsh start-up. For example, she might place her hands on her hips and in a harsh tone snarl, "What is wrong with you? Are you going to watch television all night?" Her husband hears her criticism and responds to it, unaware of her tender primary emotions of sadness and longing to be close to him for the evening. He then defends himself while she ups the ante in an attempt to persuade him that a real problem exists in the relationship. In reaction, he withdraws, concluding that he can't persuade her otherwise. If a couple is unable to repair the conflict, they get stuck in a negative and rigid pursue-withdraw cycle, leaving each hurt and protective, unable to be emotionally engaged or responsive to each other's attachment needs and longings. Over time this creates an insecure attachment bond between the couple.

EFCT is the most well-researched and empirically validated marital model. In a meta-analysis (Johnson, Hunsley, Greenberg, & Schindler, 1999), EFCT showed an effect size of 1.3, where 90% of couples reported a significant improvement and a 70% to 73% recovery rate from marital distress in only 10 to 12 couple-counseling sessions. This is meaningful in contrast to the 35% recovery rate for those receiving couples counseling based on behavioral interventions (Jacobson & Addis, 1993). Research has also found that couples continued to improve even after counseling ended.

The goal in EFCT is to access and reprocess emotional responses to create new interactional patterns that foster a safe and secure attachment bond (Johnson & Greenberg, 1994). This is accomplished by focusing on the here-and-now experiences of a couple and skillfully moving within each spouse's experience (intrapsychic) and the systemic patterns between the couple (interpersonal). Each person's inner emotional experiences are used to choreograph new interactional patterns, ones that promote a more secure attachment bond.

**Nine-Step Model.** There are nine clear yet fluid steps to guide a counselor through the therapeutic process.

1. To begin, a thorough history of the couple is gathered while the therapeutic relationship is developed. Suitability for EFT is assessed because EFT is not effective if there is abuse, incompatible agendas, or inability to take responsibility for oneself.

2. As a couple interacts, their issues and their interactional pattern (the cycle they get stuck in) are identified.

3. Primary emotions and unexpressed feelings that fuel the interactional pattern are accessed. An angry pursuer often fears rejection, abandonment, worthlessness, and insecurity. A cold withdrawer fears inadequacy, helplessness, and shame.

4. The relationship conflict and problems are expanded and reframed not as the other person's faulty character but rather as part of the rigid cycle hindering each person's attachment needs from being met. This reframing defuses much of the hurt, fear, and anger.

5. The withdrawn partner enters this process first, with the pursuer following. Both partners connect to their primary emotions and fears and take responsibility for their ways of dealing with these fears. This awareness moves them to new, more accessible positions, allowing them to risk sharing their attachment needs and vulnerabilities.

6. Each partner has had years of hurt and disappointment, so sharing a new, more vulnerable experience can be disorienting to the spouse. Fostering acceptance is key to this step.

7. In this step, needs and wants are expressed, and each spouse is able to ask for comfort from a more vulnerable position. In this way the pursuer softens and the withdrawer engages.

8. From a more accessible and responsive position, the couple is able to explore solutions to their problems.

9. The new interactional pattern is solidified as the couple constructs a testimony of their journey from distress to a safe haven.

Sharon G. May

## REFERENCES

Elliott R., Watson, J., Goldman, R., & Greenberg, L. (2004). *Learning Emotion Focused Therapy.* Washington, DC. American Psychological Association.

Gottman, J. (2011). *The Science of Trust: Emotional Attunement for Couples.* New York, NY: Norton.

Greenberg, L. (2002). *Emotion-Focused Therapy: Coaching Clients to Work Through Feelings.* Washington, DC. American Psychological Association Press.

Greenberg, L. S., & Goldman, R. (2008). *Emotion-Focused Couples Therapy: The Dynamics of Emotion, Love and Power.* Washington, DC: American Psychological Association.

Jacobson, N. S., & Addis, M. E. (1993). Research on couples and couples therapy: What do we know? Where are we going? *Journal of Consulting and Clinical Psychology, 61,* 85-93.

Jacobson, N. S., & Christensen, A. (1998). *Acceptance and Change in Couple Therapy: A Therapist's Guide to Transforming Relationships.* New York, NY: Norton.

Johnson, S. M. (2004). *The Practice of Emotionally Focused Marital Therapy: Creating Connection* (2nd ed.). New York, NY: Brunner/Routledge.

Johnson, S. M., Bradley, B., Furrow, J., Lee, A., Palmer, G. (2005). *Becoming an Emotionally Focused Couple Therapist: The Work Book.* New York, NY: Brunner/Routledge.

Johnson, S., & Greenberg, L. (Eds.). (1994). *The Heart of the Matter: Emotion in Marriage and Marital Therapy.* New York, NY: Bruner Mazel.

Johnson, S. M., Hunsley, J., Greenberg, L., & Schindler, D. (1999). Emotionally focused couples therapy: Status & challenges. *Clinical Psychology: Science & Practice, 6,* 67-79.

May, S., & Hart, A. D. (2004). *Safe Haven Marriage: Building a Relationship You Want to Come Home To.* Nashville, TN: Nelson

## INTERPERSONAL PSYCHOTHERAPY

Interpersonal psychotherapy (IPT) is a relatively brief (less than 20 sessions), highly structured and manualized treatment developed by Gerald Klerman and Myrna Weissman in the 1980s and originally designed as a treatment for depression (Weissman, Prusoff, & DiMascio, 1979). Unlike Aaron Beck's cognitive therapy for depression, which focuses on identifying and restructuring cognitive distortions, IPT focuses on addressing interpersonal issues involved in depression. IPT has no specific psychological theory but instead draws from theorists such as Sullivan (1968), Meyer (2004), and Bowlby (1969), whose theories discuss the role of disordered relationship factors in psychopathology. Bowlby and other attachment theorists address the role of unresolved loss and grief in the development and maintenance of depression.

**Four Domains.** The specific focus of IPT is on conceptualizing the client's psychopathology (such as depression or bulimia) in terms of four types of social functioning problem domains:

1. *Interpersonal disputes* have to do with relationship conflicts. These conflicts are usually within the realm of close relationships, such as with friends, parents, romantic partners, or associates in the workplace. Some conflicts can be overt, filled with open hostility, arguments, and criticism. Other conflicts are more covert, with unspoken anger and resentment. In a third kind of dispute, someone emotionally and/or physically separates from another person, refusing to even speak to that person.

2. *Role transitions* identify and address positive and negative life events. Positive events can be normal developmental transitions, such as graduating from high school or college, getting married, or having children. Negative events include dropping out of high school or college, getting divorced, or losing a job. Either type of event can trigger feelings of insecurity and sadness, which may eventuate in a full-blown depression.

3. *Unresolved grief* is a sense of loss due to the death of a loved one. Many people do not allow themselves to fully grieve and experience the accompanying sadness and feelings of loss associated with death. In some cases, the depression may not start until several years after the death, when another stressor (interpersonal dispute or role transition) triggers the unresolved grief. For instance, a client may come to therapy with depression that appears to be directly tied to a recent dispute

with her mother, but in reality, the dispute triggered the unresolved loss she had from losing her grandfather six months prior.

4. *Interpersonal deficits* relate to impoverishments in close relationships that can be both the cause and the consequences of depression. The deficits can be related to difficulties with using assertiveness, good communication skills, and micro-communication skills, such as reading and responding to others' nonverbal signals.

**Therapy Techniques.** Interpersonal psychotherapy focuses on helping patients identify which of the four interpersonal issues should be the focus of therapy. The focus usually targets one area, and therapists develop a collaborative therapeutic alliance. The treatment relationship is an important component of the therapy process; however, virtually no attention is directed to addressing therapeutic resistance or dealing with negative transference issues. IPT uses a variety of therapy techniques, many of which are borrowed from cognitive therapy, behavioral therapy, and crisis intervention approaches (Elkin et al., 1989). Skills include collaborative agenda setting, clarification, empathic listening, role playing, communication analysis, and the encouragement of affect. This last skill is very important for helping clients deal with anger, resentment, and especially unresolved grief and loss.

**Effectiveness.** IPT has been researched in a number of large-scale outcome studies and has been shown to be effective for both depression and bulimia (Fairburn, Jones, Peveler, Hope, & O'Connor, 1993; Kupfer et al., 1992; Frank et al., 1990). With depression, it has gone head-to-head with both cognitive therapy and antidepressants and been found to be at least as effective as the other two treatments. The effects with bulimia were not quite as robust as for depression, but it still looks promising.

Gary A. Sibcy

### REFERENCES

Bowlby, J. (1969). Attachment. *Attachment and Loss* (Vol. 1, 2nd ed.). New York, NY: Basic Books.

Elkin, I., Shea, M. T., Watkins, J. T., Imber, S. D., Sotsky, S. M., Collins, J. F.,...Docherty, J. P. (1989). National institute of mental health treatment of depression collaborative research program: General effectiveness of treatments. *Archives of General Psychiatry, 46*, 971-982.

Fairburn C. G., Jones R., Peveler, R. C., Hope R. A., & O'Connor, M. (1993). Psychotherapy and bulimia nervosa: the longer term effects of interpersonal psychotherapy, behavior therapy, and cognitive behavior therapy. *Archives of General Psychiatry, 50*, 419-428.

Frank, E., Kupfer, D. J., Perel, J. M., Cornes, C., Jarrett, D. B., Mallinger, A. G.,...Grochocinski, V. J. (1990). Three-year outcomes for maintenance therapies in recurrent depression. *Archives of General Psychiatry, 47*, 1093-1099.

Kupfer, D. J., Frank, E., Perel, J. M., Cornes, C., Mallinger, A. G., Thase, M. E.,...Grochocinski, V. J. (1992). Five-year outcomes for maintenance therapies in recurrent depression. *Archives of General Psychiatry, 49*, 769-773.

Meyer, D. G. (2004). Theories of emotion. *Psychology* (7th ed.). New York, NY: Worth.

Sullivan, H. S. (1968). *The Interpersonal Theory of Psychiatry.* New York, NY: Norton.

Weissman M. M., Prusoff , B. A., & DiMascio, A. (1979). The efficacy of drugs and psychotherapy in the treatment of acute depressive episodes. *American Journal of Psychiatry, 136*, 555-558.

## EMDR PRACTICE

Eye movement desensitization and reprocessing (EMDR) is a successful method for treating trauma. It rapidly and effectively releases anxiety, disturbing emotions, and negative thoughts associated with trauma. "It is a complex and powerful method of psychotherapy that integrates many of the most successful elements of a wide range of therapeutic approaches. In addition, it uses eye movements or other forms of rhythmical stimulation, such as hand taps or tones, in a way that seems to assist the brain's information processing system to proceed at a rapid rate" (Shapiro & Forrest, 2004, pp. 4-5). EMDR therapists are trained to focus on potential dangers of unexpected flashbacks or overload. It is a powerful tool that creates connections between current anxiety and childhood or adult trauma, and it should be conducted only by trained therapists.

**History.** EMDR was developed by Francine Shapiro in 1989, when she "noticed that the upsetting emotions accompanying disturbing thoughts disappeared as her eyes moved rapidly back and forth" (Shapiro & Forrest, 2004, p. 270). Researchers performed neuroimaging on patients with posttraumatic stress disorder (PTSD) and consistently found structural and functional changes in the brain regions associated with emotions and memory (Gurvits, Shenton, Hokama, & Ohta, 1996; Bremner, 1999; Hull, 2002; Gilbertson et al., 2002; Francati, Vermetten, & Bremner, 2007). EMDR stimulates cerebellar processing and activates the dorso-lateral and orbito-frontal cortices via the optical region (Bergmann, 2000). This region is responsible for sensory interpretation and involved with memory and emotional processing associated in the hippocampus and amygdala (Carlson, 2007). EMDR permits neutral processing by low-frequency stimulation of the brain, thus modifying memories in a safe environment (Rasolkhani-Kalhorn & Harper, 2006). After EMDR, brain scans found increased activity in both the anterior cingulated gyrus and the left prefrontal cortex in patients, which are responsible for discriminating between imagined and real fears (Levin, Lazrove, & van der Kolk, 1999; Oh & Choi, 2007). Therefore, the objective evidence of brain scans shows the effectiveness of EMDR in reprocessing traumatic events effectively.

**Treatment.** Two research psychiatrists who have focused on trauma and brain functioning, Bessel van der Kolk and Daniel Amen, have both demonstrated the efficacy of EMDR, documenting case studies of clients with PTSD who were treated with EMDR and displayed "marked normalization" of brain activity (Amen, 1998, p. 183). Van der Kolk also conducted neuroimaging after cognitive-behavioral therapy without EMDR and demonstrated its failure to create significant brain activity changes (van der Kolk, 2002).

Some have questioned if EMDR elicits accurate childhood memories. To date, there has not been sufficient research to validate the truth of memories. Because perceptions of trauma create the disturbance, information is only as accurate as the individual's discernment. Anxiety can originate from fears rather than from actual incidents. Therefore, memories may be a combination of fears and events and are not to be taken as literal or accurate without validation. There has been no evidence that EMDR implants false memories. In fact, there is no therapeutic method that is less suggestive, because all of the initial information and the ongoing connections come from the client (McDonald, 1995). Some people have equated EMDR to hypnosis as an altered state of consciousness, which would make it inadmissible in court. However, it is often advisable to delay EMDR until court proceedings are completed because the lack of anxiety and reaction to a trauma may decrease the believability of a testimony.

By 2004, approximately 20,000 psychotherapists had been trained in EMDR, and more than one million individuals had been helped (Shapiro & Forrest, 2004). Shapiro found that 84% to 90% of PTSD clients suffering from the trauma of rape, natural disasters, loss of a child, catastrophic illness, and the like no longer meet the criteria for PTSD after three EMDR sessions. Other psychological methods addressing trauma achieved 55% success rate in seven to fifteen sessions (Shapiro & Forrest, 2004).

**Biblical and Spiritual Issues.** EMDR poses no spiritual challenges. On the contrary, EMDR can be used by trained therapists through the power and direction of the Holy Spirit. "The Spirit of the Lord God is upon me, because the Lord has anointed me to bring good news to the suffering and afflicted. He has sent me to comfort the broken-hearted, to announce liberty to captives.... he will give: beauty for ashes; joy instead of mourning; praise instead of heaviness" (Is. 61:1,3 TLB). (Editor's note: The clinical practice of EMDR is not approved by the American Psychological Association. Visit www.apa.org for more information.)

**Arlys McDonald**

## REFERENCES


Amen, D. G. (1998). *Change Your Brain, Change Your Life: The Breakthrough Program for Conquering Anxiety, Depression, Obsessiveness, Anger, and Impulsiveness.* New York, NY: Random House.

Bergmann, U. (2000). Further thought on the neurobiology of EMDR: The role of the cerebellum in accelerated information processing. *Traumatology, 6,* 175-200.

Bremner, J. (1999). Does stress damage the brain? *Biological Psychiatry, 45*(7), 797-805.

Carlson, N. R. (2007). *Physiology of Behavior* (9th ed.). Boston, MA: Allyn & Bacon.

Francati, V. V., Vermetten, E. E., & Bremner, J. D. (2007). Functional neuroimaging studies in posttraumatic stress disorder: Review of current methods and findings. *Depression & Anxiety, 24*(3), 202-218.

Gilbertson, M. W., Shenton, M. E., Ciszewski, A., Kasai, K., Lasko, N. B., Orr, S. P., & Pitman, R. K. (2002). Smaller hippocampal volume predicts pathologic vulnerability to psychological trauma. *Nature Neuroscience, 5*(11), 1242.

Gurvits, T. V., Shenton, M. E., Hokama, H., & Ohta, H. (1996). Magnetic resonance imaging study of hippocampal volume in chronic, combat-related posttraumatic stress disorder. *Biological Psychiatry, 40*(11), 1091-1099.

Hull, A. M. (2002). Neuroimaging findings in posttraumatic stress. *British Journal of Psychiatry, 181*(2), 102-110.

Levin, P., Lazrove, S., & van der Kolk, B. (1999). What psychological testing and neuroimaging tell us about the treatment of posttraumatic stress disorder by eye movement desensitization and reprocessing. *Journal of Anxiety Disorders, 13*(1-2), 159-172.

McDonald, A. N. (1995). *Repressed Memories: Can You Trust Them?* Grand Rapids, MI: Revell.

Oh, D., & Choi, J. (2007). Changes in the regional cerebral perfusion after eye movement desensitization and reprocessing: A SPECT study of two cases. *Journal of EMDR Practice and Research, 1*(1), 24-30.

Rasolkhani-Kalhorn, T., & Harper, M. L. (2006). EMDR and low frequency stimulation of the brain. *Traumatology, 12*(1), 9-24.

Shapiro, F., & Forrest, M. S. (2004). *EMDR: The Breakthrough Therapy for Overcoming Anxiety, Stress, and Trauma* (pp. 4-8, 270-271). New York, NY: Basic Books.

Van der Kolk, B. A. (2002). Posttraumatic therapy in the age of neuroscience. *Psychoanalytic Dialogues, 12*(3), 381.


## ECLECTICISM

**Description.** Eclecticism refers to the metatheoretical integration of the best principles embedded in the many schools of psychotherapy that have proliferated over the past quarter-century. *Merriam-Webster's Collegiate Dictionary* defines eclecticism as the "method of selecting what seems best from various systems." Brammer and Shostrom (1982) defined therapeutic eclecticism as the "process of selecting concepts, methods, and strategies from a variety of current theories which work" (p. 35). It has become a serious research challenge in the 21st century—delineating both specified techniques and common relationship factors—fueled by the desire to bring about the best outcomes for particular clients. In fact, it could be argued that the major difference between eclecticism and schoolism (see below) is that schoolism attempts to fit the patient to one's preferred model of therapy, while eclecticism, at its best, involves fitting the therapy to the particular needs of the client.

*Schoolism* is the adherence to one primary theory of understanding in treating clients. It dominated the early field of psychotherapy. By the 1980s, hundreds of theories were present. When justifying the need for the periodic revision of his classic textbook, *Current Psychotherapies*, Corsini (2007) maintained that the field of psychotherapy was in constant ferment. Systems of psychotherapy were constantly fading, changing, splitting, and synthesizing. He went on to say, "New ideas, new concepts, new views which amount to complete new systems, arise" (p. ix). Prochaska and Norcross (2010, p. 1) count more than 400 systems of psychotherapy.

Norcross and Wogan (1983) expressed some concern regarding the burgeoning number of theories and models but concluded that there was something healthy about this pluralism because of all the people being helped. Evidence has accumulated that psychotherapy is effective (Cavanagh, 1982; Beutler, 1983; Norcross, 1986), but with this knowledge of effectiveness has come appreciation for the fact that different treatment strategies have essentially the same impact on a wide variety of clients (Beutler). Additionally, Fiedler's (1950a, 1950b) classic studies indicated that although experienced psychotherapists identified theoretically with one school or another, in practice they all did virtually the same thing with their clients. Smith and Glass (1977) surveyed a large number of research studies devoted to the theoretical differences between schools of psychotherapy and concluded that the results of research demonstrate negligible differences in the effects produced by different therapy types. Unconditional judgments of the superiority of one type or another of psychotherapy, and all that these claims imply about treatment and training policy, are unjustified (p. 760).

This appreciation of equivalent impact and shared methodologies has led researchers to split their efforts, exemplified by the differing agendas of Division 12 (specifying empirically supported practice or techniques) and Division 29 (delineating the various common factors of the psychotherapy relationship) of the American Psychological Association. The cutting-edge research in the field has effectively moved from schools of therapy to the specification of different treatment effects and to the discovery of the various relationship elements that are held in common by various theories and techniques.

In summary, wholesale commitment to a particular school of therapy is becoming a rarity. The sibling rivalry among orientations that characterized the early schoolism of psychotherapy, and generated what Larson (1980) called a "dogma eat dogma" environment, has become largely a thing of the past. This shift has given birth to eclecticism. "Clinicians of all persuasions are increasingly seeking a rapprochement of various systems and an integration of therapeutic intervention. Eclecticism has become the modal orientation of psychologists, with between one-third and one-half ascribing to it" (Norcross, 1986, p. 4). Nicholson and Golsan (1983) maintained that "eclecticism is an essential perspective for dealing with the complexity of human problems" (p. 25). Eclecticism has provided a breadth of orientation that is vital for counselors who seek to service a diverse clientele. The need for such breadth has been cited by many current writers.

**Application.** Brammer (1969) cautioned, "Using the term *eclectic* to label one's counseling point of view is still likely to incur accusations from some colleagues of being naïve, lazy, confused, or deluded" (p. 192). Smith (1982) suggested, "Although the eclectic model allows for openness and flexibility, it also encourages an indiscriminate selection of bits and pieces from diverse sources that results in a hodgepodge of inconsistent concepts and techniques" (p. 802). Ward (1983) cautioned therapists about the dangers inherent in operating "without guidelines to structure counseling and to govern the appropriate selection and application of theoretical demands, strategies, and techniques" (p. 23).

Many leaders have cautioned against an indiscriminate, hodgepodge approach to selecting whatever seems useful for a particular client. Beutler (1983) maintained, "While the current movement toward eclecticism is an improvement over earlier approaches to psychotherapy, it will still be some years before research can validate the many approaches advocated for working with specific clients" (p. 3). Corey (2005) warned, "An undisciplined eclectic approach can be an excuse for failing to develop a sound rationale for systematically adhering to certain concepts and to the techniques that are extensions of them" (p. 2). He feared therapists would pick and choose pieces from a variety of therapies that merely served to support their own biases. Egan (1986) shared this concern about counselors randomly borrowing ideas. He maintained, "Helpers need a conceptual framework that enables them to borrow ideas, methods, and techniques systematically from all theories, schools, and approaches and integrate them into their own theory and practice of helping" (p. 9).

Although the influence of eclecticism continues to grow, such cautions have given rise to the desire to replace the term *eclecticism* with other terms. Smith (1982) stated, "There seems to be a growing dissatisfaction with the traditional label 'eclecticism.' Current literature on counseling and psychotherapy indicates a trend in the direction of creative synthesis, masterful or theoretical integration, and systematic eclecticism" (p. 802). Ivey (1980) predicted that within five years both theoretical exclusiveness and lazy eclecticism would lose favor, giving way to systematic metatheoretical approaches that stressed matching therapies with individual differences and conditions.

Lazarus (1993) called for the development of a responsible eclecticism that is tied to clinical research—to fit the therapy to the client rather than the other way around. He maintained that multimodal therapists constantly ask, "What works, for whom, and under which particular circumstances?" (as cited in Corsini & Wedding, 2007, p. 373). Lazarus (1993) felt that this was not what most practitioners actually did. The client usually got what the therapist usually administered and thought best, but this could, in fact, be exactly what the client did *not* need. Multimodal therapists deliberately attempted to determine what type of interactive posture would best fit the particular client, placing a heavy emphasis on therapeutic flexibility. No single way could be viewed as the best approach to all clients.

**Biblical and spiritual issues.** Christian counselors—especially generalist practitioners—have often embraced eclecticism to increase their capacities for serving a widening variety of clients. McMinn & Campbell (2007) point out a potential danger for Christians possessed by the eclectic spirit when they remind us, "It was not uncommon to read that psychology and theology should both have an equal footing for true integration to occur" (p. 25). So how should the counselor who wishes to be true to the Bible and yet utilize insights from psychology proceed? Jones and Butman (1991) insist, "It is reasonable at this point in history for Christian counselors to be eclectic in their approach, drawing first on the faith for the foundation of a view of persons and then elaborating on that view with conceptions taken from secular psychology" (p. 380). Christians may benefit greatly from a thoughtful eclecticism when the effort is based on the foundation that "Christianity—informed by scripture and responsible theological appraisal—is trump" (McMinn & Campbell, p. 25).

**Ron Hawkins**
**George Ohlschlager**

## REFERENCES

Beutler, L. E. (1983). *Eclectic Psychotherapy: A Systematic Approach.* New York, NY: Pergamon.

Brammer, L. M. (1969). Eclecticism revised. *Personnel and Guidance Journal, 48,* 192-197.

Brammer, L. M., & Shostrom, E. L. (1982). *Therapeutic Psychology: Fundamentals of Counseling and Psychotherapy* (4th ed.). Englewood Cliffs, NJ: Prentice-Hall.

Cavanagh, M. (1982). *The Counseling Experience: A Theoretical and Practical Approach.* Pacific Grove, CA: Brooks/Cole.

Corey, G. (2005). *Theory and Practice of Counseling and Psychotherapy.* Monterey, CA: Brooks/Cole.

Corsini, R. J. (2007). *Current Psychotherapies.* Itasca, IL: F. E. Peacock.

Corsini, R. J., & Wedding, D. (2007). *Current Psychotherapies* (8th ed.). Belmont, CA: Brooks/Cole.

Egan, G. (1986). *The Skilled Helper* (3rd ed.). Monterey, CA: Brooks/Cole.

Fiedler, F. E. (1950a). The concept of the ideal therapeutic relationship. *Journal of Consulting Psychology, 14,* 239-245.

Fiedler, F. E. (1950b). A comparison of therapeutic relationships in psychoanalytic, non-directive and Adlerian therapy. *Journal of Consulting Psychology, 14,* 436-445.

Garfield, S. L. (1980). *Psychotherapy: An Eclectic Approach.* Hoboken, NJ: Wiley & Sons.

Ivey, A. (1980). Counseling 2000: Time to take charge! *The Counseling Psychologist, 8*(4), 12-16.

Jones, S. L., & Butman, R. E. (1991). *Modern Psychotherapies.* Downers Grove, IL: InterVarsity Press.

Larson, D. (1980). Therapeutic schools, styles, and schoolism: A national survey. *Journal of Humanistic Psychology, 20,* 3-20.

Lazarus, A. A. (1993). Tailoring the therapeutic relationship, or being an authentic chameleon. *Psychotherapy, 30*(3), 404-407.

McMinn, M. R., & Campbell, C. D. (2007). *Integrative Psychotherapy: Toward a Comprehensive Christian Approach.* Downers Grove, IL: InterVarsity Press.

Nicholson, J. A., & Golsan, G. (1983). *The Creative Counselor.* New York, NY: McGraw-Hill.

Norcross, J. C. (Ed.). (1986). *Handbook of Eclectic Psychotherapy.* New York, NY: Brunner/Mazel.

Norcross, J. C., & Wogan, M. (1983). Relationship of behavior therapists' characteristics, activities, and clients to reported practices in therapy. *Professional Psychology: Research and Practice, 14*(1), 44-56. doi:10.1037/0735-7028.14.1.44

Prochaska, J. O., & Norcross, J. C. (2010). *Systems of Psychotherapy: A Transtheoretical Analysis* (7th ed.). Pacific Grove, CA: Brooks/Cole.

Smith, D. (1982). Trends in counseling and psychotherapy. *American Psychologist, 37*(7) 802-809. doi: 10.1037/0003-066X.37.7.802

Smith, M. L., & Glass, G. V. (1977). Meta-analysis of psychotherapy outcome studies. *American Psychologist, 32,* 752-760.

Ward, D. E. (1983). The trend toward eclecticism and the development of a comprehensive model to guide counseling and psychotherapy. *Personnel and Guidance Journal, 62,* 154-157.

## THINKING/FEELING/ACTING PARADIGM

**Description.** The thinking/feeling/acting (TFA) model is a heuristic attribution model of the person—one that facilitates personal or intrapsychic change in the application of counseling or psychotherapy. First proposed by Alfred Adler (1963) and popularized into counselor education by the systematic counseling model of David Hutchins (1984), the TFA model has been used in a wide variety of counseling modes and applications. Recently, in response to the fourth wave of multiculturalism, the model has been expanded by some as the TFAC model—in which C stands for cultural context.

TFA concepts have gained a highly prominent place in the model building and writing of many counselor theoreticians and educators, and also among some of the prominent builders of models of personality. TFA is sometimes viewed as a more useful form of *systematic eclecticism,* and model builders of all kinds of theoretical persuasions have found referencing thoughts, feelings, and behavior to be a near-universal language that is commonly understood in psychotherapy and, more broadly, in the behavioral and social sciences (Hawkins, 1988; Hutchins, 1984; Seligman, 2004).

**TFA in Assessment.** In its simplest form, TFA is understood as the causal chain—and as the description of the *systemic cycle of action*—whereby what one thinks influences one's behavior, which influences what one feels (Seligman & Reichenberg, 2009). Systemically, actions may loop around to influence thinking—and the cycle goes on and on.

For example, the disclosure of depression by a client often reveals these components of the TFA model:

- *feelings*: anxiety or numbness or dread
- *action*: psychomotor retardation, withdrawal, listlessness
- *thinking*: worthless/helpless/hopeless triad—"I am worthless." "I can't do this." "The situation is hopeless."

**Treatment applications.** If thinking is targeted for intervention, you might train clients to increase awareness and intervene with themselves when they catch the triad of depressive thinking in their self-talk. For instance, they might dispute worthless talk by saying out loud, "I *feel* worthless, but the

Bible says that I'm greatly loved and cherished by God," or "I can't do this, but in Christ, I'm strong, and can learn to do this in his power."

Used prominently in addictions work and as a part of the A.A. rendition of "stinkin' thinkin'," the TFA model may look like this:

- *feelings*: euphoria and escape; then, crash and despondency
- *action*: repetitive ritual around obtaining/preparing/abusing alcohol or drugs
- *thinking*: automatic thoughts triggered by external, unresolved stressor or relationship problem—"I can't stand this," or "I've got to get outta here," or "I need a fix."

Awareness of these automatic thoughts can be taught as cues for coping behavior of a different sort: "Uh-oh, I'd better call my sponsor right now," or "Wow, that's my cue to go to the Y and find a pickup game of basketball."

The TFA model is an excellent tool for assessment and analysis that assist clients to a greater understanding of their patterns of addiction or ritual behaviors. Instead of viewing the "vicious cycle" or the "fog of addiction" as a single noninterrupted experience, both counselor and client are helped by the TFA model to break out the cycle or process in an understandable way. Such analysis also gives both counselor and client ideas for breaking into and changing that cycle at any point of thought/feelings/behavior that is amenable to change.

As the client takes change-related action, the TFA model can then be used to show the effects of such action on each part of the system. This is why this model is so heuristic—it is very practical, understandable, and adaptable across a wide range of interventions and action strategies. This is also why it has been applied in so many fields beyond counseling, including education and business.

Ron Hawkins
George Ohlschlager

## REFERENCES

Adler, A. (1963). *The Practice and Theory of Individual Psychology*. Patterson, NJ: Littlefield.

Clinton, T., & Ohlschlager, G. (2002). *Competent Christian Counseling: Foundations and Practice of Compassionate Soul Care*. Colorado Springs, CO: WaterBrook Press.

Hawkins, R. (1988). *The Assessment of Behavior Patterns, Personality Characteristics, and Theoretical Orientations for Master's Level Counseling Students* (Unpublished doctoral dissertation). Blacksburg, VA: Virginia Polytechnic Institute and State University.

Hutchins. D. (1984). Improving the counseling relationship. *The Personnel and Guidance Journal, 62*(10), 572-575.

Seligman, L. (2004). *Treatment Planning in Counseling* (3rd ed.). New York, NY: Kluwer Academic/Plenum.

Seligman, L., & Reichenberg, L. W. (2009). *Theories of Counseling and Psychotherapy: Systems, Strategies and Skills*. Saddle River, NJ: Prentice Hall.

## MULTIMODAL THERAPY

**Description.** The multimodal framework emphasizes the discrete and interactive impact of seven modalities—behavior, affect, sensation, imagery, cognition, interpersonal relationships, and drugs (and other biological interventions)—which can be easily remembered using the mnemonic acronym BASIC ID (taken from the initial letters of the modalities). Multimodal therapists will employ empirically supported techniques or refer out to experts, when feasible and necessary, to implement a specific procedure. The aim, however, is to think in BASIC ID terms to ensure thorough and comprehensive assessment and treatment coverage.

**History of Cognitive Restructuring.** The behavioral treatment repertoire during the 1950s and 1960s glossed over or completely disregarded many dysfunctional cognitive variables, untoward sensory responses, intrusive mental images, and disruptive interpersonal factors. Follow-ups on a variety of clients who had received standard behavioral therapy revealed that many clients were apt to suffer setbacks within six months to a year. Investigations into the reasons for this lack of durability revealed that treatment omissions (leaving several response deficits untreated) lay behind most of the relapses. For example, agoraphobic clients received relaxation training, imaginal and in vivo desensitization, and between-session homework assignments to consolidate and augment whatever gains ensued, but virtually no attention was paid to cognitive mediation (negative automatic thoughts, dichotomous reasoning, unrealistic expectations, and other self-defeating beliefs). Similarly, interpersonal processes (other than unassertive behaviors) were given short shrift (including marital discord, familial tensions, the impact of authority figures, or sibling rivalry). Unaddressed and untreated, these issues, when triggered, retained the power to undermine whatever treatment gains had accrued.

By the mid-1970s, cognitive behavior therapy had replaced behavior therapy as the accepted designation, and the field became trimodal, emphasizing affect, behavior, and cognition (ABC). This remains true to this day. Nevertheless, Lazarus (1971, 2006, 2008) has contended that equal weight should be given to imagery, sensation, interpersonal relationships, and biological considerations, operating from the seven-point multimodal perspective described above.

**Benefits.** Using this approach, most clients are likely to show positive gains when receiving a broad-spectrum treatment in which salient issues are addressed. Follow up studies that have been conducted since 1973 have consistently suggested that durable outcomes are in direct proportion to the number of modalities deliberately traversed (see Lazarus, 1997, 2008). Although there is obviously a point of diminishing returns, it is a multimodal maxim that the more that people learn in therapy, the less likely they are to relapse. To reiterate, it appears that lacunae or gaps in people's coping responses were responsible for many relapses.

**Contraindications.** People in crisis require therapists to focus immediately on the precipitating circumstances and events. There is often simply no time to dwell on the vicissitudes and nuances of the BASIC ID. These clients require, and may demand, instantaneous relief from their presenting anxiety and depression. Less acute issues and much less dramatic problem areas may call for unimodal or bimodal interventions. For example, clients in a smoking cessation group are likely to adhere and respond to structured methods of habit control more than they are to a broad band of assessments and interventions. And when dealing with frankly psychotic (e.g., schizophrenic) individuals or those who are in the manic stage of a bipolar disorder, the first inroad should probably consist of supportive treatment and biopsychiatric interventions. When appropriate medications have taken effect, a multimodal treatment program may then be instituted to remedy excesses and deficits that may precipitate or aggravate patients' initial or major complaints.

**Theory and Mechanism.** The BASIC ID or multimodal framework rests on a broad social and cognitive learning theory (e.g., Bandura, 1977, 1986) because its tenets are open to verification or disproof. Instead of postulating putative unconscious forces, social learning theory rests on testable developmental factors (such as modeling, observational learning, the acquisition of expectancies, operant and respondent conditioning, and various self-regulatory mechanisms). It must be emphasized that while drawing on effective methods from any discipline, the multimodal therapist does not embrace divergent theories but remains consistently within social-cognitive learning theory. The virtues of *technical eclecticism* (Lazarus, 2008) as opposed to the dangers of *theoretical integration* have been emphasized in several publications (e.g., Lazarus, 1989, 1995). The major criticism of theoretical integration is that it often blends incompatible notions and breeds confusion.

The main claim for a multimodal approach is that by assessing clients across the BASIC ID, one is less apt to overlook subtle but important problems that call for correction, and the overall problem identification process is significantly expedited.

ARNOLD A. LAZARUS

## REFERENCES


Bandura, A. (1977). *Social Learning Theory.* Englewood Cliffs, NJ: Prentice Hall.

Bandura, A. (1986). *Social Foundations of Thought and Action: A Social Cognitive Theory.* Englewood Cliffs, NJ: Prentice Hall.

Lazarus, A. A. (1971). *Behavior Therapy and Beyond.* New York, NY: McGraw-Hill.

Lazarus, A. A. (1976). *Multimodal Behavior Therapy.* New York, NY: Springer.

Lazarus, A. A. (1989). *The Practice of Multimodal Therapy.* Baltimore, MD: Johns Hopkins University Press.

Lazarus, A. A. (1995). Different types of eclecticism and integration: Let's be aware of the dangers. *Journal of Psychotherapy Integration, 5,* 27-39.

Lazarus, A. A. (1997). *Brief but Comprehensive Psychotherapy: The Multimodal Way.* New York, NY: Springer.

Lazarus, A. A. (2006). Multimodal therapy: A seven-point integration. In G. Stricker & J. Gold (Eds.), *A Casebook of Psychotherapy Integration* (pp. 17-28). Washington, DC: APA Books.

Lazarus, A. A. (2008). Multimodal therapy. In R. J. Corsini & D. Wedding (Eds.), *Current Psychotherapies* (8th ed., pp. 368-401). Belmont, CA: Thomson Brooks/Cole.


## THEORETICAL INTEGRATION

**DESCRIPTION.** In the counseling world, *theoretical integration* refers to the productive combination of aspects of one or more psychological theories for the purpose of a more comprehensive understanding and treatment of clients (Thompson, 2003). There are at least two ways integration can be practiced. One is to combine two or more of the primary ideas from at least two different theories into a hybrid, which is usually idiosyncratic to the individual counselor. Such hybrids then serve as the templates, or new pairs of theoretical glasses, for counselors as they work with their clients.

The second way to practice theoretical integration is to loosen counseling strategies from their theoretical roots and compile a "bigger toolbox" of ideas that can be accessed according to the particular need of the client (Dobson, 2010). Another term for this approach is *eclecticism.* This concept is further subdivided into *responsible eclecticism*—having a proper understanding and respect for the theories from which the ideas or strategies emerge—and *irresponsible eclecticism*—a pragmatic and sometimes haphazard use of whatever theory or strategy might produce some kind of change (Jones & Butman, 1991).

**HISTORY.** The construction of psychological theories themselves is a relatively new enterprise. In light of the pervasive impact of the various theories, it is difficult to remember that the earliest psychological theories, those of Sigmund Freud, have been around less than a century and a half. When Freud's work began to permeate the intellectual world in the early 20th century, he was the only one trying to figure out the workings of the psyche, or human mind.

A few decades later a contradictory theory emerged, focusing not on the internal workings of the soul but rather the external stimulus of behavior. These two theories had little in common and were viewed as competitors rather than complementary. The same holds true for the emergence of humanistic theories that focused on the individual, such as the theories of Maslow and Rogers, and the contrasting development of family systems theories, constructed by a diverse group of thinkers who agreed that seeing people in relationships was much more informative and therapeutic than seeing them individually. Other theories continued to enter the scene throughout the latter half of the 20th century, and soon enough theories existed to warrant whole textbooks summarizing them for students (Corey, 2008; Murdock, 2008).

**IN PRACTICE.** A common feature of such textbooks is a summary chapter attempting to address the question, so which theory is right? For most, the answers are "none of them" and "all of them." The central project of theoretical integration is to find benefit from all of the theoretical work done in the 20th century. There are several advantages to such an endeavor. First, it removes the limits of looking at clients through one monochrome set of glasses. Different theories ask different questions, and this diversity has the potential to glean more information and understanding than does limiting oneself to the glasses provided by just one theory. Second, integration tries to fit appropriate theories to individual clients rather than imposing one theory on all clients (Kottler & Shepard, 2011).

Some risks accompany these benefits. First, the expanded toolbox approach can totally disregard each tool's theoretical "instruction manual." This can lead to a pragmatic approach at best and a harmful effect at worst. Second, there can be a favoring of those tools or strategies that produce the most dramatic effect, with the assumption that this dramatic effect is evidence of true productive change.

**Spiritual Issues.** For the Christian counselor, the task becomes even more complicated. To whatever degree the Bible presents a view of human nature, that view is nonnegotiable. It is one thing to pick and choose from views whose authority rests mainly on the assumptions of their founders. It is quite another to compromise with inspired Scripture (Jones & Butman, 1991). Likewise, when it comes to techniques, Christian counselors must think carefully about what type of eclecticism they will practice (Sells & Yarhouse, 2008). Can prayer, for example, be separated from its biblical and theological moorings in order to take its place alongside systematic desensitization in the Christian counselor's toolbox?

Finally, can the process of theoretical integration be used as a model in which the views of the Christian faith can be merged or combined with the best psychology has to offer? This remains to be seen.

**Bryan N. Maier**

## REFERENCES


Corey, G. (2008). *Theories and Practice of Counseling and Psychotherapy.* Florence, KY: Thomson Brooks/Cole.

Dobson, K. S. (2010). *Handbook of Cognitive-Behavioral Therapies* (3rd ed.). New York, NY: Guilford Press.

Jones, S. L., & Butman, R. E. (1991). *Modern Psychotherapies: A Comprehensive Christian Appraisal.* Downers Grove, IL: InterVarsity Press.

Kottler, J. A., & Shepard, D. S. (2011). *Introduction to Counseling: Voices from the Field.* Belmont, CA: Brooks/Cole.

Murdock, N. L. (2008). *Theories of Counseling and Psychotherapy: A Case Approach* (2nd ed.). Upper Saddle River, NJ: Prentice Hall.

Sells, J. N., & Yarhouse, M. A. (2008). *Family Therapies: A Comprehensive Christian Appraisal.* Downers Grove, IL: InterVarsity Press.

Thompson, R. A. (2003). *Counseling Techniques: Improving Relationships with Others, Ourselves, Our Families, and Our Environment* (2nd ed.). New York, NY: Taylor & Francis.


## CAREER COUNSELING

Career counseling involves "a formal relationship in which the professional counselor assists a client or group of clients to cope more effectively with career concerns" (Niles & Harris-Bowlsby, 2009, p. 13).

**History.** The development of career counseling in the United States has been tied to social, economic, and political factors. Beginning in the late 1890s, early career counseling, called "vocational guidance," centered primarily on job placement. This was in response to increasing immigration and shifts from an agricultural to industrial economy and from a rural to urban society (Herr, 2001). The end of World War I and the advent of the Great Depression brought about social reform inside and outside the government. Vocational guidance was further expanded into schools and governmental agencies and programs as jobs were created to put Americans back to work (Pope, 2000).

The end of World War II spurred on further development of the profession with an increasing number of jobless returning veterans. The GI Bill, providing veterans with tuition for college education, opened the door for many soldiers to return to college and created the need for career counselors to assist with career guidance and development (Pope, 2000).

Increasing social consciousness and the human potential movement of the 1960s changed the views and expectations of a generation of young people. Work was no longer viewed as a means to earn income; instead, it was seen as a means to change the world for the better and to bring about personal meaning in one's life (Pope, 2000).

Career counseling continued to be important in the 1980s as American society shifted from an industrial to an informational and technological age. American workers were forced to leave behind their industrial jobs and learn new skills for the new information age (Niles & Harris-Bowlsby, 2009).

Globalization of the job market, industry downsizing, mobilization of American society, and the launching of the Internet are all forces currently impacting the direction of career counseling as the profession strives to address the ever-changing career needs of modern society (Zunker, 2006).

**Theoretical Development.** Career development theories have evolved to reflect the historical development of career counseling. The evolution of theories can be placed in four categories. Early *differential* theories emphasized matching a person's traits to job factors. This was followed by *developmental* theories, which emphasized the role of human growth and development over the life span and the need to place one's career in the larger context of multiple life roles. *Social* and *cognitive* theories came onto the scene and emphasized the wider social influences and internal cognitions that influence career development. The most recent theories are the *constructivist* theories, which emphasize personal values and meaning making in understanding career development in the individual (Hartung, 2010; Sharf, 2010).

**Application.** Though career counselors may differ on theoretical approaches to career counseling, the career counseling process remains the same: establish a therapeutic alliance with the client, assess the career concern, determine the goals of the client, and provide effective interventions to meet the goals and terminate (Brown, 2007). According to the National Career Development Association (1997), competent career counselors require knowledge and training in career development theory, individual and group counseling skills, individual and group assessment, information and resources, program management and implementation, consultation, diverse populations, supervision, ethical and legal issues, research and evaluation, and technology.

**Career Counseling and the Christian.** Career counseling with Christian clients is particularly important as clients seek to serve God throughout their lives. It is important to help clients understand their interests, talents, values, and skills and how these factors can be used to develop a vocation. Helping Christian clients make decisions regarding career must also take into account the larger underlying beliefs of the clients. What do clients believe about calling and how God leads a person's life? What do they believe regarding the will of God and how to determine that will? These questions must be explored with clients in order to assist them in their decision making.

Theological positions on decision making and the will of God tend to fall into distinct categories. The first position, known as the *traditional* view, contends that God has one life plan for each Christian, and each Christian has the responsibility to determine that will. Determining God's will, according to this view, involves the spiritual discipline of prayer for guidance. Proponents of this view often contend that people can know they have made the right decision regarding God's will by the "inner peace" they experience (LaHaye, 2001; Stanley, 1995).

The *wisdom* view contends that a person determines the will of God by using the spiritual discipline of Bible study. Some people within this school of thought posit that through the content of the Scriptures alone, people can determine God's will for their lives. Others within this camp state that people should also use reasoning, an understanding of their talents and giftedness, and the advice of wise counsel (McArthur, 1977; Swindoll, 2001).

The *pragmatic wisdom* view holds that God does not have one specific will for Christians' lives. Instead, Christians should seek to do God's general will of loving others in any vocation of their choice. According to this view, what people do is less important than who people are (Keshgegian, 2008).

Similar to this view is the *relationship-formation* approach. Like the pragmatic view, this approach does not posit one specific will for each Christian's life. However, unlike the pragmatic wisdom view, this view contends that God is involved in the Christian's decision making. In this view, God provides guidance, but he also expects Christians to mature in their decision-making abilities (Main, 2007; Willard, 1993).

**Conclusion.** Career counseling has a long history and many theoretical approaches. However, the counseling techniques used in career counseling are similar to the techniques of regular counseling. In working with Christians, it is important to integrate their personal views of how God leads and how a Christian determines the will of God in order to successfully help them make decisions.

Denise Daniel

## REFERENCES


Brown, D. (2007). *Career Information, Career Counseling and Career Development* (9th ed.). Boston, MA: Allyn & Bacon.

Hartung, P. J. (2010). Annual review: Practice and research in career counseling and development—2009. *The Career Development Quarterly, 59,* 98-142.

Herr, E. L. (2001). Career development and its practice: A historical perspective. *The Career Development Quarterly, 49,* 196-211.

Keshgegian, F. A. (2008). *God Reflected: Metaphors for Life.* Minneapolis, MN: Fortress Press.

LaHaye, T. (2001). *Finding the Will of God in a Crazy, Mixed-Up World.* Grand Rapids, MI: Zondervan.

Main, B. (2007). *Holy Hunches: Responding to the Promptings of God.* Grand Rapids, MI: Baker Books.

McArthur, J., Jr. (1977). *Found: God's Will* (Rev. ed.). Colorado Springs, CO: Victor Books.

National Career Development Association (1997). *Career Counseling Competencies.* Retrieved February 21, 2011 from http://ncda.org

Niles, S. G., & Harris-Bowlsby, J. H. (2009). *Career Development Interventions in the 21st Century* (3rd ed.). Upper Saddle River, NJ: Prentice Hall.

Pope, M. (2000). A brief history of career counseling in the United States. *The Career Development Quarterly, 48,* 194-211.

Sharf, R. S. (2010). *Applying Career Development Theory to Counseling* (5th ed.). Belmont, CA: Brooks/Cole.

Stanley, C. F. (1995). *Discerning God's Will.* Wheaton, IL: Victor Books.

Swindoll, C. R. (2001). *The Mystery of God's Will.* Waco, TX: Word.

Willard, D. (1993). *In Search of Guidance: Developing a Conversational Relationship with God.* New York, NY: Harper Collins.

Zunker, V. G. (2006). *Career Counseling: A Holistic Approach* (7th ed.). Belmont, CA: Brooks/Cole.


## SCHOOL COUNSELING

School counseling is the field in which a licensed or certified professional counselor who has completed the specialized training established by a state to serve in an educational environment performs a variety of educationally related counseling and administrative functions.

**Licensure and Certification Requirements.** These vary from state to state but normally require a minimum of a master's degree in school counseling from a state-approved program at a regionally accredited institution. Typical components of this program as described by the American School Counselor Association include a professional orientation to the field and studies in human growth and development, counseling theories, individual and group counseling methodologies, social and cultural foundations, administration and interpretation of school-related testing and appraisal instruments, career development and guidance, and issues regarding special-needs populations. These lead to a supervised practicum and internship. Although states vary in the stipulated demands for licensure/certification, many require the successful completion of a standardized instrument, such as the PRAXIS II School Guidance and Counseling Exam (Code 0420), as well as two years of successful educational experience as a classroom teacher or school counselor with a provisional license. The license/certification is usually but not always for pre-K through 12 and is valid in most states for five years. Renewal usually requires completion of additional training or study, often measured in continuing education units (CEUs).

**History.** The roots of school counseling as a profession date from the late 19th and early 20th centuries, when teachers engaged in vocational guidance counseling to help students transition into the workforce (Gysbers & Henderson, 2004). Some countries continue to add counseling-related tasks to some classroom teachers' duties, but the United States and some other nations utilize specialists. The term *guidance* was common at first, but the current preferred title omits this and stands as *school counseling*. In response to a call for nationwide standardization of training and expectations for practitioners, the American School Counselor Association released in 2003 (and revised in 2005) a manual for the profession. *The ASCA National Model: A Framework for School Counseling Programs* has been widely hailed as seminal for the progression of the field. Legislation, such as the No Child Left Behind Act of 2001, continues to shape the future of the profession.

**Duties.** The duties of the school counselor vary according to a number of factors. The level of the students served (elementary, middle, or high school), state and school district policies, rural or urban setting, area of the country, and the like all affect the school counselors' daily tasks. In general, these tasks include some combination of individual and group counseling, academically related administrative tasks (scheduling, transcript evaluation, enrollment and withdrawal), consultation (with parents, teachers and other counselors, and community agencies), appraisal (standardized national and local tests), and assisting with special populations (by means of individualized instruction plans and 504 plans). Together with parents, teachers, and administrators, school counselors continue to prepare each new generation for the tasks that lie ahead.

**Edgar E. Barker**

## RECOMMENDED ADDITIONAL SOURCES

American School Counselor Association (2005). *School Counseling Principles: Foundation and Basics.* Alexandria, VA: Author.

American School Counselor Association (2005). *The ASCA National Model: A Framework for School Counseling Programs*, Second Edition. Alexandria, VA: Author.

Franklin, C., Harris, M. B., & Allen-Meares, P. (Eds.). (2006). *The School Services Sourcebook: A Guide for School-Based Professionals.* New York, NY: Oxford University Press.

Gysbers, N. C., & Henderson, P. (2004). Comprehensive guidance and counseling programs: A rich history and a bright future. *Professional School Counseling, 4*(4), 246-257.

Kerr, M. M. (2009). *School Crisis Prevention and Intervention.* Upper Saddle River, NJ: Prentice Hall.

Knapp, S. E. (Ed.). (2003). *The School Counseling and School Social Work Homework Planner.* Hoboken, NJ: Wiley & Sons.

Knapp, S. E., & Jongsma, A. E. (Eds.). (2002). *The School Counseling and School Social Work Treatment Planner.* Hoboken, NJ: Wiley & Sons.

## GERONTOLOGICAL COUNSELING

Gerontology is a multidisciplinary field that includes physicians, biologists, nurses, social workers, pharmacists, psychologists, counselors, and economists because the issues of aging cross all of these disciplines. Other counseling fields emerged in the early part of the 20th century, but aging was largely ignored. The literature published from 1950 to 1960 was equal to the prior 115 years of aging studies, and the *Journal of Gerontology* did not launch until 1946. Even today, gerontology remains the new kid on the block in psychological and social research.

For psychologists, professional counselors, and pastoral counselors, gerontological counseling has the common thread of helping older adults successfully move through the final Eriksonian stage (integrity versus despair) to the end of their lives. In recent years the emphasis on *active aging* (World Health Organization, 2002) brought attention to the quality-of-life issues for older adults.

**Counseling Issues.** Older adults have the same problems as other adults: depression, anxiety, substance abuse, personality disorders, somatization disorders, and grief (Benner & Hill, 1999). Too often the psychological problems of older adults are blamed on aging, and they are not treated as actively as they are in younger adults. Memory impairment can increase to such an extent that assessment for Alzheimer's or dementia is needed.

Older adults often experience a series of losses within a short period, such as ceasing to drive, mobility limitations, illness, death of spouses and friends and siblings, and the need to move to assisted living or to another state to be cared for by adult children. The grief and impact of these changes becomes an adjustment issue that often turns to depression if not treated.

Prescription drug abuse both accidentally and by choice is a growing problem among older adults. As the Baby Boomer generation continues to age, the demand for substance abuse treatment for Americans over age 50 is expected to double by 2020 (Substance Abuse & Mental Health Administration, 2010).

Suicide is an increasing problem, particularly among white males over age 85. Every 97 minutes an older adult commits suicide. The major risk factors for elderly suicide include recent death of a spouse, prolonged illness, social isolation, and an inability to adjust to retirement, economic decline, or other role changes (American Association of Suicidology, 2007).

Homicide-suicide is also increasing in the elderly. Cohen's (2002) research describes the "husband killing the wife before killing himself." Risk factors for this problem include the husband as sole caregiver for a wife with dementia or long-term illness, couples in which the husband and wife both have major illnesses, and couples with history of social isolation as well as lack of caregiving support.

**The Future of Gerontological Counseling.** In 2011, the middle group among 78 million Baby Boomers reached age 60. By 2029, one in five Americans will be 65 or older (Hooyman & Unützer, 2010). In 2032, these older adults will outnumber children under 15. These drastic demographic changes mean that every counselor needs training in and acute awareness of aging issues. Additionally, the proliferation of multigenerational households will place new pressures on relationships in the family system.

Maples and Abney (2006) point to the

increased need for "preretirement to end-of-life counselors," thus opening new practice options for professional counselors and identifying more areas where pastoral counselors and lay counseling ministries can serve. As Baby Boomers redefine aging and retirement, their counseling concerns are expected to be more like those of middle adults: work frustrations, stress, relationship changes, self-image, and personal growth. Overall the Baby Boomers are considered less resistant to counseling than the prior older generation, so the potential to focus on counseling niches related to Baby Boomers may become more common as gerontological counseling rides the aging population wave to prominence in the mental-health field.

**Spiritual Issues.** Life regrets and fear of aging and death are critical spiritual issues that often arise in gerontological counseling. From a biblical perspective, aging and death are understood as realities of life in a fallen world. The psalmist writes, "The length of our days is seventy years—or eighty, if we have the strength; yet their span is but trouble and sorrow, for they quickly pass, and we fly away.... Teach us to number our days aright, that we may gain a heart of wisdom" (Ps. 90:9-10,12). The challenge of gerontological counseling is to help clients come to grips with the brevity of life and the reality of death while finding hope, joy, and meaning in their daily existence. Christians' hope is found in the promise of heaven because Jesus' sacrifice has overcome the sting of death and sin (1 Cor. 15).

Responsible aging is the goal of much of gerontological counseling. As people age, they often lose much of their freedom and capacity to engage in activities that gave them joy and purpose. As a result, many older clients struggle with feelings of hopelessness and worthlessness. But God's Word says, "Even to your old age and gray hairs I am he, I am he who will sustain you. I have made you and I will carry you; I will sustain you and I will rescue you" (Is. 46:4). God treasures and delights in all of his children because they are his. He promises to carry and sustain his people through the difficult challenges of aging, health problems, and loss. Scripture honors old age (Pr. 16:31), and gerontological counseling should help clients address spiritual issues and find purpose and joy through relationships with God and others.

Kathie T. Erwin

## REFERENCES

American Association of Suicidology. (2007). *USA Suicide: 2007 Official Final Data.* Retrieved January 29, 2011, from http://www.suicidology.org/c/document_library/get_file?folderId=232&name=DLFE-232.pdf

Benner, D. G., & Hill, P. C. (Eds.). (1999). *Baker Encyclopedia of Psychology and Counseling.* Grand Rapids, MI: Baker Books.

Cohen, D. (2002). *Homicide-Suicide in Older Persons: How You Can Help Prevent a Tragedy.* Tampa, FL: Florida Mental Health Institute at the University of South Florida.

Erikson, E. H. (1950). *Childhood and Society.* New York, NY: Norton.

Hayutin, A. D., Dietz, M., & Mitchell, L. (2010). *New Realities of an Older America.* Stanford, CA: Stanford Center on Longevity.

Hooyman, N., & Unützer, J. (2010). A perilous arc of supply and demand: How can America meet the multiplying mental health care needs of an aging populace? *Journal of American Society on Aging, 34*(4), 36-42.

Maples, M. F., & Abney, P. C. (2006, Winter). Baby Boomers mature and gerontological counseling comes of age. *Journal of Counseling & Development, 84,* 3-9. Retrieved January 29, 2011 from http://gerontology.unlv.edu/pdf/boomers-article.pdf

Substance Abuse & Mental Health Administration. (2010, January 8). *SAMHSA News Release: Increasing Substance Abuse Levels Among Older Adults.* Retrieved from http://www.samhsa.gov/newsroom/advisories/1001073150.aspx

World Health Organization. (2002). *Active Ageing: A Policy Framework.* Retrieved from http://whqlibdoc.who.int/hq/2002/who_nmh_nph_02.8.pdf

# CHRISTIAN COGNITIVE AND STRENGTH-BASED THERAPY

## CHRISTIAN COGNITIVE THERAPY

**Description.** Cognitive therapy, or CT, founded by Aaron Beck (see Beck & Weishaar, 2008), is a major part of cognitive-behavior therapy, or CBT. CT focuses on how distorted or dysfunctional thinking that is negative, irrational, extreme, unreasonable, or maladaptive leads to problem feelings such as anxiety, depression, and anger, and to problem behaviors.

Christian cognitive therapy, developed by several Christian cognitive therapists, focuses more specifically on unbiblical thinking as the root of the problem feelings and behaviors. For example, William Backus calls unbiblical, erroneous thoughts "misbeliefs" and has developed misbelief therapy as a specific Christian CT approach that uses the Bible to challenge misbeliefs and replace them with biblical truth (Backus, 1985).

Similarly, Chris Thurman's Christian CT approach, based on Albert Ellis' rational-emotive behavior therapy (REBT), uses scriptural truth to challenge irrational, unbiblical beliefs or the lies we believe (Thurman, 1989). Examples of such lies, and the Scriptures that can be used to challenge and replace them, include these: "Because I am a Christian, God will protect me from pain and suffering" (see Jn. 16:33; Phil. 1:29; 1 Pet. 4:12-13). "A good Christian doesn't feel angry, anxious, or depressed" (see Mk. 11:15-16; 14:32-34; Jn. 11:33-35; Eph. 4:26).

Larry Crabb's biblical counseling is another Christian approach to CT or REBT that emphasizes the need to identify problem thinking and replace it with biblical thinking to deal with problem behavior and problem feelings (Crabb, 1977). A final example of a Christian CT approach is what Mark McMinn has described as a more relational version of CT, which focuses on restructuring of distorted or unbiblical thinking, but in the context of a warm and caring collaborative relationship with the client (McMinn, 1991; McMinn & Campbell, 2007).

**Examples of Distorted Thinking.** Some examples of distorted thinking or cognitive distortions in one's automatic thoughts that have logical errors include the following (see Beck & Weishaar, 2008, p. 272):

- *Arbitrary inference*: coming to a conclusion without enough evidence or even with contradictory evidence. A working mother concludes, "I'm an awful mother" after a very demanding and stressful day.
- *Selective abstraction*: making a conclusion based on a particular detail while ignoring other important information, thus taking it out of context. A man gets angry and jealous because he sees his girlfriend at a party conversing with another man, who turns out to be her cousin.
- *Overgeneralization*: applying a general rule from particular incidents to other unrelated situations. After being unsuccessful at getting a date, a man concludes, "I'll never get a date with any woman."

- *Magnification* or *catastrophizing*: seeing something as significantly greater than it really is. A student says, "If I fail this exam, it'll be horrible and the end of the world for me."
- *Personalization*: connecting external events to oneself without any firm evidence to support such a causal relationship. A man waves at a friend in a crowded subway station without receiving any response and concludes, "I must have done something that offended my friend because he's avoiding me."
- *Dichotomous thinking*: seeing things in one of two extreme categories, such as complete success or total failure. A student says, "If I don't get an *A* on this test, then I am a total failure."

**Challenging and Replacing Distorted Thoughts and Misbeliefs.** Standard questions often used in Beck's CT approach to challenging and replacing distorted thoughts with more accurate, reasonable, rational, and adaptive thoughts include these:

- "On what basis do you say this? Where is the evidence for your conclusion?"
- "Is there another way of looking at this?"
- "If your conclusion is true, what does it mean to you?"

Christian CT will also include other questions, such as "What do you think the Bible has to say about this?" or "What do you think God has to say about this?" (see Tan, 2007, p. 108).

The proper use of Scripture is crucial in Christian CT to help clients restructure or change their unbiblical beliefs or misbeliefs to biblical beliefs.

Christian CT, like standard CT, often includes some behavioral interventions, such as relaxation techniques, scheduling of daily events that are pleasurable or that provide a sense of mastery or accomplishment, exposure to anxiety-provoking situations, assertiveness training, and the use of reinforcement contingencies or rewards. It is therefore more appropriate to describe CT as a form of CBT, and Christian CT as Christian CBT.

**A Biblical Approach to CBT.** Tan (1987, pp. 108-109) has noted that a biblical or Christian approach to CBT or CT will do these things:

1. Emphasize the primacy of agape love (1 Cor. 13) and the need to develop a warm, empathic, and genuine relationship with the client.
2. Deal more adequately with the past, especially unresolved developmental issues or childhood traumas, and use inner healing or healing of memories judiciously and appropriately.
3. Pay attention to the meaning of spiritual, experiential, and even mystical aspects of life and faith, according to God's wisdom as revealed in Scriptures and by the Holy Spirit's teaching ministry (Jn. 14:26). It will not overemphasize the rational, thinking dimension, although biblical, propositional truth will be given its rightful place of importance. The possibility of demonic involvement in some cases will be seriously considered and appropriately dealt with.
4. Focus on how problems in thought and behavior may often (*not* always, because of other factors, e.g., organic or biological) underlie problem feelings (Rom. 12:1-2; Eph. 4:22-24; Phil. 4:8), and use biblical truth (Jn. 8:32), not relativistic, empirically oriented values in conducting cognitive restructuring and behavioral change interventions.
5. Emphasize the Holy Spirit's ministry

in bringing about inner healing as well as cognitive, behavioral, and emotional change. It will use prayer and affirmation of God's Word in facilitating dependence on the Lord to produce deep and lasting personality change and will be cautious not to inadvertently encourage sinful self-sufficiency.

6. Pay more attention to larger contextual factors like familial, societal, religious, and cultural influences and therefore utilize appropriate community resources in therapeutic intervention, including the church as a body of believers.
7. Use only those techniques that are consistent with biblical truth and not simplistically use whatever techniques seem to work.
8. Utilize rigorous outcome research methodology before making definitive statements about the superiority of cognitive-behavior therapy.

**Conclusion.** Standard CT or CBT is one of the most empirically supported treatments for a wide range of problems and disorders (Butler, Chapman, Forman, & Beck, 2006; Tan, 2011). Christian CT or CBT has recently received more empirical support for its efficacy. Based on 18 randomized clinical trials of spiritually oriented CBT, Christian CT, or CBT for depression was found to be an empirically supported treatment that is efficacious, and Christian devotional meditation for anxiety and Christian group CBT for marital discord to be possibly efficacious (Hook et al., 2010).

Siang-Yang Tan

## REFERENCES


Backus, W. (1985). *Telling the Truth to Troubled People.* Minneapolis, MN: Bethany House.

Beck, A. T., & Weishaar, M. E. (2008). Cognitive therapy. In R. J. Corsini & D. Wedding (Eds.), *Current Psychotherapies* (8th ed., pp. 263-294). Belmont, CA: Brooks/Cole.

Butler, A. C., Chapman, J. E., Forman, E. M., & Beck, A. T. (2006). The empirical status of cognitive-behavioral therapy: A review of meta-analyses. *Clinical Psychological Review, 26,* 17-31.

Crabb, L. J., Jr. (1977). *Effective Biblical Counseling.* Grand Rapids, MI: Zondervan.

Hook, J. N., Worthington, E. L., Jr., David, D. E., Jennings, D. J., II, Gartner, A. L., & Hook, N. (2010). Empirically supported religious and spiritual therapies. *Journal of Clinical Psychology, 66,* 46-72.

McMinn, M. R. (1991). *Cognitive Therapy Techniques in Christian Counseling.* Dallas, TX: Word.

McMinn, M. R., & Campbell, C. D. (2007). *Integrative Psychotherapy: Toward a Comprehensive Christian Approach.* Downers Grove, IL: IVP Academic.

Tan, S.-Y. (1987). Cognitive-behavior therapy: A biblical approach and critique. *Journal of Psychology and Theology, 15,* 103-112.

Tan, S.-Y. (2007). Use of prayer and Scripture in cognitive-behavioral therapy. *Journal of Psychology and Christianity, 26,* 101-111.

Tan, S.-Y. (2011). *Counseling and Psychotherapy: A Christian Perspective.* Grand Rapids, MI: Baker Academic.

Thurman, C. (1989). *The Lies We Believe.* Nashville, TN: Thomas Nelson.


## CORE BELIEFS AND SCHEMAS

Schemas are ways of cognitively organizing experiences. They involve beliefs, values, memories, thought-action tendencies, goals, and plans, which can be either explicit or implicit (Metcalf & Jacobs, 1998; Smith & Kosslyn, 2007). Core beliefs, on the other hand, are the propositional beliefs that are central to experience.

**History.** Jean Piaget was a biologist who observed his children develop and posited a theory about how their cognitive abilities developed in stages (Myers & Jeeves, 2003). In the first stage, children employed sensorimotor schemas. *Schemas* were organized patterns of motor behavior that occurred in response to sensations. When the child neared the age of two, *mental schemas*, or representations of the world—verbal, spatial, and imaginal—developed. In the earliest preoperational stage, the child learned the rudiments of manipulating schemas. In the concrete operational stage, the child could apply a mental scheme (i.e., cognitive manipulation) to a mental schema (i.e., a concrete representation). In the formal operational stage, the schemas evolved beyond concrete representations to the abstract.

Cognitive therapy, developed in the 1960s, was based in part on the theory that children formed beliefs in early childhood that became fundamental and often unarticulated ways of viewing themselves and their identity (Beck, 1995). These core beliefs, as they came to be called, along with schemas form the basis for how one views the world and are often tenaciously held even in the face of discounting evidence.

**Assessment.** Different psychotherapies have different ways of assessing cognitive schemas and core beliefs. Clients reveal aspects of their implicit schemas through behaviors not fully within their awareness. An impartial psychotherapist can help the client notice, articulate, and take some control over those schemas and core beliefs.

**Treatment.** Cognitive therapy (CT) and cognitive-behavioral therapy (CBT) use a cognitive paradigm to help clients change maladaptive patterns of functioning. The underlying premise of cognitive theory is that people act and feel the way they do because of cognitive thoughts, beliefs, values, and processes. CT and CBT theories suggest that people's awareness of their cognition will help them choose more adaptive ways to act and feel. Often, psychotherapists explore both conscious and unconscious schemas and core beliefs to bring consistencies and inconsistencies to clients' consciousness. In this way, clients can choose what is in line with their values and beliefs rather than be controlled by their early childhood experiences.

Usually, psychotherapy involves learning a conceptual schema that guides the therapeutic process. Cognitive therapists and cognitive-behavioral therapists explicitly teach the cognitive paradigm to clients to raise their awareness of the connection between their thoughts and other cognition and their feelings and behaviors. Often, specific techniques are used to help clients compare their schemas and core beliefs. Inconsistencies are pointed out and called to attention by the psychotherapist, and client self-discovery is promoted through teaching clients to use the cognitive paradigm on themselves. Additionally, counselors often interpret repeated behavior patterns.

**Biblical and Spiritual Issues.** Many of the beliefs and behaviors in religion are due to schemas (Coe & Hall, 2010). The God-image can be thought of as (an often unconscious) mental representation of God (Moriarty & Davis, in press), which is often similar to a valued adult parent-figure in early life. The person has reacted emotionally to the figure with a sense of attachment. Because the actual parent is not always around, the person might transfer the emotional attachments to a God-concept or God-image. Importantly, the person might later develop core beliefs about God. Usually, those core beliefs—which are important to the organization of the entire personality—are often somewhat consistent with the schema of God. This is not always the case, and much emotional dissonance can be experienced when the God schema and core beliefs disagree. Christian counselors often help sort out the dissonance, especially when it interferes with the emotional equanimity of clients or prevents them from achieving important goals.

Everett L. Worthington Jr.
Aubrey L. Gartner
David J. Jennings II

## REFERENCES

Beck, J. (1995). *Cognitive Therapy: Basics and Beyond.* New York, NY: Guilford Press.

Coe, J. H., & Hall, T. W. (2010). *Psychology in the Spirit: Contours in a Transformational Psychology.* Downers Grove, IL: InterVarsity Press.

Metcalf, J., & Jacobs, W. J. (1998). Emotional memory: The effects of stress on "cool" and "hot" memory systems. In D. L. Medin (Ed.), *The Psychology of Learning and Motivation*. Vol. 38, *Advances in Research and Theory* (pp. 187-222). San Diego, CA: Academic Press.

Moriarty, G. L., & Davis, E. B. (in press). Client God images: Theory, research, and clinical practice. In J. D. Aten, K. D. O'Grady, & E. L. Worthington, Jr. (Eds.), *The Psychology of Religion and Spirituality for Clinicians: Using Research in Your Practice*. New York, NY: Brunner-Routledge.

Myers, D. G., & Jeeves, M. A. (2003). *Psychology Through the Eyes of Faith* (Rev. ed.). San Francisco, CA: HarperCollins.

Smith, E. E., & Kosslyn, S. M. (2007). *Cognitive Psychology: Mind and Brain*. Upper Saddle River, NJ: Prentice Hall.

## SELF-TALK

Self-talk is an important component of cognitive therapy and refers to clients' internal dialogue that allows them to (a) interpret their feelings and experiences, (b) evaluate thoughts and actions, and (c) make decisions about how to respond to their world (Hackfort & Schwenkmezger, 1993). Simply put, self-talk is an internal monologue that is important for self-awareness and self-regulation (DePape, Hakim-Larson, Voelker, Page, & Jackson, 2006).

**History.** Cognitive therapy emerged in the early 1960s, fueled largely by the work of Albert Ellis and Aaron Beck. Since its inception, an important aspect of cognitive therapy has been the link between self-talk and thoughts, emotions, and behavior (Theodorakis, Hatzigeorgiadis, & Chroni, 2008). From the late 1980s to early 1990s, many researchers and clinicians focused on merging traditional cognitive therapy with religious perspectives, and several modified forms of cognitive therapy emerged that were based on Christian principles (Hathaway & Tan, 2009).

**Assessment.** Self-talk is an innate, daily activity that is not necessarily maladaptive. However, when self-talk becomes largely negative or distorted, psychological problems, such as depression and anxiety, may arise. Researchers and counselors have turned to self-report questionnaires to better understand individuals' internal dialogue. Structured questionnaires such as the Self-Talk Scale (Brinthaupt, Hein, & Kramer, 2009) and the Self-Verbalization Questionnaire (Duncan & Cheyne, 1999) are available. Each is a self-report inventory that focuses on the frequency of self-talk. The Self-Talk Scale asks questions about when and why a person engages in self-talk, and the Self-Verbalization Questionnaire targets the number of times certain self-talk statements are made (Brinthaupt et al., 2009). Many counselors also assess self-talk through the clinical interview.

**Treatment.** The use of self-talk in treatment typically occurs in the context of cognitive therapy. Individuals who seek counseling often have distorted or dysfunctional thought patterns that can negatively impact their behavior and mood (Madewell & Shaughnessy, 2009). These negative thoughts influence the way a person views the world and can contribute to development disorders such as depression and anxiety. One of the primary aims of treatment with cognitive therapy is to identify these negative thoughts and deliberately replace them with positive self-talk statements (Madewell & Shaughnessy).

Cognitive therapy is often short-term and systematic. Once the client's presenting problem has been clarified, the focus of counseling is to help the client recognize the connection between his or her thoughts and emotions (Kellogg & Young, 2008). These thoughts can occur so frequently and unconsciously that the person is often unaware of them. Positive and negative self-talk statements can become like an audio track playing on repeat. During counseling, these self-talk statements are explored and linked to emotional and behavioral responses. The counselor works with the client to replace distorted, maladaptive, or negative self-talk (e.g., "I am worthless and unlovable") with positive and adaptive self-talk statements (e.g., "I am worthy of love and respect").

**Spiritual Issues.** Cognitive therapy in general and self-talk in particular are typically viewed as consistent with a Christian worldview. Several studies have been conducted to investigate cognitive therapies that are tailored for use with Christians. These treatments have been found to be at least as effective as standard versions of cognitive therapy (Hook et al., 2010). The spiritual disciplines of prayer and reflection often include examining one's thoughts and aligning these thoughts with biblical teachings.

Examples of using self-talk to help alleviate distress and maintain a proper perspective are seen throughout the Bible. In the Old Testament, the psalmist notes that he is "fearfully and wonderfully made" (Ps. 139:14). The writer of Proverbs also discusses the importance and centrality of thoughts in influencing our whole being (Pr. 23:7). In the New Testament, Paul teaches that we are transformed by the renewing of our mind (Rom. 12:2).

Stephanie D. Womack
Joshua N. Hook

## REFERENCES

Brinthaupt, T. M., Hein, M. B., & Kramer, T. E. (2009). The self-talk scale: Development, factor analysis, and validation. *Journal of Personality Assessment, 91*, 82-92.

DePape, A. R., Hakim-Larson, J., Voelker, S., Page, S., & Jackson, D. L. (2006). Self-talk and emotional intelligence in university students. *Canadian Journal of Behavioural Science, 38*, 250-260.

Duncan, R. M., & Cheyne, J. A. (1999). Incidence and functions of self-reported private speech in young adults: A self-verbalization questionnaire. *Canadian Journal of Behavioural Science, 31*, 133-136.

Hackfort, D., & Schwenkmezger, P. (1993). Anxiety. In R. N. Singer, M. Murphy, & L. K. Tennant (Eds.), *Handbook of Research on Sport Psychology* (pp. 328-364). New York, NY: Macmillan.

Hathaway, W., & Tan, E. (2009). Religiously oriented mindfulness-based cognitive therapy. *Journal of Clinical Psychology: In Session, 65*, 158-171.

Hook, J. N., Worthington, E. L., Jr., Davis, D. E., Gartner, A. L., Jennings, D. J., II, & Hook, J. P. (2010). Empirically supported religious and spiritual therapies. *Journal of Clinical Psychology, 66*, 46-72.

Kellogg, S. H., & Young, J. E. (2008). Cognitive therapy. In J. L. Lebow (Ed.), *Twenty-First-Century Psychotherapies* (pp. 43-79). Hoboken, NJ: Wiley & Sons.

Madewell, J., & Shaughnessy, M. F. (2009). An interview with Judith Beck about cognitive therapy. *North American Journal of Psychology, 11*, 29-36.

Theodorakis, Y., Hatzigeorgiadis, A., & Chroni, S. (2008). Self-talk: It works, but how? Development and preliminary validation of the functions of self-talk questionnaire. *Measurement in Physical Education and Exercise Science, 12*, 10-30.

## EMOTIONAL REASONING

**Description.** Beck, Emery, and Greenberg (1985) first identified emotional reasoning as a form of interpretation bias in which feelings are given prominence. They noted that anxious clients used their feelings to validate their thoughts and subsequently created a vicious circle. A cognitive error occurred because feelings were the determining factor in understanding reality. In emotional reasoning, the person believes subjective experience accurately reflects the larger reality and that one's emotions reflect the way things really are. Feelings, then, become the organizing and guiding factor in the person's thinking process and actions. Because emotions are variable, unreliable, and undependable, these perceptions contrast with logical reasoning, in which knowledge and judgment are the basis of interpreting reality. Though emotions should be considered in understanding the world, they are not meant to dominate the process.

Consider the following examples of emotional reasoning: "I feel terrified about going on airplanes. It must be very dangerous to fly." Or "I feel guilty. I must be a rotten person." Or "I feel angry. This proves I'm being treated unfairly." Or "I feel inferior. This means I'm a second-rate person." Or "I feel hopeless. I must really be" (Burns, 1999, p. 9). Because a world governed by emotions rather than rational laws is chaotic, using personal feelings to validate thoughts and relying on that information for understanding a situation remarkably increases the likelihood of misinterpreting and making poor decisions. In fact, people who live by their emotions are more prone to make decisions completely on impulse without the mediation of sound judgment. Like all cognitive distortions, emotional reasoning prevents a person from objectively examining circumstances.

**Assessment.** Arntz, Rauner, and van den Hout (1995) view emotional reasoning as bidirectional thinking. They state that although it is true that danger brings concomitant feelings of anxiety, anxiety does not necessarily indicate danger. Because emotional reasoning spawns irrationality, it has been linked to mood (Beck et al., 1985) and anxiety (Muris, 2008) disorders, gambling addiction (Ciarrocchi, 2001), antisocial behavior and psychopathy (Brannen, 2007), and relationship difficulties (Burns, 2008), among others. The distortion has been noted in both children (Muris, Merckelbach, & van Spauwen, 2003) and adults (Arntz et al., 1995).

**Treatment.** Cognitive therapy effectively addresses the problem of emotional reasoning. The cognitive counselor desires to move the client to a nonjudgmental and objective perspective of interpreting circumstances. The counselor is tasked with educating clients about the difference between facts and feelings, helping clients identify thinking errors, encouraging them to examine the evidence for their emotionally based beliefs, challenging such beliefs, and formulating alternative beliefs that are more balanced, rational, and biblically sound.

**Biblical and Spiritual Issues.** God is the author of human reason and feeling. Although mankind bears his image, both intellect and emotions are corrupted by the Fall. Still, each provides valuable input for daily functioning. Though emotions provide us with energy and enrich our daily existence, they are poor measures of reality and must be balanced with logical processes.

Sadly, when clients live in a reality fashioned by their own subjective emotions, they fail to live in God's reality. At the Fall of mankind, God cursed the world and everything in it, creating a reality that births painful emotions that will either propel us toward God or toward a life of self-sufficiency. As Allender (1996) notes, "Feeling the effects of living in a fallen world compels us to wrestle with God" (p. 34). Godly living requires that we experience reality in its fullest. Our view of circumstances should not be distorted by our cognitions or by our emotions, but fully apprehended. The objective of healthy and godly living is not to live in the tension between emotion and cognition, but to live in the center of God's grace.

John C. Thomas

## REFERENCES


Allender, D. (1996). Emotions and the pathway to God. *Christian Counseling Today, 4*(1), 32-35.

Arntz, A., Rauner, M., & van den Hout, M. (1995). If I feel anxious, there must be danger: *Ex-consequentia* reasoning in inferring danger in anxiety disorders. *Behavior Research Therapy, 33*, 917-925.

Beck, A. T., Emery, G., & Greenberg, R. L. (1985). *Anxiety Disorders and Phobias: A Cognitive Perspective.* New York, NY: Basic Books.

Brannen, D. N. (2007). *The Role of Emotional Reasoning and Antisocial Behavior in Successful Psychopathy* (Doctoral dissertation). Available from ProQuest Dissertations & Theses database. (Publication number 3286140)

Burns, D. (1999). *The Feeling Good Handbook* (Rev. ed.). New York, NY: A Plume Book.

Burns, D. (2008). *Feeling Good Together: The Secret to Making Troubled Relationships Work.* New York, NY: Broadway Books.

Ciarrocchi, J. W. (2001). *Counseling Problem Gamblers: A Self-Regulation Manual for Individual and Family Therapy.* San Diego, CA: Academic Press.

Muris, P. (2008). Distorted cognition and pathological anxiety in children and adolescents. *Cognition and Emotion 22*(3),395-421.

Muris, P., Merckelbach, & van Spauwen, I. (2003). The emotional reasoning heuristic in children. *Behavior Research Therapy, 41*, 261-272.

## RENEWING YOUR MIND

There are a number of ways Christian counselors can help people overcome their problems and "become mature, attaining to the whole measure of the fullness of Christ" (Eph. 4:13). One of the most important ways is to help people "be made new in the attitude of [their] minds" (Eph. 4:23).

Changing faulty beliefs is an integral part of enabling people to become who God intends them to be. We are told in the Bible, "Be transformed by the renewing of your mind" (Rom. 12:2), and "Set your minds on things above, not on earthly things" (Col. 3:2). Also, "whatever is true, whatever is noble, whatever is right, whatever is pure, whatever is lovely, whatever is admirable—if anything is excellent or praiseworthy—think about such things" (Phil. 4:8), and "Your attitude should be the same as that of Christ Jesus" (Phil. 2:5). For clients to grow into spiritually and psychologically healthier individuals, we must help them change the unbiblical views, the lies that are at the core of the problems they struggle with.

**The Lies People Believe.** What are the lies people believe? Here is just a small sampling of the most destructive lies that Satan, the father of lies (Jn. 8:44), has in his arsenal to "kill, steal, and destroy" (Jn. 10:10) the abundant life God wants us to have.

*I must be perfect.* This lie is the belief that we can and should be God's equal. The truth is that perfection is reserved for God, that we humans "fall short of the glory of God" (Rom. 3:23), and that our focus needs to be on becoming more like Christ over time (Eph. 4:23).

*My unhappiness is somebody else's fault.* This lie leads to blaming people for how we feel, depending on others for our emotional well-being, and falling into bitterness and unforgiveness toward people when they treat us badly. Someday, everyone will "give an account of himself to God" (Rom. 14:12), and blaming others for how we feel and act will come to an abrupt end.

*My worth as a person is determined by my performance.* This lie anchors worth in our day-to-day successes and failures rather than in our being made by God in his image. As David said, "You created me in my inmost being; you knit me together in my mother's womb. I praise you because I am fearfully and wonderfully made; your works are wonderful, I know that full well" (Ps. 139:13-14).

*I must have everyone's approval.* This lie leads us to have the fear of man, which ensnares us into self-destructive people pleasing (Pr. 29:25), rather than the fear of God, which gives birth to living life wisely (Pr. 1:7). Paul noted, "If I were still trying to please men, I would not be a servant of Christ" (Gal. 1:10).

*God's love must be earned.* According to this lie, God's love depends on our moral behavior rather than the central expression of who he is. God's love "endures forever" (Ps. 118:2). Nothing can keep us from it (Rom. 8:39), and God loves us regardless of who we are or what we do.

These are just some of the destructive lies that many of the people who come for counseling have fallen into. God offers direction and assistance in overcoming the lies we believe.

**The Work of God and the Work of Man.** God the Holy Spirit plays a key role in renewing our minds by guiding us into knowing and living out truth (Jn. 16:13-14). The Holy Spirit is our divine counselor and does inside of us what we cannot do for ourselves. As MacArthur (1994) puts it, "As a divinely indwelling teacher, the Spirit of truth fills a function that no human counselor can even approach. He is constantly there, pointing the way to truth, applying truth directly to our hearts, prompting us to conform to truth—in short, sanctifying us in the truth" (Jn. 17:17).

Our part in being transformed by the renewal of our minds is to regularly practice the various spiritual disciplines. Foster (1988) describes the "inward disciplines" (meditation, prayer, fasting, and study), the "outward disciplines" (simplicity, solitude, submission, and service), and the "corporate disciplines" (confession, worship, guidance, and celebration), and he describes how God uses our practice of these disciplines to make us more Christlike. The spiritual disciplines are the means by which the Holy Spirit can help us develop the character of Christ and experience the fruit of the Spirit: love, joy, peace, patience, kindness, goodness, faithfulness, gentleness, and self-control (Gal. 5:22).

Christian counselors who have written on the topic of renewing our minds include Backus and Chapian (2000), Thurman (2003), McMinn (2008), and Stoop (2003). Their books go into much greater depth about the process of developing the mind of Christ.

**Conclusion.** Counseling that is truly Christian involves many perspectives and approaches, but it certainly includes helping people to "take captive every thought to make it obedient to Christ" (2 Cor. 10:5-6). It is an incredible blessing to be instruments in the hands of God to help people know and live out truth so that they can be set free by it.

Chris Thurman

### REFERENCES

Backus, W., & Chapian, M. (2000). *Telling Yourself the Truth.* Bloomington, MN: Bethany.

Foster, R. (1988). *Celebration of Discipline: The Path to Spiritual Growth.* San Francisco, CA: SanFranciscoHarper.

MacArthur, J. (1994). The work of the Spirit in biblical counseling. In J. MacArthur and W. Mack (Eds.), *Introduction to Biblical Counseling.* Dallas, TX: Word.

McMinn, M. (2008). *Cognitive Therapy Techniques in Christian Counseling.* Dallas, TX: Word.

Stoop, D. (2003). *You Are What You Think.* Old Tappan, NJ: Revell.

Thurman, C. (2003). *The Lies We Believe.* Nashville, TN: Nelson.

## BRIEF THERAPY

Brief therapy, sometimes called time-sensitive or time-limited therapy, may be practiced in a number of forms but has a common emphasis in encouraging positive practical gains in a relatively short period of time. The goal is to return counselees to optimal functioning as quickly as possible. To do so, therapists rely heavily on counselee strengths, choice of goals, and desired solutions. Traditional goals of insight, character development, or cure may be less of a focus with this mode of therapy.

**Description.** What constitutes brief therapy? For some, anything short of classic analysis (multiple sessions each week for years at a time) would be considered brief. However, counting hours in session is not a good indicator of brief therapy (Budman & Gurman, 1983). Rather, "The therapist hopes to help the patient achieve maximum benefit with the lowest investment of therapist time and patient cost, both financial and psychological" (p. 277).

This mode of therapy, at its theoretical heart, has a "de-emphasis on the past" and etiology of problems (Cepeda & Davenport, 2010, p. 2). Instead of the counselor treating a patient, the client is the primary expert who works to reframe a complex problem and determine what will produce optimal change in the shortest amount of time. The therapist accepts a coaching, consulting, or cheerleading role and eschews the role of expert. Further, therapy is viewed less as the primary place of change but more of a catalyst of future change.

**History.** The genesis of this view of problems and clients is found in the work of Jay Haley and his strategic family-therapy model (1987) and fleshed out in the later work of John Weakland, Paul Watzlawick, and their fellow researchers (1974).

Some of the current drive for briefer therapies may be the result of rising health care costs and reduced mental-health care insurance coverage, producing a goal to achieve rapid progress with limited counselor-client contact. Some counselors view this trend toward briefer therapies with a wary eye and raise additional questions regarding the soundness of the research supporting the efficacy of time-limited therapy (Miller, 1996).

**Application.** To date, no single model of brief therapy exists, and few graduate students receive specific training in this form of therapy (Levenson & Davidovitz, 2000). Michael Hoyt's 2009 overview provides an excellent starting point for interested readers. Current models include brief psychodynamic therapy (Levenson, 2010), solution-focused therapy (Bannink, 2010), solution-focused couples therapy (Nims, 2007; Ziegler & Hiller, 2007), and short-term group therapy for complicated grief (Piper, Ogrodniczuk, Joyce, & Weideman, 2010). Sometimes included in lists of brief therapies are single-session interventions, such as crisis interventions for traumatic events (e.g., critical incident stress debriefing).

Each of these models of brief therapy share common first-session attributes. Counselors explore the nature of the problem (frequency, intensity, and duration), prior attempts to solve the problem, desired or hoped-for solutions, and first signs of progress ("If we are able to solve this problem, what might be one of the first signs we are making progress?"). Exploring each of these areas enables the client to take the lead role in identifying the problem and solving it. Brief therapists refer back to these questions during subsequent sessions in order to keep the problem in focus, identify progress, and adjust strategy.

**Biblical and Spiritual Issues.** The concept of brief therapy fits nicely with two central themes of the Christian faith. First, Christians mature (become sanctified) in their faith in a lifelong progressive trajectory. Brief therapy also assumes that therapy does not solve all client problems at once; rather, people grow throughout their lives, solving problems as necessary. Therapy, viewed from this model, is episodic and cyclical rather than continual or exhaustive.

Second, Christianity is a community faith in which all are equal before the Creator. Pastors and parishioners alike need discipleship and mutual edification. Brief therapy also assumes a collegial relationship between counselors and clients and rejects an expert-patient view of healing and growth.

**Additional Issues.** If counselors wish to practice brief therapy, it is essential for them to develop competency before employing techniques. Ethical treatment requires that counselors (a) do not promote themselves as competent in brief therapy without education, training, and supervision, (b) inform clients of possible positive and negative consequences of brief therapy as well as its limits, and (c) avoid overpromising treatment results without supporting evidence.

**Philip G. Monroe**

## REFERENCES


Bannink, F. (2010). *1001 Solution-Focused Questions: Handbook for Solution-Focused Interviewing.* New York, NY: Norton.

Budman, S. H., & Gurman, A. S. (1983). The practice of brief therapy. *Professional Psychology: Research & Practice, 14,* 277-292.

Cepeda, L. M., & Davenport, D. S. (2010). Person-centered therapy and solution-focused brief therapy: An integration of present and future awareness. *Psychotherapy: Theory, Research, Practice, Training, 43,* 1-12.

Haley, J. (1987). *Problem-Solving Therapy: New Strategies for Effective Family Therapy* (2nd ed.). San Francisco, CA: Jossey-Bass.

Hoyt, M. F. (2009). *Brief Psychotherapies: Principles and Practices.* Phoenix: Zeig, Tucker & Theisen.

Levenson, H. (2010). *Brief Dynamic Therapy.* Washington, DC: American Psychological Association.

Levenson, H., & Davidovitz, D. (2000). Brief therapy prevalence and training: A national survey of psychologists. *Psychotherapy: Theory, Research, Practice, Training, 37,* 335-340.

Miller, I. J. (1996). Time-limited brief therapy has gone

too far: The result is invisible rationing. *Professional Psychology: Research & Practice, 27*, 567-576.

Nims, D. R. (2007). Integrating play therapy techniques into solution-focused brief therapy. *International Journal of Play Therapy, 16*, 54-68.

Piper, W. E., Ogrodniczuk, J. S., Joyce, A. S., & Weideman, R. (2010). *Short-Term Group Therapies for Complicated Grief: Two Research-Based Models*. Washington, DC: American Psychological Association.

Weakland, J. H., Watzlawick, P. Fisch, R., & Bodin, A. (1974). Brief therapy: Focused problem resolution. *Family Process, 13*, 141-168.

Ziegler, P., & Hiller, T. (2007). Solution-focused therapy with couples. In T. S. Nelson & F. N. Thomas (Eds.), *Handbook of Solution-Focused Therapy: Clinical Applications*. New York, NY: Haworth Press.

## SOLUTION-FOCUSED COUNSELING

**Description.** More than 50 approaches to brief therapy exist. The publication of numerous books and articles as well as the growing attendance at seminars and workshops worldwide suggest that some of the most popular brief therapies are those that emphasize finding solutions more than focusing on problems. Some of the names are solution-focused, solution-oriented, solution-centered, or solution-directed. However, the best known is the solution-focused brief therapy (SFBT) approach developed by Steve deShazer and Insoo Kim Berg at the Brief Family Therapy Center in Milwaukee, Wisconsin.

In doing therapy, deShazer and Berg found that focusing on problems wasn't always helpful and believed that other approaches focused too much on pathology and the past (Macdonald, 2007). They found there were times in clients' experience when their problems weren't as bad or didn't exist at all. They also discovered that if exceptions to the problems were identified, therapists could help clients expand these pockets of problem absence. With these observations, they began to place more emphasis on helping clients identify when the problem wasn't as bad or was absent and identify what was different during those times (Lipchik, 2002). As they spent more time encouraging clients to search for those exceptions, they discovered that solutions could be developed by building on and doing more of what was already working (Connie, 2009).

> The basic premise of this model is that exceptions to problems offer keys and clues to solving problems and that it is more profitable to pay attention to the activities that center around successful solutions than to the problems. These exceptions become the pathway to future solutions (Berg, 1994).

DeShazer and Berg found that by helping clients capitalize on their existing strengths and resources, meaningful change could take place. If both the client and therapist can reorient themselves in the direction of strengths—exceptions to the problem, clarified goals, and strategies to achieve them—then in most cases therapy can be quite brief.

**Philosophy.** Solution-focused therapy is as much a way of looking at change as it is a group of techniques for change (Connie, 2009). It represents a major paradigmatic shift in looking at how people can change. Some theories start by looking at what's not working and how to fix it. This approach chooses to focus on what is right and how to use it. The therapist focuses more on the strengths and resources that clients bring to therapy than on their weaknesses or limitations. The orientation toward solutions is an attempt to create an atmosphere in which people's strengths can move out of the shadows and into the foreground.

Solution-focused therapists emphasize collaborating with people rather than directing or coercing them (Macdonald, 2007). Therapists help clients discover their own solutions rather than trying to impose solutions. Therapists and clients work together on identifying resources and cocreating solutions for what is problematic in the here and now and what needs to happen so that the situation can improve. Solution-focused therapy is a great application of the old discipleship slogan, "Give me a fish and I'll eat for a day. Teach me to fish and I'll eat for a lifetime."

**Techniques.** These are some common techniques used in solution-focused therapy.

*Scaling questions.* Clients are asked to create a scale, with one representing the problem at its worst and ten representing things going so well they no longer need to come in for counseling. They are then asked, "Where are you now?" That can be followed up with a question such as, "What would need to happen for you to be half a point higher on your scale?" Scaling uses language to create a kind of visual image, a spatial component that gives clients a way to notice change while reinforcing the idea that no change is too small or insignificant.

*Exception-finding question.* Central to a solution-focused approach is the hypothesis that no problem happens all of the time or with the same frequency, intensity, and duration. There are always exceptions to the problem. Exceptions are those times when the expected problem doesn't occur or doesn't happen the same way. The basic principle appears simple: Increase what works and decrease what doesn't. What are the exceptions to the problem? What are clients doing differently at those times when they aren't anxious or depressed? What has worked before? What strengths can they apply? What would be a useful solution? How can they construct it?

Exceptions can become building blocks to help clients construct their own solutions. The times when clients are not experiencing the problem becomes very important both for deconstructing the problem and for constructing a solution. An example of an exception-finding question would be, "Tell me about the most recent time the problem didn't occur."

*The miracle question.* "Suppose you were to go home tonight, and while you were asleep, a miracle happened, and the problem that brought you here was solved. How will you and those around you know the miracle happened? What will be different? What would you do different? What would your spouse notice you were doing different?" The miracle question helps clients imagine a future in which meaningful change has taken place. It also helps the therapist determine how realistic their goals are and what change will look like.

The key to success in the miracle question is to help the client expand all of the possibilities, to give a specific, realistic, detailed, and achievable picture of what change might look like at home, at work, at play, at church, and so on. Encourage them to describe inner feelings as well as outward signs.

**Conclusion.** There is a need for additional research to examine the strengths and limitations of solution-focused therapy, but the existing literature demonstrates that making solutions the primary focus of treatment is an effective approach to change. However, therapists learning this approach must beware of becoming solution-*forced* rather than solution-*focused.* The challenge is staying solution-*oriented* rather than solution-*obsessed.*

Solution-focused brief therapy is both a way of looking at change and a way of doing therapy. It isn't the treatment of choice for every situation, but in the hands of a well-trained therapist, it can be a powerful and effective tool for helping people change.

Gary J. Oliver

## REFERENCES

Berg, I. K. (1994). *Family-Based Services: A Solution-Focused Approach* (p. x). New York, NY: Norton.

Connie, E. (2009). Overview of solution focused therapy. In E. Connie & L. Metcalf, *The Art of Solution-Focused Therapy.* New York, NY: Springer.

Lipchik, E. (2002). *Beyond Technique in Solution-Focused Therapy: Working with Emotions and the Therapeutic Relationship.* New York, NY: Guilford Press.

Macdonald, A. J. (2007). *Solution-Focused Therapy: Theory, Research and Practice.* London, England: Sage.

## STRENGTH-BASED COUNSELING

The mental-health field has a long history of focusing on weaknesses, pathologies, mental illnesses, problem behaviors, and deficits. Doctors have studied disease to learn about health, psychologists have investigated depression to learn about happiness, and researchers have scrutinized divorce to learn about happy marriages (Buckingham & Clifton, 2001). And yet within the last 30 years, researchers and practitioners have questioned this problem-focused or deficit-based approach and are moving toward a strength-based model of treating individuals, couples, and families.

Rather than focusing on fixing clients' deficits, *strength-based counseling* focuses on helping clients to identify and use their strengths, assets, skills, talents, abilities, and competencies to confront their challenges. Strength-based therapists encourage clients to articulate what they are hopeful about, what they are already doing well, what character traits can be used in the solution, and what solutions are already proving useful. A strength-based therapist understands that all people have strengths and that individuals' motivations may be enhanced when those around them highlight their strengths.

**Description.** The strength-based model of counseling is a conceptual framework that combines other clinical approaches such as positive psychology, family systems, cognitive-behavioral therapies, and solution-focused therapy (Magyar-Moe, 2009). Implementation of the strength-based approach may vary, but clinicians using a strength-based approach tend to emphasize individual competencies and strengths and employ solution-focused techniques, such as encouraging, instilling hope, and reframing (University of California, 2009).

**History.** The book *Soar with Your Strengths* (Clifton & Nelson, 1992) revealed Donald Clifton's long-standing interest in helping people identify and utilize "their best." After the turn of the millennia, Clifton and his protégé at the Gallup Organization, Marcus Buckingham, became the face of the strengths movement with their bestselling book *Now, Discover Your Strengths* (Buckingham & Clifton, 2001). As these authors took the corporate world by storm, rumblings were occurring in the field of psychology. In the late 1990s, at the dawn of his appointment as the president of the American Psychological Association, Martin Seligman and his colleague Mihaly Csikszentmihalyi launched a new approach called *positive psychology* that helped to redefine strengths in a new way by studying what has gone right rather than wrong in both individuals and societies (Seligman & Csikszentmihalyi, 2000).

**Assessment.** Clinicians working within a strength-based framework emphasize strength-based assessment as a critical first step toward seeing the strengths and competencies of the individual. Strength-based assessment is defined as the measurement of those emotional and behavioral skills, competencies, and characteristics that create a sense of personal accomplishment; contribute to satisfying relationships with family members, peers, and adults; and enhance one's personal, social, and academic development (Epstein & Sharma, 1998).

One of the most popular methods available to help people identify their talents and strengths is the Clifton StrengthsFinder (available at www.strengthsfinder.com). In 1998 the Gallup Organization designed this Web-based assessment to measure 34 of the most common talents within an individual. After people complete the 30-minute online assessment, they receive a customized report that lists their top five talent themes and action items for development and suggestions about how they can use their talents to achieve academic, vocational, and personal success.

**Application.** In her article *The Strength-Based Counseling Model: A Paradigm Shift in Psychology*, Elsie Smith provides a good overview of the stages of strength-based counseling. The first stages are focused on helping clients to identify their strengths and competencies and to use those assets to effectively manage their difficulties. To accomplish this, strength-based therapists might utilize the Clifton StrengthsFinder assessment or teach the clients to uncover strengths using the many categories developed by Christopher Peterson and Martin Seligman in their excellent book *Character Strengths and Virtues: A Handbook and Classification* (2004).

### Stages of Strength-Based Counseling

1. creating the therapeutic alliance
2. identifying strengths
3. assessing present problems
4. encouraging and instilling hope
5. framing solutions
6. building strength and competence
7. empowering
8. changing
9. building resilience
10. evaluating and terminating

In the middle stages, strength-based counselors encourage a sense of hope in clients by focusing on their efforts or improvements rather than the outcomes of their efforts. Therapists also help clients focus on solutions rather than the problems themselves to build confidence and competence as clients realize they have the power to effect important change in their lives.

The final stages of strength-based counseling are designed to help clients view change as a process and to utilize strengths to facilitate change. Clients are also encouraged to view mistakes as opportunities for growth and learning rather than as failures. Clients are also reminded that they have the ability to choose how they will view their adversities in life. "We also glory in our sufferings, because we know that suffering produces perseverance; perseverance, character; and character, hope" (Rom. 5:3-4).

**Biblical and Spiritual Issues.** The Bible is full of verses and stories about how God gifted certain individuals with abilities that would make them effective in carrying out God's work. "Every good and perfect gift is from above, coming down from the Father of the heavenly lights" (Jas. 1:17). The strength-based therapist helps clients to clearly understand that, as a loving Father, God created us with natural abilities, talents, and strengths. "The Lord said to Moses, 'See, I have chosen Bezalel...and I have filled him with the Spirit of God, with wisdom, with understanding, with knowledge in all kinds of skills'" (Ex. 31:1-3). And then, on top of that, God has bestowed spiritual gifts as well (Rom. 12:4-8; 1 Cor. 12:1-11; 14:1-33; Eph. 4:1-13). God granted us strengths and abilities so we can love him and bring glory to his name and also so we can love and serve others. Many good online spiritual-gifts assessments are available to help clients better understand their unique spiritual strengths.

**Conclusion.** Strength-based counseling does not ignore or overlook problems, but instead focuses on what is right about people and strives to help clients understand their strengths and abilities. The therapist and client are solution-focused, working together to discover past and present successes and then using these to address today's challenges. As Paul wrote the believers in Philippi, "Whatever is true, whatever is noble, whatever is right, whatever is pure, whatever is lovely, whatever is admirable—if anything is excellent or praiseworthy—think about such things" (Phil. 4:8).

Greg Smalley

## REFERENCES


Buckingham, M., & Clifton, D. O. (2001). *Now, Discover Your Strengths*. New York, NY: Free Press.

Clifton, D., & Nelson, P. (1992). *Soar with Your Strengths*. New York, NY: Delacorte Press.

Epstein, M. H., & Sharma, J. M. (1998). *Behavioral and Emotional Rating Scale: A Strength-Based Approach to Assessment*. Austin, TX: PRO-ED.

Magyar-Moe, J. L. (2009). *Therapist's Guide to Positive Psychological Interventions*. Burlington, MA: Academic Press.

Peterson, C., & Seligman, M. (2004). *Character Strengths and Virtues: A Handbook and Classification*. New York, NY: Oxford University Press.

Seligman, M., & Csikszentmihalyi, M. (2000). Positive psychology: An introduction. *American Psychologist, 55*, 5-14.

University of California. (2009). *A Strengths Based Approach to Working with Youth and Families: A Review of Research*. Retrieved from http://humanservices.ucdavis.edu/academy/pdf/strength_based.pdf


## TRUTH MODEL OF COUNSELING

The TRUTH principle is a Christian cognitive-behavioral counseling model (Vernick, 2003) that equips therapists to grasp the person-problem dynamic and provides a road map for competent and wise biblical counseling.

**Description.** The TRUTH principle uses the acronym TRUTH to describe a five-step process that moves a person toward greater spiritual, mental, relational, and emotional growth. Each step of the TRUTH principle builds a diagnostic template that assesses how clients see self, others, the world, and God, as well as reveals what solutions they use to cope with their difficulties and where specific changes are needed.

Briefly, the goal of each step is to help individuals

1. gain a new perspective on the *troubles* God allows in their lives
2. come to better understand their *responses* to those trials
3. discover the *underlying* idols, beliefs, and lies that keep them stuck or hamper their efforts to grow or change
4. learn to discern the *truth* of God's Word
5. develop a *heart* response that draws them closer to God in love and obedience.

**Assessment and Treatment.** As Christian counselors, we are called to more than alleviating distressing symptoms. "Christian counselors typically have counseling goals that are fundamentally distinct. Beyond mere alleviation of discomfort—often the sole focus of their secular counterparts—Christian counselors recognize their work as redemptive and restorative in nature" (Johnson & Johnson, 1997). Competent Christian counseling involves both symptom reduction and helping clients think differently, external change and inner redemption and restoration (Vernick & Thurman, 2002).

The stated beliefs of many Christians don't always translate into real-life application, especially when life goes wrong. These are most often the times when people consult pastors and counselors for help. Some of the therapeutic questions and treatment goals this model provides are as follows.

*Trouble.* What is the client's presenting trouble? Clients come to counseling because they have a felt need. The goal in this step is to listen attentively (Pr. 18:13), not only to how people define the problem but also how they see God in the midst of their difficulties.

Listening carefully while the client describes her story enables the counselor to provide empathy, compassion, and care, which are essential to building the therapeutic relationship (Cormier & Cormier, 1997). Listening helps the counselor discern whether the client is looking for growth or merely relief. Is there a sense of hope? And what is that hope in?

Therapeutically, this step helps engage the client in treatment. What does she want to change by coming to counseling? It also presents an opportunity for the counselor to help the client see her present difficulty as an opportunity to grow and trust God more in the midst of her suffering.

*Response.* What is the client's response to his troubles? Specifically, the counselor is listening for the client's automatic thoughts and self-talk, feelings, and behaviors in response to the presenting problem and other life stressors. Does he have a vocabulary for describing internal feelings?

Therapeutic movement looks at whether the client blames others for his response to difficult situations or takes personal responsibility. Clinically and spiritually, we help a person understand how thoughts impact emotions (Ps. 55:2). In addition, it's important for the client to grasp that although thoughts and feelings are powerful, they don't always tell the truth. To facilitate understanding, have the client maintain a journal describing the stressful situation and concurrent feelings, automatic thoughts, and behaviors.

*Underlying idols, beliefs, and lies.* In this step we search for deeper heart themes that are repeated in different stories and situations. How one acts, lives, and thinks flows out of one's heart (Lk. 6:43). Is the client a people pleaser? Someone who craves power and control over others? A perfectionist? A lover of pleasure instead of a lover of God?

Jesus told us that the two greatest commandments are to love God and love others (Mk. 12:30-31). In this step we expose the underlying idols, false gods, deeply held beliefs, and lies that keep clients stuck and unable to make progress, unable to freely choose love and truth.

Therapeutic questions helpful in this step include these: What does she want, love, or fear the most? Often these desires, fears, and false loves have become idolatrous and cluster around the themes of security and comfort; approval, admiration, and affection; and power and control. For example, clients often sigh, "I just want to be happy," or "I just want him to love me." Legitimate needs and feelings have become her functional god, or what she believes she *needs* for life instead of trusting God.

*Truth.* There are many diverse psychotherapy approaches, each asserting its own version of the truth (Gilligan, 2001). In this step we continue to bring the client back to the good news—not only what God says but also who God is. He not only tells us the truth; he is the truth (Jn. 8:32). As Christian counselors, our role is not simply to impart biblical truth. As our clients' false loves are exposed, we invite them to find lasting love with the one who is true—Christ.

*Heart.* Biblical repentance goes much deeper than a change of outward actions. We're looking for a change of heart, a redirection of one's affections. Therapeutically, it's crucial to distinguish between two kinds of sorrow that clients may experience when wrong thinking or sin is exposed. One kind of sorrow leads to death (self-hatred and self-conscious introspection), and the other leads to Christ (repentance) (2 Cor. 7:10). Judas and Peter are excellent examples of each type (Mt. 26–27).

Biblical repentance involves turning from sin and turning to God. A person first does this in his heart, and then he learns to express this change of heart in his daily habits.

**Conclusion.** The five steps of the TRUTH principle, although discussed individually, overlap and are holistic in application. Any gains in therapy must also be practiced outside the office to produce lasting change.

**Leslie Vernick**

## REFERENCES

Cormier, W., & Cormier, L. S. (1997). *Interviewing Strategies for Helpers: Fundamental Skills and Cognitive Behavioral Intervention* (3rd ed.). Pacific Grove, CA: Brooks/Cole.

Gilligan, S. (2001). Getting to the core. In *Family Therapy Network, 25*(1), 22-29, 54-55.

Johnson, W. B., & Johnson, W. L. (1997). A wedding

of faith and practice. *Christian Counseling Today, 5*(1), 15, 52-53.

Vernick, L. (2003). *How to Live Right When Your Life Goes Wrong*. New York, NY: Random House.

Diller, J. V. (2011). *Cultural Diversity: A Primer for the Human Services* (4th ed.). Belmont, CA: Brooks/Cole.

Vernick, L., & Thurman, C. (2002). Change in process: Working from a biblical model of TRUTH in action. In T. Clinton & G. Ohlschlager (Eds.), *Competent Christian Counseling: Foundations and Practice of Compassionate Soul Care* (pp. 376-377). Colorado Springs, CO: WaterBrook Press.

## COGNITIVE CHANGE TECHNIQUES

During the past 30 years, cognitive therapy (also known as cognitive-behavioral therapy or CBT) has become one of the most prominent approaches to psychotherapy. Clinical research has consistently shown its effectiveness in treating many emotional conditions, such as anxiety and depression.

**Principles of Cognitive Therapy.** The philosophy of cognitive therapy is quite simple: Our emotions arise from how we think about any particular situation. The situation itself is not the cause of our distress; our distress comes from our own unique interpretations, evaluations, judgments, and expectations. For example, if I am stuck in traffic and think, "This is terrible! I hate all this traffic. Why doesn't the government do something about this?" I will feel very upset. On the other hand, if I think, "I don't like this traffic, but there's nothing I can do about it," I will feel better and respond more appropriately. Fortunately, we can change how we think so we are not doomed to be victims of emotional distress.

Pioneers in cognitive therapy, such as Aaron Beck, identified certain habits of thinking that cause our distress. They use the term *cognitive distortions*, but I believe this term is too negative and implies that the person is stupid, irrational, or crazy. I prefer the term *automatic negative thoughts* (ANTS). These thoughts are automatic because they come into our minds without our conscious intent. In fact, we might not even notice them until later, when we have had a chance to reflect on our inner experience. Because we really can't control our ANTS, we need not feel bad for having them. As I tell my clients, "I got ANTS, you got ANTS, all God's children got ANTS."

Even though we can't control or eliminate our ANTS, we can control our responses to them. Do we believe them and take them to heart? Or do we challenge their validity and try to replace them with more helpful thoughts? That is what cognitive therapy is all about: claiming the freedom to choose our emotional response to any situation.

**Typical Negative Thinking Habits.** There are several common varieties of ANTS. One of the most common is *all or nothing thinking*. An example would be feeling like a complete failure if one's performance is not perfect. Another example would be thinking that people completely hate you if they make mildly negative comments. All or nothing thinking is often the basis of depression and low self-esteem.

Another common variety is *fortune-telling*. This involves predicting that a bad event is definitely going to happen even if there is little evidence to suggest that it will. For example, a person in the middle of a panic attack will think he is going crazy, and a person might avoid seeing a doctor, thinking, "He might tell me something is wrong." Fortune-telling is the major culprit behind most anxiety.

A third common ANT is *mind reading*. This is assuming that others are thinking negatively about us. If I am at a party and I think, "These people don't like me. They think I'm boring," I am bound to be very uncomfortable. Mind reading is the cause of all social anxiety.

There are several other common varieties of ANTS, such as overgeneralization, discounting the positive, "should" statements, labeling, and emotional reasoning. It is helpful to give clients a list of these ANTS so they will know what to look for.

**Techniques of Cognitive Therapy.** The actual technique of cognitive therapy involves several steps.

First, ask the client to describe a specific event that triggered a high level of distress (e.g., he was late for an appointment, he was criticized by his boss, or he was turned down for a date).

Second, help the client identify any negative thoughts he had concerning the situation. Often clients will say, "I wasn't thinking anything. I was just so anxious." Comments like these are accepted but then followed by questions such as, "If you were thinking something, what might it have been?" Or "What do you think someone else in that situation might have thought?" Encourage the client to write out his thoughts. Often he makes self-critical comments, such as "I know it's stupid to think that way," or "Rationally, I know that's not true, but I can't help feeling it." Encourage the client to write out these thoughts as well.

Third, ask permission to explore his thoughts and ask questions about them. "People often find it helpful to take an objective look at their thoughts to see if they might want to change them. To help you with that, would it be okay to ask you a few questions about your thoughts?"

Fourth, having been given permission, ask questions that encourage your client to explore his thoughts in depth.

- "What type of ANT might that thought be?"
- "What is the evidence that this thought is true, and what is the evidence that it is not true?"
- "What might someone else think about this?"
- "Can you think of any alternative ways to think about this?"
- "What are the advantages of thinking of this, and what are the disadvantages?"
- "What would you say to a good friend who was thinking like this?"

Finally, invite the client to see if there is a different way to think about the situation, one that would be more helpful and cause less distress. "I am a failure because I made a 90 on the test" turns into "I wish I had made a 100, but a 90 is okay, and I'll work to do better next time."

Assume an attitude of humble curiosity about a client's thoughts and feelings. Do not argue or try to convince him that his thoughts are irrational or wrong. If the client cannot see a different way to think about the situation, you might suggest one, but don't force it. It is more important to maintain the therapeutic relationship than to convince a client to think differently.

**Spiritual Issues.** In their delightful book *Telling Yourself the Truth*, William Backus and Marie Chapian integrate cognitive therapy with solid biblical principles. Because we are made in God's image, our ANTS cannot be true reflections of who we are. As we learn to think more positively, we affirm that we are unconditionally loved by God and that our worth comes from him.

**Stanley E. Hibbs**

## REFERENCES

Backus, W., & Clark, M. (2000). *Telling Yourself the Truth*. Minneapolis, MN: Bethany House.

Burns, D. (1989). *The Feeling Good Handbook*. New York, NY: Penguin Books.

Clark, D. A., & Beck, A. T. (2010). *Cognitive Therapy of Anxiety Disorders*. New York, NY: Guilford Press.

Hibbs, S. E. (2007). *Anxiety Gone: The Three C's of Anxiety Recovery*. Mustang, OK: Dare2Dream Books.

*Part 6*

# Systemic and Ethical Issues, Education, and Research

# 23

# MULTICULTURALISM, DIVERSITY, AND OTHER CHALLENGING ISSUES

## ASSIMILATION AND ACCULTURATION

**Description.** The goal of counseling is change, and ways to bring about change are culturally dependent. An ethnic minority's reaction to counseling, the counseling process, and the counselor are all influenced by ethnicity and cultural identity. Therefore, increased awareness and knowledge of different ethnic groups and development of skills for effective counseling relationships across cultures must be part of the professional growth process for all counselors. Understanding assimilation and acculturation are necessary for studying the experiences of ethnic groups in the United States and the world.

*Acculturation* is a term that describes both the process of contacts between different cultures and also the customs of such contacts. As the process of contact between cultures, acculturation may involve either direct social interaction or exposure to other cultures by means of the mass media (Berry, 1988, 1992, 1994). As the outcome of such contact, acculturation is the assimilation by one group of the culture of another, which modifies the existing culture and so changes group identity. There may be tension between old and new cultures, leading to the adapting of the new as well as the old.

Assimilation is a process of integration whereby members of an ethno-cultural community (such as immigrants or ethnic minorities) are absorbed into another, generally larger, community. This implies the loss of the characteristics of the absorbed group, such as language, customs, ethnicity, and self-identity (Berry, 1988, 1992, 1994).

**History.** As counselors incorporate a greater awareness of their clients' culture into their theory and practice, they must realize that historically, cultural differences have been viewed as deficits. Adherence to white cultural values has brought about a naive imposition of narrowly defined criteria for normality on culturally diverse people. Multicultural counseling, however, seeks to rectify this imbalance by acknowledging cultural diversity, appreciating the value of the culture, and using it to aid the client (Sue & Sue, 2008).

**Assessment.** Using the two-dimensional model, J. W. Berry (1997) has suggested four possible outcomes of the acculturation process: assimilation (movement toward the dominant culture), integration (synthesis of the two cultures), rejection (reaffirmation of the traditional culture), or marginalization (alienation from both cultures). Similarly, Sodowsky, Lai, and Plake (1991) have defined three dimensions of acculturation: assimilation, biculturalism (the ability to live in both worlds, with denial of neither), and observance of traditionality (rejection of the dominant culture).

Counselors can use questions such as these to assess acculturation.

1. What language do you speak?
2. What language do you prefer?
3. How do you self-identify?
4. Which ethnic identification do (did) your mother and father use?

5. What was the ethnic origin of the friends and peers you had as a child?
6. With whom do you now associate in the outside community?
7. What music, television shows, and movies do you prefer?
8. Where were you born?
9. Where were you raised?
10. What food do you prefer?
11. In what language do you read? Write? Think?
12. How much pride do you have in your ethnic group?

These are some of the characteristics of acculturation:

- *Integrated individuals.* Individuals want to maintain their identity with home culture but also want to take on some characteristics of the new culture.
- *Assimilated individuals.* These people do not want to keep their identity from their home culture, but would rather take on all of the characteristics of the new culture.
- *Separated individuals.* They want to separate themselves from the dominant culture. It can be called segregation if it is forced separation.
- *Marginalized individuals.* These individuals don't want anything to do with either the new culture or the old culture.

**Treatment.** A major assumption for culturally effective counseling and psychotherapy is that we can acknowledge our own basic tendencies, the ways we comprehend other cultures, and the limits our culture places on our comprehension (Sue & Sue, 2008). It is essential to understand our own cultural heritage and worldview before we set about understanding and assisting other people. This understanding includes an awareness of one's own philosophies of life and capabilities, a recognition of different structures of reasoning, and an understanding of their effects on one's communication and helping style. Lack of such understanding may hinder effective intervention.

Part of this self-awareness is the acknowledgement that the "counselor culture" has at its core a set of white cultural values and norms by which clients are judged (Katz, 1985; Lauver, 1986). This acculturation is simultaneously general, professional, and personal. Underlying assumptions about a cultural group, personal stereotypes or racism, and traditional counseling approaches may all signal acquiescence to white culture. Identification of specific white cultural values and their influence on counseling will help to counter the effects of this framework (Katz, 1985). Effective counselors must investigate their clients' cultural background and be open to flexible definitions of appropriate or correct behavior.

Another counseling barrier is language. Language differences may be perhaps the most important stumbling block to effective multicultural counseling and assessment (Sue & Sue, 2008). Language barriers impede the counseling process when clients cannot express the complexity of their thoughts and feelings or resist discussing affectively charged issues.

**Biblical Issues.** In Galatians 3:28, Paul wrote, "There is neither Jew nor Greek, neither slave nor free, nor is there male and female, for you are all one in Christ Jesus." The first thing to understand in this discussion is that there is only one race—the human race. God does not show partiality or favoritism (Dt. 10:17; Acts 10:34; Rom. 2:11; Eph. 6:9), and neither should we. James 2:4 describes those who discriminate as "judges with evil thoughts." Instead, we are to love our neighbors as ourselves (Jas.

2:8). In the Old Testament, God divided humanity into two "racial" groups: Jews and Gentiles. God's intent was for the Jews to be a kingdom of priests, ministering to the Gentile nations. Instead, for the most part, walls grew between Jews and Gentiles. Jesus Christ put an end to this, destroying the dividing wall of hostility (Eph. 2:14). All forms of racism, prejudice, and discrimination are affronts to the work of Christ on the cross.

**Conclusion.** There is always the danger of stereotyping clients and of confusing other influences, especially race and socioeconomic status, with cultural influences. The most obvious danger in counseling is to oversimplify the client's social system by emphasizing the most obvious aspects of her background. Universal categories are necessary to understand human experience, but losing sight of specific individual factors would lead to ethical violations. Individual clients are influenced by race, ethnicity, national origin, life stage, educational level, social class, and sex roles. Counselors must view the identity and development of culturally diverse people in terms of multiple interactive factors rather than a strictly cultural framework. A pluralistic counselor considers all facets of the client's personal history, family history, and social and cultural orientation.

Mark J. Crear

## REFERENCES

Berry, J. W. (1988). Psychology of acculturation: Understanding individuals moving between cultures. In J. W. Berry & R. C. Annis (Eds.), *Ethnic Psychology: Research and Practice with Immigrants, Refugees, Native Peoples, Ethnic Groups and Sojourners* (pp. 1-40). Lisse, the Netherlands: Swets & Zeitlinger.

Berry, J. W. (1992). Acculturation and adaptation in a new society. *International Migration Review, 30*, 69-85.

Berry, J. W. (1994). Acculturation and psychological adaptation: An overview. In A. M. Bouvy, F. J. R. van de Vijver, P. Boski, & P. Schmitz (Eds.), *Journeys into Cross-Cultural Psychology* (pp. 129-141). Lisse, the Netherlands: Swets & Zeitlinger.

Berry, J. W. (1997). Immigration, acculturation, and adaptation. *Applied Psychology, 46*(1), 5-34.

Katz, J. H. (1985).The sociopolitical nature of counseling. *The Counseling Psychologist, 13*, 615-623.

Lauver, P. J. (1986). Extending counseling cross-culturally: Invisible barriers. Paper presented at the annual meeting of the California Association for Counseling and Development, San Francisco, CA. (ED 274 937). In J. G. Ponterotto, J. M. Casas, L. A. Suzuki, & C. M. Alexander (Eds.), *Handbook of Multicultural Counseling* (pp. 155-180). Thousand Oaks, CA: Sage.

Sodowsky, G. R., Lai, E. M., & Plake, B. S. (1991). Moderating effects on sociocultural variables on acculturation attitudes of Hispanics and Asian Americans. *Journal of Counseling and Development, 70*, 194-204.

Sue, W. S., & Sue, D. (2008). *Counseling the Culturally Diverse: Theory and Practice* (5th ed). Hoboken, NY: Wiley & Sons.

## CULTURAL COMPETENCE AND MINORITY GROUPS

**Description.** The United States is ever changing. Census data suggest Latinos now make up at least 14% of its population. African-Americans account for 13%; Asian Americans, 4%; Whites, 65%; and other races, 4%. By 2050, minority groups are projected to account for more than half of the U.S. population. Dramatic demographic changes, however, are not just limited to ethnic groups. For example, the fastest-growing demographic group is the elderly. Also, the differences between the rich, the middle class, and lower socioeconomic groups continue to grow. More religions and denominational diversity are also seen. With this complexity, the previous emphasis on "minority groups" has transformed to "multiple identities" (Roysircar, Dobbins, & Malloy, 2010, p. 181). Given these substantial shifts, Christian counselors must possess high levels of cultural competence to work effectively with increasingly diverse clients. Therapists need a biblical framework for cultural competence so they can identify counseling mistakes related to culture, consider biblical social justice, and utilize competencies from mental-health professional organizations.

**Biblical Framework for Cultural Competence.** The multicultural literature emphasizes a postmodern, social constructionist worldview. In this worldview, ethics and values are relative. All values from different cultures are equal. Significant logical problems result. For example, how does one justify the statement that racism is wrong when some cultural groups see racism (and perhaps even genocide) as one of their significant cultural values to be respected? Some values obviously must be better than others, but postmodernism offers no clear standard for making those judgments.

A biblical framework begins with God's Word as the standard. Racism is wrong because all people are created in God's image (*imago Dei*), we are called to treat others as we want to be treated (Mt. 7:12), and loving one another is the second-most important thing we can do in all of life (Mk. 12:28-31). In counseling, to love other people means we must see the world through our clients' eyes and understand their perspectives. Thus, we adopt a learner's perspective with our clients as opposed to an expert when it comes to their culture. We must also endeavor to see each client through God's eyes, with his compassion, grace, standards, and wisdom. Both starting points are critical to prevent counseling miscues.

**Common Counseling Errors.** Counselors who develop cultural competence avoid many mistakes. Three common errors include pathologizing reasonable mistrust, misreading cultural communication, and stereotyping.

At the beginning of treatment, clients who live in the inner city or have experienced racism might display high levels of mistrust. Clinicians sometimes classify this as pathological paranoia when it is actually an effective survival strategy. Specifically, the inner city is filled with danger. Trusting too easily will get you killed. Likewise, clients who have experienced blatant and subtle forms of discrimination learn to constantly read people, testing them to see who can be trusted. Accordingly, the therapist will be tested too.

Clinicians sometimes misread cultural communication. This is especially common for clients from collectivistic cultures. For example, an enculturated adult Chinese client may consider it impolite to tell the therapist directly when a homework assignment is problematic, but the clinician might interpret the homework noncompliance as resistance. The Chinese client also might feel compelled to discuss life decisions with grandparents and parents. The clinician might interpret this as enmeshment.

In stereotyping, the therapist makes assumptions about the client that are not accurate. Negative assumptions can arise from many sources, including harmful majority culture portrayals of the group, hurtful previous experiences, personal biases, and overgeneralizing from clinical chapters about the client's cultural group. Clinician self-awareness and individualized client assessment reduce this danger.

**Biblical Social Justice.** Secular social-justice models seek to help disadvantaged groups through systemically altering government policies, changing laws, and modifying private organizational procedures. These models have some merit, but they categorize people along oppressor and victim categories, which may create defensiveness in those classified as oppressors and entitlement in those classified as victims. Secular social-justice proponents themselves also may develop a prideful elitism that can justify, in its extreme form, harming those classified as oppressors. One can examine communism's history to view an example of this.

Biblical social justice does not start with the social system. It starts with God's broken heart for suffering people and his anger at injustice (see, for example, Ps. 10). It continues with individuals and their responsibilities. People make up systems and people possess a fallen nature, which naturally leads to the development of discriminatory social systems. Oppressor, victim, and social-justice proponents alike are called to recognition of personal sin, individual repentance, and a tangible responsibility to help the needy. All therefore are called to help the suffering. Those who are suffering are responsible to seek the Lord and make choices to improve their situation. Therefore, although there is a place for government programs, the Bible emphasizes the importance of spiritual renewal and individual actions. In addition, the church is called to develop ministries to help (both tangibly and spiritually) those in need. We are our brothers' keepers (Gen. 4:9).

**Professionally Recognized Essential Competencies.** All major mental-health organizations have adopted standards for cultural competence. In professional counseling, the Association for Multicultural Development recommends three key domains in which counselors must develop knowledge, attitudes, and skills for cultural competence (Arredondo et al., 1996).

These domains interconnect for effective therapy. Counselors must be aware of their own cultural values and biases. From a Christian point of view, bias is a by-product of the fallen nature, so self-awareness is consistent with a biblical emphasis on self-examination and repentance. Counselors must also seek to understand the client's worldview. Seeing the world through the client's eyes is a part of loving our neighbors as ourselves. Finally, counselors seek to develop culturally appropriate intervention strategies for their individual clients. This mirrors Paul's emphasis in evangelism on becoming all things to all people that he might win some to Christ (1 Cor. 9:22).

**Summary.** As Christian therapists work with an increasingly diverse client population, the need for cultural competence becomes more apparent. These perceptions and skills can reduce significant counseling errors. Mental-health organizations now have developed cultural competencies for clinical practice. Secular multicultural frameworks adopt a postmodern perspective filled with pitfalls, but the Bible provides a distinctively Christian approach to cultural competence and social justice.

Fernando Garzon

### REFERENCES

Arredondo, P., Toporek, R., Brown, S., Jones, J., Locke, D. C., Sanchez, J., & Stadler, H. (1996). Operationalization of the multicultural counseling competencies. *Journal of Multicultural Counseling and Development, 24*(1), 42-78.

Roysircar, G., Dobbins, J., & Malloy, K. (2010). Diversity competence in training and clinical practice. Competency-based education for professional psychology. In M. Kenkel & R. Peterson (Eds.), *Competency-Based Education for Professional Psychology* (pp. 179-197). Washington, DC: American Psychological Association.

## ETHNICITY

**Description.** The United States is one of the most diverse nations in the world (McAuliffe, 2008). The U.S. Census Bureau predicts that the minority population will comprise fully half the U.S. population by the year 2050 (Ethnic Majority, 2010). To fully grasp the human diversity of the United States or any other country, it is important to first understand the social constructs used for making group distinctions. In America, gender, ethnicity, and race are three visual characteristics used to categorize people.

For social scientists, ethnicity is the preferred concept for describing cultural group membership. Race is used to describe groups of people based on physical appearances. The terms *ethnicity* and *ethnic group* refer to groups of people that share ancestry, geography, cultural roots or tribal affiliations, language, and a sense of identity, which define gender roles and determine the food they eat, the way they communicate, the music they enjoy, parenting practices, and their celebration rituals. Individuals within ethnic groups may or may not share the same physical features (McAuliffe, 2008). The United States recognizes several broad ethnic groups, including European American, Latino/Latinas, African-American, Asian-American, and Native American (Lee, Blando, Mizelle, & Orozco, 2007).

**History.** Despite the diverse realities that make up the United States, perceptions of cultural superiority and theories based on a Eurocentric perspective have dominated the counseling profession (McAuliffe, 2008). For many years, counselors ignored cultural differences and counseled all clients as if they were of the same ethnic background. Consequently, clients from nondominant ethnic groups often did not find counseling to be helpful. In the wake of the civil rights movement, counselors began to recognize the impact of sociocultural experiences on human development and well-being. New ideas about counseling emerged to address multicultural issues.

**Awareness and Assessment.** Counselors who work with clients from nondominant ethnic groups, especially immigrants, need to assess their clients' levels of acculturation and enculturation. *Enculturation* is the way individuals learn the distinct, unique behaviors and values of a culture through interactions with parents, family, and peer groups and through education and media (McAuliffe, 2008; Schmidt, 2006). The "melting pot theory" was a myth that taught that nondominant groups abandon their ethnic values and completely assimilate to the U.S. culture in order to live successfully in the dominant culture. *Acculturation*, contrasted with assimilation, is the process of taking on some of the manners and values of the dominant culture while maintaining some of the original cultural expressions and norms. Individuals who are highly acculturated and highly enculturated feel connected to both cultures; they pick and choose aspects of each to internalize into their self-concept (Lee et al., 2007).

A counselor cannot know people's levels of acculturation and enculturation by their ethnic labels alone. Counselors can assess them by gathering information about the clients' choice of friends, participation in cultural activities, language use, attitudes and beliefs about social relations and gender roles, knowledge of historically significant events, and ethnic identity.

Ethnic identity is an important component of a person's self-concept and strongly influences self-perception. Ethnic identity can be positive, negative, or ambivalent. Individuals with a positive ethnic identity accept and celebrate their ethnic identity. Negative identifiers tend to deny or reject their ethnic group, sometimes to the point of accepting the dominant culture's prejudices and stereotypes about their ethnic group. Ambivalent identifiers waver between both rejecting and accepting their ethnic identity. Positive identifiers tend to be healthier psychologically and better adjusted, but negative and ambivalent identifiers tend to harbor feelings of self-depreciation and a poor self-image (Diller, 2010).

**Biblical and Spiritual Issues.** Christian counselors cannot ignore God's master plan of variety and still call themselves culturally competent. Genesis describes the creation of a diverse world. Humans were created in God's image, and he pronounced man as "very good" (Gen. 1:31). Therefore, all races and ethnic groups have the same status, dignity, and worth that result from bearing the image of God. Churches can demonstrate that they openly welcome all cultural groups through written media, decor, music choice, and openness to different expressions of worship. Those who counsel multiethnic congregations should learn as much as they can about their clients' culture before meeting with them.

Ignoring ethnicity diminishes the importance of the unique differences God placed in humankind. Ethnic superiority or ethnic inferiority is in direct disobedience to God's command in John 13:34 to love others and the value of the image of God in every person (Lee, 2010). Christian counselors must help clients address negative self-images related to their ethnic identity. Cultural sensitivity is loving and serving all of God's people; cultural competence is using biblically based strategies that are responsive to ethnic values. Cultural awareness is compassionate soul care.

JACQUELINE SMITH

## REFERENCES

Diller, J. V. (2010). *Cultural Diversity: A Primer for the Human Services* (2nd ed.). Belmont, CA: Brooks/Cole.

Ethnic Majority. (2010). *Demographics: African, Hispanic, and Asian American Demographics* [Data file]. Retrieved from http://www.ethnicmajority.com/demographics_home.htm

Lee, H. (2010). Building a community of shalom: What the Bible says about multicultural education. *A Journal of the International Christian Community for Teacher Education, 5*(2).

Lee, W. M., Blando, J. A., Mizelle, N. D., & Orozco, G. L. (2007). *Introduction to Multicultural Counseling for Helping Professionals* (2nd ed.). New York, NY: Taylor & Francis.

McAuliffe, G. (2008). What is culturally alert counseling? In G. McAuliffe & Associates, *Culturally Alert Counseling: A Comprehensive Introduction* (pp. 2-44). Thousand Oaks, CA: Sage.

Schmidt, J. J. (2006). *Social and Cultural Foundations of Counseling and Human Services: Multiple Influences on Self-Concept Development.* Boston, MA: Prentice Hall.

## MULTICULTURAL COUNSELING

**DEFINITION.** Multicultural counseling—sometimes also referred to as cross-cultural counseling—is a helping relationship intentionally attentive to the diversity of experiences and cultural realities of the individuals involved as they delineate goals and strategies for the healing process (Sue & Torino, 2005). As the United States continues to become more diverse, groups labeled as minorities are quickly growing. In fact, they are on the verge of becoming a "colorful" majority. Today, counseling and psychology have recognized the need for more culturally sensitive professionals who are better trained to respond to their needs and goals for treatment. This approach challenges the assumption that everyone fits into a European American model—a position known as *etic*, or culturally universal or neutral—and calls for training programs and practitioners to intentionally consider and address the uniqueness of ethnically and culturally different clients—a position known as *emic*, or culturally specific.

Although there is no consistency in the literature, one key difference between multicultural counseling and cross-cultural counseling is that the latter seems to be more focused on universal and indigenous models, approaches, and techniques that facilitate healing in other countries worldwide, rather than just in the United States of America (Gerstein, Heppner, Ægisdóttir, Leung, & Norsworthy, 2009). Some of the most prominent promoters of multicultural counseling advocate a balanced use of theories and techniques relevant to various cultures and realities, as well as culture-specific techniques, when crafting treatments to promote health and growth in individuals and communities in the United States (Sue & Sue, 2008). An important assumption is that the effectiveness of the therapeutic relationship is mediated by the counselor's ability to be contextually congruent to the client's reality and story (Augsburger, 1986).

**APPLICATION.** Two main positions dominate the conversation about multicultural counseling. On the one hand, a strong movement in the fields of counseling and psychology stresses the need for a culturally competent clinician, someone who, by developing a number of competencies or by following very specific standards and guidelines, is equipped to educate and practice in a diverse context (Sue, Arredondo, & McDavis, 1992; Arredondo, 1999; American Psychological Association, 2003). On the other hand, there is a position challenging the culturally competent counselor model, stating that all counseling is multicultural because we live in a multicultural society. This position argues that competent counselors are already equipped with a set of skills intended to effectively provide a therapeutic relationship, which is the main condition for effectively engaging clients from a variety of contexts and cultures (Patterson, 2004; also see Weinrach & Thomas, 2002). This so-called "universal" system—based on client-centered therapy by Carl Rogers—proposes five basic qualities any counselor should have: respect for the client; genuineness; empathic understanding; communication of empathy, respect, and genuineness; and structuring of the counselor's role (see Rogers, 1957, 1961; Pedersen, 1976). These qualities guarantee effectiveness when working with clients from any culture or ethnicity.

**A Culturally Competent Counselor.** The supporters of a multicultural model identify some essential dimensions and goals for every culturally competent counselor (Sue, et al., 1992; Arredondo, 1999; Sue & Sue, 2008).

First, culturally competent counselors are intentionally and constantly aware of their own assumptions, values, and biases and how they may interfere with or facilitate effective work with clients from all backgrounds but especially those who are culturally and ethnically different. Counselors should be cognizant of how their cultural background informs their views of clients, their emotional responses to them, their ability to form alliances or invite resistance as the therapeutic relationship develops, and their diagnostic conceptualization and treatment planning.

Second, culturally competent counselors search for understanding about the worldview of their culturally diverse clients. In pursuit of a true therapeutic relationship, counselors invest in learning about their clients' culture and unique ways of experiencing the world. This competency requires and also stimulates an open mind, making counselors more receptive to ideas, beliefs, and assumptions that may be radically different from their own.

Third, culturally competent counselors intentionally learn and practice relevant interventions, strategies, and techniques for working with clients from a culturally diverse background. The effectiveness of a particular treatment will be significantly enhanced by the integration of therapeutic modalities consistent with the cultural realities, experiences, and values of their clients.

**Multicultural Counseling and the Bible.** Diversity is at the core of multiculturalism. Clearly, humanity has much in common. Many shared characteristics make us part of the human race. It is not possible to deny, however, that many differences make us unique as well. The Bible acknowledges those differences and shows how God—who is three persons in one substance—values the distinctiveness of everyone he created.

The God of creation took the time to carefully imprint uniqueness in every part of his creation, but even more when he created human beings (Gen. 1:27). The psalmist expresses this with poetic beauty by saying, "Oh yes, you shaped me first inside, then out; you formed me in my mother's womb.... You know exactly how I was made, bit by bit, how I was sculpted from nothing into something" (Ps. 139:13,15 MSG). Every human being received the same dedication, attention, and exclusivity in God's act of creation, so everyone is unique and different from the rest.

As part of the kingdom of God, Christian counselors have a mandate to recognize their own uniqueness and reflect on how this individuality interacts with the uniqueness of the client, who also has particular ways of experiencing life. A multicultural

Christian counselor is one who appreciates the diversity of God's creation, respects the unique imprint in everyone, and thrives in practice by developing the competencies needed to better serve those in need of healing and growth.

**Conclusion.** Multicultural counseling acknowledges the fact that there is not a single way of healing. This form of counseling expects professionals to be able to use tested and familiar resources to treat clients as they also understand how cultural differences play an important role in the therapeutic relationship and develop competencies that facilitate their work with others.

J. Javier Sierra

## REFERENCES

American Psychological Association. (2003). Guidelines on multicultural education, training, research, practice and organizational change for psychologists. *American Psychologist, 58,* 377-402.

Arredondo, P. (1999). Multicultural counseling competencies as tools to address oppression and racism. *Journal of Counseling & Development, 77,* 102-109.

Augsburger, D. W. (1986). *Pastoral Counseling Across Cultures.* Philadelphia, PA: Westminster Press.

Gerstein, L. H., Heppner, P. P., Ægisdóttir, S., Leung, S. A., & Norsworthy, K. L. (2009). Cross-cultural counseling: History, challenges and rationale. In L. H. Gerstein, P. P. Heppner, S. Ægisdóttir, S. A. Leung, & K. L. Norsworthy (Eds.), *International Handbook of Cross-Cultural Counseling: Cultural Assumptions and Practices Worldwide.* Thousand Oaks, CA: Sage.

Patterson, C. H. (2004). Do we need multicultural counseling competencies? *Journal of Mental Health Counseling, 26,* 67-73.

Pedersen, P. (1976). The field of intercultural counseling. In P. Pedersen, W. J. Lonner, & J. G. Draguns (Eds.), *Counseling Across Cultures.* Honolulu. HI: University Press of Hawaii.

Rogers, C. R. (1957). The necessary and sufficient conditions of therapeutic personality change. *Journal of Consulting Psychology, 21,* 95-103.

Rogers, C. R. (1961). *On Becoming a Person.* Boston, MA: Houghton Mifflin.

Sue, D. W., Arredondo, P., & McDavis, R. J. (1992). Multicultural counseling competencies and standards: A call to the profession. *Journal of Counseling & Development, 70,* 477-486.

Sue, D. W., & Sue, D. (2008). *Counseling the Culturally Diverse* (5th ed.). Hoboken, NJ: Wiley & Sons.

Sue, D. W., & Torino, G. C. (2005). Racial-cultural competence: Awareness, knowledge and skills. In R. T. Carter (Ed.), *Handbook of Racial-Cultural Psychology and Counseling.* Hoboken, NJ: Wiley & Sons.

Weinrach, S. G., & Thomas, K. R. (2002). A critical analysis of the multicultural counseling competencies: Implications for the practice of mental health counseling. *Journal of Mental Health Counseling, 24*(1), 20-35.

## RACIAL IDENTITY

**Description.** Every counseling encounter is a cross-cultural interaction between two complex, multidimensional human beings. All of us are part of the human race, but physical characteristics such as hair type, color of eyes and skin, and ancestry have been used to dominate, oppress, and marginalize groups of people. For this reason, counselors cannot ignore the powerful influence race has on the way individuals think about themselves and others.

Much of multicultural counseling has focused on differences between races (*inter*cultural differences), giving little attention to the differences within racial and ethnic groups (*intra*cultural differences). Research indicates that there is often more diversity within a racial group than between racial groups (Lee, Blando, Mizelle, & Orozco, 2007). Racial-identity development models help to explain the differences within racial groups. They provide a framework for understanding the psychological aspect of race and racism on the individual's developing self-concept and well-being. One of the values of these models is that they explain how individuals at different stages of development may exhibit different needs and feel differently about what defines supportive counseling.

**History.** Racial identity models emerged in the counseling and psychology literature in the 1970s. Separate racial identity models exist for each racial group. Some models differ in the name and number of stages, the content of each stage, and process of movement from one stage to the next; however, the general process of racial identity development is the same for all people of color (POC).

**Assessment, Awareness, and Application.** Diller (2011) stated that racial identification has two processes. The first is the connection that individuals feel to their racial group or origin, and the second is their awareness or consciousness of the impact that race has had on their life process. These points summarize some of the most prominent theories of racial and ethnic identity development for POC:

1. In the first stage, POC value the dominant race over their own race. Both consciously and subconsciously, they tend to devalue or have a neutral attitude toward their own racial group. POC clients in this stage are likely to prefer a white counselor.

2. In the second stage, POC experience a state of internal conflict between their self-depreciating attitudes and exposure to positive attributes about their racial group. They also witness racism and feel a sense of having been "had." White counselors will experience anxiety trying to appear competent in the face of the client's ambivalence with them.

3. In stage three, POC completely endorse views of their racial group and reject the dominant society. White counselors should expect clients of color to be suspicious of them and prefer a counselor of their race.

4. In stage four, POC move toward greater individual autonomy, questioning their rigidly held negative beliefs of the dominant culture and the unequivocal appreciation of their own racial group. They also become sensitive to other racial groups. White or same-race counselors can partner with clients of color as they evaluate their ideas.

5. In the fifth stage, POC experience a sense of self-fulfillment and appreciation for their own cultural background and selectively trust members of the dominant group. They have no racial preference for a counselor but prefer counselors who are culturally aware (Atkinson, 2004; Crethar & Vargas, 2007; Erwin, Huang, & Lin, 2002).

Racial identity is not limited to people of color. Helms' model of white racial identity development allows white Americans to assess their own beliefs and identity development. They move from being oblivious to the influence of race on others' lives or their own, to recognizing they have negative attitudes and prejudices about POC, to a desire to understand racism, to an awareness of white privilege, and finally, to a nonracist identity. White counselors in the early stages may discount experiences of racism or refuse to work with clients of color. In the last stages, the white counselor is able to address issues of race with clients of color and ultimately promote actions to increase equity for all people (Crethar & Vargas, 2007; McAuliffe, 2008; Schmidt, 2006).

**Biblical and Spiritual Issues.** Physical characteristics are not a part of God's evaluation of man. When God sent Samuel to find a new king for his people, the prophet was surprised when God didn't select the first of Jesse's sons. God told Samuel, "The Lord does not look at the things people look at. People look at the outward appearance, but the Lord looks at the heart" (1 Samuel l6:7). The instruction applies to us too as we consider the people God puts in our paths.

Unfortunately, we live in a fallen world, where racism and discrimination damage people's souls. When assessing stages of identity development, Christian counselors may uncover bitterness, unforgiveness, or prejudice. Christian counselors must help people forgive others in their hearts (Col. 3:13). To heal racial divisions and facilitate emotional and spiritual freedom, they can share biblical insights (Lk. 6:27-28; Acts 8:2-23; Jas. 2:8-9), empathize with injustice, acknowledge unconfessed sin, pray for forgiveness, and facilitate spiritual-formation activities.

**Jacqueline Smith**

## REFERENCES


Atkinson, D. R. (2004). Within-group differences among ethnic minorities. In D. R. Atkinson, *Counseling American Minorities* (6th ed., pp. 27-56). New York, NY: McGraw-Hill.

Crethar, H. C., & Vargas, L. A. (2007). Multicultural intricacies in professional counseling. In Gregoire, J., & Jungers, C. (Eds.), *The Counselor's Companion: What Every Beginning Counselor Needs to Know* (pp. 52-71). Mahwah, NJ: Lawrence Erlbaum.

Diller, J. V. (2011). *Cultural Diversity: A Primer for the Human Services* (4th ed.). Belmont, CA: Brooks/Cole.

Erwin, K. T., Huang, W. J., & Lin, D. L. S. (2002). The world at our doorstep: Multicultural counseling and special populations. In T. Clinton & G. Ohlschlager (Eds.), *Competent Christian Counseling: Foundations and Practice of Compassionate Soul Care* (Vol. 1, pp. 615-637). Colorado Springs, CO: WaterBrook Press.

Lee, W. M., Blando, J. A., Mizelle, N. D., & Orozco, G. L. (2007). *Introduction to Multicultural Counseling for Helping Professionals* (2nd ed.). New York, NY: Taylor & Francis.

McAuliffe, G. (2008). What is culturally alert counseling? In G. M. Associates, *Culturally Alert Counseling: A Comprehensive Introduction* (pp. 2-44). Thousand Oaks: Sage.

Schmidt, J. J. (2006). *Social and Cultural Foundations of Counseling and Human Services: Multiple Influences on Self-Concept Development.* Boston, MA: Prentice Hall.

# ETHICAL AND LEGAL COUNSELING ISSUES

## ACCOUNTABILITY

Christian counselors and caregivers are uniquely positioned to demonstrate the affirmation of life, the upholding of human dignity, the cultivation of love for others, and the sacrifice and service of self-denial. This reality carries with it both a profound opportunity and a responsibility to authentically represent Christ as his ambassadors. Guarding of this sacred trust requires the practice of true accountability. As the adage observes, people rarely do what is expected, but what is inspected. The apostle Paul stated, "It is required of stewards that one be found trustworthy" (1 Cor. 4:2 NASB). Usually, godly leaders have first learned to be good followers. Following is where faithfulness is developed, but only when one is close enough to be observed and provided with feedback.

Most training in ethics attempts to address the kinds of problems that licensing and other regulatory boards frequently investigate and render decisions on when an alleged violation occurs. This includes theoretical models and decision-making paradigms that focus on issues such as confidentiality, dual relationships, scope of practice, informed consent, duty to warn, and recordkeeping, to name a few (Hill, 2004). Yet in a comprehensive review of ethical violations in nearly every state in the country between 2000 and 2007, it was discovered that regulatory boards continue to investigate cases and either suspend or revoke practice licenses for these same issues year after year. What is missing?

Some research suggests that significant deficiencies regarding ethics preparation still exist in counselor education programs, partly because of poor modeling by supervisors who compromise dual relationship boundaries with their own students during the instructional period (Downs, 2003). Ethics is not and should not be viewed merely as a single course to be taken in concert with a systemic program of study, but as a broader and more comprehensive orientation to every facet of a counselor's practice or ministry. Awareness is critical on many different levels. Ongoing supervision and accountability, even between peer-level colleagues, still appears to be the single determining factor in helping reduce unhealthy isolation and unnecessary risk-taking among counselors (McLaurin & Ricci, 2003).

Every year since 1991, the American Counseling Association has summarized and published the activities of their Ethics Committee. Many similar organizations, including state licensing boards, record and track ethical violations as well as the official rulings that are adjudicated from their investigative processes. Severe disciplinary action can include suspension and revocation. The counselor may be asked to complete additional coursework or training, enter into personal therapy, or maintain a certain level of clinical supervision before seeking reinstatement. These determinations are often viewed as potentially effective deterrents for practitioners because most violations eventually become matters of public record. Due to the upward trend of ethical misconduct, most states that now require continuing education units for mental-health practitioners specifically mandate that a certain number of contact hours be devoted to this critical area.

A far-reaching qualitative study identified nine specific ethics-related values that help set apart a "master therapist" (Jennings, Sovereign, Bottorff, Mussell, & Vye, 2005). Five of these qualities resonate with a committed sense of accountability: *relational connection* (the ability to form healthy relationships with clients and colleagues), *competence* (a commitment to the value of being exceptionally skilled), *humility* (an awareness of personal limitations and weaknesses), *professional growth* (the continual seeking of formal and informal learning opportunities), and *self-awareness* (attending to one's own emotional needs as well as unfinished personal business).

True oversight, an invitation to accept practical and clinical supervision, and the freedom to allow others to give honest feedback are marks of an ethically oriented counselor as well as one who is humble enough to value such a process. Whether discussing issues of confidentiality, consent, or competence, there must be a continued honing of skills and overall awareness level, and it should be done with the input of colleagues and peers. Isolation—leading to closed ears, a closed mind, and a closed spirit—is the mortal enemy of ethical practice and results in unnecessary risk taking.

Accountability is a lost spiritual discipline for many. Christian counselors have been tasked with not crossing a line that would violate the tenets of compassionate and professional caregiving. Solomon's wisdom is helpful: "Two are better than one...For if either of them falls, the one will lift up his companion. But woe to the one who falls when there is not another to lift him up... And if one can overpower him who is alone, two can resist him" (Eccl. 4:9-10,12 NASB).

ERIC SCALISE

## REFERENCES


Downs, L. (2003). A preliminary survey of relationships between counselor educators' ethics education and ensuing pedagogy and responses to attractions with counseling students. *Counseling and Values, 48*(1), 2-10.

Hill, A. (2004). Ethics education: Recommendations for an evolving discipline. *Counseling and Values, 48*(3), 183-204.

Jennings, L., Sovereign, A., Bottorff, N., Mussell, M., & Vye, C. (2005). Nine ethical values of master therapists. *Journal of Mental Health Counseling, 27*(1), 32-47.

McLaurin, S. L., & Ricci, R. J. (2003). Ethical issues and at-risk behaviors in marriage and family therapy: A qualitative study of awareness. *Contemporary Family Therapy, 25*(4), 453-466.


## CONFIDENTIALITY AND EXCEPTIONS

Among the big three "C" ethical principles in counseling—competence, consent, and confidentiality—many clients consider confidentiality the most important. Trust in counseling is grounded on counselors' dedication to keep secret clients' secrets. Many clients come to professional counseling with questions about therapists' commitment to confidentiality because their privacy was not kept in prior counseling experiences. The text of the AACC Christian Counseling Code of Ethics is self-explanatory on why this ethic is so critical.

### ES1-400 Confidentiality, Privacy, and Privileged Communication

*1-410 Maintaining Client Confidentiality*

Christian counselors maintain client confidentiality to the fullest extent allowed by law, professional ethics, and church or organizational rules. Confidential client communications include all verbal, written, telephonic, audio or videotaped, or electronic communications arising within the helping relationship. Apart from the exceptions below, Christian counselors shall not disclose confidential client communications without first discussing the intended disclosure and securing written consent from the client or client representative.

*1-411 Discussing the Limits of Confidentiality and Privilege*

Clients should be informed about both

the counselor's commitment to confidentiality and its limits before engaging in counseling. Christian counselors avoid stating or implying that confidentiality is guaranteed or absolute. We will discuss the limits of confidentiality and privacy with clients at the outset of counseling.

*1-420 Asserting Confidentiality or Privilege Following Demands for Disclosure*

Protecting confidential communications, including the assertion of privilege in the face of legal or court demands, shall be the first response of counselors to demands or requests for client communications and records.

*1-421 Disclosure of Confidential Client Communications*

Christian counselors disclose only that client information they have written permission from the client to disclose or that which is required by legal or ethical mandates. The counselor shall maintain confidentiality of client information outside the bounds of that narrowly required to fulfill the disclosure and shall limit disclosures only to those people having a direct professional interest in the case. In the face of a subpoena, counselors shall neither deny nor immediately comply with disclosure demands, but will assert privilege in order to give the client time to consult with a lawyer to direct disclosures.

*1-430 Protecting Persons from Deadly Harm: The Rule of Mandatory Disclosure*

Christian counselors accept the limits of confidentiality when human life is imperiled or abused. We will take appropriate action, including necessary disclosures of confidential information, to protect life in the face of client threats of suicide, homicide, and/or the abuse of children, elders, and dependent persons.

*1-431 The Duty to Protect Others*

The duty to take protective action is triggered when the counselor (1) has reasonable suspicion, as stated in your state statute, that a minor child (under 18 years), elder person (65 years and older), or dependent adult (regardless of age) has been harmed by the client; or (2) has direct client admissions of serious and imminent suicidal threats; or (3) has direct client admissions of harmful acts or threatened action that is serious, imminent, and attainable against a clearly identified third person or group of persons.

*1-432 Guidelines to Ethical Disclosure and Protective Action*

Action to protect life, whether your client or a third-person, shall be that which is reasonably necessary to stop or forestall deadly or harmful action in the present situation. This could involve hospitalizing the client, intensifying clinical intervention to the degree necessary to reasonably protect against harmful action, consultation and referral with other professionals, or disclosure of harm or threats to law enforcement, protective services, identifiable third-persons, and/or family members able to help with protective action.

*1-433 Special Guidelines When Violence Is Threatened Against Others*

Action to protect third-persons from client violence may involve or, in states that have a third-person protection (*Tarasoff*) duty, require disclosure of imminent harm to the intended victim, to their family or close friends, and to law enforcement. When child abuse or elder abuse or abuse of dependent adults exists, as defined by state law, Christian counselors shall report to child or elder protective services, or to any designated agency established for protective services. We shall also attempt to defuse the situation and/or take preventive action by whatever means are available and appropriate.

When clients threaten serious and imminent homicide or violence against an identifiable third-person, the Christian counselor shall inform appropriate law enforcement, and/or medical-crisis personnel, and the at-risk person or close family member of the threat, except when precluded by compelling circumstances or by state law.

When the client threat is serious but not

imminent, the Christian counselor shall take preventive clinical action that seeks to forestall any further escalation of threat toward violent behavior.

*1-440 Disclosures in Cases of Third-Party Payment and Managed Care*

Christian counselors are diligent to protect client confidences in relations with insurance and third-party payers, employee assistance programs, and managed care groups. We are cautious about demands for confidential client information that exceed the need for validation of services rendered or continued care. We do not disclose or submit session notes and details of client admissions solely on demand of third-party payers. We will narrowly disclose information that the client has given written authorization only after we have discussed and are assured that the client understands the full implications of authorizations signed or contemplated to sign.

*1-450 Disclosures for Supervision, Consultation, Teaching, Preaching, and Publication*

Christian counselors do not disclose confidential client communications in any supervisory, consultation, teaching, preaching, publishing, or other activity without written or other legal authorization by the client. Counselors under supervision will disclose that fact to their clients. We will adequately disguise client identifiers by various means when presenting cases in group or in public forums. We will not presume that disguise alone is sufficient client protection, but will consider seeking client authorization when client identity is hard to conceal.

*1-460 Maintaining Privacy and Preserving Written Records*

Christian counselors will preserve, store, and transfer written records of client communications in a way that protects client confidentiality and privacy rights. This requires, at minimum, keeping records files in locked storage with access given only to those persons with a direct professional interest in the materials.

*1-461 Maintaining Privacy in Electronic Databases*

Christian counselors take special precautions to protect client privacy rights with records stored and transferred by electronic means. This requires, at minimum, use of password entry into all electronic client files and/or coded files that do not use client names or easy identifiers. Client information transferred electronically—FAX, e-mail, or other computerized network transfer—shall be done only after the counselor determines that the process of transmission and reception of data is reasonably protected from interception and unauthorized disclosures.

*1-470 Advocacy for Privacy Rights Against Intrusive Powers*

Christian counselors hear the most private and sensitive details of client lives—information that must be zealously guarded from public disclosure. Rapidly expanding and interlocking electronic information networks are increasingly threatening client privacy rights. Though federal and state laws exist to protect client privacy, these laws are weak, are routinely violated at many levels, and the record of privacy right enforcement is dismal. Accordingly, Christian counselors are called to wisely protect and assertively advocate for privacy protection on behalf of our clients against the pervasive intrusion of personal, corporate, governmental, even religious powers.

George Ohlschlager

## REFERENCES

American Association of Christian Counselors. (2004). *AACC Christian Counseling Code of Ethics*. Forest, VA: Author.

Clinton, T., & Ohlschlager, G. (2002). *Competent Christian Counseling: Foundations and Practice of Compassionate Soul Care*. Colorado Springs, CO: WaterBrook Press.

## DOCUMENTATION AND RECORDS

**Description.** For counselors, hosting a dialogue with another human being on critical matters of life and faith is an honor, a blessing, and a profound responsibility. Clients become vulnerable as they express needs, share cherished stories, and take courageous steps of change. They open windows into their souls. In turn, counselors demonstrate suitable respect by treating the information appropriately and by competently handling all crucial arrangements that ensure that the communication is secure, intentional, meaningful, and consistent with reasonable standards of care. Developing a system to record the significant aspects of client care is an expectation in our contemporary age of accountability. The principles of documentation are essential in professional care and make extremely good sense in ministry settings where the intention is to honor not only clients but also our Lord (Col. 3:17).

**Professional Requirements.** Licensed mental-health and medical professionals develop skills through prescribed training to assess, conceptualize, and document client interactions. The level of detail must be sufficient to display the quality, effectiveness, and legality of the service. Routine documentation is an expectation of state boards, which issue licenses, as well as professional guilds, which establish ethical codes and standards of care. Third-party payers, generally insurance companies, anticipate that the client treatment record will plainly show that any treatment provided was medically necessary to address the symptoms and diagnosis that fit established criteria for an actual condition. The paper or electronic record kept by helping professionals will include documents that relate to the following aspects of care:

- evidence of informed consent
- permission to release information or make recordings
- initial assessment details and diagnosis
- treatment plans directly linked to presenting concerns and identified medical issues
- intervention procedures
- status updates and ongoing progress
- outside referrals, consultations, and supervision
- termination summaries describing outcomes and recommendations for aftercare

This list represents the main categories of documentation, but it is not a comprehensive checklist. There are substantial details in each category. Consult a reputable source for a thorough explanation. Donald E. Wiger provides examples of acceptable styles of documentation and offers templates for forms in *The Psychotherapy Documentation Primer* (1999) and *The Clinical Documentation Sourcebook* (2005). Once a comprehensive record exists, there are definitive expectations for securely storing, sharing, transmitting, transferring, and disposing of records.

Expectations for routine progress notes have changed considerably in recent years. The bar is high. Notes should be legible and consistently cover all essential aspects of the entire episode of treatment. Clinicians are advised to stay current on standards and not slip into careless habits. Applying a variation of a data assessment plan (DAP) outline is a useful way to organize essential information, themes, interpersonal movements, and the behavioral outcomes of the session (Cameron & Turtle-Song, 2002). Spiritual formation activities included in sessions should be documented in a manner that transparently indicates the relationship between the client's request, presenting concern, plain and fully informed consent, and receptivity. Such practices are worthy tools, yet inclusion of spiritual practices cannot overshadow the main thrust of the case as detailed in the treatment plan.

Any discussion of documentation can

provoke anxiety about potential liability and possible repercussions. That tactic is not the intent in this brief explanation. The appeal here is to a different level of motivation. Extensive supervision and academic mentoring has confirmed that reasonable documentation facilitates thoughtful, deliberate, and valuable case conceptualization (Falvey & Cohen, 2003; Prieto & Scheel, 2002). The practice of record keeping is not the price one pays to enjoy the privilege of client relationships. Instead, it is a central method to advance quality care for valued counselees.

**Pastoral and Lay Ministry Practices.** Pastoral or lay counselors may not hold credentials or association memberships that obligate direct adherence to an explicit secular code of professional ethics. There may be no financial arrangements that determine documentation duties to outsider payers or clients. Nonetheless, it is reasonable to predict that if client assistance is offered under the designation of *counseling* or if pastoral care procedures substantially resemble this professionally regulated service, essential features of generally accepted requirements should inform customary documentation practice in this area. Most lay counseling ministries are presented to constituents as a method to extend the impact of the pastoral staff. Therefore, procedures and training instituted to promote excellence in soul care should include specific and explicit expectations for record keeping as well as secure access. Policies for supervisory oversight of the counselors should be transparent to counselees.

The following three recommendations are offered as *minimal* starting points for the development of pastoral record-keeping procedures. First, basic demographic data should be gathered along with dates of contact. Next, include a brief and succinct statement of the general nature of the request. Third, recommendations directly presented are noted. If referral to another helper is necessary, provide a list of credible resources so that the client can make an informed choice.

State regulations have specific procedures for reporting child abuse or neglect, elder abuse, and/or domestic violence. Counseling records should substantiate adherence to these regulations. Special procedures should be formulated and implemented when a client signals that there is a credible risk of harm to self or others. Compassion, common sense, and concern for the community point to a prevailing principle that these are not the type of disclosures that can be kept in confidence, even within a ministry setting.

**Christian Application.** The Gospel of Matthew records a memorable occasion when the Pharisees set out to entrap Jesus into making a statement regarding civil disobedience in the matter of paying taxes to Rome (Mt. 22:15-22). Jesus refused to be cornered and asserted that in matters of ethical practice, Christ followers respect civil authority and honor God. Service to the Lord does not excuse disobedience to standard laws and expectations. When it comes to the complexities of helping people, Christians have to evaluate worldview, cultural, governmental, and professional expectations in light of a full range of biblical instruction. Record keeping and documentation in counseling demonstrates the use of customary procedures and delivery of quality care. In services that are uniquely Christian, there is no theological rationale to reject these currently respected standards of care. Instead, good documentation helps to focus the caregiver's plans, increases effectiveness, and may provide important information needed in the future.

**Stephen P. Greggo**

## REFERENCES

Cameron, S., & Turtle-Song, I. (2002). Learning to write case notes using the SOAP format. *Journal of Counseling & Development, 80*(3), 286.

Falvey, J., & Cohen, C. R. (2003). The buck stops here: Documenting clinical supervision. *Clinical Supervisor, 22*(2), 63-80. doi:10.1300/J001v22n02_05

Prieto, L. R., & Scheel, K. R. (2002). Using case documentation to strengthen counselor trainees' case conceptualization skills. *Journal of Counseling & Development, 80*(1), 11.

Wiger, D. E. (1999). *The Psychotherapy Documentation Primer.* New York, NY: Wiley & Sons.

Wiger, D. E. (2005). *The Clinical Documentation Sourcebook: The Complete Paperwork Resource for Your Mental Health Practice* (3rd ed.), Hoboken, NJ: Wiley & Sons.

## DUAL RELATIONSHIPS (ETHICS)

**Description.** Ethics can be understood as values in action. They are the practical rules and boundaries that guide professional or ministerial moral behavior. Regulatory or statutory law can be distinguished by a set of codified ethics that are deemed so important by a particular state or the federal government that civil and criminal penalties are applied when these rules are broken. Various professional organizations, such as the American Psychological Association, the American Counseling Association, the National Association of Social Workers, the National Association of Alcoholism and Drug Abuse Counselors, the American Association of Marriage and Family Therapy, and the American Association of Christian Counselors have established comprehensive codes of ethics to which members must strictly adhere. The "big three"—confidentiality, consent, and competence—remain the focus of most ethics training, but the subject of dual or multiple relationships is often at the forefront of many disciplinary investigations (Corey, Corey, & Callanan, 2003).

**Application.** The most egregious example of "crossing the line" involves sexual misconduct. It has been estimated that 5% to 10% of all psychotherapists in the United States have engaged in some form of sexual or erotic contact with their clients (more than half of those have multiple incidents). Over 50% of all lawsuits and licensure revocation actions against counselors in the United States are for sexual misconduct. Plaintiffs routinely win over two-thirds of the lawsuits. On a more positive note, even in secular schools, there is an increased focus on the need for an integrated, morally based philosophy in ethics training (Urofsky & Engels, 2003).

While some differences exist among various state-based regulations and the ethical codes of professional associations, there is still broad consistency when it comes to the inappropriateness of intimate, dual, or sexual relationships with *current* clients. Greater variation in codes is seen with regard to sexual intimacies or dual relationships with *former* clients. Nevertheless, since sexual or romantic relationships are potentially manipulative, practitioners are expected to bear the burden of demonstrating that there has been no exploitation. A client's consent to the initiation of or participation in sexual behavior or involvement with a practitioner does not change the nature of the conduct or necessarily lift any regulatory prohibition. Emotionally unhealthy individuals may enter into intimate relationships with a former therapist for inappropriate reasons and with unrealistic expectations.

Regulatory and ethical codes addressing issues of non-intimate dual relationships are less obvious and require even more careful examination by the therapist in assessing any potential for harm (Corey, et al., 2003). The relationship between a counselor and a client (whether current or past) is unique and by its nature can lead to possible exploitation. The therapy itself may progress well and be non-harmful, but the potential for negative outcomes must be kept in mind. When counselors begin therapy relationships with clients with whom they have another relationship, one of the two relationships is always in jeopardy of being compromised. Clearly, the dynamics and expectations of the relationship will interfere with the critical need for therapeutic objectivity and honesty.

Many counselors live and work in the

same communities as their client base. Obviously they will occasionally come into contact with clients, former clients, and future clients out of the office. Assessing potential for harm becomes more difficult, but nonetheless, it remains the responsibility of the therapist to examine carefully the what-ifs. In some cases, it is also important to consider whether there may be potential for harm to other clients or even to the profession's standing within the community. The power differential inherent in the counselor-client relationship makes clients more dependent and vulnerable, so the responsibility clearly lies with the counselor.

The following guidelines may be helpful when facing a dual relationship dilemma.

1. Define clearly the nature of the dual relationship from the onset.
2. Examine very carefully any potential risk of harm to the most vulnerable persons.
3. Anticipate possible consequences, both positive and negative, before proceeding.
4. Study regulations and ethical codes for help and clarification.
5. Earnestly seek professional consultation to process the issues.

**Biblical and Spiritual Issues.** In summary, the helping profession must be seen, whether in a ministerial or professional clinical setting, for the high calling that it is and as an absolutely sacred trust. Christian leadership flows from core values such as compassion, sacrifice, stewardship, and servanthood. When taken together, these help define one's moral and ethical compass. As God's ambassadors of reconciliation, counselors should endeavor at all times to faithfully represent his kingdom in all things and be above reproach, for "a trustworthy envoy brings healing" (Pr. 13:17).

Eric Scalise

### REFERENCES

Corey, G., Corey, M. S., & Callanan, P. (2003). *Issues and Ethics in the Helping Professions* (6th ed.). Pacific Grove, CA: Brooks/Cole.

Urofsky, R. I., & Engels, D. W. (2003). Philosophy, moral philosophy, and counseling ethics: Not an abstraction. *Counseling and Values, 47*(1), 118-130.

## INFORMED CONSENT

**Description.** Psychotherapy is grounded in the fragile human endeavor of relationships, and time and experience have ushered in the necessity for checks and balances to ensure client rights and protection. *Informed consent* is one such restraint which, when provided rightly, empowers clients to purposefully, intelligently, and responsibly take ownership of and participate in their treatment.

Informed consent can be defined as the counselor's opportunity to educate clients about the details of their therapy so they can make knowledgeable decisions about initiating and engaging in it. Informed consent communicates to clients that they will be respected and honored as equals in the context of their therapy and will be expected to collaborate with the therapist to meet their personal goals (Snyder & Barnett, 2006).

Because therapy is an unfolding process, obtaining informed consent should occur as early as possible and throughout the therapy (Barnett & Johnson, 2010; Pomerantz, 2005). Informed consent can be viewed as a multifaceted tool with ethical, legal, and clinical aspects (Corey, Corey, & Callanan, 2011). Most importantly, informing clients about the intricate details of their treatment in clear, understandable language and obtaining voluntary consent for each of these aspects of treatment is an ethical issue and is part of our commitment to do no harm to the clients we are privileged to work with. As such, it is required by our field's ethics codes (American Psychological Association [APA], 2002; American Counseling Association [ACA], 2005; American Association of Christian Counselors [AACC], 2004).

In addition to the ethical premise, there

are legal reasons for the utilization of informed consent. The statutes, rules, and regulations governing the practice of mental health in each state remind us that informed consent is not only ethically obligatory but also a necessary risk-management strategy. Those who do not practice ethically and responsibly are subject to discipline by their state boards. Finally, positive clinical outcomes have been related to therapies that are more collaborative and promote autonomy (Fisher & Oransky, 2008).

**Application.** Obtaining voluntary consent for treatment can take place after an open, informal discussion of the expectations and limitations of the therapy. It is wise to provide information about these details in a written document or brochure ("Informed Consent Form") that is read aloud and carefully reviewed in session. Clients can be encouraged to ask any and all questions that may arise about the information on the form during this conversation and at any time in the future. When client and therapist are confident there is full understanding on the part of the client regarding the parameters and expectations of the treatment, the client assents to working with the therapist within the bounds of these parameters by signing the consent form, often witnessed by another party (Barnett & Johnson, 2010; Corey et al., 2011).

When the client is a couple or family, all adult members are informed and provide consent to the treatment. In the case of children, adolescents, and those unable to assent to treatment, informed consent should be ascertained from legal guardians in keeping with the laws that govern professional practice in each state. Additionally, a developmentally appropriate, collaborative, and respectful discussion of the details of therapy should be provided to these clients, and assent for their treatment in writing, if possible, can also be ascertained (Corey et al., 2011; Kleist & Bitter, 2009).

Although recommendations regarding the content of informed consent vary, in general clients should be informed in detail about these items:

- organization, procedures, and processes involved in psychotherapy, including the therapist's professional background, credentials, training, and worldview
- session duration and out-of-session access to the therapist
- fees for services
- diagnostic information and rights related to diagnostic classification
- estimated length of the therapy
- termination procedures
- clear explanation of the treatments provided, their effectiveness, and alternative options to these treatments
- consultation and supervision procedures
- benefits and risks of treatments
- emergency, interruption, and client-therapist disagreement procedures
- whether there will be audio and/or video recording of sessions
- access to files
- the nature, purpose, and limitations of confidentiality (APA, 2002; ACA, 2005; AACC, 2004)

**Conclusion.** The *AACC Code of Ethics* states that "Christian counselors secure client consent for all counseling and related services" (p. 10). Informed consent is one means of honoring our brothers and sisters and illustrates God's command that we are to love our neighbor as ourselves (Mt. 19:19). When we utilize informed consent in therapy, we are treating our clients with the dignity and respect they deserve as God's image bearers, giving them the opportunity to experience a taste of his grace and a nuance of his truth, building the therapeutic alliance, and promoting hope for the healing journey.

LISA S. SOSIN

## REFERENCES


American Association of Christian Counselors. (2004). *AACC Christian Counseling Code of Ethics*. Forest, VA: Author. Retrieved from www.aacc.net/about-us/code-of-ethics/

American Counseling Association (2005). *Code of Ethics and Standard of Practice*. Alexandria, VA: Author. Retrieved from http://www.counseling.org/Resources/CodeofEthics/TP/Home/CT2.aspx

American Psychological Association. (2002). *APA Code of Ethics*. Washington, DC: Author. Retrieved from www.apa.org/ethics/Code2002.html#principle_a

Barnett, J. E., & Johnson, W. B. (2010). *Ethics Desk Reference for Counselors*. Alexandria, VA: American Counseling Association.

Corey, G., Corey, M., & Callanan, P. (2011). *Issues and Ethics in the Helping Professions*. Belmont, CA: Brooks/Cole, Cengage Learning.

Fisher, C., & Oransky, M. (2008). Informed consent to psychotherapy: Protecting the dignity and respecting the autonomy of patients. *Journal of Clinical Psychology, 64*, 576-588.

Kleist, D., & Bitter, J. R. (2009). Virtue, ethics, and legality in family practice. In J. R. Bitter (Ed.), *Theory and Practice of Family Therapy and Counseling* (pp. 43-65). Belmont, CA: Brooks/Cole, Cengage Learning.

Pomerantz, A. (2005). Increasingly informed consent: Discussing distinct aspects of psychotherapy at different points of time. *Ethics & Behavior, 15*, 351-360.

Snyder, F. A., & Barnett, J. E. (2006). Informed consent and the psychotherapy process. *Psychotherapy Bulletin, 41*(2), 37-42.


## LEGAL ISSUES IN COUNSELING

**DESCRIPTION.** Counselors face multiple legal risks that can be minimized by a well-planned risk management program. The most frequent legal risks arise from these issues:

- dual relationships, especially sexual misconduct
- deviation from professional practice guidelines
- violations of laws or regulations,
- behavior affecting a client's civil rights
- confidentiality and responsibility for suicide and homicidal threats to third parties
- reparative therapy

One survey regarding ethical problems in counseling revealed that the problematic issues often involved sex, money, boundary violations, dual roles, confidentiality, unfinished business, and retention of clients in therapy for longer than necessary (Sanders, 2007, p. 103).

State licensing laws and professional boards responsible for enforcing ethical codes of conduct may pose a risk to Christian counselors, particularly with respect to reparative therapy. Many state ethical codes of conduct are modeled after the ethical codes promulgated by a variety of private professional counseling associations. In some states, the reliance on these ethical codes is such that the state law would change if the association changed the ethical code. Most ethical code provisions contain commonsense guidelines designed to ensure professionalism, but other rules promote politically driven values, some of which collide with religious and moral convictions.

**FIDUCIARY DUTY.** "A fiduciary relation exists between two persons when one of them is under a duty to act for or to give advice for the benefit of another upon matters within the scope of the relation." (Restatement [Second] of Torts § 874 comment a [1977]). The existence of a counseling relationship increasingly establishes a fiduciary duty—a stronger duty than a contractual relationship—between the counselor and the client (Bourdeau & Muskus, 2010). A fiduciary duty, however, rarely exists between a counselor and a third party, except in instances involving a duty to warn.

**MALPRACTICE AND PROFESSIONAL LIABILITY.** *Malpractice.* Negligence or incompetence on the part of a professional is considered malpractice (Garner, 2009). In general, the failure to exercise the degree of care and skill that another professional of the same specialty would use under similar circumstances gives rise to liability. The risk of potentially litigious clients requires counselors to consider every encounter in light of the possible legal liability (Syverud, 1993). Every state has various mental-health licensing boards that set standards and investigate ethics complaints for counselors (Bricklin, Bennett, & Carroll, 2003). A counselor may face ethical code violations without any corresponding civil or criminal liability.

*Liability insurance.* Financial protection can be obtained through insurance coverage for counselors and for their employers. Additional coverage may be obtained to cover legal expenses involved in defending ethics complaints, although all liability insurers in the United States have stopped coverage for sexual misconduct. Good risk management should include adequate insurance provision for both professional employees and employers.

**Confidentiality and Privilege.** All professional counselors are bound to maintain client confidentiality and to disclose the three major exceptions at the onset of counseling relations—child or elder abuse, suicide risk, and homicidal threats to identifiable third parties (see next section; Ohlschlager & Mosgofian, 1992). Moreover, when faced with a subpoena or other legal demands for client records, counselors are bound to assert privilege, which is the legal form of the ethic of confidentiality.

*Asserting privilege.* Many states have a privilege statute for mental-health professionals, and it is also stated in the section ES1-400 of the AACC Christian Counseling Code of Ethics (American Association of Christian Counselors [AACC], 2004). Asserting privilege gives the counselor time to consult with the client's lawyer regarding which parts of the client record to disclose and which parts to keep secret. Courts and lawyers have a right to only those parts of the record that are relevant to the case at hand. Turning over the entire record is usually a breach of confidentiality in those parts not relevant to the case and can be embarrassing and legally damaging to your client.

*Duty to warn or protect.* Licensed counselors in many states are sometimes held to a different standard regarding the duty to warn of a pending threat of suicide or homicide against an identifiable third party. The famous *Tarasoff* case stands for the principle that a licensed therapist is not immune from liability for his failure to warn others when his client confided his intention to kill others (*Tarasoff v. Regents of Univ. of California*, 1976). Thirty-five years later, more than half the states have adopted *Tarasoff* or close variants, so this is clearly the trend in the law. (The AACC Christian Counseling Code of Ethics has adopted *Tarasoff* due to its clear policy that human life trumps client confidences when the two principles clash.) However, this same California court held that a pastoral counselor who was not licensed had no duty to refer a potentially suicidal client to professional therapists, even in the face of numerous mistakes by those counselors (*Nally v. Grace Community Church*, 1988; Ohlschlager & Mosgofian, 1992).

**Dual Relationships.** Counselors should avoid relationships where the contractual counselor-client relationship is complicated by adding other relationships not specifically related to therapy. These relations can take a number of forms, including social or intimate relationships with the patient's relatives or friends, and may constitute additional concerns for liability or malpractice. One court held that even when the record does not substantiate a finding that the dual relationship was of a sexual nature, a violation may still exist with proof of a social and friendship relationship (*Towbin v. Board of Examiners of Psychologists*, 2002).

However, as the AACC code delineates, the professions are returning to the issue of whether any harm or exploitation ensued as a result of the relationship, as some dual relations are not harmful and in fact may be unavoidable in small communities. Thus, Christian counselors should be cognizant of dual relationships surrounding clientele and avoid or minimize any actions that could complicate the counseling relationship.

*Sexual misconduct liability.* Another clear trend in dual relations law is that the states are increasingly criminalizing sexual misconduct, including in the case of Wisconsin, by those who hold themselves out to the public as counselors, licensed or not. In most states, licensed counselors and pastors have different liabilities for sexual misconduct, but the trends in all cases are toward easier proof of wrongdoing and more severe penalties for wrongdoing. A California court did not hold a pastor to the same duty of care as a licensed marriage counselor in a situation involving sexual involvement with a parishioner's wife. (*Jacqueline R. v. Household of Faith Family Church*, 2002).

Conversely, a case in Texas held that a suit against a minister who was sexually engaged with church employees he was counseling was actionable for professional negligence (*Sanders v. Casa View Baptist Church*, 1995). One can infer that professional counselors may be held to a slightly higher standard than nonlicensed clergy regarding sexual misconduct liability and malpractice. Regardless of the difference in legal treatment, Christian counselors should hold themselves beyond reproach and flee from any hint of sexual or ethical immorality.

**Risk-Managed Practice.** Professional counselors and pastoral leadership can minimize the risk of liability through several avenues.

First, establish and maintain firm, appropriate, and clearly stated boundaries between counselors and clients. Communicate these boundary lines with documentation up front to help avoid misconceptions.

Second, professional counselors and pastoral leaders alike should do everything possible to provide an accurate assessment of the situation. In the *Tarasoff* and *Nally* cases, failing to assess accurately the seriousness of the situation and take the appropriate steps resulted in death.

Third, pastors and professional counselors must go beyond what is necessary to ensure that staff training and written policies within the organization are clear on expected and prohibited conduct. If necessary, draw organizational lines not to be crossed and solidify those through written policies. Counseling the opposite sex should automatically raise concerns and require specific precautions, such as having a person of the same sex as the counselee when that is clinically appropriate. In church settings, pursuing safety without violating confidentiality (which is a continual problem in the church) suggests doing conjoint counseling with an added helper of the opposite sex. Schedule appointments with opposite-sex clients during church day hours and with other staff present and easily called upon outside your office.

Finally, maintaining sufficient liability insurance is paramount for protecting the counselor and the employer, church, or nonprofit organization. Regardless of how careful a counselor is or how detailed the precautions taken, emotional people seek counseling, and they do not always act rationally. If the client *perceives* that the counselor acted inappropriately or failed to act, the client may complain.

A common legal adage is that anyone can sue anyone for anything. Whether a suit will be successful is a different matter, but given inconvenience and risks inherent with lawsuits, counselors should be vigilant about recognizing and minimizing risks (see Tarvydas & Johnston, 2009). If a client files a complaint with a licensing board or with a court, a counselor should hire an attorney rather than attempting to navigate the legal waters alone (see Shapiro, Walker, Manosevitz, Peterson, & Williams, 2008).

**Biblical Issues.** The Bible speaks clearly about several of the issues addressed. Similar to acquiring the preparation and security that liability insurance provides, Joseph prepared for a seven-year famine by storing up grain to sustain Egypt and much of the world surrounding Egypt at the time (Gen. 41). Regarding improper relationships and drawing clear lines, Paul said to flee from sexual immorality because our bodies are temples of the Holy Spirit—the idea of "to flee" here is to run away and create distance from it, to do whatever it takes to prevent sexual immorality. Remember that we were bought with an incalculable price and we are not our own (1 Cor. 6:17-20). The Bible commands pastors and church leaders to be above reproach (1 Tim. 3:2).

**Conclusion.** There are a myriad of other issues surrounding the legal regulation of the counseling professions, but the major concerns for both clinical professionals and pastoral counselors have been covered here. Combining the proper personal and organizational precautions with the appropriate liability insurance can help prevent legal pitfalls that can precipitate professional catastrophes.

Mat Staver

## REFERENCES

American Association of Christian Counselors. (2004). *AACC Christian Counseling Code of Ethics.* Forest, VA: Author.

American Law Institute. (1977). *Restatement [Second] of Torts,* § 874, comment a. Philadelphia, PA: American Law Institute.

Bourdeau, J., & Muskus, T. (2010). Tort liability—Counseling. In West Publishing, *Corpus Juris Secundum.* Vol. 77, *Religious Societies* § 70.

Bricklin, P., Bennett, B., & Carroll, W. (2003). *Understanding Licensing Board Disciplinary Procedures.* Washington, DC: American Psychological Association. Retrieved from www.apapracticecentral.org/ce/state/disciplinary-procedures.pdf

Garner, B. A. *Black's Law Dictionary* (9th ed.). (2009). St. Paul, MN: West.

Jacqueline R. v. Household of Faith Family Church, Inc. 97 Cal. App. 4th 198, 118 Cal. Rptr.2d 264, 2002.

Nally v. Grace Community Church, 763 P.2d 948 (Cal. 1988).

Ohlschlager, G., & Mosgofian, P. (1992). *Law for the Christian Counselor: A Guidebook for Clinicians and Pastors.* Nashville, TN: Word Books.

Sanders, R. K. (2007). *Christian Counseling Ethics: A Handbook for Therapists, Pastors & Counselors.* Downers Grove, IL: InterVarsity Press.

Sanders v. Casa View Baptist Church, 898 F. Supp. 1169 (Tex, 1995).

Sanders v. Casa View Baptist Church, 134 F. 3d 331 (5th Cir. 1998).

Shapiro, D., Walker, L., Manosevitz, M., Peterson, M., & Williams, M. (2008). *Surviving a Licensing Board Complaint: What to Do, What Not to Do,* Phoenix, AZ: Zeig, Tucker, & Theisen.

Syverud, K. D. (1993). The logic of liability insurance purchases. *Texas Law Review, 72,* 1629.

Tarasoff v. Regents of University of California, 551 P.2d 334, 350 (Cal. 1976).

Tarvydas, V. M., & Johnston, S.P. (2009). Managing risk in ethical and legal situations. In Marini, I., & Stebnicki, M. A. (Eds.), *The Professional Counselor's Desk Reference.* New York, NY: Springer.

Towbin v. Board of Examiners of Psychologists, 801 A.2d 851, 857, 861 (Conn. App. Ct. 2002).

## CONSULTATION AND REFERRAL

**Description.** Duties to consult and refer arise commonly in counseling as counselors are faced with case difficulties they have not seen before or for which they are barely competent in service delivery (Hill, 2009). For the clients' sake, the general rule is to consult first to avoid the hassle for the clients of starting over with newly referred counselors. If consultation is not adequate or does not work, by all means refer clients to those who can address their primary concerns (Corey, Corey, & Callanan, 2007). These duties are part of the rules on Competence, for which the text of the American Association of Christian Counselors code is as follows.

### ES1-200 Competence in Christian Counseling

*1-210 Honoring the Call to Competent Christian Counseling*

Christian counselors maintain the highest standards of competence with integrity.

We know and respect the boundaries of competence in ourselves and others, especially those under our supervision. We make only truthful, realistic statements about our identity, education, experience, credentials, and about counseling goals and process, avoiding exaggerated and sensational claims. We do not offer services or work beyond the limits of our competence and do not aid or abet the work of Christian counseling by untrained, unqualified, or unethical helpers.

*1-220 Duties to Consult and/or Refer*

Christian counselors consult with and/or refer to more competent colleagues or supervisors when these limits of counseling competence are reached: (1) when facing issues not dealt with before or not experienced in handling, (2) when clients need further help outside the scope of our training and practice, (3) when either counselor or clients are feeling stuck or confused about counseling and neither is clear what to do about it, or (4) when counselees are deteriorating or making no realistic gain over a number of sessions. Christian counselors shall honor the client's goals and confidential privacy interests in all consultations and referrals.

*1-221 Consultation Practice*

When counseling help is needed, and with client consent, consultation may be attempted first, when in the client's best interest and to improve helper's knowledge and skill where some competence exists. Counselors shall take all reasonable action to apply consultative help to the case in order to gain/maintain ground toward client objectives. The consultant shall maintain a balanced concern for the client discussed and the practice/education needs of the consultee, directing the counselor-consultee to further training or special resources, if needed.

*1-222 Referral Practice*

Referral shall be made in situations where client need is beyond the counselor's ability or scope of practice or when consultation is inappropriate, unavailable, or unsuccessful. Referrals should be done only after the client is provided with informed choices among referral sources. As much as possible, counselors referred to shall honor prior commitments between client and referring counselor or church.

*1-223 Seek Christian Help, If Available*

When consulting or referring, Christian counselors seek out the best Christian help at a higher level of knowledge, skill, and expertise. If Christian help is not available, or when professional skill is more important than the professional's beliefs, Christian counselors shall use the entire network of professional services available.

*1-224 Avoid Counsel Against Professional Treatment*

Christian counselors do not counsel or advise against professional counseling, medical or psychiatric treatment, the use of medications, legal counsel, or other forms of professional service merely because we believe such practice is per se wrong or because the provider may not be a Christian.

*1-230 Duties to Study and Maintain Expertise*

Christian counselors keep abreast of and, whenever possible, contribute to new knowledge, issues, and resources in Christian counseling and our respective fields. We maintain an active program of study, continuing education, and personal/professional growth to improve helping effectiveness and ethical practice. We seek out specialized training, supervision, and/or advanced certification if we choose to gain expertise and before we practice and advertise in recognized specialty areas of counseling and clinical practice.

*1-240 Maintaining Integrity in Work, Reports, and Relationships*

Christian counselors maintain the highest standards of integrity in all their work, in professional reports, and in all professional relationships. We delegate to employees, supervisees, and other subordinates only work that these persons can competently perform, meeting the client's best interest and done with appropriate supervision.

*1-250 Protective Action When Personal Problems Interfere*

Christian counselors acknowledge that sin, illnesses, mental disorders, interpersonal crises, distress, and self-deception still influence us personally—and that these problems can adversely affect our clients and parishioners. When personal problems flare to a level that harm to one's clients is realized or is highly likely, the Christian counselor will refrain from or reduce those particular professional-ministerial activities that are or could be harmful. During such times, the counselor will seek out and use those reparative resources that will allow for problem resolution and a return to a fully functioning ministry, if possible.

George Ohlschlager

## REFERENCES

American Association of Christian Counselors, (2004). *AACC Christian Counseling Code of Ethics.* Forest, VA: Author.

Clinton, T., & Ohlschlager, G. (2002). *Competent Christian Counseling: Foundations and Practice of Compassionate Soul Care.* Colorado Springs, CO: WaterBrook Press.

Corey, G., Corey, M., & Callanan, P. (2007). *Issues and Ethics in the Helping Professions* (7th ed.). Pacific Grove, CA: Brooks/Cole.

Hill, C. E. (2009). *Helping Skills: Facilitating Exploration, Insight, and Action* (3rd ed.). Washington, DC: American Psychological Association.

## TERMINATION

**Description.** In many counseling programs, much emphasis is placed upon developing a therapeutic relationship, being present with the client or group, conducting an accurate diagnosis, and implementing an appropriate treatment plan. Little emphasis however is placed upon termination, which can be one of the most difficult tasks in the therapeutic process (Clinton & Ohlschlager, 2002). Termination, like other stages in the counseling process, is a phase that indicates that one set of conditions has been achieved and another set is in order (Gladding, 2008, 2011). The counselor is wise to see the importance of client health when moving into termination with a client, a family, or groups.

**Conditions for Termination.** In all types of professional counseling processes, clients have the right to end counseling at any time. Through the use of a consent form, they should have an understanding that counseling should and will terminate when certain conditions have been met (Corey, Corey, & Callanan, 2011). Professional ethics and Christian ethics govern counselors in best practice procedures for termination. The AACC Christian Counseling Code of Ethics lists these conditions for termination: (a) counseling goals have been achieved, (b) the client no longer wants or does not return to counseling, (c) the client is no longer benefiting from counseling, or (d) counseling is harmful to the client (American Association of Christian Counselors, 2004; Clinton & Ohlschlager, 2002, p. 371). It is the hope of every Christian counselor that clients mature and feel that they have adequately achieved their established goals as they allow the Spirit of Christ to guide them into a greater closeness with him and a healthier lifestyle for him.

**Process of Termination.** Termination happens on two basic levels: within the individual counseling session and after the total number of sessions. When one of the four conditions has occurred, the counselor will need to engage in four steps: orientation, summarizing, discussing past and future goals, and follow-up (Epstein & Bishop, 1981; Gladding, 2008, 2011).

In the *orientation* step, the counselor reminds the client that termination is coming—especially in an era where HMOs and managed care often limit the number of available counseling sessions. This stresses the importance for counselors to make clients aware of the upcoming termination (Corey et al., 2011). A counselor might say, "We only have three more sessions together, so I'd like to discuss...." In this way the counselor orients the client (or therapeutic group) to where they are in the counseling process.

In *summarizing*, the counselor recaps what has been discussed or discovered in the session. If clients are capable and self-aware, the counselor may ask them to summarize the session. What were the learning points or truths learned?

*Goal setting* and *evaluating set goals* is a consistent and ongoing process in counseling; however, in this step the counselor focuses on how people will continue their progress after the sessions have ended, protecting the advancements they have made and setting goals for their future (Yalom & Leszcz, 2005).

The last step is one of no less importance: *follow-up*. This kind of follow-up need not be confused with session-by-session follow-up that occurs at the beginning of the next session with homework assignments or discussion of the previous week's goals. Follow-up in termination can be done in various ways, including planned follow-up appointments three or four weeks out and phone conversations at an agreed upon time. Some individuals or groups may decide that a meeting in two weeks, then four weeks, and then three months is a good way to implement this follow-up process. These kinds of sessions may be seen as check-ups or reunions (Gladding, 2008). The purpose of follow-up is to encourage clients' continued growth and progress.

**The Example of Christ.** We see wonderful examples of these four steps in our Lord's ministry. In Matthew 26, Christ orients his disciples to the sobering fact of his upcoming betrayal and crucifixion (v. 2). He then tells them that he will not be with them always (v. 11). Christ was seeking to prepare, or orient, the disciples for what would be their toughest crisis of faith. After his death, the disciples are in Jerusalem when Jesus appears to them, showing them his hands and feet. Later that very evening we hear him summarizing, "These are the words which I spoke to you while I was still with you, that all things must be fulfilled which were written in the Law of Moses and the Prophets and the Psalms concerning Me" (Lk. 24:44 NKJV). There are several locations that we witness Christ reminding, or summarizing, what had happened or what he had taught the disciples. Christ, the counselor, discussed goals that had been established through his three years of training the disciples in Matthew 28:18-20. This Great Commission encapsulated the goals of the gospel of Christ. The last step of termination is follow-up, and can be seen in Mark 16:9-14; Luke 24:36-39; and John 20. The best picture of personal follow-up from Christ could be John 21. In this beautiful and touching passage, we see our Lord following up with those who had been devastated by what has happened to their Master, whom they had followed for three years. Christ meets them where they are (fishing), engages in an intimate campfire breakfast, addresses their feelings of failure, and then encourages them to move forward and follow him. This is a beautiful picture of care for his disciples.

**Victor Hinson**

## REFERENCES


American Association of Christian Counselors. (2004). *AACC Christian Counseling Code of Ethics*. Forest, VA: Author.

Clinton, T., & Ohlschlager, G. (2002). *Competent Christian Counseling: Foundations and Practice of Compassionate Soul Care*. Colorado Springs, CO: Waterbrook.

Corey, G. (2005). *Theory and Practice of Counseling and Psychotherapy* (7th ed.). Belmont, CA: Brooks/Cole.

Corey, G., Corey, M. S., & Callanan, P. (2011). *Issues and Ethics in the Helping Professions* (8th ed.). Belmont, CA: Brooks/Cole.

Corey, M. S., & Corey, G. (2010). *Group Process and Practice* (8th ed.). Belmont, CA: Brooks/Cole.

Epstein, N. B., & Bishop, D. S. (1981). Problem centered systems therapy of the family. *Journal of Marital and Family Therapy, 7*, 23-31.

Gladding, S. (2008). *Groups: A Counseling Specialty* (5th ed.). Upper Saddle River, NJ: Prentice Hall.

Gladding, S. (2011). *The Counseling Dictionary: Concise Definitions of Frequently Used Terms* (3rd ed.). Upper Saddle River, NJ: Prentice Hall.

Yalom, I. D., & Leszcz, M. (2005). *The Theory and Practice of Group Psychotherapy* (5th ed.). New York, NY: Basic Books.

## COMPASSION FATIGUE, BURNOUT, AND SELF-CARE

**Description.** Counselors and those who work in the caregiving professions are often considered to be compassionate people. Indeed, many who feel called to the mental-health professions readily identify with the compassion of Christ as he related to outcasts and hurting people around him. The challenge is to remain salt and light in the face of the painful issues people bring when seeking guidance and help. But the impact of caring for others can overwhelm even the most capable and mature practitioners. In reality, counselors focus on self-care when it pertains to their clients, but they struggle to apply the same lessons to their own lives.

Neglect and inattention in this area can have serious repercussions when counselors experience stress from constantly giving.

1. *Developing a preoccupation with stress-producing people or situations.* Some counselors choose to remain in the intensity of the stress-filled environment and become adrenaline junkies—always moving, always busy, appearing as human *doings* rather than human *beings*.

2. *Indulging in escape behaviors.* Some counselors are tired of being discouraged, lonely, or in pain, so they choose a way to self-medicate by means of certain substances or behaviors.

3. *Avoiding intimate relationships with one's spouse or close friends and substituting fantasy over reality.* Relational intimacy requires time and effort, so a counselor who is emotionally and spiritually drained by caring for clients may be unable to make the necessary investment in other relationships.

4. *Seeking to control everything and everyone as a means of coping.* This becomes a survival tool designed to lower the risk for further pain.

5. *Justifying actions by blaming other things and/or other people.* Blame-shifting is an attempt to avoid responsibility and accountability by making issues primarily about someone or something else. This strategy is designed to separate one's self from the emotional and practical aftermath.

**History.** Dr. Hans Selye (1956), a Canadian endocrinologist who is considered the father of stress research, began exploring the phenomena of stress overload during the mid-1930s in what he called the *general adaptation syndrome*. The normal pattern is for the body to cycle through a three-step process: alarm, resistance, and exhaustion. He defined stress as the "non-specific response of the body to any demand." The implication is that almost any demand placed on the body (including the mind and spirit), has the potential to create a stress response with both a psychosocial (within the environment) and a biogenic (within the body) orientation.

*Eustress*, which is a normal part of everyday life, is necessary for keeping one alert and active. It enables a person to be productive and creative and assists with decision-making activities. However, a chronically high level of stress becomes *distress* and exacerbates a rapidly downward spiral in day-to-day functioning. The two primary stress hormones that begin this roller coaster ride are adrenaline and cortisol.

**Causes of the Stress Response.** According to noted stress expert Archibald Hart, the stress cycle starts in the brain (Hart & Weber, 2005). When a stressor is detected as a threat, the amygdala, hypothalamus, and pituitary glands trigger the fight-or-flight stress response. The sympathetic nervous system activates several different physical responses to mobilize for action. The adrenal glands increase the output of adrenaline (also called epinephrine), cortisol, and other glucocorticoids, which tighten and contract the muscles and sharpen the senses. The body also forms free radicals that are associated with degenerative diseases, illnesses, and an acceleration of the aging process.

When excessive amounts of adrenaline and cortisol enter the bloodstream, the cumulative effects over time can be harmful. These include a narrowing of the capillaries and other blood vessels leading into and out of the heart, a decrease in the flexibility and dilation properties of blood vessels and their linings, a decrease in the body's ability to flush harmful (LDL) cholesterol out of its system, an increase in the overall production of blood cholesterol, an increase in the blood's tendency to clot, and increased deposits of plaque on arterial walls.

According to the American Institute on Stress, 80% to 90% of all doctor's visits today are stress-related. The American Heart Association further states that more than 50 million Americans suffer from high blood pressure and nearly 60 million suffer from some form of cardiovascular disease, resulting in more than one million deaths each year (two out of every five who die, or one death every 32 seconds). Heart disease has been the leading cause of death every year since 1900 and crosses all racial, gender, socioeconomic, and age barriers. Finally, the U.S. Dept. of Health and Human Services recently reported that 25% of all prescriptions written in the United States are for tranquilizers, sleep aids, antidepressants, and antianxiety medication.

**Stress and Self-Care.** In addition to being susceptible to increased levels of stress, counselors are called to love and serve others, which can lead to *compassion fatigue*. Compassion fatigue can be understood as a comprehensive exhaustion that takes place over time when people are constantly giving and lose their ability and motivation to experience joy or satisfaction or to feel and care for others. It is sometimes referred to as secondary or vicarious traumatic stress associated with the emotional residue related to the cause of caring.

Every caregiver should consider what goes into a good stress-prevention or self-care plan. The following are a few principles that may be helpful. They should be prayerfully developed into a personalized approach tailored to each individual's needs and situation.

- Learn how to recognize the stress-producing areas in life that might need attention, and take ownership of what needs to be done.
- Learn how to renew the mind and walk in God's truth.
- Learn to rest, because the nature of God has much to do with rest.
- Learn to be silent and still.
- Learn to give daily burdens to God.
- Learn to triage personal stresses and then prioritize daily and life events.
- Learn to resolve those things that can be attended to easily and quickly.
- Learn to manage time by saying no, or needs will dominate the schedule.
- Learn to incorporate a balanced lifestyle (diet, exercise, and sleep).
- Learn to delegate to others whenever, wherever, and however it is appropriate.
- Learn to value authentic relationship and find one or two key people in life to be accountable to.

**Conclusion.** Christian counseling is a high and sacred calling—to humbly, yet transparently represent Christ as his ambassadors to a lost and hurting world. In order to "run with endurance the race that is set before us" (Heb. 12:1 NASB), caregivers must be deliberate when it comes to their own self-care. Only then can they put on the compassion of Christ and consistently manifest his grace, truth, and love to all who so desperately need his touch.

**Eric Scalise**

## REFERENCES

Figley, C. (2002). *Treating Compassion Fatigue.* New York, NY: Brunner-Routledge.

Hart, H., & Weber, C. H. (2005). *Caring for People God's Way: Stress and Anxiety.* Nashville, TN: Nelson.

Selye, H. (1956). *The Stress of Life.* New York, NY: McGraw-Hill.

# EDUCATION, SUPERVISION, AND RESEARCH

## COUNSELOR EDUCATION

**Description.** Counseling programs and counselor education have seen many significant changes over the past few decades. Most significantly, all 50 states now have standards for licensure for professional counselors. At the time of this writing, the Council for Accreditation of Counseling and Related Educational Programs endorses more than 200 institutions with more than 500 programs of study (Mobley & Myers, 2010). The American Counseling Association (2005) Code of Ethics (Section F.2.a., Supervisor Preparation) mandates that counselors must be trained in supervision methods and techniques prior to offering clinical supervision. The purpose of this relationship is to help supervisees develop the attitudes and skills that will enable them to function effectively with clients (Brown, Pryzwansky, & Schulte, 2011; Clinton & Ohlschlager, 2002). Although pre- and postgraduate supervision is a requirement for licensure in most states, definitive guidelines for supervision and its regulation beyond basic skills and areas of knowledge content fall beyond the scope of regulatory boards. Research and programs of study, however, have created many different approaches to the supervision process to provide some structure, and this field continues to grow.

**History.** The Association for Counselor Education and Supervision (ACES) is the primary national organization that serves to promote quality education and supervision of counselors in all settings (ACES, 2011). ACES was originally founded in the 1940s as the National Association for Guidance Supervisors (NAGS), which later became known as the National Association of Guidance Supervisors and Counselor Trainers (NAGSCT). It assumed its present name in 1961 as a result of the expanding job market and need for counselors in settings beyond school guidance (Elmore, 1985).

**Practical Application.** Although licensing boards regulate the areas of professional development to be supervised, the style and manner in which supervision takes place is an individual process. Through the process of education, future supervisors can define which methods work best for them. Models of education and supervision typically incorporate methods of interaction based on theory-driven models, such as cognitive-behavioral, behavioral, and solution-focused approaches. As would be expected, these forms of supervision operate much like their therapeutic counterparts. However, little research exists on which models prove more effective (Brown et al., 2011).

Supervisors have a tendency to oversee and train beginning counselors based on the orientation they take in the counseling process (Stoltenberg, 1993). Regardless of the model used, the relationship between the supervisee and supervisor is a central component to bring about change in the supervisee, just as it is in the counseling process. Although there are many theories and techniques, the driving force behind change is the nature of the relationship (Howgego,

Yellowlees, Owen, Meldrum, & Dark, 2003; Ries, Jaffe, Comtois, & Kitchell, 1999).

**Biblical and Spiritual Issues.** Our effectiveness in living the Christian life is built on the process of mentoring and discipleship. This strong, life-giving relationship should also serve as the model of supervision. Being a disciple is being a learner. A central requirement for a disciple is the willingness to submit to another for the sake learning. As seen in Matthew 19:16-22 in Jesus' encounter with the rich young man, the cost of discipleship is submission. In supervision, this relationship is a two-way street. The supervisor must have an attitude that reflects patience, a passion to work with beginning counselors, and a willingness to pass their knowledge and skills on to others. Likewise, supervisees need to be open and willing to devote themselves to the task of learning insights and gaining skills. Paul tells his readers to follow his example as he follows the example of Christ (1 Cor.11:1). He lays it out for them simply: "Do as I do." As Paul set out to mentor the Corinthian believers through his example and lead them into a healthy lifestyle and relationship with Christ, the believers also had an obligation to follow. The responsibility of a learner is to be teachable. Erchul and Schulte (2009) acknowledge the second part of this relationship by indicating that the premise behind such a union is for the supervisee to assume as much responsibility for the process as possible. We see through these examples that the goal of supervision is accomplished through the quality of the relationship and the underlying commitment of the supervisor and supervisee to each other and the process. This is the heart of discipleship, and it is the essence of supervision.

Timothy H. Barclay

## REFERENCES


American Counseling Association. (2005). *ACA Code of Ethics.* Washington, DC: Author.

Association for Counselor Education and Supervision. (2011). *About the Association for Counselor Education and Supervision.* Retrieved from http://www.acesonline.net/about-aces/

Brown, D., Pryzwansky, W. B., & Schulte, A. C. (2011). *Psychological Consultation and Collaboration: Introduction to Theory and Practice.* Boston, MA: Prentice Hall.

Clinton, T., & Ohlschlager, G. (2002). *Competent Christian Counseling: Foundations and Practice of Compassionate Soul Care* (Vol. 1). New York, NY: Waterbrook.

Elmore, T. M. (1985). The era of ACES: Tradition, transformation, and the possible dream. *Journal of Counseling and Development, 63,* 411-415.

Erchul, W. P., & Schulte, A. C. (2009). Behavioral consultation. In A. Akin-Little, S. G. Little, M. A. Bray, & T. J. Kehle (Eds.), *Behavioral Interventions in Schools: Evidence Based Positive Strategies* (pp. 13-25). Washington, DC: American Psychological Association.

Howgego, I. M., Yellowlees, P., Owen, C., Meldrum, L., & Dark, F. (2003). The therapeutic alliance: The key to effective patient outcome? A descriptive review of the evidence in community mental health case management. *Australian and New Zealand Journal of Psychiatry, 37*(2), 169-183.

Mobley, A. K., & Myers, J. E. (Eds.). (2010). *Developing and Maintaining Counselor Education Laboratories* (2nd ed.). Alexandria, VA: Association for Counselor Education and Supervision.

Ries, R. K., Jaffe, C., Comtois, K. A., & Kitchell, M. (1999). Treatment satisfaction compared with outcome in severe dual disorders. *Community Mental Health Journal, 35,* 213-221.

Stoltenberg, C. D. (1993). Supervising consultants in training: An application of a model of supervision. *Journal of Counseling & Development, 72*(2), 131-136.


## CONTINUING EDUCATION

**Definition.** Listed with consent and confidentiality, competence is often seen as the third rail of ethical training and practice in professional counseling. Competence implies that the mental-health professional or caregiver is qualified to render certain services based on appropriate education, training, and supervised or professional experience. This can occur as a generalist or a specialist. Every state regulating mental-health practice has set minimum initial standards for practitioners to function independently. However, a more comprehensive understanding of competence suggests that the construct is an ongoing process of continuing education and professional development as opposed to simply achieving a one-time level of proficiency.

Continuing education is considered an all-encompassing term that applies to obtaining contact hours across a broad spectrum of undergraduate learning activities and programs. Some examples include degree credit courses, nondegree career training, self-directed learning, experiential learning, seminars, workshops, webinars, conference presentations, and classroom lectures. The method and format of delivery may be face-to-face, distance/online learning, printed texts and workbooks, or the use of recorded material. As evidence-based practices become more widely disseminated, all providers need access to information on the latest treatments to better serve their clients. Additionally, new technologies and delivery systems, especially those that utilize the Internet, have significantly enhanced available opportunities.

**Application.** Individual professions have different ways of measuring the accumulation of sufficient training hours, but the most widely accepted standard, developed by the International Association for Continuing Education & Training, is that ten contact hours equals one Continuing Education Unit (CEU). Nevertheless, not all disciplines use this convention. For example, the American Psychological Association, in contrast to the CEU, accredits sponsors of continuing education simply by awarding one continuing education (CE) credit for each hour of actual contact, including on a fractional basis.

Most regulatory agencies require CE hours for mental-health licensure renewal, and practitioners must be able to document their attendance or participation in training events. These requirements are intended to encourage professionals to expand their knowledge base and remain current with innovative developments in their respective field and with the diverse or special populations they serve. Even though there is a lack of high-quality research demonstrating clear connections between continuing education and positive treatment results, a number of studies seem to provide evidence on the efficacy of continuing education (Wilcock, Janes, & Chambers, 2009). The implications demonstrate a certain level of effectiveness in achieving and maintaining increased knowledge, changing attitudes, improved skills, evolving practice behavior, and improved clinical outcomes.

Continuing competencies can also provide a measure of consumer protection to those who seek services. By requiring ongoing learning, consumers are assured that behavioral-health professionals have worked on improving their skills. Most clients might not think to ask if a clinician has remained current with his or her training. A competency-based model requires professionals to assess their own skills, develop a plan for improvement, and demonstrate therapeutic fitness and aptitude in that area (Luke et al., 2009). Furthermore, continued training enhances the quality of health care and reduces malpractice issues. The general correlation between ongoing training and changes in practice excellence is imperfect, but the process helps ensure that clinicians give adequate attention to updating their knowledge and skills.

Kirkpatrick (1994) identifies four outcome measures upon which continuing education programs are typically evaluated: (a) participant satisfaction, (b) the acquisition and retention of knowledge and skills, (c) the transfer of training to professional practice, and (d) the wider impact on the clients receiving care. This can be a helpful paradigm when considering the mode and goals of training. Individual practitioners have an ethical responsibility not only to maintain their skill set but also to be committed to and initiate continued quality improvement (Corey, Corey, & Callanan, 2003).

**Biblical and Spiritual Issues.** From a Christian perspective, biblically oriented professionals and caregivers are encouraged to pursue excellence in all things. The apostle Paul exhorts Timothy, "Be diligent to present yourself approved to God as a workman who does not need to be ashamed, accurately handling the word of truth" (2 Tim. 2:15 NASB). The role and identity of *Christian counselor* involves significant responsibility and rightfully so. The mental-health world is watching, some seeking to undermine what is accomplished and some intrigued and attracted to the reality of Christ in the movement. The challenge is to consistently demonstrate sufficient credibility, professionalism, and counseling excellence in order to ensure a seat at the table. To accomplish this task, those who offer services should always endeavor to offer their very best.

**Eric Scalise**

## REFERENCES

Corey, G., Corey, M. S., & Callanan, P. (2003). *Issues and Ethics in the Helping Professions* (6th ed.). Pacific Grove, CA: Brooks/Cole.

Kirkpatrick, D. L. (1994). *Evaluating Training Programs: The Four Levels.* San Francisco, CA: Berrett-Koehler.

Luke, R., Solomon, P., Baptiste, S., Hall, P., Orchard, C., & Ruckholm, E. (2009). Online interprofessional health sciences education: From theory to practice. *The Journal of Continuing Education in the Health Professions, 29*(3), 161-169.

Wilcock, P. M., Janes, G., & Chambers, A. (2009). Health care improvement and continuing interprofessional development to improve patient outcomes. *The Journal of Continuing Education in the Health Professions, 29*(2), 84-91.

## SUPERVISION

**Description.** In much the same way that various studies have examined the relational dynamics between counselors and their clients, researchers have likewise developed theoretical models that describe the interactions between mental-health practitioners—including students and interns—and their clinical supervisors. At its core, *supervision* is defined as an educational process that occurs interpersonally in which one individual oversees the ongoing personal and professional development of another (Ladany & Bradley, 2010). It can certainly be a complex undertaking. Within the counseling field, supervision includes several key components, such as the promotion of basic and advanced counselor competencies, knowledge and skill acquisition, professional identity, ethical practice, and maintaining appropriate standards of accountability. Effective supervision provides a secure foundation upon which emerging counselors can safely and ethically become proficient therapists who are capable of practicing independently.

**History.** Historically, a large number of supervisors in the field had never received any formal education or training regarding this critical role (Watkins, 1997). The increased potential risk of doing harm to those seeking out professional services has led many states to require evidence of preparation for clinical supervisors so that they are qualified to render the necessary oversight for less experienced clinicians. This takes on added significance because supervisors usually carry legal and liability responsibility for the professional work and conduct of their supervisees. According to Ladany and Bradley (2010), the essence of supervision and hence the essence of counselor supervision training includes four broad constructs: consultation, counseling, training and instruction, and evaluation. Each of these focal points implies that supervision takes place within a relational context as a learning alliance between junior and senior professionals, though the ideal mode of their implementation is still the subject of some debate (Watkins, 1997).

**Application.** Due to the relationship-based nature of all supervisory environments, supervisors must incorporate much of the same skill set that is employed during any therapeutic process (Hess, Hess, & Hess, 2008). This includes accurate empathy, respect, concreteness, genuineness, immediacy, and confrontation. As with therapy, the focus is on positive growth and change. However, throughout the process, both supervisees and supervisors must typically address issues of trust, performance expectations, potential anxiety, interaction patterns, and goal-setting priorities (Ladany & Bradley, 2010). Demographics (age, gender, ethnicity, and the like), personality variables, therapeutic styles, cultural factors, and the general theoretical orientation of each individual may also impact the overall dynamic of supervision. By virtue of professional maturity and competency, supervisors must be intentional and proactive in exploring these themes early on with their supervisees. Adjustments and interventions are made throughout the course of supervision depending on the developmental growth of the supervisees.

Over the past several decades, various approaches to supervision have been identified that draw from most of the major theoretical models (psychodynamic, cognitive-behavioral, interpersonal, experiential, and systemic). Each approach has its own presuppositions that shape the supervisory milieu, establish desired goals, and help determine measureable outcomes (Hess et al., 2008). Additionally, most of these pedagogical models have also developed the essential modalities through which the supervision actually takes place (Watkins, 1997). Examples include feedback, formal and informal instruction, modeling, collaborative supervision, behavioral rehearsal and role play, and skill generalization and transfer.

**Ethical Guidelines.** As when treating clients, supervisors must adhere to ethical guidelines that commit to doing no harm to their supervisees while avoiding potential dual relationships and exploitation. The American Association of Christian Counselor's Code of Ethics identifies a number of these important considerations, including the following standards (from ES2-100 and ES2-200):

- to maintain the highest levels of clinical knowledge, professional skill, and ethical excellence
- to receive adequate training and experience in teaching and supervision methods
- to not exploit supervisees
- to not engage in romantic relations or other dual relationships with supervisees
- to not provide direct psychotherapy services to supervisees
- to acknowledge the professional contributions of supervisees
- to ensure that supervision programs integrate theory and practice while training counselors to respect client rights and promote client welfare
- to provide supervisees with a varied counseling experience
- to maintain overall responsibility of supervisees' clinical work
- to meet regularly with supervisees for the purpose of feedback and consultation
- to maintain awareness and knowledge of professional licensure and certification requirements

**Conclusion.** Within a Christian framework, supervisors must take responsibility for the development and maturation of the Christian counseling profession, for serving as active and ethical role models, and for raising up the next generation of Christian counselors, educators, and leaders.

**Eric Scalise**

## REFERENCES

Hess, A. K., Hess, K. D., & Hess, T. H. (Eds.). (2008). *Psychotherapy Supervision: Theory, Research, and Practice* (2nd ed.). Hoboken, NJ: Wiley & Sons.

Ladany, N., & Bradley, L. J. (Eds.). (2010). *Counselor*

*Supervision* (4th ed.). New York, NY: Rutledge, Taylor & Francis.

Watkins, C. E. (1997). *Handbook of Psychotherapy Supervision.* New York, NY: Wiley & Sons.

## EFFECTIVENESS OF PSYCHOTHERAPY

**Description.** In the 20th century, two important innovations advanced the treatment of psychological disorders. One has been the rapid growth of psychopharmacology—the study of medications that decrease psychological symptoms by adjusting a person's brain chemistry. The other has been the rise of efficacy research in psychotherapy. In the past 50 years, research on psychotherapy has become much more rigorous. We now have a lot to say about what is effective in psychotherapy.

Treatments are said to be *efficacious* if they perform better than an alternative treatment in a *randomized clinical trial* (RCT). RCTs attempt to increase internal validity, controlling as many extraneous variables as possible. Participants are randomly assigned to a particular treatment, control, or alternative condition. Randomization helps lower the chances that participants in each condition systematically differ from each other on other variables (e.g., gender, beginning severity of symptoms, or any other variable that might influence the outcome). In addition, clinical trials are typically guided by manuals that prescribe what can and cannot be done by the psychotherapist during counseling. A problem with RCTs is that controlling many variables may sacrifice external validity, creating conditions in the RCT that diverge from conditions in real-world settings (e.g., therapist experience, comorbid disorders, participants are not paid to participate, and so on).

*Effectiveness studies*, on the other hand, were developed to test whether a treatment works in the field with real counselors and real clients. One problem with such dissemination studies is that counselors inevitably drift from the original treatment when adherence is not monitored closely. To reduce drift, practitioners are often trained and certified in a method, taught to operate according to a manual, and given regular supervision. Typically, in dissemination trials, a specific treatment is compared to treatment as usual in that setting.

**History.** From the beginning of psychotherapy, clinicians sought to use scientific methods to see if psychotherapy was effective. In 1952, a study by Hans Eysenck (a respected personality theorist, genetics researcher, and clinician) dealt a devastating blow to the field of psychotherapy research. This study found that patients treated with psychoanalytic psychotherapy were cured at a slower rate than patients in a control sample that received no treatment at all! There were many, many problems with that study—such as different types of clients, treatments, settings, motives of hospitals, and failure to compare similar patients on similar treatments. A radical behavior therapist, Eysenck was beating a political drum (debunking psychoanalytic treatments) and opening the door for behavioral treatments that appeared on the scene in the 1950s (see, for example, Wolpe, 1958). Eysenck's stunt electrified the field. In response, psychologists began to rely on randomized clinical trials (RCTs) as the gold standard for debating the effectiveness of psychotherapy.

The real advance in psychotherapy research came with the application of meta-analysis to make sense of outcome data across studies. Individual studies, no matter how rigorous, can only say so much. In addition, qualitative reviews can only subjectively pose reasons for why results may differ across studies. Meta-analyses, in contrast, are able to estimate the typical effect size (e.g., changes in standard scores on an outcome variable) across a set of studies. Moderator variables can also be tested. For example, meta-analytic research might test to see whether studies using one form of psychotherapy performed better than did studies with another form of psychotherapy.

There have been a few other major developments in psychotherapy outcome research. In the mid-1980s, the arrival of managed mental-health care fueled dose-response research that showed most gains in psychotherapy occurred early in the process (Howard, Kopta, Krause, & Orlinsky, 1986). By the mid-1980s, the demand for accountability had led to a large number of RCTs, summarized by many qualitative reviews and a few good meta-analyses (Smith & Glass, 1977). Only in recent years have big effectiveness trials occurred (McHugh & Barlow, 2010).

**Application.** The number of explicitly Christian-tailored therapies is relatively small, compared to the massive number of outcome studies on secular psychotherapies. Most are adaptations of secular treatments. Typically, they take something like Beck's cognitive therapy and present it to the client as consistent with Christian principles and Scripture, modifying any aspects that might seem incompatible with beliefs and values of the targeted Christian community. A meta-analysis by Worthington, Hook, Davis, and McDaniel (2011) found that Christian-accommodated approaches are equally efficacious to similar secular approaches in removing psychological symptoms, though they tend to produce better spiritual outcomes.

Everett L. Worthington Jr.
Don E. Davis

### REFERENCES


Aten, J. D., Johnson, E. L., Worthington, E. L., Jr., & Hook, J. N. (Eds.). (In press). *Evidence-Based Practices for Christian Counseling and Psychotherapy.* Downers Grove, IL: InterVarsity Press.

Bergin, A. E., & Garfield, S. L. (Eds.). (1971). *Handbook of Psychotherapy and Behavior Change.* New York, NY: Wiley & Sons.

Eysenck, H. J. (1952). The effects of psychotherapy: An evaluation. *Journal of Consulting Psychology, 16,* 319-324.

Howard, K. I., Kopta, S. M., Krause, M. S., & Orlinsky, D. E. (1986). The dose-effect relationship in psychotherapy. *American Psychologist, 41,* 159-164.

McHugh, R. K., & Barlow, D. H. (2010). The dissemination and implementation of evidence-based psychological treatments: A review of current efforts. *American Psychologist, 65*(2), 73-84.

Smith, M. L., & Glass, G. V. (1977). Meta-analysis of psychotherapy outcome studies. *American Psychologist, 32,* 752-760.

Wolpe, J. (1958). *Psychotherapy by Reciprocal Inhibition.* Stanford, CA: Stanford University Press.

Worthington, E. L., Jr. (2010). *Coming to Peace with Psychology: What Christians Can Learn from Psychological Science.* Downers Grove, IL: InterVarsity Press.

Worthington, E. L., Jr., Hook, J. N., Davis, D. E., & McDaniel, M. (2011). Religion and spirituality. *Journal of Clinical Psychology: In Session, 67*(4), 204-214.


## EVALUATION IN COUNSELING

**Description.** British Prime Minister Winston Churchill observed, "True genius resides in the capacity for evaluation of uncertain, hazardous, and conflicting information." Reaching therapeutic goals requires having a systematic method in place for accurate diagnosis and treatment planning. Trends involving general inflation of prices in the economy and health-care cost increases have led to insurance companies requiring higher levels of accountability for counseling services. In order for Christian counselors in private practice to receive reimbursement for services from these companies, counseling methods must be articulated and justified. Therefore, evaluating the counseling process has become a necessity.

**Specific and Measurable.** Successful evaluation is more likely when counseling goals are clearly stated in specific and measurable terms (Steenbarger & Smith, 1996). Additionally, it is in the best interest of the client to use the time in therapy efficiently and to evaluate the effectiveness of the therapeutic process. Seligman and Reichenberg (2007) outlined four categories of variables that impact treatment outcomes. These are four adaptations of these variables:

- Therapist characteristics, including demographics, personality, educational level, ability to exhibit empathy, and unconditional positive regard (Wampold, 2001; Wampold & Brown, 2005).
- Client-related factors, such as demographics, diagnosis and symptoms, and motivation levels.
- Factors related to the therapeutic alliance and client-counselor match.
- Treatment factors, such as interventions, medication, setting frequency, and duration of contact (Nathan & Gorman, 2002).

Evaluation procedures should target all four areas to be comprehensive. Factors that are under the control of the therapist may be easily enhanced. For example, therapists can invest time and attention in establishing rapport, showing interest and empathy, and cultivating positive therapist characteristics.

**Evaluating Outcomes.** There are two different ways of evaluating outcomes in counseling. One method is for therapists to determine whether the practices carried out in counseling are effective. The other is the scientist-practitioner model. This method involves the practitioner who conducts research and uses research to inform practice and practice to inform research. The scientist-practitioner seeks to determine causal relationships between variables, such as interventions and outcomes.

One example of a Christian scientist-practitioner is Christian psychology professor Ev Worthington. He conducts studies utilizing Christian universities to run Christian psycho-educational forgiveness groups, and he evaluates the process through research (Worthington & Scherer, 2004). In college counseling centers, school counseling centers, residential facilities, and similar settings, program evaluations serve as methods of examining the effectiveness of the services provided based on such criteria as predetermined goals and objectives.

For the practitioner who wants a step-by-step process for examining outcomes in counseling (Collins, Kayser, & Platt, 1994), a set of procedures is outlined to help practitioners examine whether therapy has helped clients improve their level of functioning:

- articulating the problem
- stating specific treatment goals
- developing methods of measurement for those goals
- measuring and evaluating progress toward goals on an ongoing basis
- using the feedback to assess therapy and make modifications and changes as needed (Blythe, 1990)

Similarly, Jongsma (2006) describes six steps for utilizing a treatment plan:

1. select the most urgent primary problem to address
2. define the problem and use terminology consistent with the *Diagnostic and Statistical Manual of Mental Disorders* (*DSM-IV-TR*)
3. develop goals that represent broad desirable outcomes for counseling
4. construct objectives in specific and measurable terms
5. pair interventions with objectives
6. as is required for third-party payers (despite theoretical objections to diagnosis), consider the bio-psycho-social presentation of the clients and compare this with the *DSM-IV-TR* criteria to reach a diagnosis

In addition to correctly diagnosing problems and creating appropriate goals, objectives, and interventions, another method to increase the likelihood of positive outcomes in evaluation is to use evidence-based treatments (EBTs), which have demonstrated effectiveness in research trials (Jongsma, Peterson, & Bruce, 2006).

**Conclusion.** The American Association of Christian Counselors' *AACC Christian Counseling Code of Ethics* addresses those who participate in the evaluation of the counseling process (researchers and writers): "These leaders are responsible for the development and maturation of the Christian counseling profession, for serving as active and ethical role models, and for raising up the next generation of Christian counselors and leaders." Evaluation in counseling provides an opportunity to examine the effectiveness of one's work and share the findings with others to enrich and enhance their work. For Christian counselors, the ultimate goal for pursuing evaluation data is not to satisfy insurance companies or even to measure effectiveness, but rather to work to glorify the Lord and show Christ's love to others. Colossians 3:23 states, "Whatever you do, work at it with all your heart, as working for the Lord, not for men."

Anita M. Knight

## REFERENCES


Blythe, B. J. (1990). Applying practice research methods in intensive family preservation services. In J. K. Whittaker, J. Kinney, E. M. Tracy, & C. Booth (Eds.), *Reaching High-Risk Families: Intensive Family Preservation in Human Services* (pp. 147-164). New York, NY: Aldine de Gruyter.

Collins, P. M., Kayser, K., & Platt, S. (1994). Conjoint marital therapy: A practitioner's approach to single-system evaluation. *Families in Society, 75*(3), 131.

Henderson, S. (2009, January 1). Assessment tools in brief: Assessment of personal goals: An online tool for personal counseling, coaching, and business consulting. *Measurement and Evaluation in Counseling and Development, 41*(4), 244.

Henderson, S. J., Hill, C. E., Thompson, B. J., & Williams, E. N. (1997). A guide to conducting consensual qualitative research. *The Counseling Psychologist, 25*(4), 517-572.

Johnson, W. B., & Ridley, C. R. (2005). Sources of gain in Christian counseling and psychotherapy. *The Counseling Psychologist, 20*(1), 159-175.

Jongsma, A. E., Peterson, L. M., & Bruce, T. J. (Eds.). (2006). *The Complete Adult Psychotherapy Treatment Planner* (4th ed.). Hoboken, NJ: Wiley & Sons.

Nathan, P. E., & Gorman, J. M. (2002). *A Guide to Treatments That Work* (2nd ed.). New York, NY: Oxford University Press.

Seligman, L., & Reichenberg, L. W. (2007). *Selecting Effective Treatments: A Comprehensive, Systematic Guide to Treating Mental Disorders* (3rd ed.). San Francisco, CA: Jossey Bass.

Steenbarger, B. N., & Smith, H. B. (1996). Assessing the quality of counseling services: Developing accountable helping systems. *Journal of Counseling & Development, 75,* 145-150.

Wampold, B. E. (2001). *The Great Psychotherapy Debate: Models, Methods, and Findings.* Mahwah, NJ: Erlbaum.

Wampold, B. E., & Brown, G. S. (2005). Estimating therapist variability: A naturalistic study of outcomes in managed care. *Journal of Consulting and Clinical Psychology, 73,* 914-923.

Worthington, E. L., Jr., & Scherer, M. (2004). Forgiveness is an emotion-focused coping strategy that can reduce health risks and promote health resiliency: Theory, review, and hypotheses. *Journal of Psychology and Health, 19*(3), 385-405.


## EMPIRICALLY SUPPORTED TREATMENTS

**Description.** Empirically supported treatments (ESTs) were originally termed *empirically validated treatments*, the first list of which was published in 1995 by a task force of Division 12 (Society of Clinical Psychology) of the American Psychological Association (APA), but not officially by the APA.

**Criteria for ESTs.** The following are the original criteria for defining ESTs as well-established efficacious treatments (Task Force, 1995):

1. At least two good between-group design experiments demonstrating efficacy in one or more of the following ways: (a) superior (with statistical significance) to pill or psychological placebo or to another treatment, and (b) equivalent to an already established treatment in experiments with sufficiently large sample sizes, or

2. A large series of single case design experiments (nine or more) demonstrating efficacy. These experiments must have (a) used good experimental

designs and (b) compared the intervention to another treatment (as in 1a), or

3. Experiments must be conducted with treatment manuals.
4. Characteristics of the client samples must be clearly specified.
5. Effects must have been demonstrated by at least two different investigators or teams.

The following criteria for defining ESTs as *probably efficacious treatments* were also provided:

1. Two experiments showing the treatment gives superior results (with statistical significance) compared to a waiting-list control group.
2. One or more experiments meeting the well-established treatment criteria 1a or 1b, 3, and 4.
3. A small series of single-case design experiments (three or more) otherwise meeting well-established treatment criteria 2, 3, and 4.

Other attempts to compile lists of ESTs have used these criteria or some modified version of them. For example, Chambless and Ollendick (2001) provided a list of 145 well-established efficacious and probably efficacious treatments (37 for children and 108 for adults). Today, the list of ESTs has grown beyond even that number, and it is difficult to keep track of the latest count, as updated versions continue to be published with slightly different criteria and lists (e.g. Nathan & Gorman, 2007).

**Examples of ESTs.** Some examples of ESTs in the list provided by Chambless and Ollendick (2001) included mainly behavioral, cognitive-behavioral, and cognitive interventions, but also brief dynamic therapy, interpersonal therapy, hypnosis, family-systems therapy, emotion-focused couples therapy, insight-oriented marital therapy, systemic therapy, long-term family therapy, and functional-family therapy for a variety of disorders (see also Tan, 2001).

More recently, Hook et al. (2010) reviewed empirically supported religious and spiritual therapies using criteria for ESTs provided by Chambless and Hollon (1998). They evaluated 24 outcome studies for only mental-health problems and made the following conclusions: Christian-accommodative cognitive-behavioral therapy (CBT) for depression and 12-step facilitation for alcoholism were efficacious, and Muslim CBT for depression as well as anxiety were efficacious when combined with medication. Treatments that were probably efficacious included Christian devotional meditation for anxiety, Taoist cognitive therapy for anxiety, Christian accommodative group treatment for unforgiveness, spiritual group treatment for unforgiveness, Christian accommodative group CBT for marital discord, Christian lay counseling for general psychological problems, spiritual group therapy for eating disorders when combined with existing inpatient treatment, and Buddhist accommodative cognitive therapy for anger in a prison setting.

**Critique of ESTs.** Several criticisms have been made of ESTs, including whether they are effective in real-life clinical settings, whether they focus too much on technique when other therapy relationship factors may also be crucial for effective outcomes, and whether they are effective with ethnic minority clients (see Tan, 2011, pp. 394-395). The assumptions and findings of randomized clinical trials (RCTs) used for substantiating ESTs have also been critically questioned (Westen, Novotny, & Thompson-Brenner, 2004), with recommendations for greater use of meta-analyses and development of empirically informed therapies.

**Beyond ESTs: ESRs, ESPs, and EBPP.** In reaction to the EST movement, another task force was formed in 1999 by APA Division 20 (Psychotherapy) to focus on empirically supported therapy relationships (ESRs). For example, ESRs that are demonstrably effective with regard to general elements of the therapy relationship include the following factors: therapeutic alliance, cohesion in group therapy, empathy, and goal consensus (Norcross, 2002).

Empirically informed or empirically based principles of therapeutic change are another approach to dealing with the efficacy of psychotherapy. They have also been termed empirically supported principles (ESPs) of therapeutic change. Castonguay and Beutler (2006) have published the results of another task force in an edited volume on such broader principles of therapeutic change that work or empirically based principles of therapeutic change that go beyond single-theory views or techniques.

More recently, yet another task force took an even broader approach to effective psychotherapy by focusing on evidence-based practice in psychology (EBPP), defined as the integration of the best available research (including ESTs, ESRs, and ESPs) with clinical expertise in the context of patient or client characteristics, culture, and preferences (APA Presidential Task Force, 2006; see also Kazdin, 2008).

**A Biblical Perspective on ESTs, ESRs, ESPs, and EBPP.** A biblical perspective on ESTs, ESRs, ESPs, and EBPP, while appreciative of good, sound empirical research, will emphasize the primacy of agape love (1 Cor. 13) as the foundation of all effective counseling and the need to use empirically supported approaches only if they are consistent with biblical truth, ethics, and values (See Tan, 2011, pp. 398-399).

Siang-Yang Tan

## REFERENCES


APA Presidential Task Force on Evidence-Based Practice. (2006). Evidence-based practice in psychology. *American Psychologist, 61*, 271-285.

Castonguay, L. G., & Beutler, L. E. (Eds.). (2006). *Principles of Therapeutic Change That Work.* New York, NY: Oxford University Press.

Chambless, D. L., & Hollon, S. D. (1998). Defining empirically supported therapies. *Journal of Consulting and Clinical Psychology, 66*, 7-18.

Chambless, D. L., & Ollendick, T. H. (2001). Empirically supported psychological interventions: Controversies and evidence. *Annual Review of Psychology, 52*, 685-716.

Hook, J. N., Worthington, E. L., Jr., Davis, D. E., Jennings, D. J., II, Gartner, A. L., & Hook, J. P. (2010). Empirically supported religious and spiritual therapies. *Journal of Clinical Psychology, 66*, 46-72.

Kazdin, A. E. (2008). Evidence-based treatment and practice: New opportunities to bridge clinical research and practice, enhance the knowledge base, and improve patient care. *American Psychologist, 63*, 146-159.

Nathan, P. E., & Gorman, J. M. (Eds.). (2007). *A Guide to Treatments That Work* (3rd ed.). New York, NY: Oxford University Press.

Norcross, J. C. (Ed.). (2002). *Psychotherapy Relationships That Work.* New York, NY: Oxford University Press.

Tan, S.-Y. (2001). Empirically supported treatments. *Journal of Psychology and Christianity, 20*, 282-286.

Tan, S.-Y. (2011). *Counseling and Psychotherapy: A Christian Perspective.* Grand Rapids, MI: Baker Academic.

Task Force on Promotion & Dissemination of Psychological Procedures. (1995). Training in and dissemination of empirically validated psychological treatments: Report and recommendations. *Clinical Psychologist, 48*, 3-23.

Westen, D., Novotny, C., & Thompson-Brenner, H. (2004). The empirical status of empirically supported psychotherapies: Assumptions, findings, and reporting in controlled clinical trials. *Psychological Bulletin, 130*, 631-663.


## META-ANALYSIS AND THEORY

**Description.** A slightly jaded person suggested, "Never trust a psychological study." Psychological researchers function with high integrity, but studies—no matter how well controlled—inherently possess bias (Polanyi, 1958). Researchers decide what to measure, how to measure it, which questionnaires to use, which interventions to test against which control conditions, how to conduct the interventions, how to monitor the study, how to analyze the data, and how to interpret it. Even more, psychological studies sample people from a population, and those people respond to the study in a way that might sample from their own many moods.

Psychology is loaded with subjectivity. So when a highly acclaimed study is written up in the *New York Times* as the end-all to psychotherapy research, treat it as it deserves to be treated—with respect but not with an assumption that Truth with a capital *T* has been suddenly revealed.

If we are wise not to put much credence in a single study, can science tell us anything useful? Yes, but it must do so by carefully examining a body of literature through a qualitative or quantitative review of the research literature. If different theorists and experimentalists with different methods, different ways of analyzing data, different measures, and (most importantly) different samples of people arrive at similar findings, we ought to be able to trust it.

*Meta-analysis* is a quantitative method of reviewing research that converts outcomes into a standard score—like *d*, the number of standard deviations that a sample changes on a measure, or the number of standard deviations a treatment might exceed a control treatment. The score is *standardized*, meaning that a treatment that showed one standard deviation of change in a physiological measure could be compared with a treatment that showed a standard deviation of change in a behavioral or questionnaire measure. Thus, studies with different methods can be meaningfully compared. If we can document that a treatment is effective across many studies, we can have some confidence that the treatment is actually working.

Treatments are usually based on some clinical theory. A theory in the scientific sense is not like a theory in casual conversation, which typically means "not a fact." In science, a general psychological theory explains and ties together many well-supported models, which themselves make sense out of many studies.

Clinical theories are more speculative than psychological theories. When a counselor works with a client using, for instance, cognitive theory, the counselor is saying, "If I can get the client to think with me in a certain way—namely, that it is what a person thinks that causes his or her emotions and behaviors, not the situations—then it is likely that this client will improve." Meta-analyses or qualitative reviews of research can establish that cognitive theories help clients change.

**History.** Meta-analysis is actually an old statistical technique first used around 1900. However, it was first applied to make sense of psychotherapy research by Smith and Glass (1977). They concluded that psychotherapy was more successful than control conditions and the average *d* for psychotherapy was about 0.8, though it depended on the type of psychotherapy being studied. Since then, meta-analysis has become increasingly accepted as perhaps the most important way to determine whether treatments are really effective. Most high-level journals that publish reviews of empirical research now require meta-analyses rather than qualitative reviews.

**Assessment.** Counselors want to use effective treatments and effective clinical theories to help people change from problematic emotions and behaviors to more positive lives. Clinical theories that are supported by meta-analytic summaries of many research studies are important to that decision making.

**Treatment.** Treatment can often be based on which clinical theories really work. Two recent articles summarize research on spiritually oriented psychotherapies. Hook et al. (2010) reviewed psychotherapy studies qualitatively for empirically supported status. Worthington, Hook, Davis, and McDaniel (2011) reviewed a broader selection of studies using meta-analysis. Those two approaches show some of the differences in the qualitative and meta-analytic approaches to making sense of research. Hook et al. found specific treatments effective. Worthington et al. found that larger groupings of treatments were effective. Both review approaches help counselors make good decisions about which therapy approaches to use with their clients.

**Biblical and Spiritual Issues.** Some people argue that a biblical worldview should determine choice of counseling theory. Others argue that "all truth is God's truth" and that whatever *reliable* science (i.e., not a single study, but a body of studies) turns up is the nature of reality. There are weaknesses and strengths in both of the extreme positions. Believers will find themselves on both sides of the issue. It seems prudent to pay close attention to the research but also to keep a critical eye on the assumptions and biases of the investigators in light of Scripture.

**Everett L. Worthington Jr.**

## REFERENCES


Hook, J. N., Worthington, E. L., Jr., Davis, D. E., Gartner, A. L., Jennings, J., & Hook, J. P. (2010). Empirically supported religious and spiritual therapies. *Journal of Clinical Psychology, 66*(1), 46-72.

Polanyi, M. (1958). *Personal Knowledge: Towards a Post-Critical Philosophy*. Chicago, IL: University of Chicago Press.

Smith, M. L., & Glass, G. V. (1977). Meta-analysis of psychotherapy outcome studies. *American Psychologist, 32*(9), 752-760.

Worthington, E. L., Jr., Hook, J. N., Davis, D. E., & McDaniel, M. (2011). Religion and spirituality. *Journal of Clinical Psychology: In Session, 67*(2), 204-214.


## OUTCOME RESEARCH

**Description.** Outcome research investigates the extent to which a particular therapy (e.g., cognitive therapy for depression) works. Four important aspects of outcome research include efficacy, effectiveness, specificity, and efficiency (Chambless & Hollon, 1998). *Efficacy* refers to the extent to which a particular therapeutic technique works in a highly controlled research setting. The gold-standard approach to demonstrate efficacy is through the use of a randomized clinical trial (RCT), in which participants are randomly assigned to the treatment condition and one or more comparison conditions. The comparison condition could be a wait-list control or an alternate treatment. A treatment is labeled as *efficacious* if at least two independent research teams determine that the treatment either (a) outperformed a control condition or (b) was equivalent to a treatment that already has been deemed efficacious. A treatment is labeled *possibly efficacious* if only one study supports its efficacy, or if all the studies supporting the treatment's efficacy are from one research team.

*Effectiveness* refers to the extent to which a therapeutic technique works in actual clinical practice (Chambless & Hollon, 1998). Effectiveness research is usually conducted in naturalistic settings with real counselors and clients and is typically conducted after a treatment is determined to be efficacious. Even though the terms *efficacy* and *effectiveness* are discussed separately, a sharp distinction is usually not drawn between the two concepts. These concepts mirror the relationship between internal and external validity. Efficacy studies stress internal validity whereas effectiveness studies stress external validity.

*Specificity* involves examining whether a specific type of treatment works better than an alternate treatment for a specific disorder or type of client (Chambless & Hollon, 1998). As with efficacy, for a treatment to be labeled *specific*, a minimum of two research teams must demonstrate that a treatment outperforms an alternate treatment in at least two RCTs. An important question regarding specificity in relation to Christian counseling is whether Christian clients attending Christian therapies report more improvement than do Christian clients attending secular therapies. In general, most research has found that individuals attending religious therapies report equivalent levels of improvement as those attending secular therapies (Hook et al., 2010; McCullough, 1999), although there may be an added benefit for spiritual outcomes (e.g., greater spiritual well-being) for those attending religious therapies (Worthington, Hook, Davis, & McDaniel, 2011).

Other important aspects in outcomes research are efficiency, treatment acceptance, and compliance. *Efficiency* refers to the extent that a therapeutic technique is cost-effective (Chambless & Hollon, 1998). A therapy may have evidence supporting its efficacy and effectiveness, but if it proves too costly, it is less likely to be utilized by counselors and clients. Similarly, acceptance and compliance to treatment must be established. Again, if a treatment has evidence supporting its efficacy and effectiveness but is not likely to be accepted or adhered to by clients, the treatment will not be beneficial.

**Application.** When deciding which type of treatment to use, we encourage Christian counselors to examine outcome research. This research can inform counselors about (a) which type of treatment is best for a specific population and disorder and (b) whether a treatment of interest has demonstrated evidence of efficacy and effectiveness. With the arrival of managed care and increased attention and focus on evidence-based therapies, it is important for counselors to use counseling strategies that have been supported by evidence in order to best serve their clients. We encourage counselors to maintain competence by keeping up with the latest research on treatment outcomes. This information will educate counselors on the best treatment options for specific clients.

**Spiritual Issues.** In general, outcome research on Christian counseling has lagged behind similar research on secular counseling. This lack of research base may contribute to some secular counselors' negative opinions toward the incorporation of religion and spirituality into counseling. One problematic issue is that some Christian counselors may be disinterested in outcome research because they believe either (a) the scientific method is inadequate to understand the complexities of spiritual processes in counseling, or (b) outcome research is unnecessary because their theories are grounded in Scripture and faith (as opposed to empirical data; Johnson, 1993). We believe that all truth is God's truth, and it is important that Christian counseling strategies be both grounded in Scripture and supported by empirical evidence. We encourage researchers and clinicians to collaborate to continue to produce high-quality outcome research.

**Megan M. Purser**
**Joshua N. Hook**

### REFERENCES

Chambless, D. L., & Hollon, S. D. (1998). Defining empirically supported therapies. *Journal of Consulting and Clinical Psychology, 66*, 7-18.

Hook, J. N., Worthington, E. L., Jr., Davis, D. E., Gartner, A. L., Jennings, D. J., II, & Hook, J. P. (2010). Empirically supported religious and spiritual therapies. *Journal of Clinical Psychology, 66*, 46-72.

Johnson, W. B. (1993). Outcome research and religious psychotherapies: Where are we and where are we going? *Journal of Psychology and Theology, 21*, 297-308.

McCullough, M. E. (1999). Research on religion-accommodative counseling: Review and meta-analysis. *Journal of Counseling Psychology, 46*, 92-98.

Worthington, E. L., Jr., Hook, J. N., Davis, D. E., & McDaniel, M. A. (2011). Religion and spirituality. *Journal of Clinical Psychology: In Session, 67*, 204-214.

## QUALITATIVE RESEARCH

**Description.** At its most basic level, qualitative research, like all research, is simply a way of finding answers to questions. Qualitative research is different from quantitative approaches in that it focuses more on the *why* of a question or topic than on the *how*. In a qualitative study, the researcher investigates an issue or problem from the participant's perspective. As Creswell (2009) explains, qualitative research is a way of "exploring and understanding the meaning individuals or groups ascribe to a social or human problem" (p. 232).

Because the focus is on meaning (but not necessarily the *right* meaning), qualitative research looks at a complex, incomplete picture. Therefore, dealing with qualitative data can be messy, time consuming, and even frustrating. The upside, however, is that the data is often full of meaning, providing rich, thick descriptions of the phenomenon under investigation. This is a core component of qualitative research because "depth is what gives the phenomenon or lived experience...its meaning [and ultimately enhances] our fuller understanding" (van Manen, 1990, p. 152).

**Research Process.** Qualitative research is further distinguished by the highly emergent research process it follows. This process begins when textual data—which can come from a variety of sources, including field observations, document analysis of participant writings, and extensive interviews—is collected in the participants' setting. That data is then analyzed inductively (from particulars to more general themes), interpreted by the researcher, and reported in a flexible written structure (Creswell, 2009, p. 232). To be truly qualitative, the final write-up should include a generous sample of participant voices (van Manen, 1990) and ultimately tell the reader a story (Riessman, 1993).

In addition to this highly emergent research process, the qualitative investigator has at her disposal a variety of research strategies/methods (Creswell, 2009, p. 12), including these four commonly used ones:

- *Phenomenology.* From the Greek word meaning "to bring to light." This method seeks to provide understanding of phenomena from the perspective of those who have experienced them.
- *Grounded theory.* A theory is developed inductively, grounded in a body of qualitative data (primarily observation) that is acquired by the researcher (see Strauss & Corbin, 1990).
- *Ethnography.* The researcher studies and seeks to interpret a specific group or culture in its natural setting, which requires prolonged field activity.
- *Case study.* An in-depth examination of a single example (case) of the phenomenon of interest. The case can be an individual person, an event, a group, or an institution (see Yin, 2003).

**Biblical and Spiritual Issues.** One of the appealing features of qualitative inquiry is its narrative or storied nature. It provides the researcher with the opportunity to collect and relay the stories of participants, and the end product is itself a story, told by and about the researcher (Milacci, 2003; Riessman, 1993).

For Christian researchers, this storied nature is particularly relevant because one of the Bible's dominant writing styles is narrative literature, where "the writer's chief aim is to tell a story, not to develop a theological argument" (Ryken, 2007, p. 12). As with qualitative research, the utility of such an approach is that it "incarnates the precept in an example—an example that does not simply illustrate the truth but is itself the meaning" (Ryken, p. 13).

A second biblical and spiritual issue is related to research ethics. Because qualitative inquiry is first and foremost research on *human* subjects, it is essential that the rights and welfare of participants are protected. For that reason, most professional organizations have published ethics codes that should be consulted before any research project is initiated. Furthermore, researchers must also closely adhere to the federal guidelines established by the Office of Human Research Protections (OHRP).

Beyond these professional and federal

guidelines, Christians have a higher ethical standard to uphold, rooted in the belief that all human beings are created in the image of God, and thus have infinite value and worth (Gen. 1–2). In practical terms, this means that Christian researchers should obey the command "love your neighbor [i.e. participant] as yourself" (Mk. 12:31), treat them as you would want to be treated (Mt. 7:12), and ensure that participants' interests—and not just your professional/research ones—are protected (Phil. 2:4).

**Conclusion.** Qualitative research is not easy. It can be complicated, labor-intensive, and fraught with ambiguity—much like real life. But for researchers interested in asking why and understanding meaning, or who have a special affinity for stories, the results of a qualitative approach may be well worth the challenges.

**Fred Milacci**

## REFERENCES

Creswell, J. (2007). *Qualitative Inquiry and Research Design: Choosing Among Five Approaches* (2nd ed.). Thousand Oaks, CA: Sage.

Creswell, J. (2009). *Research Design: Qualitative, Quantitative, and Mixed-Methods Design* (3rd ed.). Thousand Oaks, CA: Sage.

Milacci, F. (2003). *A Step Towards Faith: The Limitations of Spirituality in Adult Education Practice* (Unpublished doctoral dissertation). University Park, PA: Pennsylvania State University.

Riessman, C. (1993). *Narrative Analysis*. Newbury Park, CA: Sage.

Ryken, L. (2007). *Words of Delight: A Literary Introduction to the Bible* (2nd ed.) Grand Rapids, MI: Baker.

Strauss, A., & Corbin, J. (1990). *Basics of Qualitative Research: Grounded Theory Procedures and Techniques* (1st ed.). Newbury Park, CA: Sage.

Van Manen, M. (1990). *Researching Lived Experience: Human Science for an Action Sensitive Pedagogy*. Albany, NY: State University of New York Press.

Yin, R. (2003). *Case Study Research Design and Methods*. Thousand Oaks: Sage Publications.

## QUANTITATIVE RESEARCH

**Description.** *Quantitative research* is a type of scientific investigation that records observations in a numerical or codified system. It uses such methods as surveys and experimental designs to reduce empirical observation to mathematical representations (e.g., statistics, tables, graphs) in order to identify (a) any differences among groups and (b) any correlational or causal associations. Together with other forms of social research (e.g., historical, qualitative, inductive, and deductive), quantitative analysis attempts to collect information systematically in order to discover and understand the nature of human behavior and relationships (Babbie, 2001). These forms of research can provide us with tools for studying God's creation, including the codifying of observations and the testing of theories, beliefs, and claims of reality. Sound Christian counseling recognizes both the value and the limitations of such research.

**History.** God gave humans the ability and authority to observe, control, and name all living things (Gen. 1:28; 2:19-20). When we observe his creation, we see his glory (Ps. 19:1-7). Quantitative research provides us with a tool for studying God's world, but one of the consequences of sin, the Fall, and the curse (Gen. 3:17-19) is enmity toward God, resulting in failure to fully comprehend the created order. The limitations of science include deficiencies in objectivity and reliability, observational bias, skewing of sensory data, and finitude of perception. In addition, "temporal, logical, cultural, spatial, and empirical limitations" impede the ability of science to arrive at any absolute truth (Brush, 2005). Therefore, observational research and counseling theories should be treated with suspicion. However, we are still able to learn about God by studying what he has made (Rom. 1:20) (Jones, 2002). Paul's challenge to test all things and "hold on to what is good" (1 Th. 5:21) can be applied to all fields of study, including theology and counseling. Theologians and scientists face similar challenges concerning interpretation and fallibility in understanding. Sound epistemology (the study of knowledge) and biblical interpretation require a comprehension of the basic methods of organizing and codifying information found in scientific research (O'Connor, 2005).

**Awareness and Application.** Quantitative research can assist Christian counselors in a number of ways. It can (a) give us new ways of looking at an issue (e.g., the basis for a happy marriage [Gottman, 1994; Worthington, Davis, Hook, & Miller, 2007]), (b) help explain or emphasize principles identified in Scripture (e.g., the nature, value, and process of forgiveness), (c) provide insight for improving relationships, such as marriages, (d) assist in predicting outcomes (e.g., identifying factors that contribute to divorce), (e) correct false or misleading information, and (f) provide a means of testing or measuring the effectiveness of counseling approaches and techniques (Jones, 2002).

**Biblical and Spiritual Issues.** The Bible challenges us to study and learn from the world around us (Pr. 6:6-11). Quantitative observation and investigation of human behavior provide information and basic principles for living (Pr. 24:30-34). Daniel used a form of investigation that we would recognize as quantitative research today to convince his overseers to allow him to maintain a diet that honored his God (Dan. 1:11-16). His analysis included a set time frame, control group (those who consumed Babylonian food and drink), and posttest with a clear standard of measure (physical difference in appearance between the Babylonian group and Daniel's group). Here, we see research being used to reveal the true God, affirm a godly lifestyle, and illustrate the reward found in obedience to the will of God. The Bible also stresses the importance of honest scales and accurate measurements (Lev. 19:35; Dt. 25:15; Pr. 16:11; 20:10) and ultimate obedience to God rather than dependence on numerical assessments (1 Chron. 21:1-8).

**Additional Issues.** Over the years, there has been a call for more research in Christian counseling (Collins, 1983; Ripley & Worthington, 1998; Worthington, 2006). Research contributes to our knowledge base and our understanding of God's creation, but it is also a language of communication among scientists and the general population. As such, it provides an opportunity for evangelism and for influencing secular institutions and competing "equally with secular voices in the press, government grant panels, and highest caliber journals" (Worthington). Recent attention has focused on the value in Christian marital counseling of empirically supported techniques based on rigorous quantitative research that has been replicated by at least two independent investigators—a more stringent form of research than evidence-based approaches (Worthington et al., 2007). In summary, quantitative research can inform Christian counseling; however, the criterion for use should not be that such methods work but that "they are consistent with biblical truth, ethics, and values. Whatever contradicts the Bible and its teachings, even if empirically supported, should not be accepted or applied in clinical practice by Christian therapists" (Tan, 2011).

Ian Jones

## REFERENCES

Babbie, E. (2001). *The Practice of Social Research* (9th ed.). Belmont, CA: Wadsworth/Thomson Learning.

Brush, N. (2005). *The Limitations of Scientific Truth: Why Science Can't Answer Life's Ultimate Questions*. Grand Rapids, MI: Kregel Academic & Professional.

Collins, G. R. (1983). Moving through the jungle: A decade of integration. *Journal of Psychology and Theology, 11*, 2-7.

Gottman, J. (1994). *Why Marriages Succeed or Fail... And How You Can Make Yours Last*. New York, NY: Simon & Schuster.

Jones, I. F. (2002). Research in Christian counseling: Proving and promoting our valued cause. In T. Clinton & G. Ohlschlager (Eds.), *Competent Christian Counseling: Foundations & Practice of Compassionate Soul Care* (Vol. 1, pp. 641-657). Colorado Springs, CO: WaterBrook Press.

O'Connor, R. (2005). The Bible and Science. In K. Vanhoozer (Ed.), *Dictionary for Theological Interpretation of the Bible* (pp. 722-724). Grand Rapids, MI: Baker Academic.

Ripley, J. S., & Worthington, E. L., Jr. (1998). What the journals reveal about Christian marital counseling: An inadequate (but emerging) scientific base. *Marriage and Family: A Christian Journal, 1,* 375-396.

Tan, S.-Y. (2011). *Counseling and Psychotherapy: A Christian Perspective.* Grand Rapids, MI: Baker Academic.

Worthington, E. L., Jr. (2006). Trends & needs in Christian counseling research: What you need to know, even if you don't plan to conduct research. *Christian Counseling Today 14*(4), 20-23.

Worthington, E. L., Jr., Davis, D. E., Hook, J. N., & Miller, A. J. (2007). Recent research in marital and sex therapy. *Christian Counseling Today 15*(4), 28-31.

# 26

# NEW DEVELOPMENTS IN CHRISTIAN COUNSELING

## COACHING

**Description.** Coaching is a profession focused on helping people identify, work toward, and achieve their goals. It is ongoing intimate partnership for those making important life changes by exploring and identifying their dreams, hopes, and fears, and taking actions to achieve their personal and professional goals. Coaching focuses on positive change and emphasizes results. It is a client-centered process, honoring clients as the experts in their lives, believing that they are creative, resourceful, and whole (International Coach Federation [ICF], 2011). The roles of coaches are to come alongside of individuals to (a) help them explore, identify, and clarify goals, (b) encourage self-exploration, (c) facilitate clients' discovery of new solutions and strategies, and (d) be accountable to their change process (ICF).

**Distinction Between Coaching and Counseling.** Coaching and counseling both involve bringing about transformational life change in clients; however, they are not the same discipline (Ellis, 2006). First, coaching is future oriented; it finds creative ways to reach one's potential in the future, whereas counseling is often characterized by recovery from the past. Second, coaching focuses on positive growth, such as fulfillment of one's potential and life purpose and dreams. In contrast, counseling often deals with pain, struggles, and problems. This distinction reflects the difference in assumptions: The assumption in coaching is that the major problems in life are already stabilized, whereas counseling is considered as a process to stabilize clients' lives. Third, coaching is solution and action oriented, while the counseling process is often focused on emotion regulation or inner change. In other words, a goal of coaching is to build healthy patterns characterized accountability; whereas the aim of counseling is building emotional and relational health (Hillman, 2001). Fourth, there is much difference in credential requirements between the two disciplines. There are state-specific educational and licensing requirements (i.e., examination, residency with supervisions) for counselors that take many years to complete. In addition, licensed counselors are required to seek consultation and continual education for their professional development. For coaching, there are some credentials and certifications (see ICF; International Christian Coaching Association); however, there is no licensing requirement for coaches.

**Opportunities for Coaches.** Coaching is birthed from the positive psychology movement, which does not ask, "What is wrong with you?" but rather, "What is right with you?" This change in focus involves exploring and learning to use gifts, talents, strengths, and skills that individuals already have for positive change. In recent years, coaching has become very popular as people increasingly search for positive change and fulfilled lives. With the demand for positive change comes the plethora of life issues that coaching now addresses, including life-skill coaching, business coaching, executive coaching, sport coaching, nutritional coaching, and educational coaching (Zeus & Skiffington, 2005). In addition, there are coaches specialized for ministry, marriage and relationships, health and wellness, life purpose, women, stress, time management, and many other areas.

**Christian Coaching.** The Bible has a great deal to say about maximizing and stretching to reach your God-given potential with the guidance and wisdom of others. Listen to the theme of these Scriptures as you meditate about the value of coaching. "For lack of guidance a nation falls, but victory is won through many advisers" (Pr. 11:14). "Plans fail for lack of counsel, but with many advisers they succeed" (Pr. 15:22). "The wise prevail through great power, and those who have knowledge muster their strength. Surely you need guidance to wage war, and victory is won through many advisers" (Pr. 24:5-6). Christian coaching must be a God-centered approach, helping others to find God's vision and will in their lives (Collins, 2009). Christian coaching must join God in helping others find the good works that he has already started in their lives, for Ephesians 2:9 says, "We are God's handiwork, created in Christ Jesus to do good works, which God prepared in advance for us to do."

**Conclusion.** If people want to experience biblical growth, they must have other people who challenge them to become God's best—people who will take on the confrontational role of "iron sharpening iron" (Pr. 27:17) to stretch and develop them to reach their potential. Christian coaching provides that extra push. It often produces rapid results when people are on track with trusted guides who are focused on helping them reach their goals. Here is the foundational question: Do you want to help people past the stress in their lives to move them forward to experience lasting spiritual strength? Then become your best as both a trusted counselor and as a wise coach. God's people need both of those very different disciplines.

Dwight Bain
Christopher McCluskey

## REFERENCES


Collins, G. (2009). *Christian Coaching: Helping Others Turn Potential into Reality.* (2nd ed.). Colorado Springs, CO: NavPress.

Ellis, David. (2006). *Life Coaching: A Manual for Helping Professionals.* Bethel, CT: Crown House.

Hillman, M. (2001). Perspectives on coaching. *Journal of Management Development, 20*(5).

International Christian Coaching Association. (2011). *Building Professionalism and Unity in Christian Coaching.* Retrieved March 22, 2011 from http://www.iccaonline.net/about

International Coach Federation. (2011). *Code of Ethics.* Retrieved March 20, 2011 from http://www.coachfederation.org/about-icf/ethics-&-regulation/icf-code-of-ethics/

Zeus, P., & Skiffington, S. (2005). *The Complete Guide to Coaching at Work.* Roseville, Australia: McGraw Hill Australia.


## CYBER-COUNSELING

Over the years, mental-health counseling has undergone many theoretical shifts. However, a recent shift concerns not therapeutic theory but the medium through which counseling is provided. Counseling relationships have historically developed through a series of in-person communications between counselor and client, but now telephone and online communications offer new avenues for the formation of those relationships.

**Description.** Cyber-counseling (also known as eCounseling, online counseling, or online therapy) is the provision of professional counseling through electronic communication. Common modalities for cyber-counseling include telephone, secure e-mail, online text chat, and videoconference.

A growing number of therapists are offering cyber-counseling, but these services constitute only a small fraction of the counseling market. Client demand for online services is comparatively small compared to demand for in-person care. For example, in June 2010, a Google search for *counselor* received approximately 60,500 hits. In contrast, there were merely 480 hits for the term *online counselor*.

**Purpose.** There are numerous reasons why cyber-counseling could be a desirable alternative to in-person counseling.

- *Safety.* Cyber-counseling may increase a client's sense of safety because clients are able to receive help from their own "safe space."
- *Assertiveness.* A study investigating a co-ed online discussion found that females who took a passive role in face-to-face interactions spoke more assertively online.
- *Anonymity.* Some online programs offer anonymous care. Founded in 1986 at Cornell University, one of the first online counseling services, called "Dear Uncle Ezra," accepts queries from anonymous students. In addition, over the Internet, people can "communicate without the distractions of race, gender, age, size, or physical deformity or impairment" (Worona, 2003).
- *Social stigma.* Cyber-counseling eliminates client risk of meeting persons from their community in their counselor's waiting room.
- *Selection.* Cyber-counseling may provide clients a greater selection of therapists to choose from.
- *Accessibility.* Cyber-counseling websites often offer 24-hour service availability.

**Ethical and Professional Challenges.** Cyber-counseling services have raised ethical, legal, and clinical questions:

- *Ethics and legality.* Areas of particular concern include confidentiality of electronic communications, HIPAA compliance, the effective handling of suicidal or dangerous clients, crisis response, and counseling clients across state lines.
- *Rapport.* Traditional views contend that distance communication—especially text-based communication—is a deficient modality for developing rapport due to the inability of users to read body language and hear emotional cues.
- *Clinical efficacy.* Some studies have found client improvement with various online modalities to be equal to, and in some cases greater than, in-person services, but other studies suggest cyber-counseling efficacy to be inferior to in-person treatment.

**Ethical Codes.** In review of cyber-counseling, ethical statements have been written by the American Psychological Association (APA), American Counseling Association (ACA), National Board of Certified Counselors (NBCC), the American Association of Christian Counselors (AACC), the Clinical Social Work Federation (CSWF), and others.

The sentiment of nearly every organization that has addressed cyber-counseling is similar: Counselors can practice cyber-counseling if it can be provided with competence and if counselors maintain their ethical responsibilities. The NBCC states that "telephone counseling has been available and widely used for some time...and use of the Internet to deliver information and foster communication has resulted in the creation of new forms of counseling." (National Board for Certified Counselors, 2001).

The APA writes, "The Ethics Code...has no rules prohibiting such services" (American Psychological Association, 1997).

The ACA stipulates, "Professional counselors ensure that clients are intellectually, emotionally, and physically capable of using the online counseling services, and of understanding the potential risks and/or limitations of such services" (American Counseling Association Governing Council, 1999).

In contrast, The CSWF has written a statement in opposition of text-based cyber-counseling services (one of several cyber-counseling modalities). They write, "Psychotherapy services cannot be delivered online [specifically via text] because of the inherent nature of the service and, therefore, the federation is opposed to the practice of Internet-based treatment."

However, others involved in the research and practice of online counseling disagree (Fenichel, 2001). Proprietors of text-based counseling identify numerous advantages to the text modality:

- Clients have the ability to frame and reflect on their ideas through writing.
- They may be less inhibited in treatment, communicating in a less restricted manner by text because they are less affected by the positive or negative leads of a therapist.
- They benefit from increased client and counselor accountability.
- They have a permanent text-record of their treatment progress.

**Conclusion.** Cyber-counseling is not an ideal modality of care for everyone. For example, persons with major mental illness or acute crises or who do not communicate well through the described methods may not be good candidates for cyber-counseling. However, for many clients, cyber-counseling could be a new and viable method of seeking guidance, support, and counsel.

There are many studies that can be done on the various proposed advantages and disadvantages of cyber-counseling. If good research, honest appraisals, and open attitudes continue to develop in the manner that they have for the past ten years, cyber-counseling will continue to establish itself as an accepted and perhaps invaluable tool to bring help and healing to persons with a spectrum of needs in a variety of settings.

Anthony Centore

## REFERENCES


American Counseling Association Governing Council. (1999). *American Counseling Association Code of Ethics* (A.3.a., A.3.b.). Alexandria, VA: American Counseling Association.

American Psychological Association. (1997). APA statement on services by telephone, teleconference, and Internet: A statement by the ethics committee of the American Psychological Association. Retrieved from http://www.apa.org/ethics/education/telephone-statement.aspx

Fenichel, M. (2001). A response to the clinical social work federation position paper on internet text-based therapy. International Society for Mental Health Online. Retrieved from http://www.ismho.org/response_to_cswf.asp

National Board for Certified Counselors. (2001). Standards for the ethical practice of Web counseling. Retrieved from http://www.nbcc.org/Assets/Ethics/nbcc-codeofethics.pdf

Worona, S. (2003). Privacy, security, and anonymity: An evolving balance. *Educause Review, 38*(3), 62-63.


## FORENSIC PSYCHOLOGY

Forensic psychology has been defined many ways. The Latin root for *forensic* means "forum," where the Romans conducted legal trials. The Committee on Ethical Guidelines for Forensic Psychologists (1991) defines the field of forensic psychology as "all forms of professional conduct when acting, with definable knowledge, as a psychological expert on explicitly psychological issues in direct assistance to the courts, to legal proceedings, correctional and forensic mental health facilities, and administrative, judicial, and legislative agencies acting in a judicial capacity" (p. 657).

Objectivity is a difficult ethical issue for forensic psychologists. And no professional is completely free of bias. "Even the most ethical, experienced, and conscientious forensic examiner is subject to such 'unintended bias' through the process of forensic identification with the retaining side or party" (American Psychiatric Association, 2001, p. 68).

I recently received a call from an attorney, asking if I would evaluate a man currently in jail for attempted murder. Specifically, this attorney asked me to address his client's ability to understand the moral nature of his offense.

"Did he understand right from wrong, and furthermore, was his attempt to murder this man premeditated? I would like to propose the insanity plea," the attorney continued. He paused, letting his request sink in. "I have all the records showing he has been crazy for a long time, and I think he was crazy at the time of the offense."

The attorney, confident, friendly, and perhaps a bit solicitous, had referred other cases to me for evaluation, and on this day had paid for an hour of office time to discuss the case. He also made it clear that sufficient funds would be available for my services to adequately evaluate his client and offer an opinion. He wanted the opinion to be verbal only until such time as he determined that my opinion would assist his case.

The task of any expert witness is to offer expert opinion without partiality and within the expert's area of expertise. Though there are many threats to objectivity, my challenge in this case was to maintain objectivity and offer the attorney and the court a professional opinion. The task may have seemed straightforward, but it had its challenges.

The attorney shared the background of the case with me. Indeed, his presentation sounded as though his client was psychotic and did not fully appreciate the moral nature of his actions. But this had to be conclusively determined. I made it clear that I could not guarantee any outcome but would do my best to provide an accurate diagnosis and determination about his client's ability to determine right from wrong at the time of the offense.

As the attorney left my office, I thoughtfully considered the work I was about to do. Could I truly be objective—free from partiality—given that he was paying me a fee to not only talk to him about his client, but to interview and evaluate his client? I knew he sought a certain outcome. Believing I could be objective, without bias or partiality, I agreed to do the evaluation. I considered, however, some of the dangers I've learned about the ways objectivity can easily be compromised.

1. The desire to maintain a favorable impression with the referring party, especially if they have referred to you before and are likely to refer to you again.
2. Subsequent short-term and perhaps long-term economic incentives to form an opinion favorable to the attorney.
3. Forensic countertransference, whereby one forms a favorable opinion about the attorney and wants the admiration of the attorney.
4. Selection bias on the part of the attorney in selecting someone (myself) who he presumes will support his position.
5. Outcome bias, whereby one skews the data to support what he may already have been told or concluded about the person being evaluated.
6. The desire to win a case or look good and even exhibitionism.
7. Adversarial bias to win against an opposing professional point of view.

These are only a few of the ways objectivity can be compromised. Evidence has repeatedly shown that many who espouse objectivity, claiming to bring new and impartial evidence before the court, have in actuality succumbed to temptation of being hired guns in the case. Studies have shown that attorneys have purposely withheld information from their expert witness in an effort to unduly influence them.

When this happens, objectivity is compromised, and the truthful waters of the case are muddied rather than clarified. This creates a dangerous and tragic situation in which the defendant is deprived of a fair and unbiased clinical assessment. If a psychiatrist is aware of risk of bias because of personal or relational reasons, he or she should refer the client to another colleague rather than run the risk of losing objectivity (Weiner & Goldstein, 2003).

The American Academy of Psychiatry and the Law (2005) outlines specific ethical guidelines for forensic psychologists and psychiatrists, including confidentiality, informed consent, and honesty and striving for objectivity. Professionals in the field of forensic psychology should take their ethical responsibility seriously and clarify their legal role in each unique situation (Kapardis, 2010). The following considerations may be helpful in developing personal ethics.

1. *True impartiality is nearly impossible.* At times we all want to impress others, maintain sources of revenue, and even seek to win against our professional colleagues.
2. *Be aware of your biases, seeking to keep them in the front of your mind so you are not unconsciously influenced.* Pay attention to the efforts made by others to drive an outcome. Recognize your own vulnerabilities to please others, win, or show off.
3. *Maintain professional detachment from the referring party and person being evaluated.* Without detachment you cannot maintain objectivity. You will gradually begin to advocate for a person, lessening your objectivity.
4. *Guard against becoming overly dependent upon any single referral source for revenue.* As you develop a broad-based practice, you will more easily be able to refuse certain referrals or offer opinions certain to be unpopular.
5. *Function within your area of expertise.* As tempting as it may be, refuse to practice outside the scope of your expertise. Seek consultation when dealing with a particularly challenging case.
6. *Seek objective data rather than subjective and anecdotal evidence.* When possible, refer to objective psychological testing, replete with validity scales, to support your opinion. Offer specific information when rendering a diagnosis, consistent with factors generally agreed within your profession to support your conclusions.
7. *Doubt yourself and maintain humility.* We don't know it all and must remind ourselves of this fact. A strong dose of humility is needed in the forensic arena. Solomon, the wisest man of his day, tells us, "There is a way that appears to be right, but in the end it leads to death" (Pr. 16:25). The apostle Paul warns, "For the wisdom of this world is foolishness in God's sight" (1 Cor. 3:19). Our only source of true wisdom is God.

The forensic field is an exciting and challenging one and offers many opportunities. There are many chances to utilize your skills and expertise in a most challenging field, render an opinion in the face of adversity, and discover the satisfaction of a job well done. But there are dangers to consider. Understanding the limits of your expertise, the questions and demands made of you, and potential pitfalls will assist you in providing invaluable *objective* information to the courts while enjoying the challenges of the work.

David Hawkins

## REFERENCES

American Academy of Psychiatry and the Law. (2005). *Ethics Guidelines for the Practice of Forensic Psychiatry.* Retrieved from http://www.aapl.org/ethics.htm

American Psychiatric Association (2001). *Ethics Primer of the American Psychiatric Association.* Washington, DC: Author.

Committee on Ethical Guidelines for Forensic Psychologists. (1991). Specialty guidelines for forensic psychologists. *Law and Human Behavior, 15,* 655-665.

Kapardis, A. (2010). *Psychology and Law: A Critical Introduction.* New York, NY: Cambridge University Press.

Weiner, I. B., & Goldstein, A. M. (Eds.). (2003). *Handbook of Psychology: Forensic Psychology.* Hoboken, NJ: Wiley & Sons.

## LEADERSHIP AND ORGANIZATIONAL PSYCHOLOGY

**Description.** Leadership is a universal occurrence in the human population. There are multiple (and sometimes ambiguous) definitions of this phenomenon, and its impact incorporates the concept that leaders are agents of change within the context of relationships. Over the past century, leadership dynamics and psychology has become one of the most studied constructs in human behavior, and numerous classifications for this quality have emerged. Various writers have described leadership as charismatic, servant-oriented, transactional vs. transformational, inspirational, and visionary. Overall, leaders "have a vision or mission with which they infuse the group" (Messick & Kramer, 2005, p. 54). Recent years have seen a wealth of research on the impact of leaders on businesses, organizations, and the global community. Waite (2008) reports that more than 3,000 leadership studies have been conducted in the past 70 years.

**History.** The initial focus of research was on notable leaders. "The great-man theory" held that leaders are born great and that great men determine the direction of history and culture. "Without Moses...the Jews would have remained in Egypt; without Winston Churchill, the British would have given up in 1940; without Bill Gates, there would have been no firm like Microsoft" (Bass & Bass, 2008, p. 49).

When the United States moved from an agrarian society to an industrialized one, theoretical constructs began to investigate related economic factors. Attention later shifted to the task of classifying certain personality attributes patterned around effective leaders. Support for trait theory waned, and the dimension of situational factors as a causal variable were studied. From this approach, a more relational model soon evolved as social learning theories examined leader-follower exchanges (Bass, 1990). Most recently, charismatic-transformational leadership theory and servant leadership theories have gained prominence (Bass & Bass, 2008). These approaches emphasize leaders as individuals who "are able to motivate followers to work for collective goals that transcend self-interest and transform organizations" (Messick & Kramer, 2005, p. 54).

**Application.** Researchers continue to explore the various dynamics that exert influence on the development of leadership, but today's increasingly globalized and technological society, combined with strong economic pressures and the desire to maximize bottom-line profitability, have created an increased risk for mission drift and a departure from an organization's core values. The result has contributed to an all-too-frequent ethical and moral crisis of leadership in corporate governance worldwide. The church, as the body of Christ, is no exception.

Can values and leadership be separated? Some scholars have tended to side with a value-free connotation of leadership, but for people of faith, all of life is value-laden, and one would have to be dead in order to be truly value-neutral. Ethics and values provide an organization with much-needed structure, but a position of behavioral integrity remains the critical ingredient for transformational leadership to flourish. In other words, having an organizational or personal value system becomes essentially meaningless until it is consistently demonstrated in the real world through a leader's actions.

Management by values offers a strategic and timely tool with which leaders can examine and potentially redesign organizational culture. Successful people and enterprises often rise and fall on the basis of core values and their foundational integration with the sense of mission. Throughout history, leadership legacies have been forged with values such as compassion, courage, wisdom, sacrifice, stewardship, and servanthood, which, when taken together, help any organization remain committed to moral and ethical practice (Farling, Stone, & Winston, 1999). These are the essential principles that chart a leader's course, much like a map and a compass for a navigator. Core values and attributes can enhance business excellence and efficiencies, with compassion or the quality of humaneness anchoring the organization in a safe harbor.

**Biblical and Spiritual Issues.** Compassionate leadership seems to contradict the secular commandment of satisfying individual needs first. A mind-set of humility wants the best for others rather than for one's self. The concept of compassion is also a deeply biblical one. Integrating faith with management has shed some of its taboo status in recent years; bringing spirituality into the workplace embraces the notion of compassion as working from one's soul. In part, this is because a leader's demonstrated faith typically provides a comprehensive foundation for a values-based worldview. A compassion-oriented leader seeks the greatest good for others while pursuing the success of the mission. Some may argue that the politics of compassion have become a matter of debate, sometimes converted from a spiritual virtue to a secular one, but the need to practice the love of Christ as a principle of "kingdom" leadership is not in question.

Values and beliefs consequently play a significant role in leadership function and are influenced by one's faith, education, cognitive style, culture, family norms, and societal developments. Today, there seems to be two predominant value cultures: One has a short-term perspective motivated by personal, material, or monetary gain, and the other is spiritually and morally driven. Most Christians believe that transformation flows from a servant-leadership orientation that depends on the leader's principles, values, beliefs, and worldview. Robert Greenleaf (1977) first coined the term "servant-leadership" in 1970 after reading Herman Hesse's novel *Journey to the East*. He felt the main character of the story exemplified the desire to serve others, drawing the conclusion that genuine leadership emerges from those who possess this profound desire—that a servant-leader is a servant first.

Sadly, there has been a shift in society from the premodern era to the modern, and now the postmodern. Organizational structures, and to some extent, leadership styles, have simultaneously undergone a metamorphosis. The end of the Industrial Revolution and the ushering in of advanced technologies have forced organizations and their leaders to adapt or risk extinction. Along with the enormous changes engulfing the postmodern world, philosophical perspectives now embrace pluralism, naturalism, and pantheism, with an attempt to deconstruct a Judeo-Christian heritage and create a morally relativistic society. From the Enlightenment through the modern age, there has been an expectation that religion would eventually become extinct. However, as long as mankind bears the *imago Dei*, the existence of God cannot be denied. The Lord himself proclaimed, "Heaven and earth will pass away, but my words will never pass away" (Mt. 24:35).

**Conclusion.** Good biblically based leaders will produce followers, but a truly transformational leader creates new cadres of leaders because they understand that the goal of empowerment is to not merely reproduce themselves but to see people become more Christlike. The words of the apostle Paul echo this call: "The things you have heard me say in the presence of many witnesses entrust to reliable witnesses who will also be qualified to teach others" (2 Tim. 2:2).

**Eric Scalise**

### REFERENCES


Bass, B. M. (1990). *Bass and Stogdill's Handbook of Leadership: Theory, Research, and Managerial Applications* (3rd ed.). New York, NY: Free Press.

Bass, B. M., & Bass. R. (2008). *The Bass Handbook of Leadership: Theory, Research, and Managerial Applications.* New York, NY: Simon & Schuster.

Farling, M. L., Stone, A. G., & Winston, B. E. (1999, Winter-Spring). Servant leadership: Setting the stage for empirical research. *Journal of Leadership Studies,* 49-63.

Greenleaf, R. K. (1977). *Servant Leadership: A Journey into the Nature of Legitimate Power and Greatness.* New York, NY: Paulist Press.

Messick, D. M., & Kramer, R. M. (2005). *The Psychology of Leadership: New Perspectives and Research.* Mahwah, NJ: Lawrence Erlbaum.

Waite, M. R. (2008). *Fire Service Leadership: Theories and Practices.* Sudbury, MA: Jones and Bartlett.


## POSITIVE PSYCHOLOGY AND HUMAN FLOURISHING

*Health psychology* and its intellectual antecedent, behavioral medicine, began in the 1970s and has burgeoned during the past 25 years into a major scientific and clinical discipline that promotes health and well-being as well as prevention and treatment of illness and disease (Peterson, 2006). Other terms that are sometimes used interchangeably with *health psychology* are *medical psychology* and *behavioral medicine.*

**Description and Prevalence.** Health psychology is a specialty area that is concerned with how illness and health are results of a combination of biological, psychological, and social factors that impact various medical conditions and overall well-being. Health psychologists specialize in the psychology behind why we get sick, how we stay well, how we react to illness, and how we can better relate to the health-care system and health-care providers (Straub, 2011).

This whole-person approach is known as a *bio-psycho-social model.*

Biological factors include inherited personality traits and genetic predisposition and conditions. Psychological and behavioral factors are considered, such as lifestyle, personality characteristics, health beliefs, and stress levels. Social factors take into account such things as social support systems, family relationships, and cultural influence and beliefs.

Although health psychology originates from and is closely tied to clinical psychology, there are several different divisions within health psychology and one allied field that has developed over time. The four historical divisions are clinical health psychology, public health psychology, community health psychology, and critical health psychology. Most recently, research advances are being incorporated into the emergence of positive health psychology. The allied field is occupational health psychology (Straub, 2011).

*Positive health psychology* reminds us that health is more than the absence of illness. Research in positive psychology and positive health has identified factors—especially faith practices, stress management, purpose, good nutrition, physical activity, and healthy relationship connections—that can help people live longer, healthier, and happier lives (Buettner, 2009). Lifestyle changes that facilitate health throughout the life span are encouraged, along with practical ways to build those changes into everyday life, such as prayer, nutrition, and exercise (Hart Weber, 2010).

*Clinical health psychology* (ClHP) is a major contributor to the psychiatric field of behavioral medicine. Clinical practice includes education, the techniques of behavior change, and psychotherapy. In some countries, with additional training, a clinical health psychologist can become a medical psychologist and earn prescription privileges.

*Public health psychology* (PHP) primarily investigates potential causal links between psychosocial factors and health in the general population. Public-health psychologists present research results to educators, policy makers, and health-care providers in order to promote better public health. PHP is allied to other public-health disciplines including epidemiology, nutrition, genetics, and biostatistics.

*Community health psychology* (CoHP) investigates community factors that contribute to the health and well-being of individuals who live in communities. CoHP also develops community-level interventions that are designed to combat disease and promote physical and mental health. The community *often* serves as the level of analysis and is frequently sought as a partner in health-related interventions.

*Critical health psychology* (CrHP) is concerned with the distribution of power and the impact of power differentials on health experience and behavior, health-care systems, and health policy. CrHP prioritizes social justice and the universal right to health for people of all races, genders, ages, and socioeconomic positions. A major concern is health inequalities.

**Assessment.** Health psychologists work with individuals, groups, and communities to assess for these risk factors, decrease risk for illness, and improve overall health and well-being.

Since the early 1900s, the majority of deaths were due to public or community health problems such as pneumonia, tuberculosis, and diarrhea. In the 20th and 21st centuries, most deaths have been attributed to preventable diseases associated with individual behavior and lifestyle (Brannon, 2010).

Health psychologists assess and apply research and psychological theories that influence the practice of health behaviors, especially those factors that may help people change behaviors known to compromise health leading to diseases such as heart disease, cancer, stroke, obesity, infectious diseases, infant mortality, HIV/AIDS, respiratory disease, and diabetes. These behaviors include alcohol abuse, stress, smoking, poor diet, and lack of exercise (Brannon, 2010).

Health psychologists also assess how these diseases affect individuals' psychological and overall well-being. When people become seriously ill or injured, they face many additional stressors such as medical and other bills, getting proper care when home from the hospital, challenges caring for dependents, not being able to be self-reliant, or having a new, unwanted identity as a sick person. These additional stressors can lead to depression, reduced self-esteem, and many other problems (Straub, 2011).

**Treatment.** Health psychologists focus on prevention research and treatment interventions designed to promote health and reduce the risk of disease. More than half of health psychologists provide clinical services, often working alongside other medical professionals (chaplains, physicians, physician assistants, nurses, and physical and occupational therapists) to build better communication, improve adherence to treatment plans, manage pain, and enhance overall wellness.

Health psychologists treat a wide variety of health-related issues; the following are just a few of the current areas of treatment that focus on changing health behaviors, promoting health, increasing compliance with treatment regimens, and preventing illness:

- stress
- sleep problems
- headaches
- alcohol problems
- obesity
- smoking
- poor nutrition
- risky sexual behaviors
- end-of life issues

Other health psychologists function in nonclinical roles, promoting change in public health promotion, lifestyle medicine, empowering communities to improve quality of life, teaching at universities, and conducting research.

Research in health psychology aims to identify behaviors and experiences that promote health, cause illness, and increase the effectiveness of health care. Health psychology also considers contextual factors such as economic, cultural, community, social, and lifestyle factors that influence health. A broad range of health psychology studies includes cardiac psychology, high-risk behaviors, religious beliefs, social support, and emotional states, which provide recommended ways to improve health care and health-care policy (Straub, 2011).

Health psychologists also aim at educating other health professionals in communicating effectively with patients in ways that overcome barriers to understanding, remembering, and implementing effective strategies for reducing exposures to risk factors and making health-enhancing behavior changes.

**Spiritual Issues.** Integrative health psychologists expand the bio-psycho-social model to include the whole person as well as the spiritual aspects of our being (Hart Weber, 2010). God has created us for *shalom*—for well-being and wholeness in every area of our lives. The Judeo-Christian faith offers the best foundational principles and practices for a healthy bio-psycho-social-spiritual lifestyle.

For example, research has shown that those who are actively involved in practicing their faith and attending faith-based services four times a month are healthier and can add 4 to 14 years in life expectancy (Buettner, 2009).

Christian health psychologists integrate proven principles and practices of the Judeo-Christian faith that (a) foster a personal relationship with God and others and (b) build the psychological immune system, which enhances our ability to overcome stress and boost hope, optimism, mental hygiene, and community connections. Spiritual practices such as prayer, meditation, altruism, gratitude, and healthy relationships have proven to be very effective in body-mind health and well-being (Hart Weber, 2010). Physical self-care is foundational in lifestyle medicine but can also be considered a spiritual practice. Exercise, good nutrition, adequate sleep, relaxation, and keeping the Sabbath are essential for overall health.

**Conclusion.** Health psychologists aim to understand how biological, behavioral, psychological, and social factors influence health, wellness, and illness. People are living longer and healthier lives than ever before. Today, the most common causes of death are strongly related to preventable factors and unhealthy behaviors such as smoking cigarettes, poor diet, sedentary lifestyle, and poor stress-coping skills. Fortunately, we can learn ways to control our negative thoughts and behaviors. With the help of health psychologists, we can learn scientifically proven lifestyle skills to make positive, healthy changes in our lives (Hart Weber, 2010).

Catherine Hart Weber

## REFERENCES


Brannon, L. (2010). *Health Psychology: An Introduction to Behavior and Health.* Belmont, CA: Wadsworth.

Buettner, D. (2009). *The Blue Zones: Lessons for Living Longer from the People Who've Lived the Longest.* Washington, DC: National Geographic Society.

Hart Weber, C. (2010). *Flourish: Discover the Daily Joy of Abundant Vibrant Living.* Minneapolis, MN: Bethany House.

Peterson, C. (2006). *A Primer in Positive Psychology.* New York, NY: Oxford Press.

Straub, R. (2011). *Health Psychology* (3rd ed.). New York, NY: Worth.


## MANAGED CARE

**Definition.** *Managed care* (MC) is the general term for a wide range of enforced procedures by health-care system payers (insurance companies) intended to curtail escalating costs and ensure the quality of supplied services (Davis & Meier, 2001). Insurance plans often position a primary care provider (PCP) in the role of gatekeeper. Patients obtain access to specialty medical care, surgery, or physical therapy through a PCP. An alternative MC strategy is to have insurance representatives or a contracted medical group exercise administrative oversight over the type, frequency, and level of health care service. Mental-health care may be "carved out," meaning that a managed behavioral health organization (MBHO) authorizes all treatment for behavioral care and substance abuse.

Financial incentives or direct restrictions in MC may direct patients toward approved network providers. These "in-network" mental-health professionals (MHPs) sign agreements that specify reimbursement rates, restrict co-pays, and solidify a common set of practice arrangements. Published provider panel listings may give plan members information about MHP interest areas, such as marriage and family, pediatric, grief, trauma, spiritually sensitive, or even Christian counseling. Typically, a plan member can do a quick review of any special instructions on a standard insurance card to discover if an MBHO has administrative control over inpatient or outpatient mental-health services. In short, MC reduces plan expense by placing an assortment of intermediaries between the patient and the health-care professional.

**Historical Background.** Health Maintenance Organizations (HMOs) were an early form of MC that grew in popularity following World War II. HMOs are groups of physicians who band together to offer coordinated care with a preventative focus for a predetermined fee. HMOs sparked the beginning of serious interest in MC (Austad & Berman, 1991). The rapid rise in health-care costs in subsequent decades brought MC to the forefront of political and social-justice debates. In the 1970s, critical government policies and incentives fueled further interest in MC. An extensive range of options emerged, such as preferred provider organizations (PPOs), in which an alliance of health-care professionals joins with insurance companies to streamline referrals and lower costs. The MC revolution dramatically impacted mental-health care in the 1990s and has remained a significant force. Controversy over MC cost-control activities has often been heated (Greggo, 1997, 2001, 2007). It is legitimate to consider the ethical conflict that is apparent when increased profitability for an insurance company can be realized by rationing care to its policyholders (Greggo, 1998). On another front, those who pay for policies have a vested interest in lower premiums and high-quality service. Currently, various MC formats represent the majority of mainstream practice in medically reimbursable mental-health care. When payment for services is supplied from a third party, regulated practice through a variation of MC will continue to be the norm.

**Trends.** In recent years, the emphasis in MC in behavioral/mental-health care has been on ensuring service consistency and quality. Procedures involve a combination of reviews: prospective (reporting initial session results), concurrent (treatment plans and progress reports), or retrospective (peer evaluation of the entire case record). Essentially, MHPs are required to diagnose according to prevailing standards, document symptom severity and reduced functional domains, demonstrate medical necessity, and offer empirically supported treatments (ESTs) by means of defined treatment plans to remediate clearly identified presenting problems. Demonstration of reliable and valid therapeutic care according to "best practice" criteria, regardless of outside oversight, is the best approach for MHPs (Bobbitt, 2006).

The impact of MC on Christian counseling has everything to do with the definition and distinctions of what comprises *Christian* mental-health care. Christian approaches that are compatible with a medical illness intervention model will have a different response from those exclusively rooted in pastoral-care traditions. Christian helpers may have unity regarding a biblical worldview but not agree on how to participate with the medically and behaviorally focused frameworks of MC.

**Christian Counselor Responses.** Christian MHPs are in the prime position to coach clients through the maze of MC with compassion. An MHP fulfills duties of fidelity by taking responsibility to assist clients in understanding their needs, interests, and options. The counselor-client partnership is cultivated by informing, guiding, and equipping on matters of selecting a suitable professional, the criteria of medical necessity, treatment possibilities, and cost contemplation. Clinicians disclose methods and risks in an effort to support client autonomy, secure reasonable mental-health gains, and establish realistic outcomes.

A key professional expectation is the documentation of symptom data, how diagnostic criteria were met, treatment plans, and interventions in sessions. These procedures can be streamlined through the use of checklists, psychological screening measures, targeted questionnaires, and standardized forms.

Christian counselors accept the notion that although a professional helping relationship is the catalyst for change, it is not an exclusive, "curative" affiliation (Worthington, 1996). Limiting monitored care by means of MC opens the door to encourage Christian counselors to refer out to ministry-support opportunities. Aftercare plans may strategically include support groups, discipleship guides, Stephen Ministers, lay biblical helpers, educational seminars, pastoral staff, marriage mentors, and accountability or prayer partners. Solid treatment plans accepted by MC reviewers may include such adjunct resources as appropriate for chief concerns and client values.

Stephen P. Greggo

## REFERENCES


Austad, C. S., & Berman, W. H. (Eds.). (1991). *Psychotherapy in Managed Health Care: The Optimal Use of Time and Resources.* Washington, DC: American Psychological Association.

Bobbitt, B. L. (2006). The importance of professional psychology: A view from managed care. *Professional Psychology: Research and Practice. 37*(6), 590-597.

Davis, S. R., & Meier, S. T. (2001). *The Elements of Managed Care: A Guide for Helping Professionals.* Belmont, CA: Wadsworth.

Greggo, S. P. (1997). The alphabet soup of managed care. *Christian Counseling Today, 5*(4), 12-13, 50-52.

Greggo, S. P. (1998). Therapeutic relationship in managed mental health care. In J. F. Kilner, R. D. Orr, & J. A. Shelly (Eds.), *The Changing Face of Health Care: A Christian Appraisal of Managed Care, Resource Allocation, and Patient-Caregiver Relationships* (pp. 177-191). Grand Rapids, MI: Eerdmans.

Greggo, S. P. (2001). Practitioner attitudes regarding managed mental health care: A survey of Christian Association for Psychological Studies (CAPS) practitioners. *Journal of Psychology and Christianity, 20*(1), 66-79.

Greggo, S. P. (2007). Mending mangled care: The pursuit of Christian service within managed care. *Christian Counseling Today, 15*(2), 45-47.

Worthington, E. L., Jr. (1996). Speculations about new directions in helping marriages and families that arise from pressures of managed mental healthcare. *Journal of Psychology and Christianity 25*(3), 197-212.

# CONTRIBUTORS

**Beth Ackerman, Ed.D.**
Associate Dean of Education, Liberty University

**Gregg Albers, M.D., FAAFP**
Light Medical, Lynchburg, VA

**Larry Anderson, Ph.D.**
Professor of Psychology, Liberty University

**David W. Appleby, Ph.D., Ph.D.**
President, Spiritual Interventions, Inc.

**Matthew E. Appleby, B.S.**
graduate student, Liberty University

**Dwight Bain, M.A.**
Executive Director, International Christian Coaching Association; Founder, The Life Works Group

**Steve Baker, LPC, CAC**
The Change Group

**Tim Barclay, Ph.D.**
Center for Counseling and Family Studies, Liberty University

**Ed Barker, Ph.D.**
Professor, Center for Counseling and Family Studies, Liberty University

**Jeanne Brooks, Ph.D.**
Assistant Professor of Counseling, Center for Counseling and Family Studies, Liberty University

**Theresa Burke, Ph.D.**
Founder, Rachel's Vineyard Ministries

**Ryan A. Carboneau, M.A.**
Director of Member Care, American Association of Christian Counselors; doctoral student in Professional Counseling, Liberty University

**David Carder, M.A., M.A.**
Counseling Pastor, Fullerton Evangelical Free Church

**Anthony Centore, Ph.D.**
Founder, Thrive Boston Counseling

**Gary Chapman, Ph.D.**
President, Marriage & Family Life Consultants, Inc.

**Carolyn Childerston, M.A.**
Sex Therapist & Practice Administrator, James K. Childerston & Associates

**James Childerston, Ph.D.**
Psychologist and Sex Therapist; Director, James K. Childerston & Associates

**Jennifer Cisney, M.A.**
Institute for Compassionate Care

**Todd Clements, M.D.**
Diplomate, American Board of Psychiatry and Neurology; Diplomate, American Board of Addiction Medicine; Medical Director, The Clements Clinic

**Tim Clinton, Ed.D., LPC, LMFT**
President, American Association of Christian Counselors; Professor of Counseling and Pastoral Care, Liberty University

**Henry Cloud, Ph.D.**
Cofounder, Cloud-Townsend Resources

**Mark Crear, Ph.D.**
President, Mark Crear Ministries; Director, Black African American Christian Counselors, a division of the American Association of Christian Counselors

**Jim Cress, M.A., LPC, CSAT**
Radio talk show host; Licensed Professional Counselor, Certified Sex Addiction Therapist

**Denise Daniel, Ph.D**
Director, M.A. Counseling Program, Center for Counseling and Family Studies, Liberty University

**Don Davis, Ph.D.**
Virginia Commonwealth University

**Ron Deal, M.MFT.**
President, Smart Stepfamilies

**Bob Dees, M.S., P.E.**
Major General U.S. Army (Retired); President, RFD, LLC

**Robert DeVries, D.Min., Ph.D.**
Professor of Church Education, Calvin Theological Seminary

**Fred DiBlasio, Ph.D.**
Professor, School of Social Work, University of Maryland

**Sandra Dopf, B.S.**
Founder & CEO, Emerge Victorious, LLC

**Karin Dumont, Ph.D., NCC, LPC, LCAS, CCCJS**
Assistant Professor and Clinical Consultant, Center for Counseling and Family Studies, Liberty University

**Marian Eberly, R.N., MSW, LCSW**
Remuda Ranch

**Kevin Ellers, D.Min.**
President, Institute for Compassionate Care

**Heidi Erickson, B.A.**
graduate student, Regent University

**Tiffany Erspamer, B.A.**
graduate student, Regent University

**Kathie Erwin, Ph.D.**
Assistant Professor of Clinical Mental Health Counseling, Regent University

**Laura Faidley, B.S., B.A.**
Associate Director of Member Care and Associate Editor, American Association of Christian Counselors; graduate student, Liberty University

**Amy Feigel, M.A., LPC, LMFT**
Director, Extraordinary Women; Licensed Professional Counselor, Light Counseling

**Marnie C. Ferree, M.A., LMFT, CSAT**
Executive Director, Bethesda Workshops

**Brianne Friberg, Ph.D.**
Assistant Professor of Psychology, Liberty University

**Aubrey Gartner, M.S.**
doctoral student, Virginia Commonwealth University

**Fernando Garzon, Psy.D.**
Assistant Professor of Counseling, Center for Counseling and Family Studies, Liberty University

**Fred Gingrich, D.Min.**
Professor of Counseling and Division Chair, Denver Seminary

**Heather Davediuk Gingrich, Ph.D.**
Associate Professor of Counseling, Denver Seminary

**Chelsea Greer, M.S., M.A.**
doctoral student, Virginia Commonwealth University

**Rev. Stephen P. Greggo, Psy.D.**
Professor of Counseling, Trinity Evangelical Divinity School

**Gary Habermas, Ph.D.**
Distinguished Research Professor, Liberty University

**Archibald Hart, Ph.D.**
Senior Professor of Psychology & Dean Emeritus, Graduate School of Psychology, Fuller Theological Seminary

**David Hawkins, ACSW, Ph.D., LCP**
Director, The Marriage Recovery Center

**Ron Hawkins, D.Min., Ed.D.**
Vice Provost, Professor of Counseling and Practical Theology, Liberty University and Liberty Baptist Theological Seminary; Executive Board Member, American Association of Christian Counselors

**Scott Hawkins, Ph.D.**
Associate Dean, Center for Counseling and Family Studies, Liberty University

**Stanley Hibbs, Ph.D.**
Psychologist, Atlanta Network for Individual and Family Therapy

**Kristina High, B.A.**
graduate student, Regent University

**Ed Hindson, Th.D., D.Min., D.Phil.**
Distinguished Professor of Religion, Liberty University

**Victor Hinson, Ed.D.**
Chair, Center for Counseling and Family Studies, Liberty University

**Joshua N. Hook, Ph.D.**
Assistant Professor of Psychology, University of North Texas

**June Hunt, M.A.**
CEO & CSO (Chief Servant Officer), Hope for the Heart

**Philip Jamieson, Ph.D.**
Assistant Professor of Pastoral Theology, University of Dubuque Theological Seminary

**Gregg Jantz, Ph.D.**
The Center, Inc.

**David E. Jenkins, Psy.D.**
Coordinator of Ph.D. Clinical Training, Center for Counseling and Family Studies, Liberty University

**David J. Jennings, II, M.S., M.A.**
doctoral student, Virginia Commonwealth University

**Timothy R. Jennings, M.D.**
Psychiatric Foundations

**Eric Johnson, Ph.D.**
Lawrence and Charlotte Hoover Professor of Pastoral Care, Southern Baptist Theological Seminary

**Paula Johnson, R.N., MFT, Psy.D.**
McDonald Therapy Center

**Ian Jones, Ph.D, Ph.D.**
Professor of Psychology and Counseling, New Orleans Baptist Theological Seminary; Director, Biblical Counseling and Spiritual Formation Network, a division of the American Association of Christian Counselors

**Anita Knight, Ph.D.**
Assistant Professor of Counseling, Center for Counseling and Family Studies, Liberty University

**E. John Kuhnley, M.D.**
Child and Adolescent Psychiatrist, Central Virginia Community Services; Adjunct Professor, Liberty University

**Mark Laaser, Ph.D.**
Founder and President, Faithful and True Ministries

**Diane Langberg, Ph.D.**
Director, Diane Langberg and Associates; Executive Board Chair, American Association of Christian Counselors

**Peter Larson, Ph.D.**
President, Life Innovations

**Arnold Lazarus, Ph.D.**
Executive Director, The Lazarus Institute

**Yin Lin**
Doctoral Student, Virginia Commonwealth University

**Michael Lyles, M.D.**
Lyles & Crawford Clinical Consulting; Executive Board Member, American Association of Christian Counselors

**Chad M. Magnuson, Ph.D.**
Assistant Professor of Psychology, Liberty University

**Bryan Maier, Psy.D.**
Associate Professor of Counseling and Psychology, Biblical Seminary

**Hitomi Makino, Ph.D.**
Professional Development and Research Assistant, American Association of Christian Counselors

**Sharon G. May, Ph.D.**
Director & Cofounder, Marriage, Family & Relationship Institute; Adjunct Professor, Azusa Pacific University & Denver Seminary

**Christopher McCluskey, MSW, PCC, CMCC**
Founder & President, Professional Christian Coaching Institute

**Arlys McDonald, Ph.D.**
Psychologist, Director, McDonald Therapy Center; Adjunct Professor, Bethel University and Southern California Seminary

**Fred Milacci, D.Ed.**
Associate Professor, Center for Counseling and Family Studies, Liberty University

**Frank Minirth, M.D.**
President, The Minirth Clinic

**Linda Mintle, Ph.D., LMFT, LCSW**
Assistant Professor of Clinical Pediatrics, Eastern Virginia Medical School

**Dan Mitchell, Th.D.**
Liberty Baptist Theological Seminary

**Philip G. Monroe, Psy.D.**
Professor of Counseling and Psychology, Biblical Theological Seminary

**Norman Moore, M.D.**
Chief Editor, *Clinical EEG & Neuroscience*; Professor of Psychiatry, Quillen College Medicine

**Mark Myers, ABD**
Online Chair, Center for Counseling and Family Studies, Liberty University

**Amy Newmeyer, M.D.**
Director, Nationwide Children's Hospital; Clinical Associate Professor of Pediatrics, The Ohio State University College of Medicine

**Mark Newmeyer, Ed.D.**
Assistant Professor, Regent University

**Carmela O'Hare, Psy.D.**
Associate Professor of Counseling, Liberty University

**George Ohlschlager, M.A., M.S.W., J.D.**
Chairman, AACC Law & Ethics Committee; Executive Consultant, American Association of Christian Counselors

**Gary Oliver, Ph.D.**
Executive Director, Center for Relationship Enrichment, John Brown University; Executive Board Member, American Association of Christian Counselors

**David Olson, Ph.D.**
Founder & CEO, Life Innovations

**Miriam Stark Parent, Ph.D.**
Associate Professor of Counseling, Trinity Evangelical Divinity School, Trinity International University

**Stephen Parker, Ph.D.**
Professor, School of Psychology and Counseling, Regent University

**Cliff Penner, Ph.D.**
Passionate Commitment

**Joyce Penner, R.N., M.N.**
Passionate Commitment

**Clay Peters, Ed.D.**
Director, M.A. in Human Services Program, Center for Counseling and Family Studies, Liberty University

**Megan Purser, M.A.**
doctoral student in Clinical Health Psychology and Behavioral Medicine, Texas State University

**M. Katherine Quigley, Ed.D.**
Adjunct Professor, Liberty University; Special Education Teacher

**Jennifer Ripley, Ph.D.**
Director, Psy.D. Clinical Psychology Program, Regent University

**Lynn Robinson, M.S.**
Child Custody Investigator; Therapeutic Journaling Facilitator; Guest Lecturer, Troy University

**Beverly Rodgers, Ph.D.**
Owner, Rogers Christian Counseling, Institute for Soul Healing Love

**Tom Rodgers, Ph.D.**
Owner, Rogers Christian Counseling, Institute for Soul Healing Love

**Doug Rosenau, Ed.D.**
Psychologist, Sex Therapist; Cofounder, Sexual Wholeness, Inc.

**Gene Alan Sale, Ed.D., LPC**
Dean, School of Education and Behavioral Studies, Associate Professor of Psychology, Graduate Counseling Psychology Program, Palm Beach Atlantic University

**Steven Sandage, Ph.D.**
Professor of Marriage and Family Studies, Bethel University

**John Sandy, M.S.J., M.A.B.C., J.D.**
Senior Corporate Attorney for Brotherhood

Mutual Insurance Company; Ordained Minister; Certified Christian and Pastoral Counselor

**Eric Scalise, Ph.D.**
Vice President of Professional Development, American Association of Christian Counselors; Vice President for Academic Affairs, Light University Online; Executive Director, International Board of Christian Care

**Kathryn Scott-Young, Ph.D., LMFT**
Director, SEB Health

**Dan Seaborn, M.A.**
Founder & President, Winning at Home

**J. Mark Shadoan, Ed.D., LCSW**
Clinical Director, Light Counseling, Inc., Lynchburg, VA

**Lynette Shadoan, M.A., LPC, LMFT**
Director, Light Counseling, Lynchburg, VA

**LeRon Shults, Ph.D.**
Professor of Theology and Philosophy, University of Agder

**Georgia Shaffer, M.A.**
PA Licensed Psychologist

**Gary Sibcy, II, Ph.D.**
Director, Ph.D. Program, Center for Counseling and Family Studies, Liberty University; Licensed Clinical Psychologist, Piedmont Psychiatric Center

**Jose Javier Sierra, Psy.D., LMHC, LMFT**
Associate Professor of Counseling, Asbury Theological Seminary

**Greg Smalley, Psy.D.**
Executive Director, Marriage and Family Formation, Focus on the Family

**Jacqueline Smith, Ed.D.**
Northern Kentucky University

**Sam Smith, Ed.D.**
Associate Professor, Liberty University

**Lisa Sosin, Ph.D.**
Associate Director, Ph.D. Program, Center for Counseling and Family Studies, Liberty University

**Anita Staver, J.D.**
President, Liberty Counsel

**Mathew D. Staver, J.D.**
Founder & Chairman, Liberty Counsel; Dean and Professor of Law, Liberty University, Liberty University School of Law

**David Stoop, Ph.D.**
Founder & CEO, A Promise Kept Ministries; Executive Board Member, American Association of Christian Counselors

**Joshua D. Straub, Ph.D.**
Senior Director of Executive Projects and Member Care, American Association of Christian Counselors; Adjunct Professor, Liberty University

**Daniel Sweeney, Ph.D.**
Founder & Director, Northwest Center for Play Therapy Studies, George Fox University

**Michael Sytsma, Ph.D.**
Sex Therapist; President, Building Intimate Marriages, Inc.

**Joni Eareckson Tada**
Founder & CEO, Joni & Friends, International Disability Center

**Siang-Yang Tan, Ph.D.**
Professor of Psychology, Fuller Theological Seminary; Senior Pastor, First Evangelical Church Glendale, Glendale, CA

**Debra Taylor, M.A.**
Sex Therapist, Sexual Wholeness, Inc.

**John C. Thomas, Ph.D, Ph.D.**
Associate Professor, Center for Counseling and Family Studies, Liberty University

**Warren Throckmorton, Ph.D.**
Associate Professor of Psychology, Grove City College

**Chris Thurman, Ph.D.**
Private Practice

**Elmer L. Towns, D.Min.**
Dean, Liberty Baptist Theological Seminary; Dean, School of Religion; Cofounder, Liberty University

**John Townsend, Ph.D.**
Owner, John Townsend, Ph.D. Consulting

**John Trent, Ph.D.**
President, Strong Families

**Daryl R. Van Tongeren, Ph.D.**
Virginia Commonwealth University

**Leslie Vernick, MSW**
Private Practice

**Catherine Hart Weber, Ph.D.**
Founder, Flourish in Life and Relationships Center; Director, Hart Institute

**Allison Wilkerson, M.Ed.**
doctoral student, University of North Texas

**Richard Winter, M.D.**
Professor of Practical Theology and Counseling, Covenant Theological Seminary

**Shannon Wolf, Ph.D., LPC-S**
Assistant Professor of Counseling, Dallas Baptist University

**Stephanie Womack, B.M.**
graduate student, University of North Texas

**Everett Worthington Jr., Ph.D.**
Professor of Counseling Psychology, Virginia Commonwealth University

**R. Kirby Worthington, M.S.**
Virginia Commonwealth University

**Mark A. Yarhouse, Psy.D.**
Professor of Psychology and Endowed Chair, Regent University

**Sarah Young, M.A.**
Sexual Therapy Specialist

**Susan Zonnebelt-Smeenge, Ed.D.**
Pine Rest Christian Mental Health Services

# ALPHABETIZED INDEX OF ARTICLES